The Oxford Colour German Dictionary Plus

The Oxford Colour German Dictionary Plus

Second edition

GERMAN–ENGLISH
ENGLISH–GERMAN

DEUTSCH–ENGLISCH
ENGLISCH–DEUTSCH

OXFORD
UNIVERSITY PRESS

OXFORD
UNIVERSITY PRESS

Great Clarendon Street, Oxford OX2 6DP

Oxford University Press is a department of the University of Oxford.
It furthers the University's objective of excellence in research, scholarship,
and education by publishing worldwide in

Oxford New York

Athens Auckland Bangkok Bogotá Buenos Aires Calcutta
Cape Town Chennai Dar es Salaam Delhi Florence Hong Kong Istanbul
Karachi Kuala Lumpur Madrid Melbourne Mexico City Mumbai
Nairobi Paris São Paulo Shanghai Singapore Taipei Tokyo Toronto Warsaw

with associated companies in Berlin Ibadan

Oxford is a registered trade mark of Oxford University Press
in the UK and in certain other countries

British Library Cataloguing in Publication Data

Data available

Library of Congress Cataloging in Publication Data

Data available

ISBN 0–19–864561–9
ISBN 0–19–864565–1 (US edition)
ISBN 0–19–968017–5 (educational edition)

10 9 8 7 6 5 4 3 2

Typeset by Morton
Word Processing Ltd
Printed in Spain by
Book Print S.L.

Contents

Preface

The Oxford Colour German Dictionary Plus is a dictionary
designed primarily for students of German. Its clear presentation and use of colour headwords make it easily accessible. It
contains completely new sections, not found in the *Oxford
Colour German Dictionary*, on German life and culture, letter-
writing, and German grammar, making it even more useful for
students up to intermediate level.

List of contributors

Second Edition

Editors:

Roswitha Morris
Robin Sawers

Supplementary Material:

Robin Sawers
Neil and Roswitha Morris
Valerie Grundy
Eva Vennebusch

Data Capture:

Susan Wilkin
Anne McConnell
Anna Cotgreave

Proof-reading:

Andrew Hodgson

First Edition

Editors:

Gunhild Prowe
Jill Schneider

Introduction

The text of this dictionary reflects recent changes to the spelling of German ratified in July 1996. The symbol * has been introduced to refer from the old spelling to the new, preferred one:

> **As*** *nt* -ses, -se *s.* **Ass**
> **dasein*** *vi sep* (*sein*) **da sein,** *s.* **da**
> **Schiffahrt*** *f s.* **Schifffahrt**

Where both the old and new forms are valid, an equals sign = is used to refer to the preferred form:

> **aufwändig** *a* = **aufwendig**
> **Tunfisch** *m* = **Thunfisch**

When such forms follow each other alphabetically, they are given with commas, with the preferred form in first place:

> **Panther, Panter** *m* -s, -
> panther

In phrases, *od* (oder) is used:

> ...**deine(r,s)** *poss pron* yours;
> **die D~en** *od* **d~en** *pl* your family *sg*

On the English–German side, only the preferred German form is given.

- A swung dash ~ represents the headword or that part of the headword preceding a vertical bar |. The initial letter of a German headword is given to show whether or not it is a capital.
- The vertical bar | follows the part of the headword which is not repeated in compounds or derivatives.
- Square brackets [ ] are used for optional material.
- Angled brackets < > are used after a verb translation to indicate the object; before a verb translation to indicate the subject; before an adjective to indicate a typical noun which it qualifies.

- Round brackets ( ) are used for field or style labels (see list on pages xxiii–xxv), and for explanatory matter.

- A box □ indicates a new part of speech within an entry.

- *od* (oder) and *or* denote that words or portions of a phrase are synonymous. An oblique stroke / is used where there is a difference in usage or meaning.

- ≈ is used where no exact equivalent exists in the other language.

- A dagger † indicates that a German verb is irregular and that the parts can be found in the verb table on pages 601–606. Compound verbs are not listed there as they follow the pattern of the basic verb.

- The stressed vowel is marked in a German headword by ‗ (long) or . (short). A phonetic transcription is only given for words which do not follow the normal rules of pronunciation. These rules can be found on page xi.

- German headword nouns are followed by the gender and, with the exception of compound nouns, by the genitive and plural. These are only given at compound nouns if they present some difficulty. Otherwise the user should refer to the final element.

- Nouns that decline like adjectives are entered as follows: **-e(r)** *m/f*, **-e(s)** *nt*.

- Adjectives which have no undeclined form are entered in the feminine form with the masculine and neuter in brackets **-e(r,s)**.

- The reflexive pronoun **sich** is accusative unless marked (*dat*).

Proprietary terms

This dictionary includes some words which are, or are asserted to be, proprietary names or trademarks. Their inclusion does not imply that they have acquired for legal purposes a non-proprietary or general significance, nor is any other judgement implied concerning their legal status. In cases where the editor has some evidence that a word is used as a proprietary name or trademark this is indicated by the letter (P), but no judgement concerning the legal status of such words is made or implied thereby.

Phonetic symbols used for German words

a	Hand	hant	ŋ	lang	laŋ
a:	Bahn	ba:n	o	Moral	mo'ra:l
ɐ	Ober	'o:bɐ	o:	Boot	bo:t
ɐ̯	Uhr	u:ɐ̯	o̯	loyal	lo̯a'ja:l
ã	Conférencier	kõferã'si̯e:	õ	Konkurs	kõ'kʊrs
ã:	Abonnement	abɔnə'mã:	õ:	Ballon	ba'lõ:
ai̯	weit	vai̯t	ɔ	Post	pɔst
au̯	Haut	hau̯t	ø	Ökonom	øko'no:m
b	Ball	bal	ø:	Öl	ø:l
ç	ich	ɪç	œ	göttlich	'gœtliç
d	dann	dan	ɔy̯	heute	'hɔy̯tə
dʒ	Gin	dʒɪn	p	Pakt	pakt
e	Metall	me'tal	r	Rast	rast
e:	Beet	be:t	s	Hast	hast
ɛ	mästen	'mɛstən	ʃ	Schal	ʃa:l
ɛ:	wählen	'vɛ:lən	t	Tal	ta:l
ɛ̃	Cousin	ku'zɛ̃:	ts	Zahl	tsa:l
ə	Nase	'na:zə	tʃ	Couch	kau̯tʃ
f	Faß	fas	u	Kupon	ku'põ:
g	Gast	gast	u:	Hut	hu:t
h	haben	'ha:bən	u̯	aktuell	ak'tu̯ɛl
i	Rivale	ri'va:lə	ʊ	Pult	pʊlt
i:	viel	fi:l	v	was	vas
i̯	Aktion	ak'tsi̯o:n	x	Bach	bax
ɪ	Birke	'bɪrkə	y	Physik	fy'zi:k
j	ja	ja:	y:	Rübe	'ry:bə
k	kalt	kalt	y̯	Nuance	'ny̯ã:sə
l	Last	last	Y	Fülle	'fYlə
m	Mast	mast	z	Nase	'na:zə
n	Naht	na:t	ʒ	Regime	re'ʒi:m

ʔ Glottal stop, e.g. Koordination / koʔɔrdina'tsi̯on /.

: length sign after a vowel, e.g. Chrom / kro:m /.

' Stress mark before stressed syllable, e.g. Balkon / bal'kõ:/.

Guide to German pronunciation

Consonants

Produced as in English with the following exceptions:

b	as	p	
d	as	t	*at the end of a word or syllable*
g	as	k	

ch	as in Scottish lo<u>ch</u>	*after a, o, u, au*
	like an exaggerated h as in <u>h</u>uge	*after i, e, ä, ö, ü, eu, ei*

-chs	as	x	(as in bo<u>x</u>)
-ig	as	-ich / ɪç /	*when a suffix*
j	as	y	(as in <u>y</u>es)
ps			the p is pronounced
pn			
qu	as	k + v	
s	as	z	(as in <u>z</u>ero) *at the beginning of a word*
	as	s	(as in bu<u>s</u>) *at the end of a word or syllable, before a consonant, or when doubled*
sch	as	sh	
sp	as	shp	*at the beginning of a word*
st	as	sht	*at the beginning of a word*
v	as	f	(as in <u>f</u>or)
	as	v	(as in <u>v</u>ery) *within a word*
w	as	v	(as in <u>v</u>ery)
z	as	ts	

Vowels

Approximately as follows:

a	short	as	u	(as in b<u>u</u>t)
	long	as	a	(as in c<u>a</u>r)
e	short	as	e	(as in p<u>e</u>n)
	long	as	a	(as in p<u>a</u>per)
i	short	as	i	(as in b<u>i</u>t)
	long	as	ee	(as in qu<u>ee</u>n)
o	short	as	o	(as in h<u>o</u>t)
	long	as	o	(as in p<u>o</u>pe)
u	short	as	oo	(as in f<u>oo</u>t)
	long	as	oo	(as in b<u>oo</u>t)

Vowels are always short before a double consonant, and long when followed by an h or when double

ie	is pronounced	ee	(as in k<u>ee</u>p)

Diphthongs

au	as	ow	(as in h<u>ow</u>)
ei ai	as	y	(as in m<u>y</u>)
eu äu	as	oy	(as in b<u>oy</u>)

Pronunciation of the alphabet

English/Englisch		*German/Deutsch*
eɪ	a	aː
biː	b	beː
siː	c	t͜seː
diː	d	deː
iː	e	eː
ef	f	ɛf
dʒiː	g	geː
eɪtʃ	h	haː
aɪ	i	iː
dʒeɪ	j	jɔt
keɪ	k	kaː
el	l	ɛl
em	m	ɛm
en	n	ɛn
əʊ	o	oː
piː	p	peː
kjuː	q	kuː
aː(r)	r	ɛr
es	s	ɛs
tiː	t	teː
juː	u	uː
viː	v	faʊ
ˈdʌbljuː	w	veː
eks	x	ɪks
waɪ	y	ˈʏpsilɔn
zed	z	t͜sɛt
eɪ umlaut	ä	ɛː
əʊ umlaut	ö	øː
juː umlaut	ü	yː
esˈzed	ß	ɛsˈt͜sɛt

Glossary of grammatical terms

Abbreviation A shortened form of a word or phrase: etc. = usw.

Accusative The case of a direct object; some German prepositions take the accusative

Active In the active form the subject of the verb performs the action: he asked = er hat gefragt

Adjective A word describing a noun: a *red* pencil = ein *roter* Stift

Adverb A word that describes or changes the meaning of a verb, an adjective, or another adverb: she sings *beautifully* = sie singt *schön*

Article The definite article, the = der/die/das, and indefinite article, a/an = ein/eine/ein, used in front of a noun

Attributive An adjective or noun is attributive when it is used directly before a noun: the *black* dog = der *schwarze* Hund; *farewell* speech = Abschiedsrede

Auxiliary verb One of the verbs – as German haben, sein, werden – used to form the perfect or future tense: I will help = ich werde helfen

Cardinal number A whole number representing a quantity: one/two/three = eins/zwei/drei

Case The form of a noun, pronoun, adjective, or article that shows the part it plays in a sentence; there are four cases in German – nominative, accusative, genitive, and dative

Clause A self-contained section of a sentence that contains a subject and a verb

Collective noun A noun that is singular in form but refers to a group of individual persons or things, e.g. royalty, grain

Collocate A word that regularly occurs with another; in German, Buch is a typical collocate of the verb lesen

Comparative The form of an adjective or adverb that makes it "more": smaller = kleiner, more clearly = klarer

Compound adjective An adjective formed from two or more separate words: selbstbewusst (selbst + bewusst) = self-confident

Compound noun A noun formed from two or more separate words: der Flughafen (Flug+ Hafen) = airport

Compound verb A verb formed by adding a prefix to a simple verb; in German, some compound verbs are separable (an|fangen), and some are inseparable (verlassen)

Conditional tense A tense of a verb that expresses what would happen if something else occurred: he would go = er würde gehen

Conjugation Variation of the form of a verb to show tense, person, mood, etc.

Conjunction A word used to join clauses together: **and = und, because = weil**

Dative The case of an indirect object; many German prepositions take the dative

Declension The form of a noun, pronoun, or adjective that corresponds to a particular case, number, or gender; some German nouns decline like adjectives, e.g. **Beamte, Taube**

Definite article: the = **der/die/das**

Demonstrative pronoun A pronoun indicating the person or thing referred to; *this* is my bicycle = *das* ist mein Fahrrad

Direct object The noun or pronoun directly affected by the verb: he caught *the ball* = er fing *den Ball*

Direct speech A speaker's actual words or the use of these in writing

Ending Letters added to the stem of verbs, as well as to nouns and adjectives, according to tense, case, etc.

Feminine One of the three noun genders in German: **die Frau = the woman**

Future tense The tense of a verb that refers to something that will happen in the future: I will go = **ich werde gehen**

Gender One of the three groups of nouns in German: masculine, feminine, or neuter

Genitive The case that shows possession; some prepositions in German take the genitive

Imperative A form of a verb that expresses a command: **go away! = geh weg!**

Imperfect tense The tense of a verb that refers to an uncompleted or a habitual action in the past: I went there every Friday = **ich ging jeden Freitag dorthin**

Impersonal verb A verb in English used only with 'it', and in German only with 'es': it is raining = **es regnet**

Indeclinable adjective An adjective that has no inflected forms, as German **klasse, Moskauer**

Indefinite article: a/an = **ein/eine/ein**

Indefinite pronoun A pronoun that does not identify a specific person or object: one = **man, something = etwas**

Indicative form The form of a verb used when making a statement of fact or asking questions of fact: he is just coming = **er kommt gleich**

Indirect object The noun or pronoun indirectly affected by the verb, at which the direct object is aimed: I gave *him* the book = **ich gab *ihm* das Buch**

Indirect speech A report of what someone has said which does not reproduce the exact words

Infinitive The basic part of a verb: to play = **spielen**

Inflect To change the ending

or form of a word to show its tense or its grammatical relation to other words: **gehe** and **gehst** are inflected forms of the verb **gehen**

Inseparable verb A verb with a prefix that can never be separated from it: **verstehen, ich verstehe**

Interjection A sound, word, or remark expressing a strong feeling such as anger, fear, or joy: **oh!** = **ach!**

Interrogative pronoun A pronoun that asks a question: **who?** = **wer?**

Intransitive verb A verb that does not have a direct object: **he died suddenly** = **er ist plötzlich gestorben**

Irregular verb A verb that does not follow one of the set patterns and has its own individual forms

Masculine One of the three noun genders in German: **der Mann** = **the man, der Stuhl** = **the chair**

Modal verb A verb that is used with another verb (not a model) to express permission, obligation, possibility, etc., as German **können, sollen**, English **might, should**

Negative expressing refusal or denial; **there aren't any** = **es gibt keine**

Neuter One of the three noun genders in German: **das Buch** = **the book, das Kind** = **the child**

Nominative The case of the subject of a sentence; in sentences with **sein** and **werden** the noun after the verb is in the nominative: **that is my car** = **das ist mein Auto**

Noun A word that names a person or a thing

Number The state of being either singular or plural

Object The word or words naming the person or thing acted upon by a verb or preposition, as 'Buch' in **er las das Buch** or 'ihm' in **ich traue ihm**

Ordinal number A number that shows a person's or thing's position in a series: the *twenty-first* century = **das** *einundzwanzigste* **Jahrhundert**, the *second* door on the left = **die** *zweite* **Tür links**

Part of speech A grammatical term for the function of a word; noun, verb, adjective, etc., are parts of speech.

Passive In the passive form the subject of the verb experiences the action rather than performs it: **he was asked** = **er wurde gefragt**

Past participle The part of a verb used to form past tenses: **she had** *gone*, **er hat** *gelogen*

Perfect tense The tense of a verb that refers to a completed action in the past or an action that started in the past and is still going on: **I have already eaten** = **ich habe schon gegessen; I have been reading all day** = **ich habe den ganzen Tag gelesen**

Person Any of the three groups of personal pronouns

and forms taken by verbs; the **first person** (e.g. **I/ich**) refers to the person(s) speaking, the **second person** (e.g. **you/du**) refers to the person(s) spoken to; the **third person** (e.g. **he/er**) refers to the persons spoken about

Personal pronoun A pronoun that refers to a person or thing: **he/she/it = er/sie/es**

Phrasal verb A verb in English combined with a preposition or an adverb to have a particular meaning: **run away = weglaufen**

Phrase A self-contained section of a sentence that does not contain a full verb

Pluperfect tense The tense of a verb that refers to something that happened before a particular point in the past: **als ich ankam, *war* er schon *losgefahren* = when I arrived, he *had* already *left***

Plural Of nouns etc., referring to more than one: **the trees = die Bäume**

Possessive adjective An adjective that shows possession, belonging to someone or something; **my = mein/meine/mein**

Possessive pronoun A pronoun that shows possession, belonging to someone or something: **mine = meiner/meine/meins**

Predicate The part of a sentence that says something about the **subject**, e.g. **went home** in **John went home**

Predicative An adjective is predicative when it comes after a verb such as **be** or **become** in English, or after **sein** or **werden** in German: **she is beautiful = sie ist schön**

Prefix A letter or group of letters added to the beginning of a word to change its meaning; in German, the prefix can move from separable verbs (**an|fangen**), but stays fixed to inseparable verbs (**verlassen**)

Preposition A word that stands in front of a noun or pronoun, relating it to the rest of the sentence; in German prepositions are always followed by a particular case, usually either the accusative or dative, but occasionally the genitive: **with = mit (+ dative)**, **for = für (+ accusative)**, **because of = wegen (+ genitive)**

Present participle The part of a verb that in English ends in –**ing**, and in German adds –**d** to the infinitive: **asking = fragend**

Present tense The tense of a verb that refers to something happening now: **I make = ich mache**

Pronoun A word that stands instead of a noun: **he = er, she = sie, mine = meiner/meine/meins**

Proper noun A name of a person, place, institution, etc., in English written with a capital letter at the start; **Germany**, the **Atlantic**, **Karl**, **Europa** are all proper nouns

Reflexive pronoun A pronoun that goes with a

reflexive verb: in German **mich, dich, sich, uns, euch, sich**

Reflexive verb A verb whose object is the same as its subject; in German, it is used with a reflexive pronoun: **du sollst dich waschen** = **you should wash yourself**

Regular verb A verb that follows a set pattern in its different forms

Relative pronoun A pronoun that introduces a subordinate clause, relating to a person or thing mentioned in the main clause: **the man *who* visited us** = **der Mann, *der* uns besucht hat**

Reported Speech Another name for **Indirect speech**

Sentence A sequence of words, with a subject and a verb, that can stand on their own to make a statement, ask a question, or give a command

Separable verb A verb with a prefix that can be separated from it in some tenses: **anfangen, anzufangen, angefangen**, but **ich fange an, du fingst an**

Singular Of nouns etc., referring to just one: **the tree** = **der Baum**

Stem The part of a verb to which endings are added; **fahr-** is the stem of **fahren**

Subject In a clause or sentence, the noun or pronoun that causes the action of the verb: ***he* caught the ball** = ***er* fing den Ball**

Subjunctive A verb form that is used to express doubt or unlikelihood: **if I were to tell you that ...** = **wenn ich dir sagen würde, dass ...**

Subordinate clause A clause which adds information to the main clause of a sentence but cannot be used as a sentence by itself

Suffix A letter or group of letters joined to the end of a word to make another word, as –heit in **Schönheit**

Superlative The form of an adjective or adverb that makes it "most": **the *smallest* house** = **das *kleinste* Haus**, **most clearly** = **am klarsten**

Tense The form of a verb that tells when the action takes place: present, future, imperfect, perfect, pluperfect

Transitive verb A verb that is used with a direct object: **she read the book** = **sie las das Buch**

Verb A word or group of words that describes an action: **the children *are playing*** = **die Kinder *spielen***

Abbreviations/Abkürzungen

adjective	*a*	Adjektiv
abbreviation	*abbr*	Abkürzung
accusative	*acc*	Akkusativ
Administration	*Admin*	Administration
adverb	*adv*	Adverb
American	*Amer*	amerikanisch
Anatomy	*Anat*	Anatomie
Archaeology	*Archaeol*	Archäologie
Architecture	*Archit*	Architektur
Astronomy	*Astr*	Astronomie
attributive	*attrib*	attributiv
Austrian	*Aust*	österreichisch
Motor vehicles	*Auto*	Automobil
Aviation	*Aviat*	Luftfahrt
Biology	*Biol*	Biologie
Botany	*Bot*	Botanik
Chemistry	*Chem*	Chemie
collective	*coll*	Kollektivum
Commerce	*Comm*	Handel
conjunction	*conj*	Konjunktion
Cookery	*Culin*	Kochkunst
dative	*dat*	Dativ
definite article	*def art*	bestimmter Artikel
demonstrative	*dem*	Demonstrativ-
dialect	*dial*	Dialekt
Electricity	*Electr*	Elektrizität
something	*etw*	etwas
feminine	*f*	Femininum
figurative	*fig*	figurativ
genitive	*gen*	Genitiv
Geography	*Geog*	Geographie
Geology	*Geol*	Geologie
Geometry	*Geom*	Geometrie
Grammar	*Gram*	Grammatik
Horticulture	*Hort*	Gartenbau
impersonal	*impers*	unpersönlich
indefinite article	*indef art*	unbestimmter Artikel
indefinite pronoun	*indef pron*	unbestimmtes Pronomen
infinitive	*inf*	Infinitiv

inseparable	*insep*	untrennbar
interjection	*int*	Interjektion
invariable	*inv*	unveränderlich
irregular	*irreg*	unregelmäßig
someone	*jd*	jemand
someone	*jdm*	jemandem
someone	*jdn*	jemanden
someone's	*jds*	jemandes
Journalism	*Journ*	Journalismus
Law	*Jur*	Jura
Language	*Lang*	Sprache
literary	*liter*	dichterisch
masculine	*m*	Maskulinum
Mathematics	*Math*	Mathematik
Medicine	*Med*	Medizin
Meteorology	*Meteorol*	Meteorologie
Military	*Mil*	Militär
Mineralogy	*Miner*	Mineralogie
Music	*Mus*	Musik
noun	*n*	Substantiv
Nautical	*Naut*	nautisch
North German	*N Ger*	Norddeutsch
nominative	*nom*	Nominativ
neuter	*nt*	Neutrum
or	*od*	oder
Proprietary term	*P*	Warenzeichen
pejorative	*pej*	abwertend
Photography	*Phot*	Fotografie
Physics	*Phys*	Physik
plural	*pl*	Plural
Politics	*Pol*	Politik
possessive	*poss*	Possessiv-
past participle	*pp*	zweites Partizip
predicative	*pred*	prädikativ
prefix	*pref*	Präfix
preposition	*prep*	Präposition
present	*pres*	Präsens
present participle	*pres p*	erstes Partizip
pronoun	*pron*	Pronomen
Psychology	*Psych*	Psychologie
past tense	*pt*	Präteritum
Railway	*Rail*	Eisenbahn
reflexive	*refl*	reflexiv
regular	*reg*	regelmäßig
relative	*rel*	Relativ-
Religion	*Relig*	Religion

see	*s.*	siehe
School	*Sch*	Schule
separable	*sep*	trennbar
singular	*sg*	Singular
South German	*S Ger*	Süddeutsch
someone	*s.o.*	jemand
something	*sth*	etwas
Technical	*Techn*	Technik
Telephone	*Teleph*	Telefon
Textiles	*Tex*	Textilien
Theatre	*Theat*	Theater
Television	*TV*	Fernsehen
Typography	*Typ*	Typographie
University	*Univ*	Universität
auxiliary verb	*v aux*	Hilfsverb
intransitive verb	*vi*	intransitives Verb
reflexive verb	*vr*	reflexives Verb
transitive verb	*vt*	transitives Verb
vulgar	*vulg*	vulgär
Zoology	*Zool*	Zoologie
familiar	🄸	familiär
slang	✖	Slang
old spelling	*	alte Schreibung

German–English Dictionary

Aa

al *m* -[e]s, -e eel

as *nt* -es carrion; swine

prep (+ *dat*) from ● *adv* off;
weg) away; (*auf Fahrplan*)
eparts; **ab und zu** now and then;
uf und ab up and down

ändern *vt sep* alter;
abwandeln) modify

bbau *m* dismantling; (*Kohlen-*)
ining. **a~en** *vt sep* dismantle;
ine <*Kohle*>

beißen† *vt sep* bite off

beizen *vt sep* strip

berufen† *vt sep* recall

bestellen *vt sep* cancel; **jdn a~**
ut s.o. off

biegen† *vi sep* (*sein*) turn off;
nach] **links a~** turn left

bbildung *f* -, -en illustration

blättern *vi sep* (*sein*) flake off

blend|en *vt/i sep* (*haben*) **[die**
cheinwerfer] a~en dip one's
eadlights. **A~licht** *nt* dipped
eadlights *pl*

brechen† *v sep* ● *vt* break off;
abreißen) demolish ● *vi* (*sein/*
aben) break off

brennen† *v sep* ● *vt* burn off;
niederbrennen) burn down ● *vi*
sein) burn down

bringen† *vt sep* dissuade (**von**
rom)

bbruch *m* demolition; (*Beenden*)
reaking off

buchen *vt sep* debit

bürsten *vt sep* brush down;
entfernen) brush off

danken *vi sep* (*haben*) resign;
Herrscher:> abdicate

decken *vt sep* uncover;
abnehmen) take off; (*zudecken*)
over; **den Tisch a~** clear the
able

dichten *vt sep* seal

abdrehen *vt sep* turn off

Abdruck *m* (*pl* ⁻e) impression.
a~en *vt sep* print

abdrücken *vt/i sep* (*haben*) fire;
sich a~ leave an impression

Abend *m* -s, -e evening; **am A~** in
the evening; **heute A~** this
evening, tonight; **gestern A~**
yesterday evening, last night.
A~brot *nt* supper. **A~essen** *nt*
dinner; (*einfacher*) supper.
A~mahl *nt* (*Relig*) [Holy]
Communion. **a~s** *adv* in the
evening

Abenteuer *nt* -s,- adventure;
(*Liebes-*) affair. **a~lich** *a*
fantastic

aber *conj* but; **oder a~** or else
● *adv* (*wirklich*) really

Aber|glaube *m* superstition.
a~gläubisch *a* superstitious

abfahr|en† *v sep* ● *vi* (*sein*) leave;
<*Auto:*> drive off ● *vt* take away;
(*entlangfahren*) drive along; use
<*Fahrkarte*>; **abgefahrene Reifen**
worn tyres. **A~t** *f* departure;
(*Talfahrt*) descent; (*Piste*) run;
(*Ausfahrt*) exit

Abfall *m* refuse, rubbish; (*auf der*
Straße) litter; (*Industrie-*) waste

abfallen† *vi sep* (*sein*) drop, fall;
(*übrig bleiben*) be left (**für** for);
(*sich neigen*) slope away. **a~d** *a*
sloping

Abfallhaufen *m* rubbish-dump

abfällig *a* disparaging

abfangen† *vt sep* intercept

abfärben *vi sep* (*haben*) <*Farbe:*>
run; <*Stoff:*> not be colour-fast

abfassen *vt sep* draft

abfertigen *vt sep* attend to;
(*zollamtlich*) clear; **jdn kurz a~** !
give s.o. short shrift

abfeuern *vt sep* fire

abfind|en† vt sep pay off; (entschädigen) compensate; **sich a~en mit** come to terms with. **A~ung** f -, -en compensation

abfliegen† vi sep (sein) fly off; (Aviat) take off

abfließen† vi sep (sein) drain or run away

Abflug m (Aviat) departure

Abfluss m drainage; (Öffnung) drain. **A~rohr** nt drain-pipe

abfragen vt sep jdn od jdm Vokabeln a~ test s.o. on vocabulary

Abfuhr f - removal; (fig) rebuff

abführ|en vt sep take or lead away. **A~mittel** nt laxative

abfüllen vt sep auf od in Flaschen a~ bottle

Abgase ntpl exhaust fumes

abgeben† vt sep hand in; (abliefern) deliver; (verkaufen) sell; (zur Aufbewahrung) leave; (Fußball) pass; (ausströmen) give off; (abfeuern) fire; (verlauten lassen) give; cast <Stimme>; **jdm etw a~** give s.o. a share of sth

abgehen† v sep ● vi (sein) leave; (Theat) exit; (sich lösen) come off; (abgezogen werden) be deducted ● vt walk along

abgehetzt a harassed. **abgelegen** a remote. **abgeneigt** a etw (dat) **nicht abgeneigt sein** not be averse to sth. **abgenutzt** a worn.

Abgeordnete(r) m/f deputy; (Pol) Member of Parliament.

abgepackt a pre-packed

abgeschieden a secluded

abgeschlossen a (fig) complete; <Wohnung> self-contained.

abgesehen prep apart (from von). **abgespannt** a exhausted. **abgestanden** a stale. **abgestorben** a dead; <Glied> numb. **abgetragen** a worn. **abgewetzt** a threadbare

abgewinnen† vt sep win (jdm from s.o.); etw (dat) Geschmack a~ get a taste for sth

abgewöhnen vt sep jdm/sich da Rauchen a~ cure s.o. of/ give u smoking

abgießen† vt sep pour off; drai <Gemüse>

Abgott m idol

abgöttisch adv a~ lieben idoliz

abgrenz|en vt sep divide off; (f define. **A~ung** f - demarcation

Abgrund m abyss; (fig) depths

abgucken vt sep 🔲 copy

Abguss m cast

abhacken vt sep chop off

abhaken vt sep tick off

abhalten† vt sep keep off; (hindern) keep, prevent (von from); (veranstalten) hold

abhanden adv a~ kommen get lost

Abhandlung f treatise

Abhang m slope

abhängen¹ vt sep (reg) take down; (abkuppeln) uncouple

abhäng|en² vi sep (haben) depend (von on). **a~ig** a dependent (von on). **A~igkeit** dependence

abhärten vt sep toughen up

abheben† v sep ● vt take off; (vom Konto) withdraw; **sich a~** stand out (gegen against) ● vi (haben)·(Cards) cut [the cards] (Aviat) take off; <Rakete:> lift

abheften vt sep file

Abhilfe f remedy

abholen vt sep collect

abhör|en vt sep listen to; (überwachen) tap; jdn od jdm Vokabeln a~en test s.o. on vocabulary. **A~gerät** nt buggir device

Abitur nt -s ≈ A levels pl

abkaufen vt sep buy (dat from)

abklingen† vi sep (sein) die aw (nachlassen) subside

abkochen vt sep boil

kommen† vi sep (sein) a~ von tray from; (aufgeben) give up. ~ nt -s,- agreement

kömmling m -s, -e descendant

kratzen vt sep scrape off

kühlen vt/i sep (sein) cool; sich ~ cool [down]

kunft f - origin

kuppeln vt sep uncouple

kürz|en vt sep shorten; abbreviate <Wort>. A~ung f short cut; (Wort) abbreviation

laden vt sep unload

lage f shelf; (für Akten) tray

lager|n vt sep deposit. A~ung f -en deposit

lassen vt sep drain [off]; let ff <Dampf>

lauf m drain; (Verlauf) course; Ende) end; (einer Frist) expiry. ~en† v sep ● vi (sein) run or rain off; (verlaufen) go off; enden) expire; <Zeit:> run out; Uhrwerk:> run down ● vi walk long; (absuchen) scour (nach r)

leg|en v sep ● vt put down; iscard <Karte>; (abheften) file; uszuziehen) take off; sit, take Prüfung>; abgelegte Kleidung ast-offs pl ● vi (haben) take off ne's coat; (Naut) cast off. A~er -s,- (Bot) cutting; (Schössling) hoot

lehn|en vt sep refuse; missbilligen) reject. A~ung f -, en refusal; rejection

leit|en vt sep divert; sich a~en e derived (von/aus from). ~ung f derivation; (Wort) erivative

lenk|en vt sep deflect; divert Aufmerksamkeit>. A~ung f -, -en istraction

lesen† vt sep read

licht|en vt sep photocopy. ~ung f photocopy

liefern vt sep deliver

ablös|en vt sep detach; (abwechseln) relieve; sich a~en come off; (sich abwechseln) take turns. **A~ung** f relief

abmach|en vt sep remove; (ausmachen) arrange; (vereinbaren) agree. **A~ung** f -, -en agreement

abmager|n vi sep (sein) lose weight. **A~ungskur** f slimming diet

abmelden vt sep cancel; (im Hotel) check out

abmessen† vt sep measure

abmühen (sich) vr sep struggle

Abnäher m -s,- dart

abnehm|en† v sep ● vt take off, remove; pick up <Hörer>; jdm etw a~en take/(kaufen) buy sth from s.o. ● vi (haben) decrease; (nachlassen) decline; <Person:> lose weight; <Mond:> wane. **A~er** m -s,- buyer

Abneigung f dislike (gegen of)

abnorm a abnormal

abnutz|en vt sep wear out. **A~ung** f - wear [and tear]

Abon|nement /abonə'mã:/ nt -s, -s subscription. **A~nent** m -en, -en subscriber. **a~nieren** vt take out a subscription to

Abordnung f -, -en deputation

abpassen vt sep wait for; gut a~ time well

abraten† vi sep (haben) jdm von etw a~ advise s.o. against sth

abräumen vt/i (haben) clear away

abrechn|en v sep ● vt deduct ● vi (haben) settle up. **A~ung** f settlement; (Rechnung) account

Abreise f departure. **a~n** vi sep (sein) leave

abreißen† v sep ● vt tear off; (demolieren) pull down ● vi (sein) come off

abrichten vt sep train

Abriss m demolition; (Übersicht) summary

abrufen† *vt sep* call away; (*Computer*) retrieve

abrunden *vt sep* round off

abrüst|en *vi sep* (*haben*) disarm. **A~ung** *f* disarmament

abrutschen *vi sep* (*sein*) slip

Absage *f* -, -n cancellation; (*Ablehnung*) refusal. **a~n** *v sep* ● *vt* cancel ● *vi* (*haben*) [jdm] **a~n** cancel an appointment [with s.o.]; (*auf Einladung*) refuse [s.o.'s invitation]

Absatz *m* heel; (*Abschnitt*) paragraph; (*Verkauf*) sale

abschaffen *vt sep* abolish; get rid of <*Auto, Hund*>

abschalten *vt/i sep* (*haben*) switch off

Abscheu *m* - revulsion

abscheulich *a* revolting

abschicken *vt sep* send off

Abschied *m* -[e]s, -e farewell; (*Trennung*) parting; **A~ nehmen** say goodbye (**von** to)

abschießen† *vt sep* shoot down; (*abfeuern*) fire; launch <*Rakete*>

abschirmen *vt sep* shield

abschlagen† *vt sep* knock off; (*verweigern*) refuse

Abschlepp|dienst *m* breakdown service. **a~en** *vt sep* tow away. **A~seil** *nt* tow-rope

abschließen† *v sep* ● *vt* lock; (*beenden, abmachen*) conclude; make <*Wette*>; balance <*Bücher*> ● *vi* (*haben*) lock up; (*enden*) end. **a~d** *adv* in conclusion

Abschluss *m* conclusion. **A~zeugnis** *nt* diploma

abschmecken *vt sep* season

abschmieren *vt sep* lubricate

abschneiden† *v sep* ● *vt* cut off ● *vi* (*haben*) **gut/schlecht a~** do well/badly

Abschnitt *m* section; (*Stadium*) stage; (*Absatz*) paragraph

abschöpfen *vt sep* skim off

abschrauben *vt sep* unscrew

abschreck|en *vt sep* deter; (*Culin*) put in cold water <*Ei*>. **a~end** *a* repulsive. **A~ungsmittel** *nt* deterrent

abschreib|en† *v sep* ● *vt* copy; (*Comm & fig*) write off ● *vi* (*haben*) copy. **A~ung** *f* (*Comm*) depreciation

Abschrift *f* copy

Abschuss *m* shooting down; (*Abfeuern*) firing; (*Raketen-*) launch

abschüssig *a* sloping; (*steil*) steep

abschwellen† *vi sep* (*sein*) go down

abseh|bar *a* in **a~barer Zeit** in the foreseeable future. **a~en**† *vt/i sep* (*haben*) copy; (*voraussehen*) foresee; **a~en von** disregard; (*aufgeben*) refrain from

abseits *adv* apart; (*Sport*) offside ● *prep* (+ *gen*) away from. **A~** - (*Sport*) offside

absend|en† *vt sep* send off. **A~** *m* sender

absetzen *v sep* ● *vt* put *or* set down; (*ablagern*) deposit; (*abnehmen*) take off; (*abbrechen* stop; (*entlassen*) dismiss; (*verkaufen*) sell; (*abziehen*) deduct ● *vi* (*haben*) pause

Absicht *f* -, -en intention; **mit A~** intentionally, on purpose

absichtlich *a* intentional

absitzen† *v sep* ● *vi* (*sein*) dismount ● *vt* 🇮 serve <*Strafe*>

absolut *a* absolute

absolvieren *vt* complete; (*bestehen*) pass

absonder|n *vt sep* separate; (*ausscheiden*) secrete. **A~ung** *f* -en secretion

absorbieren *vt* absorb

abspeisen *vt sep* fob off (**mit** with)

absperr|en *vt sep* cordon off; (*abstellen*) turn off; (*SGer*) lock **A~ung** *f* -, -en barrier

spielen *vt sep* play; (*Fußball*)
ass; **sich a~** take place
sprache *f* agreement
sprechen† *vt sep* arrange; **sich
~** agree
springen† *vi sep* (*sein*) jump
ff; (*mit Fallschirm*) parachute;
bgehen) come off
sprung *m* jump
spülen *vt sep* rinse
stamm|en *vi sep* (*haben*) be
escended (**von** from). **A~ung** *f* -
escent
stand *m* distance; (*zeitlich*)
aterval; **A~ halten** keep one's
istance
statten *vt sep* **jdm einen Besuch
~** pay s.o. a visit
stecher *m -s,-* detour
stehen† *vi sep* (*haben*) stick
ut
steigen† *vi sep* (*sein*)
ismount; (*niedersteigen*)
escend; (*Fußball*) be relegated
stell|en *vt sep* put down;
agern) store; (*parken*) park;
bschalten) turn off. **A~gleis** *nt*
ding. **A~raum** *m* box-room
sterben† *vi sep* (*sein*) die;
efühllos werden) go numb
stieg *m -[e]s, -e* descent;
ʃuβball) relegation
stimm|en *v sep* ●*vi* (*haben*)
ote (**über** + *acc* on) ●*vt*
oordinate (**auf** + *acc* with).
~ung *f* vote
stinenzler *m -s, -* teetotaller
stoßen† *vt sep* knock off;
erkaufen) sell; (*fig: ekeln*) repel.
~d *a* repulsive
streiten† *vt sep* deny
strich *m* (*Med*) smear
stufen *vt sep* grade
sturz *m* fall; (*Aviat*) crash
stürzen *vi sep* (*sein*) fall;
Aviat) crash
suchen *vt sep* search
surd *a* absurd
szess *m -es, -e* abscess

Abt *m -[e]s,-̈e* abbot
abtasten *vt sep* feel; (*Techn*) scan
abtauen *vt/i sep* (*sein*) thaw;
(*entfrosten*) defrost
Abtei *f -, -en* abbey
Abteil *nt* compartment
Abteilung *f -, -en* section; (*Admin,
Comm*) department
abtragen† *vt sep* clear; (*einebnen*)
level; (*abnutzen*) wear out
abträglich *a* detrimental (*dat* to)
abtreib|en† *vt sep* (*Naut*) drive
off course; **ein Kind a~en lassen**
have an abortion. **A~ung** *f -, -en*
abortion
abtrennen *vt sep* detach;
(*abteilen*) divide off
Abtreter *m -s,-* doormat
abtrocknen *vt/i sep* (*haben*) dry;
sich a~ dry oneself
abtropfen *vi sep* (*sein*) drain
abtun† *vt sep* (*fig*) dismiss
abwägen† *vt sep* (*fig*) weigh
abwandeln *vt sep* modify
abwarten *v sep* ●*vt* wait for ●*vi*
(*haben*) wait [and see]
abwärts *adv* down[wards]
Abwasch *m -[e]s* washing-up;
(*Geschirr*) dirty dishes *pl.* **a~en**†
v sep ●*vt* wash; wash up
<*Geschirr*>; (*entfernen*) wash off
●*vi* (*haben*) wash up. **A~lappen**
m dishcloth
Abwasser *nt -s,-̈* sewage.
A~kanal *m* sewer
abwechseln *vi/r sep* (*haben*)
[**sich**] **a~** alternate; <*Personen:*>
take turns. **a~d** *a* alternate
Abwechslung *f -, -en* change; **zur
A~** for a change
abwegig *a* absurd
Abwehr *f -* defence; (*Widerstand*)
resistance; (*Pol*) counter-
espionage. **a~en** *vt sep* ward off.
A~system *nt* immune system
abweich|en† *vi sep* (*sein*)
deviate/(*von Regel*) depart (**von**
from); (*sich unterscheiden*) differ
(**von** from). **a~end** *a* divergent;

(*verschieden*) different. **A~ung** *f* -, -en deviation

abweis|en† *vt sep* turn down; turn away <*Person*>. **a~end** *a* unfriendly. **A~ung** *f* rejection

abwenden† *vt sep* turn away; (*verhindern*) avert

abwerfen† *vt sep* throw off; throw <*Reiter*>; (*Aviat*) drop; (*Kartenspiel*) discard; shed <*Haut, Blätter*>; yield <*Gewinn*>

abwert|en *vt sep* devalue. **A~ung** *f* -, -en devaluation

Abwesenheit *f* - absence; absent-mindedness

abwickeln *vt sep* unwind; (*erledigen*) settle

abwischen *vt sep* wipe

abzahlen *vt sep* pay off

abzählen *vt sep* count

Abzahlung *f* instalment

Abzeichen *nt* badge

abzeichnen *vt sep* copy

Abzieh|bild *nt* transfer. **a~en†** *v sep* ● *vt* pull off; take off <*Laken*>; strip <*Bett*>; (*häuten*) skin; (*Phot*) print; run off <*Kopien*>; (*zurückziehen*) withdraw; (*abrechnen*) deduct ● *vi* (*sein*) go away, <*Rauch:*> escape

Abzug *m* withdrawal; (*Abrechnung*) deduction; (*Phot*) print (*Korrektur-*) proof; (*am Gewehr*) trigger; (*A~söffnung*) vent; **A~e** *pl* deductions

abzüglich *prep* (+ *gen*) less

Abzugshaube *f* [cooker] hood

abzweig|en *v sep* ● *vi* (*sein*) branch off ● *vt* divert. **A~ung** *f* -, -en junction; (*Gabelung*) fork

ach *int* oh; **a~ je!** oh dear! **a~ so** I see

Achse *f* -, -n axis; (*Rad-*) axle

Achsel *f* -, -n shoulder. **A~höhle** *f* armpit. **A~zucken** *nt* -s shrug

acht *inv a*, **A~** *f* -, -en eight

Acht *f* **A~ geben** be careful; **A~ geben auf** (+ *acc*) look after; **außer**

A~ lassen disregard; **sich in A~ nehmen** be careful

acht|e(r,s) *a* eighth. **a~eckig** *a* octagonal. **A~el** *nt* -s,- eighth.

achten *vt* respect ● *vi* (*haben*) **a~ auf** (+ *acc*) pay attention to; (*aufpassen*) look after

Achterbahn *f* roller-coaster

achtlos *a* careless

achtsam *a* careful

Achtung *f* - respect (**vor** + *dat* for); **A~!** look out!

acht|zehn *inv a* eighteen. **a~zehnte(r,s)** *a* eighteenth. **a~zig** *a inv* eighty. **a~zigste(r,s)** *a* eightieth

Acker *m* -s,- field. **A~bau** *m* agriculture. **A~land** *nt* arable land

addieren *vt/i* (*haben*) add

Addition /-'tsio:n/ *f* -, -en addition

ade *int* goodbye

Adel *m* -s nobility

Ader *f* -, -n vein

Adjektiv *nt* -s, -e adjective

Adler *m* -s,- eagle

adlig *a* noble. **A~e(r)** *m* nobleman

Administration /-'tsio:n/ *f* - administration

Admiral *m* -s,-e admiral

adop|tieren *vt* adopt. **A~tion** /-'tsio:n/ *f* -, -en adoption. **A~tiveltern** *pl* adoptive parents. **A~tivkind** *nt* adopted child

Adrenalin *nt* -s adrenalin

Adres|se *f* -, -n address. **a~sieren** *vt* address

Adria *f* - Adriatic

Adverb *nt* -s, -ien /-ia:n/ adverb

Affäre *f* -, -n affair

Affe *m* -n, -n monkey; (*Menschen-*) ape

affektiert *a* affected

affig *a* affected; (*eitel*) vain

Afrika *nt* -s Africa

Afrikan|er(in) *m* -s,- (*f* -, -nen) African. **a~isch** *a* African

After *m* -s,- anus

gen|t(in) *m* -en, -en (*f* -, -nen)
gent. **A~tur** *f* -, -en agency
ggres|sion *f* -, -en aggression.
~siv *a* aggressive
gnostiker *m* -s,- agnostic
gypt|en /ɛˈɡʏptən/ *nt* -s Egypt.
~er(in) *m* -s,- (*f* -, -nen)
;gyptian. **ä~isch** *a* Egyptian
hneln *vi* (*haben*) (+ *dat*)
esemble; **sich ä~** be alike
hnen *vt* have a presentiment of;
vermuten) suspect
hnen *mpl* ancestors.
~forschung *f* genealogy
hnlich *a* similar; **jdm s~ sehen**
esemble s.o. **Ä~keit** *f* -, -en
;imilarity; resemblance
hnung *f* -, -en premonition;
Vermutung) idea, hunch
horn *m* -s, -e maple
hre *f* -, -n ear [of corn]
ids /eːt͡s/ *nt* - Aids
kademie *f* -, -n academy
kadem|iker(in) *m* -s,- (*f* -, -nen)
:niversity graduate. **a~isch** *a*
:cademic
kklimatisieren (sich) *vr* become
:cclimatized
kkord *m* -[e]s, -e (*Mus*) chord.
~arbeit *f* piece-work
kkordeon *nt* -s, -s accordion
kkumul|ator *m* -s, -en /-ˈtoːrən/
Electr) accumulator
kkusativ *m* -s, -e accusative
~objekt *nt* direct object
krobat|(in) *m* -en, -en (*f* -, -nen)
:crobat. **a~isch** *a* acrobatic
kt *m* -[e]s, -e act; (*Kunst*) nude
kte *f* -, -n file; **A~n** documents.
~ntasche *f* briefcase
ktie /ˈaktsːiə/ *f* -, -n (*Comm*)
:hare. **A~ngesellschaft** *f* joint-
:tock company
ktion /akˈtsːioːn/ *f* -, -en action.
~är *m* -s, -e shareholder
ktiv *a* active
ktuell *a* topical; (*gegenwärtig*)
:urrent
kupunktur *f* - acupuncture

Akustik *f* - acoustics *pl*
akut *a* acute
Akzent *m* -[e]s, -e accent
akzept|abel *a* acceptable.
a~ieren *vt* accept
Alarm *m* -s alarm; (*Mil*) alert.
a~ieren *vt* alert; (*beunruhigen*)
alarm
Albdruck *m* nightmare
albern *a* silly ● *vi* (*haben*) play
the fool
Albtraum *m* nightmare
Album *nt* -s, -ben album
Algebra *f* - algebra
Algen *fpl* algae
Algerien /-iən/ *nt* -s Algeria
Alibi *nt* -s, -s alibi
Alimente *pl* maintenance *sg*
Alkohol *m* -s alcohol. **a~frei** *a*
non-alcoholic
Alkohol|iker(in) *m* -s,- (*f* -, -nen)
alcoholic. **a~isch** *a* alcoholic
all *inv pron* all das/mein Geld all
the/my money; **all dies** all this
All *nt* -s universe
alle *pred a* finished
all|e(r,s) *pron* all; (*jeder*) every;
a~es everything, all; (*alle Leute*)
everyone; **a~e** *pl* all; **a~es Geld**
all the money; **a~e beide** both [of
them/us]; **a~e Tage** every day;
a~e drei Jahre every three years;
ohne a~en Grund without any
reason; **vor a~em** above all; **a~es
in a~em** all in all; **a~es
aussteigen!** all change!
Allee *f* -, -n avenue
allein *adv* alone; (*nur*) only; **a~
stehend** single; **a~ der Gedanke**
the mere thought; **von a~[e]** of
its/<*Person*>'s one's own accord;
(*automatisch*) automatically
● *conj* but. **A~erziehende(r)** *m/f*
single parent. **a~ig** *a* sole.
A~stehende *pl* single people
allemal *adv* every time; (*gewiss*)
certainly
allenfalls *adv* at most; (*eventuell*)
possibly

aller|beste(r,s) a very best; **am a~besten** best of all. **a~dings** adv indeed; (zwar) admittedly.

a~erste(r,s) a very first

Allergie f -, -n allergy

allergisch a allergic (**gegen** to)

Aller|heiligen nt -s All Saints Day. **a~höchstens** adv at the very most. **a~lei** inv a all sorts of ● pron all sorts of things.

a~letzte(r,s) a very last.

a~liebste(r,s) a favourite ● adv **am a~liebsten** for preference; **am a~liebsten haben** like best of all.

a~meiste(r,s) a most ● adv **am a~meisten** most of all. **A~seelen** nt -s All Souls Day.

a~wenigste(r,s) a very least ● adv **am a~wenigsten** least of all

allgemein a general, adv -ly; **im A~en (a~en)** in general. **A~heit** f - community; (Öffentlichkeit) general public

Allianz f -, -en alliance

Alligator m -s, -en /-ˈtoːrən/ alligator

alliiert a allied; **die A~en** pl the Allies

all|jährlich a annual. **a~mählich** a gradual

Alltag m working day; **der A~** (fig) everyday life

alltäglich a daily; (gewöhnlich) everyday; <Mensch> ordinary

alltags adv on weekdays

allzu adv [far] too; **a~ oft** all too often; **a~ vorsichtig** over-cautious

Alm f -, -en alpine pasture

Almosen ntpl alms

Alpdruck m = Albdruck

Alpen pl Alps

Alphabet nt -[e]s, -e alphabet. **a~isch** a alphabetical, adv -ly

Alptraum m = Albtraum

als conj as; (zeitlich) when; (mit Komparativ) than; **nichts als** nothing but; **als ob** as if or though

also adv & conj so; **a~ gut** all right then; **na a~!** there you are

alt a old; (gebraucht) second-hand; (ehemalig) former; **alt werden** grow old

Alt m -s (Mus) contralto

Altar m -s, -̈e altar

Alt|e(r) m/f old man/woman; **die A~en** old people. **A~eisen** nt scrap iron. **A~enheim** nt old people's home

Alter nt -s,- age; (Bejahrtheit) old age; **im A~ von** at the age of

älter a older; **mein ä~er Bruder** m elder brother

altern vi (sein) age

Alternative f -, -n alternative

Alters|grenze f age limit. **A~heim** nt old people's home. **A~rente** f old-age pension. **a~schwach** a old and infirm

Alter|tum nt -s,-̈er antiquity. **a~tümlich** a old; (altmodisch) old-fashioned

altklug a precocious

alt|modisch a old-fashioned. **A~papier** nt waste paper. **A~warenhändler** m second-han dealer

Alufolie f [aluminium] foil

Aluminium nt -s aluminium, (Amer) aluminum

am prep = an dem; **am Montag** on Monday; **am Morgen** in the morning; **am besten** [the] best

Amateur /-ˈtøːɐ/ m -s, -e amateur

Ambition /-ˈtsi̯oːn/ f -, -en ambition

Amboss m -es, -e anvil

ambulan|t a out-patient ... ● ad **a~t behandeln** treat as an out-patient. **A~z** f -, -en out-patients department

Ameise f -, -n ant

amen int, **A~** nt -s amen

Amerika nt -s America

Amerikan|er(in) m -s,- (f -, -nen) American. **a~isch** a American

Ammoniak nt -s ammonia

Amnestie *f* -, -n amnesty
amoralisch *a* amoral
Ampel *f* -, -n traffic lights *pl*
Amphitheater *nt* amphitheatre
Amput|ation /-'tsi̯o:n/ *f* -, -en
amputation. **a~ieren** *vt* amputate
Amsel *f* -, -n blackbird
Amt *nt* -[e]s, ̈er office; (*Aufgabe*)
task; (*Teleph*) exchange. **a~lich** *a*
official. **A~szeichen** *nt* dialling
tone
Amulett *nt* -[e]s, -e [lucky] charm
amüs|ant *a* amusing. **a~ieren** *vt*
amuse; **sich a~ieren** be amused
(**über** + *acc* at); (*sich vergnügen*)
enjoy oneself

an

preposition (+ *dative*)
! Note that **an** plus **dem** can
  become **am**
⋯▶ (*räumlich*) on; (*Gebäude, Ort*)
at. **an der Wand** on the wall.
Frankfurt an der Oder Frankfurt
on [the] Oder. **an der Ecke** at the
corner. **am Bahnhof** at the
station. **an ... vorbei** past
⋯▶ (*zeitlich*) on. **am Montag** on
Monday. **an jedem Sonntag** every
Sunday. **am 24. Mai** on May 24th
⋯▶ (*sonstige Verwendungen*)
arm/reich an Vitaminen low/rich
in vitamins. **jdn an etw erkennen**
recognize s.o. by sth. **an etw**
leiden suffer from sth. **an einer**
Krankheit sterben die of a
disease. **an [und für] sich** actually
preposition (+ *accusative*)
! Note that **an** plus **das** can
  become **ans**
⋯▶ to. **schicke es an deinen Bruder**
send it to your brother. **er ging**
ans Fenster he went to the
window
⋯▶ (*auf, gegen*) on. **etw an die**
Wand hängen to hang sth on the
wall. **lehne es an den Baum** lean
it on *or* against the tree

⋯▶ (*sonstige Verwendungen*) an
etw/jdn glauben believe in sth/
s.o. **an etw denken** think of sth.
sich an etw erinnern remember
sth
● *adverb*
⋯▶ (*auf Fahrplan*) Köln an: 9.15
arriving Cologne 09.15
⋯▶ (*angeschaltet*) on. **die**
Waschmaschine/der Fernseher/das
Licht/das Gas ist an the washing
machine/television/light/gas is
on
⋯▶ (*ungefähr*) around; about. **an**
[die] 20 000 DM around *or* about
20,000 DM
⋯▶ (*in die Zukunft*) von heute an
from today (onwards)

analog *a* analogous; (*Computer*)
analog. **A~ie** *f* -, -n analogy
Analphabet *m* -en, -en illiterate
person. **A~entum** *nt* -s illiteracy
Analy|se *f* -, -n analysis. **a~sieren**
vt analyse. **A~tiker** *m* -s,- analyst.
a~tisch *a* analytical
Anämie *f* - anaemia
Ananas *f* -, -[se] pineapple
Anatomie *f* - anatomy
Anbau *m* cultivation; (*Gebäude*)
extension. **a~en** *vt sep* build on;
(*anpflanzen*) cultivate, grow
anbei *adv* enclosed
anbeißen† *v sep* ● *vt* take a bite
of ● *vi* (*haben*) <*Fisch:*> bite
anbeten *vt sep* worship
Anbetracht *m* in A~ (+ *gen*) in
view of
anbieten† *vt sep* offer; **sich a~**
offer (**zu** to)
anbinden† *vt sep* tie up
Anblick *m* sight. **a~en** *vt sep* look
at
anbrechen† *v sep* ● *vt* start on;
break into <*Vorräte*> ● *vi* (*sein*)
begin; <*Tag:*> break; <*Nacht:*>
fall
anbrennen† *v sep* ● *vt* light ● *vi*
(*sein*) burn

anbringen† *vt sep* bring [along]; (*befestigen*) fix

Anbruch *m* (*fig*) dawn; **bei A~ des Tages/der Nacht** at daybreak/nightfall

Andacht *f* -, -en reverence; (*Gottesdienst*) prayers *pl*

andächtig *a* reverent; (*fig*) rapt

andauern *vi sep* (*haben*) last; (*anhalten*) continue. **a~d** *a* persistent; (*ständig*) constant

Andenken *nt* -s,- memory; (*Souvenir*) souvenir

ander|e(r,s) *a* other; (*verschieden*) different; (*nächste*) next; **ein a~er, eine a~e** another ● *pron* **der a~e/die a~en** the other/others; **ein a~er** another [one]; (*Person*) someone else; **kein a~er** no one else; **einer nach dem a~en** one after the other; **alles a~e/nichts a~es** everything/nothing else; **unter a~em** among other things. **a~enfalls** *adv* otherwise. **a~erseits** *adv* on the other hand. **a~mal** *adv* **ein a~mal** another time

ändern *vt* alter; (*wechseln*) change; **sich ä~** change

andernfalls *adv* otherwise

anders *pred a* different; **a~ werden** change ● *adv* differently; (*riechen, schmecken*) different; (*sonst*) else; **jemand a~** someone else

anderseits *adv* on the other hand

andersherum *adv* the other way round

anderthalb *inv a* one and a half; **a~ Stunden** an hour and a half

Änderung *f* -, -en alteration; (*Wechsel*) change

andeut|en *vt sep* indicate; (*anspielen*) hint at. **A~ung** *f* -, -en indication; hint

Andrang *m* rush (*nach* for); (*Gedränge*) crush

androhen *vt sep* **jdm etw a~** threaten s.o. with sth

aneignen *vt sep* **sich** (*dat*) **a~** appropriate; (*lernen*) learn

aneinander *adv & pref* together; (*denken*) of one another; **a~ vorbei** past one another; **a~ geraten** quarrel

Anekdote *f* -, -n anecdote

anerkannt *a* acknowledged

anerkenn|en† *vt sep* acknowledge, recognize; (*würdigen*) appreciate. **a~end** *a* approving. **A~ung** *f* - acknowledgement, recognition; appreciation

anfahren† *v sep* ● *vt* deliver; (*streifen*) hit ● *vi* (*sein*) start

Anfall *m* fit, attack. **a~en**† *v sep* ● *vt* attack ● *vi* (*sein*) arise; (*Zinsen:*) accrue

anfällig *a* susceptible (**für** to); (*zart*) delicate

Anfang *m* -s,¨e beginning, start; **z** *od* **am A~** at the beginning; (*anfangs*) at first. **a~en**† *vt/i sep* (*haben*) begin, start; (*tun*) do

Anfänger(in) *m* -s,- (*f* -, -nen) beginner

anfangs *adv* at first. **A~buchstabe** *m* initial letter. **A~gehalt** *nt* starting salary

anfassen *vt sep* touch; (*behandeln*) treat; tackle (*Arbeit*); **sich a~** hold hands

anfechten† *vt sep* contest

anfertigen *vt sep* make

anfeuchten *vt sep* moisten

anflehen *vt sep* implore, beg

Anflug *m* (*Avia*) approach

anforder|n *vt sep* demand; (*Comm*) order. **A~ung** *f* demand

Anfrage *f* enquiry. **a~n** *vi sep* (*haben*) enquire, ask

anfreunden (sich) *vr sep* make friends (**mit** with)

anfügen *vt sep* add

anfühlen *vt sep* feel; **sich weich a~** feel soft

anführ|en *vt sep* lead; (*zitieren*) quote; (*angeben*) give. **A~er** *m* eader. **A~ungszeichen** *ntpl* quotation marks

ngabe *f* statement; (*Anweisung*) instruction; (*Tennis*) service; *ähere* A~n particulars

ngeb|en† *v sep* ● *vt* state; give ⟨*Namen, Grund*⟩; (*anzeigen*) indicate; set ⟨*Tempo*⟩ ● *vi* (*haben*) (*Tennis*) serve; (🗉 *rotzen*) show off. **A~er(in)** *m* -s,-*f* -, -nen) 🗉 show-off. **A~erei** *f* - 🗉 showing-off

ngeblich *a* alleged

ngeboren *a* innate; (*Med*) congenital

ngebot *nt* offer; (*Auswahl*) range; A~ und Nachfrage supply and demand

ngebracht *a* appropriate

ngeheiratet *a* ⟨*Onkel, Tante*⟩ by marriage

ngeheitert *a* 🗉 tipsy

ngehen† *v sep* ● *vi* (*sein*) begin, start; ⟨*Licht, Radio:*⟩ come on; (*anwachsen*) take root; a~ gegen ight ● *vt* attack; tackle ⟨*Arbeit*⟩; (*bitten*) ask (um for); (*betreffen*) concern

ngehör|en *vi sep* (*haben*) (+ *dat*) belong to. **A~ige(r)** *m/f* relative

ngeklagte(r) *m/f* accused

ngel *f* -, -n fishing-rod; (*Tür-*) hinge

ngelegenheit *f* matter

ngel|haken *m* fish-hook. **a~n** *vi* (*haben*) fish (nach for); a~n gehen go fishing ● *vt* (*fangen*) catch. **A~rute** *f* fishing-rod

ngelsächsisch *a* Anglo-Saxon

ngemessen *a* commensurate (*dat* with); (*passend*) appropriate

ngenehm *a* pleasant; (*bei Vorstellung*) a~! delighted to meet you!

ngeregt *a* animated

ngesehen *a* respected; ⟨*Firma*⟩ reputable

ngesichts *prep* (+ *gen*) in view of

angespannt *a* intent; ⟨*Lage*⟩ tense

Angestellte(r) *m/f* employee

angewandt *a* applied

angewiesen *a* dependent (auf + *acc* on); auf sich selbst a~ on one's own

angewöhnen *vt sep* jdm etw a~ get s.o. used to sth; sich (*dat*) etw a~ get into the habit of doing sth

Angewohnheit *f* habit

Angina *f* - tonsillitis

angleichen† *vt sep* adjust (*dat* to)

anglikanisch *a* Anglican

Anglistik *f* - English [language and literature]

Angorakatze *f* Persian cat

angreif|en† *vt sep* attack; tackle ⟨*Arbeit*⟩; (*schädigen*) damage. **A~er** *m* -s,- attacker; (*Pol*) aggressor

angrenzen *vi sep* (*haben*) adjoin (an etw *acc* sth). a~d *a* adjoining

Angriff *m* attack; in A~ nehmen tackle. **a~slustig** *a* aggressive

Angst *f* -,-̈e fear; (*Psych*) anxiety; (*Sorge*) worry (um about); A~ haben be afraid (vor + *dat* of); (*sich sorgen*) be worried (um about); jdm A~ machen frighten s.o.

ängstigen *vt* frighten; (*Sorge machen*) worry; sich ä~ be frightened; be worried (um about)

ängstlich *a* nervous; (*scheu*) timid; (*verängstigt*) frightened, scared; (*besorgt*) anxious

angucken *vt sep* 🗉 look at

angurten (sich) *vr sep* fasten one's seat-belt

anhaben† *vt sep* have on; er/es kann mir nichts a~ (*fig*) he/it cannot hurt me

anhalt|en† *v sep* ● *vt* stop; hold ⟨*Atem*⟩; jdn zur Arbeit a~en urge s.o. to work ● *vi* (*haben*) stop; (*andauern*) continue. **a~end** *a* persistent. **A~er(in)** *m* -s,- (*f* -,

-nen hitchhiker; **per A~er fahren** hitchhike. **A~spunkt** *m* clue

anhand *prep* (+ *gen*) with the aid of

Anhang *m* appendix

anhängen[1] *vt sep* (*reg*) hang up; (*befestigen*) attach

anhäng|en[2]† *vi* (*haben*) be a follower of. **A~er** *m* **-s,-** follower; (*Auto*) trailer; (*Schild*) [tie-on] label; (*Schmuck*) pendant. **A~erin** *f* **-, -nen** follower. **a~lich** *a* affectionate

anhäufen *vt sep* pile up

Anhieb *m* **auf A~** straight away

Anhöhe *f* hill

anhören *vt sep* listen to; **sich gut a~** sound good

animieren *vt* encourage (**zu** to)

Anis *m* **-es** aniseed

Anker *m* **-s,-** anchor; **vor A~ gehen** drop anchor. **a~n** *vi* (*haben*) anchor; (*liegen*) be anchored

anketten *vt sep* chain up

Anklage *f* accusation; (*Jur*) charge; (*Ankläger*) prosecution. **A~bank** *f* dock. **a~n** *vt sep* accuse (*gen* of); (*Jur*) charge (*gen* with)

Ankläger *m* accuser; (*Jur*) prosecutor

anklammern *vt sep* clip on; **sich a~** cling (**an** + *acc* to)

ankleben *v sep* ●*vt* stick on ●*vi* (*sein*) stick (**an** + *dat* to)

anklopfen *vi sep* (*haben*) knock

anknipsen *vt sep* 🔲 switch on

ankommen† *vi sep* (*sein*) arrive; (*sich nähern*) approach; **gut a~** arrive safely; (*fig*) go down well (**bei** with); **nicht a~ gegen** (*fig*) be no match for; **a~ auf** (+ *acc*) depend on; **das kommt darauf an it** [all] depends

ankreuzen *vt sep* mark with a cross

ankündig|en *vt sep* announce. **A~ung** *f* announcement

Ankunft *f* **-** arrival

ankurbeln *vt sep* (*fig*) boost

anlächeln *vt sep* smile at

anlachen *vt sep* smile at

Anlage *f* **-, -n** installation; (*Industrie-*) plant; (*Komplex*) complex; (*Geld-*) investment; (*Plan*) layout; (*Beilage*) enclosure; (*Veranlagung*) aptitude; (*Neigung*) predisposition; **[öffentliche] A~n** [public] gardens; **als A~** enclose

Anlass *m* **-es,-̈e** reason; (*Gelegenheit*) occasion; **A~ gebe** **zu** give cause for

anlass|en† *vt sep* (*Auto*) start; 🔲 leave on <*Licht*>; keep on <*Mantel*>. **A~er** *m* **-s,-** starter

anlässlich *prep* (+ *gen*) on the occasion of

Anlauf *m* (*Sport*) run-up; (*fig*) attempt. **a~en**† *v sep* ●*vi* (*sein*) start; (*beschlagen*) mist up; <*Metall:*> tarnish; **rot a~en** blush ●*vt* (*Naut*) call at

anlegen *v sep* ●*vt* put (**an** + *acc* against); put on <*Kleidung, Verband*>; lay back <*Ohren*>; ai <*Gewehr*>; (*investieren*) invest; (*ausgeben*) spend (**für** on); draw up <*Liste*>; **es darauf a~** (*fig*) air (**zu** to) ●*vi* (*haben*) <*Schiff:*> moor; **a~ auf** (+ *acc*) aim at

anlehnen *vt sep* lean (**an** + *acc* against); **sich a~** lean (**an** + *acc* on)

Anleihe *f* **-, -n** loan

anleit|en *vt sep* instruct. **A~ung** *f* instructions *pl*

anlernen *vt sep* train

Anliegen *nt* **-s,-** request; (*Wunsch* desire

anlieg|en† *vi sep* (*haben*) **[eng] a~en** fit closely; **[eng] a~end** close-fitting. **A~er** *mpl* resident. **'A~er frei'** 'access for residents only'

anlügen† *vt sep* lie to

nmachen vt sep Ⓘ fix; (anschalten) turn on; dress <Salat>

nmalen vt sep paint

nmarsch m (Mil) approach

nmeld|en vt sep announce; (Admin) register; **sich a~en** say that one is coming; (Admin) register; (Sch) enrol; (im Hotel) check in; (beim Arzt) make an appointment. **A~ung** f announcement; (Admin) registration; (Sch) enrolment; (Termin) appointment

nmerk|en vt sep mark; **sich** (dat) **etw a~en lassen** show sth. **A~ung** f -, -en note

nmut f - grace; (Charme) charm

nmutig a graceful

nnähen vt sep sew on

nnäher|nd a approximate. **A~ungsversuche** mpl advances

nnahme f -, -n acceptance; (Adoption) adoption; (Vermutung) assumption

nnehm|bar a acceptable. **a~en**† vt sep accept; (adoptieren) adopt; acquire <Gewohnheit>; (sich zulegen, vermuten) assume; **angenommen, dass** assuming that. **A~lichkeiten** fpl comforts

Anno adv **A~ 1920** in the year 1920

Annon|ce /a'nõ:sə/ f -, -n advertisement. **a~cieren** /-'si:-/ vt/i (haben) advertise

nnullieren vt annul; cancel

Anomalie f -, -n anomaly

nonym a anonymous

Anorak m -s, -s anorak

nordn|en vt sep arrange; (befehlen) order. **A~ung** f arrangement; order

norganisch a inorganic

normal a abnormal

npass|en vt sep try on; (angleichen) adapt (dat to); **sich a~** adapt (dat to). **A~ung** f - adaptation. **a~ungsfähig** a

adaptable. **A~ungsfähigkeit** f adaptability

Anpfiff m (Sport) kick-off

Anprall m -[e]s impact. **a~en** vi sep (sein) strike (an etw acc sth)

anpreisen† vt sep commend

Anprob|e f fitting. **a~ieren** vt sep try on

anrechnen vt sep count (als as); (berechnen) charge for; (verrechnen) allow <Summe>

Anrecht nt right (auf + acc to)

Anrede f [form of] address. **a~n** vt sep address; speak to

anreg|en vt sep stimulate; (ermuntern) encourage (zu to); (vorschlagen) suggest. **a~end** a stimulating. **A~ung** f stimulation; (Vorschlag) suggestion

Anreise f journey; (Ankunft) arrival. **a~n** vi sep (sein) arrive

Anreiz m incentive

Anrichte f -, -n sideboard. **a~n** vt sep (Culin) prepare; (garnieren) garnish (mit with); (verursachen) cause

anrüchig a disreputable

Anruf m call. **A~beantworter** m -s,- answering machine. **a~en**† v sep ● vt call to; (bitten) call on (um for); (Teleph) ring ● vi (haben) ring (bei jdm s.o.)

anrühren vt sep touch; (verrühren) mix

ans prep = **an das**

Ansage f announcement. **a~n** vt sep announce

ansamm|eln vt sep collect; (anhäufen) accumulate; **sich a~eln** collect; (sich häufen) accumulate; <Leute:> gather. **A~lung** f collection; (Menschen-) crowd

ansässig a resident

Ansatz m beginning; (Versuch) attempt

anschaffen vt sep [**sich** dat] **etw a~** acquire/(kaufen) buy sth

anschalten vt sep switch on

ạnschau|en *vt sep* look at. **a~lich** *a* vivid, *adv* -ly. **A~ung** *f* -, -en (*fig*) view

Ạnschein *m* appearance. **a~end** *adv* apparently

ạnschirren *vt sep* harness

Ạnschlag *m* notice; (*Vor-*) estimate; (*Überfall*) attack (**auf** + *acc* on); (*Mus*) touch; (*Techn*) stop. **a~en†** *v sep* ● *vt* put up <*Aushang*>; strike <*Note, Taste*>; cast on <*Masche*>; (*beschädigen*) chip ● *vi* (*haben*) strike/(*stoßen*) knock (**an** + *acc* against); (*wirken*) be effective ● *vi* (*sein*) knock (**an** + *acc* against)

ạnschließen† *v sep* ● *vt* connect (**an** + *acc* to); (*zufügen*) add; **sich a~ an** (+ *acc*) (*anstoßen*) adjoin; (*folgen*) follow; (*sich anfreunden*) become friendly with; **sich jdm a~** join s.o. ● *vi* (*haben*) **a~ an** (+ *acc*) adjoin; (*folgen*) follow. **a~d** *a* adjoining; (*zeitlich*) following ● *adv* afterwards

Ạnschluss *m* connection; (*Kontakt*) contact; **A~ finden** make friends; **im A~ an** (+ *acc*) after

ạnschmiegsam *a* affectionate

ạnschmieren *vt sep* smear

ạnschnallen *vt sep* strap on; **sich a~** fasten one's seat-belt

ạnschneiden† *vt sep* cut into; broach <*Thema*>

ạnschreiben† *vt sep* write (**an** + *acc* on); (*Comm*) put on s.o.'s account; (*sich wenden*) write to

Ạnschrift *f* address

ạnschuldig|en *vt sep* accuse. **A~ung** *f* -, -en accusation

ạnschwellen† *vi sep* (*sein*) swell

ạnsehen† *vt sep* look at; (*einschätzen*) regard (**als** as); [**sich** *dat*] **etw a~** look at sth; (*TV*) watch sth. **A~** *nt* -**s** respect; (*Ruf*) reputation

ạnsehnlich *a* considerable

ạnsetzen *v sep* ● *vt* join (**an** + *acc* to); (*veranschlagen*) estimate ● *vi* (*haben*) (*anbrennen*) burn; **zum Sprung a~** get ready to jump

Ạnsicht *f* view; **meiner A~ nach** in my view; **zur A~** (*Comm*) on approval. **A~s[post]karte** *f* picture postcard. **A~ssache** *f* matter of opinion

ạnsiedeln (sich) *vr sep* settle

ạnsonsten *adv* apart from that

ạnspannen *vt sep* hitch up; (*anstrengen*) strain; tense <*Muskel*>

Ạnspielung *f* -, -en allusion; hint

Ạnspitzer *m* -**s**,- pencil-sharpener

Ạnsprache *f* address

ạnsprechen† *v sep* ● *vt* speak to; (*fig*) appeal to ● *vi* (*haben*) respond (**auf** + *acc* to)

ạnspringen† *v sep* ● *vt* jump at ● *vi* (*sein*) (*Auto*) start

Ạnspruch *m* claim/(*Recht*) right (**auf** + *acc* to); **A~ haben** be entitled (**auf** + *acc* to); **in A~ nehmen** make use of; (*erfordern*) demand; take up <*Zeit*>; occupy <*Person*>; **hohe A~e stellen** be very demanding. **a~slos** *a* undemanding. **a~svoll** *a* demanding; (*kritisch*) discriminating; (*vornehm*) up-market

ạnstacheln *vt sep* (*fig*) spur on

Ạnstalt *f* -, -en institution

Ạnstand *m* decency; (*Benehmen*) [good] manners *pl*

ạnständig *a* decent; (*ehrbar*) respectable; (*richtig*) proper

ạnstandslos *adv* without any trouble

ạnstarren *vt sep* stare at

anstạtt *conj & prep* (+ *gen*) instead of

ạnsteck|en *v sep* ● *vt* pin (**an** + *acc* to/on); put on <*Ring*>; (*anzünden*) light; (*in Brand stecken*) set fire to; (*Med*) infect; **sich a~en** catch an infection (**bei**

from) ● vi (haben) be infectious.
a~end a infectious. A~ung f -,
-en infection

nstehen† vi sep (haben) queue

nstelle prep (+ gen) instead of

nstell|en vt sep put, stand (an +
acc against); (einstellen) employ;
(anschalten) turn on; (tun) do;
sich a~en queue [up]. A~ung f
employment; (Stelle) job

nstieg m -[e]s, -e climb; (fig) rise

nstiften vt sep cause; (anzetteln)
instigate

nstoß m (Anregung) impetus;
(Stoß) knock; (Fußball) kick-off;
A~ erregen give offence (an + dat
at). a~en† v sep ● vt knock; (mit
dem Ellbogen) nudge ● vi (sein)
knock (an + acc against) ● vi
(haben) adjoin (an etw acc sth);
a~en auf (+ acc) drink to; mit der
Zunge a~en lisp

nstößig a offensive

nstrahlen vt sep floodlight

nstreichen† vt sep paint;
(anmerken) mark

nstreng|en vt sep strain;
(ermüden) tire; sich a~en exert
oneself; (sich bemühen) make an
effort (zu to). a~end a strenuous;
(ermüdend) tiring. A~ung f -, -en
strain; (Mühe) effort

nstrich m coat [of paint]

nsturm m rush; (Mil) assault

nsuchen nt -s,- request

ntarktis f - Antarctic

nteil m share; A~ nehmen take
an interest (an + dat in).
A~nahme f - interest (an + dat
in); (Mitgefühl) sympathy

ntenne f -, -n aerial

nthologie f -, -n anthology

nthropologie f - anthropology

nti|alkoholiker m teetotaller.
A~biotikum nt -s, -ka antibiotic

ntik a antique. A~e f -
[classical] antiquity

ntikörper m antibody

ntilope f -, -n antelope

Antipathie f - antipathy

Antiquariat nt -[e]s, -e antiquarian
bookshop

Antiquitäten fpl antiques.
A~händler m antique dealer

Antrag m -[e]s, -̈e proposal; (Pol)
motion; (Gesuch) application.
A~steller m -s,- applicant

antreffen† vt sep find

antreten† v sep ● vt start; take up
<Amt> ● vi (sein) line up

Antrieb m urge; (Techn) drive;
aus eigenem A~ of one's own
accord

Antritt m start; bei A~ eines Amtes
when taking office

antun† vt sep jdm etw a~ do sth
to s.o.; sich (dat) etwas a~ take
one's own life

Antwort f -, -en answer, reply (auf
+ acc to). a~en vt/i (haben)
answer (jdm s.o.)

anvertrauen vt sep entrust/
(mitteilen) confide (jdm to s.o.)

Anwalt m -[e]s, -̈e, Anwältin f -,
-nen lawyer; (vor Gericht) counsel

Anwandlung f -, -en fit (von of)

Anwärter(in) m(f) candidate

anweis|en† vt sep assign (dat to);
(beauftragen) instruct. A~ung f
instruction; (Geld-) money order

anwend|en vt sep apply (auf + acc
to); (gebrauchen) use. A~ung f
application; use

anwerben† vt sep recruit

Anwesen nt -s,- property

anwesen|d a present (bei at); die
A~den those present. A~heit f -
presence

anwidern vt sep disgust

Anwohner mpl residents

Anzahl f number

anzahl|en vt sep pay a deposit on.
A~ung f deposit

anzapfen vt sep tap

Anzeichen nt sign

Anzeige f -, -n announcement;
(Inserat) advertisement; A~
erstatten gegen jdn report s.o. to

the police. **a~n** *vt sep* announce; (*inserieren*) advertise; (*melden*) report [to the police]; (*angeben*) indicate

anziehen|en† *vt sep* ●*vt* attract; (*festziehen*) tighten; put on <*Kleider, Bremse*>; (*ankleiden*) dress; **sich a~en** get dressed. **a~end** *a* attractive. **A~ungskraft** *f* attraction; (*Phys*) gravity

Anzug *m* suit

anzüglich *a* suggestive

anzünden *vt sep* light; (*in Brand stecken*) set fire to

anzweifeln *vt sep* question

apart *a* striking

Apathie *f* - apathy

apathisch *a* apathetic

Aperitif *m* -s, -s aperitif

Apfel *m* -s,∵ apple

Apfelsine *f* -, -n orange

Apostel *m* -s,- apostle

Apostroph *m* -s, -e apostrophe

Apothek|e *f* -, -n pharmacy. **A~er(in)** *m* -s,- (*f* -, -nen) pharmacist, [dispensing] chemist

Apparat *m* -[e]s, -e device; (*Phot*) camera; (*Radio, TV*) set; (*Teleph*) telephone; **am A~!** speaking!

Appell *m* -s, -e appeal; (*Mil*) roll-call. **a~ieren** *vi* (*haben*) appeal (*an* + *acc* to)

Appetit *m* -s appetite; **guten A~!** enjoy your meal! **a~lich** *a* appetizing

Applaus *m* -es applause

Aprikose *f* -, -n apricot

April *m* -[s] April

Aquarell *nt* -s, -e water-colour

Aquarium *nt* -s, -ien aquarium

Äquator *m* -s equator

Ära *f* - era

Araber(in) *m* -s,- (*f* -, -nen) Arab

arabisch *a* Arab; (*Geog*) Arabian; <*Ziffer*> Arabic

Arbeit *f* -, -en work; (*Anstellung*) employment, job; (*Aufgabe*) task; (*Sch*) [written] test; (*Abhandlung*) treatise; (*Qualität*) workmanship;

sich an die A~ machen set to work; sich (*dat*) viel A~ machen go to a lot of trouble. **a~en** *v sep* ●*vi* (*haben*) work (**an** + *dat* on) ●*vt* make. **A~er(in)** *m* -s,- (*f* -, -nen) worker; (*Land-, Hilfs-*) labourer. **A~erklasse** *f* working class

Arbeit|geber *m* -s,- employer. **A~nehmer** *m* -s,- employee

Arbeits|amt *nt* employment exchange. **A~erlaubnis, A~genehmigung** *f* work permit. **A~kraft** *f* worker. **a~los** *a* unemployed; **~los sein** be out of work. **A~lose(r)** *m/f* unemployed person; **die A~losen** the unemployed *pl*. **A~losenunterstützung** *f* unemployment benefit. **A~losigkeit** *f* - unemployment

arbeitsparend *a* labour-saving

Arbeitsplatz *m* job

Archäo|loge *m* -n, -n archaeologist. **A~logie** *f* - archaeology

Arche *f* - die A~ Noah Noah's Ark

Architek|t(in) *m* -en, -en (*f* -, -nen) architect. **a~tonisch** *a* architectural. **A~tur** *f* - architecture

Archiv *nt* -s, -e archives *pl*

Arena *f* -, -nen arena

arg *a* bad; (*groß*) terrible

Argentin|ien /-iən/ *nt* -s Argentina. **a~isch** *a* Argentinian

Ärger *m* -s annoyance; (*Unannehmlichkeit*) trouble. **ä~lich** *a* annoyed; (*leidig*) annoying; **ä~lich sein** be annoyed. **ä~n** *vt* annoy; (*necken*) tease; **sich ä~n** get annoyed (**über** jdn/etw with s.o./ about sth). **Ä~nis** *nt* -ses, -se annoyance; **öffentliches Ä~nis** public nuisance

Arglist *f* - malice

arglos *a* unsuspecting

Argument *nt* -[e]s, -e argument. **a~ieren** *vi* (*haben*) argue (**dass** that)

Arie /'a:riə/ *f* -, -n aria

Aristo|krat *m* -en, -en aristocrat. **A~kratie** *f* - aristocracy. **a~kratisch** *a* aristocratic

Arkt|is *f* - Arctic. **a~isch** *a* Arctic

arm *a* poor

Arm *m* -[e]s, -e arm; **jdn auf den Arm nehmen** 🛈 pull s.o.'s leg

Armaturenbrett *nt* instrument panel; (*Auto*) dashboard

Armband *nt* (*pl* -bänder) bracelet; (*Uhr*-) watch-strap. **A~uhr** *f* wrist-watch

Arm|e(r) *m/f* poor man/woman; **die A~en** the poor *pl*

Armee *f* -, -n army

Ärmel *m* -s, - sleeve. **Ä~kanal** *m* [English] Channel. **ä~los** *a* sleeveless

Arm|lehne *f* arm. **A~leuchter** *m* candelabra

ärmlich *a* poor; (*elend*) miserable

armselig *a* miserable

Armut *f* - poverty

Arran|gement /arãʒə'mã:/ *nt* -s, -s arrangement. **a~gieren** /-'ʒi:rən/ *vt* arrange

arrogant *a* arrogant

Arsch *m* -[e]s, ̈-e (*vulg*) arse

Arsen *f* -, -n arsenic

Art *f* -, -en manner; (*Weise*) way; (*Natur*) nature; (*Sorte*) kind; (*Biol*) species; **auf diese Art** in this way

Arterie /-iə/ *f* -, -n artery

Arthritis *f* - arthritis

artig *a* well-behaved

Artikel *m* -s, - article

Artillerie *f* - artillery

Artischocke *f* -, -n artichoke

Arznei *f* -, -en medicine

Arzt *m* -[e]s, ̈-e doctor

Ärzt|in *f* -, -nen [woman] doctor. **ä~lich** *a* medical

As* *nt* -ses, -se *s*. **Ass**

Asbest *m* -[e]s asbestos

Asche *f* - ash. **A~nbecher** *m* ashtray. **A~rmittwoch** *m* Ash Wednesday

Asiat|(in) *m* -en, -en (*f* -, -nen) Asian. **a~isch** *a* Asian

Asien /'a:ziən/ *nt* -s Asia

asozial *a* antisocial

Aspekt *m* -[e]s, -e aspect

Asphalt *m* -[e]s asphalt. **a~ieren** *vt* asphalt

Ass *nt* -es, -e ace

Assistent(in) *m* -en, -en (*f* -, -nen) assistant

Ast *m* -[e]s, ̈-e branch

ästhetisch *a* aesthetic

Asthma *nt* -s asthma. **a~matisch** *a* asthmatic

Astro|loge *m* -n, -n astrologer. **A~logie** *f* - astrology. **A~naut** *m* -en, -en astronaut. **A~nomie** *f* - astronomy

Asyl *nt* -s, -e home; (*Pol*) asylum. **A~ant** *m* -en, -en asylum-seeker

Atelier /-'lie:/ *nt* -s, -s studio

Atem *m* -s breath. **a~los** *a* breathless. **A~zug** *m* breath

Atheist *m* -en, -en atheist

Äther *m* -s ether

Äthiopien /-iən/ *nt* -s Ethiopia

Athlet|(in) *m* -en, -en (*f* -, -nen) athlete. **a~isch** *a* athletic

Atlant|ik *m* -s Atlantic. **a~isch** *a* Atlantic; **der A~ische Ozean** the Atlantic Ocean

Atlas *m* -lasses, -lanten atlas

atmen *vt/i* (*haben*) breathe

Atmosphäre *f* -, -n atmosphere

Atmung *f* - breathing

Atom *nt* -s, -e atom. **A~bombe** *f* atom bomb. **A~krieg** *m* nuclear war

Atten|tat *nt* -[e]s, -e assassination attempt. **A~täter** *m* assassin

Attest *nt* -[e]s, -e certificate

Attrak|tion /-'tsi̯o:n/ *f* -, -en attraction. **a~tiv** *a* attractive

Attribut *nt* -[e]s, -e attribute

ätzen vt corrode; (*Med*) cauterize; (*Kunst*) etch. **ä~d** a corrosive; <*Spott*> caustic

au int ouch; **au fein!** oh good!

Aubergine /oɛbɛr'ʒiːnə/ f -, -n aubergine

auch adv & conj also, too; (*außerdem*) what's more; (*selbst*) even; **a~ wenn** even if; **sie weiß es a~ nicht** she doesn't know either; **wer/wie/was a~ immer** whoever/ however/whatever

Audienz f -, -en audience

audiovisuell a audio-visual

Auditorium nt -s, -ien (*Univ*) lecture hall

─────────

auf
● *preposition (+ dative)*
····▸ (*nicht unter*) on. **auf dem Tisch** on the table. **auf Deck** on deck. **auf der Erde** on earth. **auf der Welt** in the world. **auf der Straße** in the street
····▸ (*bei Institution, Veranstaltung usw.*) at; (*bei Gebäude, Zimmer*) in. **auf der Schule/Uni** at school/ university. **auf einer Party/ Hochzeit** at a party/wedding. **Geld auf der Bank haben** have money in the bank. **sie ist auf ihrem Zimmer** she's in her room. **auf Urlaub** on holiday
● *preposition (+ accusative)*
····▸ (*nicht unter*) on[to]. **er legte das Buch auf den Tisch** he laid the book on the table. **auf eine Mauer steigen** climb onto a wall. **auf die Straße gehen** go [out] into the street
····▸ (*bei Institution, Veranstaltung usw.*) to. **auf eine Party/die Toilette gehen** go to a party/the toilet. **auf die Schule/Uni gehen** go to school/university. **auf Urlaub schicken** send on holiday
····▸ (*bei Entfernung*) **auf 10 km [Entfernung] zu sehen/hören**

visible/audible for [a distance of] 10 km
····▸ (*zeitlich*) (*wie lange*) for; (*bis*) until; (*wann*) on. **auf Jahre [hinaus]** for years [to come]. **auf ein paar Tage** for a few days. **etw auf nächsten Mittwoch verschieben** postpone sth until next Wednesday. **das fällt auf einen Montag** it falls on a Monday
····▸ (*Art und Weise*) in. **auf diese [Art und] Weise** in this way. **auf Deutsch/Englisch** in German/ English
····▸ (*aufgrund*) **auf Wunsch** on request. **auf meine Bitte** on or at my request. **auf Befehl** on command
····▸ (*Proportion*) to. **ein Teelöffel auf einen Liter Wasser** one teaspoon to one litre of water. **auf die Sekunde/den Millimeter [genau]** [precise] to the nearest second/millimetre
····▸ (*Toast*) to. **auf deine Gesundheit!** your health!
● *adverb*
····▸ (*aufgerichtet, aufgestanden*) up. **auf!** (*steh auf!*) up you get! **auf und ab** (*hin und her*) up and down
····▸ (*aufsetzen*) **Helm/Hut/Brille auf!** helmet/hat/glasses on!
····▸ (*geöffnet, offen*) open. **Fenster/Mund auf!** open the window/your mouth!

aufatmen vi sep (haben) heave a sigh of relief

aufbahren vt sep lay out

Aufbau m construction; (*Struktur*) structure. **a~en** v sep ● vt construct, build; (*errichten*) erect; (*schaffen*) build up; (*arrangieren*) arrange; **sich a~en** (*fig*) be based (**auf** + dat on) ● vi (haben) be based (**auf** + dat on)

aufbauschen vt sep puff out; (*fig*) exaggerate

A

aufbekommen† *vt sep* get open; (*Sch*) be given [as homework]

aufbessern *vt sep* improve; (*erhöhen*) increase

aufbewahr|en *vt sep* keep; (*lagern*) store. **A~ung** *f* - safe keeping; storage; (*Gepäck-*) left-luggage office

aufblas|bar *a* inflatable. **a~en**† *vt sep* inflate

aufbleiben† *vi sep* (*sein*) stay open; <*Person:*> stay up

aufblenden *vt/i sep* (*haben*) (*Auto*) switch to full beam

aufblühen *vi sep* (*sein*) flower

aufbocken *vt sep* jack up

aufbrauchen *vt sep* use up

aufbrechen† *v sep* ● *vt* break open ● *vi* (*sein*) <*Knospe:*> open; (*sich aufmachen*) set out, start

aufbringen† *vt sep* raise <*Geld*>; find <*Kraft*>

Aufbruch *m* start, departure

aufbrühen *vt sep* make <*Tee*>

aufbürden *vt sep* jdm etw a~ (*fig*) burden s.o. with sth

aufdecken *vt sep* (*auflegen*) put on; (*abdecken*) uncover; (*fig*) expose

aufdrehen *vt sep* turn on

aufdringlich *a* persistent

aufeinander *adv* one on top of the other; <*schießen*> at each other; <*warten*> for each other; **a~ folgend** successive; <*Tage*> consecutive.

Aufenthalt *m* stay; **10 Minuten A~ haben** <*Zug:*> stop for 10 minutes. **A~serlaubnis, A~sgenehmigung** *f* residence permit. **A~sraum** *m* recreation room; (*im Hotel*) lounge

Auferstehung *f* - resurrection

aufessen† *vt sep* eat up

auffahr|en† *vi sep* (*sein*) drive up; (*aufprallen*) crash, run (**auf** + *acc* into). **A~t** *f* drive; (*Autobahn-*) access road, slip road; (*Bergfahrt*) ascent

auffallen† *vi sep* (*sein*) be conspicuous; **unangenehm a~** make a bad impression

auffällig *a* conspicuous

auffangen† *vt sep* catch; pick up

auffass|en *vt sep* understand; (*deuten*) take. **A~ung** *f* understanding; (*Ansicht*) view

auffordern *vt sep* ask; (*einladen*) invite. **A~ung** *f* request; invitation

auffrischen *v sep* ● *vt* freshen up; revive <*Erinnerung*>; **seine Englischkenntnisse a~** brush up one's English

aufführ|en *vt sep* perform; (*angeben*) list; **sich a~en** behave. **A~ung** *f* performance

auffüllen *vt sep* fill up

Aufgabe *f* task; (*Rechen-*) problem; (*Verzicht*) giving up; **A~n** (*Sch*) homework *sg*

Aufgang *m* way up; (*Treppe*) stairs *pl*; (*Astr*) rise

aufgeben† *v sep* ● *vt* give up; post <*Brief*>; send <*Telegramm*>; place <*Bestellung*>; register <*Gepäck*>; put in the paper <*Annonce*>; **jdm eine Aufgabe a~** set s.o. a task; **jdm Suppe a~** serve s.o. with soup ● *vi* (*haben*) give up

Aufgebot *nt* contingent (**an** + *dat* of); (*Relig*) banns *pl*

aufgedunsen *a* bloated

aufgehen† *vi sep* (*sein*) open; (*sich lösen*) come undone; <*Teig, Sonne:*> rise; <*Saat:*> come up; (*Math*) come out exactly; **in Flammen a~** go up in flames

aufgelegt *a* **gut/schlecht a~ sein** be in a good/bad mood

aufgeregt *a* excited; (*erregt*) agitated

aufgeschlossen *a* (*fig*) openmindedly

aufgeweckt *a* (*fig*) bright

aufgießen† *vt sep* pour on; (*aufbrühen*) make <*Tee*>

aufgreifen† vt sep pick up; take up <Vorschlag, Thema>

aufgrund prep (+ gen) on the strength of

Aufguss m infusion

aufhaben† v sep ● vt have on; **den Mund a~** have one's mouth open; **viel a~** (Sch) have a lot of homework ● vi (haben) be open

aufhalten† vt sep hold up; (anhalten) stop; (abhalten) keep; (offenhalten) hold open; hold out <Hand>; **sich a~** stay; (sich befassen) spend one's time (mit on)

aufhäng|en vt/i sep (haben) hang up; (henken) hang; **sich a~en** hang oneself. **A~er** m -s,- loop

aufheben† vt sep pick up; (hochheben) raise; (aufbewahren) keep; (beenden) end; (rückgängig machen) lift; (abschaffen) abolish; (Jur) quash <Urteil>; repeal <Gesetz>; (ausgleichen) cancel out; **gut aufgehoben sein** be well looked after

aufheitern vt sep cheer up; **sich a~** <Wetter:> brighten up

aufhellen vt sep lighten; **sich a~** <Himmel:> brighten

aufhetzen vt sep incite

aufholen v sep ● vt make up ● vi (haben) catch up; (zeitlich) make up time

aufhören vi sep (haben) stop

aufklappen vt/i sep (sein) open

aufklär|en vt sep solve; **jdn a~en** enlighten s.o.; **sich a~en** be solved; <Wetter:> clear up. **A~ung** f solution; enlightenment; (Mil) reconnaissance; **sexuelle A~ung** sex education

aufkleb|en vt sep stick on. **A~er** m -s,- sticker

aufknöpfen vt sep unbutton

aufkochen v sep ● vt bring to the boil ● vi (sein) come to the boil

aufkommen† vi sep (sein) start; <Wind:> spring up; <Mode:> come in

aufkrempeln vt sep roll up

aufladen† vt sep load; (Electr) charge

Auflage f impression; (Ausgabe) edition; (Zeitungs-) circulation

auflassen† vt sep leave open; leave on <Hut>

Auflauf m crowd; (Culin) ≈ soufflé

auflegen v sep ● vt apply (auf + acc to); put down <Hörer>; **neu a~** reprint ● vi (haben) ring off

auflehn|en (sich) vr sep (fig) rebel. **A~ung** f - rebellion

auflesen† vt sep pick up

aufleuchten vi sep (haben) light up

auflös|en vt sep dissolve; close <Konto>; **sich a~en** dissolve; <Nebel:> clear. **A~ung** f dissolution; (Lösung) solution

aufmach|en v sep ● vt open; (lösen) undo; **sich a~en** set out (nach for) ● vi (haben) open; **jdm a~en** open the door to s.o. **A~ung** f -, -en get-up

aufmerksam a attentive; **a~ werden auf** (+ acc) notice; **jdn a~ machen auf** (+ acc) draw s.o.'s attention to. **A~keit** f -, -en attention; (Höflichkeit) courtesy

aufmuntern vt sep cheer up

Aufnahme f -, -n acceptance; (Empfang) reception; (in Klub, Krankenhaus) admission; (Einbeziehung) inclusion; (Beginn) start; (Foto) photograph; (Film-) shot; (Mus) recording; (Band-) tape recording. **a~fähig** a receptive. **A~prüfung** f entrance examination

aufnehmen† vt sep pick up; (absorbieren) absorb; take <Nahrung, Foto>; (fassen) hold; (annehmen) accept; (leihen) borrow; (empfangen) receive; (in

A

Klub, Krankenhaus) admit;
beherbergen, geistig erfassen)
ake in; (*einbeziehen*) include;
niederschreiben) take down;
filmen) film, shoot; (*Mus*) record;
uf Band a~ tape[-record]

ufopfer|n *vt sep* sacrifice; **sich
~n** sacrifice oneself. **A~ung** *f*
self-sacrifice

ufpassen *vi sep* (*haben*) pay
attention; (*sich vorsehen*) take
care; **a~ auf** (+ *acc*) look after

ufprall *m* -[e]s impact. **a~en** *vi
sep* (*sein*) **a~en auf** (+ *acc*) hit

ufpumpen *vt sep* pump up,
inflate

ufputsch|en *vt sep* incite.
A~mittel *nt* stimulant

ufquellen† *vi sep* (*sein*) swell

ufraffen *vt sep* pick up; **sich a~**
pick oneself up; (*fig*) pull oneself
together

ufragen *vi sep* (*sein*) rise [up]

ufräumen *vt/i sep* (*haben*) tidy
up; (*wegräumen*) put away

ufrecht *a & adv* upright.
a~erhalten† *vt sep* (*fig*) maintain

ufreg|en *vt* excite; (*beunruhigen*)
upset; (*ärgern*) annoy; **sich a~en**
get excited; (*sich erregen*) get
worked up. **a~end** *a* exciting.
A~ung *f* excitement

ufreiben† *vt sep* chafe; (*fig*)
wear down. **a~d** *a* trying

ufreißen† *v sep* ● *vt* tear open;
dig up <*Straße*>; open wide
<*Augen, Mund*> ● *vi* (*sein*) split
open

ufrichtig *a* sincere. **A~keit** *f* -
sincerity

ufrollen *vt sep* roll up;
(*entrollen*) unroll

ufrücken *vi sep* (*sein*) move up;
(*fig*) be promoted

ufruf *m* appeal (**an** + *dat* to).
a~en† *vt sep* call out <*Namen*>;
jdn a~en call s.o.'s name

Aufruhr *m* -s, -e turmoil;
(*Empörung*) revolt

aufrühr|en *vt sep* stir up. **A~er** *m*
-s,- rebel. **a~erisch** *a*
inflammatory; (*rebellisch*)
rebellious

aufrunden *vt sep* round up

aufrüsten *vt sep* (*haben*) arm

aufsagen *vt sep* recite

aufsässig *a* rebellious

Aufsatz *m* top; (*Sch*) essay

aufsaugen† *vt sep* soak up

aufschauen *vi sep* (*haben*) look
up (**zu** at/(*fig*) to)

aufschichten *vt sep* stack up

aufschieben† *vt sep* slide open;
(*verschieben*) put off, postpone

Aufschlag *m* impact; (*Tennis*)
service; (*Hosen-*) turn-up;
(*Ärmel-*) upturned cuff; (*Revers*)
lapel; (*Comm*) surcharge. **a~en†**
v sep ● *vt* open; crack <*Ei*>;
(*hochschlagen*) turn up;
(*errichten*) put up; (*erhöhen*)
increase; cast on <*Masche*>; **sich**
(*dat*) **das Knie a~en** cut [open]
one's knee ● *vi* (*haben*) hit (**auf
etw** *acc*/*dat* sth); (*Tennis*) serve;
(*teurer werden*) go up

aufschließen† *v sep* ● *vt* unlock
● *vi* (*haben*) unlock the door

aufschlussreich *a* revealing;
(*lehrreich*) informative

aufschneiden† *v sep* ● *vt* cut
open; (*in Scheiben*) slice ● *vi*
(*haben*) 🛈 exaggerate

Aufschnitt *m* sliced sausage, cold
meat [and cheese]

aufschrauben *vt sep* screw on;
(*abschrauben*) unscrew

Aufschrei *m* [sudden] cry

aufschreiben† *vt sep* write down;
jdn a~ <*Polizist:*> book s.o.

Aufschrift *f* inscription; (*Etikett*)
label

Aufschub *m* delay; (*Frist*) grace

aufschürfen *vt sep* **sich** (*dat*) **das
Knie a~** graze one's knee

aufschwingen† (**sich**) *vr sep* find the energy (**zu** for)

Aufschwung *m* (*fig*) upturn

aufsehen† *vi sep* (*haben*) look up (**zu** at/(*fig*) to). **A∼** *nt* -**s A∼ erregen** cause a sensation; **A∼ erregend** sensational

Aufseher(in) *m* -**s,-** (*f* -, -**nen**) supervisor; (*Gefängnis*-) warder

aufsetzen *vt sep* put on; (*verfassen*) draw up; (*entwerfen*) draft; **sich a∼** sit up

Aufsicht *f* supervision; (*Person*) supervisor. **A∼srat** *m* board of directors

aufsperren *vt sep* open wide

aufspielen *v sep* ● *vi* (*haben*) play ● *vr* **sich a∼** show off

aufspießen *vt sep* spear

aufspringen† *vi sep* (*sein*) jump up; (*aufprallen*) bounce; (*sich öffnen*) burst open

aufspüren *vt sep* track down

aufstacheln *vt sep* incite

Aufstand *m* uprising, rebellion

aufständisch *a* rebellious

aufstehen† *vi sep* (*sein*) get up; (*offen sein*) be open; (*fig*) rise up

aufsteigen† *vi sep* (*sein*) get on; <*Reiter:*> mount; <*Bergsteiger:*> climb up; (*hochsteigen*) rise [up]; (*fig: befördert werden*) rise (**zu** to); (*Sport*) be promoted

aufstell|en *vt sep* put up; (*Culin*) put on; (*postieren*) post; (*in einer Reihe*) line up; (*nominieren*) nominate; (*Sport*) select <*Mannschaft*>; make out <*Liste*>; lay down <*Regel*>; make <*Behauptung*>; set up <*Rekord*>. **A∼ung** *f* nomination; (*Liste*) list

Aufstieg *m* -[e]s, -e ascent; (*fig*) rise; (*Sport*) promotion

Aufstoßen *nt* -**s** burping

aufstrebend *a* (*fig*) ambitious

Aufstrich *m* [sandwich] spread

aufstützen *vt sep* rest (**auf** + *acc* on); **sich a∼** lean (**auf** + *acc* on)

Auftakt *m* (*fig*) start

auftauchen *vi sep* (*sein*) emerge (*fig*) turn up; <*Frage:*> crop up

auftauen *vt/i sep* (*sein*) thaw

aufteil|en *vt sep* divide [up]. **A∼ung** *f* division

auftischen *vt sep* serve [up]

Auftrag *m* -[e]s,"-e task; (*Kunst*) commission; (*Comm*) order; **im A∼** (+ *gen*) on behalf of. **a∼en†** *vt sep* apply; (*servieren*) serve; (*abtragen*) wear out; **jdm a∼en** instruct s.o. (**zu** to). **A∼ geber** *m* -**s,-** client

auftrennen *vt sep* unpick, undo

auftreten† *vi sep* (*sein*) tread; (*sich benehmen*) behave, act; (*Theat*) appear; (*die Bühne betreten*) enter; (*vorkommen*) occur

Auftrieb *m* buoyancy; (*fig*) boost

Auftritt *m* (*Theat*) appearance; (*auf die Bühne*) entrance; (*Szene*) scene

aufwachen *vi sep* (*sein*) wake up

aufwachsen† *vi sep* (*sein*) grow up

Aufwand *m* -[e]s expenditure; (*Luxus*) extravagance; (*Mühe*) trouble; **A∼ treiben** be extravagant

aufwändig *a* = aufwendig

aufwärmen *vt sep* heat up; (*fig*) rake up; **sich a∼** warm oneself; (*Sport*) warm up

Aufwartefrau *f* cleaner

aufwärts *adv* upwards; (*bergauf*) uphill; **es geht a∼ mit jdm/etw** s.o./sth is improving

Aufwartung *f* - cleaner

aufwecken *vt sep* wake up

aufweichen *v sep* ● *vt* soften ● *vi* (*sein*) become soft

aufweisen† *vt sep* have, show

aufwend|en† *vt sep* spend; **Mühe a∼en** take pains. **a∼ig** *a* lavish; (*teuer*) expensive

aufwert|en *vt sep* revalue. **A∼ung** *f* revaluation

ufwickeln vt sep roll up; ⟨*auswickeln*⟩ unwrap

ufwiegler m -s,- agitator

ufwisch|en vt sep wipe up; wash ⟨*Fußboden*⟩. **A~lappen** m floorcloth

ufwühlen vt sep churn up

ufzähl|en vt sep enumerate, list. **A~ung** f list

ufzeichn|en vt sep record; ⟨*zeichnen*⟩ draw. **A~ung** f recording; **A~ungen** notes

ufziehen† v sep ● vt pull up; hoist ⟨*Segel*⟩; ⟨*öffnen*⟩ open; draw ⟨*Vorhang*⟩; ⟨*großziehen*⟩ bring up; rear ⟨*Tier*⟩; mount ⟨*Bild*⟩; thread ⟨*Perlen*⟩; wind up ⟨*Uhr*⟩; (🗆 *necken*) tease ● vi ⟨*sein*⟩ approach

ufzug m hoist; (*Fahrstuhl*) lift, (*Amer*) elevator; (*Prozession*) procession; (*Theat*) act

ugapfel m eyeball

uge nt -s, -n eye; (*Punkt*) spot; **vier A~n werfen** throw a four; **gute A~n** good eyesight; **unter vier A~n** in private; **im A~ behalten** keep in sight; (*fig*) bear in mind

ugenblick m moment; **A~!** just a moment! **a~lich** a immediate; ⟨*derzeitig*⟩ present ● adv immediately; ⟨*derzeit*⟩ at present

Augen|braue f eyebrow. **A~höhle** f eye socket. **A~licht** nt sight. **A~lid** nt eyelid

ugust m -[s] August

uktion /-'ţs:io:n/ f -, -en auction

ula f -, -len (*Sch*) [assembly] hall

u-pair-Mädchen /o'pɛːr-/ nt aupair

us prep (+ dat) out of; (*von*) from; (*bestehend*) [made] of; **aus Angst** from or out of fear; **aus Spaß** for fun ● adv out; ⟨*Licht, Radio*⟩ off; **aus sein auf** (+ acc) be after; **aus und ein** in and out; **von sich aus** of one's own accord; **von mir aus** as far as I'm concerned

usarbeiten vt sep work out

ausarten vi sep ⟨*sein*⟩ degenerate (**in** + acc into)

ausatmen vt/i sep ⟨*haben*⟩ breathe out

ausbauen vt sep remove; (*vergrößern*) extend; (*fig*) expand

ausbedingen† vt sep **sich** (dat) **a~** insist on; (*zur Bedingung machen*) stipulate

ausbesser|n vt sep mend, repair. **A~ung** f repair

ausbeulen vt sep remove the dents from; (*dehnen*) make baggy

ausbild|en vt sep train; (*formen*) form; (*entwickeln*) develop; **sich a~en** train (**als/zu** as); (*entstehen*) develop. **A~ung** f training; (*Sch*) education

ausbitten† vt sep **sich** (dat) **a~** ask for; (*verlangen*) insist on

ausblasen† vt sep blow out

ausbleiben† vi sep ⟨*sein*⟩ fail to appear/ ⟨*Erfolg:*⟩ materialize; (*nicht heimkommen*) stay out

Ausblick m view

ausbrech|en† vi sep ⟨*sein*⟩ break out; ⟨*Vulkan:*⟩ erupt; (*fliehen*) escape; **in Tränen a~en** burst into tears. **A~er** m runaway

ausbreit|en vt sep spread [out]. **A~ung** f spread

Ausbruch m outbreak; (*Vulkan-*) eruption; (*Wut-*) outburst; (*Flucht*) escape, break-out

ausbrüten vt sep hatch

Ausdauer f perseverance; (*körperlich*) stamina. **a~nd** a persevering; (*unermüdlich*) untiring

ausdehnen vt sep stretch; (*fig*) extend; **sich a~** stretch; (*Phys & fig*) expand; (*dauern*) last

ausdenken† vt sep **sich** (dat) **a~** think up; (*sich vorstellen*) imagine

Ausdruck m expression; (*Fach-*) term; (*Computer*) printout. **a~en** vt sep print

ausdrücken vt sep squeeze out; squeeze <Zitrone>; stub out <Zigarette>; (äußern) express

ausdrucks|los a expressionless. **a~voll** a expressive

auseinander adv apart; (entzwei) in pieces; **a~ falten** unfold; **a~ gehen** part; <Linien, Meinungen:> diverge; <Ehe:> break up; **a~ halten** tell apart; **a~ nehmen** take apart or to pieces; **a~ setzen** explain (jdm to s.o.); **sich a~ setzen** sit apart; (sich aussprechen) have it out (mit jdm with s.o.); come to grips (mit einem Problem with a problem). **A~setzung** f -, -en discussion; (Streit) argument

auserlesen a select, choice

Ausfahrt f drive; (Autobahn-, Garagen-) exit

Ausfall m failure; (Absage) cancellation; (Comm) loss. **a~en†** vi sep (sein) fall out; (versagen) fail; (abgesagt werden) be cancelled; **gut/schlecht a~en** turn out to be good/poor

ausfallend, ausfällig a abusive

ausfertig|en vt sep make out. **A~ung** f -, -en in doppelter **A~ung** in duplicate

ausfindig a **a~ machen** find

Ausflug m excursion, outing

Ausflügler m -s,- [day-]tripper

Ausfluss m outlet; (Abfluss) drain; (Med) discharge

ausfragen vt sep question

Ausfuhr f -, -en (Comm) export

ausführ|en vt sep take out; (Comm) export; (erklären) explain. **a~lich** a detailed ● adv in detail. **A~ung** f execution; (Comm) version; (äußere) finish; (Qualität) workmanship; (Erklärung) explanation

Ausgabe f issue; (Buch-) edition; (Comm) version

Ausgang m way out, exit; (Flugsteig) gate; (Ende) end; (Ergebnis) outcome. **A~spunkt** starting-point. **A~ssperre** f curfew

ausgeben† vt sep hand out; issu <Fahrkarten>; spend <Geld>; sic **a~ als** pretend to be

ausgebildet a trained

ausgebucht a fully booked; <Vorstellung> sold out

ausgefallen a unusual

ausgefranst a frayed

ausgeglichen a [well-]balanced

ausgeh|en vi sep (sein) go out; <Haare:> fall out; <Vorräte, Geld:> run out; (verblassen) fade **gut/schlecht a~en** end well/badly **davon a~en, dass** assume that. **A~verbot** nt curfew

ausgelassen a high-spirited

ausgemacht a agreed

ausgenommen conj except; **a~ wenn** unless

ausgeprägt a marked

ausgeschlossen pred a out of the question

ausgeschnitten a low-cut

ausgesprochen a marked ● adv decidedly

ausgestorben a extinct; [wie] **a~** <Straße:> deserted

Ausgestoßene(r) m/f outcast

ausgezeichnet a excellent

ausgiebig a extensive; (ausgedehnt) long; **a~ Gebrauch machen von** make full use of

ausgießen† vt sep pour out

Ausgleich m -[e]s balance; (Entschädigung) compensation. **a~en†** v sep ● vt balance; even out <Höhe>; (wettmachen) compensate for; **sich a~en** balance out ● vi (haben) (Sport) equalize. **A~streffer** m equalizer

ausgrab|en† vt sep dig up; (Archaeol) excavate. **A~ung** f -, -en excavation

Ausguss m [kitchen] sink

aushaben† vt sep have finished <Buch>

ushalten† vt sep bear, stand; hold <Note>; (Unterhalt zahlen für) keep; **nicht auszuhalten, nicht um A~** unbearable

ushändigen vt sep hand over

ushängen¹ vt sep (reg) display; ake off its hinges <Tür>

ushäng|en² vi sep (haben) be displayed. **A~eschild** nt sign

usheben† vt sep excavate

ushecken vt sep (fig) hatch

ushelfen† vi sep (haben) help out (jdm s.o.)

ushilf|e f [temporary] assistant; ur A~e to help out. **A~skraft** f emporary worker. **a~sweise** adv emporarily

ushöhlen vt sep hollow out

uskennen† (sich) vr sep know one's way around; **sich mit/in etw** (dat) a~ know all about sth

uskommen† vi sep (sein) manage (mit/ohne with/without); (sich vertragen) get on (gut well)

uskugeln vt sep sich (dat) den Arm a~ dislocate one's shoulder

uskühlen vt/i sep (sein) cool

uskundschaften vt sep spy out

uskunft f -, ⸚e information; (A~sstelle) information desk/ (Büro) bureau; (Teleph) enquiries pl; **eine A~** a piece of information

uslachen vt sep laugh at

uslage f [window] display; **A~n** expenses

usland nt im/ins A~ abroad

usländ|er(in) m -s,- (f -, -nen) foreigner. **a~isch** a foreign

uslandsgespräch nt international call

uslass|en† vt sep let out; let down <Saum>; (weglassen) leave out; (versäumen) miss; (Culin) melt; (fig) vent <Ärger> (an + dat on). **A~ungszeichen** nt apostrophe

uslauf m run. **a~en**† vi sep (sein) run out; <Farbe:> run;

(Naut) put to sea; <Modell:> be discontinued

ausleeren vt sep empty [out]

ausleg|en vt sep lay out; display <Waren>; (auskleiden) line (mit with); (bezahlen) pay; (deuten) interpret. **A~ung** f -, -en interpretation

ausleihen† vt sep lend; sich (dat) a~ borrow

Auslese f - selection; (fig) pick; (Elite) elite

ausliefer|n vt sep hand over; (Jur) extradite. **A~ung** f handing over; (Jur) extradition; (Comm) distribution

ausloggen vi sep log off or out

auslosen vt sep draw lots for

auslös|en vt sep set off, trigger; (fig) cause; arouse <Begeisterung>; (einlösen) redeem; pay a ransom for <Gefangene>. **A~er** m -s,- trigger; (Phot) shutter release

Auslosung f draw

auslüften vt/i sep (haben) air

ausmachen vt sep put out; (abschalten) turn off; (abmachen) arrange; (erkennen) make out; (betragen) amount to; (wichtig sein) matter

Ausmaß nt extent; **A~e** dimensions

Ausnahm|e f -, -n exception. **A~ezustand** m state of emergency. **a~slos** adv without exception. **a~sweise** adv as an exception

ausnehmen† vt sep take out; gut <Fisch>; sich gut a~ look good. **a~d** adv exceptionally

ausnutz|en, ausnütz|en vt sep exploit. **A~ung** f exploitation

auspacken vt sep unpack; (auswickeln) unwrap

ausplaudern vt sep let out, blab

ausprobieren vt sep try out

Auspuff m -s exhaust [system].
A~gase ntpl exhaust fumes.
A~rohr nt exhaust pipe

auspusten vt sep blow out

ausradieren vt sep rub out

ausrauben vt sep rob

ausräuchern vt sep smoke out;
fumigate <Zimmer>

ausräumen vt sep clear out

ausrechnen vt sep work out

Ausrede f excuse. a~n v sep ● vi
(haben) finish speaking ● vt jdm
etw a~ talk s.o. out of sth

ausreichen vi sep (haben) be
enough. a~d a adequate

Ausreise f departure. a~n vi sep
(sein) leave the country.
A~visum nt exit visa

ausreißen† v sep ● vt pull or tear
out ● vi (sein) 🔢 run away

ausrenken vt sep dislocate

ausrichten vt sep align;
(bestellen) deliver; (erreichen)
achieve; jdm a~ tell s.o. (dass
that); ich soll Ihnen Grüße von X
a~ X sends [you] his regards

ausrotten vt sep exterminate;
(fig) eradicate

Ausruf m exclamation. a~en† vt
sep exclaim; call out <Namen>;
(verkünden) proclaim; jdn a~en
lassen have s.o. paged.
A~ezeichen nt exclamation mark

ausruhen vt/i sep (haben) rest;
sich a~ have a rest

ausrüst|en vt sep equip. A~ung f
equipment; (Mil) kit

ausrutschen vi sep (sein) slip

Aussage f -, -n statement; (Jur)
testimony, evidence; (Gram)
predicate. a~n vt/i sep (haben)
state; (Jur) give evidence, testify

ausschalten vt sep switch off

Ausschank m sale of alcoholic
drinks; (Bar) bar

Ausschau f - A~ halten nach look
out for

ausscheiden† vi sep (sein) leave
(Sport) drop out; (nicht in Frage
kommen) be excluded

ausschenken vt sep pour out

ausscheren vi sep (sein) (Auto)
pull out

ausschildern vt sep signpost

ausschimpfen vt sep tell off

ausschlafen† vi/r sep (haben)
[sich] a~ get enough sleep;
(morgens) sleep late

Ausschlag m (Med) rash; den A~
geben (fig) tip the balance.
a~gebend a decisive

ausschließ|en† vt sep lock out;
(fig) exclude; (entfernen) expel.
a~lich a exclusive

ausschlüpfen vi sep (sein) hatch

Ausschluss m exclusion;
expulsion; unter A~ der
Öffentlichkeit in camera

ausschneiden† vt sep cut out

Ausschnitt m excerpt, extract;
(Zeitungs-) cutting; (Hals-)
neckline

ausschöpfen vt sep ladle out;
(Naut) bail out; exhaust
<Möglichkeiten>

ausschreiben† vt sep write out;
(ausstellen) make out;
(bekanntgeben) announce; put
out to tender <Auftrag>

Ausschreitungen fpl riots;
(Exzesse) excesses

Ausschuss m committee; (Comm)
rejects pl

ausschütten vt sep tip out;
(verschütten) spill; (leeren) empt

aussehen† vi sep (haben) look;
wie sieht er/es aus? what does
he/it look like? A~ nt -s
appearance

außen adv [on the] outside; nach
a~ outwards. A~bordmotor m
outboard motor. A~handel m
foreign trade. A~minister m
Foreign Minister. A~politik f
foreign policy. A~seite f outside
A~seiter m -s,- outsider; (fig)

misfit. **A~stände** *mpl* outstanding debts

ußer *prep* (+ *dat*) except [for], apart from; (*außerhalb*) out of; **a~ sich** (*fig*) beside oneself ● *conj* except; **a~ wenn** unless. **a~dem** *adv* in addition, as well ● *conj* moreover

ußer|e(r,s) *a* external; <*Teil, Schicht*> outer. **Ä~e(s)** *nt* exterior; (*Aussehen*) appearance

ußerehelich *a* extramarital.

a~gewöhnlich *a* exceptional.

a~halb *prep* (+ *gen*) outside ● *adv* **a~halb wohnen** live outside town

ußer|lich *a* external; (*fig*) outward. **ä~n** *vt* express; **sich ä~n** comment; (*sich zeigen*) manifest itself

ußerordentlich *a* extraordinary

ußerst *adv* extremely

ußerste(r,s) *a* outermost; (*weiteste*) furthest; (*höchste*) utmost, extreme; (*letzte*) last; (*schlimmste*) worst. **Ä~s(s)** *nt* **das Ä~** the limit; (*Schlimmste*) the worst; **sein Ä~s tun** do one's utmost; **aufs Ä~** extremely

Äußerung *f* -, -en comment; (*Bemerkung*) remark

aussetzen *v sep* ● *vt* expose (*dat* to); abandon <*Kind*>; launch <*Boot*>; offer <*Belohnung*>; **etwas auszusetzen haben an** (+ *dat*) find fault with ● *vi* (*haben*) stop; <*Motor:*> cut out

Aussicht *f* -, -en view/(*fig*) prospect (**auf** + *acc* of); **weitere A~en** further outlook *sg*. **a~slos** *a* hopeless

ausspannen *v sep* ● *vt* spread out; unhitch <*Pferd*> ● *vi* (*haben*) rest

aussperren *vt sep* lock out

ausspielen *v sep* ● *vt* play <*Karte*>; (*fig*) play off (**gegen** against) ● *vi* (*haben*) (*Kartenspiel*) lead

Aussprache *f* pronunciation; (*Gespräch*) talk

aussprechen† *vt sep* pronounce; (*äußern*) express; **sich a~** talk; come out (**für/gegen** in favour of/against)

Ausspruch *m* saying

ausspucken *v sep* ● *vt* spit out ● *vi* (*haben*) spit

ausspülen *vt sep* rinse out

ausstatt|en *vt sep* equip. **A~ung** *f* -, -en equipment; (*Innen-*) furnishings *pl*; (*Theat*) scenery and costumes *pl*

ausstehen† *v sep* ● *vt* suffer; **Angst a~** be frightened; **ich kann sie nicht a~** I can't stand her ● *vi* (*haben*) be outstanding

aussteigen† *vi sep* (*sein*) get out; (*aus Bus, Zug*) get off; **alles a~!** all change!

ausstell|en *vt sep* exhibit; (*Comm*) display; (*ausfertigen*) make out; issue <*Pass*>. **A~ung** *f* exhibition; (*Comm*) display

aussterben† *vi sep* (*sein*) die out; (*Biol*) become extinct

Aussteuer *f* trousseau

Ausstieg *m* -[e]s, -e exit

ausstopfen *vt sep* stuff

ausstoßen† *vt sep* emit; utter <*Fluch*>; heave <*Seufzer*>; (*ausschließen*) expel

ausstrahl|en *vt/i sep* (*sein*) radiate, emit; (*Radio, TV*) broadcast. **A~ung** *f* radiation

ausstrecken *vt sep* stretch out; put out <*Hand*>

ausstreichen† *vt sep* cross out

ausströmen *v sep* ● *vi* (*sein*) pour out; (*entweichen*) escape ● *vt* emit; (*ausstrahlen*) radiate

aussuchen *vt sep* pick, choose

Austausch *m* exchange. **a~bar** *a* interchangeable. **a~en** *vt sep* exchange; (*auswechseln*) replace

austeilen *vt sep* distribute

Auster *f* -, -n oyster

austragen† *vt sep* deliver; hold <*Wettkampf*>; play <*Spiel*>
Austral|ien /-ian/ *nt* **-s** Australia. **A~ier(in)** *m* **-s,-** (*f* **-, -nen**) Australian. **a~isch** *a* Australian
austreiben† *vt sep* drive out; (*Relig*) exorcize
austreten† *v sep* ● *vt* stamp out; (*abnutzen*) wear down ● *vi* (*sein*) come out; (*ausscheiden*) leave (**aus etw** sth); **[mal] a~** 🔲 go to the loo
austrinken† *vt/i sep* (*haben*) drink up; (*leeren*) drain
Austritt *m* resignation
austrocknen *vt/i sep* (*sein*) dry out
ausüben *vt sep* practise; carry on <*Handwerk*>; exercise <*Recht*>; exert <*Druck, Einfluss*>
Ausverkauf *m* [clearance] sale. **a~t** *a* sold out
Auswahl *f* choice, selection; (*Comm*) range; (*Sport*) team
auswählen *vt sep* choose, select
Auswander|er *m* emigrant. **a~n** *vi sep* (*sein*) emigrate. **A~ung** *f* emigration
auswärt|ig *a* non-local; (*ausländisch*) foreign. **a~s** *adv* outwards; (*Sport*) away. **A~sspiel** *nt* away game
auswaschen† *vt sep* wash out
auswechseln *vt sep* change; (*ersetzen*) replace; (*Sport*) substitute
Ausweg *m* (*fig*) way out
ausweichen† *vi sep* (*sein*) get out of the way; **jdm/etw a~en** avoid/ (*sich entziehen*) evade s.o./sth
Ausweis *m* **-es, -e** pass; (*Mitglieds-, Studenten-*) card. **a~en**† *vt sep* deport; **sich a~en** prove one's identity. **A~papiere** *ntpl* identification papers. **A~ung** *f* deportation
auswendig *adv* by heart
auswerten *vt sep* evaluate
auswickeln *vt sep* unwrap

auswirk|en (sich) *vr sep* have an effect (**auf** + *acc* on). **A~ung** *f* effect; (*Folge*) consequence
auswringen *vt sep* wring out
auszahlen *vt sep* pay out; (*entlohnen*) pay off; (*abfinden*) buy out; **sich a~** (*fig*) pay off
auszählen *vt sep* count; (*Boxen*) count out
Auszahlung *f* payment
auszeichn|en *vt sep* (*Comm*) price; (*ehren*) honour; (*mit einer Preis*) award a prize to; (*Mil*) decorate; **sich a~en** distinguish oneself. **A~ung** *f* honour; (*Preis*) award; (*Mil*) decoration; (*Sch*) distinction
ausziehen† *v sep* ● *vt* pull out; (*auskleiden*) undress; take off <*Mantel, Schuhe*> ● *vi* (*sein*) move out; (*sich aufmachen*) set out
Auszug *m* departure; (*Umzug*) move; (*Ausschnitt*) extract; (*Bank-*) statement
Auto *nt* **-s, -s** car; **A~ fahren** drive/ (*mitfahren*) go in the car. **A~bahn** *f* motorway
Autobiographie *f* autobiography
Auto|bus *m* bus. **A~fahrer(in)** *m(f)* driver, motorist. **A~fahrt** *f* drive
Autogramm *nt* **-s, -e** autograph
Automat *m* **-en, -en** automatic device; (*Münz-*) slot-machine; (*Verkaufs-*) vending-machine; (*Fahrkarten-*) machine; (*Techn*) robot. **A~ik** *f* - automatic mechanism; (*Auto*) automatic transmission
automatisch *a* automatic
Autonummer *f* registration number
Autopsie *f* **-, -n** autopsy
Autor *m* **-s, -en** /-'to:rən/ author
Auto|reisezug *m* Motorail. **A~rennen** *nt* motor race
Autorin *f* **-, -nen** author[ess]

Autori|sation /-'ts:io:n/ f -
authorization. **A~tät** f -, -en
authority
Auto|schlosser m motor
mechanic. **A~skooter** /-sku:tɐ/ m
-s,- dodgem. **A~stopp** m -s per
A~stopp fahren hitch-hike.
A~verleih m car hire [firm].
A~waschanlage f car wash
autsch int ouch
Axt f -, -̈e axe

B, b /be:/ nt - (Mus) B flat
Baby /'be:bi/ nt -s, -s baby.
B~ausstattung f layette. **B~-
sitter** /-sɪtɐ/ m -s,- babysitter
Bach m -[e]s, -̈e stream
Backbord nt -[e]s port [side]
Backe f -, -n cheek
backen vt/i† (haben) bake;
(braten) fry
Backenzahn m molar
Bäcker m -s,- baker. **B~ei** f -, -en,
B~laden m baker's shop
Back|obst nt dried fruit. **B~ofen**
m oven. **B~pfeife** f 🔊 slap in the
face. **B~pflaume** f prune.
B~pulver nt baking-powder.
B~stein m brick
Bad nt -[e]s, -̈er bath; (Zimmer)
bathroom; (Schwimm-) pool;
(Ort) spa
Bade|anstalt f swimming baths
pl. **B~anzug** m swim-suit.
B~hose f swimming trunks pl.
B~kappe f bathing-cap.
B~mantel m bathrobe. **b~n** vi
(haben) have a bath; (im Meer)
bathe ● vt bath; (waschen) bathe.
B~ort m seaside resort.

B~wanne f bath. **B~zimmer** nt
bathroom
Bagger m -s,- excavator; (Nass-)
dredger. **B~see** m flooded
gravel-pit
Bahn f -, -en path; (Astr) orbit;
(Sport) track; (einzelne) lane;
(Rodel-) run; (Stoff-) width;
(Eisen-) railway; (Zug) train;
(Straßen-) tram. **b~brechend** a
(fig) pioneering. **B~hof** m
[railway] station. **B~steig** m -[e]s,
-e platform. **B~übergang** m level
crossing
Bahre f -, -n stretcher
Baiser /bɛ'ze:/ nt -s, -s meringue
Bake f -, -n (Naut, Aviat) beacon
Bakterien /-iən/ fpl bacteria
Balanc|e /ba'lã:sə/ f - balance.
b~ieren vt/i (haben/sein) balance
bald adv soon; (fast) almost
Baldachin /-xi:n/ m -s, -e canopy
bald|ig a early; <Besserung>
speedy. **b~möglichst** adv as soon
as possible
Balg nt & m -[e]s, -̈er 🔊 brat
Balkan m -s Balkans pl
Balken m -s,- beam
Balkon /bal'kõ:/ m -s, -s balcony;
(Theat) circle
Ball¹ m -[e]s, -̈e ball
Ball² m -[e]s, -̈e (Tanz) ball
Ballade f -, -n ballad
Ballast m -[e]s ballast. **B~stoffe**
mpl roughage sg
Ballen m -s,- bale; (Anat) ball of
the hand/(Fuß-) foot; (Med)
bunion
Ballerina f -, -nen ballerina
Ballett nt -s, -e ballet
Ballon /ba'lõ:/ m -s, -s balloon
Balsam m -s balm
Balt|ikum nt -s Baltic States pl.
b~isch a Baltic
Bambus m -ses, -se bamboo
banal a banal
Banane f -, -n banana
Banause m -n, -n philistine

Band¹ *nt* -[e]s,⸚er ribbon; (*Naht-, Ton-, Ziel-*) tape; **am laufenden B~** Ⓘ non-stop

Band² *m* -[e]s,⸚e volume

Band³ *nt* -[e]s, -e (*fig*) bond

Band⁴ /bɛnt/ *f* -, -s [jazz] band

Bandag|e /ban'da:ʒə/ *f* -, -n bandage. **b~ieren** *vt* bandage

Bande *f* -, -n gang

bändigen *vt* control, restrain; (*zähmen*) tame

Bandit *m* -en, -en bandit

Band|maß *nt* tape-measure. **B~scheibe** *f* (*Anat*) disc. **B~wurm** *m* tapeworm

Bang|e *f* **B~e haben** be afraid; **jdm B~e machen** frighten s.o. **b~en** *vi* (*haben*) fear (**um** for)

Banjo *nt* -s, -s banjo

Bank¹ *f* -,⸚e bench

Bank² *f* -, -en (*Comm*) bank. **B~einzug** *m* direct debit

Bankett *nt* -s, -e banquet

Bankier /baŋ'kie:/ *m* -s, -s banker

Bankkonto *nt* bank account

Bankrott *m* -s, -s bankruptcy. **b~** *a* bankrupt

Bankwesen *nt* banking

Bann *m* -[e]s, -e (*fig*) spell. **b~en** *vt* exorcize; (*abwenden*) avert; **[wie] gebannt** spellbound

Banner *nt* -s,- banner

bar *a* (*rein*) sheer; <*Gold*> pure; **b~es Geld** cash; **[in] bar bezahlen** pay cash

Bar *f* -, -s bar

Bär *m* -en, -en bear

Baracke *f* -, -n (*Mil*) hut

Barb|ar *m* -en, -en barbarian. **b~arisch** *a* barbaric

bar|fuß *adv* barefoot. **B~geld** *nt* cash

barmherzig *a* merciful

barock *a* baroque. **B~** *nt & m* -[s] baroque

Barometer *nt* -s,- barometer

Baron *m* -s, -e baron. **B~in** *f* -, -nen baroness

Barren *m* -s,- (*Gold-*) bar, ingot; (*Sport*) parallel bars *pl*. **B~gold** *nt* gold bullion

Barriere *f* -, -n barrier

Barrikade *f* -, -n barricade

barsch *a* gruff

Barsch *m* -[e]s, -e (*Zool*) perch

Bart *m* -[e]s,⸚e beard; (*der Katze*) whiskers *pl*

bärtig *a* bearded

Barzahlung *f* cash payment

Basar *m* -s, -e bazaar

Base¹ *f* -, -n [female] cousin

Base² *f* -, -n (*Chem*) alkali, base

Basel *nt* -s Basle

basieren *vi* (*haben*) be based (**auf** + *dat* on)

Basilikum *nt* -s basil

Basis *f* -,**Basen** base; (*fig*) basis

basisch *a* (*Chem*) alkaline

Bask|enmütze *f* beret. **b~isch** *a* Basque

Bass *m* -es,⸚e bass

Bassin /ba'sɛ̃:/ *nt* -s, -s pond; (*Brunnen-*) basin; (*Schwimm-*) pool

Bassist *m* -en, -en bass player; (*Sänger*) bass

Bast *m* -[e]s raffia

basteln *vt* make ● *vi* (*haben*) do handicrafts

Batterie *f* -, -n battery

Bau¹ *m* -[e]s, -e burrow; (*Fuchs-*) earth

Bau² *m* -[e]s, -ten construction; (*Gebäude*) building; (*Auf-*) structure; (*Körper-*) build; (*B~stelle*) building site. **B~arbeiten** *fpl* building work *sg*; (*Straßen-*) road-works

Bauch *m* -[e]s, Bäuche abdomen, belly; (*Magen*) stomach; (*Bauchung*) bulge. **b~ig** *a* bulbous. **B~nabel** *m* navel. **B~redner** *m* ventriloquist. **B~schmerzen** *mpl* stomach-ache *sg*. **B~speicheldrüse** *f* pancreas

bauen *vt* build; (*konstruieren*) construct ● *vi* (*haben*) build (**an**

~tw *dat* sth); **b~ auf** (+ *acc*) (*fig*) rely on

auer¹ *m* -s, -n farmer; (*Schach*) pawn

auer² *nt* -s,- [bird]cage

äuerlich *a* rustic

auern|haus *nt* farmhouse. **B~hof** *m* farm

au|fällig *a* dilapidated. **B~genehmigung** *f* planning permission. **B~gerüst** *nt* scaffolding. **B~jahr** *nt* year of construction. **B~kunst** *f* architecture. **b~lich** *a* structural

aum *m* -[e]s, Bäume tree

aumeln *vi* (*haben*) dangle

äumen (sich) *vr* rear [up]

aum|schule *f* [tree] nursery. **B~wolle** *f* cotton

ausch *m* -[e]s, Bäusche wad; in **B~ und Bogen** (*fig*) wholesale. **b~en** *vt* puff out

au|sparkasse *f* building society. **B~stein** *m* building brick. **B~stelle** *f* building site; (*Straßen-*) roadworks *pl*. **B~unternehmer** *m* building contractor

Bayer|(in) *m* -s, -n (*f* -, -nen) Bavarian. **B~n** *nt* -s Bavaria

bay[e]risch *a* Bavarian

Bazillus *m* -, -len bacillus

beabsichtig|en *vt* intend. **b~t** *a* intended; intentional

beacht|en *vt* take notice of; (*einhalten*) observe; (*folgen*) follow; **nicht b~en** ignore. **b~lich** *a* considerable. **B~ung** *f* - observance; **etw** (*dat*) **keine B~ung schenken** take no notice of sth

Beamte(r) *m*, **Beamtin** *f* -, -nen official; (*Staats-*) civil servant; (*Schalter-*) clerk

beanspruchen *vt* claim; (*erfordern*) demand

beanstand|en *vt* find fault with; (*Comm*) make a complaint about. **B~ung** *f* -, -en complaint

beantragen *vt* apply for

beantworten *vt* answer

bearbeiten *vt* work; (*weiter-*) process; (*behandeln*) treat (**mit** with); (*Admin*) deal with; (*redigieren*) edit; (*Theat*) adapt; (*Mus*) arrange

Beatmungsgerät *nt* ventilator

beaufsichtig|en *vt* supervise. **B~ung** *f* - supervision

beauftragen *vt* instruct; commission <*Künstler*>

bebauen *vt* build on; (*bestellen*) cultivate

beben *vi* (*haben*) tremble

Becher *m* -s,- beaker; (*Henkel-*) mug; (*Joghurt-, Sahne-*) carton

Becken *nt* -s,- basin; pool; (*Mus*) cymbals *pl*; (*Anat*) pelvis

bedacht *a* careful; **darauf b~** anxious (**zu** to)

bedächtig *a* careful; slow

bedanken (sich) *vr* thank (**bei jdm** s.o.)

Bedarf *m* -s need/(*Comm*) demand (**an** + *dat* for); **bei B~** if required. **B~shaltestelle** *f* request stop

bedauer|lich *a* regrettable. **b~licherweise** *adv* unfortunately. **b~n** *vt* regret; (*bemitleiden*) feel sorry for; **bedaure! sorry! b~nswert** *a* pitiful; (*bedauerlich*) regrettable

bedeckt *a* covered; <*Himmel*> overcast

bedenken† *vt* consider; (*überlegen*) think over. **B~** *pl* misgivings; **ohne B~** without hesitation

bedenklich *a* doubtful; (*verdächtig*) dubious; (*ernst*) serious

bedeut|en *vi* (*haben*) mean. **b~end** *a* important; (*beträchtlich*) considerable. **B~ung** *f* -, -en meaning; (*Wichtigkeit*) importance. **b~ungslos** *a* meaningless; (*unwichtig*)

unimportant. **b~ungsvoll** *a*
significant; (*vielsagend*)
meaningful

bedien|en *vt* serve; (*betätigen*)
operate; **sich [selbst] b~en** help
oneself. **B~ung** *f* -, -en service;
(*Betätigung*) operation; (*Kellner*)
waiter; (*Kellnerin*) *f* waitress.
B~ungsgeld *nt* service charge

Bedingung *f* -, -en condition;
B~en conditions; (*Comm*) terms.
b~slos *a* unconditional

bedroh|en *vt* threaten. **b~lich** *a*
threatening. **B~ung** *f* threat

bedrücken *vt* depress

bedruckt *a* printed

bedürf|en† *vi* (*haben*) (+ *gen*)
need. **B~nis** *nt* -ses, -se need

Beefsteak /'bi:fste:k/ *nt* -s, -s
steak; **deutsches B~** hamburger

beeilen (sich) *vr* hurry; hasten
(**zu** to)

beeindrucken *vt* impress

beeinflussen *vt* influence

beeinträchtigen *vt* mar;
(*schädigen*) impair

beengen *vt* restrict

beerdig|en *vt* bury. **B~ung** *f* -, -en
funeral

Beere *f* -, -n berry

Beet *nt* -[e]s, -e (*Hort*) bed

Beete *f* -, -n **rote B~** beetroot

befähig|en *vt* enable;
(*qualifizieren*) qualify. **B~ung** *f* -
qualification; (*Fähigkeit*) ability

befahrbar *a* passable

befallen† *vt* attack; <Angst:> seize

befangen *a* shy; (*gehemmt*) self-
conscious; (*Jur*) biased. **B~heit** *f*
- shyness; self-consciousness;
bias

befassen (sich) *vr* concern
oneself/(*behandeln*) deal (**mit**
with)

Befehl *m* -[e]s, -e order; (*Leitung*)
command (**über** + *acc* of). **b~en†**
vt **jdm etw b~en** order s.o. to do
sth ● *vi* (*haben*) give the orders.

B~sform *f* (*Gram*) imperative.
B~shaber *m* -s,- commander

befestigen *vt* fasten (**an** + *dat* to);
(*Mil*) fortify

befeuchten *vt* moisten

befinden† (sich) *vr* be. **B~** *nt* -s
[state of] health

beflecken *vt* stain

befolgen *vt* follow

beförder|n *vt* transport; (*im Rang*)
promote. **B~ung** *f* -, -en
transport; promotion

befragen *vt* question

befrei|en *vt* free; (*räumen*) clear
(**von** of); (*freistellen*) exempt (**von**
from); **sich b~en** free oneself.
B~er *m* -s,- liberator. **B~ung** *f* -
liberation; exemption

befreunden (sich) *vr* make
friends; **befreundet sein** be friends

befriedig|en *vt* satisfy. **b~end** *a*
satisfying; (*zufrieden stellend*)
satisfactory. **B~ung** *f* -
satisfaction

befrucht|en *vt* fertilize. **B~ung** *f* -
fertilization; **künstliche B~ung**
artificial insemination

Befugnis *f* -, -se authority

Befund *m* result

befürcht|en *vt* fear. **B~ung** *f* -, -er
fear

befürworten *vt* support

begab|t *a* gifted. **B~ung** *f* -, -en
gift, talent

begeben† (sich) *vr* go; **sich in
Gefahr b~** expose oneself to
danger

begegn|en *vi* (*sein*) **jdm/etw b~en**
meet s.o./sth. **B~ung** *f* -, -en
meeting

begehr|en *vt* desire. **b~t** *a*
sought-after

begeister|n *vt* **jdn b~n** arouse
s.o.'s enthusiasm. **b~t** *a*
enthusiastic; (*eifrig*) keen.
B~ung *f* - enthusiasm

Begierde *f* -, -n desire

Beginn *m* -s beginning. **b~en†**
vt/i (*haben*) start, begin

eglaubigen vt authenticate

egleichen† vt settle

egleit|en vt accompany. **B~er** m
-s, - companion; (Mus)
accompanist. **B~ung** f -, -en
company; (Mus) accompaniment

eglück|en vt make happy.
~wünschen vt congratulate (**zu**
on)

egnadig|en vt (Jur) pardon.
B~ung f -, -en (Jur) pardon

egraben† vt bury

egräbnis n -ses, -se burial;
(Feier) funeral

egreif|en† vt understand; **nicht
zu b~en** incomprehensible.
~lich a understandable

egrenz|en vt form the boundary
of; (beschränken) restrict. **b~t** a
limited. **B~ung** f -, -en restriction;
(Grenze) boundary

egriff m -[e]s, -e concept;
(Ausdruck) term; (Vorstellung)
idea

egründ|en vt give one's reason
for. **b~et** a justified. **B~ung** f -,
-en reason

egrüß|en vt greet; (billigen)
welcome. **b~enswert** a welcome.
B~ung f - greeting; welcome

egünstigen vt favour

egütert a wealthy

ehaart a hairy

ehäbig a portly

ehag|en vi (haben) please (**jdm**
s.o.). **B~en** nt -s contentment;
(Genuss) enjoyment. **b~lich** a
comfortable. **B~lichkeit** f -
comfort

ehalten† vt keep; (sich merken)
remember

Behälter m -s,- container

ehand|eln vt treat; (sich
befassen) deal with. **B~lung** f
treatment

eharr|en vi (haben) persist (**auf** +
dat in). **b~lich** a persistent

ehaupt|en vt maintain;
(vorgeben) claim; (sagen) say;

(bewahren) retain; **sich b~en** hold
one's own. **B~ung** f -, -en
assertion; claim; (Äußerung)
statement

beheben† vt remedy

behelf|en† (sich) vr make do (**mit**
with). **b~smäßig** a make-shift
● adv provisionally

beherbergen vt put up

beherrsch|en vt rule over;
(dominieren) dominate; (meistern,
zügeln) control; (können) know.
b~t a self-controlled. **B~ung** f -
control

beherzigen vt heed

behilflich a **jdm b~ sein** help s.o.

behinder|n vt hinder; (blockieren)
obstruct. **b~t** a handicapped;
(schwer) disabled. **B~te(r)** m/f
handicapped/disabled person.
B~ung f -, -en obstruction; (Med)
handicap; disability

Behörde f -, -n [public] authority

behüte|n vt protect. **b~t** a
sheltered

behutsam a careful; (zart) gentle

bei
● preposition (+ dative)
! Note that **bei** plus **dem** can
become **beim**
····➤ (nahe) near; (dicht an, neben)
by; (als Begleitung) with. **wer
steht da bei ihm?** who is standing
there next to or with him? **etw
bei sich haben** have sth with or
on one. **bleiben Sie beim Gepäck/
bei den Kindern** stay with the
luggage/the children. **war heute
ein Brief für mich bei der Post?**
was there a letter for me in the
post today?
····➤ (an) by. **jdn bei der Hand
nehmen** take s.o. by the hand
····➤ (in der Wohnung von) at …'s
home or house/flat. **bei mir [zu
Hause]** at my home or 🇬🇧 place.
bei seinen Eltern leben live with
one's parents. **wir sind bei Ulrike**

eingeladen we have been invited to Ulrike's. **bei Schmidt** at the Schmidts'; (*Geschäft*) at Schmidts'; (*auf Briefen*) c/o Schmidt. **bei jdm/einer Firma arbeiten** work for s.o./a firm. **bei uns tut man das nicht** we don't do that where I come from.

····➤ (*gegenwärtig*) at; (*verwickelt*) in. **bei einer Hochzeit/einem Empfang** at a wedding/reception. **bei einem Unfall** in an accident

····➤ (*im Falle von*) in the case of, with; (*bei Wetter*) in. **wie bei den Römern** as with the Romans. **bei Nebel** in fog, if there is fog. **bei dieser Hitze** in this heat

····➤ (*angesichts*) with; (*trotz*) in spite of. **bei deinen guten Augen** with your good eyesight. **bei all seinen Bemühungen** in spite of *or* despite all his efforts

····➤ (*Zeitpunkt*) at, on. **bei diesen Worten errötete er** he blushed at this *or* on hearing this. **bei seiner Ankunft** on his arrival. **bei Tag/ Nacht** by day/night.

····➤ (*Gleichzeitigkeit, mit Verbalsubstantiv*) **beim ...en** while *or* when ...ing. **beim Spazierengehen im Walde** while walking in the woods. **beim Überqueren der Straße** when crossing the road. **sie war beim Lesen** she was reading. **wir waren beim Frühstück** we were having breakfast

beibehalten† *vt sep* keep

beibringen† *vt sep* **jdm etw b~** teach s.o. sth; (*mitteilen*) break sth to s.o.; (*zufügen*) inflict sth on s.o.

Beicht|e *f* -, -n confession. **b~en** *vt/i* (*haben*) confess. **B~stuhl** *m* confessional

beide *a & pron* both; **b~s** both; **dreißig b~** (*Tennis*) thirty all.

b~rseitig *a* mutual. **b~rseits** *adv & prep* (+ *gen*) on both sides (of)

beieinander *adv* together

Beifahrer(in) *m(f)* [front-seat] passenger; (*Motorrad*) pillion passenger

Beifall *m* -[e]s applause; (*Billigung*) approval; **B~ klatschen** applaud

beifügen *vt sep* add; (*beilegen*) enclose

beige /bε:ʒ/ *inv a* beige

beigeben† *vt sep* add

Beihilfe *f* financial aid; (*Studien-*) grant; (*Jur*) aiding and abetting

Beil *nt* -[e]s, -e hatchet, axe

Beilage *f* supplement; (*Gemüse*) vegetable

beiläufig *a* casual

beilegen *vt sep* enclose; (*schlichten*) settle

Beileid *nt* condolences *pl.* **B~sbrief** *m* letter of condolence

beiliegend *a* enclosed

beim *prep* = bei dem; **b~ Militär** in the army; **b~ Frühstück** at breakfast

beimessen† *vt sep* (*fig*) attach (*dat* to)

Bein *nt* -[e]s, -e leg; **jdm ein B~ stellen** trip s.o. up

beinah[e] *adv* nearly, almost

Beiname *m* epithet

beipflichten *vi sep* (*haben*) agree (*dat* with)

Beirat *m* advisory committee

beisammen *adv* together; **b~ sein** be together

Beisein *nt* presence

beiseite *adv* aside; (*abseits*) apart; **b~ legen** put aside; (*sparen*) put by

beisetz|en *vt sep* bury. **B~ung** *f* - -en funeral

Beispiel *nt* example; **zum B~** for example. **b~sweise** *adv* for example

eißen† vt/i (haben) bite; ‹brennen› sting; sich b~ ‹Farben:› clash

ei|stand m -[e]s help. **~stehen†** vi sep (haben) jdm **~stehen** help s.o.

eistimmen vi sep (haben) agree

eistrich m comma

eitrag m -[e]s,-̈e contribution; (Mitglieds-) subscription; (Versicherungs-) premium; (Zeitungs-) article. **b~en†** vt/i ‹ep (haben) contribute

ei|treten† vi sep (sein) (+ dat) ‹oin. **~tritt** m joining

eize f -, -n (Holz-) stain

eizeiten adv in good time

eizen vt stain ‹Holz›

ejahen vt answer in the affirmative; (billigen) approve of

ejahrt a aged, old

ekämpf|en vt fight. **B~ung** f fight (gen against)

ekannt a well-known; (vertraut) familiar; jdn b~ machen introduce s.o.; etw b~ machen od geben announce sth; b~ werden become known. **B~e(r)** m/f acquaintance; (Freund) friend. **B~gabe** f announcement. **b~lich** adv as is well known. **B~machung** f -, -en announcement; (Anschlag) notice. **B~schaft** f acquaintance; (Leute) acquaintances pl; (Freunde) friends pl

ekehr|en vt convert. **B~ung** f -, -en conversion

ekenn|en† vt confess, profess ‹Glauben›; sich [für] schuldig b~en admit one's guilt. **B~tnis** nt -ses, -se confession; (Konfession) denomination

eklag|en vt lament; (bedauern) deplore; sich b~en complain. **b~enswert** a unfortunate. **B~te(r)** m/f (Jur) defendant

ekleid|en vt hold ‹Amt›. **B~ung** f clothing

Beklemmung f -, -en feeling of oppression

bekommen† vt get; have ‹Baby›; catch ‹Erkältung› ● vi (sein) jdm gut b~ do s.o. good; ‹Essen:› agree with s.o.

beköstig|en vt feed. **B~ung** f board; (Essen) food

bekräftigen vt reaffirm

bekreuzigen (sich) vr cross oneself

bekümmert a troubled; (besorgt) worried

bekunden vt show

Belag m -[e]s,-̈e coating; (Fußboden-) covering; (Brot-) topping; (Zahn-) tartar; (Brems-) lining

belager|n vt besiege. **B~ung** f -, -en siege

Belang m von B~ of importance; **B~e** pl interests. **B~los** a irrelevant; (unwichtig) trivial

belassen† vt leave; es dabei b~ leave it at that

belasten vt load; (fig) burden; (beanspruchen) put a strain on; (Comm) debit; (Jur) incriminate

belästigen vt bother; (bedrängen) pester; (unsittlich) molest

Belastung f -, -en load; (fig) strain; (Comm) debit. **B~smaterial** nt incriminating evidence. **B~szeuge** m prosecution witness

belaufen† (sich) vr amount (auf + acc to)

belauschen vt eavesdrop on

beleb|en vt (fig) revive; (lebhaft machen) enliven. **b~t** a lively; ‹Straße› busy

Beleg m -[e]s, -e evidence; (Beispiel) instance (für of); (Quittung) receipt. **b~en** vt cover/(garnieren) garnish (mit with); (besetzen) reserve; (Univ) enrol for; (nachweisen) provide evidence for; den ersten Platz b~en (Sport) take first place.

B~schaft *f* -, -en work-force. **b~t** *a* occupied; <*Zunge*> coated; <*Stimme*> husky; **b~te Brote** open sandwiches

belehren *vt* instruct

beleidig|en *vt* offend; (*absichtlich*) insult. **B~ung** *f* -, -en insult

belesen *a* well-read

beleucht|en *vt* light; (*anleuchten*) illuminate. **B~ung** *f* -, -en illumination

Belg|ien /-iən/ *nt* -s Belgium. **B~ier(in)** *m* -s,- (*f* -, -nen) Belgian. **b~isch** *a* Belgian

belichten *vt* (*Phot*) expose. **B~ung** *f* - exposure

Belieb|en *nt* -s **nach B~en** [just] as one likes. **b~ig** *a* **eine b~ige Zahl** any number you like ● *adv* **b~ig oft** as often as one likes. **b~t** *a* popular

bellen *vi* (*haben*) bark

belohn|en *vt* reward. **B~ung** *f* -, -en reward

belustig|en *vt* amuse. **B~ung** *f* -, -en amusement

bemalen *vt* paint

bemängeln *vt* criticize

bemannt *a* manned

bemerk|bar *a* **sich b~bar machen** attract attention. **b~en** *vt* notice; (*äußern*) remark. **b~ enswert** *a* remarkable. **B~ung** *f* -, -en remark

bemitleiden *vt* pity

bemüh|en *vt* trouble; **sich b~en** try (**zu** to; **um etw** to get sth); (*sich kümmern*) attend (**um** to); **b~t sein** endeavour (**zu** to). **B~ung** *f* -, -en effort

benachbart *a* neighbouring

benachrichtig|en *vt* inform; (*amtlich*) notify. **B~ung** *f* -, -en notification

benachteiligen *vt* discriminate against; (*ungerecht sein*) treat unfairly

benehmen† (**sich**) *vr* behave. **B~ nt** -s behaviour

beneiden *vt* envy (**um etw** sth)

Bengel *m* -s,- boy; (*Rüpel*) lout

benötigen *vt* need

benutz|en, (SGer**) benütz|en** *vt* use; take <*Bahn*> **B~ung** *f* use

Benzin *nt* -s petrol

beobacht|en *vt* observe. **B~er** *m* -s,- observer. **B~ung** *f* -, -en observation

bequem *a* comfortable; (*mühelos*) easy; (*faul*) lazy. **b~en (sich)** *vr* deign (**zu** to). **B~lichkeit** *f* -, -en comfort; (*Faulheit*) laziness

berat|en† *vt* advise; (*überlegen*) discuss; **sich b~en** confer ● *vi* (*haben*) discuss (**über etw** *acc* sth); (*beratschlagen*) confer. **B~er(in)** *m* -s,-, (*f* -, -nen) adviser. **B~ung** *f* -, -en guidance; (*Rat*) advice; (*Besprechung*) discussion; (*Med, Jur*) consultation

berechn|en *vt* calculate; (*anrechnen*) charge for; (*abfordern*) charge. **B~ung** *f* calculation

berechtig|en *vt* entitle; (*befugen*) authorize; (*fig*) justify. **b~t** *a* justified, justifiable. **B~ung** *f* -, -en authorization; (*Recht*) right; (*Rechtmäßigkeit*) justification

bered|en *vt* talk about; **sich b~en** talk. **B~samkeit** *f* - eloquence

beredt *a* eloquent

Bereich *m* -[e]s, -e area; (*fig*) realm; (*Fach-*) field

bereichern *vi* enrich

bereit *a* ready. **b~en** *vt* prepare; (*verursachen*) cause; give <*Überraschung*>. **b~halten†** *sep* have/(*ständig*) keep ready. **b~legen** *vt sep* put out [ready]. **b~machen** *vt sep* get ready. **b~s** *adv* already

Bereitschaft *f* -, -en readiness; (*Einheit*) squad. **B~sdienst** *m* **B~sdienst haben** (*Mil*) be on

tand-by; <*Arzt:*> be on call.
B~spolizei f riot police
ereit|stehen† vi sep (haben) be
eady. **b~stellen** vt sep put out
eady; (*verfügbar machen*) make
available. **B~ung** f - preparation.
~willig a willing
ereuen vt regret
erg m -[e]s, -e mountain;
(*Anhöhe*) hill; **in den B~en** in the
mountains. **b~ab** adv downhill.
~arbeiter m miner. **b~auf** adv
uphill. **B~bau** m -[e]s mining
ergen† vt recover; (*Naut*)
salvage; (*retten*) rescue
erg|führer m mountain guide.
~ig a mountainous. **B~kette** f
mountain range. **B~mann** m (pl
~leute) miner. **B~steiger(in)** m -s,-
(f -, -nen) mountaineer, climber
ergung f - recovery; (*Naut*)
salvage; (*Rettung*) rescue
erg|wacht f mountain rescue
service. **B~werk** nt mine
ericht m -[e]s, -e report; (*Reise-*)
account. **b~en** vt/i (haben)
report; (*erzählen*) tell (**von** of).
B~erstatter(in) m -s,- (f -, -nen)
reporter
erichtigen vt correct
eriesel|n vt irrigate.
B~ungsanlage f sprinkler
system
Berlin nt -s Berlin. **B~er** m -s,-
Berliner
Bernhardiner m -s,- St Bernard
Bernstein m amber
erüchtigt a notorious
erücksichtigen vt take into
consideration. **B~ung** f -
consideration
Beruf m profession; (*Tätigkeit*)
occupation; (*Handwerk*) trade.
b~en† vt appoint; **sich b~en**
refer (**auf** + acc to); (*vorgeben*)
plead (**auf etw** acc sth); ● a
competent; **b~en sein** be
destined (**zu** to). **b~lich** a
professional; <*Ausbildung*>

vocational ● adv professionally;
b~lich tätig sein work, have a job.
B~sberatung f vocational
guidance. **b~smäßig** adv
professionally. **B~sschule** f
vocational school. **B~ssoldat** m
regular soldier. **b~stätig** a
working; **b~stätig sein** work, have
a job. **B~stätige(r)** m/f working
man/woman. **B~ung** f -, -en
appointment; (*Bestimmung*)
vocation; (*Jur*) appeal; **B~ung
einlegen** appeal. **B~ungsgericht**
nt appeal court
beruhen vi (haben) be based (**auf**
+ dat on)
beruhig|en vt calm [down];
(*zuversichtlich machen*) reassure.
b~end a calming; (*tröstend*)
reassuring; (*Med*) sedative.
B~ung f - calming; reassurance;
(*Med*) sedation. **B~ungsmittel** nt
sedative; (*bei Psychosen*)
tranquillizer
berühmt a famous. **B~heit** f -, -en
fame; (*Person*) celebrity
berühr|en vt touch; (*erwähnen*)
touch on. **B~ung** f -, -en touch;
(*Kontakt*) contact
besänftigen vt soothe
Besatz m -es,¨e trimming
Besatzung f -, -en crew; (*Mil*)
occupying force
beschädig|en vt damage. **B~ung**
f -, -en damage
beschaffen vt obtain, get ● a **so
b~ sein, dass** be such that.
B~heit f - consistency
beschäftig|en vt occupy;
<*Arbeitgeber:*> employ; **sich b~en**
occupy oneself. **b~t** a busy;
(*angestellt*) employed (**bei** at).
B~ung f -, -en occupation;
(*Anstellung*) employment
beschämt a ashamed; (*verlegen*)
embarrassed
beschatten vt shade;
(*überwachen*) shadow

Bescheid *m* -[e]s information; jdm B~ **sagen** *od* **geben** let s.o. know; B~ **wissen** know

bescheiden *a* modest. **B~heit** *f* - modesty

bescheinen† *vt* shine on; **von der Sonne beschienen** sunlit

bescheinig|en *vt* certify. **B~ung** *f* -, -en [written] confirmation; (*Schein*) certificate

beschenken *vt* give a present/ presents to

Bescherung *f* -, -en distribution of Christmas presents

beschildern *vt* signpost

beschimpf|en *vt* abuse, swear at. **B~ung** *f* -, -en abuse

beschirmen *vt* protect

Beschlag *m* in **B~ nehmen** monopolize. **b~en**† *vt* shoe ● *vi* (*sein*) steam *or* mist up ● *a* steamed *or* misted up. **B~nahme** *f* -, -n confiscation; (*Jur*) seizure. **b~nahmen** *vt* confiscate; (*Jur*) seize

beschleunig|en *vt* hasten; (*schneller machen*) speed up <*Schritt*> ● *vi* (*haben*) accelerate. **B~ung** *f* - acceleration

beschließen† *vt* decide; (*beenden*) end ● *vi* (*haben*) decide (**über** + *acc* about)

Beschluss *m* decision

beschmutzen *vt* make dirty

beschneid|en† *vt* trim; (*Hort*) prune; (*Relig*) circumcise. **B~ung** *f* - circumcision

beschnüffeln *vt* sniff at

beschönigen *vt* (*fig*) gloss over

beschränken *vt* limit, restrict; **sich b~ auf** (+ *acc*) confine oneself to

beschrankt *a* <*Bahnübergang*> with barrier[s]

beschränk|t *a* limited; (*geistig*) dull-witted. **B~ung** *f* -, -en limitation, restriction

beschreib|en† *vt* describe. **B~ung** *f* -, -en description

beschuldig|en *vt* accuse. **B~ung** *f* -, -en accusation

beschummeln *vt* 🔲 cheat

Beschuss *m* (*Mil*) fire; (*Artillerie-*) shelling

beschütz|en *vt* protect. **B~er** *m* -s,- protector

Beschwer|de *f* -, -n complaint; **B~den** (*Med*) trouble *sg*. **b~en** *vt* weight down; **sich b~en** complain. **b~lich** *a* difficult

beschwindeln *vt* cheat (**um** out of); (*belügen*) lie to

beschwipst *a* 🔲 tipsy

beseitig|en *vt* remove. **B~ung** *f* - removal

Besen *m* -s,- broom

besessen *a* obsessed (**von** by)

besetz|en *vt* occupy; fill <*Posten*>; (*Theat*) cast <*Rolle*>; (*verzieren*) trim (**mit** with). **b~t** *a* occupied; <*Toilette, Leitung*> engaged; <*Zug, Bus*> full up; **der Platz ist b~t** this seat is taken. **B~tzeichen** *nt* engaged tone. **B~ung** *f* -, -en occupation; (*Theat*) cast

besichtig|en *vt* look round <*Stadt*>; (*prüfen*) inspect; (*besuchen*) visit. **B~ung** *f* -, -en visit; (*Prüfung*) inspection; (*Stadt-*) sightseeing

besiedelt *a* **dünn/dicht b~** sparsely/densely populated

besiegen *vt* defeat

besinn|en (**sich**) *vr* think, reflect; (*sich erinnern*) remember (**auf jdn/etw** s.o./sth). **B~ung** *f* - reflection; (*Bewusstsein*) consciousness; **bei/ohne B~ung** conscious/unconscious. **b~ungslos** *a* unconscious

Besitz *m* possession; (*Eigentum, Land-*) property; (*Gut*) estate. **b~en**† *vt* own, possess; (*haben*) have. **B~er(in)** *m* -s,- (*f* -, -nen) owner; (*Comm*) proprietor

besoffen *a* 🗵 drunken; **b~ sein** be drunk

B

esonder|e(r,s) *a* special/ (*bestimmt*) particular; (*gesondert*) separate. **b~s** *adv* [e]specially, particularly; (*gesondert*) separately

esonnen *a* calm

esorg|en *vt* get; (*kaufen*) buy; (*erledigen*) attend to; (*versorgen*) look after. **b~t** *a* worried/ (*bedacht*) concerned (**um** about). **B~ung** *f* -, -en errand; **B~ungen machen** do shopping

espitzeln *vt* spy on

esprech|en† *vt* discuss; (*rezensieren*) review. **B~ung** *f* -, -en discussion; review; (*Konferenz*) meeting

esser *a & adv* better. **b~n** *vt* improve; **sich b~n** get better. **B~ung** *f* - improvement; **gute B~ung!** get well soon!

estand *m* -[e]s,ᵉe existence; (*Vorrat*) stock (**an** + *dat* of)

eständig *a* constant; <*Wetter*> settled; **b~ gegen** resistant to

Bestand|saufnahme *f* stocktaking. **B~teil** *m* part

estätig|en *vt* confirm; acknowledge <*Empfang*>; **sich b~en** prove to be true. **B~ung** *f* -, -en confirmation

estatt|en *vt* bury. **B~ung** *f* -, -en funeral

Bestäubung *f* - pollination

estaunen *vt* gaze at in amazement; (*bewundern*) admire

est|e(r,s) *a* best; **b~en Dank!** many thanks! **B~e(r,s)** *m/f/nt* best; **sein B~es tun** do one's best

estech|en† *vt* bribe; (*bezaubern*) captivate. **b~end** *a* captivating. **b~lich** *a* corruptible. **B~ung** *f* - bribery. **B~ungsgeld** *nt* bribe

Besteck *nt* -[e]s, -e [set of] knife, fork and spoon; (*coll*) cutlery

estehen† *vi* (*haben*) exist; (*fortdauern*) last; (*bei Prüfung*) pass; **~ aus** consist/(*gemacht sein*) be made of; **~ auf** (+ *dat*) insist on ● *vt* pass <*Prüfung*>

besteig|en† *vt* climb; (*aufsteigen*) mount; ascend <*Thron*>. **B~ung** *f* ascent

bestell|en *vt* order; (*vor-*) book; (*ernennen*) appoint; (*bebauen*) cultivate; (*ausrichten*) tell; **zu sich b~en** send for; **b~t sein** have an appointment; **kann ich etwas b~en?** can I take a message? **B~schein** *m* order form. **B~ung** *f* order; (*Botschaft*) message; (*Bebauung*) cultivation

besteuer|n *vt* tax. **B~ung** *f* - taxation

Bestie /'bɛstiə/ *f* -, -n beast

bestimm|en *vt* fix; (*entscheiden*) decide; (*vorsehen*) intend; (*ernennen*) appoint; (*ermitteln*) determine; (*definieren*) define; (*Gram*) qualify ● *vi* (*haben*) be in charge (**über** + *acc* of). **b~t** *a* definite; (*gewiss*) certain; (*fest*) firm,. **B~ung** *f* fixing; (*Vorschrift*) regulation; (*Ermittlung*) determination; (*Definition*) definition; (*Zweck*) purpose; (*Schicksal*) destiny. **B~ungsort** *m* destination

Bestleistung *f* (*Sport*) record

bestraf|en *vt* punish. **B~ung** *f* -, -en punishment

Bestrahlung *f* radiotherapy

Bestreb|en *nt* -s endeavour; (*Absicht*) aim. **B~ung** *f* -, -en effort

bestreiten† *vt* dispute; (*leugnen*) deny; (*bezahlen*) pay for

bestürz|t *a* dismayed; (*erschüttert*) stunned. **B~ung** *f* - dismay, consternation

Bestzeit *f* (*Sport*) record [time]

Besuch *m* -[e]s, -e visit; (*kurz*) call; (*Schul-*) attendance; (*Gast*) visitor; (*Gäste*) visitors *pl*; **B~ haben** have a visitor/visitors; **bei jdm zu** *od* **auf B~ sein** be staying with s.o. **b~en** *vt* visit; (*kurz*) call

on; (teilnehmen) attend; go to
<Schule, Ausstellung>. **B~er(in)**
m -s,- (f -, -nen) visitor; caller.
B~zeit f visiting hours pl

betagt a aged, old

betätig|en vt operate; **sich b~en**
work (als as). **B~ung** f -, -en
operation; (Tätigkeit) activity

betäub|en vt stun; <Lärm:>
deafen; (Med) anaesthetize;
(lindern) ease; deaden
<Schmerz>; **wie b~t** dazed.
B~ung f - daze; (Med)
anaesthesia. **B~ungsmittel** nt
anaesthetic

Bete f -, -n **Rote B~** beetroot

beteilig|en vt give a share to; **sich
b~en** take part (**an** + dat in);
(beitragen) contribute (**an** + dat
to). **b~t a b~t sein** take part/(an
Unfall) be involved/(Comm) have
a share (**an** + dat in); **alle B~ten**
all those involved. **B~ung** f -, -en
participation; involvement;
(Anteil) share

beten vi (haben) pray

Beton /be'tɔŋ/ m -s concrete

betonen vt stressed, emphasize

beton|t a stressed; (fig) pointed.
B~ung f -, -en stress

Betracht m in **B~ ziehen** consider;
außer B~ lassen disregard; **nicht
in B~ kommen** be out of the
question. **b~en** vt look at; (fig)
regard (als as)

beträchtlich a considerable

Betrachtung f -, -en
contemplation; (Überlegung)
reflection

Betrag m -[e]s,ⁿe amount. **b~en†**
vt amount to; **sich b~en** behave.
B~en nt -s behaviour; (Sch)
conduct

betreff|en† vt affect; (angehen)
concern. **b~end** a relevant. **b~s**
prep (+ gen) concerning

betreiben† vt (leiten) run;
(ausüben) carry on

betreten† vt step on; (eintreten)
enter; 'B~ verboten' 'no entry';
(bei Rasen) 'keep off [the grass]'

betreu|en vt look after. **B~er(in)**
m -s,- (f -, -nen) helper;
(Kranken-) nurse. **B~ung** f - care

Betrieb m business; (Firma) firm;
(Treiben) activity; (Verkehr)
traffic; **außer B~** not in use;
(defekt) out of order

**Betriebs|anleitung,
B~anweisung** f operating
instructions pl. **B~ferien** pl
firm's holiday. **B~leitung** f
management. **B~rat** m works
committee. **B~störung** f
breakdown

betrinken† (sich) vr get drunk

betroffen a disconcerted; **b~ sein**
be affected (**von** by)

betrüb|en vt sadden. **b~t** a sad

Betrug m -[e]s deception; (Jur)
fraud

betrüg|en† vt cheat, swindle;
(Jur) defraud; (in der Ehe) be
unfaithful to. **B~er(in)** m -s,- (f -,
-nen) swindler. **B~erei** f -, -en
fraud

betrunken a drunken; **b~ sein** be
drunk. **B~e(r)** m drunk

Bett nt -[e]s, -en bed. **B~couch** f
sofa-bed. **B~decke** f blanket;
(Tages-) bedspread

Bettel|ei f - begging. **b~n** vi
(haben) beg

Bettler(in) m -s,- (f -, -nen) beggar

Bettpfanne f bedpan

Betttuch (Bettuch) nt sheet

Bett|wäsche f bed linen. **B~zeu**g
nt bedding

betupfen vt dab (**mit** with)

beug|en vt bend; (Gram) decline;
conjugate <Verb>; **sich b~en**
bend; (lehnen) lean; (sich fügen)
submit (**dat** to). **B~ung** f -, -en
(Gram) declension; conjugation

Beule f -, -n bump; (Delle) dent

beunruhig|en vt worry; **sich b~e**n
worry. **B~ung** f - worry

B

beurlauben vt give leave to
beurteil|en vt judge. **B~ung** f -,
-en judgement; (Ansicht) opinion
Beute f - booty, haul; (Jagd-) bag;
(eines Raubtiers) prey
Beutel m -s,- bag; (Tabak- & Zool)
pouch. **B~tier** nt marsupial
Bevölkerung f -, -en population
bevollmächtigen vt authorize
bevor conj before; **b~ nicht** until
bevormunden vt treat like a child
bevorstehen† vi sep (haben)
approach; (unmittelbar) be
imminent. **b~d** a approaching,
forthcoming; **unmittelbar b~d**
imminent
bevorzug|en vt prefer;
(begünstigen) favour. **b~t** a
privileged; <Behandlung>
preferential
bewachen vt guard
Bewachung f - guard; **unter B~**
under guard
bewaffn|en vt arm. **b~et** a
armed. **B~ung** f - armament;
(Waffen) arms pl
bewahren vt protect (**vor** + dat
from); (behalten) keep; **die Ruhe
b~** keep calm
bewähren (sich) vr prove one's/
<Ding:> its worth; (erfolgreich
sein) prove a success
bewähr|t a reliable; (erprobt)
proven. **B~ung** f - (Jur)
probation. **B~ungsfrist** f [period
of] probation. **B~ungsprobe** f
(fig) test
bewältigen vt cope with;
(überwinden) overcome
bewässer|n vt irrigate. **B~ung** f -
irrigation
bewegen¹ vt (reg) move; **sich b~**
move; (körperlich) take exercise
bewegen²† vt **jdn dazu b~, etw zu
tun** induce s.o. to do sth
Beweg|grund m motive. **b~lich** a
movable, mobile; (wendig) agile.
B~lichkeit f - mobility; agility.
B~ung f -, -en movement; (Phys)

motion; (Rührung) emotion;
(Gruppe) movement; **körperliche
B~ung** physical exercise.
b~ungslos a motionless
Beweis m -es, -e proof; (Zeichen)
token; **B~e** evidence sg. **b~en†**
vt prove; (zeigen) show; **sich
b~en** prove oneself/<Ding:>
itself. **B~material** nt evidence
bewerb|en (sich) vr apply (**um**
for; **bei** to). **B~er(in)** m -s,- (f -,
-nen) applicant. **B~ung** f -, -en
application
bewerten vt value; (einschätzen)
rate; (Sch) mark, grade
bewilligen vt grant
bewirken vt cause; (herbeiführen)
bring about
bewirt|en vt entertain. **B~ung** f -
hospitality
bewohn|bar a habitable. **b~en** vt
inhabit, live in. **B~er(in)** m -s,- (f
-, -nen) resident, occupant;
(Einwohner) inhabitant
bewölk|en (sich) vr cloud over;
b~t cloudy. **B~ung** f - clouds pl
bewunder|n vt admire. **b~nswert**
a admirable. **B~ung** f -
admiration
bewusst a conscious (gen of);
(absichtlich) deliberate. **b~los** a
unconscious. **B~losigkeit** f -
unconsciousness; **B~sein** nt -s
consciousness; (Gewissheit)
awareness; **bei B~sein** conscious
bezahl|en vt/i (haben) pay; pay
for <Ware, Essen>. **B~ung** f -
payment; (Lohn) pay.
B~fernsehen nt pay television;
pay TV
bezaubern vt enchant
bezeichn|en vt mark; (bedeuten)
denote; (beschreiben, nennen)
describe (**als** as). **b~end** a
typical. **B~ung** f marking;
(Beschreibung) description (**als**
as); (Ausdruck) term; (Name)
name
bezeugen vt testify to

bezichtigen vt accuse (gen of)
bezieh|en† vt cover; (einziehen) move into; (beschaffen) obtain; (erhalten) get; (in Verbindung bringen) relate (auf + acc to); sich b~en (bewölken) cloud over; sich b~en auf (+ acc) refer to; das Bett frisch b~en put clean sheets on the bed. **B~ung** f -, -en relation; (Verhältnis) relationship; (Bezug) respect; B~ungen haben have connections. **b~ungsweise** adv respectively; (vielmehr) or rather
Bezirk m -[e]s, -e district
Bezug m cover; (Kissen-) case; (Beschaffung) obtaining; (Kauf) purchase; (Zusammenhang) reference; **B~̈e** pl earnings; B~ nehmen refer (auf + acc to); in B~ auf (+ acc) regarding
bezüglich prep (+ gen) regarding
● a relating (auf + acc to)
bezwecken vt (fig) aim at
bezweifeln vt doubt
BH /be:'ha:/ m -[s], -[s] bra
Bibel f -, -n Bible
Biber m -s,- beaver
Biblio|thek f -, -en library. **B~thekar(in)** m -s,- (f -, -nen) librarian
biblisch a biblical
bieg|en† vt bend; sich b~en bend
● vi (sein) curve (nach to); um die Ecke b~en turn the corner. **b~sam** a flexible, supple. **B~ung** f -, -en bend
Biene f -, -n bee. **B~nstock** m beehive. **B~nwabe** f honey-comb
Bier nt -s, -e beer. **B~deckel** m beer-mat. **B~krug** m beer-mug
bieten† vt offer; (bei Auktion) bid
Bifokalbrille f bifocals pl
Bigamie f - bigamy
bigott a over-pious
Bikini m -s, -s bikini
Bilanz f -, -en balance sheet; (fig) result; die B~ ziehen (fig) draw conclusions (aus from)

Bild nt -[e]s, -er picture; (Theat) scene
bilden vt form; (sein) be; (erziehen) educate
Bild|erbuch nt picture-book. **B~fläche** f screen. **B~hauer** m -s,- sculptor. **b~lich** a pictorial; (figurativ) figurative. **B~nis** nt -ses, -se portrait. **B~schirm** m (TV) screen. **B~schirmgerät** nt visual display unit, VDU. **b~schön** a very beautiful
Bildung f - formation; (Erziehung) education; (Kultur) education
Billard /'bɪljart/ nt -s billiards sg. **B~tisch** m billiard table
Billett /bɪl'jɛt/ nt -[e]s, -e & -s ticket
Billiarde f -, -n thousand million million
billig a cheap; (dürftig) poor; recht und b~ right and proper. **b~en** vt approve. **B~ung** f - approval
Billion /bɪlio:n/ f -, -en million million, billion
Bimsstein m pumice stone
Binde f -, -n band; (Verband) bandage; (Damen-) sanitary towel. **B~hautentzündung** f conjunctivitis. **b~n**† vt tie (an + acc to); make <Strauß>; bind <Buch>; (fesseln) tie up; (Culin) thicken; sich b~n commit oneself. **B~strich** m hyphen. **B~wort** nt (pl -wörter) (Gram) conjunction
Bind|faden m string. **B~ung** f -, -en (fig) tie; (Beziehung) relationship; (Verpflichtung) commitment; (Ski-) binding; (Tex) weave
binnen prep (+ dat) within. **B~handel** m home trade
Bio- pref organic
Bio|chemie f biochemistry. **b~dynamisch** m organic. **B~graphie, B~grafie** f -, -n biography

B

Bio|hof m organic farm. **B~laden** m health-food store

Biolog|e m -n, -n biologist. **B~ie** f - biology. **b~isch** a biological; **b~ischer Anbau** organic farming; **b~isch angebaut** organically grown

Birke f -, -n birch [tree]

Birma nt -s Burma. **b~anisch** a Burmese

Birn|baum m pear-tree. **B~e** f -, -n pear; (*Electr*) bulb

bis prep (+ acc) as far as, [up] to; (*zeitlich*) until, till; (*spätestens*) by; **bis zu** up to; **bis auf** (+ acc) (*einschließlich*) [down] to; (*ausgenommen*) except [for]; **drei bis vier Mark** three to four marks; **bis morgen!** see you tomorrow! ● conj until

Bischof m -s, ̈-e bishop

bisher adv so far, up to now

Biskuit|rolle /bɪsˈkviːt-/ f Swiss roll. **B~teig** m sponge mixture

Biss m -es, -e bite

bisschen inv pron **ein b~** a bit, a little; **kein b~** not a bit

Biss|en m -s,- bite, mouthful. **b~ig** a vicious; (*fig*) caustic

bisweilen adv from time to time

bitte adv please; (*nach Klopfen*) come in; (*als Antwort auf 'danke'*) don't mention it, you're welcome; **wie b~e?** pardon? **B~e** f -, -n request/(*dringend*) plea (**um** for). **b~en†** vt/i (*haben*) ask/ (*dringend*) beg (**um** for); (*einladen*) invite, ask. **b~end** a pleading

bitter a bitter. **B~keit** f - bitterness. **b~lich** adv bitterly

Bittschrift f petition

bizarr a bizarre

bläh|en vt swell; <*Vorhang, Segel:*> billow ● vi (*haben*) cause flatulence. **B~ungen** fpl flatulence sg, ⊞ wind sg

Blamage /blaˈmaːʒə/ f -, -n humiliation; (*Schande*) disgrace

blamieren vt disgrace; **sich b~** disgrace oneself; (*sich lächerlich machen*) make a fool of oneself

blanchieren /blãˈʃiːrən/ vt (*Culin*) blanch

blank a shiny. **B~oscheck** m blank cheque

Blase f -, -n bubble; (*Med*) blister; (*Anat*) bladder. **b~n†** vt/i (*haben*) blow; play <*Flöte*>. **B~nentzündung** f cystitis

Blas|instrument nt wind instrument. **B~kapelle** f brass band

blass a pale; (*schwach*) faint

Blässe f - pallor

Blatt nt -[e]s, ̈-er (*Bot*) leaf; (*Papier*) sheet; (*Zeitung*) paper

Blattlaus f greenfly

blau a, **B~** nt -s,- blue; **b~er Fleck** bruise; **b~es Auge** black eye; **b~ sein** ⊞ be tight; **Fahrt ins B~e** mystery tour. **B~beere** f bilberry. **B~licht** nt blue flashing light

Blech nt -[e]s, -e sheet metal; (*Weiß-*) tin; (*Platte*) metal sheet; (*Back-*) baking sheet; (*Mus*) brass; (⊞ *Unsinn*) rubbish. **B~schaden** m (*Auto*) damage to the bodywork

Blei nt -[e]s lead

Bleibe f - place to stay. **b~n†** vi (*sein*) remain, stay; (*übrig-*) be left; **ruhig b~n** keep calm; **bei etw b~n** (*fig*) stick to sth; **b~n Sie am Apparat** hold the line; **etw b~n lassen** not to do sth. **b~nd** a permanent; (*anhaltend*) lasting

bleich a pale. **b~en†** vi (*sein*) bleach; (*ver-*) fade ● vt (*reg*) bleach. **B~mittel** nt bleach

blei|ern a leaden. **b~frei** a unleaded. **b~stift** m pencil. **B~stiftabsatz** m stiletto heel. **B~stiftspitzer** m -s,- pencil sharpener

Blende f -, -n shade, shield; (*Sonnen-*) [sun] visor; (*Phot*)

diaphragm; (*Öffnung*) aperture; (*an Kleid*) facing. **b~n** *vt* dazzle, blind

Blick *m* -[e]s, -e look; (*kurz*) glance; (*Aussicht*) view; **auf den ersten B~** at first sight. **b~en** *vi* (*haben*) look/(*kurz*) glance (**auf +** *acc* at). **B~punkt** *m* (*fig*) point of view

blind *a* blind; (*trübe*) dull; **b~er Alarm** false alarm; **b~er Passagier** stowaway. **B~darm** *m* appendix. **B~darmentzündung** *f* appendicitis. **B~e(r)** *m/f* blind man/woman; **die B~en** the blind *pl*. **B~enhund** *m* guidedog. **B~enschrift** *f* braille. **B~gänger** *m* -s,- (*Mil*) dud. **B~heit** *f* - blindness

blink|en *vi* (*haben*) flash; (*funkeln*) gleam; (*Auto*) indicate. **B~er** *m* -s,- (*Auto*) indicator. **B~licht** *nt* flashing light

blinzeln *vi* (*haben*) blink

Blitz *m* -es, -e [flash of] lightning; (*Phot*) flash. **B~ableiter** *m* lightning-conductor. **b~artig** *a* lightning ... ● *adv* like lightning. **b~en** *vi* (*haben*) flash; (*funkeln*) sparkle; **es hat geblitzt** there was a flash of lightning. **B~licht** *nt* (*Phot*) flash. **b~sauber** *a* spick and span. **b~schnell** *a* lightning ... ● *adv* like lightning

Block *m* -[e]s,¨e block ● -[e]s, -s & ¨e pad; (*Häuser-*) block

Blockade *f* -, -n blockade

Blockflöte *f* recorder

blockieren *vt* block; (*Mil*) blockade

Blockschrift *f* block letters *pl*

blöd[e] *a* feeble-minded; (*dumm*) stupid

Blödsinn *m* -[e]s idiocy; (*Unsinn*) nonsense

blöken *vi* (*haben*) bleat

blond *a* fair-haired; <*Haar*> fair

bloß *a* bare; (*alleinig*) mere ● *adv* only, just

bloß|legen *vt sep* uncover. **b~stellen** *vt sep* compromise

Bluff *m* -s, -s bluff. **b~en** *vt/i* (*haben*) bluff

blühen *vi* (*haben*) flower; (*fig*) flourish. **b~d** *a* flowering; (*fig*) flourishing, thriving

Blume *f* -, -n flower; (*vom Wein*) bouquet. **B~nbeet** *nt* flower-bed. **B~ngeschäft** *nt* flower-shop, florist's. **B~nkohl** *m* cauliflower. **B~nmuster** *nt* floral design. **B~nstrauß** *m* bunch of flowers. **B~ntopf** *m* flowerpot; (*Pflanze*) pot plant. **B~nzwiebel** *f* bulb

blumig *a* (*fig*) flowery

Bluse *f* -, -n blouse

Blut *nt* -[e]s blood. **b~arm** *a* anaemic. **B~bahn** *f* blood-stream. **B~bild** *nt* blood count. **B~druck** *m* blood pressure. **b~dürstig** *a* bloodthirsty

Blüte *f* -, -n flower, bloom; (*vom Baum*) blossom; (*B~zeit*) flowering period; (*Baum-*) blossom time; (*Höhepunkt*) peak, prime

Blut|egel *m* -s,- leech. **b~en** *vi* (*haben*) bleed

Blüten|blatt *nt* petal. **B~staub** *m* pollen

Blut|er *m* -s,- haemophiliac. **B~erguss** *m* bruise. **B~gefäß** *nt* blood-vessel. **B~gruppe** *f* blood group. **b~ig** *a* bloody. **B~körperchen** *nt* -s,- corpuscle. **B~probe** *f* blood test. **b~rünstig** *a* (*fig*) bloody, gory. **B~schande** *f* incest. **B~spender** *m* blood donor. **B~sturz** *m* haemorrhage. **B~transfusion, B~übertragung** *f* blood transfusion. **B~ung** *f* -, -en bleeding; (*Med*) haemorrhage; (*Regel-*) period. **b~unterlaufen** *a* bruised; <*Auge*> bloodshot. **B~vergiftung** *f* blood-poisoning. **B~wurst** *f* black pudding

Bö *f* -, -en gust; (*Regen-*) squall

Bob *m* -s, -s bob[-sleigh]

Bock m -[e]s,⸚e buck; (*Ziege*) billy goat; (*Schaf*) ram; (*Gestell*) support. **b~ig** a 🛈 stubborn. **B~springen** nt leap-frog

Boden m -s,⸚ ground; (*Erde*) soil; (*Fuß-*) floor; (*Grundfläche*) bottom; (*Dach-*) loft, attic. **B~satz** m sediment. **B~schätze** mpl mineral deposits. **B~see** (der) Lake Constance

Bogen m -s,⸚ & ⸚ curve; (*Geom*) arc; (*beim Skilauf*) turn; (*Archit*) arch; (*Waffe, Geigen-*) bow; (*Papier*) sheet; **einen großen B~ um jdn/etw machen** 🛈 give s.o./sth a wide berth. **B~schießen** nt archery

Bohle f -, -n [thick] plank

Böhm|en nt -s Bohemia. **b~isch** a Bohemian

Bohne f -, -n bean; **grüne B~n** French beans

bohner|n vt polish. **B~wachs** nt floor-polish

bohr|en vt/i (*haben*) drill (**nach** for); drive <*Tunnel*>; sink <*Brunnen*>; <*Insekt:*> bore. **B~er** m -s,- drill. **B~insel** f [offshore] drilling rig. **B~turm** m derrick

Boje f -, -n buoy

Böllerschuss m gun salute

Bolzen m -s,- bolt; (*Stift*) pin

bombardieren vt bomb; (*fig*) bombard (**mit** with)

Bombe f -, -n bomb. **B~nangriff** m bombing raid. **B~nerfolg** m huge success

Bon /bɔŋ/ m -s, -s voucher; (*Kassen-*) receipt

Bonbon /bɔŋˈbɔŋ/ m & nt -s, -s sweet

Bonus m -[sses], -[sse] bonus

Boot nt -[e]s, -e boat. **B~ssteg** m landing-stage

Bord¹ nt -[e]s, -e shelf

Bord² m (*Naut*) **an B~** aboard, on board; **über B~** overboard. **B~buch** nt log[-book]

Bordell nt -s, -e brothel

Bordkarte f boarding-pass

borgen vt borrow; **jdm etw b~** lend s.o. sth

Borke f -, -n bark

Börse f -, -n purse; (*Comm*) stock exchange. **B~nmakler** m stockbroker

Borst|e f -, -n bristle. **b~ig** a bristly

Borte f -, -n braid

Böschung f -, -en embankment

böse a wicked, evil; (*unartig*) naughty; (*schlimm*) bad; (*zornig*) cross; **jdm** od **auf jdn b~ sein** be cross with s.o.

bos|haft a malicious, spiteful. **B~heit** f -, -en malice; spite; (*Handlung*) spiteful act/ (*Bemerkung*) remark

böswillig a malicious

Botani|k f - botany. **B~ker(in)** m -s,- (f -, -nen) botanist

Bot|e m -n, -n messenger. **B~engang** m errand. **B~schaft** f -, -en message; (*Pol*) embassy. **B~schafter** m -s,- ambassador

Bouillon /bʊlˈjɔŋ/ f -, -s clear soup. **B~würfel** m stock cube

Bowle /ˈboːlə/ f -, -n punch

box|en vi (*haben*) box ●vt punch. **B~en** nt -s boxing. **B~er** m -s,- boxer

brachliegen† vi sep (*haben*) lie fallow

Branche /ˈbrãːʃə/ f -, -n [line of] business. **B~nverzeichnis** nt (*Teleph*) classified directory

Brand m -[e]s,⸚e fire; (*Med*) gangrene; (*Bot*) blight; **in B~ geraten** catch fire; **in B~ setzen** od **stecken** set on fire. **B~bombe** f incendiary bomb

Brand|stifter m arsonist. **B~stiftung** f arson

Brandung f - surf

Brand|wunde f burn. **B~zeichen** nt brand

Branntwein m spirit; (*coll*) spirits pl. **B~brennerei** f distillery

B

bras|ilianisch a Brazilian. **B~ilien** /-iən/ nt -s Brazil

Brat|apfel m baked apple. **b~en†** vt/i (haben) roast; (in der Pfanne) fry. **B~en** m -s,- roast; (B~stück) joint. **b~fertig** a oven-ready. **B~hähnchen** nt roasting chicken. **B~kartoffeln** fpl fried potatoes. **B~pfanne** f frying-pan

Bratsche f -, -n (Mus) viola

Bratspieß m spit

Brauch m -[e]s,Bräuche custom. **b~bar** a usable; (nützlich) useful. **b~en** vt need; (ge-, verbrauchen) use; take <Zeit>; er b~t es nur zu sagen he only has to say

Braue f -, -n eyebrow

brau|en vt brew. **B~er** m -s,- brewer. **B~erei** f -, -en brewery

braun a, **B~** nt -s,- brown; b~ werden <Person:> get a tan; b~ [gebrannt] sein be [sun-]tanned

Bräune f - [sun-]tan. **b~n** vt/i (haben) brown; (in der Sonne) tan

Braunschweig nt -s Brunswick

Brause f -, -n (Dusche) shower; (an Gießkanne) rose; (B~limonade) fizzy drink

Braut f -,-̈e bride; (Verlobte) fiancée

Bräutigam m -s, -e bridegroom; (Verlobter) fiancé

Brautkleid nt wedding dress

Brautpaar nt bridal couple; (Verlobte) engaged couple

brav a good; (redlich) honest ●adv dutifully; (redlich) honestly

bravo int bravo!

BRD abbr (Bundesrepublik Deutschland) FRG

Brech|eisen nt jemmy; (B~stange) crowbar. **b~en†** vt break; (Phys) refract <Licht>; (erbrechen) vomit; sich b~en <Wellen:> break; <Licht:> be refracted; sich (dat) den Arm b~en break one's arm ●vi (sein) break ●vi (haben) vomit, be sick.

B~reiz m nausea. **B~stange** f crowbar

Brei m -[e]s, -e paste; (Culin) purée; (Hafer-) porridge

breit a wide; <Schultern, Grinsen> broad. **B~e** f -, -n width; breadth; (Geog) latitude. **b~en** vt spread (über + acc over). **B~engrad** m [degree of] latitude. **B~enkreis** m parallel

Bremse¹ f -, -n horsefly

Bremse² f -, -n brake. **b~n** vt slow down; (fig) restrain ●vi (haben) brake

Bremslicht nt brake-light

brenn|bar a combustible; leicht b~bar highly [in]flammable. **b~en†** vi (haben) burn; <Licht:> be on; <Zigarette:> be alight; (weh tun) smart, sting **vt** burn; (rösten) roast; (im Brennofen) fire; (destillieren) distil. **b~end** a burning; (angezündet) lighted; (fig) fervent **B~erei** f -, -en distillery

Brennessel* f s. Brennnessel

Brenn|holz nt firewood. **B~ofen** m kiln. **B~nessel** f stinging nettle. **B~punkt** m (Phys) focus. **B~spiritus** m methylated spirits. **B~stoff** m fuel

Bretagne /bre'tanjə/ (die) - Brittany

Brett nt -[e]s, -er board; (im Regal) shelf; schwarzes B~ notice board. **B~spiel** nt board game

Brezel f -, -n pretzel

Bridge /brɪtʃ/ nt - (Spiel) bridge

Brief m -[e]s, -e letter. **B~beschwerer** m -s,- paperweight. **B~freund(in)** m(f) pen-friend. **B~kasten** m letter-box. **B~kopf** m letter-head. **b~lich** a & adv by letter. **B~marke** f [postage] stamp. **B~öffner** m paper-knife. **B~papier** nt notepaper. **B~tasche** f wallet. **B~träger** m postman. **B~umschlag** m

B

envelope. **B~wahl** *f* postal vote. **B~wechsel** *m* correspondence

Brikett *nt* -s, -s briquette

Brillant *m* -en, -en [cut] diamond

Brille *f* -, -n glasses *pl*, spectacles *pl*; (*Schutz-*) goggles *pl*; (*Klosett-*) toilet seat

bringen† *vt* bring; (*fort-*) take; (*ein-*) yield; (*veröffentlichen*) publish; (*im Radio*) broadcast; show <*Film*>; ins Bett b~ put to bed; jdn nach Hause b~ take/ (*begleiten*) see s.o. home; um etw b~ deprive of sth; jdn dazu b~, etw zu tun get s.o. to do sth; es weit b~ (*fig*) go far

Brise *f* -, -n breeze

Brit|e *m* -n, -n, **B~in** *f* -, -nen Briton. **b~isch** *a* British

Bröck|chen *nt* -s, - (*Culin*) crouton. **b~elig** *a* crumbly; <*Gestein*> friable. **b~eln** *vt/i* (*haben/sein*) crumble

Brocken *m* -s, - chunk; (*Erde, Kohle*) lump

Brokat *m* -[e]s, -e brocade

Brokkoli *pl* broccoli *sg*

Brombeere *f* blackberry

Bronchitis *f* - bronchitis

Bronze /'brõːsə/ *f* -, -n bronze

Brosch|e *f* -, -n brooch. **b~iert** *a* paperback. **B~üre** *f* -, -n brochure; (*Heft*) booklet

Brösel *mpl* (*Culin*) breadcrumbs

Brot *n* -[e]s, -e bread; ein B~ a loaf [of bread]; (*Scheibe*) a slice of bread

Brötchen *n* -s, - [bread] roll

Brotkrümel *m* breadcrumb

Bruch *m* -[e]s,̈ -e break; (*Brechen*) breaking; (*Rohr-*) burst; (*Med*) fracture; (*Eingeweide-*) rupture, hernia; (*Math*) fraction; (*fig*) breach; (*in Beziehung*) break-up

brüchig *a* brittle

Bruch|landung *f* crash-landing. **B~rechnung** *f* fractions *pl*. **B~stück** *nt* fragment. **B~teil** *m* fraction

Brücke *f* -, -n bridge; (*Teppich*) rug

Bruder *m* -s,̈ brother

brüderlich *a* brotherly, fraternal

Brügge *nt* -s Bruges

Brüh|e *f* -, -n broth, stock. **B~würfel** *m* stock cube

brüllen *vt/i* (*haben*) roar

brumm|eln *vt/i* (*haben*) mumble. **b~en** *vi* (*haben*) <*Insekt:*> buzz; <*Bär:*> growl; <*Motor:*> hum; (*murren*) grumble **B~er** *m* -s, - 🗊 bluebottle. **b~ig** *a* 🗊 grumpy

brünett *a* dark-haired

Brunnen *m* -s, - well; (*Spring-*) fountain; (*Heil-*) spa water

brüsk *a* brusque

Brüssel *nt* -s Brussels

Brust *f* -,̈ -e chest; (*weibliche, Culin: B~stück*) breast. **B~bein** *nt* breastbone

brüsten (sich) *vr* boast

Brust|fellentzündung *f* pleurisy. **B~schwimmen** *nt* breaststroke

Brüstung *f* -, -en parapet

Brustwarze *f* nipple

Brut *f* -, -en incubation

brutal *a* brutal

brüten *vi* (*haben*) sit (*on eggs*); (*fig*) ponder (*über* + *dat* over)

Brutkasten *m* (*Med*) incubator

brutto *adv*, **B~-** *pref* gross

Bub *m* -en, -en (*SGer*) boy. **B~e** *m* -n, -n (*Karte*) jack, knave

Buch *nt* -[e]s,̈ -er book; B~ führen keep a record (*über* + *acc* of); die B~̈er führen keep the accounts

Buche *f* -, -n beech

buchen *vt* book; (*Comm*) enter

Bücher|ei *f* -, -en library. **B~regal** *nt* bookcase, bookshelves *pl*. **B~schrank** *m* bookcase

Buchfink *m* chaffinch

Buch|führung *f* bookkeeping. **B~halter(in)** *m* -s, - (*f* -, -nen) bookkeeper, accountant. **B~haltung** *f* bookkeeping, accountancy; (*Abteilung*)

accounts department.
B~handlung f bookshop
Büchse f -, -n box; (Konserven-)
tin, can
Buch|stabe m -n, -n letter.
b~stabieren vt spell [out].
b~stäblich adv literally
Bucht f -, -en (Geog) bay
Buchung f -, -en booking,
reservation; (Comm) entry
Buckel m -s,- hump; (Beule)
bump; (Hügel) hillock
bücken (sich) vr bend down
bucklig a hunchbacked
Bückling m -s, -e smoked herring
Buddhis|mus m - Buddhism.
B~t(in) m -en, -en (f -, -nen)
Buddhist. **b~tisch** a Buddhist
Bude f -, -n hut; (Kiosk) kiosk;
(Markt-) stall; (🔢 Zimmer) room
Budget /by'dʒe:/ nt -s, -s budget
Büfett nt -[e]s, -e sideboard;
(Theke) bar; **kaltes B~** cold buffet
Büffel m -s,- buffalo
Bügel m -s,- frame; (Kleider-)
coathanger; (Steig-) stirrup;
(Brillen-) sidepiece. **B~brett** nt
ironing-board. **B~eisen** nt iron.
B~falte f crease. **b~frei** a non-
iron. **b~n** vt/i (haben) iron
Bühne f -, -n stage. **B~nbild** nt
set. **B~neingang** m stage door
Buhrufe mpl boos
Bukett nt -[e]s, -e bouquet
Bulgarien /-iən/ nt -s Bulgaria
Bull|auge nt (Naut) porthole.
B~dogge f bulldog. **B~dozer**
/-do:zɐ/ m -s,- bulldozer. **B~e** m
-n, -n bull; (🔢 Polizist) cop
Bummel m -s,- 🔢 stroll. **B~lei** f -
🔢 dawdling
bummel|ig a 🔢 slow; (nachlässig)
careless. **b~n** vi (sein) 🔢 stroll
● vi (haben) 🔢 dawdle. **B~streik**
m go-slow. **B~zug** m 🔢 slow
train
Bums m -es, -e 🔢 bump, thump
Bund[1] nt -[e]s, -e bunch

Bund[2] m -[e]s,ِ-e association;
(Bündnis) alliance; (Pol)
federation; (Rock-, Hosen-)
waistband; **der B~** the Federal
Government
Bündel nt -s,- bundle. **b~n** vt
bundle [up]
Bundes|- pref Federal.
B~genosse m ally. **B~kanzler** m
Federal Chancellor. **B~land** nt
[federal] state; (Aust) province.
B~liga f German national
league. **B~rat** m Upper House of
Parliament. **B~regierung** f
Federal Government. **B~republik**
f **die B~republik Deutschland** the
Federal Republic of Germany.
B~tag m Lower House of
Parliament. **B~wehr** f [Federal
German] Army
bünd|ig a & adv **kurz und b~ig**
short and to the point. **B~nis** nt
-sses, -sse alliance
Bunker m -s,- bunker;
(Luftschutz-) shelter
bunt a coloured; (farbenfroh)
colourful; (grell) gaudy;
(gemischt) varied; (wirr)
confused; **b~e Platte** assorted
cold meats. **B~stift** m crayon
Bürde f -, -n (fig) burden
Burg f -, -en castle
Bürge m -n, -n guarantor. **b~n** vi
(haben) **b~n für** vouch for; (fig)
guarantee
Bürger|(in) m -s,- (f -, -nen)
citizen. **B~krieg** m civil war.
b~lich a civil; <Pflicht> civic;
(mittelständisch) middle-class.
B~liche(r) m/f commoner.
B~meister m mayor. **B~rechte**
npl civil rights. **B~steig** m -[e]s,
-e pavement
Bürgschaft f -, -en surety
Burgunder m -s,- (Wein)
Burgundy
Büro nt -s, -s office.
B~angestellte(r) m/f office-
worker. **B~klammer** f paper-clip.

B∼kratie *f* -, -n bureaucracy.
b∼kratisch *a* bureaucratic
Bursche *m* -n, -n lad, youth
Bürste *f* -, -n brush. b∼n *vt* brush.
B∼nschnitt *m* crew cut
Bus *m* -ses, -se bus; (*Reise-*) coach
Busch *m* -[e]s,¨e bush
Büschel *nt* -s,- tuft
buschig *a* bushy
Busen *m* -s,- bosom
Bussard *m* -s, -e buzzard
Buße *f* -, -n penance; (*Jur*) fine
Bußgeld *nt* (*Jur*) fine
Büste *f* -, -n bust; (*Schneider-*)
dummy. B∼nhalter *m* -s,- bra
Butter *f* - butter. B∼blume *f*
buttercup. B∼brot *nt* slice of
bread and butter. B∼milch *f*
buttermilk. b∼n *vt* butter
b.w. *abbr* (bitte wenden) P.T.O.

ca. *abbr* (circa) about
Café /ka'fe:/ *nt* -s, -s café
camp|en /'kɛmpn/ *vi* (*haben*) go
camping. C∼ing *nt* -s camping.
C∼ingplatz *m* campsite
Caravan /'ka[:]ravan/ *m* -s, -s
(*Auto*) caravan; (*Kombi*) estate
car
CD /tsɛ:'de:/ *f* -, -s compact disc,
CD. **CD-ROM** /tsɛ:e:de:'rɔm/ *f* -,-(s)
CD-ROM
Cell|ist(in) /tʃɛ'lɪst(ɪn)/ *m* -en, -en
(*f* -, -nen) cellist. C∼o /'tʃɛlo/ *nt* -,
-los & -li cello
Celsius /'tsɛlziʊs/ *inv* Celsius,
centigrade
Champagner /ʃam'panjɐ/ *m* -s
champagne

Champignon /'ʃampɪnjɔŋ/ *m* -s, -s
[field] mushroom
Chance /'ʃã:s[ə]/ *f* -, -n chance
Chaos /'ka:ɔs/ *nt* - chaos
Charakter /ka'raktɐ/ *m* -s, -e
/-'te:rə/ character. c∼isieren *vt*
characterize. c∼istisch *a*
characteristic (**für** of)
charm|ant /ʃar'mant/ *a* charming.
C∼e /ʃarm/ *m* -s charm
Charter|flug /'tʃ-, 'ʃartɐ-/ *m*
charter flight. c∼n *vt* charter
Chassis /ʃa'si:/ *nt* -,- /-'si:[s], -'si:s/
chassis
Chauffeur /ʃɔ'føːɐ/ *m* -s, -e
chauffeur; (*Taxi-*) driver
Chauvinist /ʃovi'nɪst/ *m* -en, -en
chauvinist
Chef /ʃɛf/ *m* -s, -s head; 🄸 boss
Chemie /çe'mi:/ *f* -chemistry
Chem|iker(in) /'çe:-/ *m* -s,- (*f* -,
-nen) chemist. c∼isch *a*
chemical; c∼ische Reinigung
dry-cleaning; (*Geschäft*) dry-
cleaner's
Chicorée /'ʃikore:/ *m* -s chicory
Chiffre /'ʃɪfɐ, 'ʃɪfrə/ *f* -, -n cipher
Chile /'çi:le/ *nt* -s Chile
Chin|a /'çi:na/ *nt* -s China. C∼ese
m -n, -n, C∼esin *f* -, -nen Chinese.
c∼esisch *a* Chinese. C∼esisch
nt -[s] (*Lang*) Chinese
Chip /tʃɪp/ *m* -s, -s [micro]chip.
C∼s *pl* crisps
Chirurg /çi'rʊrk/ *m* -en, -en
surgeon. C∼ie /-'gi:/ *f* - surgery
Chlor /klo:ɐ/ *nt* -s chlorine
Choke /tʃo:k/ *m* -s, -s (*Auto*)
choke
Cholera /'ko:lera/ *f* - cholera
cholerisch /ko'le:rɪʃ/ *a* irascible
Cholesterin /ço-, kolɛste'ri:n/ *nt* -s
cholesterol
Chor /ko:ɐ/ *m* -[e]s,¨e choir
Choreographie, Choreografie
/koreogra'fi:/ *f* -, -n choreography
Christ /krɪst/ *m* -en, -en Christian.
C∼baum *m* Christmas tree.

C~entum nt -s Christianity
c~lich a Christian
Christus /'krɪstʊs/ m -ti Christ
Chrom /kro:m/ nt -s chromium
Chromosom /kromo'zo:m/ nt -s,
-en chromosome
Chronik /'kro:nɪk/ f -, -en
chronicle
chronisch /'kro:nɪʃ/ a chronic
Chrysantheme /kryzan'te:mə/ f -,
-n chrysanthemum
circa /'ʦɪrka/ adv about
Clique /'klɪkə/ f -, -n clique
Clou /klu:/ m -s, -s highlight, ▯
high spot
Clown /klaun/ m -s, -s clown
Club /klʊp/ m -s, -s club
Cocktail /'kɔkteːl/ m -s, -s cocktail
Code /'koːt/ m -s, -s code
Comic-Heft /'kɔmɪk-/ nt comic
Computer /kɔm'pju:tə/ m -s,-
computer. **c~isieren** vt
computerize. **C~spiel** nt
computer game
Conférencier /kõ'ferã'sjeː/ m -s,-
compère
Cord /kɔrt/ m -s, **C~samt** m
corduroy
Couch /kau:tʃ/ f -, -es settee
Cousin /ku'zẽ:/ m -s, -s [male]
cousin. **C~e** /-'zi:nə/ f -, -n
[female] cousin
Creme /kre:m/ f -, -s cream;
(Speise) cream dessert
Curry /'kari, 'kœri/ nt & m -s curry
powder ● nt -s, -s (Gericht) curry

da adv there; (hier) here; (zeitlich)
then; (in dem Fall) in that case;
von da an from then on; **da sein**

be there/(hier) here; (existieren)
exist; **wieder da sein** be back
● conj as, since
dabei (emphatic: **dabei**) adv
nearby; (daran) with it;
(eingeschlossen) included;
(hinsichtlich) about it;
(währenddem) during this;
(gleichzeitig) at the same time;
(doch) and yet; **dicht d~** close by;
d~ sein be present; (mitmachen)
be involved; **d~ sein, etw zu tun**
be just doing sth
Dach nt -[e]s,̈-er roof. **D~boden** m
loft. **D~luke** f skylight. **D~rinne** f
gutter
Dachs m -es, -e badger
Dachsparren m -s,- rafter
Dackel m -s,- dachshund
dadurch (emphatic: **dadurch**) adv
through it/them; (Ursache) by it;
(deshalb) because of that; **d~,
dass** because
dafür (emphatic: **dafür**) adv for it/
them; (anstatt) instead; (als
Ausgleich) but [on the other
hand]; **d~, dass** considering that;
ich kann nichts dafür it's not my
fault
dagegen (emphatic: **dagegen**) adv
against it/them; (Mittel, Tausch)
for it; (verglichen damit) by
comparison; (jedoch) however;
hast du was d~? do you mind?
daheim adv at home
daher (emphatic: **daher**) adv from
there; (deshalb) for that reason;
das kommt d~, weil that's because
● conj that is why
dahin (emphatic: **dahin**) adv there;
bis d~ up to there; (bis dann)
until/(Zukunft) by then; **jdn
d~bringen, dass er etw tut** get s.o.
to do sth
dahinten adv back there
dahinter (emphatic: **dahinter**) adv
behind it/them; **d~ kommen** (fig)
get to the bottom of it
Dahlie /-ิə/ f -, -n dahlia

dalassen† vt sep leave there

daliegen† vi sep (haben) lie there

damalig a at that time; **der d~e Minister** the then minister

damals adv at that time

Damast m -es, -e damask

Dame f -, -n lady; (Karte, Schach) queen; (D~spiel) draughts sg. **d~haft** a ladylike

damit (emphatic: **damit**) adv with it/them; (dadurch) by it; **hör auf d~!** stop it! ● conj so that

Damm m -[e]s,—e dam

dämmer|ig a dim. **D~licht** nt twilight. **d~n** vi <haben> <Morgen:> dawn; **es d~t** it is getting light/(abends) dark. **D~ung** f dawn; (Abend-) dusk

Dämon m -s, -en /-'mo:nən/ demon

Dampf m -es,—e steam; (Chem) vapour. **d~en** vi (haben) steam

dämpfen vt (Culin) steam; (fig) muffle <Ton>; lower <Stimme>

Dampf|er m -s,- steamer. **D~kochtopf** m pressure-cooker. **D~maschine** f steam engine. **D~walze** f steamroller

danach (emphatic: **danach**) adv after it/them; <suchen> for it/them; <riechen> of it; (später) afterwards; (entsprechend) accordingly; **es sieht d~ aus** it looks like it

Däne m -n, -n Dane

daneben (emphatic: **daneben**) adv beside it/them; (außerdem) in addition; (verglichen damit) by comparison

Dän|emark nt -s Denmark. **D~in** f -, -nen Dane. **d~isch** a Danish

Dank m -es thanks pl; **vielen D~!** thank you very much! **d~** prep (+ dat or gen) thanks to. **d~bar** a grateful; (erleichtert) thankful; (lohnend) rewarding. **D~barkeit** f - gratitude. **d~e** adv **d~e [schön od sehr]!** thank you [very much]! **d~en** vi (haben) thank (jdm s.o.);

(ablehnen) decline; **nichts zu d~en!** don't mention it!

dann adv then; **selbst d~, wenn** even if

daran (emphatic: **daran**) adv on it/them; at it/them; <denken> of it; **nahe d~** on the point (**etw zu tun** of doing sth). **d~setzen** vt sep **alles d~setzen** do one's utmost (**zu** to)

darauf (emphatic: **darauf**) adv on it/them; <warten> for it; <antworten> to it; (danach) after that; (d~hin) as a result. **d~hin** adv as a result

daraus (emphatic: **daraus**) adv out of or from it/them; **er macht sich nichts d~** he doesn't care for it

darlegen vt sep expound; (erklären) explain

Darlehen nt -s,- loan

Darm m -[e]s,—e intestine

darstell|en vt sep represent; (bildlich) portray; (Theat) interpret; (spielen) play; (schildern) describe. **D~er** m -s,- actor. **D~erin** f -, -nen actress. **D~ung** f representation; interpretation; description

darüber (emphatic: **darüber**) adv over it/them; (höher) above it/them; <sprechen, lachen, sich freuen> about it; (mehr) more; **d~ hinaus** beyond [it]; (dazu) on top of that

darum (emphatic: **darum**) adv round it/them; <bitten, kämpfen> for it; (deshalb) that is why; **d~, weil** because

darunter (emphatic: **darunter**) adv under it/them; (tiefer) below it/them; (weniger) less; (dazwischen) among them

das def art & pron s. der

dasein* vi sep (sein) da sein, s. da. **D~** nt -s existence

dass conj that

dasselbe pron s. derselbe

Daten|sichtgerät *nt* visual display unit, VDU. **D~verarbeitung** *f* data processing

datieren *vt/i* (*haben*) date

Dativ *m* -s, -e dative. **D~objekt** *nt* indirect object

Dattel *f* -, -n date

Datum *nt* s, -ten date; **Daten** dates; (*Angaben*) data

Dauer *f* - duration, length; (*Jur*) term; **auf die D~** in the long run. **D~auftrag** *m* standing order. **d~haft** *a* lasting, enduring; (*fest*) durable. **D~karte** *f* season ticket. **d~n** *vi* (*haben*) last; **lange d~n** take a long time. **d~nd** *a* lasting; (*ständig*) constant. **D~welle** *f* perm

Daumen *m* -s,- thumb; **jdm den D~ drücken** *od* **halten** keep one's fingers crossed for s.o.

Daunen *fpl* down *sg*. **D~decke** *f* [down-filled] duvet

davon (*emphatic:* **davon**) *adv* from it/them; (*dadurch*) by it; (*damit*) with it/them; (*darüber*) about it; (*Menge*) of it/them; **das kommt d~!** it serves you right! **d~kommen†** *vi sep* (*sein*) escape (**mit dem Leben** with one's life). **d~laufen†** *vi sep* (*sein*) run away. **d~machen (sich)** *vr sep* 🛈 make off. **d~tragen†** *vt sep* carry off; (*erleiden*) suffer; (*gewinnen*) win

davor (*emphatic:* **davor**) *adv* in front of it/them; <*sich fürchten*> of it; (*zeitlich*) before it/them

dazu (*emphatic:* **dazu**) *adv* to it/ them; (*damit*) with it/them; (*dafür*) for it; **noch d~** in addition to that; **jdn d~ bringen, etw zu tun** get s.o. to do sth; **ich kam nicht d~** I didn't get round to [doing] it. **d~kommen†** *vi sep* (*sein*) arrive [on the scene]; (*hinzukommen*) be added. **d~rechnen** *vt sep* add to it/them

dazwischen (*emphatic:* **dazwischen**) *adv* between them; in between; (*darunter*) among them. **d~kommen†** *vi sep* (*sein*) (*fig*) crop up; **wenn nichts d~kommt** if all goes well

Deba|tte *f* -, -n debate; **zur D~te stehen** be at issue. **d~tieren** *vt/i* (*haben*) debate

Debüt /de'by:/ *nt* -s, -s début

Deck *nt* -[e]s, -s (*Naut*) deck; **an D~** on deck. **D~bett** *nt* duvet

Decke *f* -, -n cover; (*Tisch-*) table-cloth; (*Bett-*) blanket; (*Reise-*) rug; (*Zimmer-*) ceiling; **unter einer D~stecken** 🛈 be in league

Deckel *m* -s,- lid; (*Flaschen-*) top; (*Buch-*) cover

decken *vt* cover; tile <*Dach*>; lay <*Tisch*>; (*schützen*) shield; (*Sport*) mark; meet <*Bedarf*>; **jdn d~** (*fig*) cover up for s.o.; **sich d~** (*fig*) cover oneself (**gegen** against); (*übereinstimmen*) coincide

Deckname *m* pseudonym

Deckung *f* - (*Mil*) cover; (*Sport*) defence; (*Mann-*) marking; (*Boxen*) guard; (*Sicherheit*) security; **in D~ gehen** take cover

defin|ieren *vt* define. **D~ition** /-'tsio:n/ *f* -, -en definition

Defizit *nt* -s, -e deficit

deformiert *a* deformed

deftig *a* 🛈 <*Mahlzeit*> hearty; <*Witz*> coarse

Degen *m* -s,- sword; (*Fecht-*) épée

degeneriert *a* (*fig*) degenerate

degradieren *vt* (*Mil*) demote; (*fig*) degrade

dehn|bar *a* elastic. **d~en** *vt* stretch; lengthen <*Vokal*>; **sich d~en** stretch

Deich *m* -[e]s, -e dike

dein *poss pron* your. **d~e(r,s)** *poss pron* yours; **die D~en** *od* **d~en** *pl* your family *sg*. **d~erseits** *adv* for your part.

d~etwegen *adv* for your sake; (*wegen dir*) because of you, on your account. **d~etwillen** *adv* um d~**etwillen** for your sake. **d~ige** *poss pron* der/die/das d~**ige** yours. **d~s** *poss pron* yours

Dekan *m* -s, -e dean

Deklin|ation /-'tsio:n/ *f* -, -en declension. **d~ieren** *vt* decline

Dekolleté, Dekolletee /dekɔl'te:/ *nt* -s, -s low neckline

Dekor *m & nt* -s decoration. **D~ateur** /-'tø:ɐ̯/ *m* -s, -e interior decorator; (*Schaufenster-*) window-dresser. **D~ation** /-'tsio:n/ *f* -, -en decoration; (*Schaufenster-*) window-dressing; (*Auslage*) display. **d~ativ** *a* decorative. **d~ieren** *vt* decorate; dress <*Schaufenster*>

Delegation /-'tsio:n/ *f* -, -en delegation. **D~ierte(r)** *m/f* delegate

delikat *a* delicate; (*lecker*) delicious; (*taktvoll*) tactful. **D~essengeschäft** *nt* delicatessen

Delikt *nt* -[e]s, -e offence

Delinquent *m* -en, -en offender

Delle *f* -, -n dent

Delphin *m* -s, -e dolphin

Delta *nt* -s, -s delta

dem *def art & pron s.* der

dementieren *vt* deny

dem|entsprechend *a* corresponding; (*passend*) appropriate ●*adv* accordingly; (*passend*) appropriately. **d~nächst** *adv* soon; (*in Kürze*) shortly

Demokrat *m* -en, -en democrat. **D~ie** *f* -, -n democracy. **d~isch** *a* democratic

demolieren *vt* wreck

Demonstr|ant *m* -en, -en demonstrator. **D~ation** /-'tsio:n/ *f* -, -en demonstration. **d~ieren** *vt/i* (*haben*) demonstrate

demontieren *vt* dismantle

Demoskopie *f* - opinion research

Demut *f* - humility

den *def art & pron s.* der. **d~en** *pron s.* der

denk|bar *a* conceivable. **d~en**† *vt/i* (*haben*) think (an + *acc* of); (*sich erinnern*) remember (an etw *acc* sth); **das kann ich mir d~en** I can imagine [that]; **ich d~e nicht daran** I have no intention of doing it. **D~mal** *nt* memorial; (*Monument*) monument. **d~würdig** *a* memorable

denn *conj* for; **besser/mehr d~ je** better/more than ever ●*adv* wie/wo d~? but how/where? **warum d~ nicht?** why ever not? **es sei d~ [, dass]** unless

dennoch *adv* nevertheless

Denunz|iant *m* -en, -en informer. **d~ieren** *vt* denounce

Deodorant *nt* -s, -s deodorant

deplaciert, deplatziert /-'tsi:ɐ̯t/ *a* (*fig*) out of place

Deponie *f* -, -n dump. **d~ren** *vt* deposit

deportieren *vt* deport

Depot /de'po:/ *nt* -s, -s depot; (*Lager*) warehouse; (*Bank-*) safe deposit

Depression *f* -, -en depression

deprimieren *vt* depress

---

der, die, das, *pl* **die**
● *definite article*
  (*acc* **den, die, das,** *pl* **die;** *gen* **des, der, des,** *pl* **der;** *dat* **dem, der, dem,** *pl* **den**)
····▸ the. **der Mensch** the person; (*als abstrakter Begriff*) man. **die Natur** nature. **das Leben** life. **das Lesen/Tanzen** reading/dancing. **sich** (*dat*) **das Gesicht/die Hände waschen** wash one's face/hands. **5 Mark das Pfund** 5 marks a pound
● *pronoun*
  (*acc* **den, die, das,** *pl* **die;** *gen* **dessen, deren, dessen,** *pl*

deren; *dat* dem, der, dem, *pl* denen)

● *demonstrative pronoun*

····▸ that; (*pl*) those

····▸ (*attributiv*) der Mann war es it was 'that man

····▸ (*substantivisch*) he, she, it; (*pl*) they. der war es it was 'him. die da (*person*) that woman/girl; (*thing*) that one

● *relative pronoun*

····▸ (*Person*) who. der Mann, der/ dessen Sohn hier arbeitet the man who/whose son works here. die Frau, mit der ich Tennis spiele the woman with whom I play tennis, the woman I play tennis with. das Mädchen, das ich gestern sah the girl I saw yesterday

····▸ (*Ding*) which, that. ich sah ein Buch, das mich interessierte I saw a book that interested me. die CD, die ich mir anhöre the CD I am listening to. das Auto, mit dem wir nach Deutschland fahren the car we are going to Germany in *or* in which we are going to Germany

derb *a* tough; (*kräftig*) strong; (*grob*) coarse; (*unsanft*) rough

deren *pron s.* der

dergleichen *inv a* such ● *pron* such a thing/such things

der-/die-/dasselbe, *pl* dieselben *pron* the same; ein- und dasselbe one and the same thing

derzeit *adv* at present

des *def art s.* der

Desert|eur /-'tø:ɐ̯/ *m* -s, -e deserter. **d~ieren** *vi* (*sein/haben*) desert

desgleichen *adv* likewise ● *pron* the like

deshalb *adv* for this reason; (*also*) therefore

Designer(in) /di'zai:nɐ, -nərɪn/ *m* -s,- (*f*, -, -nen) designer

Desin|fektion /dɛsʔɪnfɛk'tsi̯o:n/ *f* disinfecting. **D~fektionsmittel** *nt* disinfectant. **d~fizieren** *vt* disinfect

dessen *pron s.* der

Destill|ation /-'tsi̯o:n/ *f* - distillation. **d~ieren** *vt* distil

desto *adv* je mehr d~ besser the more the better

deswegen *adv* = deshalb

Detektiv *m* -s, -e detective

Deton|ation /-'tsi̯o:n/ *f* -, -en explosion. **d~ieren** *vi* (*sein*) explode

deut|en *vt* interpret; predict <*Zukunft*> ● *vi* (*haben*) point (auf + *acc* at/(*fig*) to). **d~lich** *a* clear; (*eindeutig*) plain

deutsch *a* German. **D~** *nt* -[s] (*Lang*) German; auf D~ in German. **D~e(r)** *m/f* German. **D~land** *nt* -s Germany

Deutung *f* -, -en interpretation

Devise *f* -, -n motto. **D~n** *pl* foreign currency *or* exchange *sg*

Dezember *m* -s,- December

dezent *a* unobtrusive; (*diskret*) discreet

Dezernat *nt* -[e]s, -e department

Dezimalzahl *f* decimal

d.h. *abbr* (*das heißt*) i.e.

Dia *nt* -s, -s (*Phot*) slide

Diabet|es *m* - diabetes. **D~iker** *m* -s,- diabetic

Diadem *nt* -s, -e tiara

Diagnose *f* -, -n diagnosis

diagonal *a* diagonal. **D~e** *f* -, -n diagonal

Diagramm *nt* -s, -e diagram; (*Kurven-*) graph

Diakon *m* -s, -e deacon

Dialekt *m* -[e]s, -e dialect

Dialog *m* -[e]s, -e dialogue

Diamant *m* -en, -en diamond

Diapositiv *nt* -s, -e (*Phot*) slide

Diaprojektor *m* slide projector

Diät *f* -, -en (*Med*) diet; **D~** leben be on a diet

ich *pron (acc of* du) you; *(refl)* yourself

icht *a* dense; *(dick)* thick; *(undurchlässig)* airtight; *(wasser-)* watertight ● *adv* densely; *(nahe)* close (**bei** to). **D~e** density. **d~en**¹ *vt* make watertight

icht|en² *vi (haben)* write poetry. ● *vt* write. **D~er(in)** *m* -s,- *(f* -, -en) poet. **d~erisch** *a* poetic. **D~ung**¹ *f* -, -en poetry; *(Gedicht)* poem

ichtung² *f* -, -en seal; *(Ring)* washer; *(Auto)* gasket

ick *a* thick; *(beleibt)* fat; *(geschwollen)* swollen; *(fam; eng)* close; **d~ machen** be fattening. **d~flüssig** *a* thick; *(Phys)* viscous. **D~kopf** *m* [!] stubborn person; **einen D~kopf haben** be stubborn

die *def art & pron s.* der

Dieb|(in) *m* -[e]s, -e *(f* -, -nen) thief. **d~isch** *a* thieving; *<Freude>* malicious. **D~stahl** *m* -[e]s,¨e theft

Diele *f* -, -n floorboard; *(Flur)* hall

dien|en *vi (haben)* serve. **D~er** *m* -s,- servant; *(Verbeugung)* bow. **D~erin** *f* -, -nen maid, servant

Dienst *m* -[e]s, -e service; *(Arbeit)* work; *(Amtsausübung)* duty; **außer D~** off duty; *(pensioniert)* retired; **D~ haben** work; *<Soldat, Arzt>* be on duty

Dienstag *m* Tuesday. **d~s** *adv* on Tuesdays

Dienst|bote *m* servant. **d~frei** *a* **d~freier Tag** day off; **d~frei haben** have time off; *<Soldat, Arzt>* be off duty. **D~grad** *m* rank. **D~leistung** *f* service. **d~lich** *a* official ● *adv* **d~lich verreist** away on business. **D~mädchen** *nt* maid. **D~reise** *f* business trip. **D~stelle** *f* office. **D~stunden** *fpl* office hours

dies *inv pron* this. **d~bezüglich** *a* relevant ● *adv* regarding this

matter. **d~e(r,s)** *pron* this; *(pl)* these; *(substantivisch)* this [one]; *(pl)* these; **d~e Nacht** tonight; *(letzte)* last night

dieselbe *pron s.* derselbe

Dieselkraftstoff *m* diesel [oil]

diesmal *adv* this time

Dietrich *m* -s, -e skeleton key

Diffamation /-'ʦɪ̯oːn/ *f* - defamation

Differential* /-'ʦɪ̯aːl/ *nt* -s, -e *s.* Differenzial

Differenz *f* -, -en difference. **D~ial** *nt* -s, -e differential. **d~ieren** *vt/i (haben)* differentiate (**zwischen** + *dat* between)

Digital- *pref* digital. **D~uhr** *f* digital clock/watch

Dikt|at *nt* -[e]s, -e dictation. **D~ator** *m* -s, -en /-'toːrən/ dictator. **D~atur** *f* -, -en dictatorship. **d~ieren** *vt/i (haben)* dictate

Dill *m* -s dill

Dimension *f* -, -en dimension

Ding *nt* -[e]s, -e & [!] -er thing; **guter D~e sein** be cheerful; **vor allen D~en** above all

Dinosaurier /-iɐ̯/ *m* -s,- dinosaur

Diözese *f* -, -n diocese

Diphtherie *f* - diphtheria

Diplom *nt* -s, -e diploma; *(Univ)* degree

Diplomat *m* -en, -en diplomat

dir *pron (dat of* du) [to] you; *(refl)* yourself; **ein Freund von dir** a friend of yours

direkt *a* direct ● *adv* directly; *(wirklich)* really. **D~ion** /-'ʦɪ̯oːn/ *f* - management; *(Vorstand)* board of directors. **D~or** *m* -s, -en /-'toːrən/, **D~orin** *f* -, -nen director; *(Bank-, Theater-)* manager; *(Sch)* head; *(Gefängnis)* governor. **D~übertragung** *f* live transmission

Dirig|ent *m* -en, -en *(Mus)* conductor. **d~ieren** *vt* direct; *(Mus)* conduct

Dirndl nt -s,- dirndl [dress]
Diskette f -, -n floppy disc
Disko f -, -s 🔟 disco. **D~thek** f -, -en discothèque
diskret a discreet
Diskus m -, -se & **Disken** discus
Disku|ssion f -, -en discussion. **d~tieren** vt/i (haben) discuss
disponieren vi (haben) make arrangements; **d~ [können] über** (+ acc) have at one's disposal
Disqualifi|kation /-'tsio:n/ f disqualification. **d~zieren** vt disqualify
Dissertation /-'tsio:n/ f -, -en dissertation
Dissident m -en, -en dissident
Distanz f -, -en distance. **d~ieren (sich)** vr dissociate oneself (**von** from). **d~iert** a aloof
Distel f -, -n thistle
Disziplin f -, -en discipline. **d~arisch** a disciplinary. **d~iert** a disciplined
dito adv ditto
diverse attrib a pl various
Divid|ende f -, -en dividend. **d~ieren** vt divide (**durch** by)
Division f -, -en division
DJH abbr (**Deutsche Jugendherberge**) [German] youth hostel
DM abbr (**Deutsche Mark**) DM
doch conj & adv but; (dennoch) yet; (trotzdem) after all; **wenn d~** ...! if only ...! **nicht d~!** don't!
Docht m -[e]s, -e wick
Dock nt -s, -s dock. **d~en** vt/i (haben) dock
Dogge f -, -n Great Dane
Dogm|a nt -s, -men dogma. **d~atisch** a dogmatic
Dohle f -, -n jackdaw
Doktor m -s, -en /-'to:rən/ doctor. **D~arbeit** f [doctoral] thesis
Dokument nt -[e]s, -e document. **D~arbericht** m documentary. **D~arfilm** m documentary film
Dolch m -[e]s, -e dagger

Dollar m -s,- dollar
dolmetsch|en vt/i (haben) interpret. **D~er(in)** m -s,- (f -, -nen) interpreter
Dom m -[e]s, -e cathedral
Domino nt -s, -s dominoes sg. **D~stein** m domino
Dompfaff m -en, -en bullfinch
Donau f - Danube
Donner m -s thunder. **d~n** vi (haben) thunder
Donnerstag m Thursday. **d~s** adv on Thursdays
doof a 🔟 stupid
Doppel nt -s,- duplicate; (Tennis) doubles pl. **D~bett** nt double bed. **D~decker** m -s,- doubledecker [bus]. **d~deutig** a ambiguous. **D~gänger** m -s,- double. **D~kinn** nt double chin. **D~name** m double-barrelled name. **D~punkt** m (Gram) colon. **D~stecker** m two-way adaptor. **d~t** a double; <Boden> false; **in d~ter Ausfertigung** in duplicate; **die d~te Menge** twice the amount ● adv doubly; (zweimal) twice; **d~t so viel** twice as much. **D~zimmer** nt double room
Dorf nt -[e]s,-er village. **D~bewohner** m villager
dörflich a rural
Dorn m -[e]s, -en thorn. **d~ig** a thorny
Dorsch m -[e]s, -e cod
dort adv there. **d~ig** a local
Dose f -, -n tin, can
dösen vi (haben) doze
Dosen|milch f evaporated milk. **D~öffner** m tin or can opener
dosieren vt measure out
Dosis f -, **Dosen** dose
Dot-com-Firma f dot-com (company)
Dotter m & nt -s,- [egg] yolk
Dozent(in) m -en, -en (f -, -nen) (Univ) lecturer
Dr. abbr (**Doktor**) Dr

rache m -n, -n dragon. **D∼n** m -s,- kite. **D∼nfliegen** nt hang-gliding

raht m -[e]s,¨e wire; **auf D∼** 🔲 on the ball. **D∼seilbahn** f cable railway

ram|a nt -s, -men drama. **D∼atik** f - drama. **D∼atiker** m -s,- dramatist. **d∼atisch** a dramatic

ran adv 🔲 = daran; **gut/schlecht d∼ sein** be well off/in a bad way; **ich bin d∼** it's my turn

rang m -[e]s urge; (Druck) pressure

räng|eln vt/i (haben) push; (bedrängen) pester. **d∼en** vt push; (bedrängen) urge; **sich d∼en** crowd (um round) ● vi (haben) push; (eilen) be urgent; **d∼en auf** (+ acc) press for

ran|halten† (sich) vr sep hurry. **d∼kommen†** vi sep (sein) have one's turn

rauf adv 🔲 = darauf; **d∼ und dran sein** be on the point (etw zu tun of doing sth). **D∼gänger** m -s,- daredevil

raußen adv outside; (im Freien) out of doors

rechseln vt (Techn) turn

Dreck m -s dirt; (Morast) mud

Dreh m -s 🔲 knack; **den D∼ heraushaben** have got the hang of it. **D∼bank** f lathe. **D∼bleistift** m propelling pencil. **D∼buch** nt screenplay, script. **d∼en** vt turn; (im Kreis) rotate; (verschlingen) twist; roll <Zigarette>; shoot <Film>; **lauter/leiser d∼en** turn up/down; **sich d∼en** turn; (im Kreis) rotate; (schnell) spin; <Wind:> change; **sich d∼en um** revolve around; (sich handeln) be about ● vi (haben) turn; <Wind:> change; **an etw** (dat) **d∼en** turn sth. **D∼stuhl** m swivel chair. **D∼tür** f revolving door. **D∼ung** f -, -en turn; (im Kreis) rotation. **D∼zahl** f number of revolutions

drei inv a, **D∼** f -, -en three; (Sch) ≈ pass. **D∼eck** nt -[e]s, -e triangle. **d∼eckig** a triangular. **d∼erlei** inv a three kinds of ● pron three things. **d∼fach** a triple. **d∼mal** adv three times. **D∼rad** nt tricycle

dreißig inv a thirty. **d∼ste(r,s)** a thirtieth

dreiviertel* inv a **drei viertel**, s. **viertel. D∼stunde** f three-quarters of an hour

dreizehn inv a thirteen **d∼te(r,s)** a thirteenth

dreschen† vt thresh

dress|ieren vt train. **D∼ur** f - training

dribbeln vi (haben) dribble

Drill m -[e]s (Mil) drill. **d∼en** vt drill

Drillinge mpl triplets

dringlich a urgent

Drink m -[s], -s [alcoholic] drink

drinnen adv inside

dritt adv **zu d∼** in threes; **wir waren zu d∼** there were three of us. **d∼e(r,s)** a third; **ein D∼er** a third person. **d∼el** inv a third. **D∼el** nt -s,- third. **d∼ens** adv thirdly. **d∼rangig** a third-rate

Drog|e f -, -n drug. **D∼enabhängige(r)** m/f drug addict. **D∼erie** f -, -n chemist's shop. **D∼ist** m -en, -en chemist

drohen vi (haben) threaten (jdm s.o.)

dröhnen vi (haben) resound; (tönen) boom

Drohung f -, -en threat

drollig a funny; (seltsam) odd

Drops m -,- [fruit] drop

Drossel f -, -n thrush

drosseln vt (Techn) throttle; (fig) cut back

drüben adv over there

Druck¹ m -[e]s,¨e pressure; **unter D∼ setzen** (fig) pressurize

Druck² *m* -[e]s, -e printing;
(*Schrift, Reproduktion*) print.
D~buchstabe *m* block letter
drucken *vt* print
drücken *vt/i* (*haben*) press; (*aus-*)
squeeze; <*Schuh:*> pinch;
(*umarmen*) hug; **Preise d~** force
down prices; (*an Tür*) **d~** push;
sich d~ 𝕀 make oneself scarce;
sich d~ vor (+ *dat*) 𝕀 shirk. **d~d**
a heavy; (*schwül*) oppressive
Drucker *m* -s,- printer
Druckerei *f* -, -en printing works
Druck|fehler *m* misprint.
D~knopf *m* press-stud. **D~luft** *f*
compressed air. **D~sache** *f*
printed matter. **D~schrift** *f* type;
(*Veröffentlichung*) publication; in
D~schrift in block letters *pl*
Druckstelle *f* bruise
Drüse *f* -, -n (*Anat*) gland
Dschungel *m* -s,- jungle
du *pron* (*familiar address*) you; **auf
Du und Du** on familiar terms
Dübel *m* -s,- plug
Dudelsack *m* bagpipes *pl*
Duell *nt* -s, -e duel
Duett *nt* -s, -e [vocal] duet
Duft *m* -[e]s, ̈-e fragrance, scent;
(*Aroma*) aroma. **d~en** *vi* (*haben*)
smell (*nach of*)
dulden *vt* tolerate; (*erleiden*)
suffer ● *vi* (*haben*) suffer
dumm *a* stupid; (*unklug*) foolish;
(𝕀 *lästig*) awkward; **wie d~!**.
d~erweise *adv* stupidly; (*leider*)
unfortunately. **D~heit** *f* -, -en
stupidity; (*Torheit*) foolishness;
(*Handlung*) folly. **D~kopf** *m* 𝕀
fool.
dumpf *a* dull
Düne *f* -, -n dune
Dung *m* -s manure
Dünge|mittel *nt* fertilizer. **d~en**
vt fertilize. **D~er** *m* -s,- fertilizer
dunk|el *a* dark; (*vage*) vague;
(*fragwürdig*) shady; **d~les Bier**
brown ale; **im D~eln** in the dark

Dunkel|heit *f* - darkness.
D~kammer *f* dark-room. **d~n** *vi*
(*haben*) get dark
dünn *a* thin; <*Buch*> slim;
(*spärlich*) sparse; (*schwach*) weak
Dunst *m* -es, ̈-e mist, haze;
(*Dampf*) vapour
dünsten *vt* steam
dunstig *a* misty, hazy
Duo *nt* -s, -s [instrumental] duet
Duplikat *nt* -[e]s, -e duplicate
Dur *nt* - (*Mus*) major [key]
durch *prep* (+ *acc*) through;
(*mittels*) by; [geteilt] **d~** (*Math*)
divided by ● *adv* **die Nacht d~**
throughout the night; **d~ und d~**
nass wet through
durchaus *adv* absolutely; **d~ nicht**
by no means
durchblättern *vt sep* leaf through
durchblicken *vi sep* (*haben*) look
through; **d~ lassen** (*fig*) hint at
Durchblutung *f* circulation
durchbohren *vt insep* pierce
durchbrechen¹† *vt/i sep* (*haben*)
break [in two]
durchbrechen²† *vt insep* break
through; break <*Schallmauer*>
durchbrennen† *vi sep* (*sein*) burn
through; <*Sicherung:*> blow
Durchbruch *m* breakthrough
durchdrehen *v sep* ● *vt* mince
● *vi* (*haben/sein*) 𝕀 go crazy
durchdringen† *vi sep* (*sein*)
penetrate; (*sich durchsetzen*) get
one's way. **d~d** *a* penetrating;
<*Schrei*> piercing
durcheinander *adv* in a muddle;
<*Person*> confused; **d~ bringen**
muddle [up]; confuse <*Person*>;
d~ geraten get mixed up; **d~
reden** all talk at once. **D~** *nt* -s
muddle
durchfahren *vi sep* (*sein*) drive
through; <*Zug:*> go through
Durchfahrt *f* journey/drive
through; **auf der D~** passing
through; 'D~ verboten' 'no
thoroughfare'

urchfall m diarrhoea. **d∼en†** vi sep (sein) fall through; (🗉 versagen) flop; (bei Prüfung) fail

urchfuhr f - (Comm) transit

urchführ|bar a feasible. **d∼en** vt sep carry out

urchgang m passage; (Sport) round; 'D∼ verboten' 'no entry'. **D∼sverkehr** m through traffic

urchgeben† vt sep pass through; (übermitteln) transmit; (Radio, TV) broadcast

urchgebraten a gut d∼ well done

urchgehen† vi sep (sein) go through; (davonlaufen) run away; <Pferd:> bolt; jdm etw d∼ lassen let s.o. get away with sth. **d∼d** a continuous; **d∼d** geöffnet open all day; **d∼der** Zug through train

urchgreifen† vi sep (haben) reach through; (vorgehen) take drastic action. **d∼d** a drastic

urchhalte|n† v sep (fig) ● vi (haben) hold out ● vt keep up. **D∼vermögen** nt stamina

urchkommen† vi sep (sein) come through; (gelangen, am Telefon) get through

urchlassen† vt sep let through

urchlässig a permeable; (undicht) leaky

urchlauferhitzer m -s,- geyser

urchlesen† vt sep read through

urchleuchten vt insep X-ray

urchlöchert a riddled with holes

urchmachen vt sep go through; (erleiden) undergo

urchmesser m -s,- diameter

urchnässt a wet through

urchnehmen† vt sep (Sch) do

urchnummeriert a numbered consecutively

urchpausen vt sep trace

urchqueren vt insep cross

urchreiche f -, -n hatch

Durchreise f journey through; auf der D∼ passing through. **d∼n** vi sep (sein) pass through

durchreißen† vt/i sep (sein) tear

Durchsage f -, -n announcement. **d∼n** vt sep announce

Durchschlag m carbon copy; (Culin) colander. **d∼en†** v sep ● vt (Culin) rub through a sieve; sich **d∼en** (fig) struggle through ● vi (sein) <Sicherung:> blow

durchschlagend a (fig) effective; <Erfolg> resounding

durchschneiden† vt sep cut

Durchschnitt m average; im D∼ on average. **d∼lich** a average ● adv on average. **D∼s-** pref average

Durchschrift f carbon copy

durchsehen† v sep ● vi (haben) see through ● vt look through

durchseihen vt sep strain

durchsetzen vt sep force through; sich d∼ assert oneself; <Mode:> catch on

Durchsicht f check

durchsichtig a transparent

durchsickern vi sep (sein) seep through; <Neuigkeit:> leak out

durchstehen† vt sep (fig) come through

durchstreichen† vt sep cross out

durchsuch|en vt insep search. **D∼ung** f -, -en search

durchwachsen a <Speck> streaky; (🗉 gemischt) mixed

durchwählen vi sep (haben) (Teleph) dial direct

durchweg adv without exception

durchwühlen vt insep rummage through; ransack <Haus>

Durchzug m through draught

dürfen†
● transitive & auxiliary verb
····► (Erlaubnis haben zu) be allowed; may, can. etw [tun] dürfen be allowed to do sth. **darf ich das tun?** may or can I do

that? **nein, das darfst du nicht** no you may not or cannot [do that]. **er sagte mir, ich dürfte sofort gehen** he told me I could go at once. **hier darf man nicht rauchen** smoking is prohibited here. **sie darf/durfte es nicht sehen** she must not/was not allowed to see it.

····▸ (in Höflichkeitsformeln) may. **darf ich rauchen?** may I smoke? **darf/dürfte ich um diesen Tanz bitten?** may/might I have the pleasure of this dance?

····▸ **dürfte** (sollte) should, ought. **jetzt dürften sie dort angekommen sein** they should or ought to be there by now. **das dürfte nicht allzu schwer sein** that should not be too difficult. **ich hätte es nicht tun/sagen dürfen** I ought not to have done/said it

● intransitive verb

····▸ (irgendwohin gehen dürfen) be allowed to go; may go; can go. **darf ich nach Hause?** may or can I go home? **sie durfte nicht ins Theater** she was not allowed to go the theatre

dürftig a poor; <Mahlzeit> scanty
dürr a dry; <Boden> arid; (mager) skinny. **D~e** f -, -n drought
Durst m -[e]s thirst; **D~ haben** be thirsty. **d~ig** a thirsty
Dusche f -, -n shower. **d~n** vi/r (haben) [sich] d~n have a shower
Düse f -, -n nozzle. **D~nflugzeug** nt jet
Dutzend nt -s, -e dozen. **d~weise** adv by the dozen
duzen vt jdn d~ call s.o. 'du'
Dynamik f - dynamics sg; (fig) dynamism. **d~isch** a dynamic
Dynamit nt -es dynamite
Dynamo m -s, -s dynamo
Dynastie f -, -n dynasty
D-Zug /'de:-/ m express [train]

Ee

Ebbe f -, -n low tide
eben a level; (glatt) smooth; **zu e~er Erde** on the ground floor ●adv just; (genau) exactly; **e~ noch** only just; (gerade vorhin) just now; **das ist es e~!** that's just it! **E~bild** nt image
Ebene f -, -n (Geog) plain; (Geom) plane; (fig: Niveau) level
eben|falls adv also; **danke, e~falls** thank you, [the] same to you. **E~holz** nt ebony. **e~so** adv just the same; (ebenso sehr) just as much; **e~so gut** just as good; adv just as well; **e~so sehr** just as much; **e~so viel** just as much/many; **e~so wenig** just as little/few; (noch) no more
Eber m -s,- boar
ebnen vt level; (fig) smooth
Echo nt -s, -s echo
echt a genuine, real; authentic ●adv Ⅰ really; typically. **E~heit** f - authenticity
Eck|ball m (Sport) corner. **E~e** f -, -n corner; **um die E~e bringen** Ⅰ bump off. **e~ig** a angular; <Klammern> square; (unbeholfen) awkward. **E~zahn** m canine tooth
Ecu, ECU /e'ky:/ m -[s], -[s] ecu
edel a noble; (wertvoll) precious; (fein) fine. **e~mütig** a magnanimous. **E~stahl** m stainless steel. **E~stein** m precious stone
Efeu m -s ivy
Effekt m -[e]s, -e effect. **E~en** pl securities. **e~iv** a actual, adv -ly; (wirksam) effective
EG f - abbr (Europäische Gemeinschaft) EC

gal *a* **das ist mir e~** ⊡ it's all the same to me ● *adv* **e~ wie/wo** no matter how/where

gge *f* -, -n harrow

go|ismus *m* - selfishness. **E~ist(in)** *m* -en, -en (*f* -, -nen) egoist. **e~istisch** *a* selfish

h *adv* (*Aust, fam*) anyway

he *conj* before; **ehe nicht** until

he *f* -, -n marriage. **E~bett** *nt* double bed. **E~bruch** *m* adultery. **E~frau** *f* wife. **e~lich** *a* marital; <*Recht*> conjugal; <*Kind*> legitimate

hemalig *a* former. **e~s** *adv* formerly

he|mann *m* (*pl* -**männer**) husband. **E~paar** *nt* married couple

her *adv* earlier, sooner; (*lieber, vielmehr*) rather; (*mehr*) more

hering *m* wedding ring

Ehr|e *f* -, -n honour. **e~en** *vt* honour. **e~enamtlich** *a* honorary ● *adv* in an honorary capacity. **E~engast** *m* guest of honour. **e~enhaft** *a* honourable. **E~ensache** *f* point of honour. **E~enwort** *nt* word of honour. **e~erbietig** *a* deferential. **E~furcht** *f* reverence; (*Scheu*) awe. **e~fürchtig** *a* reverent. **E~gefühl** *nt* sense of honour. **E~geiz** *m* ambition. **e~geizig** *a* ambitious. **e~lich** *a* honest. **e~lich gesagt** to be honest. **E~lichkeit** *f* - honesty. **e~los** *a* dishonourable. **e~würdig** *a* venerable; (*als Anrede*) Reverend

Ei *nt* -[e]s, -er egg

Eibe *f* -, -n yew

Eiche *f* -, -n oak. **E~l** *f* -, -n acorn

eichen *vt* standardize

Eichhörnchen *nt* -s,- squirrel

Eid *m* -[e]s, -e oath

Eidechse *f* -, -n lizard

eidlich *a* sworn ● *adv* on oath

Eidotter *m & nt* egg yolk

Eier|becher *m* egg-cup. **E~kuchen** *m* pancake; (*Omelett*) omelette. **E~schale** *f* eggshell. **E~schnee** *m* beaten egg-white. **E~stock** *m* ovary

Eifer *m* -s eagerness. **E~sucht** *f* jealousy. **e~süchtig** *a* jealous

eifrig *a* eager

Eigelb *nt* -[e]s, -e [egg] yolk

eigen *a* own; (*typisch*) characteristic (*dat* of); (*seltsam*) odd; (*genau*) particular. **E~art** *f* peculiarity. **e~artig** *a* peculiar. **e~händig** *a* personal; <*Unterschrift*> own. **E~heit** *f* -, -en peculiarity. **E~name** *m* proper name. **e~nützig** *a* selfish. **e~s** *adv* specially. **E~schaft** *f* -, -en quality; (*Phys*) property; (*Merkmal*) characteristic; (*Funktion*) capacity. **E~schaftswort** *nt* (*pl* -**wörter**) adjective. **E~sinn** *m* obstinacy. **e~sinnig** *a* obstinate

eigentlich *a* actual, real; (*wahr*) true ● *adv* actually, really; (*streng genommen*) strictly speaking

Eigen|tor *nt* own goal. **E~tum** *nt* -s property. **E~tümer(in)** *m* -s,- (*f* -, -nen) owner. **E~tumswohnung** *f* freehold flat. **e~willig** *a* self-willed; <*Stil*> highly individual

eignen (sich) *vr* be suitable

Eil|brief *m* express letter. **E~e** *f* - hurry; **E~e haben** be in a hurry; <*Sache:*> be urgent. **e~en** *vi* (*sein*) hurry ● (*haben*) (*drängen*) be urgent. **e~ig** *a* hurried; (*dringend*) urgent; **es e~ig haben** be in a hurry. **E~zug** *m* semi-fast train

Eimer *m* -s,- bucket; (*Abfall-*) bin

ein

● *indefinite article*

····▸ a, (*vor Vokal*) an. **ein Kleid/Apfel/Hotel/Mensch** a dress/an apple/a[n] hotel/a human being.

so ein such a. **was für ein ...** (*Frage*) what kind of a ...? (*Ausruf*) what a ...!

● *adjective*

····▶ (*Ziffer*) one. **eine Mark** one mark. **wir haben nur eine Stunde** we only have an/(*betont*) one hour. **eines Tages/Abends** one day/evening

····▶ (*derselbe*) the same. **einer Meinung sein** be of the same opinion. **mit jdm in einem Zimmer schlafen** sleep in the same room as s.o.

einander *pron* one another
Einäscherung *f* -, -en cremation
einatmen *vt/i sep* (*haben*) inhale, breathe in
Einbahnstraße *f* one-way street
einbalsamieren *vt sep* embalm
Einband *m* binding
Einbau *m* installation; (*Montage*) fitting. **e~en** *vt sep* install; (*montieren*) fit. **E~küche** *f* fitted kitchen
einbegriffen *pred a* included
Einberufung *f* call-up
Einbettzimmer *nt* single room
einbeulen *vt sep* dent
einbeziehen† *vt sep* [mit] e~ include; (*berücksichtigen*) take into account
einbiegen† *vi sep* (*sein*) turn
einbild|en *vt sep* sich (*dat*) etw e~en imagine sth; sich (*dat*) viel e~en be conceited. **E~ung** *f* imagination; (*Dünkel*) conceit. **E~ungskraft** *f* imagination
einblenden *vt sep* fade in
Einblick *m* insight
einbrech|en† *vi sep* (*haben/sein*) break in; **bei uns ist eingebrochen worden** we have been burgled. **E~er** *m* burglar
einbringen† *vt sep* get in; bring in <*Geld*>
Einbruch *m* burglary; **bei E~ der Nacht** at nightfall

einbürger|n *vt sep* naturalize. **E~ung** *f* - naturalization
einchecken /-tʃɛkən/ *vt/i sep* (*haben*) check in
eindecken (sich) *vr sep* stock up
eindeutig *a* unambiguous; (*deutlich*) clear
eindicken *vt sep* (*Culin*) thicken
eindringen† *vi sep* (*sein*) e~en in (+ *acc*) penetrate into; (*mit Gewalt*) force one's/<*Wasser:*> its way into; (*Mil*) invade
Eindruck *m* impression
eindrücken *vt sep* crush
eindrucksvoll *a* impressive
ein|e(r,s) *pron* one; (*jemand*) someone; (*man*) one, you
einebnen *vt sep* level
eineiig *a* <*Zwillinge*> identical
eineinhalb *inv a* one and a half; **e~ Stunden** an hour and a half
Einelternfamilie *f* one-parent family
einengen *vt sep* restrict
Einer *m* -s,- (*Math*) unit. **e~** *pron s.* eine(r,s). **e~lei** *inv a* ● *attrib* one kind of; (*eintönig, einheitlich*) the same ● *pred a* 🔢 immaterial; **es ist mir e~lei** it's all the same to me. **e~seits** *adv* on the one hand
einfach *a* simple; <*Essen*> plain; <*Fahrt, Fahrt*> single; **e~er Soldat** private. **E~heit** *f* - simplicity
einfädeln *vt sep* thread; (*fig: arrangieren*) arrange
einfahr|en† *v sep* ● *vi* (*sein*) arrive; <*Zug:*> pull in ● *vt* (*Auto*) run in. **E~t** *f* arrival; (*Eingang*) entrance, way in; (*Auffahrt*) drive; (*Autobahn-*) access road; **keine E~t** no entry
Einfall *m* idea; (*Mil*) invasion. **e~en**† *vi sep* (*sein*) collapse; (*eindringen*) invade; **jdm e~en** occur to s.o.; **was fällt ihm ein!** what does he think he is doing!
Einfalt *f* - naïvety

infarbig *a* of one colour; *<Stoff, Kleid>* plain

infass|en *vt sep* edge; set *<Edelstein>*. **E~ung** *f* border, edging

infetten *vt sep* grease

influss *m* influence. **e~reich** *a* influential

införmig *a* monotonous. **E~keit** *f* - monotony

infrieren† *vt/i sep* (*sein*) freeze

infügen *vt sep* insert; (*einschieben*) interpolate; **sich e~** fit in

einfühlsam *a* sensitive

Einfuhr *f* -, -en import

einführ|en *vt sep* introduce; (*einstecken*) insert; (*einweisen*) initiate; (*Comm*) import. **e~end** *a* introductory. **E~ung** *f* introduction; (*Einweisung*) initiation

Eingabe *f* petition; (*Computer*) input

Eingang *m* entrance, way in; (*Ankunft*) arrival

eingebaut *a* built-in; *<Schrank>* fitted

eingeben† *vt sep* hand in; (*Computer*) feed in

eingebildet *a* imaginary; (*überheblich*) conceited

Eingeborene(r) *m/f* native

eingehen† *v sep* ● *vi* (*sein*) come in; (*ankommen*) arrive; (*einlaufen*) shrink; (*sterben*) die; *<Zeitung, Firma:>* fold; (*acc*) **e~** go into sth; (*annehmen*) agree to sth ● *vt* enter into; contract *<Ehe>*; make *<Wette>*; take *<Risiko>*

eingemacht *a* (*Culin*) bottled

eingenommen *pred a* (*fig*) taken (*von* with); prejudiced (*gegen* against)

eingeschneit *a* snowbound

eingeschrieben *a* registered

Einge|ständnis *nt* admission. **e~stehen**† *vt sep* admit

eingetragen *a* registered

Eingeweide *pl* bowels, entrails

eingewöhnen (sich) *vr sep* settle in

eingießen† *vt sep* pour in; (*einschenken*) pour

eingleisig *a* single-track

einglieder|n *vt sep* integrate. **E~ung** *f* integration

eingravieren *vt sep* engrave

eingreifen† *vi sep* (*haben*) intervene. **E~** *nt* -s intervention

Eingriff *m* intervention; (*Med*) operation

einhaken *vt/r sep* jdn **e~** *od* sich bei jdm **e~** take s.o.'s arm

einhalten† *v sep* ● *vt* keep; (*befolgen*) observe ● *vi* (*haben*) stop

einhändigen *vt sep* hand in

einhängen *vt sep* hang; put down *<Hörer>*

einheimisch *a* local; (*eines Landes*) native; (*Comm*) homeproduced. **E~e(r)** *m/f* local native

Einheit *f* -, -en unity; (*Maß-, Mil*) unit. **e~lich** *a* uniform. **E~spreis** *m* standard price; (*Fahrpreis*) flat fare

einholen *vt sep* catch up with; (*aufholen*) make up for; (*erbitten*) seek; (*einkaufen*) buy

einhüllen *vt sep* wrap

einhundert *inv a* one hundred

einig *a* united; [sich (*dat*)] **e~ sein** be in agreement

einig|e(r,s) *pron* some; (*ziemlich viel*) quite a lot of; (*substantivisch*) **e~e** *pl* some; (*mehrere*) several; (*ziemlich viele*) quite a lot; **e~es** *sg* some things; **vor e~er Zeit** some time ago

einigen *vt* unite; unify *<Land>*; **sich e~** come to an agreement

einigermaßen *adv* to some extent; (*ziemlich*) fairly; (*ziemlich gut*) fairly well

E

Einigkeit *f* - unity; (*Übereinstimmung*) agreement

einjährig *a* one-year-old; **e~e Pflanze** annual

einkalkulieren *vt sep* take into account

einkassieren *vt sep* collect

Einkauf *m* purchase; (*Einkaufen*) shopping; **Einkäufe machen** do some shopping. **e~en** *vt sep* buy; **e~en gehen** go shopping. **E~swagen** *m* shopping trolley

einklammern *vt sep* bracket

Einklang *m* harmony; **in E~ stehen** be in accord (**mit** with)

einkleben *vt sep* stick in

einkleiden *vt sep* fit out

einklemmen *vt sep* clamp

einkochen *v sep* ●*vi* (*sein*) boil down ●*vt* preserve, bottle

Einkommen *nt* **-s** income. **E~[s]steuer** *f* income tax

Einkünfte *pl* income *sg*; (*Einnahmen*) revenue *sg*

einlad|en† *vt sep* load; (*auffordern*) invite; (*bezahlen für*) treat. **E~ung** *f* invitation

Einlage *f* enclosure; (*Schuh-*) arch support; (*Programm-*) interlude; (*Comm*) investment; (*Bank-*) deposit; **Suppe mit E~** soup with noodles/dumplings

Ein|lass *m* **-es** admittance. **e~lassen†** *vt sep* let in; run <*Bad, Wasser*>; **sich auf etw** (*acc*) **e~lassen** get involved in sth

einleben (sich) *vr sep* settle in

Einlege|arbeit *f* inlaid work. **e~n** *vt sep* put in; lay in <*Vorrat*>; lodge <*Protest*>; (*einfügen*) insert; (*Auto*) engage <*Gang*>; (*Culin*) pickle; (*marinieren*) marinade; **eine Pause e~n** have a break. **E~sohle** *f* insole

einleit|en *vt sep* initiate; (*eröffnen*) begin. **E~ung** *f* introduction

einleuchten *vi sep* (*haben*) be clear (*dat* to). **e~d** *a* convincing

einliefer|n *vt sep* take (**ins Krankenhaus** to hospital). **E~ung** *f* admission

einlösen *vt sep* cash <*Scheck*>; redeem <*Pfand*>; (*fig*) keep

einmachen *vt sep* preserve

einmal *adv* once; (*eines Tages*) one *or* some day; **noch/schon e~** again/before; **noch e~ so teuer** twice as expensive; **auf e~** at the same time; (*plötzlich*) suddenly; **nicht e~** not even. **E~eins** *nt* - [multiplication] tables *pl*. **e~ig** *a* (*einzigartig*) unique; (🄸 *großartig*) fantastic

einmarschieren *vi sep* (*sein*) march in

einmisch|en (sich) *vr sep* interfere. **E~ung** *f* interference

Einnahme *f* -, **-n** taking; (*Mil*) capture; **E~n** *pl* income *sg*; (*Einkünfte*) revenue *sg*; (*Comm*) receipts; (*eines Ladens*) takings

einnehmen† *vt sep* take; have <*Mahlzeit*>; (*Mil*) capture; take up <*Platz*>

einordnen *vt sep* put in its proper place; (*klassifizieren*) classify; **sich e~** fit in; (*Auto*) get in lane

einpacken *vt sep* pack

einparken *vt sep* park

einpflanzen *vt sep* plant; implant <*Organ*>

einplanen *vt sep* allow for

einprägen *vt sep* impress (**jdm** [up]on s.o.); **sich** (*dat*) **etw e~en** memorize sth.

einrahmen *vt sep* frame

einrasten *vi sep* (*sein*) engage

einräumen *vt sep* put away; (*zugeben*) admit; (*zugestehen*) grant

einrechnen *vt sep* include

einreden *v sep* ●*vt* **jdm/sich** (*dat*) **etw e~** persuade s.o./oneself of sth.

einreiben† *vt sep* rub (**mit** with)

einreichen *vt sep* submit; **die Scheidung e~** file for divorce

inreih|er *m* **-s,-** single-breasted
suit. **e~ig** *a* single-breasted
inreise *f* entry. **e~n** *vi sep* (*sein*)
enter (**nach Irland** Ireland)
inrenken *vt sep* (*Med*) set
inricht|en *vt sep* fit out;
(*möblieren*) furnish; (*anordnen*)
arrange; (*Med*) set <*Bruch*>;
(*eröffnen*) set up; **sich e~en**
furnish one's home; (*sich
einschränken*) economize; (*sich
vorbereiten*) prepare (**auf** + *acc*
for). **E~ung** *f* furnishing; (*Möbel*)
furnishings *pl*; (*Techn*)
equipment; (*Vorrichtung*) device;
(*Eröffnung*) setting up;
(*Institution*) institution;
(*Gewohnheit*) practice
inrosten *vi sep* (*sein*) rust; (*fig*)
get rusty
ins *inv a & pron* one; **noch e~**
one thing; **mir ist alles e~**
🔟 it's all the same to me. **E~** *f* **-,
-en** one; (*Sch*) ≈ A
insam *a* lonely; (*allein*) solitary;
(*abgelegen*) isolated. **E~keit** *f* **-**
loneliness; solitude; isolation
insammeln *vt sep* collect
insatz *m* use; (*Mil*) mission;
(*Wett-*) stake; (*E~teil*) insert; **im
E~** in action
inschalt|en *vt sep* switch on;
(*einschieben*) interpolate; (*fig:
beteiligen*) call in; **sich e~en** (*fig*)
intervene. **E~quote** *f* (*TV*)
viewing figures *pl*; ≈ ratings *pl*
inschätzen *vt sep* assess;
(*bewerten*) rate
inschenken *vt sep* pour
inscheren *vi sep* (*sein*) pull in
inschicken *vt sep* send in
inschieben† *vt sep* push in;
(*einfügen*) insert
inschiff|en (sich) *vr sep* embark.
E~ung *f* **-** embarkation
inschlafen† *vi sep* (*sein*) go to
sleep; (*aufhören*) peter out

einschläfern *vt sep* lull to sleep;
(*betäuben*) put out; (*töten*) put to
sleep. **e~d** *a* soporific
Einschlag *m* impact. **e~en†** *v sep*
●*vt* knock in; (*zerschlagen*)
smash; (*drehen*) turn; take
<*Weg*>; take up <*Laufbahn*> ●*vi*
(*haben*) hit/<*Blitz:*> strike (**in etw**
acc sth); (*Erfolg haben*) be a hit
einschleusen *vt sep* infiltrate
einschließ|en† *vt sep* lock in;
(*umgeben*) enclose; (*einkreisen*)
surround; (*einbeziehen*) include;
sich e~en lock oneself in;
Bedienung eingeschlossen service
included. **e~lich** *adv* inclusive
●*prep* (+ *gen*) including
einschneiden† *vt/i sep* (*haben*)
[**in**] **etw** *acc* **e~** cut into sth. **e~d**
a (*fig*) drastic
Einschnitt *m* cut; (*Med*) incision;
(*Lücke*) gap; (*fig*) decisive event
einschränk|en *vt sep* restrict;
(*reduzieren*) cut back; **sich e~en**
economize. **E~ung** *f* **-, -en**
restriction; (*Reduzierung*)
reduction; (*Vorbehalt*)
reservation
Einschreib|[e]brief *m* registered
letter. **e~en†** *vt sep* enter;
register <*Brief*>; **sich e~en** put
one's name down; (*sich
anmelden*) enrol. **E~en** *nt*
registered letter/packet; **als** *od*
per E~en by registered post
einschüchtern *vt sep* intimidate
Einsegnung *f* **-, -en** confirmation
einsehen† *vt sep* inspect; (*lesen*)
consult; (*begreifen*) see
einseitig *a* one-sided; (*Pol*)
unilateral ●*adv* on one side; (*fig*)
one-sidedly; (*Pol*) unilaterally
einsenden† *vt sep* send in
einsetzen *v sep* ●*vt* put in;
(*einfügen*) insert; (*verwenden*)
use; put on <*Zug*>; call out
<*Truppen*>; (*Mil*) deploy;
(*ernennen*) appoint; (*wetten*)
stake; (*riskieren*) risk ●*vi*

E

(haben) start; *<Winter, Regen:>* set in

Einsicht *f* insight; *(Verständnis)* understanding; *(Vernunft)* reason. **e~ig** *a* understanding

Einsiedler *m* hermit

einsinken† *vi sep (sein)* sink in

einspannen *vt sep* harness; **jdn e~** 🔲 rope s.o. in

einsparen *vt sep* save

einsperren *vt sep* shut/*(im Gefängnis)* lock up

einsprachig *a* monolingual

einspritzen *vt sep* inject

Einspruch *m* objection; **E~ erheben** object; *(Jur)* appeal

einspurig *a* single-track; *(Auto)* single-lane

einst *adv* once; *(Zukunft)* one day

Einstand *m (Tennis)* deuce

einstecken *vt sep* put in; post *<Brief>*; *(Electr)* plug in; (🔲 *behalten)* pocket; (🔲 *hinnehmen)* take; suffer *<Niederlage>*; **etw e~** put sth in one's pocket

einsteigen† *vi sep (sein)* get in; *(in Bus/Zug)* get on

einstell|en *vt sep* put in; *(anstellen)* employ; *(aufhören)* stop; *(regulieren)* adjust, set; *(Optik)* focus; tune *<Motor, Zündung>*; tune to *<Sender>*; **sich e~en** turn up; *<Schwierigkeiten:>* arise; **sich e~en auf** *(+ acc)* adjust to; *(sich vorbereiten)* prepare for. **E~ung** *f* employment; *(Regulierung)* adjustment; *(TV, Auto)* tuning; *(Haltung)* attitude

einstig *a* former

einstimmig *a* unanimous. **E~keit** *f* - unanimity

einstöckig *a* single-storey

einstudieren *vt sep* rehearse

einstufen *vt sep* classify

Ein|sturz *m* collapse. **e~stürzen** *vi sep (sein)* collapse

einstweilen *adv* for the time being; *(inzwischen)* meanwhile

eintasten *vt sep* key in

eintauchen *vt/i sep (sein)* dip in

eintauschen *vt sep* exchange

eintausend *inv a* one thousand

einteil|en *vt sep* divide (**in** + *acc* into); *(Biol)* classify; **sich** *(dat)* **seine Zeit gut e~en** organize one's time well. **e~ig** *a* one piece. **E~ung** *f* division

eintönig *a* monotonous. **E~keit** *f* - monotony

Eintopf *m*, **E~gericht** *nt* stew

Eintracht *f* - harmony

Eintrag *m* -[e]s,ᵉe entry. **e~en**† *vt sep* enter; *(Admin)* register; **sich e~en** put one's name down

einträglich *a* profitable

Eintragung *f* -, -en registration

eintreffen† *vi sep (sein)* arrive; *(fig)* come true

eintreiben† *vt sep* drive in; *(einziehen)* collect

eintreten† *v sep* ● *vi (sein)* enter; *(geschehen)* occur; **in einen Klub e~** join a club; **e~ für** *(fig)* stand up for ● *vt* kick in

Eintritt *m* entrance; *(zu Veranstaltung)* admission; *(Beitritt)* joining; *(Beginn)* beginning. **E~skarte** *f* [admission] ticket

einüben *vt sep* practise

einundachtzig *inv a* eighty-one

Einvernehmen *nt* -s understanding; *(Übereinstimmung)* agreement

einverstanden *a* **e~ sein** agree

Einverständnis *nt* agreement; *(Zustimmung)* consent

Einwand *m* -[e]s,ᵉe objection

Einwander|er *m* immigrant. **e~n** *vi sep (sein)* immigrate. **E~ung** *f* immigration

einwandfrei *a* perfect

einwärts *adv* inwards

einwechseln *vt sep* change

einwecken *vt sep* preserve, bottl[e]

Einweg- *pref* non-returnable

einweichen *vt sep* soak

inweih|en vt sep inaugurate; (Relig) consecrate; (einführen) initiate; **in ein Geheimnis e~en** let into a secret. **E~ung** f -, -en inauguration; consecration; initiation

inweisen† vt sep direct; (einführen) initiate; **ins Krankenhaus e~** send to hospital

inwerfen† vt sep insert; post <Brief>; (Sport) throw in

inwickeln vt sep wrap [up]

inwillig|en vi sep (haben) consent, agree (in + acc to). **E~ung** f - consent

inwohner|(in) m -s,- (f -, -nen) inhabitant. **E~zahl** f population

inwurf m interjection; (Einwand) objection; (Sport) throw-in; (Münz-) slot

Einzahl f (Gram) singular

inzahl|en vt sep pay in. **E~ung** f payment; (Einlage) deposit

inzäunen vt sep fence in

inzel nt -s,- (Tennis) singles pl. **E~bett** nt single bed. **E~gänger** m -s,- loner. **E~haft** f solitary confinement. **E~handel** m retail trade. **E~händler** m retailer. **E~haus** nt detached house. **E~heit** f -, -en detail. **E~karte** f single ticket. **E~kind** nt only child

inzeln a single; (individuell) individual; (gesondert) separate; odd <Handschuh, Socken>; **e~e Fälle** some cases. **E~e(r,s)** pron der/die **E~e** the individual; **E~e** pl some; **im E~en** in detail

Einzel|teil nt [component] part. **E~zimmer** nt single room

inziehen† v sep ● vt pull in; draw in <Atem, Krallen>; (Zool, Techn) retract; indent <Zeile>; (aus dem Verkehr ziehen) withdraw; (beschlagnahmen) confiscate; (eintreiben) collect; make <Erkundigungen>; (Mil) call

up ● vi (sein) enter; (umziehen) move in; (eindringen) penetrate

einzig a only; (einmalig) unique; **eine e~e Frage** a a single question ● adv only; **e~ und allein** solely. **E~e(r,s)** pron der/die/das **E~e** the only one; **ein/kein E~er** a/not a single one; **das E~e, was mich stört** the only thing that bothers me

Eis nt -es ice; (Speise-) ice-cream; **Eis am Stiel** ice lolly; **Eis laufen** skate. **E~bahn** f ice rink. **E~bär** m polar bear. **E~becher** m ice-cream sundae. **E~berg** m iceberg. **E~diele** f ice-cream parlour

Eisen nt -s,- iron. **E~bahn** f railway

eisern a iron; (fest) resolute; **e~er Vorhang** (Theat) safety curtain; (Pol) Iron Curtain

Eis|fach nt freezer compartment. **e~gekühlt** a chilled. **e~ig** a icy. **E~kaffee** m iced coffee. **E~lauf** m skating. **E~läufer(in)** m(f) skater. **E~pickel** m ice-axe. **E~scholle** f ice-floe. **E~vogel** m kingfisher. **E~würfel** m icecube. **E~zapfen** m icicle. **E~zeit** f ice age

eitel a vain; (rein) pure. **E~keit** f - vanity

Eiter m -s pus. **e~n** vi (haben) discharge pus

Eiweiß nt -es, -e egg-white

Ekel m -s disgust; (Widerwille) revulsion. **e~haft** a nauseating; (widerlich) repulsive. **e~n** vt/i (haben) **mich** od **mir e~t [es] davor** it makes me feel sick ● vr sich **e~n vor** (+ dat) find repulsive

eklig a disgusting, repulsive

Ekzem nt -s, -e eczema

elastisch a elastic; (federnd) springy; (fig) flexible

Elch m -[e]s, -e elk

Elefant m -en, -en elephant

elegan|t a elegant. **E~z** f - elegance
Elektri|ker m -s,- electrician. **e~sch** a electric
Elektrizität f - electricity. **E~swerk** nt power station
Elektr|oartikel mpl electrical appliances. **E~ode** f -, -n electrode. **E~onik** f - electronics sg. **e~onisch** a electronic
Elend nt -s misery; (Armut) poverty. **e~** a miserable; (krank) poorly; (gemein) contemptible. **E~sviertel** nt slum
elf nt a, **E~** f -, -en eleven
Elfe f -, -n fairy
Elfenbein nt ivory
Elfmeter m (Fußball) penalty
elfte(r,s) a eleventh
Ell[en]bogen m elbow
Ellip|se f -, -n ellipse. **e~tisch** a elliptical
Elsass nt - Alsace
elsässisch a Alsatian
Elster f -, -n magpie
elter|lich a parental. **E~n** pl parents. **e~nlos** a orphaned. **E~nteil** m parent
Email /e'mai:/ nt -s, -s, **E~le** /e'maljə/ f -, -n enamel
E-Mail /'i:meɪl/ f -, -s e-mail; e-mail message
Emanzi|pation /-'tsːioːn/ f - emancipation. **e~piert** a emancipated
Embargo nt -s, -s embargo
Embryo m -s, -s embryo
Emigr|ant(in) m -en, -en (f -, -nen) emigrant. **E~ation** /-'tsːioːn/ f - emigration. **e~ieren** vi (sein) emigrate
Empfang m -[e]s,ːe reception; (Erhalt) receipt; in **E~ nehmen** receive; (annehmen) accept. **e~en†** vt receive; (Biol) conceive
Empfäng|er m -s,- recipient; (Post-) addressee; (Zahlungs-) payee; (Radio, TV) receiver. **E~nis** f - (Biol) conception

Empfängnisverhütung f contraception. **E~smittel** nt contraceptive
Empfangs|bestätigung f receipt. **E~dame** f receptionist. **E~halle** f [hotel] foyer
empfehl|en† vt recommend. **E~ung** f -, -en recommendation; (Gruß) regards pl
empfind|en† vt feel. **e~lich** a sensitive (gegen to); (zart) delicate. **E~lichkeit** f - sensitivity; delicacy; tenderness; touchiness. **E~ung** f -, -en sensation; (Regung) feeling
empor adv (liter) up[wards]
empören vt incense; **sich e~** be indignant; (sich auflehnen) rebel
Emporkömmling m -s, -e upstart
empör|t a indignant. **E~ung** f - indignation; (Auflehnung) rebellion
Ende nt -s, -n end; (eines Films, Romans) ending; (⊞ Stück) bit; **zu E~ sein** be finished; **etw zu E~ schreiben** finish writing sth; **am E~** at the end; (schließlich) in the end; (⊞ vielleicht) perhaps; (⊞ erschöpft) at the end of one's tether
end|en vi (haben) end. **e~gültig** a final; (bestimmt) definite
Endivie /-iə/ f -, -n endive
end|lich adv at last, finally; (schließlich) in the end. **e~los** a endless. **E~station** f terminus. **E~ung** f -, -en (Gram) ending
Energie f - energy
energisch a resolute; (nachdrücklich) vigorous
eng a narrow; (beengt) cramped; (anliegend) tight; (nah) close; **e~ anliegend** tight-fitting
Engagement /ãgaʒəˈmãː/ nt -s, -s (Theat) engagement; (fig) commitment
Engel m -s,- angel
England nt -s England

ɪgländer *m* -s,- Englishman;
(*Techn*) monkey-wrench; **die E~**
ɪe English *pl.* **E~in** *f* -, -nen
nglishwoman
ɪglisch *a* English. **E~** *nt* -[s]
Lang) English; **auf E~** in English
ɪgpass *m* (*fig*) bottle-neck
ɪ gros /ã'gro:/ *adv* wholesale
ɪkel *m* -s,- grandson; **E~** *pl*
randchildren. **E~in** *f* -, -nen
randdaughter. **E~kind** *nt*
randchild. **E~sohn** *m* grandson.
ɪ~tochter *f* granddaughter
ɪsemble /ã'sã:bəl/ *nt* -s, -s
nsemble; (*Theat*) company
ɪtạrt|en *vi* (*sein*) degenerate.
ɪ~et *a* degenerate
ɪtbehren *vt* do without;
vermissen) miss
ɪtbịnd|en† *vt* release (**von** from);
Med) deliver (**von** of) ● *vi*
haben) give birth. **E~ung** *f*
ɪelivery. **E~ungsstation** *f*
naternity ward
ɪtdẹck|en *vt* discover. **E~er** *m*
·s,- discoverer; (*Forscher*)
xplorer. **E~ung** *f* -, -en discovery
ɪnte *f* -, -n duck
ɪntehren *vt* dishonour
ɪnteignen *vt* dispossess;
xpropriate <*Eigentum*>
ɪnterben *vt* disinherit
ɪnterich *m* -s, -e drake
ɪntfạllen† *vi* (*sein*) not apply; **auf**
dn e~ be s.o.'s share
ɪntfẹrn|en *vt* remove; **sich e~en**
eave. **e~t** *a* distant; (*schwach*)
ague; **2 Kilometer e~t** 2
ɪilometres away; (*fig*) verwandt
ɪistantly related. **E~ung** *f* -, -en
emoval; (*Abstand*) distance;
Reichweite) range
ɪntfliehen† *vi* (*sein*) escape
ɪntfrẹmden *vt* alienate
ɪntfrọsten *vt* defrost
ɪntführ|en *vt* abduct, kidnap;
ɪijack <*Flugzeug*>. **E~er** *m*
ɪbductor, kidnapper; hijacker.

E~ung *f* abduction, kidnapping;
hijacking
entgegen *adv* towards ● *prep* (+
dat) contrary to. **e~gehen**† *vi sep*
(*sein*) (+ *dat*) go to meet; (*fig*) be
heading for. **e~gesetzt** *a*
opposite; (*gegensätzlich*)
opposing. **e~kommen**† *vi sep*
(*sein*) (+ *dat*) come to meet;
(*zukommen auf*) come towards;
(*fig*) oblige. **E~kommen** *nt* -s
helpfulness; (*Zugeständnis*)
concession. **e~kommend** *a*
approaching; <*Verkehr*>
oncoming; (*fig*) obliging.
e~nehmen† *vt sep* accept.
e~wirken *vi sep* (*haben*) (+ *dat*)
counteract; (*fig*) oppose
entgegn|en *vt* reply (**auf** + *acc* to).
E~ung *f* -, -en reply
entgehen† *vi sep* (*sein*) (+ *dat*)
escape; **jdm e~** (*unbemerkt
bleiben*) escape s.o.'s notice; **sich**
(*dat*) **etw e~ lassen** miss sth
Entgẹlt *nt* -[e]s payment; **gegen**
E~ for money
entgleis|en *vi* (*sein*) be derailed;
(*fig*) make a gaffe. **E~ung** *f* -, -en
derailment; (*fig*) gaffe
entgräten *vt* fillet, bone
Enthaarungsmittel *nt* depilatory
enthạlt|en† *vt* contain; **in etw** (*dat*)
e~en sein be contained/
(*eingeschlossen*) included in sth;
sich der Stimme e~en (*Pol*)
abstain. **e~sam** *a* abstemious.
E~ung *f* (*Pol*) abstention
enthaupten *vt* behead
enthẹben† *vt* jdn seines Amtes e~
relieve s.o. of his post
Enthüllung *f* -, -en revelation
Enthusias|mus *m* - enthusiast.
E~t *m* -en, -en enthusiast
entkẹrnen *vt* stone; core <*Apfel*>
entkleiden *vt* undress; **sich e~en**
undress
entkọmmen† *vi* (*sein*) escape
entkọrken *vt* uncork

E

entladen† vt unload; (*Electr*) discharge; sich e~ discharge; <*Gewitter:*> break; <*Zorn:*> explode

entlang adv & prep (+ preceding acc or following dat) along; die Straße e~ along the road; an etw (dat) e~ along sth. **e~fahren**† vi sep (sein) drive along. **e~gehen**† vi sep (sein) walk along

entlarven vt unmask

entlass|en† vt dismiss; (aus Krankenhaus) discharge; (aus der Haft) release. **E~ung** f -, -en dismissal; discharge; release

entlast|en vt relieve the strain on; ease <*Gewissen, Verkehr*>; relieve (**von** of); (*Jur*) exonerate. **E~ung** f - relief; exoneration

entlaufen† vi (sein) run away

entleeren vt empty

entlegen a remote

entlohnen vt pay

entlüft|en vt ventilate. **E~er** m -s,- extractor fan. **E~ung** f ventilation

entmündigen vt declare incapable of managing his own affairs

entmutigen vt discourage

entnehmen† vt take (dat from); (schließen) gather (dat from)

entpuppen (sich) vr (fig) turn out (als etw to be sth)

entrahmt a skimmed

entrichten vt pay

entrinnen† vi (sein) escape

entrüst|en vt fill with indignation; sich e~en be indignant (**über** + acc at). **e~et** a indignant. **E~ung** f - indignation

entsaft|en vt extract the juice from. **E~er** m -s,- juice extractor

entsagen vi (haben) (+ dat) renounce

entschädig|en vt compensate. **E~ung** f -, -en compensation

entschärfen vt defuse

entscheid|en† vt/i (haben) decide; sich e~en decide; <*Sache:*> be decided. **e~end** a decisive; (kritisch) crucial. **E~ung** f decision

entschließen† **(sich)** vr decide, make up one's mind; sich anders e~ change one's mind

entschlossen a determined; (energisch) resolute; kurz e~ without hesitation. **E~heit** f - determination

Entschluss m decision

entschlüsseln vt decode

entschuld|bar a excusable. **e~igen** vt excuse; sich e~igen apologize (**bei** to); e~igen Sie [bitte]! sorry! (bei Frage) excuse me. **E~igung** f -, -en apology; (Ausrede) excuse; um E~igung bitten apologize

entsetz|en vt horrify. **E~en** nt -s horror. **e~lich** a horrible; (schrecklich) terrible

Entsorgung f - waste disposal

entspann|en vt relax; sich e~en relax; <*Lage:*> ease. **E~ung** f - relaxation; easing; (Pol) détente

entsprech|en† vi (haben) (+ dat) correspond to; (übereinstimmen) agree with. **e~end** a corresponding; (angemessen) appropriate; (zuständig) relevant ● adv correspondingly; appropriately; (demgemäß) accordingly ● prep (+ dat) in accordance with

entspringen† vi (sein) <*Fluss:*> rise; (fig) arise, spring (dat from)

entstammen vi (sein) come/ (abstammen) be descended (dat from)

entsteh|en† vi (sein) come into being; (sich bilden) form; (sich entwickeln) develop; <*Brand:*> start; (stammen) originate. **E~ung** f - origin; formation; development

ntstell|en vt disfigure; (*verzerren*) distort. **E~ung** f disfigurement; distortion
ntstört a (*Electr*) suppressed
nttäusch|en vt disappoint. **E~ung** f disappointment
ntwaffnen vt disarm
ntwässer|n vt drain. **E~ung** f - drainage
ntweder conj & adv either
ntwerfen† vt design; (*aufsetzen*) draft; (*skizzieren*) sketch
ntwert|en vt devalue; (*ungültig machen*) cancel. **E~er** m -s,- ticket-cancelling machine. **E~ung** f devaluation; cancelling
ntwick|eln vt develop; **sich e~eln** develop. **E~lung** f -, -en development; (*Biol*) evolution. **E~lungsland** nt developing country
ntwöhnen vt wean (*gen* from); cure <*Süchtege*>
ntwürdigend a degrading
ntwurf m design; (*Konzept*) draft; (*Skizze*) sketch
ntwurzeln vt uproot
ntzie|hen† vt take away (*dat* from); **jdm den Führerschein e~hen** disqualify s.o. from driving; **sich e~hen** (+ *dat*) withdraw from. **E~hungskur** f treatment for drug/alcohol addiction
ntziffern vt decipher
ntzug m withdrawal; (*Vorenthaltung*) deprivation
ntzünd|en vt ignite; (*anstecken*) light; (*fig: erregen*) inflame; **sich e~en** ignite; (*Med*) become inflamed. **e~et** a (*Med*) inflamed. **e~lich** a inflammable. **E~ung** f (*Med*) inflammation
ntzwei a broken
nzian m -s, -e gentian
nzyklo|pädie f -, -en encyclopaedia. **e~pädisch** a encyclopaedic
nzym nt -s, -e enzyme

Epidemie f -, -n epidemic
Epi|lepsie f - epilepsy. **E~leptiker(in)** m -s,- (f -, -nen) epileptic. **e~leptisch** a epileptic
Epilog m -s, -e epilogue
Episode f -, -n episode
Epoche f -, -n epoch
Epos nt -/Epen epic
er pron he; (*Ding, Tier*) it
erachten vt consider (**für nötig** necessary). **E~** nt -s **meines E~s** in my opinion
erbarmen (sich) vr have pity/ <*Gott:*> mercy (*gen* on). **E~** nt -s pity; mercy
erbärmlich a wretched
erbauen vt build; (*fig*) edify; **nicht erbaut von** 🄸 not pleased about
Erbe¹ m -n, -n heir
Erbe² nt -s inheritance; (*fig*) heritage. **e~n** vt inherit
erbeuten vt get; (*Mil*) capture
Erbfolge f (*Jur*) succession
erbieten (sich)† vr offer (**zu** to)
Erbin f -, -nen heiress
erbitten† vt ask for
erbittert a bitter; (*heftig*) fierce
erblassen vi (*sein*) turn pale
erblich a hereditary
erblicken vt catch sight of
erblinden vi (*sein*) go blind
erbrechen† vt vomit ● vi/r [**sich**] **e~** vomit. **E~** nt -s vomiting
Erbschaft f -, -en inheritance
Erbse f -, -n pea
Erb|stück nt heirloom. **E~teil** nt inheritance
Erd|apfel m (*Aust*) potato. **E~beben** nt -s,- earthquake. **E~beere** f strawberry
Erde f -, -n earth; (*Erdboden*) ground; (*Fußboden*) floor. **e~n** vt (*Electr*) earth
erdenklich a imaginable
Erd|gas nt natural gas. **E~geschoss** nt ground floor. **E~kugel** f globe. **E~kunde** f geography. **E~nuss** f peanut. **E~öl** nt [mineral] oil

erdrosseln vt strangle
erdrücken vt crush to death
Erd|rutsch m landslide. **E~teil** m continent
erdulden vt endure
ereignen (sich) vr happen
Ereignis nt -ses, -se event. **e~los** a uneventful. **e~reich** a eventful
Eremit m -en, -en hermit
erfahr|en† vt learn, hear; (erleben) experience ● a experienced. **E~ung** f -, -en experience; **in E~ung bringen** find out
erfassen vt seize; (begreifen) grasp; (einbeziehen) include; (aufzeichnen) record
erfind|en† vt invent. **E~er** m -s,- inventor. **e~erisch** a inventive. **E~ung** f -, -en invention
Erfolg m -[e]s, -e success; (Folge) result; **E~ haben** be successful. **e~en** vi (sein) take place; (geschehen) happen. **e~los** a unsuccessful. **e~reich** a successful
erforder|lich a required, necessary. **e~n** vt require, demand
erforsch|en vt explore; (untersuchen) investigate. **E~ung** f exploration; investigation
erfreu|en vt please. **e~lich** a pleasing. **e~licherweise** adv happily. **e~t** a pleased
erfrier|en† vi (sein) freeze to death; <Glied:> become frostbitten; <Pflanze:> be killed by the frost. **E~ung** f -, -en frostbite
erfrisch|en vt refresh. **E~ung** f -, -en refreshment
erfüll|en vt fill; (nachkommen) fulfil; serve <Zweck>; discharge <Pflicht:> **sich e~en** come true. **E~ung** f fulfilment
erfunden a invented
ergänz|en vt complement; (hinzufügen) add. **E~ung** f

complement; supplement; (Zusatz) addition
ergeben† vt produce; (zeigen) show, establish; **sich e~en** result; <Schwierigkeit:> arise; (kapitulieren) surrender; (sich fügen) submit ● a devoted; (resigniert) resigned
Ergebnis nt -ses, -se result. **e~los** a fruitless
ergiebig a productive; (fig) rich
ergreifen† vt seize; take <Maßnahme, Gelegenheit>; take up <Beruf>; (rühren) move; **die Flucht e~** flee. **e~d** a moving
ergriffen a deeply moved. **E~heit** f - emotion
ergründen vt (fig) get to the bottom of
erhaben a raised; (fig) sublime
Erhalt m -[e]s receipt. **e~en†** vt receive, get; (gewinnen) obtain; (bewahren) preserve, keep; (instand halten) maintain; (unterhalten) support; **am Leben e~en** keep alive ● a **gut/schlecht e~en** in good/bad condition; **e~en bleiben** survive
erhältlich a obtainable
Erhaltung f - preservation; maintenance
erhängen (sich) vr hang oneself
erheb|en† vt raise; levy <Steuer> charge <Gebühr>; **Anspruch e~en** lay claim (**auf** + acc to); **Protest e~en** protest; **sich e~en** rise; <Frage:> arise. **e~lich** a considerable. **E~ung** f -, -en elevation; (Anhöhe) rise; (Aufstand) uprising; (Ermittlung) survey
erheiter|n vt amuse. **E~ung** f - amusement
erhitzen vt heat
erhöh|en vt raise; (fig) increase; **sich e~en** rise, increase. **E~ung** f -, -en increase
erhol|en (sich) vr recover (**von** from); (nach Krankheit)

convalesce; (*sich ausruhen*) have a rest. **e~sam** *a* restful. **E~ung** *f* - recovery; (*Ruhe*) rest

rinner|n *vt* remind (**an** + *acc* of); **sich e~n** remember (**an jdn/etw** s.o./sth). **E~ung** *f* -, **-en** memory; (*Andenken*) souvenir

rkält|en (sich) *vr* catch a cold; **e~et sein** have a cold. **E~ung** *f* -, **-en** cold

rkenn|bar *a* recognizable; (*sichtbar*) visible. **e~en†** *vt* recognize; (*wahrnehmen*) distinguish. **E~tnis** *f* -, **-se** recognition; realization; (*Wissen*) knowledge; **die neuesten E~tnisse** the latest findings

rker *m* -s,- bay

rklär|en *vt* declare; (*erläutern*) explain; **sich bereit e~en** agree (**zu** to). **e~end** *a* explanatory. **e~lich** *a* explicable; (*verständlich*) understandable. **e~licherweise** *adv* understandably. **E~ung** *f* -, **-en** declaration; explanation; **öffentliche E~ung** public statement

rkrank|en *vi* (*sein*) fall ill; be taken ill (**an** + *dat* with). **E~ung** *f* -, **-en** illness

rkundig|en (sich) *vr* enquire (**nach jdm/etw** after s.o./about sth). **E~ung** *f* -, **-en** enquiry

rlangen *vt* attain, get

rlass *m* -es,ꞗe (*Admin*) decree; (*Befreiung*) exemption; (*Straf-*) remission

rlassen† *vt* (*Admin*) issue; **jdm etw e~** exempt s.o. from sth; let s.o. off <*Strafe*>

rlauben *vt* allow, permit; **ich kann es mir nicht e~** I can't afford it

Erlaubnis *f* - permission. **E~schein** *m* permit

rläutern *vt* explain

Erle *f* -, **-n** alder

erleb|en *vt* experience; (*mit-*) see; have <*Überraschung*>. **E~nis** *nt* **-ses, -se** experience

erledigen *vt* do; (*sich befassen mit*) deal with; (*beenden*) finish; (*entscheiden*) settle; (*töten*) kill

erleichter|n *vt* lighten; (*vereinfachen*) make easier; (*befreien*) relieve; (*lindern*) ease. **e~t** *a* relieved. **E~ung** *f* - relief

erleiden† *vt* suffer

erleuchten *vt* illuminate; **hell erleuchtet** brightly lit

erlogen *a* untrue, false

Erlös *m* -es proceeds *pl*

erlöschen† *vi* (*sein*) go out; (*vergehen*) die; (*aussterben*) die out; (*ungültig werden*) expire; **erloschener Vulkan** extinct volcano

erlös|en *vt* save; (*befreien*) release (**von** from); (*Relig*) redeem. **e~t** *a* relieved. **E~ung** *f* release; (*Erleichterung*) relief; (*Relig*) redemption

ermächtig|en *vt* authorize. **E~ung** *f* -, **-en** authorization

Ermahnung *f* exhortation; admonition

ermäßig|en *vt* reduce. **E~ung** *f* -, **-en** reduction

ermessen† *vt* judge; (*begreifen*) appreciate. **E~** *nt* -s discretion; (*Urteil*) judgement; **nach eigenem E~** at one's own discretion

ermitt|eln *vt* establish; (*herausfinden*) find out ● *vi* (*haben*) investigate (**gegen jdn** s.o.). **E~lungen** *fpl* investigations. **E~lungsverfahren** *nt* (*Jur*) preliminary inquiry

ermöglichen *vt* make possible

ermord|en *vt* murder. **E~ung** *f* -, **-en** murder

ermüd|en *vt* tire ● *vi* (*sein*) get tired. **E~ung** *f* - tiredness

ermutigen *vt* encourage. **e~d** *a* encouraging

ernähr|en *vt* feed; (*unterhalten*) support, keep; **sich e~en von**

live/<Tier:> feed on. **E~er** m -s,- breadwinner. **E~ung** f - nourishment; nutrition; (Kost) diet

ernenn|en† vt appoint. **E~ung** f -, -en appointment

erneu|ern vt renew; (auswechseln) replace; change <Verband>; (renovieren) renovate. **E~erung** f renewal; replacement; renovation. **e~t** a renewed; (neu) new ● adv again

ernst a serious; e~ nehmen take seriously; e~ m -es seriousness; im E~ seriously; mit einer Drohung E~ machen carry out a threat; **ist das dein E~?** are you serious? **e~haft** a serious. **e~lich** a serious

Ernte f -, -n harvest; (Ertrag) crop. **E~dankfest** nt harvest festival. **e~n** vt harvest; (fig) reap, win

ernüchter|n vt sober up; (fig) bring down to earth. **e~nd** a (fig) sobering

Erober|er m -s,- conqueror. **e~n** vt conquer. **E~ung** f -, -en conquest

eröffn|en vt open; jdm etw e~en announce sth to s.o. **E~ung** f opening; (Mitteilung) announcement

erörter|n vt discuss. **E~ung** f -, -en discussion

Erot|ik f - eroticism. **e~isch** a erotic

Erpel m -s,- drake

erpicht a e~auf (+ acc) keen on

erpress|en vt extort; blackmail <Person>. **E~er** m -s,- blackmailer. **E~ung** f - extortion; blackmail

erprob|en vt test. **e~t** a proven

erraten† vt guess

erreg|bar a excitable. **e~en** vt excite; (hervorrufen) arouse; **sich e~en** get worked up. **e~end** a exciting. **E~er** m -s,- (Med) germ.

e~t a agitated; (hitzig) heated. **E~ung** f - excitement

erreich|bar a within reach; <Ziel:> attainable; <Person> available. **e~en** vt reach; catch <Zug>; live to <Alter>; (durchsetzen) achieve

errichten vt erect

erringen† vt gain, win

erröten vi (sein) blush

Errungenschaft f -, -en achievement; (⚍ Anschaffung) acquisition

Ersatz m -es replacement, substitute; (Entschädigung) compensation. **E~reifen** m spare tyre. **E~teil** nt spare part

erschaffen† vt create

erschein|en† vi (sein) appear; <Buch:> be published. **E~ung** f -, -en appearance; (Person) figure; (Phänomen) phenomenon; (Symptom) symptom; (Geist) apparition

erschieß|en† vt shoot [dead]. **E~ungskommando** nt firing squad

erschlaffen vi (sein) go limp

erschlagen† vt beat to death; (tödlich treffen) strike dead; **vom Blitz e~ werden** be killed by lightning

erschließen† vt develop

erschöpf|en vt exhaust. **e~t** a exhausted. **E~ung** f - exhaustion

erschrecken† vi (sein) get a fright ● vt (reg) startle; (beunruhigen) alarm; **du hast mich erschreckt** you gave me a fright

erschrocken a frightened; (erschreckt) startled

erschütter|n vt shake; (ergreifen) upset deeply. **E~ung** f -, -en shock

erschwinglich a affordable

ersehen† vt (fig) see (aus from)

ersetzen vt replace; make good <Schaden>; refund <Kosten>; jdm etw e~ compensate s.o. for sth

ersichtlich a obvious, apparent

erspar|en vt save. **E~nis** f -, -se saving; **E~nisse** savings

erst adv (zuerst) first; (noch nicht mehr als) only; (nicht vor) not until; e~ dann only then; eben e~ [only] just

erstarren vi (sein) solidify; (gefrieren) freeze; (steif werden) go stiff; (vor Schreck) be paralysed

erstatten vt (zurück-) refund; Bericht e~ report (jdm to s.o.)

Erstaufführung f first performance, première

erstaun|en vt amaze, astonish. **E~en** nt amazement, astonishment. **e~lich** a amazing

Erst|ausgabe f first edition. **e~e(r,s)** a first; (beste) best; e~e Hilfe first aid. **E~e(r)** m/f first; (Beste) best; fürs E~e for the time being; als E~es first of all; er kam als E~er he arrived first

erstechen† vt stab to death

ersteigern vt buy at an auction

erstens adv firstly, in the first place. **e~ere(r,s)** a the former; der/die/das E~ere the former

ersticken vt suffocate; smother <Flammen> ● vi (sein) suffocate. **E~** nt -s suffocation; zum E~ stifling

erstklassig a first-class

ersuchen vt ask, request. **E~** nt -s request

ertappen vt ☒ catch

erteilen vt give (jdm s.o.)

ertönen vi (sein) sound; (erschallen) ring out

Ertrag m -[e]s,¨e yield. **e~en**† vt bear

erträglich a bearable; (leidlich) tolerable

ertränken vt drown

ertrinken† vi (sein) drown

erübrigen (sich) vr be unnecessary

erwachsen a grown-up. **E~e(r)** m/f adult, grown-up

erwäg|en† vt consider. **E~ung** f -, -en consideration; in E~ung ziehen consider

erwähn|en vt mention. **E~ung** f -, -en mention

erwärmen vt warm; sich e~ warm up; (fig) warm (für to)

erwart|en vt expect; (warten auf) wait for. **E~ung** f -, -en expectation

erweisen† vt prove; (bezeigen) do <Gefallen, Dienst, Ehre>; sich e~ als prove to be

erweitern vt widen; dilate <Pupille>; (fig) extend, expand

Erwerb m -[e]s acquisition; (Kauf) purchase; (Brot-) livelihood; (Verdienst) earnings pl. **e~en**† vt acquire; (kaufen) purchase. **e~slos** a unemployed. **e~stätig** a employed

erwidern vt reply; return <Besuch, Gruß>. **E~ung** f -, -en reply

erwirken vt obtain

erwürgen vt strangle

Erz nt -es, -e ore

erzähl|en vt tell (jdm s.o.) ● vi (haben) talk (von about). **E~er** m -s,- narrator. **E~ung** f -, -en story, tale

Erzbischof m archbishop

erzeug|en vt produce; (Electr) generate. **E~er** m -s,- producer. **E~nis** nt -ses, -se product; landwirtschaftliche E~nisse farm produce sg.

erzieh|en† vt bring up; (Sch) educate. **E~er** m -s,- [private] tutor. **E~erin** f -, -nen governess. **E~ung** f - upbringing; education

erzielen vt achieve; score <Tor>

erzogen a gut/schlecht e~ well/ badly brought up

es
● pronoun
····▸ (Sache) it; (weibliche Person) she/her; (männliche Person)

he/him. **ich bin es** it's me. **wir sind traurig, ihr seid es auch** we are sad, and so are you. **er ist es, der ...** he is the one who .... **es sind Studenten** they are students
····▸ (*impers*) it. **es hat geklopft** there was a knock. **es klingelt** someone is ringing. **es wird schöner** the weather is improving. **es geht ihm gut/ schlecht** he is well/unwell. **es lässt sich aushalten** it is bearable. **es gibt** there is *or* (*pl*) are
····▸ (*als formales Objekt*) **er hat es gut** he has it made; he's well off. **er meinte es gut** he meant well. **ich hoffe/glaube es** I hope/think so

Esche *f* -, **-n** ash
Esel *m* **-s,-** donkey; (🄳 *Person*) ass
Eskimo *m* **-[s], -[s]** Eskimo
Eskort|e *f* -, **-n** (*Mil*) escort. **e~ieren** *vt* escort
essbar *a* edible
essen† *vt/i* (*haben*) eat; **zu Mittag Abend e~** have lunch/supper; **e~ gehen** eat out. **E~** *nt* **-s,-** food; (*Mahl*) meal; (*festlich*) dinner
Esser(in) *m* **-s,-** (*f* -, **-nen**) eater
Essig *m* **-s** vinegar. **E~gurke** *f* [pickled] gherkin
Esslöffel *m* ≈ dessertspoon.
Essstäbchen *ntpl* chopsticks.
Esstisch *m* dining-table.
Esswaren *fpl* food *sg*; (*Vorräte*) provisions. **Esszimmer** *nt* dining-room
Estland *nt* **-s** Estonia
Estragon *m* **-s** tarragon
etablieren (sich) *vr* establish oneself/<*Geschäft:*> itself
Etage /e'ta:ʒə/ *f* -, **-n** storey. **E~nbett** *nt* bunk-beds *pl*. **E~nwohnung** *f* flat
Etappe *f* -, **-n** stage
Etat /e'ta:/ *m* **-s, -s** budget

Eth|ik *f* -, ethic; (*Sittenlehre*) ethics *sg*. **e~isch** *a* ethical
ethnisch *a* ethnic; **e~e Säuberung** ethnic cleansing
Etikett *nt* **-[e]s, -e[n]** label; (*Preis-*) tag. **e~ieren** *vt* label
Etui /e'tvi:/ *nt* **-s, -s** case
etwa *adv* (*ungefähr*) about; (*zum Beispiel*) for instance; (*womöglich*) perhaps; **nicht e~, dass ...** not that ...; **denkt nicht e~ ...** don't imagine ...
etwas *pron* something; (*fragend/ verneint*) anything; (*ein bisschen*) some, a little; **sonst noch e~?** anything else? **so e~ Ärgerliches!** what a nuisance! ● *adv* a bit
Etymologie *f* - etymology
euch *pron* (*acc of* **ihr** *pl*) you; (*dat*) [to] you; (*refl*) yourselves; (*einander*) each other
euer *poss pron pl* your. **e~e, e~t-s. eure, euret-**
Eule *f* -, **-n** owl
Euphorie *f* - euphoria
eur|e *poss pron pl* your. **e~e(r,s)** *poss pron* yours. **e~etwegen** *adv* for your sake; (*wegen euch*) because of you, on your account. **e~etwillen** *adv* **um e~etwillen** for your sake. **e~ige** *poss pron* **der/ die/das e~ige** yours
Euro *m* **-[s], -[s]** Euro. **E~-** *pref* Euro-
Europa *nt* **-s** Europe. **E~-** *pref* European
Europä|er(in) *m* **-s,-** (*f* -, **-nen**) European. **e~isch** *a* European
Euter *nt* **-s,-** udder
evakuier|en *vt* evacuate. **E~ung** *f* - evacuation
evan|gelisch *a* Protestant. **E~gelium** *nt* **-s, -ien** gospel
eventuell *a* possible ● *adv* possibly; (*vielleicht*) perhaps
Evolution /-'ʦio:n/ *f* - evolution
ewig *a* eternal; (*endlos*) never-ending; **e~ dauern** 🄳 take ages. **E~keit** *f* - eternity

Examen nt -s,- & -mina (Sch)
examination

Exemplar nt -s, -e specimen;
(Buch) copy. **e~isch** a exemplary

exerzieren vt/i (haben) (Mil) drill;
(üben) practise

exhumieren vt exhume

Exil nt -s exile

Existenz f -, -en existence;
(Lebensgrundlage) livelihood

existieren vi (haben) exist

exklusiv a exclusive. **e~e** prep (+
gen) excluding

exkommunizieren vt
excommunicate

Exkremente npl excrement sg

Expedition /-'ts:io:n/ f -, -en
expedition

Experiment nt -[e]s, -e
experiment. **e~ieren** vi (haben)
experiment

Experte m -n, -n expert

explo|dieren vi (sein) explode.
E~sion f -, -en explosion

Expor|t m -[e]s, -e export. **E~teur**
/-'tø:ɐ̯/ m -s, -e exporter. **e~tieren**
vt export

extra adv separately; (zusätzlich)
extra; (eigens) specially; (🄸
absichtlich) on purpose

extravagan|t a flamboyant;
(übertrieben) extravagant

extravertiert a extrovert

extrem a extreme. **E~ist** m -en,
-en extremist

Exzellenz f - (title) Excellency

Exzentr|iker m -s,- eccentric.
e~isch a eccentric

Fabel f -, -n fable. **f~haft** a 🄸
fantastic

Fabrik f -, -en factory. **F~ant** m
-en, -en manufacturer. **F~at** nt
-[e]s, -e product; (Marke) make.
F~ation /-'ts:io:n/ f - manufacture

Fach nt -[e]s,⸚er compartment;
(Schub-) drawer; (Gebiet) field;
(Sch) subject. **F~arbeiter** m
skilled worker. **F~arzt** m,
F~ärztin f specialist.
F~ausdruck m technical term

Fächer m -s,- fan

Fach|gebiet nt field. **f~kundig** a
expert. **f~lich** a technical;
(beruflich) professional. **F~mann**
m (pl -leute) expert. **f~männisch**
a expert. **F~schule** f technical
college. **F~werkhaus** nt half-
timbered house. **F~wort** nt (pl
-wörter) technical term

Fackel f -, -n torch

fade a insipid; (langweilig) dull

Faden m -s,⸚ thread; (Bohnen-)
string; (Naut) fathom

Fagott nt -[e]s, -e bassoon

fähig a capable (zu/gen of);
(tüchtig) able, competent. **F~keit**
f -, -en ability; competence

fahl a pale

fahnd|en vi (haben) search (nach
for). **F~ung** f -, -en search

Fahne f -, -n flag; (Druck-) galley
[proof]; **eine F~ haben** 🄸 reek of
alcohol. **F~nflucht** f desertion

Fahr|ausweis m ticket. **F~bahn** f
carriageway; (Straße) road. **f~bar**
a mobile

Fähre f -, -n ferry

fahren† vi (sein) go, travel;
<Fahrer:> drive; <Radfahrer:>
ride; (verkehren) run, (ab-) leave;

`<Schiff:>` sail; mit dem Auto/Zug f~en go by car/train; was ist in ihn gefahren? ⒤ what has got into him? ● vt drive; ride `<Fahrrad>`; take `<Kurve>`. f~end a moving; (f~bar) mobile; (nicht sesshaft) travelling. F~er m -s,- driver. F~erflucht f failure to stop after an accident. F~erhaus nt driver's cab. F~erin f -, -nen woman driver. F~gast m passenger. F~geld nt fare. F~gestell nt chassis; (Aviat) undercarriage. F~karte f ticket. F~kartenschalter m ticket office. f~lässig a negligent. F~lässigkeit f - negligence. F~lehrer m driving instructor. F~plan m timetable. f~planmäßig a scheduled ● adv according to/(pünktlich) on schedule. F~preis m fare. F~prüfung f driving test. F~rad nt bicycle. F~schein m ticket. F~schule f driving school. F~schüler(in) m(f) learner driver. F~stuhl m lift

Fahrt f -, -en journey; (Auto) drive; (Ausflug) trip; (Tempo) speed

Fährte f -, -n track; (Witterung) scent

Fahr|tkosten pl travelling expenses. **F~werk** nt undercarriage. **F~zeug** nt -[e]s, -e vehicle; (Wasser-) craft, vessel

fair /fɛːɐ/ a fair

Fakultät f -, -en faculty

Falke m -n, -n falcon

Fall m -[e]s,¨e fall; (Jur, Med, Gram) case; im F~[e] in case (gen of); auf jeden F~ in any case; (bestimmt) definitely; für alle F¨e just in case; auf keinen F~ on no account

Falle f -, -n trap

fallen† vi (sein) fall; (sinken) go down; [im Krieg] f~ be killed in

the war; f~ lassen drop `<etw, fig: Plan, jdn>`; make `<Bemerkung>`

fällen vt fell; (fig) pass `<Urteil>`

fällig a due; `<Wechsel>` mature; längst f~ long overdue. **F~keit** f (Comm) maturity

falls conj in case; (wenn) if

Fallschirm m parachute. **F~jäger** m paratrooper. **F~springer** m parachutist

Falltür f trapdoor

falsch a wrong; (nicht echt, unaufrichtig) false; (gefälscht) forged; `<Geld>` counterfeit; `<Schmuck>` fake ● adv wrongly; falsely; `<singen>` out of tune; f~ gehen `<Uhr:>` be wrong

fälschen vt forge, fake

Falschgeld nt counterfeit money

fälschlich a wrong; (irrtümlich) mistaken

Falsch|meldung f false report; (absichtlich) hoax report. **F~münzer** m -s,- counterfeiter

Fälschung f -, -en forgery, fake

Falte f -, -n fold; (Rock-) pleat; (Knitter-) crease; (im Gesicht) line; wrinkle

falten vt fold

Falter m -s,- butterfly; moth

faltig a creased; `<Gesicht>` lined; wrinkled

familiär a family …; (vertraut, zudringlich) familiar; (zwanglos) informal

Familie /-iə/ f -, -n family. **F~nforschung** f genealogy. **F~nname** m surname. **F~nplanung** f family planning. **F~nstand** m marital status

Fan /fɛn/ m -s, -s fan

Fana|tiker m -s,- fanatic. **f~tisch** a fanatical

Fanfare f -, -n trumpet; (Signal) fanfare

Fang m -[e]s,¨e capture; (Beute) catch; F¨e (Krallen) talons; (Zähne) fangs. **F~arm** m tentacle. **f~en**† vt catch; (ein-) capture;

gefangen nehmen take prisoner.
F~en nt -s **F~en spielen** play tag.
F~frage f catch question

Fantasie f -, -n = Phantasie

Farb|aufnahme f colour
photograph. **F~band** nt (pl
-bänder) typewriter ribbon. **F~e** f
-, -n colour; (Maler-) paint; (zum
Färben) dye; (Karten) suit.
f~echt a colour-fast

färben vt colour; dye <Textilien,
Haare> ● vi (haben) not be
colour-fast

farb|enblind a colour-blind.
f~enfroh a colourful. **F~film** m
colour film. **f~ig** a coloured
● adv in colour. **F~ige(r)** m/f
coloured man/woman. **F~kasten**
m box of paints. **f~los** a
colourless. **F~stift** m crayon.
F~stoff m dye; (Lebensmittel-)
colouring. **F~ton** m shade

Färbung f -, -en colouring

Farn m -[e]s, -e fern

Färse f -, -n heifer

Fasan m -[e]s, -e[n] pheasant

Faschierte(s) nt (Aust) mince

Fasching m -s (SGer) carnival

Faschis|mus m - fascism. **F~t** m
-en, -en fascist. **f~tisch** a fascist

Faser f -, -n fibre

Faß nt -es,̈er barrel, cask; Bier
vom F~ draught beer

Fassade f -, -n façade

faßbar a comprehensible;
(greifbar) tangible

fassen vt take [hold of], grasp;
(ergreifen) seize; (fangen) catch;
(ein-) set; (enthalten) hold; (fig:
begreifen) take in, grasp;
conceive <Plan>; make
<Entschluss>; sich kurz f~ be brief;
nicht zu f~ (fig) unbelievable ● vi
(haben) f~ an (+ acc) touch

Fassung f -, -en mount;
(Edelstein-) setting; (Electr)
socket; (Version) version;
(Beherrschung) composure; aus

der F~ bringen disconcert. **f~slos**
a shaken; (erstaunt)
flabbergasted. **F~svermögen** nt
capacity

fast adv almost, nearly; f~ nie
hardly ever

fast|en vi (haben) fast. **F~enzeit** f
Lent. **F~nacht** f Shrovetide;
(Karneval) carnival.
F~nachtsdienstag m Shrove
Tuesday

fatal a fatal; (peinlich)
embarrassing

Fata Morgana f -/- -nen mirage

fauchen vi (haben) spit, hiss ● vt
snarl

faul a lazy; (verdorben) rotten,
bad; <Ausrede> lame

faul|en vi (sein) rot; <Zahn:>
decay; (verwesen) putrefy.
f~enzen vi (haben) be lazy.
F~enzer m -s,- lazy-bones sg.
F~heit f - laziness

Fäulnis f - decay

Fauna f - fauna

Faust f -,Fäuste fist; auf eigene F~
(fig) off one's own bat.
F~handschuh m mitten.
F~schlag m punch

Fauxpas /fo'pa/ m -,- /- -[s], -s/
gaffe

Favorit(in) /favo'ri:t(in)/ m -en, -en
(f -, -nen) (Sport) favourite

Fax nt -, -[e] fax. **f~en** vt fax

Faxen fpl 🄸 antics; F~ machen
fool about

Faxgerät nt fax machine

Februar m -s, -e February

fecht|en† vi (haben) fence. **F~er**
m -s,- fencer

Feder f -, -n feather; (Schreib-)
pen; (Spitze) nib; (Techn) spring.
F~ball m shuttlecock; (Spiel)
badminton. **F~busch** m plume.
f~leicht a as light as a feather.
f~n vi (haben) be springy;
(nachgeben) give; (hoch-) bounce.
f~nd a springy; (elastisch)

elastic. **F~ung** f - (*Techn*) springs
pl; (*Auto*) suspension
Fee f -, -n fairy
Fegefeuer nt purgatory
fegen vt sweep
Fehde f -, -n feud
fehl a **f~ am Platze** out of place.
F~betrag m deficit. **f~en** vi
(*haben*) be missing/(*Sch*) absent;
(*mangeln*) be lacking; **mir f~t die
Zeit** I haven't got the time; **was
f~t ihm?** what's the matter with
him? **das hat uns noch gefehlt!**
that's all we need! **f~end** a
missing; (*Sch*) absent
Fehler m -s,- mistake, error;
(*Sport & fig*) fault; (*Makel*) flaw.
f~frei a faultless. **f~haft** a faulty.
f~los a flawless
Fehl|geburt f miscarriage. **F~griff**
m mistake. **F~kalkulation** f
miscalculation. **F~schlag** m
failure. **f~schlagen†** vi sep (sein)
fail. **F~start** m (*Sport*) false start.
F~zündung f (*Auto*) misfire
Feier f -, -n celebration;
(*Zeremonie*) ceremony; (*Party*)
party. **F~abend** m end of the
working day; **F~abend machen**
stop work. **f~lich** a solemn;
(*förmlich*) formal. **f~n** vt
celebrate; hold <*Fest*> ● vi
(*haben*) celebrate. **F~tag** m
[public] holiday; (*kirchlicher*)
feast-day; **erster/zweiter F~tag**
Christmas Day / Boxing Day.
f~tags adv on public holidays
feige a cowardly; **f~ sein** be a
coward ● adv in a cowardly way
Feige f -, -n fig
Feig|heit f - cowardice. **F~ling** m
-s, -e coward
Feile f -, -n file. **f~n** vt/i (haben)
file
feilschen vi (haben) haggle
fein a fine; (*zart*) delicate;
<*Strümpfe*> sheer; <*Unterschied*>
subtle; (*scharf*) keen; (*vornehm*)
refined; (*prima*) great; **sich f~**

machen dress up. **F~arbeit** f
precision work
Feind(in) m -es, -e (f -, -nen)
enemy. **f~lich** a enemy; (*f~selig*)
hostile. **F~schaft** f -, -en enmity
fein|fühlig a sensitive. **F~gefühl**
nt sensitivity; (*Takt*) delicacy.
F~heit f -, -en fineness; delicacy;
subtlety; refinement; **F~heiten**
subtleties. **F~kostgeschäft** nt
delicatessen [shop]
feist a fat
Feld nt -[e]s, -er field; (*Fläche*)
ground; (*Sport*) pitch; (*Schach-*)
square; (*auf Formular*) box.
F~bett nt camp-bed.
F~forschung f fieldwork. **F~herr**
m commander. **F~stecher** m -s,-
field-glasses pl. **F~webel** m -s,-
(*Mil*) sergeant. **F~zug** m
campaign
Felge f -, -n [wheel] rim
Fell nt -[e]s, -e (*Zool*) coat; (*Pelz*)
fur; (*abgezogen*) skin, pelt
Fels m -en, -en rock. **F~block** m
boulder. **F~en** m -s,- rock
Femininum nt -s, -na (*Gram*)
feminine
Feminist(in) m -en, -en (f -, -nen)
feminist. **f~isch** a feminist
Fenchel m -s fennel
Fenster nt -s,- window. **F~brett** nt
window-sill. **F~scheibe** f
[window-]pane
Ferien /'fe:riən/ pl holidays;
(*Univ*) vacation sg; **F~ haben** be
on holiday. **F~ort** m holiday
resort
Ferkel nt -s,- piglet
fern a distant; **der F~e Osten** the
Far East; **sich f~ halten** keep
away ● adv far away; **von f~**
from a distance ● prep (+ dat) far
[away] from. **F~bedienung** f
remote control. **F~e** f - distance;
in weiter F~e far away; (*zeitlich*)
in the distant future. **f~er** a
further ● adv (*außerdem*)
furthermore; (*in Zukunft*) in

uture. f~gelenkt a remote-controlled; <Rakete> guided. F~gespräch nt long-distance call. F~glas nt binoculars pl. F~kurs[us] m correspondence course. F~licht nt (Auto) full beam. F~meldewesen nt telecommunications pl. F~rohr nt telescope. F~schreiben nt telex

ernseh|apparat m television set. f~en† vi sep (haben) watch television. F~en nt -s television. F~er m -s,- [television] viewer; (Gerät) television set

ernsprech|amt nt telephone exchange. F~er m telephone

ernsteuerung f remote control

erse f -, -n heel

ertig a finished; (bereit) ready; (Comm) ready-made; <Gericht> ready-to-serve; f~ werden mit finish; (bewältigen) cope with; f~ sein have finished; (fig) be through (mit jdm with s.o.); (🗓 erschöpft) be all in/(seelisch) shattered; etw f~ bringen manage to do sth; (beenden) finish sth; etw/jdn f~ machen finish sth; (bereitmachen) get sth/s.o. ready; (🗓 erschöpfen) wear s.o. out; (seelisch) shatter s.o.; sich f~ machen get ready; etw f~ stellen complete sth ● adv f~ essen/lesen finish eating/reading. F~bau m (pl -bauten) prefabricated building. f~en vt make. F~gericht nt ready-to-serve meal. F~haus nt prefabricated house. F~keit f -, -en skill. F~stellung f completion. F~ung f - manufacture

fesch a 🗓 attractive

Fessel f -, -n ankle

fesseln vt tie up; tie (an + acc to); (fig) fascinate

fest a firm; (nicht flüssig) solid; (erstarrt) set; (haltbar) strong; (nicht locker) tight; (feststehend) fixed; (ständig) steady; <Anstellung> permanent; <Schlaf> sound; <Blick, Stimme> steady; f~ werden harden; <Gelee:> set; f~e Nahrung solids pl ● adv firmly; tightly; steadily; soundly; (kräftig, tüchtig) hard; f~ schlafen be fast asleep; f~ angestellt permanent

Fest nt -[e]s, -e celebration; (Party) party; (Relig) festival; frohes F~! happy Christmas!

fest|binden† vt sep tie (an + dat to). f~bleiben† vi sep (sein) (fig) remain firm. f~halten† v sep ● vt hold on to; (aufzeichnen) record; sich f~halten hold on ● vi (haben) f~halten an (+ dat) (fig) stick to; cling to <Tradition>. f~igen vt strengthen. F~iger m -s,- styling lotion/(Schaum-) mousse. F~igkeit f - firmness; solidity; strength; steadiness. F~land nt mainland; (Kontinent) continent. f~legen vt sep (fig) fix, settle; lay down <Regeln>; tie up <Geld>; sich f~legen commit oneself

festlich a festive F~keiten fpl festivities

fest|liegen† vi sep (haben) be fixed, settled. f~machen v sep ● vt fasten/(binden) tie (an + dat to); (f~legen) fix, settle ● vi (haben) (Naut) moor. F~mahl nt feast. F~nahme f -, -n arrest. f~nehmen† vt sep arrest. f~setzen vt sep fix, settle; (inhaftieren) gaol; sich f~setzen collect. f~sitzen† vi sep (haben) be firm/<Schraube:> tight; (haften) stick; (nicht weiterkommen) be stuck. F~spiele npl festival sg. f~stehen† vi sep (haben) be certain. f~stellen vt sep fix; (ermitteln) establish; (bemerken) notice; (sagen) state. F~tag m special day

Festung f -, -en fortress

Festzug m [grand] procession

Fete /'feːtə, 'fɛːtə/ f -, -n party

fett a fat; fatty; (fettig) greasy; (üppig) rich; <Druck> bold. **F~** nt -[e]s, -e fat; (flüssig) grease. **f~arm** a low-fat. **f~en** vt grease ● vi (haben) be greasy. **F~fleck** m grease mark. **f~ig** a greasy

Fetzen m -s,- scrap; (Stoff) rag

feucht a damp, moist; <Luft> humid. **F~igkeit** f - dampness; (Nässe) moisture; (Luft-) humidity. **F~igkeitscreme** f moisturizer

Feuer nt -s,- fire; (für Zigarette) light; (Begeisterung) passion; **F~machen** light a fire. **F~alarm** m fire alarm. **f~gefährlich** a [in]flammable. **F~leiter** f fire-escape. **F~löscher** m -s,- fire extinguisher. **F~melder** m -s,- fire alarm. **f~n** vi (haben) fire (auf + acc on). **F~probe** f (fig) test. **f~rot** a crimson. **F~stein** m flint. **F~stelle** f hearth. **F~treppe** f fire-escape. **F~wache** f fire station. **F~waffe** f firearm. **F~wehr** f -, -en fire brigade. **F~wehrauto** nt fire-engine. **F~wehrmann** m (pl -männer & -leute) fireman. **F~werk** nt firework display, fireworks pl. **F~zeug** nt lighter

feurig a fiery; (fig) passionate

Fiaker m -s,- (Aust) horse-drawn cab

Fichte f -, -n spruce

Fieber nt -s [raised] temperature; **F~** haben have a temperature. **f~n** vi (haben) be feverish. **F~thermometer** nt thermometer

fiebrig a feverish

Figur f -, -en figure; (Roman-, Film-) character; (Schach-) piece

Filet /fiˈleː/ nt -s, -s fillet

Filiale f -, -n (Comm) branch

Filigran nt -s filigree

Film m -[e]s, -e film; (Kino-) film; (Schicht) coating. **f~en** vt/i (haben) film. **F~kamera** f cine/ (für Kinofilm) film camera

Filter m & (Techn) nt -s,- filter; (Zigaretten-) filter-tip. **f~ern** vt filter. **F~erzigarette** f filter-tipped cigarette. **f~rieren** vt filte

Filz m -es felt. **F~stift** m felt-tipped pen

Fimmel m -s,- 🔲 obsession

Finale nt -s,- (Mus) finale; (Sport) final

Finanz f -, -en finance. **F~amt** nt tax office. **f~iell** a financial. **f~ieren** vt finance. **F~minister** n minister of finance

find|en† vt find; (meinen) think; den Tod f~en meet one's death; wie f~est du das? what do you think of that? es wird sich f~en it'll turn up; (fig) it'll be all right ● vi (haben) find one's way. **F~e** m -s,- finder. **F~erlohn** m reward **f~ig** a resourceful

Finesse f -, -n (Kniff) trick; **F~n** (Techn) refinements

Finger m -s,- finger; die F~ lassen von 🔲 leave alone. **F~abdruck** n finger-mark; (Admin) fingerprint **F~hut** m thimble. **F~nagel** m finger-nail. **F~spitze** f finger-tip **F~zeig** m -[e]s, -e hint

Fink m -en, -en finch

Finn|e m -n, -n, **F~in** f -, -nen Finn **f~isch** a Finnish. **F~land** nt -s Finland

finster a dark; (düster) gloomy; (unheildrohend) sinister. **F~nis** f darkness; (Astr) eclipse

Firma f -, -men firm, company

Firmen|wagen m company car. **F~zeichen** nt trade mark, logo

Firmung f -, -en (Relig) confirmation

Firnis m -ses, -se varnish. **f~sen** vt varnish

First m -[e]s, -e [roof] ridge

isch m -[e]s, -e fish; F~e (Astr) Pisces. **F~dampfer** m trawler. **~en** vt/i (haben) fish. **F~er** m -s,- fisherman. **F~erei** f - fishing. **F~händler** m fishmonger. **F~reiher** m heron

iskus m - der F~ the Treasury

t a fit. **Fitness** f - fitness

x a ⊞ quick; (geistig) bright; **f~e Idee** obsession; **fix und fertig** all finished; (bereit) all ready; (⊞ erschöpft) shattered. **F~er** m -s,- 🗙 junkie

ixieren vt stare at; (Phot) fix

jord m -[e]s, -e fiord

lach a flat; (eben) level; (niedrig) low; (nicht tief) shallow

läche f -, -n area; (Ober-) surface; (Seite) face. **F~nmaß** nt square measure

lachs m -es flax. **f~blond** a flaxen-haired; <Haar> flaxen

lackern vi (haben) flicker

lagge f -, -n flag

lair /flɛːɐ/ nt -s air, aura

lak f -, -[s] anti-aircraft artillery/ (Geschütz) gun

lämisch a Flemish

lamme f -, -n flame; (Koch-) burner

lanell m -s (Tex) flannel

lank|e f -, -n flank. **f~ieren** vt flank

lasche f -, -n bottle. **F~nbier** nt bottled beer. **F~nöffner** m bottle-opener

latter|haft a fickle. **f~n** vi (sein/ haben) flutter; <Segel:> flap

laum m -[e]s down. **f~ig** a downy; **f~ig rühren** (Aust Culin) cream

lauschig a fleecy; <Spielzeug> fluffy

lausen fpl ⊞ silly ideas

Flaute f -, -n (Naut) calm; (Comm) slack period; (Schwäche) low

läzen (sich) vr ⊞ sprawl

Flechte f -, -n (Med) eczema; (Bot) lichen; (Zopf) plait. **f~n†** vt plait; weave <Korb>

Fleck m -[e]s, -e[n] spot; (größer) patch; (Schmutz-) stain, mark; **blauer F~** bruise. **f~en** vi (haben) stain. **f~enlos** a spotless. **F~entferner** m -s,- stain remover. **f~ig** a stained

Fledermaus f bat

Flegel m -s,- lout. **f~haft** a loutish

flehen vi (haben) beg (um for)

Fleisch nt -[e]s flesh; (Culin) meat; (Frucht-) pulp; **F~ fressend** carnivorous. **F~er** m -s,- butcher. **F~fresser** m -s,- carnivore. **f~ig** a fleshy. **f~lich** a carnal. **F~wolf** m mincer

Fleiß m -es diligence; **mit F~** diligently; (absichtlich) on purpose. **f~ig** a diligent; (arbeitsam) industrious

fletschen vt die Zähne f~ <Tier:> bare its teeth

flex|ibel a flexible; <Einband> limp. **F~ibilität** f - flexibility

flicken vt mend; (mit Flicken) patch. **F~** m -s,- patch

Flieder m -s lilac

Fliege f -, -n fly; (Schleife) bow-tie. **f~n†** vi (sein) fly; (geworfen werden) be thrown; (⊞ fallen) fall; (⊞ entlassen werden) be fired/(von der Schule) expelled; **in die Luft f~n** blow up ● vt fly. **f~nd** a flying. **F~r** m -s,- airman; (Pilot) pilot; (⊞ Flugzeug) plane. **F~rangriff** m air raid

flieh|en† vi (sein) flee (vor + dat from); (entweichen) escape ● vt shun. **f~end** a fleeing; <Kinn, Stirn> receding

Fliese f -, -n tile

Fließ|band nt assembly line. **f~en†** vi (sein) flow; (aus Wasserhahn) run. **f~end** a flowing; <Wasser> running; <Verkehr> moving; (geläufig) fluent

F

flimmern vi (haben) shimmer; (TV) flicker

flink a nimble; (schnell) quick

Flinte f -, -n shotgun

Flirt /flœɛt/ m -s, -s flirtation. **f~en** vi (haben) flirt

Flitter m -s sequins pl. **F~wochen** fpl honeymoon sg

flitzen vi (sein) ⊞ dash

Flock|e f -, -n flake; (Wolle) tuft. **f~ig** a fluffy

Floh m -[e]s, ⸚e flea. **F~spiel** nt tiddly-winks sg

Flora f - flora

Florett nt -[e]s, -e foil

florieren vi (haben) flourish

Floskel f -, -n [empty] phrase

Floß nt -es, ⸚e raft

Flosse f -, -n fin; (Seehund-, Gummi-) flipper; (⊠ Hand) paw

Flöt|e f -, -n flute; (Block-) recorder. **f~en** vi (haben) play the flute/recorder; (⊞ pfeifen) whistle ● vt play on the flute/recorder. **F~ist(in)** m -en, -en (f -, -nen) flautist

flott a quick; (lebhaft) lively; (schick) smart

Flotte f -, -n fleet

flottmachen vt sep wieder f~ (Naut) refloat; get going again <Auto>; put back on its feet <Unternehmen>

Flöz nt -es, -e [coal] seam

Fluch m -[e]s, ⸚e curse. **f~en** vi (haben) curse, swear

Flucht f - flight; (Entweichen) escape; die F~ ergreifen take flight. **f~artig** a hasty

flücht|en vi (sein) flee (vor + dat from); (entweichen) escape ● vr sich f~en take refuge. **f~ig** a fugitive; (kurz) brief; <Blick> fleeting; <Bekanntschaft> passing; (oberflächlich) cursory; (nicht sorgfältig) careless. **f~ig kennen** know slightly.
F~igkeitsfehler m slip. **F~ling** m -s, -e fugitive; (Pol) refugee

Fluchwort nt (pl -wörter) swearword

Flug m -[e]s, ⸚e flight. **F~abwehr** f anti-aircraft defence

Flügel m -s, -, wing; (Fenster-) casement; (Mus) grand piano

Fluggast m [air] passenger

flügge a fully-fledged

Flug|gesellschaft f airline. **F~hafen** m airport. **F~lotse** m air-traffic controller. **F~platz** m airport; (klein) airfield. **F~preis** m air fare. **F~schein** m air ticket. **F~schneise** f flight path. **F~schreiber** m -s, - flight recorder. **F~schrift** f pamphlet. **F~steig** m -[e]s, -e gate. **F~zeug** nt -[e]s, -e aircraft, plane

Flunder f -, -n flounder

flunkern vi (haben) ⊞ tell fibs

Flur m -[e]s, -e [entrance] hall; (Gang) corridor

Fluss m -es, ⸚e river; (Fließen) flow; im F~ (fig) in a state of flux. **f~abwärts** adv downstream. **f~aufwärts** adv upstream

flüssig a liquid; <Lava> molten; (fließend) fluent; <Verkehr> freely moving. **F~keit** f -, -en liquid; (Anat) fluid

Flusspferd nt hippopotamus

flüstern vt/i (haben) whisper

Flut f -, -en high tide; (fig) flood

Föderation /-'tsːio:n/ f -, -en federation

Fohlen nt -s, - foal

Föhn m -s föhn [wind]; (Haartrockner) hair-drier. **f~en** vt [blow-]dry

Folg|e f -, -n consequence; (Reihe) succession; (Fortsetzung) instalment; (Teil) part. **f~en** vi (sein) follow (jdm/etw s.o./sth); (zuhören) listen (dat to); wie f~t as follows ● (haben) (gehorchen) obey (jdm s.o.). **f~end** a following; **F~endes** the following

folger|n vt conclude (**aus** from). F~ung f -, -en conclusion.
folg|lich adv consequently.
f~sam a obedient

Folie /'fo:liə/ f -, -n foil; (*Plastik-*) film

Folklore f - folklore

Folter f -, -n torture. f~n vt torture

Fön (P) m -s, -e hair-drier

Fonds /fõ:/ m -,- /-[s], -s/ fund

fönen* vt s. **föhnen**

Förder|band nt (pl -bänder) conveyor belt. f~lich a beneficial

fordern vt demand; (*beanspruchen*) claim; (*zum Kampf*) challenge

fördern vt promote; (*unterstützen*) encourage; (*finanziell*) sponsor; (*gewinnen*) extract

Forderung f -, -en demand; (*Anspruch*) claim

Förderung f - promotion; encouragement; (*Techn*) production

Forelle f -, -n trout

Form f -, -en form; (*Gestalt*) shape; (*Culin, Techn*) mould; (*Back-*) tin; [**gut**] **in F~** in good form

Formalität f -, -en formality

Format nt -[e]s, -e format; (*Größe*) size; (*fig: Bedeutung*) stature

formatieren vt format

Formel f -, -n formula

formen vt shape, mould; (*bilden*) form; **sich f~** take shape

förmlich a formal

form|los a shapeless; (*zwanglos*) informal. F~sache f formality

Formular nt -s, -e [printed] form

formulier|en vt formulate, word.
F~ung f -, -en wording

forsch|en vi (haben) search (**nach** for). f~end a searching. F~er m -s,- research scientist; (*Reisender*) explorer. F~ung f -, -en research

Forst m -[e]s, -e forest

Förster m -s,- forester

Forstwirtschaft f forestry

Fort nt -s, -s (*Mil*) fort

fort adv away; **f~ sein** be away; (*gegangen/verschwunden*) have gone; **und so f~** and so on; **in einem f~** continuously.
F~bewegung f locomotion.
F~bildung f further education/ training. f~bleiben† vi sep (*sein*) stay away. f~bringen† vt sep take away. f~fahren† vi sep (*sein*) go away ● (*haben/sein*) continue (**zu** to). f~fallen† vi sep (*sein*) be dropped/(*ausgelassen*) omitted; (*entfallen*) no longer apply; (*aufhören*) cease. f~führen vt sep continue. f~gehen† vi sep (*sein*) leave, go away; (*ausgehen*) go out; (*andauern*) go on.
f~geschritten a advanced; (*spät*) late. F~geschrittene(r) m/f advanced student. f~lassen† vt sep let go; (*auslassen*) omit.
f~laufen† vi sep (*sein*) run away; (*sich f~setzen*) continue.
f~laufend a consecutive.
f~pflanzen (sich) vr sep reproduce; <Ton, Licht:> travel.
F~pflanzung f - reproduction.
F~pflanzungsorgan nt reproductive organ. f~schicken vt sep send away; (*abschicken*) send off. f~schreiten† vi sep (*sein*) continue; (*Fortschritte machen*) progress, advance.
f~schreitend a progressive; <*Alter*> advancing. F~schritt m progress; F~schritte machen make progress. f~schrittlich a progressive. f~setzen vt sep continue; **sich f~setzen** continue.
F~setzung f -, -en continuation; (*Folge*) instalment; F~setzung **folgt** to be continued.
F~setzungsroman m serialized novel, serial. f~während a constant. f~ziehen† v sep ● vt pull away ● vi (*sein*) move away

Fossil nt -, -ien /-iən/ fossil

Foto *nt* -s, -s photo. **F~apparat** *m* camera. **F~gen** *a* photogenic

Fotograf|(in) *m* -en, -en (*f* -, -nen) photographer. **F~ie** *f* -, -n photography; (*Bild*) photograph. **f~ieren** *vt* take a photo[graph] of ● *vi* (*haben*) take photographs. **f~isch** *a* photographic

Fotokopie *f* photocopy. **f~ren** *vt* photocopy. **F~rgerät** *nt* photocopier

Fötus *m* -, -ten foetus

Foul /faul/ *nt* -s, -s (*Sport*) foul. **f~en** *vt* foul

Fracht *f* -, -en freight. **F~er** *m* -s,- freighter. **F~gut** *nt* freight. **F~schiff** *nt* cargo boat

Frack *m* -[e]s,ˌe & -s tailcoat

Frage *f* -, -n question; nicht in F~ kommen *s*. infrage. **F~bogen** *m* questionnaire. **f~n** *vt* (*haben*) ask; sich f~n wonder (ob whether). **f~nd** *a* questioning. **F~zeichen** *nt* question mark

frag|lich *a* doubtful; <*Person, Sache*> in question. **f~los** *adv* undoubtedly

Fragment *nt* -[e]s, -e fragment. **fragwürdig** *a* questionable; (*verdächtig*) dubious

Fraktion /-ˈtsi̯oːn/ *f* -, -en parliamentary party

Franken¹ *m* -s,- (*Swiss*) franc

Franken² *nt* -s Franconia

frankieren *vt* stamp, frank

Frankreich *nt* -s France

Fransen *fpl* fringe *sg*

Franz|ose *m* -n, -n Frenchman; die F~osen the French *pl.* **F~ösin** *f* -, -nen Frenchwoman. **f~ösisch** *a* French. **F~ösisch** *nt* -[s] (*Lang*) French

Fraß *m* -es feed; (*pej: Essen*) muck

Fratze *f* -, -n grotesque face; (*Grimasse*) grimace

Frau *f* -, -en woman; (*Ehe-*) wife; F~Thomas Mrs Thomas; Unsere Liebe F~ (*Relig*) Our Lady

Frauen|arzt *m*, **F~ärztin** *f* gynaecologist. **F~rechtlerin** *f* -, -nen feminist

Fräulein *nt* -s,- single woman; (*jung*) young lady; (*Anrede*) Miss

frech *a* cheeky; (*unverschämt*) impudent. **F~heit** *f* -, -en cheekiness; impudence; (*Äußerung*) impertinence

frei *a* free; (*freischaffend*) freelance; <*Künstler*> independent; (*nicht besetzt*) vacant; (*offen*) open; (*bloß*) bare; f~er Tag day off; sich (*dat*) f~ nehmen take time off; f~ machen (*räumen*) clear; vacate <*Platz*>; (*befreien*) liberate; f~ lassen leave free; ist dieser Platz f~? is this seat taken? 'Zimmer f~' 'vacancies' ● *adv* freely; (*ohne Notizen*) without notes; (*umsonst*) free

Frei|bad *nt* open-air swimming pool. **f~beruflich** *a & adv* freelance. **F~e** *nt* im F~en in the open air, out of doors. **F~gabe** *f* release. **f~geben†** *v sep* ● *vt* release; (*eröffnen*) open; jdm einen Tag f~geben give s.o. a day off ● *vi* (*haben*) jdm f~geben give s.o. time off. **f~gebig** *a* generous. **F~gebigkeit** *f* - generosity. **f~haben†** *v sep* ● *vt* eine Stunde f~haben have an hour off; (*Sch*) have a free period ● *vi* (*haben*) be off work/(*Sch*) school; (*beurlaubt sein*) have time off. **f~händig** *adv* without holding on **Freiheit** *f* -, -en freedom, liberty. **F~sstrafe** *f* prison sentence

Frei|herr *m* baron. **F~körperkultur** *f* naturism. **F~lassung** *f* - release. **F~lauf** *m* free-wheel. **f~legen** *vt sep* expose. **f~lich** *adv* admittedly; (*natürlich*) of course. **F~lichttheater** *nt* open-air theatre. **f~machen** *vt sep* (*frankieren*) frank; (*entkleiden*)

bare; **einen Tag f~machen** take a day off. **F~maurer** *m* Freemason. **f~schaffend** *a* freelance.

f~schwimmen† (sich) *v sep* pass one's swimming test.

f~sprechen† *vt sep* acquit. **F~spruch** *m* acquittal. **f~stehen†** *vi sep* stand empty; **es steht ihm f~** (*fig*) he is free (**zu** to). **f~stellen** *vt sep* exempt (**von** from); **jdm etw f~stellen** leave sth up to s.o. **F~stil** *m* freestyle. **F~stoß** *m* free kick.

Freitag *m* Friday. **f~s** *adv* on Fridays

Frei|tod *m* suicide. **F~umschlag** *m* stamped envelope. **f~weg** *adv* freely; (*offen*) openly. **f~willig** *a* voluntary. **F~willige(r)** *m/f* volunteer. **F~zeichen** *nt* ringing tone; (*Rufzeichen*) dialling tone. **F~zeit** *f* free *or* spare time; (*Muße*) leisure. **F~zeit-** *pref* leisure ... **F~zeitbekleidung** *f* casual wear. **f~zügig** *a* unrestricted; (*großzügig*) liberal

fremd *a* foreign; (*unbekannt*) strange; (*nicht das eigene*) other people's; **ein f~er Mann** a stranger; **f~e Leute** strangers; **unter f~em Namen** under an assumed name; **ich bin hier f~** I'm a stranger here. **F~e** *f* - in der **F~e** away from home; (*im Ausland*) in a foreign country. **F~e(r)** *m/f* stranger; (*Ausländer*) foreigner; (*Tourist*) tourist. **F~enführer** *m* [tourist] guide. **F~enverkehr** *m* tourism. **F~enzimmer** *nt* room [to let]; (*Gäste-*) guest room. **f~gehen†** *vi sep* (*sein*) 🛈 be unfaithful. **F~sprache** *f* foreign language. **F~wort** *nt* (*pl* -wörter) foreign word

Freske *f* -, -n, **Fresko** *nt* -s, -ken fresco

Fresse *f* -, -n 🗷 (*Mund*) gob; (*Gesicht*) mug. **f~n†** *vt/i* (*haben*)

eat. **F~n** *nt* -s feed; (🗷 *Essen*) grub

Fressnapf *m* feeding bowl

Freud|e *f* -, -n pleasure; (*innere*) joy; **mit F~en** with pleasure; **jdm eine F~e machen** please s.o. **f~ig** *a* joyful

freuen *vt* please; **sich f~** be pleased (**über** + *acc* about); **sich f~ auf** (+ *acc*) look forward to; **es freut mich** I'm glad (**dass** that)

Freund *m* -es, -e friend; (*Verehrer*) boyfriend. **F~in** *f* -, -nen friend; (*Liebste*) girlfriend. **f~lich** *a* kind; (*umgänglich*) friendly; (*angenehm*) pleasant. **f~licherweise** *adv* kindly. **F~lichkeit** *f* -, -en kindness; friendliness; pleasantness

Freund|schaft *f* -, -en friendship; **F~schaft schließen** become friends. **f~lich** *a* friendly

Frieden *m* -s peace; **F~ schließen** make peace; **im F~** in peacetime; **lass mich in F~!** leave me alone! **F~svertrag** *m* peace treaty

Fried|hof *m* cemetery. **f~lich** *a* peaceful

frieren† *vi* (*haben*) <*Person:*> be cold; *impers* **es friert/hat gefroren** it is freezing/there has been a frost; **frierst du?** are you cold? ● (*sein*) (*gefrieren*) freeze

Fries *m* -es, -e frieze

frisch *a* fresh; (*sauber*) clean; (*leuchtend*) bright; (*munter*) lively; (*rüstig*) fit; **sich f~ machen** freshen up ● *adv* freshly, newly; **ein Bett f~ beziehen** put clean sheets on a bed; **f~ gestrichen!** wet paint! **F~e** *f* - freshness; brightness; liveliness; fitness. **F~haltepackung** *f* vacuum pack

Fri|seur /fri'zø:ɐ̯/ *m* -s, -e hairdresser; (*Herren-*) barber. **F~seursalon** *m* hairdressing salon. **F~seuse** /-'zø:zə/ *f* -, -n hairdresser

frisier|en *vt* jdn/sich f~en do
s.o.'s/one's hair; **die Bilanz/einen
Motor f~en** 🆃 fiddle the
accounts/soup up an engine
Frisör *m* -s, -e = Friseur
Frist *f* -, -en period; (*Termin*)
deadline; (*Aufschub*) time; **drei
Tage F~** three days' grace. **f~los**
a instant
Frisur *f* -, -en hairstyle
frittieren *vt* deep-fry
frivol /fri'vo:l/ *a* frivolous
froh *a* happy; (*freudig*) joyful;
(*erleichtert*) glad
fröhlich *a* cheerful; (*vergnügt*)
merry. **F~keit** *f* - cheerfulness;
merriment
fromm *a* devout; (*gutartig*) docile
Frömmigkeit *f* - devoutness
Fronleichnam *m* Corpus Christi
Front *f* -, -en front. **f~al** *a* frontal;
<*Zusammenstoß*> head-on ● *adv*
from the front;
<*zusammenstoßen*> head-on.
F~alzusammenstoß *m* head-on
collision
Frosch *m* -[e]s,¨e frog. **F~laich** *m*
frog-spawn. **F~mann** *m* (*pl*
-männer) frogman
Frost *m* -[e]s,¨e frost. **F~beule** *f*
chilblain
frösteln *vi* (*haben*) shiver
frostig *a* frosty. **F~schutzmittel**
nt antifreeze
Frottee *nt* & *m* -s towelling
frottier|en *vt* rub down.
F~[hand]tuch *nt* terry towel
Frucht *f* -,¨e fruit; **F~ tragen** bear
fruit. **f~bar** *a* fertile; (*fig*)
fruitful. **F~barkeit** *f* - fertility
früh *a* early ● *adv* early;
(*morgens*) in the morning; **heute
f~** this morning; **von f~ an** *od* **auf**
from an early age. **F~aufsteher**
m -s,- early riser. **F~e** *f* - in aller
F~e bright and early; **in der F~e**
(*SGer*) in the morning. **f~er** *adv*
earlier; (*eher*) sooner; (*ehemals*)
formerly; (*vor langer Zeit*) in the

old days; **f~er oder später** sooner
or later; **ich wohnte f~er in X** I
used to live in X. **f~ere(r,s)** *a*
earlier; (*ehemalig*) former;
(*vorige*) previous; **in f~eren Zeiten**
in former times. **f~estens** *adv* at
the earliest. **F~geburt** *f*
premature birth/(*Kind*) baby.
F~jahr *nt* spring. **F~ling** *m* -s, -e
spring. **f~morgens** *adv* early in
the morning. **f~reif** *a* precocious
Frühstück *nt* breakfast. **f~en** *vi*
(*haben*) have breakfast
frühzeitig *a* & *adv* early;
(*vorzeitig*) premature
Frustr|ation /-'tsio:n/ *f* -, -en
frustration. **f~ieren** *vt* frustrate
Fuchs *m* -es,¨e fox; (*Pferd*)
chestnut. **f~en** *vt* 🆃 annoy
Füchsin *f* -, -nen vixen
Fuge¹ *f* -, -n joint
Fuge² *f* -, -n (*Mus*) fugue
füg|en *vt* fit (**in** + *acc* into); (*an-*)
join (**an** + *acc* on to); (*dazu-*) add
(**zu** to); **sich f~en** fit (**in** + *acc*
into); adjoin/(*folgen*) follow (**an**
etw *acc* sth); (*fig: gehorchen*)
submit (**dat** to). **f~sam** *a*
obedient. **F~ung** *f* -, -en **eine
F~ung des Schicksals** a stroke of
fate
fühl|bar *a* noticeable. **f~en** *vt/i*
(*haben*) feel; **sich f~en** feel
(**krank/einsam** ill/lonely); (🆃 *stolz
sein*) fancy oneself. **F~er** *m* -s,-
feeler. **F~ung** *f* - contact
Fuhre *f* -, -n load
führ|en *vt* lead; guide <*Tourist*>;
(*geleiten*) take; (*leiten*) run;
(*befehligen*) command;
(*verkaufen*) stock; bear <*Namen*>;
keep <*Liste, Bücher*>; **bei** *od* **mit
sich f~en** carry ● *vi* (*haben*) lead;
(*verlaufen*) go, run; **zu etw f~en**
lead to sth. **f~end** *a* leading.
F~er *m* -s,- leader; (*Fremden-*)
guide; (*Buch*) guide[book].
F~erhaus *nt* driver's cab.
F~erschein *m* driving licence;

den **F~erschein machen** take one's driving test. **F~erscheinentzug** m disqualification from driving.

F~ung f -, -en leadership; (*Leitung*) management; (*Mil*) command; (*Betragen*) conduct; (*Besichtigung*) guided tour; (*Vorsprung*) lead; in **F~ung gehen** go into the lead

Fuhr|unternehmer m haulage contractor. **F~werk** nt cart

Fülle f -, -n abundance, wealth (**an** + *dat* of); (*Körper-*) plumpness. **f~n** vt fill; (*Culin*) stuff

Füllen nt -s,- foal

Füll|er m -s,-, **[I]**, **F~federhalter** m fountain pen. **F~ung** f -, -en filling; (*Braten-*) stuffing

fummeln vi (*haben*) fumble (**an** + *dat* with)

Fund m -[e]s, -e find

Fundament nt -[e]s, -e foundations pl. **f~al** a fundamental

Fundbüro nt lost-property office

fünf inv a, **F~** f -, -en five; (*Sch*) ≈ fail mark. **F~linge** mpl quintuplets. **f~te(r,s)** a fifth. **f~zehn** inv a fifteen. **f~zehnte(r,s)** a fifteenth. **f~zig** inv a fifty. **f~zigste(r,s)** a fiftieth

fungieren vi (*haben*) act (**als** as)

Funk m -s radio. **F~e** m -n, -n spark. **f~eln** vi (*haben*) sparkle; <*Stern:*> twinkle. **F~en** m -s,- spark. **f~en** vt radio. **F~sprechgerät** nt walkie-talkie. **F~spruch** m radio message. **F~streife** f [police] radio patrol

Funktion /-'ts̩io:n/ f -, -en function; (*Stellung*) position; (*Funktionieren*) working; **außer F~** out of action. **F~är** m -s, -e official. **f~ieren** vi (*haben*) work

für prep (+ *acc*) for; **Schritt für Schritt** step by step; **was für [ein]** what [a]! (*fragend*) what sort of [a]? **Für** nt das **Für und Wider** the pros and cons pl

Furche f -, -n furrow

Furcht f - fear (**vor** + *dat* of); **F~ erregend** terrifying. **f~bar** a terrible

fürcht|en vt/i (*haben*) fear; **sich f~en** be afraid (**vor** + *dat* of). **f~erlich** a dreadful

füreinander adv for each other

Furnier nt -s, -e veneer. **f~t** a veneered

Fürsorg|e f care; (*Admin*) welfare; (**[I]** *Geld*) ≈ social security. **F~er(in)** m -s,- (f -, -nen) social worker. **f~lich** a solicitous

Fürst m -en, -en prince. **F~entum** nt -s,ʺer principality. **F~in** f -, -nen princess

Furt f -, -en ford

Furunkel m -s,- (*Med*) boil

Fürwort nt (pl -wörter) pronoun

Furz m -es, -e (*vulg*) fart

Fusion f -, -en fusion; (*Comm*) merger

Fuß m -es,ʺe foot; (*Aust: Bein*) leg; (*Lampen-*) base; (*von Weinglas*) stem; **zu F~** on foot; **zu Fuß gehen** walk; **auf freiem Fuß** free. **F~abdruck** m footprint. **F~abtreter** m -s,- doormat. **F~ball** m football. **F~ballspieler** m footballer. **F~balltoto** nt football pools pl. **F~bank** f footstool. **F~boden** m floor

Fussel f -, -n & m -s, -[n] piece of fluff; **F~n** fluff sg. **f~n** vi (*haben*) shed fluff

fußen vi (*haben*) be based (**auf** + *dat* on)

Fußgänger|(in) m -s,- (f -, -nen) pedestrian. **F~brücke** f footbridge. **F~zone** f pedestrian precinct

Fuß|geher m -s,- (*Aust*) = **F~gänger**. **F~gelenk** nt ankle. **F~hebel** m pedal. **F~nagel** m toenail. **F~note** f footnote. **F~pflege** f chiropody. **F~rücken** m instep. **F~sohle** f sole of the foot. **F~tritt** m kick. **F~weg** m footpath; **eine Stunde F∼weg** an hour's walk

futsch *pred a* 🔟 gone

Futter¹ *nt* -s feed; *(Trocken-)* fodder

Futter² *nt* -s,- *(Kleider-)* lining

Futteral *nt* -s, -e case

füttern¹ *vt* feed

füttern² *vt* line

Futur *nt* -s *(Gram)* future

Gabe *f* -, -n gift; *(Dosis)* dose

Gabel *f* -, -n fork. **g∼n (sich)** *vr* fork. **G∼stapler** *m* -s,- fork-lift truck. **G∼ung** *f* -, -en fork

gackern *vi (haben)* cackle

gaffen *vi (haben)* gape, stare

Gage /'gaːʒə/ *f* -, -n *(Theat)* fee

gähnen *vi (haben)* yawn

Gala *f* - ceremonial dress

Galavorstellung *f* gala performance

Galerie *f* -, -n gallery

Galgen *m* -s,- gallows *sg.* **G∼frist** *f* 🔟 reprieve

Galionsfigur *f* figurehead

Galle *f* - bile; *(G∼nblase)* gall-bladder. **G∼nblase** *f* gall-bladder. **G∼nstein** *m* gallstone

Galopp *m* -s gallop; **im G∼** at a gallop. **g∼ieren** *vi (sein)* gallop

gammeln *vi (haben)* 🔟 loaf around. **G∼ler(in)** *m* -s,- *(f* -, -nen) drop-out

Gams *f* -, -en *(Aust)* chamois

Gämse *f* -, -n chamois

Gang *m* -[e]s,⸚e walk; *(G∼art)* gait; *(Boten-)* errand; *(Funktionieren)* running; *(Verlauf, Culin)* course; *(Durch-)* passage; *(Korridor)* corridor; *(zwischen Sitzreihen)* aisle, gangway; *(Anat)* duct; *(Auto)* gear; **in G∼ bringen** get going; **im G∼e sein** be in progress; **Essen mit vier G∼en** four-course meal

gängig *a* common; *(Comm)* popular

Gangschaltung *f* gear change

Gangster /'gɛŋstɐ/ *m* -s,- gangster

Ganove *m* -n, -n 🔟 crook

Gans *f* -,⸚e goose

Gänse|blümchen *nt* -s,- daisy. **G∼füßchen** *ntpl* inverted commas. **G∼haut** *f* goose-pimples *pl.* **G∼rich** *m* -s, -e gander

ganz *a* whole, entire; *(vollständig)* complete; *(🔟 heil)* undamaged, intact; **die g∼e Zeit** all the time, the whole time; **eine g∼e Weile/Menge** quite a while/lot; *inv* **g∼ Deutschland** the whole of Germany; **wieder g∼ machen** 🔟 mend; **im Großen und G∼en** on the whole ● *adv* quite; *(völlig)* completely, entirely; *(sehr)* very; **nicht g∼** not quite; **g∼ allein** all on one's own; **g∼ und gar** completely, totally; **g∼ und gar nicht** not at all. **G∼e(s)** *nt* whole.

g∼jährig *adv* all the year round.

g∼tägig *a & adv* full-time; *<geöffnet>* all day. **g∼tags** *adv* all day; *<arbeiten>* full-time

gar¹ *a* done, cooked

gar² *adv* **gar nicht/nichts/niemand** not/nothing/no one at all

Garage /ga'raːʒə/ *f* -, -n garage

Garantie *f* -, -n guarantee. **g∼ren** *vt/i (haben)* [für] etw g∼ren guarantee sth. **G∼schein** *m* guarantee

Garderobe *f* -, -n *(Kleider)* wardrobe; *(Ablage)* cloakroom; *(Künstler-)* dressing-room. **G∼nfrau** *f* cloakroom attendant

Gardine *f* -, -n curtain

garen *vt/i (haben)* cook

ären† vi (haben) ferment; (fig) seethe

Garn nt -[e]s, -e yarn; (Näh-) cotton

Garnele f -, -n shrimp; prawn

garnieren vt decorate; (Culin) garnish

Garnison f -, -en garrison

Garnitur f -, -en set; (Möbel-) suite

Garten m -s,- garden. **G~arbeit** f gardening. **G~bau** m horticulture. **G~haus** nt, **G~laube** f summerhouse. **G~schere** f secateurs pl

Gärtner|(in) m -s,- (f -, -nen) gardener. **G~ei** f -, -en nursery

Gärung f - fermentation

Gas nt -es, -e gas; **Gas geben** ⚡ accelerate. **G~maske** f gas mask. **G~pedal** nt (Auto) accelerator

Gasse f -, -n alley; (Aust) street

Gast m -[e]s,-̈e guest; (Hotel-) visitor; (im Lokal) patron; **zum Mittag G~e haben** have people to lunch; **bei jdm zu G~ sein** be staying with s.o. **G~arbeiter** m foreign worker. **G~bett** nt spare bed

Gäste|bett nt spare bed. **G~buch** nt visitors' book. **G~zimmer** nt [hotel] room; (privat) spare room

gast|freundlich a hospitable. **G~freundschaft** f hospitality. **G~geber** m -s,- host. **G~geberin** f -, -nen hostess. **G~haus** nt, **G~hof** m inn, hotel

gastlich a hospitable

Gastronomie f - gastronomy.

Gast|spiel nt guest performance. **G~spielreise** f (Theat) tour. **G~stätte** f restaurant. **G~wirt** m landlord. **G~wirtin** f landlady. **G~wirtschaft** f restaurant.

Gas|werk nt gasworks sg. **G~zähler** m gas-meter

Gatte m -n, -n husband

Gattin f -, -nen wife

Gattung f -, -en kind; (Biol) genus; (Kunst) genre

Gaudi f - (Aust, fam) fun

Gaumen m -s,- palate

Gauner m -s,- crook, swindler. **G~ei** f -, -en swindle

Gaze /'ga:zə/ f - gauze

Gazelle f -, -n gazelle

Gebäck nt -s [cakes and] pastries pl; (Kekse) biscuits pl

Gebälk nt -s timbers pl

geballt a <Faust> clenched

Gebärde f -, -n gesture

gebär|en† vt give birth to, bear; **geboren werden** be born. **G~mutter** f womb, uterus

Gebäude nt -s,- building

Gebeine ntpl [mortal] remains

Gebell nt -s barking

geben† vt give; (tun, bringen) put; (Karten) deal; (aufführen) perform; (unterrichten) teach; **etw verloren g~** give sth up as lost; **viel/wenig g~ auf** (+ acc) set great/little store by; **sich g~** (nachlassen) wear off; (besser werden) get better; (sich verhalten) behave ● impers **es gibt** there is/are; **was gibt es Neues/zum Mittag/im Kino?** what's the news/for lunch/on at the cinema? **es wird Regen g~** it's going to rain ● vi (haben) (Karten) deal

Gebet nt -[e]s, -e prayer

Gebiet nt -[e]s, -e area; (Hoheits-) territory; (Sach-) field

gebieten† vt command; (erfordern) demand ● vi (haben) rule

Gebilde nt -s,- structure

gebildet a educated; (kultiviert) cultured

Gebirg|e nt -s,- mountains pl. **g~ig** a mountainous

Gebiss nt -es, -e teeth pl; (künstliches) false teeth pl; dentures pl, (des Zaumes) bit

geblümt a floral, flowered

gebogen a curved

geboren a born; **g~er Deutscher** German by birth; **Frau X, g~e Y** Mrs X, née Y

Gebot nt -[e]s, -e rule

gebraten a fried

Gebrauch m use; (Sprach-) usage; **Gebräuche** customs; **in G~** in use; **G~ machen von** make use of. **g~en** vt use; **zu nichts zu g~en** useless

gebräuchlich a common; <Wort> in common use

Gebrauchs|anleitung, G~anweisung f directions pl for use. **g~t** a used; (Comm) secondhand. **G~twagen** m used car

gebrechlich a frail, infirm

gebrochen a broken ● adv **g~ Englisch sprechen** speak broken English

Gebrüll nt -s roaring

Gebühr f -, -en charge, fee; **über G~** excessively; **g~end** a due; (geziemend) proper. **g~enfrei** a free ● adv free of charge. **g~enpflichtig** a & adv subject to a charge; **g~enpflichtige Straße** toll road

Geburt f -, -en birth; **von G~** by birth. **G~enkontrolle, G~enregelung** f birth-control. **G~enziffer** f birth-rate

gebürtig a native (aus of); **g~er Deutscher** German by birth

Geburts|datum nt date of birth. **G~helfer** m obstetrician. **G~hilfe** f obstetrics sg. **G~ort** m place of birth. **G~tag** m birthday. **G~urkunde** f birth certificate

Gebüsch nt -[e]s, -e bushes pl

Gedächtnis nt -ses memory; **aus dem G~** from memory

Gedanke m -ns, -n thought (an + acc of); (Idee) idea; **sich** (dat) **G~n machen** worry (über + acc about). **g~los** a thoughtless; (zerstreut) absent-minded. **G~nstrich** m dash

Gedärme ntpl intestines; (Tier-) entrails

Gedeck nt -[e]s, -e place setting; (auf Speisekarte) set meal

gedeihen† vi (sein) thrive, flourish

gedenken† vi (haben) propose (etw zu tun to do sth); **jds g~** remember s.o. **G~** nt -s memory

Gedenk|feier f commemoration. **G~gottesdienst** m memorial service

Gedicht nt -[e]s, -e poem

Gedräng|e nt -s crush, crowd. **g~t** a (knapp) concise ● adv **g~t voll** packed

Geduld f - patience; **G~ haben** be patient. **g~en (sich)** vr be patient. **g~ig** a patient. **G~[s]spiel** nt puzzle

gedunsen a bloated

geehrt a honoured; **Sehr g~er Herr X** Dear Mr X

geeignet a suitable; **im g~en Moment** at the right moment

Gefahr f -, -en danger; **in G~** in danger; **auf eigene G~** at one's own risk; **G~ laufen** run the risk (etw zu tun of doing sth)

gefähr|den vt endanger; (fig) jeopardize. **g~lich** a dangerous

gefahrlos a safe

Gefährt nt -[e]s, -e vehicle

Gefährte m -n, -n, **Gefährtin** f -, -nen companion

gefahrvoll a dangerous, perilous

Gefälle nt -s,- slope; (Straßen-) gradient

gefallen† vi (haben) **jdm g~** please s.o.; **er/es gefällt mir** I like him/it; **sich** (dat) **etw g~ lassen** put up with sth

Gefallen[1] m -s,- favour

Gefallen[2] nt -s pleasure (an + dat in); **dir zu G~** to please you

Gefallene(r) m soldier killed in the war

gefällig a pleasing; (hübsch) attractive; (hilfsbereit) obliging;

noch etwas g~? will there be anything else? G~keit f -, -en favour; (Freundlichkeit) kindness

ɡefangen|e(r) m/f prisoner. G~nahme f - capture. g~nehmen* vt sep g~ nehmen, s. fangen. G~schaft f - captivity

ɡefängnis nt -ses, -se prison; (Strafe) imprisonment. G~strafe f imprisonment; (Urteil) prison sentence. G~wärter m [prison] warder

ɡefäß nt -es, -e container; (Blut-) vessel

ɡefasst a composed; (ruhig) calm; g~ sein auf (+ acc) be prepared for

ɡefedert a sprung

ɡefeiert a celebrated

ɡefieder nt -s plumage

ɡefleckt a spotted

ɡeflügel nt -s poultry. G~klein nt -s giblets pl. g~t a winged

ɡeflüster nt -s whispering

ɡefolge nt -s retinue, entourage

ɡefragt a popular

ɡefreite(r) m lance-corporal

ɡefrier|en† vi (sein) freeze. G~fach nt freezer compartment. G~punkt m freezing point. G~schrank m upright freezer. G~truhe f chest freezer

ɡefroren a frozen

ɡefügig a compliant; (gehorsam) obedient

ɡefühl nt -[e]s, -e feeling; (Empfindung) sensation; (G~sregung) emotion; im G~ haben know instinctively. g~los a insensitive; (herzlos) unfeeling; (taub) numb. g~smäßig a emotional; (instinktiv) instinctive. G~sregung f emotion. g~voll a sensitive; (sentimental) sentimental

ɡefüllt a filled; (voll) full

ɡefürchtet a feared, dreaded

ɡefüttert a lined

ɡegeben a given; (bestehend) present; (passend) appropriate. g~enfalls adv if need be

ɡegen prep (+ acc) against; (Sport) versus; (g~über) to[-wards]; (Vergleich) compared with; (Richtung, Zeit) towards; (ungefähr) around; ein Mittel g~ a remedy for ● adv g~ 100 Leute about 100 people. G~angriff m counter-attack

ɡegend f -, -en area, region; (Umgebung) neighbourhood

ɡegeneinander adv against/ (gegenüber) towards one another

ɡegen|fahrbahn f opposite carriageway. G~gift nt antidote. G~maßnahme f countermeasure. G~satz m contrast; (Widerspruch) contradiction; (G~teil) opposite; im G~satz zu unlike. g~seitig a mutual; sich g~seitig hassen hate one another. G~stand m object; (Gram, Gesprächs-) subject. G~stück nt counterpart; (G~teil) opposite. G~teil nt opposite, contrary; im G~teil on the contrary. g~teilig a opposite

ɡegenüber prep (+ dat) opposite; (Vergleich) compared with; jdm g~ höflich sein be polite to s.o. ● adv opposite. G~ nt -s person opposite. g~liegend a opposite. g~stehen† vi sep (haben) (+ dat) face; feindlich g~stehen (+ dat) be hostile to. g~stellen vt sep confront; (vergleichen) compare

ɡegen|verkehr m oncoming traffic. G~vorschlag m counter-proposal. G~wart f - present; (Anwesenheit) presence. g~wärtig a present ● adv at present. G~wehr f - resistance. G~wert m equivalent. G~wind m head wind. g~zeichnen vt sep countersign

ɡeglückt a successful

Gegner|(in) *m* -s,- (*f* -, -nen) opponent. **g~isch** *a* opposing
Gehabe *nt* -s affected behaviour
Gehackte(s) *nt* mince
Gehalt *nt* -[e]s,-̈er salary.
  G~serhöhung *f* rise
gehässig *a* spiteful
gehäuft *a* heaped
Gehäuse *nt* -s,- case; (*TV, Radio*) cabinet; (*Schnecken-*) shell
Gehege *nt* -s,- enclosure
geheim *a* secret; **g~ halten** keep secret; **im G~en** secretly.
  G~dienst *m* Secret Service.
  G~nis *nt* -ses, -se secret.
  g~nisvoll *a* mysterious
gehemmt *a* (*fig*) inhibited

gehen†
● *intransitive verb* (*sein*)
····▸ (*sich irgendwohin begeben*) go; (*zu Fuß*) walk. **tanzen/ schwimmen/einkaufen gehen** go dancing/swimming/shopping. **schlafen gehen** go to bed. **zum Arzt gehen** go to the doctor's. **in die Schule gehen** go to school. **auf und ab gehen** walk up and down. **über die Straße gehen** cross the street
····▸ (*weggehen; fam: abfahren*) go; leave. **ich muss bald gehen** I must go soon. **Sie können gehen** you may go. **der Zug geht um zehn Uhr** 🕐 the train leaves *or* goes at ten o'clock
····▸ (*funktionieren*) work. **der Computer geht wieder/nicht mehr** the computer is working again/ has stopped working. **meine Uhr geht falsch/richtig** my watch is wrong/right
····▸ (*möglich sein*) be possible. **ja, das geht** yes, I *or* we can manage that. **das geht nicht** that can't be done; (🕐 *ist nicht akzeptabel*) it's not good enough, it's not on 🕐. **es geht einfach nicht, dass du so spät**

nach Hause kommst it simply won't do for you to come home so late
····▸ (🕐 *gerade noch angehen*) **es geht [so]** it is all right. **Wie war die Party? — Es ging so** How was the party? — Not bad *or* So-so
····▸ (*sich entwickeln*) do; go. **der Laden geht gut** the shop is doing well. **es geht alles nach Wunsch** everything is going to plan
····▸ (*impers*) **wie geht es Ihnen?** how are you? **es geht ihm gut/ schlecht** (*gesundheitlich*) he is well/not well; (*geschäftlich*) he is doing well/badly; **ein gut g~des Geschäft** a thriving business
····▸ (*impers; sich um etw handeln*) **es geht um** it concerns. **worum geht es hier?** what is this all about? **es geht ihr nur ums Geld** she is only interested in money

Geheul *nt* -s howling
Gehife *m* -n, -n, **Gehilfin** *f* -, -nen trainee; (*Helfer*) assistant
Gehirn *nt* -s brain; (*Verstand*) brains *pl* **G~erschütterung** *f* concussion. **G~hautentzündung** *f* meningitis. **G~wäsche** *f* brainwashing
gehoben *a* (*fig*) superior
Gehöft *nt* -[e]s, -e farm
Gehör *nt* -s hearing
gehorchen *vi* (*haben*) (+ *dat*) obey
gehören *vi* (*haben*) belong (*dat* to); **dazu gehört Mut** that takes courage; **es gehört sich nicht** it isn't done
gehörlos *a* deaf
Gehörn *nt* -s, -e horns *pl*; (*Geweih*) antlers *pl*
gehorsam *a* obedient. **G~** *m* -s obedience
Geh|steig *m* -[e]s, -e pavement.
  G~weg *m* = **Gehsteig**; (*Fußweg*) footpath

Geier m -s,- vulture

Geig|e f -, -n violin. **g~en** vi (haben) play the violin ● vt play on the violin. **G~er(in)** m -s,- (f -, -nen) violinist

geil a lecherous; randy; (🛈 toll) great

Geisel f -, -n hostage

Geiß f -, -en (SGer) [nanny-]goat. **G~blatt** nt honeysuckle

Geist m -[e]s, -er mind; (Witz) wit; (Gesinnung) spirit; (Gespenst) ghost; der Heilige G~ the Holy Ghost or Spirit

geistes|abwesend a absent-minded. **G~blitz** m brainwave. **g~gegenwärtig** adv with great presence of mind. **g~gestört** a [mentally] deranged. **g~krank** a mentally ill. **G~krankheit** f mental illness. **G~wissenschaften** fpl arts. **G~zustand** m mental state

geist|ig a mental; (intellektuell) intellectual. **g~lich** a spiritual; (religiös) religious; <Musik> sacred; <Tracht> clerical. **G~liche(r)** m clergyman. **G~lichkeit** f - clergy. **g~reich** a clever; (witzig) witty

Geiz m -es meanness. **g~en** vi (haben) be mean (mit with). **G~hals** m 🛈 miser. **g~ig** a mean, miserly. **G~kragen** m 🛈 miser

Gekicher nt -s giggling

geknickt a 🛈 dejected

gekonnt a accomplished ● adv expertly

gekränkt a offended, hurt

Gekritzel nt -s scribble

Gelächter nt -s laughter

geladen a loaded

gelähmt a paralysed

Geländer nt -s,- railings pl; (Treppen-) banisters

gelangen vi (sein) reach/(fig) attain (zu etw/an etw acc sth)

gelassen a composed; (ruhig) calm. **G~heit** f - equanimity; (Fassung) composure

Gelatine /ʒela-/ f - gelatine

geläufig a common, current; (fließend) fluent; jdm g~ sein be familiar to s.o.

gelaunt a gut/schlecht g~ sein be in a good/bad mood

gelb a yellow; (bei Ampel) amber; das G~e vom Ei the yolk of the egg. **G~** nt -s,- yellow. **g~lich** a yellowish. **G~sucht** f jaundice

Geld nt -es, -er money; öffentliche G~er public funds. **G~beutel** m, **G~börse** f purse. **G~geber** m -s,- backer. **g~lich** a financial. **G~mittel** ntpl funds. **G~schein** m banknote. **G~schrank** m safe. **G~strafe** f fine. **G~stück** nt coin

Gelee /ʒe'le:/ nt -s, -s jelly

gelegen a situated; (passend) convenient

Gelegenheit f -, -en opportunity, chance; (Anlass) occasion; (Comm) bargain; bei G~ some time. **G~sarbeit** f casual work. **G~skauf** m bargain

gelegentlich a occasional ● adv occasionally; (bei Gelegenheit) some time

Gelehrte(r) m/f scholar

Geleit nt -[e]s escort; freies G~ safe conduct. **g~en** vt escort

Gelenk nt -[e]s, -e joint. **g~ig** a supple; (Techn) flexible

gelernt a skilled

Geliebte(r) m/f lover

gelingen† vi (sein) succeed, be successful. **G~** nt -s success

gellend a shrill

geloben vt promise [solemnly]; das Gelobte Land the Promised Land

Gelöbnis nt -ses, -se vow

gelöst a (fig) relaxed

gelten† vi (haben) be valid; <Regel:> apply; g~ als be regarded as; etw nicht g~ lassen not accept sth; **wenig/viel g~** be worth/(*fig*) count for little/a lot; **jdm g~** be meant for s.o.; **das gilt nicht** that doesn't count. **g~d** *a* valid; <*Preise*> current; <*Meinung*> prevailing; **g~d machen** assert <*Recht, Forderung*>; bring to bear <*Einfluss*>

Geltung *f* - validity; (*Ansehen*) prestige; **zur G~ bringen** set off

Gelübde *nt* -s,- vow

gelungen *a* successful

Gelüst *nt* -[e]s, -e desire

gemächlich *a* leisurely ● *adv* in a leisurely manner

Gemahl *m* -s, -e husband. **G~in** *f* -, -nen wife

Gemälde *nt* -s,- painting. **G~galerie** *f* picture gallery

gemäß *prep* (+ *dat*) in accordance with

gemäßigt *a* moderate; <*Klima*> temperate

gemein *a* common; (*unanständig*) vulgar; (*niederträchtig*) mean; **g~er Soldat** private

Gemeinde *f* -, -n [local] community; (*Admin*) borough; (*Pfarr-*) parish; (*bei Gottesdienst*) congregation. **G~rat** *m* local council/(*Person*) councillor. **G~wahlen** *fpl* local elections

gemein|gefährlich *a* dangerous. **G~heit** *f* -, -en commonness; vulgarity; meanness; (*Bemerkung, Handlung*) mean thing [to say/do]; **so eine G~heit!** how mean! **G~kosten** *pl* overheads. **g~nützig** *a* charitable. **g~sam** *a* common ● *adv* together

Gemeinschaft *f* -, -en community. **g~lich** *a* joint; <*Besitz*> communal ● *adv* jointly; (*zusammen*) together. **G~sarbeit** *f* team-work

Gemenge *nt* -s,- mixture

Gemisch *nt* -[e]s, -e mixture. **g~t** *a* mixed

Gemme *f* -, -n engraved gem

Gemse* *f* -, -n *s.* **Gämse**

Gemurmel *nt* -s murmuring

Gemüse *nt* -s,- vegetable; (*coll*) vegetables *pl*. **G~händler** *m* greengrocer

gemustert *a* patterned

Gemüt *nt* -[e]s, -er nature, disposition; (*Gefühl*) feelings *pl*

gemütlich *a* cosy; (*gemächlich*) leisurely; (*zwanglos*) informal; <*Person*> genial; **es sich** (*dat*) **g~ machen** make oneself comfortable. **G~keit** *f* - cosiness

Gen *nt* -s, -e gene

genau *a* exact, precise; <*Waage, Messung*> accurate; (*sorgfältig*) meticulous; (*ausführlich*) detailed; **nichts G~es wissen** not know any details; **g~ genommen** strictly speaking; **g~!** exactly! **G~igkeit** *f* - exactitude; precision; accuracy; meticulousness

genauso *adv* just the same; (*g~sehr*) just as much; **g~ teuer** just as expensive; **g~ gut** just as good; *adv* just as well; **g~ sehr** just as much; **g~ viel** just as much/many; **g~ wenig** just as little/few; (*noch*) no more

Gendarm /ʒãˈdarm/ *m* -en, -en (*Aust*) policeman

Genealogie *f* - genealogy

genehmig|en *vt* grant; approve <*Plan*>. **G~ung** *f* -, -en permission; (*Schein*) permit

geneigt *a* sloping, inclined; (*fig*) well-disposed (*dat* towards)

General *m* -s,⸚e general. **G~direktor** *m* managing director. **G~probe** *f* dress rehearsal. **G~streik** *m* general strike

Generation /-ˈtsːioːn/ *f* -, -en generation

Generator *m* -s, -en /-ˈtoːrən/ generator

generell a general

genes|en† vi (sein) recover.
 G~ung f - recovery; (Erholung)
 convalescence

Genetik f - genetics sg

Genf nt -s Geneva. **G~er** a
 Geneva ...; **G~er See** Lake
 Geneva

genial a brilliant. **G~ität** f genius

Genick nt -s, -e [back of the]
 neck; **sich** (dat) **das G~ brechen**
 break one's neck

Genie /ʒeˈniː/ nt -s, -s genius

genieren /ʒeˈniːrən/ vt embarrass;
 sich g~ feel or be embarrassed

genieß|bar a fit to eat/drink.
 g~en† vt enjoy; (verzehren) eat/
 drink

Genitiv m -s, -e genitive

Genosse m -n, -n (Pol) comrade.
 G~nschaft f -, -en cooperative

genug inv a & adv enough

Genüge f **zur G~** sufficiently.
 g~n vi (haben) be enough. **g~nd**
 inv a sufficient, enough; (Sch)
 fair ● adv sufficiently, enough

Genuss m -es, ̈e enjoyment;
 (Vergnügen) pleasure; (Verzehr)
 consumption

geöffnet a open

Geo|graphie, G~grafie f -
 geography. **g~graphisch,**
 g~grafisch a geographical.
 G~logie f - geology. **g~logisch** a
 geological. **G~meter** m -s,-
 surveyor. **G~metrie** f - geometry.
 g~metrisch a geometric[al]

geordnet a well-ordered; (stabil)
 stable; **alphabetisch g~** in
 alphabetical order

Gepäck nt -s luggage, baggage.
 G~ablage f luggage-rack.
 G~aufbewahrung f left-luggage
 office. **G~schein** m left-luggage
 ticket; (Aviat) baggage check.
 G~träger m porter; (Fahrrad-)
 luggage carrier; (Dach-) roof-
 rack

Gepard m -s, -e cheetah

gepflegt a well-kept; <Person>
 well-groomed; <Hotel> first-class

gepunktet a spotted

gerade a straight; (direkt) direct;
 (aufrecht) upright; (aufrichtig)
 straightforward; <Zahl> even
 ● adv straight; directly; (eben)
 just; (genau) exactly; (besonders)
 especially; **g~ sitzen/stehen** sit/
 stand [up] straight; **g~ erst** only
 just. **G~** f -, -n straight line.
 g~aus adv straight ahead/on.
 g~heraus adv (fig) straight out.
 g~so adv just the same; **g~so**
 gut just as good; **g~ auf** just as well.
 g~stehen† vi sep (haben) (fig)
 accept responsibility (**für** for).
 g~zu adv virtually; (wirklich)
 absolutely

Geranie /-iə/ f -, -n geranium

Gerät nt -[e]s, -e tool; (Acker-)
 implement; (Küchen-) utensil;
 (Elektro-) appliance; (Radio-,
 Fernseh-) set; (Turn-) piece of
 apparatus; (coll) equipment

geraten† vi (sein) get; **in Brand g~**
 catch fire; **in Wut g~** get angry;
 gut g~ turn out well

Geratewohl nt **aufs G~** at
 random

geräuchert a smoked

geräumig a spacious, roomy

Geräusch nt -[e]s, -e noise. **g~los**
 a noiseless

gerben vt tan

gerecht a just; (fair) fair.
 g~fertigt a justified. **G~igkeit** f -
 justice; fairness

Gerede nt -s talk

geregelt a regular

gereizt a irritable

Geriatrie f - geriatrics sg

Gericht¹ nt -[e]s, -e (Culin) dish

Gericht² nt -[e]s, -e court [of law];
 vor G~ in court; **das Jüngste G~**
 the Last Judgement. **g~lich** a
 judicial; <Verfahren> legal ● adv
 g~lich vorgehen take legal action.
 G~shof m court of justice.

G

G∼smedizin f forensic medicine.
G∼ssaal m court-room.
G∼svollzieher m -s,- bailiff
gerieben a grated; (🗓 schlau) crafty
gering a small; (niedrig) low; (g∼fügig) slight. **g∼fügig** a slight. **g∼schätzig** a contemptuous; <Bemerkung> disparaging. **g∼ste(r,s)** a least; **nicht im G∼sten** not in the least
gerinnen† vi (sein) curdle; <Blut:> clot
Gerippe nt -s,- skeleton; (fig) framework
gerissen a 🗓 crafty
Germ m -[e]s & (Aust) f - yeast
German|e m -n, -n [ancient] German. **g∼isch** a Germanic. **G∼istik** f - German [language and literature]
gern[e] adv gladly; **g∼ haben** like; (lieben) be fond of; **ich tanze g∼** I like dancing; **willst du mit?—g∼!** do you want to come?—I'd love to!
Gerste f - barley. **G∼nkorn** nt (Med) stye
Geruch m -[e]s,¨e smell (von/nach of). **g∼los** a odourless. **G∼ssinn** m sense of smell
Gerücht nt -[e]s, -e rumour
gerührt a (fig) moved, touched
Gerümpel nt -s lumber, junk
Gerüst nt -[e]s, -e scaffolding; (fig) framework
gesammelt a collected; (gefasst) composed
gesamt a entire, whole. **G∼ausgabe** f complete edition. **G∼eindruck** m overall impression. **G∼heit** f - whole. **G∼schule** f comprehensive school. **G∼summe** f total
Gesandte(r) m/f envoy
Gesang m -[e]s,¨e singing; (Lied) song; (Kirchen-) hymn. **G∼verein** m choral society
Gesäß nt -es buttocks pl

Geschäft nt -[e]s, -e business; (Laden) shop, store; (Transaktion) deal; **schmutzige G∼e** shady dealings; **ein gutes G∼machen** do very well (mit out of). **g∼ig** a busy; <Treiben> bustling. **G∼igkeit** f - activity. **g∼lich** a business … ● adv on business
Geschäfts|brief m business letter. **G∼führer** m manager; (Vereins-) secretary. **G∼mann** m (pl -leute) businessman. **G∼stelle** f office; (Zweigstelle) branch. **g∼tüchtig** a **g∼tüchtig sein** be a good businessman/-woman. **G∼zeiten** fpl hours of business
geschehen† vi (sein) happen (dat to); **das geschieht dir recht!** it serves you right! **gern g∼!** you're welcome! **G∼** nt -s events pl
gescheit a clever
Geschenk nt -[e]s, -e present, gift
Geschicht|e f -, -n history; (Erzählung) story; (🗓 Sache) business. **g∼lich** a historical
Geschick nt -[e]s fate; (Talent) skill. **G∼lichkeit** f - skilfulness, skill. **g∼t** a skilful; (klug) clever
geschieden a divorced
Geschirr nt -s, -e (coll) crockery; (Porzellan) china; (Service) service; (Pferde-) harness; **schmutziges G∼** dirty dishes pl. **G∼spülmaschine** f dishwasher. **G∼tuch** nt tea-towel
Geschlecht nt -[e]s, -er sex; (Gram) gender; (Generation) generation. **g∼lich** a sexual. **G∼skrankheit** f venereal disease. **G∼steile** ntpl genitals. **G∼sverkehr** m sexual intercourse. **G∼swort** nt (pl -wörter) article
geschliffen a (fig) polished
Geschmack m -[e]s,¨e taste; (Aroma) flavour; (G∼ssinn) sense of taste; **einen guten G∼ haben** (fig) have good taste.

g~los *a* tasteless; **g~los sein** (*fig*) be in bad taste. **g~voll** *a* (*fig*) tasteful

Geschoss *nt* -es, -e missile; (*Stockwerk*) storey, floor

Geschrei *nt* -s screaming; (*fig*) fuss

Geschütz *nt* -es, -e gun, cannon

geschützt *a* protected; <*Stelle*> sheltered

Geschwader *nt* -s,- squadron

Geschwätz *nt* -es talk

geschweige *conj* **g~ denn** let alone

Geschwindigkeit *f* -, -en speed; (*Phys*) velocity. **G~sbegrenzung, G~sbeschränkung** *f* speed limit

Geschwister *pl* brother[s] and sister[s]; siblings

geschwollen *a* swollen; (*fig*) pompous

Geschworene|(r) *m/f* juror; **die G~n** the jury *sg*

Geschwulst *f* -,̈-e swelling; (*Tumor*) tumour

geschwungen *a* curved

Geschwür *nt* -s, -e ulcer

gesellig *a* sociable; (*Zool*) gregarious; (*unterhaltsam*) convivial; **g~er Abend** social evening

Gesellschaft *f* -, -en company; (*Veranstaltung*) party; **die G~** society; **jdm G~ leisten** keep s.o. company. **g~lich** *a* social. **G~sspiel** *nt* party game

Gesetz *nt* -es, -e law. **G~entwurf** *m* bill. **g~gebend** *a* legislative. **G~gebung** *f* - legislation. **g~lich** *a* legal. **g~mäßig** *a* lawful; (*gesetzlich*) legal. **g~widrig** *a* illegal

gesichert *a* secure

Gesicht *nt* -[e]s, -er face; (*Aussehen*) appearance. **G~sfarbe** *f* complexion. **G~spunkt** *m* point of view. **G~szüge** *mpl* features

Gesindel *nt* -s riff-raff

Gesinnung *f* -, -en mind; (*Einstellung*) attitude

gesondert *a* separate

Gespann *nt* -[e]s, -e team; (*Wagen*) horse and cart/carriage

gespannt *a* taut; (*fig*) tense; <*Beziehungen*> strained; (*neugierig*) eager; (*erwartungsvoll*) expectant; **g~ sein, ob** wonder whether; **auf etw g~ sein** look forward eagerly to sth

Gespenst *nt* -[e]s, -er ghost. **g~isch** *a* ghostly; (*unheimlich*) eerie

Gespött *nt* -[e]s mockery; **zum G~ werden** become a laughing-stock

Gespräch *nt* -[e]s-e conversation; (*Telefon-*) call; **ins G~ kommen** get talking; **im G~ sein** be under discussion. **g~ig** *a* talkative, **G~sthema** *nt* topic of conversation

Gestalt *f* -, -en figure; (*Form*) shape, form; **G~ annehmen** (*fig*) take shape. **g~en** *vt* shape; (*organisieren*) arrange; (*schaffen*) create; (*entwerfen*) design; **sich g~en** turn out

Geständnis *nt* -ses, -se confession

Gestank *m* -s stench, [bad] smell

gestatten *vt* allow, permit; **nicht gestattet** prohibited; **g~ Sie?** may I?

Geste /'gɛ-, 'gɛ:stə/ *f* -, -n gesture

Gesteck *nt* -[e]s, -e flower arrangement

gestehen† *vt/i* (*haben*) confess; confess to <*Verbrechen*>

Gestein *nt* -[e]s, -e rock

Gestell *nt* -[e]s, -e stand; (*Flaschen-*) rack; (*Rahmen*) frame

gesteppt *a* quilted

gestern *adv* yesterday; **g~ Nacht** last night

gestrandet *a* stranded

gestreift *a* striped

gestrichelt *a* <*Linie*> dotted

gestrichen *a* **g~er Teelöffel** level teaspoon[ful]

G

gestrig /'gɛstrɪç/ a yesterday's; **am g~en Tag** yesterday

Gestrüpp nt -s, -e undergrowth

Gestüt nt -[e]s, -e stud [farm]

Gesuch nt -[e]s, -e request; (Admin) application. **g~t** a sought-after

gesund a healthy; **g~ sein** be in good health; <Sport, Getränk:> be good for one; **wieder g~ werden** get well again

Gesundheit f - health; **G~!** (bei Niesen) bless you! **g~licher Zustand** state of health ● adv **es geht ihm g~lich gut/schlecht** he is in good/poor health. **g~sschädlich** a harmful

getäfelt a panelled

Getöse nt -s racket, din

Getränk nt -[e]s, -e drink. **G~ekarte** f wine-list

getrauen vt sich (dat) **etw g~** dare [to] do sth; **sich g~** dare

Getreide nt -s (coll) grain

getrennt a separate; **g~ leben** live apart; **g~ schreiben** write as two words

getreu a faithful ● prep (+ dat) true to. **g~lich** adv faithfully

Getriebe nt -s,- bustle; (Techn) gear; (Auto) transmission; (Gehäuse) gearbox

getrost adv with confidence

Getto nt -s, -s ghetto

Getue nt -s 🔲 fuss

Getümmel nt -s tumult

geübt a skilled

Gewächs nt -es, -e plant

gewachsen a **jdm g~ sein** be a match for s.o.

Gewächshaus nt greenhouse

gewagt a daring

gewählt a refined

gewahr a **g~ werden** become aware (acc/gen of)

Gewähr f - guarantee

gewähr|en vt grant; (geben) offer. **g~leisten** vt guarantee

Gewahrsam m -s safekeeping; (Haft) custody

Gewalt f -, -en power; (Kraft) force; (Brutalität) violence; **mit G~** by force. **G~herrschaft** f tyranny. **g~ig** a powerful; (🔲 groß) enormous; (stark) tremendous. **g~sam** a forcible; <Tod> violent. **g~tätig** a violent. **G~tätigkeit** f -, -en violence; (Handlung) act of violence

Gewand nt -[e]s,ˉer robe

gewandt a skilful. **G~heit** f - skill

Gewebe nt -s,- fabric; (Anat) tissue

Gewehr nt -s, -e rifle, gun

Geweih nt -[e]s, -e antlers pl

Gewerb|e nt -s,- trade. **g~lich** a commercial. **g~smäßig** a professional

Gewerkschaft f -, -en trade union. **G~ler(in)** m -s,- (f -, -nen) trade unionist

Gewicht nt -[e]s, -e weight; (Bedeutung) importance. **G~heben** nt -s weight-lifting

Gewinde nt -s,- [screw] thread

Gewinn m -[e]s, -e profit; (fig) gain, benefit; (beim Spiel) winnings pl; (Preis) prize; (Los) winning ticket. **G~beteiligung** f profit-sharing. **g~en†** vt win; (erlangen) gain; (fördern) extract ● vi (haben) win; **g~en an** (+ dat) gain in. **g~end** a engaging. **G~er(in)** m -s,- (f -, -nen) winner

Gewirr nt -s, -e tangle; (Straßen-) maze

gewiss a certain

Gewissen nt -s,- conscience. **g~haft** a conscientious. **g~los** a unscrupulous. **G~sbisse** mpl pangs of conscience

gewissermaßen adv to a certain extent; (sozusagen) as it were

Gewissheit f - certainty

Gewitt|er nt -s,- thunderstorm. **g~rig** a thundery

gewogen *a* (*fig*) well-disposed (*dat* towards)

gewöhnen *vt* jdn/sich g~ an (+ *acc*) get s.o. used to/get used to; **[an] jdn/etw gewöhnt sein** be used to s.o./sth

Gewohnheit *f* -, -en habit. **G~srecht** *nt* common law

gewöhnlich *a* ordinary; (*üblich*) usual; (*ordinär*) common

gewohnt *a* customary; (*vertraut*) familiar; (*üblich*) usual; **etw** (*acc*) **g~ sein** be used to sth

Gewölbe *nt* -s,- vault

Gewühl *nt* -[e]s crush

gewunden *a* winding

Gewürz *nt* -es, -e spice. **G~nelke** *f* clove

gezackt *a* serrated

gezahnt *a* serrated; <*Säge*> toothed

Gezeiten *fpl* tides

gezielt *a* specific; <*Frage*> pointed

geziert *a* affected

gezwungen *a* forced. **g~ermaßen** *adv* of necessity

Gicht *f* - gout

Giebel *m* -s,- gable

Gier *f* - greed (**nach** for). **g~ig** *a* greedy

gieß|en† *vt* pour; water <*Blumen, Garten*>; (*Techn*) cast ● *v impers* **es g~t** it is pouring [with rain]. **G~kanne** *f* watering-can

Gift *nt* -[e]s, -e poison; (*Schlangen-*) venom; (*Biol, Med*) toxin. **g~ig** *a* poisonous; <*Schlange*> venomous; (*Med, Chem*) toxic; (*fig*) spiteful. **G~müll** *m* toxic waste. **G~pilz** *m* toadstool

Gilde *f* -, -n guild

Gin /dʒɪn/ *m* -s gin

Ginster *m* -s (*Bot*) broom

Gipfel *m* -s,- summit, top; (*fig*) peak. **G~konferenz** *f* summit conference. **g~n** *vi* (*haben*) culminate (**in** + *dat* in)

Gips *m* -es plaster. **G~verband** *m* (*Med*) plaster cast

Giraffe *f* -, -n giraffe

Girlande *f* -, -n garland

Girokonto /ˈʒiːro-/ *nt* current account

Gischt *m* -[e]s & *f* - spray

Gitar|re *f* -, -n guitar. **G~rist(in)** *m* -en, -en (*f* -, -nen) guitarist

Gitter *nt* -s,- bars *pl*; (*Rost*) gratting, grid; (*Geländer, Zaun*) railings *pl*; (*Fenster-*) grille; (*Draht-*) wire screen

Glanz *m* -es shine; (*von Farbe, Papier*) gloss; (*Seiden-*) sheen; (*Politur*) polish; (*fig*) brilliance; (*Pracht*) splendour

glänzen *vi* (*haben*) shine. **g~d** *a* shining, bright; <*Papier*> glossy; (*fig*) brilliant

glanz|los *a* dull. **G~stück** *nt* masterpiece

Glas *nt* -es,¨er glass; (*Brillen-*) lens; (*Fern-*) binoculars *pl*; (*Marmeladen-*) [glass] jar. **G~er** *m* -s,- glazier

glasieren *vt* glaze; ice <*Kuchen*>

glas|ig *a* glassy; (*durchsichtig*) transparent. **G~scheibe** *f* pane

Glasur *f* -, -en glaze; (*Culin*) icing

glatt *a* smooth; (*eben*) even; <*Haar*> straight; (*rutschig*) slippery; (*einfach*) straightforward; <*Absage*> flat; **g~ streichen** smooth out; **g~ rasiert** clean-shaven; **g~ gehen** go off smoothly; **das ist g~ gelogen** it's a downright lie

Glätte *f* - smoothness; (*Rutschigkeit*) slipperiness

Glatt|eis *nt* [black] ice. **g~weg** *adv* Ⅱ outright

Glatz|e *f* -, -n bald patch; (*Voll-*) bald head; **eine G~e bekommen** go bald. **g~köpfig** *a* bald

Glaube *m* -ns belief (**an** + *acc* in); (*Relig*) faith; **G~n schenken** (+ *dat*) believe. **g~n** *vt/i* (*haben*) believe (**an** + *acc* in); (*vermuten*)

G

think; **jdm g~n** believe s.o; **nicht zu g~n** unbelievable, incredible.
G~nsbekenntnis nt creed
gläubig a religious; (vertrauend) trusting. **G~e(r)** m/f (Relig) believer; **die G~en** the faithful.
G~er m -s,- (Comm) creditor
glaub|lich a **kaum g~lich** scarcely believable. **g~würdig** a credible; <Person> reliable
gleich a same; (identisch) identical; (g~wertig) equal; **g~bleibend** constant; **2 mal 5 [ist] g~ 10** two times 5 equals 10; **das ist mir g~** it's all the same to me; **ganz g~, wo/wer** no matter where/who ●adv equally; (übereinstimmend) identically, the same; (sofort) immediately; (in Kürze) in a minute; (fast) nearly; (direkt) right. **g~altrig** a [of] the same age. **g~bedeutend** a synonymous. **g~berechtigt** a equal. **G~berechtigung** f equality
gleichen† vi (haben) **jdm/etw g~** be like or resemble s.o./sth
gleich|ermaßen adv equally.
g~falls adv also, likewise; **danke g~falls** thank you, the same to you. **G~gewicht** nt balance; (Phys & fig) equilibrium.
g~gültig a indifferent; (unwichtig) unimportant.
G~gültigkeit f indifference.
g~machen vt sep make equal; **dem Erdboden g~machen** raze to the ground. **g~mäßig** a even, regular; (beständig) constant.
G~mäßigkeit f - regularity
Gleichnis nt -ses, -se parable
Gleich|schritt m **im G~schritt** in step. **g~setzen** vt sep equate/ (g~stellen) place on a par (dat/ mit with). **g~stellen** vt sep place on a par (dat with). **G~strom** m direct current
Gleichung f -, -en equation
gleichwertig adv a of equal value. **g~zeitig** a simultaneous

Gleis nt -es, -e track; (Bahnsteig) platform; **G~ 5** platform 5
gleiten† vi (sein) glide; (rutschen) slide. **g~d** a sliding; **g~de Arbeitszeit** flexitime
Gleitzeit f flexitime
Gletscher m -s,- glacier
Glied nt -[e]s, -er limb; (Teil) part; (Ketten-) link; (Mitglied) member; (Mil) rank. **g~ern** vt arrange; (einteilen) divide. **G~maßen** fpl limbs
glitschig a slippery
glitzern vi (haben) glitter
globalisier|en vt globalize.
G~ung f -, -en globalization
Globus m - & -busses, -ben & -busse globe
Glocke f -, -n bell. **G~nturm** m bell-tower, belfry
glorreich a glorious
Glossar nt -s, -e glossary
Glosse f -, -n comment
glotzen vi (haben) stare
Glück nt -[e]s [good] luck; (Zufriedenheit) happiness; **G~ bringend** lucky; **G~/kein G~ haben** be lucky/unlucky; **zum G~** luckily, fortunately; **auf gut G~** on the off chance; (wahllos) at random. **g~en** vi (sein) succeed
glücklich a lucky, fortunate; (zufrieden) happy; (sicher) safe ●adv happily; safely. **g~erweise** adv luckily, fortunately
Glücksspiel nt game of chance; (Spielen) gambling
Glückwunsch m good wishes pl; (Gratulation) congratulations pl; **herzlichen G~!** congratulations! (zum Geburtstag) happy birthday! **G~karte** f greetings card
Glüh|birne f light-bulb. **g~en** vi (haben) glow. **g~end** a glowing; (rot-) red-hot; <Hitze> scorching; (leidenschaftlich) fervent.
G~faden m filament. **G~wein** m

mulled wine. **G~würmchen** *nt*
-s,- glow-worm
lukose *f -* glucose
lut *f -* embers *pl*; (*Röte*) glow;
(*Hitze*) heat; (*fig*) ardour
lyzinie /-iə/ *f -,* -n wisteria
imbH *abbr* (**Gesellschaft mit
beschränkter Haftung**) ≈ plc
nade *f -* mercy; (*Gunst*) favour;
(*Relig*) grace. **G~nfrist** *f* reprieve
nädig *a* gracious; (*mild*) lenient;
g~e Frau Madam
nom *m* -en, -en gnome
iobelin /gobə'lɛ̃ː/ *m* -s, -s tapestry
iold *nt* -[e]s gold. **g~en** *a* gold …;
(*g~farben*) golden. **G~fisch** *m*
goldfish. **g~ig** *a* sweet, lovely.
G~lack *m* wallflower. **G~regen**
m laburnum. **G~schmied** *m*
goldsmith
iolf[1] *m* -[e]s, -e (*Geog*) gulf
iolf[2] *nt* -s golf. **G~platz** *m* golf-
course. **G~schläger** *m* golf-club.
G~spieler(in) *m(f)* golfer
iondel *f -,* -n gondola; (*Kabine*)
cabin
iönnen *vt* jdm etw g~ not
begrudge s.o. sth; jdm etw nicht
g~ begrudge s.o. sth
iör *nt* -s, -en, **Göre** *f -,* -n 🔔 kid
iorilla *m* -s, -s gorilla
iosse *f -,* -n gutter
iot|ik *f -* Gothic. **g~isch** *a* Gothic
iott *m* -[e]s,¨er God; (*Myth*) god
iötterspeise *f* jelly
iottes|dienst *m* service.
G~lästerung *f* blasphemy
iottheit *f -,* -en deity
iöttin *f -,* -nen goddess
iöttlich *a* divine
iottlos *a* ungodly; (*atheistisch*)
godless
irab *nt* -[e]s,¨er grave
iraben† *vi* (*haben*) dig
iraben *m* -s,¨ ditch; (*Mil*) trench
irab|mal *nt* tomb. **G~stein** *m*
gravestone, tombstone
irad *m* -[e]s, -e degree
iraf *m* -en, -en count

Grafik *f -,* -en graphics *sg*; (*Kunst*)
graphic arts *pl*; (*Druck*) print
Gräfin *f -,* -nen countess
grafisch *a* graphic; **g~e
Darstellung** diagram
Grafschaft *f -,* -en county
Gram *m* -s grief
grämen (sich) *vr* grieve
Gramm *nt* -s, -e gram
Gram|matik *f -,* -en grammar.
g~matikalisch *a* grammatical
Granat *m* -[e]s, -e (*Miner.*) garnet.
G~e *f -,* -n shell; (*Hand-*) grenade
Granit *m* -s, -e granite
Gras *nt* -es,¨er grass. **g~en** *vi*
(*haben*) graze. **G~hüpfer** *m* -s,-
grasshopper
grässlich *a* dreadful
Grat *m* -[e]s, -e [mountain] ridge
Gräte *f -,* -n fishbone
Gratifikation /-'tsːioːn/ *f -,* -en
bonus
gratis *adv* free [of charge].
G~probe *f* free sample
Gratu|lant(in) *m* -en, -en (*f -,* -nen)
well-wisher. **G~lation** /-'tsːioːn/ *f*
-, -en congratulations *pl*;
(*Glückwünsche*) best wishes *pl*.
g~lieren *vi* (*haben*) jdm g~lieren
congratulate s.o. (**zu** on); (*zum
Geburtstag*) wish s.o. happy
birthday
grau *a*, **G~** *nt* -s,- grey
Gräuel *m* -s,- horror
grauen *v impers* **mir graut [es]
davor** I dread it. **G~** *nt* -s dread.
g~haft *a* gruesome; (*grässlich*)
horrible
gräulich *a* horrible
grausam *a* cruel. **G~keit** *f -,* -en
cruelty
graus|en *v impers* **mir graust davor**
I dread it. **G~en** *nt* -s horror,
dread. **g~ig** *a* gruesome
gravieren *vt* engrave. **g~d** *a* (*fig*)
serious
graziös *a* graceful

G

greifen† vt take hold of; (fangen) catch ● vi (haben) reach (nach for); um sich g~ (fig) spread

Greis m -es, -e old man. **G~in** f -, -nen old woman

grell a glaring; <Farbe> garish; (schrill) shrill

Gremium nt -s, -ien committee

Grenz|e f -, -n border; (Staats-) frontier; (Grundstücks-) boundary; (fig) limit. **g~en** vi (haben) border (an + acc on). **g~enlos** a boundless; (maßlos) infinite

Griech|e m -n, -n Greek. **G~enland** nt -s Greece. **G~in** f -, -nen Greek woman. **g~isch** a Greek. **G~isch** nt -[s] (Lang) Greek

Grieß m -es semolina

Griff m -[e]s, -e grasp, hold; (Hand-) movement of the hand; (Tür-, Messer-) handle; (Schwert-) hilt. **g~bereit** a handy

Grill m -s, -s grill; (Garten-) barbecue

Grille f -, -n (Zool) cricket

grill|en vt grill; (im Freien) barbecue ● vi (haben) have a barbecue. **G~fest** nt barbecue

Grimasse f -, -n grimace; **G~n schneiden** pull faces

grimmig a furious; <Kälte> bitter

grinsen vi (haben) grin

Grippe f -, -n influenza, 🔲 flu

grob a coarse; (unsanft, ungefähr) rough; (unhöflich) rude; (schwer) gross; <Fehler> bad; **g~ geschätzt** roughly. **G~ian** m -s, -e brute

Groll m -[e]s resentment. **g~en** vi (haben) be angry (dat with); <Donner:> rumble

Grönland nt -s Greenland

Gros nt -ses,- (Maß) gross

Groschen m -s,- (Aust) groschen; 🔲 ten-pfennig piece

groß a big; <Anzahl, Summe> large; (bedeutend, stark) great; (g~artig) grand; <Buchstabe> capital; **g~e Ferien** summer holidays; **der größte Teil** the majority or bulk; **g~ werden** <Person:> grow up; **g~ in etw** (dat) **sein** be good at sth; **G~ und Klein** young and old; **im G~en und Ganzen** on the whole ● adv <feiern> in style; (🔲 viel) much

groß|artig a magnificent. **G~aufnahme** f close-up. **G~britannien** nt -s Great Britain. **G~buchstabe** m capital letter. **G~e(r)** m/f unser **G~er** our eldest; **die G~en** the grown-ups; (fig) the great pl

Größe f -, -n size; (Ausmaß) extent; (Körper-) height; (Bedeutsamkeit) greatness; (Math) quantity; (Person) great figure

Großeltern pl grandparents

Groß|handel m wholesale trade. **G~händler** m wholesaler. **G~macht** f superpower. **g~mütig** a magnanimous. **G~mutter** f grandmother. **G~schreibung** f capitalization. **g~spurig** a pompous; (überheblich) arrogant. **G~stadt** f [large] city. **g~städtisch** a city ... **G~teil** m large proportion; (Hauptteil) bulk

größtenteils adv for the most part

groß|tun† (sich) vr sep brag. **G~vater** m grandfather. **g~ziehen**† vt sep bring up; rear <Tier>. **g~zügig** a generous. **G~zügigkeit** f - generosity

Grotte f -, -n grotto

Grübchen nt -s,- dimple

Grube f -, -n pit

grübeln vi (haben) brood

Gruft f -,-e [burial] vault

grün a green; **im G~en** out in the country; **die G~en** the Greens

Grund m -[e]s,-e ground; (Boden) bottom; (Hinter-) background; (Ursache) reason; **aus diesem**

G~e for this reason; **im G~e [genommen]** basically; **auf G~ laufen** (*Naut*) run aground; **zu G~e richten/gehen** s. zugrunde. **G~begriffe** *mpl* basics.

G~besitzer *m* landowner

ründ|en *vt* found, set up; start <*Familie*>; (*fig*) base (**auf** + *acc* on); **sich g~en** be based (**auf** + *acc* on). **G~er(in)** *m* -s,- (*f* -, -nen) founder

Grund|farbe *f* primary colour. **G~form** *f* (*Gram*) infinitive. **G~gesetz** *nt* (*Pol*) constitution. **G~lage** *f* basis, foundation

ründlich *a* thorough. **G~keit** *f* - thoroughness

Gründonnerstag *m* Maundy Thursday

Grund|regel *f* basic rule. **G~riss** *m* ground-plan; (*fig*) outline. **G~satz** *m* principle. **g~sätzlich** *a* fundamental; (*im Allgemeinen*) in principle; (*prinzipiell*) on principle; **G~schule** *f* primary school. **G~stück** *nt* plot [of land]

Gründung *f* -, -en foundation

Grün|span *m* verdigris. **G~streifen** *m* grass verge; (*Mittel-*) central reservation

grunzen *vi* (*haben*) grunt

Gruppe *f* -, -n group; (*Reise-*) party

gruppieren *vt* group

Grusel|geschichte *f* horror story. **g~ig** *a* creepy

Gruß *m* -es,̈e greeting; (*Mil*) salute; **einen schönen G~ an X** give my regards to X; **viele/ herzliche G~e** regards; **Mit freundlichen G~en** Yours sincerely/faithfully

rüßen *vt/i* (*haben*) say hallo (**jdn** to s.o.); (*Mil*) salute; **g~Sie X von mir** give my regards to X; **grüß Gott!** (*SGer, Aust*) good morning/afternoon/evening!

ucken *vi* (*haben*) 🛈 look

Guerilla /geˈrɪlja/ *f* - guerrilla warfare. **G~kämpfer** *m* guerrilla

Gulasch *nt* & *m* -[e]s goulash

gültig *a* valid

Gummi *m* & *nt* -s, -[s] rubber; (*Harz*) gum. **G~band** *nt* (*pl* -bänder) elastic *or* rubber band

gummiert *a* gummed

Gummi|knüppel *m* truncheon. **G~stiefel** *m* gumboot, wellington. **G~zug** *m* elastic

Gunst *f* - favour

günstig *a* favourable; (*passend*) convenient

Gurgel *f* -, -n throat. **g~n** *vi* (*haben*) gargle

Gurke *f* -, -n cucumber; (*Essig-*) gherkin

Gurt *m* -[e]s, -e strap; (*Gürtel*) belt; (*Auto*) safety-belt. **G~band** *nt* (*pl* -bänder) waistband

Gürtel *m* -s,- belt. **G~linie** *f* waistline. **G~rose** *f* shingles *sg*

Guss *m* -es,̈e (*Techn*) casting; (*Strom*) stream; (*Regen-*) downpour; (*Torten-*) icing. **G~eisen** *nt* cast iron

gut *a* good; <*Gewissen*> clear; (*gütig*) kind (**zu** to); **jdm gut sein** be fond of s.o.; **im G~en** amicably; **schon gut** that's all right ● *adv* well; <*schmecken, riechen*> good; (*leicht*) easily; **gut zu sehen** clearly visible; **gut drei Stunden** a good three hours

Gut *nt* -[e]s,̈er possession, property; (*Land-*) estate; **Gut und Böse** good and evil; **Güter** (*Comm*) goods

Gutacht|en *nt* -s,- expert's report. **G~er** *m* -s,- expert

gutartig *a* good-natured; (*Med*) benign

Gute|(s) *nt* etwas/nichts G~s something/nothing good; **G~s tun** do good; **alles G~!** all the best!

Güte *f* -, -n goodness, kindness; (*Qualität*) quality

Güterzug *m* goods train

gut|gehen* *vi sep* (*sein*) **gut gehen**, s. **gehen. g~gehend*** *a* **gut gehend**, s. **gehen. g~gläubig** *a* trusting. **g~haben†** *vt sep* **fünfzig Mark g~haben** have fifty marks credit (bei with). **G~haben** *nt* **-s,-** [credit] balance; (*Kredit*) credit
gut|machen *vt sep* make up for; make good <*Schaden*>. **g~mütig** *a* good-natured. **G~mütigkeit** *f* - good nature. **G~schein** *m* credit note; (*Bon*) voucher; (*Geschenk-*) gift token. **g~schreiben†** *vt sep* credit. **G~schrift** *f* credit
Guts|haus *nt* manor house
gut|tun* *vi sep* (*haben*) **gut tun**, s. **tun. g~willig** *a* willing
Gymnasium *nt* **-s, -ien** ≈ grammar school
Gymnastik *f* - [keep-fit] exercises *pl*; (*Turnen*) gymnastics *sg*
Gynäko|loge *m* **-n, -n** gynaecologist. **G~logie** *f* - gynaecology

H, h /ha:/ *nt*, **-,-** (*Mus*) B, b
Haar *nt* **-[e]s, -e** hair; **sich** (*dat*) **die Haare** *od* **das H~ waschen** wash one's hair; **um ein H~** ⚠ very nearly. **H~bürste** *f* hairbrush. **h~en** *vi* (*haben*) shed hairs; <*Tier:*> moult ● *vr* **sich h~en** moult. **h~ig** *a* hairy; ⚠ tricky. **H~klemme** *f* hair-grip. **H~nadelkurve** *f* hairpin bend. **H~schnitt** *m* haircut. **H~spange** *f* slide. **H~waschmittel** *nt* shampoo
Habe *f* - possessions *pl*

haben†
● *transitive verb*
····▸ have; (*im Präsens*) have got ⚠. **er hat kein Geld** he has no money *or* ⚠ he hasn't got any money. **ich habe/hatte die Grippe** I've got flu/had flu. **was haben Sie da?** what have you got there? **wenn ich die Zeit hätte** if I had the time
····▸ (*empfinden*) **Angst/Hunger/ Durst haben** be frightened/ hungry/thirsty. **was hat er?** what's wrong with him?
····▸ (+ *Adj., es*) **es gut/schlecht haben** be well/badly off. **es schwer haben** be having a difficult time
····▸ (+ *zu*) (*müssen*) **du hast zu gehorchen** you must obey
● *auxiliary verb*
····▸ have. **ich habe/hatte ihn eben gesehen** I have *or* I've/I had *or* I'd just seen him. **er hat es gewusst** he knew it. **er hätte ihr geholfen** he would have helped her
● *reflexive verb*
····▸ (⚠ *sich aufregen*) make a fuss. **hab dich nicht so!** don't make such a fuss!

Habgier *f* greed. **h~ig** *a* greedy
Habicht *m* **-[e]s, -e** hawk
Hachse *f* **-, -n** (*Culin*) knuckle
Hackbraten *m* meat loaf
Hacke¹ *f* **-, -n** hoe; (*Spitz-*) pick
Hacke² *f* **-, -n, Hacken** *m* **-s,-** heel
hack|en *vt* hoe; (*schlagen, zerkleinern*) chop; <*Vogel:*> peck. **H~fleisch** *nt* mince
Hafen *m* **-s,⸚** harbour; (*See-*) port. **H~arbeiter** *m* docker. **H~stadt** *f* port
Hafer *m* **-s** oats *pl*. **H~flocken** *fpl* [rolled] oats

Haft f - (*Jur*) custody; (*H~strafe*) imprisonment. **h~bar** a (*Jur*) liable. **H~befehl** m warrant

haften vi (*haben*) cling; (*kleben*) stick; (*bürgen*) vouch/(*Jur*) be liable (**für** for)

Häftling m -s, -e detainee

Haftpflicht f (*Jur*) liability. **H~versicherung** f (*Auto*) third-party insurance

Haftung f - (*Jur*) liability

Hagebutte f -, -n rose-hip

Hagel m -s hail. **h~n** vi (*haben*) hail

hager a gaunt

Hahn m -[e]s, ⸚e cock; (*Techn*) tap

Hähnchen nt -, -s (*Culin*) chicken

Hai[fisch] m -[e]s, -e shark

Häkchen nt -s, - tick

häkeln vt/i (*haben*) crochet. **H~nadel** f crochet-hook

Haken m -s, - hook; (*Häkchen*) tick; ([**i**] *Schwierigkeit*) snag. **h~** vt hook (**an** + *acc* to). **H~kreuz** nt swastika

halb a half; **auf h~em Weg** half-way ●adv half; **h~drei** half past two; **fünf [Minuten] vor/nach h~vier** twenty-five [minutes] past three/to four. **H~e(r,s)** f/m/nt half [a litre]

halber prep (+ *gen*) for the sake of; **Geschäfte h~** on business

Halbfinale nt semifinal

halbieren vt halve, divide in half; (*Geom*) bisect

Halb|insel f peninsula. **H~kreis** m semicircle. **H~kugel** f hemisphere. **h~laut** a low ●adv in an undertone. **h~mast** adv at half-mast. **H~mond** m half moon. **H~pension** f half-board. **h~rund** a semicircular. **H~schuh** m [flat] shoe. **h~tags** adv [for] half a day; **h~tags arbeiten** ≈ work part-time. **H~ton** m semitone. **h~wegs** adv half-way; (*ziemlich*) more or less. **h~wüchsig** a adolescent. **H~zeit**

f (*Sport*) half-time; (*Spielzeit*) half

Halde f -, -n dump, tip

Hälfte f -, -n half; **zur H~** half

Halfter f -, -n & nt -s, - holster

Halle f -, -n hall; (*Hotel-*) lobby; (*Bahnhofs-*) station concourse

hallen vi (*haben*) resound; (*wider-*) echo

Hallen- pref indoor

hallo int hallo

Halluzination /-'tsi̯o:n/ f -, -en hallucination

Halm m -[e]s, -e stalk; (*Gras-*) blade

Hals m -es, ⸚e neck; (*Kehle*) throat; **aus vollem H~e** at the top of one's voice; <*lachen*> out loud. **H~band** nt (*pl* -bänder) collar. **H~schmerzen** mpl sore throat sg

halt int stop! (*Mil*) halt! [**i**] wait a minute!

Halt m -[e]s, -e hold; (*Stütze*) support; (*innerer*) stability; (*Anhalten*) stop; **H~ machen** stop. **h~bar** a durable; (*Tex*) hard-wearing; (*fig*) tenable; **h~bar bis** … (*Comm*) use by …

halten† vt hold; make <*Rede*>; give <*Vortrag*>; (*einhalten, bewahren*) keep; [sich (*dat*)] etw h~ keep <*Hund*>; take <*Zeitung*>; h~ für regard as; viel h~ von think highly of; sich links h~ keep left; sich h~ an (+ *acc*) (*fig*) keep to ●vi (*haben*) hold; (*haltbar sein, bestehen bleiben*) keep; <*Freundschaft, Blumen:*> last; (*Halt machen*) stop; **auf sich** (*acc*) **h~** take pride in oneself; **zu jdm h~** be loyal to s.o.

Halte|stelle f stop. **H~verbot** nt waiting restriction; '**H~verbot**' 'no waiting'

Haltung f -, -en (*Körper-*) posture; (*Verhalten*) manner; (*Einstellung*) attitude; (*Fassung*) composure; (*Halten*) keeping

H

Hammel m -s,- ram; (*Culin*)
mutton. **H~fleisch** nt mutton
Hammer m -s,- hammer
hämmern vt/i (*haben*) hammer
Hamster m -s,- hamster. **h~n** vt/i
🛈 hoard
Hand f -,:e hand; **jdm die H~ geben**
shake hands with s.o.; **rechter/
linker H~** on the right/left; **zweiter
H~** second-hand; **unter der H~**
unofficially; (*geheim*) secretly;
H~ und Fuß haben (*fig*) be sound.
H~arbeit f manual work;
(*handwerklich*) handicraft;
(*Nadelarbeit*) needlework;
(*Gegenstand*) hand-made article.
H~ball m [German] handball.
H~bewegung f gesture.
H~bremse f handbrake. **H~buch**
nt handbook, manual
Händedruck m handshake
Handel m -s trade, commerce;
(*Unternehmen*) business;
(*Geschäft*) deal; **H~ treiben** trade.
h~n vi (*haben*) act; (*Handel
treiben*) trade (**mit** in); **von etw** od
über etw (*acc*) **h~n** deal with sth;
sich h~n um be about, concern.
H~smarine f merchant navy.
H~sschiff nt merchant vessel.
H~sschule f commercial college.
H~sware f merchandise
Hand|feger m -s,- brush.
H~fläche f palm. **H~gelenk** nt
wrist. **H~gemenge** nt -s,- scuffle.
H~gepäck nt hand-luggage.
h~geschrieben a hand-written.
h~greiflich a tangible; **h~greiflich
werden** become violent. **H~griff**
m handle
handhaben vt insep (*reg*) handle
Handikap /'hɛndikɛp/ nt -s, -s
handicap
Handkuss m kiss on the hand
Händler m -s,- dealer, trader
handlich a handy
Handlung f -, -en act; (*Handeln*)
action; (*Roman-*) plot; (*Geschäft*)
shop. **H~sweise** f conduct

Hand|schellen fpl handcuffs.
H~schlag m handshake.
H~schrift f handwriting; (*Text*)
manuscript. **H~schuh** m glove.
H~stand m handstand.
H~tasche f handbag. **H~tuch** nt
towel
Handwerk nt craft, trade. **H~er** m
-s,- craftsman; (*Arbeiter*)
workman
Handy /'hɛndi/ nt -s, -s mobile
phone
Hanf m -[e]s hemp
Hang m -[e]s,:e slope; (*fig*)
inclination
Hänge|brücke f suspension
bridge. **H~matte** f hammock
hängen[1] vt (*reg*) hang
hängen[2]† vi (*haben*) hang; **h~ an**
(+ *dat*) (*fig*) be attached to; **h~
lassen** leave
Hannover nt -s Hanover
hänseln vt tease
hantieren vi (*haben*) busy oneself
Happen m -s,- mouthful; **einen H~
essen** have a bite to eat
Harfe f -, -n harp
Harke f -, -n rake. **h~n** vt/i
(*haben*) rake
harmlos a harmless; (*arglos*)
innocent
Harmonie f -, -n harmony
Harmonika f -, -s accordion;
(*Mund-*) mouth-organ
harmonisch a harmonious
Harn m -[e]s urine. **H~blase** f
bladder
Harpune f -, -n harpoon
hart a hard; (*heftig*) violent;
(*streng*) harsh
Härte f -, -n hardness; (*Strenge*)
harshness; (*Not*) hardship. **h~n**
vt harden
Hart|faserplatte f hardboard.
h~näckig a stubborn;
(*ausdauernd*) persistent.
H~näckigkeit f - stubbornness;
persistence
Harz nt -es, -e resin

Haschee nt -s, -s (Culin) hash
Haschisch m & nt -[s] hashish
Hase m -n, -n hare
Hasel f -, -n hazel. **H∼maus** f
dormouse. **H∼nuss** f hazel-nut
Hass m -es hatred
hassen vt hate
hässlich a ugly; (unfreundlich)
nasty. **H∼keit** f - ugliness;
nastiness
Hast f - haste. **h∼ig** a hasty,
hurried
hast, hat, hatte, hätte s. haben
Haube f -, -n cap; (Trocken-)
drier; (Kühler-) bonnet
Hauch m -[e]s breath; (Luft-)
breeze; (Duft-) whiff; (Spur) tinge.
h∼dünn a very thin
Haue f -, -n pick; (🔲 Prügel)
beating. **h∼n†** vt beat; (hämmern)
knock; (meißeln) hew; **sich h∼n**
fight; **übers Ohr h∼n** 🔲 cheat ● vi
(haben) bang (auf + acc on); **jdm
ins Gesicht h∼n** hit s.o. in the
face
Haufen m -s,- heap, pile; (Leute)
crowd
häufen vt heap or pile [up]; **sich
h∼** pile up; (zunehmen) increase
häufig a frequent
Haupt nt -[e]s, Häupter head.
H∼bahnhof m main station.
H∼fach nt main subject.
H∼gericht nt main course
Häuptling m -s, -e chief
Haupt|mahlzeit f main meal
H∼mann m (pl -leute) captain.
H∼post f main post office.
H∼quartier nt headquarters pl.
H∼rolle f lead; (fig) leading role.
H∼sache f main thing; **in der
H∼sache** in the main.
h∼sächlich a main. **H∼satz** m
main clause. **H∼stadt** f capital.
H∼verkehrsstraße f main road.
H∼verkehrszeit f rush-hour.
H∼wort nt (pl -wörter) noun
Haus nt -es, Häuser house;
(Gebäude) building; (Schnecken-)

shell; **zu H∼e** at home; **nach H∼e**
home. **H∼arbeit** f housework;
(Sch) homework. **H∼arzt** m
family doctor. **H∼aufgaben** fpl
homework sg. **H∼besetzer** m -s,-
squatter
hausen vi (haben) live; (wüten)
wreak havoc
Haus|frau f housewife.
h∼gemacht a home-made.
H∼halt m -[e]s, -e household;
(Pol) budget. **h∼halten†** vi sep
(haben) **h∼halten mit** manage
carefully; conserve <Kraft>.
H∼hälterin f -, -nen housekeeper.
H∼haltsgeld nt housekeeping
[money]. **H∼haltsplan** m budget.
H∼herr m head of the
household; (Gastgeber) host
Hausierer m -s,- hawker
Hauslehrer m [private] tutor.
H∼in f governess
häuslich a domestic, <Person>
domesticated
Haus|meister m caretaker.
H∼ordnung f house rules pl.
H∼putz m cleaning. **H∼rat** m
-[e]s household effects pl.
H∼schlüssel m front-door key.
H∼schuh m slipper. **H∼suchung**
f [police] search.
H∼suchungsbefehl m search-
warrant. **H∼tier** nt domestic
animal; (Hund, Katze) pet. **H∼tür**
f front door. **H∼wirt** m landlord.
H∼wirtin f landlady
Haut f -,Häute skin; (Tier-) hide.
H∼arzt m dermatologist
häuten vt skin; **sich h∼** moult
haut|eng a skin-tight. **H∼farbe** f
colour; (Teint) complexion
Hebamme f -, -n midwife
Hebel m -s,- lever
heben† vt lift; (hoch-, steigern)
raise; **sich h∼** rise; <Nebel:> lift;
(sich verbessern) improve
hebräisch a Hebrew
hecheln vi (haben) pant
Hecht m -[e]s, -e pike

H

Heck nt -s, -s (Naut) stern; (Aviat) tail; (Auto) rear
Hecke f -, -n hedge
Heck|fenster nt rear window. **H~tür** f hatchback
Heer nt -[e]s, -e army
Hefe f - yeast
Heft nt -[e]s, -e booklet; (Sch) exercise book; (Zeitschrift) issue. **h~en** vt (nähen) tack; (stecken) pin/(klammern) clip/(mit Heftmaschine) staple (an + acc to). **H~er** m -s,- file
heftig a fierce, violent; <Regen> heavy; <Schmerz, Gefühl> intense
Heft|klammer f staple; (Büro-) paper-clip. **H~maschine** f stapler. **H~zwecke** f -, -n drawing-pin
Heide[1] m -n, -n heathen
Heide[2] f -, -n heath; (Bot) heather. **H~kraut** nt heather
Heidelbeere f bilberry
Heidin f -, -nen heathen
heikel a difficult, tricky
heil a undamaged, intact; <Person> unhurt; mit h~er Haut Ⓘ unscathed
Heil nt -s salvation
Heiland m -s (Relig) Saviour
Heil|anstalt f sanatorium; (Nerven-) mental hospital. **H~bad** nt spa. **h~bar** a curable
Heilbutt m -[e]s, -e halibut
heilen vt cure; heal <Wunde> ● vi (sein) heal
Heilgymnastik f physiotherapy
heilig a holy; (geweiht) sacred; der H~e Abend Christmas Eve; die h~e Anna Saint Anne; h~ sprechen canonize. **H~abend** m Christmas Eve. **H~e(r)** m/f saint. **H~enschein** m halo. **H~keit** f - sanctity, holiness. **H~tum** nt -s,-̈er shrine
heil|kräftig a medicinal. **H~kräuter** ntpl medicinal herbs. **H~mittel** nt remedy. **H~praktiker** m -s,- practitioner of

alternative medicine. **H~sarmee** f Salvation Army. **H~ung** f - cure
Heim nt -[e]s, -e home; (Studenten-) hostel. **h~** adv home
Heimat f -, -en home; (Land) native land. **H~stadt** f home town
heim|begleiten vt sep see home. **H~computer** m home computer. **h~fahren**† v sep ● vi (sein) go/drive home ● vt take/drive home. **H~fahrt** f way home. **h~gehen**† vi sep (sein) go home
heimisch a native, indigenous; (Pol) domestic
Heim|kehr f - return [home]. **h~kehren** vi sep (sein) return home. **h~kommen**† vi sep (sein) come home
heimlich a secret; etw h~ tun do sth secretly. **H~keit** f -, -en secrecy; **H~keiten** secrets
Heim|reise f journey home. **H~spiel** nt home game. **h~suchen** vt sep afflict. **h~tückisch** a treacherous; <Krankheit> insidious. **h~wärts** adv home. **H~weg** m way home. **H~weh** nt -s homesickness; **H~weh haben** be homesick. **H~werker** m -s,- [home] handyman. **h~zahlen** vt sep jdm etw h~zahlen (fig) pay s.o. back for sth
Heirat f -, -en marriage. **h~en** vt/i (haben) marry. **H~santrag** m proposal; jdm einen H~santrag machen propose to s.o.
heiser a hoarse. **H~keit** f - hoarseness
heiß a hot; (hitzig) heated; (leidenschaftlich) fervent
heißen† vi (haben) be called; (bedeuten) mean; wie heiße ... my name is ...; wie h~ Sie? what is your name? wie heißt ... auf Englisch? what's the English for ...? ● vt call; jdn etw tun h~ tell s.o. to do sth

heiter a cheerful; <Wetter> bright; (amüsant) amusing; **aus h~em Himmel** (fig) out of the blue

Heiz|anlage f heating; (Auto) heater. **H~decke** f electric blanket. **h~en** vt heat; light <Ofen> ●vi (haben) put the heating on; <Ofen:> give out heat. **H~gerät** nt heater. **H~kessel** m boiler. **H~körper** m radiator. **H~lüfter** m -s,- fan heater. **H~material** nt fuel. **H~ung** f -, -en heating; (Heizkörper) radiator

Hektar nt & m -s,- hectare

Held m -en, -en hero. **h~enhaft** a heroic. **H~entum** nt -s heroism. **H~in** f -, -nen heroine

helf|en† vi (haben) help (jdm s.o.); (nützen) be effective; **sich** (dat) **nicht zu h~en wissen** not know what to do; **es hilft nichts** it's no use. **H~er(in)** m -s,- (f -, -nen) helper, assistant

hell a light; (Licht ausstrahlend, klug) bright; <Stimme> clear; (🄸 völlig) utter; **h~es Bier** ≈ lager ●adv brightly

Hell|igkeit f - brightness. **H~seher(in)** m -s,- (f -, -nen) clairvoyant

Helm m -[e]s, -e helmet

Hemd nt -[e]s, -en vest; (Ober-) shirt

Hemisphäre f -, -n hemisphere

hemm|en vt check; (verzögern) impede; (fig) inhibit. **H~ung** f -, -en (fig) inhibition; (Skrupel) scruple; **H~ungen haben** be inhibited. **h~ungslos** a unrestrained

Hendl nt -s, -[n] (Aust) chicken

Hengst m -[e]s, -e stallion

Henkel m -s,- handle

Henne f -, -n hen

her adv here; (zeitlich) ago; **her mit ...!** give me ...! **von Norden/weit her** from the north/far away; **vom Thema her** as far as the subject is

concerned; **her sein** come (**von** from); **es ist schon lange her** it was a long time ago

herab adv down [here]; **von oben h~** from above; (fig) condescending

herab|lassen† vt sep let down; **sich h~** condescend (**zu** to)

herab|sehen† vi sep (haben) look down (**auf** + acc on). **h~setzen** vt sep reduce, cut; (fig) belittle

Heraldik f - heraldry

heran adv near; [**bis**] **h~ an** (+ acc) up to. **h~kommen**† vi sep (sein) approach; **h~kommen an** (+ acc) come up to; (erreichen) get at; (fig) measure up to.

h~machen (sich) vr sep **sich h~machen an** (+ acc) approach; get down to <Arbeit>.

h~wachsen† vi sep (sein) grow up. **h~ziehen**† v sep ●vt pull up (an + acc to); (züchten) raise; (h~bilden) train; (hinzuziehen) call in ●vi (sein) approach

herauf adv up [here]; **die Treppe h~** up the stairs. **h~setzen** vt sep raise, increase

heraus adv out (**aus** of); **h~ damit** od **mit der Sprache!** out with it! **h~bekommen**† vt sep get out; (ausfindig machen) find out; (lösen) solve; **Geld h~bekommen** get change. **h~finden**† v sep ●vt find out ●vi (haben) find one's way out. **h~fordern** vt sep provoke; challenge <Person>. **H~forderung** f provocation; challenge. **H~gabe** f handing over; (Admin) issue; (Veröffentlichung) publication. **h~geben**† vt sep hand over; (Admin) issue; (veröffentlichen) publish; edit <Zeitschrift>; **jdm Geld h~geben** give s.o. change ●vi (haben) give change (**auf** + acc for). **H~geber** m -s,- publisher; editor. **h~halten**† **(sich)** vr sep (fig) keep out (**aus**

of). **h~kommen**† vi sep (sein) come out; (aus Schwierigkeit, Takt) get out; **auf eins** od **dasselbe h~kommen** Ⓘ come to the same thing. **h~lassen**† vt sep let out. **h~nehmen**† vt sep take out; **sich zu viel h~nehmen** (fig) take liberties. **h~reden (sich)** vr sep make excuses. **h~rücken** v sep ● vt move out; (hergeben) hand over ● vi (sein) **h~rücken mit** hand over; (fig: sagen) come out with. **h~schlagen**† vt sep knock out; (fig) gain. **h~stellen** vt sep put out; **sich h~stellen** turn out (als to be; **dass** that). **h~ziehen**† vt sep pull out

herb a sharp; <Wein> dry; (fig) harsh

herbei adv here. **h~führen** vt sep (fig) bring about. **h~schaffen** vt sep get. **h~sehnen** vt sep long for

Herberg|e f -, -n [youth] hostel; (Unterkunft) lodging. **H~svater** m warden

herbestellen vt sep summon

herbitten† vt sep ask to come

herbringen† vt sep bring [here]

Herbst m -[e]s, -e autumn. **h~lich** a autumnal

Herd m -[e]s, -e stove, cooker

Herde f -, -n herd; (Schaf-) flock

herein adv in [here]; **h~!** come in! **h~bitten**† vt sep ask in. **h~fallen**† vi sep (sein) Ⓘ be taken in (auf + acc by). **h~kommen**† vi sep (sein) come in. **h~lassen**† vt sep let in. **h~legen** vt sep Ⓘ take for a ride

Herfahrt f journey/drive here

herfallen† vi sep (sein) ~ **über** (+ acc) attack; fall upon <Essen>

hergeben† vt sep hand over; (fig) give up

hergehen† vi sep (sein) **h~ vor** (+ dat) walk along in front of; **es ging lustig her** Ⓘ there was a lot of merriment

herholen vt sep fetch; **weit hergeholt** (fig) far-fetched

Hering m -s, -e herring; (Zeltpflock) tent-peg

her|kommen† vi sep (sein) come here; **wo kommt das her?** where does it come from? **h~kömmlich** a traditional. **H~kunft** f - origin

herleiten vt sep derive

hermachen vt sep **viel/wenig h~** be impressive/unimpressive; (wichtig nehmen) make a lot of/little fuss (von of); **sich h~ über** (+ acc) fall upon; tackle <Arbeit>

Hermelin[1] nt -s, -e (Zool) stoat

Hermelin[2] m -s, -e (Pelz) ermine

Hernie /'hɛrniə/ f -, -n hernia

Heroin nt -s heroin

heroisch a heroic

Herr m -n, -en gentleman; (Gebieter) master (über + acc of); [**Gott,**] **der H~** the Lord [God]; **H~ Meier** Mr Meier; **Sehr geehrte H~en** Dear Sirs. **H~enhaus** nt manor [house]. **h~enlos** a ownerless; <Tier> stray

Herrgott m der **H~** the Lord

herrichten vt sep prepare; **wieder h~** renovate

Herrin f -, -nen mistress

herrlich a marvellous; (großartig) magnificent

Herrschaft f -, -en rule; (Macht) power; (Kontrolle) control; **meine H~en!** ladies and gentlemen!

herrsch|en vi (haben) rule; (verbreitet sein) prevail; **es h~te Stille** there was silence. **H~er(in)** m -s,- (f -, -nen) ruler

herrühren vi sep (haben) stem (von from)

herstammen vi sep (haben) come (aus/von from)

herstell|en vt sep establish; (Comm) manufacture, make. **H~er** m -s,- manufacturer, maker. **H~ung** f - establishment; manufacture

herüber adv over [here]

herum adv im Kreis h~ [round] in a circle; falsch h~ the wrong way round; um ... h~ round ...; (ungefähr) [round] about ...; h~ sein be over. h~drehen vt sep turn round/(wenden) over; turn <Schlüssel>. h~gehen† vi sep (sein) walk around; <Zeit:> pass; h~gehen um go round. h~kommen† vi sep (sein) get about; h~kommen um get round; come round <Ecke>; um etw [nicht] h~kommen (fig) [not] get out of sth. h~sitzen† vi sep (haben) sit around; h~sitzen um sit round. h~sprechen† (sich) vr sep <Gerücht:> get about. h~treiben† (sich) vr sep hang around. h~ziehen† vi sep (sein) move around; (ziellos) wander about

herunter adv down [here]; die Treppe h~ down the stairs. h~fallen† vi fall off. h~gekommen a (fig) run-down; <Gebäude> dilapidated; <Person> down-at-heel. h~kommen† vi sep (sein) come down; (fig) go to rack and ruin; <Firma, Person:> go downhill; (gesundheitlich) get run down. h~lassen† vt sep let down, lower. h~machen vt sep 🛈 reprimand; (herabsetzen) run down. h~spielen vt sep (fig) play down

hervor adv out (aus of). h~bringen† vt sep produce; utter <Wort>. h~gehen† vi sep (sein) come/(sich ergeben) emerge/ (folgen) follow (aus from). h~heben† vt sep (fig) stress, emphasize. h~ragen vi sep (haben) jut out; (fig) stand out. h~ragend a (fig) outstanding. h~rufen† vt sep cause. h~stehen† vi sep (haben) protrude. h~treten† vi sep (sein) protrude, bulge; (fig) stand out. h~tun† (sich) vr sep (fig)

distinguish oneself; (angeben) show off
Herweg m way here
Herz nt -ens, -en heart; (Kartenspiel) hearts pl; sich (dat) ein H~ fassen pluck up courage. **H~anfall** m heart attack. **herzhaft** a hearty; (würzig) savoury
herziehen† v sep ● vt hinter sich (dat) h~ pull along [behind one] ● vi (sein) hinter jdm h~ follow along behind s.o.; über jdn h~ 🛈 run s.o. down
herz|ig a sweet, adorable. **H~infarkt** m heart attack. **H~klopfen** nt -s palpitations pl
herzlich a cordial; (warm) warm; (aufrichtig) sincere; h~en Dank! many thanks! h~e Grüße kind regards
herzlos a heartless
Herzog m -s,-̈e duke. **H~in** f -, -nen duchess. **H~tum** nt -s,-̈er duchy
Herzschlag m heartbeat; (Med) heart failure
Hessen nt -s Hesse
heterosexuell a heterosexual
Hetze f - rush; (Kampagne) virulent campaign (gegen against). **h~n** vt chase; sich h~n hurry
Heu nt -s hay
Heuchelei f - hypocrisy
heuch|eln vt feign ● vi (haben) pretend. **H~ler(in)** m -s,- (f -, -nen) hypocrite. **h~lerisch** a hypocritical
heuer adv (Aust) this year
heulen vi (haben) howl; (🛈 weinen) cry
Heu|schnupfen m hay fever. **H~schober** m -s,- haystack. **H~schrecke** f -, -n grasshopper
heut|e adv today; (heutzutage) nowadays; h~e früh od Morgen this morning; von h~e auf morgen from one day to the next. **h~ig** a

H

today's …; (*gegenwärtig*) present; der h~ige Tag today. h~zutage *adv* nowadays

Hexe *f* -, -n witch. **h~n** *vi* (*haben*) work magic. **H~nschuss** *m* lumbago

Hieb *m* -[e]s, -e blow; (*Peitschen*-) lash; **H~e** hiding *sg*

hier *adv* here; **h~ sein/bleiben/ lassen/behalten** be/stay/leave/ keep here; **h~ und da** here and there; (*zeitlich*) now and again

hier|auf *adv* on this/these; (*antworten*) to this; (*zeitlich*) after this. **h~aus** *adv* out of *or* from this/these. **h~durch** *adv* through this/these; (*Ursache*) as a result of this. **h~her** *adv* here. **h~hin** *adv* here. **h~in** *adv* in this/these. **h~mit** *adv* with this/these; (*Comm*) herewith; (*Admin*) hereby. **h~nach** *adv* after this/ these; (*demgemäß*) according to this/these. **h~über** *adv* over/ (*höher*) above this/these; <*sprechen, streiten*> about this/ these. **h~von** *adv* from this/ these; (*h~über*) about this/these; (*Menge*) of this/these. **h~zu** *adv* to this/these; (*h~für*) for this/ these. **h~zulande** *adv* here

hiesig *a* local. **H~e(r)** *m/f* local

Hilfe *f* -, -n help, aid; **um H~e rufen** call for help. **h~los** *a* helpless. **H~losigkeit** *f* - helplessness. **h~reich** *a* helpful

Hilfs|arbeiter *m* unskilled labourer. **h~bedürftig** *a* needy; **h~bedürftig sein** be in need of help. **h~bereit** *a* helpful. **H~kraft** *f* helper. **H~mittel** *nt* aid. **H~verb** *nt* auxiliary verb

Himbeere *f* raspberry

Himmel *m* -s,- sky; (*Relig & fig*) heaven; (*Bett*-) canopy; **unter freiem H~** in the open air. **H~bett** *nt* four-poster [bed]. **H~fahrt** *f* Ascension

himmlisch *a* heavenly

hin *adv* there; **hin und her** to and fro; **hin und zurück** there and back; (*Rail*) return; **hin und wieder** now and again; **an** (+ *dat*) … **hin** along; **auf** (+ *acc*) … **hin** in reply to <*Brief, Anzeige*>; on <*jds Rat*>; **zu** *od* **nach** … **hin** towards; **hin sein** 🛈 be gone; **es ist noch lange hin** it's a long time yet

hinauf *adv* up [there]. **h~gehen**† *vi sep* (*sein*) go up. **h~setzen** *vt sep* raise

hinaus *adv* out [there]; (*nach draußen*) outside; **zur Tür h~** out of the door; **auf Jahre h~** for years to come; **über etw** (*acc*) **h~** beyond sth; (*Menge*) [over and] above sth. **über etw** (*acc*) **h~ sein** (*fig*) be past sth. **h~gehen**† *vi sep* (*sein*) go out; <*Zimmer:*> face (**nach Norden** north); **h~gehen über** (+ *acc*) go beyond, exceed. **h~laufen**† *vi sep* (*sein*) run out; **h~laufen auf** (+ *acc*) (*fig*) amount to. **h~lehnen (sich)** *vr sep* lean out. **h~schieben**† *vt sep* push out; (*fig*) put off. **h~werfen**† *vt sep* throw out; (🛈 *entlassen*) fire. **h~wollen**† *vi sep* (*haben*) want to go out; **h~wollen auf** (+ *acc*) (*fig*) aim at. **h~ziehen**† *v sep* ● *vt* pull out; (*in die Länge ziehen*) drag out; (*verzögern*) delay; **sich h~ziehen** drag on; be delayed ● *vi* (*sein*) move out. **h~zögern** *vt* delay; **sich h~zögern** be delayed

Hinblick *m* **im H~ auf** (+ *acc*) in view of; (*hinsichtlich*) regarding

hinder|lich *a* awkward; **jdm h~lich sein** hamper s.o. **h~n** *vt* hamper; (*verhindern*) prevent. **H~nis** *nt* -ses, -se obstacle. **H~nisrennen** *nt* steeplechase

Hindu *m* -s, -s Hindu. **H~ismus** *m* - Hinduism

hindurch *adv* through it/them

hinein *adv* in [there]; (*nach drinnen*) inside; **h~ in** (+ *acc*) into. **h~fallen**† *vi sep* (*sein*) fall in. **h~gehen**† *vi sep* (*sein*) go in; **h~gehen** in (+ *acc*) go into. **h~reden** *vi sep* (*haben*) jdm h~reden interrupt s.o.; (*sich einmischen*) interfere in s.o.'s affairs. **h~versetzen (sich)** *vr sep* sich in jds Lage h~versetzen put oneself in s.o.'s position. **h~ziehen**† *vt sep* pull in; **h~ziehen** in (+ *acc*) pull into; **in etw** (*acc*) **h~gezogen werden** (*fig*) become involved in sth

hin|fahren† *v sep* ● *vi* (*sein*) go/drive there ● *vt* take/drive there. **H~fahrt** *f* journey/drive there; (*Rail*) outward journey. **h~fallen**† *vi sep* (*sein*) fall. **h~fliegen**† *v sep* ● *vi* (*sein*) fly there; ⊺ fall ● *vt* fly there. **H~flug** *m* flight there; (*Admin*) outward flight

Hingeb|ung *f* - devotion. **h~ungsvoll** *a* devoted

hingehen† *vi sep* (*sein*) go/(*zu Fuß*) walk there; (*vergehen*) pass; **h~ zu** go up to; **wo gehst du hin?** where are you going?

hingerissen *a* rapt; **h~ sein** be carried away (**von** by)

hinhalten† *vt sep* hold out; (*warten lassen*) keep waiting

hin|knien (sich) *vr sep* kneel down. **h~kommen**† *vi sep* (*sein*) get there; (*h~gehören*) belong, go; (⊺ *auskommen*) manage (**mit** with); (⊺ *stimmen*) be right. **h~laufen**† *vi sep* (*sein*) run/(*gehen*) walk there. **h~legen** *vt sep* lay *or* put down; **sich h~legen** lie down. **h~nehmen**† *vt sep* (*fig*) accept

hinreichen *v sep* ● *vt* hand (*dat* to) ● *vi* (*haben*) extend (**bis** to); (*ausreichen*) be adequate. **h~d** *a* adequate

Hinreise *f* journey there; (*Rail*) outward journey

hinreißen† *vt sep* (*fig*) carry away; **sich h~ lassen** get carried away. **h~d** *a* ravishing

hinricht|en *vt sep* execute. **H~ung** *f* execution

hinschreiben† *vt sep* write there; (*aufschreiben*) write down

hinsehen† *vi sep* (*haben*) look

hinsetzen *vt sep* put down; **sich h~** sit down

Hinsicht *f* - **in dieser H~** in this respect; **in finanzieller H~** financially. **h~lich** *prep* (+ *gen*) regarding

hinstellen *vt sep* put *or* set down; park <*Auto*>

hinstrecken *vt sep* hold out; **sich h~** extend

hinten *adv* at the back; **dort h~** back there; **nach/von h~** to the back/from behind. **h~herum** *adv* round the back; ⊺ by devious means

hinter *prep* (+ *dat/acc*) behind; (*nach*) after; **h~ jdm/etw herlaufen** run after s.o./sth; **h~ etw** (*dat*) **stecken** (*fig*) be behind sth; **h~ etw** (*acc*) **kommen** (*fig*) get to the bottom of sth; **etw h~ sich** (*acc*) **bringen** get sth over [and done] with

Hinterbliebene *pl* (*Admin*) surviving dependants; **die H~n** the bereaved family *sg*

hintere|(r,s) *a* back, rear; **h~s Ende** far end

hintereinander *adv* one behind/(*zeitlich*) after the other; **dreimal h~** three times in succession

Hintergedanke *m* ulterior motive

hintergehen† *vt* deceive

Hinter|grund *m* background. **H~halt** *m* -[e]s, -e ambush. **h~hältig** *a* underhand

hinterher *adv* behind, after; (*zeitlich*) afterwards

Hinter|hof *m* back yard. **H~kopf** *m* back of the head

hinterlassen† vt leave [behind]; (Jur) leave, bequeath (dat to). **H~schaft** f -, -en (Jur) estate
hinterlegen vt deposit
Hinterleib m (Zool) abdomen. **H~list** f deceit. **h~listig** a deceitful. **H~n** m -s,- ⊞ bottom, backside. **H~rad** nt rear or back wheel. **h~rücks** adv from behind. **h~ste(r,s)** a last; **h~ste Reihe** back row. **H~teil** nt ⊞ behind. **H~treppe** f back stairs pl
hinterziehen† vt (Admin) evade
hinüber adv over or across [there]; **h~ sein** (⊞ unbrauchbar, tot) have had it. **h~gehen**† vi sep (sein) go over or across; **h~gehen über** (+ acc) cross
hinunter adv down [there]. **h~gehen**† vi sep (sein) go down. **h~schlucken** vt sep swallow
Hinweg m way there
hinweg adv away, off; **h~ über** (+ acc) over; **über eine Zeit h~** over a period. **h~kommen**† vt sep (sein) **h~kommen über** (+ acc) (fig) get over. **h~sehen**† vi sep (haben) **h~sehen über** (+ acc) see over; (fig) overlook. **h~setzen** (sich) vr sep **sich h~setzen über** (+ acc) ignore
Hinweis m -es, -e reference; (Andeutung) hint; (Anzeichen) indication; **unter H~ auf** (+ acc) with reference to. **h~en**† v sep ● vi (haben) point (**auf** + acc to) ● vt **jdn auf etw** (acc) **h~en** point sth out to s.o.
hinwieder adv on the other hand
hin|zeigen vi sep (haben) point (**auf** + acc to). **h~ziehen**† vt sep pull; (fig: in die Länge ziehen) drag out; (verzögern) delay; **sich h~ziehen** drag on
hinzu adv in addition. **h~fügen** vt sep add. **h~kommen**† vt sep (sein) be added; (ankommen) arrive [on the scene]; join (**zu jdm** s.o.). **h~ziehen**† vt sep call in

Hiobsbotschaft f bad news sg
Hirn nt -s brain; (Culin) brains pl. **H~hautentzündung** f meningitis
Hirsch m -[e]s, -e deer; (männlich) stag; (Culin) venison
Hirse f - millet
Hirt m -en, -en, **Hirte** m -n, -n shepherd
hissen vt hoist
Histor|iker m -s,- historian. **h~isch** a historical; (bedeutend) historic
Hitz|e f - heat. **h~ig** a (fig) heated; <Person> hot-headed; (jähzornig) hot-tempered. **H~schlag** m heat-stroke
H-Milch /'ha:-/ f long-life milk
Hobby nt -s, -s hobby
Hobel m -s,- (Techn) plane; (Culin) slicer. **h~n** vt/i (haben) plane. **H~späne** mpl shavings
hoch a (attrib hohe(r,s)) high; <Baum, Mast> tall; <Offizier> high-ranking; <Alter> great; <Summe> large; <Strafe> heavy; **hohe Schuhe** ankle boots ● adv high; (sehr) highly; **h~ gewachsen** tall; **h~ begabt** highly gifted; **h~ gestellte Persönlichkeit** important person; **die Treppe h~** up the stairs; **sechs Mann h~** six of us/them. **H~** nt -s, -s cheer; (Meteorol) high
Hoch|achtung f high esteem. **H~achtungsvoll** adv Yours faithfully. **H~betrieb** m great activity; **in den Geschäften herrscht H~betrieb** the shops are terribly busy. **H~deutsch** nt High German. **H~druck** m high pressure. **H~ebene** f plateau. **h~fahren**† vi sep (sein) go up; (auffahren) start up; (aufbrausen) flare up. **H~gehen**† vi sep (sein) go up; (explodieren) blow up; (aufbrausen) flare up. **h~gestellt** attrib a <Zahl> superior; (fig) *h~ gestellt, s. hoch. **H~glanz** m high gloss. **h~gradig** a extreme.

h~hackig *a* high-heeled.
h~halten† *vt sep* hold up; (*fig*)
uphold. **H~haus** *nt* high-rise
building. **h~heben†** *vt sep* lift
up; raise <*Hand*>. **h~kant** *adv* on
end. **h~kommen†** *vi sep* (*sein*)
come up; (*aufstehen*) get up; (*fig*)
get on [in the world].
h~konjunktur *f* boom.
h~krempeln *vt sep* roll up.
h~leben *vi sep* (*haben*) **h~leben**
lassen give three cheers for;
H~mut *m* pride, arrogance.
h~näsig *a* 🔲 snooty. **H~ofen** *m*
blast-furnace. **h~ragen** *vi sep*
rise [up]; <*Turm:*> soar. **H~ruf** *m*
cheer. **H~saison** *f* high season.
h~schlagen† *vt sep* turn up
<*Kragen*>. **H~schule** *f* university;
(*Musik-, Kunst-*) academy.
H~sommer *m* midsummer.
H~spannung *f* high/(*fig*) great
tension. **h~spielen** *vt sep* (*fig*)
magnify. **H~sprung** *m* high jump.
öchst *adv* extremely, most

ochstapler *m* -s,- confidence
trickster

öchst|e(r,s) *a* highest; <*Baum,*
Turm> tallest; (*oberste, größte*)
top; **es ist h~e Zeit** it is high time.
h~ens *adv* at most; (*es sei denn*)
except perhaps.
H~geschwindigkeit *f* top or
maximum speed. **H~maß** *nt*
maximum. **h~persönlich** *adv* in
person. **H~preis** *m* top price.
H~temperatur *f* maximum
temperature

och|verrat *m* high treason.
H~wasser *nt* high tide;
(*Überschwemmung*) floods *pl.*
H~würden *m* -s Reverend; (*Anrede*) Father

ochzeit *f* -, -en wedding.
H~skleid *nt* wedding dress.
H~sreise *f* honeymoon [trip].
H~stag *m* wedding day/
(*Jahrestag*) anniversary

Hocke *f* - **in der H~sitzen** squat.
h~n *vi* (*haben*) squat ● *vr* **sich**
h~n squat down
Hocker *m* -s,- stool
Höcker *m* -s,- bump; (*Kamel-*)
hump
Hockey /hɔki/ *nt* -s hockey
Hode *f* -, -n, **Hoden** *m* -s,- testicle
Hof *m* -[e]s,ːe [court]yard;
(*Bauern-*) farm; (*Königs-*) court;
(*Schul-*) playground; (*Astr*) halo
hoffen *vt/i* (*haben*) hope (**auf** +
acc for). **h~tlich** *adv* I hope, let
us hope
Hoffnung *f* -, -en hope. **h~slos** *a*
hopeless. **h~svoll** *a* hopeful
höflich *a* polite. **H~keit** *f* -, -en
politeness, courtesy
hohe(r,s) *a s.* **hoch**
Höhe *f* -, -n height; (*Aviat, Geog*)
altitude; (*Niveau*) level; (*einer*
Summe) size; (*An-*) hill
Hoheit *f* -, -en (*Staats-*)
sovereignty; (*Titel*) Highness.
H~sgebiet *nt* [sovereign]
territory. **H~szeichen** *nt* national
emblem
Höhe|nlinie *f* contour line.
H~nsonne *f* sun-lamp. **H~punkt**
m (*fig*) climax, peak. **h~r** *a & adv*
higher; **h~re Schule** secondary
school
hohl *a* hollow; (*leer*) empty
Höhle *f* -, -n cave; (*Tier-*) den;
(*Hohlraum*) cavity; (*Augen-*)
socket
Hohl|maß *nt* measure of capacity.
H~raum *m* cavity
Hohn *m* -s scorn, derision
höhnen *vt* deride
holen *vt* fetch, get; (*kaufen*) buy;
(*nehmen*) take (**aus** from)
Holland *nt* -s Holland
Holländ|er *m* -s,- Dutchman; **die**
H~er the Dutch *pl.* **H~erin** *f* -,
-nen Dutchwoman. **h~isch** *a*
Dutch
Höll|e *f* - hell. **h~isch** *a* infernal;
(*schrecklich*) terrible

H

Holunder m -s (Bot) elder

Holz nt -es,˙er wood; (Nutz-) timber. **H~blasinstrument** nt woodwind instrument

hölzern a wooden

Holz|hammer m mallet. **h~ig** a woody. **H~kohle** f charcoal. **H~schnitt** m woodcut. **H~wolle** f wood shavings pl

Homöopathie f - homoeopathy

homosexuell a homosexual. **H~e(r)** m/f homosexual

Honig m -s honey. **H~wabe** f honeycomb

Hono|rar nt -s, -e fee. **h~rieren** vt remunerate; (fig) reward

Hopfen m -s hops pl; (Bot) hop

hopsen vi (sein) jump

horchen vi (haben) listen (auf + acc to); (heimlich) eavesdrop

hören vt hear; (an-) listen to ● vi (haben) hear; (horchen) listen; (gehorchen) obey; **h~ auf** (+ acc) listen to

Hör|er m -s,- listener; (Teleph) receiver. **H~funk** m radio. **H~gerät** nt hearing-aid

Horizon|t m -[e]s horizon. **h~tal** a horizontal

Hormon nt -s, -e hormone

Horn nt -s,˙er horn. **H~haut** f hard skin; (Augen-) cornea

Hornisse f -, -n hornet

Horoskop nt -[e]s, -e horoscope

Horrorfilm m horror film

Hör|saal m (Univ) lecture hall. **H~spiel** nt radio play

Hort m -[e]s, -e (Schatz) hoard; (fig) refuge. **h~en** vt hoard

Hortensie /-iə/ f -, -n hydrangea

Hose f -, -n, **Hosen** pl trousers pl. **H~nrock** m culottes pl. **H~nschlitz** m fly, flies pl. **H~nträger** mpl braces

Hostess f -, -tessen hostess; (Aviat) air hostess

Hostie /'hostiə/ f -, -n (Relig) host

Hotel nt -s, -s hotel

hübsch a pretty; (nett) nice

Hubschrauber m -s,- helicopter

Huf m -[e]s, -e hoof. **H~eisen** nt horseshoe

Hüft|e f -, -n hip. **H~gürtel** m -s,- girdle

Hügel m -s,- hill. **h~ig** a hilly

Huhn nt -s,˙er chicken; (Henne) hen

Hühn|chen nt -s,- chicken. **H~erauge** nt corn **H~erstall** m henhouse

Hülle f -, -n cover; (Verpackung) wrapping; (Platten-) sleeve. **h~n** vt wrap

Hülse f -, -n (Bot) pod; (Etui) case **H~nfrüchte** fpl pulses

human a humane. **H~ität** f - humanity

Hummel f -, -n bumble-bee

Hummer m -s,- lobster

Hum|or m -s humour; **H~or haben** have a sense of humour. **h~orvoll** a humorous

humpeln vi (sein/haben) hobble

Humpen m -s,- tankard

Hund m -[e]s, -e dog; (Jagd-) hound. **H~ehütte** f kennel

hundert inv a one/a hundred. **H~** nt -s, -e hundred; **H~e** od **h~e von** hundreds of. **H~jahrfeier** f centenary. **h~prozentig** a & adv one hundred per cent. **h~ste(r,s)** a hundredth. **H~stel** nt -s,- hundredth

Hündin f -, -nen bitch

Hüne m -n, -n giant

Hunger m -s hunger; **H~ haben** be hungry. **h~n** vi (haben) starve. **H~snot** f famine

hungrig a hungry

Hupe f -, -n (Auto) horn. **h~n** vi (haben) sound one's horn

hüpfen vi (sein) skip; <Frosch:> hop; <Grashüpfer:> jump

Hürde f -, -n (Sport & fig) hurdle; (Schaf-) pen, fold

Hure f -, -n whore

hurra int hurray

usten vi (haben) cough. **H~saft** m cough mixture

ut[1] m -[e]s,-̈e hat; (Pilz-) cap

ut[2] f - **auf der H~sein** be on one's guard (**vor** + dat against)

üten vt watch over; tend <Tiere>; (aufpassen) look after; **das Bett h~ müssen** be confined to bed; **sich h~** be on one's guard (**vor** + dat against); **sich h~, etw u tun** take care not to do sth

ütte f -,-n hut; (Hunde-) kennel; (Techn) iron and steel works.
H~nkäse m cottage cheese.
H~nkunde f metallurgy

lyäne f -,-n hyena

ydraulisch a hydraulic

ygiene /hy'gie:nə/ f - hygiene.
h~isch a hygienic

lypno|se f - hypnosis. **h~tisch** a hypnotic. **H~tiseur** /-'zø:ɐ/ m -s,-e hypnotist. **h~tisieren** vt hypnotize

lypochonder /hypo'xɔndɐ/ m -s,- hypochondriac

lypothek f -,-en mortgage

lypothese f -,-n hypothesis

lys|terie f - hysteria. **h~terisch** a hysterical

ch pron I; **ich bins** it's me. **lch** nt -[s], -[s] self; (Psych) ego

C-Zug /i'tse:-/ m inter-city train

deal a ideal. **I~** nt -s, -e ideal.
I~ismus m - idealism. **I~ist(in)** m -en, -en (f -, -nen) idealist.
i~istisch a idealistic

dee f -, -n idea; **fixe I~** obsession

dentifizieren vt identify

dentisch a identical

Ideo|logie f -, -n ideology.
i~logisch a ideological

idiomatisch a idiomatic

Idiot m -en, -en idiot. **i~isch** a idiotic

idyllisch /i'dʏlɪʃ/ a idyllic

Igel m -s,- hedgehog

ihm pron (dat of **er, es**) [to] him; (Ding, Tier) [to] it

ihn pron (acc of **er**) him; (Ding, Tier) it. **i~en** pron (dat of **sie** pl) [to] them. **I~en** pron (dat of **Sie**) [to] you

ihr pron (2nd pers pl) you ● (dat of **sie** sg) [to] her; (Ding, Tier) [to] it ●poss pron her; (Ding, Tier) its; (pl) their. **Ihr** poss pron your. **i~e(r,s)** poss pron hers; (pl) theirs. **I~e(r,s)** poss pron yours. **i~erseits** adv for her/(pl) their part. **I~erseits** adv on your part. **i~etwegen** adv for her/(Ding, Tier) its/(pl) their sake; (wegen) because of her/it/them, on her/ its/their account. **I~etwegen** adv for your sake; (wegen) because of you, on your account. **i~ige** poss pron **der/die/das i~ige** hers; (pl) theirs. **I~ige** poss pron **der/die/ das I~ige** yours; (pl) theirs. **i~s** poss pron hers; (pl) theirs. **I~s** poss pron yours

Ikone f -, -n icon

illegal a illegal

Illus|ion f -, -en illusion. **i~orisch** a illusory

Illustr|ation /-'tsi̯o:n/ f -, -en illustration. **i~ieren** vt illustrate.
I~ierte f -n, -[n] [illustrated] magazine

Iltis m -ses, -se polecat

im prep = in dem

Imbiss m snack. **I~stube** f snack-bar

Imit|ation /-'tsi̯o:n/ f -, -en imitation. **i~ieren** vt imitate

Imker m -s,- bee-keeper

Immatrikul|ation /-'ts:io:n/ f - (Univ) enrolment. **i∼ieren** vt (Univ) enrol; **sich i∼ieren** enrol

immer adv always; **für i∼** for ever; (endgültig) for good; **i∼ noch** still; **i∼ mehr** more and more; **was i∼** whatever. **i∼hin** adv (wenigstens) at least; (trotzdem) all the same; (schließlich) after all. **i∼zu** adv all the time

Immobilien /-iən/ pl real estate sg. **l∼makler** m estate agent

immun a immune (**gegen** to)

Imperialismus m - imperialism

impf|en vt vaccinate, inoculate. **l∼stoff** m vaccine. **l∼ung** f -, -en vaccination, inoculation

imponieren vi (haben) impress (**jdm** s.o.)

Impor|t m -[e]s, -e import. **l∼teur** /-'tø:ɐ/ m -s, -e importer. **i∼tieren** vt import

impoten|t a (Med) impotent. **l∼z** f - (Med) impotence

imprägnieren vt waterproof

Impressionismus m - impressionism

improvisieren vt/i (haben) improvise

imstande pred a able (**zu** to); capable (**etw zu tun** of doing sth)

in prep (+ dat) in; (+ acc) into, in; (bei Bus, Zug) on; **in der Schule** at school; **in die Schule** to school ● a **in sein** be in

Inbegriff m embodiment

indem conj (während) while; (dadurch) by (+ -ing)

Inder(in) m -s, - (f -, -nen) Indian

indessen conj while ● adv (unterdessen) meanwhile

Indian|er(in) m -s,- (f -, -nen) (American) Indian. **i∼isch** a Indian

Indien /'ɪndiən/ nt -s India

indirekt a indirect

indisch a Indian

indiskret a indiscreet

indiskutabel a out of the question

Individu|alist m -en, -en individualist. **l∼alität** f - individuality. **i∼ell** a individual

Indizienbeweis /m'di:ts:iən-/ m circumstantial evidence

industr|ialisiert a industrialized. **l∼ie** f -, -n industry. **i∼iell** a industrial

ineinander adv in/into one another

Infanterie f - infantry

Infektion /-'ts:io:n/ f -, -en infection. **l∼skrankheit** f infectious disease

infizieren vt infect; **sich i∼** become/ <Person:> be infected

Inflation /-'ts:io:n/ f - inflation. **i∼är** a inflationary

infolge prep (+ gen) as a result of. **i∼dessen** adv consequently

Inform|atik f - information science. **l∼ation** /-'ts:io:n/ f -, -en information; **l∼ationen** information sg. **i∼ieren** vt inform; **sich i∼ieren** find out (**über** + acc about)

infrage adv **etw i∼ stellen** question sth; (ungewiss machen) make sth doubtful; **nicht i∼ kommen** be out of the question

infrarot a infra-red

Ingenieur /ɪnʒe'niø:ɐ/ m -s, -e engineer

Ingwer m -s ginger

Inhaber(in) m -s,- (f -, -nen) holder; (Besitzer) proprietor; (Scheck-) bearer

inhaftieren vt take into custody

inhalieren vt/i (haben) inhale

Inhalt m -[e]s, -e contents pl; (Bedeutung, Gehalt) content; (Geschichte) story. **l∼sangabe** f summary. **l∼sverzeichnis** nt list/(in Buch) table of contents

Initiative /inits:ia'ti:və/ f -, -n initiative

inklusive prep (+ gen) including ● adv inclusive

inkonsequent a inconsistent

inkorrekt a incorrect

Inkubationszeit /-'ts:io:ns-/ f (Med) incubation period

Inland nt -[e]s home country; (Binnenland) interior. **I~sgespräch** nt inland call

inmitten prep (+ gen) in the middle of; (unter) amongst

innen adv inside; nach i~ inwards. **I~architekt(in)** m(f) interior designer. **I~minister** m Minister of the Interior; (in UK) Home Secretary. **I~politik** f domestic policy. **I~stadt** f town centre

inner|e(r,s) a inner; (Med, Pol) internal. **I~e(s)** nt interior; (Mitte) centre; (fig: Seele) inner being. **I~eien** fpl (Culin) offal sg. **i~halb** prep (+ gen) inside; (zeitlich & fig) within; (während) during ● adv i~halb von within. **i~lich** a internal

innig a sincere

innovativ a innovative

Innung f -, -en guild

ins prep = in das

Insasse m -n, -n inmate; (im Auto) occupant; (Passagier) passenger

insbesondere adv especially

Inschrift f inscription

Insekt nt -[e]s, -en insect. **I~envertilgungsmittel** nt insecticide

Insel f -, -n island

Inser|at nt -[e]s, -e [newspaper] advertisement. **i~ieren** vt/i (haben) advertise

insge|heim adv secretly. **i~samt** adv [all] in all

insofern, insoweit adv /-'zo:-/ in this respect; **i~ als** in as much as

Insp|ektion /inspɛk'ts:io:n/ f -, -en inspection. **I~ektor** m -en, -en /-'to:rən/ inspector

Install|ateur /insta'tø:ɐ/ m -s, -e fitter; (Klempner) plumber. **i~ieren** vt install

instand adv i~ halten maintain; (pflegen) look after. **I~haltung** f - maintenance, upkeep

Instandsetzung f - repair

Instanz f -st-/ f -, -en authority

Instinkt /-st-/ m -[e]s, -e instinct. **i~iv** a instinctive

Institut /-st-/ nt -[e]s, -e institute

Instrument /-st-/ nt -[e]s, -e instrument. **I~almusik** f instrumental music

Insulin nt -s insulin

inszenier|en vt (Theat) produce. **I~ung** f -, -en production

Integr|ation /-'ts:io:n/ f - integration. **i~ieren** vt integrate; **sich i~ieren** integrate

Intellekt m -[e]s intellect. **i~uell** a intellectual

intelligen|t a intelligent. **I~z** f - intelligence

Intendant m -en, -en director

Intensivstation f intensive-care unit

interaktiv a interactive

inter|essant a interesting. **I~esse** nt -s, -n interest; **I~esse haben** be interested (an + dat in). **I~essengruppe** f pressure group. **I~essent** m -en, -en interested party; (Käufer) prospective buyer. **i~essieren** vt interest; **sich i~essieren** be interested (für in)

Inter|nat nt -[e]s, -e boarding school. **i~national** a international. **I~nist** m -en, -en specialist in internal diseases. **I~pretation** /-'ts:io:n/ f -, -en interpretation. **i~pretieren** vt interpret. **I~vall** nt -s, -e interval. **I~vention** /-'ts:io:n/ f -, -en intervention

Internet nt -s, -s Internet; **im I~** on the Internet

Interview /'ɪntɐvjuː/ *nt* **-s, -s** interview. **i~en** /-'vjuːən/ *vt* interview

intim *a* intimate

intoleran|t *a* intolerant. **l~z** *f* - intolerance

intravenös *a* intravenous

Intrige *f* -, **-n** intrigue

introvertiert *a* introverted

Invalidenrente *f* disability pension

Invasion *f* -, **-en** invasion

Inven|tar *nt* **-s, -e** furnishings and fittings *pl*; (*Techn*) equipment; (*Bestand*) stock; (*Liste*) inventory. **l~tur** *f* -, **-en** stock-taking

investieren *vt* invest

inwie|fern *adv* in what way. **i~weit** *adv* how far, to what extent

Inzest *m* **-[e]s** incest

inzwischen *adv* in the meantime

Irak (der) -[s] Iraq. **i~isch** *a* Iraqi

Iran (der) -[s] Iran. **i~isch** *a* Iranian

irdisch *a* earthly

Ire *m* **-n, -n** Irishman; **die l~n** the Irish *pl*

irgend *adv* **wenn i~ möglich** if at all possible. **i~ein** *indef art* some/any; **i~ein anderer** someone/anyone else. **i~eine(r,s)** *pron* any one; (*jemand*) someone/anyone. **i~etwas** *pron* something; anything. **i~jemand** *pron* someone; anyone. **i~wann** *pron* at some time [or other]/at any time. **i~was** *pron* 🛈 something [or other]/anything. **i~welche(r,s)** *pron* any. **i~wer** *pron* someone/anyone. **i~wie** *adv* somehow [or other]. **i~wo** *adv* somewhere/anywhere

Irin *f* -, **-nen** Irishwoman

irisch *a* Irish

Irland *nt* **-s** Ireland

Ironie *f* - irony

ironisch *a* ironic

irre *a* mad, crazy; (🛈 *gewaltig*) incredible. **l~(r)** *m/f* lunatic. **i~führen** *vt sep* (*fig*) mislead

irre|machen *vt sep* confuse. **i~n** *vi/r* (*haben*) [sich] **i~n** be mistaken ●*vi* (*sein*) wander. **l~nanstalt** *f*. **l~nhaus** *nt* lunatic asylum. **i~werden†** *vi sep* (*sein*) get confused

Irrgarten *m* maze

irritieren *vt* irritate

Irr|sinn *m* madness, lunacy. **i~sinnig** *a* mad; (🛈 *gewaltig*) incredible. **l~tum** *m* **-s,¨er** mistake

Ischias *m & nt* - sciatica

Islam (der) -[s] Islam. **islamisch** *a* Islamic

Island *nt* **-s** Iceland

Isolier|band *nt* insulating tape. **i~en** *vt* isolate; (*Phys, Electr*) insulate; (*gegen Schall*) soundproof. **l~ung** *f* - isolation; insulation; soundproofing

Israel /'ɪsraeːl/ *nt* **-s** Israel. **l~eli** *m* **-[s], -s &** *f* -, **-[s]** Israeli. **i~elisch** *a* Israeli

ist *s.* sein; **er ist** he is

Ital|ien /-iən/ *nt* **-s** Italy. **l~iener(in)** *m* **-s,-** (*f* -, **-nen**) Italian. **i~ienisch** *a* Italian. **l~ienisch** *nt* **-[s]** (*Lang*) Italian

ja *adv*, **Ja** *nt* **-[s]** yes; **ich glaube ja** I think so; **ja nicht!** not on any account! **da seid ihr ja!** there you are!

Jacht *f* -, **-en** yacht

Jacke *f* -, **-n** jacket; (*Strick-*) cardigan

Jackett /ʒa'kɛt/ nt -s, -s jacket
Jade m -[s] & f -jade
Jagd f -, -en hunt; (Schießen) shoot; (Jagen) hunting; shooting; (fig) pursuit (nach of); **auf die J∼ gehen** go hunting/shooting.
J∼gewehr nt sporting gun.
J∼hund m gun-dog: (Hetzhund) hound
jagen vt hunt; (schießen) shoot; (verfolgen, wegjagen) chase; (treiben) drive; **sich j∼** chase each other; **in die Luft j∼** blow up ● vi (haben) hunt, go hunting/shooting; (fig) chase (nach after) ● vi (sein) race, dash
Jäger m -s,- hunter
Jahr nt -[e]s, -e year. **j∼elang** adv for years. **J∼eszahl** f year.
J∼eszeit f season. **J∼gang** m year; (Wein) vintage. **J∼hundert** nt century
jährlich a annual, yearly
Jahr|markt m fair. **J∼tausend** nt millennium. **J∼zehnt** nt -[e]s, -e decade
Jähzorn m violent temper. **j∼ig** a hot-tempered
Jalousie /ʒalu'zi:/ f -, -n venetian blind
Jammer m -s misery
jämmerlich a miserable; (Mitleid erregend) pitiful
jammern vi (haben) lament ● vt **jdn j∼n** arouse s.o.'s pity
Jänner m -s,- (Aust) January
Januar m -s, -e January
Jap|an nt -s Japan. **J∼aner(in)** m -s,- (f -, -nen) Japanese. **j∼anisch** a Japanese. **J∼anisch** nt -[s] (Lang) Japanese
jäten vt/i (haben) weed
jaulen vi (haben) yelp
Jause f -, -n (Aust) snack
jawohl adv yes
Jazz /jats:, dʒɛs/ m - jazz
je adv (jemals) ever; (jeweils) each; (pro) per; **je nach** according to; **seit eh und je** always ● conj **je**

mehr, desto besser the more the better ● prep (+ acc) per
Jeans /dʒi:ns/ pl jeans
jed|e(r,s) pron every; (j∼er Einzelne) each; (j∼er Beliebige) any; (substantivisch) everyone; each one; anyone; **ohne j∼en Grund** without any reason.
j∼enfalls adv in any case; (wenigstens) at least. **j∼ermann** pron everyone. **j∼erzeit** adv at any time. **j∼esmal** adv every time
jedoch adv & conj however
jemals adv ever
jemand pron someone, somebody; (fragend, verneint) anyone, anybody
jen|e(r,s) pron that; (pl) those; (substantivisch) that one; (pl) those. **j∼seits** prep (+ gen) [on] the other side of
jetzt adv now
jiddisch a, **J∼** nt -[s] Yiddish
Job /dʒɔp/ m -s, -s job. **j∼ben** vi (haben) Ⓘ work
Joch nt -[e]s, -e yoke
Jockei, Jockey /'dʒɔki/ m -s, -s jockey
Jod nt -[e]s iodine
jodeln vi (haben) yodel
Joga m & nt -[s] yoga
joggen /'dʒɔgən/ vi (haben/sein) jog
Joghurt, Jogurt m & nt -[s] yoghurt
Johannisbeere f redcurrant
Joker m -s,- (Karte) joker
Jolle f -, -n dinghy
Jongleur /ʒõ'glø:ɐ/ m -s, -e juggler
Jordanien /-iən/ nt -s Jordan
Journalis|mus /ʒʊrna'lɪsmʊs/ m - journalism. **J∼t(in)** m -en, -en (f -, -nen) journalist
Jubel m -s rejoicing, jubilation.
j∼n vi (haben) rejoice
Jubiläum nt -s,-äen jubilee; (Jahrestag) anniversary

jucken vi (haben) itch; **sich j~en** scratch; **es j~t mich** I have an itch

Jude m -n, -n Jew. **J~ntum** nt -s Judaism; (Juden) Jewry

Jüd|in f -, -nen Jewess. **j~isch** a Jewish

Judo nt -[s] judo

Jugend f - youth; (junge Leute) young people pl. **J~herberge** f youth hostel. **J~kriminalität** f juvenile delinquency. **j~lich** a youthful. **J~liche(r)** m/f young man/woman. **J~liche** pl young people. **J~stil** m art nouveau

Jugoslaw|ien /-iən/ nt -s Yugoslavia. **j~isch** a Yugoslav

Juli m -[s], -s July

jung a young; <Wein> new ● pron **J~ und Alt** young and old. **J~e** m -n, -n boy. **J~e(s)** nt young animal/bird; (Katzen-) kitten; (Bären-) cub; (Hunde-) pup; **die J~en** the young pl

Jünger m -s,- disciple

Jung|frau f virgin; (Astr) Virgo. **J~geselle** m bachelor

Jüngling m -s, -e youth

jüngst|e(r,s) a youngest; (neueste) latest; **in j~er Zeit** recently

Juni m -[s], -s June

Jura pl law sg

Jurist|(in) m -en, -en (f -, -nen) lawyer. **j~isch** a legal

Jury /ʒyˈriː/ f -, -s jury; (Sport) judges pl

Justiz f - die J~ justice

Juwel nt -s, -en & (fig) -e jewel. **J~ier** m -es, -e jeweller

Jux m -es, -e ⚠ joke; **aus Jux** for fun

Kabarett nt -s, -s & -e cabaret

Kabel nt -s,- cable. **K~fernsehen** nt cable television

Kabeljau m -s, -e & -s cod

Kabine f -, -n cabin; (Umkleide-) cubicle; (Telefon-) booth; (einer K~nbahn) car. **K~nbahn** f cable-car

Kabinett nt -s, -e (Pol) Cabinet

Kabriolett nt -s, -s convertible

Kachel f -, -n tile. **k~n** vt tile

Kadenz f -, -en (Mus) cadence

Käfer m -s,- beetle

Kaffee /ˈkafe:, kaˈfe:/ m -s, -s coffee. **K~kanne** f coffee-pot. **K~maschine** f coffee-maker. **K~mühle** f coffee-grinder

Käfig m -s, -e cage

kahl a bare; (haarlos) bald; **k~ geschoren** shaven

Kahn m -s,ːe boat; (Last-) barge

Kai m -s, -s quay

Kaiser m -s,- emperor. **K~in** f -, -nen empress. **k~lich** a imperial. **K~reich** nt empire. **K~schnitt** m Caesarean [section]

Kajüte f -, -n (Naut) cabin

Kakao /kaˈkau:/ m -s cocoa

Kakerlak m -s & -en, -en cockroach

Kaktus m -, -teen /-ˈteːən/ cactus

Kalb nt -[e]s,ːer calf. **K~fleisch** nt veal

Kalender m -s,- calendar; (Termin-) diary

Kaliber nt -s,- calibre; (Gewehr-) bore

Kalium nt -s potassium

Kalk m -[e]s, -e lime; (Kalzium) calcium. **k~en** vt whitewash. **K~stein** m limestone

Kalkul|ation /-'tsio:n/ f -, -en
calculation. **k~ieren** vt/i (haben)
calculate

Kalorie f -, -n calorie

kalt a cold; **mir ist k~** I am cold

Kälte f - cold; (Gefühls-) coldness;
10 Grad K~ 10 degrees below
zero

Kalzium nt -s calcium

Kamel nt -s, -e camel

Kamera f -, -s camera

Kamerad(in) m -en, -en (f -, -nen)
companion; (Freund) mate; (Mil,
Pol) comrade

Kameramann m (pl -männer &
-leute) cameraman

Kamille f - camomile

Kamin m -s, -e fireplace; (SGer:
Schornstein) chimney

Kamm m -[e]s, -̈e comb; (Berg-)
ridge; (Zool, Wellen-) crest

kämmen vt comb; **jdn/sich k~**
comb s.o.'s/one's hair

Kammer f -, -n small room;
(Techn, Biol, Pol) chamber.
K~musik f chamber music

Kammgarn nt (Tex) worsted

Kampagne /kam'panjə/ f -, -n
(Pol, Comm) campaign

Kampf m -es,-̈e fight; (Schlacht)
battle; (Wett-) contest; (fig)
struggle

kämpf|en vi (haben) fight; **sich
k~en durch** fight one's way
through. **K~er(in)** m -s,- (f -, -nen)
fighter

Kampfrichter m (Sport) judge

Kanada nt -s Canada

Kanad|ier(in) /-iɐ, -iɐrn/ m -s,- (f
-, -nen) Canadian. **k~isch** a
Canadian

Kanal m -s,-̈e canal; (Abfluss-)
drain, sewer; (Radio, TV)
channel; **der K~** the [English]
Channel

Kanalisation /-'tsio:n/ f -
sewerage system, drains pl

Kanarienvogel /-iən-/ m canary

Kanarisch a **K~e Inseln** Canaries

Kandidat(in) m -en, -en (f -, -nen)
candidate

kandiert a candied

Känguru nt -s, -s kangaroo

Kaninchen nt -s,- rabbit

Kanister m -s,- canister; (Benzin-)
can

Kännchen nt -s,- [small] jug;
(Kaffee-) pot

Kanne f -, -n jug; (Tee-) pot; (Öl-)
can; (große Milch-) churn

Kannibal|e m -n, -n cannibal.
K~ismus m - cannibalism

Kanon m -s, -s canon; (Lied)
round

Kanone f -, -n cannon, gun

kanonisieren vt canonize

Kantate f -, -n cantata

Kante f -, -n edge

Kanten m -s,- crust [of bread]

Kanter m -s,- canter

kantig a angular

Kantine f -, -n canteen

Kanton m -s, -e (Swiss) canton

Kanu nt -s, -s canoe

Kanzel f -, -n pulpit; (Aviat)
cockpit

Kanzler m -s,- chancellor

Kap nt -s, -s (Geog) cape

Kapazität f -, -en capacity

Kapelle f -, -n chapel; (Mus) band

kapern vt (Naut) seize

kapieren vt 🔲 understand

Kapital nt -s capital. **K~ismus** m -
capitalism. **K~ist** m -en, -en
capitalist. **k~istisch** a capitalist

Kapitän m -s, -e captain

Kapitel nt -s,- chapter

Kaplan m -s, -e curate

Kappe f -, -n cap

Kapsel f -, -n capsule; (Flaschen-)
top

kaputt a 🔲 broken; (zerrissen)
torn; (defekt) out of order;
(ruiniert) ruined; (erschöpft)
worn out. **k~gehen†** vi sep (sein)
🔲 break; (zerreißen) tear; (defekt
werden) pack up; <Ehe,
Freundschaft:> break up.

K

k~lachen (sich) vr sep I be in stitches. **k~machen** vt sep I break; (zerreißen) tear; (defekt machen) put out of order; (erschöpfen) wear out; **sich k~machen** wear oneself out

Kapuze f -, -n hood

Kapuzinerkresse f nasturtium

Karaffe f -, -n carafe; (mit Stöpsel) decanter

Karamell m -s caramel. **K~bonbon** m & nt ≈ toffee

Karat nt -[e]s, -e carat

Karawane f -, -n caravan

Kardinal m -s,-e cardinal. **K~zahl** f cardinal number

Karfreitag m Good Friday

karg a meagre; (frugal) frugal; (spärlich) sparse; (unfruchtbar) barren; (gering) scant

Karibik f - Caribbean

kariert a check[ed]; <Papier> squared; **schottisch k~** tartan

Karik|atur f -, -en caricature; (Journ) cartoon. **k~ieren** vt caricature

Karneval m -s, -e & -s carnival

Kärnten nt -s Carinthia

Karo nt -s, -s (Raute) diamond; (Viereck) square; (Muster) check (Kartenspiel) diamonds pl

Karosserie f -, -n bodywork

Karotte f -, -n carrot

Karpfen m -s,-. carp

Karren m -s,-. cart; (Hand-) barrow. **k~** vt cart

Karriere /ka'riɛːrə/ f -, -n career; **K~ machen** get to the top

Karte f -, -n card; (Eintritts-, Fahr-) ticket; (Speise-) menu; (Land-) map

Kartei f -, -en card index

Karten|spiel nt card-game; (Spielkarten) pack of cards. **K~vorverkauf** m advance booking

Kartoffel f -, -n potato. **K~brei** m nt mashed potatoes

Karton /kar'tɔŋ/ m -s, -s cardboard; (Schachtel) carton

Karussell nt -s, -s & -e roundabout

Käse m -s,- cheese

Kaserne f -, -n barracks pl

Kasino nt -s, -s casino

Kasperle nt & m -s,- Punch. **K~theater** nt Punch and Judy show

Kasse f -, -n till; (Registrier-) cash register; (Zahlstelle) cash desk; (im Supermarkt) check-out; (Theater-) box-office; (Geld) pool [of money], I kitty; (Kranken-) health insurance scheme; **knapp bei K~ sein** I be short of cash. **K~nwart** m -[e]s, -e treasurer. **K~nzettel** m receipt

Kasserolle f -, -n saucepan

Kassette f -, -n cassette; (Film-, Farbband-) cartridge. **K~nrekorder** /-rəkɔrdɐ/ m -s,- cassette recorder

kassier|en vi (haben) collect the money/(im Bus) the fares ●vt collect. **K~er(in)** m -s,- (f -, -nen) cashier

Kastanie /kas'taːniə/ f -, -n [horse] chestnut, I conker

Kasten m -s,-. box; (Brot-) bin; (Flaschen-) crate; (Brief-) letter-box; (Aust: Schrank) cupboard

kastrieren vt castrate; neuter

Katalog m -[e]s, -e catalogue

Katalysator m -s, -en /-'toːrən/ catalyst; (Auto) catalytic converter

Katapult nt -[e]s, -e catapult

Katarrh, Katarr m -s, -e catarrh

Katastrophe f -, -n catastrophe

Katechismus m - catechism

Kategorie f -, -n category

Kater m -s,- tom-cat; (I Katzenjammer) hangover

Kathedrale f -, -n cathedral

Kath|olik(in) m -en, -en (f -, -nen) Catholic. **k~olisch** a Catholic. **K~olizismus** m - Catholicism

ätzchen *nt* -s,- kitten; (*Bot*) catkin

atze *f* -, -n cat. **K~njammer** *m* [!] hangover. **K~nsprung** *m* ein **K~nsprung** [!] a stone's throw

auderwelsch *nt* -[s] gibberish

auen *vt/i* (*haben*) chew; bite <*Nägel*>

auf *m* -[e]s, Käufe purchase; **guter K~** bargain; **in K~nehmen** (*fig*) put up with. **k~en** *vt/i* (*haben*) buy; **k~en bei** shop at

Käufer(in) *m* -s,- (*f* -, -nen) buyer; (*im Geschäft*) shopper

Kauf|haus *nt* department store. **K~laden** *m* shop

äuflich *a* saleable; (*bestechlich*) corruptible; **k~ erwerben** buy

Kauf|mann *m* (*pl* -leute) businessman; (*Händler*) dealer; (*dial*) grocer. **K~preis** *m* purchase price

Kaugummi *m* chewing-gum

Kaulquappe *f* -, -n tadpole

kaum *adv* hardly

Kaution /-'tsio:n/ *f* -, -en surety; (*Jur*) bail; (*Miet-*) deposit

Kautschuk *m* -s rubber

Kauz *m* -es, Käuze owl

Kavalier *m* -s, -e gentleman

Kavallerie *f* - cavalry

Kaviar *m* -s caviare

keck *a* bold; cheeky

Kegel *m* -s,- skittle; (*Geom*) cone. **K~bahn** *f* skittle-alley. **k~n** *vi* (*haben*) play skittles

Kehl|e *f* -, -n throat; **aus voller K~e** at the top of one's voice. **K~kopf** *m* larynx. **K~kopfentzündung** *f* laryngitis

Kehr|e *f* -, -n [hairpin] bend. **k~en** *vt/i* (*haben*) (*fegen*) sweep ● *vt* sweep; (*wenden*) turn; **sich nicht k~en an** (+ *acc*) not care about. **K~icht** *m* -[e]s sweepings *pl*. **K~reim** *m* refrain. **K~seite** *f* (*fig*) drawback. **k~tmachen** *vi sep* (*haben*) turn back; (*sich umdrehen*) turn round

Keil *m* -[e]s, -e wedge

Keilriemen *m* fan belt

Keim *m* -[e]s, -e (*Bot*) sprout; (*Med*) germ. **k~en** *vi* (*haben*) germinate; (*austreiben*) sprout. **k~frei** *a* sterile

kein *pron* no; not a; **k~e fünf Minuten** less than five minutes. **k~e(r,s)** *pron* no one, nobody; (*Ding*) none, not one. **k~esfalls** *adv* on no account. **k~eswegs** *adv* by no means. **k~mal** *adv* not once. **k~s** *pron* none, not one

Keks *m* -[es], -[e] biscuit

Kelch *m* -[e]s, -e goblet, cup; (*Relig*) chalice; (*Bot*) calyx

Kelle *f* -, -n ladle; (*Maurer*) trowel

Keller *m* -s,- cellar. **K~ei** *f* -, -en winery. **K~wohnung** *f* basement flat

Kellner *m* -s,- waiter. **K~in** *f* -, -nen waitress

keltern *vt* press

keltisch *a* Celtic

Kenia *nt* -s Kenya

kenn|en† *vt* know; **k~en lernen** get to know; (*treffen*) meet; **sich k~en lernen** meet; (*näher*) get to know one another. **K~er** *m* -s,-, **K~erin** *f* -, -nen connoisseur; (*Experte*) expert. **k~tlich** *a* recognizable; **k~tlich machen** mark. **K~tnis** *f* -, -se knowledge; **zur K~tnis nehmen** take note of; **in K~tnis setzen** inform (*von* of). **K~wort** *nt* (*pl* -wörter) reference; (*geheimes*) password. **K~zeichen** *nt* distinguishing mark or feature; (*Merkmal*) characteristic; (*Markierung*) marking; (*Auto*) registration. **k~zeichnen** *vt* distinguish; (*markieren*) mark

kentern *vi* (*sein*) capsize

Keramik *f* -, -en pottery

Kerbe *f* -, -n notch

Kerker *m* -s,- dungeon; (*Gefängnis*) prison

Kerl *m* -s, -e & -s [!] fellow, bloke

K

Kern m -s, -e pip; (*Kirsch-*) stone; (*Nuss-*) kernel; (*Techn*) core; (*Atom-, Zell- & fig*) nucleus; (*Stadt-*) centre; (*einer Sache*) heart. **K~energie** f nuclear energy. **K~gehäuse** nt core. **k~los** a seedless. **K~physik** f nuclear physics sg

Kerze f -, -n candle. **K~nhalter** m -s,- candlestick

kess a pert

Kessel m -s,- kettle

Kette f -, -n chain; (*Hals-*) necklace. **k~n** vt chain (an + acc to). **K~nladen** m chain store

Ketzer|r(in) m -s,- (f -, -nen) heretic. **K~rei** f - heresy

keuch|en vi (*haben*) pant. **K~husten** m whooping cough

Keule f -, -n club; (*Culin*) leg; (*Hühner-*) drumstick

keusch a chaste

Khaki nt - khaki

kichern vi (*haben*) giggle

Kiefer[1] f -, -n pine[-tree]

Kiefer[2] m -s,- jaw

Kiel m -s, -e (*Naut*) keel

Kiemen fpl gills

Kies m -es gravel. **K~el** m -s,-, **K~elstein** m pebble

Kilo nt -s, -[s] kilo. **K~gramm** nt kilogram. **K~hertz** nt kilohertz. **K~meter** m kilometre. **K~meterstand** m ≈ mileage. **K~watt** nt kilowatt

Kind nt -es, -er child; von K~ auf from childhood

Kinder|arzt m, **K~ärztin** f paediatrician. **K~bett** nt child's cot. **K~garten** m nursery school. **K~geld** nt child benefit. **K~lähmung** f polio. **k~leicht** a very easy. **k~los** a childless. **K~mädchen** nt nanny. **K~reim** m nursery rhyme. **K~spiel** nt children's game. **K~tagesstätte** f day nursery. **K~teller** m children's menu. **K~wagen** m pram. **K~zimmer** nt child's/

children's room; (*für Baby*) nursery

Kind|heit f - childhood. **k~isch** a childish. **k~lich** a childlike

kinetisch a kinetic

Kinn nt -[e]s, -e chin. **K~lade** f jaw

Kino nt -s, -s cinema

Kiosk m -[e]s, -e kiosk

Kippe f -, -n (*Müll-*) dump; (🗓 *Zigaretten-*) fag-end. **k~n** vt tilt; (*schütten*) tip (in + acc into) ● vi (*sein*) topple

Kirch|e f -, -n church. **K~enbank** pew. **K~endiener** m verger. **K~enlied** nt hymn. **K~enschiff** nt nave. **K~hof** m churchyard. **k~lich** a church ... ● adv **k~lich** getraut werden be married in church. **K~turm** m church tower steeple. **K~weih** f -, -en [village] fair

Kirmes f -, -sen = Kirchweih

Kirsche f -, -n cherry

Kissen nt -s,- cushion; (*Kopf-*) pillow

Kiste f -, -n crate; (*Zigarren-*) box

Kitsch m -es sentimental rubbish, (*Kunst*) kitsch

Kitt m -s [adhesive] cement; (*Fenster-*) putty

Kittel m -s,- overall, smock

Kitz nt -es, -e (*Zool*) kid

Kitz|el m -s,- tickle; (*Nerven-*) thrill. **k~eln** vt/i (*haben*) tickle. **k~lig** a ticklish

kläffen vi (*haben*) yap

Klage f -, -n lament; (*Beschwerde*) complaint; (*Jur*) action. **k~n** vi (*haben*) lament; (*sich beklagen*) complain; (*Jur*) sue

Kläger(in) m -s,- (f -, -nen) (*Jur*) plaintiff

klamm a cold and damp; (*steif*) stiff. **K~** f -, -en (*Geog*) gorge

Klammer f -, -n (*Wäsche-*) peg; (*Büro-*) paper-clip; (*Heft-*) staple; (*Haar-*) grip; (*für Zähne*) brace;

Techn) clamp; (*Typ*) bracket.
k~n (sich) *vr* cling (an + *acc* to)
one

lang *m* -[e]s, ¨e sound; (*K~farbe*)
one

lapp|e *f* -, -n flap; (🎵 *Mund*)
rap. **k~en** *vt* fold; (*hoch-*) tip up
● *vi* (*haben*) 🎵 work out

lapper *f* -, -n rattle. **k~n** *vi*
(*haben*) rattle. **K~schlange** *f*
rattlesnake

lapp|rig *a* rickety; (*schwach*)
decrepit. **K~stuhl** *m* folding
chair

laps *m* -es, -e pat, smack

lar *a* clear; **sich** (*dat*) **k~ werden**
make up one's mind; (*erkennen*)
realize (**dass** that); **sich** (*dat*) **k~**
od **im K~en sein** realize (**dass**
that) ● *adv* clearly; (🎵 *natürlich*)
of course

lären *vt* clarify; **sich k~** clear;
(*fig: sich lösen*) resolve itself

Klarheit *f* -,- clarity

Klarinette *f* -, -n clarinet

lar|machen *vt sep* make clear
(*dat* to); **sich** (*dat*) **etw k~machen**
understand sth. **k~stellen** *vt sep*
clarify

Klärung *f* - clarification

Klasse *f* -, -n class; (*Sch*) class,
form; (*Zimmer*) classroom. **k~**
inv a 🎵 super. **K~narbeit** *f*
[written] test. **K~nzimmer** *nt*
classroom

Klass|ik *f* - classicism; (*Epoche*)
classical period. **K~iker** *m* -s,-
classical author/(*Mus*) composer.
k~isch *a* classical; (*typisch*)
classic

Klatsch *m* -[e]s gossip. **K~base** *f*
🎵 gossip. **k~en** *vt* slap; Beifall
k~en applaud ● *vi* (*haben*) make
a slapping sound; (*im Wasser*)
splash; (*tratschen*) gossip;
(*applaudieren*) clap. **k~nass** *a* 🎵
soaking wet

lauen *vt/i* (*haben*) 🎵 steal

Klausel *f* -, -n clause

Klaustrophobie *f* -
claustrophobia

Klausur *f* -, -en (*Univ*) paper

Klavier *nt* -s, -e piano.
K~spieler(in) *m(f)* pianist

kleb|en *vt* stick/(*mit Klebstoff*)
glue (an + *acc* to) ● *vi* (*haben*)
stick (an + *dat* to). **k~rig** *a* sticky.
K~stoff *m* adhesive, glue.
K~streifen *m* adhesive tape

Klecks *m* -es, -e stain; (*Tinten-*)
blot; (*kleine Menge*) dab. **k~en** *vi*
(*haben*) make a mess

Klee *m* -s clover

Kleid *nt* -[e]s, -er dress; **K~er**
dresses; (*Kleidung*) clothes. **k~en**
vt dress; (*gut stehen*) suit.
K~erbügel *m* coat-hanger.
K~erbürste *f* clothes-brush.
K~erhaken *m* coat-hook.
K~erschrank *m* wardrobe.
k~sam *a* becoming. **K~ung** *f* -
clothes *pl*, clothing.
K~ungsstück *nt* garment

Kleie *f* - bran

klein *a* small, little; (*von kleinem
Wuchs*) short; **k~ schneiden** cut
up small. **von k~ auf** from
childhood. **K~arbeit** *f*
painstaking work. **K~e(r,s)** *m/f/
nt* little one. **K~geld** *nt* [small]
change. **K~handel** *m* retail trade.
K~heit *f* - smallness; (*Wuchs*)
short stature. **K~holz** *nt*
firewood. **K~igkeit** *f* -, -en trifle;
(*Mahl*) snack. **K~kind** *nt* infant.
k~laut *a* subdued. **k~lich** *a* petty

klein|schreiben† *vt sep* write
with a small [initial] letter.
K~stadt *f* small town.
k~städtisch *a* provincial

Kleister *m* -s paste. **k~n** *vt* paste

Klemme *f* -, -n [hair-]grip. **k~n** *vt*
jam; **sich** (*dat*) **den Finger k~n** get
one's finger caught ● *vi* (*haben*)
jam, stick

Klempner *m* -s,- plumber

Klerus (der) - the clergy

Klette *f* -, -n burr

K

kletter|n vi (sein) climb. **K~pflanze** f climber

Klettverschluss m Velcro (P) fastening

klicken vi (haben) click

Klient(in) /kli'ɛnt(ɪn)/ m -en, -en (f -, -nen) (Jur) client

Kliff nt -[e]s, -e cliff

Klima nt -s climate. **K~anlage** f air-conditioning

klimat|isch a climatic. **k~isiert** a air-conditioned

klimpern vi (haben) jingle; **k~ auf** (+ dat) tinkle on <Klavier>; strum <Gitarre>

Klinge f -, -n blade

Klingel f -, -n bell. **k~n** vi (haben) ring; **es k~t** there's a ring at the door

klingen† vi (haben) sound

Klinik f -, -en clinic

Klinke f -, -n [door] handle

Klippe f -, -n [submerged] rock

Klips m -es, -e clip; (Ohr-) clip-on ear-ring

klirren vi (haben) rattle <Glas>; chink

Klo nt -s, -s 🆅 loo

klopfen vi (haben) knock; (leicht) tap; <Herz:> pound; **es k~te** there was a knock at the door

Klops m -es, -e meatball

Klosett nt -s, -s lavatory

Kloß m -es, ̈e dumpling

Kloster nt -s, ̈ monastery; (Nonnen-) convent

klösterlich a monastic

Klotz m -es, ̈e block

Klub m -s, -s club

Kluft f -, ̈e cleft; (fig: Gegensatz) gulf

klug a intelligent; (schlau) clever. **K~heit** f - cleverness

Klump|en m -s, - lump

knabbern vt/i (haben) nibble

Knabe m -n, -n boy. **k~nhaft** a boyish

Knäckebrot nt crispbread

knack|en vt/i (haben) crack. **K~s** m -es, -e crack

Knall m -[e]s, -e bang. **K~bonbon** m cracker. **k~en** vi (haben) go bang; <Peitsche:> crack ● vt (🆅 werfen) chuck; **jdm eine k~en** 🆅 clout s.o. **k~ig** a 🆅 gaudy

knapp a (gering) scant; (kurz) short; (mangelnd) scarce; (gerade ausreichend) bare; (eng) tight. **K~heit** f - scarcity

knarren vi (haben) creak

Knast m -[e]s 🆅 prison

knattern vi (haben) crackle; <Gewehr:> stutter

Knäuel m & nt -s,- ball

Knauf m -[e]s, Knäufe knob

knauserig a 🆅 stingy

knautschen vt 🆅 crumple ● vi (haben) crease

Knebel m -s,- gag. **k~n** vt gag

Knecht m -[e]s, -e farm-hand; (fig) slave

kneif|en† vt pinch ● vi (haben) pinch; (🆅 sich drücken) chicken out. **K~zange** f pincers pl

Kneipe f -, -n 🆅 pub

kneten vt knead; (formen) mould. **K~masse** f Plasticine(P)

Knick m -[e]s, -e bend; (Kniff) crease. **k~en** vt bend; (kniffen) fold; **geknickt sein** 🆅 be dejected

Knicks m -es, -e curtsy. **k~en** vi (haben) curtsy

Knie nt -s,- /'kni:ə/ knee

knien /'kni:ən/ vi (haben) kneel ● vr **sich k~** kneel [down]

Kniescheibe f kneecap

Kniff m -[e]s, -e pinch; (Falte) crease; (🆅 Trick) trick. **k~en** vt fold

knipsen vt (lochen) punch; (Photo) photograph ● vi (haben) take a photograph/photographs

Knirps m -es, -e 🆅 little chap; (P) (Schirm) telescopic umbrella

knirschen vi (haben) grate; <Schnee, Kies:> crunch

nistern vi (haben) crackle;
‹Papier:› rustle
nitter|falte f crease. **k~frei** a
crease-resistant. **k~n** vi (haben)
crease
nobeln vi (haben) toss (**um** for)
noblauch m -s garlic
nöchel m -s,- ankle; (Finger-)
knuckle
nochen m -s,- bone. **K~mark** nt
bone marrow
nochig a bony
nödel m -s,- (SGer) dumpling
nolle f -, -n tuber
nopf m -[e]s,¨e button; (Griff)
knob
nöpfen vt button
nopfloch nt buttonhole
norpel m -s gristle; (Anat)
cartilage
nospe f bud
noten m -s,- knot; (Med) lump;
(Haar-) bun, chignon. **k~** vt
knot. **K~punkt** m junction
nüll|en vt crumple ●vi (haben)
crease. **K~er** m -s,- Ⓘ sensation
nüpfen vt knot; (verbinden)
attach (**an** + acc to)
Knüppel m -s,- club; (Gummi-)
truncheon
nurren vi (haben) growl;
‹Magen:› rumble
nusprig a crunchy, crisp
k.o. /ka'ʔo:/ a k.o. schlagen knock
out; k.o. sein Ⓘ be worn out
Koalition /koali'ts̩ion/ f -, -en
coalition
Kobold m -[e]s, -e goblin, imp
Koch m -[e]s,¨e cook; (im
Restaurant) chef. **K~buch** nt
cookery book. **k~en** vt cook;
(sieden) boil; make ‹Kaffee, Tee›;
hart gekochtes Ei hard-boiled egg
●vi (haben) cook; (sieden) boil;
Ⓘ seethe (**vor** + dat with). **K~en**
nt -s cooking; (Sieden) boiling.
k~end a boiling. **K~herd** m
cooker, stove

Köchin f -, -nen [woman] cook
Koch|löffel m wooden spoon.
K~nische f kitchenette.
K~platte f hotplate. **K~topf** m
saucepan
Köder m -s,- bait
Koffein /kofe'i:n/ nt -s caffeine.
k~frei a decaffeinated
Koffer m -s,- suitcase. **K~kuli** m
luggage trolley. **K~raum** m
(Auto) boot
Kognak /'kɔnjak/ m -s, -s brandy
Kohl m -[e]s cabbage
Kohle f -, -n coal. **K~[n]hydrat** nt
-[e]s, -e carbohydrate.
K~nbergwerk nt coal-mine,
colliery. **K~ndioxid** nt carbon
dioxide. **K~nsäure** f carbon
dioxide. **K~nstoff** m carbon
Koje f -, -n (Naut) bunk
Kokain /koka'i:n/ nt -s cocaine
kokett a flirtatious. **k~ieren** vi
(haben) flirt
Kokon /ko'kõ:/ m -s, -s cocoon
Kokosnuss (f) coconut
Koks m -es coke
Kolben m -s,- (Gewehr-) butt;
(Mais-) cob; (Techn) piston;
(Chem) flask
Kolibri m -s, -s humming-bird
Kolik f -, -en colic
Kollaborateur /-'tø:ɐ̯/ m -s, -e
collaborator
Kolleg nt -s, -s & -ien /-i̯ən/ (Univ)
course of lectures
Kolleg|e m -n, -n, **K~in** f -, -nen
colleague. **K~ium** nt -s, -ien staff
Kollek|te f -, -n (Relig) collection.
K~tion /-'ts̩io:n/ f -, -en collection
Köln nt -s Cologne.
K~ischwasser, K~isch Wasser
nt eau-de-Cologne
Kolonie f -, -n colony
Kolonne f -, -n column; (Mil)
convoy
Koloss m -es, -e giant
Koma nt -s, -s coma
Kombi m -s, -s = **K~wagen**.
K~nation /-'ts̩io:n/ f -, -en

K

combination; (*Folgerung*) deduction; (*Kleidung*) co-ordinating outfit. **k~nieren** vt combine; (*fig*) reason; (*folgern*) deduce. **K~wagen** m estate car

Kombüse f -, -n (*Naut*) galley

Komet m -en, -en comet

Komfort /kɔm'foːɐ̯/ m -s comfort; (*Luxus*) luxury

Komik f - humour. **K~er** m -s,- comic, comedian

komisch a funny; <*Oper*> comic; (*sonderbar*) odd, funny. **k~erweise** adv funnily enough

Komitee nt -s, -s committee

Komma nt -s, -s & -ta comma; (*Dezimal-*) decimal point; **drei K~ fünf** three point five

Kommando nt -s, -s order; (*Befehlsgewalt*) command; (*Einheit*) detachment. **K~brücke** f bridge

kommen† vi (*sein*) come; (*eintreffen*) arrive; (*gelangen*) get (**nach** to); **k~ lassen** send for; **auf/hinter etw** (*acc*) **k~** think of/find out about sth; **um/zu etw k~** lose/acquire sth; **wieder zu sich k~** come round; **wie kommt das?** why is that? **k~d** a coming; **k~den Montag** next Monday

Kommen|tar m -s, -e commentary; (*Bemerkung*) comment. **k~tieren** vt comment on

kommerziell a commercial

Kommissar m -s, -e commissioner; (*Polizei-*) superintendent

Kommission f -, -en commission; (*Gremium*) committee

Kommode f -, -n chest of drawers

Kommunalwahlen fpl local elections

Kommunion f -, -en [Holy] Communion

Kommunismus m - Communism. **K~ist(in)** m -en, -en (f -, -nen)

Communist. **k~istisch** a Communist

kommunizieren vi (*haben*) receive [Holy] Communion

Komödie /ko'møːdi̯ə/ f -, -n comedy

Kompagnon /'kɔmpanjõ/ m -s, -s (*Comm*) partner

Kompanie f -, -n (*Mil*) company

Komparse m -n, -n (*Theat*) extra

Kompass m -es, -e compass

komplett a complete

Komplex m -es, -e complex

Komplikation /-'tsi̯oːn/ f -, -en complication

Kompliment nt -[e]s, -e compliment

Komplize m -n, -n accomplice

komplizier|en vt complicate. **k~t** a complicated

Komplott nt -[e]s, -e plot

kompo|nieren vt/i (*haben*) compose. **K~nist** m -en, -en composer

Kompost m -[e]s compost

Kompott nt -[e]s, -e stewed fruit

Kompromiss m -es, -e compromise; **einen K~ schließen** compromise. **k~los** a uncompromising

Konden|sation /-'tsi̯oːn/ f - condensation. **k~sieren** vt condense

Kondensmilch f evaporated/(*gesüßt*) condensed milk

Kondition /-'tsi̯oːn/ f - (*Sport*) fitness; **in K~** in form

Konditor m -s, -en /-'toːrən/ confectioner. **K~ei** f -, -en patisserie

Kondo|lenzbrief m letter of condolence. **k~lieren** vi (*haben*) express one's condolences

Kondom nt & m -s, -e condom

Konfekt nt -[e]s confectionery; (*Pralinen*) chocolates pl

Konfektion /-'tsi̯oːn/ f - ready-to-wear clothes pl

onferenz f -, -en conference; (*Besprechung*) meeting
onfession f -, -en [religious] denomination. **k~ell** a denominational
onfetti nt -s confetti
onfirm|and(in) m -en, -en (f -, nen) candidate for confirmation. **K~ation** /-'tsio:n/ f -, -en (*Relig*) confirmation. **k~ieren** vt (*Relig*) confirm
onfitüre f -, -n jam
onflikt m -[e]s, -e conflict
onföderation /-'tsio:n/ f confederation
onfus a confused
ongress m -es, -e congress
önig m -s, -e king. **K~in** f -, -nen queen. **k~lich** a royal; (*hoheitsvoll*) regal; (*großzügig*) handsome. **K~reich** nt kingdom
onjunktiv m -s, -e subjunctive
onjunktur f - economic situation; (*Hoch-*) boom
onkret a concrete
onkurren|t(in) m -en, -en (f -, nen) competitor, rival. **K~z** f - competition; **jdm K~z machen** compete with s.o. **K~zkampf** m competition, rivalry
onkurrieren vi (*haben*) compete
onkurs m -es, -e bankruptcy

önnen†
● *auxiliary verb*
····▸ (*vermögen*) be able to; (*Präsens*) can; (*Vergangenheit, Konditional*) could. **ich kann nicht schlafen** I cannot or can't sleep. **kann ich Ihnen helfen?** can I help you? **kann/könnte das explodieren?** can/could it explode? **es kann sein, dass er kommt** he may come

❗ Distinguish **konnte** and **könnte** (both can be 'could'): **er konnte sie nicht retten** he couldn't or was unable to rescue them. **er konnte sie**

noch retten he was able to rescue them. **er könnte sie noch retten, wenn ...** he could still rescue them if ...
····▸ (*dürfen*) can, may. **kann ich gehen?** can or may I go? **können wir mit[kommen]?** can or may we come too?
● *transitive verb*
····▸ (*beherrschen*) know <language>; be able to play <game>. **können Sie Deutsch?** do you know any German? **sie kann das [gut]** she can do that [well]. **ich kann nichts dafür** I can't help that, I'm not to blame
● *intransitive verb*
····▸ (*fähig sein*) **ich kann [heute] nicht** I can't [today]. **er kann nicht anders** there's nothing else he can do; (*es ist seine Art*) he can't help it. **er kann nicht mehr** ⚇ he can't go on; (*nicht mehr essen*) he can't eat any more
····▸ (*irgendwohin gehen können*) be able to go; can go. **ich kann nicht ins Kino** I can't go to the cinema. **er konnte endlich nach Florenz** at last he was able to go to Florence

konsequen|t a consistent; (*logisch*) logical. **K~z** f -, -en consequence
konservativ a conservative
Konserv|en fpl tinned or canned food sg. **K~endose** f tin, can. **K~ierungsmittel** nt preservative
Konsonant m -en, -en consonant
Konstitution /-'tsio:n/ f -, -en constitution. **k~ell** a constitutional
konstruieren vt construct; (*entwerfen*) design
Konstruk|tion /-'tsio:n/ f -, -en construction; (*Entwurf*) design. **k~tiv** a constructive
Konsul m -s, -n consul. **K~at** nt -[e]s, -e consulate

K

Konsum *m* -s consumption.
  K~güter *npl* consumer goods
Kontakt *m* -[e]s, -e contact.
  K~linsen *fpl* contact lenses.
  K~person *f* contact
kontern *vt/i* (*haben*) counter
Kontinent /'kɔn-, kɔnti'nɛnt/ *m*
-[e]s, -e continent
Konto *nt* -s, -s account. **K~auszug**
m [bank] statement. **K~nummer**
f account number. **K~stand** *m*
[bank] balance
Kontrabass *m* double-bass
Kontroll|abschnitt *m* counterfoil.
  K~e *f* -, -n control; (*Prüfung*)
check. **K~eur** /-'løːɐ̯/ *m* -s, -e
[ticket] inspector. **k~ieren** *vt*
check; inspect <*Fahrkarten*>;
(*beherrschen*) control
Kontroverse *f* -, -n controversy
Kontur *f* -, -en contour
konventionell *a* conventional
Konversationslexikon *nt*
encyclopaedia
konvert|ieren *vi* (*haben*) (*Relig*)
convert. **K~it** *m* -en, -en convert
Konzentration /-'ʦjoːn/ *f* -, -en
concentration. **K~slager** *nt*
concentration camp
konzentrieren *vt* concentrate;
sich **k~** concentrate (**auf** + *acc*
on)
Konzept *nt* -[e]s, -e [rough] draft;
jdn aus dem **K~bringen** put s.o. off
his stroke
Konzern *m* -s, -e (*Comm*) group
[of companies]
Konzert *nt* -[e]s, -e concert;
(*Klavier-*) concerto
Konzession *f* -, -en licence;
(*Zugeständnis*) concession
Konzil *nt* -s, -e (*Relig*) council
Kooperation /koʔɔpera'ʦjoːn/ *f*
co-operation
Koordin|ation /koʔɔrdina'ʦjoːn/ *f*
- co-ordination. **k~ieren** *vt* co-
ordinate
Kopf *m* -[e]s,ˇe head; ein **K~** Kohl/
Salat a cabbage/lettuce; aus dem

K~ from memory; (*auswendig*)
by heart; **auf dem K~** (*verkehrt*)
upside down; **K~ stehen** stand on
one's head; **sich** (*dat*) **den K~**
waschen wash one's hair; **sich**
(*dat*) **den K~ zerbrechen** rack
one's brains. **K~ball** *m* header
köpfen *vt* behead; (*Fußball*) head
Kopf|ende *nt* head. **K~haut** *f*
scalp. **K~hörer** *m* headphones
K~kissen *nt* pillow. **k~los** *a*
panic-stricken. **K~rechnen** *nt*
mental arithmetic. **K~salat** *m*
lettuce. **K~schmerzen** *mpl*
headache *sg.* **K~sprung** *m*
header, dive. **K~stand** *m*
headstand. **K~steinpflaster** *nt*
cobble-stones *pl.* **K~tuch** *nt*
headscarf. **K~über** *adv* head fir
(*fig*) headlong. **K~wäsche** *f*
shampoo. **K~weh** *nt* headache
Kopie *f* -, -n copy. **k~ren** *vt* copy
Koppel¹ *f* -, -n enclosure; (*Pferde*
paddock
Koppel² *nt* -s,- (*Mil*) belt. **k~n** *vt*
couple
Koralle *f* -, -n coral
Korb *m* -[e]s,ˇe basket; jdm einen
K~ geben (*fig*) turn s.o. down.
K~ball *m* [kind of] netball
Kord *m* -s (*Tex*) corduroy
Kordel *f* -, -n cord
Korinthe *f* -, -n currant
Kork *m* -s,- cork. **K~en** *m* -s,-
cork. **K~enzieher** *m* -s,-
corkscrew
Korn *nt* -[e]s,ˇer grain, (*Samen-*)
seed; (*am Visier*) front sight
Körn|chen *nt* -s,- granule. **k~ig** *a*
granular
Körper *m* -s,- body; (*Geom*) solid
K~bau *m* build, physique.
k~behindert *a* physically
disabled. **k~lich** *a* physical;
<*Strafe*> corporal. **K~pflege** *f*
personal hygiene. **K~schaft** *f* -,
-en corporation, body
korrekt *a* correct. **K~or** *m* -s, -en
/-'toːrən/ proof-reader. **K~ur** *f* -,

-en correction. **K∼urabzug** *m* proof

Korrespon|dent(in) *m* -en, -en (*f* -, -nen) correspondent. **K∼denz** *f* -, -en correspondence

Korridor *m* -s, -e corridor

korrigieren *vt* correct

Korrosion *f* - corrosion

korrup|t *a* corrupt. **K∼tion** /-'tsio:n/ *f* - corruption

Korsett *nt* -[e]s, -e corset

koscher *a* kosher

Kosename *m* pet name

Kosmet|ik *f* - beauty culture. **K∼ika** *ntpl* cosmetics. **K∼ikerin** *f* -, -nen beautician. **k∼isch** *a* cosmetic; <*Chirurgie*> plastic

kosm|isch *a* cosmic. **K∼onaut(in)** *m* -en, -en (*f* -, -nen) cosmonaut

Kosmos *m* - cosmos

Kost *f* - food; (*Ernährung*) diet; (*Verpflegung*) board

kostbar *a* precious. **K∼keit** *f* -, -en treasure

kosten¹ *vt/i* (*haben*) **[von]** etw k∼ taste sth

kosten² *vt* cost; (*brauchen*) take; **wie viel kostet es?** how much is it? **K∼** *pl* expense *sg*, cost *sg*; (*Jur*) costs; **auf meine K∼** at my expense. **K∼[vor]anschlag** *m* estimate. **k∼los** *a* free ● *adv* free [of charge]

köstlich *a* delicious; (*entzückend*) delightful

Kostprobe *f* taste; (*fig*) sample

Kostüm *nt* -s, -e (*Theat*) costume; (*Verkleidung*) fancy dress; (*Schneider-*) suit. **k∼iert** *a* k∼iert **sein** be in fancy dress

Kot *m* -[e]s excrement

Kotelett /kɔt'lɛt/ *nt* -s, -s chop, cutlet. **K∼en** *pl* sideburns

Köter *m* -s,- (*pej*) dog

Kotflügel *m* (*Auto*) wing

kotzen *vi* (*haben*) 🗙 throw up

Krabbe *f* -, -n crab, shrimp

krabbeln *vi* (*sein*) crawl

Krach *m* -[e]s, ̈e din, racket; (*Knall*) crash; (🔲 *Streit*) row; (🔲 *Ruin*) crash. **k∼en** *vi* (*haben*) crash; **es hat gekracht** there was a bang/(🔲 *Unfall*) a crash ● (*sein*) break, crack; (*auftreffen*) crash (**gegen** into)

krächzen *vi* (*haben*) croak

Kraft *f* -, ̈e strength; (*Gewalt*) force; (*Arbeits-*) worker; **in/außer K∼** in/no longer in force. **K∼fahrer** *m* driver. **K∼fahrzeug** *nt* motor vehicle. **K∼fahrzeugbrief** *m* [vehicle] registration document

kräftig *a* strong; (*gut entwickelt*) sturdy; (*nahrhaft*) nutritious; (*heftig*) hard

kraft|los *a* weak. **K∼probe** *f* trial of strength. **K∼stoff** *m* (*Auto*) fuel. **K∼wagen** *m* motor car. **K∼werk** *nt* power station

Kragen *m* -s,- collar

Krähe *f* -, -n crow

krähen *vi* (*haben*) crow

Kralle *f* -, -n claw

Kram *m* -s 🔲 things *pl*, 🔲 stuff; (*Angelegenheiten*) business. **k∼en** *vi* (*haben*) rummage about (**in** + *dat* in; **nach** for)

Krampf *m* -[e]s, ̈e cramp. **K∼adern** *fpl* varicose veins. **k∼haft** *a* convulsive; (*verbissen*) desperate

Kran *m* -[e]s, ̈e (*Techn*) crane

Kranich *m* -s, -e (*Zool*) crane

krank *a* sick; <*Knie*, *Herz*> bad; **k∼ sein/werden** be/fall ill. **K∼e(r)** *m/f* sick man/woman, invalid; **die K∼en** the sick *pl*

kränken *vt* offend, hurt

Kranken|bett *nt* sick-bed. **K∼geld** *nt* sickness benefit. **K∼gymnast(in)** *m* -en, -en (*f* -, -nen) physiotherapist. **K∼gymnastik** *f* physiotherapy. **K∼haus** *nt* hospital. **K∼kasse** *f* health insurance scheme/(*Amt*) office. **K∼pflege** *f* nursing.

K

K~saal m [hospital] ward.
K~schein m certificate of entitlement to medical treatment.
K~schwester f nurse.
K~versicherung f health insurance. **K~wagen** m ambulance
Krankheit f -, -en illness, disease
kränklich a sickly
krank|melden vt sep jdn k~melden report s.o. sick; **sich** k~melden report sick
Kranz m -es,⁺e wreath
Krapfen m -s,- doughnut
Krater m -s,- crater
kratzen vt/i (haben) scratch.
K~er m -s,- scratch
Kraul nt -s (Sport) crawl. **k~en¹** vi (haben/sein) (Sport) do the crawl
kraulen² vt tickle; **sich am Kopf** k~ scratch one's head
kraus a wrinkled; <Haar> frizzy; (verworren) muddled. **K~e** f -, -n frill
kräuseln vt wrinkle; frizz <Haar->; gather <Stoff>; **sich** k~ wrinkle; (sich kringeln) curl; <Haar:> go frizzy
Kraut nt -[e]s, Kräuter herb; (SGer) cabbage; (Sauer-) sauerkraut
Krawall m -s, -e riot; (Lärm) row
Krawatte f -, -n [neck]tie
krea|tiv /krea'ti:f/ a creative.
K~tur f -, -en creature
Krebs m -es, -e crayfish; (Med) cancer; (Astr) Cancer
Kredit m -s, -e credit; (Darlehen) loan; **auf K~** on credit. **K~karte** f credit card
Kreid|e f - chalk. **k~ig** a chalky
kreieren /kre'i:rən/ vt create
Kreis m -es, -e circle; (Admin) district
kreischen vt/i (haben) screech; (schreien) shriek
Kreisel m -s,- [spinning] top
kreis|en vi (haben) circle; revolve (um around). **k~förmig** a circular. **K~lauf** m cycle; (Med)

circulation. **K~säge** f circular saw. **K~verkehr** m [traffic] roundabout
Krem f -, -s & m -s, -e cream
Krematorium nt -s, -ien crematorium
Krempe f -, -n [hat] brim
krempeln vt turn (nach oben up)
Krepp m -s, -s & -e crêpe
Krepppapier nt crêpe paper
Kresse f -, -n cress; (Kapuziner-) nasturtium
Kreta nt -s Crete
Kreuz nt -es, -e cross; (Kreuzung) intersection; (Mus) sharp; (Kartenspiel) clubs pl; (Anat) small of the back; **über K~** crosswise; **das K~ schlagen** cros oneself. **k~en** vt cross; **sich k~e** cross; <Straßen:> intersect; <Meinungen:> clash ● vi (haben/ sein) cruise. **K~fahrt** f (Naut) cruise. **K~gang** m cloister
kreuzig|en vt crucify. **K~ung** f -, -en crucifixion
Kreuz|otter f adder, common viper. **K~ung** f -, -en intersectio (Straßen-) crossroads sg.
K~verhör nt cross-examination
k~weise adv crosswise.
K~worträtsel nt crossword [puzzle]. **K~zug** m crusade
kribbe|lig a ▣ edgy. **k~n** vi (haben) tingle; (kitzeln) tickle
kriech|en† vi (sein) crawl; (fig) grovel (vor + dat to). **K~spur** f (Auto) crawler lane. **K~tier** nt reptile
Krieg m -[e]s, -e war
kriegen vt ▣ get; **ein Kind k~** have a baby
kriegs|beschädigt a war-disabled. **K~dienstverweigerer** m -s,- conscientious objector.
K~gefangene(r) m prisoner of war. **K~gefangenschaft** f captivity. **K~gericht** nt court martial. **K~list** f stratagem.

K~rat m council of war. **K~recht** nt martial law

Krimi m -s, -s 🎬 crime story/film. **K~nalität** f - crime; (*Vorkommen*) crime rate. **K~nalpolizei** f criminal investigation department. **K~nalroman** m crime novel. **k~nell** a criminal

Krippe f -, -n manger; (*Weihnachts-*) crib; (*Kinder-*) crèche. **K~nspiel** nt Nativity play

Krise f -, -n crisis

Kristall nt -s crystal; (*geschliffen*) cut glass

Kritik f -, -en criticism; (*Rezension*) review; **unter aller K~** 🎬 abysmal

Kriti|ker m -s, - critic; (*Rezensent*) reviewer. **k~sch** a critical. **k~sieren** vt criticize; review

kritzeln vt/i (*haben*) scribble

Krokodil nt -s, -e crocodile

Krokus m -, -[se] crocus

Krone f -, -n crown; (*Baum-*) top

krönen vt crown

Kronleuchter m chandelier

Krönung f -, -en coronation; (*fig: Höhepunkt*) crowning event

Kropf m -[e]s, ‿e (*Zool*) crop; (*Med*) goitre

Kröte f -, -n toad

Krücke f -, -n crutch

Krug m -[e]s, ‿e jug; (*Bier-*) tankard

Krümel m -s, - crumb. **k~ig** a crumbly. **k~n** vt crumble ● vi (*haben*) be crumbly

krumm a crooked; (*gebogen*) curved; (*verbogen*) bent

krümmen vt bend; crook <*Finger*>; **sich k~** bend; (*sich winden*) writhe; (*vor Lachen*) double up

Krümmung f -, -en bend, curve

Krüppel m -s, - cripple

Kruste f -, -n crust; (*Schorf*) scab

Kruzifix nt -es, -e crucifix

Kuba nt -s Cuba. **k~anisch** a Cuban

Kübel m -s, - tub; (*Eimer*) bucket; (*Techn*) skip

Küche f -, -n kitchen; (*Kochkunst*) cooking; **kalte/warme K~** cold/hot food

Kuchen m -s, - cake

Küchen|herd m cooker, stove. **K~maschine** f food processor, mixer. **K~schabe** f -, -n cockroach

Kuckuck m -s, -e cuckoo

Kufe f -, -n [sledge] runner

Kugel f -, -n ball; (*Geom*) sphere; (*Gewehr-*) bullet; (*Sport*) shot. **k~förmig** a spherical. **K~lager** nt ball-bearing. **k~n** vt/i (*haben*) roll; **sich k~n** (*vor Lachen*) fall about. **K~schreiber** m -s, -, ballpoint [pen]. **k~sicher** a bullet-proof. **K~stoßen** nt -s shot-putting

Kuh f -, ‿e cow

kühl a cool; (*kalt*) chilly. **K~box** f -, -en cool-box. **K~e** f - coolness; chilliness. **k~en** vt cool; refrigerate <*Lebensmittel*>; chill <*Wein*>. **K~er** m -s, -; (*Auto*) radiator. **K~erhaube** f bonnet. **K~fach** nt frozen-food compartment. **K~raum** m cold store. **K~schrank** m refrigerator. **K~truhe** f freezer. **K~wasser** nt [radiator] water

kühn a bold

Kuhstall m cowshed

Küken nt -s, - chick; (*Enten-*) duckling

Kulissen fpl (*Theat*) scenery sg; (*seitlich*) wings; **hinter den K~** (*fig*) behind the scenes

Kult m -[e]s, -e cult

kultivier|en vt cultivate. **k~t** a cultured

Kultur f -, -en culture. **K~beutel** m toiletbag. **k~ell** a cultural. **K~film** m documentary film

Kultusminister m Minister of Education and Arts

Kümmel m -s caraway; (Getränk) kümmel

Kummer m -s sorrow, grief; (Sorge) worry; (Ärger) trouble

kümmer|lich a puny; (dürftig) meagre; (armselig) wretched. **k~n** vt concern; **sich k~n um** look after; (sich befassen) concern oneself with; (beachten) take notice of

kummervoll a sorrowful

Kumpel m -s,- 🔲 mate

Kunde m -n, -n customer. **K~ndienst** m [after-sales] service

Kundgebung f -, -en (Pol) rally

kündig|en vt cancel <Vertrag>; give notice of withdrawal for <Geld>; give notice to quit <Wohnung>; **seine Stellung k~en** give [in one's] notice ● vi (haben) give [in one's] notice; **jdm k~en** give s.o. notice. **K~ung** f -, -en cancellation; notice [of withdrawal/dismissal/to quit]; (Entlassung) dismissal. **K~ungsfrist** f period of notice

Kund|in f -, -nen customer. **K~schaft** f - clientele, customers pl

künftig a future ● adv in future

Kunst f -,¨e art; (Können) skill. **K~faser** f synthetic fibre. **K~galerie** f art gallery. **K~geschichte** f history of art. **K~gewerbe** nt arts and crafts pl. **K~griff** m trick

Künstler m -s,- artist; (Könner) master. **K~in** f -, -nen [woman] artist. **k~isch** a artistic

künstlich a artificial

Kunst|stoff m plastic. **K~stück** nt trick; (große Leistung) feat. **k~voll** a artistic; (geschickt) skilful

kunterbunt a multicoloured; (gemischt) mixed

Kupfer nt -s copper

Kupon /ku'põ:/ m -s, -s voucher; (Zins-) coupon; (Stoff-) length

Kuppe f -, -n [rounded] top

Kuppel f -, -n dome

kupp|eln vt couple (**an** + acc **to**) ● vi (haben) (Auto) operate the clutch. **K~lung** f -, -en coupling; (Auto) clutch

Kur f -, -en course of treatment, cure

Kür f -, -en (Sport) free exercise; (Eislauf) free programme

Kurbel f -, -n crank. **K~welle** f crankshaft

Kürbis m -ses, -se pumpkin

Kurier m -s, -e courier

kurieren vt cure

kurios a curious, odd. **K~ität** f -, -en oddness; (Objekt) curiosity

Kurort m health resort; (Badeort) spa

Kurs m -es, -e course; (Aktien-) price. **K~buch** nt timetable

kursieren vi (haben) circulate

kursiv a italic ● adv in italics. **K~schrift** f italics pl

Kursus m -,Kurse course

Kurswagen m through carriage

Kurtaxe f visitors' tax

Kurve f -, -n curve; (Straßen-) bend

kurz a short; (knapp) brief; (rasch) quick; (schroff) curt; **k~e Hosen** shorts; **vor k~em** a short time ago; **seit k~em** lately; **den Kürzeren ziehen** get the worst of it; **k~ vor** shortly before; **sich k~ fassen** be brief; **k~ und gut** in short; **zu k~ kommen** get less than one's fair share. **k~ärmelig** a short-sleeved. **k~atmig** a **k~atmig sein** be short of breath

Kürze f - shortness; (Knappheit) brevity; **in K~** shortly. **k~n** vt shorten; (verringern) cut

kurzfristig a short-term ● adv at short notice

kürzlich adv recently

Kurz|meldung f newsflash.
K~schluss m short circuit.
K~schrift f shorthand. **k~sichtig**
a short-sighted. **K~sichtigkeit** f -
short-sightedness.
K~streckenrakete f short-range
missile
Kürzung f -, -en shortening;
(Verringerung) cut (gen in)
Kurz|waren fpl haberdashery sg.
K~welle f short wave
uscheln (sich) vr snuggle (**an** +
acc up to)
Kusine f -, -n [female] cousin
Kuss m -es,-̈e kiss
küssen vt/i (haben) kiss; **sich k~**
kiss
Küste f -, -n coast
Küster m -s,- verger
Kutsch|e f -, -n [horse-drawn]
carriage/(geschlossen) coach.
K~er m -s,- coachman, driver
Kutte f -, -n (Relig) habit
Kutter m -s,- (Naut) cutter
Kuvert /ku've:ɐ̯/ nt -s, -s envelope

_abor nt -s, -s & -e laboratory.
L~ant(in) m -en, -en (f -, -nen)
laboratory assistant
_abyrinth nt -[e]s, -e maze,
labyrinth
_ache f -, -n puddle; (Blut-) pool
ächeln vi (haben) smile. **L~** nt -s
smile. **l~d** a smiling
achen vi (haben) laugh. **L~** nt -s
laugh; (Gelächter) laughter
ächerlich a ridiculous; **sich l~**
machen make a fool of oneself.
L~keit f -, -en ridiculousness;
(Kleinigkeit) triviality

Lachs m -es, -e salmon
Lack m -[e]s, -e varnish; (Japan-)
lacquer; (Auto) paint. **l~en** vt
varnish. **l~ieren** vt varnish;
(spritzen) spray. **L~schuhe** mpl
patent-leather shoes
laden† vt load; (Electr) charge;
(Jur: vor-) summon
Laden m -s,-̈ shop; (Fenster-)
shutter. **L~dieb** m shop-lifter.
L~schluss m [shop] closing-
time. **L~tisch** m counter
Laderaum m (Naut) hold
lädieren vt damage
Ladung f -, -en load; (Naut, Aviat)
cargo; (elektrische) charge
Lage f -, -n position, situation;
(Schicht) layer; **nicht in der L~**
sein not be in a position (**zu** to)
Lager nt -s,- camp; (L~haus)
warehouse; (Vorrat) stock;
(Techn) bearing; (Erz-, Ruhe-)
bed; (eines Tieres) lair; [**nicht**] **auf**
L~ [not] in stock. **L~haus** nt
warehouse. **l~n** vt store; (legen)
lay; **sich l~n** settle. **L~raum** m
store-room. **L~ung** f - storage
Lagune f -, -n lagoon
lahm a lame. **l~en** vi (haben) be
lame
lähmen vt paralyse
Lähmung f -, -en paralysis
Laib m -[e]s, -e loaf
Laich m -[e]s (Zool) spawn
Laie m -n, -n layman; (Theat)
amateur. **l~nhaft** a amateurish
Laken nt -s,- sheet
Lakritze f - liquorice
lallen vt/i (haben) mumble;
<Baby:> babble
Lametta nt -s tinsel
Lamm nt -[e]s,-̈er lamb
Lampe f -, -n lamp; (Decken-,
Wand-) light; (Glüh-) bulb.
L~nfieber nt stage fright
Lampion /lam'piɔ̃/ m -s, -s
Chinese lantern
Land nt -[e]s,-̈er country; (Fest-)
land; (Bundes-) state, Land;

L

(*Aust*) province; **auf dem L~e** in the country; **an L~ gehen** (*Naut*) go ashore. **L~arbeiter** *m* agricultural worker. **L~ebahn** *f* runway. **l~en** *vt/i* (*sein*) land; (🛈 *gelangen*) end up
Ländereien *pl* estates
Länderspiel *nt* international
Landesverrat *m* treason
Landkarte *f* map
ländlich *a* rural
Land|schaft *f* -, **-en** scenery; (*Geog, Kunst*) landscape; (*Gegend*) country[side]. **l~schaftlich** *a* scenic; (*regional*) regional. **L~streicher** *m* -s,- tramp. **L~tag** *m* state/(*Aust*) provincial parliament
Landung *f* -, **-en** landing
Land|vermesser *m* -s,- surveyor. **L~weg** *m* country lane; **auf dem L~weg** overland. **L~wirt** *m* farmer. **L~wirtschaft** *f* agriculture; (*Hof*) farm. **l~wirtschaftlich** *a* agricultural
lang[1] *adv & prep* (+ *preceding acc or preceding* **an** + *gen od am Fluss* **l~** along the river
lang[2] *a* long; (*groß*) tall; **seit l~em** for a long time ●*adv* **eine Stunde l~** for an hour; **mein Leben l~** all my life. **l~ärmelig** *a* long-sleeved. **l~atmig** *a* long-winded. **l~e** *adv* a long time; <*schlafen*> late; **schon l~e** [for] a long time; (*zurückliegend*) a long time ago; **l~e nicht** not for a long time; (*bei weitem nicht*) nowhere near
Länge *f* -, **-n** length; (*Geog*) longitude; **der L~nach** lengthways
Läng|engrad *m* degree of longitude. **l~er** *a & adv* longer; (*längere Zeit*) [for] some time
Langeweile *f* - boredom; **L~ haben** be bored
lang|fristig *a* long-term; <*Vorhersage*> long-range. **l~jährig** *a* long-standing; <*Erfahrung*> long

länglich *a* oblong; **l~ rund** oval
längs *adv & prep* (+ *gen/dat*) along; (*der Länge nach*) lengthways
lang|sam *a* slow. **L~samkeit** *f* - slowness
längst *adv* [schon] **l~** for a long time; (*zurückliegend*) a long time ago; **l~ nicht** nowhere near
Lang|strecken- *pref* long-distance; (*Mil, Aviat*) long-range
l~weilen *vt* bore; **sich l~weilen** b bored. **l~weilig** *a* boring
Lanze *f* -, **-n** lance
Lappalie /la'pa:liə/ *f* -, **-n** trifle
Lappen *m* -s,- cloth; (*Anat*) lobe
Lärche *f* -, **-n** larch
Lärm *m* -s noise. **l~end** *a* noisy
Larve /'larfə/ *f* -, **-n** larva; (*Maske* mask
lasch *a* listless; (*schlaff*) limp
Lasche *f* -, **-n** tab, flap
Laser /'le:-, 'la:zɐ/ *m* -s,- laser

lassen†
● *transitive verb*
····▸ (+ *inf: veranlassen*) **etw tun lassen** have *or* get sth done. **jdn etw tun lassen** make s.o. do sth.; get s.o. to do sth. **sich** *dat* **die Haare schneiden lassen** have *or* get one's hair cut. **jdn warten lassen** make *or* let s.o. wait; keep s.o. waiting. **jdn grüßen lassen** send one's regards to s.o **jdn kommen/rufen lassen** send fo s.o.
····▸ (+ *inf: erlauben*) let; allow; (*hineinlassen/herauslassen*) let *or* allow (**in** + *acc* into, **aus** + *dat* out of). **jdn etw tun lassen** let s.o do sth; allow s.o. to do sth. **er ließ mich nicht ausreden** he didn' let me finish [what I was saying]
····▸ (*belassen, bleiben lassen*) leave. **jdn in Frieden lassen** leave s.o. in peace. **etw ungesagt lasse** leave sth unsaid

···▸ (*unterlassen*) stop. **das Rauchen lassen** stop smoking. **er kann es nicht lassen, sie zu quälen** he can't stop *or* he is forever tormenting her

···▸ (*überlassen*) **jdm etw lassen** let s.o. have sth

···▸ (*als Aufforderung*) **lass/lasst uns gehen/fahren!** let's go!

● *reflexive verb*

···▸ **das lässt sich machen** that can be done. **das lässt sich nicht beweisen** it can't be proved. **die Tür lässt sich leicht öffnen** the door opens easily

● *intransitive verb*

···▸ Ⓘ **Lass mal. Ich mache das schon** Leave it. I'll do it

.ässig *a* casual. **L~keit** *f* - casualness

.asso *nt* -s, -s lasso

.ast *f* -, -en load; (*Gewicht*) weight; (*fig*) burden; **L~en** charges; (*Steuern*) taxes. **L~auto** *nt* lorry. **l~en** *vi* (*haben*) weigh heavily/(*liegen*) rest (**auf** + *dat* on)

.aster[1] *m* -s,- Ⓘ lorry

.aster[2] *nt* -s,- vice

.äster|n *vt* blaspheme ● *vi* (*haben*) make disparaging remarks (**über** + *acc* about). **L~ung** *f* -, -en blasphemy

.ästig *a* troublesome; **l~ sein/ werden** be/become a nuisance

.ast|kahn *m* barge. **L~[kraft]wagen** *m* lorry

.atein *nt* -[s] Latin. **L~amerika** *nt* Latin America. **l~isch** *a* Latin

.aterne *f* -, -n lantern; (*Straßen-*) street lamp. **L~npfahl** *m* lamp-post

.atschen *vi* (*sein*) Ⓘ traipse

.atte *f* -, -n slat; (*Tor-, Hochsprung-*) bar

.atz *m* -es,"e bib

.ätzchen *nt* -s,- [baby's] bib

.atzhose *f* dungarees *pl*

Laub *nt* -[e]s leaves *pl*; (*L~werk*) foliage. **L~baum** *m* deciduous tree

Laube *f* -, -n summer-house

Laub|säge *f* fretsaw. **L~wald** *m* deciduous forest

Lauch *m* -[e]s leeks *pl*

Lauer *f* **auf der L~ liegen** lie in wait. **l~n** *vi* (*haben*) lurk; **l~n auf** (+ *acc*) lie in wait for

Lauf *m* -[e]s, **Läufe** run; (*Laufen*) running; (*Verlauf*) course; (*Wett-*) race; (*Sport: Durchgang*) heat; (*Gewehr-*) barrel; **im L~[e]** (+ *gen*) in the course of. **L~bahn** *f* career. **l~en**† *vi* (*sein*) run; (*zu Fuß gehen*) walk; (*gelten*) be valid; **Ski/Schlittschuh l~en** ski/ skate. **l~end** *a* running; (*gegenwärtig*) current; (*regelmäßig*) regular; **auf dem L~enden sein** be up to date ● *adv* continually

Läufer *m* -s,- (*Person, Teppich*) runner; (*Schach*) bishop

Lauf|gitter *nt* play-pen. **L~masche** *f* ladder. **L~zettel** *m* circular

Lauge *f* -, -n soapy water

Laun|e *f* -, -n mood; (*Einfall*) whim; **guter L~e sein, gute L~e haben** be in a good mood. **l~isch** *a* moody

Laus *f* -,**Läuse** louse; (*Blatt-*) greenfly

lauschen *vi* (*haben*) listen

laut *a* loud; (*geräuschvoll*) noisy; **l~ lesen** read aloud; **l~er stellen** turn up ● *prep* (+ *gen/dat*) according to. **L~** *m* -es, -e sound

Laute *f* -, -n (*Mus*) lute

lauten *vi* (*haben*) <*Text:*> run, read

läuten *vt/i* (*haben*) ring

lauter *a* pure; (*ehrlich*) honest; <*Wahrheit*> plain ● *a inv* sheer; (*nichts als*) nothing but

laut|hals *adv* at the top of one's voice, <*lachen*> out loud. **l~los** *a*

L

silent, *<Stille>* hushed. **L~schrift**
f phonetics *pl*. **L~sprecher** *m*
loudspeaker. **L~stärke** *f* volume
lauwarm *a* lukewarm
Lava *f* -, -ven lava
Lavendel *m* -s lavender
lavieren *vi* (*haben*) manœuvre
Lawine *f* -, -n avalanche
Lazarett *nt* -[e]s, -e military
hospital
leasen /'li:sən/ *vt* rent
Lebehoch *nt* cheer
leben *vt/i* (*haben*) live (**von** on);
leb wohl! farewell! **L~** *nt* -s,- life,
(*Treiben*) bustle; **am L~** alive.
l~d *a* living
lebendig *a* live; (*lebhaft*) lively;
(*anschaulich*) vivid; **l~ sein** be
alive. **L~keit** *f* - liveliness;
vividness
Lebens|abend *m* old age. **L~alter**
nt age. **l~fähig** *a* viable.
L~gefahr *f* mortal danger; **in**
L~gefahr in mortal danger;
<Patient> critically ill.
l~gefährlich *a* extremely
dangerous; *<Verletzung>* critical.
L~haltungskosten *pl* cost of
living *sg*. **l~länglich** *a* life ...
● *adv* for life. **L~lauf** *m*
curriculum vitae. **L~mittel** *ntpl*
food *sg*. **L~mittelgeschäft** *nt*
food shop. **L~mittelhändler** *m*
grocer. **L~retter** *m* rescuer; (*beim*
Schwimmen) life-guard.
L~unterhalt *m* livelihood; **seinen**
L~unterhalt verdienen earn one's
living. **L~versicherung** *f* life
assurance. **L~wandel** *m* conduct.
l~wichtig *a* vital. **L~zeit** *f* **auf**
L~zeit for life
Leber *f* -, -n liver. **L~fleck** *m* mole
Lebe|wesen *nt* living being.
L~wohl *nt* -s, -s & -e farewell
leb|haft *a* lively; *<Farbe>* vivid.
L~kuchen *m* gingerbread. **l~los**
a lifeless. **L~zeiten** *fpl* **zu jds**
L~zeiten in s.o.'s lifetime

leck *a* leaking. **L~** *nt* -s, -s leak.
l~en¹ *vi* (*haben*) leak
lecken² *vi* (*haben*) lick
lecker *a* tasty. **L~ bissen** *m*
delicacy
Leder *nt* -s,- leather
ledig *a* single
leer *a* empty; (*unbesetzt*) vacant;
l~ laufen (*Auto*) idle. **l~en** *vt*
empty; **sich l~en** empty. **L~lauf**
m (*Auto*) neutral. **L~ung** *f* -, -en
(*Post*) collection
legal *a* legal. **l~isieren** *vt* legalize
L~ität *f* - legality
Legas|thenie *f* - dyslexia
L~theniker *m* -s,- dyslexic
legen *vt* put; (*hin-, ver-*) lay; set
<Haare>; **sich l~** lie down;
(*nachlassen*) subside
Legende *f* -, -n legend
leger /le'ʒeːɐ̯/ *a* casual
Legierung *f* -, -en alloy
Legion *f* -, -en legion
Legislative *f* - legislature
legitim *a* legitimate. **L~ität** *f* -
legitimacy
Lehm *m* -s clay
Lehne *f* -, -n (*Rücken-*) back;
(*Arm-*) arm. **l~en** *vt* lean (**an** +
acc against); **sich l~en** lean (**an** +
acc against) ● *vi* (*haben*) be
leaning (**an** + *acc against*)
Lehr|buch *nt* textbook. **L~e** *f* -, -n
apprenticeship; (*Anschauung*)
doctrine; (*Theorie*) theory;
(*Wissenschaft*) science;
(*Erfahrung*) lesson. **l~en** *vt/i*
(*haben*) teach. **L~er** *m* -s,-
teacher; (*Fahr-*) instructor.
L~erin *f* -, -nen teacher.
L~erzimmer *nt* staff-room.
L~fach *nt* (*Sch*) subject. **L~gang**
m course. **L~kraft** *f* teacher.
L~ling *m* -s, -e apprentice;
(*Auszubildender*) trainee. **L~plan**
m syllabus. **l~reich** *a* instructive
L~stelle *f* apprenticeship.
L~stuhl *m* (*Univ*) chair. **L~zeit** *f*
apprenticeship

Leib m -es, -er body; (*Bauch*) belly. **L~eserziehung** f (*Sch*) physical education. **L~gericht** nt favourite dish. **l~lich** a physical; (*blutsverwandt*) real, natural. **L~wächter** m bodyguard

Leiche f -, -n [dead] body; corpse. **L~nbestatter** m -s,- undertaker. **L~nhalle** f mortuary. **L~nwagen** m hearse. **L~nzug** m funeral procession, cortège

Leichnam m -s, -e [dead] body

leicht a light; <*Stoff*> lightweight; (*gering*) slight; (*mühelos*) easy; jdm l~ fallen be easy for s.o.; etw l~ machen make sth easy (**dat** for); **es sich** (*dat*) l~ machen take the easy way out; etw l~ nehmen (*fig*) take sth lightly. **L~athletik** f [track and field] athletics sg. **L~gewicht** nt (*Boxen*) lightweight. **l~gläubig** a gullible. **l~hin** adv casually. **L~igkeit** f - lightness; (*Mühelosigkeit*) ease; (*L~sein*) easiness; **mit L~igkeit** with ease. **L~sinn** m carelessness; recklessness; (*Frivolität*) frivolity. **l~sinnig** a careless; (*unvorsichtig*) reckless

Leid nt -[e]s sorrow, grief; (*Böses*) harm; **es tut mir L~** I am sorry; **er tut mir L~** I feel sorry for him. l~ a jdn/etw l~ sein/werden be/get tired of s.o./sth

Leide|form f passive. **l~n†** vt/i (*haben*) suffer (**an** + *dat* from); **jdn/etw nicht l~n können** dislike s.o./sth. **L~n** nt -s,- suffering; (*Med*) complaint; (*Krankheit*) disease. **l~nd** a suffering. **L~nschaft** f -, -en passion. **l~nschaftlich** a passionate

leider adv unfortunately; l~er ja/ nicht I'm afraid so/not

Leier kasten m barrel-organ. **l~n** vt/i (*haben*) wind; (*herunter-*) drone out

Leih|e f -, -n loan. **l~en†** vt lend; **sich** (*dat*) etw l~en borrow sth.

L~gabe f loan. **L~gebühr** f rental; lending charge. **L~haus** nt pawnshop. **L~wagen** m hire-car. **l~weise** adv on loan

Leim m -s glue. **l~en** vt glue

Leine f -, -n rope; (*Wäsche-*) line; (*Hunde-*) lead, leash

Lein|en nt -s linen. **L~wand** f linen; (*Kunst*) canvas; (*Film-*) screen

leise a quiet; <*Stimme, Berührung*> soft; (*schwach*) faint; (*leicht*) light; l~r stellen turn down

Leiste f -, -n strip; (*Holz-*) batten; (*Anat*) groin

leist|en vt achieve, accomplish; **sich** (*dat*) etw l~en treat oneself to sth; (**I** *anstellen*) get up to sth; **ich kann es mir nicht l~en** I can't afford it. **L~ung** f -, -en achievement; (*Sport, Techn*) performance; (*Produktion*) output; (*Zahlung*) payment

Leit|artikel m leader, editorial. **l~en** vt run, manage; (*an-/ hinführen*) lead; (*Mus, Techn, Phys*) conduct; (*lenken, schicken*) direct. **l~end** a leading; <*Posten*> executive

Leiter¹ f -, -n ladder

Leit|er² m -s,- director; (*Comm*) manager; (*Führer*) leader; (*Mus, Phys*) conductor. **L~erin** f -, -nen director; manageress; leader. **L~planke** f crash barrier. **L~spruch** m motto. **L~ung** f -, -en (*Führung*) direction; (*Comm*) management; (*Aufsicht*) control; (*Electr: Schnur*) lead, flex; (*Kabel*) cable; (*Telefon-*) line; (*Rohr-*) pipe; (*Haupt-*) main. **L~ungswasser** nt tap water

Lektion /-'tsi̯o:n/ f -, -en lesson

Lekt|or m -s, -en /-'to:rən/, **L~orin** f -, -nen (*Univ*) assistant lecturer; (*Verlags-*) editor. **L~üre** f -, -n reading matter

Lende f -, -n loin

lenk|en vt guide; (steuern) steer; (regeln) control; **jds Aufmerksamkeit auf sich** (acc) **l~en** attract s.o.'s attention. **L~rad** nt steering-wheel. **L~stange** f handlebars pl. **L~ung** f - steering

Leopard m -en, -en leopard

Lepra f - leprosy

Lerche f -, -n lark

lernen vt/i (haben) learn; (für die Schule) study

Lesb|ierin /'lɛsbiərɪn/ f -, -nen lesbian. **l~isch** a lesbian

les|en† vt/i (haben) read; (Univ) lecture ●vt pick, gather. **L~en** nt -s reading. **L~er(in)** m -s,- (f -, -nen) reader. **l~erlich** a legible. **L~ezeichen** nt bookmark

lethargisch a lethargic

Lettland nt - Latvia

letzt|e(r,s) a last; (neueste) latest; **in l~er Zeit** recently; **l~en Endes** in the end. **l~ens** adv recently; (zuletzt) lastly. **l~ere(r,s)** a the latter; **der/die/das L~ere** the latter

Leucht|e f -, -n light. **l~en** vi (haben) shine. **l~end** a shining. **L~er** m -s,- candlestick. **L~feuer** nt beacon. **L~rakete** f flare. **L~reklame** f neon sign. **L~röhre** f fluorescent tube. **L~turm** m lighthouse

leugnen vt deny

Leukämie f - leukaemia

Leumund m -s reputation

Leute pl people; (Mil) men; (Arbeiter) workers

Leutnant m -s, -s second lieutenant

Lexikon nt -s, -ka encyclopaedia; (Wörterbuch) dictionary

Libanon (der) -s Lebanon

Libelle f -, -n dragonfly

liberal a (Pol) Liberal

Libyen nt -s Libya

Licht nt -[e]s, -er light; (Kerze) candle; **L~ machen** turn on the light. **l~** a bright; (Med) lucid; (spärlich) sparse. **L~bild** nt [passport] photograph; (Dia) slide. **L~blick** m (fig) ray of hope. **l~en** vt thin out; **den Anker l~en** (Naut) weigh anchor; **sich l~en** become less dense; thin.

L~hupe f headlight flasher; **die L~hupe betätigen** flash one's headlights. **L~maschine** f dynamo. **L~ung** f -, -en clearing

Lid nt -[e]s, -er [eye]lid. **L~schatten** m eye-shadow

lieb a dear; (nett) nice; (artig) good; **jdn l~ haben** be fond of s.o.; (lieben) love s.o.; **es wäre mir l~er** I should prefer it (wenn if)

Liebe f -, -n love. **l~n** vt love; (mögen) like; **sich l~n** love each other; (körperlich) make love. **l~nd** a loving. **l~nswert** a lovable. **l~nswürdig** a kind. **l~nswürdigerweise** adv very kindly

lieber adv rather; (besser) better; **l~ mögen** like better; **ich trinke l~ Tee** I prefer tea

Liebes|brief m love letter. **L~dienst** m favour. **L~kummer** m heartache. **L~paar** nt [pair of] lovers pl

lieb|evoll a loving, affectionate. **L~haber** m -s,- lover; (Sammler) collector. **L~haberei** f -, -en hobby. **L~kosung** f -, -en caress. **l~lich** a lovely; (sanft) gentle; (süß) sweet. **L~ling** m -s, -e darling; (Bevorzugte) favourite. **L~lings-** pref favourite. **l~los** a loveless; <Eltern> uncaring; (unfreundlich) unkind. **L~schaft** f -, -en [love] affair. **l~ste(r,s)** a dearest; (bevorzugt) favourite ●adv **am l~sten** best [of all]; **jdn/ etw am l~sten mögen** like s.o./sth best [of all]. **L~ste(r)** m/f beloved; (Schatz) sweetheart

Lied nt -[e]s, -er song

liederlich a slovenly; (unordentlich) untidy. **L~keit** f - slovenliness; untidiness

ieferant *m* -en, -en supplier
iefer|bar *a* (*Comm*) available.
l~n *vt* supply; (*zustellen*) deliver;
(*hervorbringen*) yield. **L~ung** *f* -,
-en delivery; (*Sendung*)
consignment
iege *f* -, -n couch. **l~n†** *vi*
(*haben*) lie; (*gelegen sein*) be
situated; **l~n bleiben** remain lying
[there]; (*im Bett*) stay in bed;
<*Ding:*> be left; <*Schnee:*> settle;
<*Arbeit:*> remain undone;
(*zurückgelassen werden*) be left
behind; **l~n lassen** leave;
(*zurücklassen*) leave behind;
(*nicht fortführen*) leave undone;
l~n an (+ *dat*) (*fig*) be due to;
(*abhängen*) depend on; **jdm [nicht]
l~n** [not] suit s.o.; **mir liegt viel
daran** it is very important to me.
L~stuhl *m* deck-chair. **L~stütz**
m -es, -e press-up, (*Amer*) push-
up. **L~wagen** *m* couchette car
Lift *m* -[e]s, -e & -s lift
Liga *f* -, -gen league
Likör *m* -s, -e liqueur
lila *inv a* mauve; (*dunkel*) purple
Lilie /'li:liə/ *f* -, -n lily
Liliputaner(in) *m* -s,- (*f* -, -nen)
dwarf
Limo *f* -, -[s] 🗓, **L~nade** *f* -, -n
fizzy drink; lemonade
Limousine /limu'zi:nə/ *f* -, -n
saloon
lind *a* mild
Linde *f* -, -n lime tree
linder|n *vt* relieve, ease. **L~ung** *f* -
relief
Lineal *nt* -s, -e ruler
Linie /-iə/ *f* -, -n line; (*Zweig*)
branch; (*Bus-*) route; **L~ 4**
number 4 [bus/tram]; **in erster L~**
primarily. **L~nflug** *m* scheduled
flight. **L~nrichter** *m* linesman
lin[i]iert *a* lined, ruled
Link|e *f* -n, -n left side; (*Hand*) left
hand; (*Boxen*) left; **die L~e** (*Pol*)
the left. **l~e(r,s)** *a* left; (*Pol*)
leftwing; **l~e Masche** purl

links *adv* on the left; (*bei Stoff*) on
the wrong side; (*verkehrt*) inside
out; **l~ stricken** purl.
L~händer(in) *m* -s,- (*f* -, -nen)
lefthander. **l~händig** *a & adv*
lefthanded
Linoleum /-leum/ *nt* -s lino,
linoleum
Linse *f* -, -n lens; (*Bot*) lentil
Lippe *f* -, -n lip. **L~nstift** *m*
lipstick
Liquid|ation /-'tsi̯o:n/ *f* -, -en
liquidation. **l~ieren** *vt* liquidate
lispeln *vt/i* (*haben*) lisp
List *f* -, -en trick, ruse
Liste *f* -, -n list
listig *a* cunning, crafty
Litanei *f* -, -en litany
Litauen *nt* -s Lithuania
Liter *m & nt* -s,- litre
Literatur *f* - literature
Liturgie *f* -, -n liturgy
Litze *f* -, -n braid
Lizenz *f* -, -en licence
Lob *nt* -[e]s praise
Lobby /'lɔbi/ *f* - (*Pol*) lobby
loben *vt* praise
löblich *a* praiseworthy
Lobrede *f* eulogy
Loch *nt* -[e]s,¨er hole. **l~en** *vt*
punch a hole/holes in; punch
<*Fahrkarte*>. **L~er** *m* -s,- punch
löcherig *a* full of holes
Locke *f* -, -n curl. **l~n¹** *vt* curl; **sich
l~n** curl
locken² *vt* lure, entice; (*reizen*)
tempt. **l~d** *a* tempting
Lockenwickler *m* -s,- curler;
(*Rolle*) roller
locker *a* loose; <*Seil*> slack;
<*Erde*> light; (*zwanglos*) casual;
(*zu frei*) lax. **l~n** *vt* loosen;
slacken <*Seil*>; break up
<*Boden*>; relax <*Griff*>; **sich l~n**
become loose; <*Seil:*> slacken;
(*sich entspannen*) relax
lockig *a* curly
Lockmittel *nt* bait
Loden *m* -s (*Tex*) loden

L

Löffel *m* -s,- spoon; (*L∼ voll*) spoonful. **l∼n** *vt* spoon up

Logarithmus *m* -, -men logarithm

Logbuch *nt* (*Naut*) log-book

Loge /'lo:ʒə/ *f* -, -n lodge; (*Theat*) box

Log|ik *f* - logic. **l∼isch** *a* logical

Logo *nt* -s, -s logo

Lohn *m* -[e]s,"e wages *pl*, pay; (*fig*) reward. **L∼empfänger** *m* wage-earner. **l∼en** *vi/r* (*haben*) [**sich**] **l∼en** be worth it *or* worth while ●*vt* be worth. (*befriedigend*) rewarding. **L∼erhöhung** *f* [pay] rise. **L∼steuer** *f* income tax

Lok *f* -, -s Ⓔ = Lokomotive

Lokal *nt* -s, -e restaurant; (*Trink-*) bar

Lokomotiv|e *f* -, -n engine, locomotive. **L∼führer** *m* engine driver

London *nt* -s London. **L∼er** *a* London ... ●*m* -s,- Londoner

Lorbeer *m* -s, -en laurel. **L∼blatt** *nt* (*Culin*) bay-leaf

Lore *f* -, -n (*Rail*) truck

Los *nt* -es, -e lot; (*Lotterie-*) ticket; (*Schicksal*) fate

los *pred a* **los sein** be loose; **jdn/ etw los sein** be rid of s.o./sth; **was ist [mit ihm] los?** what's the matter [with him]? ●*adv* **los!** go on! **Achtung, fertig, los!** ready, steady, go!

lösbar *a* soluble

losbinden† *vt sep* untie

Lösch|blatt *nt* sheet of blotting-paper. **l∼en** *vt* put out, extinguish; quench <*Durst*>; blot <*Tinte*>; (*tilgen*) cancel; (*streichen*) delete

Löschfahrzeug *nt* fire-engine

lose *a* loose

Lösegeld *nt* ransom

losen *vt* (*haben*) draw lots (**um** for)

lösen *vt* undo; (*lockern*) loosen; (*entfernen*) detach; (*klären*) solve;

(*auflösen*) dissolve; cancel <*Vertrag*>; break off <*Beziehung*>; (*kaufen*) buy; **sich l∼** come off; (*sich trennen*) detach oneself/itself; (*lose werden*) come undone; (*sich klären*) resolve itself; (*sich auflösen*) dissolve

los|fahren† *vi sep* (*sein*) start; <*Auto:*> drive off; **l∼fahren auf** (+ *acc*) head for. **l∼gehen**† *vi sep* (*sein*) set off; (Ⓔ *anfangen*) start; <*Bombe:*> go off; **l∼gehen auf** (+ *acc*) head for; (*fig: angreifen*) go for. **l∼kommen**† *vi sep* (*sein*) get away (**von** from). **l∼lassen**† *vt sep* let go of; (*freilassen*) release

löslich *a* soluble

los|lösen *vt sep* detach; **sich l∼lösen** become detached; (*fig*) break away (**von** from). **l∼machen** *vt sep* detach; untie. **l∼reißen**† *vt sep* tear off; **sich l∼reißen** break free; (*fig*) tear oneself away (**von** from). **l∼schicken** *vt sep* send off. **l∼sprechen**† *vt sep* absolve (**von** from)

Losung *f* -, -en (*Pol*) slogan; (*Mil*) password

Lösung *f* -, -en solution. **L∼smittel** *nt* solvent

loswerden† *vt sep* get rid of

Lot *nt* -[e]s, -e perpendicular; (*Blei-*) plumb[-bob]. **l∼en** *vt* plumb

löt|en *vt* solder. **L∼lampe** *f* blow-lamp

lotrecht *a* perpendicular

Lotse *m* -n, -n (*Naut*) pilot. **l∼n** *vt* (*Naut*) pilot; (*fig*) guide

Lotterie *f* -, -n lottery

Lotto *nt* -s, -s lotto; (*Lotterie*) lottery

Löw|e *m* -n, -n lion; (*Astr*) Leo. **L∼enzahn** *m* (*Bot*) dandelion. **L∼in** *f* -, -nen lioness

loyal /loa'ja:l/ *a* loyal. **L∼ität** *f* - loyalty

Luchs *m* -es, -e lynx

.ücke *f* -, -n gap. **l~nhaft** *a* incomplete; <*Wissen*> patchy. **l~nlos** *a* complete; <*Folge*> unbroken

.uder *nt* -s,- ⊠ (*Frau*) bitch

.uft *f* -,⸚e air; **tief L~ holen** take a deep breath; **in die L~ gehen** explode. **L~angriff** *m* air raid. **L~aufnahme** *f* aerial photograph. **L~ballon** *m* balloon. **L~blase** *f* air bubble. **L~druck** *m* atmospheric pressure

üften *vt* air; raise <*Hut*>; reveal <*Geheimnis*>

Luft|fahrt *f* aviation. **L~fahrtgesellschaft** *f* airline. **L~gewehr** *nt* airgun. **l~ig** *a* airy; <*Kleid*> light. **L~kissenfahrzeug** *nt* hovercraft. **L~krieg** *m* aerial warfare. **l~leer** *a* **l~leerer Raum** vacuum. **L~linie** *f* 100 km **L~linie** 100 km as the crow flies. **L~matratze** *f* air-bed, inflatable mattress. **L~pirat** *m* hijacker. **L~post** *f* airmail. **L~röhre** *f* windpipe. **L~schiff** *nt* airship. **L~schlange** *f* [paper] streamer. **L~schutzbunker** *m* air-raid shelter

Lüftung *f* - ventilation

Luft|veränderung *f* change of air. **L~waffe** *f* air force. **L~zug** *m* draught

Lüg|e *f* -, -n lie. **l~en†** *vt/i* (*haben*) lie. **L~ner(in)** *m* -s,- (*f* -, -nen) liar. **l~nerisch** *a* untrue; <*Person*> untruthful

Luke *f* -, -n hatch; (*Dach-*) skylight

Lümmel *m* -s,- lout

Lump *m* -en, -en scoundrel. **L~en** *m* -s,- rag; **in L~en** in rags. **L~enpack** *nt* riff-raff. **L~ensammler** *m* rag-and-bone man. **l~ig** *a* mean, shabby

Lunge *f* -, -n lungs *pl*; (*L~nflügel*) lung. **L~nentzündung** *f* pneumonia

Lupe *f* -, -n magnifying glass

Lurch *m* -[e]s, -e amphibian

Lust *f* -,⸚e pleasure; (*Verlangen*) desire; (*sinnliche Begierde*) lust; **L~ haben** feel like (**auf etw** *acc* sth); **ich habe keine L~** I don't feel like it; (*will nicht*) I don't want to

lustig *a* jolly; (*komisch*) funny; **sich l~ machen über** (+ *acc*) make fun of

Lüstling *m* -s, -e lecher

lust|los *a* listless. **L~mörder** *m* sex killer. **L~spiel** *nt* comedy

lutsch|en *vt/i* (*haben*) suck. **L~er** *m* -s,- lollipop

Lüttich *nt* -s Liège

Luv *f* & *nt* - **nach Luv** (*Naut*) to windward

luxuriös *a* luxurious

Luxus *m* - luxury

Lymph|drüse /'lymf-/ *f*, **L~knoten** *m* lymph gland

lynchen /'lynçən/ *vt* lynch

Lyr|ik *f* - lyric poetry. **L~iker** *m* -s,- lyric poet. **l~isch** *a* lyrical

Machart *f* style

machen
● *transitive verb*
····▸ (*herstellen, zubereiten*) make <*money, beds, music, exception, etc*>. **aus Plastik/Holz gemacht** made of plastic/wood. **sich** (*dat*) **etw machen lassen** have sth made. **etw aus jdm machen** make s.o. into sth. **jdn zum Präsidenten machen** make s.o. president. **er machte sich** (*dat*) **viele Freunde/ Feinde** he made a lot of friends/ enemies. **jdm/sich** (*dat*) **[einen]**

Kaffee machen make [some] coffee for s.o./oneself. **ein Foto machen** take a photo

····▸ (*verursachen*) make, cause <*difficulties*>; cause <*pain, anxiety*>. **jdm Arbeit machen** make [extra] work for s.o., cause s.o. extra work. **jdm Mut/Hoffnung machen** give s.o. courage/hope. **das macht Hunger/Durst** this makes you hungry/thirsty. **das macht das Wetter** that's [because of] the weather

····▸ (*ausführen, ordnen*) do <*job, repair* 🗊: *room, washing, etc.*>; take <*walk, trip, exam, course*>. **sie machte mir die Haare** 🗊 she did my hair for me. **einen Besuch [bei jdm] machen** pay [s.o.] a visit

····▸ (*tun*) do <*nothing, everything*>. **was machst du [da]?** what are you doing? **so etwas macht man nicht** that [just] isn't done

····▸ **was macht ...?** (*wie ist es um ... bestellt?*) how is ...? **was macht die Gesundheit/Arbeit?** how are you keeping/how is the job [getting on]?

····▸ (*Math: ergeben*) be. **zwei mal zwei macht vier** two times two is four. **das macht 6 Mark [zusammen]** that's *or* that comes to six marks [altogether]

····▸ (*schaden*) **was macht das schon?** what does it matter? **[das] macht nichts!** 🗊 it doesn't matter

····▸ **machs gut!** 🗊 look after yourself!; (*auf Wiedersehen*) so long!

● *reflexive verb*

····▸ **sich machen** 🗊 do well

····▸ **sich an etw** (*acc*) **machen** get down to sth. **sie machte sich an die Arbeit** she got down to work

● *intransitive verb*

····▸ **das macht hungrig/durstig** it makes you hungry/thirsty. **das macht dick** it's fattening

Macht *f* -,-̈e power. **M~haber** *m* -s,- ruler

mächtig *a* powerful ● *adv* 🗊 terribly

machtlos *a* powerless

Mädchen *nt* -s,- girl; (*Dienst-*) maid. **m~haft** *a* girlish. **M~name** *m* girl's name; (*vor der Ehe*) maiden name

Made *f* -, -n maggot

madig *a* maggoty

Madonna *f* -, -nen madonna

Magazin *nt* -s, -e magazine; (*Lager*) warehouse; store-room

Magd *f* -,-̈e maid

Magen *m* -s,-̈ stomach. **M~verstimmung** *f* stomach upset

mager *a* thin; <*Fleisch*> lean; <*Boden*> poor; (*dürftig*) meagre. **M~keit** *f* - thinness; leanness. **M~sucht** *f* anorexia

Magie *f* - magic

Mag|ier /'ma:giɐ/ *m* -s,- magician. **m~isch** *a* magic

Magistrat *m* -s, -e city council

Magnet *m* -en & -[e]s, -e magnet. **m~isch** *a* magnetic

Mahagoni *nt* -s mahogany

Mäh|drescher *m* -s,- combine harvester. **m~en** *vt/i* (*haben*) mow

Mahl *nt* -[e]s,-̈er & -e meal

mahlen† *vt* grind

Mahlzeit *f* meal; **M~!** enjoy your meal!

Mähne *f* -, -n mane

mahn|en *vt/i* (*haben*) remind (**wegen** about); (*ermahnen*) admonish; (*auffordern*) urge (**zu** to). **M~ung** *f* -, -en reminder; admonition

Mai *m* -[e]s, -e May; **der Erste Mai** May Day. **M~glöckchen** *nt* -s,- lily of the valley

Mailand *nt* -s Milan

Mais *m* -es maize; (*Culin*) sweet corn

Majestät *f* -, -en majesty. **m~isch** *a* majestic

Major *m* -s, -e major

Majoran *m* -s marjoram

makaber *a* macabre

Makel *m* -s,- blemish; (*Defekt*) flaw

Makkaroni *pl* macaroni *sg*

Makler *m* -s,- (*Comm*) broker

Makrele *f* -, -n mackerel

Makrone *f* -, -n macaroon

mal *adv* (*Math*) times; (*bei Maßen*) by; (① *einmal*) once; (*eines Tages*) one day; **nicht mal** not even

Mal *nt* -[e]s, -e time; **zum ersten/ letzten Mal** for the first/last time; **ein für alle Mal** once and for all; **jedes Mal** every time; **jedes Mal, wenn** whenever

Mal|buch *nt* colouring book. **m~en** *vt/i* (*haben*) paint. **M~er** *m* -s,- painter. **M~erei** *f* -, -en painting. **M~erin** *f* -, -nen painter. **m~erisch** *a* picturesque

Mallorca /ma'lɔrka, -'jɔrka/ *nt* -s Majorca

malnehmen† *vt sep* multiply (**mit** by)

Malz *nt* -es malt

Mama /'mama, ma'ma:/ *f* -s, -s mummy

Mammut *nt* -s, -e & -s mammoth

mampfen *vt* ① munch

man *pron* one, you; (*die Leute*) people, they; **man sagt** they say, it is said

manche(r,s) *pron* many a; [**so**] **m~es Mal** many a time; **m~e Leute** some people

● (*substantivisch*) **m~er/m~e** many a man/woman; **m~e** *pl* some; (*Leute*) some people; (*viele*) many [people]; **m~es** some things; (*vieles*) many things. **m~erlei** *inv a* various ● *pron* various things

manchmal *adv* sometimes

Mandant(in) *m* -en, -en (*f* -, -nen) (*Jur*) client

Mandarine *f* -, -n mandarin

Mandat *nt* -[e]s, -e mandate; (*Jur*) brief; (*Pol*) seat

Mandel *f* -, -n almond; (*Anat*) tonsil. **M~entzündung** *f* tonsillitis

Manege /ma'ne:ʒə/ *f* -, -n ring; (*Reit-*) arena

Mangel¹ *m* -s,-̈ lack; (*Knappheit*) shortage; (*Med*) deficiency; (*Fehler*) defect

Mangel² *f* -, -n mangle

mangel|haft *a* faulty, defective; (*Sch*) unsatisfactory. **m~n¹** *vi* (*haben*) **es m~t an** (+ *dat*) there is a lack/(*Knappheit*) shortage of

mangeln² *vt* put through the mangle

Manie *f* -, -n mania

Manier *f* -, -en manner; **M~en** *pl* manners. **m~lich** *a* well-mannered ● *adv* properly

Manifest *nt* -[e]s, -e manifesto

Maniküre *f* -, -n manicure; (*Person*) manicurist. **m~n** *vt* manicure

Manko *nt* -s, -s disadvantage; (*Fehlbetrag*) deficit

Mann *m* -[e]s,-̈er man; (*Ehe-*) husband

Männchen *nt* -s,- little man; (*Zool*) male

Mannequin /'manəkɛ̃/ *nt* -s, -s model

männlich *a* male; (*Gram & fig*) masculine; (*mannhaft*) manly; <*Frau*> mannish. **M~keit** *f* - masculinity; (*fig*) manhood

Mannschaft *f* -, -en team; (*Naut*) crew

Manöv|er *nt* -s,- manœuvre; (*Winkelzug*) trick. **m~rieren** *vt/i* (*haben*) manœuvre

Mansarde *f* -, -n attic room; (*Wohnung*) attic flat

Manschette *f* -, -n cuff. **M~nknopf** *m* cuff-link

M

Mantel m -s,: coat; overcoat
Manuskript nt -[e]s, -e manuscript
Mappe f -, -n folder; (Akten-) briefcase; (Schul-) bag
Märchen nt -s,- fairy-tales
Margarine f - margarine
Marienkäfer /ma'ri:ən-/ m ladybird
Marihuana nt -s marijuana
Marine f marine; (Kriegs-) navy. m~blau a navy [blue]
marinieren vt marinade
Marionette f -, -n puppet, marionette
Mark¹ f -,- mark; **drei M~** three marks
Mark² nt -[e]s (Knochen-) marrow (Bot)pith; (Frucht-) pulp
markant a striking
Marke f -, -n token; (rund) disc; (Erkennungs-) tag; (Brief-) stamp; (Lebensmittel-) coupon; (Spiel-) counter; (Markierung) mark; (Fabrikat) make; (Tabak-) brand. **M~nartikel** m branded article
markieren vt mark; (🗌 vortäuschen) fake
Markise f -, -n awning
Markstück nt one-mark piece
Markt m -[e]s,:e market; (M~platz) market-place. **M~forschung** f market research
Marmelade f -, -n jam; (Orangen-) marmalade
Marmor m -s marble
Marokko nt -s Morocco
Marone f -, -n [sweet] chestnut
Marsch m -[e]s,:e march. **m~** int (Mil) march!
Marschall m -s,:e marshal
marschieren vi (sein) march
Marter f -, -n torture. **m~n** vt torture
Märtyrer(in) m -s,- (f -, -nen) martyr
Marxismus m - Marxism
März m -, -e March
Marzipan nt -s marzipan

Masche f -, -n stitch; (im Netz) mesh; (🗌 Trick) dodge.
M~ndraht m wire netting
Maschin|e f -, -n machine; (Flugzeug) plane; (Schreib-) typewriter; **M~e schreiben** type. **m~egeschrieben** a typewritten, typed. **m~ell** a machine ... ● adv by machine. **M~enbau** m mechanical engineering. **M~engewehr** nt machine-gun. **M~ist** m -en, -en machinist; (Naut) engineer
Masern pl measles sg
Maserung f -, -en [wood] grain
Maske f -, -n mask; (Theat) make-up
maskieren vt mask; **sich m~** dress up (als as)
maskulin a masculine
Masochist m -en, -en masochist
Maß¹ nt -es, -e measure; (Abmessung) measurement; (Grad) degree; (Mäßigung) moderation; **in hohem Maße** to a high degree
Maß² f -,- (SGer) litre [of beer]
Massage /ma'sa:ʒə/ f -, -n massage
Massaker nt -s,- massacre
Maßband nt (pl -bänder) tape-measure
Masse f -, -n mass; (Culin) mixture; (Menschen-) crowd; **eine M~ Arbeit** 🗌 masses of work. **m~nhaft** adv in huge quantities. **M~nproduktion** f mass production. **m~nweise** adv in huge numbers
Masseu|r /ma'sø:ɐ/ m -s, -e masseur. **M~se** /-'sø:zə/ f -, -n masseuse
maß|gebend a authoritative; (einflussreich) influential. **m~geblich** a decisive. **m~geschneidert** a made-to-measure
massieren vt massage
massig a massive

mäßig a moderate; (*mittelmäßig*) indifferent. **m∼en** vt moderate; **sich m∼en** moderate; (*sich beherrschen*) restrain oneself. **M∼ung** f - moderation

massiv a solid; (*stark*) heavy

Maß|krug m beer mug. **m∼los** a excessive; (*grenzenlos*) boundless; (*äußerst*) extreme. **M∼nahme** f -, -n measure

Maßstab m scale; (*Norm & fig*) standard. **m∼sgerecht, m∼sgetreu** a scale … ●adv to scale

Mast[1] m -[e]s, -en pole; (*Überland-*) pylon; (*Naut*) mast

Mast[2] f - fattening

mästen vt fatten

masturbieren vi (*haben*) masturbate

Material nt -s, -ien /-iən/ material; (*coll*) materials pl. **M∼ismus** m - materialism. **m∼istisch** a materialistic

Mathe f - 🄸 maths sg

Mathe|matik f - mathematics sg. **M∼matiker** m -s,- mathematician. **m∼matisch** a mathematical

Matinee f -, -n (*Theat*) morning performance

Matratze f -, -n mattress

Matrose m -n, -n sailor

Matsch m -[e]s mud; (*Schnee-*) slush

matt a weak; (*gedämpft*) dim; (*glanzlos*) dull; <*Politur, Farbe*> matt. **M∼** m -s (*Schach*) mate

Matte f -, -n mat

Mattglas nt frosted glass

Matura f - (*Aust*) ≈ A levels pl

Mauer f -, -n wall. **M∼werk** nt masonry

Maul nt -[e]s, Mäuler (*Zool*) mouth; **halts M∼!** 🄸 shut up! **M∼korb** m muzzle. **M∼tier** nt mule. **M∼wurf** m mole

Maurer m -s,- bricklayer

Maus f -,Mäuse mouse

Maut f -, -en (*Aust*) toll. **M∼straße** f toll road

maximal a maximum

Maximum nt -s, -ma maximum

Mayonnaise /majo'nɛːzə/ f -, -n mayonnaise

Mechan|ik /me'çaːnɪk/ f - mechanics sg; (*Mechanismus*) mechanism. **M∼iker** m -s,- mechanic. **m∼isch** a mechanical. **m∼isieren** vt mechanize. **M∼ismus** m -, -men mechanism

meckern vi (*haben*) bleat; (🄸 *nörgeln*) grumble

Medaill|e /me'daljə/ f -, -n medal. **M∼on** /-'jõː/ nt -s, -s medallion (*Schmuck*) locket

Medikament nt -[e]s, -e medicine

Medit|ation /-'tsjoːn/ f -, -en meditation. **m∼îeren** vi (*haben*) meditate

Medium nt -s, -ien medium; **die Medien** the media

Medizin f -, -en medicine. **M∼er** m -s,- doctor; (*Student*) medical student. **m∼isch** a medical; (*heilkräftig*) medicinal

Meer nt -[e]s, -e sea. **M∼busen** m gulf. **M∼enge** f strait. **M∼esspiegel** m sea-level. **M∼jungfrau** f mermaid. **M∼rettich** m horseradish. **M∼schweinchen** nt -s,- guinea-pig

Mehl nt -[e]s flour. **M∼schwitze** f (*Culin*) roux

mehr pron & adv more; **nicht m∼** no more; (*zeitlich*) no longer; **nichts m∼** no more; (*nichtsweiter*) nothing else; **nie m∼** never again. **m∼eres** pron several things pl. **m∼fach** a multiple; (*mehrmalig*) repeated ●adv several times. **M∼fahrtenkarte** f book of tickets. **M∼heit** f -, -en majority. **m∼malig** a repeated. **m∼mals** adv several times. **m∼sprachig** a multilingual. **M∼wertsteuer** f value-added tax, VAT. **M∼zahl** f

M

M~zweck- *pref* multi-purpose
meiden† *vt* avoid, shun
Meile *f* -, -n mile. **m~nweit** *adv* [for] miles
mein *poss pron* my. **m~e(r,s)** *poss pron* mine; **die M~en** *od* **m~en** *pl* my family *sg*
Meineid *m* perjury
meinen *vt* mean; (*glauben*) think; (*sagen*) say
mein|erseits *adv* for my part. **m~etwegen** *adv* for my sake; (*wegen mir*) because of me; (🚹 *von mir aus*) as far as I'm concerned
Meinung *f* -, -en opinion; jdm die **M~** sagen give s.o. a piece of one's mind. **M~sumfrage** *f* opinion poll
Meise *f* -, -n (*Zool*) tit
Meißel *m* -s,- chisel. **m~n** *vt/i* (*haben*) chisel
meist *adv* mostly; (*gewöhnlich*) usually. **m~e** *a* der/die/das **m~e** most; **die m~en Leute** most people; **am m~en** [the] most ● *pron* **das m~e** most [of it]; **die m~en** most. **m~ens** *adv* mostly; (*gewöhnlich*) usually
Meister *m* -s,- master craftsman; (*Könner*) master; (*Sport*) champion. **m~n** *vt* master. **M~schaft** *f* -, -en mastery; (*Sport*) championship
melden *vt* report; (*anmelden*) register; (*ankündigen*) announce; **sich m~en** report (**bei** to); (*zum Militär*) enlist; (*freiwillig*) volunteer; (*Teleph*) answer; (*Sch*) put up one's hand; (*von sich hören lassen*) get in touch (**bei** with). **M~ung** *f* -, -en report; (*Anmeldung*) registration
melken† *vt* milk
Melodie *f* -, -n tune, melody
melodisch *a* melodic; melodious
Melone *f* -, -n melon

Memoiren /me'moa:rən/ *pl* memoirs
Menge *f* -, -n amount, quantity; (*Menschen-*) crowd; (*Math*) set; **eine M~ Geld** a lot of money. **m~n** *vt* mix
Mensa *f* -, -sen (*Univ*) refectory
Mensch *m* -en, -en human being; **der M~** man; **die M~en** people; **jeder/kein M~** everybody/nobody. **M~enaffe** *m* ape. **m~enfeindlich** *a* antisocial. **M~enfresser** *m* -s,- cannibal; (*Zool*) man-eater. **m~enfreundlich** *a* philanthropic. **M~enleben** *nt* human life; (*Lebenszeit*) lifetime. **m~enleer** *a* deserted. **M~enmenge** *f* crowd. **M~enraub** *m* kidnapping. **M~enrechte** *ntpl* human rights. **m~enscheu** *a* unsociable. **m~enwürdig** *a* humane. **M~heit** *f* - die **M~heit** mankind, humanity. **m~lich** *a* human; (*human*) humane. **M~lichkeit** *f* - humanity
Menstru|ation /-'ts:io:n/ *f* - menstruation. **m~ieren** *vi* (*haben*) menstruate
Mentalität *f* -, -en mentality
Menü *nt* -s, -s menu; (*festes M~*) set meal
Meridian *m* -s, -e meridian
merk|bar *a* noticeable. **M~blatt** *nt* [explanatory] leaflet. **m~en** *vt* notice; **sich** (*dat*) etw **m~en** remember sth. **M~mal** *nt* feature
merkwürdig *a* odd, strange
Messe¹ *f* -, -n (*Relig*) mass; (*Comm*) [trade] fair
Messe² *f* -, -n (*Mil*) mess
messen† *vt/i* (*haben*) measure; (*ansehen*) look at; **[bei jdm] Fieber m~** take s.o.'s temperature; **sich mit jdm m~ können** be a match for s.o.
Messer *nt* -s,- knife
Messias *m* - Messiah
Messing *nt* -s brass
Messung *f* -, -en measurement

Metabolismus m - metabolism

Metall nt -s, -e metal. **m~isch** a metallic

Metamorphose f -, -n metamorphosis

metaphorisch a metaphorical

Meteor m -s, -e meteor. **M~ologie** f - meteorology

Meter m & nt -s,- metre. **M~maß** nt tape-measure

Method|e f -, -n method. **m~isch** a methodical

Metropole f -, -n metropolis

Metzger m -s,- butcher. **M~ei** f -, -en butcher's shop

Meuterei f -, -en mutiny

meutern vi (haben) mutiny; (🗆 schimpfen) grumble

Mexikan|er(in) m -s,- (f -, -nen) Mexican. **m~isch** a Mexican

Mexiko nt -s Mexico

miauen vi (haben) mew, miaow

mich pron (acc of ich) me; (refl) myself

Mieder nt -s,- bodice

Miene f -, -n expression

mies a 🗆 lousy

Miet|e f -, -n rent; (Mietgebühr) hire charge; **zur M~e wohnen** live in rented accommodation. **m~en** vt rent <Haus, Zimmer>; hire <Auto, Boot>. **M~er(in)** m -s,- (f -, -nen) tenant. **m~frei** a & adv rent-free. **M~shaus** nt block of rented flats. **M~vertrag** m lease. **M~wagen** m hire-car. **M~wohnung** f rented flat; (zu vermieten) flat to let

Migräne f -, -n migraine

Mikro|chip m microchip. **M~computer** m microcomputer. **M~film** m microfilm

Mikro|fon, M~phon nt -s, -e microphone. **M~skop** nt -s, -e microscope. **m~skopisch** a microscopic

Mikrowelle f microwave. **M~nherd** m microwave oven

Milbe f -, -n mite

Milch f - milk. **M~glas** nt opal glass. **m~ig** a milky. **M~mann** m (pl -männer) milkman. **M~straße** f Milky Way

mild a mild; (nachsichtig) lenient. **M~e** f - mildness; leniency. **m~ern** vt make milder; (mäßigen) moderate; (lindern) ease; **sich m~ern** become milder; (sich mäßigen) moderate; <Schmerz:> ease; **m~ernde Umstände** mitigating circumstances

Milieu /mi'liø:/ nt -s, -s [social] environment

Militär nt -s army; (Soldaten) troops pl; **beim M~** in the army. **m~isch** a military

Miliz f -, -en militia

Milliarde /mɪ'liardə/ f -, -n thousand million, billion

Milli|gramm nt milligram. **M~meter** m & nt millimetre. **M~meterpapier** nt graph paper

Million /mɪ'lio:n/ f -, -en million. **M~är** m -s, -e millionaire

Milz f - (Anat) spleen

mimen vt (🗆 vortäuschen) act

Mimose f -, -n mimosa

Minderheit f -, -en minority

minderjährig a (Jur) under-age. **M~e(r)** m/f (Jur) minor

mindern vt diminish; decrease

minderwertig a inferior. **M~keit** f - inferiority. **M~keitskomplex** m inferiority complex

Mindest- pref minimum. **m~e** a & pron **der/die/das M~e** od **m~e** the least; **nicht im M~en** not in the least. **m~ens** adv at least. **M~lohn** m minimum wage. **M~maß** nt minimum

Mine f -, -n mine; (Bleistift-) lead; (Kugelschreiber-) refill. **M~nräumboot** nt minesweeper

Mineral nt -s, -e & -ien /-iən/ mineral. **m~isch** a mineral. **M~wasser** nt mineral water

Miniatur f -, -en miniature

M

Minigolf nt miniature golf

minimal a minimal

Minimum nt -s, -ma minimum

Mini|ster m, -s,- minister.
m~steriell a ministerial.
M~sterium nt -s, -ien ministry

minus conj, adv & prep (+ gen)
minus. **M~** nt - deficit; (Nachteil)
disadvantage. **M~zeichen** nt
minus [sign]

Minute f -, -n minute

mir pron (dat of **ich**) [to] me; (refl)
myself

Misch|ehe f mixed marriage.
m~en vt mix; blend <Tee,
Kaffee>; toss <Salat>; shuffle
<Karten>; **sich m~en** mix;
<Person> mingle (**unter** + acc
with); **sich m~en in** (+ acc) join in
<Gespräch>; meddle in
<Angelegenheit> ● vi (haben)
shuffle the cards. **M~ling** m -s, -e
half-caste. **M~ung** f -, -en
mixture; blend

miserabel a abominable

missachten vt disregard

Miss|achtung f disregard.
M~bildung f deformity

missbilligen vt disapprove of

Miss|billigung f disapproval.
M~brauch m abuse

missbrauchen vt abuse;
(vergewaltigen) rape

Misserfolg m failure

Misse|tat f misdeed. **M~täter** m
🔲 culprit

missfallen† vi (haben) displease
(jdm s.o.)

Miss|fallen nt -s displeasure;
(Missbilligung) disapproval.
M~geburt f freak; (fig)
monstrosity. **M~geschick** nt
mishap; (Unglück) misfortune

miss|glücken vi (sein) fail.
m~gönnen vt begrudge

misshandeln vt ill-treat

Misshandlung f ill-treatment

Mission f -, -en mission

Missionar(in) m -s, -e (f -, -nen)
missionary

Missklang m discord

misslingen† vi (sein) fail; **es
misslang ihr** she failed. **M~** nt -s
failure

Missmut m ill humour. **m~ig** a
morose

missraten† vi (sein) turn out
badly

Miss|stand m abuse; (Zustand)
undesirable state of affairs.
M~stimmung f discord; (Laune)
bad mood

misstrauen vi (haben) **jdm/etw
m~** mistrust s.o./sth; (Argwohn
hegen) distrust s.o./sth

Misstrau|en nt -s mistrust;
(Argwohn) distrust. **M~ensvotur**
nt vote of no confidence. **m~isc**
a distrustful; (argwöhnisch)
suspicious

Miss|verständnis nt
misunderstanding.
m~verstehen† vt misunderstand
M~wirtschaft f mismanagement

Mist m -[e]s manure; 🔲 rubbish

Mistel f -, -n mistletoe

Misthaufen m dungheap

mit prep (+ dat) with; <sprechen>
to; (mittels) by; (inklusive)
including; (bei) at; **mit Bleistift** in
pencil; **mit lauter Stimme** in a loud
voice; **mit drei Jahren** at the age o
three ● adv (auch) as well; **mit
anfassen** (fig) lend a hand

Mitarbeit f collaboration. **m~en**
vi sep collaborate (**an** + dat on).
M~er(in) m(f) collaborator;
(Kollege) colleague; employee

Mitbestimmung f
co-determination

mitbringen† vt sep bring [along]

miteinander adv with each other

Mitesser m (Med) blackhead

mitfahren† vi sep (sein) go/come
along; **mit jdm m~** go with s.o.;
(mitgenommen werden) be given
a lift by s.o.

nitfühlen *vi sep* (*haben*)
sympathize

nitgeben† *vt sep* **jdm etw m~** give
s.o. sth to take with him

litgefühl *nt* sympathy

nitgehen† *vi sep* (*sein*) **mit jdm
m~** go with s.o.

litgift *f* -, -en dowry

litglied *nt* member. **M~schaft** *f* -
membership

nithilfe *prep* (+ *gen*) with the aid
of

Aithilfe *f* assistance

nitkommen† *vi sep* (*sein*) come
[along] too; (*fig: folgen können*)
keep up; (*verstehen*) follow

Mitlaut *m* consonant

Mitleid *nt* pity, compassion; **M~
erregend** pitiful. **m~ig** *a* pitying;
(*mitfühlend*) compassionate.
m~slos *a* pitiless

mitmachen *v sep* ● *vt* take part
in; (*erleben*) go through ● *vi*
(*haben*) join in

Mitmensch *m* fellow man

mitnehmen† *vt sep* take along;
(*mitfahren lassen*) give a lift to;
(*fig: schädigen*) affect badly;
(*erschöpfen*) exhaust; **'zum M~'**
'to take away'

mitreden *vi sep* (*haben*) join in
[the conversation]; (*mit
entscheiden*) have a say (**bei** in)

mitreißen† *vt sep* sweep along;
(*fig: begeistern*) carry away; **m~d**
rousing

mitsamt *prep* (+ *dat*) together
with

mitschreiben† *vt sep* (*haben*)
take down

Mitschuld *f* partial blame. **m~ig** *a*
m~ig sein be partly to blame

Mitschüler(in) *m(f)* fellow pupil

mitspielen *vi sep* (*haben*) join in;
(*Theat*) be in the cast; (*beitragen*)
play a part

Mittag *m* midday, noon;
(*Mahlzeit*) lunch; (*Pause*) lunch-
break; **heute/gestern M~** at

lunch-time today/yesterday; **[zu]
M~ essen** have lunch. **M~essen**
nt lunch. **m~s** *adv* at noon; (*als
Mahlzeit*) for lunch; **um 12 Uhr
m~s** at noon. **M~spause** *f*
lunch-hour; (*Pause*) lunch-break.
M~sschlaf *m* after-lunch nap

Mittäter|(in) *m(f)* accomplice.
M~schaft *f* - complicity

Mitte *f* -, -n middle; (*Zentrum*)
centre; **die goldene M~** the golden
mean; **M~ Mai** in mid-May; **in
unserer M~** in our midst

mitteil|en *vt sep* **jdm etw m~en**
tell s.o. sth; (*amtlich*) inform s.o.
of sth. **M~ung** *f* -, -en
communication; (*Nachricht*)
piece of news

Mittel *nt* -s, - means *sg*; (*Heil*)
remedy; (*Medikament*) medicine;
(*M~wert*) mean; (*Durchschnitt*)
average; **M~** *pl* (*Geld*-) funds,
resources. **m~** *pred a* medium;
(*m~mäßig*) middling. **M~alter** *nt*
Middle Ages *pl*. **m~alterlich** *a*
medieval. **M~ding** *nt* (*fig*) cross.
m~europäisch *a* Central
European. **M~finger** *m* middle
finger. **m~los** *a* destitute.
m~mäßig *a* middling; [*nur*]
m~mäßig mediocre. **M~meer** *nt*
Mediterranean. **M~punkt** *m*
centre; (*fig*) centre of attention

mittels *prep* (+ *gen*) by means of

Mittel|schule *f* = Realschule.
M~smann *m* (*pl* -männer)
intermediary, go-between.
M~stand *m* middle class.
m~ste(r,s) *a* middle. **M~streifen**
m (*Auto*) central reservation.
M~stürmer *m* centre-forward.
M~welle *f* medium wave.
M~wort *nt* (*pl* -wörter) participle

mitten *adv* **m~ in/auf** (*dat/acc*) in
the middle of. **m~durch** *adv*
[right] through the middle

Mitternacht *f* midnight

mittler|e(r,s) *a* middle; <*Größe,
Qualität*> medium;

M

(*durchschnittlich*) mean, average.
m~weile *adv* meanwhile;
(*seitdem*) by now
Mittwoch *m* -s, -e Wednesday.
m~s *adv* on Wednesdays
mitunter *adv* now and again
mitwirk|en *vi sep* (*haben*) take
part; (*helfen*) contribute. **M~ung**
f participation
mix|en *vt* mix. **M~er** *m* -s,- (*Culin*)
liquidizer, blender
Möbel *pl* furniture *sg*. **M~stück**
nt piece of furniture. **M~wagen**
m removal van
Mobiliar *nt* -s furniture
mobilisier|en *vt* mobilize. **M~ung**
f - mobilization
Mobil|machung *f* - mobilization.
M~telefon *nt* mobile phone
möblier|en *vt* furnish; **m~tes**
Zimmer furnished room
mochte, möchte *s.* mögen
Mode *f* -, -n fashion; **M~ sein** be
fashionable
Modell *nt* -s, -e model. **m~ieren** *vt*
model
Modenschau *f* fashion show
Modera|tor *m* -s, -en /-'to:rən/,
M~torin *f* -, -nen (*TV*) presenter
modern *a* modern; (*modisch*)
fashionable. **m~isieren** *vt*
modernize
Mode|schmuck *m* costume
jewellery. **M~schöpfer** *m* fashion
designer
modisch *a* fashionable
Modistin *f* -, -nen milliner
modrig *a* musty
modulieren *vt* modulate
Mofa *nt* -s, -s moped
mogeln *vi* (*haben*) 🛈 cheat

mögen†
● *transitive verb*
····▸ like. **sie mag ihn sehr [gern]**
she likes him very much.
möchten Sie ein Glas Wein? would
you like a glass of wine? **lieber**

mögen prefer. **ich möchte lieber**
Tee I would prefer tea
● *auxiliary verb*
····▸ (*wollen*) want to. **sie mochte**
nicht länger bleiben she didn't
want to stay any longer. **ich**
möchte ihn [gerne] sprechen I'd
like to speak to him. **möchtest d**
nach Hause? do you want to go
home? *or* would you like to go
home?
····▸ (*Vermutung, Möglichkeit*)
may. **ich mag mich irren** I may be
wrong. **wer/was mag das sein?**
whoever/whatever can it be?
[das] mag sein that may well be.
mag kommen, was da will come
what may

möglich *a* possible; **alle m~en** all
sorts of; **über alles M~e sprechen**
talk about all sorts of things.
m~erweise *adv* possibly. **M~keit**
f -, -en possibility. **M~keitsform** *f*
subjunctive. **m~st** *adv* if
possible; **m~st viel** as much as
possible
Mohammedan|er(in) *m* -s,- (*f* -,
-nen) Muslim. **m~isch** *a* Muslim
Mohn *m* -s poppy
Möhre, Mohrrübe *f* -, -n carrot
Mokka *m* -s mocha; (*Geschmack*)
coffee
Molch *m* -[e]s, -e newt
Mole *f* -, -n (*Naut*) mole
Molekül *nt* -s, -e molecule
Molkerei *f* -, -en dairy
Moll *nt* - (*Mus*) minor
mollig *a* cosy; (*warm*) warm;
(*rundlich*) plump
Moment *m* -s, -e moment;
M~[mal]! just a moment! **m~an** *a*
momentary; (*gegenwärtig*) at the
moment
Monarch *m* -en, -en monarch.
M~ie *f* -, -n monarchy
Monat *m* -s, -e month. **m~elang**
adv for months. **m~lich** *a & adv*
monthly

Mönch m -[e]s, -e monk
Mond m -[e]s, -e moon
mondän a fashionable
Mond|finsternis f lunar eclipse. **m~hell** a moonlit. **M~sichel** f crescent moon. **M~schein** m moonlight
monieren vt criticize
Monitor m -s, -en /-ˈtoːrən/ (Techn) monitor
Monogramm nt -s, -e monogram
Mono|log m -s, -e monologue. **M~pol** nt -s, -e monopoly. **m~ton** a monotonous
Monster nt -s,- monster
Monstrum nt -s, -stren monster
Monsun m -s, -e monsoon
Montag m Monday
Montage /mɔnˈtaːʒə/ f -, -n fitting; (Zusammenbau) assembly; (Film-) editing; (Kunst) montage
montags adv on Mondays
Montanindustrie f coal and steel industry
Monteur /mɔnˈtøːɐ̯/ m -s, -e fitter. **M~anzug** m overalls pl
montieren vt fit; (zusammenbauen) assemble
Monument nt -[e]s, -e monument. **m~al** a monumental
Moor nt -[e]s, -e bog; (Heide-) moor
Moos nt es, -e moss **m~ig** a mossy
Moped nt -s, -s moped
Mopp m -s, -s mop
Moral f - morals pl, (Selbstvertrauen) morale; (Lehre) moral. **m~isch** a moral
Mord m -[e]s, -e murder, (Pol) assassination. **M~anschlag** m murder/assassination attempt. **m~en** vt/i (haben) murder, kill
Mörder m -s,- murderer, (Pol) assassin. **M~in** f -, -nen murderess. **m~isch** a murderous; (🄸 schlimm) dreadful

morgen adv tomorrow; **m~ Abend** tomorrow evening
Morgen m -s,- morning; (Maß) ≈ acre; **am M~** in the morning; **heute/Montag M~** this/Monday morning. **M~dämmerung** f dawn. **M~rock** m dressing-gown. **M~rot** nt red sky in the morning. **m~s** a in the morning
morgig a tomorrow's; **der m~e Tag** tomorrow
Morphium nt -s morphine
morsch a rotten
Morsealphabet nt Morse code
Mörtel m -s mortar
Mosaik /mozaˈiːk/ nt -s, -e[n] mosaic
Moschee f -, -n mosque
Mosel f - Moselle
Moskau nt -s Moscow
Moskito m -s, -s mosquito
Moslem m -s, -s Muslim
Motiv nt -s, -e motive; (Kunst) motif
Motor /ˈmoːtɔr, moˈtoːɐ̯/ m -s, -en /-ˈtoːrən/ engine; (Elektro-) motor. **M~boot** nt motor boat
motorisieren vt motorize
Motor|rad nt motor cycle. **M~roller** m motor scooter
Motte f -, -n moth. **M~nkugel** f mothball
Motto nt -s, -s motto
Möwe f -, -n gull
Mücke f -, -n gnat; (kleine) midge; (Stech-) mosquito
müd|e a tired; **es m~e sein** be tired (**etw zu tun** of doing sth). **M~igkeit** f - tiredness
muffig a musty; (🄸 mürrisch) grumpy
Mühe f -, -n effort; (Aufwand) trouble; **sich** (dat) **M~ geben** make an effort; (sich bemühen) try; **nicht der M~ wert** not worth while; **mit M~ und Not** with great difficulty; (gerade noch) only just. **m~los** a effortless
muhen vi (haben) moo

M

Mühl|e f -, -n mill; (*Kaffee-*) grinder. **M~stein** m millstone

Müh|sal f -, -e (*liter*) toil; (*Mühe*) trouble. **m~sam** a laborious; (*beschwerlich*) difficult

Mulde f -, -n hollow

Müll m -s refuse. **M~abfuhr** f refuse collection

Mullbinde f gauze bandage

Mülleimer m waste bin; (*Mülltonne*) dustbin

Müller m -s,- miller

Müll|halde f [rubbish] dump. **M~schlucker** m refuse chute. **M~tonne** f dustbin

multi|national a multinational. **M~plikation** /-'tsio:n/ f -, -en multiplication. **m~plizieren** vt multiply

Mumie /'mu:miə/ f -, -n mummy

Mumm m -s ⚡ energy

Mumps m - mumps

Mund m -[e]s,ˉer mouth; **ein M~ voll Suppe** a mouthful of soup; **halt den M~!** ⊠ shut up! **M~art** f dialect. **m~artlich** a dialect

Mündel nt & m -s,- (*Jur*) ward. **m~sicher** a gilt-edged

münden vi (*sein*) flow/<*Straße:*> lead (**in** + acc into)

Mundharmonika f mouth-organ

mündig a **m~ sein/werden** (*Jur*) be/come of age. **M~keit** f - (*Jur*) majority

mündlich a verbal; **m~e Prüfung** oral

Mündung f -, -en (*Fluss-*) mouth; (*Gewehr-*) muzzle

Mundwinkel m corner of the mouth

Munition /-'tsio:n/ f - ammunition

munkeln vt/i (*haben*) talk (**von** of); **es wird gemunkelt** rumour has it (**dass** that)

Münster nt -s,- cathedral

munter a lively; (*heiter*) merry; **m~ sein** (*wach*) be wide awake ; **gesund und m~** fit and well

Münz|e f -, -n coin; (*M~stätte*) mint. **M~fernsprecher** m payphone

mürbe a crumbly; <*Obst*> mellow <*Fleisch*> tender. **M~teig** m short pastry

Murmel f -, -n marble

murmeln vt/i (*haben*) murmur; (*undeutlich*) mumble

Murmeltier nt marmot

murren vt/i (*haben*) grumble

mürrisch a surly

Mus nt -es purée

Muschel f -, -n mussel; [sea] shell

Museum /mu'ze:om/ nt -s, -seen /-'ze:ən/ museum

Musik f - music. **m~alisch** a musical

Musiker(in) m -s,- (f -, -nen) musician

Musik|instrument nt musical instrument. **M~kapelle** f band. **M~pavillon** m bandstand

musisch a artistic

musizieren vi (*haben*) make music

Muskat m -[e]s nutmeg

Muskel m -s, -n muscle. **M~kater** m stiff and aching muscles pl

muskulös a muscular

muss s. müssen

Muße f - leisure

---

müssen†

● *auxiliary verb*

⋯▸ (*gezwungen/verpflichtet/ notwendig sein*) have to; must. **er muss es tun** he must *or* has to do it; ⚡ he's got to do it. **ich musste schnell fahren** I had to drive fast. **das muss 1968 gewesen sein** it must have been in 1968. **er muss gleich hier sein** he must be here at any moment

⋯▸ (*in negativen Sätzen; ungezwungen*) **sie muss es nicht tun** she does not have to *or* ⚡ she hasn't got to do it. **es musste**

nicht so sein it didn't have to be like that
⋯► **es müsste (sollte) doch möglich sein** it ought to *or* should be possible. **du müsstest es mal versuchen** you ought to *or* should try it
● *intransitive verb*
⋯► *(irgendwohin gehen müssen)* have to *or* must go. **ich muss nach Hause/zum Arzt** I have to *or* must go home/to the doctor. **ich musste mal [aufs Klo]** I had to go [to the loo]

üßig *a* idle

nusste, müsste *s.* müssen

Μuster *nt* -s,- pattern; *(Probe)* sample; *(Vorbild)* model. **M~beispiel** *nt* typical example; *(Vorbild)* perfect example. **m~gültig, m~haft** *a* exemplary. **m~n** *vt* eye; *(inspizieren)* inspect. **M~ung** *f* -, -en inspection; *(Mil)* medical; *(Muster)* pattern

Μut *m* -[e]s courage; **jdm Mut machen** encourage s.o.; **zu M~e sein** = zumute sein, *s.* zumute

mut|ig *a* courageous. **m~los** *a* despondent

mutmaßen *vt* presume; *(Vermutungen anstellen)* speculate

Mutprobe *f* test of courage

Mutter¹ *f* -,- mother

Mutter² *f* -, -n *(Techn)* nut

Muttergottes *f* -,- madonna

Mutterland *nt* motherland

mütterlich *a* maternal; *(fürsorglich)* motherly. **m~erseits** *adv* on one's/the mother's side

Mutter|mal *nt* birthmark; *(dunkel)* mole. **M~schaft** *f* - motherhood. **m~seelenallein** *a & adv* all alone. **M~sprache** *f* mother tongue. **M~tag** *m* Mother's Day

Mütze *f* -, -n cap; **wollene M~** woolly hat

MwSt. *abbr* **(Mehrwertsteuer)** VAT

mysteriös *a* mysterious

Mystik /'mʏstɪk/ *f* - mysticism

myth|isch *a* mythical. **M~ologie** *f* - mythology

na *int* well; **na gut** all right then

Nabel *m* -s,- navel. **N~schnur** *f* umbilical cord

nach

● *preposition (+ dative)*
⋯► *(räumlich)* to. **nach London fahren** go to London. **der Zug nach München** the train to Munich; *(noch nicht abgefahren)* the train for Munich; the Munich train. **nach Hause gehen** go home. **nach Osten [zu]** eastwards; towards the east
⋯► *(zeitlich)* after; *(Uhrzeit)* past. **nach fünf Minuten/dem Frühstück** after five minutes/breakfast. **zehn [Minuten] nach zwei** ten [minutes] past two
⋯► *([räumliche und zeitliche] Reihenfolge)* after. **nach Ihnen/dir!** after you!
⋯► *(mit bestimmten Verben)* for. **greifen/streben/schicken nach** grasp/strive/send for
⋯► *(gemäß)* according to. **nach der neuesten Mode gekleidet** dressed in [accordance with] the latest fashion. **dem Gesetz nach** in accordance with the law; by law. **nach meiner Ansicht** *od* **Meinung, meiner Ansicht** *od* **Meinung nach** in my view *or*

opinion. **nach etwas schmecken/
riechen** taste/smell of sth
● *adverb*
····▸ (*zeitlich*) **nach und nach** little
by little; gradually. **nach wie vor**
still

nachahm|en *vt sep* imitate.
N∼ung *f* -, **-en** imitation
Nachbar|(in) *m* -n, -n (*f* -, -nen)
neighbour. **N∼haus** *nt* house
next door. **n∼lich** *a* neighbourly;
(*Nachbar-*) neighbouring.
N∼schaft *f* - neighbourhood
nachbestell|en *vt sep* reorder.
N∼ung *f* repeat order
nachbild|en *vt sep* copy,
reproduce. **N∼ung** *f* copy,
reproduction
nachdatieren *vt sep* backdate
nachdem *conj* after; **je n∼** it
depends
nachdenk|en† *vi sep* (*haben*)
think (**über** + *acc* about). **n∼lich** *a*
thoughtful
nachdrücklich *a* emphatic
nacheinander *adv* one after the
other
Nachfahre *m* -n, -n descendant
Nachfolg|e *f* succession. **N∼er(in)**
m -s,- (*f* -, -nen) successor
nachforsch|en *vi sep* (*haben*)
make enquiries. **N∼ung** *f*
enquiry
Nachfrage *f* (*Comm*) demand.
n∼n *vi sep* (*haben*) enquire
nachfüllen *vt sep* refill
nachgeben† *v sep* ● *vi* (*haben*)
give way: (*sich fügen*) give in,
yield ● *vt* **jdm Suppe n∼** give s.o.
more soup
Nachgebühr *f* surcharge
nachgehen† *vi sep* (*sein*) <*Uhr:*>
be slow; **jdm/etw n∼** follow s.o./
sth; follow up <*Spur,
Angelegenheit*>; pursue
<*Angelegenheit*>
Nachgeschmack *m* after-taste

nachgiebig *a* indulgent; (*gefällig*)
compliant. **N∼keit** *f* - indulgence
compliance
nachgrübeln *vi sep* (*haben*)
ponder (**über** + *acc* on)
nachhaltig *a* lasting
nachhelfen† *vi sep* (*haben*) help
nachher *adv* later; (*danach*)
afterwards; **bis n∼!** see you later
Nachhilfeunterricht *m* coaching
Nachhinein *adv* **im N∼** afterward
nachhinken *vi sep* (*sein*) (*fig*) lag
behind
nachholen *vt sep* (*später holen*)
fetch later; (*mehr holen*) get
more; (*später machen*) do later;
(*aufholen*) catch up on
Nachkomme *m* -n, -n descendant
n∼n† *vi sep* (*sein*) follow [later],
come later; **etw** (*dat*) **n∼n** (*fig*)
comply with <*Bitte*>; carry out
<*Pflicht*>. **N∼nschaft** *f* -
descendants *pl*, progeny
Nachkriegszeit *f* post-war period
Nachlass *m* -es,̈e discount; (*Jur*)
[deceased's] estate
nachlassen† *v sep* ● *vi* (*haben*)
decrease; <*Regen, Hitze:*> let up;
<*Schmerz:*> ease; <*Sturm:*> abate
<*Augen, Leistungen:*> deteriorate
● *vt* **etw vom Preis n∼** take sth off
the price
nachlässig *a* careless; (*leger*)
casual; (*unordentlich*) sloppy.
N∼keit *f* - carelessness;
sloppiness
nachlesen† *vt sep* look up
nachlöse|n *vi sep* (*haben*) pay
one's fare on the train/on arrival
N∼schalter *m* excess-fare office
nachmachen *vt sep* (*später
machen*) do later; (*imitieren*)
imitate, copy; (*fälschen*) forge
Nachmittag *m* afternoon; **heute/
gestern N∼** this/yesterday
afternoon. **n∼s** *adv* in the
afternoon

Nachnahme *f* etw per N∼ schicken send sth cash on delivery *or* COD

Nachname *m* surname

Nachporto *nt* excess postage

nachprüfen *vt sep* check, verify

Nachricht *f* -, -en [piece of] news *sg*; N∼en news *sg*; eine N∼ hinterlassen leave a message; jdm N∼ geben inform s.o. **N∼endienst** *m* (*Mil*) intelligence service

nachrücken *vi sep* (*sein*) move up

Nachruf *m* obituary

nachsagen *vt sep* repeat (jdm after s.o.); jdm Schlechtes/Gutes n∼ speak ill/well of s.o.

Nachsaison *f* late season

nachschicken *vt sep* (*später schicken*) send later; (*hinterher-*) send after (jdm s.o.); send on *<Post>* (jdm to s.o.)

nachschlagen† *v sep* ● *vt* look up ● *vi* (*haben*) in einem Wörterbuch n∼en consult a dictionary; jdm n∼en take after s.o.

Nachschrift *f* transcript; (*Nachsatz*) postscript

Nachschub *m* (*Mil*) supplies *pl*

nachsehen† *v sep* ● *vt* (*prüfen*) check; (*nachschlagen*) look up; (*hinwegsehen über*) overlook ● *vi* (*haben*) have a look; (*prüfen*) check; im Wörterbuch n∼ consult a dictionary

nachsenden† *vt sep* forward *<Post>* (jdm to s.o.); 'bitte n∼' 'please forward'

nachsichtig *a* forbearing; lenient; indulgent

Nachsilbe *f* suffix

nachsitzen† *vi sep* (*haben*) n∼ müssen be kept in [after school]; jdn n∼ lassen give s.o. detention. **N∼** *nt* -s (*Sch*) detention

Nachspeise *f* dessert, sweet

nachsprechen† *vt sep* repeat (jdm after s.o.)

nachspülen *vt sep* rinse

nächst /-çst/ *prep* (+ *dat*) next to. **n∼beste(r,s)** *a* first [available]; (*zweitbeste*) next best. **n∼e(r,s)** *a* next; (*nächstgelegene*) nearest; *<Verwandte>* closest; in n∼er Nähe close by; am n∼en sein be nearest *or* closest ● *pron* der/die/ das N∼e the next; der N∼e bitte next please; als N∼es next; fürs N∼e for the time being. **N∼e(r)** *m* fellow man

nachstehend *a* following ● *adv* below

Nächst|enliebe *f* charity. **n∼ens** *adv* shortly. **n∼gelegen** *a* nearest

nachsuchen *vi sep* (*haben*) search; n∼ um request

Nacht *f* -,∴e night; über/bei N∼ overnight/at night; morgen N∼ tomorrow night; heute N∼ tonight; (*letzte Nacht*) last night; gestern N∼ last night; (*vorletzte Nacht*) the night before last. **N∼dienst** *m* night duty

Nachteil *m* disadvantage; zum N∼ to the detriment (*gen* of)

Nacht|falter *m* moth. **N∼hemd** *nt* night-dress; (*Männer-*) night-shirt

Nachtigall *f* -, -en nightingale

Nachtisch *m* dessert

Nachtklub *m* night-club

nächtlich *a* nocturnal, night …

Nacht|lokal *nt* night-club. **N∼mahl** *nt* (*Aust*) supper

Nachtrag *m* postscript; (*Ergänzung*) supplement. **n∼en**† *vt sep* add; jdm etw n∼en (*fig*) bear a grudge against s.o. for sth. **n∼end** *a* vindictive; n∼end sein bear grudges

nachträglich *a* subsequent, later; (*verspätet*) belated ● *adv* later; (*nachher*) afterwards; (*verspätet*) belatedly

Nacht|ruhe *f* night's rest; angenehme N∼ruhe! sleep well! **n∼s** *adv* at night; 2 Uhr n∼s 2

N

o'clock in the morning.
N~schicht f night-shift. **N~tisch**
m bedside table. **N~tischlampe** f
bedside lamp. **N~topf** m
chamber-pot. **N~wächter** m
night-watchman. **N~zeit** f
night-time

Nachuntersuchung f check-up
Nachwahl f by-election
Nachweis m -es, -e proof. **n~bar**
a demonstrable. **n~en†** vt sep
prove; (aufzeigen) show;
(vermitteln) give details of; jdm
nichts n~en können have no proof
against s.o.
Nachwelt f posterity
Nachwirkung f after-effect
Nachwuchs m new generation;
(🔟 Kinder) offspring. **N~spieler**
m young player

nachzahlen vt/i sep (haben) pay
extra; (später zahlen) pay later;
Steuern n~ pay tax arrears
nachzählen vt/i sep (haben)
count again; (prüfen) check
Nachzahlung f extra/later
payment; (Gehalts-) back-
payment
nachzeichnen vt sep copy
Nachzügler m -s,- late-comer;
(Zurückgebliebener) straggler
Nacken m -s,- nape or back of the
neck
nackt a naked; (bloß, kahl) bare;
<Wahrheit> plain. **N~heit** f -
nakedness, nudity. **N~kultur** f
nudism. **N~schnecke** f slug
Nadel f -, -n needle; (Häkel-)
hook; (Schmuck-, Hut-) pin.
N~arbeit f needlework. **N~baum**
m conifer. **N~stich** m stitch; (fig)
pinprick. **N~wald** m coniferous
forest
Nagel m -s,¨ nail. **N~haut** f
cuticle. **N~lack** m nail varnish.
n~n vt nail. **n~neu** a brand-new
nagen vt/i (haben) gnaw (an + dat
at); **n~d** (fig) nagging
Nagetier nt rodent

nah a, adv & prep = nahe
Näharbeit f sewing
Nahaufnahme f close-up
nahe a nearby; (zeitlich)
imminent; (eng) close; der N~
Osten the Middle East; in n~r
Zukunft in the near future; von
n~m [from] close to; n~ sein be
close (dat to) ● adv near, close;
<verwandt> closely; n~ an (+
acc/dat) near [to], close to; n~
daran sein, etw zu tun nearly do
sth; n~ liegen be close; (fig) be
highly likely; n~ legen (fig)
recommend (dat to); jdm n~
legen, etw zu tun urge s.o. to do
sth; jdm n~ gehen (fig) affect s.o.
deeply; jdm zu n~ treten (fig)
offend s.o. ● prep (+ dat) near
[to], close to
Nähe f - nearness, proximity; aus
der N~ [from] close to; in der N~
near or close by
nahe|gehen* vi sep (sein) n~
gehen, s. nahe. **n~legen*** vt sep
n~ legen, s. nahe. **n~liegen*** vi
sep (haben) n~ liegen, s. nahe
nähen vt/i (haben) sew;
(anfertigen) make; (Med) stitch
[up]
näher a closer; <Weg> shorter;
<Einzelheiten> further ● adv
closer; (genauer) more closely;
n~ kommen come closer; (fig) get
closer (dat to); sich n~ erkundigen
make further enquiries; n~ an (+
acc/dat) nearer [to], closer to
● prep (+ dat) nearer [to], closer
to. **N~e[s]** nt [further] details pl.
n~n (sich) vr approach
nahezu adv almost
Nähgarn nt [sewing] cotton
Nahkampf m close combat
Näh|maschine f sewing machine.
N~nadel f sewing-needle
nähren vt feed; (fig) nurture
nahrhaft a nutritious
Nährstoff m nutrient

Nahrung f - food, nourishment. **N~smittel** nt food

Nährwert m nutritional value

Naht f -,-̈e seam; (Med) suture. **n~los** a seamless

Nahverkehr m local service

Nähzeug nt sewing; (Zubehör) sewing kit

naiv /naˈiːf/ a naïve. **N~ität** /-viˈtɛːt/ f - naïvety

Name m -ns, -n name; im N~n (+ gen) in the name of; <handeln> on behalf of. **n~nlos** a nameless; (unbekannt) unknown, anonymous. **N~nstag** m name-day. **N~nsvetter** m namesake. **N~nszug** m signature. **n~ntlich** adv by name; (besonders) especially

namhaft a noted; (ansehnlich) considerable; n~ machen name

nämlich adv (und zwar) namely; (denn) because

nanu int hallo

Napf m -[e]s,-̈e bowl

Narbe f -, -n scar

Narkose f -, -n general anaesthetic. **N~arzt** m anaesthetist. **N~mittel** nt anaesthetic

Narr m -en, -en fool; zum N~en halten make a fool of. **n~en** vt fool

Närr|in f -, -nen fool. **n~isch** a foolish; (🄓 verrückt) crazy (auf + acc about)

Narzisse f -, -n narcissus

naschen vt/i (haben) nibble (an + dat at)

Nase f -, -n nose

näseln vi (haben) speak through one's nose; **n~d** nasal

Nasen|bluten nt -s nosebleed. **N~loch** nt nostril

Nashorn nt rhinoceros

nass a wet

Nässe f - wet; wetness. **n~n** vt wet

Nation /naˈtsi̯oːn/ f -, -en nation. **n~al** a national. **N~alhymne** f national anthem. **N~alismus** m - nationalism. **N~alität** f -, -en nationality. **N~alspieler** m international

Natrium nt -s sodium

Natron nt -s doppeltkohlensaures N~ bicarbonate of soda

Natter f -, -n snake; (Gift-) viper

Natur f -, -en nature; von N~ aus by nature. **n~alisieren** vt naturalize. **N~alisierung** f -, -en naturalization

Naturell nt -s, -e disposition

Natur|erscheinung f natural phenomenon. **N~forscher** m naturalist. **N~kunde** f natural history

natürlich a natural ● adv naturally; (selbstverständlich) of course. **N~keit** f - naturalness

natur|rein a pure. **N~schutz** m nature conservation; unter N~schutz stehen be protected. **N~schutzgebiet** nt nature reserve. **N~wissenschaft** f [natural] science. **N~wissenschaftler** m scientist

nautisch a nautical

Navigation /-ˈtsi̯oːn/ f - navigation

Nazi m -s, -s Nazi

n.Chr. abbr (nach Christus) AD

Nebel m -s,- fog; (leicht) mist

neben prep (+ dat/acc) next to, beside; (+ dat) (außer) apart from. **n~an** adv next door

Neben|anschluss m (Teleph) extension. **N~ausgaben** fpl incidental expenses

nebenbei adv in addition; (beiläufig) casually

Neben|bemerkung f passing remark. **N~beruf** m second job

nebeneinander adv next to each other, side by side

N

Neben|eingang m side entrance. **N~fach** nt (Univ) subsidiary subject. **N~fluss** m tributary
nebenher adv in addition
nebenhin adv casually
Neben|höhle f sinus. **N~kosten** pl additional costs. **N~produkt** nt by-product. **N~rolle** f supporting role; (Kleine) minor role. **N~sache** f unimportant matter. **n~sächlich** a unimportant. **N~satz** m subordinate clause. **N~straße** f minor road; (Seiten-) side street. **N~wirkung** f side-effect. **N~zimmer** nt room next door
neblig a foggy; (leicht) misty
neck|en vt tease. **N~erei** f - teasing. **n~isch** a teasing
Neffe m -n, -n nephew
negativ a negative. **N~** nt -s, -e (Phot) negative
Neger m -s,- Negro
nehmen† vt take (dat from); sich (dat) etw n~ take sth; help oneself to <Essen>
Neid m -[e]s envy, jealousy. **n~isch** a envious, jealous (auf + acc of); auf jdn n~isch sein envy s.o.
neig|en vt incline; (zur Seite) tilt; (beugen) bend; sich n~en incline; <Boden:> slope; <Person:> bend (über + acc over) ●vi (haben) n~en zu (fig) have a tendency towards; be prone to <Krankheit>; incline towards <Ansicht>; dazu n~en, etw zu tun tend to do sth. **N~ung** f -, -en inclination; (Gefälle) slope; (fig) tendency
nein adv, **N~** nt -s no
Nektar m -s nectar
Nelke f -, -n carnation; (Culin) clove
nenn|en† vt call; (taufen) name; (angeben) give; (erwähnen) mention; sich n~en call oneself. **n~enswert** a significant

Neon nt -s neon. **N~beleuchtung** f fluorescent lighting
Nerv m -s, -en /-fən/ nerve; die N~en verlieren lose control of oneself. n~en vt jdn n~en ⊠ get on s.o.'s nerves. **N~enarzt** m neurologist. n~enaufreibend a nerve-racking. **N~enkitzel** m ⊡ thrill. **N~ensystem** nt nervous system. **N~enzusammenbruch** m nervous breakdown
nervös a nervy, edgy; (Med) nervous; n~ sein be on edge
Nervosität f - nerviness, edginess
Nerz m -es, -e mink
Nessel f -, -n nettle
Nest nt -[e]s, -er nest; (⊡ Ort) small place
nett a nice; (freundlich) kind
netto adv net
Netz nt -es, -e net; (Einkaufs-) string bag; (Spinnen-) web; (auf Landkarte) grid; (System) network; (Electr) mains pl. **N~haut** f retina. **N~karte** f area season ticket. **N~werk** nt network

neu a new; (modern) modern; wie neu as good as new; das ist mir neu it's news to me; von n~em all over again ●adv newly; (gerade erst) only just; (erneut) again; etw neu schreiben rewrite sth; neu vermähltes Paar newly-weds pl. **N~auflage** f new edition; (unverändert) reprint. **N~bau** m (pl -ten) new house/building
Neu|e(r) m/f new person, newcomer; (Schüler) new boy/girl. **N~e(s)** nt das N~e the new; etwas N~es something new; (Neuigkeit) a piece of news; was gibts N~es? what's the news?
neuerdings adv [just] recently
neuest|e(r,s) a newest; (letzte) latest; seit n~em just recently. **N~e** nt das N~e the latest thing; (Neuigkeit) the latest news sg
neugeboren a newborn

Neugier, Neugierde f - curiosity; (*Wissbegierde*) inquisitiveness

neugierig a curious (**auf** + *acc* about); (*wissbegierig*) inquisitive

Neuheit f -, -en novelty; newness

Neuigkeit f -, -en piece of news; N~en news sg

Neujahr nt New Year's Day; **über N~** over the New Year

neulich adv the other day

Neumond m new moon

neun inv a, **N~** f -, -en nine. **n~te(r,s)** a ninth. **n~zehn** inv a nineteen. **n~zehnte(r,s)** a nineteenth. **n~zig** inv a ninety. **n~zigste(r,s)** a ninetieth

Neuralgie f -, -n neuralgia

neureich a nouveau riche

Neurologe m -n, -n neurologist

Neurose f -, -n neurosis

Neuschnee m fresh snow

Neuseeland nt -s New Zealand

neuste(r,s) a = **neueste(r,s)**

neutral a neutral. **N~ität** f - neutrality

Neutrum nt -s, -tra neuter noun

neu|vermählt* a n~ vermählt, s. neu. **N~zeit** f modern times pl

nicht adv not; **ich kann n~** I cannot or can't; **er ist n~ gekommen** he hasn't come; **bitte n~!** please don't! **n~ berühren!** do not touch! **du kennst ihn doch, n~?** you know him, don't you?

Nichte f -, -n niece

Nichtraucher m non-smoker

nichts pron & a nothing; **n~ mehr** no more; **n~ ahnend** unsuspecting; **n~ sagend** meaningless; (*uninteressant*) nondescript. **N~** nt - nothingness; (*fig: Leere*) void

Nichtschwimmer m non-swimmer

nichts|nutzig a good-for-nothing; (🛈 *unartig*) naughty. **n~sagend*** a n~ sagend, s. nichts. **N~tun** nt -s idleness

Nickel nt -s nickel

nicken vi (*haben*) nod or lay down

Nickerchen nt -s,-, 🛈 nap

nie adv never

nieder a low ● adv down. **n~brennen**† vt/i sep (*sein*) burn down. **N~deutsch** nt Low German. **N~gang** m (*fig*) decline. **n~gedrückt** a (*fig*) depressed. **n~geschlagen** a dejected, despondent. **N~kunft** f -,ˆe confinement. **N~lage** f defeat

Niederlande (die) pl the Netherlands

Niederländ|er m -s,- Dutchman; **die N~er** the Dutch pl. **N~erin** f -, -nen Dutchwoman. **n~isch** a Dutch

nieder|lassen† vt sep let down; **sich n~lassen** settle; (*sich setzen*) sit down. **N~lassung** f -, -en settlement; (*Zweigstelle*) branch. **n~legen** vt sep put or lay down; resign <*Amt*>; **die Arbeit n~legen** go on strike. **n~metzeln** vt sep massacre. **N~sachsen** nt Lower Saxony. **N~schlag** m precipitation; (*Regen*) rainfall; (*radioaktiver*) fallout. **n~schlagen**† vt sep knock down; lower <*Augen*>; (*unterdrücken*) crush. **n~schmettern** vt sep (*fig*) shatter. **n~setzen** vt sep put or set down; **sich n~setzen** sit down. **n~strecken** vt sep fell; (*durch Schuss*) gun down. **n~trächtig** a base, vile. **n~walzen** vt sep flatten

niedlich a pretty; sweet

niedrig a low; (*fig: gemein*) base ● adv low

niemals adv never

niemand pron nobody, no one

Niere f -, -n kidney; **künstliche N~** kidney machine

nieseln vi (*haben*) drizzle. **N~regen** m drizzle

niesen vi (*haben*) sneeze. **N~** nt -s sneezing; (*Nieser*) sneeze

Niete¹ f -, -n rivet; (*an Jeans*) stud

N

Niete² f -, -n blank; ⊞ failure
nieten vt rivet
Nikotin nt -s nicotine
Nil m -[s] Nile. **N∼pferd** nt
hippopotamus
nimmer adv (SGer) not any more;
nie und n∼ never
nirgends, **n∼wo** adv nowhere
Nische f -, -n recess, niche
nisten vi (haben) nest
Nitrat nt -[e]s, -e nitrate
Niveau /ni'vo:/ nt -s, -s level;
(geistig, künstlerisch) standard
nix adv ⊞ nothing
Nixe f -, -n mermaid
nobel a noble; (⊞ luxuriös)
luxurious; (⊞ großzügig)
generous
noch adv still; (zusätzlich) as well;
(mit Komparativ) even; n∼ nicht
not yet; gerade n∼ only just; n∼
immer od immer n∼ still; n∼ letzte
Woche only last week; wer n∼?
who else? n∼ etwas something
else; (Frage) anything else? n∼
einmal again; n∼ ein Bier another
beer; n∼ größer even bigger; n∼
so sehr however much ●conj
weder ... n∼ neither ... nor
nochmals adv again
Nomad|e m -n, -n nomad. **n∼isch**
a nomadic
nominier|en vt nominate. **N∼ung**
f -, -en nomination
Nonne f -, -n nun. **N∼nkloster** nt
convent
Nonstopflug m direct flight
Nord m -[e]s north. **N∼amerika** nt
North America
Norden m -s north
nordisch a Nordic
nördlich a northern; <Richtung>
northerly ●adv & prep (+ gen)
n∼ [von] der Stadt [to the] north
of the town
Nordosten m north-east
Nord|pol m North Pole. **N∼see** f -
North Sea. **N∼westen** m northwest

Nörgelei f -, -en grumbling
nörgeln vi (haben) grumble
Norm f -, -en norm; (Techn)
standard; (Soll) quota
normal a normal. **n∼erweise** adv
normally
normen vt standardize
Norwe|gen nt -s Norway.
N∼ger(in) m -s, - (f -, -nen)
Norwegian. **n∼gisch** a
Norwegian
Nost|algie f - nostalgia.
n∼algisch a nostalgic
Not f -, "e need; (Notwendigkeit)
necessity; (Entbehrung) hardship;
(seelisch) trouble; **Not leiden** be in
need, suffer hardship; **Not
leidende Menschen** needy people;
zur Not if need be;
(äußerstenfalls) at a pinch
Notar m -s, -e notary public
Not|arzt m emergency doctor.
N∼ausgang m emergency exit.
N∼behelf m -[e]s, -e makeshift.
N∼bremse f emergency brake.
N∼dienst m **N∼dienst haben** be
on call
Note f -, -n note; (Zensur) mark;
ganze/halbe **N∼** (Mus) semi-
breve/minim; **N∼n lesen** read
music; persönliche **N∼** personal
touch. **N∼nblatt** nt sheet of
music. **N∼nschlüssel** m clef
Notfall m emergency; für den **N∼**
just in case. **n∼s** adv if need be
notieren vt note down; (Comm)
quote; sich (dat) etw n∼ make a
note of sth
nötig a necessary; n∼ haben need;
das **N∼ste** the essentials pl ●adv
urgently. **n∼enfalls** adv if need
be. **N∼ung** f - coercion
Notiz f -, -en note; (Zeitungs-)
item; [keine] **N∼** nehmen von take
[no] notice of. **N∼buch** nt
notebook. **N∼kalender** m diary
Not|lage f plight. **n∼landen** vi
(sein) make a forced landing.
N∼landung f forced landing.

n~**leidend*** a Not leidend, s. Not.
N~lösung f stopgap
Not|ruf m emergency call; (Naut, Aviat) distress call; (Nummer) emergency services number.
N~signal nt distress signal.
N~stand m state of emergency.
N~unterkunft f emergency accommodation. **N~wehr** f - (Jur) self-defence
notwendig a necessary; essential ● adv urgently. **N~keit** f -, -en necessity
Notzucht f - (Jur) rape
Nougat /'nu:gat/ m & nt -s nougat
Novelle f -, -n novella; (Pol) amendment
November m -s,- November
Novize m -n, -n, **Novizin** f -, -nen (Relig) novice
Nu m im Nu 𝕋 in a flash
nüchtern a sober; (sachlich) matter-of-fact; (schmucklos) bare; (ohne Würze) bland; **auf n~en Magen** on an empty stomach
Nudel f -, -n piece of pasta; **N~n** pasta sg; (Band-) noodles. **N~holz** nt rolling-pin
Nudist m -en, -en nudist
nuklear a nuclear
null inv a zero, nought; (Teleph) O; (Sport) nil; (Tennis) love; **n~ Fehler** no mistakes; **n~ und nichtig** (Jur) null and void. **N~** f -, -en nought, zero; (fig: Person) nonentity. **N~punkt** m zero
numerieren* vt s. nummerieren
Nummer f -, -n number; (Ausgabe) issue; (Darbietung) item; (Zirkus-) act; (Größe) size. **n~ieren** vt number. **N~nschild** nt number-plate
nun adv now; (na) well; (halt) just; **nun gut!** very well then!
nur adv only, just; **wo kann sie nur sein?** wherever can she be? **er soll es nur versuchen!** just let him try!

Nürnberg nt -s Nuremberg
nuscheln vt/i (haben) mumble
Nuss f -,̈e nut. **N~knacker** m -s,- nutcrackers pl
Nüstern fpl nostrils
Nut f -, **Nute** f -, -n groove
Nutte f -, -n 🅇 tart 🅇
nütz|bar a usable; **n~bar machen** utilize; cultivate <Boden>.
n~**bringend** a profitable
nutzen vt use, utilize; (aus-) take advantage of ● vi (haben) = nützen. **N~** m -s benefit; (Comm) profit; **N~ ziehen aus** benefit from; **von N~ sein** be useful
nützen vi (haben) be useful or of use (dat to); <Mittel:> be effective; **nichts n~** be useless or no use; **was nützt mir das?** what good is that to me? ● vt = nutzen
nützlich a useful. **N~keit** f - usefulness
nutz|los a useless; (vergeblich) vain. **N~losigkeit** f - uselessness. **N~ung** f - use, utilization
Nylon /'naɪlɔn/ nt -s nylon
Nymphe /'nʏmfə/ f -, -n nymph

o int o ja/nein! oh yes/no!
Oase f -, -n oasis
ob conj whether; **ob reich, ob arm** rich or poor; **und ob!** 𝕋 you bet!
Obacht f **O~ geben** pay attention; **O~!** look out!
Obdach nt -[e]s shelter. **o~los** a homeless. **O~lose(r)** m/f homeless person; **die O~losen** the homeless pl
Obduktion /-'tsi̯oːn/ f -, -en post-mortem

O-Beine ntpl ⚠ bow-legs, bandy legs

oben adv at the top; (auf der Oberseite) on top; (eine Treppe hoch) upstairs; (im Text) above; **da o~** up there; **o~ im Norden** in the north; **siehe o~** see above; **o~ auf** (+ acc/dat) on top of; **nach o~** up[wards]; (die Treppe hinauf) upstairs; **von o~** from above/upstairs; **von o~ bis unten** from top to bottom/<Person> from head to toe; **jdn von o~ bis unten mustern** look s.o. up and down; **o~ erwähnt** od **genannt** above-mentioned. **o~drein** adv on top of that

Ober m -s,- waiter

Ober|arm m upper arm. **O~arzt** m ≈ senior registrar. **O~deck** nt upper deck. **o~e(r,s)** a upper; (höhere) higher. **O~fläche** f surface. **o~flächlich** a superficial. **O~geschoss** nt upper storey. **o~halb** adv & prep (+ gen) above. **O~haupt** nt (fig) head. **O~haus** nt (Pol) upper house; (in UK) House of Lords. **O~hemd** nt [man's] shirt. **o~irdisch** a surface ... ● adv above ground. **O~kiefer** m upper jaw. **O~körper** m upper part of the body. **O~leutnant** m lieutenant. **O~lippe** f upper lip

Obers nt - (Aust) cream

Ober|schenkel m thigh. **O~schule** f grammar school. **O~seite** f upper/(rechte Seite) right side

Oberst m -en & -s, -en colonel

oberste(r,s) a top; (höchste) highest; <Befehlshaber, Gerichtshof> supreme; (wichtigste) first

Ober|stimme f treble. **O~teil** nt top. **O~weite** f chest/(der Frau) bust size

obgleich conj although

Obhut f - care

obig a above

Objekt nt -[e]s, -e object; (Haus, Grundstück) property

Objektiv nt -s, -e lens. **o~** a objective. **O~ität** f - objectivity

Oblate f -, -n (Relig) wafer

Obmann m (pl -männer) [jury] foreman; (Sport) referee

Oboe /o'bo:ə/ f -, -n oboe

Obrigkeit f - authorities pl

obschon conj although

Observatorium nt -s, -ien observatory

obskur a obscure; dubious

Obst nt -es (coll) fruit. **O~baum** m fruit-tree. **O~garten** m orchard. **O~händler** m fruiterer

obszön a obscene

O-Bus m trolley bus

obwohl conj although

Ochse m -n, -n ox

öde a desolate; (unfruchtbar) barren; (langweilig) dull. **Öde** f - desolation; barrenness; dullness

oder conj or; **du kennst ihn doch, o~?** you know him, don't you?

Ofen m -s,ː stove; (Heiz-) heater; (Back-) oven; (Techn) furnace

offen a open; <Haar> loose; <Flamme> naked; (o~herzig) frank; (o~ gezeigt) overt; (unentschieden) unsettled; **o~e Stelle** vacancy; **Wein o~ verkaufen** sell wine by the glass; **o~ bleiben** remain open; **o~ halten** hold open <Tör>; keep open <Mund, Augen>; **o~ lassen** leave open; leave vacant <Stelle>; **o~ stehen** be open; <Rechnung:> be outstanding; **jdm o~ stehen** (fig) be open to s.o.; adv **o~ gesagt** od **gestanden** to be honest. **o~bar** a obvious ● adv apparently. **o~baren** vt reveal. **O~barung** f -, -en revelation. **O~heit** f - frankness, openness. **o~sichtlich** a obvious

offenstehen* vi sep (haben) offen stehen, s. offen

ffentlich a public. **Ö~keit** f - public; **in aller Ö~keit** in public, publicly

fferte f -, -n (Comm) offer

ffiziell a official

ffizier m -s, -e (Mil) officer

ffn|en vt/i (haben) open; **sich ö~en** open. **Ö~er** m -s,- opener. **Ö~ung** f -, -en opening. **Ö~ungszeiten** fpl opening hours

ft adv often

fter adv quite often. **ö~e(r,s)** a frequent; **des Ö~en** frequently. **ö~s** adv 𝕀 quite often

h int oh!

hne prep (+ acc) without; **o~ mich!** count me out! **oben o~** topless ● conj **o~ zu überlegen** without thinking; **o~ dass ich es merkte** without my noticing it. **o~dies** adv anyway. **o~gleichen** pred a unparalleled. **o~hin** adv anyway

Ohn|macht f -, -en faint; (fig) powerlessness; **in O~macht fallen** faint. **o~mächtig** a unconscious; (fig) powerless; **o~mächtig werden** faint

Ohr nt -[e]s, -en ear

Öhr nt -[e]s, -e eye

Ohrenschmalz nt ear-wax. **O~schmerzen** mpl earache sg

Ohrfeige f slap in the face. **o~n** vt jdn **o~n** slap s.o.'s face

Ohr|läppchen nt -s,- ear-lobe. **O~ring** m ear-ring. **O~wurm** m earwig

oje int oh dear!

okay /o'ke:/ a & adv 𝕀 OK

Öko|logie f - ecology. **ö~logisch** a ecological. **Ö~nomie** f - economy; (Wissenschaft) economics sg. **ö~nomisch** a economic; (sparsam) economical

Oktave f -, -n octave

Oktober m -s,- October

ökumenisch a ecumenical

Öl nt -[e]s, -e oil; **in Öl malen** paint in oils. **Ölbaum** m olivetree. **ölen**

vt oil. **Ölfarbe** f oil-paint. **Ölfeld** nt oilfield. **Ölgemälde** nt oil-painting. **ölig** a oily

Oliv|e f -, -n olive. **O~enöl** nt olive oil

Ölmessstab m dip-stick.

Ölsardinen fpl sardines in oil. **Ölstand** m oil-level. **Öltanker** m oil-tanker. **Ölteppich** m oil-slick

Olympiade f -, -n Olympic Games pl, Olympics pl

Olymp|iasieger(in) /o'lʏmpia-/ m(f) Olympic champion. **o~isch** a Olympic; **O~ische Spiele** Olympic Games

Ölzeug nt oilskins pl

Oma f -, -s 𝕀 granny

Omnibus m bus; (Reise-) coach

onanieren vi (haben) masturbate

Onkel m -s,- uncle

Opa m -s, -s 𝕀 grandad

Opal m -s, -e opal

Oper f -, -n opera

Operation /-'tsi̯o:n/ f -, -en operation. **O~ssaal** m operating theatre

Operette f -, -n operetta

operieren vt operate on <Patient, Herz>; **sich o~ lassen** have an operation ● vi (haben) operate

Opernglas nt opera-glasses pl

Opfer nt -s,- sacrifice; (eines Unglücks) victim; **ein O~ bringen** make a sacrifice; **jdm/etw zum O~ fallen** fall victim to s.o./sth. **o~n** vt sacrifice

Opium nt -s opium

Opposition /-'tsi̯o:n/ f - opposition. **O~spartei** f opposition party

Optik f - optics sg, (𝕀 Objektiv) lens. **O~er** m -s,- optician

optimal a optimum

Optimis|mus m - optimism. **O~t** m -en, -en optimist. **o~tisch** a optimistic

optisch a optical; <Eindruck> visual

Orakel nt -s,- oracle

O

Orange /oˈrãːʒə/ f -, -n orange. **o~**
inv a orange. **O~ade** /orãˈʒaːdə/ f
-, -n orangeade. **O~nmarmelade** f
[orange] marmalade

Oratorium *nt* -s, -ien oratorio

Orchester /orˈkɛstɐ/ *nt* -s,-
orchestra

Orchidee /orçiˈdeːə/ f -, -n orchid

Orden *m* -s,- (*Ritter-, Kloster-*)
order; (*Auszeichnung*) medal,
decoration

ordentlich *a* neat. tidy;
(*anständig*) respectable;
(*ordnungsgemäß* I: *richtig*)
proper; <*Mitglied, Versammlung*>
ordinary; (I *gut*) decent; (I
gehörig) good

Order f -, -s & -n order

ordinär *a* common

Ordination /-ˈtsi̯oːn/ f -, -en (*Relig*)
ordination; (*Aust*) surgery

ordn|en *vt* put in order; tidy; (*an-*)
arrange. **O~er** *m* -s,- steward;
(*Akten-*) file

Ordnung f - order; **O~ machen**
tidy up; **in O~ bringen** put in
order; (*aufräumen*) tidy;
(*reparieren*) mend; (*fig*) put right;
in O~ sein be in order;
(*ordentlich sein*) be tidy; (*fig*) be
all right; **[geht] in O~!** OK!
o~sgemäß *a* proper. **O~sstrafe** f
(*Jur*) fine. **o~swidrig** *a* improper

Ordonnanz, Ordonanz f -, -en
(*Mil*) orderly

Organ *nt* -s, -e organ; voice

Organisation /-ˈtsi̯oːn/ f -, -en
organization

organisch *a* organic

organisieren *vt* organize; (I
beschaffen) get [hold of]

Organismus *m* -, -men organism;
(*System*) system

Organspenderkarte f donor card

Orgasmus *m* -, -men orgasm

Orgel f -, -n (*Mus*) organ.
O~pfeife f organ-pipe

Orgie /ˈɔrgi̯ə/ f -, -n orgy

Orien|t /ˈoːriɛnt/ *m* -s Orient.
o~talisch *â* Oriental

orientier|en /oriɛnˈtiːrən/ *vt*
inform (**über** + *acc* about); **sich
o~en** get one's bearings,
orientate oneself; (*unterrichten*)
inform oneself (**über** + *acc*
about). **O~ung** f - orientation; **di
O~ung verlieren** lose one's
bearings

original *a* original. **O~** *nt* -s, -e
original. **O~übertragung** f live
transmission

originell *a* original; (*eigenartig*)
unusual

Orkan *m* -s, -e hurricane

Ornament *nt* -[e]s, -e ornament

Ort *m* -[e]s, -e place; (*Ortschaft*)
[small] town; **am Ort** locally; **am
Ort des Verbrechens** at the scene
of the crime

ortho|dox *a* orthodox. **O~graphie
O~grafie** f - spelling. **O~päde** *m*
-n, -n orthopaedic specialist

örtlich *a* local

Ortschaft f -, -en [small] town;
(*Dorf*) village; **geschlossene O~**
(*Auto*) built-up area

Orts|gespräch *nt* (*Teleph*) local
call. **O~verkehr** *m* local traffic.
O~zeit f local time

Öse f -, -n eyelet; (*Schlinge*) loop;
Haken und Öse hook and eye

Ost *m* -[e]s east

Osten *m* -s east; **nach O~** east

ostentativ *a* pointed

Osteopath *m* -en, -en osteopath

Oster|ei /ˈoːstɐʔai̯:/ *nt* Easter egg.
O~fest *nt* Easter. **O~glocke** f
daffodil. **O~n** *nt* -,- Easter; **frohe
O~n!** happy Easter!

Österreich *nt* -s Austria. **Ö~er** *m*
-s,-, **Ö~erin** f -, -nen Austrian.
ö~isch *a* Austrian

östlich *a* eastern; <*Richtung*>
easterly ● *adv & prep* (+ *gen*) **ö~
[von] der Stadt** [to the] east of the
town

Ostsee f Baltic [Sea]

Otter¹ *m* -s,- otter
Otter² *f* -, -n adder
Ouverture /uvɛr'tyːrə/ *f* -, -n
overture
oval *a* oval. **O~** *nt* -s, -e oval
Oxid, Oxyd *nt* -[e]s, -e oxide
Ozean *m* -s, -e ocean
Ozon *nt* -s ozone. **O~loch** *nt* hole
in the ozone layer. **O~schicht** *f*
ozone layer

paar *pron inv* **ein p~** a few; **ein p~**
Mal a few times; **alle p~ Tage**
every few days. **P~** *nt* -[e]s, -e
pair; (*Ehe-, Liebes-*) couple.
p~en *vt* mate; (*verbinden*)
combine; **sich p~en** mate. **P~ung**
f -, -en mating. **p~weise** *adv* in
pairs, in twos
Pacht *f* -, -en lease; (*P~summe*)
rent. **p~en** *vt* lease
Pächter *m* -s,- lessee; (*eines*
Hofes) tenant
Pachtvertrag *m* lease
Päckchen *nt* -s,- package, small
packet
pack|en *vt/i* (*haben*) pack;
(*ergreifen*) seize; (*fig: fesseln*)
grip. **P~en** *m* -s,- bundle. **p~end**
a (*fig*) gripping. **P~papier** *nt*
[strong] wrapping paper. **P~ung**
f -, -en packet; (*Med*) pack
Pädagog|e *m* -n, -n educationalist;
(*Lehrer*) teacher. **P~ik** *f* -
educational science
Paddel *nt* -s,- paddle. **P~boot** *nt*
canoe. **p~n** *vt/i* (*haben/sein*)
paddle. **P~sport** *m* canoeing
Page /'paːʒə/ *m* -n, -n page
Paillette /pai'jɛtə/ *f* -, -n sequin

Paket *nt* -[e]s, -e packet; (*Post-*)
parcel
Pakist|an *nt* -s Pakistan.
P~aner(in) *m* -s,- (*f* -, -nen)
Pakistani. **p~anisch** *a* Pakistani
Palast *m* -[e]s,-e palace
Paläst|ina *nt* -s Palestine.
P~inenser(in) *m* -s,- (*f* -, -nen)
Palestinian. **p~inensisch** *a*
Palestinian
Palette *f* -, -n palette
Palme *f* -, -n palm[-tree]
Pampelmuse *f* -, -n grapefruit
Panier|mehl *nt* (*Culin*)
breadcrumbs *pl*. **p~t** *a* (*Culin*)
breaded
Panik *f* - panic
Panne *f* -, -n breakdown; (*Reifen-*)
flat tyre; (*Missgeschick*) mishap
Panther, Panter *m* -s,- panther
Pantine *f* -, -n [wooden] clog
Pantoffel *m* -s, -n slipper; mule
Pantomime¹ *f* -, -n mime
Pantomime² *m* -n, -n mime artist
Panzer *m* -s,- armour; (*Mil*) tank;
(*Zool*) shell. **p~n** *vt* armourplate.
P~schrank *m* safe
Papa /'papa, pa'paː/ *m* -s, -s daddy
Papagei *m* -s & -en, -en parrot
Papier *nt* -[e]s, -e paper. **P~korb**
m waste-paper basket.
P~schlange *f* streamer.
P~waren *fpl* stationery *sg*
Pappe *f* - cardboard
Pappel *f* -, -n poplar
pappig *a* 🄳 sticky
Papp|karton *m*, **P~schachtel** *f*
cardboard box
Paprika *m* -s, -[s] [sweet] pepper;
(*Gewürz*) paprika
Papst *m* -[e]s,-e pope
päpstlich *a* papal
Parade *f* -, -n parade
Paradies *nt* -es, -e paradise
Paraffin *nt* -s paraffin
Paragraph, Paragraf *m* -en, -en
section
parallel *a* & *adv* parallel. **P~e** *f* -,
-n parallel

P

Paranuss f Brazil nut

Parasit m -en, -en parasite

parat a ready

Parcours /parˈkuːɐ̯/ m -,- /-[s], -s/ (*Sport*) course

Pardon /parˈdõː/ int sorry!

Parfüm nt -s, -e & -s perfume, scent. **p~iert** a perfumed, scented

parieren vi (*haben*) 🛈 obey

Park m -s, -s park. **p~en** vt/i (*haben*) park. **P~en** nt -s parking; 'P~en verboten' 'no parking'

Parkett nt -[e]s, -e parquet floor; (*Theat*) stalls pl

Park|haus nt multi-storey car park. **P~lücke** f parking space. **P~platz** m car park; parking space. **P~scheibe** f parking-disc. **P~schein** m car-park ticket. **P~uhr** f parking-meter. **P~verbot** nt parking ban; 'P~verbot' 'no parking'

Parlament nt -[e]s, -e parliament. **p~arisch** a parliamentary

Parodie f -, -n parody

Parole f -, -n slogan; (*Mil*) password

Partei f -, -en (*Pol, Jur*) party; (*Miet-*) tenant; **für jdn P~ ergreifen** take s.o.'s part. **p~isch** a biased

Parterre /parˈtɛr/ nt -s, -s ground floor; (*Theat*) rear stalls pl

Partie f -, -n part; (*Tennis, Schach*) game; (*Golf*) round; (*Comm*) batch; **eine gute P~ machen** marry well

Partikel nt -s,- particle

Partitur f -, -en (*Mus*) full score

Partizip nt -s, -ien /-iən/ participle

Partner|(in) m -s,- (f̂ -, -nen) partner. **P~schaft** f -, -en partnership. **P~stadt** f twin town

Party /ˈpaːɐ̯ti/ f -, -s party

Parzelle f -, -n plot [of ground]

Pass m -es,̈-e passport; (*Geog, Sport*) pass

Passage /paˈsaːʒə/ f -, -n passage; (*Einkaufs-*) shopping arcade

Passagier /pasaˈʒiːɐ̯/ m -s, -e passenger

Passant(in) m -en, -en (f -, -nen) passer-by

Passe f -, -n yoke

passen vi (*haben*) fit; (*geeignet sein*) be right (**für** for); (*Sport*) pass the ball; (*aufgeben*) pass; **p~ zu** go [well] with; (*übereinstimmen*) match; **jdm p~** fit s.o.; (*gelegen sein*) suit s.o.; **[ich] passe** pass. **p~d** a suitable; (*angemessen*) appropriate; (*günstig*) convenient; (*übereinstimmend*) matching

passier|en vt pass; cross <*Grenze*>; (*Culin*) rub through a sieve ● vi (*sein*) happen (**jdm** to s.o.); **es ist ein Unglück p~t** there has been an accident. **P~schein** m pass

Passiv nt -s, -e (*Gram*) passive

Passstraße f pass

Paste f -, -n paste

Pastell nt -[e]s, -e pastel

Pastete f -, -n pie; (*Gänseleber-*) pâté

pasteurisieren /pastøriˈziːrən/ vt pasteurize

Pastor m -s, -en /-ˈtoːrən/ pastor

Pate m -n, -n godfather; (*fig*) sponsor; **P~n** godparents. **P~nkind** nt godchild

Patent nt -[e]s, -e patent; (*Offiziers-*) commission. **p~** a 🛈 clever; <*Person*> resourceful. **p~ieren** vt patent

Pater m -s,- (*Relig*) Father

Patholog|e m -n, -n pathologist. **p~isch** a pathological

Patience /paˈsiɑ̃ːs/ f -, -n patience

Patient(in) /paˈtsiɛnt(ɪn)/ m -en, -en (f -, -nen) patient

Patin f -, -nen godmother

Patriot|(in) m -en, -en (f -, -nen) patriot. **p~isch** a patriotic. **P~ismus** m - patriotism

Patrone f -, -n cartridge
Patrouille /pa'trʊljə/ f -, -n patrol
Patsch|e f in der P∼e sitzen ① be in a jam. **p∼nass** a ① soaking wet
Patt nt -s stalemate
Patz|er m -s,- ① slip. **p∼ig** a ① insolent
Pauk|e f -, -n kettledrum; **auf die P∼e hauen** ① have a good time; (*prahlen*) boast. **p∼en** vt/i (*haben*) ① swot
pauschal a all-inclusive; (*einheitlich*) flat-rate; (*fig*) sweeping <*Urteil*>; **p∼e Summe** lump sum. **P∼e** f -, -n lump sum. **P∼reise** f package tour. **P∼summe** f lump sum
Pause¹ f -, -n break; (*beim Sprechen*) pause; (*Theat*) interval; (*im Kino*) intermission; (*Mus*) rest; **P∼ machen** have a break
Pause² f -, -n tracing. **p∼n** vt trace
pausenlos a incessant
pausieren vi (*haben*) have a break; (*ausruhen*) rest
Pauspapier nt tracing-paper
Pavian m -s, -e baboon
Pavillon /'pavɪljõ/ m -s, -s pavilion
Pazifi|k m -s Pacific [Ocean]. **p∼sch** a Pacific
Pazifist m -en, -en pacifist
Pech nt -s pitch; (*Unglück*) bad luck; **P∼ haben** be unlucky
Pedal nt -s, -e pedal
Pedant m -en, -en pedant
Pediküre f -, -n pedicure
Pegel m -s,- level; (*Gerät*) water-level indicator. **P∼stand** m [water] level
peilen vt take a bearing on
peinigen vt torment
peinlich a embarrassing, awkward; (*genau*) scrupulous; **es war mir sehr p∼** I was very embarrassed
Peitsche f -, -n whip. **p∼n** vt whip; (*fig*) lash ● vi (*sein*) lash

(**an** + *acc* against). **P∼nhieb** m lash
Pelikan m -s, -e pelican
Pell|e f -, -n skin. **p∼en** vt peel; shell <*Ei*>; **sich p∼en** peel
Pelz m -es, -e fur
Pendel nt -s,- pendulum. **p∼n** vi (*haben*) swing ● vi (*sein*) commute. **P∼verkehr** m shuttle-service; (*für Pendler*) commuter traffic
Pendler m -s,- commuter
penetrant a penetrating; (*fig*) obtrusive
Penis m -, -se penis
Penne f -, -n ① school
Pension /pã'zio:n/ f -, -en pension; (*Hotel*) guest-house; **bei voller/halber P∼** with full/half board. **P∼är(in)** m -s, -e (f -, -nen) pensioner. **P∼at** nt -[e]s, -e boarding-school. **p∼ieren** vt retire. **P∼ierung** f - retirement
Pensum nt -s [allotted] work
Peperoni f -,- chilli
per prep (+ *acc*) by
Perfekt nt -s (*Gram*) perfect
Perfektion /-'tsio:n/ f - perfection
perforiert a perforated
Pergament nt -[e]s, -e parchment. **P∼papier** nt grease-proof paper
Period|e f -, -n period. **p∼isch** a periodic
Perl|e f -, -n pearl; (*Glas-, Holz-*) bead; (*Sekt-*) bubble. **P∼mutt** nt -s mother-of-pearl
Pers|ien /-iən/ nt -s Persia. **p∼isch** a Persian
Person f -, -en person; (*Theat*) character; **für vier P∼en** for four people
Personal nt -s personnel, staff. **P∼ausweis** m identity card. **P∼chef** m personnel manager. **P∼ien** /-iən/ pl personal particulars. **P∼mangel** m staff shortage

persönlich a personal ● adv personally, in person. **P~keit** f -, -en personality
Perücke f -, -n wig
pervers a [sexually] perverted. **P~ion** f -, -en perversion
Pessimismus m - pessimism. **P~t** m -en, -en pessimist. **p~tisch** a pessimistic
Pest f - plague
Petersilie /-iə/ f - parsley
Petroleum /-leʊm/ nt -s paraffin
Petze f -, -n 🗆 sneak. **p~n** vi (haben) 🗆 sneak
Pfad m -[e]s, -e path. **P~finder** m -s,- [Boy] Scout. **P~finderin** f -, -nen [Girl] Guide
Pfahl m -[e]s,ːe stake, post
Pfalz (die) - the Palatinate
Pfand nt -[e]s,ːe pledge; (beim Spiel) forfeit; (Flaschen-) deposit
pfänd|en vt (Jur) seize. **P~erspiel** nt game of forfeits
Pfandleiher m -s,- pawnbroker
Pfändung f -, -en (Jur) seizure
Pfann|e f -, -n [frying-]pan. **P~kuchen** m pancake
Pfarr|er m -s,- vicar, parson; (katholischer) priest. **P~haus** nt vicarage
Pfau m -s, -en peacock
Pfeffer m -s pepper. **P~kuchen** m gingerbread. **P~minze** f - (Bot) peppermint. **p~n** vt pepper; (🗆 schmeißen) chuck. **P~streuer** m -s,- pepperpot
Pfeif|e f -, -n whistle; (Tabak-, Orgel-) pipe. **p~en†** vt/i (haben) whistle; (als Signal) blow the whistle
Pfeil m -[e]s, -e arrow
Pfeiler m -s,- pillar; (Brücken-) pier
Pfennig m -s, -e pfennig
Pferch m -[e]s, -e [sheep] pen
Pferd nt -es, -e horse; zu P~e on horseback. **P~erennen** nt horse-race; (als Sport) [horse-] racing. **P~eschwanz** m horse's

tail; (Frisur) pony-tail. **P~estall** m stable. **P~estärke** f horsepower
Pfiff m -[e]s, -e whistle
Pfifferling m -s, -e chanterelle
pfiffig a smart
Pfingst|en nt -s Whitsun. **P~rose** f peony
Pfirsich m -s, -e peach
Pflanz|e f -, -n plant. **p~en** vt plant. **P~enfett** nt vegetable fat. **p~lich** a vegetable
Pflaster nt -s,- pavement; (Heft-) plaster. **p~n** vt pave
Pflaume f -, -n plum
Pflege f - care; (Kranken-) nursing; in P~ nehmen look after. (Admin) foster <Kind>. **p~bedürftig** a in need of care. **P~eltern** pl foster-parents. **P~kind** nt foster-child. **p~leicht** a easy-care. **p~n** vt look after, care for; nurse <Kranke>; cultivate <Künste, Freundschaft>. **P~r(in)** m -s,- (f -, -nen) nurse; (Tier-) keeper
Pflicht f -, -en duty; (Sport) compulsory exercise/routine. **p~bewusst** a conscientious. **P~gefühl** nt sense of duty
pflücken vt pick
Pflug m -[e]s,ːe plough
pflügen vt/i (haben) plough
Pforte f -, -n gate
Pförtner m -s,- porter
Pfosten m -s,- post
Pfote f -, -n paw
Pfropfen m -s,- stopper; (Korken-) cork. **p~** vt graft (auf + acc on [to]); (🗆 pressen) cram (in + acc into)
pfui int ugh
Pfund nt -[e]s, -e & - pound
Pfusch|arbeit f 🗆 shoddy work. **p~en** vi (haben) 🗆 botch one's work. **P~erei** f -, -en 🗆 botch-up
Pfütze f -, -n puddle
Phantasie f -, -n imagination; **P~n** fantasies; (Fieber-)

hallucinations. **p~los** *a* unimaginative. **p~ren** *vi* (*haben*) fantasize; (*im Fieber*) be delirious. **p~voll** *a* imaginative

phantastisch *a* fantastic

pharma|zeutisch *a* pharmaceutical. **P~zie** *f* -pharmacy

Phase *f* -, -n phase

Philologie *f* - [study of] language and literature

Philosoph *m* -en, -en philosopher. **P~ie** *f* -, -n philosophy

philosophisch *a* philosophical

Phobie *f* -, -n phobia

Phonet|ik *f* - phonetics *sg*. **p~isch** *a* phonetic

Phosphor *m* -s phosphorus

Photo *nt*, **Photo-** = Foto, Foto-

Phrase *f* -, -n empty phrase

Physik *f* - physics *sg*. **p~alisch** *a* physical

Physiker(in) *m* -s,- (*f* -, -nen) physicist

Physiologie *f* - physiology

physisch *a* physical

Pianist(in) *m* -en, -en (*f* -, -nen) pianist

Pickel *m* -s,- pimple, spot; (*Spitzhacke*) pick. **p~ig** *a* spotty

Picknick *nt* -s, -s picnic

piep[s]|en *vi* (*haben*) <*Vogel:*> cheep; <*Maus:*> squeak; (*Techn*) bleep. **P~er** *m* -s,- bleeper

Pier *m* -s, -e [harbour] pier

Pietät /pie'tɛ:t/ *f* - reverence. **p~los** *a* irreverent

Pigment *nt* -[e]s, -e pigment. **P~ierung** *f* - pigmentation

Pik *nt* -s, -s (*Karten*) spades *pl*

pikant *a* piquant; (*gewagt*) racy

piken *vt* 🗉 prick

pikiert *a* offended, hurt

Pilger|(in) *m* -s,- (*f* -, -nen) pilgrim. **P~fahrt** *f* pilgrimage. **p~n** *vi* (*sein*) make a pilgrimage

Pille *f* -, -n pill

Pilot *m* -en, -en pilot

Pilz *m* -es, -e fungus; (*essbarer*) mushroom

pingelig *a* 🗉 fussy

Pinguin *m* -s, -e penguin

Pinie /-iə/ *f* -, -n stone-pine

pinkeln *vi* (*haben*) 🗉 pee

Pinsel *m* -s,- [paint]brush

Pinzette *f* -, -n tweezers *pl*

Pionier *m* -s, -e (*Mil*) sapper; (*fig*) pioneer

Pirat *m* -en, -en pirate

Piste *f* -, -n (*Ski*-) run, piste; (*Renn-*) track; (*Aviat*) runway

Pistole *f* -, -n pistol

pitschnass *a* 🗉 soaking wet

pittoresk *a* picturesque

Pizza *f* -, -s pizza

Pkw /'pe:kave:/ *m* -s, -s car

plädieren *vi* (*haben*) plead (**für** for); **auf Freispruch p~** (*Jur*) ask for an acquittal

Plädoyer /plɛdoa'je:/ *nt* -s, -s (*Jur*) closing speech; (*fig*) plea

Plage *f* -, -n [hard] labour; (*Mühe*) trouble; (*Belästigung*) nuisance. **p~n** *vt* torment, plague; (*bedrängen*) pester; **sich p~n** struggle

Plakat *nt* -[e]s, -e poster

Plakette *f* -, -n badge

Plan *m* -[e]s,ˉe plan

Plane *f* -, -n tarpaulin; (*Boden-*) groundsheet

planen *vt/i* (*haben*) plan

Planet *m* -en, -en planet

planier|en *vt* level. **P~raupe** *f* bulldozer

Planke *f* -, -n plank

plan|los *a* unsystematic. **p~mäßig** *a* systematic; <*Ankunft:*> scheduled

Plansch|becken *nt* paddling pool. **p~en** *vi* (*haben*) splash about

Plantage /plan'ta:ʒə/ *f* -, -n plantation

Planung *f* - planning

plappern *vi* (*haben*) chatter ●*vt* talk <*Unsinn*>

P

plärren vi (haben) bawl

Plasma nt -s plasma

Plastik¹ f -, -en sculpture

Plast|ik² nt -s plastic. **p~isch** a three-dimensional; (formbar) plastic; (anschaulich) graphic

Plateau /pla'to:/ nt -s, -s plateau

Platin nt -s platinum

platonisch a platonic

plätschern vi (haben) splash; <Bach:> babble ● vi (sein) <Bach:> babble along

platt a & adv flat. **P~** nt -[s] (Lang) Low German

Plättbrett nt ironing-board

Platte f -, -n slab; (Druck-) plate; (Metall-, Glas-) sheet; (Fliese) tile; (Koch-) hotplate; (Tisch-) top; (Schall-) record, disc; (zum Servieren) [flat] dish, platter; **kalte P~** assorted cold meats and cheeses pl

Plätt|eisen nt iron. **p~en** vt/i (haben) iron

Plattenspieler m record-player

Platt|form f -, -en platform. **P~füße** mpl flat feet

Platz m -es, ̈e place; (von Häusern umgeben) square; (Sitz-) seat; (Sport-) ground; (Fußball-) pitch; (Tennis-) court; (Golf-) course; (freier Raum) room, space; **P~ nehmen** take a seat; **P~ machen** make room; **vom P~ stellen** (Sport) send off. **P~anweiserin** f -, -nen usherette

Plätzchen nt -s, - spot; (Culin) biscuit

platzen vi (sein) burst; (auf-) split; (🅻 scheitern) fall through; <Verlobung:> be off

Platz|karte f seat reservation ticket. **P~mangel** m lack of space. **P~patrone** f blank. **P~verweis** m (Sport) sending off. **P~wunde** f laceration

Plauderei f -, -en chat

plaudern vi (haben) chat

plausibel a plausible

pleite a 🅻 **p~ sein** be broke: <Firma:> be bankrupt. **P~** f -, -n 🅻 bankruptcy; (Misserfolg) flop; **P~ gehen** od **machen** go bankrupt

plissiert a [finely] pleated

Plomb|e f -, -n seal; (Zahn-) filling. **p~ieren** vt seal; fill <Zahn>

plötzlich a sudden

plump a plump; clumsy

plumpsen vi (sein) 🅻 fall

plündern vt/i (haben) loot

Plunderstück nt Danish pastry

Plural m -s, -e plural

plus adv, conj & prep (+ dat) plus. **P~** nt - surplus; (Gewinn) profit (Vorteil) advantage, plus. **P~punkt** m (Sport) point; (fig) plus

Po m -s, -s 🅻 bottom

Pöbel m -s mob, rabble. **p~haft** a loutish

pochen vi (haben) knock, <Herz:> pound; **p~ auf** (+ acc) (fig) insist on

pochieren /pɔ'ʃi:rən/ vt poach

Pocken pl smallpox sg

Podest nt -[e]s, -e rostrum

Podium nt -s, -ien /-iən/ platform; (Podest) rostrum

Poesie /poe'zi:/ f - poetry

poetisch a poetic

Pointe /'poɛ̃:tə/ f -, -n point (of a joke)

Pokal m -s, -e goblet; (Sport) cup

pökeln vt (Culin) salt

Poker nt -s poker

Pol m -s, -e pole. **p~ar** a polar

Polarstern m pole-star

Pole m, -n, -n Pole. **P~n** nt -s Poland

Police /po'li:sə/ f -, -n policy

Polier m -s, -e foreman

polieren vt polish

Polin f -, -nen Pole

Politesse f -, -n [woman] traffic warden

Politik f - politics sg; (Vorgehen, Maßnahme) policy

Polit|iker(in) m -s,- (f, -, -nen) politician. **p~isch** a political
Politur f -, -en polish
Polizei f - police pl. **p~lich** a police ... ● adv by the police; <sich anmelden> with the police. **P~streife** f police patrol. **P~stunde** f closing time. **P~wache** f police station
Polizist m -en, -en policeman. **P~in** f -, -nen policewoman
Pollen m -s pollen
polnisch a Polish
Polster nt -s,- pad; (Kissen) cushion; (Möbel-) upholstery. **p~n** vt pad; upholster <Möbel>. **P~ung** f - padding; upholstery
Polter|abend m wedding-eve party. **p~n** vi (haben) thump bang
Polyäthylen nt -s polythene
Polyester m -s polyester
Polyp m -en, -en polyp. **P~en** adenoids pl
Pommes frites /pɔm'fri:t/ pl chips; (dünner) French fries
Pomp m -s pomp
Pompon /põ'põ:/ m -s, -s pompon
pompös a ostentatious
Pony¹ nt -s, -s pony
Pony² m -s, -s fringe
Pop m -[s] pop
Popo m -s, -s 🗓 bottom
populär a popular
Pore f -, -n pore
Porno|graphie, Pornografie f - pornography. **p~graphisch, p~grafisch** a pornographic
Porree m -s leeks pl
Portal nt -s, -e portal
Portemonnaie /pɔrtmɔ'neː/ nt -s, -s purse
Portier /pɔr'tieː/ m -s, -s doorman, porter
Portion /-'tsɪoːn/ f -, -en helping, portion
Portmonee nt -s, -s = Portemonnaie

Porto nt -s postage. **p~frei** adv post free, post paid
Porträ|t /pɔr'trɛː/ nt -s, -s portrait. **p~tieren** vt paint a portrait of
Portugal nt -s Portugal
Portugies|e m -n, -n, **P~in** f -, -nen Portuguese. **p~isch** a Portuguese
Portwein m port
Porzellan nt -s china, porcelain
Posaune f -, -n trombone
Position /-'tsɪoːn/ f -, -en position
positiv a positive. **P~** nt -s, -e (Phot) positive
Post f - post office; (Briefe) mail, post; mit der **P~** by post
postalisch a postal
Post|amt nt post office. **P~anweisung** f postal money order. **P~bote** m postman
Posten m -s,- post; (Wache) sentry; (Waren-) batch; (Rechnungs-) item, entry
Poster nt & m -s,- poster
Postfach nt post-office or PO box
Post|karte f postcard. **p~lagernd** adv poste restante. **P~leitzahl** f postcode. **P~scheckkonto** nt ≈ National Girobank account. **P~stempel** m postmark
postum a posthumous
post|wendend adv by return of post. **P~wertzeichen** nt [postage] stamp
Potenz f -, -en potency; (Math & fig) power
Pracht f - magnificence, splendour
prächtig a magnificent; splendid
prachtvoll a magnificent
Prädikat nt -[e]s, -e rating; (Comm) grade; (Gram) predicate
prägen vt stamp (auf + acc on); emboss <Leder>; mint <Münze>; coin <Wort>; (fig) shape
prägnant a succinct
prähistorisch a prehistoric
prahl|en vi (haben) boast, brag (mit about)

P

Prakti|k f -, -en practice. **P~kant(in)** m -en, -en (f -, -nen) trainee

Prakti|kum nt -s, -ka practical training. **p~sch** a practical; (nützlich) handy; (tatsächlich) virtual; **p~scher Arzt** general practitioner ●adv practically; virtually; (in der Praxis) in practice. **p~zieren** vt/i (haben) practise; (anwenden) put into practice; (⊞ bekommen) get

Praline f -, -n chocolate

prall a bulging; (dick) plump; <Sonne> blazing ●adv **p~ gefüllt** full to bursting. **p~en** vi (sein) **p~ auf** (+ acc)/**gegen** collide with, hit; <Sonne:> blaze down on

Prämie /-iə/ f -, -n premium; (Preis) award

präm[i]ieren vt award a prize to

Pranger m -s,- pillory

Pranke f -, -n paw

Präparat nt -[e]s, -e preparation

Präsens nt - (Gram) present

präsentieren vt present

Präsenz f - presence

Präservativ nt -s, -e condom

Präsident|(in) m -en, -en (f -, -nen) president. **P~schaft** f - presidency

Präsidium nt -s presidency; (Gremium) executive committee; (Polizei-) headquarters pl

prasseln vi (haben) <Regen:> beat down; <Feuer:> crackle

Präteritum nt -s imperfect

Praxis f -, -xen practice; (Erfahrung) practical experience; (Arzt-) surgery; **in der P~** in practice

Präzedenzfall m precedent

präzis[e] a precise

predig|en vt/i (haben) preach. **P~t** f -, -en sermon

Preis m -es, -e price; (Belohnung) prize. **P~ausschreiben** nt competition

Preiselbeere f (Bot) cowberry; (Culin) ≈ cranberry

preisen† vt praise

preisgeben† vt sep abandon (dat to); reveal <Geheimnis>

preis|gekrönt a award-winning. **p~günstig** a reasonably priced ●adv at a reasonable price. **P~lage** f price range. **p~lich** a price ... ●adv in price. **P~richter** m judge. **P~schild** nt price-tag. **P~träger(in)** m(f) prize-winner. **p~wert** a reasonable

Prell|bock m buffers pl. **p~en** vt bounce; (verletzen) bruise; (⊞ betrügen) cheat. **P~ung** f -, -en bruise

Premiere /prə'miɛ:rə/ f -, -n première

Premierminister(in) /prə'mie:-/ m(f) Prime Minister

Presse f -, -n press. **p~n** vt press

Pressluftbohrer m pneumatic drill

Preuß|en nt -s Prussia. **p~isch** a Prussian

prickeln vi (haben) tingle

Priester m -s,- priest

prima inv a first-class, first-rate; (⊞ toll) fantastic

primär a primary

Primel f -, -n primula

primitiv a primitive

Prinz m -en, -en prince. **P~essin** f -, -nen princess

Prinzip nt -s, -ien /-iən/ principle. **p~iell** a <Frage> of principle ●adv on principle

Prise f -, -n **P~ Salz** pinch of salt

Prisma nt -s, -men prism

privat a private, personal. **P~adresse** f home address. **p~isieren** vt privatize

Privileg nt -[e]s, -ien /-iən/ privilege. **p~iert** a privileged

pro prep (+ dat) per. **Pro** nt - das **Pro und Kontra** the pros and cons pl

Probe f -, -n test, trial; (Menge, Muster) sample; (Theat) rehearsal; **auf die P~ stellen** put to the test; **ein Auto P~ fahren** test-drive a car. **p~n** vt/i (haben) (Theat) rehearse. **p~weise** adv on a trial basis. **P~zeit** f probationary period

probieren vt/i (haben) try; (kosten) taste; (proben) rehearse

Problem nt -s, -e problem. **p~atisch** a problematic

problemlos a problem-free ● adv without any problems

Produkt nt -[e]s, -e product

Produk|tion /-'tsio:n/ f -, -en production. **p~tiv** a productive

Produ|zent m -en, -en producer. **p~zieren** vt produce

Professor m -s, -en /-'so:rən/ professor

Profi m -s, -s (Sport) professional

Profil nt -s, -e profile; (Reifen-) tread; (fig) image

Profit m -[e]s, -e profit. **p~ieren** vi (haben) profit (**von** from)

Prognose f -, -n forecast; (Med) prognosis

Programm nt -s, -e programme; (Computer-) program; (TV) channel; (Comm: Sortiment) range. **p~ieren** vt/i (haben) (Computer) program. **P~ierer(in)** m -s,- (f -, -nen) [computer] programmer

Projekt nt -[e]s, -e project

Projektor m -s, -en /-'to:rən/ projector

Prolet m -en, -en boor. **P~ariat** nt -[e]s proletariat

Prolog m -s, -e prologue

Promenade f -, -n promenade

Promille pl ⓘ alcohol level sg in the blood; **zu viel P~ haben** ⓘ be over the limit

Prominenz f - prominent figures pl

Promiskuität f - promiscuity

promovieren vi (haben) obtain one's doctorate

prompt a prompt

Pronomen nt -s,- pronoun

Propaganda f - propaganda; (Reklame) publicity

Propeller m -s,- propeller

Prophet m -en, -en prophet

prophezei|en vt prophesy. **P~ung** f -, -en prophecy

Proportion /-'tsio:n/ f -, -en proportion

Prosa f - prose

prosit int cheers!

Prospekt m -[e]s, -e brochure; (Comm) prospectus

prost int cheers!

Prostitu|ierte f -n, -n prostitute. **P~tion** /-'tsio:n/ f - prostitution

Protest m -[e]s, -e protest

Protestant|(in) m -en, -en (f -, -nen) (Relig) Protestant. **p~isch** a (Relig) Protestant

protestieren vi (haben) protest

Prothese f -, -n artificial limb; (Zahn-) denture

Protokoll nt -s, -e record; (Sitzungs-) minutes pl; (diplomatisches) protocol

protz|en vi (haben) show off (**mit etw** sth). **p~ig** a ostentatious

Proviant m -s provisions pl

Provinz f -, -en province

Provision f -, -en (Comm) commission

provisorisch a provisional, temporary

Provokation /-'tsio:n/ f -, -en provocation

provozieren vt provoke

Prozedur f -, -en [lengthy] business

Prozent nt -[e]s, -e & - per cent; 5 **P~** 5 per cent. **P~satz** m percentage. **p~ual** a percentage …

Prozess m -es, -e process; (Jur) lawsuit; (Kriminal-) trial

Prozession f -, -en procession

P

prüde *a* prudish

prüf|en *vt* test/(*über-*) check (**auf** + *acc* for); audit <*Bücher*>; (*Sch*) examine; **p~ender Blick** searching look. **P~er** *m* -s,- inspector; (*Buch-*) auditor; (*Sch*) examiner. **P~ling** *m* -s, -e examination candidate. **P~ung** *f* -, -en examination; (*Test*) test; (*Bücher-*) audit; (*fig*) trial

Prügel *m* -s,- cudgel; **P~** *pl* hiding *sg*, beating *sg*. **P~ei** *f* -, -en brawl, fight. **p~n** *vt* beat, thrash

Prunk *m* -[e]s magnificence, splendour

Psalm *m* -s, -en psalm

Pseudonym *nt* -s, -e pseudonym

pst *int* shush!

Psychi|ater *m* -s,- psychiatrist. **P~atrie** *f* - psychiatry. **p~atrisch** *a* psychiatric

psychisch *a* psychological

Psycho|analyse *f* psychoanalysis. **P~loge** *m* -n, -n psychologist. **P~logie** *f* - psychology. **p~logisch** *a* psychological

Pubertät *f* - puberty

Publi|kum *nt* -s public; (*Zuhörer*) audience; (*Zuschauer*) spectators *pl*. **p~zieren** *vt* publish

Pudding *m* -s blancmange; (*im Wasserbad gekocht*) pudding

Pudel *m* -s,- poodle

Puder *m* & ▣ *nt* -s,- powder. **P~dose** *f* [powder] compact. **p~n** *vt* powder. **P~zucker** *m* icing sugar

Puff *m* & *nt* -s, -s ▣ brothel

Puffer *m* -s,- (*Rail*) buffer; (*Culin*) pancake. **P~zone** *f* buffer zone

Pull|i *m* -s, -s jumper. **P~over** *m* -s,- jumper; (*Herren-*) pullover

Puls *m* -es pulse. **P~ader** *f* artery

Pult *nt* -[e]s, -e desk

Pulver *nt* -s,- powder. **p~ig** *a* powdery

Pulverkaffee *m* instant coffee

pummelig *a* ▣ chubby

Pumpe *f* -, -n pump. **p~n** *vt/i* (*haben*) pump; (▣ *leihen*) lend; [**sich** (*dat*)] **etw p~n** (▣ *borgen*) borrow sth

Pumps /pœmps/ *pl* court shoes

Punkt *m* -[e]s, -e dot; (*Tex*) spot; (*Geom, Sport & fig*) point; (*Gram*) full stop, period; **P~ sechs Uhr** at six o'clock sharp

pünktlich *a* punctual. **P~keit** *f* - punctuality

Pupille *f* -, -n (*Anat*) pupil

Puppe *f* -, -n doll; (*Marionette*) puppet; (*Schaufenster-, Schneider-*) dummy; (*Zool*) chrysalis

pur *a* pure; (▣ *bloß*) sheer

Püree *nt* -s, -s purée; (*Kartoffel-*) mashed potatoes *pl*

purpurrot *a* crimson

Purzel|baum *m* ▣ somersault. **p~n** *vi* (*sein*) ▣ tumble

Puste *f* - ▣ breath. **p~n** *vt/i* (*haben*) ▣ blow

Pute *f* -, -n turkey

Putsch *m* -[e]s, -e coup

Putz *m* -es plaster; (*Staat*) finery. **p~en** *vt* clean; (*Aust*) dry-clean; (*zieren*) adorn; **sich p~en** dress up; **sich** (*dat*) **die Zähne/Nase p~en** clean one's teeth/blow one's nose. **P~frau** *f* cleaner, charwoman. **p~ig** *a* ▣ amusing, cute; (*seltsam*) odd

Puzzlespiel /'pazl-/ *nt* jigsaw

Pyramide *f* -, -n pyramid

Quacksalber *m* -s,- quack

Quadrat *nt* -[e]s, -e square. **q~isch** *a* square

quaken vi (haben) quack;
<Frosch:> croak
Quäker(in) m -s,- (f -, -nen)
Quaker
Qual f -, -en torment; (Schmerz)
agony
quälen vt torment; (foltern)
torture; (bedrängen) pester; **sich
q~** torment oneself; (leiden)
suffer; (sich mühen) struggle
Quälerei f -, -en torture
Qualifi|kation /-'tsi:o:n/ f -, -en
qualification. **q~zieren** vt qualify.
q~ziert a qualified; (fähig)
competent; <Arbeit> skilled
Qualität f -, -en quality
Qualle f -, -n jellyfish
Qualm m -s [thick] smoke
qualvoll a agonizing
Quantum nt -s, -ten quantity;
(Anteil) share, quota
Quarantäne f - quarantine
Quark m -s quark, ≈ curd cheese
Quartal nt -s, -e quarter
Quartett nt -[e]s, -e quartet
Quartier nt -s, -e accommodation;
(Mil) quarters pl
Quarz m -es quartz
quasseln vi (haben) 🔲 jabber
Quaste f -, -n tassel
Quatsch m -[e]s 🔲 nonsense,
rubbish; **Q~ machen** (Unfug
machen) fool around; (etw falsch
machen) do a silly thing. **q~en** 🔲
vi (haben) talk; <Wasser,
Schlamm:> squelch ● vt talk
Quecksilber nt mercury
Quelle f -, -n spring; (Fluss- & fig)
source
quengeln vi 🔲 whine
quer adv across, crosswise;
(schräg) diagonally; **q~ gestreift**
horizontally striped
Quere f - der Q~ nach across,
crosswise; **jdm in die Q~ kommen**
get in s.o.'s way
Quer|latte f crossbar. **Q~schiff** nt
transept. **Q~schnitt** m cross-
section. **q~schnittsgelähmt** a

paraplegic. **Q~straße** f side-
street. **Q~verweis** m cross-
reference
quetschen vt squash; (drücken)
squeeze; (zerdrücken) crush;
(Culin) mash; **sich q~ in** (+ acc)
squeeze into
Queue /kø:/ nt -s, -s cue
quieken vi (haben) squeal;
<Maus:> squeak
quietschen vi (haben) squeal;
<Tür, Dielen:> creak
Quintett nt -[e]s, -e quintet
quirlen vt mix
Quitte f -, -n quince
quittieren vt receipt <Rechnung>;
sign for <Geldsumme, Sendung>;
den Dienst q~ resign
Quittung f -, -en receipt
Quiz /kvɪs/ nt -,- quiz
Quote f -, -n proportion

Rabatt m -[e]s, -e discount
Rabatte f -, -n (Hort) border
Rabattmarke f trading stamp
Rabbiner m -s,- rabbi
Rabe m -n, -n raven
Rache f - revenge, vengeance
Rachen m -s,- pharynx
rächen vt avenge; **sich r~** take
revenge (an + dat on); <Fehler:>
cost s.o. dear
Rad nt -[e]s,-̈er wheel; (Fahr-)
bicycle, 🔲 bike; **Rad fahren** cycle
Radar m & nt -s radar
Radau m -s 🔲 din, racket
radeln vi (sein) 🔲 cycle
Rädelsführer m ringleader

radfahr|en* vi sep (sein) Rad fahren, s. Rad. R~er(in) m(f) -s,- (f -, -nen) cyclist

radier|en vt/i (haben) rub out; (Kunst) etch. R~gummi m eraser, rubber. R~ung f -, -en etching

Radieschen /-'di:sçən/ nt -s,- radish

radikal a radical, drastic

Radio nt -s, -s radio

radioaktiv a radioactive. R~ität f - radioactivity

Radius m -, -ien /-iən/ radius

Rad|kappe f hub-cap. R~ler m -s,- cyclist; (Getränk) shandy

raffen vt grab; (kräuseln) gather; (kürzen) condense

Raffin|ade f - refined sugar. R~erie f -, -n refinery. R~esse f -, -n refinement; (Schlauheit) cunning. r~iert a ingenious; (durchtrieben) crafty

ragen vi (haben) rise [up]

Rahm m -s (SGer) cream

rahmen vt frame. R~ m -s,- frame; (fig) framework; (Grenze) limits pl; (einer Feier) setting

Rakete f -, -n rocket; (Mil) missile

Rallye /'rali/ nt -s, -s rally

rammen vt ram

Rampe f -, -n ramp; (Theat) front of the stage

Ramsch m -[e]s junk

ran adv = heran

Rand m -[e]s,̈-er edge (Teller-, Gläser-, Brillen-) rim; (Zier-) border, edging; (Brief-) margin; (Stadt-) outskirts pl; (Ring) ring

randalieren vi (haben) rampage

Randstreifen m (Auto) hard shoulder

Rang m -[e]s,̈e rank; (Theat) tier; erster/zweiter R~ (Theat) dress/ upper circle; ersten R~es first-class

rangieren /raŋˈʒiːrən/ vt shunt ● vi (haben) rank (vor + dat before)

Rangordnung f order of importance; (Hierarchie) hierarchy

Ranke f -, -n tendril; (Trieb) shoo

ranken (sich) vr (Bot) trail; (in di Höhe) climb

Ranzen m -s,- (Sch) satchel

ranzig a rancid

Rappe m -n, -n black horse

Raps m -es (Bot) rape

rar a rare; er macht sich rar [!] we don't see much of him. R~ität f -, -en rarity

rasant a fast; (schnittig, schick) stylish

rasch a quick

rascheln vi (haben) rustle

Rasen m -s,- lawn

rasen vi (sein) tear [along]; <Puls:> race; <Zeit:> fly; gegen eine Mauer r~ career into a wall ● vi (haben) rave; <Sturm:> rage. r~d a furious; (tobend) raving; <Sturm, Durst> raging; <Schmerz> excruciating; <Beifall> tumultuous

Rasenmäher m lawn-mower

Rasier|apparat m razor. r~en vt shave; sich r~en shave. R~klinge f razor blade. R~wasser nt aftershave [lotion]

Raspel f -, -n rasp; (Culin) grater. r~n vt grate

Rasse f -, -n race. R~hund m pedigree dog

Rassel f -, -n rattle. r~n vi (haben) rattle; <Schlüssel:> jangle; <Kette:> clank

Rassendiskriminierung f racial discrimination

Rassepferd nt thoroughbred. **rassisch** a racial

Rassis|mus m - racism. r~tisch a racist

Rast f -, -en rest. R~platz m picnic area. R~stätte f motorway restaurant [and services]

Rasur f -, -en shave

Rat m -[e]s [piece of] advice; sich (dat) keinen Rat wissen not know what to do; zu Rat[e] ziehen = zurate ziehen, s. zurate

Rate f -, -n instalment

raten† vt guess; (empfehlen) advise ●vi (haben) guess; jdm r~ advise s.o.

Ratenzahlung f payment by instalments

Rat|geber m -s,- adviser; (Buch) guide. **R~haus** nt town hall

ratifizier|en vt ratify. **R~ung** f -, -en ratification

Ration /ra'tsi̯o:n/ f -, -en ration. **r~ell** a efficient. **r~ieren** vt ration

rat|los a helpless; **r~los sein** not know what to do. **r~sam** pred a advisable; prudent. **R~schlag** m piece of advice; **R~schläge** advice sg

Rätsel nt -s,- riddle; (Kreuzwort-) puzzle; (Geheimnis) mystery. **r~haft** a puzzling, mysterious. **r~n** vi (haben) puzzle

Ratte f -, -n rat

rau a rough; (unfreundlich) gruff; <Klima> harsh, raw; (heiser) husky; <Hals> sore

Raub m -[e]s robbery; (Menschen-) abduction; (Beute) loot, booty. **r~en** vt steal; abduct <Menschen>

Räuber m -s,- robber

Raub|mord m robbery with murder. **R~tier** nt predator. **R~vogel** m bird of prey

Rauch m -[e]s smoke. **r~en** vt/i (haben) smoke. **R~en** nt -s smoking; 'R~en verboten' 'no smoking'. **R~er** m -s, -smoker

Räucher|lachs m smoked salmon. **r~n** vt (Culin) smoke

rauf adv = herauf, hinauf

rauf|en vt pull ●vr/i (haben) [sich] r~en fight. **R~erei** f -,-en fight

rauh* a s. rau

Raum m -[e]s, Räume room; (Gebiet) area; (Welt-) space

räumen vt clear; vacate <Wohnung>; evacuate <Gebäude, Gebiet, (Mil) Stellung>; (bringen) put (in/auf + acc into/on); (holen) get (aus out of)

Raum|fahrer m astronaut. **R~fahrt** f space travel. **R~inhalt** m volume

räumlich a spatial

Raum|pflegerin f cleaner. **R~schiff** nt spaceship

Räumung f - clearing; vacating; evacuation. **R~sverkauf** m clearance/closing-down sale

Raupe f -, -n caterpillar

raus adv = heraus, hinaus

Rausch m -[e]s, Räusche intoxication; (fig) exhilaration; einen R~haben be drunk

rauschen vi (haben) <Wasser, Wind:> rush; <Bäume Blätter:> rustle ●vi (sein) rush [along]

Rauschgift nt [narcotic] drug; (coll) drugs pl. **R~süchtige(r)** m/f drug addict

räuspern (sich) vr clear one's throat

rausschmeißen† vt sep ! throw out; (entlassen) sack

Raute f -, -n diamond

Razzia f -, -ien /-i̯ən/ [police] raid

Reagenzglas nt test-tube

reagieren vi (haben) react (auf + acc to)

Reaktion /-'tsi̯o:n/ f -, -en reaction. **r~är** a reactionary

Reaktor m -s, -en /-'to:rən/ reactor

realisieren vt realize

Real|ismus m -, realism. **R~t** m -en, -en realist. **r~tisch** a realistic

Realität f -, -en reality

Realschule f ≈ secondary modern school

Rebe f -, -n vine

Rebell m -en, -en rebel. **r~ieren** vi (haben) rebel. **R~ion** f -, -en rebellion

R

rebellisch a rebellious

Rebhuhn nt partridge

Rebstock m vine

Rechen m -s- rake

Rechen|aufgabe f arithmetical problem; (Sch) sum.
R~maschine f calculator

recherchieren /reʃɛrˈʃiːrən/ vt/i (haben) investigate; (Journ) research

rechnen vi (haben) do arithmetic; (schätzen) reckon; (zählen) count (zu among; auf + acc on); r~ mit reckon with; (erwarten) expect ● vt calculate, work out; (fig) count (zu among). **R~** nt -s arithmetic

Rechner m -s,- calculator; (Computer) computer

Rechnung f -, -en bill; (Comm) invoice; (Berechnung) calculation; **R~ führen über** (+ acc) keep account of. **R~sjahr** nt financial year. **R~sprüfer** m auditor

Recht nt -[e]s, -e law; (Berechtigung) right (auf + acc to); **im R~ sein** be in the right; **R~ haben/behalten** be right; **R~ bekommen** be proved right; **jdm R~ geben** agree with s.o.; **mit od zu R~** rightly

recht a right; (wirklich) real; **ich habe keine r~e Lust** I don't really feel like it; **es jdm r~ machen** please s.o.; **jdm r~ sein** be all right with s.o. **r~ vielen Dank** many thanks

Recht|e f -n, -[n] right side; (Hand) right hand; (Boxen) right; **die R~e** (Pol) the right; **zu meiner R~en** on my right. **r~e(r,s)** a right; (Pol) right-wing; **r~e Masche** plain stitch. **R~e(r)** m/f **der/die R~e** the right man/woman; **R~e(s)** nt **das R~e** the right thing; **etwas R~es lernen** learn something useful; **nach dem R~en sehen** see that everything is all right

Rechteck nt -[e]s, -e rectangle. **r~ig** a rectangular

rechtfertigen vt justify; **sich r~er** justify oneself

recht|haberisch a opinionated. **r~lich** a legal. **r~mäßig** a legitimate

rechts adv on the right; (bei Stoff) on the right side; **von/nach r~** from/to the right; **zwei r~, zwei links stricken** knit two, purl two. **R~anwalt** m, **R~anwältin** f lawyer

Rechtschreibung f - spelling

Rechts|händer(in) m -s,- (f -, -nen) right-hander. **r~händig** a & adv right-handed. **r~kräftig** a legal. **R~streit** m law suit. **R~verkehr** m driving on the right. **r~widrig** a illegal. **R~wissenschaft** f jurisprudence

rechtzeitig a & adv in time

Reck nt -[e]s, -e horizontal bar

recken vt stretch

Redakteur /redakˈtøːɐ̯/ m -s, -e editor; (Radio, TV) producer

Redaktion /-ˈtsɪoːn/ f -, -en editing; (Radio, TV) production; (Abteilung) editorial/production department

Rede f -, -n speech; **zur R~ stellen** demand an explanation from; **nicht der R~ wert** not worth mentioning

reden vi (haben) talk (von about; mit to); (eine Rede halten) speak ● vt talk; speak <Wahrheit>. **R~sart** f saying

Redewendung f idiom

redigieren vt edit

Redner m -s,- speaker

reduzieren vt reduce

Reeder m -s,- shipowner. **R~ei** f -en shipping company

Refer|at nt -[e]s, -e report; (Abhandlung) paper; (Abteilung) section. **R~ent(in)** m -en, -en (f -, -nen) speaker; (Sachbearbeiter) expert. **R~enz** f -, -en reference

eflex m -es, -e reflex; (*Widerschein*) reflection. **R~ion** f -, -en reflection. **r~iv** a reflexive

eform f -, -en reform. **R~ation** -'tsio:n/ f - (*Relig*) Reformation

eformhaus nt health-food shop. **r~ieren** vt reform

efrain /rə'frɛ̃:/ m -s, -s refrain

egal nt -s, -e [set of] shelves pl

egatta f -, -ten regatta

ege a active; (*lebhaft*) lively; (*geistig*) alert; <*Handel*> brisk

egel f -, -n rule; (*Monats-*) period. **r~mäßig** a regular. **r~n** vt regulate; direct <*Verkehr*>; (*erledigen*) settle. **r~recht** a real, proper ● adv really. **R~ung** f -, -en regulation; settlement

egen vt move; sich r~ move; (*wach werden*) stir

Regen m -s,- rain. **R~bogen** m rainbow. **R~bogenhaut** f iris

Regener|ation /-'tsio:n/ f - regeneration. **r~ieren** vt regenerate

Regen|mantel m raincoat. **R~schirm** m umbrella. **R~tag** m rainy day. **R~wetter** nt wet weather. **R~wurm** m earthworm

Regie /re'ʒi:/ f - direction; **R~ führen** direct

egier|en vt/i (*haben*) govern, rule; <*Monarch:*> reign [over]; (*Gram*) take. **R~ung** f -, -en government; (*Herrschaft*) rule; (*eines Monarchen*) reign

Regiment nt -[e]s, -er regiment

Region f -, -en region. **r~al** a regional

Regisseur /reʒɪ'sø:ɐ̯/ m -s, -e director

Register nt -s,- register; (*Inhaltsverzeichnis*) index; (*Orgel-*) stop

Regler m -s,- regulator

reglos a & adv motionless

regn|en vi (*haben*) rain; **es r~et** it is raining. **r~erisch** a rainy

regul|är a normal; (*rechtmäßig*) legitimate. **r~ieren** vt regulate

Regung f -, -en movement; (*Gefühls-*) emotion. **r~slos** a & adv motionless

Reh nt -[e]s, -e roe-deer; (*Culin*) venison

Rehbock m roebuck

reib|en† vt rub; (*Culin*) grate ● vi (*haben*) rub. **R~ung** f - friction. **r~ungslos** a (*fig*) smooth

reich a rich (an + dat in)

Reich nt -[e]s, -e empire; (*König-*) kingdom; (*Bereich*) realm

Reiche(r) m/f rich man/woman; **die R~en** the rich pl

reichen vt hand; (*anbieten*) offer ● vi (*haben*) be enough; (*in der Länge*) be long enough; **r~ bis zu** reach [up to]; (*sich erstrecken*) extend to; **mit dem Geld r~** have enough money

reich|haltig a extensive, large <*Mahlzeit*> substantial. **r~lich** a ample; <*Vorrat*> abundant. **R~tum** m -s, -tümer wealth (an + dat of); **R~tümer** riches. **R~weite** f reach; (*Techn, Mil*) range

Reif m -[e]s [hoar-]frost

reif a ripe; (*fig*) mature; **r~ für** ready for. **r~en** vi (*sein*) ripen; <*Wein, Käse & fig*> mature

Reifen m -s,- hoop; (*Arm-*) bangle; (*Auto-*) tyre. **R~druck** m tyre pressure. **R~panne** f puncture, flat tyre

reiflich a careful

Reihe f -, -n row; (*Anzahl & Math*) series; **der R~ nach** in turn; **wer ist an der R~?** whose turn is it? **r~n (sich)** vr sich r~n an (+ acc) follow. **R~nfolge** f order. **R~nhaus** nt terraced house

Reiher m -s,- heron

Reim m -[e]s, -e rhyme. **r~en** vt rhyme; **sich r~en** rhyme

rein[1] a pure; (*sauber*) clean; <*Unsinn, Dummheit*> sheer; **ins**

R

R∼e schreiben make a fair copy of

rein² *adv* = herein, hinein

Reineclaude /rɛːnəˈkloːdə/ *f* -, -n greengage

Reinfall *m* 🔢 let-down; (*Misserfolg*) flop

Rein|gewinn *m* net profit. **R∼heit** *f* - purity

reinig|en *vt* clean; (*chemisch*) dry-clean. **R∼ung** *f* -, -en cleaning; (*chemische*) dry-cleaning; (*Geschäft*) dry cleaner's

reinlegen *vt sep* put in; 🔢 dupe; (*betrügen*) take for a ride

reinlich *a* clean. **R∼keit** *f* - cleanliness

Reis *m* -es rice

Reise *f* -, -n journey; (*See-*) voyage; (*Urlaubs-, Geschäfts-*) trip. **R∼andenken** *nt* souvenir. **R∼büro** *nt* travel agency. **R∼bus** *m* coach. **R∼führer** *m* tourist guide; (*Buch*) guide. **R∼gesellschaft** *f* tourist group. **R∼leiter(in)** *m(f)* courier. **r∼n** *vi* (*sein*) travel. **R∼nde(r)** *m/f* traveller. **R∼pass** *m* passport. **R∼scheck** *m* traveller's cheque. **R∼veranstalter** *m* -s,- tour operator. **R∼ziel** *nt* destination

Reisig *nt* -s brushwood

Reißaus *m* R∼ nehmen 🔢 run away

Reißbrett *nt* drawing-board

reißen† *vt* tear; (*weg-*) snatch; (*töten*) kill; **Witze r∼** crack jokes; **an sich** (*acc*) **r∼**snatch; seize <*Macht*>; **sich r∼ um** 🔢 fight for ●*vi* (*sein*) tear; <*Seil, Faden:*> break ●*vi* (*haben*) **r∼ an** (+ *dat*) pull at

Reißer *m* -s,- 🔢 thriller; (*Erfolg*) big hit

Reiß|nagel *m* = R∼zwecke. **R∼verschluss** *m* zip [fastener]. **R∼wolf** *m* shredder. **R∼zwecke** *f* -, -n drawing-pin

reit|en† *vt/i* (*sein*) ride. **R∼er(in)** *m* -s,- (*f* -, -nen) rider. **R∼hose** *f* riding breeches *pl*. **R∼pferd** *nt* saddle-horse. **R∼weg** *m* bridle-path

Reiz *m* -es, -e stimulus; (*Anziehungskraft*) attraction, appeal; (*Charme*) charm. **r∼bar** irritable. **R∼barkeit** *f* - irritability. **r∼en** *vt* provoke; (*Med*) irritate; (*interessieren, locken*) appeal to, attract; arouse <*Neugier*>; (*beim Kartenspiel*) bid. **R∼ung** *f* -, -en (*Med*) irritation. **r∼voll** *a* attractive

rekeln (sich) *vr* stretch

Reklamation /-ˈtsi̯oːn/ *f* -, -en (*Comm*) complaint

Reklam|e *f* -, -n advertising, publicity; (*Anzeige*) advertisement; (*TV, Radio*) commercial; R∼e machen advertise (für etw sth). **r∼ieren** *v* complain about; (*fordern*) claim ●*vi* (*haben*) complain

Rekord *m* -[e]s, -e record

Rekrut *m* -en, -en recruit

Rektor *m* -s, -en /-ˈtoːrən/ (*Sch*) head[master]; (*Univ*) vice-chancellor. **R∼torin** *f* -, -nen head, headmistress; vice-chancellor

Relais /rəˈlɛː/ *nt* -, /-s, -s/ (*Electr*) relay

relativ *a* relative

Religi|on *f* -, -en religion; (*Sch*) religious education. **r∼ös** *a* religious

Reling *f* -, -s (*Naut*) rail

Reliquie /reˈliːkvi̯ə/ *f* -, -n relic

rempeln *vt* jostle; (*stoßen*) push

Reneklode *f* -, -n greengage

Renn|bahn *f* race-track; (*Pferde-*) racecourse. **R∼boot** *nt* speed-boat. **r∼en†** *vt/i* (*sein*) run; um die Wette r∼en have a race. **R∼en** *nt* -s,- race. **R∼pferd** *nt* racehorse. **R∼sport** *m* racing. **R∼wagen** *m* racing car

enommiert a renowned; <*Hotel, Firma*> of repute

enovier|en vt renovate; redecorate <*Zimmer*>. **R~ung** f - renovation; redecoration

entabel a profitable

Rente f -, -n pension; in **R~ gehen** 🛈 retire. **R~nversicherung** f pension scheme

Rentier nt reindeer

entieren (sich) vr be profitable; (*sich lohnen*) be worth while

Rentner(in) m -s,- (f -, -nen) [old-age] pensioner

Reparatur f -, -en repair. **R~werkstatt** f repair workshop; (*Auto*) garage

reparieren vt repair, mend

Reportage /-'ta:ʒə/ f -, -n report

Reporter(in) m -s,- (f -, -nen) reporter

repräsentativ a representative (**für** of); (*eindrucksvoll*) imposing

Reprodu|ktion /-'ts:io:n/ f -, -en reproduction. **r~zieren** vt reproduce

Reptil nt -s, -ien /-iən/ reptile

Republik f -, -en republic. **r~anisch** a republican

Requisiten pl (*Theat*) properties, 🛈 props

Reservat nt -[e]s, -e reservation

Reserve f -, -n reserve; (*Mil, Sport*) reserves pl. **R~rad** nt spare wheel

reservier|en vt reserve; **r~en lassen** book. **r~t** a reserved. **R~ung** f -, -en reservation

Reservoir /rezɛr'voa:ɐ/ nt -s, -s reservoir

Residenz f -, -en residence

Resign|ation /-'ts:io:n/ f - resignation. **r~ieren** vi (*haben*) (*fig*) give up. **r~iert** a resigned

resolut a resolute

Resonanz f -, -en resonanance

Respekt /-sp-, -ʃp-/ m -[e]s respect (**vor** + *dat* for). **r~ieren** vt respect

respektlos a disrespectful

Ressort /rɛ'so:ɐ/ nt -s, -s department

Rest m -[e]s, -e remainder, rest; **R~e** remains; (*Essens-*) leftovers

Restaurant /rɛsto'rã:/ nt -s, -s restaurant

Restaur|ation /rɛstaura'ts:io:n/ f - restoration. **r~ieren** vt restore

Rest|betrag m balance. **r~lich** a remaining

Resultat nt -[e]s, -e result

rett|en vt save (**vor** + *dat* from); (*aus Gefahr befreien*) rescue; **sich r~en** save oneself; (*flüchten*) escape. **R~er** m -s,- rescuer; (*fig*) saviour

Rettich m -s, -e white radish

Rettung f -, -en rescue; (*fig*) salvation; **jds letzte R~** s.o.'s last hope. **R~sboot** nt lifeboat. **R~sdienst** m rescue service. **R~sgürtel** m lifebelt. **r~slos** adv hopelessly. **R~sring** m lifebelt. **R~swagen** m ambulance

retuschieren vt (*Phot*) retouch

Reue f - remorse; (*Relig*) repentance

Revanch|e /re'vã:ʃə/ f -, -n revenge; **R~e fordern** (*Sport*) ask for a return match. **r~ieren (sich)** vr take revenge; (*sich erkenntlich zeigen*) reciprocate (**mit** with)

Revers /re've:ɐ/ nt -,- /-[s], -s/ lapel

Revier nt -s, -e district; (*Zool & fig*) territory; (*Polizei-*) [police] station

Revision f -, -en revision; (*Prüfung*) check; (*Jur*) appeal

Revolution /-'ts:io:n/ f -, -en revolution. **r~är** a revolutionary. **r~ieren** vt revolutionize

Revolver m -s,- revolver

rezen|sieren vt review. **R~sion** f -, -en review

Rezept nt -[e]s, -e prescription; (*Culin*) recipe

Rezession f -, -en recession

R

R-Gespräch nt reverse-charge call

Rhabarber m -s rhubarb

Rhein m -s Rhine. **R~land** nt -s Rhineland. **R~wein** m hock

Rhetorik f - rhetoric

Rheum|a nt -s rheumatism. **r~atisch** a rheumatic. **R~atismus** m - rheumatism

Rhinozeros nt -[ses], -se rhinoceros

rhyth|misch /'ryt-/ a rhythmic[al]. **R~mus** m -, -men rhythm

richten vt direct (**auf** + acc at); address <Frage> (**an** + acc to); aim <Waffe> (**auf** + acc at); (einstellen) set; (vorbereiten) prepare; (reparieren) mend; **in die Höhe r~** raise [up]; **sich r~** be directed (**auf** + acc at; **gegen** against); <Blick:> turn (**auf** + acc on); **sich r~ nach** comply with <Vorschrift>; fit in with <jds Plänen>; (abhängen) depend on ● vi (haben) **r~ über** (+ acc) judge

Richter m -s,- judge

richtig a right, correct; (wirklich, echt) real; **das R~e** the right thing ● adv correctly; really; **r~ stellen** put right <Uhr>; (fig) correct <Irrtum>; **die Uhr geht r~** the clock is right

Richtlinien fpl guidelines

Richtung f -, -en direction

riechen† vt/i (haben) smell (**nach** of; **an etw** dat sth)

Riegel m -s,- bolt; (Seife) bar

Riemen m -s,- strap; (Ruder) oar

Riese m -n, -n giant

rieseln vi (sein) trickle; <Schnee:> fall lightly

riesengroß a huge, enormous

riesig a huge; (gewaltig) enormous ● adv 🗉 terribly

Riff nt -[e]s, -e reef

Rille f -, -n groove

Rind nt -es, -er ox; (Kuh) cow; (Stier) bull; (R~fleisch) beef; **R~er** cattle pl

Rinde f -, -n bark; (Käse-) rind; (Brot-) crust

Rinderbraten m roast beef

Rindfleisch nt beef

Ring m -[e]s, -e ring

ringeln (sich) vr curl

ring|en† vi (haben) wrestle; (fig) struggle (**um/nach** for) ● vt wring <Hände>. **R~er** m -s,- wrestler. **R~kampf** m wrestling match; (als Sport) wrestling

rings|herum, r~um adv all around

Rinn|e f -, -n channel; (Dach-) gutter. **r~en**† vi (sein) run; <Sand:> trickle. **R~stein** m gutter

Rippe f -, -n rib. **R~nfellentzündung** f pleurisy

Risiko nt -s, -s & -ken risk

risk|ant a risky. **r~ieren** vt risk

Riss m -es, -e tear; (Mauer-) crack; (fig) rift

rissig a cracked; <Haut> chapped

Rist m -[e]s, -e instep

Ritt m -[e]s, -e ride

Ritter m -s,- knight

Ritual nt -s, -e ritual

Ritz m -es, -e scratch. **R~e** f -, -n crack; (Fels-) cleft; (zwischen Betten, Vorhängen) gap. **r~en** vt scratch

Rival|e m -n, -n, **R~in** f -, -nen rival. **R~ität** f -, -en rivalry

Robbe f -, -n seal

Robe f -, -n gown; (Talar) robe

Roboter m -s,- robot

robust a robust

röcheln vi (haben) breathe stertorously

Rochen m -s,- (Zool) ray

Rock[1] m -[e]s,̈-e skirt; (Jacke) jacket

Rock[2] m -[s] (Mus) rock

rodeln vi (sein/haben) toboggan. **R~schlitten** m toboggan

roden vt clear <Land>; grub up <Stumpf>

Rogen m -s,- [hard] roe

Roggen m -s rye

oh *a* rough; (*ungekocht*) raw; <*Holz*> bare; (*brutal*) brutal. **R~bau** *m* -[e]s, -ten shell. **R~kost** *f* raw [vegetarian] food. **R~ling** *m* -s, -e brute. **R~öl** *nt* crude oil

Rohr *nt* -[e]s, -e pipe; (*Geschütz-*) barrel; (*Bot*) reed; (*Zucker-, Bambus-*) cane

Röhre *f* -, -n tube; (*Radio-*) valve; (*Back-*) oven

Rohstoff *m* raw material

Rokoko *nt* -s rococo

Rollbahn *f* taxiway; (*Start-/Landebahn*) runaway

Rolle *f* -, -n roll; (*Garn-*) reel; (*Draht-*) coil; (*Techn*) roller; (*Seil-*) pulley; (*Lauf-*) castor; (*Theat*) part, role; **das spielt keine R~** (*fig*) that doesn't matter. **r~n** *vt* roll; (*auf-*) roll up; **sich r~n** roll ● *vi* (*sein*) roll; <*Flugzeug:*> taxi. **R~r** *m* -s,- scooter

Roll|feld *nt* airfield. **R~kragen** *m* polo-neck. **R~mops** *m* rollmop[s] *sg*

Rollo *nt* -s, -s [roller] blind

Roll|schuh *m* roller-skate; **R~schuh laufen** roller-skate. **R~stuhl** *m* wheelchair. **R~treppe** *f* escalator

Rom *nt* -s Rome

Roman *m* -s, -e novel. **r~isch** *a* Romanesque; <*Sprache*> Romance

Romant|ik *f* -romanticism. **r~isch** *a* romantic

Röm|er(in) *m* -s, - (*f* -, -nen) Roman. **r~isch** *a* Roman

Rommé, Rommee /'rɔme:/ *nt* -s rummy

röntgen *vt* X-ray. **R~aufnahme** *f*, **R~bild** *nt* X-ray. **R~strahlen** *mpl* X-rays

rosa *inv a*, **R~** *nt* -[s],- pink

Rose *f* -, -n rose. **R~nkohl** *m* [Brussels] sprouts *pl*. **R~nkranz** *m* (*Relig*) rosary

Rosine *f* -, -n raisin

Rosmarin *m* -s rosemary

Ross *nt* -es,ˍer horse

Rost[1] *m* -[e]s, -e grating; (*Kamin-*) grate; (*Brat-*) grill

Rost[2] *m* -[e]s rust. **r~en** *vi* (*haben*) rust

rösten *vt* roast; toast <*Brot*>

rostfrei *a* stainless

rostig *a* rusty

rot *a*, **Rot** *nt* -s,- red; **rot werden** turn red; (*erröten*) go red, blush

Röte *f* - redness; (*Scham-*) blush

Röteln *pl* German measles *sg*

röten *vt* redden; **sich r~** turn red

rothaarig *a* red-haired

rotieren *vi* (*haben*) rotate

Rot|kehlchen *nt* -s,- robin. **R~kohl** *m* red cabbage

rötlich *a* reddish

Rotwein *m* red wine

Roulade /ru'la:də/ *f* -, -n beef olive. **R~leau** /-'lo:/ *nt* -s, -s [roller] blind

Routin|e /ru'ti:nə/ *f* -, -n routine; (*Erfahrung*) experience … **r~emäßig** *a* a routine … ● *adv* routinely. **r~iert** *a* experienced

Rowdy /'rau:di/ *m* -s, -s hooligan

Rübe *f* -, -n beet; **rote R~** beetroot

Rubin *m* -s, -e ruby

Rubrik *f* -, -en column

Ruck *m* -[e]s, -e jerk

ruckartig *a* jerky

rück|bezüglich *a* (*Gram*) reflexive. **R~blende** *f* flashback. **R~blick** *m* (*fig*) review (**auf** + *acc* of). **r~blickend** *adv* in retrospect. **r~datieren** *vt* (*inf & pp only*) backdate

Rücken *m* -s,- back; (*Buch-*) spine; (*Berg-*) ridge. **R~lehne** *f* back. **R~mark** *nt* spinal cord. **R~schwimmen** *nt* backstroke. **R~wind** *m* following wind; (*Aviat*) tail wind

rückerstatten *vt* (*inf & pp only*) refund

Rückfahr|karte *f* return ticket. **R~t** *f* return journey

R

Rück|fall m relapse. **R~flug** m return flight. **R~frage** f [further] query. **r~fragen** vi (haben) (inf & pp only) check (**bei** with). **R~gabe** f return. **r~gängig** a **r~gängig machen** cancel; break off <Verlobung>. **R~grat** nt -[e]s, -e spine, backbone. **R~hand** f backhand. **R~kehr** f return. **R~lagen** fpl reserves. **R~licht** nt rear-light. **R~reise** f return journey

Rucksack m rucksack

Rück|schau f review. **R~schlag** m (Sport) return; (fig) set-back. **r~schrittlich** a retrograde. **R~seite** f back; (einer Münze) reverse

Rücksicht f -, -en consideration. **R~nahme** f - consideration. **r~slos** a inconsiderate; (schonungslos) ruthless. **r~svoll** a considerate

Rück|sitz m back seat; (Sozius) pillion. **R~spiegel** m rear-view mirror. **R~spiel** nt return match. **R~stand** m (Chem) residue; (Arbeits-) backlog; **im R~stand sein** be behind. **r~ständig** a (fig) backward. **R~stau** m (Auto) tailback. **R~strahler** m -s,- reflector. **R~tritt** m resignation; (Fahrrad) back pedalling

rückwärt|ig a back ..., rear ... **r~s** adv backwards. **R~sgang** m reverse [gear]

Rückweg m way back

rück|wirkend a retrospective. **R~wirkung** f retrospective force; **mit R~wirkung vom** backdated to. **R~zahlung** f repayment

Rüde m -n, -n [male] dog

Rudel nt -s,- herd; (Wolfs-) pack; (Löwen-) pride

Ruder nt -s,- oar; (Steuer-) rudder; **am R~** (Naut & fig) at the helm. **R~boot** nt rowing boat. **r~n** vt/i (haben/sein) row

Ruf m -[e]s, -e call; (laut) shout; (Telefon) telephone number; (Ansehen) reputation. **r~en†** vt/i (haben) call (**nach** for); **r~en lassen** send for

Ruf|name m forename by which one is known. **R~nummer** f telephone number. **R~zeichen** nt dialling tone

Rüge f -, -n reprimand. **r~n** vt reprimand; (kritisieren) criticize

Ruhe f - rest; (Stille) quiet; (Frieden) peace; (innere) calm; (Gelassenheit) composure; **R~ [da]!** quiet! **r~los** a restless. **r~n** vi (haben) rest (**auf** + dat on); <Arbeit, Verkehr:> have stopped. **R~pause** f rest, break. **R~stand** m retirement; **im R~stand** retired. **R~störung** f disturbance of the peace. **R~tag** m day of rest; 'Montag R~tag' 'closed on Mondays'

ruhig a quiet; (erholsam) restful; (friedlich) peaceful; (unbewegt, gelassen) calm; **man kann r~ darüber sprechen** there's no harm in talking about it

Ruhm m -[e]s fame; (Ehre) glory. **rühmen** vt praise

ruhmreich a glorious

Ruhr f - (Med) dysentery

Rühr|ei nt scrambled eggs pl. **r~en** vt move; (Culin) stir; **sich r~en** move ●vi (haben) stir; **r~en an** (+ acc) touch; (fig) touch on. **r~end** a touching

Rührung f - emotion

Ruin m -s ruin. **R~e** f -, -n ruin; ruins pl (gen of). **r~ieren** vt ruin

rülpsen vi (haben) 🔊 belch

Rum m -s rum

Rumän|ien /-jən/ nt -s Romania. **r~isch** a Romanian

Rummel m -s 🔊 hustle and bustle; (Jahrmarkt) funfair

Rumpelkammer f junk-room

Rumpf m -[e]s,ˆe body, trunk; (Schiffs-) hull; (Aviat) fuselage

und a round ● adv approximately; **r~ um** [a]round.
R~blick m panoramic view.
R~brief m circular [letter]

Runde f -, -n round; (*Kreis*) circle; (*eines Polizisten*) beat; (*beim Rennen*) lap; **eine R~ Bier** a round of beer

Rund|fahrt f tour. **R~frage** f poll

Rundfunk m radio; **im R~** on the radio. **R~gerät** nt radio [set]

Rund|gang m round; (*Spaziergang*) walk (**durch** round). **r~heraus** adv straight out. **r~herum** adv all around. **r~lich** a rounded; (*mollig*) plump. **R~reise** f [circular] tour. **R~schreiben** nt circular. **r~um** adv all round. **R~ung** f -, -en curve

Runzel f -, -n wrinkle

runzlig a wrinkled

Rüpel m -s,- ⚞ lout

rupfen vt pull out; pluck <*Geflügel*>

Rüsche f -, -n frill

Ruß m -es soot

Russe m -n, -n Russian

Rüssel m -s,- (*Zool*) trunk

Russ|in f -, -nen Russian. **r~isch** a Russian. **R~isch** nt -[s] (*Lang*) Russian

Russland nt -s Russia

rüsten vi (*haben*) prepare (**zu/für** for) ● vr **sich r~** get ready

rüstig a sprightly

rustikal a rustic

Rüstung f -, -en armament; (*Harnisch*) armour. **R~skontrolle** f arms control

Rute f -, -n twig; (*Angel-, Wünschel-*) rod; (*zur Züchtigung*) birch; (*Schwanz*) tail

Rutsch m -[e]s, -e slide. **R~bahn** f slide. **R~e** f -, -n chute. **r~en** vt slide; (*rücken*) move ● vi (*sein*) slide; (*aus-, ab-*) slip; (*Auto*) skid. **r~ig** a slippery

rütteln vt shake ● vi (*haben*) **r~ an** (+ *dat*) rattle

Saal m -[e]s, Säle hall; (*Theat*) auditorium; (*Kranken-*) ward

Saat f -, -en seed; (*Säen*) sowing; (*Gesätes*) crop

sabbern vi (*haben*) ⚞ slobber; <*Baby:*> dribble; (*reden*) jabber

Säbel m -s,- sabre

Sabo|tage /zabo'ta:ʒə/ f - sabotage. **S~teur** /-'tø:ɐ/ m -s, -e saboteur. **s~tieren** vt sabotage

Sach|bearbeiter m expert.
S~buch nt non-fiction book

Sache f -, -n matter, business; (*Ding*) thing; (*fig*) cause

Sach|gebiet nt (*fig*) area, field.
s~kundig a expert. **s~lich** a factual; (*nüchtern*) matter-of-fact

sächlich a (*Gram*) neuter

Sachse m -n, -n Saxon. **S~n** nt -s Saxony

sächsisch a Saxon

Sach|verhalt m -[e]s facts pl.
S~verständige(r) m/f expert

Sack m -[e]s, ⸚e sack

Sack|gasse f cul-de-sac; (*fig*) impasse. **S~leinen** nt sacking

Sad|ismus m - sadism. **S~t** m -en, -en sadist

säen vt/i (*haben*) sow

Safe /ze:f/ m -s, -s safe

Saft m -[e]s, ⸚e juice; (*Bot*) sap.
s~ig a juicy

Sage f -, -n legend

Säge f -, -n saw. **S~mehl** nt sawdust

sagen vt say; (*mitteilen*) tell; (*bedeuten*) mean

sägen vt/i (haben) saw
sagenhaft a legendary
Säge|späne mpl wood shavings. **S~werk** nt sawmill
Sahn|e f - cream. **S~ebonbon** m & nt ≈ toffee. **s~ig** a creamy
Saison /zɛ'zõ:/ f -, -s season
Saite f -, -n (Mus, Sport) string. **S~ninstrument** nt stringed instrument
Sakko m & nt -s, -s sports jacket
Sakrament nt -[e]s, -e sacrament
Sakristei f -, -en vestry
Salat m -[e]s, -e salad. **S~soße** f salad-dressing
Salbe f -, -n ointment
Salbei m -s & f - sage
salben vt anoint
Saldo m -s, -dos & -den balance
Salon /za'lõ:/ m -s, -s salon
salopp a casual; <Benehmen> informal
Salto m -s, -s somersault
Salut m -[e]s, -e salute. **s~ieren** vi (haben) salute
Salve f -, -n volley; (Geschütz-) salvo, (von Gelächter) burst
Salz nt -es, -e salt. **s~en†** vt salt. **S~fass** nt salt-cellar. **s~ig** a salty. **S~kartoffeln** fpl boiled potatoes. **S~säure** f hydrochloric acid
Samen m -s,- seed; (Anat) semen, sperm
Sammel|becken nt reservoir. **s~n** vt/i (haben) collect; (suchen, versammeln) gather; **sich s~n** collect; (sich versammeln) gather; (sich fassen) collect oneself. **S~name** m collective noun
Sammler(in) m -s,- (f -, -nen) collector. **S~lung** f -, -en collection; (innere) composure
Samstag m -s, -e Saturday. **s~s** adv on Saturdays
samt prep (+ dat) together with
Samt m -[e]s velvet

sämtlich indef pron inv all. **s~e(r,s)** indef pron all the; **s~e Werke** complete works
Sanatorium nt -s, -ien sanatorium
Sand m -[e]s sand
Sandale f -, -n sandal
Sand|bank f sandbank. **S~kasten** m sand-pit. **S~papier** nt sandpaper
sanft a gentle
Sänger(in) m -s,- (f -, -nen) singer
sanieren vt clean up; redevelop <Gebiet>; (modernisieren) modernize; make profitable <Industrie, Firma>; **sich s~** become profitable
sanitär a sanitary
Sanität|er m -s,- first-aid man; (Fahrer) ambulance man; (Mil) medical orderly. **S~swagen** m ambulance
Sanktion /zaŋk'tsjo:n/ f -, -en sanction. **s~ieren** vt sanction
Saphir m -s, -e sapphire
Sardelle f -, -n anchovy
Sardine f -, -n sardine
Sarg m -[e]s, "-e coffin
Sarkasmus m - sarcasm
Satan m -s Satan; (🄳 Teufel) devil
Satellit m -en, -en satellite. **S~enfernsehen** nt satellite television. **S~enschüssel** f satellite dish
Satin /za'tɛŋ/ m -s satin
Satire f -, -n satire
satt a full; <Farbe> rich; **s~ sein** have had enough [to eat]; **etw s~ haben** 🄳 be fed up with sth
Sattel m -s,¨ saddle. **s~n** vt saddle. **S~zug** m articulated lorry
sättigen vt satisfy; (Chem & fig) saturate ● vi (haben) be filling
Satz m -es,¨-e sentence; (Teil-) clause; (These) proposition; (Math) theorem; (Mus) movement; (Tennis, Zusammengehöriges) set;

(*Boden-*) sediment; (*Kaffee-*) grounds *pl*; (*Steuer-, Zins-*) rate; (*Druck-*) setting; (*Schrift-*) type; (*Sprung-*) leap, bound.
S~aussage *f* predicate.
S~gegenstand *m* subject.
S~zeichen *nt* punctuation mark

Sau *f* -,Säue sow

sauber *a* clean; (*ordentlich*) neat; (*anständig*) decent; **s~ machen** clean. **S~keit** *f* - cleanliness; neatness

säuberlich *a* neat

Sauce /'zo:sə/ *f* -, -n sauce; (*Braten-*) gravy

Saudi-Arabien /-iən/ *nt* -s Saudi Arabia

sauer *a* sour; (*Chem*) acid; (*eingelegt*) pickled; (*schwer*) hard; **saurer Regen** acid rain

Sauerkraut *nt* sauerkraut

säuerlich *a* slightly sour

Sauerstoff *m* oxygen

saufen† *vt/i* (*haben*) drink; ☒ booze

Säufer *m* -s,- ☒ boozer

saugen† *vt/i* (*haben*) suck; (*staub-*) vacuum, hoover; **sich voll Wasser s~** soak up water

säugen *vt* suckle

Säugetier *nt* mammal

saugfähig *a* absorbent

Säugling *m* -s, -e infant

Säule *f* -, -n column

Saum *m* -[e]s,Säume hem; (*Rand*) edge

säumen *vt* hem; (*fig*) line

Sauna *f* -, -nas & -nen sauna

Säure *f* -, -n acidity; (*Chem*) acid

sausen *vi* (*haben*) rush; <*Ohren:*> buzz ● *vi* (*sein*) rush [along]

Saxophon, Saxofon *nt* -s, -e saxophone

S-Bahn *f* city and suburban railway

Scanner *m* -s,- scanner

sch *int* shush! (*fort*) shoo!

Schabe *f* -, -n cockroach

schaben *vt/i* (*haben*) scrape

schäbig *a* shabby

Schablone *f* -, -n stencil; (*Muster*) pattern; (*fig*) stereotype

Schach *nt* -s chess; **S~!** check!
S~brett *nt* chessboard

Schachfigur *f* chess-man

schachmatt *a* **s~ setzen** checkmate; **s~!** checkmate!

Schachspiel *nt* game of chess

Schacht *m* -[e]s,¨e shaft

Schachtel *f* -, -n box; (*Zigaretten-*) packet

Schachzug *m* move

schade *a* **s~ sein** be a pity *or* shame: **zu s~ für** too good for

Schädel *m* -s, skull. **S~bruch** *m* fractured skull

schaden *vi* (*haben*) (+ *dat*) damage; (*nachteilig sein*) hurt.
S~ *m* -s,¨ damage; (*Defekt*) defect; (*Nachteil*) disadvantage.
S~ersatz *m* damages *pl*.
S~freude *f* malicious glee.
s~froh *a* gloating

schädig|en *vt* damage, harm.
S~ung *f* -, -en damage

schädlich *a* harmful

Schädling *m* -s, -e pest.
S~sbekämpfungsmittel *nt* pesticide

Schaf *nt* -[e]s, -e sheep. **S~bock** *m* ram

Schäfer *m* -s,- shepherd. **S~hund** *m* sheepdog; **Deutscher S~hund** alsatian

schaffen¹† *vt* create; (*herstellen*) establish; make <*Platz*>

schaffen² *v* (*reg*) ● *vt* manage [to do]; pass <*Prüfung*>; catch <*Zug*>; (*bringen*) take

Schaffner *m* -s,- conductor; (*Zug-*) ticket-inspector

Schaffung *f* - creation

Schaft *m* -[e]s,¨e shaft; (*Gewehr-*) stock; (*Stiefel-*) leg

Schal *m* -s, -s scarf

Schale *f* -, -n skin; (*abgeschält*) peel; (*Eier-, Nuss-, Muschel-*) shell; (*Schüssel*) dish

S

schälen vt peel; **sich s~** peel

Schall m -[e]s sound. **S~dämpfer** m silencer. **s~dicht** a soundproof. **s~en** vi (haben) ring out; (nachhallen) resound. **S~mauer** f sound barrier. **S~platte** f record, disc

schalt|en vt switch ● vi (haben) switch/<Ampel:> turn (**auf** + acc to); (Auto) change gear; (I begreifen) catch on. **S~er** m -s,- switch; (Post-, Bank-) counter; (Fahrkarten-) ticket window. **S~hebel** m switch; (Auto) gear lever. **S~jahr** nt leap year. **S~ung** f -, -en circuit; (Auto) gear change

Scham f - shame; (Anat) private parts pl

schämen (sich) vr be ashamed

scham|haft a modest. **s~los** a shameless

Schampon (sich) nt -s shampoo. **s~ieren** vt shampoo

Schande f - disgrace, shame

schändlich a disgraceful

Schanktisch m bar

Schanze f, -, -n [ski-]jump

Schar f -, -en crowd; (Vogel-) flock

Scharade f -, -n charade

scharen vt um sich s~ gather round one; **sich s~ um** flock round one. **s~weise** adv in droves

scharf a sharp; (stark) strong; (stark gewürzt) hot; <Geruch> pungent; <Wind, Augen, Verstand> keen; (streng) harsh; <Galopp> hard; <Munition> live; <Hund> fierce; **s~ einstellen** (Phot) focus; **s~ sein** (Phot) be in focus; **s~ sein auf** (+ acc) I be keen on

Schärfe f sharpness; strength; hotness, pungency; keenness; harshness. **s~n** vt sharpen

Scharf|richter m executioner. **S~schütze** m marksman. **S~sinn** m astutenes

Scharlach m -s scarlet fever

Scharlatan m -s, -e charlatan

Scharnier nt -s, -e hinge

Schärpe f -, -n sash

scharren vi (haben) scrape; <Huhn> scratch ● vt scrape

Schaschlik m & nt -s, -s kebab

Schatten m -s,- shadow; (schattige Stelle) shade. **S~riss** n silhouette. **S~seite** f shady side; (fig) disadvantage

schattier|en vt shade. **S~ung** f -, -en shading

schattig a shady

Schatz m -es,¨e treasure; (Freund Freundin) sweetheart

schätzen vt estimate; (taxieren) value; (achten) esteem; (würdigen) appreciate

Schätzung f -, -en estimate; (Taxierung) valuation

Schau f -, -en show. **S~ bild** nt diagram

Schauder m -s shiver; (vor Abscheu) shudder. **s~ haft** a dreadful. **s~n** vi (haben) shiver; (vor Abscheu) shudder

schauen vi (haben) (SGer, Aust) look; **s~, dass** make sure that

Schauer m -s,- shower; (Schauder) shiver. **S~geschichte** f horror story. **s~lich** a ghastly

Schaufel f -, -n shovel; (Kehr-) dustpan. **s~n** vt shovel; (graben) dig

Schaufenster nt shop-window. **S~puppe** f dummy

Schaukel f -, -n swing. **s~n** vt rock ● vi (haben) rock; (auf einer Schaukel) swing; (schwanken) sway. **S~pferd** nt rocking-horse. **S~stuhl** m rocking-chair

Schaum m -[e]s foam; (Seifen-) lather; (auf Bier) froth; (als Frisier-, Rasiermittel) mousse

schäumen vi (haben) foam, froth <Seife:> lather

Schaum|gummi m foam rubber. **s~ig** a frothy; **s~ig rühren** (Culin

:ream. **S~stoff** m [synthetic]
oam. **S~wein** m sparkling wine
chauplatz m scene
chaurig a dreadful; (*unheimlich*)
·erie
chauspiel nt play; (*Anblick*)
pectacle. **S~er** m actor. **S~erin**
actress
check m -s, -s cheque. **S~buch,**
S~heft nt cheque-book. **S~karte**
cheque card
cheibe f -, -n disc; (*Schieß-*)
arget; (*Glas-*) pane; (*Brot-,*
Wurst-) slice. **S~nwischer** m -s,-
windscreen-wiper
cheich m -s & -s sheikh
cheide f -, -n sheath; (*Anat*)
vagina
cheid|en† vt separate;
(*unterscheiden*) distinguish;
dissolve <*Ehe*>; **sich s~en lassen**
get divorced ●vi (*sein*) leave;
(*voneinander*) part. **S~ung** f -, -en
divorce
chein m -[e]s, -e light; (*Anschein*)
appearance; (*Bescheinigung*)
certificate; (*Geld-*) note. **s~bar** a
apparent. **s~en†** vi (*haben*)
shine; (*den Anschein haben*)
seem, appear
cheinheilig a hypocritical
cheinwerfer m -s,- floodlight;
(*Such-*) searchlight; (*Auto*)
headlight; (*Theat*) spotlight
cheiße f - (*vulg*) shit. **s~n†** vi
(*haben*) (*vulg*) shit
cheit nt -[e]s, -e log
cheitel m -s,- parting
cheitern vi (*sein*) fail
chelle f -, -n bell. **s~n** vi (*haben*)
ring
chellfisch m haddock
chelm m -s, -e rogue
chelte f - scolding
chema nt -s, -mata model,
pattern; (*Skizze*) diagram
chemel m -s,- stool
chenke f -, -n tavern
chenkel m -s,- thigh

schenken vt give [as a present];
jdm Vertrauen s~ trust s.o.
Scherbe f -, -n [broken] piece
Schere f -, -n scissors pl; (*Techn*)
shears pl; (*Hummer-*) claw.
s~n† vt shear; crop <*Haar*>
scheren² vt (*reg*) 🛈 bother; **sich**
nicht s~ um not care about
Scherenschnitt m silhouette
Scherereien fpl 🛈 trouble sg
Scherz m -es, -e joke; **im/zum S~**
as a joke. **s~en** vi (*haben*) joke
scheu a shy; <*Tier:*> timid; **s~**
werden <*Pferd:*> shy
scheuchen vt shoo
scheuen vt be afraid of; (*meiden*)
shun; **keine Mühe/Kosten s~** spare
no effort/expense; **sich s~** be
afraid (**vor** + *dat* of); shrink (**etw**
zu tun from doing sth)
scheuern vt scrub; (*reiben*) rub;
[wund] s~n chafe ●vi (*haben*)
rub, chafe
Scheuklappen fpl blinkers
Scheune f -, -n barn
Scheusal nt -s, -e monster
scheußlich a horrible
Schi m -s, -er ski; **S~ fahren** od
laufen ski
Schicht f -, -en layer; (*Geol*)
stratum; (*Gesellschafts-*) class;
(*Arbeits-*) shift. **S~arbeit** f shift
work. **s~en** vt stack [up]
schick a stylish; <*Frau*> chic. **S~**
m -[e]s style
schicken vt/i (*haben*) send; **s~**
nach send for
Schicksal nt -s, -e fate.
S~sschlag m misfortune
Schieb|edach nt (*Auto*) sun-roof.
s~en† vt push; (*gleitend*) slide;
(🛈 *handeln mit*) traffic in; **etw**
s~en auf (+ *acc*) (*fig*) put sth
down to; shift <*Schuld*> on to
●vi (*haben*) push. **S~etür** f
sliding door. **S~ung** f -, -en 🛈
illicit deal; (*Betrug*) rigging,
fixing

S

Schieds|gericht *nt* panel of judges; (*Jur*) arbitration tribunal. **S~richter** *m* referee; (*Tennis*) umpire; (*Jur*) arbitrator

schief *a* crooked; (*unsymmetrisch*) lopsided; (*geneigt*) slanting, sloping; (*nicht senkrecht*) leaning; <*Winkel*> oblique; (*fig*) false; suspicious ● *adv* not straight; **s~ gehen** 🔲 go wrong

Schiefer *m* -s slate

schielen *vi* (*haben*) squint

Schienbein *nt* shin

Schiene *f* -, -n rail; (*Gleit-*) runner; (*Med*) splint. **s~n** *vt* (*Med*) put in a splint

Schieß|bude *f* shooting-gallery. **s~en†** *vt* shoot; fire <*Kugel*>; score <*Tor*> ● *vi* (*haben*) shoot, fire (**auf** + *acc* at). **S~scheibe** *f* target. **S~stand** *m* shooting-range

Schifahr|en *nt* skiing. **S~er(in)** *m*(*f*) skier

Schiff *nt* -[e]s, -e ship; (*Kirchen-*) nave; (*Seiten-*) aisle

Schiffahrt* *f s.* **Schifffahrt**

schiff|bar *a* navigable. **S~bruch** *m* shipwreck. **s~brüchig** *a* shipwrecked. **S~fahrt** *f* shipping

Schikan|e *f* -, -n harassment; **mit allen S~en** 🔲 with every refinement. **s~ieren** *vt* harass

Schi|laufen *nt* -s skiing. **S~läufer(in)** *m*(*f*) -s,- (*f* -, -nen) skier

Schild¹ *m* -[e]s, -e shield

Schild² *nt* -[e]s, -er sign; (*Nummern-*) plate; (*Mützen-*) badge; (*Etikett*) label

Schilddrüse *f* thyroid [gland]

schilder|n *vt* describe. **S~ung** *f* -, -en description

Schild|kröte *f* tortoise; (*See-*) turtle. **S~patt** *nt* -[e]s tortoiseshell

Schilf *nt* -[e]s reeds *pl*

schillern *vi* (*haben*) shimmer

Schimmel *m* -s,- mould; (*Pferd*) white horse. **s~n** *vi* (*haben*/*sein*) go mouldy

schimmern *vi* (*haben*) gleam

Schimpanse *m* -n, -n chimpanzee

schimpf|en *vi* (*haben*) grumble (**mit** at; **über** + *acc* about); scold (**mit jdm** s.o.) ● *vt* call. **S~wort** *nt* (*pl* -wörter) swear-word

Schinken *m* -s,- ham. **S~speck** *m* bacon

Schippe *f* -, -n shovel. **s~n** *vt* shovel

Schirm *m* -[e]s, -e umbrella; (*Sonnen-*) sunshade; (*Lampen-*) shade; (*Augen-*) visor; (*Mützen-*) peak; (*Ofen-, Bild-*) screen; (*fig: Schutz*) shield. **S~herrschaft** *f* patronage. **S~mütze** *f* peaked cap

schizophren *a* schizophrenic. **S~ie** *f* - schizophrenia

Schlacht *f* -, -en battle

schlachten *vt* slaughter, kill

Schlacht|feld *nt* battlefield. **S~hof** *m* abattoir

Schlacke *f* -, -n slag

Schlaf *m* -[e]s sleep; **im S~** in one's sleep. **S~anzug** *m* pyjamas *pl*

Schläfe *f* -, -n (*Anat*) temple

schlafen† *vi* (*haben*) sleep; **s~ gehen** go to bed; **er schläft noch** he is still asleep

schlaff *a* limp; <*Seil*> slack; <*Muskel*> flabby

Schlaf|lied *nt* lullaby. **s~los** *a* sleepless. **S~losigkeit** *f* - insomnia. **S~mittel** *nt* sleeping drug

schläfrig *a* sleepy

Schlaf|saal *m* dormitory. **S~sack** *m* sleeping-bag. **S~tablette** *f* sleeping-pill. **S~wagen** *m* sleeping-car, sleeper. **s~wandeln** *vi* (*haben*/*sein*) sleep-walk. **S~zimmer** *nt* bedroom

chlag *m* -[e]s,⸚e blow; (*Faust-*) ⸱unch; (*Herz-, Puls-, Trommel-*) ⸱eat; (*einer Uhr*) chime; *Glocken-, Gong- & Med*) stroke; *elektrischer*) shock; (*Art*) type; $•~e$ bekommen get a beating; **S~ uf S~** in rapid succession. $•~ader f$ artery. **S~anfall** *m* troke. **S~baum** *m* barrier

chlagen† *vt* hit, strike; (*fällen*) ⸱ell; knock <*Loch, Nagel*> (in + ⸱cc into); (*prügeln, besiegen*) ⸱eat; (*Culin*) whisk <*Eiweiß*>; ⸱hip <*Sahne*>; (*legen*) throw; ⸱wickeln) wrap; **sich s~** fight ● *vi ⸱haben*) beat; <*Tür:*> bang; <*Uhr:*> strike; (*melodisch*) chime; ⸱nit den Flügeln s~ flap its wings ● *vi* (*sein*) **in etw** (*acc*) **s~** <*Blitz, ⸱ugel*> strike sth; **nach jdm s~** *fig*) take after s.o.

chlager *m* -s,- popular song; *Erfolg*) hit

chläger *m* -s,- racket; *Tischtennis-*) bat; (*Golf-*) club; *Hockey-*) stick. **S~ei** *f* -, -en ight, brawl

chlag|fertig *a* quick-witted. **S~loch** *nt* pot-hole. **S~sahne** *f* whipped cream; (*ungeschlagen*) whipping cream. **S~seite** *f* *Naut*) list. **S~stock** *m* runcheon. **S~wort** *nt* (*pl* -worte) slogan. **S~zeile** *f* headline. **S~zeug** *nt* (*Mus*) percussion. **S~zeuger** *m* -s,- percussionist; *in Band*) drummer

chlamm *m* -[e]s mud. **s~ig** *a* nuddy

chlämpe *f* -, -n 🛈 slut. **s~en** *vi ⸱haben*) be sloppy (**bei** in). **s~ig** *a* slovenly; <*Arbeit*> sloppy

chlange *f* -, -n snake; *Menschen-, Auto-*) queue; **S~ stehen** queue

chlängeln (sich) *vr* wind; <*Person:*> weave (**durch** through)

chlank *a* slim. **S~heitskur** *f* limming diet

schlapp *a* tired; (*schlaff*) limp

schlau *a* clever; (*gerissen*) crafty; **ich werde nicht s~ daraus** I can't make head or tail of it

Schlauch *m* -[e]s,Schläuche tube; (*Wasser-*) hose[pipe]. **S~boot** *nt* rubber dinghy

Schlaufe *f* -, -n loop

schlecht *a* bad; (*böse*) wicked; (*unzulänglich*) poor; **s~ werden** go bad; <*Wetter:*> turn bad; **mir ist s~** I feel sick; **s~ machen** 🛈 run down. **s~gehen*** *vi sep* (*sein*) **s~ gehen**, *s*. **gehen**

schlecken *vt/i* (*haben*) lick (**an etw** *dat* sth); (*auf-*) lap up

Schlegel *m* -s,- (*SGer: Keule*) leg; (*Hühner-*) drumstick

schleichen† *vi* (*sein*) creep; (*langsam gehen/fahren*) crawl ● *vr* **sich s~** creep. **s~d** *a* creeping

Schleier *m* -s,- veil; (*fig*) haze

Schleife *f* -, -n bow; (*Fliege*) bowtie; (*Biegung*) loop

schleifen¹ *v* (*reg*) ● *vt* drag ● *vi* (*haben*) trail, drag

schleifen²† *vt* grind; (*schärfen*) sharpen; cut <*Edelstein, Glas*>

Schleim *m* -[e]s slime; (*Anat*) mucus; (*Med*) phlegm. **s~ig** *a* slimy

schlendern *vi* (*sein*) stroll

schlenkern *vt/i* (*haben*) swing; **s~ mit** swing; dangle <*Beine*>

Schlepp|dampfer *m* tug. **S~e** *f* -, -n train. **s~en** *vt* drag; (*tragen*) carry; (*ziehen*) tow; **sich s~en** drag oneself; (*sich hinziehen*) drag on; **sich s~en mit** carry. **S~er** *m* -s,- tug; (*Traktor*) tractor. **S~kahn** *m* barge. **S~lift** *m* T-bar lift. **S~tau** *nt* tow-rope; **ins S~tau nehmen** take in tow

Schleuder *f* -, -n catapult; (*Wäsche-*) spin-drier. **s~n** *vt* hurl; spin <*Wäsche*> ● *vi* (*sein*) skid; **ins S~n geraten** skid. **S~sitz** *m* ejector seat

S

Schleuse f -, -n lock; (*Sperre*) sluice[-gate]. **s~n** vt steer

Schliche pl tricks

schlicht a plain; simple

Schlichtung f - settlement; (*Jur*) arbitration

Schließe f -, -n clasp; buckle

schließen† vt close (*ab-*) lock; fasten <*Kleid, Verschluss*>; (*stilllegen*) close down; (*beenden, folgern*) conclude; enter into <*Vertrag*>; **sich s~** close; **etw s~ an** (+ acc) connect sth to; **sich s~ an** (+ acc) follow ●vi (*haben*) close, (*den Betrieb einstellen*) close down; (*den Schlüssel drehen*) turn the key; (*enden, folgern*) conclude

Schließ|fach nt locker. **s~lich** adv finally, in the end; (*immerhin*) after all. **S~ung** f -, -en closure

Schliff m -[e]s cut; (*Schleifen*) cutting; (*fig*) polish

schlimm a bad

Schlinge f -, -n loop; (*Henkers-*) noose; (*Med*) sling; (*Falle*) snare

Schlingel m -s,- 🄸 rascal

schlingen† vt wind, wrap; tie <*Knoten*> ●vi (*haben*) bolt one's food

Schlips m -es, -e tie

Schlitten m -s,- sledge; (*Rodel-*) toboggan; (*Pferde-*) sleigh; **S~ fahren** toboggan

schlittern vi (*haben/ sein*) slide

Schlittschuh m skate; **S~ laufen** skate. **S~läufer(in)** m(f) -s,- (f -, -nen) skater

Schlitz m -es, -e slit; (*für Münze*) slot; (*Jacken-*) vent; (*Hosen-*) flies pl. **s~en** vt slit

Schloss nt -es,̈-er lock; (*Vorhänge-*) padlock; (*Verschluss*) clasp; (*Gebäude*) castle; palace

Schlosser m -s,- locksmith; (*Auto-*) mechanic

Schlucht f -, -en ravine, gorge

schluchzen vi (*haben*) sob

Schluck m -[e]s, -e mouthful; (*klein*) sip

Schluckauf m -s hiccups pl

schlucken vt/i (*haben*) swallow

Schlummer m -s slumber

Schlund m -[e]s [back of the] throat; (*fig*) mouth

schlüpf|en vi (*sein*) slip; [aus de Ei] **s~en** hatch. **S~er** m -s,- knickers pl. **s~rig** a slippery

schlürfen vt/i (*haben*) slurp

Schluss m -es,̈e end; (*S~folgerung*) conclusion; **zum S~** finally; **S~ machen** stop (mit etw sth); finish (mit jdm with s.o

Schlüssel m -s,- key; (*Schrauben-*) spanner; (*Geheim-* code; (*Mus*) clef. **S~bein** nt collar-bone. **S~bund** m & nt bunch of keys. **S~loch** nt keyhole

Schlussfolgerung f conclusion

schlüssig a conclusive

Schluss|licht nt rear-light. **S~verkauf** m sale

schmächtig a slight

schmackhaft a tasty

schmal a narrow; (*dünn*) thin; (*schlank*) slender; (*karg*) meagr

schmälern vt diminish; (*herabsetzen*) belittle

Schmalz[1] nt -es lard; (*Ohren-*) wax

Schmalz[2] m -es 🄸 schmaltz

Schmarotzer m -s,- parasite; (*Person*) sponger

schmatzen vi (*haben*) eat noisil

schmausen vi (*haben*) feast

schmecken vi (*haben*) taste (na of); [gut] **s~** taste good ●vt tast

Schmeichelei f -, -en flattery; (*Kompliment*) compliment

schmeichel|haft a complimentary, flattering. **s~n** (*haben*) (+ dat) flatter

schmeißen† vt/i (*haben*) **s~ [mit** 🄸 chuck

Schmeißfliege f bluebottle

chmelz|en† *vt/i* (*sein*) melt; melt <*Erze*>. **S~wasser** *nt* melted snow and ice

chmerbauch *m* 🔲 paunch

chmerz *m* -es, -en pain; (*Kummer*) grief; **S~en haben** be in pain. **s~en** *vt* hurt; (*fig*) grieve ● *vi* (*haben*) hurt, be painful. **S~ensgeld** *nt* compensation for pain and suffering. **s~haft** *a* painful. **s~los** *a* painless ~**stillend** *a* pain-killing; ~**stillendes Mittel** analgesic, pain-killer. **S~tablette** *f* pain-killer

chmetterball *m* (*Tennis*) smash

chmetterling *m* -s, -e butterfly

chmettern *vt* hurl; (*Tennis*) mash; (*singen*) sing ● *vi* (*haben*) sound

chmied *m* -[e]s, -e blacksmith

chmiede *f* -, -n forge. **S~eisen** *nt* wrought iron. **s~n** *vt* forge

chmier|e *f* -, -n grease; (*Schmutz*) mess. **s~en** *vt* lubricate; (*streichen*) spread; (*schlecht schreiben*) scrawl ● *vi* (*haben*) smudge; (*schreiben*) scrawl. **S~geld** *nt* 🔲 bribe. **s~ig** *a* greasy; (*schmutzig*) grubby. **S~mittel** *nt* lubricant

chminke *f* -, -n make-up. **s~n** *vt* make up; **sich s~n** put on make-up; **sich** (*dat*) **die Lippen s~n** put on lipstick

chmirgel|n *vt* sand down. **S~papier** *nt* emery-paper

chmollen *vi* (*haben*) sulk

chmor|en *vt/i* (*haben*) braise. **S~topf** *m* casserole

chmuck *m* -[e]s jewellery; (*Verzierung*) ornament, decoration

chmücken *vt* decorate, adorn

chmuck|los *a* plain. **S~stück** *nt* piece of jewellery

chmuggel *m* -s smuggling. **s~n** *vt* smuggle. **S~ware** *f* contraband

chmuggler *m* -s,- smuggler

schmunzeln *vi* (*haben*) smile

schmusen *vi* (*haben*) cuddle

Schmutz *m* -es dirt. **s~en** *vi* (*haben*) get dirty. **s~ig** *a* dirty

Schnabel *m* -s,: beak, bill; (*eines Kruges*) lip; (*Tülle*) spout

Schnalle *f* -, -n buckle. **s~n** *vt* strap; (*zu-*) buckle

schnalzen *vi* (*haben*) **mit der Zunge s~** click one's tongue

schnapp|en *vi* (*haben*) **s~en nach** snap at; gasp for <*Luft*> ● *vt* snatch, grab; (🔲 *festnehmen*) nab. **S~schloss** *nt* spring lock. **S~schuss** *m* snapshot

Schnaps *m* -es,:e schnapps

schnarchen *vi* (*haben*) snore

schnaufen *vi* (*haben*) puff, pant

Schnauze *f* -, -n muzzle; (*eines Kruges*) lip; (*Tülle*) spout

schnäuzen (sich) *vr* blow one's nose

Schnecke *f* -, -n snail; (*Nackt-*) slug; (*Spirale*) scroll. **S~nhaus** *nt* snail-shell

Schnee *m* -s snow; (*Eier-*) beaten egg-white. **S~besen** *m* whisk. **S~brille** *f* snow-goggles *pl*. **S~fall** *m* snow-fall. **S~flocke** *f* snowflake. **S~glöckchen** *nt* -s,- snowdrop. **S~kette** *f* snow chain. **S~mann** *m* (*pl* -männer) snowman. **S~pflug** *m* snowplough. **S~schläger** *m* whisk. **S~sturm** *m* snowstorm, blizzard. **S~wehe** *f* -, -n snowdrift

Schneide *f* -, -n [cutting] edge; (*Klinge*) blade

schneiden† *vt* cut; (*in Scheiben*) slice; (*kreuzen*) cross; (*nicht beachten*) cut dead; **Gesichter s~** pull faces; **sich s~** cut oneself; (*über-*) intersect

Schneider *m* -s,- tailor. **S~in** *f* -, -nen dressmaker. **s~n** *vt* make <*Anzug, Kostüm*>

Schneidezahn *m* incisor

schneien *vi* (*haben*) snow; **es schneit** it is snowing

S

Schneise f -, -n path

schnell a quick; <*Auto, Tempo*> fast ● adv quickly; (*in s~em Tempo*) fast; (*bald*) soon; **mach s~!** hurry up! **S~igkeit** f - rapidity; (*Tempo*) speed. **S~kochtopf** m pressure-cooker. **s~stens** adv as quickly as possible. **S~zug** m express [train]

schnetzeln vt cut into thin strips

Schnipsel m & nt -s,- scrap

Schnitt m -[e]s, -e cut; (*Film-*) cutting; (*S~muster*) [paper] pattern; **im S~** (*durchschnittlich*) on average

Schnitte f -, -n slice [of bread]

schnittig a stylish; (*stromlinienförmig*) streamlined

Schnitt|lauch m chives pl. **S~muster** nt [paper] pattern. **S~punkt** m [point of] intersection. **S~wunde** f cut

Schnitzel nt -s,- scrap; (*Culin*) escalope. **s~n** vt shred

schnitzen vt/i (*haben*) carve

schnoddrig a 🔲 brash

Schnorchel m -s,- snorkel

Schnörkel m -s,- flourish; (*Kunst*) scroll. **s~ig** a ornate

schnüffeln vi (*haben*) sniff (**an** etw dat sth); (🔲 *spionieren*) snoop [around]

Schnuller m -s,- [baby's] dummy

Schnupf|en m -s,- [head] cold. **S~tabak** m snuff

schnuppern vt/i (*haben*) sniff (**an** etw dat sth)

Schnur f -,̈e string; (*Kordel*) cord; (*Electr*) flex

schnüren vt tie; lace [up] <*Schuhe*>

Schnurr|bart m moustache. **s~en** vi (*haben*) hum; <*Katze:*> purr

Schnürsenkel m [shoe-]lace

Schock m -[e]s, -s shock. **s~en** vt 🔲 shock. **s~ieren** vt shock

Schöffe m -n, -n lay judge

Schokolade f - chocolate

Scholle f -, -n clod [of earth]; (*Eis-*) [ice-]floe; (*Fisch*) plaice

schon adv already; (*allein*) just; (*sogar*) even; (*ohnehin*) anyway; **s~ einmal** before; (*jemals*) ever; **s~ immer/oft/wieder** always/ often/again; **s~ deshalb** for that reason alone; **das ist s~ möglich** that's quite possible; **ja s~, aber** well yes, but

schön a beautiful; <*Wetter*> fine; (*angenehm, nett*) nice; (*gut*) good (🔲 *beträchtlich*) pretty; **s~en Dank!** thank you very much!

schonen vt spare; (*gut behandeln*) look after. **s~d** a gentle

Schönheit f -, -en beauty. **S~sfehler** m blemish. **S~skonkurrenz** f beauty contest

Schonung f -, -en gentle care; (*nach Krankheit*) rest; (*Baum-*) plantation. **s~slos** a ruthless

Schonzeit f close season

schöpf|en vt scoop [up]; ladle <*Suppe*>; **Mut s~en** take heart. **s~erisch** a creative. **S~kelle** f. **S~löffel** m ladle. **S~ung** f -, -en creation

Schoppen m -s,- (*SGer*) ≈ pint

Schorf m -[e]s scab

Schornstein m chimney. **S~fege** m -s,- chimney-sweep

Schoß m -es,̈e lap; (*Frack-*) tail

Schössling m -s, -e (*Bot*) shoot

Schote f -, -n pod; (*Erbse*) pea

Schotte m -n, -n Scot, Scotsman

Schotter m -s gravel

schott|isch a Scottish, Scots. **S~land** nt -s Scotland

schraffieren vt hatch

schräg a diagonal; (*geneigt*) sloping; **s~ halten** tilt. **S~strich** m oblique stroke

Schramme f -, -n scratch

Schrank m -[e]s,̈e cupboard; (*Kleider-*) wardrobe; (*Akten-, Glas-*) cabinet

Schranke f -, -n barrier

Schraube f -, -n screw; (Schiffs-) propeller. **s~n** vt screw; (ab-) unscrew; (drehen) turn.
S~nschlüssel m spanner.
S~nzieher m -s,- screwdriver
Schraubstock m vice
Schreck m -[e]s, -e fright. **S~en** m -s,- fright; (Entsetzen) horror
Schreck|gespenst nt spectre. **s~haft** a easily frightened; (nervös) jumpy. **s~lich** a terrible. **S~schuss** m warning shot
Schrei m -[e]s, -e cry, shout; (gellend) scream; der letzte **S~** ! the latest thing
schreiben† vt/i (haben) write; (auf der Maschine) type; richtig/ falsch **s~en** spell right/wrong; sich **s~en** <Wort:> be spelt; (korrespondieren) correspond. **S~en** nt -s,- writing; (Brief) letter. **S~fehler** m spelling mistake. **S~heft** nt exercise book. **S~kraft** f clerical assistant; (für Maschineschreiben) typist. **S~maschine** f typewriter. **S~tisch** m desk. **S~ung** f -, -en spelling. **S~waren** fpl stationery sg.
schreien† vt/i (haben) cry; (gellend) scream; (rufen, laut sprechen) shout
Schreiner m -s,- joiner
schreiten† vi (sein) walk
Schrift f -, -en writing; (Druck-) type; (Abhandlung) paper; die Heilige **S~** the Scriptures pl. **S~führer** m secretary. **s~lich** a written ● adv in writing. **S~sprache** f written language. **S~steller(in)** m -s,- (f -, -nen) writer. **S~stück** nt document. **S~zeichen** nt character
schrill a shrill
Schritt m -[e]s, -e step; (Entfernung) pace; (Gangart) walk; (der Hose) crotch. **S~macher** m -s,- pace-maker. **s~weise** adv step by step

schroff a precipitous; (abweisend) brusque; (unvermittelt) abrupt; <Gegensatz> stark
Schrot m & nt -[e]s coarse meal; (Blei-) small shot. **S~flinte** f shotgun
Schrott m -[e]s scrap[-metal]; zu **S~** fahren ! write off. **S~platz** m scrap-yard
schrubben vt/i (haben) scrub
Schrulle f -, -n whim; alte **S~e** ! old crone. **s~ig** a cranky
schrumpfen vi (sein) shrink
schrump[e]lig a wrinkled
Schub m -[e]s,¨e (Phys) thrust; (S~fach) drawer; (Menge) batch. **S~fach** nt drawer. **S~karre** f, **S~karren** m wheelbarrow. **S~lade** f drawer
Schubs m -es, -e push, shove **s~en** vt push, shove
schüchtern a shy. **S~heit** f - shyness
Schuft m -[e]s, -e (pej) swine
Schuh m -[e]s, -e shoe. **S~anzieher** m -s,- shoehorn. **S~band** nt (pl -bänder) shoe-lace. **S~creme** f shoe-polish. **S~löffel** m shoehorn. **S~macher** m -s,- shoemaker
Schul|abgänger m -s,- schoolleaver. **S~arbeiten, S~aufgaben** fpl homework sg.
Schuld f -, -en guilt; (Verantwortung) blame; (Geld-) debt; **S~en** machen get into debt; **S~** haben be to blame (an + dat for); jdm **S~** geben blame s.o. ● **s~** sein be to blame (an + dat for). **s~en** vt owe
schuldig a guilty (gen of); (gebührend) due; jdm etw **s~** sein owe s.o. sth. **S~keit** f - duty
schuld|los a innocent. **S~ner** m -s,- debtor. **S~spruch** m guilty verdict
Schule f -, -n school; in der/die **S~** at/to school. **s~n** vt train
Schüler(in) m -s,- (f -, -nen) pupil

S

schul|frei a s~freier Tag day without school; **wir haben morgen s~frei** there's no school tomorrow. **S~hof** m [school] playground. **S~jahr** nt school year; (*Klasse*) form. **S~kind** nt schoolchild. **S~stunde** f lesson

Schulter f -, -n shoulder. **S~blatt** nt shoulder-blade

Schulung f - training

schummeln vi (*haben*) 🄸 cheat

Schund m -[e]s trash

Schuppe f -, -n scale; **S~n** pl dandruff sg. **s~n (sich)** vr flake [off]

Schuppen m -s,- shed

schürf|en vt mine; **sich** (*dat*) **das Knie s~en** graze one's knee ● vi (*haben*) **s~en nach** prospect for. **S~wunde** f abrasion, graze

Schürhaken m poker

Schurke m -n, -n villain

Schürze f -, -n apron

Schuss m -es,-̈e shot; (*kleine Menge*) dash

Schüssel f -, -n bowl; (*TV*) dish

Schuss|fahrt f (*Ski*) schuss. **S~waffe** f firearm

Schuster m -s,- = **Schuhmacher**

Schutt m -[e]s rubble. **S~abladeplatz** m rubbish dump

Schüttel|frost m shivering fit. **s~n** vt shake; **sich s~n** shake oneself/itself; (*vor Ekel*) shudder; **jdm die Hand s~n** shake s.o.'s hand

schütten vt pour; (*kippen*) tip; (*ver-*) spill ● vi (*haben*) **es schüttet** it is pouring [with rain]

Schutz m -es protection; (*Zuflucht*) shelter; (*Techn*) guard; **S~ suchen** take refuge. **S~anzug** m protective suit. **S~blech** nt mudguard. **S~brille** f goggles pl

Schütze m -n, -n marksman; (*Tor-*) scorer; (*Astr*) Sagittarius

schützen vt protect/(*Zuflucht gewähren*) shelter (**vor** + *dat* from) ● vi (*haben*) give

protection/shelter (**vor** + *dat* from)

Schutz|engel m guardian angel. **S~heilige(r)** m/f patron saint

Schützling m -s, -e charge

schutz|los a defenceless, helpless. **S~mann** m (pl -männer & -leute) policeman. **S~umschlag** m dust-jacket

Schwaben nt -s Swabia

schwäbisch a Swabian

schwach a weak; (*nicht gut*) poor; (*leicht*) faint

Schwäche f -, -n weakness. **s~n** vt weaken

schwäch|lich a delicate. **S~ling** m -s, -e weakling

Schwachsinn m mental deficiency. **s~ig** a mentally deficient; 🄸 idiotic

Schwager m -s,-̈ brother-in-law

Schwägerin f -, -nen sister-in-law

Schwalbe f -, -n swallow

Schwall m -[e]s torrent

Schwamm m -[e]s,-̈e sponge; (*SGer: Pilz*) fungus; (*essbar*) mushroom. **s~ig** a spongy

Schwan m -[e]s,-̈e swan

schwanger a pregnant

Schwangerschaft f -, -en pregnancy

Schwank m -[e]s,-̈e (*Theat*) farce

schwank|en vi (*haben*) sway; <*Boot:*> rock; (*sich ändern*) fluctuate; (*unentschieden sein*) be undecided ● vi (*sein*) stagger. **S~ung** f -, -en fluctuation

Schwanz m -es,-̈e tail

schwänzen vt 🄸 skip; **die Schule s~** play truant

Schwarm m -[e]s,-̈e swarm; (*Fisch-*) shoal; (🄸 *Liebe*) idol

schwärmen vi (*haben*) swarm; **s~ für** 🄸 adore; (*verliebt sein*) have a crush on

Schwarte f -, -n (*Speck-*) rind

schwarz a black; (🄸 *illegal*) illegal; **s~er Markt** black market; **s~ gekleidet** dressed in black; **s~**

auf weiß in black and white; **s~ sehen** (*fig*) be pessimistic; **ins S~e treffen** score a bull's-eye. **S~ nt -[e]s,-** black. **S~arbeit** *f* moonlighting. **s~arbeiten** *vi sep* (*haben*) moonlight. **S~e(r)** *m/f* black

Schwärze *f -* blackness. **s~n** *vt* blacken

Schwarz|fahrer *m* fare-dodger. **S~handel** *m* black market (**mit** in). **S~händler** *m* black marketeer. **S~markt** *m* black market. **S~wald** *m* Black Forest. **s~weiß** *a* black and white

schwatzen, (*SGer***) schwätzen** *vi* (*haben*) chat; (*klatschen*) gossip; (*Sch*) talk [in class] ●*vt* talk

Schwebe *f -* **in der S~** (*fig*) undecided. **S~bahn** *f* cable railway. **s~n** *vi* (*haben*) float; (*fig*) be undecided; <*Verfahren:*> be pending; **in Gefahr s~n** be in danger ● (*sein*) float

Schwed|e *m* **-n, -n** Swede. **S~en** *nt* **-s** Sweden. **S~in** *f* **-, -nen** Swede. **s~isch** *a* Swedish

Schwefel *m* **-s** sulphur

schweigen† *vi* (*haben*) be silent; **ganz zu s~** von let alone. **S~** *nt* **-s** silence; **zum S~ bringen** silence

schweigsam *a* silent; (*wortkarg*) taciturn

Schwein *nt* **-[e]s, -e** pig; (*Culin*) pork; (⚔ *Schuft*) swine; **S~ haben** 🎲 be lucky. **S~ebraten** *m* roast pork. **S~efleisch** *nt* pork. **S~erei** *f* **-, -en** ⚔ [dirty] mess; (*Gemeinheit*) dirty trick. **S~estall** *m* pigsty. **S~sleder** *nt* pigskin

Schweiß *m* **-es** sweat

schweißen *vt* weld

Schweiz (die) *-* Switzerland. **S~er** *a & m* **-s,-**, **S~erin** *f* **-, -nen** Swiss. **s~erisch** *a* Swiss

Schwelle *f* **-, -n** threshold; (*Eisenbahn-*) sleeper

schwell|en† *vi* (*sein*) swell. **S~ung** *f* **-, -en** swelling

schwer *a* heavy; (*schwierig*) difficult; (*mühsam*) hard; (*ernst*) serious; (*schlimm*) bad; **3 Pfund s~ sein** weigh 3 pounds ●*adv* heavily; with difficulty; (*mühsam*) hard; (*schlimm, sehr*) badly, seriously; **s~ krank/verletzt** seriously ill/injured; **s~ hören** be hard of hearing; **etw s~ nehmen** take sth seriously; **jdm s~ fallen** be hard for s.o.; **es jdm s~ machen** make it *or* things difficult for s.o.; **sich s~ tun** have difficulty (**mit** with); **s~ zu sagen** difficult *or* hard to say

Schwere *f -* heaviness; (*Gewicht*) weight; (*Schwierigkeit*) difficulty; (*Ernst*) gravity. **S~losigkeit** *f -* weightlessness

schwer|fällig *a* ponderous, clumsy. **S~gewicht** *nt* heavyweight. **s~hörig** *a* **s~hörig sein** be hard of hearing. **S~kraft** *f* (*Phys*) gravity. **s~mütig** *a* melancholic. **S~punkt** *m* centre of gravity; (*fig*) emphasis

Schwert *nt* **-[e]s, -er** sword. **S~lilie** *f* iris

Schwer|verbrecher *m* serious offender. **s~wiegend** *a* weighty

Schwester *f* **-, -n** sister; (*Kranken-*) nurse. **s~lich** *a* sisterly

Schwieger|eltern *pl* parents-in-law. **S~mutter** *f* mother-in-law. **S~sohn** *m* son-in-law. **S~tochter** *f* daughter-in-law. **S~vater** *m* father-in-law

schwierig *a* difficult. **S~keit** *f* **-, -en** difficulty

Schwimm|bad *nt* swimming-baths *pl*. **S~becken** *nt* swimming-pool. **s~en†** *vt/i* (*sein/haben*) swim; (*auf dem Wasser treiben*) float. **S~weste** *f* life-jacket

Schwindel *m* **-s** dizziness, vertigo; (🎲 *Betrug*) fraud; (*Lüge*) lie. **S~anfall** *m* dizzy spell. **s~frei** *a*

S

s~frei sein have a good head for heights. **s~n** *vi* (*haben*) lie

Schwindl|er *m* -s,- liar; (*Betrüger*) fraud, con-man. **s~ig** *a* dizzy; **mir ist** *od* **wird s~ig** I feel dizzy

schwing|en† *vi* (*haben*) swing; (*Phys*) oscillate; (*vibrieren*) vibrate ● *vt* swing; wave <*Fahne*>; (*drohend*) brandish. **S~ung** *f* -, -en oscillation; vibration

Schwips *m* -es, -e **einen S~ haben** 🛈 be tipsy

schwitzen *vi* (*haben*) sweat; **ich schwitze** I am hot

schwören† *vt/i* (*haben*) swear (**auf** + *acc* by)

schwul *a* (🛈 *homosexuell*) gay

schwül *a* close. **S~e** *f* - closeness

Schwung *m* -[e]s,¨e swing; (*Bogen*) sweep; (*Schnelligkeit*) momentum; (*Kraft*) vigour. **s~los** *a* dull. **s~voll** *a* vigorous; <*Bogen, Linie*> sweeping; (*mitreißend*) spirited

Schwur *m* -[e]s,¨e vow; (*Eid*) oath. **S~gericht** *nt* jury [court]

sechs *inv a*, **S~** *f* -, -en six; (*Sch*) ≈ fail mark. **s~eckig** *a* hexagonal. **s~te(r,s)** *a* sixth

sech|zehn *inv a* sixteen. **s~zehnte(r,s)** *a* sixteenth. **s~zig** *inv a* sixty. **s~zigste(r,s)** *a* sixtieth

See¹ *m* -s, -n /'ze:ən/ lake

See² *f* -, sea; **an die/der See** to/at the seaside; **auf See** at sea. **S~fahrt** *f* [sea] voyage; (*Schifffahrt*) navigation. **S~gang** *m* **schwerer S~gang** rough sea. **S~hund** *m* seal. **s~krank** *a* seasick

Seele *f* -, -n soul

seelisch *a* psychological; (*geistig*) mental

See|macht *f* maritime power. **S~mann** *m* (*pl* -leute) seaman, sailor. **S~not** *f* **in S~not** in distress. **S~räuber** *m* pirate.

S~reise *f* [sea] voyage. **S~rose** *f* water-lily. **S~sack** *m* kitbag. **S~stern** *m* starfish. **S~tang** *m* seaweed. **s~tüchtig** *a* seaworthy. **S~zunge** *f* sole

Segel *nt* -s,- sail. **S~boot** *nt* sailing-boat. **S~flugzeug** *nt* glider. **s~n** *vt/i* (*sein/haben*) sail. **S~schiff** *nt* sailing-ship. **S~sport** *m* sailing. **S~tuch** *nt* canvas

Segen *m* -s blessing

Segler *m* -s,- yachtsman

segnen *vt* bless

sehen† *vt* see; watch <*Fernsehsendung*>; **jdn/etw wieder s~** see s.o./sth again; **sich s~ lassen** show oneself ● *vi* (*haben*) see; (*blicken*) look (**aus** above); **gut/ schlecht s~** have good/bad eyesight; **vom S~ kennen** know by sight; **s~ nach** keep an eye on; (*betreuen*) look after; (*suchen*) look for. **s~swert, s~swürdig** *a* worth seeing. **S~swürdigkeit** *f* -, -en sight

Sehne *f* -, -n tendon; (*eines Bogens*) string

sehnen (sich) *vr* long (**nach** for)

Sehn|sucht *f* - longing (**nach** for). **s~süchtig** *a* longing; <*Wunsch*> dearest

sehr *adv* very; (*mit Verb*) very much; **so s~, dass** so much that

seicht *a* shallow

seid *s.* **sein¹**

Seide *f* -, -n silk

Seidel *nt* -s,- beer-mug

seiden *a* silk … **S~papier** *nt* tissue paper. **S~raupe** *f* silk-worm

seidig *a* silky

Seife *f* -, -n soap. **S~npulver** *nt* soap powder. **S~nschaum** *m* lather

Seil *nt* -[e]s, -e rope; (*Draht-*) cable. **S~bahn** *f* cable railway. **s~springen†** *vi* (*sein*) (*inf & pp*

only) skip. **S~tänzer(in)** *m(f)* tightrope walker

sein†¹
● *intransitive verb* (*sein*)
···▸ be. **ich bin glücklich** I am happy. **er ist Lehrer/Schwede** he is a teacher/Swedish. **bist du es?** is that you? **sei still!** be quiet! **sie waren in Paris** they were in Paris. **morgen bin ich zu Hause** I shall be at home tomorrow. **er ist aus Berlin** he is *or* comes from Berlin
···▸ (*impers* + *dat*) **mir ist kalt/besser** I am cold/better. **ihr ist schlecht** she feels sick
···▸ (*existieren*) be. **es ist/sind ...** there is/are .... **es ist keine Hoffnung mehr** there is no more hope. **es sind vier davon** there are four of them. **es war einmal ein Prinz** once upon a time there was a prince
● *auxiliary verb*
···▸ (*zur Perfektumschreibung*) have. **er ist gestorben** he has died. **sie sind angekommen** they have arrived. **sie war dort gewesen** she had been there. **ich wäre gefallen** I would have fallen
···▸ (*zur Bildung des Passivs*) be. **wir sind gerettet worden/wir waren gerettet** we were saved
···▸ (+ *zu* + *Infinitiv*) be to be. **es war niemand zu sehen** there was no one to be seen. **das war zu erwarten** that was to be expected. **er ist zu bemitleiden** he is to be pitied. **die Richtlinien sind strengstens zu beachten** the guidelines are to be strictly followed

sein² *poss pron* his; (*Ding, Tier*) its; (*nach man*) one's; **sein Glück versuchen** try one's luck. **s~e(r,s)** *poss pron* his; (*nach man*) one's own; **das S~e tun** do one's share.

s~erseits *adv* for his part. **s~erzeit** *adv* in those days. **s~etwegen** *adv* for his sake; (*wegen ihm*) because of him, on his account. **s~ige** *poss pron* **der/die/das s~ige** his

seins *poss pron* his; (*nach man*) one's own

seit *conj & prep* (+ *dat*) since; **s~ einiger Zeit** for some time [past]; **ich wohne s~ zehn Jahren hier** I've lived here for ten years. **s~dem** *conj* since ● *adv* since then

Seite *f* -, -n side; (*Buch-*) page; **zur S~ treten** step aside; **auf der einen/anderen S~** (*fig*) on the one/other hand

seitens *prep* (+ *gen*) on the part of

Seiten|schiff *nt* [side] aisle. **S~sprung** *m* infidelity. **S~stechen** *nt* -s (*Med*) stitch. **S~straße** *f* side-street. **S~streifen** *m* verge; (*Autobahn-*) hard shoulder

seither *adv* since then

seit|lich *a* side ... ● *adv* at/on the side; **s~lich von** to one side of ● *prep* (+ *gen*) to one side of. **s~wärts** *adv* on/to one side; (*zur Seite*) sideways

Sekret|är *m* -s, -e secretary; (*Schrank*) bureau. **S~ariat** *nt* -[e]s, -e secretary's office. **S~ärin** *f* -, -nen secretary

Sekt *m* -[e]s [German] sparkling wine

Sekte *f* -, -n sect

Sektor *m* -s, -en /-'to:rən/ sector

Sekunde *f* -, -n second

selber *pron* [1] = **selbst**

selbst *pron* oneself; **ich/du/er/sie s~** I myself /you yourself/ he himself/she herself; **wir/ihr/sie s~** we ourselves/you yourselves/ they themselves; **ich schneide mein Haar s~** I cut my own hair; **von s~** of one's own accord;

S

(*automatisch*) automatically; s~
gemacht home-made ● adv even
selbständig a = selbstständig.
S~keit f - = Selbstständigkeit
Selbst|bedienung f self-service.
S~befriedigung f masturbation.
s~bewusst a self-confident.
S~bewusstsein nt self-
confidence. S~bildnis nt self-
portrait. S~erhaltung f self-
preservation. s~gemacht* a s~
gemacht, s. selbst. s~haftend a
self-adhesive. S~hilfe f self-
help. s~klebend a self-adhesive.
S~kostenpreis m cost price.
S~laut m vowel. s~los a
selfless. S~mord m suicide.
S~mörder(in) m(f) suicide.
s~mörderisch a suicidal.
S~porträt nt self-portrait.
s~sicher a self-assured.
s~ständig a independent; self-
employed <*Handwerker*>; sich
s~ständig machen set up on one's
own. S~ständigkeit f -
independence. s~süchtig a
selfish. S~tanken nt self-service
(*for petrol*). s~tätig a automatic.
S~versorgung f self-catering.
s~verständlich a natural; etw für
s~ halten take sth for granted;
das ist s~ that goes without
saying; s~! of course!
S~verteidigung f self-defence.
S~vertrauen nt self-confidence.
S~verwaltung f self-government.
selig a blissfully happy; (*Relig*)
blessed; (*verstorben*) late. S~keit
f - bliss
Sellerie m -s, -s & f -,- celeriac;
(*Stangen-*) celery
selten a rare ● adv rarely,
seldom; (*besonders*)
exceptionally. S~heit f -, -en
rarity
seltsam a odd, strange.
s~erweise adv oddly
Semester nt -s,- (*Univ*) semester
Semikolon nt -s, -s semicolon

Seminar nt -s, -e seminar;
(*Institut*) department; (*Priester-*)
seminary
Semmel f -, -n [bread] roll.
S~brösel pl breadcrumbs
Senat m -[e]s, -e senate. S~or m
-s, -en /-'to:rən/ senator
senden[1]† vt send
sende|n[2] vt (*reg*) broadcast; (*über
Funk*) transmit, send. S~r m -s,-
[broadcasting] station; (*Anlage*)
transmitter. S~reihe f series
Sendung f -, -en consignment,
shipment; (*TV*) programme
Senf m -s mustard
senil a senile. S~ität f - senility
Senior m -s, -en /-'o:rən/ senior;
S~en senior citizens. S~enheim
nt old people's home
senken vt lower; bring down
<*Fieber, Preise*>; bow <*Kopf*>;
sich s~ come down, fall;
(*absinken*) subside
senkrecht a vertical. S~e f -n, -n
perpendicular
Sensation /-'tsɪo:n/ f -, -en
sensation. s~ell a sensational
Sense f -, -n scythe
sensibel a sensitive
sentimental a sentimental
September m -s,- September
Serie /'ze:riə/ f -, -n series;
(*Briefmarken*) set; (*Comm*) range.
S~nnummer f serial number
seriös a respectable; (*zuverlässig*)
reliable
Serpentine f -, -n winding road;
(*Kehre*) hairpin bend
Serum nt -s,Sera serum
Service[1] /zɛr'vi:s/ nt -[s],-
/-'vi:s[əs], -'vi:sə/ service, set
Service[2] /'zœ:ɛvɪs/ m & nt -s
/-vɪs[əs]/ (*Comm, Tennis*) service
servier|en vt/i (*haben*) serve.
S~erin f -, -nen waitress
Serviette f -, -n napkin, serviette
Servus int (*Aust*) cheerio;
(*Begrüßung*) hallo

Sessel m -s,- armchair. **S∼bahn** f,
S∼lift m chair-lift
sesshaft a settled
Set /zɛt/ nt & m -[s], -s set;
(Deckchen) place-mat
setz|en vt put; (abstellen) set
down; (hin-) sit down <Kind>;
move <Spielstein>; (pflanzen)
plant; (schreiben, wetten) put;
sich s∼en sit down; (sinken)
settle ● vi (sein) leap ● vi (haben)
s∼en back (+ acc) back
Seuche f -, -n epidemic
seufz|en vi (haben) sigh. **S∼er** m
-s,- sigh
Sex /zɛks/ m -[es] sex
Sexu|alität f - sexuality. **s∼ell** a
sexual
sezieren vt dissect
Shampoo /ʃam'puː/, **Shampoon**
/ʃam'poːn/ nt -s shampoo
siamesisch a Siamese
sich refl pron oneself; (mit er/
sie/es) himself/herself/itself; (mit
sie pl) themselves; (mit Sie)
yourself; (pl) yourselves;
(einander) each other; **s∼ kennen**
know oneself/(einander) each
other; **s∼ waschen** have a wash;
s∼ (dat) **die Haare kämmen** comb
one's hair; **s∼ wundern** be
surprised; **s∼ gut verkaufen** sell
well; **von s∼ aus** of one's own
accord
Sichel f -, -n sickle
sicher a safe; (gesichert) secure;
(gewiss) certain; (zuverlässig)
reliable; sure <Urteil>; steady
<Hand>; (selbstbewusst) self-
confident; **bist du s∼?** are you
sure? ● adv safely; securely;
certainly; reliably; self-
confidently; (wahrscheinlich)
most probably; **s∼!** certainly!
s∼gehen† vi sep (sein) (fig) be
sure
Sicherheit f - safety; (Pol, Psych,
Comm) security; (Gewissheit)
certainty; (Zuverlässigkeit)

reliability; (des Urteils) surety;
(Selbstbewusstsein) self-
confidence. **S∼sgurt** m safety-
belt; (Auto) seat-belt. **S∼snadel** f
safety-pin
sicherlich adv certainly;
(wahrscheinlich) most probably
sichern vt secure; (garantieren)
safeguard; (schützen) protect; put
the safety-catch on <Pistole>.
S∼ung f -, -en safeguard,
protection; (Gewehr-) safety-
catch; (Electr) fuse
Sicht f - view; (S∼weite) visibility;
auf lange S∼ in the long term.
s∼bar a visible. **S∼vermerk** m
visa. **S∼weite** f visibility; **außer**
S∼weite out of sight
sie pron (nom) (sg) she; (Ding,
Tier) it; (pl) they; (acc) (sg) her;
(Ding, Tier) it; (pl) them
Sie pron you; **gehen/warten Sie!**
go/wait!
Sieb nt -[e]s, -e sieve; (Tee-)
strainer. **s∼en¹** vt sieve, sift
sieben² inv a, **S∼** f -, -en seven.
S∼sachen fpl 🄸 belongings.
s∼te(r,s) a seventh
sieb|te(r,s) a seventh. **s∼zehn** inv
a seventeen. **s∼zehnte(r,s)** a
seventeenth. **s∼zig** inv a
seventy. **s∼zigste(r,s)** a
seventieth
siede|n† vt/i (haben) boil.
S∼punkt m boiling point
Siedlung f -, -en [housing] estate;
(Niederlassung) settlement
Sieg m -[e]s, -e victory
Siegel nt -s,- seal. **S∼ring** m
signet-ring
sieg|en vi (haben) win. **S∼er(in)**
m -s,- (f -, -nen) winner. **s∼reich**
a victorious
siezen vt jdn s∼ call s.o. 'Sie'
Signal nt -s, -e signal
Silbe f -, -n syllable
Silber nt -s silver. **s∼n** a silver
Silhouette /zɪˈlʊɛtə/ f -, -n
silhouette

S

Silizium *nt* -s silicon
Silo *m & nt* -s, -s silo
Silvester *nt* -s New Year's Eve
Sims *m & nt* -es, -e ledge
simultan *a* simultaneous
sind *s.* sein¹
Sinfonie *f* -, -n symphony
singen† *vt/i* (*haben*) sing
Singvogel *m* songbird
sinken† *vi* (*sein*) sink; (*nieder-*) drop; (*niedriger werden*) go down, fall; **den Mut s∼ lassen** lose courage
Sinn *m* -[e]s, -e sense; (*Denken*) mind; (*Zweck*) point; **in gewissem S∼e** in a sense; **das hat keinen S∼** it is pointless. **S∼bild** *nt* symbol
sinnlich *a* sensory; (*sexuell*) sensual; <*Genüsse*> sensuous. **S∼keit** *f* - sensuality; sensuousness
sinn|los *a* senseless; (*zwecklos*) pointless. **s∼voll** *a* meaningful; (*vernünftig*) sensible
Sintflut *f* flood
Siphon /'zi:fõ/ *m* -s, -s siphon
Sippe *f* -, -n clan
Sirene *f* -, -n siren
Sirup *m* -s, -e syrup; treacle
Sitte *f* -, -n custom; **S∼n** manners
sittlich *a* moral. **S∼keit** *f* - morality. **S∼keitsverbrecher** *m* sex offender
sittsam *a* well-behaved; (*züchtig*) demure
Situation /-'tsio:n/ *f* -, -en situation. **s∼iert** *a* **gut/schlecht s∼iert** well/badly off
Sitz *m* -es, -e seat; (*Passform*) fit
sitzen† *vi* (*haben*) sit; (*sich befinden*) be; (*passen*) fit; (𝕀 *treffen*) hit home; **[im Gefängnis] s∼** 𝕀 be in jail; **s∼ bleiben** remain seated; 𝕀 (*Sch*) stay *or* be kept down; (*nicht heiraten*) be left on the shelf; **s∼ bleiben auf** (+ *dat*) be left with
Sitz|gelegenheit *f* seat. **S∼platz** *m* seat. **S∼ung** *f* -, -en session

Sizilien /-iən/ *nt* -s Sicily
Skala *f* -, -len scale; (*Reihe*) range
Skalpell *nt* -s, -e scalpel
skalpieren *vt* scalp
Skandal *m* -s, -e scandal. **s∼ös** *a* scandalous
Skandinav|ien /-iən/ *nt* -s Scandinavia. **s∼isch** *a* Scandinavian
Skat *m* -s skat
Skelett *nt* -[e]s, -e skeleton
Skep|sis *f* - scepticism. **s∼tisch** *a* sceptical
Ski /ʃi:/ *m* -s, -er ski; **Ski fahren** *od* **laufen** ski. **S∼fahrer(in)**, **S∼läufer(in)** *m(f)* -s,- (*f* -, -nen) skier. **S∼sport** *m* skiing
Skizz|e *f* -, -n sketch. **s∼ieren** *vt* sketch
Sklav|e *m* -n, -n slave. **S∼erei** *f* - slavery. **S∼in** *f* -, -nen slave
Skorpion *m* -s, -e scorpion; (*Astr*) Scorpio
Skrupel *m* -s,-. scruple. **s∼los** *a* unscrupulous
Skulptur *f* -, -en sculpture
Slalom *m* -s, -s slalom
Slaw|e *m* -n, -n, **S∼in** *f* -, -nen Slav. **s∼isch** *a* Slav; (*Lang*) Slavonic
Slip *m* -s, -s briefs *pl*
Smaragd *m* -[e]s, -e emerald
Smoking *m* -s, -s dinner jacket
Snob *m* -s, -s snob. **S∼ismus** *m* - snobbery. **s∼istisch** *a* snobbish
so *adv* so; (*so sehr*) so much; (*auf diese Weise*) like this/that; (*solch*) such; (𝕀 *sowieso*) anyway; (𝕀 *umsonst*) free; (𝕀 *ungefähr*) about; **so viel** so much; **so gut/ bald wie** as good/soon as; **so ein Zufall!** what a coincidence! **mir ist so, als ob** I feel as if; **so oder so** in any case; **so um zehn Mark** 𝕀 about ten marks; **so?** really? ●*conj* (*also*) so; (*dann*) then; **so dass = sodass**
sobald *conj* as soon as
Söckchen *nt* -s,- [ankle] sock

Socke f -, -n sock
Sockel m -s,- plinth, pedestal
Socken m -s,- sock
sodass conj so that
Sodawasser nt soda water
Sodbrennen nt -s heartburn
soeben adv just [now]
Sofa nt -s, -s settee, sofa
sofern conj provided [that]
sofort adv at once, immediately;
(auf der Stelle) instantly
Software /ˈzɔftvɛːɐ̯/ f - software
sogar adv even
sogenannt a so-called
sogleich adv at once
Sohle f -, -n sole; (Tal-) bottom
Sohn m -[e]s, -̈e son
Sojabohne f soya bean
solange conj as long as
solch inv pron such; s∼ ein(e)
such a; s∼ einer/eine/eins one/
(Person) someone like that.
s∼e(r,s) pron such
● (substantivisch) ein s∼er/eine
s∼e/ein s∼es one/(Person)
someone like that; s∼e pl those;
(Leute) people like that
Soldat m -en, -en soldier
Söldner m -s,- mercenary
Solidarität f - solidarity
solide a solid; (haltbar) sturdy;
(sicher) sound; (anständig)
respectable
Solist(in) m -en, -en (f -, -nen)
soloist
Soll nt -s (Comm) debit;
(Produktions-) quota

sollen†
● auxiliary verb
····▸ (Verpflichtung) be [supposed
or meant] to. er soll morgen zum
Arzt gehen he is [supposed] to
go to the doctor tomorrow. die
beiden Flächen sollen fluchten the
two surfaces are meant to be or
should be in alignment. du
solltest ihn anrufen you were

meant to phone him or should
have phoned him
····▸ (Befehl) du sollst sofort damit
aufhören you're to stop that at
once. er soll hereinkommen he is
to come in; (sagen Sie es ihm)
tell him to come in
····▸ sollte (subjunctive) should;
ought to. wir sollten früher
aufstehen we ought to or should
get up earlier. das hätte er nicht
tun/sagen sollen he shouldn't
have done/said that
····▸ (Zukunft, Geplantes) be to. ich
soll die Abteilung übernehmen I
am to take over the department.
du sollst dein Geld
zurückbekommen you are to or
shall get your money back. es
soll nicht wieder vorkommen it
won't happen again. sie sollten
ihr Reiseziel nie erreichen they
were never to reach their
destination
····▸ (Ratlosigkeit) be to; shall. was
soll man nur machen? what is
one to do?; what shall I/we do?
ich weiß nicht, was ich machen soll
I don't know what I should do
or what to do
····▸ (nach Bericht) be supposed
to. er soll sehr reich sein he is
supposed or is said to be very
rich. sie soll geheiratet haben they
say or I gather she has got
married
····▸ (Absicht) be meant or
supposed to. was soll dieses Bild
darstellen? what is this picture
supposed to represent? das
sollte ein Witz sein that was
meant or supposed to be a joke
····▸ (in Bedingungssätzen) should.
sollte er anrufen, falls od wenn er
anrufen sollte should he or if he
should telephone
● intransitive verb
····▸ (irgendwohin gehen sollen) be
[supposed] to go. er soll morgen

S

zum Arzt/nach Berlin he is [supposed] to go to the doctor/ to Berlin tomorrow. **ich sollte ins Theater** I was supposed to go to the theatre

····▶ *(sonstige Wendungen)* **soll er doch!** let him! **was soll das?** what's that in aid of? Ⓘ

Solo nt -s, -los & -li solo

somit adv therefore, so

Sommer m -s,- summer. **s~lich** a summery; *(Sommer-)* summer … ●adv **s~lich warm** as warm as summer. **S~sprossen** fpl freckles

Sonate f -, -n sonata

Sonde f -, -n probe

Sonder|angebot nt special offer. **s~bar** a odd. **S~fahrt** f special excursion. **S~fall** m special case. **s~gleichen** adv **eine Gemeinheit s~gleichen** unparalleled meanness. **S~ling** m -s, -e crank. **S~marke** f special stamp

sondern conj but; **nicht nur … s~ auch** not only … but also

Sonder|preis m special price. **S~schule** f special school

Sonett nt -[e]s, -e sonnet

Sonnabend m -s, -e Saturday. **s~s** adv on Saturdays

Sonne f -, -n sun. **s~n (sich)** vr sun oneself

Sonnen|aufgang m sunrise. **s~baden** vi *(haben)* sunbathe. **S~bank** f sun-bed. **S~blume** f sunflower. **S~brand** m sun-burn. **S~brille** f sun-glasses pl. **S~energie** f solar energy. **S~finsternis** f solar eclipse. **S~milch** f sun-tan lotion. **S~öl** nt sun-tan oil. **S~schein** m sunshine. **S~schirm** m sunshade. **S~stich** m sunstroke. **S~uhr** f sundial. **S~untergang** m sunset. **S~wende** f solstice

sonnig a sunny

Sonntag m -s, -e Sunday. **s~s** adv on Sundays

sonst adv *(gewöhnlich)* usually; *(im Übrigen)* apart from that; *(andernfalls)* otherwise, or [else] **wer/was/wie/wo s~?** who/what/ how/where else? **s~ niemand** no one else; anything else? **s~ noch etwas?** anything else? **s~ noch Fragen?** any more questions? **s~ jemand** od **wer** someone/*(fragend, verneint)* anyone else; *(irgendjemand)* [just] anyone; **s~ wo** somewhere/*(fragend, verneint)* anywhere else; *(irgendwo)* [just] anywhere. **s~ig** a other

sooft conj whenever

Sopran m -s, -e soprano

Sorge f -, -n worry (um about); *(Fürsorge)* care; **sich** *(dat)* **S~n machen** worry. **s~n** vi *(haben)* **s~n für** look after, care for; *(vorsorgen)* provide for; *(sich kümmern)* see to; **dafür s~n, dass** see or make sure that ●vr **sich s~n** worry. **s~nfrei** a carefree. **s~nvoll** a worried. **S~recht** nt *(Jur)* custody

Sorg|falt f - care. **s~fältig** a careful

Sorte f -, -n kind, sort; *(Comm)* brand

sort|ieren vt sort [out]; *(Comm)* grade. **S~iment** nt -[e]s, -e range

sosehr conj however much

Soße f -, -n sauce; *(Braten-)* gravy; *(Salat-)* dressing

Souvenir /zuvəˈniːɐ̯/ nt -s, -s souvenir

souverän /zuvəˈrɛːn/ a sovereign

soviel conj however much; **s~ ich weiß** as far as I know ●adv *so viel, s.* **viel**

soweit conj as far as; *(insoweit)* [in] so far as ●adv *so weit, s.* **weit**

sowenig conj however little ●adv *so wenig, s.* **wenig**

sowie conj as well as; *(sobald)* as soon as

owieso *adv* anyway, in any case

owjet|isch *a* Soviet. **S~union** *f* - Soviet Union

owohl *adv* **s~ ... als** *od* **wie auch ... ...** as well as ...

ozial *a* social; *<Einstellung, Beruf>* caring. **S~arbeit** *f* social work. **S~demokrat** *m* social democrat. **S~hilfe** *f* social security

Sozialis|mus *m* - socialism. **S~t** *m* -en, -en socialist

Sozial|versicherung *f* National Insurance. **S~wohnung** *f* ≈ council flat

Soziologie *f* - sociology

Sozius *m* -, -se *(Comm)* partner; *(Beifahrersitz)* pillion

Spachtel *m* -s,- & *f* -, -n spatula

Spagat *m* -[e]s, -e *(Aust)* string; **S~ machen** do the splits *pl*

Spaghetti, Spagetti *pl* spaghetti *sg*

Spalier *nt* -s, -e trellis

Spalt|e *f* -, -n crack; *(Gletscher-)* crevasse; *(Druck-)* column; *(Orangen-)* segment. **s~en†** *vt* split. **S~ung** *f* -, -en splitting; *(Kluft)* split; *(Phys)* fission

Span *m* -[e]s,¨e [wood] chip

Spange *f* -, -n clasp; *(Haar-)* slide; *(Zahn-)* brace

Span|ien /-iən/ *nt* -s Spain. **S~ier** *m* -s,-, **S~ierin** *f* -, -nen Spaniard. **s~isch** *a* Spanish. **S~isch** *nt* -[s] *(Lang)* Spanish

Spann *m* -[e]s instep

Spanne *f* -, -n span; *(Zeit-)* space; *(Comm)* margin

spann|en *vt* stretch; put up *<Leine>*; *(straffen)* tighten; *(an-)* harness **(an** + *acc* to); **sich s~en** tighten ● *vi (haben)* be too tight. **s~end** *a* exciting. **S~ung** *f* -, -en tension; *(Erwartung)* suspense; *(Electr)* voltage

Spar|buch *nt* savings book. **S~büchse** *f* money-box. **s~en** *vt/i (haben)* save; *(sparsam sein)*

economize **(mit/an** + *dat* on). **S~er** *m* -s,- saver

Spargel *m* -s,- asparagus

Spar|kasse *f* savings bank. **S~konto** *nt* deposit account

sparsam *a* economical; *<Person>* thrifty. **S~keit** *f* - economy; thrift

Sparschwein *nt* piggy bank

Sparte *f* -, -n branch; *(Zeitungs-)* section; *(Rubrik)* column

Spaß *m* -es,¨e fun; *(Scherz)* joke; **im/aus/zum S~** for fun; **S~ machen** be fun; *<Person:>* be joking; **viel S~!** have a good time! **s~en** *vi (haben)* joke. **S~vogel** *m* joker

Spastiker *m* -s,- spastic

spät *a & adv* late; **wie s~ ist es?** what time is it? **zu s~ kommen** be late

Spaten *m* -s,- spade

später *a* later; *(zukünftig)* future ● *adv* later

spätestens *adv* at the latest

Spatz *m* -en, -en sparrow

Spätzle *pl (Culin)* noodles

spazieren *vi (sein)* stroll; **s~ gehen** go for a walk

Spazier|gang *m* walk; **einen S~gang machen** go for a walk. **S~gänger(in)** *m* -s,- *(f* -, -nen)* walker. **S~stock** *m* walking-stick

Specht *m* -[e]s, -e woodpecker

Speck *m* -s bacon. **s~ig** *a* greasy

Spedi|teur /ʃpediˈtøːɐ̯/ *m* -s, -e haulage/*(für Umzüge)* removals contractor. **S~tion** /-ˈtsi̯oːn/ *f* -, -en carriage, haulage; *(Firma)* haulage/*(für Umzüge)* removals firm

Speer *m* -[e]s, -e spear; *(Sport)* javelin

Speiche *f* -, -n spoke

Speichel *m* -s saliva

Speicher *m* -s,- warehouse; *(dial: Dachboden)* attic; *(Computer)* memory. **s~n** *vt* store

Speise *f* -, -n food; *(Gericht)* dish; *(Pudding)* blancmange. **S~eis** *nt*

S

ice-cream. **S~kammer** f larder.
S~karte f menu. **s~n** vi (haben)
eat ● vt feed. **S~röhre** f
oesophagus. **S~saal** m dining-
room. **S~wagen** m dining-car
Spektrum nt -s, -tra spectrum
Spekul|ant m -en, -en speculator.
s~ieren vi (haben) speculate;
s~ieren auf (+ acc) Ⓘ hope to get
Spelze f -, -n husk
spendabel a generous
Spende f -, -n donation. **s~n** vt
donate; give <Blut, Schatten>;
Beifall **s~n** applaud. **S~r** m -s,-
donor; (Behälter) dispenser
spendieren vt pay for
Sperling m -s, -e sparrow
Sperre f -, -n barrier; (Verbot)
ban; (Comm) embargo. **s~n** vt
close; (ver-) block; (verbieten)
ban; cut off <Strom, Telefon>;
stop <Scheck, Kredit>; **s~n** in (+
acc) put in <Gefängnis, Käfig>
Sperr|holz nt plywood. **S~müll** m
bulky refuse. **S~stunde** f closing
time
Spesen pl expenses
spezial|isieren (sich) vr
specialize (auf + acc in). **S~ist** m
-en, -en specialist. **S~ität** f -, -en
speciality
spicken vt (Culin) lard; gespickt
mit (fig) full of ● vi (haben) Ⓘ
crib (bei from)
Spiegel m -s,- mirror; (Wasser-,
Alkohol-) level. **S~bild** nt
reflection. **S~ei** nt fried egg. **s~n**
vt reflect; sich **s~n** be reflected
● vi (haben) reflect [the light];
(glänzen) gleam. **S~ung** f -, -en
reflection
Spiel nt -[e]s, -e game; (Spielen)
playing; (Glücks-) gambling;
(Schau-) play; (Satz) set; auf dem
S~ stehen be at stake; aufs **S~**
setzen risk. **S~automat** m fruit
machine. **S~bank** f casino.
S~dose f musical box. **s~en** vt/i
(haben) play; (im Glücksspiel)

gamble; (vortäuschen) act;
<Roman:> be set (in + dat in);
s~en mit (fig) toy with
Spieler(in) m -s,- (f -, -nen) player;
(Glücks-) gambler
Spiel|feld nt field, pitch.
S~marke f chip. **S~plan** m
programme. **S~platz** m
playground. **S~raum** m (fig)
scope; (Techn) clearance.
S~regeln fpl rules [of the game].
S~sachen fpl toys. **S~verderber**
m -s,- spoilsport. **S~waren** fpl
toys. **S~warengeschäft** nt
toyshop. **S~zeug** nt toy;
(S~sachen) toys pl
Spieß m -es, -e spear; (Brat-) spit;
skewer; (Fleisch-) kebab. **S~er** m
-s,- [petit] bourgeois. **s~ig** a
bourgeois
Spike[s]reifen /'∫pai:k[s]-/ m
studded tyre
Spinat m -s spinach
Spindel f -, -n spindle
Spinne f -, -n spider
spinn|en† vt/i (haben) spin; er
spinnt Ⓘ he's crazy.
S~[en]gewebe nt, **S~webe** f -, -n
cobweb
Spion m -s, -e spy
Spionage /∫pio'na:ʒə/ f -
espionage, spying. **S~abwehr** f
counter-espionage
spionieren vi (haben) spy
Spionin f -, -nen [woman] spy
Spirral|e f -, -n spiral. **s~ig** a spiral
Spirituosen pl spirits
Spiritus m - alcohol; (Brenn-)
methylated spirits pl. **S~kocher**
m spirit stove
spitz a pointed; (scharf) sharp;
(schrill) shrill; <Winkel> acute.
S~bube m scoundrel
Spitze f -, -n point; (oberer Teil)
top; (vorderer Teil) front; (Pfeil-,
Finger-, Nasen-) tip; (Schuh-,
Strumpf-) toe; (Zigarren-,
Zigaretten-) holder;
(Höchstleistung) maximum; (Tex)

lace; (⧉ *Anspielung*) dig; **an der S~ liegen** be in the lead

Spitzel *m* -s,- informer

spitzen *vt* sharpen; purse <*Lippen*>; prick up <*Ohren*>. **S~geschwindigkeit** *f* top speed

Spitzname *m* nickname

Spleen /ʃpliːn/ *m* -s, -e obsession

Splitter *m* -s,- splinter. **s~n** *vi* (*sein*) shatter

sponsern *vt* sponsor

Spore *f* -, -n (*Biol*) spore

Sporn *m* -[e]s, Sporen spur

Sport *m* -[e]s sport; (*Hobby*) hobby. **S~art** *f* sport. **S~ler** *m* -s,- sportsman. **S~lerin** *f* -, -nen sportswoman. **s~lich** *a* sports ...; (*fair*) sporting; (*schlank*) sporty. **S~platz** *m* sports ground. **S~verein** *m* sports club. **S~wagen** *m* sports car; (*Kinder-*) push-chair, (*Amer*) stroller

Spott *m* -[e]s mockery

spotten *vi* (*haben*) mock; **s~ über** (+ *acc*) make fun of; (*höhnend*) ridicule

spöttisch *a* mocking

Sprach|e *f* -, -n language; (*Sprechfähigkeit*) speech; **zur S~e bringen** bring up. **S~fehler** *m* speech defect. **S~labor** *nt* language laboratory. **s~lich** *a* linguistic. **s~los** *a* speechless

Spray /ʃpreː/ *nt & m* -s, -s spray. **S~dose** *f* aerosol [can]

Sprechanlage *f* intercom

sprechen† *vi* (*haben*) speak/(*sich unterhalten*) talk (**über** + *acc*/**von** about/of); **Deutsch s~** speak German ● *vt* speak; (*sagen*) say; pronounce <*Urteil*>; **schuldig s~** find guilty; **Herr X ist nicht zu s~** Mr X is not available

Sprecher(in) *m* -s,- (*f* -, -nen) speaker; (*Radio, TV*) announcer; (*Wortführer*) spokesman, *f* spokeswoman

Sprechstunde *f* consulting hours *pl*; (*Med*) surgery. **S~nhilfe** *f* (*Med*) receptionist

Sprechzimmer *nt* consulting room

spreizen *vt* spread

spreng|en *vt* blow up; blast <*Felsen*>; (*fig*) burst; (*begießen*) water; (*mit Sprenger*) sprinkle; dampen <*Wäsche*>. **S~er** *m* -s,- sprinkler. **S~kopf** *m* warhead. **S~körper** *m* explosive device. **S~stoff** *m* explosive

Spreu *f* - chaff

Sprich|wort *nt* (*pl* -wörter) proverb. **s~wörtlich** *a* proverbial

Springbrunnen *m* fountain

spring|en† *vi* (*sein*) jump; (*Schwimmsport*) dive; <*Ball:*> bounce; (*spritzen*) spurt; (*zer-*) break; (*rissig werden*) crack; (*SGer: laufen*) run. **S~er** *m* -s,- jumper; (*Kunst-*) diver; (*Schach*) knight. **S~reiten** *nt* show-jumping

Sprint *m* -s, -s sprint

Spritz|e *f* -, -n syringe; (*Injektion*) injection; (*Feuer-*) hose. **s~en** *vt* spray; (*be-, ver-*) splash; (*Culin*) pipe; (*Med*) inject ● *vi* (*haben*) splash; <*Fett:*> spit ● *vi* (*sein*) splash; (*hervor-*) spurt. **S~er** *m* -s,- splash; (*Schuss*) dash

spröde *a* brittle; (*trocken*) dry

Sprosse *f* -, -n rung

Sprotte *f* -, -n sprat

Spruch *m* -[e]s, ¨e saying; (*Denk-*) motto; (*Zitat*) quotation. **S~band** *nt* (*pl* -bänder) banner

Sprudel *m* -s,- sparkling mineral water. **s~n** *vi* (*haben/sein*) bubble

Sprüh|dose *f* aerosol [can]. **s~en** *vt* spray ● *vi* (*sein*) <*Funken:*> fly; (*fig*) sparkle

Sprung *m* -[e]s, ¨e jump, leap; (*Schwimmsport*) dive; (⧉ *Katzen-*) stone's throw; (*Riss*) crack. **S~brett** *nt* springboard.

S

S~schanze f ski-jump. **S~seil** nt skipping-rope

Spucke f - spit. **s~n** vt/i (haben) spit; (sich übergeben) be sick

Spuk m -[e]s, -e [ghostly] apparition. **s~en** vi (haben) <Geist:> walk; **in diesem Haus s~t es** this house is haunted

Spülbecken nt sink

Spule f -, -n spool

Spüle f -, -n sink

spulen vt spool

spül|en vt rinse; (schwemmen) wash; **Geschirr s~en** wash up ● vi (haben) flush [the toilet]. **S~kasten** m cistern. **S~mittel** nt washing-up liquid

Spur f -, -en track; (Fahr-) lane; (Fährte) trail; (Anzeichen) trace; (Hinweis) lead

spürbar a noticeable

spür|en vt feel; (seelisch) sense. **S~hund** m tracker dog

spurlos adv without trace

spurten vi (sein) put on a spurt

sputen (sich) vr hurry

Staat m -[e]s, -en state; (Land) country; (Putz) finery. **s~lich** a state ... ● adv by the state

Staatsangehörig|e(r) m/f national. **S~keit** f - nationality

Staats|anwalt m state prosecutor. **S~beamte(r)** m civil servant. **S~besuch** m state visit. **S~bürger(in)** m(f) national. **S~mann** m (pl -männer) statesman. **S~streich** m coup

Stab m -[e]s, ̈e rod; (Gitter-) bar (Sport) baton; (Mil) staff

Stäbchen ntpl chopsticks

Stabhochsprung m pole-vault

stabil a stable; (gesund) robust; (solide) sturdy

Stachel m -s, - spine; (Gift-) sting; (Spitze) spike. **S~beere** f gooseberry. **S~draht** m barbed wire. **S~schwein** nt porcupine

Stadion nt -s, -ien stadium

Stadium nt -s, -ien stage

Stadt f -, ̈e town; (Groß-) city

städtisch a urban; (kommunal) municipal

Stadt|mitte f town centre. **S~plan** m street map. **S~teil** m district

Staffel f -, -n team; (S~lauf) relay; (Mil) squadron

Staffelei f -, -en easel

Staffel|lauf m relay race. **s~n** vt stagger; (abstufen) grade

Stahl m -s steel. **S~beton** m reinforced concrete

Stall m -[e]s, ̈e stable; (Kuh-) shed; (Schweine-) sty; (Hühner-) coop; (Kaninchen-) hutch

Stamm m -[e]s, ̈e trunk; (Sippe) tribe; (Wort-) stem. **S~baum** m family tree; (eines Tieres) pedigree

stammeln vt/i (haben) stammer

stammen vi (haben) come/ (zeitlich) date (von/aus from)

stämmig a sturdy

Stamm|kundschaft f regulars pl. **S~lokal** nt favourite pub

stampfen vi (haben) stamp; <Maschine:> pound ● vi (sein) tramp ● vt pound; mash <Kartoffeln>

Stand m -[e]s, ̈e standing position; (Zustand) state; (Spiel-) score; (Höhe) level; (gesellschaftlich) class; (Verkaufs-) stall; (Messe-) stand; (Taxi-) rank; **auf den neuesten S~ bringen** up-date

Standard m -s, -s standard

Standbild nt statue

Ständer m -s, - stand; (Geschirr-) rack; (Kerzen-) holder

Standes|amt nt registry office. **S~beamte(r)** m registrar

standhaft a steadfast

ständig a constant; (fest) permanent

Stand|licht nt sidelights pl. **S~ort** m position; (Firmen-) location; (Mil) garrison. **S~punkt** m point of view. S~uhr f grandfather clock

Stange f -, -n bar; (Holz-) pole; (Gardinen-) rail; (Hühner-) perch; (Zimt-) stick; **von der S~** 🔟 off the peg

Stängel m -s,- stalk, stem

Stangenbohne f runner bean

Stanniol nt -s tin foil. **S~papier** nt silver paper

stanzen vt stamp; punch <Loch>

Stapel m -s,- stack, pile. **S~lauf** m launch[ing]. **s~n** vt stack or pile up

Star¹ m -[e]s, -e starling

Star² m -[e]s (Med) [grauer] S~ cataract; grüner S~ glaucoma

Star³ m -s, -s (Theat, Sport) star

stark a strong; <Motor> powerful; <Verkehr, Regen> heavy; <Hitze, Kälte> severe; (groß) big; (schlimm) bad; (dick) thick; (korpulent) stout ● adv (sehr) very much

Stärk|e f -, -n strength; power; thickness; stoutness; (Größe) size; (Mais-, Wäsche-) starch. **S~emehl** nt cornflour. **s~en** vt strengthen; starch <Wäsche>; **sich s~en** fortify oneself. **S~ung** f -, -en strengthening; (Erfrischung) refreshment

starr a rigid; (steif) stiff

starren vi (haben) stare

Starr|sinn m obstinacy. **s~sinnig** a obstinate

Start m -s, -s start; (Aviat) take-off. **S~bahn** f runway. **s~en** vi (sein) start; (Aviat) take off ● vt start; (fig) launch

Station /-'tsio:n/ f -, -en station; (Haltestelle) stop; (Abschnitt) stage; (Med) ward; **S~ machen** break one's journey. **s~är** adv as an inpatient. **s~ieren** vt station

statisch a static

Statist(in) m -en, -en (f -, -nen) (Theat) extra

Statisti|k f -, -en statistics sg; (Aufstellung) statistics pl. **s~sch** a statistical

Stativ nt -s, -e (Phot) tripod

statt prep (+ gen) instead of; **an seiner s~** in his place; **an Kindes s~ annehmen** adopt ● conj **s~ etw zu tun** instead of doing sth. **s~dessen** adv instead

statt|finden vi sep (haben) take place. **s~haft** a permitted

Statue /'ʃta:tuə/ f -, -n statue

Statur f - build, stature

Status m - status. **S~symbol** nt status symbol

Statut nt -[e]s, -en statute

Stau m -[e]s, -s congestion; (Auto) [traffic] jam; (Rück-) tailback

Staub m -[e]s dust; S~ wischen dust; **S~ saugen** vacuum, hoover

Staubecken nt reservoir

staub|ig a dusty. **s~saugen** vt/i (haben) vacuum, hoover. **S~sauger** m vacuum cleaner, Hoover (P)

Staudamm m dam

stauen vt dam up; **sich s~** accumulate; <Autos:> form a tailback

staunen vi (haben) be amazed or astonished

Stau|see m reservoir. **S~ung** f -, -en congestion; (Auto) [traffic] jam

Steak /ʃte:k, ste:k/ nt -s, -s steak

stechen† vt stick (in + acc in); (verletzen) prick; (mit Messer) stab; <Insekt:> sting; <Mücke:> bite ● vi (haben) prick; <Insekt:> sting; <Mücke:> bite; (mit Stechuhr) clock in/out; **in See s~** put to sea

Stech|ginster m gorse. **S~kahn** m punt. **S~palme** f holly. **S~uhr** f time clock

Steck|brief m 'wanted' poster. **S~dose** f socket. **s~en** vt put; (mit Nadel, Reißzwecke) pin; (pflanzen) plant ● vi (haben) be;

S

(fest-) be stuck; **s~ bleiben** get stuck; **den Schlüssel s~ lassen** leave the key in the lock

Steckenpferd *nt* hobby-horse

Steck|er *m* -s,- *(Electr)* plug. **S~nadel** *f* pin

Steg *m* -[e]s, -e foot-bridge; *(Boots-)* landing-stage; *(Brillen-)* bridge

stehen† *vi (haben)* stand; *(sich befinden)* be; *(still-)* be stationary; *<Maschine, Uhr:>* have stopped; **s~ bleiben** remain standing; *<Gebäude:>* be left standing; *(anhalten)* stop; *<Motor:>* stall; *<Zeit:>* stand still; **vor dem Ruin s~** face ruin; **zu jdm/etw s~** *(fig)* stand by s.o./sth; **jdm [gut] s~** suit s.o.; **sich gut s~** be on good terms; **es steht 3 zu 1** the score is 3–1. **s~d** *a* standing; *(sich nicht bewegend)* stationary; *<Gewässer:>* stagnant

Stehlampe *f* standing lamp

stehlen† *vt/i (haben)* steal; **sich s~** steal, creep

Steh|platz *m* standing place. **S~vermögen** *nt* stamina, staying-power

steif *a* stiff

Steig|bügel *m* stirrup. **S~eisen** *nt* crampon

steigen† *vi (sein)* climb; *(hochgehen)* rise, go up; *<Schulden, Spannung:>* mount; **s~ auf** (+ *acc*) climb on [to] *<Stuhl>*; climb *<Berg, Leiter>*; get on *<Pferd, Fahrrad>*; **s~ in** (+ *acc*) climb into; get in *<Auto>*; get on *<Bus, Zug>*; **s~ aus** climb out of; get out of *<Bett, Auto>*; get off *<Bus, Zug>*; **s~de Preise** rising prices

steiger|n *vt* increase; **sich s~n** increase; *(sich verbessern)* improve. **S~ung** *f* -, -en increase; improvement; *(Gram)* comparison

steil *a* steep. **S~küste** *f* cliffs *pl*

Stein *m* -[e]s, -e stone; *(Ziegel-)* brick; *(Spiel-)* piece. **S~bock** *m* ibex; *(Astr)* Capricorn. **S~bruch** *m* quarry. **S~garten** *m* rockery. **S~gut** *nt* earthenware. **s~ig** *a* stony. **s~igen** *vt* stone. **S~kohle** *f* [hard] coal. **S~schlag** *m* rock fall

Stelle *f* -, -n place; *(Fleck)* spot; *(Abschnitt)* passage; *(Stellung)* job, post; *(Behörde)* authority; **auf der S~** immediately

stellen *vt* put; *(aufrecht)* stand; set *<Wecker, Aufgabe>*; ask *<Frage>*; make *<Antrag, Forderung, Diagnose>*; **zur Verfügung** provide; **lauter/leiser s~** turn up/down; **kalt/warm s~** chill/keep hot; **sich s~** [go and] stand; give oneself up *(der Polizei* to the police); **sich tot s~** pretend to be dead; **gut gestellt sein** be well off

Stellen|anzeige *f* job advertisement. **S~vermittlung** *f* employment agency. **s~weise** *adv* in places

Stellung *f* -, -en position; *(Arbeit)* job; **S~ nehmen** make a statement (**zu** on). **S~suche** *f* job-hunting

Stellvertreter *m* deputy

Stelzen *fpl* stilts. **s~** *vi (sein)* stalk

stemmen *vt* press; lift *<Gewicht>*

Stempel *m* -s,- stamp; *(Post-)* post-mark; *(Präge-)* die; *(Feingehalts-)* hallmark. **s~n** *vt* stamp; hallmark *<Silber>*; cancel *<Marke>*

Stengel* *m* -s,- *s.* Stängel

Steno *f* - 🔟 shorthand

Steno|gramm *nt* -[e]s, -e shorthand text. **S~grafie** *f* - shorthand. **s~grafieren** *vt* take down in shorthand ●*vi (haben)* do shorthand

Steppdecke *f* quilt

Steppe *f* -, -n steppe

Stepptanz m tap-dance
sterben† vi (sein) die (an + dat of); im S~ liegen be dying
sterblich a mortal. **S~keit** f - mortality

stereo adv in stereo. **S~anlage** f stereo [system]
steril a sterile. **s~isieren** vt sterilize. **S~ität** f - sterility
Stern m -[e]s, -e star. **S~bild** nt constellation. **S~chen** nt -s,- asterisk. **S~kunde** f astronomy. **S~schnuppe** f -, -n shooting star. **S~warte** f -, -n observatory
stets adv always
Steuer¹ nt -s,- steering-wheel; (Naut) helm; am S~ at the wheel
Steuer² f -, -n tax
Steuerbord nt -[e]s starboard [side]. **S~erklärung** f tax return. **s~frei** a & adv tax-free. **S~mann** m (pl -leute) helmsman; (beim Rudern) cox. **s~n** vt steer; (Aviat) pilot; (Techn) control ●vi (haben) be at the wheel/(Naut) helm. **s~pflichtig** a taxable. **S~rad** nt steering-wheel. **S~ruder** nt helm. **S~ung** f - steering; (Techn) controls pl. **S~zahler** m -s,- taxpayer

Stewardess /'stju:ɐdɛs/ f -, -en air hostess, stewardess
Stich m -[e]s, -e prick; (Messer-) stab; (S~wunde) stab wound; (Bienen-) sting; (Mücken-) bite; (Schmerz) stabbing pain; (Näh-) stitch; (Kupfer-) engraving; (Kartenspiel) trick
stick|en vt/i (haben) embroider. **S~erei** f - embroidery
Stickstoff m nitrogen
Stiefel m -s,- boot
Stief|kind nt stepchild. **S~mutter** f stepmother. **S~mütterchen** nt -s,- pansy. **S~sohn** m stepson. **S~tochter** f stepdaughter. **S~vater** m stepfather
Stiege f -, -n stairs pl

Stiel m -[e]s, -e handle; (Blumen-, Gläser-) stem; (Blatt-) stalk
Stier m -[e]s, -e bull; (Astr) Taurus
Stierkampf m bullfight
Stift¹ m -[e]s, -e pin; (Nagel) tack; (Blei-) pencil; (Farb-) crayon
Stift² nt -[e]s, -e [endowed] foundation. **s~en** vt endow; (spenden) donate; create <Unheil, Verwirrung>; bring about <Frieden>. **S~ung** f -, -en foundation; (Spende) donation
Stil m -[e]s, -e style
still a quiet; (reglos, ohne Kohlensäure) still; (heimlich) secret; der S~e Ozean the Pacific; im S~en secretly. **S~e** f - quiet; (Schweigen) silence
Stilleben* nt s. Stillleben
stillen vt satisfy; quench <Durst>; stop <Schmerzen, Blutung>; breast-feed <Kind>
still|halten† vi sep (haben) keep still. **S~leben** nt still life
Still|schweigen nt silence. **S~stand** m standstill; zum S~stand bringen/kommen stop. **s~stehen**† vi sep (haben) stand still; (anhalten) stop; <Verkehr:> be at a standstill
Stimm|bänder ntpl vocal cords. **s~berechtigt** a entitled to vote. **S~bruch** m er ist im S~bruch his voice is breaking
Stimme f -, -n voice; (Wahl-) vote
stimmen vi (haben) be right; (wählen) vote ●vt tune
Stimmung f -, -en mood; (Atmosphäre) atmosphere
Stimmzettel m ballot-paper
stink|en vi (haben) smell/(stark) stink (nach of). **S~tier** nt skunk
Stipendium nt -s, -ien scholarship; (Beihilfe) grant
Stirn f -, -en forehead
stochern vi (haben) s~ in (+ dat) poke <Feuer>; pick at <Essen>

S

Stock¹ m -[e]s,-̈e stick; (*Ski-*) pole; (*Bienen-*) hive; (*Rosen-*) bush; (*Reb-*) vine

Stock² m -[e]s,- storey, floor. **S~bett** nt bunk-beds pl.

stock|en vi (*haben*) stop; <*Verkehr:*> come to a standstill; <*Person:*> falter. **S~ung** f -, -en hold-up

Stockwerk nt storey, floor

Stoff m -[e]s, -e substance; (*Tex*) fabric, material; (*Thema*) subject [matter]; (*Gesprächs-*) topic. **S~wechsel** m metabolism

stöhnen vi (*haben*) groan, moan

Stola f -, -len stole

Stollen m -s,- gallery; (*Kuchen*) stollen

stolpern vi (*sein*) stumble; **s~ über** (+ acc) trip over

stolz a proud (**auf** + acc of). **S~** m -es pride

stopfen vt stuff; (*stecken*) put; (*ausbessern*) darn ● vi (*haben*) be constipating

Stopp m -s, -s stop. **s~** int stop!

stoppelig a stubbly

stopp|en vt stop; (*Sport*) time ● vi (*haben*) stop. **S~uhr** f stop-watch

Stöpsel m -s,- plug; (*Flaschen-*) stopper

Storch m -[e]s,-̈e stork

Store /ʃtoːɐ̯/ m -s, -s net curtain

stören vt disturb; disrupt <*Rede*>; jam <*Sender*>; (*missfallen*) bother ● vi (*haben*) be a nuisance

stornieren vt cancel

störrisch a stubborn

Störung f -, -en disturbance; disruption; (*Med*) trouble; (*Radio*) interference; **technische S~** technical fault

Stoß m -es,-̈e push, knock; (*mit Ellbogen*) dig; (*Hörner-*) butt; (*mit Waffe*) thrust; (*Schwimm-*) stroke; (*Ruck*) jolt; (*Erd-*) shock; (*Stapel*) stack, pile. **S~dämpfer** m -s,- shock absorber

stoßen† vt push, knock; (*mit Füßen*) kick; (*mit Kopf*) butt; (*an-*) poke, nudge; (*treiben*) thrust; **sich s~** knock oneself; **sich** (*dat*) **den Kopf s~** hit one's head ● vi (*haben*) push; **s~ an** (acc) knock against; (*angrenzen*) adjoin ● vi (*sein*) **s~ gegen** knoc against; bump into <*Tür*>; **s~ a** (+ acc) bump into; (*entdecken*) come across; strike <*Öl*>

Stoß|stange f bumper. **S~verkehr** m rush-hour traffic. **S~zahn** m tusk. **S~zeit** f rush-hour

stottern vt/i (*haben*) stutter, stammer

Str. abbr (**Straße**) St

Strafanstalt f prison

Strafe f -, -n punishment; (*Jur & fig*) penalty; (*Geld-*) fine; (*Freiheits-*) sentence. **s~n** vt punish

straff a tight, taut. **s~en** vt tighten

Strafgesetz nt criminal law

sträf|lich a criminal. **S~ling** m -s -e prisoner

Straf|mandat nt (*Auto*) [parking/ speeding] ticket. **S~porto** nt excess postage. **S~raum** m penalty area. **S~stoß** m penalty **S~tat** f crime

Strahl m -[e]s, -en ray; (*einer Taschenlampe*) beam; (*Wasser-*) jet. **s~en** vi (*haben*) shine; (*funkeln*) sparkle; (*lächeln*) beam **S~enbehandlung** f radiotherapy **S~ung** f - radiation

Strähne f -, -n strand

stramm a tight

Strampel|höschen /-sç-/ nt -s,- rompers pl. **s~n** vi (*haben*) <*Baby:*> kick

Strand m -[e]s,-̈e beach. **s~en** vi (*sein*) run aground

Strang m -[e]s,-̈e rope

Strapaz|e f -, -n strain. **s~ieren** v be hard on; tax <*Nerven*>

Strass m - & -es paste

Straße f -, -n road; (*in der Stadt auch*) street; (*Meeres-*) strait. **S~nbahn** f tram. **S~nkarte** f road-map. **S~nsperre** f road-block

Strat|egie f -, -n strategy. **s~egisch** a strategic

Strauch m -[e]s, Sträucher bush

Strauß¹ m -es, Sträuße bunch [of flowers]; (*Bukett*) bouquet

Strauß² m -es, -e ostrich

streben vi (*haben*) strive (**nach** for) ● vi (*sein*) head (**nach/zu** for)

Streber m -s,- pushy person

Strecke f -, -n stretch, section; (*Entfernung*) distance; (*Rail*) line; (*Route*) route

strecken vt stretch; (*aus-*) stretch out; (*gerade machen*) straighten; (*Culin*) thin down; **den Kopf aus dem Fenster s~** put one's head out of the window

Streich m -[e]s, -e prank, trick

streicheln vt stroke

streichen† vt spread; (*weg-*) smooth; (*an-*) paint; (*aus-*) delete; (*kürzen*) cut ● vi (*haben*) **s~ über** (+ *acc*) stroke

Streichholz nt match

Streich|instrument nt stringed instrument. **S~käse** m cheese spread. **S~orchester** nt string orchestra. **S~ung** f -, -en deletion; (*Kürzung*) cut

Streife f -, -n patrol

streifen vt brush against; (*berühren*) touch; (*verletzen*) graze; (*fig*) touch on <*Thema*>

Streifen m -s,- stripe; (*Licht-*) streak; (*auf der Fahrbahn*) line; (*schmales Stück*) strip

Streifenwagen m patrol car

Streik m -s, -s strike; **in den S~ treten** go on strike. **S~brecher** m strike-breaker, (*pej*) scab. **s~en** vi (*haben*) strike; 🅸 refuse; (*versagen*) pack up

Streit m -[e]s, -e quarrel; (*Auseinandersetzung*) dispute. **s~en†** vr/i (*haben*) [**sich**] **s~en** quarrel. **S~igkeiten** fpl quarrels. **S~kräfte** fpl armed forces

streng a strict; <*Blick, Ton*> stern; (*rau, nüchtern*) severe; <*Geschmack*> sharp; **s~ genommen** strictly speaking. **S~e** f - strictness; sternness; severity

Stress m -es, -e stress

streuen vt spread; (*ver-*) scatter; sprinkle <*Zucker, Salz*>; **die Straßen s~** grit the roads

streunen vi (*sein*) roam

Strich m -[e]s, -e line; (*Feder-, Pinsel-*) stroke; (*Morse-, Gedanken-*) dash. **S~kode** m bar code. **S~punkt** m semicolon

Strick m -[e]s, -e cord; (*Seil*) rope

strick|en vt/i (*haben*) knit. **S~jacke** f cardigan. **S~leiter** f rope-ladder. **S~nadel** f knitting-needle. **S~waren** fpl knitwear sg. **S~zeug** nt knitting

striegeln vt groom

strittig a contentious

Stroh nt -[e]s straw. **S~blumen** fpl everlasting flowers. **S~dach** nt thatched roof. **S~halm** m straw

Strolch m -[e]s, -e 🅸 rascal

Strom m -[e]s, ̈e river; (*Menschen-, Auto-, Blut-*) stream; (*Tränen-*) flood; (*Schwall*) torrent; (*Electr*) current, power; **gegen den S~** (*fig*) against the tide. **s~abwärts** adv downstream. **s~aufwärts** adv upstream

strömen vi (*sein*) flow; <*Menschen, Blut:*> stream, pour

Strom|kreis m circuit. **s~linienförmig** a streamlined. **S~sperre** f power cut

Strömung f -, -en current

Strophe f -, -n verse

Strudel m -s,- whirlpool; (*SGer Culin*) strudel

Strumpf m -[e]s, ̈e stocking; (*Knie-*) sock. **S~band** nt (*pl*

-bänder) suspender. **S~hose** f
tights pl

Strunk m -[e]s,¨e stalk

struppig a shaggy

Stube f -, -n room. **s~nrein** a
house-trained

Stuck m -s stucco

Stück nt -[e]s, -e piece; (Zucker-)
lump; (Seife) tablet; (Theater-)
play; (Gegenstand) item;
(Exemplar) specimen; **ein S~**
(Entfernung) some way. **S~chen**
nt -s,- [little] bit. **s~weise** adv bit
by bit; (einzeln) singly

Student|(in) m -en, -en (f -, -nen)
student. **s~isch** a student …

Studie /-iə/ f -, -n study

studieren vt/i (haben) study

Studio nt -s, -s studio

Studium nt -s, -ien studies pl

Stufe f -, -n step; (Treppen-) stair;
(Raketen-) stage; (Niveau) level.
s~n vt terrace; (staffeln) grade

Stuhl m -[e]s,¨e chair; (Med) stools
pl. **S~gang** m bowel movement

stülpen vt put (über + acc over)

stumm a dumb; (schweigsam)
silent

Stummel m -s,- stump;
(Zigaretten-) butt; (Bleistift-) stub

Stümper m -s,- bungler

stumpf a blunt; <Winkel> obtuse;
(glanzlos) dull; (fig) apathetic.
S~ m -[e]s,¨e stump

Stumpfsinn m apathy; tedium

Stunde f -, -n hour; (Sch) lesson

stunden vt jdm eine Schuld s~
give s.o. time to pay a debt

Stunden|kilometer mpl
kilometres per hour. **s~lang** adv
for hours. **S~lohn** m hourly rate.
S~plan m timetable. **s~weise**
adv by the hour

stündlich a & adv hourly

stur a pigheaded

Sturm m -[e]s,¨e gale; storm; (Mil)
assault

stürm|en vi (haben) <Wind:> blow
hard ● vi (sein) rush ● vt storm;

(bedrängen) besiege. **S~er** m -s,-
forward. **s~isch** a stormy;
<Überfahrt> rough

Sturz m -es,¨e [heavy] fall;
(Preis-) sharp drop; (Pol)
overthrow

stürzen vi (sein) fall [heavily]; (in
die Tiefe) plunge; <Preise:> drop
sharply; <Regierung:> fall; (eilen)
rush ● vt throw; (umkippen) turn
upside down; turn out <Speise,
Kuchen>; (Pol) overthrow, topple
sich s~ throw oneself (aus/in +
acc out of/into)

Sturzhelm m crash-helmet

Stute f -, -n mare

Stütze f -, -n support

stützen vt support; (auf-) rest;
sich s~ auf (+ acc) lean on

stutzig a puzzled; (misstrauisch)
suspicious

Stützpunkt m (Mil) base

Substantiv nt -s, -e noun

Substanz f -, -en substance

Subvention /-'ts:io:n/ f -, -en
subsidy. **s~ieren** vt subsidize

Such|e f - search; **auf der S~e**
nach looking for. **s~en** vt look
for; (intensiv) search for; seek
<Hilfe, Rat>; 'Zimmer gesucht'
'room wanted' ● vi (haben) look,
search (nach for). **S~er** m -s,-
(Phot) viewfinder

Sucht f -,¨e addiction; (fig) mania

süchtig a addicted. **S~e(r)** m/f
addict

Süd m -[e]s south. **S~afrika** nt
South Africa. **S~amerika** nt
South America. **s~deutsch** a
South German

Süden m -s south; **nach S~** south

Süd|frucht f tropical fruit. **s~lich**
a southern; <Richtung> southerly
● adv & prep (+ gen) **s~lich der**
Stadt south of the town. **S~pol** m
South Pole. **s~wärts** adv
southwards

Sühne f -, -n atonement; (Strafe)
penalty. **s~n** vt atone for

Sultanine f -, -n sultana

Sülze f -, -n [meat] jelly

Summe f -, -n sum

summen vi (haben) hum; <Biene:> buzz ● vt hum

summieren (sich) vr add up

Sumpf m -[e]s, ̈e marsh, swamp

Sünd|e f -, -n sin. **S~enbock** m scapegoat. **S~er(in)** m -s, - (f -, -nen) sinner. **s~igen** vi (haben) sin

super inv a 🄸 great. **S~markt** m supermarket

Suppe f -, -n soup. **S~nlöffel** m soup-spoon. **S~nteller** m soup-plate. **S~nwürfel** m stock cube

Surf|brett /'sœːɐ̯f-/ nt surfboard. **S~en** nt -s surfing

surren vi (haben) whirr

süß a sweet. **S~e** f - sweetness. **s~en** vt sweeten. **S~igkeit** f -, -en sweet. **s~lich** a sweetish; (fig) sugary. **S~speise** f sweet. **S~stoff** m sweetener. **S~waren** fpl confectionery sg, sweets pl. **S~wasser-** pref freshwater ...

Sylvester nt -s = Silvester

Symbol nt -s, -e symbol. **S~ik** f - symbolism. **s~isch** a symbolic

Sym|metrie f - symmetry. **s~metrisch** a symmetrical

Sympathie f -, -n sympathy

sympathisch a agreeable; <Person:> likeable

Symptom nt -s, -e symptom. **s~atisch** a symptomatic

Synagoge f -, -n synagogue

synchronisieren /zʏnkroni'ziːrən/ vt synchronize; dub <Film>

Syndikat nt -[e]s, -e syndicate

Syndrom nt -s, -e syndrome

synonym a synonymous

Synthese f -, -n synthesis

Syrien /-iən/ nt -s Syria

System nt -s, -e system. **s~atisch** a systematic

Szene f -, -n scene

Tabak m -s, -e tobacco

Tabelle f -, -n table; (Sport) league table

Tablett nt -[e]s, -s tray

Tablette f -, -n tablet

tabu a taboo. **T~** nt -s, -s taboo

Tacho m -s, -s, **Tachometer** m & nt speedometer

Tadel m -s, - reprimand; (Kritik) censure; (Sch) black mark. **t~los** a impeccable. **t~n** vt reprimand; censure

Tafel f -, -n (Tisch, Tabelle) table; (Platte) slab; (Anschlag-, Hinweis-) board; (Gedenk-) plaque; (Schiefer-) slate; (Wand-) blackboard; (Bild-) plate; (Schokolade) bar

Täfelung f - panelling

Tag m -[e]s, -e day; unter T~e underground; es wird Tag it is getting light; guten Tag! good morning/afternoon!

Tage|buch nt diary. **t~lang** adv for days

Tages|anbruch m daybreak. **T~ausflug** m day trip. **T~decke** f bedspread. **T~karte** f day ticket; (Speise-) menu of the day. **T~licht** nt daylight. **T~mutter** f child-minder. **T~ordnung** f agenda. **T~rückfahrkarte** f day return [ticket]. **T~zeit** f time of the day. **T~zeitung** f daily [news]paper

täglich a & adv daily; zweimal t~ twice a day

tags adv by day; t~ zuvor/darauf the day before/after

tagsüber adv during the day

tag|täglich a daily ●adv every single day. **T∼ung** f -, -en meeting; conference

Taill|e /'taljə/ f -, -n waist. **t∼iert** /ta'ji:ɐt/ a fitted

Takt m -[e]s, -e tact; (Mus) bar; (Tempo) time; (Rhythmus) rhythm; **im T∼** in time

Taktik f - tactics pl.

takt|los a tactless. **T∼losigkeit** f - tactlessness. **T∼stock** m baton. **t∼voll** a tactful

Tal nt -[e]s, -e valley

Talar m -s, -e robe; (Univ) gown

Talent nt -[e]s, -e talent. **t∼iert** a talented

Talg m -s tallow; (Culin) suet

Talsperre f dam

Tampon /tam'põ:/ m -s, -s tampon

Tank m -s, -s tank. **t∼en** vt fill up with <Benzin>. ●vi (haben) fill up with petrol; (Aviat) refuel. **T∼er** m -s,- tanker. **T∼stelle** f petrol station. **T∼wart** m -[e]s, -e petrol-pump attendant

Tanne f -, -n fir [tree]. **T∼nbaum** m fir tree; (Weihnachtsbaum) Christmas tree. **T∼nzapfen** m fir cone

Tante f -, -n aunt

Tantiemen /tan'tie:mən/ pl royalties

Tanz m -es,¨e dance. **t∼en** vt/i (haben) dance

Tänzer(in) m -s,- (f -, -nen) dancer

Tapete f -, -n wallpaper

tapezieren vt paper

tapfer a brave. **T∼keit** f - bravery

Tarif m -s, -e rate; (Verzeichnis) tariff

tarn|en vt disguise; (Mil) camouflage. **T∼ung** f - disguise; camouflage

Tasche f -, -n bag; (Hosen-, Mantel-) pocket. **T∼nbuch** nt paper-back. **T∼ndieb** m pickpocket. **T∼ngeld** nt pocket-money. **T∼nlampe** f torch.

T∼nmesser nt penknife. **T∼ntuch** nt handkerchief

Tasse f -, -n cup

Tastatur f -, -en keyboard

Tast|e f -, -n key; (Druck-) push-button. **t∼en** vi (haben) feel, grope (nach for) ●vt key in <Daten>; **sich t∼en** feel one's way (zu to)

Tat f -, -en action; (Helden-) deed; (Straf-) crime; **auf frischer Tat ertappt** caught in the act

Täter(in) m -s,- (f -, -nen) culprit; (Jur) offender

tätig a active; **t∼ sein** work. **T∼keit** f -, -en activity; (Arbeit) work, job

Tatkraft f energy

Tatort m scene of the crime

tätowier|en vt tattoo. **T∼ung** f -, -en tattooing; (Bild) tattoo

Tatsache f fact. **T∼nbericht** m documentary

tatsächlich a actual

Tatze f -, -n paw

Tau¹ m -[e]s dew

Tau² nt -[e]s, -e rope

taub a deaf; (gefühllos) numb

Taube f -, -n pigeon; dove. **T∼nschlag** m pigeon-loft

Taub|heit f - deafness. **t∼stumm** a deaf and dumb

tauch|en vt dip, plunge; (unter-) duck ●vi (haben/sein) dive/(ein-) plunge (in + acc into); (auf-) appear (aus out of). **T∼er** m -s,- diver. **T∼eranzug** m diving-suit

tauen vi (sein) melt, thaw ●impers **es taut** it is thawing

Tauf|becken nt font. **T∼e** f -, -n christening, baptism. **t∼en** vt christen, baptize. **T∼pate** m godfather

taugen vi (haben) **etwas/nichts t∼** be good/no good

tauglich a suitable; (Mil) fit

Tausch m -[e]s, -e exchange, 🔁 swap. **t∼en** vt exchange/ (handeln) barter (gegen for) ●vi

äuschen (*haben*) swap (*mit etw* sth; *mit jdm* with s.o.)

äuschen vt deceive, fool; betray <*Vertrauen*>; **sich t~** delude oneself; (*sich irren*) be mistaken ● vi (*haben*) be deceptive. **t~d** a deceptive; <*Ähnlichkeit*> striking

äuschung f -, -en deception; (*Irrtum*) mistake; (*Illusion*) delusion

ausend inv a one/a thousand. **T~** nt -s, -e thousand. **T~füßler** m -s,- centipede. **t~ste(r, s)** a thousandth. **T~stel** nt -s,- thousandth

rau|tropfen m dewdrop. **T~wetter** nt thaw

Taxe f -, -n charge; (*Kur-*) tax; (*Taxi*) taxi

Taxi nt -s, -s taxi, cab

Taxi|fahrer m taxi driver. **T~stand** m taxi rank

Teakholz /'ti:k-/ nt teak

Team /ti:m/ nt -s, -s team

Techni|k f -, -en technology; (*Methode*) technique. **T~ker** m -s,- technician. **t~sch** a technical; (*technologisch*) technological; **T~sche Hochschule** Technical University

Techno|logie f -, -n technology. **t~logisch** a technological

Teddybär m teddy bear

Tee m -s, -s tea. **T~beutel** m teabag. **T~kanne** f teapot. **T~löffel** m teaspoon

Teer m -s tar. **t~en** vt tar

Tee|sieb nt tea-strainer. **T~wagen** m [tea] trolley

Teich m -[e]s, -e pond

Teig m -[e]s, -e pastry; (*Knet-*) dough; (*Rühr-*) mixture; (*Pfannkuchen-*) batter. **T~rolle** f rolling-pin. **T~waren** fpl pasta sg

Teil m -[e]s, -e part; (*Bestand-*) component; (*Jur*) party; **zum T~** partly; **zum großen/größten T~** for the most part ● m & nt -[e]s (*Anteil*) share; **ich für mein[en] T~**

for my part ● nt -[e]s, -e part; (*Ersatz-*) spare part; (*Anbau-*) unit

teil|bar a divisible. **T~chen** nt -s,- particle. **t~en** vt divide; (*auf-*) share out; (*gemeinsam haben*) share; (*Pol*) partition <*Land*>; **sich (dat) etw t~en** share sth; **sich t~en** divide; (*sich gabeln*) fork; <*Meinungen:*> differ ● vi (*haben*) share

Teilhaber m -s,- (*Comm*) partner

Teilnahme f - participation; (*innere*) interest; (*Mitgefühl*) sympathy

teilnehm|en† vi sep (*haben*) **t~en an** (+ dat) take part in; (*mitfühlen*) share [in]. **T~er(in)** m -s, (f -, -nen) participant; (*an Wettbewerb*) competitor

teil|s adv partly. **T~ung** f -, -en division; (*Pol*) partition. **t~weise** a partial ● adv partially, partly. **T~zahlung** f part-payment; (*Rate*) instalment. **T~zeitbeschäftigung** f part-time job

Teint /tɛ̃:/ m -s, -s complexion

Telefax nt fax

Telefon nt -s, -e [tele]phone. **T~anruf** m, **T~at** nt -[e]s, -e [tele]phone call. **T~buch** nt [tele]phone book. **t~ieren** vi (*haben*) [tele]phone

telefon|isch a [tele]phone ... ● adv by [tele]phone. **T~ist(in)** m -en, -en (f -, -nen) telephonist. **T~karte** f phone card. **T~nummer** f [tele]phone number. **T~zelle** f [tele]phone box

Telegraf m -en, -en telegraph. **T~enmast** m telegraph pole. **t~ieren** vi (*haben*) send a telegram. **t~isch** a telegraphic ● adv by telegram

Telegramm nt -s, -e telegram

Teleobjektiv nt telephoto lens

Telepathie f - telepathy

Teleskop nt -s, -e telescope
Telex nt -, -[e] telex. **t~en** vt telex
Teller m -s,- plate
Tempel m -s,- temple
Temperament nt -s, -e temperament; (*Lebhaftigkeit*) vivacity
Temperatur f -, -en temperature
Tempo nt -s, -s speed; **T~ [T~]!** hurry up!
Tendenz f -, -en trend; (*Neigung*) tendency
Tennis nt - tennis. **T~platz** m tennis-court. **T~schläger** m tennis-racket
Teppich m -s,e carpet. **T~boden** m fitted carpet
Termin m -s, -e date; (*Arzt-*) appointment. **T~kalender** m [appointments] diary
Terpentin nt -s turpentine
Terrasse f -, -n terrace
Terrier /'tɛriɐ/ m -s,- terrier
Terrine f -, -n tureen
Territorium nt -s, -ien territory
Terror m -s terror. **t~isieren** vt terrorize. **T~ismus** m - terrorism. **T~ist** m -en, -en terrorist
Tesafilm (P) m ≈ Sellotape (P)
Test m -[e]s, -s & -e test
Testament nt -[e]s, -e will; **Altes/Neues T~** Old/New Testament. **T~svollstrecker** m -s,- executor
testen vt test
Tetanus m - tetanus
teuer a expensive; (*lieb*) dear; **wie t~?** how much?
Teufel m -s,- devil. **T~skreis** m vicious circle
teuflisch a fiendish
Text m -[e]s, -e text; (*Passage*) passage; (*Bild-*) caption; (*Lied-*) lyrics pl. **T~er** m -s,- copy-writer; (*Schlager-*) lyricist
Textilien /-iən/ pl textiles; (*Textilwaren*) textile goods
Textverarbeitungssystem nt word processor

Theater nt -s,- theatre; (🔲 *Getue*) fuss. **T~kasse** f box-office. **T~stück** nt play
Theke f -, -n bar; (*Ladentisch*) counter
Thema nt -s, -men subject
Themse f - Thames
Theologe m -n, -n theologian. **T~gie** f - theology
theoretisch a theoretical. **T~ie** f -, -n theory
Therapeut(in) m -en, -en (f -, -nen) therapist
Therapie f -, -n therapy
Thermalbad nt thermal bath
Thermometer nt -s,- thermometer
Thermosflasche (P) f Thermos flask (P)
Thermostat m -[e]s, -e thermostat
These f -, -n thesis
Thrombose f -, -n thrombosis
Thron m -[e]s, -e throne. **t~en** vi (*haben*) sit [in state]. **T~folge** f succession. **T~folger** m -s,- heir to the throne
Thunfisch m tuna
Thymian m -s thyme
ticken vi (*haben*) tick
tief a deep; (*t~ liegend, niedrig*) low; (*t~gründig*) profound; **t~er** Teller soup-plate ● adv deep; low; (*sehr*) deeply, profoundly; <*schlafen*> soundly. **T~** nt -s, -s (*Meteorol*) depression. **T~bau** m civil engineering. **T~e** f -, -n depth. **T~garage** f underground car park. **t~gekühlt** a [deep-] frozen
Tiefkühl|fach nt freezer compartment. **T~kost** f frozen food. **T~truhe** f deep-freeze
Tiefsttemperatur f minimum temperature
Tier nt -[e]s, -e animal. **T~arzt** m, **T~ärztin** f vet, veterinary surgeon. **T~garten** m zoo. **T~kreis** m zodiac. **T~kunde** f zoology. **T~quälerei** f cruelty to animals

Tiger m -s,- tiger

tilgen vt pay off <Schuld>; (streichen) delete; (fig: auslöschen) wipe out

Tinte f -, -n ink. **T~nfisch** m squid

Tipp m -s, -s 🔲 tip

tipp|en vt 🔲 type ● vi (haben) (berühren) touch (auf/an etw acc sth); (🔲 Maschine schreiben) type; **t~en auf** (+ acc) (🔲 wetten) bet on. **T~schein** m pools/lottery coupon

tipptopp a 🔲 immaculate

Tirol nt -s [the] Tyrol

Tisch m -[e]s, -e table; (Schreib-) desk; **nach T~** after the meal. **T~decke** f table-cloth. **T~gebet** nt grace. **T~ler** m -s,- joiner; (Möbel-) cabinet-maker. **T~rede** f after-dinner speech. **T~tennis** nt table tennis

Titel m -s,- title

Toast /to:st/ m -[e]s, -e toast; (Scheibe) piece of toast. **T~er** m -s,- toaster

toben vi (haben) rave; <Sturm:> rage; <Kinder:> play boisterously

Tochter f -,: daughter. **T~gesellschaft** f subsidiary

Tod m -es death

Todes|angst f mortal fear. **T~anzeige** f death announcement; (Zeitungs-) obituary. **T~fall** m death. **T~opfer** nt fatality, casualty. **T~strafe** f death penalty. **T~urteil** nt death sentence

todkrank a dangerously ill

tödlich a fatal; <Gefahr> mortal

Toilette /toa'lɛtə/ f -, -n toilet. **T~npapier** nt toilet paper

toler|ant a tolerant. **T~anz** f - tolerance. **t~ieren** vt tolerate

toll a crazy, mad; (🔲 prima) fantastic; (schlimm) awful ● adv (sehr) very; (schlimm) badly. **t~kühn** a foolhardy. **T~wut** f rabies. **t~wütig** a rabid

Tölpel m -s,- fool

Tomate f -, -n tomato. **T~nmark** nt tomato purée

Tombola f -, -s raffle

Ton[1] m -[e]s clay

Ton[2] m -[e]s,:e tone; (Klang) sound; (Note) note; (Betonung) stress; (Farb-) shade; **der gute Ton** (fig) good form. **T~abnehmer** m -s,- pick-up. **t~angebend** a (fig) leading. **T~art** f tone [of voice]; (Mus) key. **T~band** nt (pl -bänder) tape. **T~bandgerät** nt tape recorder

tönen vi (haben) sound ● vt tint

Tonleiter f scale

Tonne f -, -n barrel, cask; (Müll-) bin; (Maß) tonne, metric ton

Topf m -[e]s,:e pot; (Koch-) pan

Topfen m -s (Aust) ≈ curd cheese

Töpferei f -, -en pottery

Topf|lappen m oven-cloth. **T~pflanze** f potted plant

Tor nt -[e]s, -e gate; (Einfahrt) gateway; (Sport) goal

Torf m -s peat

torkeln vi (sein/habe) stagger

Tornister m -s,- knapsack; (Sch) satchel

Torpedo m -s, -s torpedo

Torpfosten m goal-post

Torte f -, -n gateau; (Obst-) flan

Tortur f -, -en torture

Torwart m -s, -e goalkeeper

tot a dead; **tot geboren** stillborn; **sich tot stellen** pretend to be dead

total a total. **T~schaden** m ≈ write-off

Tote|(r) m/f dead man/woman; (Todesopfer) fatality; **die T~n** the dead pl

töten vt kill

Toten|gräber m -s,- grave-digger. **T~kopf** m skull. **T~schein** m death certificate

totfahren† vt sep run over and kill

Toto nt & m -s football pools pl. **T~schein** m pools coupon

T

tot|schießen† vt sep shoot dead. **T~schlag** m (Jur) manslaughter. **t~schlagen**† vt sep kill

Tötung f -, -en killing; **fahrlässige T~** (Jur) manslaughter

Toup|et /tu'pe:/ nt -s, -s toupee. **t~ieren** vt back-comb

Tour /tu:ɐ/ f -, -en tour; (Ausflug) trip; (Auto-) drive; (Rad-) ride; (Strecke) distance; (Techn) revolution; (🅸 Weise) way

Touris|mus /tu'rɪsmʊs/ m - tourism. **T~t** m -en, -en tourist

Tournee /tʊr'ne:/ f -, -n tour

Trab m -[e]s trot

Trabant m -en, -en satellite

traben vi (haben/sein) trot

Tracht f -, -en [national] costume

Tradition /-'tsi̯o:n/ f -, -en tradition. **t~ell** a traditional

Trag|bahre f stretcher. **t~bar** a portable; (Kleidung) wearable

tragen† vt carry; (an-/ aufhaben) wear; (fig) bear ● vi (haben) carry; **gut t~** <Baum:> produce a good crop

Träger m -s,- porter; (Inhaber) bearer; (eines Ordens) holder; (Bau-) beam; (Stahl-) girder; (Achsel-) [shoulder] strap. **T~kleid** nt pinafore dress

Trag|etasche f carrier bag. **T~flächenboot, T~flügelboot** nt hydrofoil

Trägheit f - sluggishness; (Faulheit) laziness; (Phys) inertia

Trag|ik f - tragedy. **t~isch** a tragic

Tragödie /-i̯ə/ f -, -n tragedy

Train|er /'trɛːnɐ/ m -s,- trainer; (Tennis-) coach. **t~ieren** vt/i (haben) train

Training /'trɛːnɪŋ/ nt -s training. **T~sanzug** m tracksuit. **T~s-schuhe** mpl trainers

Traktor m -s, -en /-'to:rən/ tractor

trampeln vi (haben) stamp one's feet ● vi (sein) trample (auf + acc on) ● vt trample

trampen /'trɛmpən/ vi (sein) 🅸 hitch-hike

Tranchiermesser /trã'ʃi:ɐ-/ nt carving-knife

Träne f -, -n tear. **t~n** vi (haben) water. **T~ngas** nt tear-gas

Tränke f -, -n watering-place; (Trog) drinking-trough. **t~n** vt water <Pferd>; (nässen) soak (mit with)

Trans|formator m -s, -en /-'to:rən/ transformer. **T~fusion** f -, -en [blood] transfusion

Transit /tran'zi:t/ m -s transit

Transparent nt -[e]s, -e banner; (Bild) transparency

transpirieren vi (haben) perspire

Transport m -[e]s, -e transport; (Güter-) consignment. **t~ieren** vt transport

Trapez nt -es, -e trapeze

Tratte f -, -n (Comm) draft

Traube f -, -n bunch of grapes; (Beere) grape; (fig) cluster. **T~nzucker** m glucose

trauen vi (haben) (+ dat) trust ● vt marry; **sich t~** dare (etw zu tun [to] do sth); venture (in + acc/aus into/out of)

Trauer f - mourning; (Schmerz) grief (um for); **T~ tragen** be [dressed] in mourning. **T~fall** m bereavement. **T~feier** f funeral service. **t~n** vi (haben) grieve; **t~n um** mourn [for]. **T~spiel** nt tragedy. **T~weide** f weeping willow

Traum m -[e]s, Träume dream

Trauma nt -s, -men trauma

träumen vt/i (haben) dream

traumhaft a dreamlike; (schön) fabulous

traurig a sad; (erbärmlich) sorry. **T~keit** f - sadness

Trau|ring m wedding-ring. **T~schein** m marriage certificate. **T~ung** f -, -en wedding [ceremony]

Treff nt -s, -s (Karten) spades pl

treff|en† vt hit; <Blitz:> strike; (fig: verletzen) hurt; (zusammenkommen mit) meet; take <Maßnahme>; **sich t~en** meet (mit jdm s.o.); **sich gut t~en** be convenient; **es gut/schlecht t~en** be lucky/unlucky ●vi (haben) hit the target; **t~en auf** (+ acc) meet with; (fig) meet with. **T~en** nt -s,- meeting. **T~er** m -s,- hit; (Los) winner. **T~punkt** m meeting-place

treiben† vt drive; (sich befassen mit) do; carry on <Gewerbe>; indulge in <Luxus>; get up to <Unfug>; **Handel t~** trade ●vi (sein) drift; (schwimmen) float ●vi (haben) (Bot) sprout. **T~** nt -s activity

Treib|haus nt hothouse. **T~hauseffekt** m greenhouse effect. **T~holz** nt driftwood. **T~riemen** m transmission belt. **T~sand** m quicksand. **T~stoff** m fuel

trenn|bar a separable. **t~en** vt separate/(abmachen) detach (von from); divide, split <Wort>; **sich t~en** separate; (auseinander gehen) part; **sich t~en von** leave; (fortgeben) part with. **T~ung** f -, -en separation; (Silben-) division. **T~ungsstrich** m hyphen. **T~wand** f partition

trepp|ab adv downstairs. **t~auf** adv upstairs

Treppe f -, -n stairs pl; (Außen-) steps pl. **T~ngeländer** nt banisters pl

Tresor m -s, -e safe

Tresse f -, -n braid

Treteimer m pedal bin

treten† vi (sein/haben) step; (versehentlich) tread; (ausschlagen) kick (nach at); in **Verbindung t~** get in touch ●vt tread; (mit Füßen) kick

treu a faithful; (fest) loyal. **T~e** f - faithfulness; loyalty; (eheliche)

fidelity. **T~händer** m -s,- trustee. **t~los** a disloyal; (untreu) unfaithful

Tribüne f -, -n platform; (Zuschauer-) stand

Trichter m -s,- funnel; (Bomben-) crater

Trick m -s, -s trick. **T~film** m cartoon. **t~reich** a clever

Trieb m -[e]s, -e drive, urge; (Instinkt) instinct; (Bot) shoot. **T~verbrecher** m sex offender. **T~werk** nt (Aviat) engine; (Uhr-) mechanism

triefen† vi (haben) drip; (nass sein) be dripping (von/vor + dat with)

Trigonometrie f - trigonometry

Trikot¹ /tri'ko:/ m -s (Tex) jersey

Trikot² nt -s, -s (Sport) jersey; (Fußball-) shirt

Trimester nt -s,- term

Trimm-dich nt -s keep-fit

trimmen vt trim; tune <Motor>; **sich t~** keep fit

trink|en† vt/i (haben) drink. **T~er(in)** m -s,- (f -, -nen) alcoholic. **T~geld** nt tip. **T~spruch** m toast

trist a dreary

Tritt m -[e]s, -e step; (Fuß-) kick. **T~brett** nt step

Triumph m -s, -e triumph. **t~ieren** vi (haben) rejoice

trocken a dry. **T~haube** f drier. **T~heit** f -, -en dryness; (Dürre) drought. **t~legen** vt sep change <Baby>; drain <Sumpf>. **T~milch** f powdered milk

trocknen vt/i (sein) dry. **T~er** m -s,- drier

Trödel m -s 🔲 junk. **t~n** vi (haben) dawdle

Trödler m -s,- 🔲 slowcoach; (Händler) junk-dealer

Trog m -[e]s,ᵉe trough

Trommel f -, -n drum. **T~fell** nt ear-drum. **t~n** vi (haben) drum

Trommler m -s,- drummer

T

Trompete f -, -n trumpet. **T~r** m -s,- trumpeter

Tropen pl tropics

Tropf m -[e]s, -e (Med) drip

tröpfeln vt/i (sein/haben) drip

tropfen vt/i (sein/haben) drip. **T~** m -s,- drop; (fallend) drip. **t~weise** adv drop by drop

Trophäe /troˈfɛːə/ f -, -n trophy

tropisch a tropical

Trost m -[e]s consolation, comfort

tröst|en vt console, comfort; **sich t~en** console oneself. **t~lich** a comforting

trost|los a desolate; (elend) wretched; (reizlos) dreary. **T~preis** m consolation prize

Trott m -s amble; (fig) routine

Trottel m -s,- 🗊 idiot

Trottoir /trɔˈtoaːɐ̯/ nt -s, -s pavement

trotz prep (+ gen) despite, in spite of. **T~** m -es defiance. **t~dem** adv nevertheless. **t~ig** a defiant; stubborn

trübe a dull; <Licht> dim; <Flüssigkeit> cloudy; (fig) gloomy

Trubel m -s bustle

trüben vt dull; make cloudy <Flüssigkeit>; (fig) spoil; strain <Verhältnis> **sich t~** <Flüssigkeit:> become cloudy; <Himmel:> cloud over; <Augen:> dim

Trüb|sal f - misery. **T~sinn** m melancholy. **t~sinnig** a melancholy

trügen† vt deceive ●vi (haben) be deceptive

Trugschluss m fallacy

Truhe f -, -n chest

Trümmer pl rubble sg; (T~teile) wreckage sg, (fig) ruins

Trumpf m -[e]s,¨e trump [card]. **t~en** vi (haben) play trumps

Trunk m -[e]s drink. **T~enheit** f - drunkenness; **T~enheit am Steuer** drink-driving

Trupp m -s, -s group; (Mil) squad. **T~e** f -, -n (Mil) unit; (Theat) troupe; **T~en** troops

Truthahn m turkey

Tschech|e m -n, -n, **T~in** f -, -nen Czech. **t~isch** a Czech. **T~oslowakei (die)** - Czechoslovakia

tschüs, tschüss int bye, cheerio

Tuba f -, -ben (Mus) tuba

Tube f -, -n tube

Tuberkulose f - tuberculosis

Tuch nt -[e]s,¨er cloth; (Hals-, Kopf-) scarf; (Schulter-) shawl

tüchtig a competent; (reichlich, beträchtlich) good; (groß) big ●adv competently; (ausreichend) well

Tück|e f -, -n malice. **t~isch** a malicious; (gefährlich) treacherous

Tugend f -,en virtue. **t~haft** a virtuous

Tülle f -, -n spout

Tulpe f -, -n tulip

Tümmler m -s,- porpoise

Tumor m -s, -en /-ˈmoːrən/ tumour

Tümpel m -[e]s,- pond

Tumult m -[e]s, -e commotion; (Aufruhr) riot

tun† vt do; take <Schritt, Blick>; work <Wunder>; (bringen) put (in + acc into); **sich tun** happen; **jdm etwas tun** hurt s.o.; **das tut nichts** it doesn't matter ●vi (haben) act (als ob as if); **er tut nur so** he's just pretending; **jdm/etw gut tun** do s.o./sth. good; **zu tun haben** have things/work to do; **[es] zu tun haben** mit have to deal with. **Tun** nt -s actions pl

Tünche f -, -n whitewash; (fig) veneer. **t~n** vt whitewash

Tunesien /-iən/ nt -s Tunisia

Tunfisch m = Thunfisch

Tunnel m -s,- tunnel

tupf|en vt dab ●vi (haben) **t~en an/auf** (+ acc) touch. **T~en** m -s,-

spot. **T~er** *m* -s,- spot; (*Med*)
swab

ür *f* -, -en door

urban *m* -s, -e turban

urbine *f* -, -n turbine

ürk|e *m* -n, -n Turk. **T~ei** (die) -
Turkey. **T~in** *f* -, -nen Turk

ürkis *inv a* turquoise

ürkisch *a* Turkish

urm *m* -[e]s, ̈-e tower; (*Schach*)
rook, castle

ürm|chen *nt* -s,- turret. **t~en** *vt*
pile [up]; **sich t~en** pile up

urmspitze *f* spire

urn|en *vi* (*haben*) do gymnastics.
T~en *nt* -s gymnastics *sg*; (*Sch*)
physical education, 🄸 gym.
T~er(in) *m* -s,- (*f* -, -nen) gymnast.
T~halle *f* gymnasium

Turnier *nt* -s, -e tournament;
(*Reit*-) show

Turnschuhe *mpl* gym shoes;
trainers

Türschwelle *f* doorstep,
threshold

Tusche *f* -, -n [drawing] ink

tuscheln *vt/i* (*haben*) whisper

Tüte *f* -, -n bag; (*Comm*) packet;
(*Eis*-) cornet; **in die T~ blasen** 🄸
be breathalysed

TÜV *m* - ≈ MOT [test]

Typ *m* -s, -en type; (🄸 *Kerl*) bloke.
T~e *f* -, -n type

Typhus *m* - typhoid

typisch *a* typical (**für** of)

Typus *m* -, Typen type

Tyrann *m* -en, -en tyrant. **T~ei** *f* -
tyranny. **t~isch** *a* tyrannical.
t~isieren *vt* tyrannize

U-Bahn *f* underground

übel *a* bad; (*hässlich*) nasty; **mir
ist ü~** I feel sick; **jdm etw ü~
nehmen** hold sth against s.o.
Ü~keit *f* - nausea

üben *vt/i* (*haben*) practise

über *prep* (+ *dat/acc*) over; (*höher
als*) above; (*betreffend*) about;
<*Buch, Vortrag*> on; <*Scheck,
Rechnung*> for; (*quer ü~*) across;
ü~ Köln fahren go via Cologne;
ü~ Ostern over Easter; **die Woche
ü~** during the week; **Fehler ü~
Fehler** mistake after mistake
● *adv* **ü~ und ü~** all over; **jdm ü~
sein** be better/(*stärker*) stronger
than s.o. ● *a* 🄸 **ü~ sein** be left
over; **etw ü~ sein** be fed up with
sth

überall *adv* everywhere

überanstrengen *vt insep* overtax;
strain <*Augen*>

überarbeiten *vt insep* revise; **sich
ü~en** overwork

überbieten† *vt insep* outbid;
(*übertreffen*) surpass

Überblick *m* overall view;
(*Abriss*) summary

überblicken *vt insep* overlook;
(*abschätzen*) assess

überbringen† *vt insep* deliver

überbrücken *vt insep* (*fig*) bridge

überdies *adv* moreover

überdimensional *a* oversized

Überdosis *f* overdose

überdrüssig *a* **ü~ sein/werden**
be/grow tired (*gen* of)

übereignen *vt insep* transfer

übereilt *a* over-hasty

übereinander *adv* one on top of/
above the other; <*sprechen*>
about each other

überein|kommen† vi sep (sein) agree. **Ü~kunft** f - agreement. **ü~stimmen** vi sep (haben) agree; <Zahlen:> tally; <Ansichten:> coincide; <Farben:> match. **Ü~stimmung** f agreement

überfahren† vt insep run over

Überfahrt f crossing

Überfall m attack; (Bank-) raid

überfallen† vt insep attack; raid <Bank>; (bestürmen) bombard (mit with)

Überfluss m abundance; (Wohlstand) affluence

überflüssig a superfluous

überfordern vt insep overtax

überführen vt insep transfer; (Jur) convict (gen of). **Ü~ung** f transfer; (Straße) flyover; (Fußgänger-) foot-bridge

überfüllt a overcrowded

Übergabe f handing over; transfer

Übergang m crossing; (Wechsel) transition

übergeben† vt insep hand over; (übereignen) transfer; **sich ü~** be sick

übergehen† vt insep (fig) pass over; (nicht beachten) ignore; (auslassen) leave out

Übergewicht nt excess weight; (fig) predominance; **Ü~ haben** be overweight

über|greifen† vi sep (haben) spread (auf + acc to). **Ü~griff** m infringement

über|groß a outsize; (übertrieben) exaggerated. **Ü~größe** f outsize

überhand adv **ü~ nehmen** increase alarmingly

überhäufen vt insep inundate (mit with)

überhaupt adv (im Allgemeinen) altogether; (eigentlich) anyway; (überdies) besides; **ü~ nicht/nichts** not/nothing at all

überheblich a arrogant. **Ü~keit** f - arrogance

überhollen vt insep overtake; (reparieren) overhaul. **ü~t** a out-dated. **Ü~ung** f -, -en overhaul. **Ü~verbot** nt 'Ü~verbo 'no overtaking'

überhören vt insep fail to hear; (nicht beachten) ignore

überirdisch a supernatural

überkochen vi sep (sein) boil over

überlassen† vt insep jdm etw ü~ leave sth to s.o.; (geben) let s.o. have sth; **sich** (dat) **selbst ü~ sei** be left to one's own devices

Überlauf m overflow

überlaufen† vi sep (sein) overflow; (Mil, Pol) defect

Überläufer m defector

überleben vt/i insep (haben) survive. **Ü~de(r)** m/f survivor

überlegen¹ vt sep put over

überlegen² v insep ● vt [sich dat] ü~ think over, consider; **es sich** (dat) **anders ü~** change one's mind ● vi (haben) think, reflect

überlegen³ a superior. **Ü~heit** f - superiority

Überlegung f -, -en reflection

überliefer|n vt insep hand down. **Ü~ung** f tradition

überlisten vt insep outwit

Übermacht f superiority

übermäßig a excessive

Übermensch m superman. **ü~lich** a superhuman

übermitteln vt insep convey; (senden) transmit

übermorgen adv the day after tomorrow

übermüdet a overtired

Übermut m high spirits pl. **ü~mütig** a high-spirited

übernächst|e(r,s) a next ... but one; **ü~es Jahr** the year after next

übernacht|en vi insep (haben) stay overnight. **Ü~ung** f -, -en overnight stay; **Ü~ung und Frühstück** bed and breakfast

Übernahme *f* - taking over; (*Comm*) take-over

übernatürlich *a* supernatural

übernehmen† *vt insep* take over; (*annehmen*) take on; **sich ü~** overdo things; (*finanziell*) overreach oneself

überqueren *vt insep* cross

überraschen *vt insep* surprise. **ü~end** *a* surprising; (*unerwartet*) unexpected. **Ü~ung** *f* -, -en surprise

überreden *vt insep* persuade

Überreste *mpl* remains

Überschall- *pref* supersonic

überschätzen *vt insep* overestimate

Überschlag *m* rough estimate; (*Sport*) somersault

überschlagen¹† *vt sep* cross <*Beine*>

überschlagen²† *vt insep* estimate roughly; (*auslassen*) skip; **sich ü~** somersault; <*Ereignisse:*> happen fast ● *a* tepid

überschneiden† (**sich**) *vr insep* intersect, cross; (*zusammenfallen*) overlap

überschreiten† *vt insep* cross; (*fig*) exceed

Überschrift *f* heading; (*Zeitungs-*) headline

Überschuss *m* surplus. **ü~schüssig** *a* surplus

überschwemmen *vt insep* flood; (*fig*) inundate. **Ü~ung** *f* -, -en flood

Übersee in/nach **Ü~** overseas; **aus/von Ü~** from overseas. **Ü~dampfer** *m* ocean liner. **ü~isch** *a* overseas

übersehen† *vt insep* look out over; (*abschätzen*) assess; (*nicht sehen*) overlook, miss; (*ignorieren*) ignore

übersenden† *vt insep* send

übersetzen¹ *vi sep* (*haben/sein*) cross [over]

übersetzen² *vt insep* translate. **Ü~er(in)** *m* -s,- (*f* -, -nen) translator. **Ü~ung** *f* -, -en translation

Übersicht *f* overall view; (*Abriss*) summary; (*Tabelle*) table. **ü~lich** *a* clear

Übersiedlung *f* move

überspielen *vt insep* (*fig*) cover up; **auf Band ü~** tape

überstehen† *vt insep* come through; get over <*Krankheit*>; (*überleben*) survive

übersteigen† *vt insep* climb [over]; (*fig*) exceed

überstimmen *vt insep* outvote

Überstunden *fpl* overtime *sg*; **Ü~ machen** work overtime

überstürzen *vt insep* rush; **sich ü~en** <*Ereignisse:*> happen fast. **ü~t** *a* hasty

übertragbar *a* transferable; (*Med*) infectious. **ü~en**† *vt insep* transfer; (*übergeben*) assign (*dat* to); (*Techn, Med*) transmit; (*Radio, TV*) broadcast; (*übersetzen*) translate; (*anwenden*) apply (**auf** + *acc* to) ● *a* transferred, figurative. **Ü~ung** *f* -, -en transfer; transmission; broadcast; translation, application

übertreffen† *vt insep* surpass; (*übersteigen*) exceed; **sich selbst ü~** excel oneself

übertreiben† *vt insep* exaggerate; (*zu weit treiben*) overdo. **Ü~ung** *f* -, -en exaggeration

übertreten¹† *vi sep* (*sein*) step over the line; (*Pol*) go over/(*Relig*) convert (**zu** to)

übertreten²† *vt insep* infringe; break <*Gesetz*>. **Ü~ung** *f* -, -en infringement; breach

übertrieben *a* exaggerated

übervölkert *a* overpopulated

überwachen *vt insep* supervise; (*kontrollieren*) monitor;

(*bespitzeln*) keep under surveillance

überwältigen vt insep overpower; (*fig*) overwhelm

überweis|en† vt insep transfer; refer <*Patienten*>. **Ü~ung** f transfer; (*ärztliche*) referral

überwiegen† v insep ● vi (*haben*) predominate. ● vt outweigh

überwind|en† vt insep overcome; sich ü~en force oneself. **Ü~ung** f effort

Über|zahl f majority. **ü~zählig** a spare

überzeug|en vt insep convince; sich [selbst] ü~en satisfy oneself. **ü~end** a convincing. **Ü~ung** f -, -en conviction

überziehen¹† vt sep put on

überziehen²† vt insep cover; overdraw <*Konto*>

Überzug m cover; (*Schicht*) coating

üblich a usual; (*gebräuchlich*) customary

U-Boot nt submarine

übrig a remaining; (*andere*) other; alles Ü~e [all] the rest; im Ü~en besides; (*ansonsten*) apart from that; ü~ sein od bleiben be left [over]; etw ü~ lassen leave sth [over]; uns blieb nichts anderes ü~ we had no choice

Übung f -, -en exercise; (*Üben*) practice; (*Übung*) außer od aus der Ü~ out of practice

Ufer nt -s,- shore; (*Fluss-*) bank

Uhr f -, -en clock; (*Armband-*) watch; (*Zähler*) meter; um ein U~ at one o'clock; wie viel U~ ist es? what's the time? **U~macher** m -s,- watch and clockmaker.

U~werk nt clock/watch mechanism. **U~zeiger** m [clock-/watch-]hand. **U~zeit** f time

Uhu m -s, -s eagle owl

UKW abbr (*Ultrakurzwelle*) VHF

ulkig funny (*seltsam*) odd

Ulme f -, -n elm

Ultimatum nt -s, -ten ultimatum

Ultrakurzwelle f very high frequency

Ultraschall m ultrasound

ultraviolett a ultraviolet

um prep (+ acc) [a]round; (*Uhrzeit*) at; <*bitten*> for; <*streiten*> over; <*sich sorgen*> about; <*betrügen*> out of; (*bei Angabe einer Differenz*) by; um [... herum] around, [round] about; Tag um Tag day after day; um seinetwillen for his sake ● adv (*ungefähr*) around, about; um sein ⚠ be over; <*Zeit*> be up ● conj um zu to; (*Absicht*) [in order] to; zu müde, um zu ... too tired to ...

umarm|en vt insep embrace, hug. **U~ung** f -, -en embrace, hug

Umbau m rebuilding; conversion (zu into). **u~en** vt sep rebuild; convert (zu into)

Umbildung f reorganization; (*Pol*) reshuffle

umbinden† vt sep put on

umblättern v sep ● vt turn [over] ● vi (*haben*) turn the page

umbringen† vt sep kill; sich u~ kill oneself

umbuchen v sep ● vt change; (*Comm*) transfer ● vi (*haben*) change one's booking

umdrehen v sep ● vt turn round/ (*wenden*) over; turn <*Schlüssel*>; (*umkrempeln*) turn inside out; sich u~ turn round; (*im Liegen*) turn over ● vi (*haben/sein*) turn back

Umdrehung f turn; (*Motor-*) revolution

umeinander adv around each other; sich u~ sorgen worry about each other

umfahren¹† vt sep run over

umfahren²† vt insep go round; bypass <*Ort*>

umfallen† vi sep (*sein*) fall over; <*Person:*> fall down

Umfang m girth; (*Geom*) circumference; (*Größe*) size

umfangreich a extensive; (*dick*) big

umfassen vt insep consist of, comprise; (*umgeben*) surround. **u~d** a comprehensive

Umfrage f survey, poll

umfüllen vt sep transfer

umfunktionieren vt sep convert

Umgang m [social] contact; (*Umgehen*) dealing (**mit** with)

Umgangssprache f colloquial language

umgeb|en† vt/i insep (*haben*) surround ● a **u~en** von surrounded by. **U~ung** f -, -en surroundings pl

umgehen† vt insep avoid; (*nicht beachten*) evade; <*Straße:*> bypass

umgehend a immediate

Umgehungsstraße f bypass

umgekehrt a inverse; <*Reihenfolge*> reverse; **es war u~** it was the other way round

umgraben† vt sep dig [over]

Umhang m cloak

umhauen† vt sep knock down; (*fällen*) chop down

umhören (sich) vr sep ask around

Umkehr f - turning back. **u~en** v sep ● vi (*sein*) turn back ● vt turn round; turn inside out <*Tasche:*>; (*fig*) reverse

umkippen v sep ● vt tip over; (*versehentlich*) knock over ● vi (*sein*) fall over; <*Boot:*> capsize

Umkleide|kabine f changing-cubicle. **u~n (sich)** vr sep change. **U~raum** m changing-room

umknicken v sep ● vt bend; (*falten*) fold ● vi (*sein*) bend; (*mit dem Fuß*) go over on one's ankle

umkommen† vi sep (*sein*) perish

Umkreis m surroundings pl; **im U~ von** within a radius of

umkreisen vt insep circle; (*Astr*) revolve around; <*Satellit:*> orbit

umkrempeln vt sep turn up; (*von innen nach außen*) turn inside out; (*ändern*) change radically

Umlauf m circulation; (*Astr*) revolution. **U~bahn** f orbit

Umlaut m umlaut

umlegen vt sep lay or put down; flatten <*Getreide*>; turn down <*Kragen*>; put on <*Schal*>; throw <*Hebel*>; (*verlegen*) transfer; (🅸 *töten*) kill

umleit|en vt sep divert. **U~ung** f diversion

umliegend a surrounding

umpflanzen vt sep transplant

umranden vt insep edge

umräumen vt sep rearrange

umrechn|en vt sep convert. **U~ung** f conversion

umreißen† vt insep outline

Umriss m outline

umrühren vt/i sep (*haben*) stir

ums pron = um das

Umsatz m (*Comm*) turnover

umschalten vt/i sep (*haben*) switch over; **auf Rot u~** <*Ampel:*> change to red

Umschau f **U~ halten nach** look out for

Umschlag m cover; (*Schutz-*) jacket; (*Brief-*) envelope; (*Med*) compress; (*Hosen-*) turn-up. **u~en†** v sep ● vt turn up; turn over <*Seite*>; (*fällen*) chop down ● vi (*sein*) topple over; <*Wetter:*> change; <*Wind:*> veer

umschließen† vt insep enclose

umschreiben vt insep define; (*anders ausdrücken*) paraphrase

umschulen vt sep retrain; (*Sch*) transfer to another school

Umschwung m (*fig*) change; (*Pol*) U-turn

umsehen† (sich) vr sep look round; (*zurück*) look back; **sich u~ nach** look for

U

umsein* *vi sep* um sein, *s.* um

umseitig *a & adv* overleaf

umsetzen *vt sep* move; *(umpflanzen)* transplant; *(Comm)* sell

umsied|eln *v sep* ● *vt* resettle ● *vi (sein)* move. **U~lung** *f* resettlement

umso *conj* ~ **besser/mehr** all the better/more; **je mehr,** ~ **besser** the more the better

umsonst *adv* in vain; *(grundlos)* without reason; *(gratis)* free

Umstand *m* circumstance; *(Tatsache)* fact; *(Aufwand)* fuss; *(Mühe)* trouble; **unter U~en** possibly; **jdm U~e machen** put s.o. to trouble; **in andern U~en** pregnant

umständlich *a* laborious; *(kompliziert)* involved

Umstands|kleid *nt* maternity dress. **U~wort** *nt (pl* -wörter) adverb

Umstehende *pl* bystanders

umsteigen† *vi sep (sein)* change

umstellen¹ *vt insep* surround

umstell|en² *vt sep* rearrange; transpose <Wörter>; *(anders einstellen)* reset; *(Techn)* convert; *(ändern)* change; **sich u~en** adjust. **U~ung** *f* rearrangement; transposition; resetting; conversion; change; adjustment

umstritten *a* controversial; *(ungeklärt)* disputed

umstülpen *vt sep* turn upside down; *(von innen nach außen)* turn inside out

Um|sturz *m* coup. **u~stürzen** *v sep* ● *vt* overturn; *(Pol)* overthrow ● *vi (sein)* fall over

umtaufen *vt sep* rename

Umtausch *m* exchange. **u~en** *vt sep* change; exchange (**gegen** for)

umwechseln *vt sep* change

Umweg *m* detour; **auf U~en** *(fig)* in a roundabout way

Umwelt *f* environment. **u~freundlich** *a* environmentally friendly. **U~schutz** *m* protection of the environment

umwerfen† *vt sep* knock over; *(fig)* upset <Plan>

umziehen† *v sep* ● *vi (sein)* move ● *vt* change; **sich u~** change

umzingeln *vt insep* surround

Umzug *m* move; *(Prozession)* procession

unabänderlich *a* irrevocable; <Tatsache> unalterable

unabhängig *a* independent; **u~ davon, ob** irrespective of whether. **U~keit** *f* - independence

unablässig *a* incessant

unabsehbar *a* incalculable

unabsichtlich *a* unintentional

unachtsam *a* careless

unangebracht *a* inappropriate

unangenehm *a* unpleasant; *(peinlich)* embarrassing

Unannehmlichkeiten *fpl* trouble *sg*

unansehnlich *a* shabby

unanständig *a* indecent

unappetitlich *a* unappetizing

Unart *f* -, -en bad habit. **u~ig** *a* naughty

unauffällig *a* inconspicuous; unobtrusive

unaufgefordert *adv* without being asked

unauf|haltsam *a* inexorable. **u~hörlich** *a* incessant

unaufmerksam *a* inattentive

unaufrichtig *a* insincere

unausbleiblich *a* inevitable

unausstehlich *a* insufferable

unbarmherzig *a* merciless

unbeabsichtigt *a* unintentional

unbedenklich *a* harmless ● *adv* without hesitation

unbedeutend *a* insignificant; *(geringfügig)* slight

unbedingt *a* absolute; **nicht u~** not necessarily

unbefriedig|end *a* unsatisfactory.
u~t *a* dissatisfied

unbefugt *a* unauthorized ●*adv*
without authorization

unbegreiflich *a*
incomprehensible

unbegrenzt *a* unlimited ●*adv*
indefinitely

unbegründet *a* unfounded

Unbehagen *nt* unease;
(*körperlich*) discomfort

unbekannt *a* unknown; (*nicht
vertraut*) unfamiliar. **U~e(r)** *m/f*
stranger

unbekümmert *a* unconcerned;
(*unbeschwert*) carefree

unbeliebt *a* unpopular. **U~heit** *f*
unpopularity

unbemannt *a* unmanned

unbemerkt *a* & *adv* unnoticed

unbenutzt *a* unused

unbequem *a* uncomfortable;
(*lästig*) awkward

unberechenbar *a* unpredictable

unberechtigt *a* unjustified;
(*unbefugt*) unauthorized

unberührt *a* untouched; (*fig*)
virgin; <*Landschaft*> unspoilt

unbescheiden *a* presumptuous

unbeschrankt *a* unguarded

unbeschränkt *a* unlimited ●*adv*
without limit

unbeschwert *a* carefree

unbesiegt *a* undefeated

unbespielt *a* blank

unbeständig *a* inconsistent;
<*Wetter*> unsettled

unbestechlich *a* incorruptible

unbestimmt *a* indefinite: <*Alter*>
indeterminate; (*ungewiss*)
uncertain; (*unklar*) vague

unbestritten *a* undisputed ●*adv*
indisputably

unbeteiligt *a* indifferent; **u~ an**
(+ *dat*) not involved in

unbetont *a* unstressed

unbewacht *a* unguarded

unbewaffnet *a* unarmed

unbeweglich *a* & *adv* motionless,
still

unbewohnt *a* uninhabited

unbewusst *a* unconscious

unbezahlbar *a* priceless

unbrauchbar *a* useless

und *conj* and; **und so weiter** and so
on; **nach und nach** bit by bit

Undank *m* ingratitude. **u~bar** *a*
ungrateful; (*nicht lohnend*)
thankless. **U~barkeit** *f*
ingratitude

undeutlich *a* indistinct; vague

undicht *a* leaking; **u~e Stelle** leak

Unding *nt* absurdity

undiplomatisch *a* undiplomatic

unduldsam *a* intolerant

undurch|dringlich *a*
impenetrable; <*Miene*>
inscrutable. **u~führbar** *a*
impracticable

undurch|lässig *a* impermeable.
u~sichtig *a* opaque; (*fig*)
doubtful

uneben *a* uneven. **U~heit** *f* -, -en
unevenness; (*Buckel*) bump

unecht *a* false; **u~er Schmuck**
imitation jewellery

unehelich *a* illegitimate

uneinig *a* (*fig*) divided; [**sich**
(*dat*)] **u~ sein** disagree

uneins *a* **u~ sein** be at odds

unempfindlich *a* insensitive
(**gegen** to); (*widerstandsfähig*)
tough; (*Med*) immune

unendlich *a* infinite; (*endlos*)
endless. **U~keit** *f* - infinity

unentbehrlich *a* indispensable

unentgeltlich *a* free, <*Arbeit*>
unpaid ●*adv* free of charge

unentschieden *a* undecided;
(*Sport*) drawn; **u~ spielen** draw.
U~ *nt* -s,- draw

unentschlossen *a* indecisive;
(*unentschieden*) undecided

unentwegt *a* persistent;
(*unaufhörlich*) incessant

unerfahren *a* inexperienced.
U~heit *f* - inexperience

unerfreulich *a* unpleasant
unerhört *a* enormous; (*empörend*) outrageous
unerklärlich *a* inexplicable
unerlässlich *a* essential
unerlaubt *a* unauthorized ● *adv* without permission
unerschwinglich *a* prohibitive
unersetzlich *a* irreplaceable; <*Verlust*> irreparable
unerträglich *a* unbearable
unerwartet *a* unexpected
unerwünscht *a* unwanted; <*Besuch*> unwelcome
unfähig *a* incompetent; u~, etw zu tun incapable of doing sth; (*nicht in der Lage*) unable to do sth. **U~keit** *f* incompetence; inability (zu to)
unfair *a* unfair
Unfall *m* accident. **U~flucht** *f* failure to stop after an accident. **U~station** *f* casualty department
unfassbar *a* incomprehensible
Unfehlbarkeit *f* - infallibility
unfolgsam *a* disobedient
unförmig *a* shapeless
unfreiwillig *a* involuntary; (*unbeabsichtigt*) unintentional
unfreundlich *a* unfriendly; (*unangenehm*) unpleasant. **U~keit** *f* unfriendliness; unpleasantness
Unfriede[n] *m* discord
unfruchtbar *a* infertile; (*fig*) unproductive. **U~keit** *f* infertility
Unfug *m* -s mischief; (*Unsinn*) nonsense
Ungar|(in) *m* -n, -n (*f* -, -nen) Hungarian. **u~isch** *a* Hungarian. **U~n** *nt* -s Hungary
ungeachtet *prep* (+ *gen*) in spite of; **dessen u~** notwithstanding [this]. **ungebraucht** *a* unused. **ungedeckt** *a* uncovered; (*Sport*) unmarked; <*Tisch*> unlaid
Ungeduld *f* impatience. **u~ig** *a* impatient
ungeeignet *a* unsuitable

ungefähr *a* approximate, rough
ungefährlich *a* harmless
ungeheuer *a* enormous. **U~** *nt* -s,- monster
ungehorsam *a* disobedient. **U~** *m* disobedience
ungeklärt *a* unsolved; <*Frage*> unsettled; <*Ursache*> unknown
ungelegen *a* inconvenient
ungelernt *a* unskilled
ungemütlich *a* uncomfortable; (*unangenehm*) unpleasant
ungenau *a* inaccurate; vague. **U~igkeit** *f* -, -en inaccuracy
ungeniert /'ʊnʒeniːɐt/ *a* uninhibited ● *adv* openly
ungenießbar *a* inedible; <*Getränk*> undrinkable
ungenügend *a* inadequate; (*Sch*) unsatisfactory. **ungepflegt** *a* neglected; <*Person*> unkempt.
ungerade *a* <*Zahl*> odd
ungerecht *a* unjust. **U~igkeit** *f* -, -en injustice
ungern *adv* reluctantly
ungesalzen *a* unsalted
Ungeschick|lichkeit *f* clumsiness. **u~t** *a* clumsy
ungeschminkt *a* without make-up; <*Wahrheit*> unvarnished.
ungesetzlich *a* illegal. **ungestört** *a* undisturbed. **ungesund** *a* unhealthy. **ungesüßt** *a* unsweetened. **ungetrübt** *a* perfect
Ungetüm *nt* -s, -e monster
ungewiss *a* uncertain; im Ungewissen sein/lassen be/leave in the dark. **U~heit** *f* uncertainty
ungewöhnlich *a* unusual.
ungewohnt *a* unaccustomed; (*nicht vertraut*) unfamiliar
Ungeziefer *nt* -s vermin
ungezogen *a* naughty
ungezwungen *a* informal; (*natürlich*) natural
ungläubig *a* incredulous
unglaublich *a* incredible, unbelievable

ungleich a unequal; (*verschieden*) different. **U~heit** f - inequality. **u~mäßig** a uneven

Unglück nt -s, -e misfortune; (*Pech*) bad luck; (*Missgeschick*) mishap; (*Unfall*) accident. **u~lich** a unhappy; (*ungünstig*) unfortunate. **u~licherweise** adv unfortunately

ungültig a invalid; (*Jur*) void

ungünstig a unfavourable; (*unpassend*) inconvenient

Unheil nt -s disaster; **U~ anrichten** cause havoc

unheilbar a incurable

unheimlich a eerie; (*gruselig*) creepy; (🄸 *groß*) terrific ● adv eerily; (🄸 *sehr*) terribly

unhöflich a rude. **U~keit** f rudeness

unhygienisch a unhygienic

Uni f -, -s 🄸 university

uni /y'ni:/ inv a plain

Uniform f -, -en uniform

uninteressant a uninteresting

Union f -, -en union

universell a universal

Universität f -, -en university

Universum nt -s universe

unkenntlich a unrecognizable

unklar a unclear; (*ungewiss*) uncertain; (*vage*) vague; **im U~en sein** be in the dark

unkompliziert a uncomplicated

Unkosten pl expenses

Unkraut nt weed; (*coll*) weeds pl; **U~ jäten** weed. **U~vertilgungsmittel** nt weed-killer

unlängst adv recently

unlauter a dishonest; (*unfair*) unfair

unleserlich a illegible

unleugbar a undeniable

unlogisch a illogical

Unmenge f enormous amount/ (*Anzahl*) number

Unmensch m 🄸 brute. **u~lich** a inhuman

unmerklich a imperceptible

unmittelbar a immediate; (*direkt*) direct

unmöbliert a unfurnished

unmodern a old-fashioned

unmöglich a impossible. **U~keit** f - impossibility

Unmoral f immorality. **u~isch** a immoral

unmündig a under-age

Unmut m displeasure

unnatürlich a unnatural

unnormal a abnormal

unnötig a unnecessary

unord|entlich a untidy; (*nachlässig*) sloppy. **U~nung** f disorder; (*Durcheinander*) muddle

unorthodox a unorthodox ● adv in an unorthodox manner

unparteiisch a impartial

unpassend a inappropriate; <*Moment*> inopportune

unpersönlich a impersonal

unpraktisch a impractical

unpünktlich a unpunctual ● adv late

unrealistisch a unrealistic

unrecht a wrong ● n **jdm u~ tun** do s.o. an injustice. **U~** nt wrong; **zu U~** wrongly; **U~ haben** be wrong; **jdm U~ geben** disagree with s.o. **u~mäßig** a unlawful

unregelmäßig a irregular

unreif a unripe; (*fig*) immature

unrein a impure; <*Luft*> polluted; <*Haut*> bad; **ins U~e schreiben** make a rough draft of

unrentabel a unprofitable

Unruh|e f -, -n restlessness; (*Erregung*) agitation; (*Besorgnis*) anxiety; **U~en** (*Pol*) unrest sg. **u~ig** a restless; (*laut*) noisy; (*besorgt*) anxious

uns pron (*acc/dat of* wir) us; (*refl*) ourselves; (*einander*) each other

unsauber a dirty; (*nachlässig*) sloppy

unschädlich a harmless

unscharf *a* blurred
unschätzbar *a* inestimable
unscheinbar *a* inconspicuous
unschlagbar *a* unbeatable
unschlüssig *a* undecided
Unschuld *f* - innocence;
(*Jungfräulichkeit*) virginity. **u~ig**
a innocent
unselbstständig, unselbständig *a*
dependent ● *adv* **u~ denken** not
think for oneself
unser *poss pron* our. **u~e(r,s)**
poss pron ours. **u~erseits** *adv* for
our part. **u~twegen** *adv* for our
sake; (*wegen uns*) because of us,
on our account
unsicher *a* unsafe; (*ungewiss*)
uncertain; (*nicht zuverlässig*)
unreliable; <*Schritte, Hand*>
unsteady; <*Person*> insecure
● *adv* unsteadily. **U~heit** *f*
uncertainty; unreliability;
insecurity
unsichtbar *a* invisible
Unsinn *m* nonsense. **u~ig** *a*
nonsensical, absurd
Unsitt|e *f* bad habit. **u~lich** *a*
indecent
unsportlich *a* not sporty; (*unfair*)
unsporting
uns|re(r,s) *poss pron* = unsere(r,s).
u~rige *poss pron* **der/die/das**
u~rige ours
unsterblich *a* immortal. **U~keit** *f*
immortality
Unsumme *f* vast sum
unsympathisch *a* unpleasant; **er**
ist mir u~ I don't like him
untätig *a* idle
untauglich *a* unsuitable; (*Mil*)
unfit
unten *adv* at the bottom; (*auf der*
Unterseite) underneath; (*eine*
Treppe tiefer) downstairs; (*im*
Text) below; **hier/da u~** down
here/there; **nach u~**
down[wards]; (*die Treppe*
hinunter) downstairs; **siehe u~**
see below

unter *prep* (+ *dat/acc*) under;
(*niedriger als*) below; (*inmitten,*
zwischen) among; **u~ anderem**
among other things; **u~ der**
Woche during the week; **u~ sich**
by themselves
Unter|arm *m* forearm.
U~bewusstsein *nt* subconscious
unterbieten† *vt insep* undercut;
beat <*Rekord*>
unterbinden† *vt insep* stop
unterbrech|en† *vt insep*
interrupt; break <*Reise*>. **U~ung**
f -, -en interruption, break
unterbringen† *vt sep* put;
(*beherbergen*) put up
unterdessen *adv* in the
meantime
Unterdrückung *f* - suppression;
oppression
untere(r,s) *a* lower
untereinander *adv* one below the
other; (*miteinander*) among
ourselves/yourselves/themselves
unterernähr|t *a* undernourished.
U~ung *f* malnutrition
Unterführung *f* underpass;
(*Fußgänger-*) subway
Untergang *m* (*Astr*) setting;
(*Naut*) sinking; (*Zugrundegehen*)
disappearance; (*der Welt*) end
Untergebene(r) *m/f* subordinate
untergehen† *vi sep* (*sein*) (*Astr*)
set; (*versinken*) go under;
<*Schiff:*> go down, sink;
(*zugrunde gehen*) disappear;
<*Welt:*> come to an end
Untergeschoss *nt* basement
Untergrund *m* foundation;
(*Hintergrund*) background.
U~bahn *f* underground [railway]
unterhaken *vt sep* **jdn u~** take
s.o.'s arm; **untergehakt** arm in arm
unterhalb *adv & prep* (+ *gen*)
below
Unterhalt *m* maintenance
unterhalt|en† *vt insep* maintain;
(*ernähren*) support; (*betreiben*)
run; (*erheitern*) entertain; **sich**

u~en talk; (*sich vergnügen*) enjoy oneself. **U~ung** *f* -, -en maintenance; (*Gespräch*) conversation; (*Zeitvertreib*) entertainment

Jnter|haus *nt* (*Pol*) lower house; (*in UK*) House of Commons. **U~hemd** *nt* vest. **U~hose** *f* underpants *pl*. **u~irdisch** *a & adv* underground

Jnterkiefer *m* lower jaw

interkommen† *vi sep* (*sein*) find accommodation; (*eine Stellung finden*) get a job

Jnterkunft *f* -, -künfte accommodation

Unterlage *f* pad; **U~n** papers **Unterlass** *m* ohne **U~** incessantly **Unterlassung** *f* -, -en omission **unterlegen** *a* inferior; (*Sport*) losing; **zahlenmäßig u~** outnumbered (*dat* by). **U~e(r)** *m/f* loser

Unterleib *m* abdomen

unterliegen† *vi insep* (*sein*) lose (*dat* to); (*unterworfen sein*) be subject (*dat* to)

Unterlippe *f* lower lip

Untermiete *f* zur **U~** wohnen be a lodger. **U~r(in)** *m(f)* lodger

unternehm|en† *vt insep* undertake; take <*Schritte*>; **etw/ nichts u~en** do sth/nothing. **U~en** *nt* -s,- undertaking, enterprise (*Betrieb*) concern. **U~er** *m* -s,- employer; (*Bau-*) contractor; (*Industrieller*) industrialist. **u~ungslustig** *a* enterprising

Unteroffizier *m* non-commissioned officer

unterordnen *vt sep* subordinate

Unterredung *f* -, -en talk

Unterricht *m* -[e]s teaching; (*Privat-*) tuition; (*U~sstunden*) lessons *pl*

unterrichten† *vt/i insep* (*haben*) teach; (*informieren*) inform; **sich u~** inform oneself

Unterrock *m* slip

untersagen *vt insep* forbid

Untersatz *m* mat; (*mit Füßen*) stand; (*Gläser-*) coaster

unterscheid|en† *vt/i insep* (*haben*) distinguish; (*auseinander halten*) tell apart; **sich u~en** differ. **U~ung** *f* -, -en distinction

Unterschied *m* -[e]s, -e difference; (*Unterscheidung*) distinction; **im U~ zu** ihm unlike him. **u~lich** *a* different; (*wechselnd*) varying

unterschlag|en† *vt insep* embezzle; (*verheimlichen*) suppress. **U~ung** *f* -, -en embezzlement; suppression

Unterschlupf *m* -[e]s shelter; (*Versteck*) hiding-place

unterschreiben† *vt/i insep* (*haben*) sign

Unter|schrift *f* signature; (*Bild-*) caption. **U~seeboot** *nt* submarine

Unterstand *m* shelter

unterste(r,s) *a* lowest, bottom

unterstehen† *v insep* ● *vi* (*haben*) be answerable (*dat* to); (*unterliegen*) be subject (*dat* to)

unterstellen¹ *vt sep* put underneath; (*abstellen*) store; **sich u~** shelter

unterstellen² *vt insep* place under the control (*dat* of); (*annehmen*) assume; (*fälschlich zuschreiben*) impute (*dat* to)

unterstreichen† *vt insep* underline

unterstütz|en *vt insep* support; (*helfen*) aid. **U~ung** *f* -, -en support; (*finanziell*) aid; (*regelmäßiger Betrag*) allowance; (*Arbeitslosen-*) benefit

untersuch|en *vt insep* examine; (*Jur*) investigate; (*prüfen*) test; (*überprüfen*) check; (*durchsuchen*) search. **U~ung** *f* -, -en examination; investigation; test; check; search. **U~ungshaft** *f* detention on remand

U

Untertan *m* -s & -en, -en subject
Untertasse *f* saucer
Unterteil *nt* bottom (part)
Untertitel *m* subtitle
untervermieten *vt/i insep* (*haben*) sublet
Unterwäsche *f* underwear
unterwegs *adv* on the way; (*außer Haus*) out; (*verreist*) away
Unterwelt *f* underworld
unterzeichnen *vt insep* sign
unterziehen† *vt insep* **etw einer Untersuchung/Überprüfung u~** examine/ check sth; **sich einer Operation/Prüfung u~** have an operation/take a test
Untier *nt* monster
untragbar *a* intolerable
untrennbar *a* inseparable
untreu *a* disloyal; (*in der Ehe*) unfaithful. **U~e** *f* disloyalty; infidelity
untröstlich *a* inconsolable
unübersehbar *a* obvious; (*groß*) immense
ununterbrochen *a* incessant
unveränderlich *a* invariable; (*gleichbleibend*) unchanging
unverändert *a* unchanged
unverantwortlich *a* irresponsible
unverbesserlich *a* incorrigible
unverbindlich *a* non-committal; (*Comm*) not binding ● *adv* without obligation
unverdaulich *a* indigestible
unver|gesslich *a* unforgettable. **u~gleichlich** *a* incomparable. **u~heiratet** *a* unmarried. **u~käuflich** *a* not for sale; <*Muster*> free
unverkennbar *a* unmistakable
unverletzt *a* unhurt
unvermeidlich *a* inevitable
unver|mindert *a* & *adv* undiminished. **u~mutet** *a* unexpected
Unver|nunft *f* folly. **u~nünftig** *a* foolish

unverschämt *a* insolent; (🄳 *ungeheuer*) outrageous. **U~heit** *f* -, -en insolence
unver|sehens *adv* suddenly. **u~sehrt** *a* unhurt; (*unbeschädigt*) intact·
unverständlich *a* incomprehensible; (*undeutlich*) indistinct
unverträglich *a* incompatible; <*Person*> quarrelsome; (*unbekömmlich*) indigestible
unver|wundbar *a* invulnerable. **u~wüstlich** *a* indestructible; <*Person, Humor*> irrepressible; <*Gesundheit*> robust. **u~zeihlich** *a* unforgivable
unverzüglich *a* immediate
unvollendet *a* unfinished
unvollkommen *a* imperfect; (*unvollständig*) incomplete
unvollständig *a* incomplete
unvor|bereitet *a* unprepared. **u~hergesehen** *a* unforeseen
unvorsichtig *a* careless
unvorstellbar *a* unimaginable
unvorteilhaft *a* unfavourable; (*nicht hübsch*) unattractive
unwahr *a* untrue. **U~heit** *f* -, -en untruth. **u~scheinlich** *a* unlikely; (*unglaublich*) improbable; (🄳 *groß*) incredible
unweit *adv* & *prep* (+ *gen*) not far
unwesentlich *a* unimportant
Unwetter *nt* -s,- storm
unwichtig *a* unimportant
unwider|legbar *a* irrefutable. **u~stehlich** *a* irresistible
Unwill|e *m* displeasure. **u~ig** *a* angry; (*widerwillig*) reluctant
unwirklich *a* unreal
unwirksam *a* ineffective
unwirtschaftlich *a* uneconomic
unwissen|d *a* ignorant. **U~heit** *f* - ignorance
unwohl *a* unwell; (*unbehaglich*) uneasy
unwürdig *a* unworthy (*gen* of)

Unzahl f vast number. **unzählig** a innumerable, countless

unzerbrechlich a unbreakable

unzerstörbar a indestructible

unzertrennlich a inseparable

Unzucht f sexual offence; **gewerbsmäßige U~** prostitution

unzüchtig a indecent; <*Schriften*> obscene

unzufrieden a dissatisfied; (*innerlich*) discontented. **U~heit** f dissatisfaction

unzulässig a inadmissible

unzurechnungsfähig a insane. **U~keit** f insanity

unzusammenhängend a incoherent

unzutreffend a inapplicable; (*falsch*) incorrect

unzuverlässig a unreliable

unzweifelhaft a undoubted

üppig a luxuriant; (*überreichlich*) lavish

uralt a ancient

Uran nt -s uranium

Uraufführung f first performance

Urenkel m great-grandson; (*pl*) great-grandchildren

Urgroß|mutter f great-grandmother. **U~vater** m great-grandfather

Urheber m -s,- originator; (*Verfasser*) author. **U~recht** nt copyright

Urin m -s, -e urine

Urkunde f -, -n certificate; (*Dokument*) document

Urlaub m -s holiday; (*Mil, Admin*) leave; **auf U~** on holiday/leave; **U~ haben** be on holiday/leave. **U~er(in)** m -s, - (f -, -nen) holiday-maker. **U~sort** m holiday resort

Urne f -, -n urn; (*Wahl-*) ballot-box

Ursache f cause; (*Grund*) reason; **keine U~!** don't mention it!

Ursprung m origin

ursprünglich a original; (*anfänglich*) initial; (*natürlich*) natural

Urteil nt -s, -e judgement; (*Meinung*) opinion; (*U~sspruch*) verdict; (*Strafe*) sentence. **u~en** vi (*haben*) judge

Urwald m primeval forest; (*tropischer*) jungle

Urzeit f primeval times pl

USA pl USA sg

usw. abbr (**und so weiter**) etc.

utopisch a Utopian

Vakuum /'va:kuʊm/ nt -s vacuum. **v~verpackt** a vacuum-packed

Vanille /va'nɪljə/ f - vanilla

variieren vt/i (*haben*) vary

Vase /'va:zə/ f -, -n vase

Vater m -s,- father. **V~land** nt fatherland

väterlich a paternal; (*fürsorglich*) fatherly. **v~erseits** adv on one's/the father's side

Vater|schaft f - fatherhood; (*Jur*) paternity. **V~unser** nt -s,- Lord's Prayer

v. Chr. abbr (**vor Christus**) BC

Vegetar|ier(in) /vege'ta:riɐ, -jərɪn/ m(f) -s,- (f -, -nen) vegetarian. **v~isch** a vegetarian

Veilchen nt -s, -n violet

Vene /'ve:nə/ f -, -n vein

Venedig /ve'ne:dɪç/ nt -s Venice

Ventil /vɛn'ti:l/ nt -s, -e valve. **V~ator** m -s, -en /-'to:rən/ fan

verabred|en vt arrange; **sich [mit jdm]** **v~en** arrange to meet [s.o.]. **V~ung** f -, -en arrangement; (*Treffen*) appointment

verabschieden vt say goodbye to; (*aus dem Dienst*) retire; pass <Gesetz>; **sich v~** say goodbye

verachten vt despise

Verachtung f - contempt

verallgemeinern vt/i (haben) generalize

veränder|lich a changeable; (*Math*) variable. **v~n** vt change; **sich v~n** change; (*beruflich*) change one's job. **V~ung** f change

verängstigt a frightened, scared

verankern vt anchor

veranlag|t a künstlerisch/ musikalisch **v~t sein** have an artistic/a musical bent; **praktisch v~t** practically minded. **V~ung** f -, -en disposition; (*Neigung*) tendency; (*künstlerisch*) bent

veranlassen vt (reg) arrange for; (*einleiten*) institute; **jdn v~** prompt s.o. (**zu** to)

veranschlagen vt (reg) estimate

veranstalt|en vt organize; hold, give <Party>; make <Lärm>. **V~er** m -s,- organizer. **V~ung** f -, -en event

verantwort|lich a responsible; **v~lich machen** hold responsible. **V~ung** f - responsibility. **v~ungsbewusst** a responsible. **v~ungslos** a irresponsible. **v~ungsvoll** a responsible

verarbeiten vt use; (*Techn*) process; (*verdauen & fig*) digest

verärgern vt annoy

verausgaben (sich) vr spend all one's money

veräußern vt sell

Verb /vɛrp/ nt -s, -en verb

Verband m -[e]s,·̈e association; (*Mil*) unit; (*Med*) bandage; (*Wund-*) dressing. **V~szeug** nt first-aid kit

verbann|en vt exile; (fig) banish. **V~ung** f - exile

verbergen† vt hide; **sich v~** hide

verbesser|n vt improve; (*berichtigen*) correct. **V~ung** f -, -en improvement; correction

verbeug|en (sich) vr bow. **V~ung** f bow

verbeulen vt dent

verbiegen† vt bend

verbieten† vt forbid; (*Admin*) prohibit, ban

verbillig|en vt reduce [in price]. **v~t** a reduced

verbinden† vt connect (**mit** to); (*zusammenfügen*) join; (*verknüpfen*) combine; (*in Verbindung bringen*) associate; (*Med*) bandage; dress <Wunde>; **jdm verbunden sein** (fig) be obliged to s.o.

verbindlich a friendly; (*bindend*) binding

Verbindung f connection; (*Verknüpfung*) combination; (*Kontakt*) contact; (*Vereinigung*) association; **chemische V~** chemical compound; **in V~ stehen/sich in V~ setzen** be/get in touch

verbissen a grim

verbitter|n vt make bitter. **v~t** a bitter. **V~ung** f - bitterness

verblassen vi (sein) fade

Verbleib m -s whereabouts pl

verbleit a <Benzin> leaded

verblüff|en vt amaze, astound. **V~ung** f - amazement

verblühen vi (sein) wither, fade

verbluten vi (sein) bleed to death

verborgen vt lend

Verbot nt -[e]s, -e ban. **v~en** a forbidden; (*Admin*) prohibited

Verbrauch m -[e]s consumption. **v~en** vt use; consume <Lebensmittel>; (*erschöpfen*) use up. **V~er** m -s,- consumer

Verbrechen nt -s,- crime

Verbrecher m -s,- criminal

verbreit|en vt spread. **v~et** a widespread. **V~ung** f - spread; (*Verbreiten*) spreading

verbrenn|en† vt/i (sein) burn; cremate <Leiche>. **V~ung** f -, -en burning; cremation; (Wunde) burn

verbringen† vt spend

verbrühen vt scald

verbuchen vt enter

verbünd|en (sich) vr form an alliance. **V~ete(r)** m/f ally

verbürgen vt guarantee; **sich v~ für** vouch for

Verdacht m -[e]s suspicion; **in** or **im V~ haben** suspect

verdächtig a suspicious. **v~en** vt suspect (gen of). **V~te(r)** m/f suspect

verdamm|en vt condemn; (Relig) damn. **v~t** a & adv ✖ damned; **v~t!** damn!

verdampfen vt/i (sein) evaporate

verdanken vt owe (dat to)

verdau|en vt digest. **v~lich** a digestible. **V~ung** f - digestion

Verdeck nt -[e]s, -e hood; (Oberdeck) top deck

verderb|en† vi (sein) spoil; <Lebensmittel:> go bad ● vt spoil; **ich habe mir den Magen verdorben** I have an upset stomach. **V~en** nt -s ruin. **v~lich** a perishable; (schädlich) pernicious

verdien|en vt/i (haben) earn; (fig) deserve. **V~er** m -s,- wage-earner

Verdienst[1] m -[e]s earnings pl

Verdienst[2] nt -[e]s, -e merit

verdient a well-deserved

verdoppeln vt double

verdorben a spoilt, ruined; <Magen> upset; (moralisch) corrupt; (verkommen) depraved

verdreh|en vt twist; roll <Augen>; (fig) distort. **v~t** a 🗓 crazy

verdreifachen vt treble, triple

verdrücken vt crumple; (🗓 essen) polish off; **sich v~** 🗓 slip away

Verdruss m -es annoyance

verdünnen vt dilute; **sich v~** taper off

verdunst|en vi (sein) evaporate. **V~ung** f - evaporation

verdursten vi (sein) die of thirst

veredeln vt refine; (Hort) graft

verehr|en vt revere; (Relig) worship; (bewundern) admire; (schenken) give. **V~er(in)** m -s,- (f -, -nen) admirer. **V~ung** f - veneration; worship; admiration

vereidigen vt swear in

Verein m -s, -e society; (Sport-) club

vereinbar a compatible. **v~en** vt arrange. **V~ung** f -, -en agreement

vereinfachen vt simplify

vereinheitlichen vt standardize

vereinig|en vt unite; merge <Firmen>; **wieder v~en** reunite; reunify <Land>; **sich v~en** unite; **V~te Staaten [von Amerika]** United States sg [of America]. **V~ung** f -, -en union; (Organisation) organization

vereinzelt a isolated ● adv occasionally

vereist a frozen; <Straße> icy

vereitert a septic

verenden vi (sein) die

verengen vt restrict; **sich v~** narrow; <Pupille:> contract

vererb|en vt leave (dat to); (Biol & fig) pass on (dat to). **V~ung** f - heredity

verfahren† vi (sein) proceed; **v~ mit** deal with ● vr **sich v~** lose one's way ● a muddled. **V~** nt -s,- procedure; (Techn) process; (Jur) proceedings pl

Verfall m decay; (eines Gebäudes) dilapidation; (körperlich & fig) decline; (Ablauf) expiry. **v~en**† vi (sein) decay; <Person, Sitten:> decline; (ablaufen) expire; **v~en in** (+ acc) lapse into; **v~en auf** (+ acc) hit on <Idee>

verfärben (sich) vr change colour; <Stoff:> discolour

verfass|en vt write; (Jur) draw up; (entwerfen) draft. **V~er** m -s,- author. **V~ung** f (Pol) constitution; (Zustand) state

verfaulen vi (sein) rot, decay

verfechten† vt advocate

verfehlen vt miss

verfeinde|n (sich) vr become enemies; **v~t sein** be enemies

verfeinern vt refine; (verbessern) improve

verfilmen vt film

verfluch|en vt curse. **v~t** a & adv 🛈 damned; **v~t!** damn!

verfolg|en vt pursue; (folgen) follow; (bedrängen) pester; (Pol) persecute; **strafrechtlich v~en** prosecute. **V~er** m -s,- pursuer. **V~ung** f - pursuit; persecution

verfrüht a premature

verfügbar a available

verfüg|en vt order; (Jur) decree ● vi (haben) **v~en über** (+ acc) have at one's disposal. **V~ung** f -, -en order; (Jur) decree; **jdm zur V~ung stehen** be at s.o.'s disposal

verführ|en vt seduce; tempt. **V~ung** f seduction; temptation

vergangen a past; (letzte) last. **V~heit** f - past; (Gram) past tense

vergänglich a transitory

vergas|en vt gas. **V~er** m -s,- carburettor

vergeb|en† vt award (an + dat to); (weggeben) give away; (verzeihen) forgive. **v~lich** a futile, vain ● adv in vain. **V~ung** f - forgiveness

vergehen† vi (sein) pass; **sich v~** violate (gegen etw sth). **V~** nt -s,- offence

vergelt|en† vt repay. **V~ung** f - retaliation; (Rache) revenge

vergessen† vt forget; (liegen lassen) leave behind

vergesslich a forgetful. **V~keit** f - forgetfulness

vergeuden vt waste, squander

vergewaltig|en vt rape. **V~ung** f -, -en rape

vergießen† vt spill; shed <Tränen, Blut>

vergift|en vt poison. **V~ung** f -, -en poisoning

Vergissmeinnicht nt -[e]s, -[e] forget-me-not

vergittert a barred

verglasen vt glaze

Vergleich m -[e]s, -e comparison; (Jur) settlement. **v~bar** a comparable. **v~en†** vt compare (mit with/to)

vergnüg|en (sich) vr enjoy oneself. **V~en** nt -s,- pleasure; (Spaß) fun; **viel V~en!** have a good time! **v~t** a cheerful; (zufrieden) happy. **V~ungen** fpl entertainments

vergolden vt gild; (plattieren) gold-plate

vergraben† vt bury

vergriffen a out of print

vergrößer|n vt enlarge; <Linse:> magnify; (vermehren) increase; (erweitern) extend; expand <Geschäft>; **sich v~n** grow bigger; <Firma:> expand; (zunehmen) increase. **V~ung** f -, -en magnification; increase; expansion; (Phot) enlargement. **V~ungsglas** nt magnifying glass

vergüt|en vt pay for; **jdm etw v~en** reimburse s.o. for sth. **V~ung** f -, -en remuneration; (Erstattung) reimbursement

verhaft|en vt arrest. **V~ung** f -, -en arrest

verhalten† (sich) vr behave; (handeln) act; (beschaffen sein) be. **V~** nt -s behaviour, conduct

Verhältnis nt -ses, -se relationship; (Liebes-) affair; (Math) ratio; **V~se** circumstances; conditions. **v~mäßig** adv comparatively, relatively

verhand|eln vt discuss; (Jur) try ● vi (haben) negotiate. **V~lung** f (Jur) trial; **V~lungen** negotiations

Verhängnis nt -ses fate, doom

verhärten vt/i (sein) harden

verhasst a hated

verhätscheln vt spoil

verhauen† vt 🔢 beat; make a mess of <Prüfung>

verheilen vi (sein) heal

verheimlichen vt keep secret

verheirat|en (sich) vr get married (mit to); **sich wieder v~en** remarry. **v~et** a married

verhelfen† vi (haben) jdm zu etw v~ help s.o. get sth

verherrlichen vt glorify

verhexen vt bewitch

verhinder|n vt prevent; **v~t sein** be unable to come

Verhör nt -s, -e interrogation; **ins V~ nehmen** interrogate. **v~en** vt interrogate; **sich v~en** mishear

verhungern vi (sein) starve

verhüt|en vt prevent. **V~ung** f - prevention. **V~ungsmittel** nt contraceptive

verirren (sich) vr get lost

verjagen vt chase away

verjüngen vt rejuvenate

verkalkt a 🔢 senile

verkalkulieren (sich) vr miscalculate

Verkauf m sale; **zum V~** for sale. **v~en** vt sell; **zu v~en** for sale

Verkäufer(in) m(f) seller; (im Geschäft) shop assistant

Verkehr m -s traffic; (Kontakt) contact; (Geschlechts-) intercourse; **aus dem V~ ziehen** take out of circulation. **v~en** vi (haben) operate; <Bus, Zug:> run; (Umgang haben) associate, mix (mit with); (Gast sein) visit (bei jdm s.o.)

Verkehrs|ampel f traffic lights pl. **V~unfall** m road accident. **V~verein** m tourist office. **V~zeichen** nt traffic sign

verkehrt a wrong; **v~ herum** adv the wrong way round; (links) inside out

verklagen vt sue (auf + acc for)

verkleid|en vt disguise; (Techn) line; **sich v~en** disguise oneself; (für Kostümfest) dress up. **V~ung** f -, -en disguise; (Kostüm) fancy dress; (Techn) lining

verkleiner|n vt reduce [in size]. **V~ung** f - reduction

verknittern vt/i (sein) crumple

verknüpfen vt knot together

verkommen† vi (sein) be neglected; (sittlich) go to the bad; (verfallen) decay; <Haus:> fall into disrepair; <Gegend:> become run-down; <Lebensmittel:> go bad ● a neglected; (sittlich) depraved; <Haus> dilapidated; <Gegend> run-down

verkörpern vt embody, personify

verkraften vt cope with

verkrampft a (fig) tense

verkriechen† (sich) vr hide

verkrümmt a crooked, bent

verkrüppelt a crippled; <Glied> deformed

verkühl|en (sich) vr catch a chill. **V~ung** f -, -en chill

verkümmern vi (sein) waste/ <Pflanze:> wither away

verkünden vt announce; pronounce <Urteil>

verkürzen vt shorten; (verringern) reduce; (abbrechen) cut short; while away <Zeit>

Verlag m -[e]s, -e publishing firm

verlangen vt ask for; (fordern) demand; (berechnen) charge. **V~** nt -s desire; (Bitte) request

verlänger|n vt extend; lengthen <Kleid>; (zeitlich) prolong; renew <Pass, Vertrag>; (Culin) thin down. **V~ung** f -, -en extension; renewal. **V~ungsschnur** f extension cable

verlassen† vt leave; (im Stich lassen) desert; **sich v~ auf** (+ acc)

rely or depend on ● a deserted.
V~heit f - desolation
verlässlich a reliable
Verlauf m course; im V~ (+ gen)
in the course of. **v~en†** vi (sein)
run; (ablaufen) go; gut v~en go
[off] well ● vr sich v~en lose
one's way
verlegen vt move; (verschieben)
postpone; (vor-) bring forward;
(verlieren) mislay; (versperren)
block; (legen) lay <Teppich,
Rohre>; (veröffentlichen) publish;
sich v~ auf (+ acc) take up
<Beruf>; resort to <Bitten> ● a
embarrassed. **V~heit** f -
embarrassment
Verleger m -s,- publisher
verleihen† vt lend; (gegen
Gebühr) hire out; (überreichen)
award, confer; (fig) give
verlernen vt forget
verletz|en vt injure; (kränken)
hurt; (verstoßen gegen) infringe;
violate <Grenze>. **v~end** a
hurtful, wounding. **V~te(r)** m/f
injured person; (bei Unfall)
casualty. **V~ung** f -, -en (Verstoß)
infringement; violation
verleugnen vt deny; disown
<Freund>
verleumd|en vt slander;
(schriftlich) libel. **v~erisch** a
slanderous; libellous. **V~ung** f -,
-en slander; (schriftlich) libel
verlieben (sich) vr fall in love (in
+ acc with); verliebt sein be in
love (in + acc with)
verlier|en† vt lose; shed <Laub>
● vi (haben) lose (an etw dat sth).
V~er m -s,- loser
verlob|en (sich) vr get engaged
(mit to); **v~t sein** be engaged.
V~te(r) f fiancée. **V~te(r)** m fiancé.
V~ung f -, -en engagement
verlock|en vt tempt. **V~ung** f
-, -en temptation
verloren a lost; v~ gehen get lost

verlos|en vt raffle. **V~ung** f -, -en
raffle; (Ziehung) draw
Verlust m -[e]s, -e loss
vermachen vt leave, bequeath
Vermächtnis nt -ses, -se legacy
vermähl|en (sich) vr marry.
V~ung f -, -en marriage
vermehren vt increase; propagate
<Pflanzen>; sich v~ increase;
(sich fortpflanzen) breed
vermeiden† vt avoid
Vermerk m -[e]s, -e note. **v~en**
note [down]
vermessen† vt measure; survey
<Gelände> ● a presumptuous
vermiet|en vt let, rent [out]; hire
out <Boot, Auto>; zu v~en to let;
<Boot:> for hire. **V~er** m
landlord. **V~erin** f landlady
vermindern vt reduce
vermischen vt mix
vermissen vt miss
vermisst a missing
vermitteln vi (haben) mediate
● vt arrange; (beschaffen) find;
place <Arbeitskräfte>
Vermittl|er m -s,- agent;
(Schlichter) mediator. **V~ung** f
-, -en arrangement; (Agentur)
agency; (Teleph) exchange;
(Schlichtung) mediation
Vermögen nt -s,- fortune. **v~d** a
wealthy
vermut|en vt suspect; (glauben)
presume. **v~lich** a probable
● adv presumably. **V~ung** f -, -en
supposition; (Verdacht) suspicion
vernachlässigen vt neglect
vernehm|en† vt hear; (verhören)
question; (Jur) examine. **V~ung** f
-, -en questioning
verneigen (sich) vr bow
vernein|en vt answer in the
negative; (ablehnen) reject.
v~end a negative. **V~ung** f -, -en
negative answer
vernicht|en vt destroy; (ausrotten)
exterminate. **V~ung** f -
destruction; extermination

Vernunft *f* - reason

vernünftig *a* reasonable, sensible

veröffentlich|en *vt* publish. **V~ung** *f* -, **-en** publication

verordn|en *vt* prescribe (*dat* for). **V~ung** *f* -, **-en** prescription; (*Verfügung*) decree

verpachten *vt* lease [out]

verpack|en *vt* pack; (*einwickeln*) wrap. **V~ung** *f* packaging; wrapping

verpassen *vt* miss; (🆘 *geben*) give

verpfänden *vt* pawn

verpflanzen *vt* transplant

verpfleg|en *vt* feed: **sich selbst v~en** cater for oneself. **V~ung** *f* - board; (*Essen*) food; **Unterkunft und V~ung** board and lodging

verpflicht|en *vt* oblige; (*einstellen*) engage; (*Sport*) sign; **sich v~en** undertake/(*versprechen*) promise (**zu** to); (*vertraglich*) sign a contract. **V~ung** *f* -, **-en** obligation, commitment

verprügeln *vt* beat up, thrash

Verputz *m* **-es** plaster. **v~en** *vt* plaster

Verrat *m* **-[e]s** betrayal, treachery. **v~en†** *vt* betray; give away <*Geheimnis*>

Verräter *m* **-s,-** traitor

verrech|nen *vt* settle; clear <*Scheck*>; **sich v~nen** make a mistake; (*fig*) miscalculate. **V~nungsscheck** *m* crossed cheque

verreisen *vi* (*sein*) go away; **verreist sein** be away

verrenken *vt* dislocate

verrichten *vt* perform, do

verriegeln *vt* bolt

verringer|n *vt* reduce; **sich v~n** decrease. **V~ung** *f* - reduction; decrease

verrost|en *vi* (*sein*) rust. **v~et** *a* rusty

verrückt *a* crazy, mad. **V~e(r)** *m/f* lunatic, **V~heit** *f* -, **-en** madness; (*Torheit*) folly

verrühren *vt* mix

verrunzelt *a* wrinkled

verrutschen *vt* (*sein*) slip

Vers /fɛrs/ *m* **-es, -e** verse

versag|en *vi* (*haben*) fail ● *vt* **sich etw v~en** deny oneself sth. **V~en** *nt* **-s,-** failure. **V~er** *m* **-s,-** failure

versalzen† *vt* put too much salt in/on; (*fig*) spoil

versamm|eln *vt* assemble. **V~lung** *f* assembly, meeting

Versand *m* **-[e]s** dispatch. **V~haus** *nt* mail-order firm

versäumen *vt* miss; lose <*Zeit*>; (*unterlassen*) neglect; **[es] v~, etw zu tun** fail to do sth

verschärfen *vt* intensify; tighten <*Kontrolle*>; increase <*Tempo*>; aggravate <*Lage*>; **sich v~** intensify; increase; <*Lage:*> worsen

verschätzen (sich) *vr* **sich v~ in** (+ *dat*) misjudge

verschenken *vt* give away

verscheuchen *vt* shoo/(*jagen*) chase away

verschicken *vt* send; (*Comm*) dispatch

verschieb|en† *vt* move; (*aufschieben*) put off, postpone; **sich v~en** move, shift; (*verrutschen*) slip; (*zeitlich*) be postponed. **V~ung** *f* shift; postponement

verschieden *a* different; **v~e** *pl* different; (*mehrere*) various; **V~es** some things; (*dieses und jenes*) various things; **das ist v~** it varies ● *adv* differently; **v~ groß** of different sizes. **v~artig** *a* diverse

verschimmel|n *vi* (*sein*) go mouldy. **v~t** *a* mouldy

verschlafen† *vi* (*haben*) oversleep ● *vt* sleep through

V

<Tag>; sich v~ oversleep ● *a* sleepy

verschlagen† *vt* lose <Seite>; jdm die Sprache/den Atem v~ leave s.o. speechless/take s.o.'s breath away ● *a* sly

verschlechter|n *vt* make worse; sich v~n get worse, deteriorate. V~ung *f* -, -en deterioration

Verschleiß *m* -es wear and tear

verschleppen *vt* carry off; (*entführen*) abduct; spread <Seuche>; neglect <Krankheit>; (*hinausziehen*) delay

verschleudern *vt* sell at a loss

verschließen† *vt* close; (*abschließen*) lock; (*einschließen*) lock up

verschlimmer|n *vt* make worse; aggravate <Lage>; sich v~n get worse, deteriorate. V~ung *f* -, -en deterioration

verschlossen *a* reserved. V~heit *f* - reserve

verschlucken *vt* swallow; sich v~ choke (an + *dat* on)

Verschluss *m* -es,⸚e fastener, clasp; (Koffer-) catch; (Flaschen-) top; (*luftdicht*) seal; (Phot) shutter

verschlüsselt *a* coded

verschmelzen† *vt/i* (sein) fuse

verschmerzen *vt* get over

verschmutz|en *vt* soil; pollute <Luft> ● *vi* (sein) get dirty. V~ung *f* - pollution

verschneit *a* snow-covered

verschnörkelt *a* ornate

verschnüren *vt* tie up

verschollen *a* missing

verschonen *vt* spare

verschossen *a* faded

verschränken *vt* cross

verschreiben† *vt* prescribe; sich v~ make a slip of the pen

verschulden *vt* be to blame for. V~ *nt* -s fault

verschuldet *a* v~ sein be in debt

verschütten *vt* spill; (*begraben*) bury

verschweigen† *vt* conceal, hide

verschwend|en *vt* waste. V~ung *f* - extravagance; (*Vergeudung*) waste

verschwiegen *a* discreet

verschwind|en† *vi* (sein) disappear; [mal] v~ 🔳 spend a penny

verschwommen *a* blurred

verschwör|en† (sich) *vr* conspire. V~ung *f* -, -en conspiracy

versehen† *vt* perform; hold <Posten>; keep <Haushalt>; v~ mit provide with; sich v~ make a mistake. V~ *nt* -s,- oversight; (*Fehler*) slip; aus V~ by mistake. v~tlich *adv* by mistake

Versehrte(r) *m* disabled person

versengen *vt* singe; (*stärker*) scorch

versenken *vt* sink

versessen *a* keen (auf + *acc* on)

versetz|en *vt* move; transfer <Person>; (Sch) move up; (*verpfänden*) pawn; (*verkaufen*) sell; (*vermischen*) blend; jdn v~en (🔳 warten lassen) stand s.o. up; jdm in Angst/Erstaunen v~en frighten/astonish s.o.; sich in jds Lage v~en put oneself in s.o.'s place. V~ung *f* -, -en move; transfer; (Sch) move to a higher class

verseuchen *vt* contaminate

versicher|n *vt* insure; (*bekräftigen*) affirm; jdm v~n assure s.o (dass that). V~ung *f* -, -en insurance; assurance

versiegeln *vt* seal

versiert /vɛrˈziːɐt/ *a* experienced

versilbert *a* silver-plated

Versmaß /ˈfɛrs-/ *nt* metre

versöhn|en *vt* reconcile; sich v~en become reconciled. V~ung *f* -, -en reconciliation

versorg|en *vt* provide, supply (mit with); provide for <Familie>;

(betreuen) look after. **V~ung** f - provision, supply; *(Betreuung)* care

verspät|en (sich) vr be late. **v~et** a late; *<Zug>* delayed; *<Dank>* belated. **V~ung** f - lateness; **V~ung haben** be late

versperren vt block; bar *<Weg>*

verspiel|en vt gamble away. **v~t** a playful

verspotten vt mock, ridicule

versprech|en† vt promise; **sich v~en** make a slip of the tongue; **sich** *(dat)* **viel v~en von** have high hopes of; **ein viel v~ender Anfang** a promising start. **V~en** nt -s,- promise. **V~ungen** fpl promises

verstaatlich|en vt nationalize. **V~ung** f - nationalization

Verstand m -[e]s mind; *(Vernunft)* reason; **den V~ verlieren** go out of one's mind

verständig a sensible; *(klug)* intelligent. **v~en** vt notify, inform; **sich v~en** communicate; *(sich verständlich machen)* make oneself understood. **V~ung** f - notification; communication; *(Einigung)* agreement

verständlich a comprehensible; *(deutlich)* clear; *(begreiflich)* understandable; **sich v~ machen** make oneself understood. **v~erweise** adv understandably

Verständnis nt -ses understanding

verstärk|en vt strengthen, reinforce; *(steigern)* intensify, increase; amplify *<Ton>*. **V~er** m -s,- amplifier. **V~ung** f reinforcement; increase; amplification; *(Truppen)* reinforcements pl

verstaubt a dusty

verstauchen vt sprain

Versteck nt -[e]s, -e hiding-place; **V~ spielen** play hide-and-seek. **v~en** vt hide; **sich v~en** hide

verstehen† vt understand; *(können)* know; **falsch v~** misunderstand; **sich v~** understand one another; *(auskommen)* get on

versteiger|n vt auction. **V~ung** f auction

versteinert a fossilized

verstell|en vt adjust; *(versperren)* block; *(verändern)* disguise; **sich v~en** pretend. **V~ung** f - pretence

versteuern vt pay tax on

verstimm|t a disgruntled; *<Magen>* upset; *(Mus)* out of tune. **V~ung** f - ill humour; *(Magen-)* upset

verstockt a stubborn

verstopf|en vt plug; *(versperren)* block; **v~t** blocked; *<Person>* constipated. **V~ung** f -, -en blockage; *(Med)* constipation

verstorben a late, deceased. **V~e(r)** m/f deceased

verstört a bewildered

Verstoß m infringement. **v~en**† vt disown ● vi *(haben)* **v~en gegen** contravene, infringe

verstreuen vt scatter

verstümmeln vt mutilate; garble *<Text>*

Versuch m -[e]s, -e attempt; *(Experiment)* experiment. **v~en** vt/i *(haben)* try; **v~t sein** be tempted (**zu** to). **V~ung** f -, -en temptation

vertagen vt adjourn; *(aufschieben)* postpone; **sich v~** adjourn

vertauschen vt exchange; *(verwechseln)* mix up

verteidig|en vt defend. **V~er** m -s,- defender; *(Jur)* defence counsel. **V~ung** f -, -en defence

verteil|en vt distribute; *(zuteilen)* allocate; *(ausgeben)* hand out; *(verstreichen)* spread. **V~ung** f - distribution; allocation

vertief|en vt deepen; **v~t sein in** (+ acc) be engrossed in. **V~ung** f -, -en hollow, depression

vertikal /vɛrtiˈkaːl/ a vertical

vertilgen vt exterminate; kill [off] <Unkraut>

vertippen (sich) vr make a typing mistake

vertonen vt set to music

Vertrag m -[e]s,⸚e contract; (Pol) treaty

vertragen† vt tolerate, stand; take <Kritik, Spaß>; **sich v~** get on

vertraglich a contractual

verträglich a good-natured; (bekömmlich) digestible

vertrauen vi (haben) trust (**jdm/ etw** s.o./sth; **auf** + acc in). **V~** nt -s trust, confidence (**zu** in). **im V~** in confidence. **v~swürdig** a trustworthy

vertraulich a confidential; (intim) familiar

vertraut a intimate; (bekannt) familiar. **V~heit** f - intimacy; familiarity

vertreib|en† vt drive away; drive out <Feind>; (Comm) sell; **sich** (dat) **die Zeit v~en** pass the time. **V~ung** f -, -en expulsion

vertret|en† vt represent; (einspringen für) stand in or deputize for; (verfechten) support; hold <Meinung>; **sich** (dat) **den Fuß v~en** twist one's ankle. **V~er** m -s,- representative; deputy; (Arzt-) locum; (Verfechter) supporter. **V~ung** f -, -en representation; (Person) deputy; (eines Arztes) locum; (Handels-) agency

Vertrieb m -[e]s (Comm) sale

vertrocknen vi (sein) dry up

verüben vt commit

verunglücken vi (sein) be involved in an accident; (Ⅰ missglücken) go wrong; **tödlich v~** be killed in an accident

verunreinigen vt pollute; (verseuchen) contaminate

verursachen vt cause

verurteil|en vt condemn; (Jur) convict (**wegen** of); sentence (**zum Tode** to death). **V~ung** f - condemnation; (Jur) conviction

vervielfachen vt multiply

vervielfältigen vt duplicate

vervollständigen vt complete

verwählen (sich) vr misdial

verwahren vt keep; (verstauen) put away

verwahrlost a neglected; <Haus> dilapidated

Verwahrung f - keeping; **in V~ nehmen** take into safe keeping

verwaist a orphaned

verwalt|en vt administer; (leiten) manage; govern <Land>. **V~er** m -s,- administrator; manager. **V~ung** f -, -en administration; management; government

verwandt a transform, change (**in** + acc into) **sich v~eln** change, turn (**in** + acc into). **V~lung** f transformation

verwandt a related (**mit** to). **V~e(r)** m/f relative. **V~schaft** f - relationship; (Menschen) relatives pl

verwarn|en vt warn, caution. **V~ung** f warning, caution

verwechs|eln vt mix up, confuse; (halten für) mistake (**mit** for). **V~lung** f -, -en mix-up

verweigern vt/i (haben) refuse (**jdm etw** s.o sth). **V~ung** f refusal

Verweis m -es, -e reference (**auf** + acc to); (Tadel) reprimand; **v~en†** vt refer (**auf/an** + acc to); (tadeln) reprimand; **von der Schule v~en** expel

verwelken vi (sein) wilt

verwend|en† vt use; spend <Zeit, Mühe>. **V~ung** f use

verwerten vt utilize, use

verwesen vi (sein) decompose

verwick|eln vt involve (in + acc in); **sich v~eln** get tangled up. **v~elt** a complicated

verwildert a wild; <Garten> overgrown; <Aussehen> unkempt

verwinden† vt (fig) get over

verwirklichen vt realize

verwirr|en vt tangle up; (fig) confuse; **sich v~en** get tangled; (fig) become confused. **v~t** a confused. **V~ung** f - confusion

verwischen vt smudge

verwittert a weathered

verwitwet a widowed

verwöhn|en vt spoil. **v~t** a spoilt

verworren a confused

verwund|bar a vulnerable. **v~en** vt wound

verwunder|lich a surprising. **v~n** vt surprise; **sich v~n** be surprised. **V~ung** f - surprise

Verwund|ete(r) m wounded soldier; **die V~eten** the wounded pl. **V~ung** f -, -en wound

verwüst|en vt devastate, ravage. **V~ung** f -, -en devastation

verzählen (sich) vr miscount

verzaubern vt bewitch; (fig) enchant; **v~ in** (+ acc) turn into

Verzehr m -s consumption. **v~en** vt eat

verzeih|en† vt forgive; **v~en Sie!** excuse me! **V~ung** f - forgiveness; **um V~ung bitten** apologize; **V~ung!** sorry! (bei Frage) excuse me!

Verzicht m -[e]s renunciation (auf + acc of). **v~en** vi (haben) do without; **v~en auf** (+ acc) give up; renounce <Recht, Erbe>

verziehen† vt pull out of shape; (verwöhnen) spoil; **sich v~** lose shape; <Holz:> warp; <Gesicht:> twist; (verschwinden) disappear; <Nebel:> pass ● vi (sein) move [away]

verzier|en vt decorate. **V~ung** f -, -en decoration

verzinsen vt pay interest on

verzöger|n vt delay; (verlangsamen) slow down. **V~ung** f -, -en delay

verzollen vt pay duty on; **haben Sie etwas zu v~?** have you anything to declare?

verzweif|eln vi (sein) despair. **v~elt** a desperate. **V~lung** f - despair; (Ratlosigkeit) desperation

verzweigen (sich) vr branch [out]

Veto /'ve:to/ nt -s, -s veto

Vetter m -s, -n cousin

vgl. abbr (vergleiche) cf.

Viadukt /via'dʊkt/ nt -[e]s, -e viaduct

Video /'vi:deo/ nt -s, -s video. **V~kassette** f video cassette. **V~recorder** /-rəkɔrdɐ/ m -s,- video recorder

Vieh nt -[e]s livestock; (Rinder) cattle pl; (🅵 Tier) creature

viel pron a great deal/🅵 a lot of; (pl) many, 🅵 a lot of; (substantivisch) **v~[es]** much, 🅵 a lot; **nicht/so/wie/zu v~** not/so/how/too much/ (pl) many; **v~e** pl many; **das v~e Geld** all that money ● adv much, 🅵 a lot; **v~ mehr/weniger** much more/less; **v~ zu groß/klein** much or far too big/small; **so v~ wie möglich** as much as possible; **so/zu v~ arbeiten** work so/too much

viel|deutig a ambiguous. **v~fach** a multiple ● adv many times; (🅵 oft) frequently. **V~falt** f - diversity, [great] variety

vielleicht adv perhaps, maybe; (🅵 wirklich) really

vielmals adv very much

vielmehr adv rather; (im Gegenteil) on the contrary

vielseitig a varied; <Person> versatile. **V~keit** f - versatility

vielversprechend* a viel versprechend, s. versprechen

vier inv a, **V~** f -, -en four; (Sch) ≈ fair. **V~eck** nt -[e]s, -e oblong,

rectangle; (*Quadrat*) square.
v~eckig a oblong, rectangular;
square. **V~linge** mpl quadruplets
viertel /'fɪrtəl/ *inv a* quarter; **um**
v~ neun at [a] quarter past eight;
um drei v~ neun at [a] quarter to
nine. **V~** nt -s,- quarter; (*Wein*)
quarter litre; **V~ vor/nach sechs**
[a] quarter to/past six. **V~finale**
nt quarter-final. **V~jahr** nt three
months pl; (*Comm*) quarter.
v~jährlich a & adv quarterly.
V~stunde f quarter of an hour
vier|zehn /'fɪr-/ *inv a* fourteen.
v~zehnte(r,s) a fourteenth.
v~zig *inv a* forty. **v~zigste(r,s)** a
fortieth
Villa /'vɪla/ f -, -len villa
violett /vio'lɛt/ a violet
Vio|line /vio'li:nə/ f -, -n violin.
V~linschlüssel m treble clef
Virus /'vi:rʊs/ nt -, -ren virus
Visier /vi'zi:ɐ/ nt -s, -e visor
Visite /vi'zi:tə/ f -, -n round; **V~**
machen do one's round
Visum /'vi:zʊm/ nt -s, -sa visa
Vitamin /vita'mi:n/ nt -s, -e
vitamin
Vitrine /vi'tri:nə/ f -, -n display
cabinet/(*im Museum*) case
Vizepräsident /'fi:tsə-/ m vice
president
Vogel m -s,- bird; **einen V~ haben**
🛈 have a screw loose.
V~scheuche f -, -n scarecrow
Vokabeln /vo'ka:bəln/ fpl
vocabulary sg
Vokal /vo'ka:l/ m -s, -e vowel
Volant /vo'lã:/ m -s, -s flounce
Volk nt -[e]s,-er people sg;
(*Bevölkerung*) people pl
Völker|kunde f ethnology.
V~mord m genocide. **V~recht** nt
international law
Volks|abstimmung f plebiscite.
V~fest nt public festival.
V~hochschule f adult education
classes pl/(*Gebäude*) centre.
V~lied nt folk-song. **V~tanz** m

folk-dance. **v~tümlich** a popular
V~wirt m economist.
V~wirtschaft f economics sg.
V~zählung f [national] census
voll a full (**von** od **mit** of); <*Haar*>
thick; <*Erfolg, Ernst*> complete;.
<*Wahrheit*> whole; **v~ machen** fill
up; **v~ tanken** fill up with petrol
● adv (*ganz*) completely;
<*arbeiten*> full-time; <*auszahlen*>
in full; **v~ und ganz** completely
Vollblut nt thoroughbred
vollende|n vt insep complete. **v~t**
a perfect
Vollendung f completion;
(*Vollkommenheit*) perfection
voller inv a full of
Volleyball /'vɔli-/ m volleyball
vollführen vt insep perform
vollfüllen vt sep fill up
Vollgas nt **V~ geben** put one's
foot down; **mit V~** flat out
völlig a complete
volljährig a **v~ sein** (*Jur*) be of
age. **V~keit** f - (*Jur*) majority
Vollkaskoversicherung f fully
comprehensive insurance
vollkommen a perfect; (*völlig*)
complete
Voll|kornbrot nt wholemeal
bread. **V~macht** f -, -en authority;
(*Jur*) power of attorney. **V~mond**
m full moon. **V~pension** f full
board
vollständig a complete
vollstrecken vt insep execute;
carry out <*Urteil*>
volltanken* vi sep (*haben*) **voll**
tanken, s. **voll**
Volltreffer m direct hit
vollzählig a complete
vollziehen† vt insep carry out;
perform <*Handlung*>;
consummate <*Ehe*>; **sich v~** take
place
Volt /vɔlt/ nt -[s],- volt
Volumen /vo'lu:mən/ nt -s,-
volume
vom prep = **von dem**

von

● *preposition (+ dative)*

! Note that **von dem** can become **vom**

····▶ (*räumlich*) from; (*nach Richtungen*) of. **von hier an** from here on[ward]. **von Wien aus** [starting] from Vienna. **nördlich/südlich von Mannheim** [to the] north/south of Mannheim. **rechts/links von mir** to the right/left of me; on my right/left

····▶ (*zeitlich*) from. **von jetzt an** from now on. **von heute/morgen an** [as] from today/tomorrow; starting today/tomorrow

····▶ (*zur Angabe des Urhebers, der Ursache; nach Passiv*) by. **der Roman ist von Fontane** the novel is by Fontane. **sie hat ein Kind von ihm**. she has a child by him. **er ist vom Blitz erschlagen worden** he was killed by lightning

····▶ (*anstelle eines Genitivs; Zugehörigkeit, Beschaffenheit, Menge etc.*) of. **ein Stück von dem Kuchen** a piece of the cake. **einer von euch** one of you. **eine Fahrt von drei Stunden** a drive of three hours; a three-hour drive. **das Brot von gestern** yesterday's bread. **ein Tal von erstaunlicher Schönheit** a valley of extraordinary beauty

····▶ (*betreffend*) about. **handeln/wissen/erzählen** *od* **reden von …** be/know/talk about …. **eine Geschichte von zwei Elefanten** a story about *or* of two elephants

voneinander *adv* from each other; <*abhängig*> on each other

vonseiten *prep* (+ *gen*) on the part of

vonstatten *adv* **v~ gehen** take place

vor *prep* (+ *dat/acc*) in front of; (*zeitlich, Reihenfolge*) before; (+ *dat*) (*bei Uhrzeit*) to; <*warm, sich fürchten*> of; <*schützen, davonlaufen*> from; <*Respekt haben*> for; **vor Angst zittern** tremble with fear; **vor drei Tagen** three days ago; **vor allen Dingen** above all ● *adv* forward; **vor und zurück** backwards and forwards

Vorabend *m* eve

voran *adv* at the front; (*voraus*) ahead; (*vorwärts*) forward. **v~gehen**† *vi sep* (*sein*) lead the way; (*Fortschritte machen*) make progress. **v~kommen**† *vi sep* (*sein*) make progress; (*fig*) get on

Vor|anschlag *m* estimate. **V~anzeige** *f* advance notice. **V~arbeiter** *m* foreman

voraus *adv* ahead (*dat* of); (*vorn*) at the front; (*vorwärts*) forward ● **im Voraus** in advance. **v~bezahlen** *vt sep* pay in advance. **v~gehen**† *vi sep* (*sein*) go on ahead; **jdm/etw v~gehen** precede s.o./sth. **V~sage** *f* -, -n prediction. **v~sagen** *vt sep* predict

voraussetz|en *vt sep* take for granted; (*erfordern*) require; **vorausgesetzt, dass** provided that. **V~ung** *f* -, -en assumption; (*Erfordernis*) prerequisite

voraussichtlich *a* anticipated, expected ● *adv* probably

Vorbehalt *m* -[e]s, -e reservation

vorbei *adv* past (**an** *jdm/etw* s.o./sth); (*zu Ende*) over. **v~fahren**† *vi sep* (*sein*) drive/go past. **v~gehen**† *vi sep* (*sein*) go past; (*verfehlen*) miss; (*vergehen*) pass; (**I** *besuchen*) drop in (**bei** on)

vorbereit|en *vt sep* prepare; prepare for <*Reise*>; **sich v~en** prepare [oneself] (**auf** + *acc* for). **V~ung** *f* -, -en preparation

vorbestellen *vt sep* order/(*im Theater, Hotel*) book in advance

vorbestraft *a* v∼ sein have a [criminal] record

Vorbeugung *f* - prevention

Vorbild *nt* model. **v∼lich** *a* exemplary, model ● *adv* in an exemplary manner

vorbringen† *vt sep* put forward; offer <*Entschuldigung*>

vordatieren *vt sep* post-date

Vorder|bein *nt* foreleg. **v∼e(r,s)** *a* front. **V∼grund** *m* foreground. **V∼rad** *nt* front wheel. **V∼seite** *f* front; (*einer Münze*) obverse. **v∼ste(r,s)** *a* front, first. **V∼teil** *nt* front

vor|drängeln (sich) *vr sep* Ⓘ jump the queue. **v∼drängen (sich)** *vr sep* push forward. **v∼dringen**† *vi sep* (sein) advance

voreilig *a* rash

voreingenommen *a* biased, prejudiced. **V∼heit** *f* - bias

vorenthalten† *vt sep* withhold

vorerst *adv* for the time being

Vorfahr *m* -en, -en ancestor

Vorfahrt *f* right of way; 'V∼ beachten' 'give way'. **V∼sstraße** *f* ≈ major road

Vorfall *m* incident. **v∼en**† *vi sep* (sein) happen

vorfinden† *vt sep* find

Vorfreude *f* [happy] anticipation

vorführ|en *vt sep* present, show; (*demonstrieren*) demonstrate; (*aufführen*) perform. **V∼ung** *f* presentation; demonstration; performance

Vor|gabe *f* (*Sport*) handicap. **V∼gang** *m* occurrence; (*Techn*) process. **V∼gänger(in)** *m* -s,- (*f* -, -nen) predecessor

vorgehen† *vi sep* (sein) go forward; (*voraus-*) go on ahead; <*Uhr:*> be fast; (*wichtig sein*) take precedence; (*verfahren*) act, proceed; (*geschehen*) happen, go on. **V∼** *nt* -s action

vor|geschichtlich *a* prehistoric. **V∼geschmack** *m* foretaste.

V∼gesetzte(r) *m/f* superior.

v∼gestern *adv* the day before yesterday; **v∼gestern Abend** the evening before last

vorhaben† *vt sep* propose, intend (zu to); **etw v∼** have sth planned. **V∼** *nt* -s,- plan

Vorhand *f* (*Sport*) forehand

vorhanden *a* existing; **v∼ sein** exist; be available

Vorhang *m* curtain

Vorhängeschloss *nt* padlock

vorher *adv* before[hand]

vorhergehend *a* previous

vorherrschend *a* predominant

Vorher|sage *f* -, -n prediction: (*Wetter-*) forecast. **v∼sagen** *vt sep* predict; forecast <*Wetter*>. **v∼sehen**† *vt sep* foresee

vorhin *adv* just now

vorige(r,s) *a* last, previous

Vor|kehrungen *fpl* precautions. **V∼kenntnisse** *fpl* previous knowledge *sg*

vorkommen† *vi sep* (sein) happen; (*vorhanden sein*) occur; (*nach vorn kommen*) come forward; (*hervorkommen*) come out; (*zu sehen sein*) show; **jdm bekannt v∼** seem familiar to s.o.

Vorkriegszeit *f* pre-war period

vorlad|en† *vt sep* (*Jur*) summons. **V∼ung** *f* summons

Vorlage *f* model; (*Muster*) pattern; (*Gesetzes-*) bill

vorlassen† *vt sep* admit; **jdn v∼** Ⓘ let s.o. pass; (*den Vortritt lassen*) let s.o. go first

Vor|lauf *m* (*Sport*) heat. **V∼läufer** *m* forerunner. **v∼läufig** *a* provisional; (*zunächst*) for the time being. **v∼laut** *a* forward. **V∼leben** *nt* past

vorleg|en *vt sep* put on <*Kette*>; (*unterbreiten*) present; (*vorzeigen*) show. **V∼er** *m* -s,- mat; (*Bett-*) rug

vorles|en† *vt sep* read [out]; **jdm v∼en** read to s.o. **V∼ung** *f* lecture

vorletzte(r,s) *a* last … but one;
v~es Jahr the year before last
Vorliebe *f* preference
vorliegen† *vt sep* (*haben*) be
present/(*verfügbar*) available;
(*bestehen*) exist, be
vorlügen† *vt sep* lie (*dat* to)
vormachen *vt sep* put up; put on
⟨*Kette*⟩; push ⟨*Riegel*⟩; (*zeigen*)
demonstrate; **jdm etwas v~** (🇮 *täuschen*) kid s.o.
Vormacht *f* supremacy
vormals *adv* formerly
vormerken *vt sep* make a note of;
(*reservieren*) reserve
Vormittag *m* morning; **gestern/
heute V~** yesterday/this morning.
v~s *adv* in the morning
Vormund *m* -[e]s, -munde &
-münder guardian
vorn *adv* at the front; **nach v~** to
the front; **von v~** from the front/
(*vom Anfang*) beginning; **von v~
anfangen** start afresh
Vorname *m* first name
vorne *adv* = vorn
vornehm *a* distinguished; smart
vornehmen† *vt sep* carry out; **sich**
(*dat*) **v~, etw zu tun** plan to do sth
vornherein *adv* **von v~herein** from
the start
Vor|ort *m* suburb. **V~rang** *m*
priority, precedence (**vor** + *dat*
over). **V~rat** *m* -[e]s, ¨e supply,
stock (**an** + *dat* of). **v~rätig** *a*
available; **v~rätig haben** have in
stock. **V~ratskammer** *f* larder.
V~recht *nt* privilege. **V~richtung**
f device
Vorrunde *f* qualifying round
vorsagen *vt/i sep* (*haben*) recite;
jdm v~ tell s.o. the answer
Vor|satz *m* resolution. **v~sätzlich**
a deliberate; (*Jur*) premeditated
Vorschau *f* preview; (*Film-*)
trailer
Vorschein *m* **zum V~kommen**
appear

Vorschlag *m* suggestion,
proposal. **v~en†** *vt sep* suggest,
propose
vorschnell *a* rash
vorschreiben† *vt sep* lay down;
dictate (*dat* to); **vorgeschriebene
Dosis** prescribed dose
Vorschrift *f* regulation;
(*Anweisung*) instruction; **jdm
V~en machen** tell s.o. what to do.
v~smäßig *a* correct
Vorschule *f* nursery school
Vorschuss *m* advance
vorseh|en† *v sep* ● *vt* intend
(**für/als** for/as); (*planen*) plan; **sich
v~en** be careful (**vor** + *dat* of)
● *vi* (*haben*) peep out. **V~ung** *f* -
providence
Vorsicht *f* - care; (*bei Gefahr*)
caution; **V~!** careful! (*auf Schild*)
'caution'. **v~ig** *a* careful;
cautious. **V~smaßnahme** *f*
precaution
Vorsilbe *f* prefix
Vorsitz *m* chairmanship; **den V~
führen** be in the chair. **V~ende(r)**
m/f chairman
Vorsorge *f* **V~ treffen** take
precautions; make provisions (**für**
for). **v~n** *vi sep* (*haben*) provide
(**für** for)
Vorspeise *f* starter
Vorspiel *nt* prelude. **v~en** *v sep*
● *vt* perform; (*Mus*) play (*dat*
for) ● *vi* (*haben*) audition
vorsprechen† *v sep* ● *vt* recite;
(*zum Nachsagen*) say (*dat* to) ● *vi*
(*haben*) (*Theat*) audition; **bei jdm
v~** call on s.o.
Vor|sprung *m* projection; (*Fels-*)
ledge; (*Vorteil*) lead (**vor** + *dat*
over). **V~stadt** *f* suburb.
V~stand *m* board [of directors];
(*Vereins-*) committee; (*Partei-*)
executive
vorsteh|en† *vi sep* (*haben*)
project, protrude; **einer Abteilung
v~en** be in charge of a
department. **V~er** *m* -s,- head

vorstell|en vt sep put forward <Bein, Uhr>; (darstellen) represent; (bekanntmachen) introduce; **sich v~en** introduce oneself; (als Bewerber) go for an interview; **sich** (dat) **etw v~en** imagine sth. **V~ung** f introduction; (bei Bewerbung) interview; (Aufführung) performance; (Idee) idea; (Phantasie) imagination. **V~ungsgespräch** nt interview

Vorstoß m advance

Vorstrafe f previous conviction

Vortag m day before

vortäuschen vt sep feign, fake

Vorteil m advantage. **v~haft** a advantageous; flattering

Vortrag m -[e]s,-̈e talk; (wissenschaftlich) lecture. **v~en**† vt sep perform; (aufsagen) recite; (singen) sing; (darlegen) present (dat to)

vortrefflich a excellent

Vortritt m precedence; **jdm den V~ lassen** let s.o. go first

vorüber adv v~ sein be over; **an etw** (dat) **v~** past sth. **v~gehend** a temporary

Vor|urteil nt prejudice. **V~verkauf** m advance booking

vorverlegen vt sep bring forward

Vor|wahl[nummer] f dialling code. **V~wand** m -[e]s,-̈e pretext; (Ausrede) excuse

vorwärts adv forward[s]; **v~kommen** make progress; (fig) get on or ahead

vorwegnehmen† vt sep anticipate

vorweisen† vt sep show

vorwiegend adv predominantly

Vorwort nt (pl -worte) preface

Vorwurf m reproach; **jdm Vorwürfe machen** reproach s.o. **v~svoll** a reproachful

Vorzeichen nt sign; (fig) omen

vorzeigen vt sep show

vorzeitig a premature

vorziehen† vt sep pull forward; draw <Vorhang>; (lieber mögen) prefer; favour

Vor|zimmer nt ante-room; (Büro) outer office. **V~zug** m preference; (gute Eigenschaft) merit, virtue; (Vorteil) advantage

vorzüglich a excellent

vulgär /vʊlˈgɛːɐ̯/ a vulgar ● adv in a vulgar way

Vulkan /vʊlˈkaːn/ m -s, -e volcano

Waage f -, -n scales pl; (Astr) Libra. **w~recht** a horizontal

Wabe f -, -n honeycomb

wach a awake; (aufgeweckt) alert; **w~ werden** wake up

Wach|e f -, -n guard; (Posten) sentry; (Dienst) guard duty; (Naut) watch; (Polizei-) station; **W~e halten** keep watch. **W~hund** m guard-dog

Wacholder m -s juniper

Wachposten m sentry

Wachs nt -es wax

wachsam a vigilant. **W~keit** f - vigilance

wachsen† vi (sein) grow

wachs|en² vt (reg) wax. **W~figur** f waxwork

Wachstum nt -s growth

Wächter m -s,- guard; (Park-) keeper; (Parkplatz-) attendant

Wacht|meister m [police] constable. **W~posten** m sentry

wackel|ig a wobbly; <Stuhl> rickety; <Person> shaky. **W~kontakt** m loose connection. **w~n** vi (haben) wobble; (zittern) shake

Wade f -, -n (*Anat*) calf
Waffe f -, -n weapon; **W~n** arms
Waffel f -, -n waffle; (*Eis-*) wafer
Waffen|ruhe f cease-fire.
W~schein m firearms licence.
W~stillstand m armistice
Wagemut m daring
wagen vt risk; **es w~**, **etw zu tun**
dare [to] do sth; **sich w~** (*gehen*)
venture
Wagen m -s,- cart; (*Eisenbahn-*)
carriage, coach; (*Güter-*) wagon;
(*Kinder-*) pram; (*Auto*) car.
W~heber m -s,- jack
Waggon /va'gõː/ m -s, -s wagon
Wahl f -, -en choice; (*Pol, Admin*)
election; (*geheime*) ballot; **zweite**
W~ (*Comm*) seconds pl
wähl|en vt/i (*haben*) choose; (*Pol,*
Admin) elect; (*stimmen*) vote;
(*Teleph*) dial. **W~er(in)** m -s,-
(f -, -nen) voter. **w~erisch** a
choosy, fussy
Wahl|fach nt optional subject.
w~frei a optional. **W~kampf** m
election campaign. **W~kreis** m
constituency. **W~lokal** nt
polling-station. **w~los** a
indiscriminate
Wahl|spruch m motto. **W~urne** f
ballot-box
Wahn m -[e]s delusion; (*Manie*)
mania
Wahnsinn m madness. **w~ig** a
mad, insane; (🆎 *unsinnig*) crazy;
(🆎 *groß*) terrible; **w~ig werden** go
mad ● adv 🆎 terribly. **W~ige(r)**
m/f maniac
wahr a true; (*echt*) real; **du**
kommst doch, nicht w~? you are
coming, aren't you?
während prep (+ gen) during
● conj while; (*wohingegen*)
whereas
Wahrheit f -, -en truth.
w~sgemäß a truthful
wahrnehm|en† vt sep notice;
(*nutzen*) take advantage of;
exploit <*Vorteil*>; look after

<*Interessen*>. **W~ung** f -, -en
perception
Wahrsagerin f -, -nen fortune
teller
wahrscheinlich a probable.
W~keit f - probability
Währung f -, -en currency
Wahrzeichen nt symbol
Waise f -, -n orphan. **W~nhaus** nt
orphanage. **W~nkind** nt orphan
Wal m -[e]s, -e whale
Wald m -[e]s,¨er wood; (*groß*)
forest. **w~ig** a wooded
Walis|er m -s,- Welshman.
w~isch a Welsh
Wall m -[e]s,¨e mound
Wallfahr|er(in) m(f) pilgrim. **W~t**
f pilgrimage
Walnuss f walnut
Walze f -, -n roller. **w~n** vt roll
Walzer m -s,- waltz
Wand f -,¨e wall; (*Trenn-*)
partition; (*Seite*) side; (*Fels-*) face
Wandel m -s change
Wander|er m -s,-, **W~in** f -, -nen
hiker, rambler. **w~n** vi (*sein*)
hike, ramble; (*ziehen*) travel;
(*gemächlich gehen*) wander;
(*ziellos*) roam. **W~schaft** f -
travels pl. **W~ung** f -, -en hike,
ramble. **W~weg** m footpath
Wandlung f -, -en change,
transformation
Wand|malerei f mural. **W~tafel** f
blackboard. **W~teppich** m
tapestry
Wange f -, -n cheek
wann adv when
Wanne f -, -n tub
Wanze f -, -n bug
Wappen nt -s,- coat of arms.
W~kunde f heraldry
war, wäre s. sein[1]
Ware f -, -n article; (*Comm*)
commodity; (*coll*) merchandise;
W~n goods. **W~nhaus** nt
department store. **W~nprobe** f
sample. **W~nzeichen** nt
trademark

warm a warm; <Mahlzeit> hot;
w~ machen heat ● adv warmly;
w~ essen have a hot meal
Wärm|e f - warmth; (Phys) heat;
10 Grad W~e 10 degrees above
zero. w~en vt warm; heat
<Essen, Wasser>. W~flasche f
hot-water bottle
Warn|blinkanlage f hazard
[warning] lights pl. w~en vt/i
(haben) warn (vor + dat of).
W~ung f -, -en warning
Warteliste f waiting list
warten vi (haben) wait (auf + acc
for) ● vt service
Wärter(in) m -s,- (f -, -nen) keeper;
(Museums-) attendant;
(Gefängnis-) warder; (Kranken-)
orderly
Warte|raum, W~saal m
waiting-room. W~zimmer nt
(Med) waiting-room
Wartung f - (Techn) service
warum adv why
Warze f -, -n wart
was pron what ● rel pron that;
alles, was ich brauche all [that] I
need ● indef pron (🅵 etwas)
something; (fragend, verneint)
anything; so was Ärgerliches!
what a nuisance! ● adv 🅵
(warum) why; (wie) how
wasch|bar a washable.
W~becken nt wash-basin
Wäsche f - washing; (Unter-)
underwear
waschecht a colour-fast
Wäscheklammer f clothes-peg
waschen† vt wash; sich w~ have
a wash; W~ und Legen shampoo
and set ● vi (haben) do the
washing
Wäscherei f -, -en laundry
Wäsche|schleuder f spin-drier.
W~trockner m tumble-drier
Wasch|küche f laundry-room.
W~lappen m face-flannel.
W~maschine f washing
machine. W~mittel nt detergent.

W~pulver nt washing-powder.
W~salon m launderette.
W~zettel m blurb
Wasser nt -s water. W~ball m
beach-ball; (Spiel) water polo.
w~dicht a watertight;
<Kleidung> waterproof. W~fall m
waterfall. W~farbe f water-
colour. W~hahn m tap. W~kraft
f water-power. W~kraftwerk nt
hydroelectric power-station.
W~leitung f water-main; aus der
W~leitung from the tap.
W~mann m (Astr) Aquarius
wässern vt soak; (begießen) water
● vi (haben) water
Wasser|ski nt -s water-skiing.
W~stoff m hydrogen. W~straße
f waterway. W~waage f spirit-
level
wässrig a watery
watscheln vi (sein) waddle
Watt nt -s,- (Phys) watt
Watt|e f - cotton wool. w~iert a
padded; (gesteppt) quilted
WC /ve:'tse:/ nt -s, -s WC
web|en vt/i (haben) weave. W~er
m -s,- weaver. W~stuhl m loom
Website /web'sait/ f -s, -s web site
Wechsel m -s,- change; (Tausch)
exchange; (Comm) bill of
exchange. W~geld nt change.
w~haft a changeable. W~jahre
npl menopause sg. W~kurs m
exchange rate. w~n vt change;
(tauschen) exchange ● vi (haben)
change; vary. w~nd a changing;
varying. W~strom m alternating
current. W~stube f bureau de
change
weck|en vt wake [up]; (fig)
awaken ● vi (haben) <Wecker:>
go off. W~er m -s,- alarm [clock]
wedeln vi (haben) wave; mit dem
Schwanz w~ wag its tail
weder conj w~ ... noch neither ...
nor

Weg *m* **-[e]s, -e** way; (*Fuß-*) path; (*Fahr-*) track; (*Gang*) errand; **sich auf den Weg machen** set off

weg *adv* away, off; (*verschwunden*) gone; **weg sein** be away; (*gegangen/verschwunden*) have gone; **Hände weg!** hands off!

wegen *prep* (+ *gen*) because of; (*um ... willen*) for the sake of; (*bezüglich*) about

weg|fahren† *vi sep* (*sein*) go away; (*abfahren*) leave. **w~fallen**† *vi sep* (*sein*) be dropped/(*ausgelassen*) omitted; (*entfallen*) no longer apply. **w~geben**† *vt sep* give away. **w~gehen**† *vi sep* (*sein*) leave, go away; (*ausgehen*) go out. **w~kommen**† *vi sep* (*sein*) get away; (*verloren gehen*) disappear; **schlecht w~kommen** 🛈 get a raw deal. **w~lassen**† *vt sep* let go; (*auslassen*) omit. **w~laufen**† *vi sep* (*sein*) run away. **w~räumen** *vt sep* put away; (*entfernen*) clear away. **w~schicken** *vt sep* send away; (*abschicken*) send off. **w~tun**† *vt sep* put away; (*wegwerfen*) throw away

Wegweiser *m* **-s,-** signpost

weg|werfen† *vt sep* throw away. **w~ziehen**† *v sep* ● *vt* pull away ● *vi* (*sein*) move away

weh *a* sore; **weh tun** hurt; <*Kopf, Rücken:*> ache; **jdm weh tun** hurt s.o.

wehe *int* alas; **w~ [dir/euch]!** (*drohend*) don't you dare!

wehen *vi* (*haben*) blow; (*flattern*) flutter ● *vt* blow

Wehen *fpl* contractions

Wehr¹ *nt* **-[e]s, -e** weir

Wehr² *f* **sich zur W~ setzen** resist. **W~dienst** *m* military service. **W~dienstverweigerer** *m* **-s,-** conscientious objector

wehren (sich) *vr* resist; (*gegen Anschuldigung*) protest; (*sich sträuben*) refuse

wehr|los *a* defenceless. **W~macht** *f* armed forces *pl*. **W~pflicht** *f* conscription

Weib *nt* **-[e]s, -er** woman; (*Ehe-*) wife. **W~chen** *nt* **-s,-** (*Zool*) female. **w~lich** *a* feminine; (*Biol*) female

weich *a* soft; (*gar*) done

Weiche *f* **-, -n** (*Rail*) points *pl*

Weich|heit *f* **-** softness. **w~lich** *a* soft; <*Charakter*> weak. **W~spüler** *m* **-s,-** (*Tex*) conditioner. **W~tier** *nt* mollusc

Weide¹ *f* **-, -n** (*Bot*) willow

Weide² *f* **-, -n** pasture. **w~n** *vt/i* (*haben*) graze

weiger|n (sich) *vr* refuse. **W~ung** *f* **-, -en** refusal

Weihe *f* **-, -n** consecration; (*Priester-*) ordination. **w~n** *vt* consecrate; (*zum Priester*) ordain

Weiher *m* **-s,-** pond

Weihnacht|en *nt* **-s & *pl*** Christmas. **w~lich** *a* Christmassy. **W~sbaum** *m* Christmas tree. **W~slied** *nt* Christmas carol. **W~smann** *m* (*pl* -männer) Father Christmas. **W~stag** *m* **erster/zweiter W~stag** Christmas Day/Boxing Day

Weih|rauch *m* incense. **W~wasser** *nt* holy water

weil *conj* because; (*da*) since

Weile *f* **-** while

Wein *m* **-[e]s, -e** wine; (*Bot*) vines *pl*; (*Trauben*) grapes *pl*. **W~bau** *m* wine-growing. **W~berg** *m* vineyard. **W~brand** *m* **-[e]s** brandy

weinen *vt/i* (*haben*) cry, weep

Wein|glas *nt* wineglass. **W~karte** *f* wine-list. **W~lese** *f* grape harvest. **W~liste** *f* wine-list. **W~probe** *f* wine-tasting. **W~rebe** *f*, **W~stock** *m* vine. **W~stube** *f* wine-bar. **W~traube** *f* bunch of grapes; (*W~beere*) grape

weise *a* wise

Weise *f* -, -n way; (*Melodie*) tune
Weisheit *f* -, -en wisdom.
  W~szahn *m* wisdom tooth
weiß *a*, **W~** *nt* -, -white
weissag|en *vt/i insep* (*haben*)
  prophesy. **W~ung** *f* -, -en
  prophecy
Weiß|brot *nt* white bread. **W~e(r)**
  m/f white man/woman. **w~en** *vt*
  whitewash. **W~wein** *m* white
  wine
Weisung *f* -, -en instruction;
  (*Befehl*) order
weit *a* wide; (*ausgedehnt*)
  extensive; (*lang*) long ● *adv*
  widely; <*offen, öffnen*> wide;
  (*lang*) far; **von w~em** from a
  distance; **bei w~em** by far; **w~**
  und breit far and wide; **ist es noch**
  w~? is it much further? **so w~**
  wie möglich as far as possible; **ich**
  bin so w~ I'm ready; **w~**
  verbreitet widespread; **w~**
  reichende Folgen far-reaching
  consequences
Weite *f* -, -n expanse; (*Entfernung*)
  distance; (*Größe*) width. **w~n** *vt*
  widen; stretch <*Schuhe*>
weiter *a* further ● *adv* further;
  (*außerdem*) in addition;
  (*anschließend*) then; (*leicht*) easily
  go on doing sth; **w~ nichts/**
  niemand nothing/no one else; **und**
  so w~ and so on
weiter|e(r,s) *a* further; **ohne w~es**
  just like that; (*leicht*) easily
weiter|erzählen *vt sep* go on
  with; (*w~sagen*) repeat.
  w~fahren† *vi sep* (*sein*) go on.
  w~geben† *vt sep* pass on. **w~hin**
  adv (*immer noch*) still; (*in*
  Zukunft) in future; (*außerdem*)
  furthermore; **etw w~hin tun** go on
  doing sth. **w~machen** *vi sep*
  (*haben*) carry on
weit|gehend *a* extensive ● *adv* to
  a large extent. **w~sichtig** *a*
  long-sighted; (*fig*) far-sighted.
  W~sprung *m* long jump

w~verbreitet* *a* **w~ verbreitet**, *s.*
  weit
Weizen *m* -s wheat
welch *inv pron* what; **w~ ein(e)**
  what a. **w~e(r,s)** *pron* which; **um**
  w~e Zeit? at what time? ● *rel*
  pron which; (*Person*) who ● *indef*
  pron some; (*fragend*) any; **was für**
  w~e? what sort of?
Wellblech *nt* corrugated iron
Well|e *f* -, -n wave; (*Techn*) shaft.
  W~enlänge *f* wavelength.
  W~enlinie *f* wavy line.
  W~enreiten *nt* surfing.
  W~ensittich *m* -s, -e budgerigar.
  w~ig *a* wavy
Welt *f* -, -en world; **auf der W~** in
  the world; **auf die** *od* **zur W~**
  kommen be born. **W~all** *nt*
  universe. **w~berühmt** *a* world-
  famous. **w~fremd** *a* unworldly.
  W~kugel *f* globe. **w~lich** *a*
  worldly; (*nicht geistlich*) secular
Weltmeister|(in) *m(f)* world
  champion. **W~schaft** *f* world
  championship
Weltraum *m* space. **W~fahrer** *m*
  astronaut
Weltrekord *m* world record
wem *pron* (*dat of* **wer**) to whom
wen *pron* (*acc of* **wer**) whom
Wende *f* -, -n change. **W~kreis** *m*
  (*Geog*) tropic
Wendeltreppe *f* spiral staircase
wenden[1] *vt* (*reg*) turn ● *vi*
  (*haben*) turn [round]
wenden[2]† (& *reg*) *vt* turn; **sich w~**
  turn; **sich an jdn w~** turn/
  (*schriftlich*) write to s.o.
Wend|epunkt *m* (*fig*) turning-
  point. **W~ung** *f* -, -en turn;
  (*Biegung*) bend; (*Veränderung*)
  change
wenig *pron* little; (*pl*) few; **so/zu**
  w~ so/too little/(*pl*) few; **w~e** *pl*
  few ● *adv* little; (*kaum*) not
  much; **so w~ wie möglich** as little
  as possible. **w~er** *pron* less; (*pl*)
  fewer; **immer w~er** less and less

● adv & conj less. **w~ste(r,s)**
least; **am w~sten** least [of all].
w~stens adv at least
wenn conj if; (sobald) when;
immer w~ whenever; **w~ nicht** od
außer w~ unless; **w~ auch** even
though
wer pron who; (🔲 jemand)
someone; (fragend) anyone
Verbe|agentur f advertising
agency. **w~n†** vt recruit; attract
<Kunden, Besucher> ● vi (haben)
w~n für advertise; canvass for
<Partei>. **W~spot** /-sp-/ m
-s, -s commercial
Verbung f - advertising

werden†
● intransitive verb (sein)
····➤ (+ adjective) become; get;
(allmählich) grow. **müde/alt/**
länger werden become or get/
grow tired/old/longer. **taub/**
blind/wahnsinnig werden go
deaf/blind/mad. **blass werden**
become or turn pale. **krank**
werden become or fall ill. **es wird**
warm/dunkel it is getting warm/
dark. **mir wurde schlecht/**
schwindlig I began to feel sick/
dizzy
····➤ (+ noun) become. **Arzt/Lehrer/**
Mutter werden become a doctor/
teacher/mother. **er will Lehrer**
werden he wants to be a teacher.
was ist aus ihm geworden? what
has become of him?
····➤ **werden zu** become; turn into.
das Erlebnis wurde zu einem
Albtraum the experience became
or turned into a nightmare. **zu**
Eis werden turn into ice
● auxiliary verb
····➤ (Zukunft) will; shall. **er wird**
bald hier sein he will or he'll
soon be here. **wir werden sehen**
we shall see. **es wird bald regnen**
it's going to rain soon

····➤ (Konjunktiv) **würde(n)** would.
ich würde es kaufen, wenn ... I
would buy it if .... **würden Sie so**
nett sein? would you be so kind?
····➤ (beim Passiv; pp **worden**) be.
geliebt/geboren werden be loved/
born. **du wirst gerufen** you are
being called. **er wurde gebeten** he
was asked. **es wurde gemunkelt** it
was rumoured. **mir wurde gesagt,**
dass ... I was told that .... **das**
Haus ist soeben/1995 renoviert
worden the house has just been
renovated/was renovated in
1995

werfen† vt throw; cast <Blick,
Schatten>; **sich w~** <Holz:> warp
Werft f -, -en shipyard
Werk nt -[e]s, -e work; (Fabrik)
works sg, factory; (Trieb-)
mechanism. **W~en** nt -s (Sch)
handicraft. **W~statt** f -,-en
workshop; (Auto-) garage.
W~tag m weekday. **w~tags** adv
on weekdays. **w~tätig** a working
Werkzeug nt tool; (coll) tools pl
Wermut m -s vermouth
wert a viel **w~** worth a lot; nichts
w~ sein be worthless; jds **w~ sein**
be worthy of s.o. **W~** m -[e]s, -e
value; (Nenn-) denomination. im
W~ von worth. **w~en** vt rate
Wert|gegenstand m object of
value. **w~los** a worthless.
W~minderung f depreciation.
W~papier nt (Comm) security.
W~sachen fpl valuables. **w~voll**
a valuable
Wesen nt -s,- nature; (Lebe-)
being; (Mensch) creature
wesentlich a essential;
(grundlegend) fundamental ● adv
considerably, much
weshalb adv why
Wespe f -, -n wasp
wessen pron (gen of wer) whose
westdeutsch a West German
Weste f -, -n waistcoat

Westen m -s west

Western m -[s],- western

Westfalen nt -s Westphalia

Westindien nt West Indies pl

westlich a western; <Richtung> westerly ● adv & prep (+ gen) w~lich [von] die Stadt [to the] west of the town. **w~wärts** adv westwards

weswegen adv why

Wettbewerb m -s, -e competition

Wette f -, -n bet; um die W~ laufen race (mit jdm s.o.)

wetten vt/i (haben) bet (auf + acc on); mit jdm w~ have a bet with s.o.

Wetter nt -s,- weather; (Un-) storm. **W~bericht** m weather report. **W~vorhersage** f weather forecast. **W~warte** f -, -n meteorological station

Wett|kampf m contest. **W~kämpfer(in)** m(f) competitor. **W~lauf** m race. **W~rennen** nt race. **W~streit** m contest

Whisky m -s whisky

wichtig a important; w~ nehmen take seriously. **W~keit** f - importance

Wicke f -, -n sweet pea

Wickel m -s,- compress

wickeln vt wind; (ein-) wrap; (bandagieren) bandage; ein Kind frisch w~ change a baby

Widder m -s,- ram; (Astr) Aries

wider prep (+ acc) against; (entgegen) contrary to; w~ Willen against one's will

widerlegen vt insep refute

wider|lich a repulsive. **W~rede** f contradiction; keine W~rede! don't argue!

widerrufen† vt/i insep (haben) retract; revoke <Befehl>

Widersacher m -s,- adversary

widersetzen (sich) vr insep resist (jdm/etw s.o./sth)

widerspiegeln vt sep reflect

widersprechen† vi insep (haben) contradict (jdm/etw s.o./sth)

Wider|spruch m contradiction; (Protest) protest. **w~sprüchlich** a contradictory. **w~spruchslos** ad without protest

Widerstand m resistance; W~ leisten resist. **w~sfähig** a resistant; (Bot) hardy

widerstehen† vi insep (haben) resist (jdm/etw s.o/sth); (anwidern) be repugnant (jdm to s.o.)

Widerstreben nt -s reluctance

widerwärtig a disagreeable

Widerwill|e m aversion, repugnance. **w~ig** a reluctant

widm|en vt dedicate (dat to); (verwenden) devote (dat to); sich w~en (+ dat) devote oneself to. **W~ung** f -, -en dedication

wie adv how; wie viel how much/ (pl) many; um wie viel Uhr? at what time? wie viele? how many wie ist Ihr Name? what is your name? wie ist das Wetter? what is the weather like? ● conj as; (gleich wie) like; (sowie) as well as; (als) when, as; so gut wie as good as; nichts wie nothing but

wieder adv again; jdn/etw w~ erkennen recognize s.o./sth; etw w~ verwenden/verwerten reuse/ recycle sth; etw w~ gutmachen make up for <Schaden>; redress <Unrecht>; (bezahlen) pay for sth

Wiederaufbau m reconstruction

wieder|bekommen† vt sep get back. **W~belebung** f - resuscitation. **w~bringen†** vt sep bring back. **w~erkennen*** vt sep w~ erkennen, s. wieder.

w~geben† vt sep give back, return; (darstellen) portray; (ausdrücken, übersetzen) render; (zitieren) quote. **W~geburt** f reincarnation

Wiedergutmachung f - reparation; (*Entschädigung*) compensation

wiederherstellen vt sep re-establish; restore <*Gebäude*>; restore to health <*Kranke*>

wiederhol|en vt insep repeat; (*Sch*) revise; **sich w~en** recur; <*Person:*> repeat oneself. **w~t** a repeated. **W~ung** f -, -en repetition; (*Sch*) revision

Wieder|hören nt **auf W~hören!** goodbye! **W~käuer** m -s,- ruminant. **W~kehr** f - return; (*W~holung*) recurrence. **w~kommen†** vi sep (sein) come back

wiedersehen* vt sep **wieder sehen**, s. **sehen**. **W~** nt -s,- reunion; **auf W~!** goodbye!

wiedervereinig|en* vt sep **wieder vereinigen**, s. **vereinigen**. **W~ung** f reunification

wieder|verwenden* vt sep **w~ verwenden**, s. **wieder**. **w~verwerten*** vt sep **w~ verwerten**, s. **wieder**

Wiege f -, -n cradle

wiegen¹† vt/i (haben) weigh

wiegen² vt (reg) rock. **W~lied** nt lullaby

wiehern vi (haben) neigh

Wien nt -s Vienna. **W~er** a Viennese ● m -s,- Viennese ● f -,- ≈ frankfurter. **w~erisch** a Viennese

Wiese f -, -n meadow

Wiesel nt -s,- weasel

wieso adv why

wieviel* pron **wie viel**, s. **wie**. **w~te(r,s)** a which; **der W~te ist heute?** what is the date today?

wieweit adv how far

wild a wild; <*Stamm*> savage; **w~er Streik** wildcat strike; **w~ wachsen** grow wild. **W~** nt -[e]s game; (*Rot-*) deer; (*Culin*) venison. **W~e(r)** m/f savage

Wilder|er m -s,- poacher. **w~n** vt/i (haben) poach

Wild|heger, W~hüter m -s,- gamekeeper. **W~leder** nt suede. **W~nis** f - wilderness. **W~schwein** nt wild boar. **W~westfilm** m western

Wille m -ns will

Willenskraft f will-power

willig a willing

willkommen a welcome; **w~ heißen** welcome. **W~** nt -s welcome

wimmeln vi (haben) swarm

wimmern vi (haben) whimper

Wimpel m -s,- pennant

Wimper f -, -n [eye]lash; **W~ntusche** f mascara

Wind m -[e]s, -e wind

Winde f -, -n (*Techn*) winch

Windel f -, -n nappy

winden† vt wind; make <*Kranz*>; **in die Höhe w~** winch up; **sich w~** wind (um round); (*sich krümmen*) writhe

Wind|hund m greyhound. **w~ig** a windy. **W~mühle** f windmill. **W~pocken** fpl chickenpox sg. **W~schutzscheibe** f windscreen. **W~stille** f calm. **W~stoß** m gust of wind. **W~surfen** nt windsurfing

Windung f -, -en bend; (*Spirale*) spiral

Winkel m -s,- angle; (*Ecke*) corner. **W~messer** m -s,- protractor

winken vi (haben) wave

Winter m -s,- winter. **w~lich** a wintry; (*Winter-*) winter ... **W~schlaf** m hibernation; **W~sport** m winter sports pl

Winzer m -s,- winegrower

winzig a tiny, minute

Wipfel m -s,- [tree-]top

Wippe f -, -n see-saw

wir pron we; **wir sind es** it's us

Wirbel m -s,- eddy; (*Drehung*) whirl; (*Trommel-*) roll; (*Anat*)

vertebra; (*Haar-*) crown; (*Aufsehen*) fuss. **w~n** *vt/i* (*sein/haben*) whirl. **W~säule** *f* spine. **W~sturm** *m* cyclone. **W~tier** *nt* vertebrate. **W~wind** *m* whirlwind **wird** *s.* **werden**

wirken *vi* (*haben*) have an effect (**auf** + *acc* on); (*zur Geltung kommen*) be effective; (*tätig sein*) work; (*scheinen*) seem ● *vt* (*Tex*) knit

wirklich *a* real. **W~keit** *f* -, -en reality

wirksam *a* effective

Wirkung *f* -, -en effect. **w~slos** *a* ineffective. **w~svoll** *a* effective

wirr *a* tangled; <*Haar*> tousled; (*verwirrt, verworren*) confused

Wirt *m* -[e]s, -e landlord. **W~in** *f* -, -nen landlady

Wirtschaft *f* -, -en economy; (*Gast-*) restaurant; (*Kneipe*) pub. **w~en** *vi* (*haben*) manage one's finances. **w~lich** *a* economic; (*sparsam*) economical. **W~sgeld** *nt* housekeeping [money]. **W~sprüfer** *m* auditor

Wirtshaus *nt* inn; (*Kneipe*) pub

wischen *vt/i* (*haben*) wipe; wash <*Fußboden*>

wissen† *vt/i* (*haben*) know; **weißt du noch?** do you remember? **nichts w~ wollen von** not want anything to do with. **W~** *nt* -s knowledge; **meines W~s** to my knowledge

Wissenschaft *f* -, -en science. **W~ler** *m* -s,- academic; (*Natur-*) scientist. **w~lich** *a* academic; scientific

wissenswert *a* worth knowing

wittern *vt* scent; (*ahnen*) sense. **W~ung** *f* -, scent; (*Wetter*) weather

Witwe *f* -, -n widow. **W~r** *m* -s,- widower

Witz *m* -es, -e joke; (*Geist*) wit. **W~bold** *m* -[e]s, -e joker. **w~ig** *a* funny; witty

wo *adv* where; (*als*) when; (*irgendwo*) somewhere; **wo immer** wherever; (*obwohl*) although; (*wenn*) if

woanders *adv* somewhere else

wobei *adv* how; (*relativ*) during the course of which

Woche *f* -, -n week. **W~nende** *nt* weekend. **W~nkarte** *f* weekly ticket. **w~nlang** *adv* for weeks. **W~ntag** *m* day of the week; (*Werktag*) weekday. **w~ntags** *adv* on weekdays

wöchentlich *a & adv* weekly

Wodka *m* -s vodka

wofür *adv* what ... for; (*relativ*) for which

Woge *f* -, -n wave

woher *adv* where from; **woher weißt du das?** how do you know that? **wohin** *adv* where [to]; **wohin gehst du?** where are you going?

wohl *adv* well; (*vermutlich*) probably; (*etwa*) about; (*zwar*) perhaps; **w~ kaum** hardly; **sich w~ fühlen** feel well/(*behaglich*) comfortable; **jdm w~ tun** do s.o. good. **W~** *nt* -[e]s welfare, well-being; **zum W~** (+ *gen*) for the good of; **zum W~!** cheers!

Wohl|befinden *nt* well-being. **W~behagen** *nt* feeling of well-being. **W~ergehen** *nt* -s welfare. **w~erzogen** *a* well brought-up

Wohlfahrt *f* - welfare. **W~sstaat** *m* Welfare State

wohl|habend *a* prosperous, well-to-do. **w~ig** *a* comfortable. **w~schmeckend** *a* tasty

Wohlstand *m* prosperity. **W~sgesellschaft** *f* affluent society

Wohltat *f* [act of] kindness; (*Annehmlichkeit*) treat; (*Genuss*) bliss

Wohltät|er *m* benefactor. **w~ig** *a* charitable

wohl|tuend *a* agreeable. **w~tun***
vi sep (*haben*) **w~ tun**, *s.* **wohl**
Wohlwollen *nt* -s goodwill;
(*Gunst*) favour. **w~d** *a*
benevolent

Wohn|block *m* block of flats.
w~en *vi* (*haben*) live;
(*vorübergehend*) stay. **W~gegend**
f residential area. **w~haft** *a*
resident. **W~haus** *nt* house.
W~heim *nt* hostel; (*Alten-*)
home. **w~lich** *a* comfortable.
W~mobil *nt* -s, -e camper. **W~ort**
m place of residence. **W~sitz** *m*
place of residence

Wohnung *f* -, -en flat; (*Unterkunft*)
accommodation. **W~snot** *f*
housing shortage

Wohn|wagen *m* caravan.
W~zimmer *nt* living-room
wölb|en *vt* curve; arch <*Rücken*>.
W~ung *f* -, -en curve; (*Archit*)
vault
Wolf *m* -[e]s,¨e wolf; (*Fleisch-*)
mincer; (*Reiß-*) shredder
Wolk|e *f* -, -n cloud. **W~enbruch**
m cloudburst. **W~enkratzer** *m*
skyscraper. **w~enlos** *a* cloudless.
w~ig *a* cloudy
Woll|decke *f* blanket. **W~e** *f* -, -n
wool

wollen†¹
● *auxiliary verb*
····▸ (*den Wunsch haben*) want to.
ich will nach Hause gehen I want
to go home. **ich wollte Sie fragen,
ob ...** I wanted to ask you if ...
····▸ (*im Begriff sein*) be about to.
wir wollten gerade gehen we were
just about to go
····▸ (*sich in der gewünschten
Weise verhalten*) will not. **will nicht
refuses to. der Motor will nicht
ansprechen** the engine won't *or*
refuses to start
● *intransitive verb*

····▸ want to. **ob du willst oder nicht**
whether you want to or not.
ganz wie du willst just as you like
····▸ (🛈 *irgendwohin zu gehen
wünschen*) **ich will nach Hause** I
want to go home. **zu wem wollen
Sie?** who[m] do you want to
see?
····▸ (🛈 *funktionieren*) will not. **will nicht**
won't go. **meine Beine wollen
nicht mehr** my legs are giving up
🛈
● *transitive verb*
····▸ want; (*beabsichtigen*) intend.
er will nicht, dass du ihm hilfst he
does not want you to help him.
das habe ich nicht gewollt I never
intended *or* meant that to
happen

wollen² *a* woollen. **w~ig** *a*
woolly. **W~sachen** *fpl* woollens.
womit *adv* what ... with; (*relativ*)
with which. **wonach** *adv* what ...
after/<*suchen*> for/<*riechen*> of;
(*relativ*) after/for/of which
woran *adv* what ... on/<*denken,
sterben*> of; (*relativ*) on/of which;
woran hast du ihn erkannt? how
did you recognize him? **worauf**
adv what ... on/<*warten*> for;
(*relativ*) on/for which;
(*woraufhin*) whereupon. **woraus**
adv what ... from; (*relativ*) from
which
Wort *nt* -[e]s,¨er & -e word; **jdm ins
W~ fallen** interrupt s.o.
Wörterbuch *nt* dictionary
Wort|führer *m* spokesman.
w~getreu *a* & *adv* word-for-
word. **w~karg** *a* taciturn. **W~laut**
m wording
wörtlich *a* literal; (*wortgetreu*)
word-for-word
wort|los *a* silent ● *adv* without a
word. **W~schatz** *m* vocabulary.
W~spiel *nt* pun, play on words
worüber *adv* what ... over/<*lachen,
sprechen*> about; (*relativ*) over/

about which. **worum** adv what … round/<bitten, kämpfen> for; (relativ) round/for which; **worum geht es?** what is it about? **wovon** adv what … from/<sprechen> about; (relativ) from/about which. **wovor** adv what … in front of; <sich fürchten> what … of; (relativ) in front of which; of which. **wozu** adv what … to/ <brauchen, benutzen> for; (relativ) to/for which; **wozu?** what for?

Wrack nt -s, -s wreck

wringen† vt wring

Wucher|preis m extortionate price. **W~ung** f -, -en growth

Wuchs m -es growth; (Gestalt) stature

Wucht f - force

wühlen vi (haben) rummage; (in der Erde) burrow ● vt dig

Wulst m -[e]s,̈e bulge; (Fett-) roll

wund a sore; **w~ reiben** chafe; **sich w~ liegen** get bedsores. **W~brand** m gangrene

Wunde f -, -n wound

Wunder nt -s,- wonder, marvel; (übernatürliches) miracle; **kein W~!** no wonder! **w~bar** a miraculous; (herrlich) wonderful. **W~kind** nt infant prodigy. **w~n** vt surprise; **sich w~n** be surprised (über + acc at). **w~schön** a beautiful

Wundstarrkrampf m tetanus

Wunsch m -[e]s,̈e wish; (Verlangen) desire; (Bitte) request

wünschen vt want; **sich** (dat) **etw w~** want sth; (bitten um) ask for sth; **jdm Glück/gute Nacht w~** wish s.o. luck/good night; **Sie w~?** can I help you? **w~swert** a desirable

Wunschkonzert nt musical request programme

wurde, würde s. werden

Würde f -, -n dignity; (Ehrenrang) honour. **w~los** a undignified.

W~nträger m dignitary. **w~voll** a dignified ● adv with dignity

würdig a dignified; (wert) worthy

Wurf m -[e]s,̈e throw; (Junge) litter

Würfel m -s,- cube; (Spiel-) dice; (Zucker-) lump. **w~n** vi (haben) throw the dice; **w~n um** play dice for ● vt throw; (in Würfel schneiden) dice. **W~zucker** m cube sugar

würgen vt choke ● vi (haben) retch; choke (an + dat on)

Wurm m -[e]s,̈er worm; (Made) maggot. **w~en** vi (haben) jdn **w~en** 𝔽 rankle [with s.o.]

Wurst f -,̈e sausage; **das ist mir W~** 𝔽 I couldn't care less

Würze f -, -n spice; (Aroma) aroma

Wurzel f -, -n root; **W~n schlagen** take root. **w~n** vi (haben) root

würz|en vt season. **w~ig** a tasty; (aromatisch) aromatic; (pikant) spicy

wüst a chaotic; (wirr) tangled; (öde) desolate; (wild) wild; (schlimm) terrible

Wüste f -, -n desert

Wut f - rage, fury. **W~anfall** m fit of rage

wüten vi (haben) rage. **w~d** a furious; **w~d machen** infuriate

x /ɪks/ inv a (Math) x; 𝔽 umpteen. **X-Beine** ntpl knock-knees. **x-beinig, X-beinig** a knock-kneed. **x-beliebig** a 𝔽 any. **x-mal** adv 𝔽 umpteen times

Yoga /'jo:ga/ *m & nt* -[s] yoga

Zack|e *f* -, -n point; (*Berg-*) peak; (*Gabel-*) prong. **z~ig** *a* jagged; (*gezackt*) serrated

zaghaft *a* timid; (*zögernd*) tentative

zäh *a* tough; (*hartnäckig*) tenacious. **z~flüssig** *a* viscous; <*Verkehr*> slow-moving. **Z~igkeit** *f* - toughness; tenacity

Zahl *f* -, -en number; (*Ziffer, Betrag*) figure

zahlen *vt/i* (*haben*) pay; (*bezahlen*) pay for; **bitte z~!** the bill please!

zählen *vi* (*haben*) count; **z~ zu** (*fig*) be one/(*pl*) some of ● *vt* count; **z~ zu** add to; (*fig*) count among

zahlenmäßig *a* numerical

Zähler *m* -s,- meter

Zahl|grenze *f* fare-stage. **Z~karte** *f* paying-in slip. **z~los** *a* countless. **z~reich** *a* numerous; <*Anzahl, Gruppe*> large ● *adv* in large numbers. **Z~ung** *f* -, -en payment; **in Z~ung nehmen** take in part-exchange

Zählung *f* -, -en count

Zahlwort *nt* (*pl* -wörter) numeral

zahm *a* tame

zähmen *vt* tame; (*fig*) restrain

Zahn *m* -[e]s,-̈e tooth; (*am Zahnrad*) cog. **Z~arzt** *m*, **Z~ärztin** *f* dentist. **Z~belag** *m* plaque. **Z~bürste** *f* toothbrush. **Z~fleisch** *nt* gums *pl*. **z~los** *a* toothless. **Z~pasta** *f* -, -en toothpaste. **Z~rad** *nt* cog-wheel. **Z~schmelz** *m* enamel. **Z~schmerzen** *mpl* toothache *sg*. **Z~spange** *f* brace. **Z~stein** *m* tartar. **Z~stocher** *m* -s,- toothpick

Zange *f* -, -n pliers *pl*; (*Kneif-*) pincers *pl*; (*Kohlen-, Zucker-*) tongs *pl*; (*Geburts-*) forceps *pl*

Zank *m* -[e]s squabble. **z~en** *vr* **sich z~en** squabble

Zäpfchen *nt* -s,- (*Anat*) uvula; (*Med*) suppository

zapfen *vt* tap, draw. **Z~streich** *m* (*Mil*) tattoo

Zapf|hahn *m* tap. **Z~säule** *f* petrol-pump

zappeln *vi* (*haben*) wriggle; <*Kind:*> fidget

zart *a* delicate; (*weich, zärtlich*) tender; (*sanft*) gentle. **Z~gefühl** *nt* tact

zärtlich *a* tender; (*liebevoll*) loving. **Z~keit** *f* -, -en tenderness; (*Liebkosung*) caress

Zauber *m* -s magic; (*Bann*) spell. **Z~er** *m* -s,- magician. **z~haft** *a* enchanting. **Z~künstler** *m* conjuror. **z~n** *vi* (*haben*) do magic; (*Zaubertricks ausführen*) do conjuring tricks ● *vt* produce as if by magic. **Z~stab** *m* magic wand. **Z~trick** *m* conjuring trick

Zaum *m* -[e]s,Zäume bridle

Zaun *m* -[e]s,Zäune fence

z.B. *abbr* (**zum Beispiel**) e.g.

Zebra *nt* -s, -s zebra. **Z~streifen** *m* zebra crossing

Zeche *f* -, -n bill; (*Bergwerk*) pit

zechen *vi* (*haben*) Ⓘ drink

Zeder *f* -, -n cedar

Zeh *m* -[e]s, -en toe. **Z~e** *f* -, -n toe; (*Knoblauch-*) clove

Z

zehn inv a, **Z~** f -, -en ten. **z~te(r,s)** a tenth. **Z~tel** nt -s,- tenth

Zeichen nt -s,- sign; (Signal) signal. **Z~setzung** f - punctuation. **Z~trickfilm** m cartoon

zeichn|en vt/i (haben) draw; (kenn-) mark; (unter-) sign. **Z~ung** f -, -en drawing

Zeige|finger m index finger. **z~n** vt show; **sich z~n** appear; (sich herausstellen) become clear ● vi (haben) point (auf + acc to). **Z~r** m -s,- pointer; (Uhr-) hand

Zeile f -, -n line; (Reihe) row

Zeit f -, -en time; **sich** (dat) **Z~ lassen** take one's time; **es hat Z~** there's no hurry; **mit der Z~** in time; **in nächster Z~** in the near future; **zur Z~** (rechtzeitig) in time; *(derzeit) s.* **zurzeit**; **eine Z~ lang** for a time or while

Zeit|alter nt age, era. **z~gemäß** a modern, up-to-date. **Z~genosse** m, **Z~genossin** f contemporary. **z~genössisch** a contemporary. **z~ig** a & adv early

zeitlich a <Dauer> in time; <Folge> chronological. ● adv **z~ begrenzt** for a limited time

zeit|los a timeless. **Z~lupe** f slow motion. **Z~punkt** m time. **z~raubend** a time-consuming. **Z~raum** m period. **Z~schrift** f magazine, periodical.

Zeitung f -, -en newspaper. **Z~spapier** nt newspaper

Zeit|verschwendung f waste of time. **Z~vertreib** m pastime. **z~weise** adv at times. **Z~wort** nt (pl -wörter) verb. **Z~zünder** m time fuse

Zelle f -, -n cell; (Telefon-) box

Zelt nt -[e]s, -e tent; (Fest-) marquee. **z~en** vi (haben) camp. **Z~en** nt -s camping. **Z~plane** f tarpaulin. **Z~platz** m campsite

Zement m -[e]s cement

zen|sieren vt (Sch) mark; censor <Presse, Film>. **Z~sur** f -, -en (Sch) mark; (Presse-) censorship

Zentimeter m & nt centimetre. **Z~maß** nt tape-measure

Zentner m -s,- [metric] hundredweight (50 kg)

zentral a central. **Z~e** f -, -n central office; (Partei-) headquarters pl; (Teleph) exchange. **Z~heizung** f central heating

Zentrum nt -s, -tren centre

zerbrech|en† vt/i (sein) break. **z~lich** a fragile

zerdrücken vt crush

Zeremonie f -, -n ceremony

Zerfall m disintegration; (Verfall) decay. **z~en†** vi (sein) disintegrate; (verfallen) decay

zergehen† vi (sein) melt; (sich auflösen) dissolve

zerkleinern vt chop/(schneiden) cut up; (mahlen) grind

zerknüllen vt crumple [up]

zerkratzen vt scratch

zerlassen† vt melt

zerlegen vt take to pieces, dismantle; (zerschneiden) cut up; (tranchieren) carve

zerlumpt a ragged

zermalmen vt crush

zermürben vt (fig) wear down

zerplatzen vi (sein) burst

zerquetschen vt squash; crush

Zerrbild nt caricature

zerreißen† vt tear; (in Stücke) tear up; break <Faden, Seil> ● vi (sein) tear; break

zerren vt drag; pull <Muskel> ● vi (haben) pull (**an** + dat at)

zerrissen a torn

zerrütten vt ruin, wreck; shatter <Nerven>

zerschlagen† vt smash; smash up <Möbel>; **sich z~** (fig) fall through; <Hoffnung:> be dashed

zerschmettern vt/i (sein) smash

zerschneiden† vt cut; (in Stücke) cut up

zersplittern vi (sein) splinter; <Glas:> shatter ● vt shatter

zerspringen† vi (sein) shatter; (bersten) burst

Zerstäuber m -s,- atomizer

zerstör|en vt destroy; (zunichte machen) wreck. **Z~er** m -s,- destroyer. **Z~ung** f destruction

zerstreu|en vt scatter; disperse <Menge>; dispel <Zweifel>; **sich z~en** disperse; (sich unterhalten) amuse oneself. **z~t** a absent-minded

Zertifikat nt -[e]s, -e certificate

zertrümmern vt smash [up]; wreck <Gebäude, Stadt>

Zettel m -s,- piece of paper; (Notiz) note; (Bekanntmachung) notice

Zeug nt -s 🛈 stuff; (Sachen) things pl; (Ausrüstung) gear; **dummes Z~** nonsense

Zeuge m -n, -n witness. **z~n** vi (haben) testify; **z~n von** (fig) show ● vt father. **Z~naussage** f testimony. **Z~nstand** m witness box

Zeugin f -, -nen witness

Zeugnis nt -ses, -se certificate; (Sch) report; (Referenz) reference; (fig: Beweis) evidence

Zickzack m -[e]s, -e zigzag

Ziege f -, -n goat

Ziegel m -s,- brick; (Dach-) tile. **Z~stein** m brick

ziehen† vt pull; (sanfter; zücken; zeichnen) draw; (heraus-) pull out; extract <Zahn>; raise <Hut>; put on <Bremse>; move <Schachfigur>; (dehnen) stretch; make <Grimasse, Scheitel>; (züchten) breed; grow <Rosen>; **nach sich z~** (fig) entail ● vr **sich z~** (sich erstrecken) run; (sich verziehen) warp ● vi (haben) pull (an + dat on/at); <Tee, Ofen:> draw; (Culin) simmer; **es zieht**

there is a draught; **solche Filme z~ nicht mehr** films like that are no longer popular ● vi (sein) (um-) move (nach to): <Menge:> march; <Vögel:> migrate; <Wolken, Nebel:> drift

Ziehharmonika f accordion

Ziehung f -, -en draw

Ziel nt -[e]s, -e destination; (Sport) finish; (Z~scheibe & Mil) target; (Zweck) aim, goal. **z~bewusst** a purposeful. **z~en** vi (haben) aim (auf + acc at). **z~los** a aimless. **Z~scheibe** f target

ziemlich a 🛈 fair ● adv rather, fairly

Zier|de f -, -n ornament. **z~en** vt adorn

zierlich a dainty

Ziffer f -, -n figure, digit; (Zahlzeichen) numeral. **Z~blatt** nt dial

Zigarette f -, -n cigarette

Zigarre f -, -n cigar

Zigeuner(in) m -s,- (f -, -nen) gypsy

Zimmer nt -s,- room. **Z~mädchen** nt chambermaid. **Z~mann** m (pl -leute) carpenter. **Z~nachweis** m accommodation bureau. **Z~pflanze** f house plant

Zimt m -[e]s cinnamon

Zink nt -s zinc

Zinn m -s tin; (Gefäße) pewter

Zins|en mpl interest sg; **Z~en tragen** earn interest. **Z~eszins** m -es, -en compound interest. **Z~fuß** m, **Z~satz** m interest rate

Zipfel m -s,- corner; (Spitze) point

zirka adv about

Zirkel m -s,- [pair of] compasses pl; (Gruppe) circle

Zirkul|ation /-'tsi̯o:n/ f - circulation. **z~ieren** vi (sein) circulate

Zirkus m -, -se circus

zirpen vi (haben) chirp

zischen vi (haben) hiss; <Fett:> sizzle ● vt hiss

Z

Zit|at nt -[e]s, -e quotation.
z~ieren vt/i (haben) quote
Zitr|onat nt -[e]s candied lemon-peel. **Z~one** f -, -n lemon
zittern vi (haben) tremble; (vor Kälte) shiver; (beben) shake
zittrig a shaky
Zitze f -, -n teat
zivil a civilian; <Ehe, Recht> civil. **Z~** nt -s civilian clothes pl.
Z~dienst m community service
Zivili|sation /-'ts:io:n/ f -, -en civilization. **z~sieren** vt civilize.
z~siert a civilized ● adv in a civilized manner
Zivilist m -en, -en civilian
zögern vi (haben) hesitate. **Z~** nt -s hesitation. **z~d** a hesitant
Zoll¹ m -[e]s,- inch
Zoll² m -[e]s,¨e [customs] duty; (Behörde) customs pl.
Z~abfertigung f customs clearance. **Z~beamte(r)** m customs officer. **z~frei** a & adv duty-free. **Z~kontrolle** f customs check
Zone f -, -n zone
Zoo m -s, -s zoo
zoologisch a zoological
Zopf m -[e]s,¨e plait
Zorn m -[e]s anger. **z~ig** a angry

zu
● preposition (+ dative)
! Note that **zu dem** can become **zum** and **zu der** zur
····➤ (Richtung) to; (bei Beruf) into. **wir gehen zur Schule** we are going to school. **ich muss zum Arzt** I must go to the doctor's. **zu ... hin** towards. **er geht zum Theater/Militär** he is going into the theatre/army
····➤ (zusammen mit) with. **zu dem Käse gab es Wein** there was wine with the cheese. **zu etw passen** go with sth
····➤ (räumlich; zeitlich) at. **zu Hause** at home. **zu ihren Füßen** at her feet. **zu Ostern** at Easter. **zur Zeit** (+ gen) at the time of
····➤ (preislich) at; for. **zum halben Preis** at half price. **das Stück zu zwei Mark** at or for two marks each. **eine Marke zu 60 Pfennig** a 60-pfennig stamp
····➤ (Zweck, Anlass) for. **zu diesem Zweck** for this purpose. **zum Spaß** for fun. **zum Lesen** for reading. **zum Geburtstag bekam ich ...** for my birthday I got .... **zum ersten Mal** for the first time
····➤ (Art und Weise) **zu meinem Erstaunen/Entsetzen** to my surprise/horror. **zu Fuß/Pferde** on foot/horseback. **zu Dutzenden** by the dozen. **wir waren zu dritt/viert** there were three/four of us
····➤ (Zahlenverhältnis) to. **es steht 5 zu 3** the score is 5–3
····➤ (Ziel, Ergebnis) into. **zu etw werden** turn into sth
····➤ (gegenüber) to; towards. **freundlich/hässlich zu jdm sein** be friendly/nasty to s.o.
····➤ (über) on; about. **sich zu etw äußern** to comment on sth
● adverb
····➤ (allzu) too. **zu groß/viel/weit** too big/much/far
····➤ (Richtung) towards. **nach dem Fluss zu** towards the river
····➤ (geschlossen) closed; (an Schalter, Hahn) off. **zu sein** be closed. **Augen zu!** close your eyes! **Tür zu!** shut the door!
● conjunction
····➤ to. **etwas zu essen** something to eat. **nicht zu glauben** unbelievable. **zu erörternde Probleme** problems to be discussed

zualler|erst adv first of all.
z~letzt adv last of all
Zubehör nt -s accessories pl

zubereit|en vt sep prepare. **Z~ung** f - preparation; (in Rezept) method

zubinden† vt sep tie [up]

zubring|en† vt sep spend. **Z~er** m **-s,-** access road; (Bus) shuttle

Zucchini /tsuːˈkiːni/ pl courgettes

Zucht f -, -en breeding; (Pflanzen-) cultivation; (Art, Rasse) breed; (von Pflanzen) strain; (Z~farm) farm; (Pferde-) stud

zücht|en vt breed; cultivate, grow <Rosen>. **Z~er** m **-s,-** breeder; grower

Zuchthaus nt prison

Züchtung f -, -en breeding; (Pflanzen-) cultivation; (Art, Rasse) breed; (von Pflanzen) strain

zucken vi (haben) twitch; (sich z~d bewegen) jerk; <Blitz:> flash; <Flamme:> flicker ● vt die **Achseln z~** shrug one's shoulders

Zucker m **-s** sugar. **Z~dose** f sugar basin. **Z~guss** m icing. **z~krank** a diabetic. **Z~krankheit** f diabetes. **z~n** vt sugar. **Z~rohr** nt sugar cane. **Z~rübe** f sugar beet. **Z~watte** f candyfloss

zudecken vt sep cover up; (im Bett) tuck up; cover <Topf>

zudem adv moreover

zudrehen vt sep turn off

zueinander adv to one another; **z~ passen** go together; **z~ halten** (fig) stick together

zuerkennen† vt sep award (dat to)

zuerst adv first; (anfangs) at first

zufahr|en† vi sep (sein) **z~en auf** (+ acc) drive towards. **Z~t** f access; (Einfahrt) drive

Zufall m chance; (Zusammentreffen) coincidence. **durch Z~** by chance/coincidence. **z~en†** vi sep (sein) close, shut; **jdm z~en** <Aufgabe:> fall/<Erbe:> go to s.o.

zufällig a chance, accidental ● adv by chance

Zuflucht f refuge; (Schutz) shelter

zufolge prep (+ dat) according to

zufrieden a contented; (befriedigt) satisfied; **sich z~ geben** be satisfied; **jdn z~ lassen** leave s.o. in peace; **jdn z~ stellen** satisfy s.o.; **z~ stellend** satisfactory. **Z~heit** f - contentment; satisfaction

zufrieren† vi sep (sein) freeze over

zufügen vt sep inflict (dat on); do <Unrecht> (dat to)

Zufuhr f - supply

Zug m **-[e]s,̈e** train; (Kolonne) column; (Um-) procession; (Mil) platoon; (Vogelschar) flock; (Ziehen, Zugkraft) pull; (Wandern, Ziehen) migration; (Schluck, Luft-) draught; (Atem-) breath; (beim Rauchen) puff; (Schach-) move; (beim Schwimmen, Rudern) stroke; (Gesichts-) feature; (Wesens-) trait

Zugabe f (Geschenk) [free] gift; (Mus) encore

Zugang m access

zugänglich a accessible; <Mensch:> approachable

Zugbrücke f drawbridge

zugeben† vt sep add; (gestehen) admit; (erlauben) allow

zugehen† vi sep (sein) close; **jdm z~** be sent to s.o.; **z~ auf** (+ acc) go towards; **dem Ende z~** draw to a close; <Vorräte:> run low; **auf der Party ging es lebhaft zu** the party was pretty lively

Zugehörigkeit f - membership

Zügel m **-s,-** rein

zugelassen a registered

zügel|los a unrestrained. **z~n** vt rein in; (fig) curb

Zuge|ständnis nt concession. **z~stehen†** vt sep grant

zügig a quick

Z

Zugkraft f pull; (fig) attraction
zugleich adv at the same time
Zugluft f draught
zugreifen† vi sep (haben) grab it/them; (bei Tisch) help oneself; (bei Angebot) jump at it; (helfen) lend a hand
zugrunde adv z~ richten destroy; z~ gehen be destroyed; (sterben) die; z~ liegen form the basis (dat of)
zugunsten prep (+ gen) in favour of; <Sammlung> in aid of
zugute adv jdm/etw z~ kommen benefit s.o./sth
Zugvogel m migratory bird
zuhalten† v sep ● vt keep closed; (bedecken) cover; sich (dat) die Nase z~ hold one's nose
Zuhälter m -s,- pimp
zuhause = zu Hause, s. Haus. Z~ nt -s,- home
zuhör|en vi sep (haben) listen (dat to). Z~er(in) m(f) listener
zujubeln vi sep (haben) jdm z~ cheer s.o.
zukleben vt sep seal
zuknöpfen vt sep button up
zukommen† vi sep (sein) z~ auf (+ acc) come towards; (sich nähern) approach; z~ lassen send (jdm s.o.); devote <Pflege> (dat to); jdm z~ be s.o.'s right
Zukunft f - future. **zukünftig** a future ● adv in future
zulächeln vi sep (haben) smile (dat at)
zulangen vi sep (haben) help oneself
zulassen† vt sep allow, permit; (teilnehmen lassen) admit; (Admin) license, register; (geschlossen lassen) leave closed; leave unopened <Brief>
zulässig a permissible
Zulassung f -, -en admission; registration; (Lizenz) licence
zuleide adv jdm etwas z~ tun hurt s.o.

zuletzt adv last; (schließlich) in the end
zuliebe adv jdm/etw z~ for the sake of s.o./sth
zum prep = zu dem; zum Spaß for fun; etw zum Lesen sth to read
zumachen v sep ● vt close, shut; do up <Jacke>; seal <Umschlag>; turn off <Hahn>; (stilllegen) close down ● vi (haben) close, shut; (stillgelegt werden) close down
zumal adv especially ● conj especially since
zumindest adv at least
zumutbar a reasonable
zumute adv mir ist nicht danach z~ I don't feel like it
zumut|en vt sep jdm etw z~en ask or expect sth of s.o.; sich (dat) zu viel z~en overdo things. Z~ung f - imposition
zunächst adv first [of all]; (anfangs) at first; (vorläufig) for the moment ● prep (+ dat) nearest to
Zunahme f -, -n increase
Zuname m surname
zünd|en vt/i (haben) ignite. Z~er m -s,- detonator, fuse. Z~holz nt match. Z~kerze f sparking-plug. Z~schlüssel m ignition key. Z~schnur f fuse. Z~ung f -, -en ignition
zunehmen† vi sep (haben) increase (an + dat in); <Mond:> wax; (an Gewicht) put on weight. z~d a increasing
Zuneigung f - affection
Zunft f -,-e guild
Zunge f -, -n tongue. Z~nbrecher m tongue-twister
zunutze a sich (dat) etw z~ machen make use of sth; (ausnutzen) take advantage of sth
zuoberst adv right at the top
zuordnen vt sep assign (dat to)
zupfen vt/i (haben) pluck (an + dat at); pull out <Unkraut>

zur *prep* = zu der; **zur Schule** to school; **zur Zeit** at present

zurate *adv* **z~ ziehen** consult

zurechnungsfähig *a* of sound mind

zurecht|finden† (sich) *vr sep* find one's way. **z~kommen†** *vi sep* (*sein*) cope (**mit** with); (*rechtzeitig kommen*) be in time. **z~legen** *vt sep* put out ready; **sich** (*dat*) **eine Ausrede z~legen** have an excuse all ready. **z~machen** *vt sep* get ready. **Z~weisung** *f* reprimand

zureden *vi sep* (*haben*) **jdm z~** try to persuade s.o.

zurichten *vt sep* prepare; (*beschädigen*) damage; (*verletzen*) injure

zuriegeln *vt sep* bolt

zurück *adv* back; **Berlin, hin und z~** return to Berlin. **z~bekommen†** *vt sep* get back. **z~bleiben†** *vi sep* (*sein*) stay behind; (*nicht mithalten*) lag behind. **z~bringen†** *vt sep* bring back; (*wieder hinbringen*) take back. **z~erstatten** *vt sep* refund. **z~fahren†** *v sep* ● *vt* drive back ● *vi* (*sein*) return, go back; (*im Auto*) drive back; (*z~weichen*) recoil. **z~finden†** *vi sep* (*haben*) find one's way back. **z~führen** *v sep* ● *vt* take back; (*fig*) attribute (**auf** + *acc* to) ● *vi* (*haben*) lead back. **z~geben†** *vt sep* give back, return. **z~geblieben** *a* retarded. **z~gehen†** *vi sep* (*sein*) go back, return; (*abnehmen*) go down; **z~gehen auf** (+ *acc*) (*fig*) go back to

zurückgezogen *a* secluded. **Z~heit** *f* - seclusion

zurückhalt|en† *vt sep* hold back; (*abhalten*) stop; **sich z~en** restrain oneself. **z~end** *a* reserved. **Z~ung** *f* - reserve

zurück|kehren *vi sep* (*sein*) return. **z~kommen†** *vi sep* (*sein*) come back, return; (*ankommen*)

get back. **z~lassen†** *vt sep* leave behind; (*z~kehren lassen*) allow back. **z~legen** *vt sep* put back; (*reservieren*) keep; (*sparen*) put by; cover <*Strecke*>. **z~liegen†** *vi sep* (*haben*) be in the past; (*Sport*) be behind; **das liegt lange zurück** that was long ago. **z~melden (sich)** *vr sep* report back. **z~schicken** *vt sep* send back. **z~schlagen** *v sep* ● *vi* (*haben*) hit back ● *vt* hit back; (*umschlagen*) turn back. **z~schrecken†** *vi sep* (*sein*) shrink back, recoil; (*fig*) shrink (**vor** + *dat* from). **z~stellen** *vt sep* put back; (*reservieren*) keep; (*fig*) put aside; (*aufschieben*) postpone. **z~stoßen†** *v sep* ● *vt* push back ● *vi* (*sein*) reverse, back. **z~treten†** *vi sep* (*sein*) step back; (*vom Amt*) resign; (*verzichten*) withdraw. **z~weisen†** *vt sep* turn away; (*fig*) reject. **z~zahlen** *vt sep* pay back. **z~ziehen†** *vt sep* draw back; (*fig*) withdraw; **sich z~ziehen** withdraw; (*vom Beruf*) retire

Zuruf *m* shout. **z~en†** *vt sep* shout (*dat* to)

zurzeit *adv* at present

Zusage *f* -, -n acceptance; (*Versprechen*) promise. **z~n** *v sep* ● *vt* promise ● *vi* (*haben*) accept

zusammen *adv* together; (*insgesamt*) altogether; **z~ sein** be together. **Z~arbeit** *f* co-operation. **z~arbeiten** *vi sep* (*haben*) co-operate. **z~bauen** *vt sep* assemble. **z~bleiben†** *vi sep* (*sein*) stay together. **z~brechen†** *vi sep* (*sein*) collapse. **z~bruch** *m* collapse; (*Nerven- & fig*) breakdown. **z~fallen†** *vi sep* (*sein*) collapse; (*zeitlich*) coincide. **z~fassen** *vt sep* summarize, sum up. **Z~fassung** *f* summary.

Z

z~**fügen** vt sep fit together.
z~**gehören** vi sep (haben) belong together; (z~passen) go together.
z~**gesetzt** a (Gram) compound.
z~**halten**† v sep ● vt hold together; (beisammenhalten) keep together ● vi (haben) (fig) stick together. **Z~hang** m connection; (Kontext) context. z~**hanglos** a incoherent. z~**klappen** v sep ● vt fold up ● vi (sein) collapse.
z~**kommen**† vi sep (sein) meet; (sich sammeln) accumulate.
Z~kunft f -,ˮe meeting. z~**laufen**† vi sep (sein) gather; (Flüssigkeit:) collect; (Linien:) converge. z~**leben** vi sep (haben) live together. z~**legen** v sep ● vt put together; (z~falten) fold up; (vereinigen) amalgamate; pool (Geld) ● vi (haben) club together. z~**nehmen**† vt sep gather up; summon up (Mut); collect (Gedanken); sich z~nehmen pull oneself together. z~**passen** vi sep (haben) go together, match. **Z~prall** m collision. z~**rechnen** vt sep add up. z~**schlagen**† vt sep smash up; (prügeln) beat up. z~**schließen**† (sich) vr sep join together; (Firmen:) merge. **Z~schluss** m union; (Comm) merger
Zusammensein nt -s get-together
zusammensetz|en vt sep put together; (Techn) assemble; sich z~en sit [down] together; (bestehen) be made up (aus from). **Z~ung** f -, -en composition; (Techn) assembly; (Wort) compound
zusammen|stellen vt sep put together; (gestalten) compile.
Z~stoß m collision; (fig) clash.
z~**treffen**† vi sep (sein) meet; (zeitlich) coincide. z~**zählen** vt sep add up. z~**ziehen**† v sep ● vt draw together; (addieren) add up;

(konzentrieren) mass; sich z~ziehen contract; (Gewitter:) gather ● vi (sein) move in together; move in (mit with)
Zusatz m addition; (Jur) rider; (Lebensmittel-) additive.
zusätzlich a additional ● adv in addition
zuschau|en vi sep (haben) watch.
Z~er(in) m -s,- (f -, -nen) spectator; (TV) viewer
Zuschlag m surcharge; (D-Zug-) supplement. z~**pflichtig** a (Zug) for which a supplement is payable
zuschließen† v sep ● vt lock ● vi (haben) lock up
zuschneiden† vt sep cut out; cut to size (Holz)
zuschreiben† vt sep attribute (dat to); jdm die Schuld z~ blame s.o.
Zuschrift f letter; (auf Annonce) reply
zuschulden adv sich (dat) etwas z~ kommen lassen do wrong
Zuschuss m contribution; (staatlich) subsidy
zusehends adv visibly
zusein* vi sep (sein) zu sein, s. zu
zusenden† vt sep send (dat to)
zusetzen v sep ● vt add; (einbüßen) lose
zusicher|n vt sep promise. **Z~ung** f promise.
zuspielen vt sep (Sport) pass
zuspitzen (sich) vr sep (fig) become critical
Zustand m condition, state
zustande adv z~ bringen/kommen bring/come about
zuständig a competent; (verantwortlich) responsible
zustehen† vi sep (haben) jdm z~ be s.o.'s right; (Urlaub:) be due to s.o.
zusteigen† vi sep (sein) get on; noch jemand zugestiegen? tickets please; (im Bus) any more fares please?

zustell|en vt sep block; (bringen) deliver. **Z~ung** f delivery

zusteuern v sep ● vi (sein) head (auf + acc for) ● vt contribute

zustimm|en vi sep (haben) agree; (billigen) approve (dat of). **Z~ung** f consent; approval

zustoßen† vi sep (sein) happen (dat to)

Zustrom m influx

Zutat f (Culin) ingredient

zuteil|en vt sep allocate; assign <Aufgabe>. **Z~ung** f allocation

zutiefst adv deeply

zutragen† vt sep carry/(fig) report (dat to); **sich z~** happen

zutrau|en vt sep jdm etw z~ believe s.o. capable of sth. **Z~en** nt -s confidence

zutreffen† vi sep (haben) be correct; **z~ auf** (+ acc) apply to

Zutritt m admittance

zuunterst adv right at the bottom

zuverlässig a reliable. **Z~keit** f - reliability

Zuversicht f - confidence. **z~lich** a confident

zuviel* pron & adv zu viel, s. viel

zuvor adv before; (erst) first

zuvorkommen† vi sep (sein) (+ dat) anticipate. **z~d** a obliging

Zuwachs m -es increase

zuwege adv **z~ bringen** achieve

zuweilen adv now and then

zuweisen† vt sep assign

Zuwendung f donation; (Fürsorge) care

zuwenig* pron & adv zu wenig, s. wenig

zuwerfen† vt sep slam <Tür>; jdm etw z~ throw s.o. sth

zuwider adv jdm z~ sein be repugnant to s.o. ● prep (+ dat) contrary to

zuzahlen vt sep pay extra

zuziehen† v sep ● vt pull tight; draw <Vorhänge>; (hinzu-) call in; **sich** (dat) **etw z~** contract <Krankheit>; sustain

<Verletzung>; incur <Zorn> ● vi (sein) move into the area

zuzüglich prep (+ gen) plus

Zwang m -[e]s,-̈e compulsion; (Gewalt) force; (Verpflichtung) obligation

zwängen vt squeeze

zwanglos a informal. **Z~igkeit** f - informality

Zwangsjacke f straitjacket

zwanzig inv a twenty. **z~ste(r,s)** a twentieth

zwar adv admittedly

Zweck m -[e]s, -e purpose; (Sinn) point. **z~los** a pointless. **z~mäßig** a suitable; (praktisch) functional

zwei inv a, **Z~** f -, -en two; (Sch) ≈ B. **Z~bettzimmer** nt twin-bedded room

zweideutig a ambiguous

zweierlei inv a two kinds of ● pron two things. **z~fach** a double

Zweifel m -s,- doubt. **z~haft** a doubtful; (fragwürdig) dubious. **z~los** adv undoubtedly. **z~n** vi (haben) doubt (**an etw** dat sth)

Zweig m -[e]s, -e branch. **Z~stelle** f branch [office]

Zwei|kampf m duel. **z~mal** adv twice. **z~reihig** a <Anzug> double-breasted. **z~sprachig** a bilingual

zweit adv zu z~ in twos; wir waren zu z~ there were two of us. **z~beste(r,s)** a second-best. **z~e(r,s)** a second

zweitens adv secondly

Zwerchfell nt diaphragm

Zwerg m -[e]s, -e dwarf

Zwickel m -s,- gusset

zwicken vt/i (haben) pinch

Zwieback m -[e]s,-̈e rusk

Zwiebel f -, -n onion; (Blumen-)bulb

Zwielicht nt half-light; (Dämmerlicht) twilight. **z~ig** a shady

Z

Zwiespalt m conflict
Zwilling m -s, -e twin; **Z~e** (*Astr*) Gemini
zwingen† vt force; **sich z~** force oneself. **z~d** a compelling
Zwinger m -s,- run; (*Zucht-*) kennels pl
zwinkern vi (*haben*) blink; (*als Zeichen*) wink
Zwirn m -[e]s button thread
zwischen prep (+ dat/acc) between; (*unter*) among[st]. **Z~bemerkung** f interjection. **z~durch** adv in between; (*in der Z~zeit*) in the meantime. **Z~fall** m incident. **Z~landung** f

stopover. **Z~raum** m gap, space. **Z~wand** f partition. **Z~zeit** f in der Z~zeit in the meantime
Zwist m -[e]s, -e discord; (*Streit*) feud
zwitschern vi (*haben*) chirp
zwo inv a two
zwölf inv a twelve. **z~te(r,s)** a twelfth
Zylind|er m -s,- cylinder; (*Hut*) top hat. **z~risch** a cylindrical
Zyn|iker m -s,- cynic. **z~isch** a cynical. **Z~ismus** m - cynicism
Zypern nt -s Cyprus
Zypresse f -, -n cypress
Zyste /'tsʏstə/ f -, -n cyst

Test yourself with word games

This section contains a number of word games which will help you to use your dictionary more effectively and to build up your knowledge of German vocabulary and usage an entertaining way. You will find answers to all puzzles and games at the end of the section.

1 Join Up the Nouns

These German nouns are all made up of two separate words, but they have split apart. Draw a line between two pieces of paper that make up a noun. Watch out: one of the first words goes with two of the second words!

When you've made all the German words, do the same for the English translations and match them up with the German.

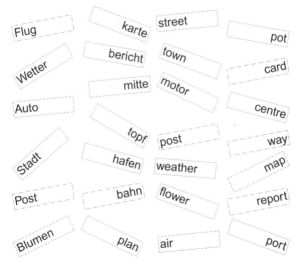

2 Wordsearch

Fifteen German words are hidden among the letters in the grid. Can you find them all? Watch out: six of the words read downwards, while all the others read across.

To help you, here are the English meanings of the German words. You can tick them off as you find the German.

ace	rough
almost	save
also	speak
better	ten
daughter	under
opera	village
powder	wide
quay	

M	W	N	B	U	N	T	E	R	V
Z	E	H	N	C	X	Z	L	K	J
H	I	G	F	P	U	L	V	E	R
D	T	O	C	H	T	E	R	S	A
D	S	P	R	E	C	H	E	N	P
O	B	E	S	S	E	R	A	O	I
R	U	R	K	U	F	A	S	T	A
F	Y	T	A	R	E	W	S	Q	U
Z	X	C	I	V	B	R	A	U	C
N	R	E	T	T	E	N	M	L	H

3 Odd Meaning Out

One word can have several different meanings. In the
following exercise, only two of the three English translations
given for each German word are correct. Use the dictionary to
spot the odd one out, and then look up the right German
translation for it:

fordern	demand challenge convince	**Pilz**	mushroom fungus beer
Schnee	snow icing beaten egg-white	**schwer**	swift difficult heavy
patent	obvious resourceful clever	**gerade**	straight grand even
Haken	tick hake hook	**drehen**	turn shoot catch
Brause	bruise fizzy drink shower	**Strom**	power storm stream
neben	next to apart from foggy	**Blase**	blanket blister bladder

4 Troubleshooting

Our computer has developed some annoying little problems.
Can you help put them right?

First, when we type any three-letter word beginning with d,
the computer shows three d's on the screen! The problem
words are all highlighted in our "Recipe of the Week".
Can you correct them in the box above each word?

Ddd Rezept ddd Woche

Für ddd Kuchenteig ddd Butter in Stückchen schneiden und

mit ddd Mehl vermischen. Ddd Gemisch mit ddd Honig und

ddd Milch zu einem festen Teig verarbeiten. Ddd Äpfel

waschen, halbieren und in ddd Pfanne mit ddd Butter, ddd

Zimt und ddd Zitronensaft aufkochen lassen. Ddd Teig in

ddd Form geben und mit ddd Obst belegen. Ddd Kuchen in

ddd Backofen schieben und 35 Minuten backen.

5 Crossword

If you need to, you can use the dictionary to solve this crossword. Just translate the clues into German, and write the translations in capital letters.

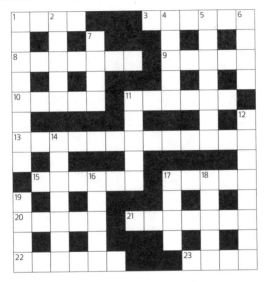

Across
1 mature (4)
3 journeys (6)
8 advertisement, small ad (7)
9 pale (adjective) (5)
10 to hurry (5)
11 few (6)
13 a (male) industrialist (13)
15 to catch (6)
17 (male) Russian (5)
20 price or prize (5)
21 bags or pockets (7)
22 saddle (noun) (6)
23 stove (4)

Down
1 (female) rider (8)
2 island (5)
4 heiress (5)
5 asparagus (7)
6 nest (4)
7 crane (machine) (4)
11 goods, or (they) were (5)
12 to appoint (8)
14 dialect (7)
16 alley (5)
17 pink (4)
18 sheep (5)
19 epic (noun) (4)

6 Curly Words

One word is missing in each of the curly lists. Which day, month, capital city, and number are missing?

Can you write out the four lists in the right order?

7 Sporting Links

Can you match each piece of sporting equipment to the right sport?
Can you translate the sports into German?

das Seil	**archery**
die Zielscheibe	**tennis**
der Schlittschuh	**skittles**
der Tennisschläger	**surfing**
der Kegel	**mountaineering**
der Ski	**football**
der Federball	**swimming**
das Segel	**golf**
die Kugel	**skating**
der Fußball	**riding**
die Flosse	**cycling**
der Zügel	**gymnastics**
das Sprungbrett	**skiing**
das Fahrrad	**fencing**
der Golfschläger	**diving**
die Turnschuhe	**shot-put**
das Florett	**sailing**
das Surfbrett	**badminton**

Answers

1

Flughafen	airport
Wetterbericht	weather report
Autobahn	motorway
Stadtmitte	town centre
Stadtplan	street map
Postkarte	postcard
Blumentopf	flowerpot

2

Ass	ace	rau	rough
fast	almost	retten	save
auch	also	sprechen	speak
besser	better	zehn	ten
Tochter	daughter	unter	under
Oper	opera	Dorf	village
Pulver	powder	weit	wide
Kai	quay		

3

convince	überzeugen
icing	Zuckerguss
obvious	offensichtlich
hake	Seehecht
bruise	blauer Fleck
foggy	neblig
beer	Bier
swift	schnell
grand	großartig
catch	fangen
storm	Sturm
blanket	Decke

4

Das Rezept *der* Woche

Für *den* Kuchenteig *die* Butter in Stückchen schneiden und mit *dem* Mehl vermischen. *Das* Gemisch mit *dem* Honig und *der* Milch zu einem festen Teig verarbeiten. *Die* Äpfel waschen, halbieren und in *der* Pfanne mit der Butter, *dem* Zimt und *dem* Zitronensaft aufkochen lassen. *Den* Teig in *die* Form geben und mit *dem* Obst belegen. *Den* Kuchen in *den* Backofen schieben und 35 Minuten backen.

5

6

Freitag; Sonntag, Montag, Dienstag, Mittwoch, Donnerstag, Freitag,
  Samstag;
November; Januar, Februar, März, April, Mai, Juni, Juli, August,
  September, Oktober, November, Dezember;
Rom; Deutschland/Berlin, Österreich/Wien, die Schweiz/Bern,
  Frankreich/Paris, Italien/Rom;
zehn; eins, zwei, drei, vier, fünf, sechs, sieben, acht, neun, zehn, elf, zwölf.

7

das Fahrrad	bicycle	cycling	das Radfahren
der Federball	shuttlecock	badminton	der Federball
das Florett	foil	fencing	das Fechten
die Flosse	flipper	swimming	das Schwimmen
der Fußball	football	football	der Fußball
der Golfschläger	golf-club	golf	das Golf
der Kegel	skittle	skittles	das Kegeln
die Kugel	shot	shot-put	das Kugelstoßen
der Schlittschuh	ice-skate	skating	das Eislaufen
das Segel	sail	sailing	der Segelsport
das Seil	rope	mountaineering	das Bergsteigen
der Ski	ski	skiing	das Skilaufen
das Sprungbrett	springboard	diving	das Kunstspringen
das Surfbrett	surfboard	surfing	das Surfen
der Tennisschläger	tennis-racket	tennis	das Tennis
die Turnschuhe	gym shoes	gymnastics	das Turnen
die Zielscheibe	target	archery	das Bogenschießen
der Zügel	rein	riding	das Reiten

Calendar of traditions, festivals, and holidays in German-speaking countries

January
1 8 15 22 29
2 9 16 23 30
3 10 17 24 31
4 11 18 25
5 12 19 26
6 13 20 27
7 14 21 28

February
1 8 15 22
2 9 16 23
3 10 17 24
4 11 18 25
5 12 19 26
6 13 20 27
7 **14** 21 28

March
1 8 15 22 29
2 9 16 23 30
3 10 17 24 31
4 11 18 25
5 12 19 26
6 13 20 27
7 14 21 28

April
1 8 15 22 29
2 9 16 23 30
3 10 17 24 31
4 11 18 25
5 12 19 26
6 13 20 27
7 14 21 28

May
1 8 15 22 29
2 9 16 23 30
3 10 17 24 31
4 11 18 25
5 12 19 26
6 13 20 27
7 14 21 28

June
1 8 15 22 29
2 9 16 23 30
3 10 17 24
4 11 18 25
5 12 19 26
6 13 20 27
7 14 21 28

July
1 8 15 22 29
2 9 16 23 30
3 10 17 24 31
4 11 18 25
5 12 19 26
6 13 20 27
7 14 21 28

August
1 8 15 22 29
2 9 16 23 30
3 10 17 24 31
4 11 18 25
5 12 19 26
6 13 20 27
7 14 21 28

September
1 8 15 22 29
2 9 16 23 30
3 10 17 24
4 11 18 25
5 12 19 26
6 13 20 27
7 14 21 28

October
1 8 15 22 29
2 9 16 23 30
3 10 17 24 **31**
4 11 18 25
5 12 19 **26**
6 13 20 27
7 14 21 28

November
1 8 15 22 29
2 9 16 23 30
3 10 17 24
4 **11** 18 25
5 12 19 26
6 13 20 27
7 14 21 28

December
1 8 15 22 29
2 9 16 23 30
3 10 17 **24 31**
4 11 18 **25**
5 12 19 **26**
6 13 20 27
7 14 21 28

1 January

Neujahr New Year's Day is always a public holiday and tends to be a quiet day when people are recovering from the *Silvester* celebrations.

6 January

Heilige Drei Könige Epiphany or Twelfth Night is a public holiday in Austria and some parts of southern Germany. In some areas, children dressed up as the Three Kings go from house to house to bless the homes for the coming year and collect money for charity. This is also traditionally the day when the Christmas tree is taken down.

2 February

Mariä Lichtmess Candlemas is celebrated in the Catholic church but is not a public holiday.

1 April

Erster April April Fool's Day is the time to make an April fool of your family and friends (*jdn. in den April schicken*) or to play an April fool trick (*Aprilscherz*).

1 May

Erster Mai May Day is a public holiday in Germany, Austria, and Switzerland. It is celebrated by trade unions as *Labour Day*, often with rallies and demonstrations. Many people simply use the day for a family outing or picnic, and in rural areas maypoles are put up in the villages.

3 October

Tag der deutschen Einheit Germany's national holiday, the *Day of German Unity* commemorates German reunification on 3 October 1990.

26 October

Nationalfeiertag Austria's national holiday.

31 October

Reformationstag Reformation Day is a public holiday in some mainly Protestant parts of Germany and commemorates the Reformation.

1 November

Allerheiligen All Saints' Day is a public holiday in Catholic parts of Germany and Austria.

2 November

Allerseelen All Souls' Day is the day when Catholics remember their dead by visiting the cemeteries to pray and place wreaths, flowers, and lighted candles on the graves. This is often done on 1 November as *Allerseelen* is not a public holiday.

11 November

Martinstag St Martin's day is not a public holiday, but in Catholic areas the charitable Saint is commemorated with processions where children carry lanterns and sing songs. Traditional food includes the *Martinsgans* (roast goose) and *Martinsbrezel* (a kind of soft pretzel).

6 December

Nikolaustag On the eve of St Nicholas' Day, children put out their boots in the hope of finding presents and fruit, nuts, and sweets in the morning. The Saint may also turn up in person, looking much like Santa Claus or Father Christmas.

24 December

Heiligabend Christmas Eve is not a public holiday but many firms and shops close early for the Christmas period. This is the day when traditionally the Christmas tree is put up and decorated. Christmas presents are given in the evening, and many people attend midnight mass.

25 December

Erster Weihnachtstag Christmas Day is a public holiday in Germany, Austria, and Switzerland. It tends to be a quiet day for family get-togethers, often with a traditional lunch of goose or carp.

26 December

Zweiter Weihnachtstag Boxing Day is a public holiday in Germany, Austria, and Switzerland. In Austria and Switzerland it is called *Stephanstag* (St Stephen's day).

31 December

Silvester New Year's Eve is not a bank holiday, but firms and shops tend to close early. A party, or at least a meal with friends, is a must for *Silvester* evening. At midnight, the new year is toasted in Sekt (German sparkling wine), and everybody goes outside to admire the fireworks.

Movable feasts

Rosenmontag The day before Shrove Tuesday is not an official public holiday but many people, especially in the Rhineland, get the day off work or school to take part in the *Karneval* celebrations, which involve masked balls, fancy-dress parties, and parades. The street parades in Düsseldorf, Cologne, Mainz, and other cities are attended by thousands of revellers and shown live on television.

Faschingsdienstag Shrove Tuesday is the final day of *Fasching* (Carnival) in Southern Germany, with processions and fancy dress parties similar to Rosenmontag in the Northwest. In the far south, ancient customs to drive out the winter with bells and drums survive. The pre-Lent carnival in and around the Rhineland is called Karneval. Almost every town has its own carnival prince and princess, and organizes a street parade with decorated floats, which is watched by thousands of revellers in fancy dress.

Aschermittwoch Ash Wednesday marks the end of the carnival season and the beginning of Lent. This day is celebrated in the Catholic Church but is not a public holiday.

Karfreitag Good Friday is a public holiday and generally a very quiet day. Catholics traditionally eat fish on this day.

Ostern Easter traditions include hiding Easter eggs (often dyed hardboiled eggs, or the chocolate variety) in the garden for the children. The *Osterhase* (Easter bunny) is supposed to have brought them. Ostermontag (Easter Monday) is also a public holiday.

Weißer Sonntag (Sunday after Easter) In the Catholic Church, first communion is traditionally taken on this Sunday.

Muttertag (second Sunday in May) On Mothers' Day, children of all ages give their mothers small gifts, cards, or flowers.

Christi Himmelfahrt (40 days after Easter) Ascension day is a public holiday in Germany, Austria, and Switzerland. This day is also Fathers' day when fathers traditionally go out on daytrips or pub crawls.

Pfingsten (seventh Sunday after Easter) As *Pfingstmontag* (Whit Monday) is also a public holiday in Germany, Austria, and Switzerland, Whitsun is a popular time to have a long weekend away.

Fronleichnam (second Thursday after Whitsun) Corpus Christi is a public holiday in Austria and in parts of Germany and Switzerland. In Catholic areas, processions and open-air masses are held.

Buß- und Bettag (third Wednesday in November, 11 days before the first Advent Sunday) This 'day of repentance and prayer' is a public holiday only in some parts of Germany.

Volkstrauertag (second Sunday before the beginning of Advent) In Germany, this is a national day of mourning to commemorate the dead of both world wars, and the victims of the Nazis.

Totensonntag (last Sunday before the beginning of Advent) Protestants remember their dead on this day.

Advent The four weeks leading up to Christmas, beginning with the **1. Adventssonntag** (first Sunday in Advent) in late November or early December, still have a special significance in Germany, even for non-religious people. An Advent wreath with four candles is present in almost every German household during this time, and on each Sunday of Advent one more candle is lit.

A–Z of German life and culture

Abendbrot, Abendessen

For most Germans, MITTAGESSEN is still the main meal of the day. *Abendbrot* or *Abendessen* normally consists of bread, cheese, meats, perhaps a salad, and a hot drink. It is eaten by the whole family at about 6 or 7 p.m. *Abendessen* can also refer to a cooked meal, especially for people who are out at work all day.

Abitur

This is the final exam taken by pupils at a GYMNASIUM, usually when they are about 19. The result is based on continuous assessment during the last two years before the *Abitur*, plus examinations in four subjects. The *Abitur* is the obligatory qualification for university entrance.

Ampel-Koalition

A term describing any coalition between the SPD (the party colour is red), the FDP (yellow), and the Green Party. This type of coalition has become increasingly common in local government over the last ten years, with some LÄNDER ruled in this way.

AOK - Allgemeine Ortskrankenkasse

The largest health insurance organization in Germany. Foreign visitors to Germany who need medical assistance can get the necessary forms at the local *AOK* office.

Arbeitsamt

The local employment office to be found in every German town. It provides career guidance, helps the unemployed find new jobs, and processes all claims for ARBEITSLOSENGELD and related benefits. Unemployed people have to report to the *Arbeitsamt* once every three months to prove they are still looking for work.

Arbeitslosengeld

This is the benefit paid to all unemployed people who are looking for a new job and have already made a minimum contribution to the ARBEITSLOSENVERSICHERUNG. The benefit is a proportion of the person's previous pay, and is higher for people supporting children. After one year, it is reduced and called *Arbeitslosenhilfe*.

Arbeitslosenversicherung

This is the compulsory state-run insurance against unemployment. All *Arbeiter* and *Angestellte* have to pay into this scheme and in return are entitled to ARBEITSLOSENGELD and related benefits. This area has been subject to wide-ranging reforms in recent years.

ARD

An umbrella organization for the regional broadcasting stations of the various German LÄNDER, financed by licence fees plus a certain amount of advertising. The *ARD* broadcasts DAS ERSTE.

Autobahn

Germany's motorway network is very extensive and not subject to a general speed limit, other than a recommended limit of about 80 mph. Many motorways have only two lanes. To ease congestion, lorries are not allowed to use the *Autobahn* on Sundays.

BAföG - Bundesausbildungsförderungsgesetz

The grant which about a quarter of German students receive from the state. Whether they are entitled to *BAföG*, and how much they get, depends on the students'

and their parents' financial circumstances. Half of the money is given in the form of a loan which has to be repaid later.

Bayern

Bayern (Bavaria), Germany's largest and southernmost LAND, is known for its beautiful scenery (the Alps and their foothills, as well as forests, rivers, and lakes, picturesque towns and villages), its excellent beer and food, and its lively cosmopolitan capital München (Munich). The Bavarians are said to be warm and hospitable, but also fiercely independent and very conservative.

Beamte

This term covers civil servants and other officials, but also occupations like teachers and lecturers. *Beamte* are legally obliged to support the democratic system in Germany and are not allowed to go on strike. In return, they enjoy many privileges, such as total job security, private health insurance, and exemption from social security contributions.

Berlin

After WIEDERVEREINIGUNG, Berlin took over from Bonn as

the capital of Germany, but the German government did not start moving there until 1998. This vibrant city in the heart of Europe lies on the river Spree. It has about 3.5 million inhabitants and is a major cultural and industrial centre.

Berufsausbildung
▶ LEHRE.

Berufsschule
A college for young people who are doing a LEHRE. They attend *Berufsschule* 2 days a week (or sometimes in blocks of several weeks) to continue their general education and receive formal training in their chosen type of job.

Biergarten
A rustic open-air pub which is traditional in Bavaria but can now be found throughout Germany. It is usually set up for the summer in the yard of a pub or restaurant. A *Biergarten* is the best place to enjoy a beer and a simple meal on a summer's day.

Bild Zeitung
Germany's largest-selling daily newspaper, *Bild* is a typical tabloid with huge headlines, lots of photos, scandal stories, gossip, and nude models. It is known for its right-wing views. *Bild* sells about 4.5 million copies every day, almost eight times more than any other newspaper in Germany. Its Sunday edition is called *Bild am Sonntag*.

Bodensee
This is the German name for Lake Constance, Germany's biggest lake, bordered by Germany, Switzerland, and Austria. The river Rhine flows through it. This popular recreation area enjoys a particularly mild climate, especially on the three islands Lindau, Mainau, and Reichenau.

Bonn
Bonn was the capital of the Federal Republic of Germany from 1949 until BERLIN was made the capital of a reunified Germany and it remains home to a number of government institutions. This relatively small, quiet city of about 300,000 inhabitants enjoys a picturesque location on the river Rhine.

Bund
This term refers to the federal state as the top level of government, as opposed to the individual LÄNDER which make up the Federal Republic. *Bund* and *Länder* have different responsibilities, with the *Bund* in charge of foreign policy, defence,

transport, health, employment, etc.

Bundesbank

Properly called the *Deutsche Bundesbank*, Germany's central bank is located in Frankfurt/Main. With the introduction of the Euro in 1999, some of its functions have passed to the European Central Bank (also in Frankfurt).

Bundeskanzler

The Chancellor is the head of government in Germany and Austria. The German chancellor is normally elected for 4 years by the MPs in the BUNDESTAG after being proposed by the BUNDESPRÄSIDENT. He chooses the ministers and decides on government policies.

Bundesland

▶ LAND.

Bundespräsident

The President is the head of state in Germany and Austria. The German president is elected for 5 years by the MPs and delegates from the LÄNDER. He (so far there have not been any women) acts mainly as a figurehead, representing Germany abroad, and does not get involved in party politics, although he often takes a moral lead in major issues like the reform of the education system.

Bundesrat

This is the upper house of the German parliamentary system, where the LÄNDER are represented. The *Bundesrat* members are appointed by the Länder governments. It has to approve laws affecting the *Länder*, and also any changes to the GRUNDGESETZ. Sometimes the opposition parties actually hold a majority in the *Bundesrat*, which allows them to influence German legislation.

Bundestag

The lower house of the German parliament, which is elected every four years by the German people. The *Bundestag* is responsible for federal legislation, the federal budget, and electing the BUNDESKANZLER. Half of the MPs are elected directly and half by proportional representation, in a complicated voting system where each voter has two votes.

Bundeswehr

This is the name for the German armed forces, which come under the control of the defence minister. The

Bundeswehr consists of professional soldiers and conscripts serving their WEHRDIENST. Until 1994, the GRUNDGESETZ did not allow German forces to be deployed abroad, but they now take part in certain operations, notably UN peacekeeping missions.

Bündnis 90/Die Grünen

This party came into being in 1993 as the result of a merger of the West German Green party and civil rights movements of the former GDR. It is the third largest force in the German parliament, committed to environmental and social issues.

CDU - Christlich-Demokratische Union

One of the main German political parties. It was founded in 1945 and is committed to Christian and conservative values. The *CDU* is not active in Bavaria.
▶ CSU.

Christkind

Traditionally, it is *Das Christkind* (the Christ Child) who brings Christmas presents to children on Christmas Eve. The concept of *der Weihnachtsmann* (Father Christmas) is relatively new in Germany.

CSU - Christlich-Soziale Union

The Bavarian sister party of the CDU. It was founded in 1946 and has enjoyed an absolute majority in Bavaria for over 30 years. Politically, it stands to the right of the *CDU*.

Das Erste

Also called ERSTES PROGRAMM, this is the first German public TV channel, broadcast by ARD. Programming includes news, information, films, and entertainment. There is a limited amount of advertising, which is concentrated in 'blocks' at certain times of day and not after 8 p.m.

Der Spiegel

One of Germany's best-selling weekly news and current affairs magazines, *Der Spiegel* was founded in 1947 and is published in Hamburg. It has a liberal to left-wing outlook and has become synonymous with investigative journalism in Germany, as it has brought to light a number of major scandals in German business and politics over the years.

Deutsche Post

The previously state-run German postal system has undergone wide-ranging reforms in recent years which will effectively remove the *Deutsche Post* monopoly by

2002. The number of post offices has been reduced, but small post office agencies can now be found in shops, newsagents, and petrol stations. German letter boxes are yellow. Postal charges are relatively high, but the service is very reliable.

Deutsche Telekom

The previously state-run German telecommunications service has undergone extensive reforms and gradual privatization and is now a public limited company. Since 1998 when the market was opened up to competition, *Deutsche Telekom* has ceased to have a monopoly.

Deutsche Welle

The German equivalent of the BBC World Service, this radio station is financed and controlled by the German government and broadcasts programmes on German politics, business, arts, and culture, aimed at listeners abroad.

Die Republikaner

This ultra right-wing party was founded in 1983 and quickly became notorious for its xenophobic and nationalistic aims. After some success in the early 90s it now has very little support and is not represented in the BUNDESTAG.

Die Welt

A national daily newspaper which was founded in 1946 and is published in Hamburg. It has a large business section and is considered to be right-wing in its views.

Die Zeit

Germany's 'heaviest' weekly newspaper is published in Hamburg and is considered essential reading for academics and intellectuals. Former BUNDESKANZLER Helmut Schmidt is a joint editor. The paper offers in-depth analysis of current issues in politics, society, culture, and the arts.

Drittes Programm

One of the eight regional television channels run by the ARD and focussing on regional affairs and educational programmes.

Duales System

This is a waste disposal and recycling system which was introduced in Germany in 1993 and is operated by the private company *DSD*. All packaging materials marked with the GRÜNER PUNKT symbol are collected separately, and sorted into plastics, glass, paper, and metal for recycling. Non-recyclable and compostable waste is still collected by the local refuse collection service.

Eigenheim

The level of home ownership in Germany is rising but still far lower than in Britain. Many people happily live in rented flats or houses, but most dream of buying or building their *Eigenheim* (own home) one day and save up towards it through the system of BAUSPAREN. German houses tend to be large and solidly built, usually with cellars, and are therefore relatively expensive. First-time buyers are usually middle-aged and expect to stay in their home for the rest of their lives.

Einwohnermeldeamt

Anybody who moves to Germany or relocates within Germany is legally obliged to register their address with the *Einwohnermeldeamt* within a week.

Entwerter

When travelling on buses and trams in Germany it is important to remember that you have to cancel (*entwerten*) your ticket in one of the *Entwerter* machines located inside the bus or tram. Your ticket, even if you have just bought it from the driver, is not valid without the stamp from the *Entwerter*.

Erste, Das

▶ DAS ERSTE.

Eurocheque

The Eurocheque is the standard cheque issued by banks in Germany. It is backed up by the *Eurochequekarte* which can also be used at cash machines and for payments in shops. Although plastic cards have become more popular in Germany, many people (and shops and restaurants) still prefer cash.

Fachhochschule

This type of university provides shorter, more vocational and practically-based courses than those available at a HOCHSCHULE.

Fahrschule

Learner drivers in Germany have to take lessons from a qualified driving instructor at a *Fahrschule* (driving school) in a specially adapted car with dual controls. It is quite common to have 20 or 30 driving lessons before sitting the driving test, as there is no other way of getting driving practice on the road.

FDP - Freie Demokratische Partei

The German Liberal party, which was founded in 1948. This relatively small party tends to gain only 5 to 10% of the vote at general elections, but it has held the balance of power in various coalition governments both with the SPD and the CDU/CSU. It supports a free-market economy and the freedom of the individual.

Focus

A relatively new weekly news and current affairs magazine published in Munich. It was set up in 1993 and is aimed at a centre-right readership, especially businesspeople and professionals. *Focus* has become a serious competitor of DER SPIEGEL, with shorter, easier-to-read articles and a more modern presentation.

Frankfurter Allgemeine Zeitung (FAZ)

One of Germany's most serious and widely respected daily newspapers. It was founded in 1945 and is published in Frankfurt/Main. It tends to have a centre-left to liberal outlook.

Frühstück

Breakfast in Germany typically consists of strong coffee, slices of bread or fresh rolls with butter, jam, honey, sliced cheese and meat, and maybe a boiled egg. For working people and schoolchildren, who have little time for breakfast first thing in the morning, a *zweites Frühstück* is common at around 10 a.m.

Gastarbeiter

The term used for foreign workers from southern European countries, mainly Turkey, former Yugoslavia, and Italy, many of whom came to Germany in the 60s and 70s. Despite the time that they have lived in Germany and the fact that their children have grown up there, integration is still a widely discussed issue.

Gemeinde

The lowest level of local government, run by a local council chaired by the *Bürgermeister* (mayor). *Gemeinden* have their own budget, with income from local taxes. They pass local legislation and administer local affairs.

Gesamthochschule

A type of university established in some LÄNDER following reforms in the 60s and combining HOCHSCHULE and FACHHOCHSCHULE under one roof, thereby offering greater flexibility and a wider choice of subjects to the student.

Gesamtschule

A comprehensive secondary school introduced in the 70s and designed to replace the traditional division into GYMNASIUM, REALSCHULE, and HAUPTSCHULE. Pupils are taught different subjects at their own level and may take any of the school-leaving exams, including the ABITUR.

Goethe-Institut

An organization for promoting German language and culture abroad. It is based in Munich and runs about 140 institutes in over 70 countries, offering German language classes, cultural events such as exhibitions, films and seminars, and a library of German books and magazines and other documentation, which is open to the public.

Grundgesetz

The written German constitution which came into force in May 1949. It lays down the basic rights of German citizens, the relationship between BUND and LÄNDER, and the legal framework of the German state.

Grundschule

The primary school which all German children attend for four years from the age of 6 (some children do not start until they are 7). Lessons are intense but pupils only attend school for about 4 hours a day. At the end of the Grundschule, teachers and parents decide

together which type of secondary school the child should attend.

Grüner Punkt

A symbol used to mark packaging materials which can be recycled. Any packaging carrying this logo is collected separately under the DUALES SYSTEM recycling scheme. Manufacturers have to buy a licence from the recycling company DSD to entitle them to use this symbol.

Gymnasium

The secondary school which prepares pupils for the ABITUR. The Gymnasium is attended after the GRUNDSCHULE by the most academically-inclined pupils. They spend nine years at this school, and during the last three years, they have some choice as to which subjects they study.
▶ SCHULE.

Hauptschule

The secondary school which prepares pupils for the HAUPTSCHULABSCHLUSS (school-leaving certificate). The Hauptschule aims to give the least academically-inclined children a sound educational grounding. Pupils stay at the Hauptschule for 5 or 6 years after the

GRUNDSCHULE. ▶ SCHULE, LEHRE.

Hochschule

German *Hochschulen* (universities) do not charge fees, and anybody who has passed the ABITUR is entitled to go to university (except for some subjects which have a NUMERUS CLAUSUS). They tend to be very large and impersonal institutions. Students may receive a BAFÖG grant and often take more than the minimum 8 semesters (4 years) to complete their course.

ICE - Intercityexpresszug

This high-speed train runs at two-hour intervals on a number of main routes in Germany, offering shorter journey times and better facilities than ordinary trains. A futuristic new *ICE* station has been built at Frankfurt airport.

Internet

A wealth of useful information on German politics, culture, and so on can be obtained on the Internet, which is very popular in Germany. All the main German newspapers have web sites (e.g. http://www.focus.de), as do the television channels (e.g. http://www.ard.de) and

organizations like the *Goethe-Institut* (http://goethe.de). In addition, many German towns and cities have web sites (e.g. http://www.berlin.de).

Kaffee

This refers not only to coffee as a drink but also to the small meal taken at about 4 in the afternoon, consisting of coffee and cakes or biscuits. It is often a social occasion as it is common to invite family or friends for *Kaffee und Kuchen* (rather than for lunch or dinner), especially on birthdays and other family occasions.

Kanton

The name for the individual autonomous states that make up Switzerland. There are 26 *Kantone*, with the largest having just over 1 million inhabitants. Each *Kanton* has its own government and its own constitution.

Kindergarten

Every German pre-school child has the right to attend *Kindergarten* (nursery or play school) between the ages of 3 and 6. Kindergarten concentrates on play, crafts, singing etc., and aims to foster the child's social and emotional development. There is no formal teaching at all, this being reserved for the

GRUNDSCHULE

Kindertagesstätte
Often called *Kita* for short, this is a day nursery intended for the children of working parents. The age range is usually from babies to 6, although some *Kitas* also offer after-school care for older children.

Krankenkasse
There are many different health insurance organizations in Germany with the AOK being the largest. Contributions are high, due to the high standard (and cost) of health care in Germany. The *Krankenkassen* issue their members with plastic cards which entitle them to treatment by the doctor of their choice.

Ladenschlusszeit
The strict regulations governing shop closing times in Germany were relaxed in 1996. Shops are allowed to stay open until 8 p.m. on weekdays and 4 p.m. on Saturdays, and bakeries may open for 3 hours on Sundays. However, the actual opening times vary, depending on the location and size of the shop.

Land
Germany is a federal republic consisting of 16 member states called *Länder* or *Bundesländer*. Five so-called neue *Bundesländer* were added after reunification in 1990. The Land has a degree of autonomy and is responsible for all educational and cultural affairs, the police, the environment, and local government. Austria is a federal state consisting of 9 *Länder*, and the Swiss equivalent is a KANTON

Landtag
The parliament of a LAND, which is elected every 4 to 5 years using a similar mixed system of voting as for the BUNDESTAG elections.

Lehre
This type of apprenticeship is still the normal way to learn a trade or train for a practical career in Germany. A *Hauptschulabschluss* is the minimum requirement, although many young people with a *Realschulabschluss* or even *Lehre* opt to train in this way. A Lehre takes about 2 to 3 years and involves practical training by a MEISTER(IN) backed up by lessons at a BERUFSSCHULE, with an exam at the end.

Love Parade
A festival of techno music and dance which takes place in Berlin every summer, with

about 1 million mainly young people attending. Originally a celebration of youth culture, it has become a major tourist attraction.

Markt

Weekly markets are still held in most German cities and towns, usually laid out very attractively in the picturesque market squares. Fresh fruit and vegetables, flowers, eggs, cheese and other dairy products, bread, meat and fish are available directly from the producer. Many Germans still buy most of their provisions *auf dem Markt*.

Meister(in)

A master craftsman or craftswoman who has completed rigorous training in his/her trade or vocation and has passed a final exam after several years' experience in a job. A *Meister(in)* is allowed to set up in business and train young people who are doing their LEHRE.

Mittagessen

This is a cooked meal eaten in the middle of the day and is the main meal of the day for most Germans. Schoolchildren come home from school in time for *Mittagessen* and most large companies have canteens where hot meals are served at lunchtime. On a Sunday, *Mittagessen* might consist of a starter like a clear broth, followed by a roast with gravy, boiled potatoes and vegetables, and a dessert.

Namenstag

This day is celebrated by many Germans, especially Catholics, in the same way as a birthday. It is the day dedicated to the saint whose name the person carries so, for example, someone called Martin would celebrate their *Namenstag* on *Martinstag* (November 11).

Numerus clausus

The *Numerus clausus* system is used to limit the number of students studying certain oversubscribed subjects such as medicine at German universities. It means that only those students who have achieved a minimum average mark in their ABITUR are admitted.

Orientierungsstufe

The name given to the first two years at a HAUPTSCHULE, a REALSCHULE, or a GYMNASIUM. During this time pupils can find out if they are suited to the type of school they are attending, and at the end of the two years they may transfer to a different school.

Ossi

A colloquial and sometimes derogatory term for someone from East Germany, as opposed to a WESSI (someone from West Germany).

Polterabend

This is Germany's answer to stag and hen nights. The *Polterabend* usually takes place a few days before the wedding and takes the form of a large party for the family and friends of both bride and groom. Traditionally, the guests smash some crockery, as this is supposed to bring luck to the couple.

Post

▶ DEUTSCHE POST.

Premiere

Germany's main Pay-TV channel was introduced in 1991 and can be received via satellite or cable. *Premiere* subscribers can watch the latest feature films, sports events, cultural programmes, and documentaries uninterrupted by advertising.

Realschule

The secondary school which prepares pupils for the *Realschulabschluss* (school-leaving certificate). This type of school is in between HAUPTSCHULE and GYMNASIUM, catering for less academic children who will probably train for a practical career. Pupils stay at the *Realschule* for 6 years after the GRUNDSCHULE. ▶ SCHULE, LEHRE.

Rechtschreibreform

After much controversy, a reform aiming to simplify the strict rules governing German spelling and punctuation was finally implemented in 1998. The old spelling is still acceptable for a transitional period until 2005, but most newspapers and some new books already use the new spelling.

Reichstag

This historic building in the centre of Berlin became the seat of the BUNDESTAG in 1999. The refurbishment of the *Reichstag* included the addition of a glass cupola, with a walkway open to visitors, which provides a spectacular viewing platform and addition to the Berlin skyline.

Republikaner

▶ DIE REPUBLIKANER.

RTL

Germany's largest privately-owned television channel is the market leader in commercial television. It broadcasts films, sport, news, and entertainment and regularly achieves the highest viewing figures.

SAT 1
Germany's second largest privately-owned television channel broadcasts films, news, sport, and entertainment. It was the first commercial channel in the country.

3SAT
This satellite TV channel is run jointly by ARD, ZDF, and Swiss and Austrian TV.

Schule
German children do not start school until they are 6, and they are not allowed to leave school until they are at least 15. All children attend the GRUNDSCHULE for four years (six in Berlin) and either a HAUPTSCHULE, REALSCHULE, GYMNASIUM, or GESAMTSCHULE, depending on their ability. Some students stay at school until they are over 20 due to the system of "SITZEN BLEIBEN".

Schultag - 1. Schultag
The first day at school is a big event for a German child, involving a ceremony at school and sometimes at church. The child is given a *Schultüte*, a large cardboard cone containing pens, small gifts, and sweets, to mark this special occasion.

Schützenfest
An annual festival celebrated in most towns, involving a shooting competition, parade, and fair. The winners of the shooting competition are crowned *Schützenkönig* and *Schützenkönigin* for the year.

Schwarzwald
This is the German name for the Black Forest, a mountainous area in south-western Germany and a popular holiday destination for Germans and foreign tourists alike. The name refers to the large coniferous forests in the area.

sitzen bleiben
If German pupils fail more than one subject in their end-of-year school report, they have to repeat the year. This is colloquially referred to as *sitzen bleiben*, and it means that some pupils do not manage to sit their ABITUR until they are 20.

Skat
A popular card game for three players playing with 32 German cards. Keen players meet regularly for a game or even join a *Skat* club.

Sozialabgaben
This term refers to the contributions every German taxpayer has to make towards

the four main state insurance schemes: pension, health, nursing care, and unemployment. Altogether this amounts to over 40% of gross income, with employee and employer paying half each.

SPD - Sozialdemokratische Partei Deutschlands

One of the main German political parties and the party with the biggest membership. Re-formed after the war in 1945, it is a workers' party supporting social democratic values.

Spiegel

▶ DER SPIEGEL.

Stammtisch

A large table reserved for regulars in most German pubs. The word is also used to refer to the group of people who meet around this table for a drink and lively discussion.

Stasi - Staatssicherheitsdienst

The secret service in the former GDR. With the help of an extensive network of informers, the *Stasi* built up personal files on over 6 million people, that is one third of the population. It was disbanded a year before re-unification.

▶ IM.

Süddeutsche Zeitung

This respected daily national newspaper was founded in 1945 and is published in Munich. It has a liberal outlook and is read mainly in southern Germany.

Volkshochschule (VHS)

A local adult education centre that can be found in every German town. The *VHS* offers low-cost daytime and evening classes in a wide range of subjects, including crafts, languages, music, and exercise.

Waldorfschule

An increasingly popular type of private school originally founded by the Austrian anthroposophist Rudolf Steiner in the 1920s. The main aim of these schools is to develop pupils' creative and cognitive abilities through music, art, and crafts.

Wehrdienst

Compulsory military service for young men in Germany (10 months), Switzerland (3 months), and Austria (6 months). Young Germans are generally called up when they are 19, although there are certain exemptions. Conscientious objectors may apply to do ZIVILDIENST instead.

Weihnachtsmarkt

During the weeks of Advent, these Christmas markets take place in most German towns, selling Christmas decorations, handmade toys and crib figures, traditional Christmas biscuits, and mulled wine to sustain the shoppers.

Weinstube

A cosy wine bar which offers a wide choice of wines and usually also serves a few dishes which are considered to go well with wine. A *Weinstube* tends be more upmarket than an ordinary pub, or else fairly rustic, especially in wine-growing areas.

Welt

▶ DIE WELT.

Wende

This word can refer to any major political or social change or turning point, but it is used especially to refer to the collapse of Communism in 1989, which was symbolized by the fall of the Berlin wall and eventually led to the WIEDERVEREINIGUNG in 1990.

Wessi

A colloquial and sometimes derogatory term for someone from West Germany, as opposed to an OSSI. The expression *Besserwessi*, a pun on *Besserwisser* ('know-all') is used by East Germans to describe a *Wessi* who thinks he knows it all.

Westdeutsche Allgemeine Zeitung (WAZ)

Germany's highest-circulation serious national paper. It was founded in 1948 and is published in Essen, catering mainly for the densely populated Ruhr area.

Wiedervereinigung

This is the German word for the reunification of Germany which officially took place on 3 October 1990, when the former GDR was incorporated into the Federal Republic. The huge financial and social costs of reunification are still being felt throughout Germany.

ZDF - Zweites Deutsches Fernsehen

The second German public TV channel which was founded in 1961 and broadcasts the *Zweites Programm* with entertainment, news, information, and a limited amount of advertising.

Zeit

▶ DIE ZEIT.

Zivildienst

Community service which recognized conscientious

objectors in Germany and Austria can choose to carry out instead of WEHRDIENST. It lasts 3 months longer than *Wehrdienst* (2 months longer in Austria) and usually involves caring for children, the elderly, the disabled, or the sick.

Letter-writing in German

Holiday postcard

- Beginnings (informal): *'Lieber'* here because it's a man; if it's a woman, use e.g. *Liebe Elke.*

  To two people, repeat *'Liebe(r)'*: *Lieber Hans, liebe Elke.*

  To a family: *Liebe Schmidts, Liebe Familie Schmidt,* or just *Liebe Leute.*

- Address: Note that the title (*Herrn, Frau, Fräulein*) stands on the line above the name. *Herr* always has an n on the end in addresses.

  The house number comes after the street name.

  The postcode comes before the place, and if you're writing from outside the country put a D- for Germany, A- for Austria or CH- for Switzerland in front of it.

Heidelberg, den 6. 8. 2001

Lieber Hans!

Einen schönen Gruß aus Alt-Heidelberg! Wir sind erst zwei Tage hier, aber schon sehr angetan von der Stadt und Umgebung, trotz der vielen Touristen. Wir waren gestern abend in einem Konzert im Schlosshof, eine wunderbare Stimmung! Morgen machen wir eine Bootsfahrt, dann geht's am Donnerstag wieder nach Hause. Hoffentlich ist deine Mutter inzwischen wieder gesund.

Bis bald

Max und Sophie

Herrn

Hans Matthäus

Brucknerstr. 26

91052 Erlangen

- Endings (informal): *Herzlich* or *Herzlichst, Herzliche Grüße;* more affectionately: *Alles Liebe; Bis bald* = See you soon .

Christmas and New Year wishes

On a card:

Frohe Weihnachten und viel Glück im neuen Jahr

A bit more formal: Ein gesegnetes Weihnachtsfest und die besten Wünsche zum neuen Jahr

A bit less formal: Fröhliche Weihnachten und einen guten Rutsch ins neue Jahr

In a letter:

- On most personal letters German speakers don't put their address at the top, but just the name of the place and the date

Würzburg, den 20.12.2001

Liebe Karin, lieber Ferdinand,

euch und euren Kindern wünschen wir von Herzen frohe Weihnachten und ein glückliches neues Jahr. Wir hoffen, es geht euch allen gut, und dass wir uns bald mal wieder sehen werden. Es kommt uns so vor, als hätten wir uns eine Ewigkeit nicht gesehen.

Das vergangene Jahr war für uns sehr ereignisreich. Thomas hatte im Sommer einen Unfall mit dem Fahrrad, und brach sich den Arm und das Schlüsselbein. Sabine hat das Abitur gerade noch bestanden und ist jetzt an der Uni in Erlangen, studiert Sport. Der arme Michael ist im Oktober arbeitslos geworden und sucht immer noch nach einer Stelle.

Ihr müsst unbedingt vorbeikommen, wenn ihr das nächste Mal in der Gegend seid. Ruft doch einfach ein paar Tage vorher an, damit wir etwas ausmachen können.

Mit herzlichen Grüßen

Eure Gabi und Michael

Invitation (informal)

Hamm, den 22.4.2001

Liebe Jennie,

... wäre es möglich, dass du 1 in den Sommerferien zu uns kommst? Katrin und Gottfried würden sich riesig freuen (ich und mein Mann natürlich auch). Wir planen eine Reise zum Bodensee Ende Juli/Anfang August, du 1 könntest gerne mitfahren. Es ist wirklich sehr schön dort unten. Wir werden wahrscheinlich zelten – hoffentlich hast du 1 nichts dagegen!

Schreib bald, ob das für dich 1 in Frage kommt.

Herzliche Grüße

Monika Pfortner

- Beginning: if you put a comma after the name on the first line (which is usual), the letter proper should start with a small letter.

1 *du, dich, dein* etc.: although many people still write these with a capital in letters, this is not necessary. But the formal *Sie, Ihnen, Ihr* must always have a capital.

Invitation (formal)

Invitations to parties are usually by word of mouth, while for weddings, announcements rather than invitations are usually sent out:

Irene Brinkmann   Stefan Hopf

Wir heiraten am Samstag, den 20. April
2001, um 14 Uhr in der Pfarrkirche
Landsberg.

Goethestraße 12   Ulrichsweg 4

Landsberg   Altötting

Accepting an invitation

Edinburgh, den 2.5.2001

Liebe Frau Pfortner,

recht herzlichen Dank für Ihre liebe Einladung. Da ich noch keine
festen Pläne für die Sommerferien habe, möchte ich sie sehr gerne
annehmen. Allerdings darf ich nicht mehr als vier bis fünf Tage
weg sein, da es meiner Mutter nicht sehr gut geht. Sie **1** müssen
mir sagen, was ich mitbringen soll (außer Edinburgh Rock!). Ist
es sehr warm am Bodensee? Kann man im See schwimmen?

Natürlich habe ich nichts gegen Zelten. Auch hier in Schottland
bei Wind und Regen macht es mir Spaß!

Ich freue mich auf ein baldiges Wiedersehen.

Herzliche Grüße

Jennie Stewart

1 Since this is a letter from a younger person writing to the mother of
a friend, she uses the formal *Sie* form and possessive *Ihr* (always
with capitals), and writes to her as "*Frau Pfortner*". On the other
hand it was quite natural for Frau Pfortner to use the *du* form to her.

Enquiry to a tourist office

■ A simple business-style letter. The recipient's address is on the left and the sender's on the right, with the date below.

■ The subject of the letter is centred.

Verkehrsverein Heidelberg e.V.
Friedrich-Ebert-Anlage 2
69117 Heidelberg

Silvia Sommer
Tannenweg 23
48149 Münster

24. April 2001

Hotels und Pensionen in Heidelberg

Sehr geehrte Damen und Herren,

würden Sie mir bitte freundlicherweise eine Liste der Hotels und Pensionen (der mittleren Kategorie) am Ort zusenden?

Ich möchte bitte auch Informationen über Busfahrten zu den Sehenswürdigkeiten der Umgebung in der zweiten Augusthälfte haben.

Mit freundlichen Grüßen

Silvia Sommer

■ This is the standard formula for starting a business letter addressed to a firm or organization, and not to a particular person.

■ "*Mit freundlichen Grüßen*" is the standard ending for a formal or business letter; another possibility is "*Mit besten Grüßen*".

Booking a hotel room

Hotel Goldener Pflug
Ortsstraße 7
69235 Steinbach
Baden

Tobias Schwarz
Gartenstr. 19
76530 Baden-

16. Juli 2001

Sehr geehrte Damen und Herren,

Ich wurde durch die Broschüre "Hotels und Pensionen im Naturpark Odenwald (Ausgabe 2000)" auf ihr Hotel aufmerksam.

Ich möchte für mich und meine Frau für die Zeit vom 2. bis 11. August (neun Nächte) ein ruhiges Doppelzimmer mit Dusche reservieren, sowie ein Einzelzimmer für unseren Sohn.

Falls Sie für diese Zeit etwas Passendes haben, informieren Sie mich doch bitte über den Preis und darüber, ob Sie eine Anzahlung wünschen.

Mit freundlichen Grüßen

Tobias Schwarz

Booking a campsite

■ For a business letter to a particular person, use "*Sehr geehrte(r)*"
and the name. (If this letter were to a man, it would start "*Sehr
geehrter Herr Sattler*").

Camilla Stumpf
Saalgasse 10
60311 Frankfurt

Camping am See
Frau Bettina Sattler
Auweg 6-10
87654 Waldenkirchen   Frankfurt, den 16.04.2001

Sehr geehrte Frau Sattler,

Ihr Campingplatz wurde mir von Herrn Stephan Seidel
empfohlen, der schon mehrmals bei Ihnen war. **1** Ich würde nun
gerne vom 18. bis 25. Juli mit zwei Freunden eine Woche bei Ihnen
verbringen. Könnten Sie uns bitte einen Zeltplatz **2** möglichst
in unmittelbarer Nähe des Sees **3** reservieren?

Würden Sie mir freundlicherweise mitteilen, ob Sie meine
Reservierung annehmen können und ob Sie eine Anzahlung
wünschen?

Außerdem wäre ich Ihnen dankbar für eine kurze
Wegbeschreibung von der Autobahn.

Mit vielem Dank im Voraus und freundlichen Grüßen

Camilla Stumpf

---

1 Or if you have found the campsite in a guide, say e.g.: "*Ich habe Ihre
Anschrift dem ACDA-Campingführer 2000 entnommen*".

2 Or if you have a caravan: "*einen Stellplatz für einen Wohnwagen*".

3 Alternatives: "*in schattiger/geschützter Lage*".

Cancelling a reservation

Herrn
Hans Knauer
Gasthaus Sonnenblick
Hauptstr. 6
D-94066 Bad Füssing
Germany   Aberdeen, den 2.6.2001

Sehr geehrter Herr Knauer,

leider muss ich meine Reservierung für die
Woche vom 7. bis 13. August **1** rückgängig
machen. Wegen unvorhergesehener Umstände
2 muss ich auf meinen Urlaub verzichten.

Es tut mir aufrichtig Leid, dass ich so spät
abbestellen muss, und hoffe, dass Sie
deswegen keine Unannehmlichkeiten haben.

Mit freundlichen Grüßen

Robert McDonald

1 Or: "*für die Zeit vom 7. bis 20. August*" etc.
2 Or more precisely: "*Durch den überraschenden Tod meines
Vaters/die Krankheit meines Mannes*" etc.

Sending an e-mail

The illustration shows a typical interface for sending e-mail.

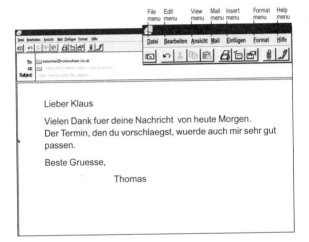

English–German Dictionary

a

vor einem Vokal **an**
● *indefinite article*

····▶ ein (*m*), eine (*f*), ein (*nt*). **a problem** ein Problem. **an apple** ein Apfel. **a cat** eine Katze. **have you got a pencil?** hast du einen Bleistift? **I gave it to a beggar** ich gab es einem Bettler

❗ There are some cases where a is not translated, such as when talking about people's professions or nationalities: **she is a lawyer** sie ist Rechtsanwältin. **he's an Italian** er ist Italiener

····▶ (*with 'not'*) kein (*m*), keine (*f*), kein (*nt*), keine (*pl*). **that's not a problem/not a good idea** das ist kein Problem/keine gute Idee. **there was not a chance that ...** es bestand keine Möglichkeit, dass .... **she did not say a word** sie sagte kein Wort. **I didn't tell a soul** ich habe es keinem Menschen gesagt

····▶ (*per; each*) pro. **£300 a week** 300 Pfund pro Woche. **30 miles an hour** 30 Meilen pro Stunde. (*in prices*) **it costs 90p a pound** es kostet 90 Pence das Pfund.

aback *adv* **be taken ~** verblüfft sein

abandon *vt* verlassen; (*give up*) aufgeben

abate *vi* nachlassen

abattoir *n* Schlachthof *m*

abb|ey *n* Abtei *f*. **~ot** *n* Abt *m*

abbreviat|e *vt* abkürzen. **~ion** *n* Abkürzung *f*

abdicat|e *vi* abdanken. **~ion** *n* Abdankung *f*

abdom|en *n* Unterleib *m*. **~inal** *a* Unterleibs-

abduct *vt* entführen. **~ion** *n* Entführung *f*

aberration *n* Abweichung *f*; (*mental*) Verwirrung *f*

abeyance *n* **in ~** [zeitweilig] außer Kraft

abhor *vt* (*pt/pp* abhorred) verabscheuen. **~rent** *a* abscheulich

abid|e *vt* (*pt/pp* abided) (*tolerate*) aushalten; ausstehen <*person*>

ability *n* Fähigkeit *f*; (*talent*) Begabung *f*

abject *a* erbärmlich; (*humble*) demütig

ablaze *a* in Flammen

able *a* (**-r, -st**) fähig; **be ~ to do sth** etw tun können. **~-bodied** *a* körperlich gesund

ably *adv* gekonnt

abnormal *a* anormal; (*Med*) abnorm. **~ity** *n* Abnormität *f*. **~ly** *adv* ungewöhnlich

aboard *adv* & *prep* an Bord (+ *gen*)

abol|ish *vt* abschaffen. **~ition** *n* Abschaffung *f*

abominable *a*, **-bly** *adv* abscheulich

aborigines *npl* Ureinwohner *pl*

abort *vt* abtreiben. **~ion** *n* Abtreibung *f*. **~ive** *a* <*attempt*> vergeblich

about *adv* umher, herum; (*approximately*) ungefähr; **be ~** (*in circulation*) umgehen; (*in existence*) vorhanden sein; **be ~ to do sth** im Begriff sein, etw zu tun; **there was no one ~** es war kein Mensch da; **run/play ~** herumlaufen/-spielen ● *prep* um (+ *acc*) [… herum]; (*concerning*)

über (+ *acc*); **what is it ~?** worum
geht es? *<book:>* wovon handelt
es? **I know nothing ~ it** ich weiß
nichts davon; **talk/know ~**
reden/wissen von

about: **~-face** *n*, **-turn** *n*
Kehrtwendung *f*
above *adv* oben ● *prep* über (+
dat/*acc*); **~ all** vor allem
above: **~-board** *a* legal. **~-
mentioned** *a* oben erwähnt
abrasive *a* Scheuer-; *<remark>*
verletzend ● *n* Scheuermittel *nt*;
(Techn) Schleifmittel *nt*
abreast *adv* nebeneinander; **keep
~ of** Schritt halten mit
abridge *vt* kürzen
abroad *adv* im Ausland; **go ~** ins
Ausland fahren
abrupt *a*, **-ly** *adv* abrupt; *(sudden)*
plötzlich; *(curt)* schroff
abscess *n* Abszess *m*
absence *n* Abwesenheit *f*
absent *a* abwesend; **be ~** fehlen
absentee *n* Abwesende(r) *m/f*
absent-minded *a*, **-ly** *adv*
geistesabwesend; *(forgetful)*
zerstreut
absolute *a*, **-ly** *adv* absolut
absorb *vt* absorbieren,
aufsaugen; **~ed in** vertieft in (+
acc). **~ent** *a* saugfähig
absorption *n* Absorption *f*
abstain *vi* sich enthalten (**from**
gen)
abstemious *a* enthaltsam
abstention *n* *(Pol)*
[Stimm]enthaltung *f*
abstract *a* abstrakt ● *n*
(summary) Abriss *m*
absurd *a*, **-ly** *adv* absurd. **~ity** *n*
Absurdität *f*
abundan|ce *n* Fülle *f* (**of** an +
dat). **~t** *a* reichlich
abuse¹ *vt* missbrauchen; *(insult)*
beschimpfen
abus|e² *n* Missbrauch *m*; *(insults)*
Beschimpfungen *pl*. **~ive** *a*
ausfallend

abysmal *a* 🔲 katastrophal
abyss *n* Abgrund *m*
academic *a*, **-ally** *adv* akademisch
academy *n* Akademie *f*
accelerat|e *vt/i* beschleunigen.
~ion *n* Beschleunigung *f*. **~or** *n*
(Auto) Gaspedal *nt*
accent *n* Akzent *m*
accept *vt* annehmen; *(fig)*
akzeptieren ● *vi* zusagen. **~able**
a annehmbar. **~ance** *n*
Annahme *f*; *(of invitation)* Zusage
f
access *n* Zugang *m*. **~ible** *a*
zugänglich
accessor|y *n* *(Jur)*
Mitschuldige(r) *m/f*; **~ies** *pl*
(fashion) Accessoires *pl*; *(Techn)*
Zubehör *nt*
accident *n* Unfall *m*; *(chance)*
Zufall *m*; **by ~** zufällig;
(unintentionally) versehentlich.
~al *a*, **-ly** *adv* zufällig;
(unintentional) versehentlich
acclaim *vt* feiern (**as** als)
acclimatize *vt* **become ~d** sich
akklimatisieren
accommodat|e *vt* unterbringen.
~ing *a* entgegenkommend. **~ion**
n *(rooms)* Unterkunft *f*
accompan|iment *n* Begleitung *f*.
~ist *n* *(Mus)* Begleiter(in) *m(f)*
accompany *vt* *(pt/pp* **-ied)**
begleiten
accomplice *n* Komplize/-zin *m/f*
accomplish *vt* erfüllen *<task>*;
(achieve) erreichen. **~ed** *a* fähig.
~ment *n* Fertigkeit *f*;
(achievement) Leistung *f*
accord *n* **of one's own ~** aus
eigenem Antrieb. **~ance** *n* **in
~ance with** entsprechend (+ *dat*)
according *adv* **~ to** nach (+ *dat*).
~ly *adv* entsprechend
accordion *n* Akkordeon *nt*
account *n* Konto *nt*; *(bill)*
Rechnung *f*; *(description)*
Darstellung *f*; *(report)* Bericht *m*;
~s *pl* *(Comm)* Bücher *pl*; **on ~ of**

wegen (+ *gen*); **on no ~** auf keinen Fall; **take into ~** in Betracht ziehen, berücksichtigen ● *vi* **~ for** Rechenschaft ablegen für; (*explain*) erklären

accountant *n* Buchhalter(in) *m(f)*; (*chartered*) Wirtschaftsprüfer *m*

accumulat|e *vt* ansammeln, anhäufen ● *vi* sich ansammeln, sich anhäufen. **~ion** *n* Ansammlung *f*, Anhäufung *f*

accura|cy *n* Genauigkeit *f*. **~te** *a*, **-ly** *adv* genau

accusation *n* Anklage *f*

accusative *a & n* **~ [case]** (*Gram*) Akkusativ *m*

accuse *vt* (*Jur*) anklagen (**of** *gen*); **~ s.o. of doing sth** jdn beschuldigen, etw getan zu haben

accustom *vt* gewöhnen (**to** an + *dat*); **grow** *or* **get ~ed to** sich gewöhnen an (+ *acc*). **~ed** *a* gewohnt

ace *n* (*Cards, Sport*) Ass *nt*

ache *n* Schmerzen *pl* ● *vi* weh tun, schmerzen

achieve *vt* leisten; (*gain*) erzielen; (*reach*) erreichen. **~ment** *n* (*feat*) Leistung *f*

acid *a* sauer; (*fig*) beißend ● *n* Säure *f*. **~ity** *n* Säure *f*. **~ rain** *n* saurer Regen *m*

acknowledge *vt* anerkennen; (*admit*) zugeben; erwidern <*greeting*>; **~ receipt of** den Empfang bestätigen (+ *gen*). **~ment** *n* Anerkennung *f*; (*of letter*) Empfangsbestätigung *f*

acne *n* Akne *f*

acorn *n* Eichel *f*

acoustic *a*, **-ally** *adv* akustisch. **~s** *npl* Akustik *f*

acquaint *vt* **be ~ed with** kennen; vertraut sein mit <*fact*>. **~ance** *n* (*person*) Bekannte(r) *m/f*; **make s.o.'s ~ance** jdn kennen lernen

acquire *vt* erwerben

acquisit|ion *n* Erwerb *m*; (*thing*) Erwerbung *f*. **~ive** *a* habgierig

acquit *vt* (*pt/pp* **acquitted**) freisprechen

acre *n* ≈ Morgen *m*

acrimonious *a* bitter

acrobat *n* Akrobat(in) *m(f)*. **~ic** *a* akrobatisch

across *adv* hinüber/herüber; (*wide*) breit; (*not lengthwise*) quer; (*in crossword*) waagerecht; **come ~ sth** auf etw (*acc*) stoßen; **go ~** hinübergehen; **bring ~** herüberbringen ● *prep* über (+ *acc*); (*on the other side of*) auf der anderen Seite (+ *gen*)

act *n* Tat *f*; (*action*) Handlung *f*; (*law*) Gesetz *nt*; (*Theat*) Akt *m*; (*item*) Nummer *f* ● *vi* handeln; (*behave*) sich verhalten; (*Theat*) spielen; (*pretend*) sich verstellen; **~ as** fungieren als ● *vt* spielen <*role*>. **~ing** *a* (*deputy*) stellvertretend ● *n* (*Theat*) Schauspielerei *f*

action *n* Handlung *f*; (*deed*) Tat *f*; (*Mil*) Einsatz *m*; (*Jur*) Klage *f*; (*effect*) Wirkung *f*; (*Techn*) Mechanismus *m*; **out of ~** <*machine:*> außer Betrieb; **take ~** handeln; **killed in ~** gefallen

activate *vt* betätigen

activ|e *a*, **-ly** *adv* aktiv; **on ~e service** im Einsatz. **~ity** *n* Aktivität *f*

act|or *n* Schauspieler *m*. **~ress** *n* Schauspielerin *f*

actual *a*, **-ly** *adv* eigentlich; (*real*) tatsächlich

acupuncture *n* Akupunktur *f*

acute *a* scharf; <*angle*> spitz; <*illness*> akut. **~ly** *adv* sehr

ad *n* 🔲 = **advertisement**

AD *abbr* (**Anno Domini**) n.Chr.

adamant *a* **be ~ that** darauf bestehen, dass

adapt *vt* anpassen; bearbeiten <*play*> ● *vi* sich anpassen. **~able** *a* anpassungsfähig

adaptation n (*Theat*) Bearbeitung f

add vt hinzufügen; (*Math*) addieren ● vi zusammenzählen, addieren; ~ **to** hinzufügen zu; (*fig: increase*) steigern; (*compound*) verschlimmern. ~ **up** vt zusammenzählen <*figures*> ● vi zusammenzählen, addieren

adder n Kreuzotter f

addict n Süchtige(r) m/f

addict|ed a süchtig; ~**ed to drugs** drogensüchtig. ~**ion** n Sucht f

addition n Hinzufügung f; (*Math*) Addition f; (*thing added*) Ergänzung f; **in** ~ zusätzlich. ~**al** a, -**ly** adv zusätzlich

additive n Zusatz m

address n Adresse f, Anschrift f; (*speech*) Ansprache f ● vt adressieren (**to** an + *acc*); (*speak to*) anreden <*person*>; sprechen vor (+ *dat*) <*meeting*>. ~**ee** n Empfänger m

adequate a, -**ly** adv ausreichend

adhere vi kleben/(*fig*) festhalten (**to** an + *dat*)

adhesive a klebend ● n Klebstoff m

adjacent a angrenzend

adjective n Adjektiv nt

adjoin vt angrenzen an (+ *acc*). ~**ing** a angrenzend

adjourn vt vertagen (**until** auf + *acc*) ● vi sich vertagen. ~**ment** n Vertagung f

adjudicate vi (*in competition*) Preisrichter sein

adjust vt einstellen; (*alter*) verstellen ● vi sich anpassen (**to** *dat*). ~**able** a verstellbar. ~**ment** n Einstellung f; Anpassung f

ad lib adv aus dem Stegreif ● vi (*pt/pp* **ad libbed**) 🅘 improvisieren

administer vt verwalten; verabreichen <*medicine*>

administration n Verwaltung f; (*Pol*) Regierung f

admirable a bewundernswert

admiral n Admiral m

admiration n Bewunderung f

admire vt bewundern. ~**r** n Verehrer(in) m(f)

admission n Eingeständnis nt; (*entry*) Eintritt m

admit vt (*pt/pp* **admitted**) (*let in*) hereinlassen; (*acknowledge*) zugeben; ~ **to sth** etw zugeben. ~**tance** n Eintritt m. ~**tedly** adv zugegebenermaßen

admonish vt ermahnen

adolescen|ce n Jugend f, Pubertät f. ~**t** a Jugend-; <*boy, girl*> halbwüchsig ● n Jugendliche(r) m/f

adopt vt adoptieren; ergreifen <*measure*>; (*Pol*) annehmen <*candidate*>. ~**ion** n Adoption f

ador|able a bezaubernd. ~**ation** n Anbetung f

adore vt (*worship*) anbeten; (🅘 *like*) lieben

adorn vt schmücken. ~**ment** n Schmuck m

Adriatic a & n ~ **[Sea]** Adria f

adrift a **be** ~ treiben

adroit a, -**ly** adv gewandt, geschickt

adulation n Schwärmerei f

adult n Erwachsene(r) m/f

adulterate vt verfälschen; panschen <*wine*>

adultery n Ehebruch m

advance n Fortschritt m; (*Mil*) Vorrücken nt; (*payment*) Vorschuss m; **in** ~ im Voraus ● vi vorankommen; (*Mil*) vorrücken; (*make progress*) Fortschritte machen ● vt fördern <*cause*>; vorbringen <*idea*>; vorschießen <*money*>. ~**d** a fortgeschritten; (*progressive*) fortschrittlich. ~**ment** n Förderung f; (*promotion*) Beförderung f

advantage n Vorteil m; **take** ~ **of** ausnutzen. ~**ous** a vorteilhaft

adventur|e n Abenteuer nt. **~er** n Abenteurer m. **~ous** a abenteuerlich; <person> abenteuerlustig

adverb n Adverb nt

adverse a ungünstig

advert n ▣ = advertisement

advertise vt Reklame machen für; (by small ad) inserieren ● vi Reklame machen; inserieren

advertisement n Anzeige f; (publicity) Reklame f; (small ad) Inserat nt

advertis|er n Inserent m. **~ing** n Werbung f

advice n Rat m

advisable a ratsam

advis|e vt raten (s.o. jdm); (counsel) beraten; (inform) benachrichtigen; **~e s.o. against sth** jdm von etw abraten ● vi raten. **~er** n Berater(in) m(f). **~ory** a beratend

advocate¹ n (supporter) Befürworter m

advocate² vt befürworten

aerial a Luft- ● n Antenne f

aerobics n Aerobic nt

aero|drome n Flugplatz m. **~plane** n Flugzeug nt

aerosol n Spraydose f

aesthetic a ästhetisch

affair n Angelegenheit f, Sache f; (scandal) Affäre f; **[love-]~** [Liebes]verhältnis nt

affect vt sich auswirken auf (+ acc); (concern) betreffen; (move) rühren; (pretend) vortäuschen. **~ation** n Affektiertheit f. **~ed** a affektiert

affection n Liebe f. **~ate** a, **-ly** adv liebevoll

affirm vt behaupten

affirmative a bejahend ● n Bejahung f

afflict vt be **~ed with** behaftet sein mit. **~ion** n Leiden nt

affluen|ce n Reichtum m. **~t** a wohlhabend. **~t society** n Wohlstandsgesellschaft f

afford vt be able to **~ sth** sich (dat) etw leisten können. **~able** a erschwinglich

affront n Beleidigung f ● vt beleidigen

afloat a be **~** <ship:> flott sein; **keep ~** <person:> sich über Wasser halten

afraid a be **~** Angst haben (of vor + dat); **I'm ~ not** leider nicht; **I'm ~ so** [ja] leider

Africa n Afrika nt. **~n** a afrikanisch ● n Afrikaner(in) m(f)

after adv danach ● prep nach (+ dat); **~ that** danach; **~ all** schließlich; **the day ~ tomorrow** übermorgen; **be ~** aus sein auf (+ acc) ● conj nachdem

after: **~-effect** n Nachwirkung f. **~math** n Auswirkungen pl. **~noon** n Nachmittag m; **good ~noon!** guten Tag! **~-sales service** n Kundendienst m. **~shave** n Rasierwasser nt. **~thought** n nachträglicher Einfall m. **~wards** adv nachher

again adv wieder; (once more) noch einmal; **~ and ~** immer wieder

against prep gegen (+ acc)

age n Alter nt; (era) Zeitalter nt; **~s** ▣ ewig; **under ~** minderjährig; **of ~** volljährig; **two years of ~** zwei Jahre alt ● v (pres p ageing) ● vt älter machen ● vi altern; (mature) reifen

aged¹ a **~ two** zwei Jahre alt

aged² a betagt ● n **the ~** pl die Alten

ageless a ewig jung

agency n Agentur f; (office) Büro nt

agenda n Tagesordnung f

agent n Agent(in) m(f); (Comm) Vertreter(in) m(f); (substance) Mittel nt

aggravat|e vt verschlimmern; (🗓 annoy) ärgern. **~ion** n 🗓 Ärger m

aggregate a gesamt ● n Gesamtzahl f; (sum) Gesamtsumme f

aggress|ion n Aggression f. **~ive** a, **-ly** adv aggressiv. **~or** n Angreifer(in) m(f)

aggro n 🗓 Ärger m

aghast a entsetzt

agil|e a flink, behände; <mind> wendig. **~ity** n Flinkheit f, Behändigkeit f

agitat|e vt bewegen; (shake) schütteln ● vi (fig) **~ for** agitieren für. **~ed** a, **-ly** adv erregt. **~ion** n Erregung f; (Pol) Agitation f

ago adv vor (+ dat); **a long time ~** vor langer Zeit; **how long ~ is it?** wie lange ist es her?

agony n Qual f; **be in ~** furchtbare Schmerzen haben

agree vt vereinbaren; (admit) zugeben; **~ to do sth** sich bereit erklären, etw zu tun ● vi <people, figures:> übereinstimmen; (reach agreement) sich einigen; (get on) gut miteinander auskommen; (consent) einwilligen (**to** in + acc); **~ with s.o.** jdm zustimmen; <food:> jdm bekommen; **~ with sth** (approve of) mit etw einverstanden sein

agreeable a angenehm

agreed a vereinbart

agreement n Übereinstimmung f; (consent) Einwilligung f; (contract) Abkommen nt; **reach ~** sich einigen

agricultur|al a landwirtschaftlich. **~e** n Landwirtschaft f

aground a gestrandet; **run ~** <ship:> stranden

ahead adv straight **~** geradeaus; **be ~ of s.o./sth** vor jdm/etw sein; (fig) voraus sein; **go on ~** vorgehen; **get ~** vorankommen; **go ~!** 🗓 bitte! **look/plan ~** vorausblicken/-planen

aid n Hilfe f; (financial) Unterstützung f; **in ~ of** zugunsten (+ gen) ● vt helfen (+ dat)

Aids n Aids nt

aim n Ziel nt; **take ~** zielen ● vt richten (**at** auf + acc); ● vi zielen (**at** auf + acc); **~ to do sth** beabsichtigen, etw zu tun. **~less** a, **-ly** adv ziellos

air n Luft f; (expression) Miene f; (appearance) Anschein m; **be on the ~** <programme:> gesendet werden; <person:> auf Sendung sein; **by ~** auf dem Luftweg; (airmail) mit Luftpost ● vt lüften; vorbringen <views>

air: **~-conditioned** a klimatisiert. **~-conditioning** n Klimaanlage f. **~craft** n Flugzeug nt. **~field** n Flugplatz m. **~ force** n Luftwaffe f. **~ freshener** n Raumspray nt. **~gun** n Luftgewehr nt. **~ hostess** n Stewardess f. **~ letter** n Aerogramm nt. **~line** n Fluggesellschaft f. **~mail** n Luftpost f. **~man** n Flieger m. **~plane** n (Amer) Flugzeug nt. **~port** n Flughafen m. **~-raid** n Luftangriff m. **~-raid shelter** n Luftschutzbunker m. **~ship** n Luftschiff nt. **~ ticket** n Flugschein m. **~tight** a luftdicht. **~-traffic controller** n Fluglotse m

airy a (-ier, -iest) luftig; <manner> nonchalant

aisle n Gang m

ajar a angelehnt

alarm n Alarm m; (device) Alarmanlage f; (clock) Wecker m; (fear) Unruhe f ● vt erschrecken

alas int ach!

album n Album nt

alcohol n Alkohol m. **~ic** a
alkoholisch ● n Alkoholiker(in)
m(f). **~ism** n Alkoholismus m
alert a aufmerksam ● n Alarm m
algebra n Algebra f
Algeria n Algerien nt
alias n Deckname m ● adv alias
alibi n Alibi nt
alien a fremd ● n Ausländer(in)
m(f)
alienate vt entfremden
alight[1] vi aussteigen (**from** aus)
alight[2] a be ~ brennen; **set** ~
anzünden
align vt ausrichten. **~ment** n
Ausrichtung f
alike a & adv ähnlich; (same)
gleich; **look** ~ sich (dat) ähnlich
sehen
alive a lebendig; **be** ~ leben; **be** ~
with wimmeln von

all
● adjective
····▶ (plural) alle. **all [the] children**
alle Kinder. **all our children** alle
unsere Kinder. **all the books** alle
Bücher. **all the others** alle
anderen
····▶ (singular = whole) ganz. **all
the wine** der ganze Wein. **all the
town** die ganze Stadt. **all my
money** mein ganzes Geld; all
mein Geld. **all day** den ganzen
Tag. **all Germany** ganz
Deutschland
● pronoun
····▶ (plural = all persons/things)
alle. **all are welcome** alle sind
willkommen. **they all came** sie
sind alle gekommen. **are we all
here?** sind wir alle da? **the best
pupils of all** die besten Schüler
(von allen). **the most beautiful of
all** der/die/das schönste von
allen
····▶ (singular = everything) alles.
that is all das ist alles. **all that I
possess** alles, was ich besitze

····▶ **all of** ganz; (with plural) alle.
all of the money das ganze Geld.
all of the paintings alle Gemälde.
all of you/them Sie/sie alle
····▶ (in phrases) **all in all** alles in
allem. **in all** insgesamt. **most of
all** am meisten. **once and for all**
ein für alle Mal. **not at all** gar
nicht
● adverb
····▶ (completely) ganz. **she was all
alone** sie war ganz allein. **I was
all dirty** ich war ganz schmutzig
····▶ (in scores) **four** all vier zu vier
····▶ **all right** (things) in Ordnung.
is everything all right? ist alles in
Ordnung? **is that all right for you?**
passt das Ihnen? **I'm all right** mir
geht es gut. **did you get home all
right?** sind Sie gut nach Hause
gekommen? **is it all right to go in?**
kann ich reingehen? **yes, all right**
ja, gut. **work out all right** gut
gehen; klappen 🎧
····▶ (in phrases) **all but** (almost)
fast. **all at once** auf einmal. **all the
better** umso besser. **all the same**
(nevertheless) trotzdem

allege vt behaupten
allegiance n Treue f
allerg|ic a allergisch (**to** gegen).
~y n Allergie f
alleviate vt lindern
alley n Gasse f; (for bowling)
Bahn f
alliance n Verbindung f; (Pol)
Bündnis nt
allied a alliiert
alligator n Alligator m
allocat|e vt zuteilen; (share out)
verteilen. **~ion** n Zuteilung f
allot vt (pt/pp allotted) zuteilen
(s.o. jdm)
allow vt erlauben; (give) geben;
(grant) gewähren; (reckon)
rechnen; (agree, admit) zugeben;
~ **for** berücksichtigen; ~ **s.o. to**

do sth jdm erlauben, etw zu tun; **be ~ed to do sth** etw tun dürfen

allowance *n* [finanzielle] Unterstützung *f*; **make ~s for** berücksichtigen

alloy *n* Legierung *f*

allude *vi* anspielen (**to** auf + *acc*)

allusion *n* Anspielung *f*

ally[1] *n* Verbündete(r) *m/f*; **the Allies** *pl* die Alliierten

ally[2] *vt* (*pt/pp* **-ied**) verbinden; **~ oneself with** sich verbünden mit

almighty *a* allmächtig; (**[I]** *big*) Riesen-. ●*n* **the A~** der Allmächtige

almond *n* (*Bot*) Mandel *f*

almost *adv* fast, beinahe

alone *a & adv* allein; **leave me ~** lass mich in Ruhe; **leave that ~!** lass die Finger davon! **let ~** ganz zu schweigen von

along *prep* entlang (+ *acc*); **~ the river** den Fluss entlang ●*adv* **~ with** zusammen mit; **all ~** die ganze Zeit; **come ~** komm doch; **I'll bring it ~** ich bringe es mit

alongside *adv* daneben ●*prep* neben (+ *dat*)

aloud *adv* laut

alphabet *n* Alphabet *nt*. **~ical** *a*, **-ly** *adv* alphabetisch

alpine *a* alpin; **A ~** Alpen-

Alps *npl* Alpen *pl*

already *adv* schon

Alsace *n* Elsass *nt*

Alsatian *n* (*dog*) [deutscher] Schäferhund *m*

also *adv* auch

altar *n* Altar *m*

alter *vt* ändern ●*vi* sich verändern. **~ation** *n* Änderung *f*

alternate[1] *vi* [sich] abwechseln ●*vt* abwechseln

alternate[2] *a*, **-ly** *adv* abwechselnd; **on ~ days** jeden zweiten Tag

alternative *a* andere(r,s); **~ medicine** Alternativmedizin *f* ●*n* Alternative *f*. **~ly** *adv* oder aber

although *conj* obgleich, obwohl

altitude *n* Höhe *f*

altogether *adv* insgesamt; (*on the whole*) alles in allem

aluminium *n*, (*Amer*) **aluminum** *n* Aluminium *nt*

always *adv* immer

am *see* be

a.m. *abbr* (**ante meridiem**) vormittags

amass *vt* anhäufen

amateur *n* Amateur *m* ●*attrib* Amateur-; (*Theat*) Laien-. **~ish** *a* laienhaft

amaze *vt* erstaunen. **~d** *a* erstaunt. **~ment** *n* Erstaunen *nt*

amazing *a*, **-ly** *adv* erstaunlich

ambassador *n* Botschafter *m*

amber *n* Bernstein *m* ●*a* (*colour*) gelb

ambigu|ity *n* Zweideutigkeit *f*. **~ous** *a* **-ly** *adv* zweideutig

ambiti|on *n* Ehrgeiz *m*; (*aim*) Ambition *f*. **~ous** *a* ehrgeizig

amble *vi* schlendern

ambulance *n* Krankenwagen *m*. **~ man** *n* Sanitäter *m*

ambush *n* Hinterhalt *m* ●*vt* aus dem Hinterhalt überfallen

amen *int* amen

amend *vt* ändern. **~ment** *n* Änderung *f*

amenities *npl* Einrichtungen *pl*

America *n* Amerika *nt*. **~n** *a* amerikanisch ●*n* Amerikaner(in) *m(f)*. **~nism** *n* Amerikanismus *m*

amiable *a* nett

amicable *a*, **-bly** *adv* freundschaftlich; <*agreement*> gütlich

amid[st] *prep* inmitten (+ *gen*)

ammonia *n* Ammoniak *nt*

ammunition *n* Munition *f*

amnesty *n* Amnestie *f*

among[st] *prep* unter (+ *dat/acc*); **~ yourselves** untereinander

amoral *a* amoralisch

amorous *a* zärtlich

amount n Menge f; (sum of money) Betrag m; (total) Gesamtsumme f • vi ~ **to** sich belaufen auf (+ acc); (fig) hinauslaufen auf (+ acc)
amphibi|an n Amphibie f. ~**ous** a amphibisch
amphitheatre n Amphitheater nt
ample a (-r, -st), -**ly** adv reichlich; (large) füllig
amplif|ier n Verstärker m. ~**y** vt (pt/pp -ied) weiter ausführen; verstärken <sound>
amputat|e vt amputieren. ~**ion** n Amputation f
amuse vt amüsieren, belustigen; (entertain) unterhalten. ~**ment** n Belustigung f; Unterhaltung f
amusing a amüsant
an see a
anaem|ia n Blutarmut f, Anämie f. ~**ic** a blutarm
anaesthetic n Narkosemittel nt, Betäubungsmittel nt; **under [an]** ~ in Narkose
anaesthetist n Narkosearzt m
analogy n Analogie f
analyse vt analysieren
analysis n Analyse f
analyst n Chemiker(in) m(f); (Psych) Analytiker m
analytical a analytisch
anarch|ist n Anarchist m. ~**y** n Anarchie f
anatom|ical a, -**ly** adv anatomisch. ~**y** n Anatomie f
ancest|or n Vorfahr m. ~**ry** n Abstammung f
anchor n Anker m • vi ankern • vt verankern
ancient a alt
and conj und; ~ **so on** und so weiter; **six hundred** ~ **two** sechshundertzwei; **more** ~ **more** immer mehr; **nice** ~ **warm** schön warm
anecdote n Anekdote f
angel n Engel m. ~**ic** a engelhaft

anger n Zorn m • vt zornig machen
angle n Winkel m; (fig) Standpunkt m; **at an** ~ schräg
angler n Angler m
Anglican a anglikanisch • n Anglikaner(in) m(f)
Anglo-Saxon a angelsächsich • n Angelsächsisch nt
angry a (-ier, -iest), -**ily** adv zornig; **be** ~ **with** böse sein auf (+ acc)
anguish n Qual f
angular a eckig; <features> kantig
animal n Tier nt • a tierisch
animat|e vt beleben. ~**ed** a lebhaft
animosity n Feindseligkeit f
ankle n [Fuß]knöchel m
annex[e] n Nebengebäude nt; (extension) Anbau m
annihilate vt vernichten
anniversary n Jahrestag m
annotate vt kommentieren
announce vt bekannt geben; (over loudspeaker) durchsagen; (at reception) ankündigen; (Radio, TV) ansagen; (in newspaper) anzeigen. ~**ment** n Bekanntgabe f, Bekanntmachung f; Durchsage f; Ansage f; Anzeige f. ~**r** n Ansager(in) m(f)
annoy vt ärgern; (pester) belästigen; **get** ~**ed** sich ärgern. ~**ance** n Ärger m. ~**ing** a ärgerlich
annual a, -**ly** adv jährlich • n (book) Jahresalbum nt
anonymous a, -**ly** adv anonym
anorak n Anorak m
anorexi|a n Magersucht f. ~**c** a **be** ~**c** an Magersucht leiden
another a & pron ein anderer/ eine andere/ein anderes; (additional) noch ein(e); ~ **[one]** noch einer/eine/eins; ~ **time** ein andermal; **one** ~ einander
answer n Antwort f; (solution) Lösung f • vt antworten (**s.o.** jdm); beantworten <question,

letter>; ~ **the door/telephone** an die Tür/ans Telefon gehen ● *vi* antworten; (*Teleph*) sich melden; ~ **back** eine freche Antwort geben. ~**ing machine** *n* (*Teleph*) Anrufbeantworter *m*

ant *n* Ameise *f*

antagonis|m *n* Antagonismus *m*. ~**tic** *a* feindselig

Antarctic *n* Antarktis *f*

antelope *n* Antilope *f*

antenatal *a* ~ **care** Schwangerschaftsfürsorge *f*

antenna *n* Fühler *m*; (*Amer: aerial*) Antenne *f*

anthem *n* Hymne *f*

anthology *n* Anthologie *f*

anthropology *n* Anthropologie *f*

antibiotic *n* Antibiotikum *nt*

anticipat|e *vt* vorhersehen; (*forestall*) zuvorkommen (+ *dat*); (*expect*) erwarten. ~**ion** *n* Erwartung *f*

anticlimax *n* Enttäuschung *f*

anticlockwise *a & adv* gegen den Uhrzeigersinn

antics *npl* Mätzchen *pl*

antidote *n* Gegengift *nt*

antifreeze *n* Frostschutzmittel *nt*

antipathy *n* Abneigung *f*, Antipathie *f*

antiquated *a* veraltet

antique *a* antik ● *n* Antiquität *f*. ~ **dealer** *n* Antiquitätenhändler *m*

antiquity *n* Altertum *nt*

antiseptic *a* antiseptisch ● *n* Antiseptikum *nt*

antisocial *a* asozial; 🛈 ungesellig

antlers *npl* Geweih *nt*

anus *n* After *m*

anvil *n* Amboss *m*

anxiety *n* Sorge *f*

anxious *a*, **-ly** *adv* ängstlich; (*worried*) besorgt; **be** ~ **to do sth** etw gerne machen wollen

any *a* irgendein(e); *pl* irgendwelche; (*every*) jede(r,s); *pl* alle; (*after negative*) kein(e); *pl* keine; ~ **colour/number you like** eine beliebige Farbe/Zahl; **have you** ~ **wine/apples?** haben Sie Wein/Äpfel? ● *pron* [irgend]einer/eine/eins; *pl* [irgend]welche; (*some*) welche(r,s); *pl* welche; (*all*) alle *pl*; (*negative*) keiner/keine/keins; *pl* keine; **I don't want** ~ **of it** ich will nichts davon; **there aren't** ~ es gibt keine ● *adv* noch; ~ **quicker/slower** noch schneller/langsamer; **is it** ~ **better?** geht es etwas besser? **would you like** ~ **more?** möchten Sie noch [etwas]? **I can't eat** ~ **more** ich kann nichts mehr essen

anybody *pron* [irgend]jemand; (*after negative*) niemand; ~ **can do that** das kann jeder

anyhow *adv* jedenfalls; (*nevertheless*) trotzdem; (*badly*) irgendwie

anyone *pron* = **anybody**

anything *pron* [irgend]etwas; (*after negative*) nichts; (*everything*) alles

anyway *adv* jedenfalls; (*in any case*) sowieso

anywhere *adv* irgendwo; (*after negative*) nirgendwo; <*be, live*> überall; <*go*> überallhin

apart *adv* auseinander; **live** ~ getrennt leben; ~ **from** abgesehen von

apartment *n* Zimmer *nt*; (*flat*) Wohnung *f*

ape *n* [Menschen]affe *m* ● *vt* nachäffen

aperitif *n* Aperitif *m*

apologetic *a*, **-ally** *adv* entschuldigend; **be** ~ sich entschuldigen

apologize *vi* sich entschuldigen (**to** bei)

apology *n* Entschuldigung *f*

apostle *n* Apostel *m*

apostrophe *n* Apostroph *m*

appal vt (pt/pp **appalled**)
entsetzen. ~**ling** a entsetzlich
apparatus n Apparatur f; (Sport)
Geräte pl; (single piece) Gerät nt
apparent a offenbar; (seeming)
scheinbar. ~**ly** adv offenbar,
anscheinend
appeal n Appell m, Aufruf m;
(request) Bitte f; (attraction) Reiz
m; (Jur) Berufung f ● vi
appellieren (**to** an + acc); (ask)
bitten (**for** um); (be attractive)
zusagen (**to** dat); (Jur) Berufung
einlegen. ~**ing** a ansprechend
appear vi erscheinen; (seem)
scheinen; (Theat) auftreten.
~**ance** n Erscheinen nt; (look)
Aussehen nt; **to all** ~**ances** allem
Anschein nach
appendicitis n
Blinddarmentzündung f
appendix n (pl **-ices**) (of book)
Anhang m ● (pl **-es**) (Anat)
Blinddarm m
appetite n Appetit m
appetizing a appetitlich
applau|d vt/i Beifall klatschen (+
dat). ~**se** n Beifall m
apple n Apfel m
appliance n Gerät nt
applicable a anwendbar (**to** auf +
acc); (on form) **not** ~ nicht
zutreffend
applicant n Bewerber(in) m(f)
application n Anwendung f;
(request) Antrag m; (for job)
Bewerbung f; (diligence) Fleiß m
applied a angewandt
apply vt (pt/pp **-ied**) auftragen
<paint>; anwenden <force, rule>
● vi zutreffen (**to** auf + acc); ~ **for**
beantragen; sich bewerben um
<job>
appoint vt ernennen; (fix)
festlegen. ~**ment** n Ernennung f;
(meeting) Verabredung f; (at
doctor's, hairdresser's) Termin m;
(job) Posten m; **make an** ~**ment**
sich anmelden

appreciable a merklich;
(considerable) beträchtlich
appreciat|e vt zu schätzen
wissen; (be grateful for) dankbar
sein für; (enjoy) schätzen;
(understand) verstehen ● vi
(increase in value) im Wert
steigen. ~**ion** n (gratitude)
Dankbarkeit f. ~**ive** a dankbar
apprehens|ion n Festnahme f;
(fear) Angst f. ~**ive** a ängstlich
apprentice n Lehrling m. ~**ship** n
Lehre f
approach n Näherkommen nt; (of
time) Nahen nt; (access) Zugang
m; (road) Zufahrt f ● vi sich
nähern; <time:> nahen ● vt sich
nähern (+ dat); (with request)
herantreten an (+ acc); (set
about) sich heranmachen an (+
acc). ~**able** a zugänglich
appropriate a angebracht,
angemessen
approval n Billigung f; **on** ~ zur
Ansicht
approv|e vt billigen ● vi ~**e of**
sth/s.o. mit etw/jdm
einverstanden sein. ~**ing** a, **-ly**
adv anerkennend
approximate a, **-ly** adv ungefähr
approximation n Schätzung f
apricot n Aprikose f
April n April m; **make an** ~ **fool of**
in den April schicken
apron n Schürze f
apt a, **-ly** adv passend; **be** ~ **to do**
sth dazu neigen, etw zu tun
aqualung n Tauchgerät nt
aquarium n Aquarium nt
aquatic a Wasser-
Arab a arabisch ● n Araber(in)
m(f). ~**ian** a arabisch
Arabic a arabisch
arbitrary a, **-ily** adv willkürlich
arbitrat|e vi schlichten. ~**ion** n
Schlichtung f
arc n Bogen m
arcade n Laubengang m; (shops)
Einkaufspassage f

arch n Bogen m; (of foot) Gewölbe nt ● vt ~ its back <cat:> einen Buckel machen

archaeological a archäologisch

archaeolog|ist n Archäologe m/-login f. ~**y** n Archäologie f

archaic a veraltet

archbishop n Erzbischof m

archer n Bogenschütze m. ~**y** n Bogenschießen nt

architect n Architekt(in) m(f). ~**ural** a, **-ly** adv architektonisch

architecture n Architektur f

archives npl Archiv nt

archway n Torbogen m

Arctic a arktisch ● n the ~ die Arktis

ardent a, **-ly** adv leidenschaftlich

ardour n Leidenschaft f

arduous a mühsam

are see be

area n (surface) Fläche f; (Geom) Flächeninhalt m; (region) Gegend f; (fig) Gebiet nt

arena n Arena f

Argentina n Argentinien nt

Argentin|e, ~ian a argentinisch

argue vi streiten (about über + acc); <two people:> sich streiten; (debate) diskutieren; don't ~! keine Widerrede! ● vt (debate) diskutieren; (reason) ~ that argumentieren, dass

argument n Streit m, Auseinandersetzung f; (reasoning) Argument nt; have an ~ sich streiten. ~**ative** a streitlustig

aria n Arie f

arise vi (pt arose, pp arisen) sich ergeben (from aus)

aristocracy n Aristokratie f

aristocrat n Aristokrat(in) m(f). ~**ic** a aristokratisch

arithmetic n Rechnen nt

arm n Arm m; (of chair) Armlehne f; ~**s** pl (weapons) Waffen pl; (Heraldry) Wappen nt ● vt bewaffnen

armament n Bewaffnung f; ~**s** pl Waffen pl

armchair n Sessel m

armed a bewaffnet; ~ **forces** Streitkräfte pl

armour n Rüstung f. ~**ed** a Panzer-

armpit n Achselhöhle f

army n Heer nt; (specific) Armee f; join the ~ zum Militär gehen

aroma n Aroma nt, Duft m. ~**tic** a aromatisch

arose see arise

around adv [all] ~ rings herum; he's not ~ er ist nicht da; travel ~ herumreisen ● prep um (+ acc) … herum; (approximately) gegen

arouse vt aufwecken; (excite) erregen

arrange vt arrangieren; anordnen <furniture, books>; (settle) abmachen. ~**ment** n Anordnung f; (agreement) Vereinbarung f; (of flowers) Gesteck nt; make ~**ments** Vorkehrungen treffen

arrest n Verhaftung f; under ~ verhaftet ● vt verhaften

arrival n Ankunft f; new ~**s** pl Neuankömmlinge pl

arrive vi ankommen; ~ **at** (fig) gelangen zu

arrogan|ce n Arroganz f. ~**t** a, **-ly** adv arrogant

arrow n Pfeil m

arse n (vulg) Arsch m

arson n Brandstiftung f. ~**ist** n Brandstifter m

art n Kunst f; work of ~ Kunstwerk nt; ~**s and crafts** pl Kunstgewerbe nt; A~**s** pl (Univ) Geisteswissenschaften pl

artery n Schlagader f, Arterie f

art gallery n Kunstgalerie f

arthritis n Arthritis f

artichoke n Artischocke f

article n Artikel m; (object) Gegenstand m; ~ **of clothing** Kleidungsstück nt

artificial a, **-ly** adv künstlich

A

artillery n Artillerie f
artist n Künstler(in) m(f)
artiste n (Theat) Artist(in) m(f)
artistic a, **-ally** adv künstlerisch
as conj (because) da; (when) als; (while) während ● prep als; **as a child/foreigner** als Kind/ Ausländer ● adv as well auch; **as soon as** sobald; **as much as** so viel wie; **as quick as you** so schnell wie du; **as you know** wie Sie wissen; **as far as I'm concerned** was mich betrifft
asbestos n Asbest m
ascend vi [auf]steigen ● vt besteigen <throne>
ascent n Aufstieg m
ascertain vt ermitteln
ash[1] n (tree) Esche f
ash[2] n Asche f
ashamed a beschämt; **be ~** sich schämen (of über + acc)
ashore adv an Land
ashtray n Aschenbecher m
Asia n Asien nt. **~n** a asiatisch ● n Asiat(in) m(f). **~tic** a asiatisch
aside adv beiseite
ask vt/i fragen; stellen <question>; (invite) einladen; **~ for** bitten um; verlangen <s.o.>; **~ after** sich erkundigen nach; **~ s.o. in** jdn hereinbitten; **~ s.o. to do sth** jdn bitten, etw zu tun
asleep a **be ~** schlafen; **fall ~** einschlafen
asparagus n Spargel m
aspect n Aspekt m
asphalt n Asphalt m
aspire vi **~ to** streben nach
ass n Esel m
assail vt bestürmen. **~ant** n Angreifer(in) m(f)
assassin n Mörder(in) m(f). **~ate** vt ermorden. **~ation** n [politischer] Mord m
assault n (Mil) Angriff m; (Jur) Körperverletzung f ● vt [tätlich] angreifen

assemble vi sich versammeln ● vt versammeln; (Techn) montieren
assembly n Versammlung f; (Sch) Andacht f; (Techn) Montage f. **~ line** n Fließband nt
assent n Zustimmung f
assert vt behaupten; **~ oneself** sich durchsetzen. **~ion** n Behauptung f
assess vt bewerten; (fig & for tax purposes) einschätzen: schätzen <value>. **~ment** n Einschätzung f; (of tax) Steuerbescheid m
asset n Vorteil m; **~s** pl (money) Vermögen nt; (Comm) Aktiva pl
assign vt zuweisen (**to** dat). **~ment** n (task) Aufgabe f
assist vt/i helfen (+ dat). **~ance** n Hilfe f. **~ant** a Hilfs- ● n Assistent(in) m(f); (in shop) Verkäufer(in) m(f)
associate[1] vt verbinden; (Psych) assoziieren ● vi **~ with** verkehren mit. **~ion** n Verband m
associate[2] a assoziiert ● n Kollege m/-gin f
assort|ed a gemischt. **~ment** n Mischung f
assum|e vt annehmen; übernehmen <office>; **~ing that** angenommen, dass
assumption n Annahme f; **on the ~** in der Annahme (**that** dass)
assurance n Versicherung f; (confidence) Selbstsicherheit f
assure vt versichern (s.o. jdm); I **~ you [of that]** das versichere ich Ihnen. **~d** a sicher
asterisk n Sternchen nt
asthma n Asthma nt
astonish vt erstaunen. **~ing** a erstaunlich. **~ment** n Erstaunen nt
astray adv go **~** verloren gehen; <person:> sich verlaufen
astride adv rittlings ● prep rittlings auf (+ dat/acc)

astrolog|er n Astrologe m/-gin f.
~**y** n Astrologie f
astronaut n Astronaut(in) m(f)
astronom|er n Astronom m.
~**ical** a astronomisch. ~**y** n
Astronomie f
astute a scharfsinnig
asylum n Asyl nt; [lunatic] ~
Irrenanstalt f

at
● *preposition*
····▸ (*expressing place*) an (+ *dat*).
at the station am Bahnhof. **at the
end** am Ende. **at the corner** an
der Ecke. **at the same place** an
der gleichen Stelle
····▸ (*at s.o.'s house or shop*) bei (+
dat). **at Lisa's** bei Lisa. **at my
uncle's** bei meinem Onkel. **at the
baker's/butcher's** beim Bäcker/
Fleischer
····▸ (*inside a building*) in (+ *dat*).
at the theatre/supermarket im
Theater/Supermarkt. **we spent
the night at a hotel** wir
übernachteten in einem Hotel.
he is still at the office er ist noch
im Büro
····▸ (*expressing time*) (*with clock
time*) um; (*with main festivals*)
zu. **at six o'clock** um sechs Uhr.
at midnight um Mitternacht. **at
midday** um zwölf Uhr mittags. **at
Christmas/Easter** zu
Weihnachten/Ostern
····▸ (*expressing age*) mit. **at [the
age of] forty** mit vierzig; im Alter
von vierzig
····▸ (*expressing price*) zu. **at £2.50
[each]** zu *od* für [je] 2,50 Pfund
····▸ (*expressing speed*) mit. **at 30
m.p.h.** mit dreißig Meilen pro
Stunde
····▸ (*in phrases*) **good/bad at
languages** gut/schlecht in
Sprachen. **two at a time** zwei auf
einmal. **at that** (*at that point*)
dabei; (*at that provocation*)

daraufhin; (*moreover*) noch
dazu

ate *see* **eat**
atheist n Atheist(in) m(f)
athlet|e n Athlet(in) m(f). ~**ic** a
sportlich. ~**ics** n Leichtathletik f
Atlantic a & n **the** ~ **[Ocean]** der
Atlantik
atlas n Atlas m
atmosphere n Atmosphäre f
atom n Atom nt. ~ **bomb** n
Atombombe f
atomic a Atom-
atrocious a abscheulich
atrocity n Gräueltat f
attach vt befestigen (**to** an + *dat*);
beimessen <*importance*> (**to** *dat*);
be ~**ed to** (*fig*) hängen an (+ *dat*)
attack n Angriff m; (*Med*) Anfall
m ● vt/i angreifen. ~**er** n
Angreifer m
attain vt erreichen. ~**able** a
erreichbar
attempt n Versuch m ● vt
versuchen
attend vt anwesend sein bei; (*go
regularly to*) besuchen; (*take part
in*) teilnehmen an (+ *dat*);
(*accompany*) begleiten; <*doctor:*>
behandeln ● vi anwesend sein;
(*pay attention*) aufpassen; ~ **to**
sich kümmern um; (*in shop*)
bedienen. ~**ance** n Anwesenheit
f; (*number*) Besucherzahl f. ~**ant**
n Wärter(in) m(f); (*in car park*)
Wächter m
attention n Aufmerksamkeit f; ~!
(*Mil*) stillgestanden! **pay** ~
aufpassen; **pay** ~ **to** beachten,
achten auf (+ *acc*)
attentive a, **-ly** adv aufmerksam
attic n Dachboden m
attitude n Haltung f
attorney n (*Amer: lawyer*)
Rechtsanwalt m; **power of** ~
Vollmacht f
attract vt anziehen; erregen
<*attention*>; ~ **s.o.'s attention** jds

Aufmerksamkeit auf sich (*acc*) lenken. ~**ion** *n* Anziehungskraft *f*; (*charm*) Reiz *m*; (*thing*) Attraktion *f*. ~**ive** *a*, **-ly** *adv* attraktiv

attribute *vt* zuschreiben (**to** *dat*)

aubergine *n* Aubergine *f*

auburn *a* kastanienbraun

auction *n* Auktion *f*, Versteigerung *f* ● *vt* versteigern. ~**eer** *n* Auktionator *m*

audaci|ous *a*, **-ly** *adv* verwegen. ~**ty** *n* Verwegenheit *f*; (*impudence*) Dreistigkeit *f*

audible *a*, **-bly** *adv* hörbar

audience *n* Publikum *nt*; (*Theat, TV*) Zuschauer *pl*; (*Radio*) Zuhörer *pl*; (*meeting*) Audienz *f*

audit *n* Bücherrevision *f* ● *vt* (*Comm*) prüfen

audition *n* (*Theat*) Vorsprechen *nt*; (*Mus*) Vorspielen *nt*; (*for singer*) Vorsingen *nt* ● *vi* vorsprechen; vorspielen; vorsingen

auditor *n* Buchprüfer *m*

auditorium *n* Zuschauerraum *m*

August *n* August *m*

aunt *n* Tante *f*

au pair *n* ~ **[girl]** Au-pair-Mädchen *nt*

aura *n* Fluidum *nt*

auspicious *a* günstig; <*occasion*> freudig

auster|e *a* streng; (*simple*) nüchtern. ~**ity** *n* Strenge *f*; (*hardship*) Entbehrung *f*

Australia *n* Australien *nt*. ~**n** *a* australisch ● *n* Australier(in) *m(f)*

Austria *n* Österreich *nt* ~**n** *a* österreichisch ● *n* Österreicher(in) *m(f)*

authentic *a* echt, authentisch. ~**ate** *vt* beglaubigen. ~**ity** *n* Echtheit *f*

author *n* Schriftsteller *m*, Autor *m*; (*of document*) Verfasser *m*

authoritarian *a* autoritär

authoritative *a* maßgebend

authority *n* Autorität *f*; (*public*) Behörde *f*; **in** ~ verantwortlich

authorization *n* Ermächtigung *f*

authorize *vt* ermächtigen <*s.o.*>; genehmigen <*sth*>

autobiography *n* Autobiographie *f*

autograph *n* Autogramm *nt*

automatic *a*, **-ally** *adv* automatisch

automation *n* Automation *f*

automobile *n* Auto *nt*

autonom|ous *a* autonom. ~**y** *n* Autonomie *f*

autumn *n* Herbst *m*. ~**al** *a* herbstlich

auxiliary *a* Hilfs- ● *n* Helfer(in) *m(f)*, Hilfskraft *f*

avail *n* **to no** ~ vergeblich

available *a* verfügbar; (*obtainable*) erhältlich

avalanche *n* Lawine *f*

avenge *vt* rächen

avenue *n* Allee *f*

average *a* Durchschnitts-, durchschnittlich ● *n* Durchschnitt *m*; **on** ~ im Durchschnitt, durchschnittlich ● *vt* durchschnittlich schaffen

averse *a* **not be** ~**e to sth** etw (*dat*) nicht abgeneigt sein

avert *vt* abwenden

aviary *n* Vogelhaus *nt*

aviation *n* Luftfahrt *f*

avocado *n* Avocado *f*

avoid *vt* vermeiden; ~ **s.o.** jdm aus dem Weg gehen. ~**able** *a* vermeidbar. ~**ance** *n* Vermeidung *f*

await *vt* warten auf (+ *acc*)

awake *a* wach; **wide** ~ hellwach ● *vi* (*pt* **awoke**, *pp* **awoken**) erwachen

awaken *vt* wecken ● *vi* erwachen. ~**ing** *n* Erwachen *nt*

award *n* Auszeichnung *f*; (*prize*) Preis *m* ● *vt* zuerkennen (**to s.o.** *dat*); verleihen <*prize*>

aware *a* **become ~** gewahr werden (**of** *gen*); **be ~ that** wissen, dass. **~ness** *n* Bewusstsein *nt*

away *adv* weg, fort; (*absent*) abwesend; **four kilometres ~** vier Kilometer entfernt; **play ~** (*Sport*) auswärts spielen. **~ game** *n* Auswärtsspiel *nt*

awful *a*, **-ly** *adv* furchtbar

awkward *a* schwierig; (*clumsy*) ungeschickt; (*embarrassing*) peinlich; (*inconvenient*) ungünstig. **~ly** *adv* ungeschickt; (*embarrassedly*) verlegen

awning *n* Markise *f*

awoke(n) *see* **awake**

axe *n* Axt *f* ● *vt* (*pres p* **axing**) streichen

axle *n* (*Techn*) Achse *f*

B *n* (*Mus*) H *nt*

baboon *n* Pavian *m*

baby *n* Baby *nt*; (*Amer* 🅵) Schätzchen *nt*

baby: **~ish** *a* kindisch. **~-sit** *vi* babysitten. **~-sitter** *n* Babysitter *m*

bachelor *n* Junggeselle *m*

back *n* Rücken *m*; (*reverse*) Rückseite *f*; (*of chair*) Rückenlehne *f*; (*Sport*) Verteidiger *m*; **at**/(*Auto*) **in the ~** hinten; **on the ~** auf der Rückseite; **~ to front** verkehrt ● *a* Hinter- ● *adv* zurück; **~ here/there** hier/da hinten; **~ at home** zu Hause; **go/pay ~** zurückgehen/-zahlen ● *vt* (*support*) unterstützen; (*with money*) finanzieren; (*Auto*) zurücksetzen; (*Betting*) [Geld] setzen auf (+ *acc*); (*cover the back of*) mit einer Verstärkung versehen ● *vi* (*Auto*) zurücksetzen. **~ down** *vi* klein beigeben. **~ in** *vi* rückwärts hineinfahren. **~ out** *vi* rückwärts hinaus-/herausfahren; (*fig*) aussteigen (**of** aus). **~ up** *vt* unterstützen; (*confirm*) bestätigen ● *vi* (*Auto*) zurücksetzen

back: **~ache** *n* Rückenschmerzen *pl*. **~biting** *n* gehässiges Gerede *nt*. **~bone** *n* Rückgrat *nt*. **~date** *vt* rückdatieren; **~dated to** rückwirkend von. **~ door** *n* Hintertür *f*

backer *n* Geldgeber *m*

back: **~fire** *vi* (*Auto*) fehlzünden; (*fig*) fehlschlagen. **~ground** *n* Hintergrund *m*; **family ~ground** Familienverhältnisse *pl*. **~hand** *n* (*Sport*) Rückhand *f*. **~handed** *a* <*compliment*> zweifelhaft

backing *n* (*support*) Unterstützung *f*; (*material*) Verstärkung *f*

back: **~lash** *n* (*fig*) Gegenschlag *m*. **~log** *n* Rückstand *m* (**of** an + *dat*). **~pack** *n* Rucksack *m*. **~ seat** *n* Rücksitz *m*. **~side** *n* 🅵 Hintern *m*. **~stroke** *n* Rückenschwimmen *nt*. **~-up** *n* Unterstützung *f*; (*Amer: traffic jam*) Stau *m*

backward *a* zurückgeblieben; <*country*> rückständig ● *adv* rückwärts. **~s** rückwärts; **~s and forwards** hin und her

back yard *n* Hinterhof *m*; **not in my ~ yard** 🅵 nicht vor meiner Haustür

bacon *n* [Schinken]speck *m*

bacteria *npl* Bakterien *pl*

bad *a* (**worse, worst**) schlecht; (*serious*) schwer, schlimm; (*naughty*) unartig; **~ language**

gemeine Ausdrucksweise f; **feel ~** sich schlecht fühlen; (*feel guilty*) ein schlechtes Gewissen haben

badge n Abzeichen nt

badger n Dachs m ● vt plagen

badly adv schlecht; (*seriously*) schwer; **~ off** schlecht gestellt; **~ behaved** unerzogen; **want ~** sich (*dat*) sehnsüchtig wünschen; **need ~** dringend brauchen

bad-mannered a mit schlechten Manieren

badminton n Federball m

bad-tempered a schlecht gelaunt

baffle vt verblüffen

bag n Tasche f; (*of paper*) Tüte f; (*pouch*) Beutel m; **~s of** 🛈 jede Menge ● vt (🛈 *reserve*) in Beschlag nehmen

baggage n [Reise]gepäck nt

baggy a <*clothes*> ausgebeult

bagpipes npl Dudelsack m

bail n Kaution f; **on ~** gegen Kaution ● vt **~ s.o. out** jdn gegen Kaution freibekommen; (*fig*) jdm aus der Patsche helfen

bait n Köder m ● vt mit einem Köder versehen; (*fig: torment*) reizen

bake vt/i backen

baker n Bäcker m; **~'s [shop]** Bäckerei f. **~y** n Bäckerei f

baking n Backen nt. **~-powder** n Backpulver nt

balance n (*equilibrium*) Gleichgewicht nt, Balance f; (*scales*) Waage f; (*Comm*) Saldo m; (*outstanding sum*) Restbetrag m; **[bank] ~** Kontostand m; **in the ~** (*fig*) in der Schwebe ● vt balancieren; (*equalize*) ausgleichen; (*Comm*) abschließen <*books*> ● vi balancieren; (*fig & Comm*) sich ausgleichen. **~d** a ausgewogen

balcony n Balkon m

bald a (-er, -est) kahl; <*person*> kahlköpfig

bald|ly adv unverblümt. **~ness** n Kahlköpfigkeit f

ball¹ n Ball m; (*Billiards, Croquet*) Kugel f; (*of yarn*) Knäuel m & nt; **on the ~** 🛈 auf Draht

ball² n (*dance*) Ball m

ball-bearing n Kugellager nt

ballerina n Ballerina f

ballet m Ballett nt. **~ dancer** n Balletttänzer(in) m(f)

balloon n Luftballon m; (*Aviat*) Ballon m

ballot n [geheime] Wahl f; (*on issue*) [geheime] Abstimmung f. **~-box** n Wahlurne f. **~-paper** n Stimmzettel m

ball: **~point [pen]** n Kugelschreiber m. **~room** n Ballsaal m

balm n Balsam m

balmy a (-ier, -iest) a sanft

Baltic a & n the **~ [Sea]** die Ostsee

bamboo n Bambus m

ban n Verbot nt ● vt (*pt/pp* banned) verbieten

banal a banal. **~ity** n Banalität f

banana n Banane f

band n Band nt; (*stripe*) Streifen m; (*group*) Schar f; (*Mus*) Kapelle f

bandage n Verband m; (*for support*) Bandage f ● vt verbinden; bandagieren <*limb*>

b. & b. abbr of **bed and breakfast**

bandit n Bandit m

band: **~stand** n Musikpavillon m. **~wagon** n **jump on the ~wagon** (*fig*) sich einer erfolgreichen Sache anschließen

bang n (*noise*) Knall m; (*blow*) Schlag m ● adv **go ~** knallen ● int bums! peng! ● vt knallen; (*shut noisily*) zuknallen; (*strike*) schlagen auf (+ *acc*); **~ one's head** sich (*dat*) den Kopf stoßen (**on** an + *acc*) ● vi schlagen; <*door:*> zuknallen

banger n (*firework*) Knallfrosch m; (🆄 *sausage*) Wurst f; old ~ (🆄 *car*) Klapperkiste f

bangle n Armreifen m

banish vt verbannen

banisters npl [Treppen]geländer nt

banjo n Banjo nt

bank[1] n (*of river*) Ufer nt; (*slope*) Hang m ● vi (*Aviat*) in die Kurve gehen

bank[2] n Bank f ● ~ on vt sich verlassen auf (+ acc)

bank account n Bankkonto nt

banker n Bankier m

bank: ~ holiday n gesetzlicher Feiertag m. ~ing n Bankwesen nt. ~note n Banknote f

bankrupt a bankrott; go ~ Bankrott machen ● n Bankrotteur m ● vt Bankrott machen. ~cy n Bankrott m

banner n Banner nt; (*carried by demonstrators*) Transparent nt, Spruchband nt

banquet n Bankett nt

baptism n Taufe f

baptize vt taufen

bar n Stange f; (*of cage*) [Gitter]stab m; (*of gold*) Barren m; (*of chocolate*) Tafel f; (*of soap*) Stück nt; (*long*) Riegel m; (*café*) Bar f; (*counter*) Theke f; (*Mus*) Takt m; (*fig: obstacle*) Hindernis nt; parallel ~s (*Sport*) Barren m; behind ~s 🆄 hinter Gittern ● vt (*pt/pp barred*) versperren <*way, door*>; ausschließen <*person*>

barbar|ic a barbarisch. ~ity n Barbarei f. ~ous a barbarisch

barbecue n Grill m; (*party*) Grillfest nt ● vt [im Freien] grillen

barbed a ~ wire Stacheldraht m

barber n [Herren]friseur m

bar code n Strichkode m

bare a (-r, -st) nackt, bloß; <*tree*> kahl; (*empty*) leer; (*mere*) bloß

bare: ~back adv ohne Sattel. ~faced a schamlos. ~foot adv barfuß. ~headed a mit unbedecktem Kopf

barely adv kaum

bargain n (*agreement*) Geschäft nt; (*good buy*) Gelegenheitskauf m; into the ~ noch dazu; make a ~ sich einigen ● vi handeln; (*haggle*) feilschen; ~ for (*expect*) rechnen mit

barge n Lastkahn m; (*towed*) Schleppkahn m ● vi ~ in 🆄 hereinplatzen

baritone n Bariton m

bark[1] n (*of tree*) Rinde f

bark[2] n Bellen nt ● vi bellen

barley n Gerste f

bar: ~maid n Schankmädchen nt. ~man n Barmann m

barmy a 🆄 verrückt

barn n Scheune f

barometer n Barometer nt

baron n Baron m. ~ess n Baronin f

barracks npl Kaserne f

barrage n (*in river*) Wehr nt; (*Mil*) Sperrfeuer nt; (*fig*) Hagel m

barrel n Fass nt; (*of gun*) Lauf m; (*of cannon*) Rohr nt. ~-organ n Drehorgel f

barren a unfruchtbar; <*landscape*> öde

barricade n Barrikade f ● vt verbarrikadieren

barrier n Barriere f; (*across road*) Schranke f; (*Rail*) Sperre f; (*fig*) Hindernis nt

barrow n Karre f, Karren m

base n Fuß m; (*fig*) Basis f; (*Mil*) Stützpunkt m ● vt stützen (on auf + acc); be ~d on basieren auf (+ dat)

base: ~ball n Baseball m. ~less a unbegründet. ~ment n Kellergeschoss nt

bash n Schlag m; have a ~! 🆄 probier es mal! ● vt hauen

B

basic *a* Grund-; (*fundamental*) grundlegend; (*essential*) wesentlich; (*unadorned*) einfach; **the ~s** das Wesentliche. **~ally** *adv* grundsätzlich

basin *n* Becken *nt*; (*for washing*) Waschbecken *nt*; (*for food*) Schüssel *f*

basis *n* (*pl* **-ses**) Basis *f*

bask *vi* sich sonnen

basket *n* Korb *m*. **~ball** *n* Basketball *m*

Basle *n* Basel *nt*

bass *a* Bass-; **~ voice** Bassstimme *f* ● *n* Bass *m*; (*person*) Bassist *m*

bassoon *n* Fagott *nt*

bastard *n* ✕ Schuft *m*

bat¹ *n* Schläger *m*; **off one's own ~** ⊞ auf eigene Faust ● *vt* (*pt/pp* **batted**) schlagen; **not ~ an eyelid** (*fig*) nicht mit der Wimper zucken

bat² *n* (*Zool*) Fledermaus *f*

batch *n* (*of people*) Gruppe *f*; (*of papers*) Stoß *m*; (*of goods*) Sendung *f*; (*of bread*) Schub *m*

bath *n* (*pl* **-s**) Bad *nt*; (*tub*) Badewanne *f*; **~s** *pl* Badeanstalt *f*; **have a ~** baden

bathe *n* Bad *nt* ● *vt/i* baden. **~r** *n* Badende(r) *m/f*

bathing *n* Baden *nt*. **~cap** *n* Bademütze *f*. **~costume** *n* Badeanzug *m*

bath: **~-mat** *n* Badematte *f*. **~room** *n* Badezimmer *nt*. **~towel** *n* Badetuch *nt*

battalion *n* Bataillon *nt*

batter *n* (*Culin*) flüssiger Teig *m* ● *vt* schlagen. **~ed** *a* <*car*> verbeult; <*wife*> misshandelt

battery *n* Batterie *f*

battle *n* Schlacht *f*; (*fig*) Kampf *m* ● *vi* (*fig*) kämpfen (**for** um)

battle: **~field** *n* Schlachtfeld *nt*. **~ship** *n* Schlachtschiff *nt*

batty *a* ⊞ verrückt

Bavaria *n* Bayern *nt*. **~n** *a* bayrisch ● *n* Bayer(in) *m(f)*

bawl *vt/i* brüllen

bay¹ *n* (*Geog*) Bucht *f*; (*Archit*) Erker *m*

bay² *n* (*Bot*) [echter] Lorbeer *m*. **~-leaf** *n* Lorbeerblatt *nt*

bayonet *n* Bajonett *nt*

bay window *n* Erkerfenster *nt*

bazaar *n* Basar *m*

BC *abbr* (**before Christ**) v. Chr.

be

(*pres* **am, are, is**, *pl* **are**; *pt* **was**, *pl* **were**; *pp* **been**)

● *intransitive verb*

····► (*expressing identity, nature, state, age etc.*) sein. **he is a teacher** er ist Lehrer. **she is French** sie ist Französin. **he is very nice** er ist sehr nett. **I am tall** ich bin groß. **you are thirty** du bist dreißig. **it was very cold** es war sehr kalt

····► (*expressing general position*) sein; (*lie*) liegen; (*stand*) stehen. **where is the bank?** wo ist die Bank? **the book is on the table** das Buch liegt auf dem Tisch. **the vase is on the shelf** die Vase steht auf dem Brett

····► (*feel*) **I am cold/hot** mir ist kalt/heiß. **I am ill** ich bin krank. **I am well** mir geht es gut. **how are you?** wie geht es Ihnen?

····► (*date*) **it is the 5th today** heute haben wir den Fünften

····► (*go, come, stay*) sein. **I have been to Vienna** ich bin in Wien gewesen. **have you ever been to London?** bist du schon einmal in London gewesen? **has the postman been?** war der Briefträger schon da? **I've been here for an hour** ich bin seit einer Stunde hier

····► (*origin*) **where are you from?** woher stammen *od* kommen Sie? **she is from Australia** sie stammt *od* ist aus Australien

····➤ (cost) kosten. **how much are the eggs?** was kosten die Eier?

····➤ (in calculations) **two threes are six** zweimal drei ist od sind sechs

····➤ (exist) **there is/are** es gibt (+ acc). **there's no fish left** es gibt keinen Fisch mehr

● auxiliary verb

····➤ (forming continuous tenses: not translated) **I'm working** ich arbeite. **I'm leaving tomorrow** ich reise morgen [ab]. **they were singing** sie sangen. **they will be coming on Tuesday** sie kommen am Dienstag

····➤ (forming passive) werden. **the child was found** das Kind wurde gefunden. **German is spoken here** hier wird Deutsch gesprochen; hier spricht man Deutsch

····➤ (expressing arrangement, obligation, destiny) sollen. **I am to go/inform you** ich soll gehen/Sie unterrichten. **they were to fly today** sie sollten heute fliegen. **you are to do that immediately** das sollst du sofort machen. **you are not to ...** (prohibition) du darfst nicht .... **they were never to meet again** (destiny) sie sollten sich nie wieder treffen

····➤ (in short answers) **Are you disappointed? — Yes I am** Bist du enttäuscht? — Ja. (negating previous statement) **Aren't you coming? — Yes I am!** Kommst du nicht? — Doch!

····➤ (in tag questions) **isn't it? wasn't she? aren't they?** etc. nicht wahr. **it's a beautiful house, isn't it?** das Haus ist sehr schön, nicht wahr?

beach n Strand m
bead n Perle f
beak n Schnabel m

beam n Balken m; (of light) Strahl m ● vi strahlen. ~**ing** a [freude]strahlend
bean n Bohne f
bear[1] n Bär m
bear[2] vt/i (pt bore, pp borne) tragen; (endure) ertragen; gebären <child>; ~ **right** sich rechts halten. ~**able** a erträglich
beard n Bart m. ~**ed** a bärtig
bearer n Träger m; (of news, cheque) Überbringer m; (of passport) Inhaber(in) m(f)
bearing n Haltung f; (Techn) Lager nt; **get one's** ~**s** sich orientieren
beast n Tier nt; (🛈 person) Biest nt
beastly a (-ier, -iest) 🛈 scheußlich; <person> gemein
beat n Schlag m; (of policeman) Runde f; (rhythm) Takt m ● vt/i (pt beat, pp beaten) schlagen; (thrash) verprügeln; klopfen <carpet>; (hammer) hämmern (on an + acc); ~ **it!** 🛈 hau ab! **it** ~**s me** 🛈 das begreife ich nicht. ~ **up** vt zusammenschlagen
beat|en a off the ~**en track** abseits. ~**ing** n Prügel pl
beauti|ful a, -**ly** adv schön. ~**fy** vt (pt/pp -ied) verschönern
beauty n Schönheit f. ~ **parlour** n Kosmetiksalon m. ~ **spot** n Schönheitsfleck m; (place) landschaftlich besonders reizvolles Fleckchen nt.
beaver n Biber m
became see **become**
because conj weil ● adv ~ **of** wegen (+ gen)
become vt/i (pt became, pp become) werden. ~**ing** a <clothes> kleidsam
bed n Bett nt; (layer) Schicht f; (of flowers) Beet nt; **in** ~ im Bett; **go to** ~ ins od zu Bett gehen; ~ **and breakfast** Zimmer mit Frühstück.

∼**clothes** *npl*, ∼**ding** *n* Bettzeug *nt*. ∼**room** *n* Schlafzimmer *nt*

bedside *n* at his ∼ an seinem Bett. ∼ **lamp** *n* Nachttischlampe *f*. ∼ **table** *n* Nachttisch *m*

bed: ∼**sitter** *n*, ∼**sitting-room** *n* Wohnschlafzimmer *nt*. ∼**spread** *n* Tagesdecke *f*. ∼**time** *n* at ∼**time** vor dem Schlafengehen

bee *n* Biene *f*

beech *n* Buche *f*

beef *n* Rindfleisch *nt*. ∼**burger** *n* Hamburger *m*

bee: ∼**hive** *n* Bienenstock *m*. ∼**line** *n* make a ∼**line for** 🔲 zusteuern auf (+ *acc*)

been *see* be

beer *n* Bier *nt*

beet *n* (*Amer: beetroot*) Rote Bete *f*, **[sugar]** ∼ Zuckerrübe *f*

beetle *n* Käfer *m*

beetroot *n* Rote Bete *f*

before *prep* vor (+ *dat/acc*); **the day** ∼ **yesterday** vorgestern; ∼ **long** bald ● *adv* vorher; (*already*) schon; **never** ∼ noch nie; ∼ **that** davor ● *conj* (*time*) ehe, bevor. ∼**hand** *adv* vorher, im Voraus

beg *v* (*pt/pp* **begged**) ● *vi* betteln ● *vt* (*entreat*) anflehen; (*ask*) bitten (**for** um)

began *see* begin

beggar *n* Bettler(in) *m(f)*; 🔲 Kerl *m*

begin *vt/i* (*pt* began, *pp* begun, *pres p* **beginning**) anfangen, beginnen; **to** ∼ **with** anfangs. ∼**ner** *n* Anfänger(in) *m(f)*. ∼**ning** *n* Anfang *m*, Beginn *m*

begun *see* begin

behalf *n* on ∼ of im Namen von; **on my** ∼ meinetwegen

behave *vi* sich verhalten; ∼ **oneself** sich benehmen

behaviour *n* Verhalten *nt*; **good/ bad** ∼ gutes/schlechtes Benehmen *nt*

behind *prep* hinter (+ *dat/acc*); **be** ∼ **sth** hinter etw (*dat*) stecken

● *adv* hinten; (*late*) im Rückstand; **a long way** ∼ weit zurück ● *n* 🔲 Hintern *m*. ∼**hand** *adv* im Rückstand

beige *a* beige

being *n* Dasein *nt*; **living** ∼ Lebewesen *nt*; **come into** ∼ entstehen

belated *a*, **-ly** *adv* verspätet

belfry *n* Glockenstube *f*; (*tower*) Glockenturm *m*

Belgian *a* belgisch ● *n* Belgier(in) *m(f)*

Belgium *n* Belgien *nt*

belief *n* Glaube *m*

believable *a* glaubhaft

believe *vt/i* glauben (**s.o.** jdm; **in** an + *acc*). ∼**r** *n* (*Relig*) Gläubige(r) *m/f*

belittle *vt* herabsetzen

bell *n* Glocke *f*; (*on door*) Klingel *f*

bellow *vt/i* brüllen

belly *n* Bauch *m*

belong *vi* gehören (**to** *dat*); (*be member*) angehören (**to** *dat*). ∼**ings** *npl* Sachen *pl*

beloved *a* geliebt ● *n* Geliebte(r) *m/f*

below *prep* unter (+ *dat/acc*) ● *adv* unten; (*Naut*) unter Deck

belt *n* Gürtel *m*; (*area*) Zone *f*; (*Techn*) [Treib]riemen *m* ● *vi* (🔲 *rush*) rasen ● *vt* (🔲 *hit*) hauen

bench *n* Bank *f*; (*work-*) Werkbank *f*

bend *n* Biegung *f*; (*in road*) Kurve *f*; **round the** ∼ 🔲 verrückt ● *v* (*pt/pp* **bent**) ● *vt* biegen; beugen <*arm, leg*> ● *vi* sich bücken; <*thing:*> sich biegen; <*road:*> eine Biegung machen. ∼ **down** *vi* sich bücken. ∼ **over** *vi* sich vornüberbeugen

beneath *prep* unter (+ *dat/acc*); ∼ **him** (*fig*) unter seiner Würde ● *adv* darunter

benefactor *n* Wohltäter(in) *m(f)*

beneficial *a* nützlich

benefit n Vorteil m; (allowance) Unterstützung f; (insurance) Leistung f; **sickness** ~ Krankengeld nt ● v (pt/pp -fited, pres p -fiting) ● vt nützen (+ dat) ● vi profitieren (from von)

benevolen|ce n Wohlwollen nt. ~t a, -ly adv wohlwollend

bent see bend ● a <person> gebeugt; (distorted) verbogen; (⊞ dishonest) korrupt; **be** ~ **on doing sth** darauf erpicht sein, etw zu tun ● n Hang m, Neigung f (for zu); **artistic** ~ künstlerische Ader f

bequeath vt vermachen (**to** dat)

bereave|d n the ~d pl die Hinterbliebenen

beret n Baskenmütze f

Berne n Bern nt

berry n Beere f

berth n (on ship) [Schlaf]koje f; (ship's anchorage) Liegeplatz m; **give a wide** ~ **to** ⊞ einen großen Bogen machen um

beside prep neben (+ dat/acc); ~ **oneself** außer sich (dat)

besides prep außer (+ dat) ● adv außerdem

besiege vt belagern

best a & n the ~ der/die/das Beste; **at** ~ bestenfalls; **all the** ~! alles Gute! **do one's** ~ sein Bestes tun; **the** ~ **part of a year** fast ein Jahr; **to the** ~ **of my knowledge** so viel ich weiß; **make the** ~ **of it** das Beste daraus machen ● adv am besten; **as** ~ **I could** so gut ich konnte. ~ **man** n ≈ Trauzeuge m. ~**seller** n Bestseller m

bet n Wette f ● v (pt/pp bet or betted) ● vt ~ **s.o. £5** mit jdm um £5 wetten ● vi wetten; ~ **on** [Geld] setzen auf (+ acc)

betray vt verraten. ~**al** n Verrat m

better a besser; **get** ~ sich bessern; (after illness) sich

erholen ● adv besser; ~ **off** besser dran; ~ **not** lieber nicht; **all the** ~ umso besser; **the sooner the** ~ je eher, desto besser; **think** ~ **of it** sich eines Besseren besinnen; **you'd** ~ **stay** du bleibst am besten hier ● vt (do better than) übertreffen; ~ **oneself** sich verbessern

between prep zwischen (+ dat/acc); ~ **you and me** unter uns; ~ **us** (together) zusammen ● adv [**in**] ~ dazwischen

beware vi sich in Acht nehmen (**of** vor + dat); ~ **of the dog!** Vorsicht, bissiger Hund!

bewilder vt verwirren. ~**ment** n Verwirrung f

bewitch vt verzaubern; (fig) bezaubern

beyond prep über (+ acc) … hinaus; (further) weiter als; ~ **reach** außer Reichweite; ~ **doubt** ohne jeden Zweifel; **it's** ~ **me** ⊞ das geht über meinen Horizont ● adv darüber hinaus

bias n Voreingenommenheit f; (preference) Vorliebe f; (Jur) Befangenheit f ● vt (pt/pp biased) (influence) beeinflussen. ~**ed** a voreingenommen; (Jur) befangen

bib n Lätzchen nt

Bible n Bibel f

biblical a biblisch

bibliography n Bibliographie f

bicycle n Fahrrad nt ● vi mit dem Rad fahren

bid n Gebot nt; (attempt) Versuch m ● vt/i (pt/pp bid, pres p bidding) bieten (**for** auf + acc); (Cards) reizen

bidder n Bieter(in) m(f)

bide vt ~ **one's time** den richtigen Moment abwarten

big a (bigger, biggest) groß ● adv **talk** ~ ⊞ angeben

bigam|ist n Bigamist m. ~**y** n Bigamie f

big-headed a ⊞ eingebildet

bigot n Eiferer m. ~ed a engstirnig

bigwig n 🅸 hohes Tier nt

bike n 🅸 [Fahr]rad nt

bikini n Bikini m

bile n Galle f

bilingual a zweisprachig

bilious a (Med) ~ attack verdorbener Magen m

bill¹ n Rechnung f; (poster) Plakat nt; (Pol) Gesetzentwurf m; (Amer: note) Banknote f; ~ of exchange Wechsel m ● vt eine Rechnung schicken (+ dat)

bill² n (beak) Schnabel m

billfold n (Amer) Brieftasche f

billiards n Billard m

billion n (thousand million) Milliarde f; (million million) Billion f

bin n Mülleimer m; (for bread) Kasten m

bind vt (pt/pp bound) binden (to an + acc); (bandage) verbinden; (Jur) verpflichten; (cover the edge of) einfassen. ~ing a verbindlich ● n Einband m; (braid) Borte f; (on ski) Bindung f

binge n 🅸 go on the ~ eine Sauftour machen

binoculars npl [pair of] ~ Fernglas nt

bio|chemistry n Biochemie f. ~degradable a biologisch abbaubar

biograph|er n Biograph(in) m(f). ~y n Biographie f

biological a biologisch

biolog|ist n Biologe m. ~y n Biologie f

birch n Birke f; (whip) Rute f

bird n Vogel m; (🅸 girl) Mädchen nt; kill two ~s with one stone zwei Fliegen mit einer Klappe schlagen

Biro (P) n Kugelschreiber m

birth n Geburt f

birth: ~ certificate n Geburtsurkunde f. ~control n

Geburtenregelung f. ~day n Geburtstag m. ~-rate n Geburtenziffer f

biscuit n Keks m

bishop n Bischof m

bit¹ n Stückchen nt; (for horse) Gebiss nt; (Techn) Bohreinsatz m; a ~ ein bisschen; ~ by ~ nach und nach; a ~ of bread ein bisschen Brot; do one's ~ sein Teil tun

bit² see bite

bitch n Hündin f; 🗙 Luder nt. ~y a gehässig

bit|e n Biss m; [insect] ~ Stich m; (mouthful) Bissen m ● vt/i (pt bit, pp bitten) beißen; <insect:> stechen; kauen <one's nails>. ~ing a beißend

bitten see bite

bitter a, -ly adv bitter; ~ly cold bitterkalt ● n bitteres Bier nt. ~ness n Bitterkeit f

bitty a zusammengestoppelt

bizarre a bizarr

black a (-er, -est) schwarz; be ~and blue grün und blau sein ● n Schwarz nt; (person) Schwarze(r) m/f ● vt schwärzen; boykottieren <goods>

black: ~berry n Brombeere f. ~bird n Amsel f. ~board n (Sch) [Wand]tafel f. ~currant n schwarze Johannisbeere f

blacken vt/i schwärzen

black: ~ eye n blaues Auge nt. B~ Forest n Schwarzwald m. ~ ice n Glatteis nt. ~list vt auf die schwarze Liste setzen. ~mail n Erpressung f ● vt erpressen. ~mailer n Erpresser(in) m(f). ~ market n schwarzer Markt m. ~-out n have a ~-out (Med) das Bewusstsein verlieren. ~ pudding n Blutwurst f

bladder n (Anat) Blase f

blade n Klinge f; (of grass) Halm m

blame n Schuld f • vt die Schuld geben (+ dat); **no one is to ~** keiner ist schuld daran. **~less** a schuldlos

bland a (-er, -est) mild

blank a leer; <look> ausdruckslos • n Lücke f; (cartridge) Platzpatrone f. **~ cheque** n Blankoscheck m

blanket n Decke f; **wet ~** ⚇ Spielverderber(in) m(f)

blare vt/i schmettern

blasé a blasiert

blast n (gust) Luftstoß m; (sound) Schmettern nt; (of horn) Tuten nt • vt sprengen • int ⊠ verdammt. **~ed** a ⊠ verdammt

blast-off n (of missile) Start m

blatant a offensichtlich

blaze n Feuer nt • vi brennen

blazer n Blazer m

bleach n Bleichmittel nt • vt/i bleichen

bleak a (-er, -est) öde; (fig) trostlos

bleary-eyed a mit trüben/(on waking up) verschlafenen Augen

bleat vi blöken

bleed v (pt/pp bled) • vi bluten • vt entlüften <radiator>

bleep n Piepton m • vi piepsen • vt mit dem Piepser rufen. **~er** n Piepser m

blemish n Makel m

blend n Mischung f • vt mischen • vi sich vermischen

bless vt segnen. **~ed** a heilig; ⊠ verflixt. **~ing** n Segen m

blew see **blow²**

blight n (Bot) Brand m

blind a blind; <corner> unübersichtlich; **~ man/woman** Blinde(r) m/f • n [roller] **~** Rouleau nt • vt blenden

blind: ~ alley n Sackgasse f. **~fold** a & adv mit verbundenen Augen • n Augenbinde f • vt die Augen verbinden (+ dat). **~ly** adv blindlings. **~ness** n Blindheit f

blink vi blinzeln; <light:> blinken

bliss n Glückseligkeit f. **~ful** a glücklich

blister n (Med) Blase f

blitz n ⊡ Großaktion f

blizzard n Schneesturm m

bloated a aufgedunsen

blob n Klecks m

block n Block m; (of wood) Klotz m; (of flats) [Wohn]block m • vt blockieren. **~ up** vt zustopfen

blockade n Blockade f • vt blockieren

blockage n Verstopfung f

block: ~head n ⊡ Dummkopf m. **~ letters** npl Blockschrift f

bloke n ⊡ Kerl m

blonde a blond • n Blondine f

blood n Blut nt

blood: ~-curdling a markerschütternd. **~ donor** n Blutspender m. **~ group** n Blutgruppe f. **~hound** n Bluthund m. **~-poisoning** n Blutvergiftung f. **~ pressure** n Blutdruck m. **~shed** n Blutvergießen nt. **~shot** a blutunterlaufen. **~ sports** npl Jagdsport m. **~-stained** a blutbefleckt. **~ test** n Blutprobe f. **~thirsty** a blutdürstig. **~-vessel** n Blutgefäß nt

bloody a (-ier, -iest) blutig; ⊠ verdammt. **~-minded** a ⊠ stur

bloom n Blüte f • vi blühen

blossom n Blüte f • vi blühen

blot n [Tinten]klecks m; (fig) Fleck m • **~ out** vt (fig) auslöschen

blotch n Fleck m. **~y** a fleckig

blotting-paper n Löschpapier nt

blouse n Bluse f

blow¹ n Schlag m

blow² v (pt blew, pp blown) • vt blasen; (fam; squander) verpulvern; **~ one's nose** sich (dat) die Nase putzen • vi blasen; <fuse:> durchbrennen. **~ away** vt wegblasen • vi

wegfliegen. **∼ down** *vt* umwehen
● *vi* umfallen. **∼ out** *vt*
(*extinguish*) ausblasen. **∼ over** *vi*
umfallen; (*fig: die down*)
vorübergehen. **∼ up** *vt* (*inflate*)
aufblasen; (*enlarge*) vergrößern;
(*shatter by explosion*) sprengen
● *vi* explodieren

●lowlamp *n* Lötlampe *f*

●lown *see* **blow²**

●lowtorch *n* (*Amer*) Lötlampe *f*

●lowy *a* windig

blue *a* (**-r, -st**) blau; **feel ∼**
deprimiert sein ● *n* Blau *nt*; **have
the ∼s** deprimiert sein; **out of the
∼** aus heiterem Himmel

blue: ∼bell *n* Sternhyazinthe *f*.
∼berry *n* Heidelbeere *f*. **∼bottle**
n Schmeißfliege *f*. **∼ film** *n*
Pornofilm *m*. **∼print** *n* (*fig*)
Entwurf *m*

bluff *n* Bluff *m* ● *vi* bluffen

blunder *n* Schnitzer *m* ● *vi* einen
Schnitzer machen

blunt *a* stumpf; <*person*>
geradeheraus. **∼ly** *adv*
unverblümt, geradeheraus

blur *n* **it's all a ∼** alles ist
verschwommen ● *vt* (*pt/pp*
blurred) verschwommen machen;
∼red verschwommen

blush *n* Erröten *nt* ● *vi* erröten

bluster *n* Großtuerei *f*. **∼y** *a*
windig

boar *n* Eber *m*

board *n* Brett *nt*; (*for notices*)
schwarzes Brett *nt*; (*committee*)
Ausschuss *m*; (*of directors*)
Vorstand *m*; **on ∼** an Bord; **full ∼**
Vollpension *f*; **∼ and lodging**
Unterkunft und Verpflegung *pl*
● *vt* einsteigen in (+ *acc*); (*Naut,
Aviat*) besteigen ● *vi* an Bord
gehen. **∼ up** *vt* mit Brettern
verschlagen

boarder *n* Pensionsgast *m*; (*Sch*)
Internatsschüler(in) *m(f)*

board: ∼-game *n* Brettspiel *nt*.
∼ing-house *n* Pension *f*. **∼ing-
school** *n* Internat *nt*

boast *vt* sich rühmen (+ *gen*) ● *vi*
prahlen (**about** mit). **∼ful** *a*, **-ly**
adv prahlerisch

boat *n* Boot *nt*; (*ship*) Schiff *nt*

bob *vi* (*pt/pp* **bobbed**) **∼ up and
down** sich auf und ab bewegen

bob-sleigh *n* Bob *m*

bodily *a* körperlich ● *adv*
(*forcibly*) mit Gewalt

body *n* Körper *m*; (*corpse*) Leiche
f; (*corporation*) Körperschaft *f*.
∼guard *n* Leibwächter *m*. **∼work**
n (*Auto*) Karosserie *f*

bog *n* Sumpf *m*

bogus *a* falsch

boil¹ *n* Furunkel *m*

boil² *n* **bring/come to the ∼** zum
Kochen bringen/kommen ● *vt/i*
kochen; **∼ed potatoes**
Salzkartoffeln *pl*. **∼ down** *vi* (*fig*)
hinauslaufen (**to** auf + *acc*). **∼
over** *vi* überkochen

boiler *n* Heizkessel *m*

boiling point *n* Siedepunkt *m*

boisterous *a* übermütig

bold *a* (**-er, -est**), **-ly** *adv* kühn;
(*Typ*) fett. **∼ness** *n* Kühnheit *f*

bolster *n* Nackenrolle *f* ● *vt* **∼ up**
Mut machen (+ *dat*)

bolt *n* Riegel *m*; (*Techn*) Bolzen *m*
● *vt* schrauben (**to** an + *acc*);
verriegeln <*door*>;
hinunterschlingen <*food*> ● *vi*
abhauen; <*horse:*> durchgehen

bomb *n* Bombe *f* ● *vt*
bombardieren

bombard *vt* beschießen; (*fig*)
bombardieren

bombastic *a* bombastisch

bomber *n* (*Aviat*) Bomber *m*;
(*person*) Bombenleger(in) *m(f)*

bond *n* (*fig*) Band *nt*; (*Comm*)
Obligation *f*

bone *n* Knochen *m*; (*of fish*)
Gräte *f* ● *vt* von den Knochen

lösen <*meat*>; entgräten <*fish*>.
~-dry *a* knochentrocken
bonfire *n* Gartenfeuer *nt*;
(*celebratory*) Freudenfeuer *nt*
bonus *n* Prämie *f*; (*gratuity*)
Gratifikation *f*; (*fig*) Plus *nt*
bony *a* (**-ier, -iest**) knochig; <*fish*>
grätig
boo *int* buh! ● *vt* ausbuhen ● *vi*
buhen
boob *n* (Ⅰ *mistake*) Schnitzer *m*
book *n* Buch *nt*; (*of tickets*) Heft
nt; **keep the ~s** (*Comm*) die
Bücher führen ● *vt/i* buchen;
(*reserve*) [vor]bestellen; (*for
offence*) aufschreiben
book: ~case *n* Bücherregal *nt*.
~-ends *npl* Buchstützen *pl*.
~ing-office *n* Fahrkartenschalter
m. **~keeping** *n* Buchführung *f*.
~let *n* Broschüre *f*. **~maker** *n*
Buchmacher *m*. **~mark** *n*
Lesezeichen *nt*. **~seller** *n*
Buchhändler(in) *m(f)*. **~shop** *n*
Buchhandlung *f*. **~stall** *n*
Bücherstand *m*
boom *n* (*Comm*) Hochkonjunktur
f; (*upturn*) Aufschwung *m* ● *vi*
dröhnen; (*fig*) blühen
boon *n* Segen *m*
boost *n* Auftrieb *m* ● *vt* Auftrieb
geben (+ *dat*)
boot *n* Stiefel *m*; (*Auto*)
Kofferraum *m*
booth *n* Bude *f*; (*cubicle*) Kabine *f*
booty *n* Beute *f*
booze *n* (Ⅰ) Alkohol *m* ● *vi* Ⅰ
saufen
border *n* Rand *m*; (*frontier*)
Grenze *f*; (*in garden*) Rabatte *f*
● *vi* **~ on** grenzen an (+ *acc*).
~line case *n* Grenzfall *m*
bore¹ *see* **bear²**
bor|e² *n* (*of gun*) Kaliber *nt*;
(*person*) langweiliger Mensch *m*;
(*thing*) langweilige Sache *f* ● *vt*
langweilen; **be ~ed** sich
langweilen. **~edom** *n* Langeweile
f. **~ing** *a* langweilig

born *pp* **be ~** geboren werden ●
geboren
borne *see* **bear²**
borrow *vt* [sich (*dat*)] borgen *od*
leihen (**from** von)
bosom *n* Busen *m*
boss *n* Ⅰ Chef *m* ● *vt*
herumkommandieren. **~y** *a*
herrschsüchtig
botanical *a* botanisch
botan|ist *n* Botaniker(in) *m(f)*. **~**
n Botanik *f*
both *a & pron* beide; **~[of] the
children** beide Kinder; **~ of them**
beide [von ihnen] ● *adv* **~ men
and women** sowohl Männer als
auch Frauen
bother *n* Mühe *f*; (*minor trouble*)
Ärger *m* ● *int* Ⅰ verflixt! ● *vt*
belästigen; (*disturb*) stören ● *vi*
sich kümmern (**about** um)
bottle *n* Flasche *f* ● *vt* auf
Flaschen abfüllen; (*preserve*)
einmachen
bottle: ~neck *n* (*fig*) Engpass *m*.
~-opener *n* Flaschenöffner *m*
bottom *a* unterste(r,s) ● *n* (*of
container*) Boden *m*; (*of river*)
Grund *m*; (*of page, hill*) Fuß *m*;
(*buttocks*) Hintern *m*; **at the ~**
unten; **get to the ~ of sth** (*fig*)
hinter etw (*acc*) kommen
bought *see* **buy**
bounce *vi* [auf]springen;
<*cheque:*> Ⅰ nicht gedeckt sein
● *vt* aufspringen lassen <*ball*>
bouncer *n* Ⅰ Rausschmeißer *m*
bound¹ *n* Sprung *m* ● *vi* springen
bound² *see* **bind** ● *a* **~ for** <*ship*>
mit Kurs auf (+ *acc*); **be ~ to do
sth** etw bestimmt machen;
(*obliged*) verpflichtet sein, etw zu
machen
boundary *n* Grenze *f*
bounds *npl* (*fig*) Grenzen *pl*; **out
of ~** verboten
bouquet *n* [Blumen]strauß *m*; (*of
wine*) Bukett *nt*
bourgeois *a* (*pej*) spießbürgerlich

out n (Med) Anfall m; (Sport) Kampf m;

bow¹ n (weapon & Mus) Bogen m; (knot) Schleife f

bow² n Verbeugung f ● vi sich verbeugen ● vt neigen <head>

bow³ n (Naut) Bug m

bowel n Darm m. ~s pl Eingeweide pl

bowl¹ n Schüssel f; (shallow) Schale f

bowl² n (ball) Kugel f ● vt/i werfen. ~ over vt umwerfen

bowler n (Sport) Werfer m

bowling n Kegeln nt. ~-alley n Kegelbahn f

bowls n Bowlsspiel nt

bow-tie n Fliege f

box¹ n Schachtel f; (wooden) Kiste f; (cardboard) Karton m; (Theat) Loge f

box² vt/i (Sport) boxen

box|er n Boxer m. ~ing n Boxen nt. **B~ing Day** n zweiter Weihnachtstag m

box: ~-office n (Theat) Kasse f. ~-room n Abstellraum m

boy n Junge m

boycott n Boykott m ● vt boykottieren

boy: ~friend n Freund m. ~ish a jungenhaft

bra n BH m

brace n Strebe f, Stütze f; (dental) Zahnspange f; ~s npl Hosenträger mpl

bracelet n Armband nt

bracing a stärkend

bracket n Konsole f; (group) Gruppe f; (Typ) round/square ~s runde/eckige Klammern ● vt einklammern

brag vi (pt/pp bragged) prahlen (about mit)

braille n Blindenschrift f

brain n Gehirn nt; ~s (fig) Intelligenz f

brain: ~less a dumm. ~wash vt einer Gehirnwäsche unterziehen. ~wave n Geistesblitz m

brainy a (-ier, -iest) klug

brake n Bremse f ● vt/i bremsen. ~-light n Bremslicht nt

bramble n Brombeerstrauch m

branch n Ast m; (fig) Zweig m; (Comm) Zweigstelle f; (shop) Filiale f ● vi sich gabeln

brand n Marke f ● vt (fig) brandmarken als

brandish vt schwingen

brand-new a nagelneu

brandy n Weinbrand m

brash a nassforsch

brass n Messing nt; (Mus) Blech nt; **top ~** 🄸 hohe Tiere pl. ~ **band** n Blaskapelle f

brassy a (-ier, -iest) 🄸 ordinär

brat n (pej) Balg nt

bravado n Forschheit f

brave a (-r, -st), -ly adv tapfer ● vt die Stirn bieten (+ dat). ~ry n Tapferkeit f

bravo int bravo!

brawl n Schlägerei f

brawn n (Culin) Sülze f

brawny a muskulös

bray vi iahen

brazen a unverschämt

Brazil n Brasilien nt. ~ian a brasilianisch. ~ nut n Paranuss f

breach n Bruch m; (Mil & fig) Bresche f; ~ **of contract** Vertragsbruch m

bread n Brot nt; **slice of ~ and butter** Butterbrot nt. ~crumbs npl Brotkrümel pl; (Culin) Paniermehl nt

breadth n Breite f

break n Bruch m; (interval) Pause f; (interruption) Unterbrechung f; (🄸 chance) Chance f ● v (pt broke, pp broken) ● vt brechen; (smash) zerbrechen; (damage) kaputtmachen 🄸; (interrupt) unterbrechen; ~ **one's arm** sich (dat) den Arm brechen ● vi brechen; <*day:*> anbrechen; <*storm:*> losbrechen; <*thing:*> kaputtgehen ⬚; <*rope, thread:*> reißen; <*news:*> bekannt werden; **his voice is ~ing** er ist im Stimmbruch. **~ away** *vi* sich losreißen/(*fig*) sich absetzen (**from** von). **~ down** *vi* zusammenbrechen; (*Techn*) eine Panne haben; <*negotiations:*> scheitern ● *vt* aufbrechen <*door*>; aufgliedern <*figures*>. **~ in** *vi* einbrechen ● *vt* /*i* abbrechen; lösen <*engagement*>. **~ out** *vi* ausbrechen. **~ up** *vt* zerbrechen ● *vi* <*crowd:*> sich zerstreuen; <*marriage, couple:*> auseinander gehen; (*Sch*) Ferien bekommen

break|able *a* zerbrechlich. **~age** *n* Bruch *m*. **~down** *n* (*Techn*) Panne *f*; (*Med*) Zusammenbruch *m*; (*of figures*) Aufgliederung *f*. **~er** *n* (*wave*) Brecher *m*

breakfast *n* Frühstück *nt*

break: ~through *n* Durchbruch *m*. **~water** *n* Buhne *f*

breast *n* Brust *f*. **~bone** *n* Brustbein *nt*. **~-feed** *vt* stillen. **~-stroke** *n* Brustschwimmen *nt*

breath *n* Atem *m*; **out of ~** außer Atem; **under one's ~** vor sich (*acc*) hin

breathe *vt*/*i* atmen. **~ in** *vt*/*i* einatmen. **~ out** *vt*/*i* ausatmen

breathing *n* Atmen *nt*

breath: : ~less *a* atemlos. **~-taking** *a* atemberaubend

bred *see* **breed**

breed *n* Rasse *f* ● *v* (*pt*/*pp* **bred**) ● *vt* züchten; (*give rise to*) erzeugen ● *vi* sich vermehren. **~er** *n* Züchter *m*. **~ing** *n* Zucht *f*; (*fig*) [gute] Lebensart *f*

breez|e *n* Lüftchen *nt*; (*Naut*) Brise *f*. **~y** *a* windig

brevity *n* Kürze *f*

brew *n* Gebräu *nt* ● *vt* brauen; kochen <*tea*>. **~er** *n* Brauer *m*. **~ery** *n* Brauerei *f*

bribe *n* (*money*) Bestechungsgeld *nt* ● *vt* bestechen. **~ry** *n* Bestechung *f*

brick *n* Ziegelstein *m*, Backstein *m*

bricklayer *n* Maurer *m*

bridal *a* Braut-

bride *n* Braut *f*. **~groom** *n* Bräutigam *m*. **~smaid** *n* Brautjungfer *f*

bridge¹ *n* Brücke *f*; (*of nose*) Nasenrücken *m*; (*of spectacles*) Steg *m*

bridge² *n* (*Cards*) Bridge *nt*

bridle *n* Zaum *m*

brief¹ *a* (**-er, -est**) kurz; **be ~** <*person:*> sich kurz fassen

brief² *n* Instruktionen *pl*; (*Jur: case*) Mandat *nt*. **~case** *n* Aktentasche *f*

brief|ing *n* Informationsgespräch *nt*. **~ly** *adv* kurz. **~ness** *n* Kürze *f*

briefs *npl* Slip *m*

brigade *n* Brigade *f*

bright *a* (**-er, -est**), **-ly** *adv* hell; <*day*> heiter; **~ red** hellrot

bright|en *v* **~en** [**up**] ● *vt* aufheitern ● *vi* sich aufheitern. **~ness** *n* Helligkeit *f*

brilliance *n* Glanz *m*; (*of person*) Genialität *f*

brilliant *a*, **-ly** *adv* glänzend; <*person*> genial

brim *n* Rand *m*; (*of hat*) Krempe *f*

bring *vt* (*pt*/*pp* **brought**) bringen; **~ them with you** bring sie mit; **I can't ~ myself to do it** ich bringe es nicht fertig. **~ about** *vt* verursachen. **~ along** *vt* mitbringen. **~ back** *vt* zurückbringen. **~ down** *vt* herunterbringen; senken <*price*>. **~ off** *vt* vollbringen. **~ on** *vt* (*cause*) verursachen. **~ out** *vt* herausbringen. **~ round** *vt*

vorbeibringen; (*persuade*)
überreden; wieder zum
Bewusstsein bringen
<*unconscious person*>. **~ up** *vt*
heraufbringen; (*vomit*)
erbrechen; aufziehen <*children*>;
erwähnen <*question*>

brink *n* Rand *m*

brisk *a* (**-er, -est,**) **-ly** *adv* lebhaft;
(*quick*) schnell

bristle *n* Borste *f*

Brit|ain *n* Großbritannien *nt*.
~ish *a* britisch; **the ~ish** die
Briten *pl*. **~on** *n* Brite *m*/Britin *f*

Brittany *n* die Bretagne

brittle *a* brüchig, spröde

broad *a* (**-er, -est**) breit; <*hint*>
deutlich; **in ~ daylight** am
helllichten Tag. **~ beans** *npl*
dicke Bohnen *pl*

broadcast *n* Sendung *f* ● *vt/i*
(*pt/pp* **-cast**) senden. **~er** *n*
Rundfunk- und
Fernsehpersönlichkeit *f*. **~ing** *n*
Funk und Fernsehen *pl*

broaden *vt* verbreitern; (*fig*)
erweitern ● *vi* sich verbreitern

broadly *adv* breit; **~ speaking**
allgemein gesagt

broadminded *a* tolerant

broccoli *n inv* Brokkoli *pl*

brochure *n* Broschüre *f*

broke *see* **break** ● *a* 🛈 pleite

broken *see* **break** ● *a* zerbrochen,
🛈 kaputt. **~-hearted** *a*
untröstlich

broker *n* Makler *m*

brolly *n* 🛈 Schirm *m*

bronchitis *n* Bronchitis *f*

bronze *n* Bronze *f*

brooch *n* Brosche *f*

brood *vi* (*fig*) grübeln

broom *n* Besen *m*; (*Bot*) Ginster
m

broth *n* Brühe *f*

brothel *n* Bordell *nt*

brother *n* Bruder *m*

brother: **~-in-law** *n* (*pl* **-s-in-law**)
Schwager *m*. **~ly** *a* brüderlich

brought *see* **bring**

brow *n* Augenbraue *f*; (*forehead*)
Stirn *f*; (*of hill*) [Berg]kuppe *f*

brown *a* (**-er, -est**) braun; **~ paper**
Packpapier *nt* ● *n* Braun *nt* ● *vt*
bräunen ● *vi* braun werden

browse *vi* (*read*) schmökern; (*in
shop*) sich umsehen

bruise *n* blauer Fleck *m* ● *vt*
beschädigen <*fruit*>; **~ one's arm**
sich (*dat*) den Arm quetschen

brunette *n* Brünette *f*

brush *n* Bürste *f*; (*with handle*)
Handfeger *m*; (*for paint, pastry*)
Pinsel *m*; (*bushes*) Unterholz *nt*;
(*fig: conflict*) Zusammenstoß *m*
● *vt* bürsten; putzen <*teeth*>; **~
against** streifen [gegen]; **~ aside**
(*fig*) abtun. **~ off** *vt* abbürsten. **~
up** *vt/i* (*fig*) **~ up [on]** auffrischen

brusque *a*, **-ly** *adv* brüsk

Brussels *n* Brüssel *nt*. **~ sprouts**
npl Rosenkohl *m*

brutal *a*, **-ly** *adv* brutal. **~ity** *n*
Brutalität *f*

brute *n* Unmensch *m*. **~ force** *n*
rohe Gewalt *f*

bubble *n* [Luft]blase *f* ● *vi*
sprudeln

buck[1] *n* (*deer & Gym*) Bock *m*;
(*rabbit*) Rammler *m* ● *vi* <*horse:*>
bocken

buck[2] *n* (*Amer* 🛈) Dollar *m*

buck[3] *n* **pass the ~** die
Verantwortung abschieben

bucket *n* Eimer *m*

buckle *n* Schnalle *f* ● *vt*
zuschnallen ● *vi* sich verbiegen

bud *n* Knospe *f*

buddy *n* 🛈 Freund *m*

budge *vt* bewegen ● *vi* sich [von
der Stelle] rühren

budget *n* Budget *nt*; (*Pol*)
Haushaltsplan *m*; (*money
available*) Etat *m* ● *vi* (*pt/pp*
budgeted) **~ for sth** etw
einkalkulieren

buff *a* (*colour*) sandfarben ● *n* Sandfarbe *f*; Ⓘ Fan *m* ● *vt* polieren

buffalo *n* (*inv or pl* **-es**) Büffel *m*

buffer *n* (*Rail*) Puffer *m*

buffet[1] *n* Büfett *nt*; (*on station*) Imbissstube *f*

buffet[2] *vt* (*pt/pp* **buffeted**) hin und her werfen

bug *n* Wanze *f*; (Ⓘ *virus*) Bazillus *m*; (Ⓘ *device*) Abhörgerät *nt*, Ⓘ Wanze *f* ● *vt* (*pt/pp* **bugged**) Ⓘ verwanzen <*room*>; abhören <*telephone*>; (*Amer: annoy*) ärgern

bugle *n* Signalhorn

build *n* (*of person*) Körperbau *m* ● *vt/i* (*pt/pp* **built**) bauen. ~ **on** *vt* anbauen (**to** an + *acc*). ~ **up** *vt* aufbauen ● *vi* zunehmen

builder *n* Bauunternehmer *m*

building *f* *n* Gebäude *nt*. ~ **site** *n* Baustelle *f*. ~ **society** *n* Bausparkasse *f*

built *see* **build**. ~**-in** *a* eingebaut. ~**-in cupboard** *n* Einbauschrank *m*. ~**-up area** *n* bebautes Gebiet *nt*; (*Auto*) geschlossene Ortschaft *f*

bulb *n* [Blumen]zwiebel *f*; (*Electr*) [Glüh]birne *f*

bulbous *a* bauchig

Bulgaria *n* Bulgarien *nt*

bulg|e *n* Ausbauchung *f* ● *vi* sich ausbauchen. ~**ing** *a* prall; <*eyes*> hervorquellend

bulk *n* Masse *f*; (*greater part*) Hauptteil *m*. ~**y** *a* sperrig; (*large*) massig

bull *n* Bulle *m*, Stier *m*

bulldog *n* Bulldogge *f*

bulldozer *n* Planierraupe *f*

bullet *n* Kugel *f*

bulletin *n* Bulletin *nt*

bullet-proof *a* kugelsicher

bullfight *n* Stierkampf *m*. ~**er** *n* Stierkämpfer *m*

bullfinch *n* Dompfaff *m*

bullock *n* Ochse *m*

bull: ~**ring** *n* Stierkampfarena *f*. ~'**s-eye** *n* **score a** ~'**s-eye** ins Schwarze treffen

bully *n* Tyrann *m* ● *vt* tyrannisieren

bum *n* ⊠ Hintern *m*

bumble-bee *n* Hummel *f*

bump *n* Bums *m*; (*swelling*) Beule *f*; (*in road*) holperige Stelle *f* ● *vt* stoßen; ~ **into** stoßen gegen; (*meet*) zufällig treffen. ~ **off** *vt* Ⓘ um die Ecke bringen

bumper *a* Rekord- ● *n* (*Auto*) Stoßstange *f*

bumpy *a* holperig

bun *n* Milchbrötchen *nt*; (*hair*) [Haar]knoten *m*

bunch *n* (*of flowers*) Strauß *m*; (*of radishes, keys*) Bund *m*; (*of people*) Gruppe *f*; ~ **of grapes** [ganze] Weintraube *f*

bundle *n* Bündel *nt* ● *vt* ~ [**up**] bündeln

bungalow *n* Bungalow *m*

bungle *vt* verpfuschen

bunk *n* [Schlaf]koje *f*. ~**-beds** *npl* Etagenbett *nt*

bunker *n* Bunker *m*

bunny *n* Ⓘ Kaninchen *nt*

buoy *n* Boje *f*

buoyan|cy *n* Auftrieb *m*. ~**t** *a* **be** ~**t** schwimmen

burden *n* Last *f*

bureau *n* (*pl* **-x** *or* **-s**) (*desk*) Sekretär *m*; (*office*) Büro *nt*

bureaucracy *n* Bürokratie *f*

bureaucratic *a* bürokratisch

burger *n* Hamburger *m*

burglar *n* Einbrecher *m*. ~ **alarm** *n* Alarmanlage *f*

burglary *n* Einbruch *m*

burgle *vt* einbrechen in (+ *acc*); **they have been** ~**d** bei ihnen ist eingebrochen worden

burial *n* Begräbnis *nt*

burly *a* (**-ier, -iest**) stämmig

Burm|a *n* Birma *nt*. ~**ese** *a* birmanisch

burn n Verbrennung f; (on skin) Brandwunde f; (on material) Brandstelle f ● v (pt/pp burnt or burned) ● vt verbrennen ● vi brennen; <food:> anbrennen. ~ **down** vt/i niederbrennen

burnt see **burn**

burp vi 🔢 aufstoßen

burrow n Bau m ● vi wühlen

burst n Bruch m; (surge) Ausbruch m ● v (pt/pp burst) ● vt platzen machen ● vi platzen; <bud:> aufgehen; ~ **into tears** in Tränen ausbrechen

bury vt (pt/pp -ied) begraben; (hide) vergraben

bus n [Auto]bus m

bush n Strauch m; (land) Busch m. ~**y** a (-ier, -iest) buschig

busily adv eifrig

business n Angelegenheit f; (Comm) Geschäft nt; **on ~** geschäftlich; **he has no ~** er hat kein Recht (**to** zu); **mind one's own ~** sich um seine eigenen Angelegenheiten kümmern; **that's none of your ~** das geht Sie nichts an. ~**like** a geschäftsmäßig. ~**man** n Geschäftsmann m

bus-stop n Bushaltestelle f

bust[1] n Büste f

bust[2] a 🔢 kaputt; **go ~** Pleite gehen ● v (pt/pp busted or bust) 🔢 ● vt kaputtmachen ● vi kaputtgehen

busy a (-ier, -iest) beschäftigt; <day> voll; <street> belebt; (with traffic) stark befahren; (Amer Teleph) besetzt; **be ~** zu tun haben ● vt ~ **oneself** sich beschäftigen (**with** mit)

but conj aber; (after negative) sondern ● prep außer (+ dat); ~ **for** (without) ohne (+ acc); **the last ~ one** der/die/das vorletzte; **the next ~ one** der/die/das übernächste ● adv nur

butcher n Fleischer m, Metzger m; ~**'s [shop]** Fleischerei f, Metzgerei f ● vt [ab]schlachten

butler n Butler m

butt n (of gun) [Gewehr]kolben m; (fig: target) Zielscheibe f; (of cigarette) Stummel m; (for water) Regentonne f ● vi ~ **in** unterbrechen

butter n Butter f ● vt mit Butter bestreichen. ~ **up** vt 🔢 schmeicheln (+ dat)

butter: ~**cup** a Butterblume f, Hahnenfuß m. ~**fly** n Schmetterling m

buttocks npl Gesäß nt

button n Knopf m ● vt ~ **[up]** zuknöpfen. ~**hole** n Knopfloch nt

buy n Kauf m ● vt (pt/pp bought) kaufen. ~**er** n Käufer(in) m(f)

buzz n Summen nt ● vi summen

buzzer n Summer m

by prep (close to) bei (+ dat); (next to) neben (+ dat/acc); (past) an (+ dat) ... vorbei; (to the extent of) um (+ acc); (at the latest) bis; (by means of) durch; **by Mozart/ Dickens** von Mozart/Dickens; ~ **oneself** allein; ~ **the sea** am Meer; ~ **car/bus** mit dem Auto/Bus; ~ **sea** mit dem Schiff; ~ **day/night** bei Tag/Nacht; ~ **the hour** pro Stunde; ~ **the metre** meterweise; **six metres ~ four** sechs mal vier Meter; **win ~ a length** mit einer Länge Vorsprung gewinnen; **miss the train ~ a minute** den Zug um eine Minute verpassen ● adv ~ **and large** im Großen und Ganzen; **put ~** beiseite legen; **go/pass ~** vorbeigehen

bye int 🔢 tschüs

by: ~**-election** n Nachwahl f. ~**pass** n Umgehungsstraße f; (Med) Bypass m ● vt umfahren. ~**-product** n Nebenprodukt m. ~**stander** n Zuschauer(in) m(f)

cab n Taxi nt; (of lorry, train) Führerhaus nt
cabaret n Kabarett nt
cabbage n Kohl m
cabin n Kabine f; (hut) Hütte f
cabinet n Schrank m; [display] ~ Vitrine f; **C~** (Pol) Kabinett nt
cable n Kabel nt; (rope) Tau nt. ~ **railway** n Seilbahn f. ~ **television** n Kabelfernsehen nt
cackle vi gackern
cactus n (pl -ti or -tuses) Kaktus m
cadet n Kadett m
cadge vt/i ▣ schnorren
Caesarean a & n ~ [section] Kaiserschnitt m
café n Café nt
cafeteria n Selbstbedienungsrestaurant nt
cage n Käfig m
cagey a ▣ be ~ mit der Sprache nicht herauswollen
cake n Kuchen m; (of soap) Stück nt. ~**d** a verkrustet (**with** mit)
calamity n Katastrophe f
calculat|e vt berechnen; (estimate) kalkulieren. ~**ing** a (fig) berechnend. ~**ion** n Rechnung f, Kalkulation f. ~**or** n Rechner m
calendar n Kalender m
calf¹ n (pl calves) Kalb nt
calf² n (pl calves) (Anat) Wade f
calibre n Kaliber nt
call n Ruf m; (Teleph) Anruf m; (visit) Besuch m ● vt rufen; (Teleph) anrufen; (wake) wecken; ausrufen <strike>; (name) nennen; **be ~ed** heißen ● vi rufen; ~ **[in or round]** vorbeikommen. ~ **back** vt zurückrufen ● vi noch einmal vorbeikommen. ~ **for** vt rufen nach; (demand) verlangen; (fetch) abholen. ~ **off** vt zurückrufen <dog>; (cancel) absagen. ~ **on** vt bitten (**for** um); (appeal to) appellieren an (+ acc); (visit) besuchen. ~ **out** vt rufen; aufrufen <names> ● vi rufen. ~ **up** vt (Mil) einberufen; (Teleph) anrufen
call: ~-box n Telefonzelle f. ~**er** n Besucher m; (Teleph) Anrufer m. ~**ing** n Berufung f. ~-**up** n (Mil) Einberufung f
calm a (-er, -est), -**ly** adv ruhig ● n Ruhe f ~ [down] beruhigen ● vi ~ **down** sich beruhigen. ~**ness** n Ruhe f; (of sea) Stille f
calorie n Kalorie f
calves npl see calf¹ & ²
came see come
camel n Kamel nt
camera n Kamera f
camouflage n Tarnung f ● vt tarnen
camp n Lager nt ● vi campen; (Mil) kampieren
campaign n Feldzug m; (Comm, Pol) Kampagne f ● vi (Pol) im Wahlkampf arbeiten
camp: ~-bed n Feldbett nt. ~**er** n Camper m; (Auto) Wohnmobil nt. ~**ing** n Camping nt. ~**site** n Campingplatz m
can¹ n (for petrol) Kanister m; (tin) Dose f, Büchse f; **a ~ of beer** eine Dose Bier

can²

pres can, *pt* could
● *auxiliary verb*
····▶ (be able to) können. **I can't** or **cannot go** ich kann nicht gehen. **she couldn't** or **could not go** (was unable to) sie konnte nicht gehen; (would not be able to) sie könnte nicht gehen. **he could go if he had time** er könnte gehen,

wenn er Zeit hätte. **if I could go** wenn ich gehen könnte. **that cannot be true** das kann nicht stimmen

····► (*know how to*) können. **can you swim?** können Sie schwimmen? **she can drive** sie kann Auto fahren

····► (*be allowed to*) dürfen. **you can't smoke here** hier dürfen Sie nicht rauchen. **can I go?** kann *od* darf ich gehen?

····► (*in requests*) können. **can I have a glass of water, please?** kann ich ein Glas Wasser haben, bitte? **could you ring me tomorrow?** könnten Sie mich morgen anrufen?

····► **could** (*expressing possibility*) könnte. **that could be so** das könnte *od* kann sein. **I could have killed him** ich hätte ihn umbringen können

Canad|a n Kanada nt. **~ian** a kanadisch ● n Kanadier(in) m(f)
canal n Kanal m
canary n Kanarienvogel m
cancel vt/i (pt/pp **cancelled**) absagen; abbestellen <*newspaper*>; **be ~led** ausfallen. **~lation** n Absage f
cancer n, & (*Astr*) **C~** Krebs m. **~ous** a krebsig
candid a, **-ly** adv offen
candidate n Kandidat(in) m(f)
candle n Kerze f. **~stick** n Kerzenständer m, Leuchter m
candy n (*Amer*) Süßigkeiten pl; **[piece of]** ~ Bonbon m
cane n Rohr nt; (*stick*) Stock m ● vt mit dem Stock züchtigen
canine a Hunde-. ~ **tooth** n Eckzahn m
cannabis n Haschisch nt
canned a Dosen-, Büchsen-
cannibal n Kannibale m. **~ism** n Kannibalismus m
cannon n inv Kanone f

cannot *see* **can²**
canoe n Paddelboot nt; (*Sport*) Kanu nt
can-opener n Dosenöffner m
can't = **cannot**. See **can²**
canteen n Kantine f; ~ **of cutlery** Besteckkasten m
canter n Kanter m ● vi kantern
canvas n Segeltuch nt; (*Art*) Leinwand f; (*painting*) Gemälde nt
canvass vi um Stimmen werben
canyon n Cañon m
cap n Kappe f, Mütze f; (*nurse's*) Haube f; (*top, lid*) Verschluss m
capability n Fähigkeit f
capable a, **-bly** adv fähig; **be ~ of doing sth** fähig sein, etw zu tun
capacity n Fassungsvermögen nt; (*ability*) Fähigkeit f; **in my ~ as** in meiner Eigenschaft als
cape¹ n (*cloak*) Cape nt
cape² n (*Geog*) Kap nt
capital a <*letter*> groß ● n (*town*) Hauptstadt f; (*money*) Kapital nt; (*letter*) Großbuchstabe m
capital|ism n Kapitalismus m. **~ist** a kapitalistisch ● n Kapitalist m. ~ **letter** n Großbuchstabe m. ~ **punishment** n Todesstrafe f
capsize vi kentern ● vt zum Kentern bringen
captain n Kapitän m; (*Mil*) Hauptmann m ● vt anführen <*team*>
caption n Überschrift f; (*of illustration*) Bildtext m
captivate vt bezaubern
captiv|e a **hold/take ~e** gefangen halten/nehmen ● n Gefangene(r) m/f. **~ity** n Gefangenschaft f
capture n Gefangennahme f ● vt gefangen nehmen; [ein]fangen <*animal*>; (*Mil*) einnehmen <*town*>
car n Auto nt, Wagen m; **by ~** mit dem Auto *od* Wagen
caramel n Karamell m

C

carat n Karat nt
caravan n Wohnwagen m; (procession) Karawane f
carbon n Kohlenstoff m; (paper) Kohlepapier nt; (copy) Durchschlag m
carbon: ~ **copy** n Durchschlag m. ~ **paper** n Kohlepapier nt
carburettor n Vergaser m
carcass n Kadaver m
card n Karte f
cardboard n Pappe f, Karton m. ~ **box** n Pappschachtel f; (large) [Papp]karton m
card-game n Kartenspiel nt
cardigan n Strickjacke f
cardinal a Kardinal- ● n (Relig) Kardinal m
card index n Kartei f
care n Sorgfalt f; (caution) Vorsicht f; (protection) Obhut f; (looking after) Pflege f; (worry) Sorge f; ~ **of** (on letter abbr **c/o**) bei; **take** ~ vorsichtig sein; **take into** ~ in Pflege nehmen; **take** ~ **of** sich kümmern um ● vi ~ **for** (like) mögen; (look after) betreuen; **I don't** ~ das ist mir gleich
career n Laufbahn f; (profession) Beruf m ● vi rasen
care: ~**free** a sorglos. ~**ful** a, **-ly** adv sorgfältig; (cautious) vorsichtig. ~**less** a, **-ly** adv nachlässig. ~**lessness** n Nachlässigkeit f
caretaker n Hausmeister m
car ferry n Autofähre f
cargo n (pl **-es**) Ladung f
Caribbean n the ~ die Karibik
caricature n Karikatur f ● vt karikieren
caring a <parent> liebevoll; <profession, attitude> sozial
carnation n Nelke f
carnival n Karneval m
carol n [Christmas] ~ Weihnachtslied nt
carp¹ n inv Karpfen m

carp² vi nörgeln
car park n Parkplatz m; (multi-storey) Parkhaus nt; (underground) Tiefgarage f
carpent|er n Zimmermann m; (joiner) Tischler m. ~**ry** n Tischlerei f
carpet n Teppich m
carriage n Kutsche f; (Rail) Wagen m; (of goods) Beförderung f; (cost) Frachtkosten pl; (bearing) Haltung f
carrier n Träger(in) m(f); (Comm) Spediteur m; ~ **[-bag]** Tragetasche f
carrot n Möhre f, Karotte f
carry vt/i (pt/pp **-ied**) tragen; **be carried away** ⊞ hingerissen sein. ~ **off** vt wegtragen; gewinnen <prize>. ~ **on** vi weitermachen; ~ **on with** ⊞ eine Affäre haben mit ● vt führen; (continue) fortführen. ~ **out** vt hinaus-/ heraustragen; (perform) ausführen
cart n Karren m; **put the** ~ **before the horse** das Pferd beim Schwanz aufzäumen ● vt karren; (⊞ carry) schleppen
carton n [Papp]karton m; (for drink) Tüte f; (of cream, yoghurt) Becher m
cartoon n Karikatur f; (joke) Witzzeichnung f; (strip) Comic Strips pl; (film) Zeichentrickfilm m. ~**ist** n Karikaturist m
cartridge n Patrone f; (for film) Kassette f
carve vt schnitzen; (in stone) hauen; (Culin) aufschneiden
carving n Schnitzerei f. ~**-knife** n Tranchiermesser nt
car wash n Autowäsche f; (place) Autowaschanlage f
case¹ n Fall m; **in any** ~ auf jeden Fall; **just in** ~ für alle Fälle; **in** ~ **he comes** falls er kommt

case² n Kasten m; (crate) Kiste f; (for spectacles) Etui nt; (suitcase) Koffer m; (for display) Vitrine f

cash n Bargeld nt; **pay [in]** ~ [in] bar bezahlen; ~ **on delivery** per Nachnahme ● vt einlösen <cheque>. ~ **desk** n Kasse f

cashier n Kassierer(in) m(f)

cash register n Registrierkasse f

cassette n Kassette f. ~ **recorder** n Kassettenrecorder m

cast n (mould) Form f; (model) Abguss m; (Theat) Besetzung f; **[plaster]** ~ (Med) Gipsverband m ● vt (pt/pp cast) (throw) werfen; (shed) abwerfen; abgeben <vote>; gießen <metal>; (Theat) besetzen <role>. ~ **off** vi (Naut) ablegen

castle n Schloss nt; (fortified) Burg f; (Chess) Turm m

cast-offs npl abgelegte Kleidung f

castor n (wheel) [Lauf]rolle f

castor sugar n Streuzucker m

casual a, **-ly** adv (chance) zufällig; (offhand) lässig; (informal) zwanglos; (not permanent) Gelegenheits-; ~ **wear** Freizeitbekleidung f

casualty n [Todes]opfer nt; (injured person) Verletzte(r) m/f; ~ **[department]** Unfallstation f

cat n Katze f

catalogue n Katalog m ● vt katalogisieren

catapult n Katapult nt ● vt katapultieren

cataract n (Med) grauer Star m

catarrh n Katarrh m

catastroph|e n Katastrophe f. ~**ic** a katastrophal

catch n (of fish) Fang m; (fastener) Verschluss m; (on door) Klinke f; (🔲 snag) Haken m 🔲 ● v (pt/pp caught) ● vt fangen; (be in time for) erreichen; (travel by) fahren mit; bekommen <illness>; ~ **a cold** sich erkälten; ~ **sight of**

erblicken; ~ **s.o. stealing** jdn beim Stehlen erwischen; ~ **one's finger in the door** sich (dat) den Finger in der Tür [ein]klemmen ● vi (burn) anbrennen; (get stuck) klemmen. ~ **on** vi 🔲 (understand) kapieren; (become popular) sich durchsetzen. ~ **up** vt einholen ● vi aufholen; ~ **up with** einholen <s.o.>; nachholen <work>

catching a ansteckend

catch: ~**-phrase** n, ~**word** n Schlagwort nt

catchy a (-ier, -iest) einprägsam

categor|ical a, **-ly** adv kategorisch. ~**y** n Kategorie f

cater vi ~ **for** beköstigen; <firm:> das Essen liefern für <party>; (fig) eingestellt sein auf (+ acc). ~**ing** n (trade) Gaststättengewerbe nt

caterpillar n Raupe f

cathedral n Dom m, Kathedrale f

Catholic a katholisch ● n Katholik(in) m(f). **C** ~**ism** n Katholizismus m

cattle npl Vieh nt

catty a (-ier, -iest) boshaft

caught see **catch**

cauliflower n Blumenkohl m

cause n Ursache f; (reason) Grund m; **good** ~ gute Sache f ● vt verursachen; ~ **s.o. to do sth** jdn veranlassen, etw zu tun

caution n Vorsicht f; (warning) Verwarnung f ● vt (Jur) verwarnen

cautious a, **-ly** adv vorsichtig

cavalry n Kavallerie f

cave n Höhle f ● vi ~ **in** einstürzen

cavern n Höhle f

caviare n Kaviar m

cavity n Hohlraum m; (in tooth) Loch nt

CD abbr (compact disc) CD f; ~**-ROM** CD-ROM f

cease vt/i aufhören. ~-**fire** n
Waffenruhe f. ~**less** a, -**ly** adv
unaufhörlich
cedar n Zeder f
ceiling n [Zimmer]decke f; (fig)
oberste Grenze f
celebrat|e vt/i feiern. ~**ed** a
berühmt (**for** wegen). ~**ion** n
Feier f
celebrity n Berühmtheit f
celery n [Stangen]sellerie m & f
cell n Zelle f
cellar n Keller m
cellist n Cellist(in) m(f)
cello n Cello nt
Celsius a Celsius
Celt n Kelte m/ Keltin f. ~**ic** a
keltisch
cement n Zement m; (adhesive)
Kitt m
cemetery n Friedhof m
censor n Zensor m ● vt
zensieren. ~**ship** n Zensur f
census n Volkszählung f
cent n (coin) Cent m
centenary n, (Amer) **centennial** n
Hundertjahrfeier f
center n (Amer) = **centre**
centi|grade a Celsius. ~**metre** n
Zentimeter m & nt
central a, -**ly** adv zentral. ~
heating n Zentralheizung f. ~**ize**
vt zentralisieren
centre n Zentrum nt; (middle)
Mitte f ● v (pt/pp **centred**) ● vt
zentrieren. ~-**forward** n
Mittelstürmer m
century n Jahrhundert nt
ceramic a Keramik-
cereal n Getreide nt; (breakfast
food) Frühstücksflocken pl
ceremon|ial a, -**ly** adv
zeremoniell, feierlich ● n
Zeremoniell nt. ~**ious** a, -**ly** adv
formell
ceremony n Zeremonie f, Feier f
certain a sicher; (not named)
gewiss; **for** ~ mit Bestimmtheit;
make ~ (check) sich vergewissern

(that dass); (ensure) dafür sorgen
(that dass); **he is** ~ **to win** er wird
ganz bestimmt siegen. ~**ly** adv
bestimmt, sicher; ~**ly not!** auf
keinen Fall! ~**ty** n Sicherheit f,
Gewissheit f; **it's a** ~**ty** es ist
sicher
certificate n Bescheinigung f;
(Jur) Urkunde f; (Sch) Zeugnis nt
certify vt (pt/pp -**ied**)
bescheinigen; (declare insane) für
geisteskrank erklären
cf. abbr (compare) vgl.
chafe vt wund reiben
chaffinch n Buchfink m
chain n Kette f ● vt ketten (**to** an
+ acc). ~ **up** vt anketten
chain: ~ **reaction** n
Kettenreaktion f. ~-**smoker** n
Kettenraucher m. ~ **store** n
Kettenladen m
chair n Stuhl m; (Univ) Lehrstuhl
m; (Adm) Vorsitzende(r) m/f. ~-
lift n Sessellift m. ~-**man** n
Vorsitzende(r) m/f
chalet n Chalet nt
chalk n Kreide f
challeng|e n Herausforderung f;
(Mil) Anruf m ● vt
herausfordern; (Mil) anrufen;
(fig) anfechten <statement>. ~**er**
n Herausforderer m. ~**ing** a
herausfordernd; (demanding)
anspruchsvoll
chamber n Kammer f; **C~ of
Commerce** Handelskammer f. ~
music n Kammermusik f
chamber music n Kammermusik
f
chamois n ~-[**-leather**] Ledertuch
nt
champagne n Champagner m
champion n (Sport) Meister(in)
m(f); (of cause) Verfechter m ● vt
sich einsetzen für. ~**ship** n
(Sport) Meisterschaft f
chance n Zufall m; (prospect)
Chancen pl; (likelihood) Aussicht
f; (opportunity) Gelegenheit f; **by**

~ zufällig; **take a ~** ein Risiko eingehen; **give s.o. a ~** jdm eine Chance geben ● *attrib* zufällig ● *vt* ~ **it** es riskieren

chancellor *n* Kanzler *m*; (*Univ*) Rektor *m*

chancy *a* riskant

change *n* Veränderung *f*; (*alteration*) Änderung *f*; (*money*) Wechselgeld *nt*; **for a ~** zur Abwechslung ● *vt* wechseln; (*alter*) ändern; (*exchange*) umtauschen (**for** gegen); (*transform*) verwandeln; trocken legen <*baby*>; ~ **one's clothes** sich umziehen; ~ **trains** umsteigen ● *vi* sich verändern; (~ *clothes*) sich umziehen; (~ *trains*) umsteigen; **all ~!** alles aussteigen!

changeable *a* wechselhaft

changing-room *n* Umkleideraum *m*

channel *n* Rinne *f*; (*Radio, TV*) Kanal *m*; (*fig*) Weg *m*; **the [English] C~** der Ärmelkanal; **the C~ Islands** die Kanalinseln

chant *vt* singen; <*demonstrators*:> skandieren

chao|s *n* Chaos *nt*. **~tic** *a* chaotisch

chap *n* 🗊 Kerl *m*

chapel *n* Kapelle *f*

chaplain *n* Geistliche(r) *m*

chapped *a* <*skin*> aufgesprungen

chapter *n* Kapitel *nt*

character *n* Charakter *m*; (*in novel, play*) Gestalt *f*; (*Typ*) Schriftzeichen *nt*; **out of ~** uncharakteristisch; **quite a ~** 🗊 ein Original

characteristic *a*, **-ally** *adv* charakteristisch (**of** für) ● *n* Merkmal *nt*

characterize *vt* charakterisieren

charge *n* (*price*) Gebühr *f*; (*Electr*) Ladung *f*; (*attack*) Angriff *m*; (*Jur*) Anklage *f*; **free of ~** kostenlos; **be in ~** verantwortlich

sein (**of** für); **take ~** die Aufsicht übernehmen (**of** über ● *acc*) ● *vt* berechnen <*fee*>; (*Electr*) laden; (*attack*) angreifen; (*Jur*) anklagen (**with** *gen*); ~ **s.o. for sth** jdm etw berechnen

charitable *a* wohltätig; (*kind*) wohlwollend

charity *n* Nächstenliebe *f*; (*organization*) wohltätige Einrichtung *f*; **for ~** für Wohltätigkeitszwecke

charm *n* Reiz *m*; (*of person*) Charme *f*; (*object*) Amulett *nt* ● *vt* bezaubern. **~ing** *a*, **-ly** *adv* reizend; <*person, smile*> charmant

chart *n* Karte *f*; (*table*) Tabelle *f*

charter *n* ~ **[flight]** Charterflug *m* ● *vt* chartern; **~ed accountant** Wirtschaftsprüfer(in) *m(f)*

chase *n* Verfolgungsjagd *f* ● *vt* jagen, verfolgen. ~ **away** or **off** *vt* wegjagen

chassis *n* (*pl* **chassis**) Chassis *nt*

chaste *a* keusch

chat *n* Plauderei *f*; **have a ~ with** plaudern mit ● *vi* (*pt/pp* **chatted**) plaudern. ~ **show** *n* Talkshow *f*

chatter *n* Geschwätz *nt* ● *vi* schwatzen; <*child:*> plappern; <*teeth:*> klappern. **~box** *n* 🗊 Plappermaul *nt*

chatty *a* (**-ier, -iest**) geschwätzig

chauffeur *n* Chauffeur *m*

cheap *a* & *adv* (**-er, -est**), **-ly** *adv* billig. **~en** *vt* entwürdigen

cheat *n* Betrüger(in) *m(f)*; (*at games*) Mogler *m* ● *vt* betrügen ● *vi* (*at games*) mogeln 🗊

check¹ *a* (*squared*) kariert ● *n* Karo *nt*

check² *n* Überprüfung *f*; (*inspection*) Kontrolle *f*; (*Chess*) Schach *nt*; (*Amer: bill*) Rechnung *f*; (*Amer: cheque*) Scheck *m*; (*Amer: tick*) Haken *m*; **keep a ~ on** kontrollieren ● *vt* [über]prüfen; (*inspect*) kontrollieren; (*restrain*) hemmen; (*stop*) aufhalten ● *vi* [go and] ~ nachsehen. ~ **in** *vi* sich anmelden; (*Aviat*) einchecken ● *vt* abfertigen; einchecken. ~ **out** *vi* sich abmelden. ~ **up** *vi* prüfen, kontrollieren; ~ **up on** überprüfen

checked *a* kariert

check: ~**out** *n* Kasse *f.* ~**room** *n* (*Amer*) Garderobe *f.* ~**up** *n* (*Med*) [Kontroll]untersuchung *f*

cheek *n* Backe *f*; (*impudence*) Frechheit *f.* ~**y** *a*, **-ily** *adv* frech

cheer *n* Beifallsruf *m*; **three** ~**s** ein dreifaches Hoch (**for** auf + *acc*); ~**s!** prost! (*goodbye*) tschüs! ● *vt* zujubeln (+ *dat*) ● *vi* jubeln. ~ **up** *vt* aufmuntern; aufheitern ● *vi* munterer werden. ~**ful** *a*, **-ly** *adv* fröhlich. ~**fulness** *n* Fröhlichkeit *f*

cheerio *int* 🔟 tschüs!

cheese *n* Käse *m.* ~**cake** *n* Käsekuchen *m*

chef *n* Koch *m*

chemical *a*, **-ly** *adv* chemisch ● *n* Chemikalie *f*

chemist *n* (*pharmacist*) Apotheker(in) *m(f)*; (*scientist*) Chemiker(in) *m(f)*; ~**'s [shop]** Drogerie *f*; (*dispensing*) Apotheke *f.* ~**ry** *n* Chemie *f*

cheque *n* Scheck *m.* ~**book** *n* Scheckbuch *nt.* ~ **card** *n* Scheckkarte *f*

cherish *vt* lieben; (*fig*) hegen

cherry *n* Kirsche *f* ● *attrib* Kirsch-

chess *n* Schach *nt*

chess: ~**board** *n* Schachbrett *nt.* ~**man** *n* Schachfigur *f*

chest *n* Brust *f*; (*box*) Truhe *f*

chestnut *n* Esskastanie *f*, Marone *f*; (*horse-*) [Ross]kastanie *f*

chest of drawers *n* Kommode *f*

chew *vt* kauen. ~**ing-gum** *n* Kaugummi *m*

chick *n* Küken *nt*

chicken *n* Huhn *nt* ● *attrib* Hühner- ● *a* 🔟 feige

chief *a* Haupt- ● *n* Chef *m*; (*of tribe*) Häuptling *m.* ~**ly** *adv* hauptsächlich

child *n* (*pl* ~**ren**) Kind *nt*

child: ~**birth** *n* Geburt *f.* ~**hood** *n* Kindheit *f.* ~**ish** *a* kindisch. ~**less** *a* kinderlos. ~**like** *a* kindlich. ~**minder** *n* Tagesmutter *f*

children *npl see* **child**

Chile *n* Chile *nt*

chill *n* Kälte *f*; (*illness*) Erkältung *f* ● *vt* kühlen

chilly *a* kühl; **I felt** ~ mich fröstelte [es]

chime *vi* läuten; <*clock:*> schlagen

chimney *n* Schornstein *m.* ~**pot** *n* Schornsteinaufsatz *m.* ~**sweep** *n* Schornsteinfeger *m*

chin *n* Kinn *nt*

china *n* Porzellan *nt*

Chin|a *n* China *nt.* ~**ese** *a* chinesisch ● *n* (*Lang*) Chinesisch *nt*; **the** ~**ese** *pl* die Chinesen

chink[1] *n* (*slit*) Ritze *f*

chink[2] *n* Geklirr *nt* ● *vi* klirren; <*coins:*> klimpern

chip *n* (*fragment*) Span *m*; (*in china, paintwork*) angeschlagene Stelle *f*; (*Computing, Gambling*) Chip *m*; ~**s** *pl* (*Culin*) Pommes frites *pl*; (*Amer: crisps*) Chips *pl* ● *vt* (*pt/pp* **chipped**) (*damage*) anschlagen. ~**ped** *a* angeschlagen

chirp *vi* zwitschern; <*cricket:*> zirpen. ~**y** *a* 🔟 munter

chit *n* Zettel *m*

chocolate *n* Schokolade *f*; (*sweet*) Praline *f*

choice *n* Wahl *f*; (*variety*) Auswahl *f* ● *a* auserlesen

choir *n* Chor *m.* ~**boy** *n* Chorknabe *m*

choke *n* (*Auto*) Choke *m* ● *vt* würgen; (*to death*) erwürgen ● *vi* sich verschlucken; **~ on** [fast] ersticken an (+ *dat*)

choose *vt/i* (*pt* **chose**, *pp* **chosen**) wählen; (*select*) sich (*dat*) aussuchen; **~ to do/go** [freiwillig] tun/gehen; **as you ~** wie Sie wollen

choos[e]y *a* 🅸 wählerisch

chop *n* (*blow*) Hieb *m*; (*Culin*) Kotelett *nt* ● *vt* (*pt/pp* **chopped**) hacken. **~ down** *vt* abhacken; fällen <*tree*>. **~ off** *vt* abhacken

chop|per *n* Beil *nt*; 🅸 (*helicopter*) Hubschrauber *m*. **~py** *a* kabbelig

chopsticks *npl* Essstäbchen *pl*

choral *a* Chor-

chord *n* (*Mus*) Akkord *m*

chore *n* lästige Pflicht *f*; [household] **~s** Hausarbeit *f*

chorus *n* Chor *m*; (*of song*) Refrain *m*

chose, chosen *see* **choose**

Christ *n* Christus *m*

christen *vt* taufen

Christian *a* christlich ● *n* Christ(in) *m(f)*. **~ity** *n* Christentum *nt*. **~ name** *n* Vorname *m*

Christmas *n* Weihnachten *nt*. **~ card** *n* Weihnachtskarte *f*. **~ Day** *n* erster Weihnachtstag *m*. **~ Eve** *n* Heiligabend *m*. **~ tree** *n* Weihnachtsbaum *m*

chrome, chromium *n* Chrom *nt*

chronic *a* chronisch

chronicle *n* Chronik *f*

chrysanthemum *n* Chrysantheme *f*

chubby *a* (**-ier, -iest**) mollig

chuck *vt* 🅸 schmeißen. **~ out** *vt* 🅸 rausschmeißen

chuckle *vi* in sich (*acc*) hineinlachen

chum *n* Freund(in) *m(f)*

chunk *n* Stück *nt*

church *n* Kirche *f*. **~yard** *n* Friedhof *m*

churn *vt* **~ out** am laufenden Band produzieren

cider *n* ≈ Apfelwein *m*

cigar *n* Zigarre *f*

cigarette *n* Zigarette *f*

cine-camera *n* Filmkamera *f*

cinema *n* Kino *nt*

cinnamon *n* Zimt *m*

circle *n* Kreis *m*; (*Theat*) Rang *m* ● *vt* umkreisen ● *vi* kreisen

circuit *n* Runde *f*; (*racetrack*) Rennbahn *f*; (*Electr*) Stromkreis *m*. **~ous** *a* **~ route** Umweg *m*

circular *a* kreisförmig ● *n* Rundschreiben *nt*. **~ saw** *n* Kreissäge *f*. **~ tour** *n* Rundfahrt *f*

circulat|e *vt* in Umlauf setzen ● *vi* zirkulieren. **~ion** *n* Kreislauf *m*; (*of newspaper*) Auflage *f*

circumference *n* Umfang *m*

circumstance *n* Umstand *m*; **~s** *pl* Umstände *pl*; (*financial*) Verhältnisse *pl*

circus *n* Zirkus *m*

cistern *n* (*tank*) Wasserbehälter *m*; (*of WC*) Spülkasten *m*

cite *vt* zitieren

citizen *n* Bürger(in) *m(f)*. **~ship** *n* Staatsangehörigkeit *f*

citrus *n* **~ [fruit]** Zitrusfrucht *f*

city *n* [Groß]stadt *f*

civic *a* Bürger-

civil *a* bürgerlich; <*aviation, defence*> zivil; (*polite*) höflich. **~ engineering** *n* Hoch- und Tiefbau *m*

civilian *a* Zivil-; **in ~ clothes** in Zivil ● *n* Zivilist *m*

civiliz|ation *n* Zivilisation *f*. **~e** *vt* zivilisieren

civil: ~servant *n* Beamte(r) *m*/ Beamtin *f*. **C~ Service** *n* Staatsdienst *m*

claim *n* Anspruch *m*; (*application*) Antrag *m*; (*demand*) Forderung *f*; (*assertion*) Behauptung *f* ● *vt* beanspruchen; (*apply for*) beantragen; (*demand*) fordern; (*assert*) behaupten; (*collect*) abholen

clam *n* Klaffmuschel *f*

clamber vi klettern

clammy a (-ier, -iest) feucht

clamour n Geschrei nt ● vi ~ **for** schreien nach

clamp n Klammer f ● vt [ein]spannen ● vi 🗓 ~ **down on** vorgehen gegen

clan n Clan m

clang n Schmettern nt. ~**er** n 🗓 Schnitzer m

clank vi klirren

clap n **give s.o. a** ~ jdm Beifall klatschen; ~ **of thunder** Donnerschlag m ● vt/i (pt/pp **clapped**) Beifall klatschen (+ dat); ~ **one's hands** [in die Hände] klatschen

clari|fication n Klärung f. ~**fy** vt/i (pt/pp -ied) klären

clarinet n Klarinette f

clarity n Klarheit f

clash n Geklirr nt; (fig) Konflikt m ● vi klirren; <colours:> sich beißen; <events:> ungünstig zusammenfallen

clasp n Verschluss m ● vt ergreifen; (hold) halten

class n Klasse f; **travel first/second** ~ erster/zweiter Klasse reisen ● vt einordnen

classic a klassisch ● n Klassiker m. ~**al** a klassisch

classi|fication n Klassifikation f. ~**fy** vt (pt/pp -ied) klassifizieren

classroom n Klassenzimmer nt

classy a (-ier, -iest) 🗓 schick

clatter n Geklapper nt ● vi klappern

clause n Klausel f; (Gram) Satzteil m

claw n Kralle f; (of bird of prey & Techn) Klaue f; (of crab, lobster) Schere f ● vt kratzen

clay n Lehm m; (pottery) Ton m

clean a (-er, -est) sauber ● adv glatt ● vt sauber machen; putzen <shoes, windows>; ~ **one's teeth** sich (dat) die Zähne putzen; **have** sth ~**ed** etw reinigen lassen. ~ **up** vt sauber machen

cleaner n Putzfrau f; (substance) Reinigungsmittel nt; **[dry]** ~'s chemische Reinigung f

cleanliness n Sauberkeit f

cleanse vt reinigen

clear a (-er, -est), -**ly** adv klar; (obvious) eindeutig; (distinct) deutlich; <conscience:> rein; (without obstacles) frei; **make sth** ~ etw klarmachen (**to** dat) ● adv **stand** ~ zurücktreten; **keep** ~ **of** aus dem Wege gehen (+ dat) ● vt räumen; abräumen <table>; (acquit) freisprechen; (authorize) genehmigen; (jump over) überspringen; ~ **one's throat** sich räuspern ● vi <fog:> sich auflösen. ~ **away** vt wegräumen. ~ **off** vi 🗓 abhauen. ~ **out** vt ausräumen ● vi 🗓 abhauen. ~ **up** vt (tidy) aufräumen; (solve) aufklären ● vi <weather:> sich aufklären

clearance n Räumung f; (authorization) Genehmigung f; (customs) [Zoll]abfertigung f; (Techn) Spielraum m. ~ **sale** n Räumungsverkauf m

clench vt ~ **one's fist** die Faust ballen; ~ **one's teeth** die Zähne zusammenbeißen

clergy npl Geistlichkeit f. ~**man** n Geistliche(r) m

clerk n Büroangestellte(r) m/f; (Amer: shop assistant) Verkäufer(in) m(f)

clever a (-er, -est), -**ly** adv klug; (skilful) geschickt

cliché n Klischee nt

click vi klicken

client n Kunde m/ Kundin f; (Jur) Klient(in) m(f)

cliff n Kliff nt

climate n Klima nt

climax n Höhepunkt m

climb n Aufstieg m ● vt besteigen <mountain>; steigen auf (+ acc)

C

<ladder, tree> ● *vi* klettern; *(rise)* steigen; *<road:>* ansteigen. **~ down** *vi* hinunter-/ herunterklettern; *(from ladder, tree)* heruntersteigen; Ⅱ nachgeben

climber *n* Bergsteiger *m*; *(plant)* Kletterpflanze *f*

cling *vi (pt/pp* **clung)** sich klammern (**to** an + *acc*); *(stick)* haften (**to** an + *dat*). **~ film** *n* Sichtfolie *f* mit Hafteffekt

clinic *n* Klinik *f*. **~al** *a*, **-ly** *adv* klinisch

clink *vi* klirren

clip¹ *n* Klammer *f*; *(jewellery)* Klipp *m* ● *vt (pt/pp* **clipped)** anklammern (**to** an + *acc*)

clip² *n (extract)* Ausschnitt *m* ● *vt* schneiden; knipsen *<ticket>*. **~ping** *n (extract)* Ausschnitt *m*

cloak *n* Umhang *m*. **~room** *n* Garderobe *f*; *(toilet)* Toilette *f*

clobber *n* Ⅱ Zeug *nt* ● *vt* (Ⅱ *hit, defeat)* schlagen

clock *n* Uhr *f*; (Ⅱ *speedometer)* Tacho *m* ● *vi* **~ in/out** stechen

clock: ~wise *a & adv* im Uhrzeigersinn. **~work** *n* Uhrwerk *nt*; *(of toy)* Aufziehmechanismus *m*; **like ~work** Ⅱ wie am Schnürchen

clod *n* Klumpen *m*

clog *vt/i (pt/pp* **clogged)** **~ [up]** verstopfen

cloister *n* Kreuzgang *m*

close¹ *a* (**-r, -st)** nah[e] (**to** *dat*); *<friend>* eng; *<weather>* schwül; **have a ~ shave** Ⅱ mit knapper Not davonkommen ● *adv* nahe ● *n (street)* Sackgasse *f*

close² *n* Ende *nt*; **draw to a ~** sich dem Ende nähern ● *vt* zumachen, schließen; *(bring to an end)* beenden; sperren *<road>* ● *vi* sich schließen; *<shop:>* schließen, zumachen; *(end)* enden. **~ down** *vt* schließen; stilllegen *<factory>* ● *vi*

schließen; *<factory:>* stillgelegt werden

closely *adv* eng, nah[e]; *(with attention)* genau

closet *n (Amer)* Schrank *m*

close-up *n* Nahaufnahme *f*

closure *n* Schließung *f*; *(of factory)* Stilllegung *f*; *(of road)* Sperrung *f*

clot *n* [Blut]gerinnsel *nt*; (Ⅱ *idiot)* Trottel *m*

cloth *n* Tuch *nt*

clothe *vt* kleiden

clothes *npl* Kleider *pl*. **~-line** *n* Wäscheleine *f*

clothing *n* Kleidung *f*

cloud *n* Wolke *f* ● *vi* **~ over** sich bewölken

cloudy *a* (**-ier, -iest)** wolkig, bewölkt; *<liquid>* trübe

clout *n* Ⅱ Schlag *m*; *(influence)* Einfluss *m*

clove *n* [Gewürz]nelke *f*; **~ of garlic** Knoblauchzehe *f*

clover *n* Klee *m*. **~ leaf** *n* Kleeblatt *nt*

clown *n* Clown *m* ● *vi* **~ [about]** herumalbern

club *n* Klub *m*; *(weapon)* Keule *f*; *(Sport)* Schläger *m*; **~s** *pl (Cards)* Kreuz *nt*, Treff *nt*

clue *n* Anhaltspunkt *m*; *(in crossword)* Frage *f*; **I haven't a ~** Ⅱ ich habe keine Ahnung

clump *n* Gruppe *f*

clumsiness *n* Ungeschicklichkeit *f*

clumsy *a* (**-ier, -iest)**, **-ily** *adv* ungeschickt; *(unwieldy)* unförmig

clung *see* **cling**

clutch *n* Griff *m*; *(Auto)* Kupplung *f*; **be in s.o.'s ~es** Ⅱ in jds Klauen sein ● *vt* festhalten; *(grab)* ergreifen ● *vi* **~ at** greifen nach

clutter *n* Kram *m* ● *vt* **~ [up]** vollstopfen

c/o *abbr* (**care of**) bei

coach n [Reise]bus m; (Rail) Wagen m; (horse-drawn) Kutsche f; (Sport) Trainer m ● vt Nachhilfestunden geben (+ dat); (Sport) trainieren

coal n Kohle f

coalition n Koalition f

coal-mine n Kohlenbergwerk nt

coarse a (-r, -st), **-ly** adv grob

coast n Küste f ● vi (freewheel) im Freilauf fahren; (Auto) im Leerlauf fahren. **~er** n (mat) Untersatz m

coast: **~guard** n Küstenwache f. **~line** n Küste f

coat n Mantel m; (of animal) Fell nt; (of paint) Anstrich m; **~ of arms** Wappen nt ● vt überziehen; (with paint) streichen. **~-hanger** n Kleiderbügel m. **~-hook** n Kleiderhaken m

coating n Überzug m, Schicht f; (of paint) Anstrich m

coax vt gut zureden (+ dat)

cobble[1] n Kopfstein m; **~s** pl Kopfsteinpflaster nt

cobble[2] vt flicken. **~r** n Schuster m

cobweb n Spinnengewebe nt

cock n Hahn m; (any male bird) Männchen nt ● vt <animal:> **~ its ears** die Ohren spitzen; **~ the gun** den Hahn spannen

cockerel n [junger] Hahn m

cockney n (dialect) Cockney nt; (person) Cockney m

cock: **~pit** n (Aviat) Cockpit nt. **~roach** n Küchenschabe f. **~tail** n Cocktail m. **~-up** n 🗵 **make a ~-up** Mist bauen (of bei)

cocky a (-ier, -iest) 🔡 eingebildet

cocoa n Kakao m

coconut n Kokosnuß f

cod n inv Kabeljau m

COD abbr (cash on delivery) per Nachnahme

coddle vt verhätscheln

code n Kode m; (Computing) Code m; (set of rules) Kodex m. **~d** a verschlüsselt

coerc|e vt zwingen. **~ion** n Zwang m

coffee n Kaffee m

coffee: **~-grinder** n Kaffeemühle f. **~-pot** n Kaffeekanne f. **~-table** n Couchtisch m

coffin n Sarg m

cogent a überzeugend

coherent a zusammenhängend; (comprehensible) verständlich

coil n Rolle f; (Electr) Spule f; (one ring) Windung f ● vt **~[up]** zusammenrollen

coin n Münze f ● vt prägen

coincide vi zusammenfallen; (agree) übereinstimmen

coinciden|ce n Zufall m. **~tal** a, **-ly** adv zufällig

coke n Koks m

Coke (P) n (drink) Cola f

cold a (-er, -est) kalt; **I am** or **feel ~** mir ist kalt ● n Kälte f; (Med) Erkältung f

cold: **~-blooded** a kaltblütig. **~-hearted** a kaltherzig. **~ly** adv (fig) kalt, kühl. **~ness** n Kälte f

collaborat|e vi zusammenarbeiten (with mit); **~e on sth** mitarbeiten bei etw. **~ion** n Zusammenarbeit f, Mitarbeit f; (with enemy) Kollaboration f. **~or** n Mitarbeiter(in) m(f); Kollaborateur m

collaps|e n Zusammenbruch m; Einsturz m ● vi zusammenbrechen; <roof, building> einstürzen. **~ible** a zusammenklappbar

collar n Kragen m; (for animal) Halsband nt. **~-bone** n Schlüsselbein nt

colleague n Kollege m/Kollegin f

collect vt sammeln; (fetch) abholen; einsammeln <tickets>; einziehen <taxes> ● vi sich

[an]sammeln ●*adv* call ~ (*Amer*)
ein R-Gespräch führen
collection *n* Sammlung *f*; (*in
church*) Kollekte *f*; (*of post*)
Leerung *f*; (*designer's*) Kollektion
f
collector *n* Sammler(in) *m(f)*
college *n* College *nt*
collide *vi* zusammenstoßen
colliery *n* Kohlengrube *f*
collision *n* Zusammenstoß *m*
colloquial *a*, **-ly** *adv*
umgangssprachlich
Cologne *n* Köln *nt*
colon *n* Doppelpunkt
colonel *n* Oberst *m*
colonial *a* Kolonial-
colony *n* Kolonie *f*
colossal *a* riesig
colour *n* Farbe *f*; (*complexion*)
Gesichtsfarbe *f*; (*race*) Hautfarbe
f; off ~ 🔲 nicht ganz auf der
Höhe ●*vt* färben; ~ **[in]**
ausmalen
colour: ~**blind** *a* farbenblind.
~**ed** *a* farbig ●*n* (*person*)
Farbige(r) *m/f*. ~**fast** *a* farbecht.
~ **film** *n* Farbfilm *m*. ~**ful** *a*
farbenfroh. ~**less** *a* farblos. ~
photo[graph] *n* Farbaufnahme *f*.
~ **television** *n* Farbfernsehen *nt*
column *n* Säule *f*; (*of soldiers,
figures*) Kolonne *f*; (*Typ*) Spalte *f*;
(*Journ*) Kolumne *f*
comb *n* Kamm *m* ●*vt* kämmen;
(*search*) absuchen; ~ **one's hair**
sich (*dat*) [die Haare] kämmen
combat *n* Kampf *m*
combination *n* Kombination *f*
combine¹ *vt* verbinden ●*vi* sich
verbinden; <*people*:> sich
zusammenschließen
combine² *n* (*Comm*) Konzern *m*
combustion *n* Verbrennung *f*
come *vi* (*pt* came, *pp* come)
kommen; (*reach*) reichen (to an +
acc); that ~ **s to £10** das macht
£10; ~ **into money** zu Geld
kommen; ~ **true** wahr werden; ~

in two sizes in zwei Größen
erhältlich sein; **the years to** ~ die
kommenden Jahre; **how** ~? 🔲
wie das? ~ **about** *vi* geschehen.
~ **across** *vi* herüberkommen; 🔲
klar werden ●*vt* stoßen auf (+
acc). ~ **apart** *vi* sich auseinander
nehmen lassen; (*accidentally*)
auseinander gehen. ~ **away** *vi*
weggehen; <*thing*:> abgehen. ~
back *vi* zurückkommen. ~ **by** *vi*
vorbeikommen ●*vt* (*obtain*)
bekommen. ~ **in** *vi*
hereinkommen. ~ **off** *vi*
abgehen; (*take place*) stattfinden;
(*succeed*) klappen 🔲. ~ **out** *vi*
herauskommen; <*book*:>
erscheinen; <*stain*:>
herausgehen. ~ **round** *vi*
vorbeikommen; (*after fainting*)
[wieder] zu sich kommen;
(*change one's mind*) sich
umstimmen lassen. ~ **to** *vi*
[wieder] zu sich kommen. ~ **up**
vi heraufkommen; <*plant*:>
aufgehen; (*reach*) reichen (**to**
bis); ~ **up with** sich (*dat*)
einfallen lassen
come-back *n* Comeback *nt*
comedian *n* Komiker *m*
come-down *n* Rückschritt *m*
comedy *n* Komödie *f*
comet *n* Komet *m*
comfort *n* Bequemlichkeit *f*;
(*consolation*) Trost *m* ●*vt* trösten
comfortable *a*, **-bly** *adv* bequem
comfort station *n* (*Amer*)
öffentliche Toilette *f*
comfy *a* 🔲 bequem
comic *a* komisch ●*n* Komiker *m*;
(*periodical*) Comic-Heft *nt*
coming *a* kommend ●*n* Kommen
nt
comma *n* Komma *nt*
command *n* Befehl *m*; (*Mil*)
Kommando *nt*; (*mastery*)
Beherrschung *f* ●*vt* befehlen (+
dat); kommandieren <*army*>

command|er n Befehlshaber m. **~ing officer** n Befehlshaber m

commemorat|e vt gedenken (+ gen). **~ion** n Gedenken nt

commence vt/i anfangen, beginnen

commend vt loben; (recommend) empfehlen (to dat)

comment n Bemerkung f; **no ~!** kein Kommentar! ● vi sich äußern (on zu); **~ on** (Journ) kommentieren

commentary n Kommentar m; **[running] ~** (Radio, TV) Reportage f

commentator n Kommentator m; (Sport) Reporter m

commerce n Handel m

commercial a, **-ly** adv kommerziell ● n (Radio, TV) Werbespot m

commission n (order for work) Auftrag m; (body of people) Kommission f; (payment) Provision f; (Mil) [Offiziers]patent nt; **out of ~** außer Betrieb ● vt beauftragen <s.o.>; in Auftrag geben <thing>; (Mil) zum Offizier ernennen

commit vt (pt/pp committed) begehen; (entrust) anvertrauen (to dat); (consign) einweisen (to in + acc); **~ oneself** sich festlegen; (involve oneself) sich engagieren. **~ment** n Verpflichtung f; (involvement) Engagement nt. **~ted** a engagiert

committee n Ausschuss m, Komitee nt

common a (-er, -est) gemeinsam; (frequent) häufig; (ordinary) gewöhnlich; (vulgar) ordinär ● n Gemeindeland nt; **have in ~** gemeinsam haben; **House of C~s** Unterhaus nt

common: ~ly adv allgemein. **C~ Market** n Gemeinsamer Markt m. **~place** a häufig. **~-room** n

Aufenthaltsraum m. **~ sense** n gesunder Menschenverstand m

commotion n Tumult m

communal a gemeinschaftlich

communicate vt mitteilen (to dat); übertragen <disease> ● vi sich verständigen

communication n Verständigung f; (contact) Verbindung f; (message) Mitteilung f; **~s** pl (technology) Nachrichtenwesen nt

communicative a mitteilsam

Communion n **[Holy] ~** das [heilige] Abendmahl; (Roman Catholic) die [heilige] Kommunion

communis|m n Kommunismus m. **~t** a kommunistisch ● n Kommunist(in) m(f)

community n Gemeinschaft f; **local ~** Gemeinde f

commute vi pendeln. **~r** n Pendler(in) m(f)

compact a kompakt

companion n Begleiter(in) m(f). **~ship** n Gesellschaft f

company n Gesellschaft f; (firm) Firma f; (Mil) Kompanie f; (🆒 guests) Besuch m. **~ car** n Firmenwagen m

comparable a vergleichbar

comparative a vergleichend; (relative) relativ ● n (Gram) Komparativ m. **~ly** adv verhältnismäßig

compare vt vergleichen (with/to mit) ● vi sich vergleichen lassen

comparison n Vergleich m

compartment n Fach nt; (Rail) Abteil nt

compass n Kompass m

compassion n Mitleid nt. **~ate** a mitfühlend

compatible a vereinbar; <drugs> verträglich; (Techn) kompatibel; **be ~** <people:> [gut] zueinander passen

compatriot n Landsmann m /-männin f

compel vt (pt/pp **compelled**) zwingen

compensat|e vt entschädigen. **~ion** n Entschädigung f; (fig) Ausgleich m

compete vi konkurrieren; (take part) teilnehmen (in an + dat)

competen|ce n Fähigkeit f. **~t** a fähig

competition n Konkurrenz f; (contest) Wettbewerb m; (in newspaper) Preisausschreiben nt

competitive a (Comm) konkurrenzfähig

competitor n Teilnehmer m; (Comm) Konkurrent m

compile vt zusammenstellen

complacen|cy n Selbstzufriedenheit f. **~t** a, **-ly** adv selbstzufrieden

complain vi klagen (**about/of** über + acc); (formally) sich beschweren. **~t** n Klage f; (formal) Beschwerde f; (Med) Leiden nt

complement¹ n Ergänzung f; **full ~** volle Anzahl f

complement² vt ergänzen

complete a vollständig; (finished) fertig; (utter) völlig ● vt vervollständigen; (finish) abschließen; (fill in) ausfüllen. **~ly** adv völlig

completion n Vervollständigung f; (end) Abschluss m

complex a komplex ● n Komplex m

complexion n Teint m; (colour) Gesichtsfarbe f

complexity n Komplexität f

complicat|e vt komplizieren. **~ed** a kompliziert. **~ion** n Komplikation f

compliment n Kompliment nt; **~s** pl Grüße pl ● vt ein Kompliment machen (+ dat)

~ary a schmeichelhaft; (given free) Frei-

comply vi (pt/pp -**ied**) **~ with** nachkommen (+ dat)

compose vt verfassen; (Mus) komponieren; **be ~d of** sich zusammensetzen aus. **~r** n Komponist m

composition n Komposition f; (essay) Aufsatz m

compost n Kompost m

composure n Fassung f

compound a zusammengesetzt; <fracture> kompliziert ● n (Chem) Verbindung f; (Gram) Kompositum nt

comprehen|d vt begreifen, verstehen. **~sible** a, **-bly** adv verständlich. **~sion** n Verständnis nt

comprehensive a & n umfassend; **~ [school]** Gesamtschule f. **~ insurance** n (Auto) Vollkaskoversicherung f

compress vt zusammenpressen; **~ed air** Druckluft f

comprise vt umfassen, bestehen aus

compromise n Kompromiss m ● vt kompromittieren <person> ● vi einen Kompromiss schließen

compuls|ion n Zwang m. **~ive** a zwanghaft. **~ory** a obligatorisch

comput|er n Computer m. **~er game** n Computerspiel. **~erize** vt computerisieren <data>; auf Computer umstellen <firm>. **~-literate** a mit Computern vertraut. **~ing** n Computertechnik f

comrade n Kamerad m; (Pol) Genosse m/Genossin f

con¹ see **pro**

con² n 🛈 Schwindel m ● vt (pt/pp **conned**) 🛈 beschwindeln

concave a konkav

conceal vt verstecken; (keep secret) verheimlichen

concede vt zugeben; (give up) aufgeben

conceit n Einbildung f. ~ed a eingebildet

conceivable a denkbar

conceive vt (Biol) empfangen; (fig) sich (dat) ausdenken ● vi schwanger werden

concentrat|e vt konzentrieren ● vi sich konzentrieren. ~ion n Konzentration f

concern n Angelegenheit f; (worry) Sorge f; (Comm) Unternehmen nt ● vt (be about, affect) betreffen; (worry) kümmern; be ~ed about besorgt sein um; ~ oneself with sich beschäftigen mit; as far as I am ~ed was mich angeht od betrifft. ~ing prep bezüglich (+ gen)

concert n Konzert nt

concerto n Konzert nt

concession n Zugeständnis nt; (Comm) Konzession f; (reduction) Ermäßigung f

concise a, -ly adv kurz

conclude vt/i schließen

conclusion n Schluss m; in ~ abschließend, zum Schluss

conclusive a schlüssig

concoct vt zusammenstellen; (fig) fabrizieren. ~ion n Zusammenstellung f; (drink) Gebräu nt

concrete a konkret ● n Beton m ● vt betonieren

concurrently adv gleichzeitig

concussion n Gehirnerschütterung f

condemn vt verurteilen; (declare unfit) für untauglich erklären. ~ation n Verurteilung f

condensation n Kondensation f

condense vt zusammenfassen

condescend vi sich herablassen (to zu). ~ing a, -ly adv herablassend

condition n Bedingung f; (state) Zustand m; ~s pl Verhältnisse pl; on ~ that unter der Bedingung, dass ● vt (Psych) konditionieren. ~al a bedingt ● n (Gram) Konditional m. ~er n Pflegespülung f; (for fabrics) Weichspüler m

condolences npl Beileid nt

condom n Kondom nt

condominium n (Amer) ≈ Eigentumswohnung f

conduct¹ n Verhalten nt; (Sch) Betragen nt

conduct² vt führen; (Phys) leiten; (Mus) dirigieren. ~or n Dirigent m; (of bus) Schaffner m; (Phys) Leiter m

cone n Kegel m; (Bot) Zapfen m; (for ice-cream) [Eis]tüte f; (Auto) Leitkegel m

confectioner n Konditor m. ~y n Süßwaren pl

conference n Konferenz f

confess vt/i gestehen; (Relig) beichten. ~ion n Geständnis nt; (Relig) Beichte f

confetti n Konfetti nt

confide vt anvertrauen ● vi ~ in s.o. sich jdm anvertrauen

confidence n (trust) Vertrauen nt; (self-assurance) Selbstvertrauen nt; (secret) Geheimnis nt; in ~ im Vertrauen. ~ trick n Schwindel m

confident a, -ly adv zuversichtlich; (self-assured) selbstsicher

confidential a, -ly adv vertraulich

confine vt beschränken (to auf + acc). ~d a (narrow) eng

confirm vt bestätigen; (Relig) konfirmieren; (Roman Catholic) firmen. ~ation n Bestätigung f; Konfirmation f; Firmung f

confiscat|e vt beschlagnahmen. ~ion n Beschlagnahme f

conflict¹ n Konflikt m

conflict² vi im Widerspruch stehen (with zu). ~ing a widersprüchlich

conform vi <person:> sich anpassen; <thing:> entsprechen (to dat). ~ist n Konformist m

confounded a 🛈 verflixt

confront vt konfrontieren. ~ation n Konfrontation f

confus|e vt verwirren; (mistake for) verwechseln (with mit). ~ing a verwirrend. ~ion n Verwirrung f; (muddle) Durcheinander nt

congenial a angenehm

congest|ed a verstopft; (with people) überfüllt. ~ion n Verstopfung f; Überfüllung f

congratulat|e vt gratulieren (+ dat) (on zu). ~ions npl Glückwünsche pl; ~ions! [ich] gratuliere!

congregation n (Relig) Gemeinde f

congress n Kongress m. ~man n Kongressabgeordnete(r) m

conical a kegelförmig

conifer n Nadelbaum m

conjecture n Mutmaßung f

conjunction n Konjunktion f; in ~ with zusammen mit

conjur|e vi zaubern ● vt ~e up heraufbeschwören. ~or n Zauberkünstler m

conk vi ~ out 🛈 <machine:> kaputtgehen

conker n 🛈 Kastanie f

con-man n 🛈 Schwindler m

connect vt verbinden (to mit); (Electr) anschließen (to an + acc); be ~ed with zu tun haben mit; (be related to) verwandt sein mit ● vi verbunden a 🛈 <train:> Anschluss haben (with an + acc)

connection n Verbindung f; (Rail, Electr) Anschluss m; in ~ with in Zusammenhang mit. ~s npl Beziehungen pl

connoisseur n Kenner m

conquer vt erobern; (fig) besiegen. ~or n Eroberer m

conquest n Eroberung f

conscience n Gewissen nt

conscientious a, -ly adv gewissenhaft

conscious a, -ly adv bewusst; [fully] ~ bei [vollem] Bewusstsein; be/become ~ of sth sich (dat) etw (gen) bewusst sein/werden. ~ness n Bewusstsein nt

conscript n Einberufene(r) m

consecrat|e vt weihen; einweihen <church>. ~ion n Weihe f; Einweihung f

consecutive a aufeinanderfolgend. -ly adv fortlaufend

consent n Einwilligung f, Zustimmung f ● vi einwilligen (to in + acc), zustimmen (to dat)

consequen|ce n Folge f. ~t a daraus folgend. ~tly adv folglich

conservation n Erhaltung f, Bewahrung f. ~ist n Umweltschützer m

conservative a konservativ; <estimate> vorsichtig. C~ (Pol) a konservativ ● n Konservative(r) m/f

conservatory n Wintergarten m

conserve vt erhalten, bewahren; sparen <energy>

consider vt erwägen; (think over) sich (dat) überlegen; (take into account) berücksichtigen; (regard as) betrachten als; ~ doing sth erwägen, etw zu tun. ~able a, -bly adv erheblich

consider|ate a, -ly adv rücksichtsvoll. ~ation n Erwägung f; (thoughtfulness) Rücksicht f; (payment) Entgelt nt; take into ~ation berücksichtigen. ~ing prep wenn man bedenkt (that dass)

consist vi ~ of bestehen aus

consisten|cy n Konsequenz f; (density) Konsistenz f. ~t a konsequent; (unchanging) gleichbleibend. ~tly adv konsequent; (constantly) ständig

consolation n Trost m. ~ **prize** n
Trostpreis m
console vt trösten
consonant n Konsonant m
conspicuous a auffällig
conspiracy n Verschwörung f
constable n Polizist m
constant a, **-ly** adv beständig;
(continuous) ständig
constipat|ed a verstopft. ~**ion** n
Verstopfung f
constituency n Wahlkreis m
constitut|e vt bilden. ~**ion** n (Pol)
Verfassung f; (of person)
Konstitution f
constraint n Zwang m;
(restriction) Beschränkung f;
(strained manner)
Gezwungenheit f
construct vt bauen. ~**ion** n Bau
m; (Gram) Konstruktion f;
(interpretation) Deutung f; **under**
~**ion** im Bau
consul n Konsul m. ~**ate** n
Konsulat nt
consult vt [um Rat] fragen;
konsultieren <doctor>;
nachschlagen in (+ dat) <book>.
~**ant** n Berater m; (Med)
Chefarzt m. ~**ation** n Beratung f;
(Med) Konsultation f
consume vt verzehren; (use)
verbrauchen. ~**r** n Verbraucher
m
consumption n Konsum m; (use)
Verbrauch m
contact n Kontakt m; (person)
Kontaktperson f ● vt sich in
Verbindung setzen mit. ~ **lenses**
npl Kontaktlinsen pl
contagious a direkt übertragbar
contain vt enthalten; (control)
beherrschen. ~**er** n Behälter m;
(Comm) Container m
contaminat|e vt verseuchen.
~**ion** n Verseuchung f
contemplat|e vt betrachten;
(meditate) nachdenken über (+

acc). ~**ion** n Betrachtung f;
Nachdenken nt
contemporary a zeitgenössisch
● n Zeitgenosse m/ -genossin f
contempt n Verachtung f; **beneath**
~ verabscheuungswürdig. ~**ible**
a verachtenswert. ~**uous** a, **-ly**
adv verächtlich
content¹ n & **contents** pl Inhalt m
content² a zufrieden ● n **to one's
heart's** ~ nach Herzenslust ● vt
~ **oneself** sich begnügen (with
mit). ~**ed** a, **-ly** adv zufrieden
contentment n Zufriedenheit f
contest n Kampf m; (competition)
Wettbewerb m. ~**ant** n
Teilnehmer m
context n Zusammenhang m
continent n Kontinent m
continental a Kontinental-. ~
breakfast n kleines Frühstück nt.
~ **quilt** n Daunendecke f
continual a, **-ly** adv dauernd
continuation n Fortsetzung f
continue vt fortsetzen; ~ **doing** or
to do sth fortfahren, etw zu tun;
to be ~**d** Fortsetzung folgt ● vi
weitergehen; (doing sth)
weitermachen; (speaking)
fortfahren; <weather:> anhalten
continuity n Kontinuität f
continuous a, **-ly** adv anhaltend,
ununterbrochen
contort vt verzerren. ~**ion** n
Verzerrung f
contour n Kontur f; (line)
Höhenlinie f
contracep|tion n
Empfängnisverhütung f. ~**tive** n
Empfängnisverhütungsmittel nt
contract¹ n Vertrag m
contract² vi sich
zusammenziehen. ~**or** n
Unternehmer m
contradict vt widersprechen (+
dat). ~**ion** n Widerspruch m.
~**ory** a widersprüchlich
contralto n Alt m; (singer)
Altistin f

contraption *n* 🔢 Apparat *m*

contrary *a & adv*
entgegengesetzt; ~ **to** entgegen
(+ *dat*) ● *n* Gegenteil *nt*; **on the** ~
im Gegenteil

contrast[1] *n* Kontrast *m*

contrast[2] *vt* gegenüberstellen
(**with** *dat*) ● *vi* einen Kontrast
bilden (**with** zu). ~**ing** *a*
gegensätzlich; <*colour*> Kontrast-

contribut|e *vt/i* beitragen;
beisteuern <*money*>; (*donate*)
spenden. ~**ion** *n* Beitrag *m*;
(*donation*) Spende *f*. ~**or** *n*
Beitragende(r) *m/f*

contrivance *n* Vorrichtung *f*

control *n* Kontrolle *f*; (*mastery*)
Beherrschung *f*; (*Techn*) Regler
m; ~**s** *pl* (*of car, plane*)
Steuerung *f*; **get out of** ~ außer
Kontrolle geraten ● *vt* (*pt/pp*
controlled) kontrollieren;
(*restrain*) unter Kontrolle halten;
~ **oneself** sich beherrschen

controvers|ial *a* umstritten. ~**y** *n*
Kontroverse *f*

convalesce *vi* sich erholen.
~**nce** *n* Erholung *f*

convalescent *a* ~ **home** *n*
Erholungsheim *nt*

convenience *n* Bequemlichkeit *f*;
[public] ~ öffentliche Toilette *f*;
with all modern ~**s** mit allem
Komfort

convenient *a*, **-ly** *adv* günstig; **be**
~ **for s.o.** jdm gelegen sein, jdm
passen; **if it is** ~ **[for you]** wenn es
Ihnen passt

convent *n* [Nonnen]kloster *nt*

convention *n* (*custom*) Brauch *m*,
Sitte *f*. ~**al**, **-ly** *adv*
konventionell

converge *vi* zusammenlaufen

conversation *n* Gespräch *nt*;
(*Sch*) Konversation *f*

conversion *n* Umbau *m*; (*Relig*)
Bekehrung *f*; (*calculation*)
Umrechnung *f*

convert[1] *n* Bekehrte(r) *m/f*,
Konvertit *m*

convert[2] *vt* bekehren <*person*>;
(*change*) umwandeln (**into** in +
acc); umbauen <*building*>;
(*calculate*) umrechnen; (*Techn*)
umstellen. ~**ible** *a* verwandelbar
● *n* (*Auto*) Kabrio[lett] *nt*

convex *a* konvex

convey *vt* befördern; vermitteln
<*idea, message*>. ~**or belt** *n*
Förderband *nt*

convict[1] *n* Sträfling *m*

convict[2] *vt* verurteilen (**of**
wegen). ~**ion** *n* Verurteilung *f*;
(*belief*) Überzeugung *f*; **previous**
~**ion** Vorstrafe *f*

convinc|e *vt* überzeugen. ~**ing** *a*,
-ly *adv* überzeugend

convoy *n* Konvoi *m*

convulse *vt* **be** ~**ed** sich
krümmen (**with** vor + *dat*)

coo *vi* gurren

cook *n* Koch *m*/ Köchin *f* ● *vt/i*
kochen; **is it** ~**ed?** ist es gar? ~
the books 🔢 die Bilanz frisieren.
~**book** *n* (*Amer*) Kochbuch *nt*

cooker *n* [Koch]herd *m*; (*apple*)
Kochapfel *m*. ~**y** *n* Kochen *nt*.
~**y book** *n* Kochbuch *nt*

cookie *n* (*Amer*) Keks *m*

cool *a* (**-er, -est**), **-ly** *adv* kühl ● *n*
Kühle *f* ● *vt* kühlen ● *vi*
abkühlen. ~**-box** *n* Kühlbox *f*.
~**ness** *n* Kühle *f*

coop *vt* ~ **up** einsperren

co-operat|e *vi*
zusammenarbeiten. ~**ion** *n*
Kooperation *f*

co-operative *a* hilfsbereit ● *n*
Genossenschaft *f*

cop *n* 🔢 Polizist *m*

cope *vi* 🔢 zurechtkommen; ~
with fertig werden mit

copious *a* reichlich

copper[1] *n* Kupfer *nt* ● *a* kupfern

copper[2] *n* 🔢 Polizist *m*

copper beech *n* Blutbuche *f*

coppice *n*, **copse** *n* Gehölz *nt*

copy n Kopie f; (book) Exemplar nt ● vt (pt/pp -ied) kopieren; (imitate) nachahmen; (Sch) abschreiben

copy: ~**right** n Copyright nt. ~**writer** n Texter m

coral n Koralle f

cord n Schnur f; (fabric) Cordsamt m; ~**s** pl Cordhose f

cordial a, -ly adv herzlich ● n Fruchtsirup m

cordon n Kordon m ● vt ~ off absperren

corduroy n Cordsamt m

core n Kern m; (of apple, pear) Kerngehäuse nt

cork n Kork m; (for bottle) Korken m. ~**screw** n Korkenzieher m

corn¹ n Korn nt; (Amer: maize) Mais m

corn² n (Med) Hühnerauge nt

corned beef n Cornedbeef nt

corner n Ecke f; (bend) Kurve f; (football) Eckball m ● vt (fig) in die Enge treiben; (Comm) monopolisieren <market>. ~**stone** n Eckstein m

cornet n (Mus) Kornett nt; (for ice-cream) [Eis]tüte f

corn: ~**flour** n, (Amer) ~**starch** n Stärkemehl nt

corny a 🄵 abgedroschen

coronation n Krönung f

coroner n Beamte(r) m, der verdächtige Todesfälle untersucht

corporal n (Mil) Stabsunteroffizier m

corps n (pl corps) Korps nt

corpse n Leiche f

correct a, -ly adv richtig; (proper) korrekt ● vt verbessern; (Sch, Typ) korrigieren. ~**ion** n Verbesserung f; (Typ) Korrektur f

correspond vi entsprechen (to dat); <two things:> sich entsprechen; (write) korrespondieren. ~**ence** n Briefwechsel m; (Comm) Korrespondenz f. ~**ent** n Korrespondent(in) m(f). ~**ing** a, -ly adv entsprechend

corridor n Gang m; (Pol, Aviat) Korridor m

corro|de vt zerfressen ● vi rosten. ~**sion** n Korrosion f

corrugated a gewellt. ~ **iron** n Wellblech nt

corrupt a korrupt ● vt korrumpieren; (spoil) verderben. ~**ion** n Korruption f

corset n & -s pl Korsett nt

Corsica n Korsika nt

cosh n Totschläger m

cosmetic a kosmetisch ● n ~**s** pl Kosmetika pl

cosset vt verhätscheln

cost n Kosten pl; ~**s** pl (Jur) Kosten; at all ~**s** um jeden Preis ● vt (pt/pp cost) kosten; it ~ me £20 es hat mich £20 gekostet ● vt (pt/pp costed) ~ [out] die Kosten kalkulieren für

costly a (-ier, -iest) teuer

cost: ~ **of living** n Lebenshaltungskosten pl. ~ **price** n Selbstkostenpreis m

costume n Kostüm nt; (national) Tracht f. ~ **jewellery** n Modeschmuck m

cosy a (-ier, -iest) gemütlich ● n (tea-, egg-) Wärmer m

cot n Kinderbett nt; (Amer: camp bed) Feldbett nt

cottage n Häuschen nt. ~ **cheese** n Hüttenkäse m

cotton n Baumwolle f; (thread) Nähgarn nt ● a baumwollen ● vi ~ **on** 🄵 kapieren

cotton wool n Watte f

couch n Liege f

couchette n (Rail) Liegeplatz m

cough n Husten m ● vi husten. ~ **up** vt/i husten; (🄵 pay) blechen

cough mixture n Hustensaft m

could see can²

council n Rat m; (*Admin*) Stadtverwaltung f; (*rural*) Gemeindeverwaltung f. ~ **house** n ≈ Sozialwohnung f

councillor n Ratsmitglied nt

council tax n Gemeindesteuer f

count¹ n Graf m

count² n Zählung f; **keep** ~ zählen ● vt/i zählen. ~ **on** vt rechnen auf (+ acc)

counter¹ n (*in shop*) Ladentisch m; (*in bank*) Schalter m; (*in café*) Theke f; (*Games*) Spielmarke f

counter² a Gegen- ● vt/i kontern (+ dat)

counteract vt entgegenwirken (+ dat)

counterfeit a gefälscht

counterfoil n Kontrollabschnitt m

counterpart n Gegenstück nt

counter-productive a be ~ das Gegenteil bewirken

countersign vt gegenzeichnen

countess n Gräfin f

countless a unzählig

country n Land nt; (*native land*) Heimat f; (*countryside*) Landschaft f; **in the** ~ auf dem Lande. ~**man** n [fellow] ~**man** Landsmann m. ~**side** n Landschaft f

county n Grafschaft f

coup n (*Pol*) Staatsstreich m

couple n Paar nt; **a** ~ **of** (*two*) zwei ● vt verbinden

coupon n Kupon m; (*voucher*) Gutschein m; (*entry form*) Schein m

courage n Mut m. ~**ous** a, **-ly** adv mutig

courgettes npl Zucchini pl

courier n Bote m; (*diplomatic*) Kurier m; (*for tourists*) Reiseleiter(in) m(f)

course n (*Naut, Sch*) Kurs m; (*Culin*) Gang m; (*for golf*) Platz m; ~ **of treatment** (*Med*) Kur f; **of** ~ natürlich, selbstverständlich; **in the** ~ **of** im Lauf[e] (+ gen)

court n Hof m; (*Sport*) Platz m; (*Jur*) Gericht nt

courteous a, **-ly** adv höflich

courtesy n Höflichkeit f

court: ~ **martial** n (pl ~s martial) Militärgericht nt. ~**yard** n Hof m

cousin n Vetter m, Cousin m; (*female*) Kusine f

cove n kleine Bucht f

cover n Decke f; (*of cushion*) Bezug m; (*of umbrella*) Hülle f; (*of typewriter*) Haube f; (*of book, lid*) Deckel m; (*of magazine*) Umschlag m; (*protection*) Deckung f, Schutz m; **take** ~ Deckung nehmen; **under separate** ~ mit getrennter Post ● vt bedecken; beziehen <*cushion*>; decken <*costs, needs*>; zurücklegen <*distance*>; (*Journ*) berichten über (+ acc); (*insure*) versichern. ~ **up** vt zudecken; (*fig*) vertuschen

coverage n (*Journ*) Berichterstattung f (**of** über + acc)

cover: ~**ing** n Decke f; (*for floor*) Belag m. ~-**up** n Vertuschung f

cow n Kuh f

coward n Feigling m. ~**ice** n Feigheit f. ~**ly** a feige

cowboy n Cowboy m; Ⅱ unsolider Handwerker m

cower vi sich [ängstlich] ducken

cowshed n Kuhstall m

cox n, **coxswain** n Steuermann m

coy a (-er, -est) gespielt schüchtern

crab n Krabbe f

crack n Riss m; (*in china, glass*) Sprung m; (*noise*) Knall m; (Ⅱ *joke*) Witz m; (Ⅱ *attempt*) Versuch m ● a Ⅱ erstklassig ● vt knacken <*nut, code*>; einen Sprung machen in (+ acc) <*china, glass*>; Ⅱ reißen <*joke*>; Ⅱ lösen <*problem*> ● vi <*china, glass:*> springen; <*whip:*>

knallen. **~ down** vi 🗌 durchgreifen

cracked a gesprungen; <rib> angebrochen; (🗌 crazy) verrückt

cracker n (biscuit) Kräcker m; (firework) Knallkörper m; [Christmas] ~ Knallbonbon m. **~s** a **be ~s** 🗌 einen Knacks haben

crackle vi knistern

cradle n Wiege f

craft n Handwerk nt; (technique) Fertigkeit f. **~sman** n Handwerker m

crafty a (-ier, -iest), **-ily** adv gerissen

crag n Felszacken m

cram v (pt/pp **crammed**) ● vt hineinstopfen (into in + acc); vollstopfen (with mit) ● vi (for exams) pauken

cramp n Krampf m. **~ed** a eng

cranberry n (Culin) Preiselbeere f

crane n Kran m; (bird) Kranich m

crank n 🗌 Exzentriker m

crankshaft n Kurbelwelle f

crash n (noise) Krach m; (Auto) Zusammenstoß m; (Aviat) Absturz m ● vi krachen (into gegen); <cars:> zusammenstoßen; <plane:> abstürzen ● vt einen Unfall haben mit <car>

crash: ~-helmet n Sturzhelm m. **~-landing** n Bruchlandung f

crate n Kiste f

crater n Krater m

crawl n (Swimming) Kraul nt; **do the ~** kraulen; **at a ~** im Kriechtempo ● vi kriechen; <baby:> krabbeln; **~ with** wimmeln von

crayon n Wachsstift m; (pencil) Buntstift m

craze n Mode f

crazy a (-ier, -iest) verrückt; **be ~ about** verrückt sein nach

creak vi knarren

cream n Sahne f; (Cosmetic, Med, Culin) Creme f ● a (colour) cremefarben ● vt (Culin) cremig rühren. **~y** a sahnig; (smooth) cremig

crease n Falte f; (unwanted) Knitterfalte f ● vt falten; (accidentally) zerknittern ● vi knittern

creat|e vt schaffen. **~ion** n Schöpfung f. **~ive** a schöpferisch. **~or** n Schöpfer m

creature n Geschöpf nt

crèche n Kinderkrippe f

credibility n Glaubwürdigkeit f

credible a glaubwürdig

credit n Kredit m; (honour) Ehre f ● vt glauben; **~ s.o. with sth** (Comm) jdm etw gutschreiben; (fig) jdm etw zuschreiben. **~able** a lobenswert

credit: ~ card n Kreditkarte f. **~or** n Gläubiger m

creep vi (pt/pp **crept**) schleichen ● n 🗌 fieser Kerl m; **it gives me the ~s** es ist mir unheimlich. **~er** n Kletterpflanze f. **~y** a gruselig

cremat|e vt einäschern. **~ion** n Einäscherung f

crêpe n Krepp m. **~ paper** n Krepppapier n

crept see creep

crescent n Halbmond m

cress n Kresse f

crest n Kamm m; (coat of arms) Wappen nt

crew n Besatzung f; (gang) Bande f. **~ cut** n Bürstenschnitt m

crib¹ n Krippe f

crib² vt/i (pt/pp **cribbed**) 🗌 abschreiben

cricket n Kricket nt. **~er** n Kricketspieler m

crime n Verbrechen nt; (rate) Kriminalität f

criminal a kriminell, verbrecherisch; <law, court> Straf- ● n Verbrecher m

crimson a purpurrot

crinkle vt/i knittern

cripple n Krüppel m ● vt zum Krüppel machen; (fig) lahmlegen. **~d** a verkrüppelt

crisis n (pl **-ses**) Krise f

crisp a (**-er, -est**) knusprig. **~bread** n Knäckebrot nt. **~s** npl Chips pl

criss-cross a schräg gekreuzt

criterion n (pl **-ria**) Kriterium nt

critic n Kritiker m. **~al** a kritisch. **~ally** adv kritisch; **~ally ill** schwer krank

criticism n Kritik f

criticize vt kritisieren

croak vi krächzen; <frog:> quaken

crockery n Geschirr nt

crocodile n Krokodil nt

crocus n (pl **-es**) Krokus m

crony n Kumpel m

crook n (stick) Stab m; (🗉 criminal) Schwindler m, Gauner m

crooked a schief; (bent) krumm; (🗉 dishonest) unehrlich

crop n Feldfrucht f; (harvest) Ernte f ● v (pt/pp **cropped**) ● vt stutzen ● vi **~ up** 🗉 zur Sprache kommen; (occur) dazwischenkommen

croquet n Krocket nt

cross a, **-ly** adv (annoyed) böse (**with** auf + acc); **talk at ~ purposes** aneinander vorbeireden ● n Kreuz nt; (Bot, Zool) Kreuzung f ● vt kreuzen <cheque, animals>; überqueren <road>; **~ oneself** sich bekreuzigen; **~ one's arms** die Arme verschränken; **~ one's legs** die Beine übereinander schlagen; **keep one's fingers ~ed for s.o.** jdm die Daumen drücken; **it ~ed my mind** es fiel mir ein ● vi (go across) hinübergehen/ -fahren; <lines:> sich kreuzen. **~ out** vt durchstreichen

cross: ~-country n (Sport) Crosslauf m. **~-eyed** a schielend; **be ~-eyed** schielen. **~fire** n Kreuzfeuer nt. **~ing** n Übergang m; (sea journey) Überfahrt f. **~roads** n [Straßen]kreuzung f. **~-section** n Querschnitt m. **~wise** adv quer. **~word** n **~word [puzzle]** Kreuzworträtsel nt

crotchety a griesgrämig

crouch vi kauern

crow n Krähe f; **as the ~ flies** Luftlinie

crowd n [Menschen]menge f ● vi sich drängen. **~ed** a [gedrängt] voll

crown n Krone f ● vt krönen; überkronen <tooth>

crucial a höchst wichtig; (decisive) entscheidend (**to** für)

crude a (**-r, -st**) primitiv; (raw) roh

cruel a (**crueller, cruellest**), **-ly** adv grausam (**to** gegen). **~ty** n Grausamkeit f

cruis|e n Kreuzfahrt f ● vi kreuzen; <car:> fahren. **~er** n (Mil) Kreuzer m; (motor boat) Kajütboot nt

crumb n Krümel m

crumble vt/i krümeln; (collapse) einstürzen

crumple vt zerknittern ● vi knittern

crunch n 🗉 **when it comes to the ~** wenn es [wirklich] drauf ankommt ● vt mampfen ● vi knirschen

crusade n Kreuzzug m; (fig) Kampagne f. **~r** n Kreuzfahrer m; (fig) Kämpfer m

crush n (crowd) Gedränge nt ● vt zerquetschen; zerknittern <clothes>; (fig: subdue) niederschlagen

crust n Kruste f

crutch n Krücke f

cry n Ruf m; (shout) Schrei m; **a far ~ from** (fig) weit entfernt von ● vi (pt/pp **cried**) (weep) weinen; <baby:> schreien; (call) rufen

crypt n Krypta f. **~ic** a rätselhaft

crystal n Kristall m; (glass) Kristall nt

cub n (Zool) Junge(s) nt

Cuba n Kuba nt

cubby-hole n Fach nt

cub|e n Würfel m. **~ic** a Kubik-

cubicle n Kabine f

cuckoo n Kuckuck m. **~ clock** n Kuckucksuhr f

cucumber n Gurke f

cuddl|e vt herzen ● vi **~e up to** sich kuscheln an (+ acc). **~y** a kuschelig

cue[1] n Stichwort nt

cue[2] n (Billiards) Queue nt

cuff n Manschette f; (Amer: turn-up) [Hosen]aufschlag m; (blow) Klaps m; **off the ~** 🛈 aus dem Stegreif. **~-link** n Manschettenknopf m

cul-de-sac n Sackgasse f

culinary a kulinarisch

culprit n Täter m

cult n Kult m

cultivate vt anbauen <crop>; bebauen <land>

cultural a kulturell

culture n Kultur f. **~d** a kultiviert

cumbersome a hinderlich; (unwieldy) unhandlich

cunning a listig ● n List f

cup n Tasse f; (prize) Pokal m

cupboard n Schrank m

Cup Final n Pokalendspiel nt

curable a heilbar

curate n Vikar m; (Roman Catholic) Kaplan m

curb vt zügeln

curdle vi gerinnen

cure n [Heil]mittel nt ● vt heilen; (salt) pökeln; (smoke) räuchern; gerben <skin>

curiosity n Neugier f; (object) Kuriosität f

curious a, **-ly** adv neugierig; (strange) merkwürdig, seltsam

curl n Locke f ● vt locken ● vi sich locken

curly a (-ier, -iest) lockig

currant n (dried) Korinthe f

currency n Geläufigkeit f; (money) Währung f; **foreign ~** Devisen pl

current a augenblicklich, gegenwärtig; (in general use) geläufig, gebräuchlich ● n Strömung f; (Electr) Strom m. **~ affairs** or **events** npl Aktuelle(s) nt. **~ly** adv zurzeit

curriculum n Lehrplan m. **~ vitae** n Lebenslauf m

curry n Curry nt & m; (meal) Currygericht nt

curse n Fluch m ● vt verfluchen ● vi fluchen

cursory a flüchtig

curt a, **-ly** adv barsch

curtain n Vorhang m

curtsy n Knicks m ● vi (pt/pp -ied) knicksen

curve n Kurve f ● vi einen Bogen machen; **~ to the right/left** nach rechts/links biegen. **~d** a gebogen

cushion n Kissen nt ● vt dämpfen; (protect) beschützen

cushy a (-ier, -iest) 🛈 bequem

custard n Vanillesoße f

custom n Brauch m; (habit) Gewohnheit f; (Comm) Kundschaft f. **~ary** a üblich; (habitual) gewohnt. **~er** n Kunde m/Kundin f

customs npl Zoll m. **~ officer** n Zollbeamte(r) m

cut n Schnitt m; (Med) Schnittwunde f; (reduction) Kürzung f; (in price) Senkung f; **~ [of meat]** [Fleisch]stück nt ● vt/i (pt/pp cut, pres p cutting) schneiden; (mow) mähen; abheben <cards>; (reduce) kürzen; senken <price>; **~ one's finger** sich in den Finger schneiden; **~ s.o.'s hair** jdm die Haare schneiden; **~ short** abkürzen. **~ back** vt zurückschneiden; (fig) einschränken, kürzen. **~ down** vt fällen; (*fig*) einschränken. **~ off** vt abschneiden; (*disconnect*) abstellen; **be ~ off** (*Teleph*) unterbrochen werden. **~ out** vt ausschneiden; (*delete*) streichen; **be ~ out for** Ⓘ geeignet sein zu. **~ up** vt zerschneiden; (*slice*) aufschneiden

cut-back n Kürzung f

cute a (-r, -st) Ⓘ niedlich

cut glass n Kristall nt

cutlery n Besteck nt

cutlet n Kotelett nt

cut-price a verbilligt

cutting a <*remark*> bissig ● n (*from newspaper*) Ausschnitt m; (*of plant*) Ableger m

CV abbr of **curriculum vitae**

cycl|e n Zyklus m; (*bicycle*) [Fahr]rad nt ● vi mit dem Rad fahren. **~ing** n Radfahren nt. **~ist** n Radfahrer(in) m(f)

cylind|er n Zylinder m. **~rical** a zylindrisch

cynic n Zyniker m. **~al** a, **-ly** adv zynisch. **~ism** n Zynismus m

Cyprus n Zypern nt

Czech a tschechisch; **~ Republic** Tschechische Republik f ● n Tscheche m/ Tschechin f

dab n Tupfer m; (*of butter*) Klecks m

dabble vi **~ in sth** (*fig*) sich nebenbei mit etw befassen

dachshund n Dackel m

dad[dy] n Ⓘ Vati m

daddy-long-legs n [Kohl]schnake f; (*Amer: spider*) Weberknecht m

daffodil n Osterglocke f, gelbe Narzisse f

daft a (-er, -est) dumm

dagger n Dolch m

dahlia n Dahlie f

daily a & adv täglich

dainty a (-ier, -iest) zierlich

dairy n Molkerei f; (*shop*) Milchgeschäft nt. **~ products** pl Milchprodukte pl

daisy n Gänseblümchen nt

dam n [Stau]damm m ● vt (pt/pp dammed) eindämmen

damage n Schaden m (to an + dat); **~s** pl (*Jur*) Schadenersatz m ● vt beschädigen; (*fig*) beeinträchtigen

damn a, int & adv Ⓘ verdammt ● n **I don't care** or **give a ~** Ⓘ ich schere mich einen Dreck darum ● vt verdammen. **~ation** n Verdammnis f

damp a (-er, -est) feucht ● n Feuchtigkeit f

damp|en vt anfeuchten; (*fig*) dämpfen. **~ness** n Feuchtigkeit f

dance n Tanz m; (*function*) Tanzveranstaltung f ● vt/i tanzen. **~ music** n Tanzmusik f

dancer n Tänzer(in) m(f)

dandelion n Löwenzahn m

dandruff n Schuppen pl

Dane n Däne m/Dänin f

danger n Gefahr f; **in/out of ~** in/ außer Gefahr. **~ous** a, **-ly** adv gefährlich; **~ously ill** schwer erkrankt

dangle vi baumeln ● vt baumeln lassen

Danish a dänisch. **~ pastry** n Hefeteilchen nt

Danube n Donau f

dare vt/i (*challenge*) herausfordern (to zu); **~ [to] do sth** [es] wagen, etw zu tun. **~devil** n Draufgänger m

daring a verwegen ● n Verwegenheit f

D

dark a (-er, -est) dunkel; ~ blue/ brown dunkelblau/ -braun; ~ horse (fig) stilles Wasser nt ● n Dunkelheit f; after ~ nach Einbruch der Dunkelheit; in the ~ im Dunkeln

dark|en vt verdunkeln ● vi dunkler werden. ~ness n Dunkelheit f

dark-room n Dunkelkammer f

darling a allerliebst ● n Liebling m

darn vt stopfen

dart n Pfeil m; ~s sg (game) [Wurf]pfeil m ● vi flitzen

dash n (Typ) Gedankenstrich m; a ~ of milk ein Schuss Milch ● vi rennen ● vt schleudern. ~ off vi losstürzen ● vt (write quickly) hinwerfen

dashboard n Armaturenbrett nt

data npl & sg Daten pl. ~ processing n Datenverarbeitung f

date¹ n (fruit) Dattel f

date² n Datum nt; 🆃 Verabredung f; to ~ bis heute; out of ~ überholt; (expired) ungültig; be up to ~ auf dem Laufenden sein ● vt/i datieren; (Amer 🆃: go out with) ausgehen mit

dated a altmodisch

dative a & n (Gram) ~ [case] Dativ m

daub vt beschmieren (with mit); schmieren <paint>

daughter n Tochter f. ~-in-law (pl ~s-in-law) Schwiegertochter f

dawdle vi trödeln

dawn n Morgendämmerung f; at ~ bei Tagesanbruch ● vi anbrechen; it ~ed on me (fig) es ging mir auf

day n Tag m; ~ by ~ Tag für Tag; ~ after ~ Tag um Tag; these ~s heutzutage; in those ~s zu der Zeit

day: ~-dream n Tagtraum m ● vi [mit offenen Augen] träumen. ~light n Tageslicht nt. ~time n in the ~time am Tage

daze n in a ~ wie benommen. ~d a benommen

dazzle vt blenden

dead a tot; <flower> verwelkt; (numb) taub; ~ body Leiche f; ~ centre genau in der Mitte ● adv ~ tired todmüde; ~ slow sehr langsam ● n the ~ pl die Toten; in the ~ of night mitten in der Nacht

deaden vt dämpfen <sound>; betäuben <pain>

dead: ~ end n Sackgasse f. ~ heat n totes Rennen nt. ~line n [letzter] Termin m

deadly a (-ier, -iest) tödlich; (🆃 dreary) sterbenslangweilig

deaf a (-er, -est) taub; ~ and dumb taubstumm

deaf|en vt betäuben; (permanently) taub machen. ~ening a ohrenbetäubend. ~ness n Taubheit f

deal n (transaction) Geschäft nt; whose ~? (Cards) wer gibt? a good or great ~ eine Menge; get a raw ~ 🆃 schlecht wegkommen ● v (pt/pp dealt) ● vt (Cards) geben; ~ out austeilen ● vi ~ in handeln mit; ~ with zu tun haben mit; (handle) sich befassen mit; (cope with) fertig werden mit; (be about) handeln von; that's been dealt with das ist schon erledigt

dealer n Händler m

dean n Dekan m

dear a (-er, -est) lieb; (expensive) teuer; (in letter) liebe(r,s)/ (formal) sehr geehrte(r,s) ● n Liebe(r) m/f ● int oh ~! oje! ~ly adv <love> sehr; <pay> teuer

death n Tod m; three ~s drei Todesfälle. ~ certificate n Sterbeurkunde f

deathly a ~ **silence** Totenstille f
● adv ~ **pale** totenblass
death: ~ **penalty** n Todesstrafe f.
~**-trap** n Todesfalle f
debatable a strittig
debate n Debatte f ● vt/i
debattieren
debauchery n Ausschweifung f
debit n ~ **[side]** Soll nt ● vt (pt/pp
debited) belasten; abbuchen
<sum>
debris n Trümmer pl
debt n Schuld f; **in** ~ verschuldet.
~ **or** n Schuldner m
debut n Debüt nt
decade n Jahrzehnt nt
decaden|ce n Dekadenz f. ~**t** a
dekadent
decaffeinated a koffeinfrei
decay n Verfall m; (rot)
Verwesung f; (of tooth)
Zahnfäule f ● vi verfallen; (rot)
verwesen; <tooth:> schlecht
werden
deceased a verstorben ● n **the**
~**d** der/die Verstorbene
deceit n Täuschung f. ~**ful** a, **-ly**
adv unaufrichtig
deceive vt täuschen; (be
unfaithful to) betrügen
December n Dezember m
decency n Anstand m
decent a, **-ly** adv anständig
decept|ion n Täuschung f; (fraud)
Betrug m. ~**ive** a, **-ly** adv
täuschend
decide vt entscheiden ● vi sich
entscheiden (**on** für)
decided a, **-ly** adv entschieden
decimal a Dezimal- ● n
Dezimalzahl f. ~ **point** n Komma
nt
decipher vt entziffern
decision n Entscheidung f;
(firmness) Entschlossenheit f
decisive a ausschlaggebend;
(firm) entschlossen
deck¹ vt schmücken

deck² n (Naut) Deck nt; **on** ~ an
Deck; ~ **of cards** (Amer)
[Karten]spiel nt. ~**-chair** n
Liegestuhl m
declaration n Erklärung f
declare vt erklären; angeben
<goods>; **anything to** ~? etwas zu
verzollen?
decline n Rückgang m; (in health)
Verfall m ● vt ablehnen; (Gram)
deklinieren ● vi ablehnen; (fall)
sinken; (decrease) nachlassen
décor n Ausstattung f
decorat|e vt (adorn) schmücken;
verzieren <cake>; (paint)
streichen; (wallpaper) tapezieren;
(award medal to) einen Orden
verleihen (+ dat). ~**ion** n
Verzierung f; (medal) Orden m;
~**ions** pl Schmuck m. ~**ive** a
dekorativ. ~**or** n **painter and** ~**or**
Maler und Tapezierer m
decoy n Lockvogel m
decrease¹ n Verringerung f; (in
number) Rückgang m
decrease² vt verringern;
herabsetzen <price> ● vi sich
verringern; <price:> sinken
decrepit a altersschwach
dedicat|e vt widmen; (Relig)
weihen. ~**ed** a hingebungsvoll;
<person> aufopfernd. ~**ion** n
Hingabe f; (in book) Widmung f
deduce vt folgern (**from** aus)
deduct vt abziehen
deduction n Abzug m;
(conclusion) Folgerung f
deed n Tat f; (Jur) Urkunde f
deep a (-er, -est), **-ly** adv tief; **go
off the** ~ **end** [T] auf die Palme
gehen ● adv tief
deepen vt vertiefen
deep-freeze n Gefriertruhe f;
(upright) Gefrierschrank m
deer n inv Hirsch m; (roe) Reh nt
deface vt beschädigen
default n **win by** ~ (Sport)
kampflos gewinnen

defeat n Niederlage f; (defeating) Besiegung f; (rejection) Ablehnung f ●vt besiegen; ablehnen <motion>; (frustrate) vereiteln

defect n Fehler m; (Techn) Defekt m. ~**ive** a fehlerhaft; (Techn) defekt

defence n Verteidigung f. ~**less** a wehrlos

defend vt verteidigen; (justify) rechtfertigen. ~**ant** n (Jur) Beklagte(r) m/f; (in criminal court) Angeklagte(r) m/f

defensive a defensiv

defer vt (pt/pp deferred) (postpone) aufschieben

deferen|ce n Ehrerbietung f. ~**tial** a, -**ly** adv ehrerbietig

defian|ce n Trotz m; in ~**ce** of zum Trotz (+ dat). ~**t** a, -**ly** adv aufsässig

deficien|cy n Mangel m. ~**t** a mangelhaft

deficit n Defizit nt

define vt bestimmen; definieren <word>

definite a, -**ly** adv bestimmt; (certain) sicher

definition n Definition f; (Phot, TV) Schärfe f

definitive a endgültig; (authoritative) maßgeblich

deflat|e vt die Luft auslassen aus. ~**ion** n (Comm) Deflation f

deflect vt ablenken

deform|ed a missgebildet. ~**ity** n Missbildung f

defraud vt betrügen (of um)

defray vt bestreiten

defrost vt entfrosten; abtauen <fridge>; auftauen <food>

deft a (-er, -est), -**ly** adv geschickt. ~**ness** n Geschicklichkeit f

defuse vt entschärfen

defy vt (pt/pp -ied) trotzen (+ dat); widerstehen (+ dat) <attempt>

degrading a entwürdigend

degree n Grad m; (Univ) akademischer Grad m; **20** ~**s** 20 Grad

de-ice vt enteisen

deity n Gottheit f

dejected a, -**ly** adv niedergeschlagen

delay n Verzögerung f; (of train, aircraft) Verspätung f; without ~ unverzüglich ●vt aufhalten; (postpone) aufschieben ●vi zögern

delegate¹ n Delegierte(r) m/f

delegat|e² vt delegieren. ~**ion** n Delegation f

delet|e vt streichen. ~**ion** n Streichung f

deliberate a, -**ly** adv absichtlich; (slow) bedächtig

delicacy n Feinheit f; Zartheit f; (food) Delikatesse f

delicate a fein; <fabric, health> zart; <situation> heikel; <mechanism> empfindlich

delicatessen n Delikatessengeschäft nt

delicious a köstlich

delight n Freude f ●vt entzücken ●vi ~ in sich erfreuen an (+ dat). ~**ed** a hocherfreut; be ~**ed** sich sehr freuen. ~**ful** a reizend

delinquent a straffällig ●n Straffällige(r) m/f

deli|rious a be ~**rious** im Delirium sein. ~**rium** n Delirium nt

deliver vt liefern; zustellen <post, newspaper>; halten <speech>; überbringen <message>; versetzen <blow>; (set free) befreien; ~ a baby ein Kind zur Welt bringen. ~**y** n Lieferung f; (of post) Zustellung f; (Med) Entbindung f; cash on ~**y** per Nachnahme

delta n Delta nt

deluge n Flut f; (heavy rain) schwerer Guss m

delusion n Täuschung f

de luxe a Luxus-

D

demand n Forderung f; (Comm) Nachfrage f; **in ~** gefragt; **on ~** auf Verlangen ● vt verlangen, fordern (**of/from** von). **~ing** a anspruchsvoll

demented a verrückt

demister n (Auto) Defroster m

demo n (pl **~s**) ⓘ Demonstration f

democracy n Demokratie f

democrat n Demokrat m. **~ic** a, **-ally** adv demokratisch

demo|lish vt abbrechen; (destroy) zerstören. **~lition** n Abbruch m

demon n Dämon m

demonstrat|e vt beweisen; vorführen <appliance> ● vi (Pol) demonstrieren. **~ion** n Vorführung f; (Pol) Demonstration f

demonstrator n Vorführer m; (Pol) Demonstrant m

demoralize vt demoralisieren

demote vt degradieren

demure a, **-ly** adv sittsam

den n Höhle f; (room) Bude f

denial n Leugnen nt; **official ~** Dementi nt

denim n Jeansstoff m; **~s** pl Jeans pl

Denmark n Dänemark nt

denounce vt denunzieren; (condemn) verurteilen

dens|e a (**-r, -st**), **-ly** adv dicht; (ⓘ stupid) blöd[e]. **~ity** n Dichte f

dent n Delle f, Beule f ● vt einbeulen; **~ed** verbeult

dental a Zahn-; <treatment> zahnärztlich. **~ floss** n Zahnseide f. **~ surgeon** n Zahnarzt m

dentist n Zahnarzt m/-ärztin f. **~ry** n Zahnmedizin f

denture n Zahnprothese f; **~s** pl künstliches Gebiss nt

deny vt (pt/pp **-ied**) leugnen; (officially) dementieren; **~ s.o. sth** jdm etw verweigern

deodorant n Deodorant nt

depart vi abfahren; (Aviat) abfliegen; (go away) weggehen/-fahren; (deviate) abweichen (**from** von)

department n Abteilung f; (Pol) Ministerium nt. **~ store** n Kaufhaus nt

departure n Abfahrt f; (Aviat) Abflug m; (from rule) Abweichung f

depend vi abhängen (**on** von); (rely) sich verlassen (**on** auf + acc); **it all ~s** das kommt darauf an. **~able** a zuverlässig. **~ant** n Abhängige(r) m/f. **~ence** n Abhängigkeit f. **~ent** a abhängig (**on** von)

depict vt darstellen

deplor|able a bedauerlich. **~e** vt bedauern

deploy vt (Mil) einsetzen

depopulate vt entvölkern

deport vt deportieren, ausweisen. **~ation** n Ausweisung f

depose vt absetzen

deposit n Anzahlung f; (against damage) Kaution f; (on bottle) Pfand nt; (sediment) Bodensatz m; (Geol) Ablagerung f ● vt (pt/pp **deposited**) legen; (for safety) deponieren; (Geol) ablagern. **~ account** n Sparkonto nt

depot n Depot nt; (Amer: railway station) Bahnhof m

deprave vt verderben. **~d** a verkommen

depreciat|e vi an Wert verlieren. **~ion** n Wertminderung f; (Comm) Abschreibung f

depress vt deprimieren; (press down) herunterdrücken. **~ed** a deprimiert. **~ing** a deprimierend. **~ion** n Vertiefung f; (Med) Depression f; (Meteorol) Tief nt

deprivation n Entbehrung f

deprive vt **~ s.o. of sth** jdm etw entziehen. **~d** a benachteiligt

depth *n* Tiefe *f*; in ~ gründlich; in the ~s of winter im tiefsten Winter

deputize *vi* ~ for vertreten

deputy *n* Stellvertreter *m* ● *attrib* stellvertretend

derail *vt* be ~ed entgleisen. ~ment *n* Entgleisung *f*

derelict *a* verfallen; (*abandoned*) verlassen

derisory *a* höhnisch; <*offer*> lächerlich

derivation *n* Ableitung *f*

derivative *a* abgeleitet ● *n* Ableitung *f*

derive *vt/i* (*obtain*) gewinnen (from aus); be ~d from <*word:*> hergeleitet sein aus

derogatory *a* abfällig

derv *n* Diesel[kraftstoff] *m*

descend *vt/i* hinunter-/ heruntergehen; <*vehicle, lift:*> hinunter-/herunterfahren; be ~ed from abstammen von. ~ant *n* Nachkomme *m*

descent *n* Abstieg *m*; (*lineage*) Abstammung *f*

describe *vt* beschreiben

descrip|tion *n* Beschreibung *f*; (*sort*) Art *f*. ~tive *a* beschreibend; (*vivid*) anschaulich

desecrate *vt* entweihen

desert[1] *n* Wüste *f*. ~ island verlassene Insel *f*

desert[2] *vt* verlassen ● *vt* desertieren. ~ed *a* verlassen. ~er *n* (*Mil*) Deserteur *m*. ~ion *n* Fahnenflucht *f*

deserv|e *vt* verdienen. ~edly *adv* verdientermaßen. ~ing *a* verdienstvoll

design *n* Entwurf *m*; (*pattern*) Muster *nt*; (*construction*) Konstruktion *f*; (*aim*) Absicht *f* ● *vt* entwerfen; (*construct*) konstruieren; be ~ed for bestimmt sein für

designer *n* Designer *m*; (*Techn*) Konstrukteur *m*; (*Theat*) Bühnenbildner *m*

desirable *a* wünschenswert; (*sexually*) begehrenswert

desire *n* Wunsch *m*; (*longing*) Verlangen *nt* (for nach); (*sexual*) Begierde *f* ● *vt* [sich (*dat*)] wünschen; (*sexually*) begehren

desk *n* Schreibtisch *m*; (*Sch*) Pult *nt*

desolat|e *a* trostlos. ~ion *n* Trostlosigkeit *f*

despair *n* Verzweiflung *f*; in ~ verzweifelt ● *vi* verzweifeln

desperat|e *a*, **-ly** *adv* verzweifelt; (*urgent*) dringend; be ~e for dringend brauchen. ~ion *n* Verzweiflung *f*

despicable *a* verachtenswert

despise *vt* verachten

despite *prep* trotz (+ *gen*)

despondent *a* niedergeschlagen

dessert *n* Dessert *nt*, Nachtisch *m*. ~ spoon *n* Dessertlöffel *m*

destination *n* [Reise]ziel *nt*; (*of goods*) Bestimmungsort *m*

destiny *n* Schicksal *nt*

destitute *a* völlig mittellos

destroy *vt* zerstören; (*totally*) vernichten. ~er *n* (*Naut*) Zerstörer *m*

destruc|tion *n* Zerstörung *f*; Vernichtung *f*. **-tive** *a* zerstörerisch; (*fig*) destruktiv

detach *vt* abnehmen; (*tear off*) abtrennen. ~able *a* abnehmbar. ~ed *a* ~ed house Einzelhaus *nt*

detail *n* Einzelheit *f*, Detail *nt*; in ~ ausführlich ● *vt* einzeln aufführen. ~ed *a* ausführlich

detain *vt* aufhalten; <*police:*> in Haft behalten; (*take into custody*) in Haft nehmen

detect *vt* entdecken; (*perceive*) wahrnehmen. ~ion *n* Entdeckung *f*

detective *n* Detektiv *m*. ~ story *n* Detektivroman *m*

detention n Haft f; (Sch) Nachsitzen nt

deter vt (pt/pp **deterred**) abschrecken; (prevent) abhalten

detergent n Waschmittel nt

deteriorat|e vi sich verschlechtern. ~**ion** n Verschlechterung f

determination n Entschlossenheit f

determine vt bestimmen. ~**d** a entschlossen

deterrent n Abschreckungsmittel nt

detest vt verabscheuen. ~**able** a abscheulich

detonate vt zünden

detour n Umweg m

detract vi ~ from beeinträchtigen

detriment n to the ~ (of) zum Schaden (+ gen). ~**al** a schädlich (to dat)

deuce n (Tennis) Einstand m

devaluation n Abwertung f

devalue vt abwerten <currency>

devastat|e vt verwüsten. ~**ing** a verheerend. ~**ion** n Verwüstung f

develop vt entwickeln; bekommen <illness>; erschließen <area> ● vi sich entwickeln (into zu). ~**er** n Umweg m [property] ~**er** Bodenspekulant m

development n Entwicklung f

deviat|e vi abweichen. ~**ion** n Abweichung f

device n Gerät nt; (fig) Mittel nt

devil n Teufel m. ~**ish** a teuflisch

devious a verschlagen

devise vt sich (dat) ausdenken

devot|e vt widmen (to dat). ~**ed** a, **-ly** adv ergeben; <care> liebevoll; be ~**ed** to s.o. sehr an jdm hängen

devotion n Hingabe f

devour vt verschlingen

devout a fromm

dew n Tau m

dexterity n Geschicklichkeit f

diabet|es n Zuckerkrankheit f. ~**ic** n Diabetiker(in) m(f)

diabolical a teuflisch

diagnose vt diagnostizieren

diagnosis n (pl -oses) Diagnose f

diagonal a, **-ly** adv diagonal ● n Diagonale f

diagram n Diagramm nt

dial n (of clock) Zifferblatt nt; (Techn) Skala f; (Teleph) Wählscheibe f ● vt/i (pt/pp **dialled**) (Teleph) wählen; ~ **direct** durchwählen

dialect n Dialekt m

dialling n ~ **code** n Vorwahlnummer f. ~ **tone** n Amtszeichen nt

dialogue n Dialog m

diameter n Durchmesser m

diamond n Diamant m; (cut) Brillant m; (shape) Raute f; ~**s** pl (Cards) Karo nt

diaper n (Amer) Windel f

diarrhoea n Durchfall m

diary n Tagebuch nt; (for appointments) [Termin]kalender m

dice n inv Würfel m

dictat|e vt/i diktieren. ~**ion** n Diktat nt

dictator n Diktator m. ~**ial** a diktatorisch. ~**ship** n Diktatur f

dictionary n Wörterbuch nt

did see **do**

didn't = did not

die¹ n (Techn) Prägestempel m; (metal mould) Gussform f

die² vi (pres p **dying**) sterben (of an + dat); <plant, animal:> eingehen; <flower:> verwelken; be **dying to do sth** 🔼 darauf brennen, etw zu tun; be **dying for sth** 🔼 sich nach etw sehnen. ~ **down** vi nachlassen; <fire:> herunterbrennen. ~ **out** vi aussterben

diesel n Diesel m. ~ **engine** n Dieselmotor m

D

diet n Kost f; (restricted) Diät f; (for slimming) Schlankheitskur f; **be on a ~** Diät leben; eine Schlankheitskur machen ●vi diät leben; eine Schlankheitskur machen

differ vi sich unterscheiden; (disagree) verschiedener Meinung sein

differen|ce n Unterschied m; (disagreement) Meinungsverschiedenheit f. **~t** a andere(r,s); (various) verschiedene; **be ~t** anders sein (from als)

differential a Differenzial- ●n Unterschied m; (Techn) Differenzial nt

differentiate vt/i unterscheiden (between zwischen + dat)

differently adv anders

difficult a schwierig, schwer. **~y** n Schwierigkeit f

diffiden|ce n Zaghaftigkeit f. **~t** a zaghaft

dig n (poke) Stoß m; (remark) spitze Bemerkung f; (Archaeol) Ausgrabung f ●vt/i (pt/pp dug, pres p digging) graben; umgraben <garden>. **~ out** vt ausgraben. **~ up** vt ausgraben; umgraben <garden>; aufreißen <street>

digest vt verdauen. **~ible** a verdaulich. **~ion** n Verdauung f

digit n Ziffer f; (finger) Finger m; (toe) Zehe f

digital a Digital-

dignified a würdevoll

dignity n Würde f

dilapidated a baufällig

dilatory a langsam

dilemma n Dilemma nt

dilettante n Dilettant(in) m(f)

diligen|ce n Fleiß m. **~t** a, **-ly** adv fleißig

dilute vt verdünnen

dim a (dimmer, dimmest). **-ly** adv (weak) schwach; (dark) trüb[e]; (indistinct) undeutlich; (🅸 stupid) dumm, 🅸 doof ●v (pt/pp dimmed) ●vt dämpfen

dime n (Amer) Zehncentstück nt

dimension n Dimension f; **~s** pl Maße pl

diminutive a winzig ●n Verkleinerungsform f

dimple n Grübchen nt

din n Krach m, Getöse nt

dine vi speisen. **~r** n Speisende(r) m/f; (Amer: restaurant) Esslokal nt

dinghy n Dinghi nt; (inflatable) Schlauchboot nt

dingy a (-ier, -iest) trübe

dining: ~-car n Speisewagen m. **~-room** n Esszimmer nt. **~-table** n Esstisch m

dinner n Abendessen nt; (at midday) Mittagessen nt; (formal) Essen nt. **~-jacket** n Smoking m

dinosaur n Dinosaurier m

diocese n Diözese f

dip n (in ground) Senke f; (Culin) Dip m ●v (pt/pp dipped) vt [ein]tauchen; **~ one's headlights** (Auto) [die Scheinwerfer] abblenden ●vi sich senken

diploma n Diplom nt

diplomacy n Diplomatie f

diplomat n Diplomat m. **~ic** a, **-ally** adv diplomatisch

dip-stick n (Auto) Ölmessstab m

dire a (-r, -st) bitter; <consequences> furchtbar

direct a & adv direkt ●vt (aim) richten (at auf / (fig) an + acc); (control) leiten; (order) anweisen; **~ a film/play** bei einem Film/ Theaterstück Regie führen

direction n Richtung f; (control) Leitung f; (of play, film) Regie f; **~s** pl Anweisungen pl; **~s for use** Gebrauchsanweisung f

directly adv direkt; (at once) sofort

director n (Comm) Direktor m; (of play, film) Regisseur m

directory n Verzeichnis nt; (Teleph) Telefonbuch nt

dirt n Schmutz m; (soil) Erde f; ~ **cheap** 🔲 spottbillig

dirty a (-ier, -iest) schmutzig

dis|ability n Behinderung f. ~**abled** a [körper]behindert

disadvantage n Nachteil m; **at a** ~ im Nachteil. ~**d** a benachteiligt

disagree vi nicht übereinstimmen (with mit); I ~ ich bin anderer Meinung; **oysters** ~ **with me** Austern bekommen mir nicht

disagreeable a unangenehm

disagreement n Meinungsverschiedenheit f

disappear vi verschwinden. ~**ance** n Verschwinden nt

disappoint vt enttäuschen. ~**ment** n Enttäuschung f

disapproval n Missbilligung f

disapprove vi dagegen sein; ~ **of** missbilligen

disarm vt entwaffnen ● vi (Mil) abrüsten. ~**ament** n Abrüstung f. ~**ing** a entwaffnend

disast|er n Katastrophe f; (accident) Unglück nt. ~**rous** a katastrophal

disbelief n Ungläubigkeit f; **in** ~ ungläubig

disc n Scheibe f; (record) [Schall]platte f; (CD) CD f

discard vt ablegen; (throw away) wegwerfen

discerning a anspruchsvoll

discharge[1] n Ausstoßen nt; (Naut, Electr) Entladung f; (dismissal) Entlassung f; (Jur) Freispruch m; (Med) Ausfluss m

discharge[2] vt ausstoßen; (Naut, Electr) entladen; (dismiss) entlassen; (Jur) freisprechen <accused>

disciplinary a disziplinarisch

discipline n Disziplin f ● vt Disziplin beibringen (+ dat); (punish) bestrafen

disc jockey n Diskjockey m

disclaim vt abstreiten. ~**er** n Verzichterklärung f

disclos|e vt enthüllen. ~**ure** n Enthüllung f

disco n 🔲 Disko f

discolour vt verfärben ● vi sich verfärben

discomfort n Beschwerden pl; (fig) Unbehagen nt

disconnect vt trennen; (Electr) ausschalten; (cut supply) abstellen

discontent n Unzufriedenheit f. ~**ed** a unzufrieden

discontinue vt einstellen; (Comm) nicht mehr herstellen

discord n Zwietracht f; (Mus & fig) Missklang m

discothèque n Diskothek f

discount n Rabatt m

discourage vt entmutigen; (dissuade) abraten (+ dat)

discourteous a, **-ly** adv unhöflich

discover vt entdecken. ~**y** n Entdeckung f

discreet a, **-ly** adv diskret

discretion n Diskretion f; (judgement) Ermessen nt

discriminat|e vi unterscheiden (between zwischen + dat); ~**e against** diskriminieren. ~**ing** a anspruchsvoll. ~**ion** n Diskriminierung f

discus n Diskus m

discuss vt besprechen; (examine critically) diskutieren. ~**ion** n Besprechung f; Diskussion f

disdain n Verachtung f

disease n Krankheit f

disembark vi an Land gehen

disenchant vt ernüchtern

disengage vt losmachen

disentangle vt entwirren

disfigure vt entstellen

D

disgrace n Schande f; **in ~** in
Ungnade ● vt Schande machen
(+ dat). **~ful** a schändlich

disgruntled a verstimmt

disguise n Verkleidung f; **in ~**
verkleidet ● vt verkleiden;
verstellen <voice>

disgust n Ekel m; **in ~** empört
● vt anekeln; (appal) empören.
~ing a eklig; (appalling)
abscheulich

dish n Schüssel f; (shallow)
Schale f; (small) Schälchen nt;
(food) Gericht nt. **~ out** vt
austeilen. **~ up** vt auftragen

dishcloth n Spültuch nt

dishearten vt entmutigen

dishonest a **-ly** adv unehrlich. **~y**
n Unehrlichkeit f

dishonour n Schande f. **~able** a,
-bly adv unehrenhaft

dishwasher n
Geschirrspülmaschine f

disillusion vt ernüchtern. **~ment**
n Ernüchterung f

disinfect vt desinfizieren. **~ant** n
Desinfektionsmittel nt

disinherit vt enterben

disintegrate vi zerfallen

disjointed a
unzusammenhängend

disk n = disc

dislike n Abneigung f ● vt nicht
mögen

dislocate vt ausrenken

dislodge vt entfernen

disloyal a, **-ly** adv illoyal. **~ty** n
Illoyalität f

dismal a trüb[e]; <person>
trübselig

dismantle vt auseinander
nehmen; (take down) abbauen

dismay n Bestürzung f. **~ed** a
bestürzt

dismiss vt entlassen; (reject)
zurückweisen. **~al** n Entlassung
f; Zurückweisung f

disobedien|ce n Ungehorsam m.
~t a ungehorsam

disobey vt/i nicht gehorchen (+
dat); nicht befolgen <rule>

disorder n Unordnung f; (Med)
Störung f. **~ly** a unordentlich

disorganized a unorganisiert

disown vt verleugnen

disparaging a, **-ly** adv abschätzig

dispassionate a, **-ly** adv gelassen;
(impartial) unparteiisch

dispatch n (Comm) Versand m;
(Mil) Nachricht f; (report) Bericht
m ● vt [ab]senden; (kill) töten

dispel vt (pt/pp dispelled)
vertreiben

dispensary n Apotheke f

dispense vt austeilen; **~ with**
verzichten auf (+ acc). **~r** n
(device) Automat m

disperse vt zerstreuen ● vi sich
zerstreuen

dispirited a entmutigt

display n Ausstellung f; (Comm)
Auslage f; (performance)
Vorführung f ● vt zeigen;
ausstellen <goods>

displease vt missfallen (+ dat)

displeasure n Missfallen nt

disposable a Wegwerf-;
<income> verfügbar

disposal n Beseitigung f; **be at
s.o.'s ~** jdm zur Verfügung
stehen

dispose vi **~ of** beseitigen; (deal
with) erledigen

disposition n Veranlagung f;
(nature) Wesensart f

disproportionate a, **-ly** adv
unverhältnismäßig

disprove vt widerlegen

dispute n Disput m; (quarrel)
Streit m ● vt bestreiten

disqualification n
Disqualifikation f

disqualify vt disqualifizieren; **~
s.o. from driving** jdm den
Führerschein entziehen

disregard vt nicht beachten

disrepair n **fall into ~** verfallen

disreputable a verrufen

disrepute n Verruf m

disrespect n Respektlosigkeit f.
~**ful** a, **-ly** adv respektlos

disrupt vt stören. ~**ion** n Störung
f

dissatisfaction n
Unzufriedenheit f

dissatisfied a unzufrieden

dissect vt zergliedern; (Med)
sezieren. ~**ion** n Zergliederung f;
(Med) Sektion f

dissent n Nichtübereinstimmung
f ● vi nicht übereinstimmen

dissident n Dissident m

dissimilar a unähnlich (**to** dat)

dissociate vt ~ **oneself** sich
distanzieren (**from** von)

dissolute a zügellos; <life>
ausschweifend

dissolve vt auflösen ● vi sich
auflösen

dissuade vt abbringen (**from** von)

distance n Entfernung f; **long/
short** ~ lange/kurze Strecke f; **in
the/from a** ~ in/aus der Ferne

distant a fern; (aloof) kühl;
<relative> entfernt

distasteful a unangenehm

distil vt (pt/pp **distilled**) brennen;
(Chem) destillieren. ~**lery** n
Brennerei f

distinct a deutlich; (different)
verschieden. ~**ion** n Unterschied
m; (Sch) Auszeichnung f. ~**ive** a
kennzeichnend; (unmistakable)
unverwechselbar. ~**ly** adv
deutlich

distinguish vt/i unterscheiden;
(make out) erkennen; ~ **oneself**
sich auszeichnen. ~**ed** a
angesehen; <appearance>
distinguiert

distort vt verzerren; (fig)
verdrehen. ~**ion** n Verzerrung f;
(fig) Verdrehung f

distract vt ablenken. ~**ion** n
Ablenkung f; (despair)
Verzweiflung f

distraught a [völlig] aufgelöst

distress n Kummer m; (pain)
Schmerz m; (poverty, danger) Not
f ● vt Kummer/Schmerz bereiten
(+ dat); (sadden) bekümmern;
(shock) erschüttern. ~**ing** a
schmerzlich; (shocking)
erschütternd

distribut|**e** vt verteilen; (Comm)
vertreiben. ~**ion** n Verteilung f;
Vertrieb m. ~**or** n Verteiler m

district n Gegend f; (Admin)
Bezirk m

distrust n Misstrauen nt ● vt
misstrauen (+ dat). ~**ful** a
misstrauisch

disturb vt stören; (perturb)
beunruhigen; (touch) anrühren.
~**ance** n Unruhe f; (interruption)
Störung f. ~**ed** a beunruhigt;
[mentally] ~**ed** geistig gestört.
~**ing** a beunruhigend

disused a stillgelegt; (empty) leer

ditch n Graben m ● vt (🄸
abandon) fallen lassen <plan>

dither vi zaudern

ditto n dito; 🄸 ebenfalls

dive n [Kopf]sprung m; (Aviat)
Sturzflug m; (🄸 place) Spelunke
f ● vi einen Kopfsprung machen;
(when in water) tauchen; (Aviat)
einen Sturzflug machen; (🄸
rush) stürzen

diver n Taucher m; (Sport)
[Kunst]springer m

diverse a verschieden

diversify vt/i (pt/pp **-ied**)
variieren; (Comm) diversifizieren

diversion n Umleitung f;
(distraction) Ablenkung f

diversity n Vielfalt f

divert vt umleiten; ablenken
<attention>; (entertain)
unterhalten

divide vt teilen; (separate)
trennen; (Math) dividieren (**by**
durch) ● vi sich teilen

dividend n Dividende f

divine a göttlich

D

diving n (Sport) Kunstspringen nt. **~-board** n Sprungbrett nt

divinity n Göttlichkeit f; (subject) Theologie f

division n Teilung f; (separation) Trennung f; (Math, Mil) Division f; (Parl) Hammelsprung m; (line) Trennlinie f; (group) Abteilung f

divorce n Scheidung f ● vt sich scheiden lassen von. **~d** a geschieden; **get ~d** sich scheiden lassen

DIY abbr of **do-it-yourself**

dizziness n Schwindel m

dizzy a (-ier, -iest) schwindlig; **I feel ~** mir ist schwindlig

do

3 sg pres tense **does**; pt **did**; pp **done**

● transitive verb

····▶ (perform) machen <homework, housework, exam, handstand etc>; tun <duty, favour, something, nothing>; vorführen <trick, dance>; durchführen <test>. **what are you doing?** was tust od machst du? **what can I do for you?** was kann ich für Sie tun? **do something!** tu doch etwas! **have you nothing better to do?** hast du nichts Besseres zu tun? **do the washing-up /cleaning** abwaschen/sauber machen

····▶ (as job) **what does your father do?** was macht dein Vater?; was ist dein Vater von Beruf?

····▶ (clean) putzen; (arrange) [zurecht]machen <hair>

····▶ (cook) kochen; (roast, fry) braten. **well done** <meat> durch[gebraten]. **the potatoes aren't done yet** die Kartoffeln sind noch nicht richtig durch

····▶ (solve) lösen <problem, riddle>; machen <puzzle>

····▶ (🔢 swindle) reinlegen. **do s.o. out of sth** jdn um etw bringen

● intransitive verb

····▶ (with as or adverb) es tun; es machen. **do as they do** mach es wie sie. **he can do as he likes** er kann tun od machen, was er will. **you did well** du hast es gut gemacht

····▶ (get on) vorankommen; (in exams) abschneiden. **do well/ badly at school** gut/schlecht in der Schule sein. **how are you doing?** wie geht's dir? **how do you do?** (formal) guten Tag!

····▶ **will do** (serve purpose) es tun; (suffice) [aus]reichen; (be suitable) gehen. **that won't do** das geht nicht. **that will do!** jetzt aber genug!

● auxiliary verb

····▶ (in questions) **do you know him?** kennst du ihn? **what does he want?** was will er?

····▶ (in negation) **I don't** or **do not wish to take part** ich will nicht teilnehmen. **don't be so noisy!** seid [doch] nicht so laut!

····▶ (as verb substitute) **you mustn't act as he does** du darfst nicht so wie er handeln. **come in, do!** komm doch herein!

····▶ (in tag questions) **don't you, doesn't he** etc. nicht wahr. **you went to Paris, didn't you?** du warst in Paris, nicht wahr?

····▶ (in short questions) **Does he live in London? — Yes, he does** Wohnt er in London? — Ja [, stimmt]

····▶ (for special emphasis) **I do love Greece** Griechenland gefällt mir wirklich gut

····▶ (for inversion) **little did he know that …** er hatte keine Ahnung, dass …

● noun

pl **do's** or **dos**

····▶ (🔢 celebration) Feier f

● phrasal verbs

● **do away with** vt abschaffen.

● **do for** vt 🔢: do for s.o. jdn fertig machen 🔢; be done for erledigt sein. ● **do in** vt (🔲 *kill*) kaltmachen 🔲. ● **do up** vt (*fasten*) zumachen; binden <shoe-lace, bow-tie>; (*wrap*) einpacken; (*renovate*) renovieren. ● **do with** vt: I could do with ... ich brauche .... ● **do without** vt: do without sth auf etw (*acc*) verzichten; vi darauf verzichten

docile a fügsam

dock¹ n (*Jur*) Anklagebank f

dock² n Dock nt ● vi anlegen. **~er** n Hafenarbeiter m. **~yard** n Werft f

doctor n Arzt m/ Ärztin f; (*Univ*) Doktor m ● vt kastrieren; (*spay*) sterilisieren

doctrine n Lehre f

document n Dokument nt. **~ary** a Dokumentar- ● n Dokumentarbericht m; (*film*) Dokumentarfilm m

dodge n 🔢 Trick m, Kniff m ● vt/i ausweichen (+ *dat*)

dodgy a (-ier, -iest) 🔢 (*awkward*) knifflig; (*dubious*) zweifelhaft

doe n Ricke f; (*rabbit*) [Kaninchen]weibchen nt

does see do

doesn't = does not

dog n Hund m

dog: **~-biscuit** n Hundekuchen m. **~-collar** n Hundehalsband nt; (*Relig* 🔢) Kragen m eines Geistlichen. **~-eared** a be ~-eared Eselsohren haben

dogged a, **-ly** adv beharrlich

dogma n Dogma nt. **~tic** a dogmatisch

do-it-yourself n Heimwerken nt. **~ shop** n Heimwerkerladen m

doldrums npl be in the ~ niedergeschlagen sein; <*business*:> daniederliegen

dole n 🔢 Stempelgeld nt; be on the ~ arbeitslos sein ● vt ~ out austeilen

doll n Puppe f ● vt 🔢 ~ oneself up sich herausputzen

dollar n Dollar m

dolphin n Delphin m

domain n Gebiet nt

dome n Kuppel f

domestic a häuslich; (*Pol*) Innen-; (*Comm*) Binnen-. **~ animal** n Haustier nt. **~ flight** n Inlandflug m

dominant a vorherrschend

dominat|e vt beherrschen ● vi dominieren. **~ion** n Vorherrschaft f

domineering a herrschsüchtig

domino n (pl -es) Dominostein m; **~es** sg (*game*) Domino nt

donat|e vt spenden. **~ion** n Spende f

done see do

donkey n Esel m; ~'s years 🔢 eine Ewigkeit. **~-work** n Routinearbeit f

donor n Spender(in) m(f)

don't = do not

doom n Schicksal nt; (*ruin*) Verhängnis nt

door n Tür f; out of ~s im Freien

door: **~man** n Portier m. **~mat** n [Fuß]abtreter m. **~step** n Türschwelle f; on the ~step vor der Tür. **~way** n Türöffnung f

dope n 🔢 Drogen pl; (🔢 *information*) Informationen pl; (🔢 *idiot*) Trottel m ● vt betäuben; (*Sport*) dopen

dormant a ruhend

dormitory n Schlafsaal m

dormouse n Haselmaus f

dosage n Dosierung f

dose n Dosis f

dot n Punkt m; on the ~ pünktlich. **~com** n Dot-com-Firma f

dote vi ~ **on** vernarrt sein in (+ *acc*)

D

dotted a ~ **line** punktierte Linie f; **be** ~ **with** bestreut sein mit

dotty a (**-ier, -iest**) 🗊 verdreht

double a & adv doppelt; <*bed, chin*> Doppel-; <*flower*> gefüllt ● n das Doppelte; (*person*) Doppelgänger m; ~**s** pl (*Tennis*) Doppel nt; ● vt verdoppeln; (*fold*) falten ● vi sich verdoppeln. ~ **up** vi sich krümmen (**with** vor + dat)

double: ~**-bass** n Kontrabass m. ~**-breasted** a zweireihig. ~**-cross** vt im Doppelspiel treiben mit. ~**-decker** n Doppeldecker m. ~ **glazing** n Doppelverglasung f. ~ **room** n Doppelzimmer nt

doubly adv doppelt

doubt n Zweifel m ● vt bezweifeln. ~**ful** a, **-ly** adv zweifelhaft; (*disbelieving*) skeptisch. ~**less** adv zweifellos

dough n [fester] Teig m; (🗊 *money*) Pinke f. ~**nut** n Berliner [Pfannkuchen] m

dove n Taube f

dowdy a (**-ier, -iest**) unschick

down[1] n (*feathers*) Daunen pl

down[2] adv unten; (*with movement*) nach unten; **go** ~ hinuntergehen; **come** ~ herunterkommen; ~ **there** da unten; **£50** ~ £50 Anzahlung; ~**!** (*to dog*) Platz! ~ **with** ...! nieder mit ...! ● $prep$ ~ **the road/stairs** die Straße/Treppe hinunter; ~ **the river** den Fluss abwärts ● vt 🗊 (*drink*) runterkippen; ~ **tools** die Arbeit niederlegen

down: ~**cast** a niedergeschlagen. ~**fall** n Sturz m; (*ruin*) Ruin m. ~**-hearted** a entmutigt. ~**hill** adv bergab. ~ **payment** n Anzahlung f. ~**pour** n Platzregen m. ~**right** a & adv ausgesprochen. ~**stairs** adv unten; <*go*> nach unten ● a im Erdgeschoss. ~**stream** adv stromabwärts. ~**-to-earth** a sachlich. ~**town** adv (*Amer*) im Stadtzentrum. ~**ward** a nach

unten; <*slope*> abfallend ● adv ~**[s]** abwärts, nach unten

doze n Nickerchen nt ● vi dösen. ~ **off** vi einnicken

dozen n Dutzend nt

Dr $abbr$ of **doctor**

draft[1] n Entwurf m; (*Comm*) Tratte f; (*Amer Mil*) Einberufung f ● vt entwerfen; (*Amer Mil*) einberufen

draft[2] n (*Amer*) = **draught**

drag n **in** ~ 🗊 <*man*> als Frau gekleidet ● vt (*pt/pp* **dragged**) schleppen; absuchen <*river*>. ~ **on** vi sich in die Länge ziehen

dragon n Drache m. ~**fly** n Libelle f

drain n Abfluss m; (*underground*) Kanal m; **the** ~**s** die Kanalisation ● vt entwässern <*land*>; ablassen <*liquid*>; das Wasser ablassen aus <*tank*>; abgießen <*vegetables*>; austrinken <*glass*> ● vi ~ [**away**] ablaufen

drain|age n Kanalisation f; (*of land*) Dränage f. ~**ing board** n Abtropfbrett nt. ~**-pipe** n Abflussrohr nt

drake n Enterich m

drama n Drama nt

dramatic a, **-ally** adv dramatisch

dramat|ist n Dramatiker m. ~**ize** vt für die Bühne bearbeiten; (*fig*) dramatisieren

drank *see* **drink**

drape n (*Amer*) Vorhang m ● vt drapieren

drastic a, **-ally** adv drastisch

draught n [Luft]zug m; ~**s** sg (*game*) Damespiel nt; **there is a** ~ es zieht

draught beer n Bier nt vom Fass

draughty a zugig

draw n Attraktion f; (*Sport*) Unentschieden nt; (*in lottery*) Ziehung f ● v (*pt* **drew**, *pp* **drawn**) ● vt ziehen; (*attract*) anziehen; zeichnen <*picture*>; abheben <*money*>; ~ **the curtains** die

Vorhänge zuziehen/ (*back*) aufziehen ● *vi* (*Sport*) unentschieden spielen. ~ **back** *vt* zurückziehen ● *vi* (*recoil*) zurückweichen. ~ **in** *vt* einziehen ● *vi* einfahren. ~ **out** *vt* herausziehen; abheben <*money*> ● *vi* ausfahren. ~ **up** *vt* aufsetzen <*document*>; herrücken <*chair*> ● *vi* [an]halten

draw: ~**back** *n* Nachteil *m*. ~**bridge** *n* Zugbrücke *f*

drawer *n* Schublade *f*

drawing *n* Zeichnung *f*

drawing: ~**-board** *n* Reißbrett *nt*. ~**-pin** *n* Reißzwecke *f*. ~**-room** *n* Wohnzimmer *nt*

drawl *n* schleppende Aussprache *f*

drawn *see* **draw**

dread *n* Furcht *f* (**of** vor + *dat*) ● *vt* fürchten. ~**ful** *a*, **-fully** *adv* fürchterlich

dream *n* Traum *m* ● *vt/i* (*pt/pp* **dreamt** *or* **dreamed**) träumen (**about/of** von)

dreary *a* (**-ier, -iest**) trüb[e]; (*boring*) langweilig

dregs *npl* Bodensatz *m*

drench *vt* durchnässen

dress *n* Kleid *nt*; (*clothing*) Kleidung *f* ● *vt* anziehen; (*Med*) verbinden; ~ **oneself, get** ~**ed** sich anziehen ● *vi* sich anziehen. ~ **up** *vi* sich schön anziehen; (*in disguise*) sich verkleiden (**as** als)

dress: ~ **circle** *n* (*Theat*) erster Rang *m*. ~**er** *n* (*furniture*) Anrichte *f*; (*Amer: dressing-table*) Frisiertisch *m*

dressing *n* (*Culin*) Soße *f*; (*Med*) Verband *m*

dressing: ~**-gown** *n* Morgenmantel *m*. ~**-room** *n* Ankleidezimmer *nt*; (*Theat*) [Künstler]garderobe *f*. ~**-table** *n* Frisiertisch *m*

dress: ~**maker** *n* Schneiderin *f*. ~ **rehearsal** *n* Generalprobe *f*

drew *see* **draw**

dried *a* getrocknet; ~ **fruit** Dörrobst *nt*

drier *n* Trockner *m*

drift *n* Abtrift *f*; (*of snow*) Schneewehe *f*; (*meaning*) Sinn *m* ● *vi* treiben; (*off course*) abtreiben; <*snow:*> Wehen bilden; (*fig*) <*person:*> sich treiben lassen

drill *n* Bohrer *m*; (*Mil*) Drill *m* ● *vt/i* bohren (**for** nach); (*Mil*) drillen

drily *adv* trocken

drink *n* Getränk *nt*; (*alcoholic*) Drink *m*; (*alcohol*) Alkohol *m* ● *vt/i* (*pt* **drank**, *pp* **drunk**) trinken. ~ **up** *vt/i* austrinken

drink|able *a* trinkbar. ~**er** *n* Trinker *m*

drinking-water *n* Trinkwasser *nt*

drip *n* Tropfen *nt*; (*drop*) Tropfen *m*; (*Med*) Tropf *m*; (🅸 *person*) Niete *f* ● *vi* (*pt/pp* **dripped**) tropfen

drive *n* [Auto]fahrt *f*; (*entrance*) Einfahrt *f*; (*energy*) Elan *m*; (*Psych*) Trieb *m*; (*Pol*) Aktion *f*; (*Sport*) Treibschlag *m*; (*Techn*) Antrieb *m* ● *v* (*pt* **drove**, *pp* **driven**) ● *vt* treiben; fahren <*car*>; (*Sport: hit*) schlagen; (*Techn*) antreiben; ~ **s.o. mad** 🅸 jdn verrückt machen; **what are you driving at?** 🅸 worauf willst du hinaus? ● *vi* fahren. ~ **away** *vt* vertreiben ● *vi* abfahren. ~ **off** *vt* vertreiben ● *vi* abfahren. ~ **on** *vi* weiterfahren. ~ **up** *vi* vorfahren

drivel *n* 🅸 Quatsch *m*

driven *see* **drive**

driver *n* Fahrer(in) *m(f)*; (*of train*) Lokführer *m*

driving: ~ **lesson** *n* Fahrstunde *f*. ~ **licence** *n* Führerschein *m*. ~ **school** *n* Fahrschule *f*. ~ **test** *n* Fahrprüfung *f*

drizzle *n* Nieselregen *m* ● *vi* nieseln

drone n (sound) Brummen nt

droop vi herabhängen

drop n Tropfen m; (fall) Fall m; (in price, temperature) Rückgang m ● v (pt/pp dropped) ● vt fallen lassen; abwerfen <bomb>; (omit) auslassen; (give up) aufgeben ● vi fallen; (fall lower) sinken; <wind:> nachlassen. **~ in** vi vorbeikommen. **~ off** vt absetzen <person> ● vi abfallen; (fall asleep) einschlafen. **~ out** vi herausfallen; (give up) aufgeben

drought n Dürre f

drove see **drive**

drown vi ertrinken ● vt ertränken; übertönen <noise>; be **~ed** ertrinken

drowsy a schläfrig

drudgery n Plackerei f

drug n Droge f ● vt (pt/pp drugged) betäuben

drug: **~ addict** n Drogenabhängige(r) m/f. **~store** n (Amer) Drogerie f; (dispensing) Apotheke f

drum n Trommel f; (for oil) Tonne f ● v (pt/pp drummed) ● vi trommeln ● vt **~sth into s.o.** Ⅰ jdm etw einbläuen. **~mer** n Trommler m; (in pop-group) Schlagzeuger m. **~stick** n Trommelschlegel m; (Culin) Keule f

drunk see **drink** ● a betrunken; get **~** sich betrinken ● n Betrunkene(r) m

drunk|ard n Trinker m. **~en** a betrunken

dry a (drier, driest) trocken ● vt/i trocknen. **~ up** vt/i austrocknen

dry: **~-clean** vt chemisch reinigen. **~-cleaner's** n (shop) chemische Reinigung f. **~ness** n Trockenheit f

dual a doppelt

dual carriageway n ≈ Schnellstraße f

dubious a zweifelhaft

duchess n Herzogin f

duck n Ente f ● vt (in water) untertauchen ● vi sich ducken

duct n Rohr nt; (Anat) Gang m

dud a Ⅰ nutzlos; <coin> falsch; <cheque> ungedeckt; (forged) gefälscht

due a angemessen; be **~** fällig sein; <baby:> erwartet werden; <train:> planmäßig ankommen; **~ to** (owing to) wegen (+ gen); be **~ to** zurückzuführen sein auf (+ acc) ● adv **~ west** genau westlich

duel n Duell nt

duet n Duo nt; (vocal) Duett nt

dug see **dig**

duke n Herzog m

dull a (-er, -est) (overcast, not bright) trüb[e]; (not shiny) matt; <sound> dumpf; (boring) langweilig; (stupid) schwerfällig

duly adv ordnungsgemäß

dumb a (-er, -est) stumm

dummy n (tailor's) [Schneider]puppe f; (for baby) Schnuller m; (Comm) Attrappe f

dump n Abfallhaufen m; (for refuse) Müllhalde f, Deponie f; (Ⅰ town) Kaff nt; be down in the **~s** Ⅰ deprimiert sein ● vt abladen

dumpling n Kloß m

dunce n Dummkopf m

dune n Düne f

dung n Mist m

dungarees npl Latzhose f

dungeon n Verlies nt

dunk vt eintunken

duo n Paar nt; (Mus) Duo nt

dupe n Betrogene(r) m/f ● vt betrügen

duplicate¹ n Doppel nt; in **~** in doppelter Ausfertigung f

duplicate² vt kopieren; (do twice) zweimal machen

durable a haltbar

duration n Dauer f

during prep während (+ gen)

dusk n [Abend]dämmerung f

dust *n* Staub *m* ● *vt* abstauben; (*sprinkle*) bestäuben (**with** mit) ● *vi* Staub wischen

dust: ~**bin** *n* Mülltonne *f*. ~**-cart** *n* Müllwagen *m*. ~**er** *n* Staubtuch *nt*. ~**jacket** *n* Schutzumschlag *m*. ~**man** *n* Müllmann *m*. ~**pan** *n* Kehrschaufel *f*

dusty *a* (-ier, -iest) staubig

Dutch *a* holländisch ● *n* (*Lang*) Holländisch *nt*; **the** ~ *pl* die Holländer. ~**man** *n* Holländer *m*

dutiful *a*, **-ly** *adv* pflichtbewusst

duty *n* Pflicht *f*; (*task*) Aufgabe *f*; (*tax*) Zoll *m*; **be on** ~ Dienst haben. ~**-free** *a* zollfrei

duvet *n* Steppdecke *f*

dwarf *n* (*pl* **-s** *or* **dwarves**) Zwerg *m*

dwell *vi* (*pt/pp* **dwelt**); ~ **on** (*fig*) verweilen bei. ~**ing** *n* Wohnung *f*

dwindle *vi* abnehmen, schwinden

dye *n* Farbstoff *m* ● *vt* (*pres p* **dyeing**) färben

dying *see* **die**²

dynamic *a* dynamisch

dynamite *n* Dynamit *nt*

dyslex|ia *n* Legasthenie *f*. ~**ic** *a* legasthenisch; **be** ~**ic** Legastheniker sein

Ee

each *a & pron* jede(r,s); (*per*) je; ~ **other** einander; **£1** ~ £1 pro Person; (*for thing*) pro Stück

eager *a*, **-ly** *adv* eifrig; **be** ~ **to do sth** etw gerne machen wollen. ~**ness** *n* Eifer *m*

eagle *n* Adler *m*

ear *n* Ohr *nt*. ~**ache** *n* Ohrenschmerzen *pl*. ~**drum** *n* Trommelfell *nt*

earl *n* Graf *m*

early *a & adv* (-ier, -iest) früh; <*reply*> baldig; **be** ~ früh dran sein

earn *vt* verdienen

earnest *a*, **-ly** *adv* ernsthaft ● *n* **in** ~ im Ernst

earnings *npl* Verdienst *m*

ear: ~**phones** *npl* Kopfhörer *pl*. ~**-ring** *n* Ohrring *m*; (*clip-on*) Ohrklips *m*. ~**shot** *n* **within/out of** ~**shot** in/außer Hörweite

earth *n* Erde *f*; (*of fox*) Bau *m* ● *vt* (*Electr*) erden

earthenware *n* Tonwaren *pl*

earthly *a* irdisch; **be no** ~ **use** 🄳 völlig nutzlos sein

earthquake *n* Erdbeben *nt*

earthy *a* erdig; (*coarse*) derb

ease *n* Leichtigkeit *f* ● *vt* erleichtern; lindern <*pain*> ● *vi* <*pain:*> nachlassen; <*situation:*> sich entspannen

easily *adv* leicht, mit Leichtigkeit

east *n* Osten *m*; **to the** ~ **of** östlich von ● *a* Ost-, ost- ● *adv* nach Osten

Easter *n* Ostern *nt* ● *attrib* Oster-. ~ **egg** *n* Osterei *nt*

east|erly *a* östlich. ~**ern** *a* östlich. ~**ward[s]** *adv* nach Osten

easy *a* (-ier, -iest) leicht; **take it** ~ 🄳 sich schonen; **go** ~ **with** 🄳 sparsam umgehen mit

easy: ~ **chair** *n* Sessel *m*. ~**going** *a* gelassen

eat *vt/i* (*pt* **ate**, *pp* **eaten**) essen; <*animal:*> fressen. ~ **up** *vt* aufessen

eatable *a* genießbar

eau-de-Cologne *n* Kölnisch Wasser *nt*

eaves *npl* Dachüberhang *m*. ~**drop** *vi* (*pt/pp* ~ **dropped**) [heimlich] lauschen

ebb n (*tide*) Ebbe f ● vi zurückgehen; (*fig*) verebben

ebony n Ebenholz nt

EC abbr (**European Community**) EG f

eccentric a exzentrisch ● n Exzentriker m

ecclesiastical a kirchlich

echo n (*pl* -es) Echo nt, Widerhall m ● v (*pt/pp* echoed, *pres p* echoing) ● vi widerhallen (with von)

eclipse n (*Astr*) Finsternis f

ecolog|ical a ökologisch. ~y n Ökologie f

economic a wirtschaftlich. ~al a sparsam. ~ally adv wirtschaftlich; (*thriftily*) sparsam. ~s n Volkswirtschaft f

economist n Volkswirt m; (*Univ*) Wirtschaftswissenschaftler m

economize vi sparen (**on** an + dat)

economy n Wirtschaft f; (*thrift*) Sparsamkeit f

ecstasy n Ekstase f

ecstatic a, -ally adv ekstatisch

eczema n Ekzem nt

eddy n Wirbel m

edge n Rand m; (*of table, lawn*) Kante f; (*of knife*) Schneide f; **on** ~ 🔲 nervös ● vt einfassen. ~ **forward** vi sich nach vorn schieben

edgy a 🔲 nervös

edible a essbar

edifice n [großes] Gebäude nt

edit vt (*pt/pp* edited) redigieren; herausgeben <*anthology, dictionary*>; schneiden <*film, tape*>

edition n Ausgabe f; (*impression*) Auflage f

editor n Redakteur m; (*of anthology, dictionary*) Herausgeber m; (*of newspaper*) Chefredakteur m; (*of film*) Cutter(in) m(f)

editorial a redaktionell, Redaktions- ● n (*Journ*) Leitartikel m

educate vt erziehen. ~**d** a gebildet

education n Erziehung f; (*culture*) Bildung f. ~**al** a pädagogisch; <*visit*> kulturell

eel n Aal m

eerie a (-ier, -iest) unheimlich

effect n Wirkung f, Effekt m; **take** ~ **in Kraft treten**

effective a, -ly adv wirksam, effektiv; (*striking*) wirkungsvoll, effektvoll; (*actual*) tatsächlich. ~**ness** n Wirksamkeit f

effeminate a unmännlich

effervescent a sprudelnd

efficiency n Tüchtigkeit f; (*of machine, organization*) Leistungsfähigkeit f

efficient a tüchtig; <*machine, organization*> leistungsfähig; <*method*> rationell. ~**ly** adv gut; <*function*> rationell

effort n Anstrengung f; **make an** ~ sich (*dat*) Mühe geben. ~**less** a, -ly adv mühelos

e.g. abbr z.B.

egalitarian a egalitär

egg n Ei nt. ~**-cup** n Eierbecher m. ~**shell** n Eierschale f

ego n Ich nt. ~**ism** n Egoismus m. ~**ist** n Egoist m. ~**tism** n Ichbezogenheit f. ~**tist** n ichbezogener Mensch m

Egypt n Ägypten nt. ~**ian** a ägyptisch ● n Ägypter(in) m(f)

eiderdown n (*quilt*) Daunendecke f

eigh|t a acht ● n Acht f; (*boat*) Achter m. ~**teen** a achtzehn. ~**teenth** a achtzehnte(r,s)

eighth a achte(r,s) ● n Achtel nt

eightieth a achtzigste(r,s)

eighty a achtzig

either a & pron ~ **[of them]** einer von [den] beiden; (*both*) beide; **on** ~ **side** auf beiden Seiten

● *adv* I don't ∼ ich auch nicht
● *conj* ∼ ... or entweder ... oder
eject *vt* hinauswerfen
elaborate *a*, **-ly** *adv* kunstvoll;
(*fig*) kompliziert
elapse *vi* vergehen
elastic *a* elastisch. ∼ **band** *n*
Gummiband *nt*
elasticity *n* Elastizität *f*
elated *a* überglücklich
elbow *n* Ellbogen *m*
elder[1] *n* Holunder *m*
eld|er[2] *a* ältere(r,s) ● *n* the ∼er
der/die Ältere. ∼**erly** *a* alt. ∼**est**
a älteste(r,s) ● *n* the ∼est der/die
Älteste
elect *vt* wählen. ∼**ion** *n* Wahl *f*
elector *n* Wähler(in) *m(f)*. ∼ **ate**
n Wählerschaft *f*
electric *a*, **-ally** *adv* elektrisch
electrical *a* elektrisch; ∼
engineering Elektrotechnik *f*
electric: ∼ **blanket** *n* Heizdecke *f*.
∼ **fire** *n* elektrischer Heizofen *m*
electrician *n* Elektriker *m*
electricity *n* Elektrizität *f*;
(*supply*) Strom *m*
electrify *vt* (*pt/pp* **-ied**)
elektrifizieren. ∼**ing** *a* (*fig*)
elektrisierend
electrocute *vt* durch einen
elektrischen Schlag töten
electrode *n* Elektrode *f*
electronic *a* elektronisch. ∼**s** *n*
Elektronik *f*
elegance *n* Eleganz *f*
elegant *a*, **-ly** *adv* elegant
elegy *n* Elegie *f*
element *n* Element *nt*. ∼**ary** *a*
elementar
elephant *n* Elefant *m*
elevat|e *vt* heben; (*fig*) erheben.
∼**ion** *n* Erhebung *f*
elevator *n* (*Amer*) Aufzug *m*,
Fahrstuhl *m*
eleven *a* elf ● *n* Elf *f*. ∼**th** *a*
elfte(r,s); **at the** ∼**th hour** 🕛 in
letzter Minute
eligible *a* berechtigt

eliminate *vt* ausschalten
élite *n* Elite *f*
elm *n* Ulme *f*
elocution *n* Sprecherziehung *f*
elope *vi* durchbrennen 🕛
eloquen|ce *n* Beredsamkeit *f*. ∼**t**
a, ∼**ly** *adv* beredt
else *adv* sonst; **nothing** ∼ sonst
nichts; **or** ∼ oder; (*otherwise*)
sonst; **someone/somewhere** ∼
jemand/irgendwo anders; **anyone**
∼ jeder andere; (*as question*)
sonst noch jemand? **anything** ∼
alles andere; (*as question*) sonst
noch etwas? ∼**where** *adv*
woanders
elucidate *vt* erläutern
elusive *a* **be** ∼ schwer zu fassen
sein
emaciated *a* abgezehrt
e-mail *n* E-Mail *f*. ∼ **address** *n*
E-Mail-Adresse *f*. ∼ **message** *n*
E-Mail *f* ● *vt* per E-Mail
übermitteln <*Ergebnisse, Datei
usw.*>; ∼ **s.o.** jdm eine E-Mail
schicken
emancipat|ed *a* emanzipiert.
∼**ion** *n* Emanzipation *f*; (*of
slaves*) Freilassung *f*
embankment *n* Böschung *f*; (*of
railway*) Bahndamm *m*
embark *vi* sich einschiffen.
∼**ation** *n* Einschiffung *f*
embarrass *vt* in Verlegenheit
bringen. ∼**ed** *a* verlegen. ∼**ing** *a*
peinlich. ∼**ment** *n* Verlegenheit *f*
embassy *n* Botschaft *f*
embellish *vt* verzieren; (*fig*)
ausschmücken
embezzle *vt* unterschlagen.
∼**ment** *n* Unterschlagung *f*
emblem *n* Emblem *nt*
embodiment *n* Verkörperung *f*
embody *vt* (*pt/pp* **-ied**)
verkörpern; (*include*) enthalten
embrace *n* Umarmung *f* ● *vt*
umarmen; (*fig*) umfassen ● *vi*
sich umarmen

embroider vt besticken; sticken
<*design*> ● vi sticken. ~**y** n
Stickerei f
embryo n Embryo m
emerald n Smaragd m
emer|ge vi auftauchen (**from** aus);
(*become known*) sich
herausstellen; (*come into being*)
entstehen. ~**gence** n Auftauchen
nt; Entstehung f
emergency n Notfall m. ~ **exit** n
Notausgang m
emigrant n Auswanderer m
emigrat|e vi auswandern. ~**ion** n
Auswanderung f
eminent a, **-ly** adv eminent
emission n Ausstrahlung f; (*of*
pollutant) Emission f
emit vt (*pt/pp* **emitted**) ausstrahlen
<*light, heat*>; ausstoßen <*smoke,*
fumes, cry>
emotion n Gefühl nt. ~**al** a
emotional; **become** ~**al** sich
erregen
empathy n Einfühlungsvermögen
nt
emperor n Kaiser m
emphasis n Betonung f
emphasize vt betonen
emphatic a, **-ally** adv
nachdrücklich
empire n Reich nt
employ vt beschäftigen; (*appoint*)
einstellen; (*fig*) anwenden. ~**ee** n
Beschäftigte(r) m/f; (*in contrast*
to employer) Arbeitnehmer m.
~**er** n Arbeitgeber m. ~**ment** n
Beschäftigung f; (*work*) Arbeit f.
~**ment agency** n
Stellenvermittlung f
empress n Kaiserin f
emptiness n Leere f
empty a leer ● vt leeren;
ausleeren <*container*> ● vi sich
leeren
emulsion n Emulsion f
enable vt ~ **s.o. to** es jdm möglich
machen, zu
enact vt (*Theat*) aufführen

enamel n Email nt; (*on teeth*)
Zahnschmelz m; (*paint*) Lack m
enchant vt bezaubern. ~**ing** a
bezaubernd. ~**ment** n Zauber m
encircle vt einkreisen
enclos|e vt einschließen; (*in*
letter) beilegen (**with** dat). ~**ure** n
(*at zoo*) Gehege nt; (*in letter*)
Anlage f
encore n Zugabe f ● int bravo!
encounter n Begegnung f ● vt
begegnen (+ *dat*); (*fig*) stoßen auf
(+ *acc*)
encourag|e vt ermutigen;
(*promote*) fördern. ~**ement** n
Ermutigung f. ~**ing** a ermutigend
encroach vi ~ **on** eindringen in
(+ *acc*) <*land*>
encyclopaed|ia n Enzyklopädie f,
Lexikon nt. ~**ic** a enzyklopädisch
end n Ende nt; (*purpose*) Zweck
m; **in the** ~ schließlich; **at the** ~ **of**
May Ende Mai; **on** ~ hochkant;
for days on ~ tagelang; **make** ~**s**
meet ⊡ [gerade] auskommen; **no**
~ **of** ⊡ unheimlich viel(e) ● vt
beenden ● vi enden; ~ **up in** (⊡
arrive at) landen in (+ *dat*)
endanger vt gefährden
endeavour n Bemühung f ● vi
sich bemühen (**to** zu)
ending n Schluss m, Ende nt;
(*Gram*) Endung f
endless a, **-ly** adv endlos
endorse vt (*Comm*) indossieren;
(*confirm*) bestätigen. ~**ment** n
(*Comm*) Indossament nt; (*fig*)
Bestätigung f; (*on driving licence*)
Strafvermerk m
endow vt stiften; **be** ~**ed with** (*fig*)
haben
endurance n
Durchhaltevermögen nt; **beyond**
~ unerträglich
endure vt ertragen
enemy n Feind m ● *attrib*
feindlich
energetic a tatkräftig; **be** ~ voller
Energie sein

energy *n* Energie *f*
enforce *vt* durchsetzen. **~d** *a* unfreiwillig
engage *vt* einstellen <*staff*>; (*Theat*) engagieren; (*Auto*) einlegen <*gear*> ● *vi* sich beteiligen (**in** an + *dat*); (*Techn*) ineinandergreifen. **~d** *a* besetzt; <*person*> beschäftigt; (*to be married*) verlobt; **get ~d** sich verloben (**to** mit). **~ment** *n* Verlobung *f*; (*appointment*) Verabredung *f*; (*Mil*) Gefecht *nt*
engaging *a* einnehmend
engine *n* Motor *m*; (*Naut*) Maschine *f*; (*Rail*) Lokomotive *f*; (*of jet plane*) Triebwerk *nt*. **~-driver** Lokomotivführer *m*
engineer *n* Ingenieur *m*; (*service, installation*) Techniker *m*; (*Naut*) Maschinist *m*; (*Amer*) Lokomotivführer *m*. **~ing** *n* [mechanical] **~ing** Maschinenbau *m*
England *n* England *nt*
English *a* englisch; **the ~ Channel** der Ärmelkanal ● *n* (*Lang*) Englisch *nt*; **in ~** auf Englisch; **into ~** ins Englische; **the ~** *pl* die Engländer. **~man** *n* Engländer *m*. **~woman** *n* Engländerin *f*
engrav|e *vt* eingravieren. **~ing** *n* Stich *m*
enhance *vt* verschönern; (*fig*) steigern
enigma *n* Rätsel *nt*. **~tic** *a* rätselhaft
enjoy *vt* genießen; **~ oneself** sich amüsieren; **~ cooking** gern kochen; **I ~ed it** es hat mir gut gefallen/ <*food:*> geschmeckt. **~able** *a* angenehm, nett. **~ment** *n* Vergnügen *nt*
enlarge *vt* vergrößern. **~ment** *n* Vergrößerung *f*
enlist *vt* (*Mil*) einziehen; **~ s.o.'s help** jdn zur Hilfe heranziehen ● *vi* (*Mil*) sich melden
enliven *vt* beleben

enmity *n* Feindschaft *f*
enormity *n* Ungeheuerlichkeit *f*
enormous *a*, **-ly** *adv* riesig
enough *a*, *adv* & *n* genug; **be ~** reichen; **funnily ~** komischerweise
enquir|e *vi* sich erkundigen (**about** nach). **~y** *n* Erkundigung *f*; (*investigation*) Untersuchung *f*
enrage *vt* wütend machen
enrich *vt* bereichern
enrol *v* (*pt/pp* **-rolled**) ● *vt* einschreiben ● *vi* sich einschreiben
ensemble *n* (*clothing* & *Mus*) Ensemble *nt*
enslave *vt* versklaven
ensue *vi* folgen; (*result*) sich ergeben (**from** aus)
ensure *vt* sicherstellen; **~ that** dafür sorgen, dass
entail *vt* erforderlich machen; **what does it ~?** was ist damit verbunden?
entangle *vt* **get ~d** sich verfangen (**in** in + *dat*)
enter *vt* eintreten/ <*vehicle:*> einfahren in (+ *acc*); einreisen in (+ *acc*) <*country*>; (*register*) eintragen; sich anmelden zu <*competition*> ● *vi* eintreten; <*vehicle:*> einfahren; (*Theat*) auftreten; (*register as competitor*) sich anmelden; (*take part*) sich beteiligen (**in** an + *dat*)
enterpris|e *n* Unternehmen *nt*; (*quality*) Unternehmungsgeist *m*. **~ing** *a* unternehmend
entertain *vt* unterhalten; (*invite*) einladen; (*to meal*) bewirten <*guest*> ● *vi* unterhalten; (*have guests*) Gäste haben. **~er** *n* Unterhalter *m*. **~ment** *n* Unterhaltung *f*
enthral *vt* (*pt/pp* **enthralled**) **be ~led** gefesselt sein (**by** von)
enthuse *vi* **~ over** schwärmen von

enthusias|m n Begeisterung f. ~t n Enthusiast m. ~tic a, -ally adv begeistert

entice vt locken. ~ment n Anreiz m

entire a ganz. ~ly adv ganz, völlig. ~ty n in its ~ty in seiner Gesamtheit

entitle vt berechtigen; ~d ... mit dem Titel ...; be ~d to sth das Recht auf etw (acc) haben. ~ment n Berechtigung f; (claim) Anspruch m (to auf + acc)

entrance[1] n Eintritt m; (Theat) Auftritt m; (way in) Eingang m; (for vehicle) Einfahrt f. ~ fee n Eintrittsgebühr f

entrant n Teilnehmer(in) m(f)

entreat vt anflehen (for um)

entrust vt ~ s.o. with sth, ~ sth to s.o. jdm etw anvertrauen

entry n Eintritt m; (into country) Einreise f; (on list) Eintrag m; no ~ Zutritt/ (Auto) Einfahrt verboten

envelop vt (pt/pp enveloped) einhüllen

envelope n [Brief]umschlag m

enviable a beneidenswert

envious a, -ly adv neidisch (of auf + acc)

environment n Umwelt f

environmental a Umwelt-. ~ist n Umweltschützer m. ~ly adv ~ly friendly umweltfreundlich

envisage vt sich (dat) vorstellen

envoy n Gesandte(r) m

envy n Neid m ● vt (pt/pp -ied) ~ s.o. sth jdn um etw beneiden

epic a episch ● n Epos nt

epidemic n Epidemie f

epilep|sy n Epilepsie f. ~tic a epileptisch ● n Epileptiker(in) m(f)

epilogue n Epilog m

episode n Episode f; (instalment) Folge f

epitome n Inbegriff m

epoch n Epoche f. ~-making a epochemachend

equal a gleich (to dat); be ~ to a task einer Aufgabe gewachsen sein ● n Gleichgestellte(r) m/f ● vt (pt/pp equalled) gleichen (+ dat); (fig) gleichkommen (+ dat). ~ity n Gleichheit f

equalize vt/i ausgleichen

equally adv gleich; <divide> gleichmäßig; (just as) genauso

equat|e vt gleichsetzen (with mit). ~ion n (Math) Gleichung f

equator n Äquator m

equestrian a Reit-

equilibrium n Gleichgewicht nt

equinox n Tagundnachtgleiche f

equip vt (pt/pp equipped) ausrüsten; (furnish) ausstatten. ~ment n Ausrüstung f; Ausstattung f

equity n Gerechtigkeit f

equivalent a gleichwertig; (corresponding) entsprechend ● n Äquivalent nt; (value) Gegenwert m; (counterpart) Gegenstück nt

era n Ära f, Zeitalter nt

eradicate vt ausrotten

erase vt ausradieren; (from tape) löschen

erect a aufrecht ● vt errichten. ~ion n Errichtung f; (building) Bau m; (Biol) Erektion f

ero|de vt <water:> auswaschen; <acid:> angreifen. ~sion n Erosion f

erotic a erotisch

errand n Botengang m

erratic a unregelmäßig; <person> unberechenbar

erroneous a falsch; <belief, assumption> irrig

error n Irrtum m; (mistake) Fehler m; in ~ irrtümlicherweise

erupt vi ausbrechen. ~ion n Ausbruch m

escalat|e vt/i eskalieren. ~or n Rolltreppe f

escape n Flucht f; (from prison) Ausbruch m; **have a narrow ~** gerade noch davonkommen ● vi flüchten; <prisoner:> ausbrechen; entkommen (**from** aus; **from s.o.** jdm); <gas:> entweichen ● vt **the name ~s me** der Name entfällt mir

escapism n Eskapismus m

escort[1] n (of person) Begleiter m; (Mil) Eskorte f

escort[2] vt begleiten; (Mil) eskortieren

Eskimo n Eskimo m

esoteric a esoterisch

especially adv besonders

espionage n Spionage f

essay n Aufsatz m

essence n Wesen nt; (Chem, Culin) Essenz f

essential a wesentlich; (indispensable) unentbehrlich ● n **the ~s** das Wesentliche; (items) das Nötigste. **~ly** adv im Wesentlichen

establish vt gründen; (form) bilden; (prove) beweisen

estate n Gut nt; (possessions) Besitz m; (after death) Nachlass m; (housing) [Wohn]siedlung f. **~ agent** n Immobilienmakler m. **~ car** n Kombi[wagen] m

esteem n Achtung f ● vt hochschätzen

estimate[1] n Schätzung f; (Comm) [Kosten]voranschlag m; **at a rough ~** grob geschätzt

estimat|e[2] vt schätzen. **~ion** n Einschätzung f

estuary n Mündung f

etc. abbr (et cetera) und so weiter, usw.

eternal a, -ly adv ewig

eternity n Ewigkeit f

ethic|al a ethisch; (morally correct) moralisch einwandfrei. **~s** n Ethik f

Ethiopia n Äthiopien nt

ethnic a ethnisch. **~ cleansing** n ethnische Säuberung

etiquette n Etikette f

EU abbr (European Union) EU f

eulogy n Lobrede f

euphemis|m n Euphemismus m. **~tic** a, -ally adv verhüllend

Euro n Euro m. **~cheque** n Euroscheck m

Europe n Europa nt

European a europäisch; **~ Union** Europäische Union f ● n Europäer(in) m(f)

evacuat|e vt evakuieren; räumen <building, area>. **~ion** n Evakuierung f; Räumung f

evade vt sich entziehen (+ dat); hinterziehen <taxes>

evaluate vt einschätzen

evange|lical a evangelisch. **~list** n Evangelist m

evaporat|e vi verdunsten. **~ion** n Verdampfung f

evasion n Ausweichen nt; **tax ~** Steuerhinterziehung f

evasive a, -ly adv ausweichend; **be ~** ausweichen

even a (level) eben; (same, equal) gleich; (regular) gleichmäßig; <number> gerade; **get ~ with** I es jdm heimzahlen ● adv sogar, selbst; **~ so** trotzdem; **not ~** nicht einmal ● vt **~ the score** ausgleichen

evening n Abend m; **this ~** heute Abend; **in the ~** abends, am Abend. **~ class** n Abendkurs m

evenly adv gleichmäßig

event n Ereignis nt; (function) Veranstaltung f; (Sport) Wettbewerb m. **~ful** a ereignisreich

eventual a **his ~ success** der Erfolg, der ihm schließlich zuteil wurde. **~ly** adv schließlich

ever adv je[mals]; **not ~** nie; **for ~** für immer; **hardly ~** fast nie; **~ since** seitdem

evergreen n immergrüner Strauch m/ (tree) Baum m

everlasting a ewig

every a jede(r,s); ~ **one** jede(r,s) Einzelne; ~ **other day** jeden zweiten Tag

every: ~**body** pron jeder[mann]; alle pl. ~**day** a alltäglich. ~ **one** pron jeder[mann]; alle pl. ~**thing** pron alles. ~**where** adv überall

evict vt [aus der Wohnung] hinausweisen. ~**ion** n Ausweisung f

eviden|ce n Beweise pl; (Jur) Beweismaterial nt; (testimony) Aussage f; give ~ce aussagen. ~**t** a, -ly adv offensichtlich

evil a böse ● n Böse nt

evoke vt heraufbeschwören

evolution n Evolution f

evolve vt entwickeln ● vi sich entwickeln

ewe n Schaf nt

exact a, -ly adv genau; not ~ly nicht gerade. ~**ness** n Genauigkeit f

exaggerat|e vt/i übertreiben. ~**ion** n Übertreibung f

exam n 🄸 Prüfung f

examination n Untersuchung f; (Sch) Prüfung f

examine vt untersuchen; (Sch) prüfen

example n Beispiel nt (of für); for ~ zum Beispiel; make an ~ of ein Exempel statuieren an (+ dat)

exasperat|e vt zur Verzweiflung treiben. ~**ion** n Verzweiflung f

excavat|e vt ausschachten; (Archaeol) ausgraben. ~**ion** n Ausgrabung f

exceed vt übersteigen. ~**ingly** adv äußerst

excel v (pt/pp excelled) vi sich auszeichnen ● vt ~ oneself sich selbst übertreffen

excellen|ce n Vorzüglichkeit f. ~**t** a, -ly adv ausgezeichnet, vorzüglich

except prep außer (+ dat); ~ **for** abgesehen von ● vt ausnehmen

exception n Ausnahme f. ~**al** a, -ly adv außergewöhnlich

excerpt n Auszug m

excess n Übermaß nt (of an + dat); (surplus) Überschuss m; ~**es** pl Exzesse pl

excessive a, -ly adv übermäßig

exchange n Austausch m; (Teleph) Fernsprechamt nt; (Comm) [Geld]wechsel m; in ~ dafür ● vt austauschen (for gegen); tauschen <places>. ~ **rate** n Wechselkurs m

excitable a [leicht] erregbar

excit|e vt aufregen; (cause) erregen. ~**ed** a, -ly adv aufgeregt; get ~**ed** sich aufregen. ~**ement** n Aufregung f; Erregung f. ~**ing** a aufregend; <story> spannend

exclaim vt/i ausrufen

exclamation n Ausruf m. ~ **mark** n, (Amer) ~ **point** n Ausrufezeichen nt

exclu|de vt ausschließen. ~**ding** prep ausschließlich (+ gen). ~**sion** n Ausschluss m

exclusive a, -ly adv ausschließlich; (select) exklusiv

excrement n Kot m

excrete vt ausscheiden

excruciating a grässlich

excursion n Ausflug m

excusable a entschuldbar

excuse¹ n Entschuldigung f; (pretext) Ausrede f

excuse² vt entschuldigen; ~ **me!** Entschuldigung!

ex-directory a be ~ nicht im Telefonbuch stehen

execute vt ausführen; (put to death) hinrichten

execution n Ausführung f; Hinrichtung f

executive a leitend ● n leitende(r) Angestellte(r) m/f; (Pol) Exekutive f

exemplary a beispielhaft

exemplify vt (pt/pp -ied) veranschaulichen

exempt a befreit ● vt befreien (from von). ~**ion** n Befreiung f

exercise n Übung f; physical ~ körperliche Bewegung f ● vt (use) ausüben; bewegen <horse> ● vi sich bewegen. ~ **book** n [Schul]heft nt

exert vt ausüben; ~ **oneself** sich anstrengen. ~**ion** n Anstrengung f

exhale vt/i ausatmen

exhaust n (Auto) Auspuff m; (fumes) Abgase pl ● vt erschöpfen. ~**ed** a erschöpft. ~**ing** a anstrengend. ~**ion** n Erschöpfung f. ~**ive** a (fig) erschöpfend

exhibit n Ausstellungsstück nt; (Jur) Beweisstück nt ● vt ausstellen

exhibition n Ausstellung f; (Univ) Stipendium nt. ~**ist** n Exhibitionist(in) m(f)

exhibitor n Aussteller m

exhilarat|ing a berauschend. ~**ion** n Hochgefühl nt

exhume vt exhumieren

exile n Exil nt; (person) im Exil Lebende(r) m/f ● vt ins Exil schicken

exist vi bestehen, existieren. ~**ence** n Existenz f; **be in** ~**ence** existieren

exit n Ausgang m; (Auto) Ausfahrt f; (Theat) Abgang m

exorbitant a übermäßig hoch

exotic a exotisch

expand vt ausdehnen; (explain better) weiter ausführen ● vi sich ausdehnen; (Comm) expandieren

expans|e n Weite f. ~**ion** n Ausdehnung f; (Techn, Pol, Comm) Expansion f

expect vt erwarten; (suppose) annehmen; **I** ~ **so** wahrscheinlich

expectan|cy n Erwartung f. ~**t** a, -**ly** adv erwartungsvoll; ~**t mother** werdende Mutter f

expectation n Erwartung f

expedient a zweckdienlich

expedite vt beschleunigen

expedition n Expedition f

expel vt (pt/pp **expelled**) ausweisen (from aus); (from school) von der Schule verweisen

expenditure n Ausgaben pl

expense n Kosten pl; **business** ~**s** pl Spesen pl; **at my** ~ auf meine Kosten

expensive a, -**ly** adv teuer

experience n Erfahrung f; (event) Erlebnis nt ● vt erleben. ~**d** a erfahren

experiment n Versuch m, Experiment nt ● vi experimentieren. ~**al** a experimentell

expert a, -**ly** adv fachmännisch ● n Fachmann m, Experte m

expertise n Sachkenntnis f

expire vi ablaufen

expiry n Ablauf m

explain vt erklären

explana|tion n Erklärung f. ~**tory** a erklärend

explicit a, -**ly** adv deutlich

explode vi explodieren ● vt zur Explosion bringen

exploit¹ n [Helden]tat f

exploit² vt ausbeuten. ~**ation** n Ausbeutung f

exploration n Erforschung f

explore vt erforschen. ~**r** n Forschungsreisende(r) m/f

explos|ion n Explosion f. ~**ive** a explosiv ● n Sprengstoff m

export¹ n Export m, Ausfuhr f

export² vt exportieren, ausführen. ~**er** n Exporteur m

expos|e vt freilegen; (to danger) aussetzen (to dat); (reveal) aufdecken; (Phot) belichten. ~**ure** n Aussetzung f; (Med) Unterkühlung f; (Phot)

Belichtung *f*; **24 ~ures** 24 Aufnahmen

express *adv* <send> per Eilpost ● *n* (*train*) Schnellzug *m* ● *vt* ausdrücken; **~ oneself** sich ausdrücken. **~ion** *n* Ausdruck *m*. **~ive** *a* ausdrucksvoll. **~ly** *adv* ausdrücklich

expulsion *n* Ausweisung *f*; (*Sch*) Verweisung *f* von der Schule

exquisite *a* erlesen

extend *vt* verlängern; (*stretch out*) ausstrecken; (*enlarge*) vergrößern ● *vi* sich ausdehnen; <*table:*> sich ausziehen lassen

extension *n* Verlängerung *f*; (*to house*) Anbau *m*; (*Teleph*) Nebenanschluss *m*

extensive *a* weit; (*fig*) umfassend. **~ly** *adv* viel

extent *n* Ausdehnung *f*; (*scope*) Ausmaß *nt*, Umfang *m*; **to a certain ~** in gewissem Maße

exterior *a* äußere(r,s) ● **the ~** das Äußere

exterminat|e *vt* ausrotten. **~ion** *n* Ausrottung *f*

external *a* äußere(r,s); **for ~ use only** (*Med*) nur äußerlich. **~ly** *adv* äußerlich

extinct *a* ausgestorben; <*volcano*> erloschen. **~ion** *n* Aussterben *nt*

extinguish *vt* löschen. **~er** *n* Feuerlöscher *m*

extort *vt* erpressen. **~ion** *n* Erpressung *f*

extortionate *a* übermäßig hoch

extra *a* zusätzlich ● *adv* extra; (*especially*) besonders ● *n* (*Theat*) Statist(in) *m*(*f*); **~s** *pl* Nebenkosten *pl*; (*Auto*) Extras *pl*

extract¹ *n* Auszug *m*

extract² *vt* herausziehen; ziehen <tooth>

extraordinary *a*, **-ily** *adv* außerordentlich; (*strange*) seltsam

extravagan|ce *n* Verschwendung *f*; **an ~ce** ein Luxus *m*. **~t** *a* verschwenderisch

extrem|e *a* äußerste(r,s); (*fig*) extrem ● *n* Extrem *nt*; **in the ~e** im höchsten Grade. **~ely** *adv* äußerst. **~ist** *n* Extremist *m*

extricate *vt* befreien

extrovert *n* extravertierter Mensch *m*

exuberant *a* überglücklich

exude *vt* absondern; (*fig*) ausstrahlen

exult *vi* frohlocken

eye *n* Auge *nt*; (*of needle*) Öhr *nt*; (*for hook*) Öse *f*; **keep an ~ on** aufpassen auf (+ *acc*) ● *vt* (*pt/pp* eyed, *pres p* ey[e]ing) ansehen

eye: ~ brow *n* Augenbraue *f*. **~lash** *n* Wimper *f*. **~lid** *n* Augenlid *nt*. **~-shadow** *n* Lidschatten *m*. **~sight** *n* Sehkraft *f*. **~sore** *n* ⊞ Schandfleck *m*. **~witness** *n* Augenzeuge *m*

fable *n* Fabel *f*

fabric *n* Stoff *m*

fabrication *n* Erfindung *f*

fabulous *a* ⊞ phantastisch

façade *n* Fassade *f*

face *n* Gesicht *nt*; (*surface*) Fläche *f*; (*of clock*) Zifferblatt *nt*; **pull ~s** Gesichter schneiden; **in the ~ of** angesichts (+ *gen*); **on the ~ of it** allem Anschein nach ● *vt/i* gegenüberstehen (+ *dat*); **~ north** <*house:*> nach Norden liegen; **~ the fact that** sich damit abfinden, dass

face: ~**-flannel** n Waschlappen m. ~**less** a anonym. ~**-lift** n Gesichtsstraffung f
facet n Facette f; (fig) Aspekt m
facetious a, **-ly** adv spöttisch
facial a Gesichts-
facile a oberflächlich
facilitate vt erleichtern
facility n Leichtigkeit f; (skill) Gewandtheit f; ~**ies** pl Einrichtungen pl
facsimile n Faksimile nt
fact n Tatsache f; **in** ~ tatsächlich; (actually) eigentlich
faction n Gruppe f
factor n Faktor m
factory n Fabrik f
factual a, **-ly** adv sachlich
faculty n Fähigkeit f; (Univ) Fakultät f
fad n Fimmel m
fade vi verblassen; <material:> verbleichen; <sound:> abklingen; <flower:> verwelken.
fag n (chore) Plage f; (🔲 cigarette) Zigarette f
fail n **without** ~ unbedingt ● vi <attempt:> scheitern; (grow weak) nachlassen; (break down) versagen; (in exam) durchfallen; ~ **to do sth** etw nicht tun ● vt nicht bestehen <exam>; durchfallen lassen <candidate>; (disappoint) enttäuschen
failing n Fehler m
failure n Misserfolg m; (breakdown) Versagen nt; (person) Versager m
faint a (-er, -est), **-ly** adv schwach; **I feel**~ mir ist schwach ● n Ohnmacht f ● vi ohnmächtig werden. ~**ness** n Schwäche f
fair[1] n Jahrmarkt m; (Comm) Messe f
fair[2] a (-er, -est) <hair> blond; <skin> hell; <weather> heiter; (just) gerecht, fair; (quite good) ziemlich gut; (Sch) genügend; **a** ~ **amount** ziemlich viel ● adv **play** ~ **fair** sein. ~**ly** adv gerecht; (rather) ziemlich. ~**ness** n Blondheit f; Helle f; Gerechtigkeit f; (Sport) Fairness f
fairy n Elfe f; **good/wicked** ~ gute/böse Fee f. ~ **story,** ~**-tale** n Märchen nt
faith n Glaube m; (trust) Vertrauen n (in zu)
faithful a, **-ly** adv treu; (exact) genau; **Yours** ~**ly** Hochachtungsvoll. ~**ness** n Treue f; Genauigkeit f
fake a falsch ● n Fälschung f; (person) Schwindler m ● vt fälschen; (pretend) vortäuschen
falcon n Falke m
fall n Fall m; (heavy) Sturz m; (in prices) Fallen nt; (Amer: autumn) Herbst m; **have a** ~ fallen ● vi (pt **fell,** pp **fallen**) fallen; (heavily) stürzen; <night:> anbrechen; ~**in love** sich verlieben; ~ **back on** zurückgreifen auf (+ acc); ~ **for s.o.** 🔲 sich in jdn verlieben; ~ **for sth** 🔲 auf etw (acc) hereinfallen. ~ **about** vi (with laughter) sich [vor Lachen] kringeln. ~ **down** vi umfallen; <thing:> herunterfallen. ~ **in** vi hineinfallen; (collapse) einfallen; (Mil) antreten; ~ **in with** sich anschließen (+ dat). ~ **off** vi herunterfallen; (diminish) abnehmen. ~ **out** vi herausfallen; <hair:> ausfallen; (quarrel) sich überwerfen. ~ **over** vi hinfallen. ~ **through** vi durchfallen; <plan:> ins Wasser fallen ●
fallacy n Irrtum m
fallible a fehlbar
fall-out n [radioaktiver] Niederschlag m
false a falsch; (artificial) künstlich. ~**hood** n Unwahrheit f. ~**ly** adv falsch

false teeth npl [künstliches] Gebiss nt

falsify vt (pt/pp **-ied**) fälschen

falter vi zögern

fame n Ruhm m.

familiar a vertraut; (known) bekannt; **too** ~ familiär. ~**ity** n Vertrautheit f. ~**ize** vt vertraut machen (**with** mit)

family n Familie f

family: ~ **doctor** n Hausarzt m. ~ **life** n Familienleben nt. ~ **planning** n Familienplanung f. ~ **tree** n Stammbaum m

famine n Hungersnot f

famished a sehr hungrig

famous a berühmt

fan[1] n Fächer m; (Techn) Ventilator m

fan[2] n (admirer) Fan m

fanatic n Fanatiker m. ~**al** a, **-ly** adv fanatisch. ~**ism** n Fanatismus m

fanciful a phantastisch; (imaginative) phantasiereich

fancy n Phantasie f; **I have taken a real** ~ **to him** er hat es mir angetan ● a ausgefallen ● vt (believe) meinen; (imagine) sich (dat) einbilden; (Ⓘ want) Lust haben auf (+ acc); ~ **that!** stell dir vor! (really) tatsächlich! ~ **dress** n Kostüm nt

fanfare n Fanfare f

fang n Fangzahn m

fan heater n Heizlüfter m

fantas|ize vi fantasieren. ~**tic** a fantastisch. ~**y** n Fantasie f

far adv weit; (much) viel; **by** ~ bei weitem; ~ **away** weit weg; **as** ~ **as I know** soviel ich weiß; **as** ~ **as the church** bis zur Kirche ● a at the ~ **end** am anderen Ende; **the** F~ **East** der Ferne Osten

farc|e n Farce f. ~**ical** a lächerlich

fare n Fahrpreis m; (money) Fahrgeld nt; (food) Kost f; **air** ~ Flugpreis m

farewell int (liter) lebe wohl! ● n Lebewohl nt

far-fetched a weit hergeholt

farm n Bauernhof m ● vi Landwirtschaft betreiben ● vt bewirtschaften <land>. ~**er** n Landwirt m

farm: ~**house** n Bauernhaus nt. ~**ing** n Landwirtschaft f. ~**yard** n Hof m

far: ~-**reaching** a weit reichend. ~-**sighted** a (fig) umsichtig; (Amer: long-sighted) weitsichtig

farther adv weiter; ~ **off** weiter entfernt

fascinat|e vt faszinieren. ~**ing** a faszinierend. ~**ion** n Faszination f

fascis|m n Faschismus m. ~**t** n Faschist m ● a faschistisch

fashion n Mode f; (manner) Art f. ~**able** a, **-bly** adv modisch

fast a & adv (**-er, -est**) schnell; (firm) fest; <colour> waschecht; **be** ~ <clock:> vorgehen; **be** ~ **asleep** fest schlafen

fasten vt zumachen; (fix) befestigen (**to an** + dat). ~**er** n, ~**ing** n Verschluss m

fastidious a wählerisch; (particular) penibel

fat a (**fatter, fattest**) dick; <meat> fett ● n Fett nt

fatal a tödlich; <error> verhängnisvoll. ~**ity** n Todesopfer nt. ~**ly** adv tödlich

fate n Schicksal nt. ~**ful** a verhängnisvoll

fat-head n Ⓘ Dummkopf m

father n Vater m; **F** ~ **Christmas** der Weihnachtsmann ● vt zeugen

father: ~**hood** n Vaterschaft f. ~**-in-law** n (pl ~**s-in-law**) Schwiegervater m. ~**ly** a väterlich

fathom n (Naut) Faden m ● vt verstehen

fatigue n Ermüdung f

fatten vt mästen <animal>
fatty a fett; <foods> fetthaltig
fatuous a, **-ly** adv albern
fault n Fehler m; (Techn) Defekt m; (Geol) Verwerfung f; at ~ im Unrecht; find ~ with etwas auszusetzen haben an (+ dat); it's your ~ du bist schuld. **~less** a, **-ly** adv fehlerfrei
faulty a fehlerhaft
favour n Gunst f; I am in ~ ich bin dafür; do s.o. a ~ jdm einen Gefallen tun ● vt begünstigen; (prefer) bevorzugen. **~able** a, **-bly** adv günstig; <reply> positiv
favourit|e a Lieblings- ● n Liebling m; (Sport) Favorit(in) m(f). **~ism** n Bevorzugung f
fawn a rehbraun ● n Hirschkalb nt
fax n Fax nt ● vt faxen (s.o. jdm). ~ **machine** n Faxgerät nt
fear n Furcht f, Angst f (of vor + dat) ● vt/i fürchten
fear|ful a besorgt; (awful) furchtbar. **~less** a, **-ly** adv furchtlos
feas|ibility n Durchführbarkeit f. **~ible** a durchführbar; (possible) möglich
feast n Festmahl nt; (Relig) Fest nt ● vi ~ [on] schmausen
feat n Leistung f
feather n Feder f
feature n Gesichtszug m; (quality) Merkmal nt; (Journ) Feature nt ● vt darstellen
February n Februar m
fed ● a be ~ up 🆄 die Nase voll haben (with von)
federal a Bundes-
federation n Föderation f
fee n Gebühr f; (professional) Honorar nt
feeble a (-r, -st), **-bly** adv schwach
feed n Futter nt; (for baby) Essen nt ● v (pt/pp fed) ● vt füttern; (support) ernähren; (into machine) eingeben; speisen

<computer> ● vi sich ernähren (on von)
feedback n Feedback nt
feel v (pt/pp felt) ● vt fühlen; (experience) empfinden; (think) meinen ● vi sich fühlen; ~ **soft**/ **hard** sich weich/hart anfühlen; I ~ **hot/ill** mir ist heiß/schlecht; **~ing** n Gefühl nt; no hard ~ings nichts für ungut
feet see foot
feline a Katzen-; (catlike) katzenartig
fell[1] vt fällen
fell[2] see fall
fellow n (🆃 man) Kerl m
fellow: **~-countryman** n Landsmann m. ~ **men** pl Mitmenschen pl
felt[1] see feel
felt[2] n Filz m. ~**[-tipped] pen** n Filzstift m
female a weiblich ● nt Weibchen nt; (pej: woman) Weib nt
femin|ine a weiblich ● n (Gram) Femininum nt. **~inity** n Weiblichkeit f. **~ist** a feministisch ● n Feminist(in) m(f)
fenc|e n Zaun m; (🆃 person) Hehler m ● vi (Sport) fechten ● vt ~e in einzäunen. **~er** n Fechter m. **~ing** n Zaun m; (Sport) Fechten nt
fender n Kaminvorsetzer m; (Naut) Fender m; (Amer: wing) Kotflügel m
ferment vi gären ● vt gären lassen
fern n Farn m
feroc|ious a wild. **~ity** n Wildheit f
ferry n Fähre f
fertile a fruchtbar. **~ity** n Fruchtbarkeit f
fertilize vt befruchten; düngen <land>. **~r** n Dünger m
fervent a leidenschaftlich
fervour n Leidenschaft f

festival n Fest nt; (Mus, Theat) Festspiele pl

festiv|e a festlich. ~**ities** npl Feierlichkeiten pl

festoon vt behängen (with mit)

fetch vt holen; (collect) abholen; (be sold for) einbringen

fetching a anziehend

fête n Fest nt ● vt feiern

feud n Fehde f

feudal a Feudal-

fever n Fieber nt. ~**ish** a fiebrig; (fig) fieberhaft

few a (-er, -est) wenige; **every ~ days** alle paar Tage ● n a ~ ein paar; **quite a ~** ziemlich viele

fiancé n Verlobte(r) m. **fiancée** n Verlobte f

fiasco n Fiasko nt

fib n kleine Lüge

fibre n Faser f

fiction n Erfindung f; [works of] ~ Erzählungsliteratur f. ~**al** a erfunden

fictitious a [frei] erfunden

fiddle n Ⓘ Geige f; (cheating) Schwindel m ● vi herumspielen (with mit) ● vt Ⓘ frisieren <accounts>

fiddly a knifflig

fidelity n Treue f

fidget vi zappeln. ~**y** a zappelig

field n Feld nt; (meadow) Wiese f; (subject) Gebiet nt

field: ~ **events** npl Sprung- und Wurfdisziplinen pl. **F~ Marshal** n Feldmarschall m

fiendish a teuflisch

fierce a (-r, -st), -**ly** adv wild; (fig) heftig. ~**ness** n Wildheit f; (fig) Heftigkeit f

fiery a (-ier, -iest) feurig

fifteen a fünfzehn ● n Fünfzehn f. ~**th** a fünfzehnte(r,s)

fifth a fünfte(r,s)

fiftieth a fünfzigste(r,s)

fifty a fünfzig

fig n Feige f

fight n Kampf m; (brawl) Schlägerei f; (between children, dogs) Rauferei f ● v (pt/pp **fought**) ● vt kämpfen gegen; (fig) bekämpfen ● vi kämpfen; (brawl) sich schlagen; <children, dogs:> sich raufen. ~**er** n Kämpfer m; (Aviat) Jagdflugzeug nt. ~**ing** n Kampf m

figurative a, -**ly** adv bildlich, übertragen

figure n (digit) Ziffer f; (number) Zahl f; (sum) Summe f; (carving, sculpture, woman's) Figur f; (form) Gestalt f; (illustration) Abbildung f; **good at** ~**s** gut im Rechnen ● vi (appear) erscheinen ● vt (Amer: think) glauben

filch vt Ⓘ klauen

file¹ n Akte f; (for documents) [Akten]ordner m ● vt ablegen <documents>; (Jur) einreichen

file² n (line) Reihe f; **in single** ~ im Gänsemarsch

file³ n (Techn) Feile f ● vt feilen

fill n **eat one's** ~ sich satt essen ● vt füllen; plombieren <tooth> ● vi sich füllen. ~ **in** vt auffüllen; ausfüllen <form>. ~ **out** vt ausfüllen <form>. ~ **up** vi sich füllen ● vt vollfüllen; (Auto) volltanken; ausfüllen <form>

fillet n Filet nt ● vt (pt/pp **filleted**) entgräten

filling n Füllung f; (of tooth) Plombe f. ~ **station** n Tankstelle f

filly n junge Stute f

film n Film m ● vt/i filmen; verfilmen <book>. ~ **star** n Filmstar m

filter n Filter m ● vt filtern

filth n Dreck m. ~**y** a (-ier, -iest) dreckig

fin n Flosse f

final a letzte(r,s); (conclusive) endgültig ● n (Sport) Endspiel nt; ~**s** pl (Univ) Abschlussprüfung f

finale n Finale nt
final|ist n Finalist(in) m(f)
final|ize vt endgültig festlegen.
~ly adv schließlich
finance n Finanz f ● vt
finanzieren
financial a, -ly adv finanziell
find n Fund m ● vt (pt/pp found)
finden; (establish) feststellen; **go
and ~ holen; try to ~** suchen. **~
out** vt herausfinden; (learn)
erfahren ● vi (enquire) sich
erkundigen
fine[1] n Geldstrafe f ● vt zu einer
Geldstrafe verurteilen
fine[2] a (-r, -st,) -ly adv fein;
<weather> schön; **he's ~** es geht
ihm gut ● adv gut; **cut it ~** 🛈 sich
(dat) wenig Zeit lassen
finesse n Gewandtheit f
finger n Finger m ● vt anfassen
finger: ~nail n Fingernagel m.
~print n Fingerabdruck m. **~tip**
n Fingerspitze f
finicky a knifflig; (choosy)
wählerisch
finish n Schluss m; (Sport) Finish
nt; (line) Ziel nt; (of product)
Ausführung f ● vt beenden; (use
up) aufbrauchen; **~ one's drink**
austrinken; **~ reading** zu Ende
lesen ● vi fertig werden;
<performance:> zu Ende sein;
<runner:> durchs Ziel gehen
Finland n Finnland nt
Finn n Finne m/ Finnin f. **~ish** a
finnisch
fir n Tanne f
fire n Feuer nt; (forest, house)
Brand m; **be on ~** brennen; **catch
~** Feuer fangen; **set ~ to**
anzünden; <arsonist:> in Brand
stecken; **under ~** unter Beschuss
● vt brennen <pottery>; abfeuern
<shot>; schießen mit <gun>; (🛈
dismiss) feuern ● vi schießen (at
auf + acc); <engine:> anspringen
fire: ~ alarm n Feuermelder m. **~
brigade** n Feuerwehr f. **~engine**

n Löschfahrzeug nt. **~
extinguisher** n Feuerlöscher m.
~man n Feuerwehrmann m.
~place n Kamin m. **~side** n **by
or at the ~side** am Kamin. **~
station** n Feuerwache f. **~wood** n
Brennholz nt. **~work** n
Feuerwerkskörper m; **~works** pl
(display) Feuerwerk nt
firm[1] n Firma f
firm[2] a (-er, -est), -ly adv fest;
(resolute) entschlossen; (strict)
streng
first a & n erste(r,s); **at ~** zuerst;
at ~ sight auf den ersten Blick;
from the ~ von Anfang an ● adv
zuerst; (firstly) erstens
first: ~ aid n erste Hilfe. **~-aid kit**
n Verbandkasten m. **~-class** a
erstklassig; (Rail) erster Klasse
● adv <travel> erster Klasse. **~
floor** n erster Stock; (Amer:
ground floor) Erdgeschoss nt. **~ly**
adv erstens. **~name** n Vorname
m. **~rate** a erstklassig
fish n Fisch m ● vt/i fischen; (with
rod) angeln
fish: ~bone n Gräte f. **~erman** n
Fischer m. **~ finger** n
Fischstäbchen nt. **~ boat** n
Fischerboot nt. **~rod** n
Angel[rute] f
fishing n Fischerei f. **~ boat** n
Fischerboot nt. **~-rod** n
Angel[rute] f
fish: ~monger n Fischhändler m.
~y a Fisch-; (🛈 suspicious)
verdächtig
fission n (Phys) Spaltung f
fist n Faust f
fit[1] n (attack) Anfall m
fit[2] a (fitter, fittest) (suitable)
geeignet; (healthy) gesund;
(Sport) fit; **~ to eat** essbar
fit[3] n (of clothes) Sitz m; **be a good
~** gut passen ● v (pt/pp fitted)
● vi (be the right size) passen
● vt anbringen (to an + dat);
(install) einbauen; **~ with**
versehen mit. **~ in** vi
hineinpassen; (adapt) sich

einfügen (**with** in + *acc*) ● *vt*
(*accommodate*) unterbringen

fit|ness *n* Eignung *f*; [**physical**]
~**ness** Gesundheit *f*; (*Sport*)
Fitness *f*. ~**ted** *a* eingebaut;
<*garment*> tailliert

fitted: ~ **carpet** *n* Teppichboden
m. ~ **kitchen** *n* Einbauküche *f*. ~
sheet *n* Spannlaken *nt*

fitting *a* passend ● *n* (*of clothes*)
Anprobe *f*; (*of shoes*) Weite *f*;
(*Techn*) Zubehörteil *nt*; ~**s** *pl*
Zubehör *nt*

five *a* fünf ● *n* Fünf *f*. ~**r** *n*
Fünfpfundschein *m*

fix *n* (⊠ *drugs*) Fix *m*; **be in a** ~ ▣
in der Klemme sitzen ● *vt*
befestigen (**to** an + *dat*);
(*arrange*) festlegen; (*repair*)
reparieren; (*Phot*) fixieren; ~ **a**
meal Essen machen

fixed *a* fest

fixture *n* (*Sport*) Veranstaltung *f*;
~**s and fittings** zu einer Wohnung
gehörende Einrichtungen *pl*

fizz *vi* sprudeln

fizzle *vi* ~ **out** verpuffen

fizzy *a* sprudelnd. ~ **drink** *n*
Brause[limonade] *f*

flabbergasted *a* **be** ~ platt sein
▣

flabby *a* schlaff

flag *n* Fahne *f*; (*Naut*) Flagge *f*

flag-pole *n* Fahnenstange *f*

flagrant *a* flagrant

flagstone *n* [Pflaster]platte *f*

flair *n* Begabung *f*

flake *n* Flocke *f* ● *vi* ~ [**off**]
abblättern

flamboyant *a* extravagant

flame *n* Flamme *f*

flan *n* [fruit] ~ Obsttorte *f*

flank *n* Flanke *f*

flannel *n* Flanell *m*; (*for washing*)
Waschlappen *m*

flap *n* Klappe *f*; **in a** ~ ▣
aufgeregt ● *v* (*pt/pp* **flapped**) *vi*
flattern; ▣ sich aufregen ● *vt* ~

its wings mit den Flügeln
schlagen

flare *n* Leuchtsignal *nt*. ● *vi* ~ **up**
auflodern; (▣ *get angry*)
aufbrausen

flash *n* Blitz *m*; **in a** ~ ▣ im Nu
● *vi* blitzen; (*repeatedly*) blinken;
~ **past** vorbeirasen

flash: ~**back** *n* Rückblende *f*. ~**er**
n (*Auto*) Blinker *m*. ~**light** *n*
(*Phot*) Blitzlicht *nt*; (*Amer: torch*)
Taschenlampe *f*. ~**y** *a* auffällig

flask *n* Flasche *f*

flat *a* (**flatter, flattest**) flach;
<*surface*> eben; <*refusal*> glatt;
<*beer*> schal; <*battery*>
verbraucht/ (*Auto*) leer; <*tyre*>
platt; (*Mus*) **A** ~ As *nt*; **B** ~ B *nt*
● *n* Wohnung *f*; (▣ *puncture*)
Reifenpanne *f*

flat: ~**ly** *adv* <*refuse*> glatt. ~
rate *n* Einheitspreis *m*

flatten *vt* platt drücken

flatter *vt* schmeicheln (+ *dat*). ~**y**
n Schmeichelei *f*

flat tyre *n* Reifenpanne *f*

flaunt *vt* prunken mit

flautist *n* Flötist(in) *m(f)*

flavour *n* Geschmack *m* ● *vt*
abschmecken. ~**ing** *n* Aroma *nt*

flaw *n* Fehler *m*. ~**less** *a* tadellos;
<*complexion*> makellos

flea *n* Floh *m*

fleck *n* Tupfen *m*

fled *see* **flee**

flee *v* (*pt/pp* **fled**) ● *vi* fliehen
(**from** vor + *dat*) ● *vt* flüchten aus

fleece *n* Vlies *nt* ● *vt* ▣
schröpfen

fleet *n* Flotte *f*; (*of cars*)
Wagenpark *m*

fleeting *a* flüchtig

Flemish *a* flämisch

flesh *n* Fleisch *nt*

flew *see* **fly²**

flex¹ *vt* anspannen <*muscle*>

flex² *n* (*Electr*) Schnur *f*

flexib|ility n Biegsamkeit f; (fig) Flexibilität f. **~le** a biegsam; (fig) flexibel

flick vt schnippen

flicker vi flackern

flier n = flyer

flight¹ n (fleeing) Flucht f

flight² n (flying) Flug m; **~ of stairs** Treppe f

flight recorder n Flugschreiber m

flimsy a (-ier, -iest) dünn; <excuse> fadenscheinig

flinch vi zurückzucken

fling vt (pt/pp flung) schleudern

flint n Feuerstein m

flip vt/i schnippen; **~ through** durchblättern

flippant a, -ly adv leichtfertig

flirt n kokette Frau f ● vi flirten

flirtat|ion n Flirt m. **~ious** a kokett

flit vi (pt/pp flitted) flattern

float n Schwimmer m; (in procession) Festwagen m; (money) Wechselgeld nt ● vi <thing:> schwimmen; <person:> sich treiben lassen; (in air) schweben

flock n Herde f; (of birds) Schwarm m ● vi strömen

flog vt (pt/pp flogged) auspeitschen; (Ⅱ sell) verkloppen

flood n Überschwemmung f; (fig) Flut f ● vt überschwemmen

floodlight n Flutlicht nt ● vt (pt/pp floodlit) anstrahlen

floor n Fußboden m; (storey) Stock m

floor: ~ board n Dielenbrett nt. **~-polish** n Bohnerwachs nt. **~ show** n Kabarettvorstellung f

flop n (Ⅱ failure) Reinfall m; (Theat) Durchfall m ● vi (pt/pp flopped) (Ⅱ fail) durchfallen

floppy a schlapp. **~ disc** n Diskette f

floral a Blumen-

florid a <complexion> gerötet; <style> blumig

florist n Blumenhändler(in) m(f)

flounder vi zappeln

flour n Mehl nt

flourish n große Geste f; (scroll) Schnörkel m ● vi gedeihen; (fig) blühen ● vt schwenken

flout vt missachten

flow n Fluss m; (of traffic, blood) Strom m ● vi fließen

flower n Blume f ● vi blühen

flower: ~-bed n Blumenbeet nt. **~pot** n Blumentopf m. **~y** a blumig

flown see fly²

flu n Ⅱ Grippe f

fluctuat|e vi schwanken. **~ion** n Schwankung f

fluent a, -ly adv fließend

fluff n Fusseln pl; (down) Flaum m. **~y** a (-ier, -iest) flauschig

fluid a flüssig, (fig) veränderlich ● n Flüssigkeit f

fluke n [glücklicher] Zufall m

flung see fling

fluorescent a fluoreszierend

fluoride n Fluor nt

flush n (blush) Erröten nt ● vi rot werden ● vt spülen ● a in einer Ebene (with mit); (Ⅱ affluent) gut bei Kasse

flustered a nervös

flute n Flöte f

flutter n Flattern nt ● vi flattern

fly¹ n (pl flies) Fliege f

fly² v (pt flew, pp flown) ● vi fliegen; <flag:> wehen; (rush) sausen ● vt fliegen; führen <flag>

fly³ n & flies pl (on trousers) Hosenschlitz m

flyer n Flieger(in) m(f); (leaflet) Flugblatt nt

foal n Fohlen nt

foam n Schaum m; (synthetic) Schaumstoff m ● vi schäumen

F

fob vt (pt/pp fobbed) ~ sth off etw andrehen (on s.o. jdm); ~ s.o. off jdn abspeisen (with mit)

focal n Brenn-

focus n Brennpunkt m; in ~ scharf eingestellt ● v (pt/pp **focused** or **focussed**) ● vt einstellen (on auf + acc) ● vi (fig) sich konzentrieren (on auf + acc)

fog n Nebel m

foggy a (**foggier, foggiest**) neblig

fog-horn n Nebelhorn nt

foible n Eigenart f

foil¹ n Folie f; (Culin) Alufolie f

foil² vt (thwart) vereiteln

foil³ n (Fencing) Florett nt

fold n Falte f; (in paper) Kniff m ● vt falten; ~ one's arms die Arme verschränken ● vi sich falten lassen; (fail) eingehen. ~ up vt zusammenfalten; zusammenklappen <chair> ● vi sich zusammenfalten/-klappen lassen; 🄸 <business:> eingehen

fold|er n Mappe f. ~**ing** a Klapp-

foliage n Blätter pl; (of tree) Laub nt

folk npl Leute pl

folk: ~**-dance** n Volkstanz m. ~**song** n Volkslied nt

follow vt/i folgen (+ dat); (pursue) verfolgen; (in vehicle) nachfahren (+ dat). ~ **up** vt nachgehen (+ dat)

follow|er n Anhänger(in) m(f). ~**ing** a folgend ● n Folgende(s) nt; (supporters) Anhängerschaft f ● prep im Anschluss an (+ acc)

folly n Torheit f

fond a (-er, -est), -ly adv liebevoll; be ~ of gern haben; gern essen <food>

fondle vt liebkosen

fondness n Liebe f (for zu)

food n Essen nt; (for animals) Futter nt; (groceries) Lebensmittel pl. ~ **poisoning** n Lebensmittelvergiftung f

food poisoning n Lebensmittelvergiftung f

fool¹ n (Culin) Fruchtcreme f

fool² n Narr m; make a ~ of oneself sich lächerlich machen ● vt hereinlegen ● vi ~ **around** herumalbern

fool|hardy a tollkühn. ~**ish** a, -ly adv dumm. ~**ishness** n Dummheit f. ~**proof** a narrensicher

foot n (pl feet) Fuß m; (measure) Fuß m (30,48 cm); (of bed) Fußende nt; on ~ zu Fuß; on one's feet auf den Beinen; put one's ~ in it 🄸 ins Fettnäpfchen treten

foot: ~**ball** n Fußball m. ~**baller** n Fußballspieler m. ~**ball pools** npl Fußballtoto nt. ~**bridge** n Fußgängerbrücke f. ~**hills** npl Vorgebirge nt. ~**hold** n Halt m. ~**ing** n Halt m. ~**lights** npl Rampenlicht nt. ~**note** n Fußnote f. ~**path** n Fußweg m. ~**print** n Fußabdruck m. ~**step** n Schritt m; follow in s.o.'s ~**steps** (fig) in jds Fußstapfen treten. ~**wear** n Schuhwerk nt

for
● preposition
····▸ (on behalf of; in place of; in favour of) für (+ acc). I did it for you ich habe es für dich gemacht. for him/for a bank ich arbeite für ihn/für eine Bank. be for doing sth dafür sein, etw zu tun. cheque/bill for £5 Scheck/Rechnung über 5 Pfund. for nothing umsonst. what have you got for a cold? was haben Sie gegen Erkältungen?

····▸ (expressing reason) wegen (+ gen); (with emotion) aus. famous for these wines berühmt wegen dieser Weine od für diese Weine. he was sentenced to death for murder er wurde wegen

Mordes zum Tode verurteilt. **were it not for you/your help** ohne dich/deine Hilfe. **for fear/love of** aus Angst vor (+ *dat*)/aus Liebe zu (+ *dat*)

····▸ (*expressing purpose*) (*with action, meal*) zu (+ *dat*); (*with object*) für (+ *acc*). **it's for washing the car** es ist zum Autowaschen. **we met for a discussion** wir trafen uns zu einer Besprechung. **for pleasure** zum Vergnügen. **meat for lunch** Fleisch zum Mittagessen. **what is that for?** wofür *od* wozu ist das? **a dish for nuts** eine Schale für Nüsse

····▸ (*expressing direction*) nach (+ *dat*); (*less precise*) in Richtung. **the train for Oxford** der Zug nach Oxford. **they were heading** *or* **making for London** sie fuhren in Richtung London

····▸ (*expressing time*) (*completed process*) … lang; (*continuing process*) seit (+ *dat*). **I lived here for two years** ich habe zwei Jahre [lang] hier gewohnt. **I have been living here for two years** ich wohne hier seit zwei Jahren. **we are staying for a week** wir werden eine Woche bleiben

····▸ (*expressing difficulty, impossibility, embarrassment etc.*) + *dat*. **it's impossible/inconvenient for her** es ist ihr unmöglich/ungelegen. **it was embarrassing for our teacher** unserem Lehrer war es peinlich

● *conjunction*

····▸ denn. **he's not coming for he has no money** er kommt nicht mit, denn er hat kein Geld

forbade *see* **forbid**

forbid *vt* (*pt* **forbade**, *pp* **forbidden**) verbieten (**s.o.** jdm). **~ding** *a* bedrohlich; (*stern*) streng

force *n* Kraft *f*; (*of blow*) Wucht *f*; (*violence*) Gewalt *f*; **in ~** gültig; (*in large numbers*) in großer Zahl; **come into ~** in Kraft treten; **the ~s** *pl* die Streitkräfte *pl* ● *vt* zwingen; (*break open*) aufbrechen

forced *a* gezwungen; **~ landing** Notlandung *f*

force: **~-feed** *vt* (*pt/pp* **-fed**) zwangsernähren. **~ful** *a*, **-ly** *adv* energisch

forceps *n inv* Zange *f*

forcible *a* gewaltsam

ford *n* Furt *f* ● *vt* durchwaten; (*in vehicle*) durchfahren

fore *a* vordere(r,s)

fore: **~arm** *n* Unterarm *m*. **~cast** *n* Voraussage *f*; (*for weather*) Vorhersage *f* ● *vt* (*pt/pp* **~cast**) voraussagen, vorhersagen. **~finger** *n* Zeigefinger *m*. **~gone** *a* **be a ~gone conclusion** von vornherein feststehen. **~ground** *n* Vordergrund *m*. **~head** *n* Stirn *f*. **~hand** *n* Vorhand *f*

foreign *a* ausländisch; *<country>* fremd; **he is ~** er ist Ausländer. **~ currency** *n* Devisen *pl*. **~er** *n* Ausländer(in) *m(f)*. **~ language** *n* Fremdsprache *f*

Foreign: **~ Office** *n* ≈ Außenministerium *nt*. **~ Secretary** *n* ≈ Außenminister *m*

fore: **~leg** *n* Vorderbein *nt*. **~man** *n* Vorarbeiter *m*. **~most** *a* führend ● *adv* **first and ~most** zuallererst. **~name** *n* Vorname *m*. **~runner** *n* Vorläufer *m*

foresee *vt* (*pt* **-saw**, *pp* **-seen**) voraussehen, vorhersehen. **~able** *a* **in the ~able future** in absehbarer Zeit

foresight *n* Weitblick *m*

forest *n* Wald *m*. **~er** *n* Förster *m*

forestry *n* Forstwirtschaft *f*

foretaste *n* Vorgeschmack *m*

forever *adv* für immer

forewarn *vt* vorher warnen

foreword n Vorwort nt

forfeit n (in game) Pfand nt ● vt verwirken

forgave see forgive

forge n Schmiede f ● vt schmieden; (counterfeit) fälschen. ~r n Fälscher m. ~ry n Fälschung f

forget vt/i (pt -got, pp -gotten) vergessen; verlernen <language, skill>. ~ful a vergesslich. ~fulness n Vergesslichkeit f. ~me-not n Vergissmeinnicht nt

forgive vt (pt -gave, pp -given) ~ s.o. for sth jdm etw vergeben od verzeihen

forgot(ten) see forget

fork n Gabel f; (in road) Gabelung f ● vi <road:> sich gabeln; ~ right rechts abzweigen

fork-lift truck n Gabelstapler m

forlorn a verlassen; <hope> schwach

form n Form f; (document) Formular nt; (bench) Bank f; (Sch) Klasse f ● vt formen (into zu); (create) bilden ● vi sich bilden; <idea:> Gestalt annehmen

formal a, -ly adv formell, förmlich. ~ity n Förmlichkeit f; (requirement) Formalität f

format n Format nt ● vt formatieren

formation n Formation f

former a ehemalig; the ~ der/die/das Erstere. ~ly adv früher

formidable a gewaltig

formula n (pl -ae or -s) Formel f

formulate vt formulieren

forsake vt (pt -sook, pp -saken) verlassen

fort n (Mil) Fort nt

forth adv back and ~ hin und her; and so ~ und so weiter

forth: ~coming a bevorstehend; (I communicative) mitteilsam. ~right a direkt

fortieth a vierzigste(r,s)

fortification n Befestigung f

fortify vt (pt/pp -ied) befestigen; (fig) stärken

fortnight n vierzehn Tage pl. ~ly a vierzehntäglich ● adv alle vierzehn Tage

fortress n Festung f

fortunate a glücklich; be ~ Glück haben. ~ly adv glücklicherweise

fortune n Glück nt; (money) Vermögen nt. ~-teller n Wahrsagerin f

forty a vierzig

forward adv vorwärts; (to the front) nach vorn ● a Vorwärts-; (presumptuous) anmaßend ● n (Sport) Stürmer m ● vt nachsenden <letter>. ~s adv vorwärts

fossil n Fossil nt

foster vt fördern; in Pflege nehmen <child>. ~-child n Pflegekind nt. ~-mother n Pflegemutter f

fought see fight

foul a (-er, -est) widerlich; <language> unflätig; ~ play (Jur) Mord m ● n (Sport) Foul nt ● vt verschmutzen; (obstruct) blockieren; (Sport) foulen

found¹ see find

found² vt gründen

foundation n (basis) Gundlage f; (charitable) Stiftung f; ~s pl Fundament nt

founder n Gründer(in) m(f)

foundry n Gießerei f

fountain n Brunnen m

four a vier ● n Vier f

four: ~teen a vierzehn ● n Vierzehn f. ~teenth a vierzehnte(r,s)

fourth a vierte(r,s)

fowl n Geflügel nt

fox n Fuchs m ● vt (puzzle) verblüffen

foyer n Foyer nt; (in hotel) Empfangshalle f

F

fraction n Bruchteil m; (Math)
Bruch m
fracture n Bruch m ● vt/i brechen
fragile a zerbrechlich
fragment n Bruchstück nt,
Fragment nt
fragran|ce n Duft m. ~**t** a
duftend
frail a (-er, -est) gebrechlich
frame n Rahmen m; (of
spectacles) Gestell nt; (Anat)
Körperbau m ● vt einrahmen;
(fig) formulieren; ✗ ein
Verbrechen anhängen (+ dat).
~**work** n Gerüst nt; (fig) Gerippe
nt
franc n (French, Belgian) Franc
m; (Swiss) Franken m
France n Frankreich nt
franchise n (Pol) Wahlrecht nt;
(Comm) Franchise nt
frank a, -**ly** adv offen
frankfurter n Frankfurter f
frantic a, -**ally** adv verzweifelt;
außer sich (dat) (with vor)
fraternal a brüderlich
fraud n Betrug m; (person)
Betrüger(in) m(f)
fray vi ausfransen
freak n Missbildung f; (person)
Missgeburt f ● a anormal
freckle n Sommersprosse f
free a (freer, freest) frei; <ticket,
copy, time> Frei-; (lavish)
freigebig; ~ **[of charge]** kostenlos;
set ~ freilassen; (rescue)
befreien ● vt (pt/pp freed)
freilassen; (rescue) befreien;
(disentangle) freibekommen
free: ~**dom** n Freiheit f. ~**hold** n
[freier] Grundbesitz m. ~**lance** a
& adv freiberuflich. ~**ly** adv frei;
(voluntarily) freiwillig;
(generously) großzügig. **F~mason**
n Freimaurer m. ~**range** a ~-
range eggs Landeier pl. ~ **sample**
n Gratisprobe f. ~**style** n Freistil
m. ~**way** n (Amer) Autobahn f

freez|e vt (pt froze, pp frozen)
einfrieren; stoppen <wages> ● vi
it's ~ing es friert. ~**er** n
Gefriertruhe f; (upright)
Gefrierschrank m. ~**ing** a eiskalt
● n below ~ing unter Null
freight n Fracht f. ~**er** n Frachter
m. ~ **train** n Güterzug m
French a französisch ● n (Lang)
Französisch nt; **the** ~ pl die
Franzosen
French: ~ **beans** npl grüne
Bohnen pl. ~ **bread** n
Stangenbrot nt. ~ **fries** npl
Pommes frites pl. ~**man** n
Franzose m. ~ **window** n
Terrassentür f. ~**woman** n
Französin f
frenzy n Raserei f
frequency n Häufigkeit f; (Phys)
Frequenz f
frequent[1] a, -**ly** adv häufig
frequent[2] vt regelmäßig besuchen
fresh a (-er, -est), -**ly** adv frisch;
(new) neu; (cheeky) frech
freshness n Frische f
freshwater a Süßwasser-
fret vi (pt/pp fretted) sich grämen.
~**ful** a weinerlich
fretsaw n Laubsäge f
friction n Reibung f; (fig)
Reibereien pl
Friday n Freitag m
fridge n Kühlschrank m
fried see fry[2] ● a gebraten; ~ **egg**
Spiegelei nt
friend n Freund(in) m(f). ~**liness**
n Freundlichkeit f. ~**ly** a (-ier,
-iest) freundlich; be ~**ly with**
befreundet mit. ~**ship** n
Freundschaft f
fright n Schreck m
frighten vt Angst machen (+ dat);
(startle) erschrecken; be ~**ed**
Angst haben (of vor + dat). ~**ing**
a Angst erregend
frightful a, -**ly** adv schrecklich
frigid a frostig; (Psych) frigide.
~**ity** n Frostigkeit f; Frigidität f

frill n Rüsche f; (paper)
Manschette f. **~y** a
rüschenbesetzt

fringe n Fransen pl; (of hair)
Pony m; (fig: edge) Rand m

frisk vi herumspringen ● vt
(search) durchsuchen

frisky a (-ier, -iest) lebhaft

fritter vt **~ [away]** verplempern ⚠

frivol|ity n Frivolität f. **~ous** a, **-ly**
adv frivol, leichtfertig

fro see **to**

frock n Kleid nt

frog n Frosch m. **~man** n
Froschmann m

frolic vi (pt/pp **frolicked**)
herumtollen

from prep von (+ dat); (out of) aus
(+ dat); (according to) nach (+
dat); **~ Monday** ab Montag; **~ that
day** seit dem Tag

front n Vorderseite f; (fig)
Fassade f; (of garment)
Vorderteil nt; (sea**~**)
Strandpromenade f; (Mil, Pol,
Meteorol) Front f; **in ~ of** vor; **in
or at the ~** vorne; **to the ~** nach
vorne ● a vordere(r,s); <page,
row> erste(r,s); <tooth, wheel>
Vorder-

front: **~ door** n Haustür f. **~
garden** n Vorgarten m

frontier n Grenze f

frost n Frost m; (hoar-**~**) Raureif
m; **ten degrees of ~** zehn Grad
Kälte. **~bite** n Erfrierung f.
~bitten a erfroren

frost|ed a **~ed glass** Mattglas nt.
~ing n (Amer Culin) Zuckerguss
m. **~y** a, **-ily** adv frostig

froth n Schaum m ● vi schäumen.
~y a schaumig

frown n Stirnrunzeln nt ● vi die
Stirn runzeln

froze see **freeze**

frozen see **freeze** ● a gefroren;
(Culin) tiefgekühlt; **I'm ~** ⚠ mir
ist eiskalt. **~ food** n Tiefkühlkost
f

frugal a, **-ly** adv sparsam; <meal>
frugal

fruit n Frucht f; (collectively) Obst
nt. **~ cake** n englischer
[Tee]kuchen m

fruitful a fruchtbar

fruit: **~ juice** n Obstsaft m. **~less**
a, **-ly** adv fruchtlos. **~ salad** n
Obstsalat m

fruity a fruchtig

frustrat|e vt vereiteln; (Psych)
frustrieren. **~ion** n Frustration f

fry vt/i (pt/pp **fried**) [in der
Pfanne] braten. **~ing-pan** n
Bratpfanne f

fuel n Brennstoff m; (for car)
Kraftstoff m; (for aircraft)
Treibstoff m

fugitive n Flüchtling m

fulfil vt (pt/pp **-filled**) erfüllen.
~ment n Erfüllung f

full a & adv (-er, -est) voll;
(detailed) ausführlich; <skirt>
weit; **~ of** voll von (+ dat), voller
(+ gen); **at ~ speed** in voller
Fahrt ● n **in ~** vollständig

full: **~ moon** n Vollmond m. **~-
scale** a <model> in
Originalgröße; <rescue, alert>
großangelegt. **~ stop** n Punkt m.
~-time a ganztägig ● adv
ganztags

fully adv völlig; (in detail)
ausführlich

fumble vi herumfummeln (**with**
an + dat)

fume vi vor Wut schäumen

fumes npl Dämpfe pl; (from car)
Abgase pl

fun n Spaß m; **for ~** aus od zum
Spaß; **make ~ of** sich lustig
machen über (+ acc); **have ~!** viel
Spaß!

function n Funktion f; (event)
Veranstaltung f ● vi
funktionieren; (serve) dienen (**as**
als). **~al** a zweckmäßig

fund n Fonds m; (fig) Vorrat m; ~s pl Geldmittel pl ● vt finanzieren
fundamental a grundlegend; (essential) wesentlich
funeral n Beerdigung f; (cremation) Feuerbestattung f
funeral: ~ **march** n Trauermarsch m. ~ **service** n Trauergottesdienst m
funfair n Jahrmarkt m
fungus n (pl -gi) Pilz m
funnel n Trichter m; (on ship, train) Schornstein m
funnily adv komisch; ~ **enough** komischerweise
funny a (-ier, -iest) komisch
fur n Fell nt; (for clothing) Pelz m; (in kettle) Kesselstein m. ~ **coat** n Pelzmantel m
furious a, -ly adv wütend (with auf + acc)
furnace n (Techn) Ofen m
furnish vt einrichten; (supply) liefern. ~ed a ~ed room möbliertes Zimmer nt. ~ings npl Einrichtungsgegenstände pl
furniture n Möbel pl
further a weitere(r,s); at the ~ end am anderen Ende; until ~ notice bis auf weiteres ● adv weiter; ~ off weiter entfernt ● vt fördern
furthest a am weitesten entfernt ● adv am weitesten
fury n Wut f
fuse¹ n (of bomb) Zünder m; (cord) Zündschnur f
fuse² n (Electr) Sicherung f ● vt/i verschmelzen; the lights have ~d die Sicherung [für das Licht] ist durchgebrannt. ~-**box** n Sicherungskasten m
fuselage n (Aviat) Rumpf m
fuss n Getue nt; make a ~ of verwöhnen; (caress) liebkosen ● vi Umstände machen
fussy a (-ier, -iest) wählerisch; (particular) penibel

futil|e a zwecklos. ~**ity** n Zwecklosigkeit f
future a zukünftig ● n Zukunft f; (Gram) [erstes] Futur nt
futuristic a futuristisch
fuzzy a (-ier, -iest) <hair> kraus; (blurred) verschwommen

gabble vi schnell reden
gable n Giebel m
gadget n [kleines] Gerät nt
Gaelic n Gälisch nt
gag n Knebel m; (joke) Witz m; (Theat) Gag m ● vt (pt/pp gagged) knebeln
gaiety n Fröhlichkeit f
gaily adv fröhlich
gain n Gewinn m; (increase) Zunahme f ● vt gewinnen; (obtain) erlangen; ~ **weight** zunehmen ● vi <clock:> vorgehen
gait n Gang m
gala n Fest nt ● attrib Gala-
galaxy n Galaxie f; the G~ die Milchstraße
gale n Sturm m
gallant a, -ly adv tapfer; (chivalrous) galant. ~**ry** n Tapferkeit f
gall-bladder n Gallenblase f
gallery n Galerie f
galley n (ship's kitchen) Kombüse f; ~ [**proof**] [Druck]fahne f
gallon n Gallone f (= 4,5 l; Amer = 3,785 l)
gallop n Galopp m ● vi galoppieren
gallows n Galgen m
galore adv in Hülle und Fülle

gamble n (risk) Risiko nt ● vi [um Geld] spielen; ~ on (rely) sich verlassen auf (+ acc). ~r n Spieler(in) m(f)

game n Spiel nt; (animals, birds) Wild nt; (Sch) Sport m ● a (brave) tapfer; (willing) bereit (for zu). ~keeper n Wildhüter m

gammon n [geräucherter] Schinken m

gang n Bande f; (of workmen) Kolonne f

gangling a schlaksig

gangrene n Wundbrand m

gangster n Gangster m

gangway n Gang m; (Naut, Aviat) Gangway f

gaol n Gefängnis nt ● vt ins Gefängnis sperren. ~er n Gefängniswärter m

gap n Lücke f; (interval) Pause f; (difference) Unterschied m

gap|e vi gaffen; ~e at anstarren. ~ing a klaffend

garage n Garage f; (for repairs) Werkstatt f; (for petrol) Tankstelle f

garbage n Müll m. ~ can n (Amer) Mülleimer m

garbled a verworren

garden n Garten m; [public] ~s pl [öffentliche] Anlagen pl ● vi im Garten arbeiten. ~er n Gärtner(in) m(f). ~ing n Gartenarbeit f

gargle n (liquid) Gurgelwasser nt ● vi gurgeln

garish a grell

garland n Girlande f

garlic n Knoblauch m

garment n Kleidungsstück nt

garnet n Granat m

garnish n Garnierung f ● vt garnieren

garrison n Garnison f

garrulous a geschwätzig

garter n Strumpfband nt; (Amer: suspender) Strumpfhalter m

gas n Gas nt; (Amer ⊞: petrol) Benzin nt ● v (pt/pp gassed) ● vt vergasen ● vi ⊞ schwatzen. ~-cooker n Gasherd m. ~ fire n Gasofen m

gash n Schnitt m; (wound) klaffende Wunde f

gasket n (Techn) Dichtung f

gas: ~ mask n Gasmaske f. ~-meter n Gaszähler m

gasoline n (Amer) Benzin nt

gasp vi keuchen; (in surprise) hörbar die Luft einziehen

gas station n (Amer) Tankstelle f

gastric a Magen-

gastronomy n Gastronomie f

gate n Tor nt; (to field) Gatter nt; (barrier) Schranke f; (at airport) Flugsteig m

gate: ~crasher n ungeladener Gast m. ~way n Tor nt

gather vt sammeln; (pick) pflücken; (conclude) folgern (from aus) ● vi sich versammeln; <storm:> sich zusammenziehen. ~ing n family ~ing Familientreffen nt

gaudy a (-ier, -iest) knallig

gauge n Stärke f; (Rail) Spurweite f; (device) Messinstrument nt

gaunt a hager

gauze n Gaze f

gave see give

gawky a (-ier, -iest) schlaksig

gay a (-er, -est) fröhlich; ⊞ homosexuell, ⊞ schwul

gaze n [langer] Blick m ● vi sehen; ~ at ansehen

GB abbr of **Great Britain**

gear n Ausrüstung f; (Techn) Getriebe nt; (Auto) Gang m; change ~ schalten

gear: ~box n (Auto) Getriebe nt. ~-lever n, (Amer) ~-shift n Schalthebel m

geese see goose

gel n Gel nt

gelatine n Gelatine f

gem n Juwel nt
gender n (Gram) Geschlecht nt
gene n Gen nt
genealogy n Genealogie f
general a allgemein ●n General m; **in** ~ im Allgemeinen. ~ **election** n allgemeine Wahlen pl
generaliz|ation n Verallgemeinerung f. ~**e** vi verallgemeinern
generally adv im Allgemeinen
general practitioner n praktischer Arzt m
generate vt erzeugen
generation n Generation f
generator n Generator m
generosity n Großzügigkeit f
generous a, **-ly** adv großzügig
Geneva n Genf nt
genial a, **-ly** adv freundlich
genitals pl [äußere] Geschlechtsteile pl
genitive a & n ~ **[case]** Genitiv m
genius n (pl **-uses**) Genie nt; (quality) Genialität f
genre n Gattung f, Genre nt
gent n Ⅱ Herr m; **the** ~**s** sg die Herrentoilette f
genteel a vornehm
gentle a (**-r, -st**) sanft
gentleman n Herr m; (well-mannered) Gentleman m
gent|leness n Sanftheit f. ~**ly** adv sanft
genuine a echt; (sincere) aufrichtig. ~**ly** adv (honestly) ehrlich
geograph|ical a, **-ly** adv geographisch. ~**y** n Geographie f, Erdkunde f
geological a, **-ly** adv geologisch
geolog|ist n Geologe m/-gin f. ~**y** n Geologie f
geometr|ic(al) a geometrisch. ~**y** n Geometrie f
geranium n Geranie f
geriatric a geriatrisch ●n geriatrischer Patient m

germ n Keim m; ~**s** pl Ⅱ Bazillen pl
German a deutsch ●n (person) Deutsche(r) m/f; (Lang) Deutsch nt; **in** ~ auf Deutsch; **into** ~ ins Deutsche
Germanic a germanisch
Germany n Deutschland nt
germinate vi keimen
gesticulate vi gestikulieren
gesture n Geste f

G

get v
  pt **got**, pp **got** (Amer also **gotten**), pres p **getting**
● transitive verb
····▸ (obtain, receive) bekommen, Ⅱ kriegen; (procure) besorgen; (buy) kaufen; (fetch) holen. **get a job/taxi for s.o.** jdm einen Job verschaffen/ein Taxi besorgen. **I must get some bread** ich muss Brot holen. **get permission** die Erlaubnis erhalten. **I couldn't get her on the phone** ich konnte sie nicht telefonisch erreichen
····▸ (prepare) machen <meal>. **he got the breakfast** er machte das Frühstück
····▸ (cause) **get s.o. to do sth** jdn dazu bringen, etw zu tun. **get one's hair cut** sich (dat) die Haare schneiden lassen. **get one's hands dirty** sich (dat) die Hände schmutzig machen
····▸ **get the bus/train** (travel by) den Bus/Zug nehmen; (be in time for, catch) den Bus/Zug erreichen
····▸ **have got** (Ⅱ have) haben. **I've got a cold** ich habe eine Erkältung
····▸ **have got to do sth** etw tun müssen. **I've got to hurry** ich muss mich beeilen
····▸ (Ⅱ understand) kapieren Ⅱ. **I don't get it** ich kapiere nicht
● intransitive verb

·····➤ (*become*) werden. **get older** älter werden. **the weather got worse** das Wetter wurde schlechter. **get to** kommen zu/ nach <*town*>; (*reach*) erreichen. **get dressed** sich anziehen. **get married** heiraten.

● *phrasal verbs*

● **get about** vi (*move*) sich bewegen; (*travel*) herumkommen; (*spread*) sich verbreiten. ● **get at** vt (*have access*) herankommen an (+ acc); (🔲 *criticize*) anmachen 🔲. (*mean*) **what are you getting at?** worauf willst du hinaus? ● **get away** vi (*leave*) wegkommen; (*escape*) entkommen. ● **get back** vi zurückkommen; vt (*recover*) zurückbekommen; **get one's own back** sich revanchieren. ● **get by** vi vorbeikommen; (*manage*) sein Auskommen haben. ● **get down** vi heruntersteigen; **get down to** sich [heran]machen an (+ acc); vt (*depress*) deprimieren. ● **get in** vi (*into bus*) einsteigen; vt (*fetch*) hereinholen. ● **get off** vi (*dismount*) absteigen; (*from bus*) aussteigen; (*leave*) wegkommen; (*Jur*) freigesprochen werden; vt (*remove*) abbekommen. ● **get on** vi (*mount*) aufsteigen; (*to bus*) einsteigen; (*be on good terms*) gut auskommen (**with** mit + dat); (*make progress*) Fortschritte machen; **how are you getting on?** wie geht's? ● **get out** vi herauskommen; (*of car*) aussteigen; **get out of** (*avoid doing*) sich drücken um; vt (*take out*) herausholen; herausbekommen <*cork, stain*>. ● **get over** vi hinübersteigen; vt (*fig*) hinwegkommen über (+ acc).

● **get round** vi herumkommen; **I never get round to it** ich komme nie dazu; vt herumkriegen; (*avoid*) umgehen. ● **get through** vi durchkommen. ● **get up** vi aufstehen

get: ~**away** n Flucht f. ~**-up** n Aufmachung f

ghastly a (**-ier, -iest**) grässlich; (*pale*) blass

gherkin n Essiggurke f

ghost n Geist m, Gespenst nt. ~**ly** a geisterhaft

ghoulish a makaber

giant n Riese m ● a riesig

gibberish n Kauderwelsch nt

giblets npl Geflügelklein nt

giddiness n Schwindel m

giddy a (**-ier, -iest**) schwindlig

gift n Geschenk nt; (*to charity*) Gabe f; (*talent*) Begabung f. ~**ed** a begabt

gigantic a riesig, riesengroß

giggle n Kichern nt ● vi kichern

gild vt vergolden

gilt a vergoldet ● n Vergoldung f. ~**-edged** a (*Comm*) mündelsicher

gimmick n Trick m

gin n Gin m

ginger a rotblond; <*cat*> rot ● n Ingwer m. ~**bread** n Pfefferkuchen m

gingerly adv vorsichtig

gipsy n = gypsy

giraffe n Giraffe f

girder n (*Techn*) Träger m

girl n Mädchen nt; (*young woman*) junge Frau f. ~**friend** n Freundin f. ~**ish** a, **-ly** adv mädchenhaft

gist n the ~ das Wesentliche

give n Elastizität f ● v (pt **gave**, pp **given**) ● vt geben/(*as present*) schenken (**to** dat); (*donate*) spenden; <*lecture*> halten; <*one's name*> angeben ● vi geben; (*yield*) nachgeben. ~ **away** vt verschenken; (*betray*) verraten; (*distribute*) verteilen. ~ **back** vt zurückgeben. ~ **in** vt einreichen ● vi (yield) nachgeben. ~ **off** vt abgeben. ~ **up** vt/i aufgeben; ~ **oneself up** sich stellen. ~ **way** vi nachgeben; (Auto) die Vorfahrt beachten

glacier n Gletscher m

glad a froh (of über + acc)

gladly adv gern[e]

glamorous a glanzvoll; <film star> glamourös

glamour n [betörender] Glanz m

glance n [flüchtiger] Blick m ● vi ~ **at** einen Blick werfen auf (+ acc). ~ **up** vi aufblicken

gland n Drüse f

glare n grelles Licht nt; (look) ärgerlicher Blick m ● vi ~ **at** böse ansehen

glaring a grell; <mistake> krass

glass n Glas nt; (mirror) Spiegel m; ~**es** pl (spectacles) Brille f. ~**y** a glasig

glaze n Glasur f

gleam n Schein m ● vi glänzen

glib a, -**ly** adv (pej) gewandt

glid|e vi gleiten; (through the air) schweben. ~**er** n Segelflugzeug nt. ~**ing** n Segelfliegen nt

glimmer n Glimmen nt ● vi glimmen

glimpse vt flüchtig sehen

glint n Blitzen nt ● vi blitzen

glisten vi glitzern

glitter vi glitzern

global a, -**ly** adv global

globaliz|e vt globalisieren. ~**ation** n Globalisierung f

globe n Kugel f; (map) Globus m

gloom n Düsterkeit f; (fig) Pessimismus m

gloomy a (-ier, -iest), -**ily** adv düster; (fig) pessimistisch

glorify vt (pt/pp -ied) verherrlichen

glorious a herrlich; <deed, hero> glorreich

glory n Ruhm m; (splendour) Pracht f ● vi ~ **in** genießen

gloss n Glanz m ● a Glanz- ● vi ~ **over** beschönigen

glossary n Glossar nt

glossy a (-ier, -iest) glänzend

glove n Handschuh m

glow n Glut f; (of candle) Schein m ● vi glühen; <candle:> scheinen. ~**ing** a glühend; <account> begeistert

glucose n Traubenzucker m, Glukose f

glue n Klebstoff m ● vt (pres p gluing) kleben (to an + acc)

glum a (glummer, glummest), -**ly** adv niedergeschlagen

glut n Überfluss m (of an + dat)

glutton n Vielfraß m

GM abbr (genetically modified); ~ **crops/food** gentechnisch veränderte Feldfrüchte/ Nahrungsmittel

gnash vt ~ **one's teeth** mit den Zähnen knirschen

gnat n Mücke f

gnaw vt/i nagen (at an + dat)

G

go

3 sg pres tense **goes**; pt **went**; pp **gone**

● intransitive verb

····▸ gehen; (in vehicle) fahren. **go by air** fliegen. **where are you going?** wo gehst du hin? **I'm going to France** ich fahre nach Frankreich. **go to the doctor's/ dentist's** zum Arzt/Zahnarzt gehen. **go to the theatre/cinema** ins Theater/Kino gehen. **I must go to Paris/to the doctor's** ich muss nach Paris/zum Arzt. **go shopping** einkaufen gehen. **go swimming** schwimmen gehen. **go to see s.o.** jdn besuchen [gehen]

····▸ (leave) weggehen; (on journey) abfahren. **I must go now** ich muss jetzt gehen. **we're going on Friday** wir fahren am Freitag

····▸ (work, function) <engine, clock> gehen

••••➤ (*become*) werden. **go deaf** taub werden. **go mad** verrückt werden. **he went red** er wurde rot

••••➤ (*pass*) <*time*> vergehen

••••➤ (*disappear*) weggehen; <*coat, hat, stain*> verschwinden. **my headache/my coat/the stain has gone** mein Kopfweh/mein Mantel/der Fleck ist weg

••••➤ (*turn out, progress*) gehen; verlaufen. **everything's going very well** alles geht *od* verläuft sehr gut. **how did the party go?** wie war die Party? **go smoothly/ according to plan** reibungslos/ planmäßig verlaufen

••••➤ (*match*) zusammenpassen. **the two colours don't go [together]** die beiden Farben passen nicht zusammen

••••➤ (*cease to function*) kaputtgehen; <*fuse*> durchbrennen. **his memory is going** sein Gedächtnis lässt nach

● *auxiliary verb*

••••➤ **be going to** werden + *inf*. **it's going to rain** es wird regnen. **I'm not going to** ich werde es nicht tun

● *noun*

pl **goes**

••••➤ (*turn*) **it's your go** du bist jetzt an der Reihe *od* dran

••••➤ (*attempt*) Versuch. **have a go at doing sth** versuchen, etw zu tun. **have another go!** versuch's noch mal!

••••➤ (*energy, drive*) Energie

••••➤ (*in phrases*) **on the go** auf Trab. **make a go of sth** das Beste aus etw machen

● *phrasal verbs*

● **go across** *vi* hinübergehen/ -fahren; *vt* überqueren. ● **go after** *vt* (*pursue*) jagen. ● **go away** *vi* weggehen/-fahren; (*on holiday or business*) verreisen. ● **go back** *vi* zurückgehen/ -fahren. ● **go back on** *vt* nicht

[ein]halten <*promise*>. ● **go by** *vi* vorbeigehen/-fahren; <*time*> vergehen. ● **go down** *vi* hinuntergehen/-fahren; <*sun, ship*> untergehen; <*prices*> fallen; <*temperature, swelling*> zurückgehen. ● **go for** *vt* holen; (Ⅰ *attack*) losgehen auf (+ *acc*). ● **go in** *vi* hineingehen/-fahren; ● **go in for** *vt* teilnehmen an (+ *dat*) <*competition*>; (*take up*) sich verlegen auf (+ *acc*). ● **go off** *vi* weggehen/-fahren; <*alarm clock*> klingeln; <*alarm, gun, bomb*> losgehen; <*light*> ausgehen; (*go bad*) schlecht werden; **go off well** gut verlaufen; *vt*: **go off sth** von etw abkommen. ● **go on** *vi* weitergehen/-fahren; <*light*> angehen; (*continue*) weitermachen; (*talking*) fortfahren; (*happen*) vorgehen. ● **go on at** *vt* Ⅰ herumnörgeln an (+ *dat*). ● **go out** *vi* (*from home*) ausgehen; (*leave*) hinausgehen/-fahren; <*fire, light*> ausgehen; **go out to work/ for a meal** arbeiten/essen gehen; **go out with s.o.** (Ⅰ *date s.o.*) mit jdm gehen Ⅰ. ● **go over** *vi* hinübergehen/-fahren; *vt* (*rehearse*) durchgehen. ● **go round** *vi* herumgehen/-fahren; (*visit*) vorbeigehen; (*turn*) sich drehen; (*be enough*) reichen. ● **go through** *vi* durchgehen/ -fahren; *vt* (*suffer*) durchmachen; (*rehearse*) durchgehen; <*bags*> durchsuchen. ● **go through with** *vt* zu Ende machen. ● **go under** *vi* untergehen/-fahren; (*fail*) scheitern. ● **go up** *vi* hinaufgehen/-fahren; <*lift*> hochfahren; <*prices*> steigen. ● **go without** *vt*: **go without sth** auf etw (*acc*) verzichten; *vi* darauf verzichten

go-ahead a fortschrittlich; (*enterprising*) unternehmend ● n (*fig*) grünes Licht nt

goal n Ziel nt; (*sport*) Tor nt. **~keeper** n Torwart m. **~post** n Torpfosten m

goat n Ziege f

gobble vt hinunterschlingen

God, god n Gott m

god: **~child** n Patenkind nt. **~daughter** n Patentochter f. **~dess** n Göttin f. **~father** n Pate m. **~mother** n Patin f. **~parents** npl Paten pl. **~send** n Segen m. **~son** n Patensohn m

goggles npl Schutzbrille f

going a <*price, rate*> gängig; <*concern*> gut gehend ● n **it is hard ~** es ist schwierig

gold n Gold nt ● a golden

golden a golden. **~ wedding** n goldene Hochzeit f

gold: **~fish** n inv Goldfisch m. **~mine** n Goldgrube f. **~plated** a vergoldet. **~smith** n Goldschmied m

golf n Golf nt

golf: **~club** n Golfklub m; (*implement*) Golfschläger m. **~course** n Golfplatz m. **~er** m Golfspieler(in) m(f)

gone see **go**

good a (better, best) gut; (*well-behaved*) brav, artig; **~ at** gut in (+ dat); **a ~ deal** ziemlich viel; **~ morning/evening** guten Morgen/Abend ● n **for ~** für immer; **do ~** Gutes tun; **do s.o. ~** jdm gut tun; **it's no ~** es ist nutzlos; (*hopeless*) da ist nichts zu machen

goodbye int auf Wiedersehen; (*Teleph, Radio*) auf Wiederhören

good: **G~ Friday** n Karfreitag m. **~-looking** a gut aussehend. **~-natured** a gutmütig

goodness n Güte f; **thank ~!** Gott sei Dank!

goods npl Waren pl. **~ train** n Güterzug m

goodwill n Wohlwollen nt; (*Comm*) Goodwill m

gooey a 🛈 klebrig

goose n (pl **geese**) Gans f

gooseberry n Stachelbeere f

goose: **~flesh** n, **~pimples** npl Gänsehaut f

gorge n (*Geog*) Schlucht f ● vt **~ oneself** sich vollessen

gorgeous a prachtvoll; 🛈 herrlich

gorilla n Gorilla m

gormless a 🛈 doof

gorse n inv Stechginster m

gory a (-ier, -iest) blutig; <*story*> blutrünstig

gosh int 🛈 Mensch!

gospel n Evangelium nt

gossip n Klatsch m; (*person*) Klatschbase f ● vi klatschen

got see **get**; **have ~** haben; **have ~ to müssen**; **have ~ to do sth** etw tun müssen

Gothic a gotisch

gotten see **get**

goulash n Gulasch nt

gourmet n Feinschmecker m

govern vt/i regieren; (*determine*) bestimmen

government n Regierung f

governor n Gouverneur m; (*on board*) Vorstandsmitglied nt; (*of prison*) Direktor m; (🛈 boss) Chef m

gown n [elegantes] Kleid nt; (*Univ, Jur*) Talar m

GP abbr of **general practitioner**

grab vt (pt/pp **grabbed**) ergreifen; **~ [hold of]** packen

grace n Anmut f; (*before meal*) Tischgebet nt; **three days' ~** drei Tage Frist. **~ful** a, **-ly** adv anmutig

gracious a gnädig; (*elegant*) vornehm

grade n Stufe f; (*Comm*) Güteklasse f; (*Sch*) Note f; (*Amer, Sch: class*) Klasse f; (*Amer*) = **gradient** ● vt einstufen; (*Comm*)

G

sortieren. **~ crossing** *n* (*Amer*)
Bahnübergang *m*
gradient *n* Steigung *f*;
(*downward*) Gefälle *nt*
gradual *a*, **-ly** *adv* allmählich
graduate *n* Akademiker(in) *m(f)*
graffiti *npl* Graffiti *pl*
graft *n* (*Bot*) Pfropfreis *nt*; (*Med*)
Transplantat *nt*; (🔲 *hard work*)
Plackerei *f*
grain *n* (*sand, salt, rice*) Korn *nt*;
(*cereals*) Getreide *nt*; (*in wood*)
Maserung *f*
gram *n* Gramm *nt*
grammar *n* Grammatik *f*. **~
school** *n* ≈ Gymnasium *nt*
grammatical *a*, **-ly** *adv*
grammatisch
grand *a* (**-er, -est**) großartig
grandad *n* 🔲 Opa *m*
grandchild *n* Enkelkind *nt*
granddaughter *n* Enkelin *f*
grandeur *n* Pracht *f*
grandfather *n* Großvater *m*. **~
clock** *n* Standuhr *f*
grandiose *a* grandios
grand: ~mother *n* Großmutter *f*.
~parents *npl* Großeltern *pl*. **~
piano** *n* Flügel *m*. **~son** *n* Enkel
m. **~stand** *n* Tribüne *f*
granite *n* Granit *m*
granny *n* 🔲 Oma *f*
grant *n* Subvention *f*; (*Univ*)
Studienbeihilfe *f* ● *vt* gewähren;
(*admit*) zugeben; **take sth for ~ed**
etw als selbstverständlich
hinnehmen
grape *n* [Wein]traube *f*; **bunch of
~s** [ganze] Weintraube *f*
grapefruit *n invar* Grapefruit *f*
graph *n* grafische Darstellung *f*
graphic *a*, **-ally** *adv* grafisch;
(*vivid*) anschaulich
graph paper *n* Millimeterpapier
nt
grapple *vi* ringen
grasp *n* Griff *m* ● *vt* ergreifen;
(*understand*) begreifen. **~ing** *a*
habgierig

grass *n* Gras *nt*; (*lawn*) Rasen *m*.
~hopper *n* Heuschrecke *f*
grassy *a* grasig
grate[1] *n* Feuerrost *m*; (*hearth*)
Kamin *m*
grate[2] *vt* (*Culin*) reiben
grateful *a*, **-ly** *adv* dankbar (**to**
dat)
grater *n* (*Culin*) Reibe *f*
gratify *vt* (*pt/pp* **-ied**) befriedigen.
~ing *a* erfreulich
gratis *adv* gratis
gratitude *n* Dankbarkeit *f*
gratuitous *a* (*uncalled for*)
überflüssig
grave[1] *a* (**-r, -st**), **-ly** *adv* ernst; **-ly**
ill schwer krank
grave[2] *n* Grab *nt*. **~-digger** *n*
Totengräber *m*
gravel *n* Kies *m*
grave: ~stone *n* Grabstein *m*.
~yard *n* Friedhof *m*
gravity *n* Ernst *m*; (*force*)
Schwerkraft *f*
gravy *n* [Braten]soße *f*
gray *a* (*Amer*) = **grey**
graze[1] *vi* <*animal:*> weiden
graze[2] *n* Schürfwunde *f* ● *vt*
<*car*> streifen; <*knee*>
aufschürfen
grease *n* Fett *nt*; (*lubricant*)
Schmierfett *nt* ● *vt* einfetten;
(*lubricate*) schmieren
greasy *a* (**-ier, -iest**) fettig
great *a* (**-er, -est**) groß; (🔲
marvellous) großartig
great: ~-aunt *n* Großtante *f*. **G~
Britain** *n* Großbritannien *nt*. **~-
grandchildren** *npl* Urenkel *pl*.
~-grandfather *n* Urgroßvater *m*.
~-grandmother *n* Urgroßmutter *f*
great|ly *adv* sehr. **~ness** *n* Größe
f
great-uncle *n* Großonkel *m*
Greece *n* Griechenland *nt*
greed *n* [Hab]gier *f*
greedy *a* (**-ier, -iest**), **-ily** *adv* gierig
Greek *a* griechisch ● *n* Grieche
m/Griechin *f*; (*Lang*) Griechisch

nt

green a (-er, -est) grün; (fig) unerfahren ● n Grün nt; (grass) Wiese f; ~s pl Kohl m; **the G~s** pl (Pol) die Grünen pl

greenery n Grün nt

green: ~**fly** n Blattlaus f. ~**grocer** n Obst- und Gemüsehändler m. ~**house** n Gewächshaus nt

Greenland n Grönland nt

greet vt grüßen; (welcome) begrüßen. ~**ing** n Gruß m; (welcome) Begrüßung f

grew see grow

grey a (-er, -est) grau ● n Grau nt ● vi grau werden. ~**hound** n Windhund m

grid n Gitter nt

grief n Trauer f

grievance n Beschwerde f

grieve vi trauern (for um)

grill n Gitter nt; (Culin) Grill m; **mixed** ~ Gemischtes nt vom Grill ● vt/i grillen; (interrogate) [streng] verhören

grille n Gitter nt

grim a (grimmer, grimmest), **-ly** adv ernst; <determination> verbissen

grimace n Grimasse f ● vi Grimassen schneiden

grime n Schmutz m

grimy a (-ier, -iest) schmutzig

grin n Grinsen nt ● vi (pt/pp grinned) grinsen

grind n (🄵 hard work) Plackerei f ● vt (pt/pp ground) mahlen; (smooth, sharpen) schleifen; (Amer: mince) durchdrehen

grip n Griff m; (bag) Reisetasche f ● vt (pt/pp gripped) ergreifen; (hold) festhalten

gripping a fesselnd

grisly a (-ier, -iest) grausig

gristle n Knorpel m.

grit n [grober] Sand m; (for roads) Streugut nt; (courage) Mut m ● vt (pt/pp gritted) streuen <road>

groan n Stöhnen nt ● vi stöhnen

grocer n Lebensmittelhändler m; ~**'s [shop]** Lebensmittelgeschäft nt. ~**ies** npl Lebensmittel pl

groin n (Anat) Leiste f

groom n Bräutigam m; (for horse) Pferdepfleger(in) m(f) ● vt striegeln <horse>

groove n Rille f

grope vi tasten (for nach)

gross a (-er, -est) fett; (coarse) derb; (glaring) grob; (Comm) brutto; <salary, weight> Brutto-. ~**ly** adv (very) sehr

grotesque a, **-ly** adv grotesk

ground[1] see grind

ground[2] n Boden m; (terrain) Gelände nt; (reason) Grund m; (Amer, Electr) Erde f; ~**s** pl (park) Anlagen pl; (of coffee) Satz m

ground: ~ **floor** n Erdgeschoss nt. ~**ing** n Grundlage f. ~**less** a grundlos. ~**sheet** n Bodenplane f. ~**work** n Vorarbeiten pl

group n Gruppe f ● vt gruppieren ● vi sich gruppieren

grouse vi 🄵 meckern

grovel vi (pt/pp grovelled) kriechen

grow v (pt grew, pp grown) ● vi wachsen; (become) werden; (increase) zunehmen ● vt anbauen. ~ **up** vi aufwachsen; <town:> entstehen

growl n Knurren nt ● vi knurren

grown see grow. ~-**up** a erwachsen ● n Erwachsene(r) m/f

growth n Wachstum nt; (increase) Zunahme f; (Med) Gewächs nt

grub n (larva) Made f; (fam: food) Essen nt

grubby a (-ier, -iest) schmuddelig

grudge|e n Groll m ● vt ~**e s.o. sth** jdm etw missgönnen. ~**ing** a, **-ly** adv widerwillig

gruelling a strapaziös

gruesome a grausig

gruff a, **-ly** adv barsch

G

grumble vi schimpfen (**at** mit)

grumpy a (**-ier, -iest**) griesgrämig

grunt n Grunzen nt ● vi grunzen

guarantee n Garantie f;
(*document*) Garantieschein m
● vt garantieren; garantieren für
<*quality, success*>

guard n Wache f; (*security*)
Wächter m; (*on train*) ≈
Zugführer m; (*Techn*) Schutz m;
be on ~ Wache stehen; **on one's**
~ auf der Hut ● vt bewachen;
(*protect*) schützen ● vi ~ **against**
sich hüten vor (+ *dat*). ~**-dog** n
Wachhund m

guarded a vorsichtig

guardian n Vormund m

guess n Vermutung f ● vt erraten
● vi raten; (*Amer: believe*)
glauben. ~**work** n Vermutung f

guest n Gast m. ~**-house** n
Pension f

guidance n Führung f, Leitung f;
(*advice*) Beratung f

guide n Führer(in) m(f); (*book*)
Führer m; [**Girl**] **G**~ Pfadfinderin
f ● vt führen, leiten. ~**book** n
Führer m

guided a ~ **tour** Führung f

guide: ~**-dog** n Blindenhund m.
~**lines** npl Richtlinien pl

guilt n Schuld f. ~**ily** adv
schuldbewusst

guilty a (**-ier, -iest**) a schuldig (**of**
gen); <*look*> schuldbewusst;
<*conscience*> schlecht

guinea-pig n Meerschweinchen
nt; (*person*) Versuchskaninchen
nt

guitar n Gitarre f. ~**ist** n
Gitarrist(in) m(f)

gulf n (*Geog*) Golf m; (*fig*) Kluft f

gull n Möwe f

gullible a leichtgläubig

gully n Schlucht f; (*drain*) Rinne f

gulp n Schluck m ● vi schlucken
● vt ~ **down** hinunterschlucken

gum¹ n & **-s** pl (*Anat*) Zahnfleisch
nt

gum² n Gummi[harz] nt; (*glue*)
Klebstoff m; (*chewing gum*)
Kaugummi m

gummed see **gum**² ● a <*label*>
gummiert

gun n Schusswaffe f; (*pistol*)
Pistole f; (*rifle*) Gewehr nt;
(*cannon*) Geschütz nt

gun: ~**fire** n Geschützfeuer
nt. ~**man** bewaffneter Bandit
m

gunner n Artillerist m

gunpowder n Schießpulver nt

gurgle vi gluckern; (*of baby*)
glucksen

gush vi strömen; (*enthuse*)
schwärmen (**over** von)

gust n (*of wind*) Windstoß m;
(*Naut*) Bö f

gusto n **with** ~ mit Schwung

gusty a böig

gut n Darm m; ~**s** pl Eingeweide
pl; (🗉 *courage*) Schneid m ● vt
(*pt/pp* **gutted**) (*Culin*)
ausnehmen; ~**ted by fire**
ausgebrannt

gutter n Rinnstein m; (*fig*) Gosse
f; (*on roof*) Dachrinne f

guy n 🗉 Kerl m

guzzle vt/i schlingen; (*drink*)
schlürfen

gym n 🗉 Turnhalle f;
(*gymnastics*) Turnen nt

gymnasium n Turnhalle f

gymnast n Turner(in) m(f). ~**ics**
n Turnen nt

gym shoes pl Turnschuhe pl

gynaecolog|ist n Frauenarzt m
/-ärztin f. ~**y** n Gynäkologie f

gypsy n Zigeuner(in) m(f)

habit n Gewohnheit f; (Relig: costume) Ordenstracht f; **be in the ∼** die Angewohnheit haben (of zu)

habitat n Habitat nt

habitation n unfit for human ∼ für Wohnzwecke ungeeignet

habitual a gewohnt; (inveterate) gewohnheitsmäßig. **∼ly** adv gewohnheitsmäßig; (constantly) ständig

hack[1] n (writer) Schreiberling m; (hired horse) Mietpferd nt

hack[2] vt hacken; **∼ to pieces** zerhacken

hackneyed a abgedroschen

hacksaw n Metallsäge f

had see have

haddock n inv Schellfisch m

haggard a abgehärmt

haggle vi feilschen (over um)

hail[1] vt begrüßen; herbeirufen <taxi> ● vi ∼ **from** kommen aus

hail[2] n Hagel m ● vi hageln. **∼stone** n Hagelkorn nt

hair n Haar nt; **wash one's ∼** sich (dat) die Haare waschen

hair: ∼brush n Haarbürste f. **∼cut** n Haarschnitt m; **have a ∼cut** sich (dat) die Haare schneiden lassen. **∼do** n 🔝 Frisur f. **∼dresser** n Friseur m/ Friseuse f. **∼drier** n Haartrockner m; (hand-held) Föhn m. **∼pin** n Haarnadel f. **∼pin bend** n Haarnadelkurve f. **∼-raising** a haarsträubend. **∼style** n Frisur f

hairy a (-ier, -iest) behaart; (excessively) haarig; (fam; frightening) brenzlig

hake n inv Seehecht m

half n (pl **halves**) Hälfte f; **cut in ∼** halbieren; **one and a ∼** eineinhalb, anderthalb; **∼ a dozen** ein halbes Dutzend; **∼ an hour** eine halbe Stunde ● a & adv halb; **∼ past two** halb drei; **[at] ∼ price** zum halben Preis

half: ∼-hearted a lustlos. **∼-term** n schulfreie Tage nach dem halben Trimester. **∼-timbered** a Fachwerk-. **∼-time** n (Sport) Halbzeit f. **∼-way** a the **∼-way** mark/stage die Hälfte ● adv auf halbem Weg

halibut n inv Heilbutt m

hall n Halle f; (room) Saal m; (Sch) Aula f; (entrance) Flur m; (mansion) Gutshaus nt; **∼ of residence** (Univ) Studentenheim nt

hallmark n [Feingehalts]stempel m; (fig) Kennzeichen nt (of für)

hallo int [guten] Tag! 🔝 hallo!

hallucination n Halluzination f

halo n (pl **-es**) Heiligenschein m; (Astr) Hof m

halt n Halt m; **come to a ∼** stehen bleiben; <traffic:> zum Stillstand kommen ● vi Halt machen; **∼!** halt! **∼ing** a, adv **-ly** zögernd

halve vt halbieren; (reduce) um die Hälfte reduzieren

ham n Schinken m

hamburger n Hamburger m

hammer n Hammer m ● vt/i hämmern (at an + acc)

hammock n Hängematte f

hamper vt behindern

hamster n Hamster m

hand n Hand f; (of clock) Zeiger m; (writing) Handschrift f; (worker) Arbeiter(in) m(f); (Cards) Blatt nt; **on the one/other ∼** einer-/andererseits; **out of ∼** außer Kontrolle; (summarily) kurzerhand; **in ∼** unter Kontrolle; (available) verfügbar; **give s.o. a ∼** jdm behilflich sein ● vt reichen (to dat). **∼ in** vt

abgeben. ~ **out** vt austeilen. ~
over vt überreichen
hand: ~**bag** n Handtasche f.
~**book** n Handbuch nt. ~**brake** n
Handbremse f. ~**cuffs** npl
Handschellen pl. ~**ful** n
Handvoll f; **be [quite] a** ~**ful** 🆃
nicht leicht zu haben sein
handicap n Behinderung f; (Sport
& fig) Handikap nt. ~**ped** a
mentally/physically ~**ped** geistig/
körperlich behindert
handkerchief n (pl ~**s** & -**chieves**)
Taschentuch nt
handle n Griff m; (of door) Klinke
f; (of cup) Henkel m; (of broom)
Stiel m ● vt handhaben; (treat)
umgehen mit; (touch) anfassen.
~**bars** npl Lenkstange f
hand: ~**made** a handgemacht.
~**shake** n Händedruck m
handsome a gut aussehend;
(generous) großzügig; (large)
beträchtlich
hand: ~**writing** n Handschrift f.
~-**written** a handgeschrieben
handy a (-ier, -iest) handlich;
<person> geschickt; **have/keep** ~
griffbereit haben/halten
hang vt/i (pt/pp hung) hängen; ~
wallpaper tapezieren ● vt (pt/pp
hanged) hängen <criminal> ● n
get the ~ **of it** 🆃 den Dreh
herauskriegen. ~ **about** vi sich
herumdrücken. ~ **on** vi sich
festhalten (**to** an + dat); (🆃 wait)
warten. ~ **out** vi heraushängen;
(🆃 live) wohnen ● vt draußen
aufhängen <washing>. ~ **up** vt/i
aufhängen
hangar n Flugzeughalle f
hanger n [Kleider]bügel m
hang: ~-**glider** n Drachenflieger
m. ~-**gliding** n Drachenfliegen nt.
~**man** n Henker m. ~**over** n 🆃
Kater m 🆃. ~-**up** n 🆃 Komplex
m
hanker vi ~ **after sth** sich (dat)
etw wünschen

hanky n 🆃 Taschentuch nt
haphazard a, -**ly** adv planlos
happen vi geschehen, passieren; I
~**ed to be there** ich war zufällig
da; **what has** ~**ed to him?** was ist
mit ihm los? (become of) was ist
aus ihm geworden? ~**ing** n
Ereignis nt
happi|ly adv glücklich;
(fortunately) glücklicherweise.
~**ness** n Glück nt
happy a (-ier, -iest) glücklich. ~-
go-lucky a sorglos
harass vt schikanieren. ~**ed** a
abgehetzt. ~**ment** n Schikane f;
(sexual) Belästigung f
harbour n Hafen m
hard a (-er, -est) hart; (difficult)
schwer; ~ **of hearing** schwerhörig
● adv hart; <work> schwer;
<pull> kräftig; <rain, snow> stark;
be ~ **up** 🆃 knapp bei Kasse sein;
be ~ **done by** 🆃 ungerecht
behandelt werden
hard: ~**back** n gebundene
Ausgabe f. ~**board** n
Hartfaserplatte f. ~-**boiled** a hart
gekocht
harden vi hart werden
hard-hearted a hartherzig
hard|ly adv kaum; ~**ly ever** kaum
[jemals]. ~**ness** n Härte f. ~**ship**
n Not f
hard: ~ **shoulder** n (Auto)
Randstreifen m. ~**ware** n
Haushaltswaren pl; (Computing)
Hardware f. ~-**wearing** a
strapazierfähig. ~-**working** a
fleißig
hardy a (-ier, -iest) abgehärtet;
<plant> winterhart
hare n Hase m
harm n Schaden m; **it won't do any**
~ es kann nichts schaden ● vt ~
s.o. jdm etwas antun. ~**ful** a
schädlich. ~**less** a harmlos
harmonious a, -**ly** adv
harmonisch

harmon|ize vi (fig) harmonieren. **~y** n Harmonie f

harness n Geschirr nt; (of parachute) Gurtwerk nt ● vt anschirren <horse>; (use) nutzbar machen

harp n Harfe f. **~ist** n Harfenist(in) m(f)

harpsichord n Cembalo nt

harrowing a grauenhaft

harsh a (-er, -est), **-ly** adv hart; <voice> rau; <light> grell. **~ness** n Härte f; Rauheit f

harvest n Ernte f ● vt ernten

has see **have**

hassle n ① Ärger m ● vt schikanieren

haste n Eile f

hasten vi sich beeilen (**to** zu); (go quickly) eilen ● vt beschleunigen

hasty a (-ier, -iest), **-ily** adv hastig; <decision> voreilig

hat n Hut m; (knitted) Mütze f

hatch¹ n (for food) Durchreiche f; (Naut) Luke f

hatch² vi **~[out]** ausschlüpfen ● vt ausbrüten

hatchback n (Auto) Modell nt mit Hecktür

hate n Hass m ● vt hassen. **~ful** a abscheulich

hatred n Hass m

haughty a (-ier, -iest), **-ily** adv hochmütig

haul n (loot) Beute f ● vt/i ziehen (**on** an + dat)

haunt n Lieblingsaufenthalt m ● vt umgehen in (+ dat); **this house is ~ed** in diesem Haus spukt es

have
  3 sg pres tense **has**; *pt and pp* **had**
● *transitive verb*
····▸ (possess) haben. **he has [got] a car** er hat ein Auto. **she has [got] a brother** sie hat einen Bruder.

we have [got] five minutes wir haben fünf Minuten

····▸ (eat) essen; (drink) trinken; (smoke) rauchen. **have a cup of tea** eine Tasse Tee trinken. **have a pizza** eine Pizza essen. **have a cigarette** eine Zigarette rauchen. **have breakfast/dinner/lunch** frühstücken/zu Abend essen/zu Mittag essen

····▸ (take esp. in shop, restaurant) nehmen. **I'll have the soup/the red dress** ich nehme die Suppe/das rote Kleid. **have a cigarette!** nehmen Sie eine Zigarette!

····▸ (get, receive) bekommen. **I had a letter from her** ich bekam einen Brief von ihr. **have a baby** ein Baby bekommen

····▸ (suffer) haben <illness, pain, disappointment>; erleiden <shock>

····▸ (organize) **have a party** eine Party veranstalten. **they had a meeting** sie hielten eine Versammlung ab

····▸ (take part in) **have a game of football** Fußball spielen. **have a swim** schwimmen

····▸ (as guest) **have s.o. to stay** jdn zu Besuch haben

····▸ **have had it** ① <thing> ausgedient haben; <person> geliefert sein. **you've had it now** jetzt ist es aus

····▸ **have sth done** etw machen lassen. **we had the house painted** wir haben das Haus malen lassen. **have a dress made** sich (dat) ein Kleid machen lassen. **have a tooth out** sich (dat) einen Zahn ziehen lassen. **have one's hair cut** sich (dat) die Haare schneiden lassen

····▸ **have to do sth** etw tun müssen. **I have to go now** ich muss jetzt gehen
● *auxiliary verb*

····▶ (*forming perfect and past perfect tenses*) haben; (*with verbs of motion and some others*) sein. **I have seen him** ich habe ihn gesehen. **he has never been there** er ist nie da gewesen. **I had gone** ich war gegangen. **if I had known ...** wenn ich gewusst hätte ...

····▶ (*in tag questions*) nicht wahr. **you've met her, haven't you?** du kennst sie, nicht wahr?

····▶ (*in short answers*) **Have you seen the film? — Yes, I have** Hast du den Film gesehen? — Ja [, stimmt]

● ● **have on** vt (*be wearing*) anhaben; (*dupe*) anführen

havoc n Verwüstung f

hawk n Falke m

hawthorn n Hagedorn m

hay n Heu nt. ~ **fever** n Heuschnupfen m. ~**stack** n Heuschober m

hazard n Gefahr f; (*risk*) Risiko nt ● vt riskieren. ~**ous** a gefährlich; (*risky*) riskant

haze n Dunst m

hazel n Haselbusch m. ~**-nut** n Haselnuss f

hazy a (-ier, -iest) dunstig; (*fig*) unklar

he pron er

head n Kopf m; (*chief*) Oberhaupt nt; (*of firm*) Chef(in) m(f); (*of school*) Schulleiter(in) m(f); (*on beer*) Schaumkrone f; (*of bed*) Kopfende nt; ~ **first** kopfüber ● vt anführen; (*Sport*) köpfen <*ball*> ● vi ~ **for** zusteuern auf (+ acc). ~**ache** n Kopfschmerzen pl

head|er n Kopfball m; (*dive*) Kopfsprung m. ~**ing** n Überschrift f

head: ~**lamp**, ~**light** n (*Auto*) Scheinwerfer m. ~**line** n Schlagzeile f. ~**long** adv kopfüber. ~**master** n Schulleiter

m. ~**mistress** n Schulleiterin f. ~**-on** a & adv frontal. ~**phones** npl Kopfhörer m. ~**quarters** npl Hauptquartier nt; (*Pol*) Zentrale f. ~**rest** n Kopfstütze f. ~**room** n lichte Höhe f. ~**scarf** n Kopftuch nt. ~**strong** a eigenwillig. ~**way** n make ~**way** Fortschritte machen. ~**word** n Stichwort nt

heady a berauschend

heal vt/i heilen

health n Gesundheit f

health: ~ **farm** n Schönheitsfarm f. ~ **foods** npl Reformkost f. ~-**food shop** n Reformhaus nt. ~ **insurance** n Krankenversicherung f

healthy a (-ier, -iest), **-ily** adv gesund

heap n Haufen m; ~**s** 🄸 jede Menge ● vt ~ [up] häufen

hear vt/i (pt/pp heard) hören; ~,~! hört, hört! **he would not ~ of it** er ließ es nicht zu

hearing n Gehör nt; (*Jur*) Verhandlung f. ~-**aid** n Hörgerät nt

hearse n Leichenwagen m

heart n Herz nt; (*courage*) Mut m; ~**s** pl (*Cards*) Herz nt; **by ~** auswendig

heart: ~**ache** n Kummer m. ~**attack** n Herzanfall m. ~**beat** n Herzschlag m. ~**-breaking** a herzzerreißend. ~**-broken** a untröstlich. ~**burn** n Sodbrennen nt. ~**en** vt ermutigen. ~**felt** a herzlich[st]

hearth n Herd m; (*fireplace*) Kamin m

heart|ily adv herzlich; <*eat*> viel. ~**less** a, **-ly** adv herzlos. ~**y** a herzlich; <*meal*> groß; <*person*> burschikos

heat n Hitze f; (*Sport*) Vorlauf m ● vt heiß machen; heizen <*room*>. ~**ed** a geheizt; <*swimming pool*> beheizt;

<discussion> hitzig. **~er** n
Heizgerät nt; (Auto) Heizanlage f
heath n Heide f
heathen a heidnisch ●n Heide
m/Heidin f
heather n Heidekraut nt
heating n Heizung f
heat wave n Hitzewelle f
heave vt/i ziehen; (lift) heben; (🖪
throw) schmeißen
heaven n Himmel m. **~ly** a
himmlisch
heavy a (-ier, -iest), **-ily** adv
schwer; <traffic, rain> stark.
~weight n Schwergewicht nt
heckle vt [durch Zwischenrufe]
unterbrechen. **~r** n
Zwischenrufer m
hectic a hektisch
hedge n Hecke f. **~hog** n Igel m
heed vt beachten
heel[1] n Ferse f; (of shoe) Absatz
m; down at **~** heruntergekommen
heel[2] vi **~ over** (Naut) sich auf die
Seite legen
hefty a (-ier, -iest) kräftig; (heavy)
schwer
height n Höhe f; (of person)
Größe f. **~en** vt (fig) steigern
heir n Erbe m. **~ess** n Erbin f.
~loom n Erbstück nt
held see hold[2]
helicopter a Hubschrauber m
hell n Hölle f; go to **~**! 🖾 geh zum
Teufel! ●int verdammt!
hello int [guten] Tag! 🖪 hallo!
helm n [Steuer]ruder nt
helmet n Helm m
help n Hilfe f; (employees)
Hilfskräfte pl; that's no **~** das
nützt nichts ●vt/i helfen (s.o.
jdm); **~** oneself to sth sich (dat)
etw nehmen; **~** yourself (at table)
greif zu; I could not **~** laughing ich
musste lachen; it cannot be **~**ed
es lässt sich nicht ändern; I can't
~ it ich kann nichts dafür
help|er n Helfer(in) m(f). **~ful** a,
-ly adv hilfsbereit; <advice>

nützlich. **~ing** n Portion f. **~less**
a, **-ly** adv hilflos
hem n Saum m ●vt (pt/pp
hemmed) säumen; **~** in
umzingeln
hemisphere n Hemisphäre f
hem-line n Rocklänge f
hen n Henne f; (any female bird)
Weibchen nt
hence adv daher; five years **~** in
fünf Jahren. **~forth** adv von nun
an
henpecked a **~** husband
Pantoffelheld m
her a ihr ●pron (acc) sie; (dat)
ihr
herald vt verkünden. **~ry** n
Wappenkunde f
herb n Kraut nt
herbaceous a **~** border
Staudenrabatte f
herd n Herde f. **~** together vt
zusammentreiben
here adv hier; (to this place)
hierher; in **~** hier drinnen;
come/bring **~** herkommen/
herbringen
hereditary a erblich
here|sy n Ketzerei f. **~tic** n
Ketzer(in) m(f)
herewith adv (Comm) beiliegend
heritage n Erbe nt
hero n (pl -es) Held m
heroic a, **-ally** adv heldenhaft
heroin n Heroin nt
hero|ine n Heldin f. **~ism** n
Heldentum nt
heron n Reiher m
herring n Hering m
hers poss pron ihre(r), ihrs; a
friend of **~** ein Freund von ihr;
that is **~** das gehört ihr
herself pron selbst; (refl) sich; by
~ allein
hesitant a, **-ly** adv zögernd
hesitat|e vi zögern. **~ion** n
Zögern nt; without **~ion** ohne zu
zögern
hexagonal a sechseckig

H

heyday n Glanzzeit f
hi int he! (hallo) Tag!
hiatus n (pl -tuses) Lücke f
hibernat|e vi Winterschlaf halten.
~**ion** n Winterschlaf m
hiccup n Hick m; (🔳 hitch) Panne
f; **have the** ~**s** den Schluckauf
haben ● vi hick machen
hid, hidden see **hide²**
hide v (pt hid, pp hidden) ● vt
verstecken; (keep secret)
verheimlichen ● vi sich
verstecken
hideous a, **-ly** adv hässlich;
(horrible) grässlich
hide-out n Versteck nt
hiding¹ n 🔳 **give s.o. a** ~ jdn
verdreschen
hiding² n **go into** ~ untertauchen
hierarchy n Hierarchie f
high a (-er, -est) hoch; attrib
hohe(r,s); <meat> angegangen;
<wind> stark; (on drugs) high; **it's**
~ **time** es ist höchste Zeit ● adv
hoch; ~ **and low** überall ● n Hoch
nt; (temperature)
Höchsttemperatur f
high: ~**brow** a intellektuell.
~**chair** n Kinderhochstuhl m. ~-
handed a selbstherrlich. ~-
heeled a hochhackig. ~ **jump** n
Hochsprung m
highlight n (fig) Höhepunkt m;
~**s** pl (in hair) helle Strähnen pl
● vt (emphasize) hervorheben
highly adv hoch; **speak** ~ **of**
loben; **think** ~ **of** sehr schätzen.
~-**strung** a nervös
Highness n Hoheit f
high: ~ **season** n Hochsaison f. ~
street n Hauptstraße f. ~ **tide** n
Hochwasser nt. ~**way** n public
~**way** öffentliche Straße f
hijack vt entführen. ~**er** n
Entführer m
hike n Wanderung f ● vi
wandern. ~**r** n Wanderer m
hilarious a sehr komisch

hill n Berg m; (mound) Hügel m;
(slope) Hang m
hill: ~**side** n Hang m. ~**y** a
hügelig
him pron (acc) ihn; (dat) ihm.
~**self** pron selbst; (refl) sich; **by**
~**self** allein
hind a Hinter-
hind|er vt hindern. ~**rance** n
Hindernis nt
hindsight n **with** ~ rückblickend
Hindu n Hindu m ● a Hindu-.
~**ism** n Hinduismus m
hinge n Scharnier nt; (on door)
Angel f
hint n Wink m, Andeutung f;
(advice) Hinweis m; (trace) Spur
f ● vi ~ **at** anspielen auf (+ acc)
hip n Hüfte f
hip pocket n Gesäßtasche f
hippopotamus n (pl -muses or
-mi) Nilpferd nt
hire vt mieten <car>; leihen
<suit>; einstellen <person>;
~[**out**] vermieten; verleihen
his a sein ● poss pron seine(r),
seins; **a friend of** ~ ein Freund
von ihm; **that is** ~ das gehört ihm
hiss n Zischen nt ● vt/i zischen
historian n Historiker(in) m(f)
historic a historisch. ~**al** a, **-ly**
adv geschichtlich, historisch
history n Geschichte f
hit n (blow) Schlag m; (🔳 success)
Erfolg m; **direct** ~ Volltreffer m
● vt/i (pt/pp hit, pres p hitting)
schlagen; (knock against, collide
with, affect) treffen; ~ **the target**
das Ziel treffen; ~ **on** (fig)
kommen auf (+ acc); ~ **it off** gut
auskommen (with mit); ~ **one's**
head on sth sich (dat) den Kopf
an etw (dat) stoßen
hitch n Problem nt; **technical** ~
Panne f ● vt festmachen (to an +
dat); ~ **up** hochziehen. ~-**hike** vi
🔳 trampen. ~-**hiker** n
Anhalter(in) m(f)
hive n Bienenstock m

hoard n Hort m ● vt horten, hamstern

hoarding n Bauzaun m; (with advertisements) Reklamewand f

hoar-frost n Raureif m

hoarse a (-r, -st), **-ly** adv heiser. ~**ness** n Heiserkeit f

hoax n übler Scherz m; (false alarm) blinder Alarm m

hobble vi humpeln

hobby n Hobby nt. ~**-horse** n (fig) Lieblingsthema nt

hockey n Hockey nt

hoe n Hacke f ● vt (pres p **hoeing**) hacken

hog vt (pt/pp **hogged**) [T] mit Beschlag belegen

hoist n Lastenaufzug m ● vt hochziehen; hissen <flag>

hold[1] n (Naut) Laderaum m

hold[2] n Halt m; (Sport) Griff m; (fig: influence) Einfluss m; **get ~ of** fassen; ([T] contact) erreichen ● v (pt/pp **held**) ● vt halten; <container:> fassen; (believe) meinen; (possess) haben; anhalten <breath> ● vi <rope:> halten; <weather:> sich halten. ~ **back** vt zurückhalten ● vi zögern. ~ **on** vi (wait) warten; (on telephone) am Apparat bleiben; ~ **on to** (keep) behalten; (cling to) sich festhalten an (+ dat). ~ **out** vt hinhalten ● vi (resist) aushalten. ~ **up** vt hochhalten; (delay) aufhalten; (rob) überfallen

hold|**all** n Reisetasche f. ~**er** n Inhaber(in) m(f); (container) Halter m. ~**-up** n Verzögerung f; (attack) Überfall m

hole n Loch nt

holiday n Urlaub m; (Sch) Ferien pl; (public) Feiertag m; (day off) freier Tag m; **go on ~** in Urlaub fahren

holiness n Heiligkeit f

Holland n Holland nt

hollow a hohl; <promise> leer ● n Vertiefung f; (in ground) Mulde f. ~ **out** vt aushöhlen

holly n Stechpalme f

holster n Pistolentasche f

holy a (-ier, -iest) heilig. **H~ Ghost** or **Spirit** n Heiliger Geist m

homage n Huldigung f; **pay ~ to** huldigen (+ dat)

home n Zuhause nt (house) Haus nt; (institution) Heim nt; (native land) Heimat f ● adv **at ~** zu Hause; **come/go ~** nach Hause kommen/gehen

home: ~ **address** n Heimatanschrift f. ~ **game** n Heimspiel nt. ~ **help** n Haushaltshilfe f. ~**land** n Heimatland nt. ~**less** a obdachlos

homely a (-ier, -iest) gemütlich; (Amer: ugly) unscheinbar

home: ~**-made** a selbst gemacht. **H~ Office** n Innenministerium nt. **H~ Secretary** Innenminister m. ~**sick** a **be ~sick** Heimweh haben (for nach). ~**sickness** n Heimweh nt. ~ **town** n Heimatstadt f. ~**work** n (Sch) Hausaufgaben pl

homosexual a homosexuell ● n Homosexuelle(r) m/f

honest a, **-ly** adv ehrlich. ~**y** n Ehrlichkeit f

honey n Honig m; ([T] darling) Schatz m

honey: ~**comb** n Honigwabe f. ~**moon** n Flitterwochen pl; (journey) Hochzeitsreise f

honorary a ehrenamtlich; <member, doctorate> Ehren-

honour n Ehre f ● vt ehren; honorieren <cheque>. ~**able** a, **-bly** adv ehrenhaft

hood n Kapuze f; (of car, pram) [Klapp]verdeck nt; (over cooker) Abzugshaube f; (Auto, Amer) Kühlerhaube f

hoof n (pl ~**s** or **hooves**) Huf m

H

hook n Haken m ● vt festhaken (to an + acc)

hook|ed a ~ed nose Hakennase f; ~ed on Ⅰ abhängig von; (keen on) besessen von. ~er n (Amer ⊠) Nutte f

hookey n **play** ~ (Amer Ⅰ) schwänzen

hooligan n Rowdy m. ~ism n Rowdytum nt

hooray int & n = hurrah

hoot n Ruf m; ~s of laughter schallendes Gelächter nt ● vi <owl:> rufen; <car:> hupen; (jeer) johlen. ~er n (of factory) Sirene f; (Auto) Hupe f

hoover n H~ (P) Staubsauger m ● vt/i [staub]saugen

hop¹ n, & ~s pl Hopfen m

hop² vi (pt/pp hopped) hüpfen; ~ it! Ⅰ hau ab!

hope n Hoffnung f; (prospect) Aussicht f (of auf + acc) ● vt/i hoffen (for auf + acc); I ~ so hoffentlich

hope|ful a hoffnungsvoll; be ~ful that hoffen, dass. ~fully adv hoffnungsvoll; (it is hoped) hoffentlich. ~less a, -ly adv hoffnungslos; (useless) nutzlos; (incompetent) untauglich

horde n Horde f

horizon n Horizont m

horizontal a, -ly adv horizontal. ~ bar n Reck nt

horn n Horn nt; (Auto) Hupe f

hornet n Hornisse f

horoscope n Horoskop nt

horrible a, -bly adv schrecklich

horrid a grässlich

horrific a entsetzlich

horrify vt (pt/pp -ied) entsetzen

horror n Entsetzen nt

hors-d'œuvre n Vorspeise f

horse n Pferd nt

horse: ~back n on ~back zu Pferde. ~man n Reiter m. ~power n Pferdestärke f. ~racing n Pferderennen nt.

~**radish** n Meerrettich m. ~**shoe** n Hufeisen nt

horticulture n Gartenbau m

hose n (pipe) Schlauch m ● vt ~ down abspritzen

hosiery n Strumpfwaren pl

hospitable a, -bly adv gastfreundlich

hospital n Krankenhaus nt

hospitality n Gastfreundschaft f

host¹ n Gastgeber m

hostage n Geisel f

hostel n [Wohn]heim nt

hostess n Gastgeberin f

hostile a feindlich; (unfriendly) feindselig

hostilit|y n Feindschaft f; ~ies pl Feindseligkeiten pl

hot a (hotter, hottest) heiß; <meal> warm; (spicy) scharf; I am or feel ~ mir ist heiß

hotel n Hotel nt

hot: ~**head** n Hitzkopf m. ~**house** n Treibhaus nt. ~**ly** adv (fig) heiß, heftig. ~**plate** n Tellerwärmer m; (of cooker) Kochplatte f. ~ **tap** n Warmwasserhahn m. ~-**tempered** a jähzornig. ~-**water bottle** n Wärmflasche f

hound n Jagdhund m ● vt (fig) verfolgen

hour n Stunde f. ~**ly** a & adv stündlich

house¹ n Haus nt; **at my** ~ bei mir

house² vt unterbringen

house: ~**breaking** n Einbruch m. ~**hold** n Haushalt m. ~**holder** n Hausinhaber(in) m(f). ~**keeper** n Haushälterin f. ~**keeping** n Hauswirtschaft f; (money) Haushaltsgeld nt. ~**plant** n Zimmerpflanze f. ~-**trained** a stubenrein. ~-**warming** n **have a** ~-**warming party** Einstand feiern. ~**wife** n Hausfrau f. ~**work** n Hausarbeit f

housing n Wohnungen pl; (Techn) Gehäuse nt

hovel n elende Hütte f
hover vi schweben. **~craft** n Luftkissenfahrzeug nt
how adv wie; **~ do you do?** guten Tag!; **and ~!** und ob!
however adv (in question) wie; (nevertheless) jedoch, aber; **~ small** wie klein es auch sein mag
howl n Heulen nt ●vi heulen; <baby:> brüllen
hub n Nabe f
huddle vi **~ together** sich zusammendrängen
huff n **in a ~** beleidigt
hug n Umarmung f ●vt (pt/pp hugged) umarmen
huge a, **-ly** adv riesig
hull n (Naut) Rumpf m
hullo int = hallo
hum n Summen nt; Brummen nt ●vt/i (pt/pp hummed) summen; <motor:> brummen
human a menschlich ●n Mensch m. **~ being** n Mensch m
humane a, **-ly** adv human
humanitarian a humanitär
humanity n Menschheit f
humble a (-r, -st), **-bly** adv demütig ●vt demütigen
humdrum a eintönig
humid a feucht. **~ity** n Feuchtigkeit f
humiliat|e vt demütigen. **~ion** n Demütigung f
humility n Demut f
humorous a, **-ly** adv humorvoll; <story> humoristisch
humour n Humor m; (mood) Laune f; **have a sense of ~** Humor haben
hump n Buckel m; (of camel) Höcker m ●vt schleppen
hunch n (idea) Ahnung f
hunchback n Bucklige(r) m/f
hundred a **one/a ~** [ein]hundert ●n Hundert nt; (written figure) Hundert f. **~th** a hundertste(r,s) ●n Hundertstel nt. **~weight** n ≈ Zentner m

hung see **hang**
Hungarian a ungarisch ●n Ungar(in) m(f)
Hungary n Ungarn nt
hunger n Hunger m. **~-strike** n Hungerstreik m
hungry a (-ier, -iest), **-ily** adv hungrig; **be ~** Hunger haben
hunt n Jagd f; (for criminal) Fahndung f ●vt/i jagen; fahnden nach <criminal>; **~ for** suchen. **~er** n Jäger m; (horse) Jagdpferd nt. **~ing** n Jagd f
hurdle n (Sport & fig) Hürde f
hurl vt schleudern
hurrah, hurray int hurra! ●n Hurra nt
hurricane n Orkan m
hurried a, **-ly** adv eilig; (superficial) flüchtig
hurry n Eile f; **be in a ~** es eilig haben ●vi (pt/pp -ied) sich beeilen; (go quickly) eilen. **~ up** vi sich beeilen ●vt antreiben
hurt n Schmerz m ●vt/i (pt/pp hurt) weh tun (+ dat); (injure) verletzen; (offend) kränken
hurtle vi **~ along** rasen
husband n [Ehe]mann m
hush n Stille f ●vt **~ up** vertuschen. **~ed** a gedämpft
husky a (-ier, -iest) heiser; (burly) stämmig
hustle vt drängen ●n Gedränge nt
hut n Hütte f
hutch n [Kaninchen]stall m
hybrid a hybrid ●n Hybride f
hydraulic a, **-ally** adv hydraulisch
hydroelectric a hydroelektrisch
hydrogen n Wasserstoff m
hygien|e n Hygiene f. **~ic** a, **-ally** adv hygienisch
hymn n Kirchenlied nt. **~-book** n Gesangbuch nt
hyphen n Bindestrich m. **~ate** vt mit Bindestrich schreiben
hypno|sis n Hypnose f. **~tic** a hypnotisch

H

hypno|tism n Hypnotik f. **~tist** n
Hypnotiseur m. **~tize** vt
hypnotisieren
hypochondriac n Hypochonder
m
hypocrisy n Heuchelei f
hypocrite n Heuchler(in) m(f)
hypodermic a & n ~ **[syringe]**
Injektionsspritze f
hypothe|sis n Hypothese f. **~tical**
a, **-ly** adv hypothetisch
hyster|ia n Hysterie f. **~ical** a, **-ly**
adv hysterisch. **~ics** npl
hysterischer Anfall m

I pron ich
ice n Eis nt ● vt mit Zuckerguss
überziehen <cake>
ice: **~berg** n Eisberg m. **~box** n
(Amer) Kühlschrank m. **~-cream**
n [Speise]eis nt. **~-cube** n
Eiswürfel m
Iceland n Island nt
ice: **~lolly** n Eis nt am Stiel. ~
rink n Eisbahn f
icicle n Eiszapfen m
icing n Zuckerguss m. ~ **sugar** n
Puderzucker m
icon n Ikone f
icy a (-ier, -iest), **-ily** adv eisig;
<road> vereist
idea n Idee f; (conception)
Vorstellung f; **I have no ~!** ich
habe keine Ahnung!
ideal a n Ideal ● n Ideal nt. **~ism** n
Idealismus m. **~ist** n Idealist(in)
m(f). **~istic** a idealistisch. **~ize**
vt idealisieren. **~ly** adv ideal; (in
ideal circumstances) idealerweise

identical a identisch; <twins>
eineiig
identi|fication n Identifizierung f;
(proof of identity)
Ausweispapiere pl. **~fy** vt (pt/pp
-ied) identifizieren
identity n Identität f. ~ **card** n
[Personal]ausweis m
idiom n [feste] Redewendung f.
~atic a, **-ally** adv idiomatisch
idiosyncrasy n Eigenart f
idiot n Idiot m. **~ic** a idiotisch
idle a (-r, -st), **-ly** adv untätig;
(lazy) faul; (empty) leer;
<machine> nicht in Betrieb ● vi
faulenzen; <engine:> leer laufen.
~ness n Untätigkeit f; Faulheit f
idol n Idol nt. **~ize** vt vergöttern
idyllic a idyllisch
i.e. abbr (**id est**) d.h.
if conj wenn; (whether) ob; **as if**
als ob
ignition n (Auto) Zündung f. ~
key n Zündschlüssel m
ignoramus n Ignorant m
ignoran|ce n Unwissenheit f. **~t**
a unwissend
ignore vt ignorieren
ill a krank; (bad) schlecht; **feel ~**
at ease sich unbehaglich fühlen
● adv schlecht
illegal a, **-ly** adv illegal
illegible a, **-bly** adv unleserlich
illegitimate a unehelich; <claim>
unberechtigt
illicit a, **-ly** adv illegal
illiterate a **be ~te** nicht lesen und
schreiben können
illness n Krankheit f
illogical a, **-ly** adv unlogisch
ill-treat vt misshandeln. **~ment** n
Misshandlung f
illuminat|e vt beleuchten. **~ion** n
Beleuchtung f
illusion n Illusion f; **be under the**
~ that sich (dat) einbilden, dass
illustrat|e vt illustrieren. **~ion** n
Illustration f
illustrious a berühmt

image n Bild nt; (statue) Standbild nt; (exact likeness) Ebenbild nt; [public] ~ Image nt

imagin|able a vorstellbar. ~**ary** a eingebildet

imagination n Fantasie f; (fancy) Einbildung f. ~**ive** a, **-ly** adv fantasievoll; (full of ideas) einfallsreich

imagine vt sich (dat) vorstellen; (wrongly) sich (dat) einbilden

imbalance n Unausgeglichenheit f

imbecile n Schwachsinnige(r) m/f; (pej) Idiot m

imitat|e vt nachahmen, imitieren. ~**ion** n Nachahmung f, Imitation f

immaculate a, **-ly** adv tadellos; (Relig) unbefleckt

immature a unreif

immediate a sofortig; (nearest) nächste(r,s). ~**ly** adv sofort; ~**ly next to** unmittelbar neben ● conj sobald

immemorial a from time ~ seit Urzeiten

immense a, **-ly** adv riesig; Ⅰ enorm

immerse vt untertauchen

immigrant n Einwanderer m

immigration n Einwanderung f

imminent a be ~ unmittelbar bevorstehen

immobile a unbeweglich

immodest a unbescheiden

immoral a, **-ly** adv unmoralisch. ~**ity** n Unmoral f

immortal a unsterblich. ~**ity** n Unsterblichkeit f. ~**ize** vt verewigen

immune a immun (to/from gegen)

immunity n Immunität f

imp n Kobold m

impact n Aufprall m; (collision) Zusammenprall m; (of bomb) Einschlag m; (fig) Auswirkung f

impair vt beeinträchtigen

impart vt übermitteln (to dat); vermitteln <knowledge>

impartial a unparteiisch. ~**ity** n Unparteilichkeit f

impassable a unpassierbar

impassioned a leidenschaftlich

impassive a, **-ly** adv unbeweglich

impatien|ce n Ungeduld f. ~**t** a, **-ly** adv ungeduldig

impeccable a, **-bly** adv tadellos

impede vt behindern

impediment n Hindernis nt; (in speech) Sprachfehler m

impel vt (pt/pp impelled) treiben

impending a bevorstehend

impenetrable a undurchdringlich

imperative a be ~ dringend notwendig sein ● n (Gram) Imperativ m

imperceptible a nicht wahrnehmbar

imperfect a unvollkommen; (faulty) fehlerhaft ● n (Gram) Imperfekt nt. ~**ion** n Unvollkommenheit f; (fault) Fehler m

imperial a kaiserlich. ~**ism** n Imperialismus m

impersonal a unpersönlich

impersonat|e vt sich ausgeben als; (Theat) nachahmen, imitieren. ~**or** n Imitator m

impertinen|ce n Frechheit f. ~**t** a frech

imperturbable a unerschütterlich

impetuous a, **-ly** adv ungestüm

impetus n Schwung m

implacable a unerbittlich

implant vt einpflanzen

implement[1] n Gerät nt

implement[2] vt ausführen

implication n Verwicklung f; ~**s** pl Auswirkungen pl; by ~ implizit

implicit a, **-ly** adv unausgesprochen; (absolute) unbedingt

implore vt anflehen

imply vt (pt/pp **-ied**) andeuten; **what are you ~ing?** was wollen Sie damit sagen?

impolite a, **-ly** adv unhöflich

import[1] n Import m, Einfuhr f

import[2] vt importieren, einführen

importan|ce n Wichtigkeit f. **~t** a wichtig

importer n Importeur m

impos|e vt auferlegen (**on** dat). ●vi sich aufdrängen (**on** dat). **~ing** a eindrucksvoll

impossibility n Unmöglichkeit f

impossible a, **-bly** adv unmöglich

impostor n Betrüger(in) m(f)

impoten|ce n Machtlosigkeit f; (Med) Impotenz f. **~t** a machtlos; (Med) impotent

impoverished a verarmt

impracticable a undurchführbar

impractical a unpraktisch

imprecise a ungenau

impress vt beeindrucken; **~ sth [up]on s.o.** jdm etw einprägen

impression n Eindruck m; (imitation) Nachahmung f; (edition) Auflage f. **~ism** n Impressionismus m

impressive a eindrucksvoll

imprison vt gefangen halten; (put in prison) ins Gefängnis sperren

improbable a unwahrscheinlich

impromptu a improvisiert ●adv aus dem Stegreif

improper a, **-ly** adv inkorrekt; (indecent) unanständig

impropriety n Unkorrektheit f

improve vt verbessern; verschönern <appearance> ●vi sich bessern; **~ [up]on** übertreffen. **~ment** n Verbesserung f; (in health) Besserung f

improvise vt/i improvisieren

imprudent a unklug

impuden|ce n Frechheit f. **~t** a, **-ly** adv frech

impuls|e n Impuls m; **on [an] ~e** impulsiv. **~ive** a, **-ly** adv impulsiv

impur|e a unrein. **~ity** n Unreinheit f

in prep in (+ dat/(into) + acc); **sit in the garden** im Garten sitzen; **go in the garden** in den Garten gehen; **in May** im Mai; **in 1992** [im Jahre] 1992; **in this heat** bei dieser Hitze; **in the evening** am Abend; **in the sky** am Himmel; **in the world** auf der Welt; **in the street** auf der Straße; **deaf in one ear** auf einem Ohr taub; **in the army** beim Militär; **in English/German** auf Englisch/Deutsch; **in ink/pencil** mit Tinte/Bleistift; **in a soft/loud voice** mit leiser/lauter Stimme; **in doing this, he ...** indem er das tut/tat, ... er ●adv (at home) zu Hause; (indoors) drinnen; **he's not in yet** er ist noch nicht da; **all in** alles inbegriffen; (🔢 exhausted) kaputt; **day in, day out** tagaus, tagein; **have it in for s.o.** 🔢 es auf jdn abgesehen haben; **send/go in** hineinschicken/ -gehen; **come/bring in** hereinkommen/-bringen ●a (🔢 in fashion) in ●n **the ins and outs** alle Einzelheiten pl

inability n Unfähigkeit f

inaccessible a unzugänglich

inaccura|cy n Ungenauigkeit f. **~te**, **-ly** adv ungenau

inac|tive a untätig. **~tivity** n Untätigkeit f

inadequate a, **-ly** adv unzulänglich

inadmissible a unzulässig

inadvertently adv versehentlich

inadvisable a nicht ratsam

inane a, **-ly** adv albern

inanimate a unbelebt

inapplicable a nicht zutreffend

inappropriate a unangebracht

inarticulate a undeutlich; **be ~** sich nicht gut ausdrücken können

inattentive a unaufmerksam

inaudible a, **-bly** adv unhörbar

inaugural a Antritts-
inauspicious a ungünstig
inborn a angeboren
inbred a angeboren
incalculable a nicht berechenbar; *(fig)* unabsehbar
incapable a unfähig; **be ~ of doing sth** nicht fähig sein, etw zu tun
incapacitate vt unfähig machen
incarnation n Inkarnation f
incendiary a & n ~ **[bomb]** Brandbombe f
incense¹ n Weihrauch m
incense² vt wütend machen
incentive n Anreiz m
incessant a, **-ly** adv unaufhörlich
incest n Inzest m, Blutschande f
inch n Zoll m ● vi ~ **forward** sich ganz langsam vorwärts schieben
incident n Zwischenfall m
incidental a nebensächlich; *<remark>* beiläufig; *<expenses>* Neben-. **~ly** adv übrigens
incinerate vt verbrennen
incision n Einschnitt m
incisive a scharfsinnig
incite vt aufhetzen. **~ment** n Aufhetzung f
inclement a rau
inclination n Neigung f
incline vt neigen; **be ~d to do sth** dazu neigen, etw zu tun ● vi sich neigen
inclu|de vt einschließen; *(contain)* enthalten; *(incorporate)* aufnehmen (**in** in + acc). **~ding** prep einschließlich (+ gen). **~sion** n Aufnahme f
inclusive a Inklusiv-; ~ **of** einschließlich (+ gen)
incognito adv inkognito
incoherent a, **-ly** adv zusammenhanglos; *(incomprehensible)* unverständlich
income n Einkommen nt. ~ **tax** n Einkommensteuer f

incoming a ankommend; *<mail, call>* eingehend
incomparable a unvergleichlich
incompatible a unvereinbar; **be ~** *<people:>* nicht zueinander passen
incompeten|ce n Unfähigkeit f. **~t** a unfähig
incomplete a unvollständig
incomprehensible a unverständlich
inconceivable a undenkbar
inconclusive a nicht schlüssig
incongruous a unpassend
inconsiderate a rücksichtslos
inconsistent a, **-ly** adv widersprüchlich; *(illogical)* inkonsequent; **be ~** *<things:>* nicht übereinstimmen
inconsolable a untröstlich
inconspicuous a unauffällig
incontinen|ce n Inkontinenz f. **~t** a inkontinent
inconvenien|ce n Unannehmlichkeit f; *(drawback)* Nachteil m. **~t** a, **-ly** adv ungünstig; **be ~t for s.o.** jdm nicht passen
incorporate vt aufnehmen; *(contain)* enthalten
incorrect a, **-ly** adv inkorrekt
incorrigible a unverbesserlich
incorruptible a unbestechlich
increase¹ n Zunahme f; *(rise)* Erhöhung f; **be on the ~** zunehmen
increas|e² vt vergrößern; *(raise)* erhöhen ● vi zunehmen; *(rise)* sich erhöhen. **~ing** a, **-ly** adv zunehmend
incredible a, **-bly** adv unglaublich
incredulous a ungläubig
incriminate vt *(Jur)* belasten
incur vt *(pt/pp incurred)* sich *(dat)* zuziehen; machen *<debts>*
incurable a, **-bly** adv unheilbar
indebted a verpflichtet (**to** dat)
indecent a, **-ly** adv unanständig

indecision n Unentschlossenheit f

indecisive a ergebnislos; <person> unentschlossen

indeed adv in der Tat, tatsächlich; **very much** ~ sehr

indefatigable a unermüdlich

indefinite a unbestimmt. ~**ly** adv unbegrenzt; <postpone> auf unbestimmte Zeit

indent vt (Typ) einrücken. ~**ation** n Einrückung f; (notch) Kerbe f

independen|ce n Unabhängigkeit f; (self-reliance) Selbstständigkeit f. ~**t** a, **-ly** adv unabhängig; selbstständig

indescribable a, **-bly** adv unbeschreiblich

indestructible a unzerstörbar

indeterminate a unbestimmt

index n Register nt

index: ~ **card** n Karteikarte f. ~ **finger** n Zeigefinger m. ~**-linked** a <pension> dynamisch

India n Indien nt. ~**n** a indisch; (American) indianisch ● n Inder(in) m(f); (American) Indianer(in) m(f)

Indian summer n Nachsommer m

indicat|e vt zeigen; (point at) zeigen auf (+ acc); (hint) andeuten; (register) anzeigen ● vi <car:> blinken. ~**ion** n Anzeichen nt

indicative n (Gram) Indikativ m

indicator n (Auto) Blinker m

indifferen|ce n Gleichgültigkeit f. ~**t** a, **-ly** adv gleichgültig; (not good) mittelmäßig

indigest|ible a unverdaulich; (difficult to digest) schwer verdaulich. ~**ion** n Magenverstimmung f

indigna|nt a, **-ly** adv entrüstet, empört. ~**tion** n Entrüstung f, Empörung f

indignity n Demütigung f

indirect a, **-ly** adv indirekt

indiscreet a indiskret

indiscretion n Indiskretion f

indispensable a unentbehrlich

indisposed a indisponiert

indisputable a, **-bly** adv unbestreitbar

indistinct a, **-ly** adv undeutlich

indistinguishable a be ~ nicht zu unterscheiden sein

individual a, **-ly** adv individuell; (single) einzeln ● n Individuum nt. ~**ity** n Individualität f

indivisible a unteilbar

indoctrinate vt indoktrinieren

indolen|ce n Faulheit f. ~**t** a faul

indomitable a unbeugsam

indoor a Innen-; <clothes> Haus-; <plant> Zimmer-; (Sport) Hallen-. ~**s** adv im Haus, drinnen; **go** ~**s** ins Haus gehen

indulge vt frönen (+ dat); verwöhnen <child> ● vi ~ **in** frönen (+ dat). ~**nce** n Nachgiebigkeit f; (leniency) Nachsicht f. ~**nt** a [zu] nachgiebig; nachsichtig

industrial a Industrie-. ~**ist** n Industrielle(r) m

industr|ious a, **-ly** adv fleißig. ~**y** n Industrie f; (zeal) Fleiß m

inebriated a betrunken

inedible a nicht essbar

ineffective a, **-ly** adv unwirksam; <person> untauglich

inefficient a unfähig; <organization> nicht leistungsfähig; <method> nicht rationell

ineligible a nicht berechtigt

inept a ungeschickt

inequality n Ungleichheit f

inertia n Trägheit f

inescapable a unvermeidlich

inestimable a unschätzbar

inevitab|le a unvermeidlich. ~**ly** adv zwangsläufig

inexact a ungenau

inexcusable a unverzeihlich

inexhaustible a unerschöpflich

inexpensive a, **-ly** adv preiswert

inexperience n Unerfahrenheit f.
~d a unerfahren
inexplicable a unerklärlich
infallible a unfehlbar
infamous a niederträchtig;
(*notorious*) berüchtigt
infan|cy n frühe Kindheit f; (*fig*)
Anfangsstadium nt. ~t n
Kleinkind nt. ~tile a kindisch
infantry n Infanterie f
infatuated a vernarrt (**with** in +
acc)
infect vt anstecken, infizieren;
become ~ed <*wound*:> sich
infizieren. ~ion n Infektion f.
~ious a ansteckend
inferior a minderwertig; (*in rank*)
untergeordnet ● n
Untergeordnete(r) m/f
inferiority n Minderwertigkeit f.
~ **complex** n
Minderwertigkeitskomplex m
infern|al a höllisch. ~o n
flammendes Inferno nt
infertile a unfruchtbar
infest vt be ~ed with befallen sein
von; <*place*> verseucht sein mit
infidelity n Untreue f
infighting n (*fig*) interne
Machtkämpfe pl
infinite a, -ly adv unendlich
infinitive n (*Gram*) Infinitiv m
infinity n Unendlichkeit f
inflame vt entzünden. ~d a
entzündet
inflammable a feuergefährlich
inflammation n Entzündung f
inflammatory a aufrührerisch
inflat|e vt aufblasen; (*with pump*)
aufpumpen. ~ion n Inflation f.
~ionary a inflationär
inflexible a starr; <*person*>
unbeugsam
inflict vt zufügen (**on** *dat*);
versetzen <*blow*> (**on** *dat*)
influen|ce n Einfluss m ● vt
beeinflussen. ~tial a
einflussreich
influenza n Grippe f

inform vt benachrichtigen;
(*officially*) informieren; ~ **s.o. of**
sth jdm etw mitteilen; **keep s.o.**
~ed jdn auf dem Laufenden
halten ● vi ~ **against**
denunzieren
informal a, -ly adv zwanglos;
(*unofficial*) inoffiziell. ~ity n
Zwanglosigkeit f
informant n Gewährsmann m
informat|ion n Auskunft f; **a piece**
of ~ion eine Auskunft. ~ive a
aufschlussreich; (*instructive*)
lehrreich
informer n Spitzel m; (*Pol*)
Denunziant m
infra-red a infrarot
infrequent a, -ly adv selten
infringe vt/i ~ [**on**] verstoßen
gegen. ~ment n Verstoß m
infuriat|e vt wütend machen.
~ing a ärgerlich
ingenious a erfinderisch; <*thing*>
raffiniert
ingenuity n Geschicklichkeit f
ingrained a eingefleischt; **be** ~
<*dirt*:> tief sitzen
ingratiate vt ~ **oneself** sich
einschmeicheln (**with** bei)
ingratitude n Undankbarkeit f
ingredient n (*Culin*) Zutat f
ingrowing a <*nail*> eingewachsen
inhabit vt bewohnen. ~ant n
Einwohner(in) m(f)
inhale vt/i einatmen; (*Med &*
when smoking) inhalieren
inherent a natürlich
inherit vt erben. ~ance n
Erbschaft f, Erbe nt
inhibit|ed a gehemmt. ~ion n
Hemmung f
inhospitable a ungastlich
inhuman a unmenschlich
inimitable a unnachahmlich
initial a anfänglich, Anfangs- ● n
Anfangsbuchstabe m; **my** ~s
meine Initialen. ~ly adv anfangs,
am Anfang

initiat|e vt einführen. **~ion** n
Einführung f

initiative n Initiative f

inject vt einspritzen, injizieren.
~ion n Spritze f, Injektion f

injur|e vt verletzen. **~y** n
Verletzung f

injustice n Ungerechtigkeit f; **do
s.o. an ~** jdm unrecht tun

ink n Tinte f

inlaid a eingelegt

inland a Binnen- ● adv
landeinwärts

in-laws npl 🄳 Schwiegereltern pl

inlay n Einlegearbeit f

inlet n schmale Bucht f; (Techn)
Zuleitung f

inmate n Insasse m

inn n Gasthaus nt

innate a angeboren

inner a innere(r,s). **~most** a
innerste(r,s)

innocen|ce n Unschuld f. **~t** a
unschuldig. **~tly** adv in aller
Unschuld

innocuous a harmlos

innovat|ion n Neuerung f. **~ive** a
innovativ. **~or** n Neuerer m

innumerable a unzählig

inoculat|e vt impfen. **~ion** n
Impfung f

inoffensive a harmlos

inoperable a nicht operierbar

inopportune a unpassend

inorganic a anorganisch

in-patient n [stationär
behandelter]
Krankenhauspatient m

input n Input m & nt

inquest n gerichtliche
Untersuchung f der
Todesursache

inquir|e vi sich erkundigen (**about**
nach); **~e into** untersuchen ● vt
sich erkundigen nach. **~y** n
Erkundigung f; (investigation)
Untersuchung f

inquisitive a, **-ly** adv neugierig

insane a geisteskrank; (fig)
wahnsinnig

insanitary a unhygienisch

insanity n Geisteskrankheit f

insatiable a unersättlich

inscription n Inschrift f

inscrutable a unergründlich;
<expression> undurchdringlich

insect n Insekt nt. **~icide** n
Insektenvertilgungsmittel nt

insecur|e a nicht sicher; (fig)
unsicher. **~ity** n Unsicherheit f

insensitive a gefühllos; **~ to**
unempfindlich gegen

inseparable a untrennbar;
(people) unzertrennlich

insert¹ n Einsatz m

insert² vt einfügen, einsetzen;
einstecken <key>; einwerfen
<coin>. **~ion** n (insert) Einsatz m;
(in text) Einfügung f

inside n Innenseite f; (of house)
Innere(s) nt ● attrib Innen-
● adv innen; (indoors) drinnen;
go ~ hineingehen; **come ~**
hereinkommen; **~ out** links
[herum]; **know sth ~ out** etw in-
und auswendig kennen ● prep **~
[of]** in (+ dat/ (into) + acc)

insight n Einblick m (**into** in +
acc); (understanding) Einsicht f

insignificant a unbedeutend

insincere a unaufrichtig

insinuat|e vt andeuten. **~ion** n
Andeutung f

insipid a fade

insist vi darauf bestehen; **~ on**
bestehen auf (+ dat) ● vt **~ that**
darauf bestehen, dass. **~ence** n
Bestehen nt. **~ent** a, **-ly** adv
beharrlich; **be ~ent** darauf
bestehen

insole n Einlegesohle f

insolen|ce n Unverschämtheit f.
~t a, **-ly** adv unverschämt

insoluble a unlöslich; (fig)
unlösbar

insolvent a zahlungsunfähig

insomnia n Schlaflosigkeit f

inspect vt inspizieren; (test) prüfen; kontrollieren <ticket>. ~ion n Inspektion f. ~or n Inspektor m; (of tickets) Kontrolleur m

inspiration n Inspiration f

inspire vt inspirieren

instability n Unbeständigkeit f; (of person) Labilität f

install vt installieren. ~ation n Installation f

instalment n (Comm) Rate f; (of serial) Fortsetzung f; (Radio, TV) Folge f

instance n Fall m; (example) Beispiel nt; in the first ~ zunächst; for ~ zum Beispiel

instant a sofortig; (Culin) Instant- ●n Augenblick m, Moment m. ~aneous a unverzüglich, unmittelbar

instant coffee n Pulverkaffee m

instantly adv sofort

instead adv statt dessen; ~ of statt (+ gen), anstelle von; ~ of me an meiner Stelle; ~ of going anstatt zu gehen

instep n Spann m, Rist m

instigat|e vt anstiften; einleiten <proceedings>. ~ion n Anstiftung f; at his ~ion auf seine Veranlassung

instil vt (pt/pp instilled) einprägen (into s.o. jdm)

instinct n Instinkt m. ~ive a, -ly adv instinktiv

institut|e n Institut nt. ~ion n Institution f; (home) Anstalt f

instruct vt unterrichten; (order) anweisen. ~ion n Unterricht m; Anweisung f; ~ions pl for use Gebrauchsanweisung f. ~ive a lehrreich. ~or n Lehrer(in) m(f); (Mil) Ausbilder m

instrument n Instrument nt. ~al a Instrumental-

insubordi|nate a ungehorsam. ~nation n Ungehorsam m; (Mil) Insubordination f

insufficient a, -ly adv nicht genügend

insulat|e vt isolieren. ~ing tape n Isolierband nt. ~ion n Isolierung f

insult¹ n Beleidigung f

insult² vt beleidigen

insur|ance n Versicherung f. ~e vt versichern

intact a unbeschädigt; (complete) vollständig

intake n Aufnahme f

intangible a nicht greifbar

integral a wesentlich

integrat|e vt integrieren ●vi sich integrieren. ~ion n Integration f

integrity n Integrität f

intellect n Intellekt m. ~ual a intellektuell

intelligen|ce n Intelligenz f; (Mil) Nachrichtendienst m; (information) Meldungen pl. ~t a, -ly adv intelligent

intelligible a verständlich

intend vt beabsichtigen; be ~ed for bestimmt sein für

intense a intensiv; <pain> stark. ~ly adv äußerst; <study> intensiv

intensify v (pt/pp -ied) ●vt intensivieren ●vi zunehmen

intensity n Intensität f

intensive a, -ly adv intensiv; be in ~ care auf der Intensivstation sein

intent a, -ly adv aufmerksam; ~ on (absorbed in) vertieft in (+ acc) ●n Absicht f

intention n Absicht f. ~al a, -ly adv absichtlich

interacti|on n Wechselwirkung f. ~ve a interaktiv

intercede vi Fürsprache einlegen (on behalf of für)

intercept vt abfangen

interchange n Austausch m; (Auto) Autobahnkreuz nt

intercom n [Gegen]sprechanlage f

intercourse n (*sexual*) Geschlechtsverkehr m

interest n Interesse nt; (*Comm*) Zinsen pl ● vt interessieren; **be ~ed** sich interessieren (**in** für). **~ing** a interessant. **~ rate** n Zinssatz m

interfere vi sich einmischen. **~nce** n Einmischung f; (*Radio, TV*) Störung f

interim a Zwischen-; (*temporary*) vorläufig

interior a innere(r,s), Innen- ● n Innere(s) nt

interject vt einwerfen. **~ion** n Interjektion f; (*remark*) Einwurf m

interlude n Pause f; (*performance*) Zwischenspiel nt

intermarry vi untereinander heiraten; <*different groups:*> Mischehen schließen

intermediary n Vermittler(in) m(f)

intermediate a Zwischen-

interminable a endlos [lang]

intermittent a in Abständen auftretend

internal a innere(r,s); <*matter, dispute*> intern. **~ly** adv innerlich; <*deal with*> intern

international a, **-ly** adv international ● n Länderspiel nt; (*player*) Nationalspieler(in) m(f)

Internet n Internet nt; **on the ~** im Internet

internment n Internierung f

interplay n Wechselspiel nt.

interpolate vt einwerfen.

interpret vt interpretieren; auslegen <*text*>; deuten <*dream*>; (*translate*) dolmetschen ● vi dolmetschen. **~ation** n Interpretation f. **~er** n Dolmetscher(in) m(f)

interrogat|e vt verhören. **~ion** n Verhör nt

interrogative a & n ~ **[pronoun]** Interrogativpronomen nt

interrupt vt/i unterbrechen; **don't ~!** red nicht dazwischen! **~ion** n Unterbrechung f

intersect vi sich kreuzen; (*Geom*) sich schneiden. **~ion** n Kreuzung f

interspersed a ~ **with** durchsetzt mit

intertwine vi sich ineinanderschlingen

interval n Abstand m; (*Theat*) Pause f; (*Mus*) Intervall nt; **at hourly ~s** alle Stunde; **bright ~s** pl Aufheiterungen pl

interven|e vi eingreifen; (*occur*) dazwischenkommen. **~tion** n Eingreifen nt; (*Mil, Pol*) Intervention f

interview n (*Journ*) Interview nt; (*for job*) Vorstellungsgespräch nt ● vt interviewen; ein Vorstellungsgespräch führen mit. **~er** n Interviewer(in) m(f)

intimacy n Vertrautheit f; (*sexual*) Intimität f

intimate a, **-ly** adv vertraut; <*friend*> eng; (*sexually*) intim

intimidat|e vt einschüchtern. **~ion** n Einschüchterung f

into prep in (+ acc); **be ~ ⊞** sich auskennen mit; **7 ~ 21** 21 [geteilt] durch 7

intolerable a unerträglich

intoleran|ce n Intoleranz f. **~t** a intolerant

intonation n Tonfall m

intoxicat|ed a betrunken; (*fig*) berauscht. **~ion** n Rausch m

intransigent a unnachgiebig

intransitive a, **-ly** adv intransitiv

intrepid a kühn, unerschrocken

intricate a kompliziert

intrigue n Intrige f ● vt faszinieren. **~ing** a faszinierend

intrinsic a ~ **value** Eigenwert m

introduce vt vorstellen; (*bring in, insert*) einführen

introduct|ion n Einführung f; (to person) Vorstellung f; (to book) Einleitung f. **~ory** a einleitend

introvert n introvertierter Mensch m

intru|de vi stören. **~der** n Eindringling m. **~sion** n Störung f

intuit|ion n Intuition f. **~ive** a, **-ly** adv intuitiv

inundate vt überschwemmen

invade vt einfallen in (+ acc). **~r** n Angreifer m

invalid¹ n Kranke(r) m/f

invalid² a ungültig

invaluable a unschätzbar; <person> unersetzlich

invariab|le a unveränderlich. **~ly** adv immer

invasion n Invasion f

invent vt erfinden. **~ion** n Erfindung f. **~ive** a erfinderisch. **~or** n Erfinder m

inventory n Bestandsliste f

invert vt umkehren. **~ed commas** npl Anführungszeichen pl

invest vt investieren, anlegen; **~ in** (☐ buy) sich (dat) zulegen

investigat|e vt untersuchen. **~ion** n Untersuchung f

invest|ment n Anlage f; **be a good ~ment** (fig) sich bezahlt machen. **~or** n Kapitalanleger m

invidious a unerfreulich; (unfair) ungerecht

invincible a unbesiegbar

inviolable a unantastbar

invisible a unsichtbar

invitation n Einladung f

invit|e vt einladen. **~ing** a einladend

invoice n Rechnung f ● vt **~ s.o.** jdm eine Rechnung schicken

involuntary a, **-ily** adv unwillkürlich

involve vt beteiligen; (affect) betreffen; (implicate) verwickeln; (entail) mit sich bringen; (mean) bedeuten; **be ~d in** beteiligt sein

an (+ dat); (implicated) verwickelt sein in (+ acc); **get ~d with s.o.** sich mit jdm einlassen. **~d** a kompliziert

invulnerable a unverwundbar; <position> unangreifbar

inward a innere(r,s). **~s** adv nach innen

iodine n Jod nt

IOU abbr Schuldschein m

Iran n der Iran

Iraq n der Irak

irascible a aufbrausend

irate a wütend

Ireland n Irland nt

iris n (Anat) Regenbogenhaut f, Iris f; (Bot) Schwertlilie f

Irish a irisch ● n **the ~** pl die Iren. **~man** n Ire m. **~woman** n Irin f

iron a Eisen-; (fig) eisern ● n Eisen nt; (appliance) Bügeleisen nt ● vt/i bügeln

ironic[al] a ironisch

ironing n Bügeln nt; (articles) Bügelwäsche f. **~-board** n Bügelbrett nt

ironmonger n **~'s [shop]** Haushaltswarengeschäft nt

irony n Ironie f

irrational a irrational

irreconcilable a unversöhnlich

irrefutable a unwiderlegbar

irregular a, **-ly** adv unregelmäßig; (against rules) regelwidrig. **~ity** n Unregelmäßigkeit f; Regelwidrigkeit f

irrelevant a irrelevant

irreparable a nicht wieder gutzumachen

irreplaceable a unersetzlich

irrepressible a unverwüstlich; **be ~** <person:> nicht unterzukriegen sein

irresistible a unwiderstehlich

irresolute a unentschlossen

irrespective a **~ of** ungeachtet (+ gen)

irresponsible *a*, **-bly** *adv*
unverantwortlich; <*person*>
verantwortungslos
irreverent *a*, **-ly** *adv* respektlos
irrevocable *a*, **-bly** *adv*
unwiderruflich
irrigat|e *vt* bewässern. **~ion** *n*
Bewässerung *f*
irritable *a* reizbar
irritant *n* Reizstoff *m*
irritat|e *vt* irritieren; (*Med*) reizen.
~ion *n* Ärger *m*; (*Med*) Reizung *f*
is *see* be
Islam *n* der Islam. **~ic** *a*
islamisch
island *n* Insel *f*. **~er** *n*
Inselbewohner(in) *m(f)*
isolat|e *vt* isolieren. **~ed** *a*
(*remote*) abgelegen; (*single*)
einzeln. **~ion** *n* Isoliertheit *f*;
(*Med*) Isolierung *f*
Israel *n* Israel *nt*. **~i** *a* israelisch
●*n* Israeli *m/f*
issue *n* Frage *f*; (*outcome*)
Ergebnis *nt*; (*of magazine,
stamps*) Ausgabe *f*; (*offspring*)
Nachkommen *pl* ●*vt* ausgeben;
ausstellen <*passport*>; erteilen
<*order*>; herausgeben <*book*>; be
~d with sth etw erhalten

it
● *pronoun*
‣ (*as subject*) er (*m*), sie (*f*), es
(*nt*); (*in impersonal sentence*) es.
**where is the spoon? it's on the
table** wo ist der Löffel? Er liegt
auf dem Tisch. **it was very kind of
you** es war sehr nett von Ihnen.
it's five o'clock es ist fünf Uhr
‣ (*as direct object*) ihn (*m*), sie
(*f*), es (*nt*). **that's my pencil — give
it to me** das ist mein Bleistift —
gib ihn mir.
‣ (*as dative object*) ihm (*m*), ihr
(*f*), ihm (*nt*). **he found a track and
followed it** er fand eine Spur und
folgte ihr.
‣ (*after prepositions*)

! Combinations such as *with it,
from it, to it* are translated
by the prepositions with the
prefix da- (damit, davon,
dazu). Prepositions beginning
with a vowel insert an 'r'
(daran, darauf, darüber). **I
can't do anything with it** ich
kann nichts damit anfangen.
don't lean on it! lehn dich
nicht daran!
‣ (*the person in question*) es. **it's
me** ich bin's. **is it you, Dad?** bist
du es, Vater? **who is it?** wer ist
da?

Italian *a* italienisch ●*n*
Italiener(in) *m(f)*; (*Lang*)
Italienisch *nt*
italics *npl* Kursivschrift *f*; in **~s**
kursiv
Italy *n* Italien *nt*
itch *n* Juckreiz *m*; **I have an ~** es
juckt mich ●*vi* jucken; **I'm ~ing**
Ⓘ es juckt mich (to zu). **~y** *a* be
~y jucken
item *n* Gegenstand *m*; (*Comm*)
Artikel *m*; (*on agenda*) Punkt *m*;
(*on invoice*) Posten *m*; (*act*)
Nummer *f*
itinerary *n* [Reise]route *f*
its *poss pron* sein; (*f*) ihr
it's = it is, it has
itself *pron* selbst; (*refl*) sich; **by ~**
von selbst; (*alone*) allein
ivory *n* Elfenbein *nt* ●*attrib*
Elfenbein-
ivy *n* Efeu *m*

jab *n* Stoß *m*; (Ⓘ *injection*) Spritze
f ●*vt* (*pt/pp* jabbed) stoßen

jabber vi plappern

jack n (Auto) Wagenheber m; (Cards) Bube m ● vt ~ up (Auto) aufbocken

jacket n Jacke f; (of book) Schutzumschlag m

jackpot n hit the ~ das große Los ziehen

jade n Jade m

jagged a zackig

jail = gaol

jam¹ n Marmelade f

jam² n Gedränge nt; (Auto) Stau m; (fam. difficulty) Klemme f ● v (pt/pp jammed) ● vt klemmen (in in + acc); stören <broadcast> ● vi klemmen

Jamaica n Jamaika nt

jangle vi klimpern ● vt klimpern mit

January n Januar m

Japan n Japan nt. ~ese a japanisch ● n Japaner(in) m(f); (Lang) Japanisch nt

jar n Glas nt; (earthenware) Topf m

jargon n Jargon m

jaunt n Ausflug m

jaunty a (-ier, -iest) -ily adv keck

javelin n Speer m

jaw n Kiefer m

jazz n Jazz m. ~y a knallig

jealous a, -ly adv eifersüchtig (of auf + acc). ~y n Eifersucht f

jeans npl Jeans pl

jeer n johlen; ~ at verhöhnen

jelly n Gelee nt; (dessert) Götterspeise f. ~fish n Qualle f

jeopar|dize vt gefährden. ~dy n in ~dy gefährdet

jerk n Ruck m ● vt stoßen; (pull) reißen ● vi rucken; <limb, muscle:> zucken. ~ily adv ruckweise. ~y a ruckartig

jersey n Pullover m; (Sport) Trikot nt; (fabric) Jersey m

jest n in ~ im Spaß

jet n (of water) [Wasser]strahl m; (nozzle) Düse f; (plane) Düsenflugzeug nt

jet: ~-black a pechschwarz. ~-propelled a mit Düsenantrieb

jetty n Landesteg m; (breakwater) Buhne f

Jew n Jude m /Jüdin f

jewel n Edelstein m; (fig) Juwel nt. ~ler n Juwelier m; ~ler's [shop] Juweliergeschäft nt. ~lery n Schmuck m

Jew|ess n Jüdin f. ~ish a jüdisch

jib vi (pt/pp jibbed) (fig) sich sträuben (at gegen)

jigsaw n ~ [puzzle] Puzzlespiel nt

jilt vt sitzen lassen

jingle n (rhyme) Verschen nt ● vi klimpern

jinx n 🅸 it's got a ~ on it es ist verhext

jittery a 🅸 nervös

job n Aufgabe f; (post) Stelle f, 🅸 Job m; be a ~ 🅸 nicht leicht sein; it's a good ~ that es ist [nur] gut, dass. ~less a arbeitslos

jockey n Jockei m

jocular a, -ly adv spaßhaft

jog n Stoß m ● v (pt/pp jogged) ● vt anstoßen; ~ s.o.'s memory jds Gedächtnis nachhelfen ● vi (Sport) joggen. ~ging n Jogging nt .

john n (Amer 🅸) Klo nt

join n Nahtstelle f ● vt verbinden (to mit); sich anschließen (+ dat) <person>; (become member of) beitreten (+ dat); eintreten in (+ acc) <firm> ● vi <roads:> sich treffen. ~ in vi mitmachen. ~ up vi (Mil) Soldat werden ● vt zusammenfügen

joint a, -ly adv gemeinsam ● n Gelenk nt; (in wood, brickwork) Fuge f; (Culin) Braten m; (🅸 bar) Lokal nt

jok|e n Scherz m; (funny story) Witz m; (trick) Streich m ● vi scherzen. ~er n Witzbold m;

(*Cards*) Joker m. ∼**ing** n ∼**ing apart** Spaß beiseite. ∼**ingly** adv im Spaß

jolly a (-ier, -iest) lustig ● adv ☐ sehr

jolt n Ruck m ● vt einen Ruck versetzen (+ dat) ● vi holpern

Jordan n Jordanien nt

jostle vt anrempeln

jot vt (pt/pp jotted) ∼ **[down]** sich (dat) notieren

journal n Zeitschrift f; (*diary*) Tagebuch nt. ∼**ese** n Zeitungsjargon m. ∼**ism** n Journalismus m. ∼**ist** n Journalist(in) m(f)

journey n Reise f

jovial a lustig

joy n Freude f. ∼**ful** a, -**ly** adv freudig, froh. ∼**ride** n ☐ Spritztour f [im gestohlenen Auto]

jubil|ant a überglücklich. ∼**ation** n Jubel m

jubilee n Jubiläum nt

judder vi rucken

judge n Richter m; (*of competition*) Preisrichter m ● vt beurteilen; (*estimate*) [ein]schätzen ● vi urteilen (**by** nach). ∼**ment** n Beurteilung f; (*Jur*) Urteil nt; (*fig*) Urteilsvermögen nt

judic|ial a gerichtlich. ∼**ious** a klug

jug n Kanne f; (*small*) Kännchen nt; (*for water, wine*) Krug m

juggle vi jonglieren. ∼**r** n Jongleur m

juice n Saft m

juicy a (-ier, -iest) saftig; ☐ <*story*> pikant

juke-box n Musikbox f

July n Juli m

jumble n Durcheinander nt ● vt ∼ **[up]** durcheinander bringen. ∼ **sale** n [Wohltätigkeits]basar m

jump n Sprung m; (*in prices*) Anstieg m; (*in horse racing*) Hindernis nt ● vi springen; (*start*) zusammenzucken; **make s.o.** ∼ jdn erschrecken; ∼ **at** (*fig*) sofort zugreifen bei <*offer*>; ∼ **to conclusions** voreilige Schlüsse ziehen ● vt überspringen. ∼ **up** vi aufspringen

jumper n Pullover m, Pulli m

jumpy a nervös

junction n Kreuzung f; (*Rail*) Knotenpunkt m

June n Juni m

jungle n Dschungel m

junior a jünger; (*in rank*) untergeordnet; (*Sport*) Junioren- ● n Junior m

junk n Gerümpel nt, Trödel m

junkie n ✕ Fixer m

junk-shop n Trödelladen m

jurisdiction n Gerichtsbarkeit f

jury n **the** ∼ die Geschworenen pl; (*for competition*) die Jury

just a gerecht ● adv gerade; (*only*) nur; (*simply*) einfach; (*exactly*) genau; ∼ **as tall** ebenso groß; **I'm** ∼ **going** ich gehe schon

justice n Gerechtigkeit f; **do** ∼ **to** gerecht werden (+ dat)

justifiab|le a berechtigt. ∼**ly** adv berechtigterweise

justi|fication n Rechtfertigung f. ∼**fy** vt (pt/pp -ied) rechtfertigen

justly adv zu Recht

jut vi (pt/pp jutted) ∼ **out** vorstehen

juvenile a jugendlich; (*childish*) kindisch ● n Jugendliche(r) m/f. ∼ **delinquency** n Jugendkriminalität f

kangaroo n Känguru nt

kebab n Spießchen nt

keel n Kiel m ● vi ~ **over** umkippen; (Naut) kentern

keen a (-er, -est) (sharp) scharf; (intense) groß; (eager) eifrig, begeistert; ~ **on** 🔟 erpicht auf (+ acc); ~ **on s.o.** von jdm sehr angetan; **be** ~ **to do sth** etw gerne machen wollen. ~**ly** adv tief. ~**ness** n Eifer m, Begeisterung f

keep n (maintenance) Unterhalt m; (of castle) Bergfried m; **for** ~**s** für immer ● v (pt/pp **kept**) ● vt behalten; (store) aufbewahren; (not throw away) aufheben; (support) unterhalten; (detain) aufhalten; freihalten <seat>; halten <promise, animals>; führen, haben <shop>; einhalten <law, rules>; ~ **s.o. waiting** jdn warten lassen; ~ **sth to oneself** etw nicht weitersagen ● vi (remain) bleiben; <food:> sich halten; ~ **left/right** sich links/ rechts halten; ~ **on doing sth** etw dauernd machen; ~ **in with** sich gut stellen mit. ~ **up** vi Schritt halten ● vt (continue) weitermachen

keep|er n Wärter(in) m(f). ~**ing** n **be in** ~**ing with** passen zu

kennel n Hundehütte f; ~**s** pl (boarding) Hundepension f; (breeding) Zwinger m

Kenya n Kenia nt

kept see **keep**

kerb n Bordstein m

kernel n Kern m

ketchup n Ketschup m

kettle n [Wasser]kessel m; **put the** ~ **on** Wasser aufsetzen

key n Schlüssel m; (Mus) Tonart f; (of piano, typewriter) Taste f ● vt ~ **in** eintasten

key: ~**board** n Tastatur f; (Mus) Klaviatur f. ~**hole** n Schlüsselloch nt. ~**-ring** n Schlüsselring m

khaki a khakifarben ● n Khaki nt

kick n [Fuß]tritt m; **for** ~**s** 🔟 zum Spaß ● vt treten; ~ **the bucket** 🔟 abkratzen ● vi <animal> ausschlagen

kid n (🔟 child) Kind nt ● vt (pt/pp **kidded**) 🔟 ~ **s.o.** jdm etwas vormachen

kidnap vt (pt/pp **-napped**) entführen. ~**per** n Entführer m. ~**ping** n Entführung f

kidney n Niere f

kill vt töten; 🔟 totschlagen <time>; ~ **two birds with one stone** zwei Fliegen mit einer Klappe schlagen. ~**er** n Mörder(in) m(f). ~**ing** n Tötung f; (murder) Mord m

killjoy n Spielverderber m

kilo n Kilo nt

kilo:: ~**gram** n Kilogramm nt. ~**metre** n Kilometer m. ~**watt** n Kilowatt nt

kilt n Schottenrock m

kind[1] n Art f; (brand, type) Sorte f; **what** ~ **of car?** was für ein Auto? ~ **of** 🔟 irgendwie

kind[2] a (-er, -est) nett; ~ **to animals** gut zu Tieren

kind|ly a (-ier, -iest) nett ● adv netterweise; (if you please) gefälligst. ~**ness** n Güte f; (favour) Gefallen m

king n König m; (Draughts) Dame f. ~**dom** n Königreich nt; (fig & Relig) Reich nt

king: ~**fisher** n Eisvogel m. ~**-sized** a extragroß

kink n Knick m. ~**y** a 🔟 pervers

kiosk n Kiosk m

kip n have a ~ 🔲 pennen ●vi
(pt/pp kipped) 🔲 pennen
kipper n Räucherhering m
kiss n Kuss m ●vt/i küssen
kit n Ausrüstung f; (tools)
Werkzeug nt; (construction ~)
Bausatz m ●vt (pt/pp kitted) ~out
ausrüsten
kitchen n Küche f ●attrib
Küchen-. ~ette n Kochnische f
kitchen: ~garden n
Gemüsegarten m. ~sink n
Spülbecken nt
kite n Drachen m
kitten n Kätzchen nt
kitty n (money) [gemeinsame]
Kasse f
knack n Trick m, Dreh m
knead vt kneten
knee n Knie nt. ~cap n
Kniescheibe f
kneel vi (pt/pp knelt) knien; ~
[down] sich [nieder]knien
knelt see kneel
knew see know
knickers npl Schlüpfer m
knife n (pl knives) Messer nt ●vt
einen Messerstich versetzen (+
dat)
knight n Ritter m; (Chess)
Springer m ●vt adeln
knit vt/i (pt/pp knitted) stricken; ~
one's brow die Stirn runzeln.
~ting n Stricken nt; (work)
Strickzeug nt. ~ting-needle n
Stricknadel f. ~wear n
Strickwaren pl
knives npl see knife
knob n Knopf m; (on door) Knauf
m; (small lump) Beule f. ~bly a
knorrig; (bony) knochig
knock n Klopfen nt; (blow) Schlag
m; there was a ~ es klopfte ●vt
anstoßen; (🔲 criticize)
heruntermachen; ~ a hole in sth
ein Loch in etw (acc) schlagen; ~
one's head sich (dat) den Kopf
stoßen (on an + dat) ●vi klopfen.
~ about vt schlagen ●vi 🔲

herumkommen. ~ down vt
herunterwerfen; (with fist)
niederschlagen; (in car)
anfahren; (demolish) abreißen;
(🔲 reduce) herabsetzen. ~ off vt
herunterwerfen; (🔲 steal)
klauen; (🔲 complete quickly)
hinhauen ●vi (🔲 cease work)
Feierabend machen. ~ out vt
ausschlagen; (make unconscious)
bewusstlos schlagen; (Boxing)
k.o. schlagen. ~ over vt
umwerfen; (in car) anfahren
knock: ~-down a ~-down prices
Schleuderpreise pl. ~er n
Türklopfer m. ~-out n (Boxing)
K.o. m
knot n Knoten m ●vt (pt/pp
knotted) knoten
know vt/i (pt knew, pp known)
wissen; kennen <person>;
können <language>; get to ~
kennen lernen ●n in the ~ 🔲 im
Bild
know: ~-all n 🔲 Alleswisser m.
~-how n 🔲 [Sach]kenntnis f.
~ing a wissend. ~ingly adv
wissend; (intentionally)
wissentlich
knowledge n Kenntnis f (of von/
gen); (general) Wissen nt;
(specialized) Kenntnisse pl.
~able a be ~able viel wissen
knuckle n [Finger]knöchel m;
(Culin) Hachse f
kosher a koscher
kudos n 🔲 Prestige nt

lab n 🔲 Labor nt

label n Etikett nt ● vt (pt/pp labelled) etikettieren

laboratory n Labor nt

laborious a, **-ly** adv mühsam

labour n Arbeit f; (workers) Arbeitskräfte pl; (Med) Wehen pl; L~ (Pol) die Labourpartei ● attrib Labour- ● vi arbeiten ● vt (fig) sich lange auslassen über (+ acc). ~**er** n Arbeiter m

labour-saving a arbeitssparend

lace n Spitze f; (of shoe) Schnürsenkel m ● vt schnüren

lack n Mangel m (of an + dat) ● vt I ~ the time mir fehlt die Zeit ● vi be ~**ing** fehlen

laconic a, **-ally** adv lakonisch

lacquer n Lack m; (for hair) [Haar]spray m

lad n Junge m

ladder n Leiter f; (in fabric) Laufmasche f

ladle n [Schöpf]kelle f ● vt schöpfen

lady n Dame f; (title) Lady f

lady: ~**bird** n, (Amer) ~**bug** n Marienkäfer m. ~**like** a damenhaft

lag¹ vi (pt/pp lagged) ~ behind zurückbleiben; (fig) nachhinken

lag² vt (pt/pp lagged) umwickeln <pipes>

lager n Lagerbier nt

laid see **lay³**

lain see **lie²**

lake n See m

lamb n Lamm nt

lame a (-r, -st) lahm

lament n Klage f; (song) Klagelied nt ● vt beklagen ● vi klagen

laminated a laminiert

lamp n Lampe f; (in street) Laterne f. ~**post** n Laternenpfahl m. ~**shade** n Lampenschirm m

lance vt (Med) aufschneiden

land n Land nt; plot of ~ Grundstück nt ● vt/i landen; ~ s.o. with sth 🛈 jdm etw aufhalsen

landing n Landung f; (top of stairs) Treppenflur m. ~**stage** n Landesteg m

land: ~**lady** n Wirtin f. ~**lord** n Wirt m; (of land) Grundbesitzer m; (of building) Hausbesitzer m. ~**mark** n Erkennungszeichen nt; (fig) Meilenstein m. ~**owner** n Grundbesitzer m. ~**scape** n Landschaft f. ~**slide** n Erdrutsch m

lane n kleine Landstraße f; (Auto) Spur f; (Sport) Bahn f; 'get in ~' (Auto) 'bitte einordnen'

language n Sprache f; (speech, style) Ausdrucksweise f

languid a, **-ly** adv träge

languish vi schmachten

lanky a (-ier, -iest) schlaksig

lantern n Laterne f

lap¹ n Schoß m

lap² n (Sport) Runde f; (of journey) Etappe f ● vi (pt/pp lapped) plätschern (against gegen)

lap³ vt (pt/pp lapped) ~ up aufschlecken

lapel n Revers nt

lapse n Fehler m; (moral) Fehltritt m; (of time) Zeitspanne f ● vi (expire) erlöschen; ~ into verfallen in (+ acc)

lard n [Schweine]schmalz nt

larder n Speisekammer f

large a (-r, -st) & adv groß; by and ~ im Großen und Ganzen; at ~ auf freiem Fuß. ~**ly** adv großenteils

lark¹ n (bird) Lerche f

lark² n (joke) Jux m ● vi ~ about herumalbern

laryngitis n Kehlkopfentzündung f

larynx n Kehlkopf m

laser n Laser m

lash n Peitschenhieb m; (*eyelash*) Wimper f ● vt peitschen; (*tie*). festbinden (**to** an + *acc*). ~ **out** vi um sich schlagen; (*spend*) viel Geld ausgeben (**on** für)

lass n Mädchen nt

lasso n Lasso nt

last a & n letzte(r,s); ~ **night** heute *od* gestern Nacht; (*evening*) gestern Abend; **at** ~ endlich; **for the** ~ **time** zum letzten Mal; **the** ~ **but one** der/die/das vorletzte ● adv zuletzt; (*last time*) das letzte Mal; **he/she went** ~ er/sie ging als Letzter/Letzte ● vi dauern; <*weather*:> sich halten; <*relationship*:> halten. ~**ing** a dauerhaft. ~**ly** adv schließlich, zum Schluss

latch n [einfache] Klinke f

late a & adv (**-r, -st**) spät; (*delayed*) verspätet; (*deceased*) verstorben; **the** ~**st news** die neuesten Nachrichten; **stay up** ~ bis spät aufbleiben; **arrive** ~ zu spät ankommen; **I am** ~ ich komme zu spät *od* habe mich verspätet; **the train is** ~ der Zug hat Verspätung. ~**comer** n Zuspätkommende(r) m/f. ~**ly** adv in letzter Zeit. ~**ness** n Zuspätkommen nt; (*delay*) Verspätung f

later a & adv später; ~ **on** nachher

lateral a seitlich

lather n [Seifen]schaum m

Latin a lateinisch ● n Latein nt. ~ **America** n Lateinamerika nt

latitude n (*Geog*) Breite f; (*fig*) Freiheit f

latter a & n **the** ~ der/die/das Letztere

Latvia n Lettland nt

laudable a lobenswert

laugh n Lachen nt; **with a** ~ lachend ● vi lachen (**at/about** über + *acc*); ~ **at s.o.** (*mock*) jdn auslachen. ~**able** a lachhaft, lächerlich

laughter n Gelächter nt

launch[1] n (*boat*) Barkasse f

launch[2] n Stapellauf m; (*of rocket*) Abschuss m; (*of product*) Lancierung f ● vt vom Stapel lassen <*ship*>; zu Wasser lassen <*lifeboat*>; abschießen <*rocket*>; starten <*attack*>; (*Comm*) lancieren <*product*>

laund(e)rette n Münzwäscherei f

laundry n Wäscherei f; (*clothes*) Wäsche f

laurel n Lorbeer m

lava n Lava f

lavatory n Toilette f

lavender n Lavendel m

lavish a, -**ly** adv großzügig; (*wasteful*) verschwenderisch ● vt ~ **sth on s.o.** jdn mit etw überschütten

law n Gesetz nt; (*system*) Recht nt; **study** ~ Jura studieren; ~ **and order** Recht und Ordnung

law: ~-**abiding** a gesetzestreu. ~ **court** n Gerichtshof m. ~**ful** a rechtmäßig. ~**less** a gesetzlos

lawn n Rasen m. ~-**mower** n Rasenmäher m

lawyer n Rechtsanwalt m /-anwältin f

lax a lax, locker

laxative n Abführmittel nt

laxity n Laxheit f

lay[1] see **lie**[2]

lay[2] vt (*pt/pp* **laid**) legen; decken <*table*>; ~ **a trap** eine Falle stellen. ~ **down** vt hinlegen; festlegen <*rules, conditions*>. ~ **off** vt entlassen <*workers*> ● vi (**f** *stop*) aufhören. ~ **out** vt hinlegen; aufbahren <*corpse*>; anlegen <*garden*>; (*Typ*) gestalten

lay-by n Parkbucht f

layer n Schicht f

lay: ~**man** n Laie m. ~**out** n Anordnung f; (design) Gestaltung f; (Typ) Layout nt

laze vi ~**[about]** faulenzen

laziness n Faulheit f

lazy a (-ier, -iest) faul. ~**-bones** n Faulenzer m

lead[1] n Blei nt; (of pencil) [Bleistift]mine f

lead[2] n Führung f; (leash) Leine f; (flex) Schnur f; (clue) Hinweis m, Spur f; (Theat) Hauptrolle f; (distance ahead) Vorsprung m; **be in the** ~ in Führung liegen ● vt/i (pt/pp **led**) führen, leiten <team>; (induce) bringen; (at cards) ausspielen; ~ **the way** vorangehen; ~ **up to sth** (fig) etw (dat) vorangehen

leader n Führer m; (of expedition, group) Leiter(in) m(f); (of orchestra) Konzertmeister m; (in newspaper) Leitartikel m. ~**ship** n Führung f; Leitung f

leading a führend; ~ **lady** Hauptdarstellerin f

leaf n (pl **leaves**) Blatt nt ● vi ~ **through sth** etw durchblättern. ~**let** n Merkblatt nt; (advertising) Reklameblatt nt; (political) Flugblatt nt

league n Liga f

leak n (hole) undichte Stelle f; (Naut) Leck nt; (of gas) Gasausfluss m ● vi undicht sein; <ship:> leck sein, lecken; <liquid:> auslaufen; <gas:> ausströmen ● vt auslaufen lassen; ~ **sth to s.o.** (fig) jdm etw zuspielen. ~**y** a undicht; (Naut) leck

lean[1] a (-er, -est) mager

lean[2] v (pt/pp **leaned** or **leant**) ● vt lehnen (against/on an + acc) ● vi <person> sich lehnen (against/on an + acc); (not be straight) sich neigen; **be** ~**ing against** lehnen an (+ dat). ~ **back** vi sich zurücklehnen. ~ **forward** vi sich

vorbeugen. ~ **out** vi sich hinauslehnen. ~ **over** vi sich vorbeugen

leaning a schief ● n Neigung f

leap n Sprung m ● vi (pt/pp **leapt** or **leaped**) springen; **he leapt at it** [!] er griff sofort zu. ~ **year** n Schaltjahr nt

learn vt/i (pt/pp **learnt** or **learned**) lernen; (hear) erfahren; ~ **to swim** schwimmen lernen

learn|ed a gelehrt. ~**er** n Anfänger m; ~**er [driver]** Fahrschüler(in) m(f). ~**ing** n Gelehrsamkeit f

lease n Pacht f; (contract) Mietvertrag m ● vt pachten

leash n Leine f

least a geringste(r,s) ● n **the** ~ das wenigste; **at** ~ wenigstens, mindestens; **not in the** ~ nicht im Geringsten ● adv am wenigsten

leather n Leder nt

leave n Erlaubnis f; (holiday) Urlaub m; **on** ~ auf Urlaub; **take one's** ~ sich verabschieden ● v (pt/pp **left**) ● vt lassen; (go out of, abandon) verlassen; (forget) liegen lassen; (bequeath) vermachen (**to** dat); ~ **it to me!** überlassen Sie es mir! **there is nothing left** es ist nichts mehr übrig ● vi [weg]gehen/-fahren; <train, bus:> abfahren. ~ **behind** vt zurücklassen; (forget) liegen lassen. ~ **out** vt liegen lassen; (leave outside) draußen lassen; (omit) auslassen

leaves see **leaf**

Lebanon n Libanon m

lecherous a lüstern

lecture n Vortrag m; (Univ) Vorlesung f; (reproof) Strafpredigt f ● vi einen Vortrag/eine Vorlesung halten (**on** über + acc) ● vt ~ **s.o.** jdm eine Strafpredigt halten. ~**r** n Vortragende(r) m/f; (Univ) Dozent(in) m(f)

led see lead²

ledge n Leiste f; (shelf, of window) Sims m; (in rock) Vorsprung m

ledger n Hauptbuch nt

leech n Blutegel m

leek n Stange f Porree; ~s pl Porree m

left¹ see leave

left² a linke(r,s) ● adv links; <go> nach links ● n linke Seite f; on the ~ links; from/to the ~ von/ nach links; the ~ (Pol) die Linke

left: ~-handed a linkshändig. ~-luggage [office] n Gepäckaufbewahrung f. ~overs npl Reste pl. ~-wing a (Pol) linke(r,s)

leg n Bein nt; (Culin) Keule f; (of journey) Etappe f

legacy n Vermächtnis nt, Erbschaft f

legal a, -ly adv gesetzlich; <matters> rechtlich; <department, position> Rechts-; be ~ [gesetzlich] erlaubt sein

legality n Legalität f

legend n Legende f. ~ary a legendär

legible a, -bly adv leserlich

legion n Legion f

legislat|e vi Gesetze erlassen. ~ion n Gesetzgebung f; (laws) Gesetze pl

legislative a gesetzgebend

legitimate a rechtmäßig; (justifiable) berechtigt

leisure n Freizeit f; at your ~ wenn Sie Zeit haben. ~ly a gemächlich

lemon n Zitrone f. ~ade n Zitronenlimonade f

lend vt (pt/pp lent) leihen (s.o. sth jdm etw)

length n Länge f; (piece) Stück nt; (of wallpaper) Bahn f; (of time) Dauer f

length|en vt länger machen ● vi länger werden. ~ways adv der Länge nach

lengthy a (-ier, -iest) langwierig

lenien|t a, -ly adv nachsichtig

lens n Linse f; (Phot) Objektiv nt; (of spectacles) Glas nt

lent see lend

Lent n Fastenzeit f

lentil n (Bot) Linse f

leopard n Leopard m

leotard n Trikot nt

lesbian a lesbisch ● n Lesbierin f

less a, adv, n & prep weniger; ~ and ~ immer weniger

lessen vt verringern ● vi nachlassen; <value:> abnehmen

lesser a geringere(r,s)

lesson n Stunde f; (in textbook) Lektion f; (Relig) Lesung f; teach s.o. a ~ (fig) jdm eine Lehre erteilen

lest conj (liter) damit ... nicht

let vt (pt/pp let, pres p letting) lassen; (rent) vermieten; ~ alone (not to mention) geschweige denn; ~ us go gehen wir; ~ me know sagen Sie mir Bescheid; ~ oneself in for sth 🗉 sich (dat) etw einbrocken. ~ down vt hinunter-/herunterlassen; (lengthen) länger machen; ~ s.o. down 🗉 jdn im Stich lassen; (disappoint) jdn enttäuschen. ~ in vt hereinlassen. ~ off vt abfeuern <gun>; hochgehen lassen <firework, bomb>; (emit) ausstoßen; (excuse from) befreien von; (not punish) frei ausgehen lassen. ~ out vt hinaus-/herauslassen; (make larger) auslassen. ~ through vt durchlassen. ~ up vi 🗉 nachlassen

let-down n Enttäuschung f, 🗉 Reinfall m

lethal a tödlich

letharg|ic a lethargisch. ~y n Lethargie f

letter n Brief m; (of alphabet) Buchstabe m. ~-**box** n Briefkasten m. ~-**head** n Briefkopf m. ~**ing** n Beschriftung f

lettuce n [Kopf]salat m

let-up n 🖪 Nachlassen nt

level a eben; (horizontal) waagerecht; (in height) auf gleicher Höhe; <spoonful> gestrichen; one's ~ **best** sein Möglichstes ●n Höhe f; (fig) Ebene f, Niveau nt; (stage) Stufe f; **on the** ~ 🖪 ehrlich ●vt (pt/pp **levelled**) einebnen

level crossing n Bahnübergang m

lever n Hebel m ●vt ~ **up** mit einem Hebel anheben. ~**age** n Hebelkraft f

lewd a (-er, -est) anstößig

liabilit|y n Haftung f; ~**ies** pl Verbindlichkeiten pl

liable a haftbar; **be** ~ **to do sth** etw leicht tun können

liaise vi 🖪 Verbindungsperson sein

liaison n Verbindung f; (affair) Verhältnis nt

liar n Lügner(in) m(f)

libel n Verleumdung f ●vt (pt/pp **libelled**) verleumden. ~**lous** a verleumderisch

liberal a, -**ly** adv tolerant; (generous) großzügig. **L**~ a (Pol) liberal ●n Liberale(r) m/f

liberat|e vt befreien. ~**ed** a <woman> emanzipiert. ~**ion** n Befreiung f. ~**or** n Befreier m

liberty n Freiheit f; **take liberties** sich (dat) Freiheiten erlauben

librarian n Bibliothekar(in) m(f)

library n Bibliothek f

Libya n Libyen nt

lice see **louse**

licence n Genehmigung f; (Comm) Lizenz f; (for TV) ≈ Fernsehgebühr f; (for driving) Führerschein m; (for alcohol) Schankkonzession f

license vt eine Genehmigung/ (Comm) Lizenz erteilen (+ dat); **be** ~**d** <car:> zugelassen sein; <restaurant:> Schankkonzession haben. ~-**plate** n (Amer) Nummernschild nt

lick n Lecken nt; **a** ~ **of paint** ein bisschen Farbe ●vt lecken; (🖪 defeat) schlagen

lid n Deckel m; (of eye) Lid nt

lie¹ n Lüge f; **tell a** ~ lügen ●vi (pt/pp **lied**, pres p **lying**) lügen; ~ **to** belügen

lie² vi (pt **lay**, pp **lain**, pres p **lying**) liegen; **here** ~**s** ... hier ruht ... ~ **down** vi sich hinlegen

lie-in n **have a** ~ [sich] ausschlafen

lieu n **in** ~ **of** statt (+ gen)

lieutenant n Oberleutnant m

life n (pl **lives**) Leben nt; **lose one's** ~ ums Leben kommen

life: ~-**boat** n Rettungsboot nt. ~-**guard** n Lebensretter m. ~-**jacket** n Schwimmweste f. ~**less** a leblos. ~**like** a naturgetreu. ~**long** a lebenslang. ~ **preserver** n (Amer) Rettungsring m. ~-**size(d)** a ... in Lebensgröße. ~**time** n Leben nt; **in s.o.'s** ~**time** zu jds Lebzeiten; **the chance of a** ~**time** eine einmalige Gelegenheit

lift n Aufzug m, Lift m; **give s.o. a** ~ jdn mitnehmen; **get a** ~ mitgenommen werden ●vt heben; aufheben <restrictions> ●vi <fog:> sich lichten. ~ **up** vt hochheben

light¹ a (-er, -est) (not dark) hell; ~ **blue** hellblau ●n Licht nt; (lamp) Lampe f; **have you [got] a** ~**?** haben Sie Feuer? ●vt (pt/pp **lit** or **lighted**) anzünden <fire, cigarette>; (illuminate) beleuchten. ~ **up** vi <face:> sich erhellen

L

light² a (-er, -est) (not heavy) leicht; ~ **sentence** milde Strafe f ● adv travel ~ mit wenig Gepäck reisen

light-bulb n Glühbirne f

lighten¹ vt heller machen

lighten² vt leichter machen <load>

lighter n Feuerzeug nt

light: ~**-hearted** a unbekümmert. ~**house** n Leuchtturm m. ~**ing** n Beleuchtung f. ~**ly** adv leicht; **get off ~ly** glimpflich davonkommen

lightning n Blitz m

lightweight a leicht ● n (Boxing) Leichtgewicht nt

like¹ a ähnlich; (same) gleich ● prep wie; (similar to) ähnlich (+ dat); ~ **this** so; **what's he ~?** wie ist er denn? ● conj (🗊 as) wie; (Amer: as if) als ob

like² vt mögen; **I should/would ~** ich möchte; **I ~ the car** das Auto gefällt mir; ~ **dancing/singing** gern tanzen/singen ● n ~**s and dislikes** pl Vorlieben und Abneigungen pl

like|able a sympathisch. ~**lihood** n Wahrscheinlichkeit f. ~**ly** a (-ier, -iest) & adv wahrscheinlich; **not ~ly!** 🗊 auf gar keinen Fall!

like-minded a gleich gesinnt

liken vt vergleichen (to mit)

like|ness n Ähnlichkeit f. ~**wise** adv ebenso

liking n Vorliebe f; **is it to your ~?** gefällt es Ihnen?

lilac n Flieder m

lily n Lilie f

limb n Glied nt

lime n (fruit) Limone f; (tree) Linde f. ~**light** n **be in the ~light** im Rampenlicht stehen

limit n Grenze f; (limitation) Beschränkung f; **that's the ~!** 🗊 das ist doch die Höhe! ● vt beschränken (to auf + acc). ~**ation** n Beschränkung f; ~**ed** a beschränkt. ~**ed company**

Gesellschaft f mit beschränkter Haftung

limousine n Limousine f

limp¹ n Hinken nt ● vi hinken

limp² a (-er, -est), -ly adv schlaff

limpid a klar

line¹ n Linie f; (length of rope, cord) Leine f; (Teleph) Leitung f; (of writing) Zeile f; (row) Reihe f; (wrinkle) Falte f; (of business) Branche f; (Amer: queue) Schlange f; **in ~ with** gemäß (+ dat) ● vt säumen <street>

line² vt füttern <garment>; (Techn) auskleiden

lined¹ a (wrinkled) faltig; <paper> liniert

lined² a <garment> gefüttert

linen n Leinen nt; (articles) Wäsche f

liner n Passagierschiff nt

linesman n (Sport) Linienrichter m

linger vi [zurück]bleiben

lingerie n Damenunterwäsche f

linguist n Sprachkundige(r) m/f

linguistic a, -ally adv sprachlich

lining n (of garment) Futter nt; (Techn) Auskleidung f

link n (of chain) Glied nt (fig) Verbindung f ● vt verbinden; ~ **arms** sich unterhaken

links n or npl Golfplatz m

lint n Verbandstoff m

lion n Löwe m; ~'**s share** (fig) Löwenanteil m. ~**ess** n Löwin f

lip n Lippe f; (edge) Rand m; (of jug) Schnabel m

lip: ~**-reading** n Lippenlesen nt. ~**-service** n **pay ~-service** ein Lippenbekenntnis ablegen (to zu). ~**stick** n Lippenstift m

liqueur n Likör m

liquid n Flüssigkeit f ● a flüssig

liquidation n Liquidation f

liquidize vt [im Mixer] pürieren. ~**r** n Mixer m

liquor n Alkohol m. ~ **store** n (Amer) Spirituosengeschäft nt

lisp n Lispeln nt ● vt/i lispeln
list[1] n Liste f ● vt aufführen
list[2] vi <ship:> Schlagseite haben
listen vi zuhören (**to** dat); ~ **to the
radio** Radio hören. ~**er** n
Zuhörer(in) m(f); (Radio)
Hörer(in) m(f)
listless a, **-ly** adv lustlos
lit see **light**[1]
literacy n Lese- und
Schreibfertigkeit f
literal a wörtlich. ~**ly** adv
buchstäblich
literary a literarisch
literate a be ~ lesen und
schreiben können
literature n Literatur f; Ⓘ
Informationsmaterial nt
lithe a geschmeidig
Lithuania n Litauen nt
litre n Liter m & nt
litter n Abfall m; (Zool) Wurf m.
~**-bin** n Abfalleimer m
little a klein; (not much) wenig
● adv & n wenig; **a** ~ ein
bisschen/wenig; ~ **by** ~ nach
und nach
live[1] a lebendig; <ammunition>
scharf; ~ **broadcast** Live-
Sendung f; **be** ~ (Electr) unter
Strom stehen
live[2] vi leben; (reside) wohnen. ~
on vt leben von; (eat) sich
ernähren von ● vi weiterleben
liveli|hood n Lebensunterhalt m.
~**ness** n Lebendigkeit f
lively a (**-ier, -iest**) lebhaft,
lebendig
liver n Leber f
lives see **life**
livid a Ⓘ wütend
living a lebend ● n earn one's ~
seinen Lebensunterhalt
verdienen. ~**-room** n
Wohnzimmer nt
lizard n Eidechse f
load n Last f; (quantity) Ladung f;
(Electr) Belastung f; ~**s of** Ⓘ jede
Menge ● vt laden <goods, gun>;

beladen <vehicle>; ~ **a camera**
einen Film in eine Kamera
einlegen. ~**ed** a beladen; (Ⓘ
rich) steinreich
loaf n (pl **loaves**) Brot nt
loan n Leihgabe f; (money)
Darlehen nt; **on** ~ geliehen ● vt
leihen (**to** dat)
loath a be ~ **to do sth** etw ungern
tun
loath|e vt verabscheuen. ~**ing** n
Abscheu m
loaves see **loaf**[1]
lobby n Foyer nt; (anteroom)
Vorraum m; (Pol) Lobby f
lobster n Hummer m
local a hiesig; <time, traffic>
Orts-; ~ **anaesthetic** örtliche
Betäubung; **I'm not** ~ ich bin
nicht von hier ● n Hiesige(r) m/f;
(Ⓘ public house) Stammkneipe f.
~ **call** n (Teleph) Ortsgespräch nt
locality n Gegend f
locally adv am Ort
locat|e vt ausfindig machen; **be**
~**ed** sich befinden. ~**ion** n Lage
f; **filmed on** ~**ion** als
Außenaufnahme gedreht
lock[1] n (hair) Strähne f
lock[2] n (on door) Schloss nt; (on
canal) Schleuse f ● vt
abschließen ● vi sich
abschließen lassen. ~ **in** vt
einschließen. ~ **out** vt
ausschließen. ~ **up** vt
abschließen; einsperren
<person>
locker n Schließfach nt; (Mil)
Spind m
lock: ~**-out** n Aussperrung f.
~**smith** n Schlosser m
locomotive n Lokomotive f
locum n Vertreter(in) m(f)
locust n Heuschrecke f
lodge n (porter's) Pförtnerhaus nt
● vt (submit) einreichen;
(deposit) deponieren ● vi zur
Untermiete wohnen (**with** bei);

L

(*become fixed*) stecken bleiben.
~r n Untermieter(in) m(f)

lodging n Unterkunft f; **~s** npl
möbliertes Zimmer nt

loft n Dachboden m

lofty a (-ier, -iest) hoch

log n Baumstamm m; (*for fire*)
[Holz]scheit nt; **sleep like a ~** 🔲
wie ein Murmeltier schlafen ●vi
~ off sich abmelden; **~ on** sich
anmelden

loggerheads npl **be at ~** 🔲 sich
in den Haaren liegen

logic n Logik f. **~al** a, **-ly** adv
logisch

logo n Symbol nt, Logo nt

loiter vi herumlungern

loll vi sich lümmeln

loll|ipop n Lutscher m. **~y** n
Lutscher m; (🔲 *money*) Moneten
pl

London n London nt ●attrib
Londoner. **~er** n Londoner(in)
m(f)

lone a einzeln. **~liness** n
Einsamkeit f

lonely a (-ier, -iest) einsam

lone|r n Einzelgänger m. **~some**
a einsam

long[1] a (-er, -est) lang; <*journey*>
weit; **a ~ time** lange; **a ~ way**
weit; **in the ~ run** auf lange Sicht;
(*in the end*) letzten Endes ●adv
lange; **all day ~** den ganzen Tag;
not ~ ago vor kurzem; **before ~**
bald; **no ~er** nicht mehr; **as** or **so
~as** solange; **so ~!** 🔲 tschüs!

long[2] vi **~ for** sich sehnen nach

long-distance a Fern-; (*Sport*)
Langstrecken-

longing a, **-ly** adv sehnsüchtig ●n
Sehnsucht f

longitude n (*Geog*) Länge f

long: ~ jump n Weitsprung m.
~-lived a langlebig. **~-range** a
(*Mil, Aviat*) Langstrecken-;
<*forecast*> langfristig. **~-sighted**
a weitsichtig. **~-sleeved** a
langärmelig. **~-suffering** a

langmütig. **~-term** a langfristig.
~ wave n Langwelle. **~-winded** a
langatmig

loo n 🔲 Klo nt

look n Blick m; (*appearance*)
Aussehen nt; **[good] ~s** pl
[gutes] Aussehen nt; **have a ~ at**
sich (*dat*) ansehen; **go and have a
~** sieh mal nach ●vi sehen;
(*search*) nachsehen; (*seem*)
aussehen; **don't ~** sieh nicht hin;
~ here! hören Sie mal! **~ at**
ansehen; **~ for** suchen; **~ forward
to** sich freuen auf (+ *acc*); **~ in on**
vorbeischauen bei; **~ into**
(*examine*) nachgehen (+ *dat*); **~
like** aussehen wie; **~ on to**
<*room:*> gehen auf (+ *acc*). **~
after** vt betreuen. **~ down** vi
hinuntersehen; **~ down on s.o.**
(*fig*) auf jdn herabsehen. **~ out**
vi hinaus-/heraussehen; (*take
care*) aufpassen; **~ out for**
Ausschau halten nach; **~ out!**
Vorsicht! **~ round** vi sich
umsehen. **~ up** vi aufblicken; **~
up to s.o.** (*fig*) zu jdm aufsehen
●vt nachschlagen <*word*>

look-out n Wache f; (*prospect*)
Aussicht f; **be on the ~ for**
Ausschau halten nach

loom[1] n Webstuhl m

loom[2] vi auftauchen

loony a 🔲 verrückt

loop n Schlinge f; (*in road*)
Schleife f. **~hole** n
Hintertürchen nt; (*in the law*)
Lücke f

loose a (-r, -st), **-ly** adv lose; (*not
tight enough*) locker; (*inexact*)
frei; **be at a ~ end** nichts zu tun
haben. **~ change** n Kleingeld nt

loosen vt lockern

loot n Beute f ●vt/i plündern.
~er n Plünderer m

lop vt (*pt/pp* lopped) stutzen

lopsided a schief

lord n Herr m; (title) Lord m; **House of L~ s** ≈ Oberhaus nt; **the L~'s Prayer** das Vaterunser

lorry n Last[kraft]wagen m

lose v (pt/pp lost) ● vt verlieren; (miss) verpassen ● vi verlieren; <clock:> nachgehen; **get lost** verloren gehen; <person> sich verlaufen. **~r** n Verlierer m

loss n Verlust m; **be at a ~** nicht mehr weiter wissen

lost see lose. **~ property office** n Fundbüro nt

lot[1] n Los nt; (at auction) Posten m; **draw ~s** losen (for um)

lot[2] n **the ~** alle; (everything) alles; **a ~ [of]** viel; (many) viele; **~s of** 🗓 eine Menge; **it has changed a ~** es hat sich sehr verändert

lotion n Lotion f

lottery n Lotterie f. **~ ticket** n Los nt

loud a (-er, -est), **-ly** adv laut; <colours> grell ● adv **[out] ~** laut. **~ speaker** n Lautsprecher m

lounge n Wohnzimmer nt; (in hotel) Aufenthaltsraum m. ● vi sich lümmeln

louse n (pl lice) Laus f

lousy a (-ier, -iest) 🗓 lausig

lout n Flegel m, Lümmel m

lovable a liebenswert

love n Liebe f; (Tennis) null; **in ~** verliebt ● vt lieben; **~ doing sth** etw sehr gerne machen. **~-affair** n Liebesverhältnis nt. **~ letter** n Liebesbrief m

lovely a (-ier, -iest) schön

lover n Liebhaber m

love: ~ song n Liebeslied nt. **~ story** n Liebesgeschichte f

loving a, **-ly** adv liebevoll

low a (-er, -est) niedrig; <cloud, note> tief; <voice> leise; (depressed) niedergeschlagen ● adv niedrig; <fly, sing> tief; <speak> leise ● n (Meteorol) Tief nt; (fig) Tiefstand m

low: ~brow a geistig anspruchslos. **~cut** a <dress> tief ausgeschnitten

lower a & adv see low ● vt niedriger machen; (let down) herunterlassen; (reduce) senken

low: ~fat a fettarm. **~lands** npl Tiefland nt. **~ tide** n Ebbe f

loyal a, **-ly** adv treu. **~ty** n Treue f

lozenge n Pastille f

Ltd abbr (Limited) GmbH

lubricant n Schmiermittel nt

lubricat|e vt schmieren. **~ion** n Schmierung f

lucid a klar. **~ity** n Klarheit f

luck n Glück nt; **bad ~** Pech nt; **good ~!** viel Glück! **~ily** adv glücklicherweise, zum Glück

lucky a (-ier, -iest) glücklich; <day, number> Glücks-; **be ~** Glück haben; <thing:> Glück bringen

lucrative a einträglich

ludicrous a lächerlich

lug vt (pt/pp lugged) 🗓 schleppen

luggage n Gepäck nt

luggage: ~rack n Gepäckablage f. **~van** n Gepäckwagen m

lukewarm a lauwarm

lull n Pause f ● vt **~ to sleep** einschläfern

lullaby n Wiegenlied nt

lumber n Gerümpel nt; (Amer: timber) Bauholz m ● vt **~ s.o. with sth** jdm etw aufhalsen. **~jack** n (Amer) Holzfäller m

luminous a leuchtend

lump n Klumpen m; (of sugar) Stück nt; (swelling) Beule f; (in breast) Knoten m; (tumour) Geschwulst f; **a ~ in one's throat** 🗓 ein Kloß im Hals

lump: ~ sugar n Würfelzucker m. **~ sum** n Pauschalsumme f

lumpy a (-ier, -iest) klumpig

lunacy n Wahnsinn m

lunar a Mond-

lunatic n Wahnsinnige(r) m/f

L

lunch *n* Mittagessen *nt* ● *vi* zu Mittag essen

luncheon *n* Mittagessen *nt*. ~ **voucher** *n* Essensbon *m*

lunch: ~**-hour** *n* Mittagspause *f*. ~**-time** *n* Mittagszeit *f*

lung *n* Lungenflügel *m*; ~**s** *pl* Lunge *f*

lunge *vi* sich stürzen (**at** auf + *acc*)

lurch[1] *n* **leave in the** ~ 🛈 im Stich lassen

lurch[2] *vi* <*person:*> torkeln

lure *vt* locken

lurid *a* grell; (*sensational*) reißerisch

lurk *vi* lauern

luscious *a* lecker, köstlich

lush *a* üppig

lust *n* Begierde *f*. ~**ful** *a* lüstern

lustre *n* Glanz *m*

lusty *a* (**-ier, -iest**) kräftig

luxuriant *a* üppig

luxurious *a*, **-ly** *adv* luxuriös

luxury *n* Luxus *m* ● *attrib* Luxus-

lying *see* lie[1], lie[2]

lynch *vt* lynchen

lyric *a* lyrisch. ~**al** *a* lyrisch; (*enthusiastic*) schwärmerisch. ~ **poetry** *n* Lyrik *f*. ~**s** *npl* [Lied]text *m*

mac *n* 🛈 Regenmantel *m*

macabre *a* makaber

macaroni *n* Makkaroni *pl*

machinations *pl* Machenschaften *pl*

machine *n* Maschine *f* ● *vt* (*sew*) mit der Maschine nähen; (*Techn*) maschinell bearbeiten. ~**-gun** *n* Maschinengewehr *nt*

machinery *n* Maschinerie *f*

mackerel *n inv* Makrele *f*

mackintosh *n* Regenmantel *m*

mad *a* (**madder, maddest**) verrückt; (*dog*) tollwütig; (*fam: angry*) böse (**at** auf + *acc*)

madam *n* gnädige Frau *f*

madden *vt* (*make angry*) wütend machen

made *see* make; ~ **to measure** maßgeschneidert

mad|ly *adv* 🛈 wahnsinnig. ~**man** *n* Irre(r) *m*. ~**ness** *n* Wahnsinn *m*

madonna *n* Madonna *f*

magazine *n* Zeitschrift *f*; (*Mil, Phot*) Magazin *nt*

maggot *n* Made *f*

magic *n* Zauber *m*; (*tricks*) Zauberkunst *f* ● *a* magisch; <*word, wand*> Zauber-. ~**al** *a* zauberhaft

magician *n* Zauberer *m*; (*entertainer*) Zauberkünstler *m*

magistrate *n* ≈ Friedensrichter *m*

magnet *n* Magnet *m*. ~**ic** *a* magnetisch. ~**ism** *n* Magnetismus *m*

magnification *n* Vergrößerung *f*

magnificen|ce *n* Großartigkeit *f*. ~**t** *a*, **-ly** *adv* großartig

magnify *vt* (*pt/pp* **-ied**) vergrößern; (*exaggerate*) übertreiben. ~**ing glass** *n* Vergrößerungsglas *nt*

magnitude *n* Größe *f*; (*importance*) Bedeutung *f*

magpie *n* Elster *f*

mahogany *n* Mahagoni *nt*

maid *n* Dienstmädchen *nt*; **old** ~ (*pej*) alte Jungfer *f*

maiden *a* <*speech, voyage*> Jungfern-. ~ **name** *n* Mädchenname *m*

mail *n* Post *f* ● *vt* mit der Post schicken

mail: ~**bag** n Postsack m. ~**box** n (Amer) Briefkasten m. ~**ing list** n Postversandliste f. ~**man** n (Amer) Briefträger m. ~**order firm** n Versandhaus nt

maim vt verstümmeln

main a Haupt- ● n (water, gas, electricity) Hauptleitung f

main: ~**land** n Festland nt. ~**ly** adv hauptsächlich. ~**stay** n (fig) Stütze f. ~ **street** n Hauptstraße f

maintain vt aufrechterhalten; (keep in repair) instand halten; (support) unterhalten; (claim) behaupten

maintenance n Aufrechterhaltung f; (care) Instandhaltung f; (allowance) Unterhalt m

maize n Mais m

majestic a, -ally adv majestätisch

majesty n Majestät f

major a größer ● n (Mil) Major m; (Mus) Dur nt ● vi ~ **in** als Hauptfach studieren

majority n Mehrheit f; **in the** ~ in der Mehrzahl

major road n Hauptverkehrsstraße f

make n (brand) Marke f ● v (pt/pp made) ● vt machen; (force) zwingen; (earn) verdienen; halten <speech>; treffen <decision>; erreichen <destination> ● vi ~ **do** vi zurechtkommen (with mit). ~ **for** vi zusteuern auf (+ acc). ~ **off** vi sich davonmachen (with mit). ~ **out** vt (distinguish) ausmachen; (write out) ausstellen; (assert) behaupten. ~ **up** vt (constitute) bilden; (invent) erfinden; (apply cosmetics to) schminken; ~ **up one's mind** sich entschließen ● vi sich versöhnen; ~ **up for sth** etw wieder gutmachen; ~ **up for lost time** verlorene Zeit aufholen

make-believe n Phantasie f

maker n Hersteller m

make: ~ **shift** a behelfsmäßig ● n Notbehelf m. ~**up** n Make-up nt

maladjusted a verhaltensgestört

male a männlich ● n Mann m; (animal) Männchen nt. ~ **nurse** n Krankenpfleger m. ~ **voice choir** n Männerchor m

malice n Bosheit f

malicious a, -ly adv böswillig

malign vt verleumden

malignant a bösartig

mallet n Holzhammer m

malnutrition n Unterernährung f

malpractice n Berufsvergehen nt

malt n Malz nt

maltreat vt misshandeln. ~**ment** n Misshandlung f

mammal n Säugetier nt

mammoth a riesig

man n (pl **men**) Mann m; (mankind) der Mensch; (chess) Figur f; (draughts) Stein m ● vt (pt/pp **manned**) bemannen <ship>; bedienen <pump>; besetzen <counter>

manage vt leiten; verwalten <estate>; (cope with) fertig werden mit; ~ **to do sth** es schaffen, etw zu tun ● vi zurechtkommen; ~ **on** auskommen mit. ~**able** a <tool> handlich; <person> fügsam. ~**ment** n Leitung f; **the** ~**ment** die Geschäftsleitung f

manager n Geschäftsführer m; (of bank) Direktor m; (of estate) Verwalter m; (Sport) [Chef]trainer m. ~**ess** n Geschäftsführerin f. ~**ial** a ~**ial staff** Führungskräfte pl

managing a ~ **director** Generaldirektor m

mandat|e n Mandat nt. ~**ory** a obligatorisch

mane n Mähne f

manful a, -ly adv mannhaft

man: ~**handle** vt grob behandeln <person>. ~**hole** n Kanalschacht

m. **~hood** *n* Mannesalter *nt*;
(*quality*) Männlichkeit *f*. **~-hour**
n Arbeitsstunde *f*. **~-hunt** *n*
Fahndung *f*

mania *n* Manie *f*. **~c** *n*
Wahnsinnige(r) *m/f*

manicure *n* Maniküre *f* ● *vt*
maniküren

manifest *a*, **-ly** *adv* offensichtlich

manifesto *n* Manifest *nt*

manifold *a* mannigfaltig

manipulat|e *vt* handhaben; (*pej*)
manipulieren. **~ion** *n*
Manipulation *f*

mankind *n* die Menschheit

manly *a* männlich

man-made *a* künstlich. **~ fibre** *n*
Kunstfaser *f*

manner *n* Weise *f*; (*kind,
behaviour*) Art *f*; [**good/bad**] **~s**
[gute/schlechte] Manieren *pl*.
~ism *n* Angewohnheit *f*

manœuvrable *a* manövrierfähig

manœuvre *n* Manöver *nt* ● *vt/i*
manövrieren

manor *n* Gutshof *m*; (*house*)
Gutshaus *nt*

manpower *n* Arbeitskräfte *pl*

mansion *n* Villa *f*

manslaughter *n* Totschlag *m*

mantelpiece *n* Kaminsims *m & nt*

manual *a* Hand- ● *n* Handbuch
nt

manufacture *vt* herstellen ● *n*
Herstellung *f*. **~r** *n* Hersteller *m*

manure *n* Mist *m*

manuscript *n* Manuskript *nt*

many *a* viele ● *n* a good/great **~**
sehr viele

map *n* Landkarte *f*; (*of town*)
Stadtplan *m*

maple *n* Ahorn *m*

mar *vt* (*pt/pp* **marred**) verderben

marathon *n* Marathon *m*

marble *n* Marmor *m*; (*for game*)
Murmel *f*

March *n* März *m*

march *n* Marsch *m* ● *vi*
marschieren ● *vt* marschieren
lassen; **~ s.o. off** jdn abführen

mare *n* Stute *f*

margarine *n* Margarine *f*

margin *n* Rand *m*; (*leeway*)
Spielraum *m*; (*Comm*) Spanne *f*.
~al, **-ly** *adv* geringfügig

marigold *n* Ringelblume *f*

marina *n* Jachthafen *m*

marine *a* Meeres- ● *n* Marine *f*;
(*sailor*) Marineinfanterist *m*

marital *a* ehelich. **~ status** *n*
Familienstand *m*

maritime *a* See-

mark¹ *n* (*currency*) Mark *f*

mark² *n* Fleck *m*; (*sign*) Zeichen
nt; (*trace*) Spur *f*; (*target*) Ziel *nt*;
(*Sch*) Note *f* ● *vt* markieren;
(*spoil*) beschädigen;
(*characterize*) kennzeichnen;
(*Sch*) korrigieren; (*Sport*) decken;
~ time (*Mil*) auf der Stelle treten;
(*fig*) abwarten. **~ out** *vt*
markieren

marked *a*, **-ly** *adv* deutlich;
(*pronounced*) ausgeprägt

market *n* Markt *m* ● *vt*
vertreiben; (*launch*) auf den
Markt bringen. **~ing** *n* Marketing
nt. **~ research** *n* Marktforschung
f

marking *n* Markierung *f*; (*on
animal*) Zeichnung *f*

marksman *n* Scharfschütze *m*

marmalade *n* Orangenmarmelade
f

maroon *a* dunkelrot

marooned *a* (*fig*) von der
Außenwelt abgeschnitten

marquee *n* Festzelt *nt*

marquetry *n* Einlegearbeit *f*

marriage *n* Ehe *f*; (*wedding*)
Hochzeit *f*. **~able** *a* heiratsfähig

married *see* **marry** ● *a* verheiratet.
~ life *n* Eheleben *nt*

marrow *n* (*Anat*) Mark *nt*;
(*vegetable*) Kürbis *m*

marr|y vt/i (pt/pp **married**) heiraten; (unite) trauen; **get ~ied** heiraten

marsh n Sumpf m

marshal n Marschall m; (steward) Ordner m

marshy a sumpfig

martial a kriegerisch. **~ law** n Kriegsrecht nt

martyr n Märtyrer(in) m(f). **~dom** n Martyrium nt

marvel n Wunder nt ● vi (pt/pp **marvelled**) staunen (at über + acc). **~lous** a, **-ly** adv wunderbar

Marxis|m n Marxismus m. **~t** a marxistisch ● n Marxist(in) m(f)

marzipan n Marzipan nt

mascot n Maskottchen nt

masculin|e a männlich ● n (Gram) Maskulinum nt. **~ity** n Männlichkeit f

mash n ①, **~ed potatoes** npl Kartoffelpüree nt

mask n Maske f ● vt maskieren

masochis|m n Masochismus m. **~t** n Masochist m

mason n Steinmetz m. **~ry** n Mauerwerk nt

mass¹ n (Relig) Messe f

mass² n Masse f ● vi sich sammeln; (Mil) sich massieren

massacre n Massaker nt ● vt niedermetzeln

massage n Massage f ● vt massieren

masseu|r n Masseur m. **~se** n Masseuse f

massive a massiv; (huge) riesig

mass: **~ media** npl Massenmedien pl. **~-produce** vt in Massenproduktion herstellen. **~ production** n Massenproduktion f

mast n Mast m

master n Herr m; (teacher) Lehrer m; (craftsman, artist) Meister m; (of ship) Kapitän m ● vt meistern; beherrschen <language>

master: **~ly** a meisterhaft. **~-mind** n führender Kopf m ● vt der führende Kopf sein von. **~piece** n Meisterwerk nt. **~y** n (of subject) Beherrschung f

mat n Matte f; (on table) Untersatz m

match¹ n Wettkampf m; (in ball games) Spiel nt; (Tennis) Match nt; (marriage) Heirat f; **be a good ~ <colours:>** gut zusammenpassen; **be no ~ for s.o.** jdm nicht gewachsen sein ● vt (equal) gleichkommen (+ dat); (be like) passen zu; (find sth similar) etwas Passendes finden zu ● vi zusammenpassen

match² n Streichholz nt. **~box** n Streichholzschachtel f

mate¹ n Kumpel m; (assistant) Gehilfe m; (Naut) Maat m; (Zool) Männchen nt; (female) Weibchen nt ● vi sich paaren

mate² n (Chess) Matt nt

material n Material nt; (fabric) Stoff m; **raw ~s** Rohstoffe pl ● a materiell

material|ism n Materialismus m. **~istic** a materialistisch. **~ize** vi sich verwirklichen

maternal a mütterlich

maternity n Mutterschaft f. **~ clothes** npl Umstandskleidung f. **~ ward** n Entbindungsstation f

mathematic|al a, **-ly** adv mathematisch. **~ian** n Mathematiker(in) m(f)

mathematics n Mathematik f

maths n ① Mathe f

matinée n (Theat) Nachmittagsvorstellung f

matrimony n Ehe f

matron n (of hospital) Oberin f; (of school) Hausmutter f

matt a matt

matted a verfilzt

matter n (affair) Sache f; (Phys: substance) Materie f; **money ~s** Geldangelegenheiten pl; **what is**

M

the ~? was ist los? ●*vi* wichtig sein; ~ **to s.o.** jdm etwas ausmachen; **it doesn't** ~ es macht nichts. ~**-of-fact** *a* sachlich

mattress *n* Matratze *f*

matur|e *a* reif; (*Comm*) fällig ●*vi* reifen; <*person:*> reifer werden; (*Comm*) fällig werden ●*vt* reifen lassen. ~**ity** *n* Reife *f*; (*Comm*) Fälligkeit *f*

mauve *a* lila

maximum *a* maximal ●*n* (*pl* **-ima**) Maximum *nt*. ~ **speed** *n* Höchstgeschwindigkeit *f*

may
pres **may**, *pt* **might**
● *auxiliary verb*
····▸ (*expressing possibility*) können. **she may come** es kann sein, dass sie kommt; es ist möglich, dass sie kommt. **she might come** (*more distant possibility*) sie könnte kommen. **it may/might rain** es könnte regnen. **I may be wrong** vielleicht irre ich mich. **he may have missed his train** vielleicht hat er seinen Zug verpasst
····▸ (*expressing permission*) dürfen. **may I come in?** darf ich reinkommen? **you may smoke** Sie dürfen rauchen
····▸ (*expressing wish*) **may the best man win!** auf dass der Beste gewinnt!
····▸ (*expressing concession*) **he may be slow but he's accurate** mag *od* kann sein, dass er langsam ist, aber dafür ist er auch genau
····▸ **may/might as well** ebenso gut können. **we may/might as well go** wir könnten eigentlich ebensogut [auch] gehen. **we might as well give up** da können wir gleich aufgeben

May *n* Mai *m*

maybe *adv* vielleicht

May Day *n* der Erste Mai

mayonnaise *n* Mayonnaise *f*

mayor *n* Bürgermeister *m*. ~**ess** *n* Bürgermeisterin *f*; (*wife of mayor*) Frau Bürgermeister *f*

maze *n* Irrgarten *m*; (*fig*) Labyrinth *nt*

me *pron* (*acc*) mich; (*dat*) mir; **it's** ~ Ⓣ ich bin es

meadow *n* Wiese *f*

meagre *a* dürftig

meal *n* Mahlzeit *f*; (*food*) Essen *nt*; (*grain*) Schrot *m*

mean¹ *a* (**-er, -est**) (*miserly*) geizig; (*unkind*) gemein; (*poor*) schäbig

mean² *a* mittlere(r,s) ●*n* (*average*) Durchschnitt *m*

mean³ *vt* (*pt/pp* **meant**) heißen; (*signify*) bedeuten; (*intend*) beabsichtigen; **I** ~ **it** das ist mein Ernst; ~ **well** es gut meinen; **be meant for** <*present:*> bestimmt sein für; <*remark:*> gerichtet sein an (+ *acc*)

meaning *n* Bedeutung *f*. ~**ful** *a* bedeutungsvoll. ~**less** *a* bedeutungslos

means *n* Möglichkeit *f*, Mittel *nt*; ~ **of transport** Verkehrsmittel *nt*; **by** ~ **of** durch; **by all** ~! aber natürlich! **by no** ~ keineswegs ●*npl* (*resources*) [Geld]mittel *pl*

meant *see* **mean³**

meantime *n* **in the** ~ in der Zwischenzeit ●*adv* inzwischen

meanwhile *adv* inzwischen

measles *n* Masern *pl*

measure *n* Maß *nt*; (*action*) Maßnahme *f* ●*vt/i* messen; ~ **up to** (*fig*) herankommen an (+ *acc*). ~**d** *a* gemessen. ~**ment** *n* Maß *nt*

meat *n* Fleisch *nt*

mechan|ic *n* Mechaniker *m*. ~**ical** *a*, **-ly** *adv* mechanisch. ~**ical engineering** Maschinenbau *m*

mechan|ism *n* Mechanismus *m*. ~**ize** *vt* mechanisieren

medal n Orden m; (*Sport*) Medaille f

medallist n Medaillengewinner(in) m(f)

meddle vi sich einmischen (**in** in + acc); (*tinker*) herumhantieren (**with** an + acc)

media see **medium** ● n pl the ~ die Medien pl

mediat|e vi vermitteln. ~**or** n Vermittler(in) m(f)

medical a medizinisch; <*treatment*> ärztlich ● n ärztliche Untersuchung f. ~ **insurance** n Krankenversicherung f. ~ **student** n Medizinstudent m

medicat|ed a medizinisch. ~**ion** n (*drugs*) Medikamente pl

medicinal a medizinisch; <*plant*> heilkräftig

medicine n Medizin f; (*preparation*) Medikament nt

medieval a mittelalterlich

mediocr|e a mittelmäßig. ~**ity** n Mittelmäßigkeit f

meditat|e vi nachdenken (**on** über + acc). ~**ion** n Meditation f

Mediterranean n Mittelmeer nt ● a Mittelmeer-

medium a mittlere(r,s); <*steak*> medium; **of** ~ **size** von mittlerer Größe ● n (pl **media**) Medium nt; (*means*) Mittel nt

medium: ~-**sized** a mittelgroß. ~ **wave** n Mittelwelle f

medley n Gemisch nt; (*Mus*) Potpourri nt

meek a (-**er**, -**est**), -**ly** adv sanftmütig; (*unprotesting*) widerspruchslos

meet v (pt/pp **met**) ● vt treffen; (*by chance*) begegnen (+ dat); (*at station*) abholen; (*make the acquaintance of*) kennen lernen; stoßen auf (+ acc) <*problem*>; bezahlen <*bill*>; erfüllen <*requirements*> ● vi sich treffen; (*for the first time*) sich kennen lernen

meeting n Treffen nt; (*by chance*) Begegnung f; (*discussion*) Besprechung f; (*of committee*) Sitzung f; (*large*) Versammlung f

megalomania n Größenwahnsinn m

megaphone n Megaphon nt

melancholy a melancholisch ● n Melancholie f

mellow a (-**er**, -**est**) <*fruit*> ausgereift; <*sound, person*> sanft ● vi reifer werden

melodious a melodiös

melodramatic a, -**ally** adv melodramatisch

melody n Melodie f

melon n Melone f

melt vt/i schmelzen

member n Mitglied nt; (*of family*) Angehörige(r) m/f; **M~ of Parliament** Abgeordnete(r) m/f. ~**ship** n Mitgliedschaft f; (*members*) Mitgliederzahl f

memento n Andenken nt

memo n Mitteilung f

memoirs n pl Memoiren pl

memorable a denkwürdig

memorial n Denkmal nt. ~ **service** n Gedenkfeier f

memorize vt sich (dat) einprägen

memory n Gedächtnis nt; (*thing remembered*) Erinnerung f; (*of computer*) Speicher m; **from** ~ auswendig; **in** ~ **of** zur Erinnerung an (+ acc)

men see **man**

menac|e n Drohung f; (*nuisance*) Plage f ● vt bedrohen. ~**ing** a, ~**ly** adv drohend

mend vt reparieren; (*patch*) flicken; ausbessern <*clothes*>

menfolk n pl Männer pl

menial a niedrig

menopause n Wechseljahre pl

mental a, -**ly** adv geistig; (🄘 *mad*) verrückt. ~ **arithmetic** n Kopfrechnen nt. ~ **illness** n Geisteskrankheit f

mentality n Mentalität f

M

mention n Erwähnung f ● vt erwähnen; **don't ~ it** keine Ursache; bitte
menu n Speisekarte f
merchandise n Ware f
merchant n Kaufmann m; (*dealer*) Händler m. ~ **navy** n Handelsmarine f
merci|ful a barmherzig. ~**fully** adv ⚐ glücklicherweise. ~**less** a, -**ly** adv erbarmungslos
mercury n Quecksilber nt
mercy n Barmherzigkeit f, Gnade f; **be at s.o.'s ~** jdm ausgeliefert sein
mere a, -**ly** adv bloß
merest a kleinste(r,s)
merge vi zusammenlaufen; (*Comm*) fusionieren
merger n Fusion f
meringue n Baiser nt
merit n Verdienst nt; (*advantage*) Vorzug m; (*worth*) Wert m ● vt verdienen
merry a (-ier, -iest) fröhlich
merry-go-round n Karussell nt
mesh n Masche f
mesmerized a (*fig*) [wie] gebannt
mess n Durcheinander nt; (*trouble*) Schwierigkeiten pl; (*something spilt*) Bescherung f ⚐; (*Mil*) Messe f; **make a ~ of** (*botch*) verpfuschen ● vt ~ **up** in Unordnung bringen; (*botch*) verpfuschen ● vi ~ **about** herumalbern; (*tinker*) herumspielen (**with** mit)
message n Nachricht f; **give s.o. a ~** jdm etwas ausrichten
messenger n Bote m
Messrs n pl see **Mr**; (*on letter*) ~ **Smith** Firma Smith
messy a (-ier, -iest) schmutzig; (*untidy*) unordentlich
met see **meet**
metal n Metall nt ● a Metall-. ~**lic** a metallisch
metaphor n Metapher f. ~**ical** a, -**ly** adv metaphorisch

meteor n Meteor m. ~**ic** a kometenhaft
meteorological a Wetter-
meteorolog|ist n Meteorologe m/ -gin f. ~**y** n Meteorologie f
meter¹ n Zähler m
meter² n (*Amer*) = **metre**
method n Methode f; (*Culin*) Zubereitung f
methodical a, -**ly** adv systematisch, methodisch
methylated a ~ **spirit[s]** Brennspiritus m
meticulous a, -**ly** adv sehr genau
metre n Meter m & n; (*rhythm*) Versmaß nt
metric a metrisch
metropolis n Metropole f
metropolitan a hauptstädtisch; (*international*) weltstädtisch
mew n Miau nt ● vi miauen
Mexican a mexikanisch ● n Mexikaner(in) m(f). **Mexico** n Mexiko nt
miaow n Miau nt ● vi miauen
mice see **mouse**
micro: ~**film** n Mikrofilm m. ~**phone** n Mikrofon nt. ~**scope** n Mikroskop nt. ~**scopic** a mikroskopisch. ~**wave [oven]** n Mikrowellenherd m
mid a ~ **May** Mitte Mai; **in ~ air** in der Luft
midday n Mittag m
middle a mittlere(r,s); **the M~ Ages** das Mittelalter; **the ~ class[es]** der Mittelstand; **the M~ East** der Nahe Osten ● n Mitte f; **in the ~ of the night** mitten in der Nacht
middle: ~-**aged** a mittleren Alters. ~-**class** a bürgerlich
midge n [kleine] Mücke f
midget n Liliputaner(in) m(f)
Midlands npl **the ~** Mittelengland n
midnight n Mitternacht f
midriff n ⚐ Taille f

midst n in the ~ of mitten in (+ dat); in our ~ unter uns

mid: ~**summer** n Hochsommer m. ~**way** adv auf halbem Wege. ~**wife** n Hebamme f. ~**winter** n Mitte f des Winters

might¹ v aux I ~ vielleicht; it ~ be true es könnte wahr sein; he asked if he ~ go er fragte, ob er gehen dürfte; you ~ have drowned du hättest ertrinken können

might² n Macht f

mighty a (-ier, -iest) mächtig

migraine n Migräne f

migrat|e vi abwandern; <birds> ziehen. ~**ion** n Wanderung f; (of birds) Zug m

mike n 🄸 Mikrofon nt

mild a (-er, -est) mild

mild|ly adv leicht; to put it ~ly gelinde gesagt. ~**ness** n Milde f

mile n Meile f (= 1,6 km); ~s too big 🄸 viel zu groß

mile|age n Meilenzahl f; (of car) Meilenstand m

militant a militant

military a militärisch. ~ **service** n Wehrdienst m

milk n Milch f ● vt melken

milk: ~**man** n Milchmann m. ~**shake** n Milchmixgetränk nt. ~**tooth** n Milchzahn m

milky a (-ier, -iest) milchig. **M~ Way** n (Astr) Milchstraße f

mill n Mühle f; (factory) Fabrik f

millennium n Jahrtausend nt

milli|gram n Milligramm m. ~**metre** n Millimeter m & nt

million n Million f; a ~ pounds eine Million Pfund. ~**aire** n Millionär(in) m(f)

mime n Pantomime f ● vt pantomimisch darstellen

mimic n Imitator m ● vt (pt/pp mimicked) nachahmen

mince n Hackfleisch nt ● vt (Culin) durchdrehen; not ~ words kein Blatt vor den Mund nehmen

mince: ~**meat** n Masse f aus Korinthen, Zitronat usw; make ~ meat of (fig) vernichtend schlagen. ~ **pie** n mit 'mincemeat' gefülltes Pastetchen nt

mincer n Fleischwolf m

mind n Geist m; (sanity) Verstand m; give s.o. a piece of one's ~ jdm gehörig die Meinung sagen; make up one's ~ sich entschließen; be out of one's ~ nicht bei Verstand sein; have sth in ~ etw im Sinn haben; bear sth in ~ an etw (acc) denken; have a good ~ to große Lust haben, zu; I have changed my ~ ich habe es mir anders überlegt ● vt aufpassen auf (+ acc); I don't ~ the noise der Lärm stört mich nicht; ~ the step! Achtung Stufe! ● vi (care) sich kümmern (about um); I don't ~ mir macht es nichts aus; never ~! macht nichts! do you ~ if? haben Sie etwas dagegen, wenn? ~ out vi aufpassen

mindless a geistlos

mine¹ poss pron meine(r), meins; a friend of ~ ein Freund von mir; that is ~ das gehört mir

mine² n Bergwerk nt; (explosive) Mine f ● vt abbauen; (Mil) verminen

miner n Bergarbeiter m

mineral n Mineral nt. ~ **water** n Mineralwasser nt

minesweeper n Minenräumboot nt

mingle vi ~ with sich mischen unter (+ acc)

miniature a Klein- ● n Miniatur f

mini|bus n Kleinbus m. ~**cab** n Kleintaxi nt

minim|al a minimal. ~**um** n (pl -ima) Minimum nt ● a Mindest-

mining n Bergbau m

miniskirt n Minirock m

minister n Minister m; (Relig) Pastor m. ~**ial** a ministeriell

ministry n (Pol) Ministerium nt

mink n Nerz m

minor a kleiner; (less important) unbedeutend ● n Minderjährige(r) m/f; (Mus) Moll nt

minority n Minderheit f

minor road n Nebenstraße f

mint¹ n Münzstätte f ● a <stamp> postfrisch; in ~ condition wie neu ● vt prägen

mint² n (herb) Minze f; (sweet) Pfefferminzbonbon m & nt

minus prep minus, weniger; (🖃 without) ohne

minute¹ n Minute f; in a ~ (shortly) gleich; ~s pl (of meeting) Protokoll nt

minute² a winzig

mirac|le n Wunder nt. ~ulous a wunderbar

mirror n Spiegel m ● vt widerspiegeln

mirth n Heiterkeit f

misadventure n Missgeschick nt

misapprehension n Missverständnis nt; be under a ~ sich irren

misbehav|e vi sich schlecht benehmen. ~iour n schlechtes Benehmen nt

miscalcu|late vt falsch berechnen ● vi sich verrechnen. ~lation n Fehlkalkulation f

miscarriage n Fehlgeburt f

miscellaneous a vermischt

mischief n Unfug m

mischievous a, -ly adv schelmisch; (malicious) boshaft

misconception n falsche Vorstellung f

misconduct n unkorrektes Verhalten nt; (adultery) Ehebruch m

miser n Geizhals m

miserable a, -bly adv unglücklich; (wretched) elend

miserly adv geizig

misery n Elend nt; (🖃 person) Miesepeter m

misfire vi fehlzünden; (go wrong) fehlschlagen

misfit n Außenseiter(in) m(f)

misfortune n Unglück nt

misgivings npl Bedenken pl

misguided a töricht

mishap n Missgeschick nt

misinform vt falsch unterrichten

misinterpret vt missdeuten

misjudge vt falsch beurteilen

mislay vt (pt/pp -laid) verlegen

mislead vt (pt/pp -led) irreführen. ~ing a irreführend

mismanage vt schlecht verwalten. ~ment n Misswirtschaft f

misnomer n Fehlbezeichnung f

misprint n Druckfehler m

misquote vt falsch zitieren

misrepresent vt falsch darstellen

miss n Fehltreffer m ● vt verpassen; (fail to hit or find) verfehlen; (fail to attend) versäumen; (fail to notice) übersehen; (feel the loss of) vermissen ● vi (fail to hit) nicht treffen. ~ out vt auslassen

Miss n (pl -es) Fräulein nt

missile n [Wurf]geschoss nt; (Mil) Rakete f

missing a fehlend; (lost) verschwunden; (Mil) vermisst; be ~ fehlen

mission n Auftrag m; (Mil) Einsatz m; (Relig) Mission f

missionary n Missionar(in) m(f)

misspell vt (pt/pp -spelt or -spelled) falsch schreiben

mist n Dunst m; (fog) Nebel m; (on window) Beschlag m ● vi ~ up beschlagen

mistake n Fehler m; by ~ aus Versehen ● vt (pt mistook, pp mistaken); ~ for verwechseln mit

mistaken a falsch; be ~ sich irren. ~ly adv irrtümlicherweise

mistletoe n Mistel f

mistress n Herrin f; (teacher) Lehrerin f; (lover) Geliebte f

mistrust n Misstrauen nt ● vt misstrauen (+ dat)

misty a (-ier, -iest) dunstig; (foggy) neblig; (fig) unklar

misunderstand vt (pt/pp -stood) missverstehen. ~ing n Missverständnis nt

misuse¹ vt missbrauchen

misuse² n Missbrauch m

mitigating a mildernd

mix n Mischung f ● vt mischen ● vi sich mischen; ~ with (associate with) verkehren mit. ~ up vt mischen; (muddle) durcheinander bringen; (mistake for) verwechseln (with mit)

mixed a gemischt; be ~ up durcheinander sein

mixer n Mischmaschine f; (Culin) Küchenmaschine f

mixture n Mischung f; (medicine) Mixtur f; (Culin) Teig m

mix-up n Durcheinander nt; (confusion) Verwirrung f; (mistake) Verwechslung f

moan n Stöhnen nt ● vi stöhnen; (complain) jammern

mob n Horde f; (rabble) Pöbel m; (🄸 gang) Bande f ● vt (pt/pp mobbed) herfallen über (+ acc); belagern <celebrity>

mobile a beweglich ● n Mobile nt; (telephone) Handy nt. ~ home n Wohnwagen m. ~ phone n Handy nt

mobility n Beweglichkeit f

mock a Schein- ● vt verspotten. ~ery n Spott m

mock-up n Modell nt

mode n [Art und] Weise f; (fashion) Mode f

model n Modell nt; (example) Vorbild nt; [fashion] ~ Mannequin nt ● a Modell-; (exemplary) Muster- ● v (pt/pp modelled) ● vt formen, modellieren; vorführen <clothes>

● vi Mannequin sein; (for artist) Modell stehen

moderate¹ vt mäßigen

moderate² a mäßig; <opinion> gemäßigt. ~ly adv mäßig; (fairly) einigermaßen

moderation n Mäßigung f; in ~ mit Maß[en]

modern a modern. ~ize vt modernisieren. ~ languages npl neuere Sprachen pl

modest a bescheiden; (decorous) schamhaft. ~y n Bescheidenheit f

modif|ication n Abänderung f. ~y vt (pt/pp -fied) abändern

moist a (-er, -est) feucht

moisten vt befeuchten

moistur|e n Feuchtigkeit f. ~izer n Feuchtigkeitscreme f

molar n Backenzahn m

mole¹ n Leberfleck m

mole² n (Zool) Maulwurf m

molecule n Molekül nt

molest vt belästigen

mollify vt (pt/pp -ied) besänftigen

mollycoddle vt verzärteln

molten a geschmolzen

mom n (Amer fam) Mutti f

moment n Moment m, Augenblick m; at the ~ im Augenblick, augenblicklich. ~ary a vorübergehend

momentous a bedeutsam

momentum n Schwung m

monarch n Monarch(in) m(f). ~y n Monarchie f

monastery n Kloster nt

Monday n Montag m

money n Geld nt

money: ~-box n Sparbüchse f. ~-lender n Geldverleiher m. ~ order n Zahlungsanweisung f

mongrel n Promenadenmischung f

monitor n (Techn) Monitor m ● vt überwachen <progress>; abhören <broadcast>

monk n Mönch m

M

monkey n Affe m

mono n Mono nt

monogram n Monogramm nt

monologue n Monolog m

monopol|ize vt monopolisieren. **~y** n Monopol nt

monosyllable n einsilbiges Wort nt

monotone n in a **~** mit monotoner Stimme

monoton|ous a, **-ly** adv eintönig, monoton; (tedious) langweilig. **~y** n Eintönigkeit f, Monotonie f

monster n Ungeheuer nt; (cruel person) Unmensch m

monstrosity n Monstrosität f

monstrous a ungeheuer; (outrageous) ungeheuerlich

month n Monat m. **~ly** a & adv monatlich ● n (periodical) Monatszeitschrift f

monument n Denkmal nt. **~al** a (fig) monumental

moo n Muh nt ● vi (pt/pp mooed) muhen

mood n Laune f; be in a good/bad **~** gute/schlechte Laune haben

moody a (-ier, -iest) launisch

moon n Mond m; over the **~** 🛈 überglücklich

moon: ~light n Mondschein m. **~lighting** n 🛈 ≈ Schwarzarbeit f. **~lit** a mondhell

moor¹ n Moor nt

moor² vt (Naut) festmachen ● vi anlegen

mop n Mopp m; **~** of hair Wuschelkopf m ● vt (pt/pp mopped) wischen. **~** up vt aufwischen

moped n Moped nt

moral a, **-ly** adv moralisch, sittlich; (virtuous) tugendhaft ● n Moral f; **~s** pl Moral f

morale n Moral f

morality n Sittlichkeit f

morbid a krankhaft; (gloomy) trübe

more a, adv & n mehr; (in addition) noch; **a few ~** noch ein paar; **any ~** noch etwas; **once ~** noch einmal; **~ or less** mehr oder weniger; **some ~ tea?** noch etwas Tee? **~ interesting** interessanter; **~ [and ~] quickly** [immer] schneller

moreover adv außerdem

morgue n Leichenschauhaus nt

morning n Morgen m; in the **~** morgens, am Morgen; (tomorrow) morgen früh

Morocco n Marokko nt

moron n 🛈 Idiot m

morose a, **-ly** adv mürrisch

morsel n Happen m

mortal a sterblich; (fatal) tödlich ● n Sterbliche(r) m/f. **~ity** n Sterblichkeit f. **~ly** adv tödlich

mortar n Mörtel m

mortgage n Hypothek f ● vt hypothekarisch belasten

mortuary n Leichenhalle f; (public) Leichenschauhaus nt; (Amer: undertaker's) Bestattungsinstitut nt

mosaic n Mosaik nt

Moscow n Moskau nt

mosque n Moschee f

mosquito n (pl **-es**) [Stech]mücke f, Schnake f; (tropical) Moskito m

moss n Moos nt. **~y** a moosig

most a der/die/das meiste; (majority) die meisten; **for the ~ part** zum größten Teil ● adv am meisten; (very) höchst; **the ~ interesting day** der interessanteste Tag; **~ unlikely** höchst unwahrscheinlich ● n das meiste; **~ of them** die meisten [von ihnen]; **at [the] ~** höchstens; **~ of the time** die meiste Zeit. **~ly** adv meist

MOT n ≈ TÜV m

motel n Motel nt

moth n Nachtfalter m; [clothes-] **~** Motte f

mothball n Mottenkugel f

mother n Mutter f

mother: ~**hood** n Mutterschaft f.
~**-in-law** n (pl ~s-in-law)
Schwiegermutter f. ~**land** n
Mutterland nt. ~**ly** a mütterlich.
~**-of-pearl** n Perlmutter f. ~**to-**
be n werdende Mutter f

mothproof a mottenfest

motif n Motiv nt

motion n Bewegung f; (proposal)
Antrag m. ~**less** a, -ly adv
bewegungslos

motivat|e vt motivieren. ~**ion** n
Motivation f

motive n Motiv nt

motor n Motor m; (car) Auto nt
● a Motor-; (Anat) motorisch ● vi
[mit dem Auto] fahren

motor: ~**bike** n Ⓘ Motorrad nt. ~
boat n Motorboot nt. ~ **car** n
Auto nt, Wagen m. ~**cycle** n
Motorrad nt. ~**cyclist** n
Motorradfahrer m. ~**ing** n
Autofahren nt. ~**ist** n
Autofahrer(in) m(f). ~ **vehicle** n
Kraftfahrzeug nt. ~**way** n
Autobahn f

mottled a gesprenkelt

motto n (pl -es) Motto nt

mould¹ n (fungus) Schimmel m

mould² n Form f ● vt formen (into
zu). ~**ing** n (Archit) Fries m

mouldy a schimmelig; (Ⓘ
worthless) schäbig

mound n Hügel m; (of stones)
Haufen m

mount n (animal) Reittier nt; (of
jewel) Fassung f; (of photo,
picture) Passepartout nt ● vt (get
on) steigen auf (+ acc); (on
pedestal) montieren auf (+ acc);
besteigen <horse>; fassen
<jewel>; aufziehen <photo,
picture> ● vi aufsteigen;
<tension:> steigen. ~ **up** vi sich
häufen; (add up) sich anhäufen

mountain n Berg m

mountaineer n Bergsteiger(in)
m(f). ~**ing** n Bergsteigen nt

mountainous a bergig, gebirgig

mourn vt betrauern ● vi trauern
(for um). ~**er** n Trauernde(r) m/f.
~**ful** a, -ly adv trauervoll. ~**ing** n
Trauer f

mouse n (pl mice) Maus f. ~**trap**
n Mausefalle f

moustache n Schnurrbart m

mouth¹ vt ~ sth etw lautlos mit
den Lippen sagen

mouth² n Mund m; (of animal)
Maul nt; (of river) Mündung f

mouth: ~**ful** n Mundvoll m; (bite)
Bissen m. ~**organ** n
Mundharmonika f. ~**wash** n
Mundwasser nt

movable a beweglich

move n Bewegung f; (fig) Schritt
m; (moving house) Umzug m; (in
board game) Zug m; on the ~
unterwegs; **get a** ~ **on** Ⓘ sich
beeilen ● vt bewegen;
(emotionally) rühren; (move
along) rücken; (in board game)
ziehen; (take away) wegnehmen;
wegfahren <car>; (rearrange)
umstellen; (transfer) versetzen
<person>; verlegen <office>;
(propose) beantragen; ~ **house**
umziehen ● vi sich bewegen;
(move house) umziehen; don't ~!
stillhalten! (stop) stillstehen! ~
along vt/i weiterrücken. ~ **away**
vt/i wegrücken; (move house)
wegziehen. ~ **in** vi einziehen. ~
off vi <vehicle:> losfahren. ~ **out**
vi ausziehen. ~ **over** vt/i [zur
Seite] rücken. ~ **up** vi aufrücken

movement n Bewegung f; (Mus)
Satz m; (of clock) Uhrwerk nt

movie n (Amer) Film m; **go to the**
~**s** ins Kino gehen

moving a beweglich; (touching)
rührend

mow vt (pt mowed, pp mown or
mowed) mähen

mower n Rasenmäher m

MP abbr see **Member of Parliament**

Mr n (pl **Messrs**) Herr m

M

Mrs *n* Frau *f*
Ms *n* Frau *f*
much *a, adv & n* viel; **as ~ as** so viel wie; **~ loved** sehr geliebt
muck *n* Mist *m*; (🗉 *filth*) Dreck *m*. **~ about** *vi* herumalbern; (*tinker*) herumspielen (**with** mit). **~ out** *vt* ausmisten. **~ up** *vt* 🗉 vermasseln; (*make dirty*) schmutzig machen
mucky *a* (**-ier, -iest**) dreckig
mud *n* Schlamm *m*
muddle *n* Durcheinander *nt*; (*confusion*) Verwirrung *f* ● *vt* **~ [up]** durcheinander bringen
muddy *a* (**-ier, -iest**) schlammig; <*shoes*> schmutzig
mudguard *n* Kotflügel *m*; (*on bicycle*) Schutzblech *nt*
muffle *vt* dämpfen
muffler *n* Schal *m*; (*Amer, Auto*) Auspufftopf *m*
mug[1] *n* Becher *m*; (*for beer*) Bierkrug *m*; (🗉 *face*) Visage *f*; (🗉 *simpleton*) Trottel *m*
mug[2] *vt* (*pt/pp* **mugged**) überfallen. **~ger** *n* Straßenräuber *m*. **~ging** *n* Straßenraub *m*
muggy *a* (**-ier, -iest**) schwül
mule *n* Maultier *nt*
mulled *a* **~ wine** Glühwein *m*
multi: ~coloured *a* vielfarbig, bunt. **~lingual** *a* mehrsprachig. **~national** *a* multinational
multiple *a* vielfach; (*with pl*) mehrere ● *n* Vielfache(s) *nt*
multiplication *n* Multiplikation *f*
multiply *v* (*pt/pp* **-ied**) ● *vt* multiplizieren (**by** mit) ● *vi* sich vermehren
multistorey *a* **~ car park** Parkhaus *nt*
mum *n* 🗉 Mutti *f*
mumble *vt/i* murmeln
mummy[1] *n* 🗉 Mutti *f*
mummy[2] *n* (*Archaeol*) Mumie *f*
mumps *n* Mumps *m*
munch *vt/i* mampfen

municipal *a* städtisch
munitions *npl* Kriegsmaterial *nt*
mural *n* Wandgemälde *nt*
murder *n* Mord *m* ● *vt* ermorden. **~er** *n* Mörder *m*. **~ess** *n* Mörderin *f*. **~ous** *a* mörderisch
murky *a* (**-ier, -iest**) düster
murmur *n* Murmeln *nt* ● *vt/i* murmeln
muscle *n* Muskel *m*
muscular *a* Muskel-; (*strong*) muskulös
museum *n* Museum *nt*
mushroom *n* [essbarer] Pilz *m*, *esp* Champignon *m* ● *vi* (*fig*) wie Pilze aus dem Boden schießen
mushy *a* breiig
music *n* Musik *f*; (*written*) Noten *pl*; **set to ~** vertonen
musical *a* musikalisch ● *n* Musical *nt*. **~ box** *n* Spieldose *f*. **~ instrument** *n* Musikinstrument *nt*
musician *n* Musiker(in) *m(f)*
music-stand *n* Notenständer *m*
Muslim *a* mohammedanisch ● *n* Mohammedaner(in) *m(f)*
must *v aux* (*nur Präsens*) müssen; (*with negative*) dürfen ● *n* **a ~** 🗉 ein Muss *nt*
mustard *n* Senf *m*
musty *a* (**-ier, -iest**) muffig
mute *a* stumm
mutilat|e *vt* verstümmeln. **~ion** *n* Verstümmelung *f*
mutin|ous *a* meuterisch. **~y** *n* Meuterei *f* ● *vi* (*pt/pp* **-ied**) meutern
mutter *n* Murmeln *nt* ● *vt/i* murmeln
mutton *n* Hammelfleisch *nt*
mutual *a* gegenseitig; (🗉 *common*) gemeinsam. **~ly** *adv* gegenseitig
muzzle *n* (*of animal*) Schnauze *f*; (*of firearm*) Mündung *f*; (*for dog*) Maulkorb *m*
my *a* mein

myself *pron* selbst; *(refl)* mich; **by ~** allein; **I thought to ~** ich habe mir gedacht

mysterious *a*, **-ly** *adv* geheimnisvoll; *(puzzling)* mysteriös, rätselhaft

mystery *n* Geheimnis *nt*; *(puzzle)* Rätsel *nt*; **~ [story]** Krimi *m*

mysti|c[al] *a* mystisch. **~cism** *n* Mystik *f*

mystified *a* **be ~** vor einem Rätsel stehen

mystique *n* geheimnisvoller Zauber *m*

myth *n* Mythos *m*; *(□ untruth)* Märchen *nt*. **~ical** *a* mythisch; *(fig)* erfunden

mythology *n* Mythologie *f*

nab *vt* *(pt/pp* **nabbed)** □ erwischen

nag¹ *n* *(horse)* Gaul *m*

nag² *vt/i* *(pp/pp* **nagged)** herumnörgeln (**s.o.** an jdm)

nail *n* *(Anat, Techn)* Nagel *m*; **on the ~** □ sofort ● *vt* nageln (**to an** + *acc*)

nail: **~-brush** *n* Nagelbürste *f*. **~-file** *n* Nagelfeile *f*. **~ scissors** *npl* Nagelschere *f*. **~ varnish** *n* Nagellack *m*

naïve *a*, **-ly** *adv* naiv. **~ty** *n* Naivität *f*

naked *a* nackt; *<flame>* offen; **with the ~ eye** mit bloßem Auge. **~ness** *n* Nacktheit *f*

name *n* Name *m*; *(reputation)* Ruf *m*; **by ~** dem Namen nach; **by the ~ of** namens; **call s.o. ~s** □ jdn beschimpfen ● *vt* nennen; *(give a name to)* einen Namen geben (+ *dat*); *(announce publicly)* den Namen bekannt geben von. **~less** *a* namenlos. **~ly** *adv* nämlich

name: **~-plate** *n* Namensschild *nt*. **~sake** *n* Namensvetter *m*/ Namensschwester *f*

nanny *n* Kindermädchen *nt*

nap *n* Nickerchen *nt*

napkin *n* Serviette *f*

nappy *n* Windel *f*

narcotic *n* *(drug)* Rauschgift *nt*

narrat|e *vt* erzählen. **~ion** *n* Erzählung *f*

narrative *n* Erzählung *f*

narrator *n* Erzähler(in) *m(f)*

narrow *a* (**-er**, **-est**) schmal; *(restricted)* eng; *<margin, majority>* knapp; **have a ~ escape** mit knapper Not davonkommen ● *vi* sich verengen. **~-minded** *a* engstirnig

nasal *a* nasal; *(Med & Anat)* Nasen-

nasty *a* (**-ier**, **-iest**) übel; *(unpleasant)* unangenehm; *(unkind)* boshaft; *(serious)* schlimm

nation *n* Nation *f*; *(people)* Volk *nt*

national *a* national; *<newspaper>* überregional; *<campaign>* landesweit ● *n* Staatsbürger(in) *m(f)*

national: **~ anthem** *n* Nationalhymne *f*. **N~ Health Service** *n* staatlicher Gesundheitsdienst *m*. **N~ Insurance** *n* Sozialversicherung *f*

nationalism *n* Nationalismus *m*

nationality *n* Staatsangehörigkeit *f*

national|ization *n* Verstaatlichung *f*. **~ize** *vt* verstaatlichen

native *a* einheimisch; *(innate)* angeboren ● *n* Eingeborene(r) *m/f*; *(local inhabitant)*

Einheimische(r) *m/f*; **a** ~ **of**
Vienna ein gebürtiger Wiener
native: ~ **land** *n* Heimatland *nt*.
~ **language** *n* Muttersprache *f*
natter *vi* 🖬 schwatzen
natural *a*, **-ly** *adv* natürlich; ~[-
coloured] naturfarben
natural: ~ **gas** *n* Erdgas *nt*. ~
history *n* Naturkunde *f*
naturalist *n* Naturforscher *m*
natural|ization *n* Einbürgerung *f*.
~**ize** *vt* einbürgern
nature *n* Natur *f*; (*kind*) Art *f*; **by**
~ von Natur aus. ~ **reserve** *n*
Naturschutzgebiet *nt*
naughty *a* (**-ier, -iest**), **-ily** *adv*
unartig; (*slightly indecent*) gewagt
nausea *n* Übelkeit *f*
nautical *a* nautisch. ~ **mile** *n*
Seemeile *f*
naval *a* Marine-
nave *n* Kirchenschiff *nt*
navel *n* Nabel *m*
navigable *a* schiffbar
navigat|e *vi* navigieren ● *vt*
befahren <*river*>. ~**ion** *n*
Navigation *f*
navy *n* [Kriegs]marine *f* ● *a* ~
[blue] marineblau
near *a* (**-er, -est**) nah[e]; **the** ~**est**
bank die nächste Bank ● *adv*
nahe; **draw** ~ sich nähern ● *prep*
nahe an (+ *dat/acc*); in der Nähe
von
near: ~**by** *a* nahe gelegen, nahe
liegend. ~**ly** *adv* fast, beinahe;
not ~**ly** bei weitem nicht. ~**ness**
n Nähe *f*. ~ **side** *n* Beifahrerseite
f. ~-**sighted** *a* (*Amer*) kurzsichtig
neat *a* (**-er, -est**), **-ly** *adv* adrett;
(*tidy*) ordentlich; (*clever*)
geschickt; (*undiluted*) pur. ~**ness**
n Ordentlichkeit *f*
necessarily *adv*
notwendigerweise; **not** ~ nicht
unbedingt
necessary *a* nötig, notwendig
necessit|ate *vt* notwendig
machen. ~**y** *n* Notwendigkeit *f*;

work from ~**y** arbeiten, weil man
es nötig hat
neck *n* Hals *m*; ~ **and** ~ Kopf an
Kopf
necklace *n* Halskette *f*
neckline *n* Halsausschnitt *m*
née *a* ~ X geborene X
need *n* Bedürfnis *nt*; (*misfortune*)
Not *f*; **be in** ~ **of** brauchen; **in case**
of ~ notfalls; **if** ~ **be** wenn nötig;
there is a ~ **for** es besteht ein
Bedarf an (+ *dat*); **there is no** ~
for that das ist nicht nötig ● *vt*
brauchen; **you** ~ **not go** du
brauchst nicht zu gehen; ~ **I**
come? muss ich kommen? **I** ~ **to**
know ich muss es wissen
needle *n* Nadel *f*
needless *a*, **-ly** *adv* unnötig; ~ **to**
say selbstverständlich, natürlich
needlework *n* Nadelarbeit *f*
needy *a* (**-ier, -iest**) bedürftig
negation *n* Verneinung *f*
negative *a* negativ ● *n*
Verneinung *f*; (*photo*) Negativ *nt*
neglect *n* Vernachlässigung *f* ● *vt*
vernachlässigen; (*omit*)
versäumen (**to** zun). ~**ed** *a*
verwahrlost. ~**ful** *a* nachlässig
negligen|ce *n* Nachlässigkeit *f*.
~**t** *a*, **-ly** *adv* nachlässig
negligible *a* unbedeutend
negotiat|e *vt* aushandeln; (*Auto*)
nehmen <*bend*> ● *vi* verhandeln.
~**ion** *n* Verhandlung *f*. ~**or** *n*
Unterhändler(in) *m(f)*
Negro *a* Neger- ● *n* (*pl* **-es**) Neger
m
neigh *vi* wiehern
neighbour *n* Nachbar(in) *m(f)*.
~**hood** *n* Nachbarschaft *f*. ~**ing** *a*
Nachbar-. ~**ly** *a* [gut]nachbarlich
neither *a & pron* keine(r, s) [von
beiden] ● *adv* ~... **nor** weder ...
noch ● *conj* auch nicht
neon *n* Neon *nt*
nephew *n* Neffe *m*
nepotism *n* Vetternwirtschaft *f*

nerve n Nerv m; (⧉ courage) Mut m; (⧉ impudence) Frechheit f. **~-racking** a nervenaufreibend

nervous a, **-ly** adv (afraid) ängstlich; (highly strung) nervös; (Anat, Med) Nerven-. **~ breakdown** n Nervenzusammenbruch m. **~ness** Ängstlichkeit f

nervy a (-ier, -iest) nervös; (Amer: impudent) frech

nest n Nest nt ● vi nisten

nestle vi sich schmiegen (against an + acc)

net¹ n Netz nt; (curtain) Store m

net² a netto; <salary, weight> Netto-

netball n ≈ Korbball m

Netherlands npl the ~ die Niederlande pl

nettle n Nessel f

network n Netz nt

neurolog|ist n Neurologe m/ -gin f. **~y** n Neurologie f

neur|osis n (pl **-oses**) Neurose f. **~otic** a neurotisch

neuter a (Gram) sächlich ● n (Gram) Neutrum nt ● vt kastrieren; (spay) sterilisieren

neutral a neutral ● n in ~ (Auto) im Leerlauf. **~ity** n Neutralität f

never adv nie, niemals; (⧉ not) nicht; ~ mind macht nichts; well I ~! ja so was! **~-ending** a endlos

nevertheless adv dennoch, trotzdem

new a (-er, -est) neu

new: ~comer n Neuankömmling m. **~fangled** a (pej) neumodisch. **~-laid** a frisch gelegt

newly adv frisch. **~-weds** npl Jungverheiratete pl

new: ~ moon n Neumond m. **~ness** n Neuheit f

news n Nachricht f; (Radio, TV) Nachrichten pl; **piece of** ~ Neuigkeit f

news: ~agent n Zeitungshändler m. **~ bulletin** n Nachrichtensendung f. **~letter** n Mitteilungsblatt nt. **~paper** n Zeitung f; (material) Zeitungspapier nt. **~reader** n Nachrichtensprecher(in) m(f)

New: ~ Year's Day n Neujahr nt. **~ Year's Eve** n Silvester nt. **~ Zealand** n Neuseeland nt

next a & n nächste(r, s); **who's** ~? wer kommt als Nächster dran? **the** ~ **best** das nächstbeste; ~ **door** nebenan; **my** ~ **of kin** mein nächster Verwandter; ~ **to nothing** fast gar nichts; **the week after** ~ übernächste Woche ● adv als Nächstes; ~ **to** neben

nib n Feder f

nibble vt/i knabbern (at an + dat)

nice a (-r, -st) nett; <day, weather> schön; <food> gut; <distinction> fein. **~ly** adv nett; (well) gut

niche n Nische f; (fig) Platz m

nick n Kerbe f; (⧉ prison) Knast m; (⧉ police station) Revier nt; in **good** ~ ⧉ in gutem Zustand ● vt einkerben; (steal) klauen; (⧉ arrest) schnappen

nickel n Nickel nt; (Amer) Fünfcentstück nt

nickname n Spitzname m

nicotine n Nikotin nt

niece n Nichte f

Nigeria n Nigeria nt. **~n** a nigerianisch ● n Nigerianer(in) m(f)

night n Nacht f; (evening) Abend m; **at** ~ nachts

night: ~-club n Nachtklub m. **~-dress** n Nachthemd nt. **~fall** n at **~fall** bei Einbruch der Dunkelheit. **~-gown** n, ⧉ **~ie** n Nachthemd nt

nightingale n Nachtigall f

night: ~-life n Nachtleben nt. **~ly** a nächtlich ● adv jede Nacht. **~mare** n Albtraum m. **~-time** n at **~-time** bei Nacht

nil n null

nimble a (-r, -st), **-bly** adv flink

nine a neun ● n Neun f. **~teen** a neunzehn. **~teenth** a neunzehnte(r, s)

ninetieth a neunzigste(r, s)

ninety a neunzig

ninth a neunte(r, s)

nip vt kneifen; (bite) beißen; ~ in the bud (fig) im Keim ersticken ● vi (⚏ run) laufen

nipple n Brustwarze f; (Amer: on bottle) Sauger m

nitwit n ⚏ Dummkopf m

no adv nein ● n (pl noes) Nein nt ● a kein(e); (pl) keine; in no time [sehr] schnell; no parking/smoking Parken/Rauchen verboten; no one = nobody

nobility n Adel m

noble a (-r, -st) edel; (aristocratic) adlig. **~man** n Adlige(r) m

nobody pron niemand, keiner ● n a ~ ein Niemand m

nocturnal a nächtlich; <animal, bird> Nacht-

nod n Nicken nt ● v (pt/pp nodded) ● vi nicken ● vt ~ one's head mit dem Kopf nicken

noise n Geräusch nt; (loud) Lärm m. **~less, -ly** adv geräuschlos

noisy a (-ier, -iest), **-ily** adv laut; <eater> geräuschvoll

nomad n Nomade m. **~ic** a nomadisch; <life, tribe> Nomaden-

nominal a, **-ly** adv nominell

nominat|e vt nominieren, aufstellen; (appoint) ernennen. **~ion** n Nominierung f; Ernennung f

nominative a & n (Gram) **~[case]** Nominativ m

nonchalant a, **-ly** adv nonchalant; <gesture> lässig

nondescript a unbestimmbar; <person> unscheinbar

none pron keine(r)/keins; ~ of it/this nichts davon ● adv ~ too nicht gerade; ~ too soon [um]

keine Minute zu früh; ~ the less dennoch

nonentity n Null f

non-existent a nicht vorhanden

non-fiction n Sachliteratur f

nonplussed a verblüfft

nonsens|e n Unsinn m. **~ical** a unsinnig

non-smoker n Nichtraucher m

non-stop adv ununterbrochen; <fly> nonstop

non-swimmer n Nichtschwimmer m

non-violent a gewaltlos

noodles npl Bandnudeln pl

noon n Mittag m; at ~ um 12 Uhr mittags

noose n Schlinge f

nor adv noch ● conj auch nicht

Nordic a nordisch

norm n Norm f

normal a normal. **~ity** n Normalität f. **~ly** adv normal; (usually) normalerweise

north n Norden m; to the ~ of nördlich von ● a Nord-, nord- ● adv nach Norden

north: N~ **America** n Nordamerika nt. **~-east** a Nordost- ● n Nordosten m

norther|ly a nördlich. **~n** a nördlich. N~n **Ireland** n Nordirland nt

north: N~ **Pole** n Nordpol m. N~ **Sea** n Nordsee f. **~ward[s]** adv nach Norden. **~-west** a Nordwest- ● n Nordwesten m

Nor|way n Norwegen nt. **~wegian** a norwegisch ● n Norweger(in) m(f)

nose n Nase f

nosebleed n Nasenbluten nt

nostalg|ia n Nostalgie f. **~ic** a nostalgisch

nostril n Nasenloch nt

nosy a (-ier, -iest) ⚏ neugierig

not
● adverb

····▸ nicht. **I don't know** ich weiß nicht. **isn't she pretty?** ist sie nicht hübsch?

····▸ **not** a kein. **he is not a doctor** er ist kein Arzt. **she didn't wear a hat** sie trug keinen Hut. **there was not a person to be seen** es gab keinen Menschen zu sehen. **not a thing** gar nichts. **not a bit** kein bisschen

····▸ (*in elliptical phrases*) **I hope not** ich hoffe nicht. **of course not** natürlich nicht. **not at all** überhaupt nicht; (*in polite reply to thanks*) keine Ursache; gern geschehen. **certainly not!** auf keinen Fall! **not I** ich nicht

····▸ **not ... but ...** nicht ... sondern .... **it was not a small town but a big one** es war keine kleine Stadt, sondern eine große

notab|le a bedeutend; (*remarkable*) bemerkenswert. **~ly** adv insbesondere

notation n Notation f; (*Mus*) Notenschrift f

notch n Kerbe f

note n (*written comment*) Notiz f, Anmerkung f; (*short letter*) Briefchen nt, Zettel m; (*bank ~*) Banknote f, Schein m; (*Mus*) Note f; (*sound*) Ton m; (*on piano*) Taste f; **half/whole ~** (*Amer*) halbe/ganze Note f; **of ~** von Bedeutung; **make a ~ of** notieren ● vt beachten; (*notice*) bemerken (**that** dass)

notebook n Notizbuch nt

noted a bekannt (**for** für)

note: **~paper** n Briefpapier nt. **~worthy** a beachtenswert

nothing n, pron & adv nichts; **for ~** umsonst; **~ but** nichts als; **~ much** nicht viel; **~ interesting** nichts Interessantes

notice n (*on board*) Anschlag m, Bekanntmachung f; (*announcement*) Anzeige f;

(*review*) Kritik f; (*termination of lease, employment*) Kündigung f; **give [in one's] ~** kündigen; **give s.o. ~** jdm kündigen; **take no ~!** ignoriere es! ● vt bemerken. **~able** a, **-bly** adv merklich. **~board** n Anschlagbrett nt

noti|fication n Benachrichtigung f. **~fy** vt (*pt/pp* -ied) benachrichtigen

notion n Idee f

notorious a berüchtigt

notwithstanding prep trotz (+ gen) ● adv trotzdem, dennoch

nought n Null f

noun n Substantiv nt

nourish vt nähren. **~ing** a nahrhaft. **~ment** n Nahrung f

novel a neu[artig] ● n Roman m. **~ist** n Romanschriftsteller(in) m(f). **~ty** n Neuheit f

November n November m

novice n Neuling m; (*Relig*) Novize m/Novizin f

now adv & conj jetzt; **~ [that]** jetzt, wo; **just ~** gerade, eben; **right ~** sofort; **~ and again** hin und wieder; **now, now!** na, na!

nowadays adv heutzutage

nowhere adv nirgendwo, nirgends

nozzle n Düse f

nuance n Nuance f

nuclear a Kern-. **~ deterrent** n nukleares Abschreckungsmittel nt

nucleus n (*pl* -lei) Kern m

nude a nackt ● n (*Art*) Akt m; **in the ~** nackt

nudge vt stupsen

nud|ist n Nudist m. **~ity** n Nacktheit f

nuisance n Ärgernis nt; (*pest*) Plage f; **be a ~** ärgerlich sein

null a **~ and void** null und nichtig

numb a gefühllos, taub ● vt betäuben

number n Nummer f; (*amount*) Anzahl f; (*Math*) Zahl f ● vt

N

nummerieren; *(include)* zählen (among zu). **~-plate** *n* Nummernschild *nt*

numeral *n* Ziffer *f*

numerical *a*, **-ly** *adv* numerisch; **in ~ order** zahlenmäßig geordnet

numerous *a* zahlreich

nun *n* Nonne *f*

nurse *n* [Kranken]schwester *f*; *(male)* Krankenpfleger *m*; **children's ~** Kindermädchen *nt* ● *vt* pflegen

nursery *n* Kinderzimmer *nt*; *(Hort)* Gärtnerei *f*; **[day] ~** Kindertagesstätte *f*. **~ rhyme** *n* Kinderreim *m*. **~ school** *n* Kindergarten *m*

nursing *n* Krankenpflege *f*. **~ home** *n* Pflegeheim *nt*

nut *n* Nuss *f*; *(Techn)* [Schrauben]mutter *f*; (🖫 *head*) Birne *f* 🖫; **be ~s** 🖫 spinnen 🖫. **~crackers** *npl* Nussknacker *m*. **~meg** *n* Muskat *m*

nutrient *n* Nährstoff *m*

nutrit|ion *n* Ernährung *f*. **~ious** *a* nahrhaft

nutshell *n* Nussschale *f*; **in a ~** *(fig)* kurz gesagt

nylon *n* Nylon *nt*

O *n (Teleph)* null

oak *n* Eiche *f*

OAP *abbr* (old-age pensioner) Rentner(in) *m(f)*

oar *n* Ruder *nt*. **~sman** *n* Ruderer *m*

oasis *n (pl* oases) Oase *f*

oath *n* Eid *m*; *(swear-word)* Fluch *m*

oatmeal *n* Hafermehl *nt*

oats *npl* Hafer *m*; *(Culin)* **[rolled] ~** Haferflocken *pl*

obedien|ce *n* Gehorsam *m*. **~t** *a*, **-ly** *adv* gehorsam

obey *vt/i* gehorchen (+ *dat*); befolgen *<instructions, rules>*

obituary *n* Nachruf *m*; *(notice)* Todesanzeige *f*

object¹ *n* Gegenstand *m*; *(aim)* Zweck *m*; *(intention)* Absicht *f*; *(Gram)* Objekt *nt*; **money is no ~** Geld spielt keine Rolle

object² *vi* Einspruch erheben (**to** gegen); *(be against)* etwas dagegen haben

objection *n* Einwand *m*; **have no ~** nichts dagegen haben. **~able** *a* anstößig; *<person>* unangenehm

objectiv|e *a*, **-ly** *adv* objektiv ● *n* Ziel *nt*. **~ity** *n* Objektivität *f*

objector *n* Gegner *m*

obligation *n* Pflicht *f*; **without ~** unverbindlich

obligatory *a* obligatorisch; **be ~** Vorschrift sein

oblig|e *vt* verpflichten; *(compel)* zwingen; *(do a small service)* einen Gefallen tun (+ *dat*). **~ing** *a* entgegenkommend

oblique *a* schräg; *<angle>* schief; *(fig)* indirekt

obliterate *vt* auslöschen

oblivion *n* Vergessenheit *f*

oblivious *a* **be ~** sich *(dat)* nicht bewusst sein (**of** *gen*)

oblong *a* rechteckig ● *n* Rechteck *nt*

obnoxious *a* widerlich

oboe *n* Oboe *f*

obscen|e *a* obszön. **~ity** *n* Obszönität *f*

obscur|e *a* dunkel; *(unknown)* unbekannt ● *vt* verdecken; *(confuse)* verwischen. **~ity** *n* Dunkelheit *f*; Unbekanntheit *f*

observa|nce *n* *(of custom)* Einhaltung *f*. **~nt** *a* aufmerksam

~**tion** n Beobachtung f; (remark) Bemerkung f

observatory n Sternwarte f

observe vt beobachten; (say, notice) bemerken; (keep, celebrate) feiern; (obey) einhalten. ~**r** n Beobachter m

obsess vt be ~**ed by** besessen sein von. ~**ion** n Besessenheit f; (persistent idea) fixe Idee f. ~**ive** a, -**ly** adv zwanghaft

obsolete a veraltet

obstacle n Hindernis nt

obstina|cy n Starrsinn m. ~**te** a, -**ly** adv starrsinnig; <refusal> hartnäckig

obstruct vt blockieren; (hinder) behindern. ~**ion** n Blockierung f; Behinderung f; (obstacle) Hindernis nt. ~**ive** a be ~**ive** Schwierigkeiten bereiten

obtain vt erhalten. ~**able** a erhältlich

obtrusive a aufdringlich; <thing> auffällig

obtuse a begriffsstutzig

obvious a, -**ly** adv offensichtlich, offenbar

occasion n Gelegenheit f; (time) Mal nt; (event) Ereignis nt; (cause) Anlass m, Grund m; **on the** ~ **of** anlässlich (+ gen)

occasional a gelegentlich. ~**ly** adv gelegentlich, hin und wieder

occult a okkult

occupant n Bewohner(in) m(f); (of vehicle) Insasse m

occupation n Beschäftigung f; (job) Beruf m; (Mil) Besetzung f; (period) Besatzung f. ~**al** a Berufs-. ~**al therapy** n Beschäftigungstherapie f

occupier n Bewohner(in) m(f)

occupy vt (pt/pp occupied) besetzen <seat, (Mil) country>; einnehmen <space>; in Anspruch nehmen <time>; (live in) bewohnen; (fig) bekleiden <office>; (keep busy) beschäftigen

occur vi (pt/pp occurred) geschehen; (exist) vorkommen, auftreten; **it** ~ **red to me that** es fiel mir ein, dass. ~**rence** n Auftreten nt; (event) Ereignis nt

ocean n Ozean m

o'clock adv [at] 7 ~ [um] 7 Uhr

octagonal a achteckig

October n Oktober m

octopus n (pl -puses) Tintenfisch m

odd a (-er, -est) seltsam, merkwürdig; <number> ungerade; (not of set) einzeln; **forty** ~ über vierzig; ~ **jobs** Gelegenheitsarbeiten pl; **the** ~ **one out** die Ausnahme; **at** ~ **moments** zwischendurch

odd|ity n Kuriosität f. ~**ly** adv merkwürdig; ~**ly enough** merkwürdigerweise ~**ment** n (of fabric) Rest m

odds npl (chances) Chancen pl; **at** ~ uneinig; ~ **and ends** Kleinkram m

ode n Ode f

odious a widerlich

odour n Geruch m. ~**less** a geruchlos

O

of

● preposition

····▶ (indicating belonging, origin) von (+ dat); genitive. **the mother of twins** die Mutter von Zwillingen. **the mother of the twins** die Mutter der Zwillinge or von den Zwillingen. **the Queen of England** die Königin von England. **a friend of mine** ein Freund von mir. **a friend of the teacher's** ein Freund des Lehrers. **the brother of her father** der Bruder ihres Vaters. **the works of Shakespeare** Shakespeares Werke. **it was nice of him** es war nett von ihm

····➤ *(made of)* aus (+ *dat*). **a dress of cotton** ein Kleid aus Baumwolle

····➤ *(following number)* **five of us** fünf von uns. **the two of us** wir zwei. **there were four of us waiting** wir waren vier, die warteten

····➤ *(followed by number, description)* (+ *dat*). **a girl of ten** ein Mädchen von zehn Jahren. **a distance of 50 miles** eine Entfernung von 50 Meilen. **a man of character** ein Mann von Charakter. **a woman of exceptional beauty** eine Frau von außerordentlicher Schönheit. **a person of strong views** ein Mensch mit festen Ansichten

! of is not translated after measures and in some other cases: **a pound of apples** ein Pfund Äpfel; **a cup of tea** eine Tasse Tee; **a glass of wine** ein Glas Wein; **the city of Chicago** die Stadt Chicago; **the fourth of January** der vierte Januar

off *prep* von (+ *dat*); ~ **the coast** vor der Küste; **get ~ the ladder/ bus** von der Leiter/aus dem Bus steigen ● *adv* weg; *<button, lid, handle>* ab; *<light>* aus; *<brake>* los; *<machine>* abgeschaltet; *<tap>* zu; *(on appliance)* **'off'** 'aus'; **2 kilometres ~** 2 Kilometer entfernt; **a long way ~** weit weg; *(time)* noch lange hin; ~ **and on** hin und wieder; **with his hat/coat ~** ohne Hut/Mantel; **20% ~** 20% Nachlass; **be ~** *(leave)* [weg]gehen; *(Sport)* starten; *<food:>* schlecht sein; **be well ~** gut dran sein; *(financially)* wohlhabend sein; **have a day ~** einen freien Tag haben

offal *n* *(Culin)* Innereien *pl*

offence *n* *(illegal act)* Vergehen *nt*; **give/take ~** Anstoß erregen/ nehmen (**at** an + *dat*)

offend *vt* beleidigen. ~**er** *n* *(Jur)* Straftäter *m*

offensive *a* anstößig; *(Mil, Sport)* offensiv ● *n* Offensive *f*

offer *n* Angebot *nt*; **on (special) ~** im Sonderangebot ● *vt* anbieten (**to** *dat*); leisten *<resistance>*; ~ **to do sth** sich anbieten, etw zu tun. ~**ing** *n* Gabe *f*

offhand *a* brüsk; *(casual)* lässig

office *n* Büro *nt*; *(post)* Amt *nt*

officer *n* Offizier *m*; *(official)* Beamte(r) *m*/ Beamtin *f*; *(police)* Polizeibeamte(r) *m*/-beamtin *f*

official *a* offiziell, amtlich ● *n* Beamte(r) *m*/ Beamtin *f*; *(Sport)* Funktionär *m*. ~**ly** *adv* offiziell

officious *a*, -**ly** *adv* übereifrig

off-licence *n* Wein und Spirituosenhandlung *f*

off-load *vt* ausladen

off-putting *a* ⚠ abstoßend

offset *vt* *(pt/pp* -**set**, *pres p* -**setting)** ausgleichen

offshoot *n* Schössling *m*; *(fig)* Zweig *m*

offshore *a* Offshore-

offside *a* *(Sport)* abseits

offspring *n* Nachwuchs *m*

offstage *adv* hinter den Kulissen

off-white *a* fast weiß

often *adv* oft; **every so ~** von Zeit zu Zeit

oh *int* oh! ach! **oh dear!** o weh!

oil *n* Öl *nt*; *(petroleum)* Erdöl *nt* ● *vt* ölen

oil: ~**field** *n* Ölfeld *nt*. ~**-painting** *n* Ölgemälde *nt*. ~ **refinery** *n* [Erd]ölraffinerie *f*. ~**-tanker** *n* Öltanker *m*. ~ **well** *n* Ölquelle *f*

oily *a* (-**ier**, -**iest**) ölig

ointment *n* Salbe *f*

OK *a & int* ⚠ in Ordnung; okay ● *adv* *(well)* gut ● *vt* *(auch* **okay**) *(pt/pp* **okayed**) genehmigen

old *a* (-er, -est) alt; (*former*) ehemalig

old: ~ **age** *n* Alter *nt*. ~-**age pensioner** *n* Rentner(in) *m(f)*. ~ **boy** *n* ehemaliger Schüler. ~-**fashioned** *a* altmodisch. ~ **girl** *n* ehemalige Schülerin *f*

olive *n* Olive *f*; (*colour*) Oliv *nt* ● *a* olivgrün. ~ **oil** *n* Olivenöl *nt*

Olympic *a* olympisch ● *n* **the** ~**s** die Olympischen Spiele *pl*

omelette *n* Omelett *nt*

ominous *a* bedrohlich

omission *n* Auslassung *f*; (*failure to do*) Unterlassung *f*

omit *vt* (*pt/pp* **omitted**) auslassen; ~ **to do sth** es unterlassen, etw zu tun

omnipotent *a* allmächtig

on *prep* auf (+ *dat*/(on to) + *acc*); (*on vertical surface*) an (+ *dat*/(on to) + *acc*); (*about*) über (+ *acc*); **on Monday** [am] Montag; **on Mondays; on the first of May** am ersten Mai; **on arriving** als ich ankam; **on one's finger** am Finger; **on the right/left** rechts/links; **on the Rhine** am Rhein; **on the radio/television** im Radio/ Fernsehen; **on the bus/train** im Bus/Zug; **go on the bus/train** mit dem Bus/Zug fahren; **on me** (*with me*) bei mir; **it's on me** Ⅰ das spendiere ich ● *adv* (*further on*) weiter; (*switched on*) an; <*brake*> angezogen; <*machine*> angeschaltet; (*on appliance*) 'on' 'ein'; **with/without his hat/coat on** mit/ohne Hut/Mantel; **be on** <*film*:> laufen; <*event*:> stattfinden; **be on at** Ⅰ bedrängen (**zu** to); **it's not on** Ⅰ das geht nicht; **on and on** immer weiter; **on and off** hin und wieder; **and so on** und so weiter

once *adv* einmal; (*formerly*) früher; **at** ~ sofort; (*at the same time*) gleichzeitig; ~ **and for all**

ein für alle Mal ● *conj* wenn; (*with past tense*) als

oncoming *a* ~ **traffic** Gegenverkehr *m*

one *a* ein(e); (*only*) einzig; **not** ~ kein(e); ~ **day/evening** eines Tages/Abends ● *n* Eins *f* ● *pron* eine(r)/eins; (*impersonal*) man; **which** ~ welche(r,s); ~ **another** einander; ~ **by** ~ einzeln; ~ **never knows** man kann nie wissen

one: ~-**parent family** *n* Einelternfamilie *f*. ~**self** *pron* selbst; (*refl*) sich; **by** ~**self** allein. ~-**sided** *a* einseitig. ~-**way** *a* <*street*> Einbahn-; <*ticket*> einfach

onion *n* Zwiebel *f*

onlooker *n* Zuschauer(in) *m(f)*

only *a* einzige(r,s); **an** ~ **child** ein Einzelkind *nt* ● *adv & conj* nur; ~ **just** gerade erst; (*barely*) gerade noch

onset *n* Beginn *m*; (*of winter*) Einsetzen *nt*

onward[s] *adv* vorwärts; **from then** ~ von der Zeit an

ooze *vi* sickern

opaque *a* undurchsichtig

open *a*, -**ly** *adv* offen; **be** ~ <*shop*:> geöffnet sein; **in the** ~ **air** im Freien ● *n* **in the** ~ im Freien ● *vt* öffnen, aufmachen; (*start, set up*) eröffnen ● *vi* sich öffnen; <*flower*:> aufgehen; <*shop*:> öffnen, aufmachen; (*be started*) eröffnet werden. ~ **up** *vt* öffnen, aufmachen

open day *n* Tag *m* der offenen Tür

opener *n* Öffner *m*

opening *n* Öffnung *f*; (*beginning*) Eröffnung *f*; (*job*) Einstiegsmöglichkeit *f*. ~ **hours** *npl* Öffnungszeiten *pl*

open: ~-**minded** *a* aufgeschlossen. ~ **sandwich** *n* belegtes Brot *nt*

O

opera n Oper f. **~-house** n Opernhaus nt. **~-singer** n Opernsänger(in) m(f)
operate vt bedienen <*machine, lift*>; betätigen <*lever, brake*>; (*fig: run*) betreiben ● vi (*Techn*) funktionieren; (*be in action*) in Betrieb sein; (*Mil & fig*) operieren; **~ [on]** (*Med*) operieren
operatic a Opern-
operation n (*see* operate) Bedienung f; Betätigung f; Operation f; **in ~** (*Techn*) in Betrieb; **come into ~** (*fig*) in Kraft treten; **have an ~** (*Med*) operiert werden. **~al** a **be ~al** in Betrieb sein; <*law:*> in Kraft sein
operative a wirksam
operator n (*user*) Bedienungsperson f; (*Teleph*) Vermittlung f
operetta n Operette f
opinion n Meinung f; **in my ~** meiner Meinung nach. **~ated** a rechthaberisch
opponent n Gegner(in) m(f)
opportun|e a günstig. **~ist** n Opportunist m
opportunity n Gelegenheit f
oppos|e vt Widerstand leisten (+ dat); (*argue against*) sprechen gegen; **be ~ed to sth** gegen etw sein; **be ~ed to** im Gegensatz zu. **~ing** a gegnerisch
opposite a entgegengesetzt; <*house, side*> gegenüberliegend; **~ number** (*fig*) Gegenstück nt; **the ~ sex** das andere Geschlecht ● n Gegenteil nt ● adv gegenüber ● prep gegenüber (+ dat)
opposition n Widerstand m; (*Pol*) Opposition f
oppress vt unterdrücken. **~ion** n Unterdrücken f. **~ive** a tyrannisch; <*heat*> drückend
opt vi **~ for** sich entscheiden für
optical a optisch
optician n Optiker m

optimis|m n Optimismus m. **~t** n Optimist m. **~tic** a, **-ally** adv optimistisch
optimum a optimal
option n Wahl f; (*Comm*) Option f. **~al** a auf Wunsch erhältlich; <*subject*> wahlfrei
opu|lence n Prunk m. **~lent** a prunkvoll
or conj oder; (*after negative*) noch; **or [else]** sonst; **in a year or two** in ein bis zwei Jahren
oral a, **-ly** adv mündlich; (*Med*) oral ● n Mündliche(s) nt
orange n Apfelsine f, Orange f; (*colour*) Orange nt ● a orangefarben
oratorio n Oratorium nt
oratory n Redekunst f
orbit n Umlaufbahn f ● vt umkreisen
orchard n Obstgarten m
orches|tra n Orchester nt. **~tral** a Orchester-. **~trate** vt orchestrieren
ordeal n (*fig*) Qual f
order n Ordnung f; (*sequence*) Reihenfolge f; (*condition*) Zustand m; (*command*) Befehl m; (*in restaurant*) Bestellung f; (*Comm*) Auftrag m; (*Relig, medal*) Orden m; **out of ~** <*machine*> außer Betrieb; **in ~ that** damit; **in ~ to help** um zu helfen ● vt (*put in ~*) ordnen; (*command*) befehlen (+ dat); (*Comm, in restaurant*) bestellen; (*prescribe*) verordnen
orderly a ordentlich; (*not unruly*) friedlich ● n (*Mil, Med*) Sanitäter m
ordinary a gewöhnlich, normal
ore n Erz nt
organ n (*Biol & fig*) Organ nt; (*Mus*) Orgel f
organic a, **-ally** adv organisch; (*without chemicals*) biodynamisch; <*crop*> biologisch

angebaut; <*food*> Bio-. **~ farming** n biologischer Anbau m

organism n Organismus m

organist n Organist m

organization n Organisation f

organize vt organisieren; veranstalten <*event*>. **~r** n Organisator m; Veranstalter m

orgy n Orgie f

Orient n Orient m. **o~al** a orientalisch ● n Orientale m/ Orientalin f

orientation n Orientierung f

origin n Ursprung m; (of person, goods) Herkunft f

original a ursprünglich; (not copied) original; (new) originell ● n Original nt. **~ity** n Originalität f. **~ly** adv ursprünglich

originate vi entstehen

ornament n Ziergegenstand m; (decoration) Verzierung f. **~al** a dekorativ

ornate a reich verziert

ornithology n Vogelkunde f

orphan n Waisenkind nt, Waise f. **~age** n Waisenhaus nt

orthodox a orthodox

ostensible a, **-bly** adv angeblich

ostentat|ion n Protzerei f 𝕀. **~ious** a protzig 𝕀

osteopath n Osteopath m

ostrich n Strauß m

other a, pron & n andere(r,s); the ~ **[one]** der/die/das andere; the ~ **two** die zwei anderen; no ~s sonst keine; any ~ questions? sonst noch Fragen? every ~ day jeden zweiten Tag; the ~ day neulich; the ~ evening neulich abends; someone/something or ~ irgendjemand/-etwas ● adv anders; ~ than him außer ihm; somehow/somewhere or ~ irgendwie/irgendwo

otherwise adv sonst; (differently) anders

ought v aux I/we ~ to stay ich sollte/wir sollten eigentlich bleiben; he ~ not to have done it er hätte es nicht machen sollen

ounce n Unze f (28, 35 g)

our a unser

ours poss pron unsere(r,s); a friend of ~ ein Freund von uns; that is ~ das gehört uns

ourselves pron selbst; (refl) uns; by ~ allein

out adv (not at home) weg; (outside) draußen; (not alight) aus; (unconscious) bewusstlos; be ~ <*sun*:> scheinen; <*flower*> blühen; <*workers*> streiken; <*calculation*:> nicht stimmen; (Sport) aus sein; (fig: not feasible) nicht infrage kommen; ~ and about unterwegs; have it ~ with s.o. 𝕀 jdn zur Rede stellen; get ~! 𝕀 raus! ~ with it! 𝕀 heraus damit! ● prep ~ of aus (+ dat); go ~ (of) the door zur Tür hinausgehen; be ~ of bed/ the room nicht im Bett/im Zimmer sein; ~ of breath/danger außer Atem/Gefahr; ~ of work arbeitslos; nine ~ of ten neun von zehn; be ~ of sugar keinen Zucker mehr haben

outboard a ~ motor Außenbordmotor m

outbreak n Ausbruch m

outbuilding n Nebengebäude nt

outburst n Ausbruch m

outcast n Ausgestoßene(r) m/f

outcome n Ergebnis nt

outcry n Aufschrei m [der Entrüstung]

outdated a überholt

outdo vt (pt **-did**, pp **-done**) übertreffen, übertrumpfen

outdoor a <*life, sports*> im Freien; ~ **swimming pool** Freibad nt

outdoors adv draußen; go ~ nach draußen gehen

outer a äußere(r,s)

O

outfit n Ausstattung f; (clothes) Ensemble nt; (🄸 organization) Laden m

outgoing a ausscheidend; <mail> ausgehend; (sociable) kontaktfreudig. **~s** npl Ausgaben pl

outgrow vi (pt **-grew**, pp **-grown**) herauswachsen aus

outing n Ausflug m

outlaw n Geächtete(r) m/f ● vt ächten

outlay n Auslagen pl

outlet n Abzug m; (for water) Abfluss m; (fig) Ventil nt; (Comm) Absatzmöglichkeit f

outline n Umriss m; (summary) kurze Darstellung f ● vt umreißen

outlive vt überleben

outlook n Aussicht f; (future prospect) Aussichten pl; (attitude) Einstellung f

outmoded a überholt

outnumber vt zahlenmäßig überlegen sein (+ dat)

out-patient n ambulanter Patient m

outpost n Vorposten m

output n Leistung f; Produktion f

outrage n Gräueltat f; (fig) Skandal m; (indignation) Empörung f. **~ous** a empörend

outright[1] a völlig, total; <refusal> glatt

outright[2] adv ganz; (at once) sofort; (frankly) offen

outset n Anfang m

outside[1] a äußere(r,s); **~ wall** Außenwand f ● n Außenseite f; from the **~** von außen; at the **~** höchstens

outside[2] adv außen; (out of doors) draußen; go **~** nach draußen gehen ● prep außerhalb (+ gen); (in front of) vor (+ dat/acc)

outsider n Außenseiter m

outsize a übergroß

outskirts npl Rand m

outspoken a offen; be **~** kein Blatt vor den Mund nehmen

outstanding a hervorragend; (conspicuous) bemerkenswert; (Comm) ausstehend

outstretched a ausgestreckt

outvote vt überstimmen

outward a äußerlich; **~ journey** Hinreise f ● adv nach außen. **~ly** adv nach außen hin, äußerlich. **~s** adv nach außen

outwit vt (pt/pp **-witted**) überlisten

oval a oval ● n Oval nt

ovation n Ovation f

oven n Backofen m

over prep über (+ acc/dat); **~ dinner** beim Essen; **~ the phone** am Telefon; **~ the page** auf der nächsten Seite ● adv (remaining) übrig; (ended) zu Ende; **~ again** noch einmal; **~ and ~** immer wieder; **~ here/there** hier/da drüben; all **~** (everywhere) überall; it's all **~** es ist vorbei; I ache all **~** mir tut alles weh

overall[1] n Kittel m; **~s** pl Overall m

overall[2] a gesamt; (general) allgemein ● adv insgesamt

overbalance vi das Gleichgewicht verlieren

overbearing a herrisch

overboard adv (Naut) über Bord

overcast a bedeckt

overcharge vt **~** s.o. jdm zu viel berechnen ● vi zu viel verlangen

overcoat n Mantel m

overcome vt (pt **-came**, pp **-come**) überwinden; be **~** by überwältigt werden von

overcrowded a überfüllt

overdo vt (pt **-did**, pp **-done**) übertreiben; (cook too long) zu lange kochen; **~** it (🄸 do too much) sich übernehmen

overdose n Überdosis f

overdraft n [Konto]überziehung f; have an **~** sein Konto überzogen haben

overdue a überfällig

overestimate vt überschätzen

overflow¹ n Überschuss m; *(outlet)* Überlauf m

overflow² vi überlaufen

overgrown a *<garden>* überwachsen

overhang¹ n Überhang m

overhang² vt/i *(pt/pp* **-hung)** überhängen (über + *acc*)

overhaul¹ n Überholung f

overhaul² vt *(Techn)* überholen

overhead¹ adv oben

overhead² a Ober-; *(ceiling)* Decken-. ~s npl allgemeine Unkosten pl

overhear vt *(pt/pp* **-heard)** mit anhören *<conversation>*

overheat vi zu heiß werden

overjoyed a überglücklich

overland a & adv auf dem Landweg; ~ route Landroute f

overlap vi *(pt/pp* **-lapped)** sich überschneiden

overleaf adv umseitig

overload vt überladen

overlook vt überblicken; *(fail to see, ignore)* übersehen

overnight¹ adv über Nacht; stay ~ übernachten

overnight² a Nacht-; ~ stay Übernachtung f

overpass n Überführung f

overpay vt *(pt/pp* **-paid)** überbezahlen

overpopulated a übervölkert

overpower vt überwältigen. ~ing a überwältigend

overpriced a zu teuer

overrated a überbewertet

overreact vi überreagieren. ~ion n Überreaktion f

overriding a Haupt-

overrule vt ablehnen; we were ~d wir wurden überstimmt

overrun vt *(pt* **-ran,** pp **-run,** pres p **-running)** überrennen; überschreiten *<time>*; be ~ with überlaufen sein von

overseas¹ adv in Übersee; go ~ nach Übersee gehen

overseas² a Übersee-

oversee vt *(pt* **-saw,** pp **-seen)** beaufsichtigen

overshadow vt überschatten

overshoot vt *(pt/pp* **-shot)** hinausschießen über (+ *acc*)

oversight n Versehen nt

oversleep vi *(pt/pp* **-slept)** [sich] verschlafen

overstep vt *(pt/pp* **-stepped)** überschreiten

overt a offen

overtake vt/i *(pt* **-took,** pp **-taken)** überholen

overthrow vt *(pt* **-threw,** pp **-thrown)** *(Pol)* stürzen

overtime n Überstunden pl ● adv work ~ Überstunden machen

overtired a übermüdet

overture n *(Mus)* Ouvertüre f; ~s pl *(fig)* Annäherungsversuche pl

overturn vt umstoßen ● vi umkippen

overweight a übergewichtig; be ~ Übergewicht haben

overwhelm vt überwältigen. ~ing a überwältigend

overwork n Überarbeitung f ● vt überfordern ● vi sich überarbeiten

overwrought a überreizt

ow|e vt schulden/ *(fig)* verdanken ([to] s.o. jdm); ~e s.o. sth jdm etw schuldig sein. ~ing a schuldig. ~ing to prep wegen (+ *gen*)

owl n Eule f

own¹ a & pron eigen; it's my ~ es gehört mir; a car of my ~ mein eigenes Auto; on one's ~ allein; get one's ~ back ⑤ sich revanchieren

own² vt besitzen; I don't ~ it es gehört mir nicht. ~ up vi es zugeben

owner n Eigentümer(in) m(f), Besitzer(in) m(f); *(of shop)*

O

Inhaber(in) m(f). **~ship** n Besitz m

oxygen n Sauerstoff m

oyster n Auster f

pace n Schritt m; (speed) Tempo nt; **keep ~ with** Schritt halten mit ● vi **~ up and down** auf und ab gehen. **~maker** n (Sport & Med) Schrittmacher m

Pacific a & n **the ~ [Ocean]** der Pazifik

pacifist n Pazifist m

pacify vt (pt/pp -ied) beruhigen

pack n Packung f; (Mil) Tornister m; (of cards) [Karten]spiel nt; (gang) Bande f; (of hounds) Meute f; (of wolves) Rudel nt; **a ~ of lies** ein Haufen Lügen ● vt/i packen; einpacken <article>; **be ~ed** (crowded) [gedrängt] voll sein. **~ up** vt einpacken ● vi 🗊 <machine:> kaputtgehen

package n Paket nt. **~ holiday** n Pauschalreise f

packet n Päckchen nt

packing n Verpackung f

pact n Pakt m

pad n Polster nt; (for writing) [Schreib]block m ● vt (pt/pp padded) polstern

padding n Polsterung f; (in written work) Füllwerk nt

paddle[1] n Paddel nt ● vt (row) paddeln

paddle[2] vi waten

paddock n Koppel f

padlock n Vorhängeschloss nt ● vt mit einem Vorhängeschloss verschließen

paediatrician n Kinderarzt m /-ärztin f

pagan a heidnisch ● n Heide m/ Heidin f

page[1] n Seite f

page[2] n (boy) Page m ● vt ausrufen <person>

paid see pay ● a bezahlt; **put ~ to** 🗊 zunichte machen

pail n Eimer m

pain n Schmerz m; **be in ~** Schmerzen haben; **take ~s** sich (dat) Mühe geben; **~ in the neck** 🗊 Nervensäge f

pain: **~ful** a schmerzhaft; (fig) schmerzlich. **~-killer** n schmerzstillendes Mittel nt. **~less** a, **-ly** adv schmerzlos

painstaking a sorgfältig

paint n Farbe f ● vt/i streichen; <artist:> malen. **~brush** n Pinsel m. **~er** n Maler m; (decorator) Anstreicher m. **~ing** n Malerei f; (picture) Gemälde nt

pair n Paar nt; **~ of trousers** Hose f ● vi **~ off** Paare bilden

pajamas n pl (Amer) Schlafanzug m

Pakistan n Pakistan nt. **~i** a pakistanisch ● n Pakistaner(in) m(f)

pal n Freund(in) m(f)

palace n Palast m

palatable a schmackhaft

palate n Gaumen m

palatial a palastartig

pale a (-r, -st) blass ● vi blass werden. **~ness** n Blässe f

Palestin|e n Palästina nt. **~ian** a palästinensisch ● n Palästinenser(in) m(f)

palette n Palette f

palm n Handfläche f; (tree, symbol) Palme f ● vt **~ sth off on s.o.** jdm etw andrehen. **P~ Sunday** n Palmsonntag m

palpable a tastbar; (perceptible) spürbar

palpitations npl Herzklopfen nt

paltry a (-ier, -iest) armselig
pamper vt verwöhnen
pamphlet n Broschüre f
pan n Pfanne f; (saucepan) Topf m; (of scales) Schale f
panacea n Allheilmittel nt
pancake n Pfannkuchen m
panda n Panda m
pandemonium n Höllenlärm m
pane n [Glas]scheibe f
panel n Tafel f, Platte f; ~ of experts Expertenrunde f; ~ of judges Jury f. ~ling n Täfelung f
pang n ~s of hunger Hungergefühl nt; ~s of conscience Gewissensbisse pl
panic n Panik f ● vi (pt/pp panicked) in Panik geraten. ~-stricken a von Panik ergriffen
panoram|a n Panorama nt. ~ic a Panorama-
pansy n Stiefmütterchen nt
pant vi keuchen; <dog:> hecheln
panther n Panther m
panties npl [Damen]slip m
pantomime n [zu Weihnachten aufgeführte] Märchenvorstellung f
pantry n Speisekammer f
pants npl Unterhose f; (woman's) Schlüpfer m; (trousers) Hose f
pantyhose n (Amer) Strumpfhose f
paper n Papier nt; (newspaper) Zeitung f; (exam ~) Testbogen m; (exam) Klausur f; (treatise) Referat nt; ~s pl (documents) Unterlagen pl; (for identification) [Ausweis]papiere pl ● vt tapezieren
paper: ~back n Taschenbuch nt. ~-clip n Büroklammer f. ~weight n Briefbeschwerer m. ~work n Schreibarbeit f
par n (Golf) Par nt; on a ~ gleichwertig (with dat)
parable n Gleichnis nt
parachut|e n Fallschirm m ● vi [mit dem Fallschirm]

abspringen. ~ist n Fallschirmspringer m
parade n Parade f; (procession) Festzug m ● vt (show off) zur Schau stellen
paradise n Paradies nt
paradox n Paradox nt. ~ical a paradox
paraffin n Paraffin nt
paragraph n Absatz m
parallel a & adv parallel ● n (Geog) Breitenkreis m; (fig) Parallele f
paralyse vt lähmen; (fig) lahmlegen
paralysis n (pl -ses) Lähmung f
paranoid a [krankhaft] misstrauisch
parapet n Brüstung f
paraphernalia n Kram m
parasite n Parasit m, Schmarotzer m
paratrooper n Fallschirmjäger m
parcel n Paket nt
parch vt austrocknen; be ~ed <person:> einen furchtbaren Durst haben
parchment n Pergament nt
pardon n Verzeihung f; (Jur) Begnadigung f; ~? ① bitte? I beg your ~ wie bitte? (sorry) Verzeihung! ● vt verzeihen; (Jur) begnadigen
parent n Elternteil m; ~s pl Eltern pl. ~al a elterlich
parenthesis n (pl -ses) Klammer f
parish n Gemeinde f. ~ioner n Gemeindemitglied nt
park n Park m ● vt/i parken
parking n Parken nt; 'no ~' 'Parken verboten'. ~-lot n (Amer) Parkplatz m. ~-meter n Parkuhr f. ~ space n Parkplatz m
parliament n Parlament nt. ~ary a parlamentarisch
parochial a Gemeinde-; (fig) beschränkt

P

parody n Parodie f ●vt (pt/pp -ied) parodieren

parole n on ~ auf Bewährung

parquet n ~ floor Parkett nt

parrot n Papagei m

parsley n Petersilie f

parsnip n Pastinake f

parson n Pfarrer m

part n Teil m; (Techn) Teil nt; (area) Gegend f; (Theat) Rolle f; (Mus) Part m; **spare** ~ Ersatzteil nt; **for my** ~ meinerseits; **on the** ~ **of** vonseiten (+ gen); **take s.o.'s** ~ für jdn Partei ergreifen; **take** ~ **in** teilnehmen an (+ dat) ●adv teils ●vt trennen; scheiteln <hair> ●vi <people:> sich trennen; ~ **with** sich trennen von

partial a Teil-; **be** ~ **to** mögen. **-ly** adv teilweise

particip|ant n Teilnehmer(in) m(f). ~**ate** vi teilnehmen (in an + dat). ~**ation** n Teilnahme f

particle n Körnchen nt; (Phys) Partikel nt; (Gram) Partikel f

particular a besondere(r,s); (precise) genau; (fastidious) penibel; **in** ~ besonders. ~**ly** adv besonders. ~**s** npl nähere Angaben pl

parting n Abschied m; (in hair) Scheitel m

partition n Trennwand f; (Pol) Teilung f ●vt teilen

partly adv teilweise

partner n Partner(in) m(f); (Comm) Teilhaber m. ~**ship** n Partnerschaft f; (Comm) Teilhaberschaft f

partridge n Rebhuhn nt

part-time a & adv Teilzeit-; **be** or **work** ~ Teilzeitarbeit machen

party n Party f, Fest nt; (group) Gruppe f; (Pol, Jur) Partei f

pass n Ausweis m; (Geog, Sport) Pass m; (Sch) ≈ ausreichend; **get a** ~ bestehen ●vt vorbeigehen/ -fahren an (+ dat); (overtake) überholen; (hand) reichen; (Sport) abgeben, abspielen; (approve) annehmen; (exceed) übersteigen; bestehen <exam>; machen <remark>; fällen <judgement>; (Jur) verhängen <sentence>; ~ **the time** sich (dat) die Zeit vertreiben; ~ **one's hand over sth** mit der Hand über etw (acc) fahren ●vi vorbeigehen/ -fahren; (get by) vorbeikommen; (overtake) überholen; <time:> vergehen; (in exam) bestehen; ~ **away** vi sterben. ~ **down** vt herunterreichen; (fig) weitergeben. ~ **out** vi ohnmächtig werden. ~ **round** vt herumreichen. ~ **up** vt heraufreichen; (🔲 miss) vorübergehen lassen

passable a <road> befahrbar; (satisfactory) passabel

passage n Durchgang m; (corridor) Gang m; (voyage) Überfahrt f; (in book) Passage f

passenger n Fahrgast m; (Naut, Aviat) Passagier m; (in car) Mitfahrer m. ~ **seat** n Beifahrersitz m

passer-by n (pl -s-by) Passant(in) m(f)

passion n Leidenschaft f. ~**ate** a, -ly adv leidenschaftlich

passive a passiv ●n Passiv nt

pass: ~port n [Reise]pass m. ~**word** n Kennwort nt; (Mil) Losung f

past a vergangene(r,s); (former) ehemalig; **that's all** ~ das ist jetzt vorbei ●n Vergangenheit f ●prep an (+ dat) ... vorbei; (after) nach; **at ten** ~ **two** um zehn nach zwei ●adv vorbei; **go** ~ vorbeigehen

pasta n Nudeln pl

paste n Brei m; (adhesive) Kleister m; (jewellery) Strass m ●vt kleistern

pastel n Pastellfarbe f; (drawing) Pastell nt ●attrib Pastell-

pastime n Zeitvertreib m
pastry n Teig m; cakes and ~ies Kuchen und Gebäck
pasture n Weide f
pasty n Pastete f
pat n Klaps m; (of butter) Stückchen nt ● vt (pt/pp patted) tätscheln; ~ s.o. on the back jdm auf die Schulter klopfen
patch n Flicken m; (spot) Fleck m; not a ~ on 🔲 gar nicht zu vergleichen mit ● vt flicken. ~ up vt [zusammen]flicken; beilegen <quarrel>
patchy a ungleichmäßig
patent n Patent nt ● vt patentieren. ~ leather n Lackleder nt
paternal a väterlich
path n (pl -s) [Fuß]weg m, Pfad m; (orbit, track) Bahn f; (fig) Weg m
pathetic a mitleiderregend; <attempt> erbärmlich
patience n Geduld f; (game) Patience f
patient a, -ly adv geduldig ● n Patient(in) m(f)
patio n Terrasse f
patriot n Patriot(in) m(f). ~ic a patriotisch. ~ism n Patriotismus m
patrol n Patrouille f ● vt/i patrouillieren [in (+ dat)]; <police:> auf Streife gehen/ fahren [in (+ dat)]. ~ car n Streifenwagen m
patron n Gönner m; (of charity) Schirmherr m; (of the arts) Mäzen m; (customer) Kunde m/ Kundin f; (Theat) Besucher m. ~age n Schirmherrschaft f
patroniz|e vt (fig) herablassend behandeln. ~ing a, -ly adv gönnerhaft
patter n (speech) Gerede nt
pattern n Muster nt
paunch n [Schmer]bauch m
pause n Pause f ● vi innehalten

pave vt pflastern; ~ the way den Weg bereiten (for dat). ~ment n Bürgersteig m
paw n Pfote f; (of large animal) Pranke f, Tatze f
pawn[1] n (Chess) Bauer m; (fig) Schachfigur f
pawn[2] vt verpfänden. ~ broker n Pfandleiher m
pay n Lohn m; (salary) Gehalt nt; be in the ~ of bezahlt werden von ● v (pt/pp paid) ● vt bezahlen; zahlen <money>; ~ s.o. a visit jdm einen Besuch abstatten; ~ s.o. a compliment jdm ein Kompliment machen ● vi zahlen; (be profitable) sich bezahlt machen; (fig) sich lohnen; ~ for sth etw bezahlen. ~ back vt zurückzahlen. ~ in vt einzahlen. ~ off vt abzahlen <debt> ● vi (fig) sich auszahlen
payable a zahlbar; make ~ to ausstellen auf (+ acc)
payment n Bezahlung f; (amount) Zahlung f
pea n Erbse f
peace n Frieden m; for my ~ of mind zu meiner eigenen Beruhigung
peace|ful a, -ly adv friedlich. ~maker n Friedensstifter m
peach n Pfirsich m
peacock n Pfau m
peak n Gipfel m; (fig) Höhepunkt m. ~ed cap n Schirmmütze f. ~ hours npl Hauptbelastungszeit f; (for traffic) Hauptverkehrszeit f
peal n (of bells) Glockengeläut nt; ~s of laughter schallendes Gelächter nt
peanut n Erdnuss f
pear n Birne f
pearl n Perle f
peasant n Bauer m
peat n Torf m
pebble n Kieselstein m

P

peck n Schnabelhieb m; (kiss) flüchtiger Kuss m ●vt/i picken/ (nip) hacken (at nach)
peculiar a eigenartig, seltsam; ~ to eigentümlich (+ dat). ~ity n Eigenart f
pedal n Pedal nt ●vt fahren <bicycle> ●vi treten
pedantic a, -ally adv pedantisch
pedestal n Sockel m
pedestrian n Fußgänger(in) m(f) ●a (fig) prosaisch. ~ **crossing** n Fußgängerüberweg m. ~ **precinct** n Fußgängerzone f
pedigree n Stammbaum m ●attrib <animal> Rasse-
pedlar n Hausierer m
peek vi 🔟 gucken
peel n Schale f ●vt schälen; ●vi <skin:> sich schälen; <paint:> abblättern. ~ings npl Schalen pl
peep n kurzer Blick m ●vi gucken. ~**hole** n Guckloch nt
peer[1] vi ~ at forschend ansehen
peer[2] n Peer m; **his** ~s pl seinesgleichen
peg n (hook) Haken m; (for tent) Pflock m, Hering m; (for clothes) [Wäsche]klammer f; **off the** ~ 🔟 von der Stange
pejorative a, -ly adv abwertend
pelican n Pelikan m
pellet n Kügelchen nt
pelt[1] n (skin) Pelz m, Fell nt
pelt[2] vt bewerfen ●vi ~ [down] <rain:> [hernieder]prasseln
pelvis n (Anat) Becken nt
pen[1] n (for animals) Hürde f
pen[2] n Federhalter m; (ballpoint) Kugelschreiber m
penal a Straf-. ~**ize** vt bestrafen; (fig) benachteiligen
penalty n Strafe f; (fine) Geldstrafe f; (Sport) Strafstoß m; (Football) Elfmeter m
penance n Buße f
pence see penny

pencil n Bleistift m ●vt (pt/pp pencilled) mit Bleistift schreiben. ~**-sharpener** n Bleistiftspitzer m
pendulum n Pendel nt
penetrat|e vt durchdringen; ~e into eindringen in (+ acc). ~**ing** a durchdringend. ~**ion** n Durchdringen nt
penfriend n Brieffreund(in) m(f)
penguin n Pinguin m
penicillin n Penizillin nt
peninsula n Halbinsel f
penis n Penis m
penitentiary n (Amer) Gefängnis nt
pen: ~**knife** n Taschenmesser nt. ~**name** n Pseudonym nt
penniless a mittellos
penny n (pl pence; single coins pennies) Penny m; (Amer) Centstück nt; **the** ~**'s dropped** 🔟 der Groschen ist gefallen
pension n Rente f; (of civil servant) Pension f. ~**er** n Rentner(in) m(f); Pensionär(in) m(f)
pensive a nachdenklich
pent-up a angestaut
people npl Leute pl, Menschen pl; (citizens) Bevölkerung f; **the** ~ das Volk; **English** ~ die Engländer; ~ **say** man sagt; **for four** ~ für vier Personen ●vt bevölkern
pepper n Pfeffer m; (vegetable) Paprika m
pepper: ~**mint** n Pfefferminz nt; (Bot) Pfefferminze f. ~**pot** n Pfefferstreuer m
per prep pro; ~ **cent** Prozent nt
percentage n Prozentsatz m; (part) Teil m
perceptible a wahrnehmbar
percept|ion n Wahrnehmung f. ~**ive** a feinsinnig
perch[1] n Stange f ●vi <bird:> sich niederlassen
perch[2] n inv (fish) Barsch m

percussion n Schlagzeug nt. ~ **instrument** n Schlaginstrument nt

perennial a <problem> immer wiederkehrend ● n (Bot) mehrjährige Pflanze f

perfect¹ a perfekt, vollkommen; (I utter) völlig ● n (Gram) Perfekt nt

perfect² vt vervollkommnen. ~ion n Vollkommenheit f; **to** ~ion perfekt

perfectly adv perfekt; (completely) vollkommen, völlig

perforated a perforiert

perform vt ausführen; erfüllen <duty>; (Theat) aufführen <play>; spielen <role> ● vi (Theat) auftreten; (Techn) laufen. ~ance n Aufführung f; (at theatre, cinema) Vorstellung f; (Techn, Sport) Leistung f. ~er n Künstler(in) m(f)

perfume n Parfüm nt; (smell) Duft m

perhaps adv vielleicht

perilous a gefährlich

perimeter n [äußere] Grenze f; (Geom) Umfang m

period n Periode f; (Sch) Stunde f; (full stop) Punkt m ● attrib <costume> zeitgenössisch; <furniture> antik. ~ic a, **-ally** adv periodisch. ~ical n Zeitschrift f

peripher|al a nebensächlich. ~y n Peripherie f

perish vi <rubber:> verrotten; <food:> verderben; (liter: die) ums Leben kommen. ~able a leicht verderblich. ~ing a (I cold) eiskalt

perjur|e vt ~e oneself einen Meineid leisten. ~y n Meineid m

perk¹ n I [Sonder]vergünstigung f

perk² vi ~ up munter werden

perm n Dauerwelle f ● vt ~ s.o.'s hair jdm eine Dauerwelle machen

permanent a ständig; <job, address> fest. ~ly adv ständig; <work, live> dauernd, permanent; <employed> fest

permissible a erlaubt

permission n Erlaubnis f

permit¹ vt (pt/pp -mitted) erlauben (s.o. jdm)

permit² n Genehmigung f

perpendicular a senkrecht ● n Senkrechte f

perpetual a, **-ly** adv ständig, dauernd

perpetuate vt bewahren; verewigen <error>

perplex vt verblüffen. ~ed a verblüfft

persecut|e vt verfolgen. ~ion n Verfolgung f

perseverance n Ausdauer f

persevere vi beharrlich weitermachen

Persia n Persien nt

Persian a persisch; <cat, carpet> Perser-

persist vi beharrlich weitermachen; (continue) anhalten; <view:> weiter bestehen; ~ **in doing sth** dabei bleiben, etw zu tun. ~ence n Beharrlichkeit f. ~ent a, **-ly** adv beharrlich; (continuous) anhaltend

person n Person f; **in** ~ persönlich

personal a, **-ly** adv persönlich. ~ **hygiene** n Körperpflege f

personality n Persönlichkeit f

personify vt (pt/pp -ied) personifizieren, verkörpern

personnel n Personal nt

perspective n Perspektive f

persp|iration n Schweiß m. ~ire vi schwitzen

persua|de vt überreden; (convince) überzeugen. ~sion n Überredung f; (powers of ~sion) Überredungskunst f

P

persuasive *a*, **-ly** *adv* beredsam; (*convincing*) überzeugend

pertinent *a* relevant (**to** für)

perturb *vt* beunruhigen

peruse *vt* lesen

perverse *a* eigensinnig. ~**ion** *n* Perversion *f*

pervert¹ *vt* verdrehen; verführen <*person*>

pervert² *n* Perverse(r) *m*

pessimism *n* Pessimismus *m*. ~**t** *n* Pessimist *m*. ~**tic** *a*, **-ally** *adv* pessimistisch

pest *n* Schädling *m*; (🄴 *person*) Nervensäge *f*

pester *vt* belästigen

pesticide *n* Schädlingsbekämpfungsmittel *nt*

pet *n* Haustier *nt*; (*favourite*) Liebling *m* ● *vt* (*pt/pp* **petted**) liebkosen

petal *n* Blütenblatt *nt*

peter *vi* ~ **out** allmählich aufhören

petition *n* Bittschrift *f*

pet name *n* Kosename *m*

petrified *a* vor Angst wie versteinert

petrol *n* Benzin *nt*

petroleum *n* Petroleum *nt*

petrol: ~**-pump** *n* Zapfsäule *f*. ~ **station** *n* Tankstelle *f*. ~ **tank** *n* Benzintank *m*

petticoat *n* Unterrock *m*

petty *a* (**-ier, -iest**) kleinlich. ~ **cash** *n* Portokasse *f*

petulant *a* gekränkt

pew *n* [Kirchen]bank *f*

pharmaceutical *a* pharmazeutisch

pharmacist *n* Apotheker(in) *m(f)*. ~**y** *n* Pharmazie *f*; (*shop*) Apotheke *f*

phase *n* Phase *f* ● *vt* ~ **in/out** allmählich einführen/abbauen

Ph.D. (*abbr of Doctor of Philosophy*) Dr. phil.

pheasant *n* Fasan *m*

phenomenal *a* phänomenal. ~**on** *n* (*pl* **-na**) Phänomen *nt*

philharmonic *n* (*orchestra*) Philharmoniker *pl*

Philippines *npl* Philippinen *pl*

philistine *n* Banause *m*

philosopher *n* Philosoph *m*. ~**ical** *a*, **-ly** *adv* philosophisch. ~**y** *n* Philosophie *f*

phlegmatic *a* phlegmatisch

phobia *n* Phobie *f*

phone *n* Telefon *nt*; **be on the** ~ Telefon haben; (*be phoning*) telefonieren ● *vt* telefonieren ● *vi* telefonieren. ~ **back** *vt/i* zurückrufen. ~ **book** *n* Telefonbuch *nt*. ~ **box** *n* Telefonzelle *f*. ~ **card** *n* Telefonkarte *f*. ~**in** *n* (*Radio*) Hörersendung *f*. ~ **number** *n* Telefonnummer *f*

phonetic *a* phonetisch. ~**s** *n* Phonetik *f*

phoney *a* (**-ier, -iest**) falsch; (*forged*) gefälscht

photo *n* Foto *nt*, Aufnahme *f*. ~**copier** *n* Fotokopiergerät *nt*. ~**copy** *n* Fotokopie *f* ● *vt* fotokopieren

photogenic *a* fotogen

photograph *n* Fotografie *f*, Aufnahme *f* ● *vt* fotografieren

photographer *n* Fotograf(in) *m(f)*. ~**ic** *a*, **-ally** *adv* fotografisch. ~**y** *n* Fotografie *f*

phrase *n* Redensart *f* ● *vt* formulieren. ~**-book** *n* Sprachführer *m*

physical *a*, **-ly** *adv* körperlich

physician *n* Arzt *m*/ Ärztin *f*

physicist *n* Physiker(in) *m(f)*. ~**s** *n* Physik *f*

physiotherapist *n* Physiotherapeut(in) *m(f)*. ~**y** *n* Physiotherapie *f*

physique *n* Körperbau *m*

pianist *n* Klavierspieler(in) *m(f)*; (*professional*) Pianist(in) *m(f)*

piano *n* Klavier *nt*

pick¹ n Spitzhacke f

pick² n Auslese f; take one's ~ sich (dat) aussuchen ● vt/i (pluck) pflücken; (select) wählen, sich (dat) aussuchen; ~ and choose wählerisch sein; ~ a quarrel einen Streit anfangen; ~ holes in ① kritisieren; ~ at one's food im Essen herumstochern. ~ on vt wählen; (① find fault with) herumhacken auf (+ dat). ~ up vt in die Hand nehmen; (off the ground) aufheben; hochnehmen <baby>; (learn) lernen; (acquire) erwerben; (buy) kaufen; (Teleph) abnehmen <receiver>; auffangen <signal>; (collect) abholen; aufnehmen <passengers>; <police:> aufgreifen <criminal>; sich holen <illness>; ① aufgabeln <girl>; ~ oneself up aufstehen ● vi (improve) sich bessern

pickaxe n Spitzhacke f

picket n Streikposten m

pickle n (Amer: gherkin) Essiggurke f; ~s pl [Mixed] Pickles pl ● vt einlegen

pick: ~pocket n Taschendieb m. ~-up n (truck) Lieferwagen m

picnic n Picknick nt ● vi (pt/pp -nicked) picknicken

picture n Bild nt; (film) Film m; as pretty as a ~ bildhübsch; put s.o. in the ~ (fig) jdn ins Bild setzen ● vt (imagine) sich (dat) vorstellen

picturesque a malerisch

pie n Pastete f; (fruit) Kuchen m

piece n Stück nt; (of set) Teil nt; (in game) Stein m; (Journ) Artikel m; a ~ of bread/paper ein Stück Brot/Papier; a ~ of news/advice eine Nachricht/ein Rat; take to ~s auseinander nehmen ● vt ~ together zusammensetzen; (fig) zusammenstückeln. ~meal adv stückweise

pier n Pier m; (pillar) Pfeiler m

pierc|e vt durchstechen. ~ing a durchdringend

pig n Schwein nt

pigeon n Taube f. ~-hole n Fach nt

piggy|back n give s.o. a ~back jdn huckepack tragen. ~ bank n Sparschwein nt

pigheaded a ① starrköpfig

pigment n Pigment nt

pig: ~skin n Schweinsleder nt. ~sty n Schweinestall m. ~tail n ① Zopf m

pilchard n Sardine f

pile¹ n (of fabric) Flor m

pile² n Haufen m ● vt ~ sth on to sth etw auf etw (acc) häufen. ~ up vt häufen ● vi sich häufen

piles npl Hämorrhoiden pl

pile-up n Massenkarambolage f

pilgrim n Pilger(in) m(f). ~age n Pilgerfahrt f, Wallfahrt f

pill n Pille f

pillar n Säule f. ~-box n Briefkasten m

pillow n Kopfkissen nt. ~case n Kopfkissenbezug m

pilot n Pilot m; (Naut) Lotse m ● vt fliegen <plane>; lotsen <ship>. ~-light n Zündflamme f

pimple n Pickel m

pin n Stecknadel f; (Techn) Bolzen m, Stift m; (Med) Nagel m; I have ~s and needles in my leg ① mein Bein ist eingeschlafen ● vt (pt/pp pinned) anstecken (to/on an + acc); (sewing) stecken; (hold down) festhalten

pinafore n Schürze f. ~ dress n Kleiderrock m

pincers npl Kneifzange f; (Zool) Scheren pl

pinch n Kniff m; (of salt) Prise f; at a ~ ① zur Not ● vt kneifen, zwicken; (fam; steal) klauen; ~ one's finger sich (dat) den Finger klemmen ● vi <shoe:> drücken

pine¹ n (tree) Kiefer f

pine² vi ~ for sich sehnen nach

P

pineapple n Ananas f
ping-pong n Tischtennis nt
pink a rosa
pinnacle n Gipfel m; (on roof)
Turmspitze f
pin: ~**point** vt genau festlegen.
~**stripe** n Nadelstreifen m
pint n Pint nt (0,57 l, Amer: 0,47 l)
pioneer n Pionier m ● vt
bahnbrechende Arbeit leisten für
pious a, **-ly** adv fromm
pip¹ n (seed) Kern m
pip² n (sound) Tonsignal nt
pipe n Pfeife f; (for water, gas)
Rohr nt ● vt in Rohren leiten;
(Culin) spritzen
pipe: ~**-dream** n Luftschloss nt.
~**line** n Pipeline f; **in the** ~**line** 🔢
in Vorbereitung
piping a ~ **hot** kochend heiß
pirate n Pirat m
piss vi 🔀 pissen
pistol n Pistole f
piston n (Techn) Kolben m
pit n Grube f; (for orchestra)
Orchestergraben m
pitch¹ n (steepness) Schräge f; (of
voice) Stimmlage f; (of sound)
[Ton]höhe f; (Sport) Feld nt; (of
street trader) Standplatz m; (fig:
degree) Grad m ● vt werfen;
aufschlagen <tent> ● vi fallen
pitch² n (tar) Pech nt. ~**-black** a
pechschwarz. ~**-dark** a
stockdunkel
piteous a erbärmlich
pitfall n (fig) Falle f
pith n (Bot) Mark nt; (of orange)
weiße Haut f
pithy a (-ier, -iest) (fig) prägnant
piti|ful a bedauernswert. ~**less** a
mitleidslos
pittance n Hungerlohn m
pity n Mitleid nt, Erbarmen nt;
[what a] ~**!** [wie] schade! **take** ~
on sich erbarmen über (+ acc)
● vt bemitleiden
pivot n Drehzapfen m ● vi sich
drehen (**on um**)

pizza n Pizza f
placard n Plakat nt
placate vt beschwichtigen
place n Platz m; (spot) Stelle f;
(town, village) Ort m; (🔢 house)
Haus nt; **out of** ~ fehl am Platze;
take ~ stattfinden ● vt setzen;
(upright) stellen; (flat) legen;
(remember) unterbringen 🔢; ~
an order eine Bestellung
aufgeben; **be** ~**d** (in race) sich
platzieren. ~**-mat** n Set nt
placid a gelassen
plague n Pest f ● vt plagen
plaice n inv Scholle f
plain a (-er, -est) klar; (simple)
einfach; (not pretty) nicht
hübsch; (not patterned) einfarbig;
<chocolate> zartbitter; **in** ~
clothes in Zivil ● adv (simply)
einfach ● n Ebene f. ~**ly** adv
klar, deutlich; (simply) einfach;
(obviously) offensichtlich
plait n Zopf m ● vt flechten
plan n Plan m ● vt (pt/pp planned)
planen; (intend) vorhaben
plane¹ n (tree) Platane f
plane² n Flugzeug nt; (Geom &
fig) Ebene f
plane³ n (Techn) Hobel m ● vt
hobeln
planet n Planet m
plank n Brett nt; (thick) Planke f
planning n Planung f
plant n Pflanze f; (Techn) Anlage
f; (factory) Werk nt ● vt pflanzen;
(place in position) setzen; ~
oneself sich hinstellen. ~**ation** n
Plantage f
plaque n [Gedenk]tafel f; (on
teeth) Zahnbelag m
plaster n Verputz m; (sticking ~)
Pflaster nt; ~ **[of Paris]** Gips m
● vt verputzen <wall>; (cover)
bedecken mit
plastic n Kunststoff m, Plastik nt
● a Kunststoff-, Plastik-;
(malleable) formbar, plastisch

plastic surgery n plastische Chirurgie f

plate n Teller m; (flat sheet) Platte f; (with name, number) Schild nt; (gold and silverware) vergoldete/versilberte Ware f; (in book) Tafel f ●vt (with gold) vergolden; (with silver) versilbern

platform n Plattform f; (stage) Podium nt; (Rail) Bahnsteig m; ~ 5 Gleis 5

platinum n Platin nt

platitude n Plattitüde f

plausible a plausibel

play n Spiel nt; [Theater]stück nt; (Radio) Hörspiel nt; (TV) Fernsehspiel nt; ~ on words Wortspiel nt ●vt/i spielen; ausspielen <card>; ~ safe sichergehen. ~ down vt herunterspielen. ~ up vi 🇬🇧 Mätzchen machen

play: ~er n Spieler(in) m(f). ~ful a, -ly adv verspielt. ~ground n Spielplatz m; (Sch) Schulhof m. ~group n Kindergarten m

playing: ~card n Spielkarte f. ~field n Sportplatz m

play: ~mate n Spielkamerad m. ~thing n Spielzeug nt. ~wright n Dramatiker m

plc abbr (public limited company) ≈ GmbH

plea n Bitte f; make a ~ for bitten um

plead vi flehen (for um); ~ guilty sich schuldig bekennen; ~ with s.o. jdn anflehen

pleasant a angenehm; <person> nett. ~ly adv angenehm; <say, smile> freundlich

pleas|e adv bitte ●vt gefallen (+ dat); ~e s.o. jdm eine Freude machen; ~e oneself tun, was man will. ~ed a erfreut; be ~ed with/ about sth sich über etw (acc) freuen. ~ing a erfreulich

pleasure n Vergnügen nt; (joy) Freude f; with ~ gern[e]

pleat n Falte f ●vt fälteln

pledge n Versprechen nt ●vt verpfänden; versprechen

plentiful a reichlich

plenty n eine Menge; (enough) reichlich; ~ of money/people viel Geld/viele Leute

pliable a biegsam

pliers npl [Flach]zange f

plight n [Not]lage f

plinth n Sockel m

plod vi (pt/pp plodded) trotten; (work) sich abmühen

plonk n 🇬🇧 billiger Wein m

plot n Komplott nt; (of novel) Handlung f; ~ of land Stück nt Land ●vt einzeichnen ●vi ein Komplott schmieden

plough n Pflug m ●vt/i pflügen

ploy n 🇬🇧 Trick m

pluck n Mut m ●vt zupfen; rupfen <bird>; pflücken <flower>; ~ up courage Mut fassen

plucky a (-ier, -iest) tapfer, mutig

plug n Stöpsel m; (wood) Zapfen m; (cotton wool) Bausch m; (Electr) Stecker m; (Auto) Zündkerze f; (🇬🇧 advertisement) Schleichwerbung f ●vt zustopfen; (🇬🇧 advertise) Schleichwerbung machen für. ~ in vt (Electr) einstecken

plum n Pflaume f

plumage n Gefieder nt

plumb|er n Klempner m. ~ing n Wasserleitungen pl

plume n Feder f

plump a (-er, -est) mollig, rundlich ●vt ~ for wählen

plunge n Sprung m; take the ~ 🇬🇧 den Schritt wagen ●vt/i tauchen

plural a pluralisch ●n Mehrzahl f, Plural m

plus prep plus (+ dat) ●a Plus- ●n Pluszeichen nt; (advantage) Plus nt

plush[y] a luxuriös

P

ply vt (pt/pp **plied**) ausüben <trade>; ~ **s.o. with drink** jdm ein Glas nach dem anderen eingießen. **~wood** n Sperrholz nt

p.m. adv (abbr of **post meridiem**) nachmittags

pneumatic a pneumatisch. ~ **drill** n Presslufthammer m

pneumonia n Lungenentzündung f

poach vt (Culin) pochieren; (steal) wildern. **~er** n Wilddieb m

pocket n Tasche f; **be out of** ~ [an einem Geschäft] verlieren ● vt einstecken. **~-book** n Notizbuch nt; (wallet) Brieftasche f. **~-money** n Taschengeld nt

pod n Hülse f

poem n Gedicht nt

poet n Dichter(in) m(f). **~ic** a dichterisch

poetry n Dichtung f

poignant a ergreifend

point n Punkt m; (sharp end) Spitze f; (meaning) Sinn m; (purpose) Zweck m; (Electr) Steckdose f; **~s** pl (Rail) Weiche f; ~ **of view** Standpunkt m; **good/bad ~s** gute/schlechte Seiten; **what is the ~?** wozu? **the** ~ **is** es geht darum; **up to a** ~ bis zu einem gewissen Grade; **be on the** ~ **of doing sth** im Begriff sein, etw zu tun ● vt richten (at auf + acc); ausfugen <brickwork> ● vi deuten (at/to auf + acc); (with finger) mit dem Finger zeigen. ~ **out** vt zeigen auf (+ acc); ~ **sth out to s.o.** jdn auf etw (acc) hinweisen

point-blank a aus nächster Entfernung; (fig) rundweg

point|ed a spitz; <question> gezielt. **~less** a zwecklos, sinnlos

poise n Haltung f

poison n Gift nt ● vt vergiften. **~ous** a giftig

poke n Stoß m ● vt stoßen; schüren <fire>; (put) stecken

poker[1] n Schüreisen nt

poker[2] n (Cards) Poker nt

poky a (-ier, -iest) eng

Poland n Polen nt

polar a Polar-. ~ **bear** n Eisbär m

Pole n Pole m/Polin f

pole[1] n Stange f

pole[2] n (Geog, Electr) Pol m

pole-vault n Stabhochsprung m

police npl Polizei f

police: ~man n Polizist m. ~ **station** n Polizeiwache f. **~woman** n Polizistin f

policy[1] n Politik f

policy[2] n (insurance) Police f

Polish a polnisch

polish n (shine) Glanz m; (for shoes) [Schuh]creme f; (for floor) Bohnerwachs m; (for furniture) Politur f; (for silver) Putzmittel nt; (for nails) Lack m; (fig) Schliff m ● vt polieren; bohnern <floor>. ~ **off** vt 🇮 verputzen <food>; erledigen <task>

polite a, **-ly** adv höflich. **~ness** n Höflichkeit f

politic|al a, **-ly** adv politisch. **~ian** n Politiker(in) m(f)

politics n Politik f

poll n Abstimmung f; (election) Wahl f; **[opinion]** [Meinungs]umfrage f

pollen n Blütenstaub m, Pollen m

polling: ~-booth n Wahlkabine f. **~-station** n Wahllokal nt

pollut|e vt verschmutzen. **~ion** n Verschmutzung f

polo n Polo nt. **~-neck** n Rollkragen m

polystyrene n Polystyrol nt; (for packing) Styropor (P) nt

polythene n Polyäthylen nt. ~ **bag** n Plastiktüte f

pomp n Pomp m

pompous a, **-ly** adv großspurig

pond n Teich m

ponder vi nachdenken

ponderous a schwerfällig

pony n Pony nt. **~tail** n Pferdeschwanz m

poodle n Pudel m

pool n [Schwimm]becken nt; (pond) Teich m; (of blood) Lache f; (common fund) [gemeinsame] Kasse f; **~s** pl [Fußball]toto nt ● vt zusammenlegen

poor a (-er, -est) arm; (not good) schlecht; in **~** health nicht gesund. **~ly** a be **~ly** krank sein ● adv ärmlich; (badly) schlecht

pop[1] n Knall m ● v (pt/pp popped) ● vt 🔟 (put) stecken (in in + acc) ● vi knallen; (burst) platzen. **~ in** vi 🔟 reinschauen. **~ out** vi 🔟 kurz rausgehen

pop[2] n 🔟 Popmusik f, Pop m ● attrib Pop-

popcorn n Puffmais m

pope n Papst m

poplar n Pappel f

poppy n Mohn m

popular a beliebt, populär; <belief> volkstümlich. **~ity** n Beliebtheit f, Popularität f

populat|e vt bevölkern. **~ion** n Bevölkerung f

porcelain n Porzellan nt

porch n Vorbau m; (Amer) Veranda f

porcupine n Stachelschwein nt

pore n Pore f

pork n Schweinefleisch nt

porn n 🔟 Porno m

pornograph|ic a pornographisch. **~y** n Pornographie f

porridge n Haferbrei m

port[1] n Hafen m; (town) Hafenstadt f

port[2] n (Naut) Backbord nt

port[3] n (wine) Portwein m

portable a tragbar

porter n Portier m; (for luggage) Gepäckträger m

porthole n Bullauge nt

portion n Portion f; (part, share) Teil nt

portrait n Porträt nt

portray vt darstellen. **~al** n Darstellung f

Portug|al n Portugal nt. **~uese** a portugiesisch ● n Portugiese m/ -giesin f

pose n Pose f ● vt aufwerfen <problem>; stellen <question> ● vi posieren; (for painter) Modell stehen

posh a 🔟 feudal

position n Platz m; (posture) Haltung f; (job) Stelle f; (situation) Lage f, Situation f; (status) Stellung f ● vt platzieren; **~ oneself** sich stellen

positive a, **-ly** adv positiv; (definite) eindeutig; (real) ausgesprochen ● n Positiv nt

possess vt besitzen. **~ion** n Besitz m; **~ions** pl Sachen pl

possess|ive a Possessiv-; be **~ive** about s.o. zu sehr an jdm hängen

possibility n Möglichkeit f

possib|le a möglich. **~ly** adv möglicherweise; not **~ly** unmöglich

post[1] n (pole) Pfosten m

post[2] n (place of duty) Posten m; (job) Stelle f

post[3] n (mail) Post f; by **~** mit der Post ● vt aufgeben <letter>; (send by **~**) mit der Post schicken; keep s.o. **~ed** jdn auf dem Laufenden halten

postage n Porto nt

postal a Post-. **~ order** n ≈ Geldanweisung f

post: ~-box n Briefkasten m. **~card** n Postkarte f; (picture) Ansichtskarte f. **~code** n Postleitzahl f. **~-date** vt vordatieren

poster n Plakat nt

posterity n Nachwelt f

posthumous a, **-ly** adv postum

post: ~man n Briefträger m. **~mark** n Poststempel m

post-mortem n Obduktion f

P

post office n Post f
postpone vt aufschieben; ~ until
verschieben auf (+ acc). ~ment n
Verschiebung f
postscript n Nachschrift f
posture n Haltung f
pot n Topf m; (for tea, coffee)
Kanne f; ~s of money I eine
Menge Geld
potato n (pl -es) Kartoffel f
potent a stark
potential a, -ly adv potenziell ● n
Potenzial nt
pot: ~hole n Höhle f; (in road)
Schlagloch nt. ~-shot n take a ~-
shot at schießen auf (+ acc)
potter n Töpfer(in) m(f). ~y n
Töpferei f; (articles) Töpferwaren
pl
potty a (-ier, -iest) I verrückt ● n
Töpfchen nt
pouch n Beutel m
poultry n Geflügel nt
pounce vi zuschlagen; ~ on sich
stürzen auf (+ acc)
pound[1] n (money & 0,454 kg)
Pfund nt
pound[2] vi <heart:> hämmern; (run
heavily) stampfen
pour vt gießen; einschenken
<drink> ● vi strömen; (with rain)
gießen. ~ out vi ausströmen ● vt
ausschütten; einschenken
<drink>
pout vi einen Schmollmund
machen
poverty n Armut f
powder n Pulver nt; (cosmetic)
Puder m ● vt pudern
power n Macht f; (strength) Kraft
f; (Electr) Strom m; (nuclear)
Energie f; (Math) Potenz f. ~ cut
n Stromsperre f. ~ed a betrieben
(by mit); ~ed by electricity mit
Elektroantrieb. ~ful a mächtig;
(strong) stark. ~less a machtlos.
~-station n Kraftwerk nt
practicable a durchführbar,
praktikabel

practical a, -ly adv praktisch. ~
joke n Streich m
practice n Praxis f; (custom)
Brauch m; (habit) Gewohnheit f;
(exercise) Übung f; (Sport)
Training nt; in ~ (in reality) in
der Praxis; out of ~ außer
Übung; put into ~ ausführen
practise vt üben; (carry out)
praktizieren; ausüben
<profession> ● vi üben; <doctor:>
praktizieren. ~d a geübt
praise n Lob nt ● vt loben.
~worthy a lobenswert
pram n Kinderwagen m
prank n Streich m
prawn n Garnele f, Krabbe f
pray vi beten. ~er n Gebet nt
preach vt/i predigen. ~er n
Prediger m
pre-arrange vt im Voraus
arrangieren
precarious a, -ly adv unsicher
precaution n
Vorsichtsmaßnahme f
precede vt vorangehen (+ dat)
preceden|ce n Vorrang m. ~t n
Präzedenzfall m
preceding a vorhergehend
precinct n Bereich m; (traffic-
free) Fußgängerzone f; (Amer:
district) Bezirk m
precious a kostbar; <style>
preziös ● adv I ~ little recht
wenig
precipice n Steilabfall m
precipitation n (Meteorol)
Niederschlag m
precis|e a, -ly adv genau. ~ion n
Genauigkeit f
precocious a frühreif
pre|conceived a vorgefasst.
~conception n vorgefasste
Meinung f
predator n Raubtier nt
predecessor n Vorgänger(in)
m(f)
predicat|e n (Gram) Prädikat nt.
~ive a, -ly adv prädikativ

predict vt voraussagen. ~able a voraussehbar; <person> berechenbar. ~ion n Voraussage f

predomin|ant a vorherrschend. ~antly adv hauptsächlich, überwiegend. ~ate vi vorherrschen

preen vt putzen

prefab n Ⓣ [einfaches] Fertighaus nt. ~ricated a vorgefertigt

preface n Vorwort nt

prefect n Präfekt m

prefer vt (pt/pp preferred) vorziehen; I ~ to walk ich gehe lieber zu Fuß; I ~ wine ich trinke lieber Wein

prefera|ble a be ~ble vorzuziehen sein (to dat). ~bly adv vorzugsweise

preferen|ce n Vorzug m. ~tial a bevorzugt

pregnan|cy n Schwangerschaft f. ~t a schwanger; <animal> trächtig

prehistoric a prähistorisch

prejudice n Vorurteil nt; (bias) Voreingenommenheit f ● vt einnehmen (against gegen). ~d a voreingenommen

preliminary a Vor-

prelude n Vorspiel nt

premature a vorzeitig; <birth> Früh-. ~ly adv zu früh

premeditated a vorsätzlich

premier a führend ● n (Pol) Premier[minister] m

premiere n Premiere f

premises npl Räumlichkeiten pl; on the ~ im Haus

premium n Prämie f; be at a ~ hoch im Kurs stehen

premonition n Vorahnung f

preoccupied a [in Gedanken] beschäftigt

preparation n Vorbereitung f; (substance) Präparat nt

preparatory a Vor-

prepare vt vorbereiten; anrichten <meal> ● vi sich vorbereiten (for auf + acc); ~d to bereit zu

preposition n Präposition f

preposterous a absurd

prerequisite n Voraussetzung f

Presbyterian a presbyterianisch ● n Presbyterianer(in) m(f)

prescribe vt vorschreiben; (Med) verschreiben

prescription n (Med) Rezept nt

presence n Anwesenheit f, Gegenwart f; ~ of mind Geistesgegenwart f

present[1] a gegenwärtig; be ~ anwesend sein; (occur) vorkommen ● n Gegenwart f; (Gram) Präsens nt; at ~ zurzeit; for the ~ vorläufig

present[2] n (gift) Geschenk nt

present[3] vt überreichen; (show) zeigen; vorlegen <cheque>; (introduce) vorstellen; ~ s.o. with sth jdm etw überreichen. ~able a be ~able sich zeigen lassen können

presentation n Überreichung f

presently adv nachher; (Amer: now) zurzeit

preservation n Erhaltung f

preservative n Konservierungsmittel nt

preserve vt erhalten; (Culin) konservieren; (bottle) einmachen ● n (Hunting & fig) Revier nt; (jam) Konfitüre f

preside vi den Vorsitz haben (over bei)

presidency n Präsidentschaft f

president n Präsident m; (Amer: chairman) Vorsitzende(r) m/f. ~ial a Präsidenten-; <election> Präsidentschafts-

press n Presse f ● vt/i drücken; drücken auf (+ acc) <button>; pressen <flower>; (iron) bügeln; (urge) bedrängen; ~ for drängen auf (+ acc); be ~ed for time in Zeitdruck sein. ~ on vi

weitergehen/-fahren; (fig)
weitermachen
press: ~ **cutting** n
Zeitungsausschnitt m. ~**ing** a
dringend
pressure n Druck m. ~**-cooker** n
Schnellkochtopf m
pressurize vt Druck ausüben auf
(+ acc). ~**d** a Druck-
prestig|e n Prestige nt. ~**ious** a
Prestige-
presumably adv vermutlich
presume vt vermuten
presumpt|ion n Vermutung f;
(boldness) Anmaßung f. ~**uous** a,
-ly adv anmaßend
pretence n Verstellung f;
(pretext) Vorwand m
pretend vt (claim) vorgeben; ~
that so tun, als ob; ~ **to be** sich
ausgeben als
pretentious a protzig
pretext n Vorwand m
pretty a (-ier, -iest), ~**ily** adv
hübsch ● adv (🄵 fairly) ziemlich
prevail vi siegen; <custom:>
vorherrschen; ~ **on s.o. to do sth**
jdn dazu bringen, etw zu tun
prevalen|ce n Häufigkeit f. ~**t** a
vorherrschend
prevent vt verhindern, verhüten;
~ **s.o. [from] doing sth** jdn daran
hindern, etw zu tun. ~**ion** n
Verhinderung f, Verhütung f.
~**ive** a vorbeugend
preview n Voraufführung f
previous a vorhergehend; ~ **to**
vor (+ dat). ~**ly** adv vorher,
früher
prey n Beute f; **bird of** ~
Raubvogel m
price n Preis m ● vt (Comm)
auszeichnen. ~**less** a
unschätzbar; (fig) unbezahlbar
prick n Stich m ● vt/i stechen
prickl|e n Stachel m; (thorn) Dorn
m. ~**y** a stachelig; <sensation>
stechend

pride n Stolz m; (arrogance)
Hochmut m ● vt ~ **oneself on**
stolz sein auf (+ acc)
priest n Priester m
prim a (primmer, primmest) prüde
primarily adv hauptsächlich, in
erster Linie
primary a Haupt-. ~ **school** n
Grundschule f
prime¹ a Haupt-; (first-rate)
erstklassig
prime² vt scharf machen <bomb>;
grundieren <surface>
Prime Minister n
Premierminister(in) m(f)
primitive a primitiv
primrose n gelbe Schlüsselblume
f
prince n Prinz m
princess n Prinzessin f
principal a Haupt- ● n (Sch)
Rektor(in) m(f)
principally adv hauptsächlich
principle n Prinzip nt, Grundsatz
m; **in/on** ~ im/aus Prinzip
print n Druck m; (Phot) Abzug m;
in ~ gedruckt; (available)
erhältlich; **out of** ~ vergriffen
● vt drucken; (write in capitals)
in Druckschrift schreiben;
(Computing) ausdrucken; (Phot)
abziehen. ~**ed matter** n
Drucksache f
print|er n Drucker m. ~**ing** n
Druck m
printout n (Computing) Ausdruck
m
prior a frühere(r,s); ~ **to** vor (+
dat)
priority n Priorität f, Vorrang m
prise vt ~ **open/up** aufstemmen/
hochstemmen
prison n Gefängnis nt. ~**er** n
Gefangene(r) m/f
privacy n Privatsphäre f; **have no**
~ nie für sich sein
private a, **-ly** adv privat;
(confidential) vertraulich; <car,
secretary, school> Privat- ● n

(*Mil*) [einfacher] Soldat *m*; **in ~** privat; (*confidentially*) vertraulich
privation *n* Entbehrung *f*
privilege *n* Privileg *nt*. **~d** *a* privilegiert
prize *n* Preis *m* ● *vt* schätzen
pro *n* Ⓘ Profi *m*; **the ~s and cons** das Für und Wider
probability *n* Wahrscheinlichkeit *f*
probable *a*, **-bly** *adv* wahrscheinlich
probation *n* (*Jur*) Bewährung *f*
probe *n* Sonde *f*; (*fig: investigation*) Untersuchung *f*
problem *n* Problem *nt*; (*Math*) Textaufgabe *f*. **~atic** *a* problematisch
procedure *n* Verfahren *nt*
proceed *vi* gehen; (*in vehicle*) fahren; (*continue*) weitergehen/ -fahren; (*speaking*) fortfahren; (*act*) verfahren
proceedings *npl* Verfahren *nt*; (*Jur*) Prozess *m*
proceeds *npl* Erlös *m*
process *n* Prozess *m*; (*procedure*) Verfahren *nt*; **in the ~** dabei ● *vt* verarbeiten; (*Admin*) bearbeiten; (*Phot*) entwickeln
procession *n* Umzug *m*, Prozession *f*
proclaim *vt* ausrufen
proclamation *n* Proklamation *f*
procure *vt* beschaffen
prod *n* Stoß *m* ● *vt* stoßen
prodigy *n* [infant] ~ Wunderkind *nt*
produce¹ *n* landwirtschaftliche Erzeugnisse *pl*
produce² *vt* erzeugen, produzieren; (*manufacture*) herstellen; (*bring out*) hervorholen; (*cause*) hervorrufen; inszenieren <*play*>; (*Radio, TV*) redigieren. **~r** *n* Erzeuger *m*, Produzent *m*; Hersteller *m*; (*Theat*) Regisseur

m; (*Radio, TV*) Redakteur(in) *m(f)*
product *n* Erzeugnis *nt*, Produkt *nt*. **~ion** *n* Produktion *f*; (*Theat*) Inszenierung *f*
productiv|e *a* produktiv; <*land, talks*> fruchtbar. **~ity** *n* Produktivität *f*
profession *n* Beruf *m*. **~al** *a*, **-ly** *adv* beruflich; (*not amateur*) Berufs-; (*expert*) fachmännisch; (*Sport*) professionell ● *n* Fachmann *m*; (*Sport*) Profi *m*
professor *n* Professor *m*
proficien|cy *n* Können *nt*. **~t** *a* **be ~t in** beherrschen
profile *n* Profil *nt*; (*character study*) Porträt *nt*
profit *n* Gewinn *m*, Profit *m* ● *vi* **~ from** profitieren von. **~able** *a*, **-bly** *adv* gewinnbringend; (*fig*) nutzbringend
profound *a*, **-ly** *adv* tief
program (*Amer & Computing*) *n* Programm *nt* ● *vt* (*pt/pp* **programmed**) programmieren
programme *n* Programm *nt*; (*Radio, TV*) Sendung *f*. **~r** *n* (*Computing*) Programmierer(in) *m(f)*
progress¹ *n* Vorankommen *nt*; (*fig*) Fortschritt *m*; **in ~** im Gange; **make ~** (*fig*) Fortschritte machen
progress² *vi* vorankommen; (*fig*) fortschreiten. **~ion** *n* Folge *f*; (*development*) Entwicklung *f*
progressive *a* fortschrittlich. **~ly** *adv* zunehmend
prohibit *vt* verbieten (s.o. jdm). **~ive** *a* unerschwinglich
project¹ *n* Projekt *nt*; (*Sch*) Arbeit *f*
project² *vt* projizieren <*film*>; (*plan*) planen ● *vi* (*jut out*) vorstehen
projector *n* Projektor *m*
prolific *a* fruchtbar; (*fig*) produktiv

P

prologue *n* Prolog *m*
prolong *vt* verlängern
promenade *n* Promenade *f* ●*vi* spazieren gehen
prominent *a* vorstehend; (*important*) prominent; (*conspicuous*) auffällig
promiscuous *a* be ~**ous** häufig den Partner wechseln
promis|e *n* Versprechen *nt* ●*vt/i* versprechen (**s.o.** jdm). ~**ing** *a* viel versprechend
promot|e *vt* befördern; (*advance*) fördern; (*publicize*) Reklame machen für; **be** ~**ed** (*Sport*) aufsteigen. ~**ion** *n* Beförderung *f*; (*Sport*) Aufstieg *m*; (*Comm*) Reklame *f*
prompt *a* prompt, unverzüglich; (*punctual*) pünktlich ●*adv* pünktlich ●*vt/i* veranlassen (**to** zu); (*Theat*) soufflieren (+ *dat*). ~**er** *n* Souffleur *m*/Souffleuse *f*. ~**ly** *adv* prompt
prone *a* be or lie ~ auf dem Bauch liegen; **be** ~ **to** neigen zu
pronoun *n* Fürwort *nt*, Pronomen *nt*
pronounce *vt* aussprechen; (*declare*) erklären. ~**d** *a* ausgeprägt; (*noticeable*) deutlich. ~**ment** *n* Erklärung *f*
pronunciation *n* Aussprache *f*
proof *n* Beweis *m*; (*Typ*) Korrekturbogen *m*. ~**-reader** *n* Korrektor *m*
prop¹ *n* Stütze *f* ●*vt* (*pt/pp* propped) ~ **against** lehnen an (+ *acc*). ~ **up** *vt* stützen
prop² *n* (*Theat* 🄸) Requisit *nt*
propaganda *n* Propaganda *f*
propel *vt* (*pt/pp* propelled) [an]treiben. ~**ler** *n* Propeller *m*
proper *a*, **-ly** *adv* richtig; (*decent*) anständig
property *n* Eigentum *nt*; (*quality*) Eigenschaft *f*; (*Theat*) Requisit *nt*; (*land*) [Grund]besitz *m*; (*house*) Haus *nt*

prophecy *n* Prophezeiung *f*
prophesy *vt* (*pt/pp* -ied) prophezeien
prophet *n* Prophet *m*. ~**ic** *a* prophetisch
proportion *n* Verhältnis *nt*; (*share*) Teil *m*; ~**s** *pl* Proportionen; (*dimensions*) Maße. ~**al** *a*, **-ly** *adv* proportional
proposal *n* Vorschlag *m*; (*of marriage*) [Heirats]antrag *m*
propose *vt* vorschlagen; (*intend*) vorhaben; einbringen <*motion*> ●*vi* einen Heiratsantrag machen
proposition *n* Vorschlag *m*
proprietor *n* Inhaber(in) *m(f)*
propriety *n* Korrektheit *f*; (*decorum*) Anstand *m*
prose *n* Prosa *f*
prosecut|e *vt* strafrechtlich verfolgen. ~**ion** *n* strafrechtliche Verfolgung *f*; **the** ~**ion** die Anklage. ~**or** *n* [Public] P~or Staatsanwalt *m*
prospect *n* Aussicht *f*
prospect|ive *a* (*future*) zukünftig. ~**or** *n* Prospektor *m*
prospectus *n* Prospekt *m*
prosper *vi* gedeihen, florieren; <*person*> Erfolg haben. ~**ity** *n* Wohlstand *m*
prosperous *a* wohlhabend
prostitut|e *n* Prostituierte *f*. ~**ion** *n* Prostitution *f*
prostrate *a* ausgestreckt
protagonist *n* Kämpfer *m*; (*fig*) Protagonist *m*
protect *vt* schützen (**from** vor + *dat*); beschützen <*person*>. ~**ion** *n* Schutz *m*. ~**ive** *a* Schutz-; (*fig*) beschützend. ~**or** *n* Beschützer *m*
protein *n* Eiweiß *nt*
protest¹ *n* Protest *m*
protest² *vi* protestieren
Protestant *a* protestantisch ●*n* Protestant(in) *m(f)*
protester *n* Protestierende(r) *m/f*
prototype *n* Prototyp *m*

protrude *vi* [her]vorstehen
proud *a*, **-ly** *adv* stolz (*of* auf + *acc*)
prove *vt* beweisen ● *vi* ~ **to be** sich erweisen als
proverb *n* Sprichwort *nt*
provide *vt* zur Verfügung stellen; spenden <*shade*>; ~ **s.o. with sth** jdn mit etw versorgen *od* versehen ● *vi* ~ **for** sorgen für
provided *conj* ~ **[that]** vorausgesetzt [dass]
providen|ce *n* Vorsehung *f.* ~**tial** *a* be ~**tial** ein Glück sein
provinc|e *n* Provinz *f;* (*fig*) Bereich *m.* ~**ial** *a* provinziell
provision *n* Versorgung *f* (*of* mit); ~**s** *pl* Lebensmittel *pl.* ~**al** *a*, **-ly** *adv* vorläufig
provocat|ion *n* Provokation *f.* ~**ive** *a*, **-ly** *adv* provozierend; (*sexually*) aufreizend
provoke *vt* provozieren; (*cause*) hervorrufen
prow *n* Bug *m*
prowl *vi* herumschleichen
proximity *n* Nähe *f*
pruden|ce *n* Umsicht *f.* ~**t** *a*, **-ly** *adv* umsichtig; (*wise*) klug
prudish *a* prüde
prune¹ *n* Backpflaume *f*
prune² *vt* beschneiden
pry *vi* (*pt/pp* **pried**) neugierig sein
psalm *n* Psalm *m*
psychiatric *a* psychiatrisch
psychiatr|ist *n* Psychiater(in) *m(f).* ~**y** *n* Psychiatrie *f*
psychic *a* übersinnlich
psycho|analysis *n* Psychoanalyse *f.* ~**analyst** *n* Psychoanalytiker(in) *m(f)*
psychological *a*, **-ly** *adv* psychologisch; <*illness*> psychisch
psycholog|ist *n* Psychologe *m/* -login *f.* ~**y** *n* Psychologie *f*
P.T.O. *abbr* (**please turn over**) b.w.
pub *n* Ⓘ Kneipe *f*
puberty *n* Pubertät *f*

public *a*, **-ly** *adv* öffentlich; **make** ~ publik machen ● *n* **the** ~ die Öffentlichkeit
publican *n* [Gast]wirt *m*
publication *n* Veröffentlichung *f*
public: ~ **holiday** *n* gesetzlicher Feiertag *m.* ~ **house** *n* [Gast]wirtschaft *f*
publicity *n* Publicity *f;* (*advertising*) Reklame *f*
publicize *vt* Reklame machen für
public: ~ **school** *n* Privatschule *f;* (*Amer*) staatliche Schule *f.* ~**spirited** *a* be ~**-spirited** Gemeinsinn haben
publish *vt* veröffentlichen. ~**er** *n* Verleger(in) *m(f);* (*firm*) Verlag *m.* ~**ing** *n* Verlagswesen *nt*
pudding *n* Pudding *m;* (*course*) Nachtisch *m*
puddle *n* Pfütze *f*
puff *n* (*of wind*) Hauch *m;* (*of smoke*) Wölkchen *nt.* ● *vt* blasen, pusten; ~ **out** ausstoßen. ● *vi* keuchen; ~ **at** paffen an (+ *dat*) <*pipe*>. ~**ed** *a* (*out of breath*) aus der Puste. ~ **pastry** *n* Blätterteig *m*
pull *n* Zug *m;* (*jerk*) Ruck *m;* (Ⓘ *influence*) Einfluss *m* ● *vt* ziehen; ziehen an (+ *dat*) <*rope*>; ~ **a muscle** sich (*dat*) einen Muskel zerren; ~ **oneself together** sich zusammennehmen; ~ **one's weight** tüchtig mitarbeiten; ~ **s.o.'s leg** Ⓘ jdn auf den Arm nehmen. ~ **down** *vt* herunterziehen; (*demolish*) abreißen. ~ **in** *vt* hereinziehen ● *vi* (*Auto*) einscheren. ~ **off** *vt* abziehen; Ⓘ schaffen. ~ **out** *vt* herausziehen ● *vi* (*Auto*) ausscheren. ~ **through** *vt* durchziehen ● *vi* (*recover*) durchkommen. ~ **up** *vt* heraufziehen; ausziehen <*plant*> ● *vi* (*Auto*) anhalten
pullover *n* Pullover *m*

P

pulp n Brei m; (of fruit) [Frucht]fleisch nt
pulpit n Kanzel f
pulse n Puls m
pulses npl Hülsenfrüchte pl
pummel vt (pt/pp pummelled) mit den Fäusten bearbeiten
pump n Pumpe f ● vt pumpen; 🄸 aushorchen. ~ **up** vt (inflate) aufpumpen
pumpkin n Kürbis m
pun n Wortspiel nt
punch[1] n Faustschlag m; (device) Locher m ● vt boxen; lochen <ticket>; stanzen <hole>
punch[2] n (drink) Bowle f
punctual a, **-ly** adv pünktlich. ~**ity** n Pünktlichkeit f
punctuat|e vt mit Satzzeichen versehen. ~**ion** n Interpunktion f
puncture n Loch nt; (tyre) Reifenpanne f ● vt durchstechen
punish vt bestrafen. ~**able** a strafbar. ~**ment** n Strafe f
punt n (boat) Stechkahn m
puny a (-ier, -iest) mickerig
pup n = puppy
pupil n Schüler(in) m(f); (of eye) Pupille f
puppet n Puppe f; (fig) Marionette f
puppy n junger Hund m
purchase n Kauf m; (leverage) Hebelkraft f ● vt kaufen. ~**r** n Käufer m
pure a (-r, -st,) **-ly** adv rein
purge n (Pol) Säuberungsaktion f ● vt reinigen
puri|fication n Reinigung f. ~**fy** vt (pt/pp -ied) reinigen
puritanical a puritanisch
purity n Reinheit f
purple a [dunkel]lila
purpose n Zweck m; (intention) Absicht f; (determination) Entschlossenheit f; on ~ absichtlich. ~**ful** a, **-ly** adv entschlossen. ~**ly** adv absichtlich
purr vi schnurren

purse n Portemonnaie nt; (Amer: handbag) Handtasche f
pursue vt verfolgen; (fig) nachgehen (+ dat). ~**r** n Verfolger m
pursuit n Verfolgung f; Jagd f; (pastime) Beschäftigung f
pus n Eiter m
push n Stoß m; get the ~ 🄸 hinausfliegen ● vt/i schieben; (press) drücken; (roughly) stoßen. ~ **off** vt hinunterstoßen ● vi (🄸 leave) abhauen. ~ **on** vi (continue) weitergehen/-fahren; (with activity) weitermachen. ~ **up** vt hochschieben; hochtreiben <price>
push: ~**button** n Druckknopf m. ~**chair** n [Kinder]sportwagen m
pushy a 🄸 aufdringlich
puss n, **pussy** n Mieze f
put vt (pt/pp put, pres p putting) tun; (place) setzen; (upright) stellen; (flat) legen; (express) ausdrücken; (say) sagen; (estimate) schätzen (at auf + acc); ~ **aside** or **by** beiseite legen ● vi ~ **to sea** auslaufen ● a stay ~ dableiben. ~ **away** vt wegräumen. ~ **back** vt wieder hinsetzen/-stellen/-legen; zurückstellen <clock>. ~ **down** vt hinsetzen/-stellen/-legen; (suppress) niederschlagen; (kill) töten; (write) niederschreiben; (attribute) zuschreiben (to dat). ~ **forward** vt vorbringen; vorstellen <clock>. ~ **in** vt hineinsetzen/ -stellen/-legen; (insert) einstecken; (submit) einreichen ● vi ~ **in for** beantragen. ~ **off** vt ausmachen <light>; (postpone) verschieben; ~ **s.o. off** jdn abbestellen; (disconcert) jdn aus der Fassung bringen. ~ **on** vt anziehen <clothes, brake>; sich (dat) aufsetzen <hat>; (Culin) aufsetzen; anmachen <light>; aufführen <play>; annehmen

<accent>; ~ **on weight** zunehmen.
~ **out** *vt* hinaussetzen/-stellen/
-legen; ausmachen *<fire, light>*;
ausstrecken *<hand>*; *(disconcert)*
aus der Fassung bringen; ~ **s.o./
oneself out** jdm/sich Umstände
machen. ~ **through** *vt*
durchstecken; *(Teleph)*
verbinden (**to** mit). ~ **up** *vt*
errichten *<building>*; aufschlagen
<tent>; aufspannen *<umbrella>*;
anschlagen *<notice>*; erhöhen
<price>; unterbringen *<guest>*
● *vi* (*at hotel*) absteigen in (+
dat); ~ **up with sth** sich (*dat*) etw
bieten lassen

putrid *a* faulig

putty *n* Kitt *m*

puzzl|e *n* Rätsel *nt*; *(jigsaw)*
Puzzlespiel *nt* ● *vt* it ~es me es
ist mir rätselhaft. ~**ing** *a*
rätselhaft

pyjamas *npl* Schlafanzug *m*

pylon *n* Mast *m*

pyramid *n* Pyramide *f*

python *n* Pythonschlange *f*

quack *n* Quaken *nt*; *(doctor)*
Quacksalber *m* ● *vi* quaken

quadrangle *n* Viereck *nt*; *(court)*
Hof *m*

quadruped *n* Vierfüßer *m*

quadruple *a* vierfach ● *vt*
vervierfachen ● *vi* sich
vervierfachen

quaint *a* (**-er, -est**) malerisch;
(odd) putzig

quake *n* ① Erdbeben *nt* ● *vi*
beben; *(with fear)* zittern

qualif|ication *n* Qualifikation *f*;
(reservation) Einschränkung *f*.
~**ied** *a* qualifiziert; *(trained)*
ausgebildet; *(limited)* bedingt

qualify *v* (*pt/pp* -**ied**) ● *vt*
qualifizieren; *(entitle)*
berechtigen; *(limit)* einschränken
● *vi* sich qualifizieren

quality *n* Qualität *f*;
(characteristic) Eigenschaft *f*

qualm *n* Bedenken *pl*

quantity *n* Quantität *f*, Menge *f*; in
~ in großen Mengen

quarantine *n* Quarantäne *f*

quarrel *n* Streit *m* ● *vi* (*pt/pp*
quarrelled) sich streiten. ~**some** *a*
streitsüchtig

quarry[1] *n* (*prey*) Beute *f*

quarry[2] *n* Steinbruch *m*

quart *n* Quart *nt*

quarter *n* Viertel *nt*; *(of year)*
Vierteljahr *nt*; *(Amer)* 25-Cent-
Stück *nt*; ~**s** *pl* Quartier *nt*; **at [a]**
~ **to six** um Viertel vor sechs ● *vt*
vierteln; *(Mil)* einquartieren (**on**
bei). ~~**final** *n* Viertelfinale *nt*

quarterly *a* & *adv* vierteljährlich

quartet *n* Quartett *nt*

quartz *n* Quarz *m*

quay *n* Kai *m*

queasy *a* **I feel** ~ mir ist übel

queen *n* Königin *f*; *(Cards, Chess)*
Dame *f*

queer *a* (**-er, -est**) eigenartig;
(dubious) zweifelhaft; *(ill)*
unwohl

quell *vt* unterdrücken

quench *vt* löschen

query *n* Frage *f*; *(question mark)*
Fragezeichen *nt* ● *vt* (*pt/pp* -**ied**)
infrage stellen; reklamieren
<bill>

quest *n* Suche *f* (**for** nach)

question *n* Frage *f*; *(for
discussion)* Thema *nt*; **out of the**
~ ausgeschlossen; **the person in**
~ die fragliche Person ● *vt*
infrage stellen; ~ **s.o.** jdn
ausfragen; *<police:>* jdn

Q

verhören. **~able** a zweifelhaft. **~ mark** n Fragezeichen nt

questionnaire n Fragebogen m

queue n Schlange f ● vi ~ [up] Schlange stehen, sich anstellen (for nach)

quibble vi Haarspalterei treiben

quick a (-er, -est), **-ly** adv schnell; be ~! mach schnell! ● adv schnell. **~en** vt beschleunigen ● vi sich beschleunigen

quick: ~sand n Treibsand m. **~- tempered** a aufbrausend

quid n inv 🇬🇧 Pfund nt

quiet a (-er, -est), **-ly** adv still; (calm) ruhig; (soft) leise; keep ~ about i nichts sagen von ● n Stille f; Ruhe f

quiet|en vt beruhigen ● vi ~en down ruhig werden. **~ness** n Stille f; Ruhe f

quilt n Steppdecke f. **~ed** a Stepp-

quintet n Quintett nt

quirk n Eigenart f

quit v (pt/pp quitted or quit) ● vt verlassen; (give up) aufgeben; ~ doing sth aufhören, etw zu tun ● vi gehen

quite adv ganz; (really) wirklich; ~ [so]! genau! ~ a few ziemlich viele

quits a quitt

quiver vi zittern

quiz n Quiz nt ● vt (pt/pp quizzed) ausfragen. **~zical** a, **-ly** adv fragend

quota n Anteil m; (Comm) Kontingent nt

quotation n Zitat nt; (price) Kostenvoranschlag m; (of shares) Notierung f. **~ marks** npl Anführungszeichen pl

quote n i = quotation; in ~s in Anführungszeichen ● vt/i zitieren

rabbi n Rabbiner m; (title) Rabbi m

rabbit n Kaninchen nt

rabid a fanatisch; <animal> tollwütig

rabies n Tollwut f

race¹ n Rasse f

race² n Rennen nt; (fig) Wettlauf m ● vi [am Rennen] teilnehmen; <athlete, horse:> laufen; (🇬🇧 rush) rasen ● vt um die Wette laufen mit; an einem Rennen teilnehmen lassen <horse>

race: ~course n Rennbahn f. **~horse** n Rennpferd nt. **~-track** n Rennbahn f

racial a, **-ly** adv rassisch; <discrimination> Rassen-

racing n Rennsport m; (horse-) Pferderennen nt. **~ car** n Rennwagen m. **~ driver** n Rennfahrer m

racis|m n Rassismus m. **~t** a rassistisch ● n Rassist m

rack¹ n Ständer m; (for plates) Gestell nt ● vt ~ one's brains sich (dat) den Kopf zerbrechen

rack² n go to ~ and ruin verfallen; (fig) herunterkommen

racket n (Sport) Schläger m; (din) Krach m; (swindle) Schwindelgeschäft nt

racy a (-ier, -iest) schwungvoll; (risqué) gewagt

radar n Radar m

radian|ce n Strahlen nt. **~t** a, **-ly** adv strahlend

radiate vt ausstrahlen ● vi <heat:> ausgestrahlt werden; <roads:> strahlenförmig ausgehen. **~ion** n Strahlung f

radiator n Heizkörper m; (Auto) Kühler m
radical a, **-ly** adv radikal ● n Radikale(r) m/f
radio n Radio nt; **by ~** über Funk ● vt funken <message>
radio|active a radioaktiv. **~activity** n Radioaktivität f
radish n Radieschen nt
radius n (pl **-dii**) Radius m, Halbmesser m
raffle n Tombola f
raft n Floß nt
rafter n Dachsparren m
rag n Lumpen m; (pej: newspaper) Käseblatt nt
rage n Wut f; **all the ~** 🔲 der letzte Schrei ● vi rasen
ragged a zerlumpt; <edge> ausgefranst
raid n Überfall m; (Mil) Angriff m; (police) Razzia f ● vt überfallen; (Mil) angreifen; <police> eine Razzia durchführen in (+ dat); (break in) eindringen in (+ acc). **~er** n Eindringling m; (of bank) Bankräuber m
rail n Schiene f; (pole) Stange f; (hand~) Handlauf m; (Naut) Reling f; **by ~** mit der Bahn
railings npl Geländer nt
railroad n (Amer) = railway
railway n [Eisen]bahn f. **~ station** n Bahnhof m
rain n Regen m ● vi regnen
rain: **~bow** n Regenbogen m. **~coat** n Regenmantel m. **~fall** n Niederschlag m
rainy a (-ier, -iest) regnerisch
raise n (Amer) Lohnerhöhung f ● vt erheben; (upright) aufrichten; (make higher) erhöhen; (lift) [hoch]heben; aufziehen <child, animal>; aufwerfen <question>; aufbringen <money>
raisin n Rosine f
rake n Harke f, Rechen m ● vt harken, rechen

rally n Versammlung f; (Auto) Rallye f; (Tennis) Ballwechsel m ● vt sammeln
ram n Schafbock m ● vt (pt/pp rammed) rammen
rambl|e n Wanderung f ● vi wandern; (in speech) irrereden. **~er** n Wanderer m; (rose) Kletterrose f. **~ing** a weitschweifig; <club> Wander-
ramp n Rampe f; (Aviat) Gangway f
rampage¹ n **be/go on the ~** randalieren
rampage² vi randalieren
ramshackle a baufällig
ran see run
ranch n Ranch f
random a willkürlich; **a ~ sample** eine Stichprobe ● n **at ~** aufs Geratewohl; <choose> willkürlich
rang see ring²
range n Serie f, Reihe f; (Comm) Auswahl f, Angebot nt (of an + dat); (of mountains) Kette f; (Mus) Umfang m; (distance) Reichweite f; (for shooting) Schießplatz m; (stove) Kohlenherd m ● vi reichen; **~ from ... to** gehen von ... bis. **~r** n Aufseher m
rank n (row) Reihe f; (Mil) Rang m; (social position) Stand m; **the ~ and file** die breite Masse ● vt/i einstufen; **~ among** zählen zu
ransack vt durchwühlen; (pillage) plündern
ransom n Lösegeld nt; **hold s.o. to ~** Lösegeld für jdn fordern
rape n Vergewaltigung f ● vt vergewaltigen
rapid a, **-ly** adv schnell. **~ity** n Schnelligkeit f
rapist n Vergewaltiger m
raptur|e n Entzücken nt. **~ous** a, **-ly** adv begeistert
rare¹ a (-r, -st), **-ly** adv selten
rare² a (Culin) englisch gebraten
rarefied a dünn

R

rarity n Seltenheit f
rascal n Schlingel m
rash¹ n (Med) Ausschlag m
rash² a (-er, -est), **-ly** adv voreilig
rasher n Speckscheibe f
raspberry n Himbeere f
rat n Ratte f; (🔲 person) Schuft m; **smell a ~** 🔲 Lunte riechen
rate n Rate f; (speed) Tempo nt; (of payment) Satz m; (of exchange) Kurs m; **~s** pl (taxes) ≈ Grundsteuer f; **at any ~** auf jeden Fall; **at this ~** auf diese Weise ● vt einschätzen; **~ among** zählen zu ● vi **~ as** gelten als
rather adv lieber; (fairly) ziemlich; **~!** und ob!
rating n Einschätzung f; (class) Klasse f; (sailor) [einfacher] Matrose m; **~s** pl (Radio, TV) ≈ Einschaltquote f
ratio n Verhältnis nt
ration n Ration f ● vt rationieren
rational a, **-ly** adv rational. **~ize** vt/i rationalisieren
rattle n Rasseln nt; (of windows) Klappern nt; (toy) Klapper f ● vi rasseln; klappern ● vt rasseln mit
raucous a rau
rave vi toben; **~ about** schwärmen von
raven n Rabe m
ravenous a heißhungrig
ravine n Schlucht f
raving a **~ mad** 🔲 total verrückt
ravishing a hinreißend
raw a (-er, -est) roh; (not processed) Roh-; <skin> wund; <weather> nasskalt; (inexperienced) unerfahren; **get a ~ deal** 🔲 schlecht wegkommen. **~ materials** npl Rohstoffe pl
ray n Strahl m
razor n Rasierapparat m. **~ blade** n Rasierklinge f
re prep betreffs (+ gen)
reach n Reichweite f; (of river) Strecke f; **within/out of ~** in/außer

Reichweite ● vt erreichen; (arrive at) ankommen in (+ dat); (**~ as far as**) reichen bis zu; kommen zu <decision, conclusion>; (pass) reichen ● vi reichen (**to** bis zu); **~ for** greifen nach
react vi reagieren (**to** auf + acc)
reaction n Reaktion f. **~ary** a reaktionär
reactor n Reaktor m
read vt/i (pt/pp read) lesen; (aloud) vorlesen (**to** dat); (Univ) studieren; ablesen <meter>. **~ out** vt vorlesen
readable a lesbar
reader n Leser(in) m(f); (book) Lesebuch nt
readily adv bereitwillig; (easily) leicht
reading n Lesen nt; (Pol, Relig) Lesung f
readjust vt neu einstellen ● vi sich umstellen (**to** auf + acc)
ready a (-ier, -iest) fertig; (willing) bereit; (quick) schnell; **get ~** sich fertig machen; (prepare to) sich bereitmachen
ready: ~-made a fertig. **~-to-wear** a Konfektions-
real a wirklich; (genuine) echt; (actual) eigentlich ● adv (Amer 🔲) echt. **~ estate** n Immobilien pl
realis|m n Realismus m. **~t** n Realist m. **~tic** a, **-ally** adv realistisch
reality n Wirklichkeit f
realization n Erkenntnis f
realize vt einsehen; (become aware) gewahr werden; verwirklichen <hopes, plans>; einbringen <price>
really adv wirklich; (actually) eigentlich
realm n Reich nt
realtor n (Amer) Immobilienmakler m
reap vt ernten

reappear vi wiederkommen

rear¹ a Hinter-; (Auto) Heck- ● n
the ~ der hintere Teil; from the ~
von hinten

rear² vt aufziehen ● vi ~ [up]
<horse:> sich aufbäumen

rearrange vt umstellen

reason n Grund m; (good sense)
Vernunft f; (ability to think)
Verstand m; within ~ in
vernünftigen Grenzen ● vi
argumentieren; ~ with vernünftig
reden mit. ~able a vernünftig;
(not expensive) preiswert. ~ably
adv (fairly) ziemlich

reassur|ance n Beruhigung f;
Versicherung f. ~e vt beruhigen;
~e s.o. of sth jdm etw (gen)
versichern

rebel¹ n Rebell m

rebel² vi (pt/pp rebelled)
rebellieren. ~lion n Rebellion f.
~lious a rebellisch

rebound¹ vi abprallen

rebound² n Rückprall m

rebuild vt (pt/pp -built) wieder
aufbauen

rebuke n Tadel m ● vt tadeln

recall n Erinnerung f ● vt
zurückrufen; abberufen
<diplomat>; (remember) sich
erinnern an (+ acc)

recant vi widerrufen

recap vt/i Ⅰ = recapitulate

recapitulate vt/i
zusammenfassen; rekapitulieren

recapture vt wieder gefangen
nehmen <person>; wieder
einfangen <animal>

reced|e vi zurückgehen. ~ing a
<forehead, chin> fliehend

receipt n Quittung f; (receiving)
Empfang m; ~s pl (Comm)
Einnahmen pl

receive vt erhalten, bekommen;
empfangen <guests>. ~r n
(Teleph) Hörer m; (of stolen
goods) Hehler m

recent a kürzlich erfolgte(r,s).
~ly adv vor kurzem

receptacle n Behälter m

reception n Empfang m; ~ [desk]
(in hotel) Rezeption f; ~ist n
Empfangsdame f

receptive a aufnahmefähig; ~ to
empfänglich für

recess n Nische f; (holiday)
Ferien pl

recession n Rezession f

recharge vt [wieder] aufladen

recipe n Rezept nt

recipient n Empfänger m

recital n (of poetry, songs)
Vortrag m; (of instrumental
music) Konzert nt

recite vt aufsagen; (before
audience) vortragen

reckless a, -ly adv leichtsinnig;
(careless) rücksichtslos. ~ness n
Leichtsinn m; (carelessness)
Rücksichtslosigkeit f

reckon vt rechnen; (consider)
glauben ● vi ~ on/with rechnen
mit

reclaim vt zurückfordern;
zurückgewinnen <land>

reclin|e vi liegen. ~ing seat n
Liegesitz m

recluse n Einsiedler(in) m(f)

recognition n Erkennen nt;
(acknowledgement) Anerkennung
f; in ~ als Anerkennung (of gen)

recognize vt erkennen; (know
again) wieder erkennen;
(acknowledge) anerkennen

recoil vi zurückschnellen; (in
fear) zurückschrecken

recollect vt sich erinnern an (+
acc). ~ion n Erinnerung f

recommend vt empfehlen.
~ation n Empfehlung f

recon|cile vt versöhnen; ~cile
oneself to sich abfinden mit.
~ciliation n Versöhnung f

reconnaissance n (Mil)
Aufklärung f

R

reconnoitre vi (pres p -tring) auf Erkundung ausgehen

reconsider vt sich (dat) noch einmal überlegen

reconstruct vt wieder aufbauen; rekonstruieren <crime>

record¹ vt aufzeichnen; (register) registrieren; (on tape) aufnehmen

record² n Aufzeichnung f; (Jur) Protokoll nt; (Mus) [Schall]platte f; (Sport) Rekord m; ~s pl Unterlagen pl; off the ~ inoffiziell; have a [criminal] ~ vorbestraft sein

recorder n (Mus) Blockflöte f

recording n Aufnahme f

re-count¹ vt nachzählen

re-count² n (Pol) Nachzählung f

recover vt zurückbekommen ●vi sich erholen. ~y n Wiedererlangung f; (of health) Erholung f

recreation n Erholung f; (hobby) Hobby nt. ~al a Freizeit-; be ~al erholsam sein

recruit n (Mil) Rekrut m; new ~ (member) neues Mitglied nt; (worker) neuer Mitarbeiter m ●vt rekrutieren; anwerben <staff>. ~ment n Rekrutierung f; Anwerbung f

rectang|le n Rechteck nt. ~ular a rechteckig

rectify vt (pt/pp -ied) berichtigen

rector n Pfarrer m; (Univ) Rektor m. ~y n Pfarrhaus nt

recur vi (pt/pp recurred) sich wiederholen; <illness:> wiederkehren

recurren|ce n Wiederkehr f. ~t a wiederkehrend

recycle vt wieder verwerten

red a (redder, reddest) rot ●n Rot nt

redd|en vt röten ●vi rot werden. ~ish a rötlich

redecorate vt renovieren; (paint) neu streichen; (wallpaper) neu tapezieren

redeem vt einlösen; (Relig) erlösen

redemption n Erlösung f

red: ~-haired a rothaarig. ~-handed a catch s.o. ~-handed jdn auf frischer Tat ertappen. ~ herring n falsche Spur f. ~-hot a glühend heiß. ~ light n (Auto) rote Ampel f. ~ness n Röte f

redo vt (pt -did, pp -done) noch einmal machen

redouble vt verdoppeln

red tape n Ⅰ Bürokratie f

reduc|e vt verringern, vermindern; (in size) verkleinern; ermäßigen <costs>; herabsetzen <price, goods>; (Culin) einkochen lassen. ~tion n Verringerung f; (in price) Ermäßigung f; (in size) Verkleinerung f

redundan|cy n Beschäftigungslosigkeit f. ~t a überflüssig; make ~t entlassen; be made ~t beschäftigungslos werden

reed n [Schilf]rohr nt; ~s pl Schilf nt

reef n Riff nt

reek vi riechen (of nach)

reel n Rolle f, Spule f ●vi (stagger) taumeln ●vt ~ off (fig) herunterrasseln

refectory n Refektorium nt; (Univ) Mensa f

refer v (pt/pp referred) ●vt verweisen (to an + acc); übergeben, weiterleiten <matter> (to an + acc) ●vi ~ to sich beziehen auf (+ acc); (mention) erwähnen; (concern) betreffen; (consult) sich wenden an (+ acc); nachschlagen in (+ dat) <book>; are you ~ring to me? meinen Sie mich?

referee n Schiedsrichter m; (Boxing) Ringrichter m; (for job) Referenz f ● vt/i (pt/pp refereed) Schiedsrichter/Ringrichter sein (bei)

reference n Erwähnung f; (in book) Verweis m; (for job) Referenz f; with ~ to in Bezug auf (+ acc); make [a] ~ to erwähnen. ~ book n Nachschlagewerk nt

referendum n Volksabstimmung f

refill¹ vt nachfüllen

refill² n (for pen) Ersatzmine f

refine vt raffinieren. ~d a fein, vornehm. ~ment n Vornehmheit f; (Techn) Verfeinerung f. ~ry n Raffinerie f

reflect vt reflektieren; <mirror:> [wider]spiegeln; be ~ed in sich spiegeln in (+ dat) ● vi nachdenken (on über + acc). ~ion n Reflexion f; (image) Spiegelbild nt; on ~ion nach nochmaliger Überlegung. ~or n Rückstrahler m

reflex n Reflex m

reflexive a reflexiv

reform n Reform f ● vt reformieren ● vi sich bessern

refrain¹ n Refrain m

refrain² vi ~ from doing sth etw nicht tun

refresh vt erfrischen. ~ing a erfrischend. ~ments npl Erfrischungen pl

refrigerat|e vt kühlen. ~or n Kühlschrank m

refuel vt/i (pt/pp -fuelled) auftanken

refuge n Zuflucht f; take ~ Zuflucht nehmen

refugee n Flüchtling m

refund¹ n get a ~ sein Geld zurückbekommen

refund² vt zurückerstatten

refusal n (see refuse¹) Ablehnung f; Weigerung f

refuse¹ vt ablehnen; (not grant) verweigern; ~ to do sth sich weigern, etw zu tun ● vi ablehnen; sich weigern

refuse² n Müll m

refute vt widerlegen

regain vt wiedergewinnen

regal a, -ly adv königlich

regard n (heed) Rücksicht f; (respect) Achtung f; ~s pl Grüße pl; with ~ to in Bezug auf (+ acc) ● vt ansehen, betrachten (as als). ~ing prep bezüglich (+ gen). ~less adv ohne Rücksicht (of auf + acc)

regatta n Regatta f

regime n Regime nt

regiment n Regiment nt. ~al a Regiments-

region n Region f; in the ~ of (fig) ungefähr. ~al a, -ly adv regional

register n Register nt; (Sch) Anwesenheitsliste f ● vt registrieren; (report) anmelden; einschicken <letter>; aufgeben <luggage> ● vi (report) sich anmelden

registrar n Standesbeamte(r) m

registration n Registrierung f; Anmeldung f. ~ number n Autonummer f

registry office n Standesamt nt

regret n Bedauern nt ● vt (pt/pp regretted) bedauern. ~fully adv mit Bedauern

regrettab|le a bedauerlich. ~ly adv bedauerlicherweise

regular a, -ly adv regelmäßig; (usual) üblich ● n (in pub) Stammgast m; (in shop) Stammkunde m. ~ity n Regelmäßigkeit f

regulat|e vt regulieren. ~ion n (rule) Vorschrift f

rehears|al n (Theat) Probe f. ~e vt proben

reign n Herrschaft f ● vi herrschen, regieren

rein n Zügel m

R

reindeer n inv Rentier nt

reinforce vt verstärken. ~**ment** n Verstärkung f; send ~**ments** Verstärkung schicken

reiterate vt wiederholen

reject vt ablehnen. ~**ion** n Ablehnung f

rejects npl (Comm) Ausschussware f

rejoic|e vi (liter) sich freuen. ~**ing** n Freude f

rejoin vt sich wieder anschließen (+ dat); wieder beitreten (+ dat) <club, party>

rejuvenate vt verjüngen

relapse n Rückfall m ● vi einen Rückfall erleiden

relate vt (tell) erzählen; (connect) verbinden

relation n Beziehung f; (person) Verwandte(r) m/f. ~**ship** n Beziehung f; (link) Verbindung f; (blood tie) Verwandtschaft f; (affair) Verhältnis nt

relative n Verwandte(r) m/f ● a relativ; (Gram) Relativ-. ~**ly** adv relativ, verhältnismäßig

relax vt lockern, entspannen ● vi sich lockern, sich entspannen. ~**ation** n Entspannung f. ~**ing** a entspannend

relay[1] vt (pt/pp -layed) weitergeben; (Radio, TV) übertragen

relay[2] n. ~ [race] n Staffel f

release n Freilassung f, Entlassung f; (Techn) Auslöser m ● vt freilassen; (let go of) loslassen; (Techn) auslösen; veröffentlichen <information>

relent vi nachgeben. ~**less** a, -ly adv erbarmungslos; (unceasing) unaufhörlich

relevan|ce n Relevanz f. ~**t** a relevant (to für)

reliab|ility n Zuverlässigkeit f. ~**le** a, -ly adv zuverlässig

relian|ce n Abhängigkeit f (on von). ~**t** a angewiesen (on auf + acc)

relic n Überbleibsel nt; (Relig) Reliquie f

relief n Erleichterung f; (assistance) Hilfe f; (replacement) Ablösung f; (Art) Relief nt

relieve vt erleichtern; (take over from) ablösen; ~ of entlasten von

religion n Religion f

religious a religiös

relinquish vt loslassen; (give up) aufgeben

relish n Genuss m; (Culin) Würze f ● vt genießen

reluctan|ce n Widerstreben nt. ~**t** a widerstrebend; be ~**t** zögern (to zu). ~**tly** adv ungern, widerstrebend

rely vi (pt/pp -ied) ~ on sich verlassen auf (+ acc); (be dependent on) angewiesen sein auf (+ acc)

remain vi bleiben; (be left) übrig bleiben. ~**der** n Rest m. ~**ing** a restlich. ~**s** npl Reste pl; [mortal] ~**s** [sterbliche] Überreste pl

remand n on ~ in Untersuchungshaft ● vt ~ in custody in Untersuchungshaft schicken

remark n Bemerkung f ● vt bemerken. ~**able** a, -bly adv bemerkenswert

remarry vi wieder heiraten

remedy n [Heil]mittel nt (for gegen); (fig) Abhilfe f ● vt (pt/pp -ied) abhelfen (+ dat); beheben <fault>

remember vt sich erinnern an (+ acc); ~ to do sth daran denken, etw zu tun ● vi sich erinnern

remind vt erinnern (of an + acc). ~**er** n Andenken nt; (letter, warning) Mahnung f

reminisce vi sich seinen Erinnerungen hingeben. ~**nces**

npl Erinnerungen *pl.* ~nt *a* be
~nt of erinnern an (+ *acc*)

remnant *n* Rest *m*

remorse *n* Reue *f.* ~ful *a,* -ly *adv*
reumütig. ~less *a,* -ly *adv*
unerbittlich

remote *a* fern; (*isolated*)
abgelegen; (*slight*) gering. ~
control *n* Fernsteuerung *f;* (*for
TV*) Fernbedienung *f*

remotely *adv* entfernt; not ~
nicht im Entferntesten

removable *a* abnehmbar

removal *n* Entfernung *f;* (*from
house*) Umzug *m.* ~ **van** *n*
Möbelwagen *m*

remove *vt* entfernen; (*take off*)
abnehmen; (*take out*)
herausnehmen

render *vt* machen; erweisen
<*service*>; (*translate*)
wiedergeben; (*Mus*) vortragen

renegade *n* Abtrünnige(r) *m/f*

renew *vt* erneuern; verlängern
<*contract*>. ~al *n* Erneuerung *f;*
Verlängerung *f*

renounce *vt* verzichten auf (+
acc)

renovat|e *vt* renovieren. ~ion *n*
Renovierung *f*

renown *n* Ruf *m.* ~ed *a* berühmt

rent *n* Miete *f* ● *vt* mieten; (*hire*)
leihen; ~ [out] vermieten;
verleihen. ~al *n* Mietgebühr *f;*
Leihgebühr *f*

renunciation *n* Verzicht *m*

reopen *vt/i* wieder aufmachen

reorganize *vt* reorganisieren

rep *n* Ⓕ Vertreter *m*

repair *n* Reparatur *f;* in good/bad
~ in gutem/schlechtem Zustand
● *vt* reparieren

repatriate *vt* repatriieren

repay *vt* (*pt/pp* -paid)
zurückzahlen; ~ s.o. for sth jdm
etw zurückzahlen. ~ment *n*
Rückzahlung *f*

repeal *n* Aufhebung *f* ● *vt*
aufheben

repeat *n* Wiederholung *f* ● *vt/i*
wiederholen; ~ after me sprechen
Sie mir nach. ~ed *a,* -ly *adv*
wiederholt

repel *vt* (*pt/pp* repelled)
abwehren; (*fig*) abstoßen. ~lent
a abstoßend

repent *vi* Reue zeigen. ~ance *n*
Reue *f.* ~ant *a* reuig

repercussions *npl* Auswirkungen
pl

repertoire, repertory *n* Repertoire
nt

repetit|ion *n* Wiederholung *f.*
~ive *a* eintönig

replace *vt* zurücktun; (*take the
place of*) ersetzen; (*exchange*)
austauschen. ~ment *n* Ersatz *m*

replay *n* (*Sport*)
Wiederholungsspiel *nt;* [action] ~
Wiederholung *f*

replenish *vt* auffüllen <*stocks*>;
(*refill*) nachfüllen

replica *n* Nachbildung *f*

reply *n* Antwort *f* (to auf + *acc*)
● *vt/i* (*pt/pp* replied) antworten

report *n* Bericht *m;* (*Sch*) Zeugnis
nt; (*rumour*) Gerücht *nt;* (*of gun*)
Knall *m* ● *vt* berichten; (*notify*)
melden; ~ s.o. to the police jdn
anzeigen; ● *vi* berichten (on über
+ *acc*); (*present oneself*) sich
melden (to bei). ~er *n*
Reporter(in) *m/f*

reprehensible *a* tadelnswert

represent *vt* darstellen; (*act for*)
vertreten, repräsentieren. ~ation
n Darstellung *f*

representative *a* repräsentativ
(of für) ● *n* Bevollmächtigte(r)
m/(f); (*Comm*) Vertreter(in) *m/(f);*
(*Amer, Pol*) Abgeordnete(r) *m/f*

repress *vt* unterdrücken. ~ion *n*
Unterdrückung *f.* ~ive *a*
repressiv

reprieve *n* Begnadigung *f;* (*fig*)
Gnadenfrist *f* ● *vt* begnadigen

reprimand *n* Tadel *m* ● *vt* tadeln

reprint[1] *n* Nachdruck *m*

Ⓕ

reprint² vt neu auflegen
reprisal n Vergeltungsmaßnahme f
reproach n Vorwurf m ● vt Vorwürfe pl machen (+ dat). ~**ful** a, -**ly** adv vorwurfsvoll
reproduc|e vt wiedergeben, reproduzieren ● vi sich fortpflanzen. ~**tion** n Reproduktion f; (Biol) Fortpflanzung f
reptile n Reptil nt
republic n Republik f. ~**an** a republikanisch ● n Republikaner(in) m(f)
repugnan|ce n Widerwille m. ~**t** a widerlich
repuls|ion n Widerwille m. ~**ive** a abstoßend, widerlich
reputable a <firm> von gutem Ruf; (respectable) anständig
reputation n Ruf m
request n Bitte f ● vt bitten
require vt (need) brauchen; (demand) erfordern; **be ~d to do sth** etw tun müssen. ~**ment** n Bedürfnis nt; (condition) Erfordernis nt
resale n Weiterverkauf m
rescue n Rettung f ● vt retten. ~**r** n Retter m
research n Forschung f ● vt erforschen; (Journ) recherchieren. ~**er** n Forscher m; (Journ) Rechercheur m
resem|blance n Ähnlichkeit f. ~**ble** vt ähneln (+ dat)
resent vt übel nehmen; einen Groll hegen gegen <person>. ~**ful** a, -**ly** adv verbittert. ~**ment** n Groll m
reservation n Reservierung f; (doubt) Vorbehalt m; (enclosure) Reservat nt
reserve n Reserve f; (for animals) Reservat nt; (Sport) Reservespieler(in) m(f) ● vt reservieren; <client:> reservieren lassen; (keep) aufheben; sich

(dat) vorbehalten <right>. ~**d** a reserviert
reservoir n Reservoir nt
reshuffle n (Pol) Umbildung f ● vt (Pol) umbilden
residence n Wohnsitz m; (official) Residenz f; (stay) Aufenthalt m
resident a ansässig (in in + dat); <housekeeper, nurse> im Haus wohnend ● n Bewohner(in) m(f); (of street) Anwohner m. ~**ial** a Wohn-
residue n Rest m; (Chem) Rückstand m
resign vt ~ **oneself to** sich abfinden mit ● vi kündigen; (from public office) zurücktreten. ~**ation** n Resignation f; (from job) Kündigung f; Rücktritt m. ~**ed** a, -**ly** adv resigniert
resilient a federnd; (fig) widerstandsfähig
resin n Harz nt
resist vt/i sich widersetzen (+ dat), (fig) widerstehen (+ dat). ~**ance** n Widerstand m. ~**ant** a widerstandsfähig
resolut|e a, -**ly** adv entschlossen. ~**ion** n Entschlossenheit f; (intention) Vorsatz m; (Pol) Resolution f
resolve n Entschlossenheit f; (decision) Beschluss m ● vt beschließen; (solve) lösen
resort n (place) Urlaubsort m; **as a last ~** wenn alles andere fehlschlägt ● vi ~ **to** (fig) greifen zu
resound vi widerhallen
resource n ~**s** pl Ressourcen pl. ~**ful** a findig
respect n Respekt m, Achtung f (for vor + dat); (aspect) Hinsicht f; **with ~ to** in Bezug auf (+ acc) ● vt respektieren, achten
respect|able a, -**bly** adv ehrbar; (decent) anständig; (considerable)

ansehnlich. **~ful** a, **-ly** adv
respektvoll

respective a jeweilig. **~ly** adv
beziehungsweise

respiration n Atmung f

respite n [Ruhe]pause f; (delay)
Aufschub m

respond vi antworten; (react)
reagieren (**to** auf + acc)

response n Antwort f; Reaktion f

responsibility n Verantwortung f;
(duty) Verpflichtung f

responsib|le a verantwortlich;
(trustworthy) verantwortungsvoll.
~ly adv verantwortungsbewusst

rest[1] n Ruhe f; (holiday) Erholung
f; (interval & Mus) Pause f; **have a
~** eine Pause machen; (rest) sich
ausruhen ● vt ausruhen; (lean)
lehnen (**on** an/auf + acc) ● vi
ruhen; (have a rest) sich
ausruhen

rest[2] n **the ~** der Rest; (people)
die Übrigen pl ● vi **it ~s with you**
es ist an Ihnen (**to** zu)

restaurant n Restaurant nt,
Gaststätte f

restful a erholsam

restive a unruhig

restless a, **-ly** adv unruhig

restoration n (of building)
Restaurierung f

restore vt wiederherstellen;
restaurieren <building>

restrain vt zurückhalten; **~
oneself** sich beherrschen. **~ed** a
zurückhaltend. **~t** n
Zurückhaltung f

restrict vt einschränken; **~ to**
beschränken auf (+ acc). **~ion** n
Einschränkung f; Beschränkung
f. **~ive** a einschränkend

rest room n (Amer) Toilette f

result n Ergebnis nt, Resultat nt;
(consequence) Folge f; **as a ~** als
Folge (**of** gen) ● vi sich ergeben
(**from** aus); **~ in** enden in (+ dat);
(lead to) führen zu

resume vt wieder aufnehmen ● vi
wieder beginnen

résumé n Zusammenfassung f

resumption n Wiederaufnahme f

resurrect vt (fig) wieder beleben.
~ion n **the R~ion** (Relig) die
Auferstehung

resuscitat|e vt wieder beleben.
~ion n Wiederbelebung f

retail n Einzelhandel m ● a
Einzelhandels- ● adv im
Einzelhandel ● vt im
Einzelhandel verkaufen ● vi **~ at**
im Einzelhandel kosten. **~er** n
Einzelhändler m

retain vt behalten

retaliat|e vi zurückschlagen. **~ion**
n Vergeltung f; **in ~ion** als
Vergeltung

retarded a zurückgeblieben

reticen|ce n Zurückhaltung f. **~t**
a zurückhaltend

retina n Netzhaut f

retinue n Gefolge nt

retire vi in den Ruhestand treten;
(withdraw) sich zurückziehen.
~d a im Ruhestand. **~ment** n
Ruhestand m

retiring a zurückhaltend

retort n scharfe Erwiderung f;
(Chem) Retorte f ● vt scharf
erwidern

retrace vt **~ one's steps**
denselben Weg zurückgehen

retrain vt umschulen ● vi
umgeschult werden

retreat n Rückzug m; (place)
Zufluchtsort m ● vi sich
zurückziehen

retrial n
Wiederaufnahmeverfahren nt

retrieve vt zurückholen; (from
wreckage) bergen; (Computing)
wieder auffinden

retrograde a rückschrittlich

retrospect n **in ~** rückblickend.
~ive a, **-ly** adv rückwirkend;
(looking back) rückblickend

R

return n Rückkehr f; (*giving back*)
Rückgabe f; (*Comm*) Ertrag m;
(*ticket*) Rückfahrkarte f; (*Aviat*)
Rückflugschein m; **by ~** [**of post**]
postwendend; **in ~** dafür; **in ~ for**
für; **many happy ~s!** herzlichen
Glückwunsch zum Geburtstag!
● vt zurückgehen/-fahren; (*come
back*) zurückkommen ● vt
zurückgeben; (*put back*)
zurückstellen/-legen; (*send back*)
zurückschicken

return ticket n Rückfahrkarte f;
(*Aviat*) Rückflugschein m

reunion n Wiedervereinigung f;
(*social gathering*) Treffen nt

reunite vt wieder vereinigen

reuse vt wieder verwenden

rev n (*Auto* 🄸) Umdrehung f
● vt/i **~** [**up**] den Motor auf
Touren bringen

reveal vt zum Vorschein bringen;
(*fig*) enthüllen. **~ing** a (*fig*)
aufschlussreich

revel vi (*pt/pp* revelled) **~ in sth**
etw genießen

revelation n Offenbarung f,
Enthüllung f

revenge n Rache f; (*fig & Sport*)
Revanche f ● vt rächen

revenue n [Staats]einnahmen pl

revere vt verehren. **~nce** n
Ehrfurcht f

Reverend a the **~ X** Pfarrer X;
(*Catholic*) Hochwürden X

reverent a, **-ly** adv ehrfürchtig

reversal n Umkehrung f

reverse a umgekehrt ● n
Gegenteil nt; (*back*) Rückseite f;
(*Auto*) Rückwärtsgang m ● vt
umkehren; (*Auto*) zurücksetzen
● vi zurücksetzen

revert vi **~ to** zurückfallen an (+
acc)

review n Rückblick m (of auf +
acc); (*re-examination*)
Überprüfung f; (*Mil*)
Truppenschau f; (*of book, play*)
Kritik f, Rezension f ● vt
zurückblicken auf (+ *acc*);
überprüfen <*situation*>;
rezensieren <*book, play*>. **~er** n
Kritiker m, Rezensent m

revis|e vt revidieren; (*for exam*)
wiederholen. **~ion** n Revision f;
(*for exam*) Wiederholung f

revival n Wiederbelebung f

revive vt wieder beleben; (*fig*)
wieder aufleben lassen ● vi
wieder aufleben

revolt n Aufstand m ● vi
rebellieren ● vt anwidern. **~ing**
a widerlich, eklig

revolution n Revolution f; (*Auto*)
Umdrehung f. **~ary** a
revolutionär. **~ize** vt
revolutionieren

revolve vi sich drehen; **~ around**
kreisen um

revolv|er n Revolver m. **~ing** a
Dreh-

revue n Revue f; (*satirical*)
Kabarett nt

revulsion n Abscheu m

reward n Belohnung f ● vt
belohnen. **~ing** a lohnend

rewrite vt (*pt* rewrote, *pp* rewritten)
noch einmal [neu] schreiben;
(*alter*) umschreiben

rhetoric n Rhetorik f. **~al** a
rhetorisch

rheumatism n Rheumatismus m,
Rheuma nt

Rhine n Rhein m

rhinoceros n Nashorn nt,
Rhinozeros nt

rhubarb n Rhabarber m

rhyme n Reim m ● vt reimen ● vi
sich reimen

rhythm n Rhythmus m. **~ic[al]** a,
-ally adv rhythmisch

rib n Rippe f

ribbon n Band nt; (*for typewriter*)
Farbband nt

rice n Reis m

rich a (**-er, -est**), **-ly** adv reich;
<*food*> gehaltvoll; (*heavy*) schwer

● *n* the ∼ *pl* die Reichen; ∼es *pl*
Reichtum *m*

ricochet *vi* abprallen

rid *vt* (*pt/pp* rid, *pres p* ridding)
befreien (of von); get ∼ of
loswerden

riddance *n* good ∼! auf
Nimmerwiedersehen!

ridden *see* ride

riddle *n* Rätsel *nt*

riddled *a* ∼ with durchlöchert mit

ride *n* Ritt *m*; (in vehicle) Fahrt *f*;
take s.o. for a ∼ ▣ jdn reinlegen
● *v* (*pt* rode, *pp* ridden) ● *vt* reiten
<*horse*>; fahren mit <*bicycle*>
● *vi* reiten; (in vehicle) fahren.
∼r *n* Reiter(in) *m*(*f*); (on bicycle)
Fahrer(in) *m*(*f*)

ridge *n* Erhebung *f*; (on roof)
First *m*; (of mountain) Grat *m*,
Kamm *m*

ridicule *n* Spott *m* ● *vt*
verspotten, spotten über (+ *acc*)

ridiculous *a*, **-ly** *adv* lächerlich

riding *n* Reiten *nt* ● *attrib* Reit-

riff-raff *n* Gesindel *nt*

rifle *n* Gewehr *nt* ● *vt* plündern;
∼ through durchwühlen

rift *n* Spalt *m*; (fig) Riss *m*

rig *n* Ölbohrturm *m*; (at sea)
Bohrinsel *f* ● *vt* (*pt/pp* rigged) ∼
out ausrüsten; ∼ up aufbauen

right *a* richtig; (not left)
rechte(r,s); be ∼ <*person*:> Recht
haben; <*clock*:> richtig gehen; put
∼ wieder in Ordnung bringen;
(fig) richtig stellen; that's ∼! das
stimmt! ● *adv* richtig; (directly)
direkt; (completely) ganz; (not
left) rechts; <*go*> nach rechts; ∼
away sofort ● *n* Recht *nt*; (not
left) rechte Seite *f*; on the ∼
rechts; from/to the ∼ von/nach
rechts; be in the ∼ Recht haben;
by ∼s eigentlich; the R∼ (Pol) die
Rechte. ∼ angle *n* rechter
Winkel *m*

rightful *a*, **-ly** *adv* rechtmäßig

right-handed *a* rechtshändig

rightly *adv* mit Recht

right-wing *a* (Pol) rechte(r,s)

rigid *a* starr; (strict) streng. ∼ity *n*
Starrheit *f*; Strenge *f*

rigorous *a*, **-ly** *adv* streng

rigour *n* Strenge *f*

rim *n* Rand *m*; (of wheel) Felge *f*

rind *n* (on fruit) Schale *f*; (on
cheese) Rinde *f*; (on bacon)
Schwarte *f*

ring[1] *n* Ring *m*; (for circus)
Manege *f*; stand in a ∼ im Kreis
stehen ● *vt* umringen

ring[2] *n* Klingeln *nt*; give s.o. a ∼
(Teleph) jdn anrufen ● *v* (*pt* rang,
pp rung) ● *vt* läuten; ∼ [up]
(Teleph) anrufen ● *vi* <*bells*:>
läuten; <*telephone*:> klingeln. ∼
back *vt/i* (Teleph) zurückrufen

ring: ∼leader *n* Rädelsführer *m*.
∼ road *n* Umgehungsstraße *f*

rink *n* Eisbahn *f*

rinse *n* Spülung *f*; (hair colour)
Tönung *f* ● *vt* spülen

riot *n* Aufruhr *m*; ∼s *pl* Unruhen
pl; run ∼ randalieren ● *vi*
randalieren. ∼er *n* Randalierer
m. ∼ous *a* aufrührerisch;
(boisterous) wild

rip *n* Riss *m* ● *vt/i* (*pt/pp* ripped)
zerreißen; ∼ open aufreißen. ∼
off *vt* ▣ neppen

ripe *a* (-r, -st) reif

ripen *vi* reifen ● *vt* reifen lassen

ripeness *n* Reife *f*

rip-off *n* ▣ Nepp *m*

ripple *n* kleine Welle *f*

rise *n* Anstieg *m*; (fig) Aufstieg *m*;
(increase) Zunahme *f*; (in wages)
Lohnerhöhung *f*; (in salary)
Gehaltserhöhung *f*; give ∼ to
Anlass geben zu ● *vi* (*pt* rose, *pp*
risen) steigen; <*ground*:>
ansteigen; <*sun, dough*:>
aufgehen; <*river*:> entspringen;
(get up) aufstehen; (fig)
aufsteigen (to zu). ∼r *n* early ∼r
Frühaufsteher *m*

rising a steigend; <sun> aufgehend ● n (revolt) Aufstand m

risk n Risiko nt; **at one's own ~** auf eigene Gefahr ● vt riskieren

risky a (-ier, -iest) riskant

rite n Ritus m

ritual a rituell ● n Ritual nt

rival a rivalisierend ● n Rivale m/Rivalin f. **~ry** n Rivalität f; (Comm) Konkurrenzkampf m

river n Fluss m

rivet n Niete f ● vt [ver]nieten; **~ed by** (fig) gefesselt von

road n Straße f; (fig) Weg m

road: ~-map n Straßenkarte f. **~ safety** n Verkehrssicherheit f. **~side** n Straßenrand m. **~way** n Fahrbahn f. **~-works** npl Straßenarbeiten pl. **~worthy** a verkehrssicher

roam vi wandern

roar n Gebrüll nt; **~s of laughter** schallendes Gelächter nt ● vi brüllen; (with laughter) schallend lachen. **~ing** a <fire> prasselnd; **do a ~ing trade** [T] ein Bombengeschäft machen

roast a gebraten, Brat-; **~ beef/ pork** Rinder-/Schweinebraten m ● n Braten m ● vt/i braten; rösten <coffee, chestnuts>

rob vt (pt/pp robbed) berauben (of gen); ausrauben <bank>. **~ber** n Räuber m. **~bery** n Raub m

robe n Robe f; (Amer: bathrobe) Bademantel m

robin n Rotkehlchen nt

robot n Roboter m

robust a robust

rock¹ n Fels m; **on the ~s** <ship> aufgelaufen; <marriage> kaputt; <drink> mit Eis

rock² vt/i schaukeln

rock³ n (Mus) Rock m

rockery n Steingarten m

rocket n Rakete f

rocking: ~-chair n Schaukelstuhl m. **~-horse** n Schaukelpferd nt

rocky a (-ier, -iest) felsig; (unsteady) wackelig

rod n Stab m; (stick) Rute f; (for fishing) Angel[rute] f

rode see ride

rodent n Nagetier nt

rogue n Gauner m

role n Rolle f

roll n Rolle f; (bread) Brötchen nt; (list) Liste f; (of drum) Wirbel m ● vi rollen; **be ~ing in money** [T] Geld wie Heu haben ● vt rollen; walzen <lawn>; ausrollen <pastry>. **~ over** vi sich auf die andere Seite rollen. **~ up** vt aufrollen; hochkrempeln <sleeves> ● vi [T] auftauchen

roller n Rolle f; (lawn, road) Walze f; (hair) Lockenwickler m. **~ blind** n Rollo nt. **~-coaster** n Berg-und-Talbahn f. **~-skate** n Rollschuh m

rolling-pin n Teigrolle f

Roman a römisch ● n Römer(in) m(f)

romance n Romantik f; (love-affair) Romanze f; (book) Liebesgeschichte f

Romania n Rumänien nt. **~n** a rumänisch ● n Rumäne m/-nin f

romantic a, **-ally** adv romantisch. **~ism** n Romantik f

Rome n Rom nt

romp vi [herum]tollen

roof n Dach nt; (of mouth) Gaumen m ● vt **~ [over]** überdachen. **~-top** n Dach nt

rook n Saatkrähe f; (Chess) Turm m

room n Zimmer nt; (for functions) Saal m; (space) Platz m. **~y** a geräumig

roost n Hühnerstange f

root¹ n Wurzel f; **take ~** anwachsen ● vi Wurzeln schlagen. **~ out** vt (fig) ausrotten

root² vi **~ about** wühlen; **~ for s.o.** [T] für jdn sein

rope n Seil nt; **know the ~s** 🔲 sich auskennen. **~ in** vt 🔲 einspannen

rose¹ n Rose f; (of watering-can) Brause f

rose² see **rise**

rostrum n Podium nt

rosy a (-ier, -iest) rosig

rot n Fäulnis f; (🔲 nonsense) Quatsch m ●vi (pt/pp rotted) [ver]faulen

rota n Dienstplan m

rotary a Dreh-; (Techn) Rotations-

rotat|e vt drehen ●vi sich drehen; (Techn) rotieren. **~ion** n Drehung f; **in ~ion** im Wechsel

rote n by **~** auswendig

rotten a faul; 🔲 mies; <person> fies

rough a (-er, -est) rau; (uneven) uneben; (coarse, not gentle) grob; (brutal) roh; (turbulent) stürmisch; (approximate) ungefähr ●adv **sleep ~** im Freien übernachten ●vt **~ it** primitiv leben. **~ out** vt im Groben entwerfen

roughage n Ballaststoffe pl

rough draft n grober Entwurf m

rough|ly adv (see rough) rau; grob; roh; ungefähr. **~ness** n Rauheit f

rough paper n Konzeptpapier nt

round a (-er, -est) rund ●n Runde f; (slice) Scheibe f; **do one's ~s** seine Runde machen ●prep um (+ acc); **~ the clock** rund um die Uhr ●adv **all ~** ringsherum; **ask s.o. ~** jdn einladen ●vt biegen um <corner>. **~ off** vt abrunden. **~ up** vt aufrunden; zusammentreiben <animals>; festnehmen <criminals>

roundabout a **~ route** Umweg m ●n Karussell nt; (for traffic) Kreisverkehr m

round trip n Rundreise f

rous|e vt wecken; (fig) erregen. **~ing** a mitreißend

route n Route f; (of bus) Linie f

routine a, **-ly** adv routinemäßig ●n Routine f; (Theat) Nummer f

row¹ n (line) Reihe f

row² vt/i rudern

row³ n 🔲 Krach m ●vi 🔲 sich streiten

rowdy a (-ier, -iest) laut

rowing boat n Ruderboot nt

royal a, **-ly** adv königlich

royal|ty n Königtum nt; (persons) Mitglieder pl der königlichen Familie; **-ies** pl (payments) Tantiemen pl

rub vt (pt/pp rubbed) reiben; (polish) polieren; **don't ~ it in** 🔲 reib es mir nicht unter die Nase. **~ off** vt abreiben ●vi abgehen. **~ out** vt ausradieren

rubber n Gummi m; (eraser) Radiergummi m. **~ band** n Gummiband nt

rubbish n Abfall m, Müll m; (🔲 nonsense) Quatsch m; (🔲 junk) Plunder m. **~ bin** n Abfalleimer m. **~ dump** n Abfallhaufen m; (official) Müllhalde f

rubble n Trümmer pl

ruby n Rubin m

rudder n [Steuer]ruder nt

rude a (-r, -st), **-ly** adv unhöflich; (improper) unanständig. **~ness** n Unhöflichkeit f

rudimentary a elementar; (Biol) rudimentär

ruffian n Rüpel m

ruffle vt zerzausen

rug n Vorleger m, [kleiner] Teppich m; (blanket) Decke f

rugged a <coastline> zerklüftet

ruin n Ruine f; (fig) Ruin m ●vt ruinieren

rule n Regel f; (control) Herrschaft f; (government) Regierung f; (for measuring) Lineal nt; **as a ~** in der Regel ●vt regieren, herrschen über (+ acc); (fig) beherrschen; (decide) entscheiden; ziehen <line> ●vi

regieren, herrschen. ~ **out** vt
ausschließen
ruled a <paper> liniert
ruler n Herrscher(in) m(f);
(measure) Lineal nt
ruling a herrschend; <factor>
entscheidend; (Pol) regierend
● n Entscheidung f
rum n Rum m
rumble n Grollen nt ● vi grollen;
<stomach:> knurren
rummage vi wühlen; ~ **through**
durchwühlen
rumour n Gerücht nt ● vt **it is** ~**ed**
that es geht das Gerücht, dass
rump n Hinterteil nt. ~ **steak** n
Rumpsteak nt
run n Lauf m; (journey) Fahrt f;
(series) Serie f, Reihe f; (Theat)
Laufzeit f; (Skiing) Abfahrt f;
(enclosure) Auslauf m; (Amer:
ladder) Laufmasche f; ~ **of bad**
luck Pechsträhne f; **be on the** ~
flüchtig sein; **in the long** ~ auf
lange Sicht ● v (pt ran, pp run,
pres p running) ● vi laufen; (flow)
fließen; <eyes:> tränen; <bus:>
verkehren; <butter, ink:>
zerfließen; <colours:> [ab]färben;
(in election) kandidieren ● vt
laufen lassen; einlaufen lassen
<bath>; (manage) führen, leiten;
(drive) fahren; eingehen <risk>;
(Journ) bringen <article>; ~ **one's**
hand over sth mit der Hand über
etw (acc) fahren. ~ **away** vi
weglaufen. ~ **down** vi hinunter-
/herunterlaufen; <clockwork:>
ablaufen; <stocks:> sich
verringern ● vt (run over)
überfahren; (reduce) verringern;
(🗉 criticize) heruntermachen. ~
in vi hinein-/hereinlaufen. ~ **off**
vi weglaufen ● vt abziehen
<copies>. ~ **out** vi hinaus-/
herauslaufen; <supplies, money:>
ausgehen; **I've** ~ **out of sugar** ich
habe keinen Zucker mehr. ~
over vt überfahren. ~ **up** vi

hinauf-/herauflaufen; (towards)
hinlaufen ● vt machen <debts>;
auflaufen lassen <bill>; (sew)
schnell nähen
runaway n Ausreißer m
run-down a <area> verkommen
rung¹ n (of ladder) Sprosse f
rung² see ring²
runner n Läufer m; (Bot)
Ausläufer m; (on sledge) Kufe f.
~ **bean** n Stangenbohne f. ~**-up**
n Zweite(r) m/f
running a laufend; <water>
fließend; **four times** ~ viermal
nacheinander ● n Laufen nt;
(management) Führung f, Leitung
f; **be/not be in the** ~ eine/keine
Chance haben
runny a flüssig
run: ~**-up** n (Sport) Anlauf m; (to
election) Zeit f vor der Wahl.
~**way** n Start- und Landebahn f
rupture n Bruch m ● vt/i brechen
rural a ländlich
ruse n List f
rush¹ n (Bot) Binse f
rush² n Hetze f; **in a** ~ in Eile ● vi
sich hetzen; (run) rasen; <water:>
rauschen ● vt hetzen, drängen.
~**-hour** n Hauptverkehrszeit f,
Stoßzeit f
Russia n Russland nt. ~**n** a
russisch ● n Russe m/Russin f;
(Lang) Russisch nt
rust n Rost m ● vi rosten
rustle vi rascheln ● vt rascheln
mit; (Amer) stehlen <cattle>. ~
up vt 🗉 improvisieren
rustproof a rostfrei
rusty a (-ier, -iest) rostig
rut n Furche f
ruthless a, **-ly** adv rücksichtslos.
~**ness** n Rücksichtslosigkeit f
rye n Roggen m

sabbath n Sabbat m
sabotage n Sabotage f ●vt sabotieren
sachet n Beutel m; (scented) Kissen nt
sack n Sack m; get the ~ 🗈 rausgeschmissen werden ●vt 🗈 rausschmeißen
sacred a heilig
sacrifice n Opfer nt ●vt opfern
sacrilege n Sakrileg nt
sad a (sadder, saddest) traurig; <loss, death> schmerzlich. ~den vt traurig machen
saddle n Sattel m ●vt satteln; ~ s.o. with sth 🗈 jdm etw aufhalsen
sadist n Sadist m. ~ic a, -ally adv sadistisch
sad|ly adv traurig; (unfortunately) leider. ~ness n Traurigkeit f
safe a (-r, -st) sicher; <journey> gut; (not dangerous) ungefährlich; ~ and sound gesund und wohlbehalten ●n Safe m. ~guard n Schutz m ●vt schützen. ~ly adv sicher; <arrive> gut
safety n Sicherheit f. ~-belt n Sicherheitsgurt m. ~-pin n Sicherheitsnadel f. ~-valve n [Sicherheits]ventil nt
sag vi (pt/pp sagged) durchhängen
saga n Saga f; (fig) Geschichte f
said see say
sail n Segel nt; (trip) Segelfahrt f ●vi segeln; (on liner) fahren; (leave) abfahren (for nach) ●vt segeln mit
sailing n Segelsport m. ~-boat n Segelboot nt. ~-ship n Segelschiff nt

sailor n Seemann m; (in navy) Matrose m
saint n Heilige(r) m/f. ~ly a heilig
sake n for the ~ of ... um ... (gen) willen; for my/your ~ um meinet-/deinetwillen
salad n Salat m. ~-dressing n Salatsoße f
salary n Gehalt nt
sale n Verkauf m; (event) Basar m; (at reduced prices) Schlussverkauf m; for ~ zu verkaufen
sales|man n Verkäufer m. ~woman n Verkäuferin f
saliva n Speichel m
salmon n Lachs m
saloon n Salon m; (Auto) Limousine f; (Amer: bar) Wirtschaft f
salt n Salz nt ●a salzig; <water, meat> Salz- ●vt salzen; (cure) pökeln; streuen <road>. ~-cellar n Salzfass nt. ~ water n Salzwasser nt. ~y a salzig
salute n (Mil) Gruß m ●vt/i (Mil) grüßen
salvage n (Naut) Bergung f ●vt bergen
salvation n Rettung f; (Relig) Heil nt
same a & pron the ~ der/die/das gleiche; (pl) die gleichen; (identical) der-/die-/dasselbe; (pl) dieselben ●adv the ~ gleich; all the ~ trotzdem
sample n Probe f; (Comm) Muster nt ●vt probieren; kosten <food>
sanatorium n Sanatorium nt
sanction n Sanktion f ●vt sanktionieren
sanctuary n (Relig) Heiligtum nt; (refuge) Zuflucht f; (for wildlife) Tierschutzgebiet nt
sand n Sand m ●vt ~ [down] [ab]schmirgeln
sandal n Sandale f

S

sand: ~**bank** n Sandbank f.
~**paper** n Sandpapier nt. ~**pit** n
Sandkasten m
sandwich n; Sandwich m ● vt
~**ed between** eingeklemmt
zwischen
sandy a (-ier, -iest) sandig; <beach,
soil> Sand-; <hair> rotblond
sane a (-r, -st) geistig normal;
(sensible) vernünftig
sang see sing
sanitary a hygienisch; <system>
sanitär. ~ **napkin** n (Amer), ~
towel n [Damen]binde f
sanitation n Kanalisation und
Abfallbeseitigung pl
sanity n [gesunder] Verstand m
sank see sink
sap n (Bot) Saft m ● vt (pt/pp
sapped) schwächen
sarcas|m n Sarkasmus m. ~**tic** a,
-**ally** adv sarkastisch
sardine n Sardine f
sash n Schärpe f
sat see sit
satchel n Ranzen m
satellite n Satellit m. ~ **television**
n Satellitenfernsehen nt
satin n Satin m
satire n Satire f
satirical a, -**ly** adv satirisch
satir|ist n Satiriker(in) m(f)
satisfaction n Befriedigung f; to
my ~ zu meiner Zufriedenheit
satisfactory a, -**ily** adv zufrieden
stellend
satisfy vt (pp/pp -ied) befriedigen;
zufrieden stellen <customer>;
(convince) überzeugen; be ~**ied**
zufrieden sein. ~**ing** a
befriedigend; <meal> sättigend
saturate vt durchtränken; (Chem
& fig) sättigen
Saturday n Samstag m
sauce n Soße f; (cheek) Frechheit
f. ~**pan** n Kochtopf m
saucer n Untertasse f
saucy a (-ier, -iest) frech
Saudi Arabia n Saudi-Arabien n

sauna n Sauna f
saunter vi schlendern
sausage n Wurst f
savage a wild; (fierce) scharf;
(brutal) brutal ● n Wilde(r) m/f.
~**ry** n Brutalität f
save n (Sport) Abwehr f ● vt
retten (**from** vor + dat); (keep)
aufheben; (not waste) sparen;
(collect) sammeln; (avoid)
ersparen; (Sport) verhindern
<goal> ● vi ~ [**up**] sparen
saver n Sparer m
saving n (see save) Rettung f;
Sparen nt; Ersparnis f; ~**s** pl
(money) Ersparnisse pl
savour n Geschmack m ● vt
auskosten. ~**y** a würzig
saw¹ see see¹
saw² n Säge f ● vt/i (pt sawed, pp
sawn or sawed) sägen
saxophone n Saxophon nt
say n Mitspracherecht nt; have
one's ~ seine Meinung sagen
● vt/i (pt/pp said) sagen;
sprechen <prayer>; that is to ~
das heißt; that goes without ~**ing**
das versteht sich von selbst.
~**ing** n Redensart f
scab n Schorf m; (pej)
Streikbrecher m
scaffolding n Gerüst nt
scald vt verbrühen
scale¹ n (of fish) Schuppe f
scale² n Skala f; (Mus) Tonleiter
f; (ratio) Maßstab m ● vt (climb)
erklettern. ~ **down** vt
verkleinern
scales npl (for weighing) Waage f
scalp n Kopfhaut f
scamper vi huschen
scan n (Med) Szintigramm nt ● v
(pt/pp scanned) ● vt absuchen;
(quickly) flüchtig ansehen; (Med)
szintigraphisch untersuchen
scandal n Skandal m; (gossip)
Skandalgeschichten pl. ~**ize** vt
schockieren. ~**ous** a skandalös

Scandinavia n Skandinavien nt.
~n a skandinavisch ● n
Skandinavier(in) m(f)

scanner n Scanner m

scanty a (-ier, -iest), **-ily** adv
spärlich; <clothing> knapp

scapegoat n Sündenbock m

scar n Narbe f

scarc|e a (-r, -st) knapp; **make
oneself** ~e 🗊 sich aus dem Staub
machen. ~ely adv kaum. ~ity n
Knappheit f

scare n Schreck m; (panic)
[allgemeine] Panik f ● vt Angst
machen (+ dat); **be** ~d Angst
haben (**of** vor + dat)

scarf n (pl scarves) Schal m;
(square) Tuch nt

scarlet a scharlachrot

scary a unheimlich

scathing a bissig

scatter vt verstreuen; (disperse)
zerstreuen ● vi sich zerstreuen.
~ed a verstreut; <showers>
vereinzelt

scatty a (-ier, -iest) 🗊 verrückt

scene n Szene f; (sight) Anblick
m; (place of event) Schauplatz m;
behind the ~s hinter den
Kulissen

scenery n Landschaft f; (Theat)
Szenerie f

scenic a landschaftlich schön

scent n Duft m; (trail) Fährte f;
(perfume) Parfüm nt. ~ed a
parfümiert

sceptic|al a, **-ly** adv skeptisch.
~ism n Skepsis f

schedule n Programm nt; (of
work) Zeitplan m; (timetable)
Fahrplan m; **behind** ~ im
Rückstand; **according to** ~
planmäßig ● vt planen

scheme n Programm nt; (plan)
Plan m; (plot) Komplott nt ● vi
Ränke schmieden

schizophrenic a schizophren

scholar n Gelehrte(r) m/f. ~ly a
gelehrt. ~ship n Gelehrtheit f;
(grant) Stipendium nt

school n Schule f; (Univ) Fakultät
f ● vt schulen

school: ~boy n Schüler m. ~girl
n Schülerin f. ~ing n
Schulbildung f. ~master n
Lehrer m. ~mistress n Lehrerin
f. ~-teacher n Lehrer(in) m(f)

scien|ce n Wissenschaft f. ~tific
a wissenschaftlich. ~tist n
Wissenschaftler m

scissors npl Schere f; **a pair of** ~
eine Schere

scoff¹ vi ~ **at** spotten über (+ acc)

scoff² vt 🗊 verschlingen

scold vt ausschimpfen

scoop n Schaufel f; (Culin)
Portionierer m; (Journ)
Exklusivmeldung f ● vt ~ **out**
aushöhlen; (remove) auslöffeln

scooter n Roller m

scope n Bereich m; (opportunity)
Möglichkeiten pl

scorch vt versengen. ~ing a
glühend heiß

score n [Spiel]stand m;
(individual) Punktzahl f; (Mus)
Partitur f; (Cinema) Filmmusik f;
on that ~ was das betrifft ● vt
erzielen; schießen <goal>; (cut)
einritzen ● vi Punkte erzielen;
(Sport) ein Tor schießen; (keep
score) Punkte zählen. ~r n
Punktezähler m; (of goals)
Torschütze m

scorn n Verachtung f ● vt
verachten. ~ful a, **-ly** adv
verächtlich

Scot n Schotte m/Schottin f

Scotch a schottisch ● n (whisky)
Scotch m

Scot|land n Schottland nt. ~s,
~tish a schottisch

scoundrel n Schurke m

scour vt (search) absuchen;
(clean) scheuern

S

scout n (Mil) Kundschafter m; [Boy] S~ Pfadfinder m

scowl n böser Gesichtsausdruck m ● vi ein böses Gesicht machen

scram vi 🄴 abhauen

scramble n Gerangel nt ● vi klettern; ~ for sich drängen nach. ~d egg[s] n[pl] Rührei nt

scrap¹ n (🄴 fight) Rauferei f ● vi sich raufen

scrap² n Stückchen nt; (metal) Schrott m; ~s pl Reste; not a ~ kein bisschen ● vt (pt/pp scrapped) aufgeben

scrapbook n Sammelalbum nt

scrape vt schaben; (clean) abkratzen; (damage) [ver]schrammen. ~ through vi gerade noch durchkommen. ~ together vt zusammenkriegen

scrappy a lückenhaft

scrapyard n Schrottplatz m

scratch n Kratzer m; start from ~ von vorne anfangen; not be up to ~ zu wünschen übrig lassen ● vt/i kratzen; (damage) zerkratzen

scrawl n Gekrakel nt ● vt/i krakeln

scream n Schrei m ● vt/i schreien

screech n Kreischen nt ● vt/i kreischen

screen n Schirm m; (Cinema) Leinwand f; (TV) Bildschirm m ● vt schützen; (conceal) verdecken; vorführen <film>; (examine) überprüfen; (Med) untersuchen

screw n Schraube f ● vt schrauben. ~ up vt festschrauben; (crumple) zusammenknüllen; zusammenkneifen <eyes>; (🄴 bungle) vermasseln

screwdriver n Schraubenzieher m

scribble n Gekritzel nt ● vt/i kritzeln

script n Schrift f; (of speech, play) Text m; (Radio, TV) Skript nt; (of film) Drehbuch nt

scrounge vt/i schnorren. ~r n Schnorrer m

scrub¹ n (land) Buschland nt, Gestrüpp nt

scrub² vt/i (pt/pp scrubbed) schrubben

scruff n by the ~ of the neck beim Genick

scruffy a (-ier, -iest) vergammelt

scrum n Gedränge nt

scruple n Skrupel m

scrupulous a, -ly adv gewissenhaft

scuffle n Handgemenge nt

sculpt|or n Bildhauer(in) m(f). ~ure n Bildhauerei f; (piece of work) Skulptur f, Plastik f

scum n Schmutzschicht f; (people) Abschaum m

scurry vi (pt/pp -ied) huschen

scuttle¹ vt versenken <ship>

scuttle² vi schnell krabbeln

sea n Meer nt, See f; at ~ auf See; by ~ mit dem Schiff. ~food n Meeresfrüchte pl. ~gull n Möwe f

seal¹ n (Zool) Seehund m

seal² n Siegel nt ● vt versiegeln; (fig) besiegeln. ~ off vt abriegeln

sea-level n Meeresspiegel m

seam n Naht f; (of coal) Flöz nt

seaman n Seemann m; (sailor) Matrose m

seance n spiritistische Sitzung f

search n Suche f; (official) Durchsuchung f ● vt durchsuchen; absuchen <area> ● vi suchen (for nach). ~ing a prüfend, forschend

search: ~light n [Such]scheinwerfer m. ~-party n Suchmannschaft f

sea: ~sick a seekrank. ~side n at/to the ~side am/ans Meer

season n Jahreszeit f; (social, tourist, sporting) Saison f ● vt *(flavour)* würzen. **~al** *a* Saison-. **~ing** *n* Gewürze *pl*

season ticket *n* Dauerkarte *f*

seat *n* Sitz *m*; *(place)* Sitzplatz *m*; *(bottom)* Hintern *m*; **take a ~** Platz nehmen ● *vt* setzen; *(have seats for)* Sitzplätze bieten (+ *dat*); **remain ~ed** sitzen bleiben. **~-belt** *n* Sicherheitsgurt *m*; **fasten one's ~-belt** sich anschnallen

sea: ~weed *n* [See]tang *m*. **~worthy** *a* seetüchtig

seclu|ded *a* abgelegen. **~sion** *n* Zurückgezogenheit *f*

second *a* zweite(r,s); **on ~ thoughts** nach weiterer Überlegung ● *n* Sekunde *f*; *(Sport)* Sekundant *m*; **~s** *pl* *(goods)* Waren zweiter Wahl ● *adv* *(in race)* an zweiter Stelle ● *vt* unterstützen *<proposal>*

secondary *a* zweitrangig; *(Phys)* Sekundär-. **~ school** *n* höhere Schule *f*

second: ~-best *a* zweitbeste(r,s). **~ class** *adv* *<travel, send>* zweiter Klasse. **~-class** *a* zweitklassig

second hand *n* *(on clock)* Sekundenzeiger *m*

second-hand *a* gebraucht ● *adv* aus zweiter Hand

secondly *adv* zweitens

second-rate *a* zweitklassig

secrecy *n* Heimlichkeit *f*

secret *a* geheim; *<agent, police>* Geheim-; *<drinker, lover>* heimlich ● *n* Geheimnis *nt*

secretarial *a* Sekretärinnen-; *<work, staff>* Sekretariats-

secretary *n* Sekretär(in) *m(f)*

secretive *a* geheimtuerisch

secretly *adv* heimlich

sect *n* Sekte *f*

section *n* Teil *m*; *(of text)* Abschnitt *m*; *(of firm)* Abteilung *f*; *(of organization)* Sektion *f*

sector *n* Sektor *m*

secular *a* weltlich

secure *a*, **-ly** *adv* sicher; *(firm)* fest; *(emotionally)* geborgen ● *vt* sichern; *(fasten)* festmachen; *(obtain)* sich *(dat)* sichern

securit|y *n* Sicherheit *f*; *(emotional)* Geborgenheit *f*; **~ies** *pl* Wertpapiere *pl*

sedan *n* *(Amer)* Limousine *f*

sedate *a*, **-ly** *adv* gesetzt

sedative *a* beruhigend ● *n* Beruhigungsmittel *nt*

sediment *n* [Boden]satz *m*

seduce *vt* verführen

seduct|ion *n* Verführung *f*. **~ive** *a*, **-ly** *adv* verführerisch

see *v* *(pt* **saw**, *pp* **seen)** ● *vt* sehen; *(understand)* einsehen; *(imagine)* sich *(dat)* vorstellen; *(escort)* begleiten; **go and ~** nachsehen; *(visit)* besuchen; **~ you later!** bis nachher! **~ing that** da ● *vi* sehen; *(check)* nachsehen; **~ about** sich kümmern um. **~ off** *vt* verabschieden; *(chase away)* vertreiben. **~ through** *vt* *(fig)* durchschauen *<person>*

seed *n* Samen *m*; *(of grape)* Kern *m*; *(fig)* Saat *f*; *(Tennis)* gesetzter Spieler *m*; **go to ~** Samen bilden; *(fig)* herunterkommen. **~ed** *a* *(Tennis)* gesetzt

seedy *a* (**-ier, -iest**) schäbig; *<area>* heruntergekommen

seek *vt* *(pt/pp* **sought)** suchen

seem *vi* scheinen

seen *see* **see¹**

seep *vi* sickern

seethe *vi* **~ with anger** vor Wut schäumen

see-through *a* durchsichtig

segment *n* Teil *m*; *(of worm)* Segment *nt*; *(of orange)* Spalte *f*

segregat|e *vt* trennen. **~ion** *n* Trennung *f*

seize *vt* ergreifen; *(Jur)* beschlagnahmen; **~ s.o. by the arm** jdn am Arm packen. **~ up** *vi* *(Techn)* sich festfressen

seldom *adv* selten

S

select *a* ausgewählt; (*exclusive*) exklusiv ● *vt* auswählen; aufstellen <*team*>. ~**ion** *n* Auswahl *f*

self *n* (*pl* **selves**) Ich *nt*

self: ~**-assurance** *n* Selbstsicherheit *f.* ~**-assured** *a* selbstsicher. ~**-catering** *n* Selbstversorgung *f.* ~**-centred** *a* egozentrisch. ~**-confidence** *n* Selbstbewusstsein *nt,* Selbstvertrauen *nt.* ~**-confident** *a* selbstbewusst. ~**-conscious** *a* befangen. ~**-contained** *a* <*flat*> abgeschlossen. ~**-control** *n* Selbstbeherrschung *f.* ~**-defence** *n* Selbstverteidigung *f;* (*Jur*) Notwehr *f.* ~**-employed** selbstständig. ~**-esteem** *n* Selbstachtung *f.* ~**-evident** *a* offensichtlich. ~**-indulgent** *a* maßlos. ~**-interest** *n* Eigennutz *m*

self|ish *a,* **-ly** *adv* egoistisch, selbstsüchtig. ~**less** *a,* **-ly** *adv* selbstlos

self: ~**-pity** *n* Selbstmitleid *nt.* ~**-portrait** *n* Selbstporträt *nt.* ~**-respect** *n* Selbstachtung *f.* ~**-righteous** *a* selbstgerecht. ~**-sacrifice** *n* Selbstaufopferung *f.* ~**-satisfied** *a* selbstgefällig. ~**-service** *n* Selbstbedienung *f* ● *attrib* Selbstbedienungs-. ~**-sufficient** *a* selbstständig

sell *v* (*pt/pp* **sold**) ● *vt* verkaufen; **be sold out** ausverkauft sein ● *vi* sich verkaufen. ~ **off** *vt* verkaufen

seller *n* Verkäufer *m*

Sellotape (P), *n* ≈ Tesafilm (P) *m*

sell-out *n* **be a** ~ ausverkauft sein; (📧 *betrayal*) Verrat sein

selves *see* **self**

semester *n* (*Amer*) Semester *nt*

semi|breve *n* (*Mus*) ganze Note *f.* ~**circle** *n* Halbkreis *m.* ~**circular** *a* halbkreisförmig. ~**colon** *n* Semikolon *nt.* ~**-detached** *a &* n

~**-detached** [**house**] Doppelhaushälfte *f.* ~**-final** *n* Halbfinale *nt*

seminar *n* Seminar *nt*

senat|e *n* Senat *m.* ~**or** *n* Senator *m*

send *vt/i* (*pt/pp* **sent**) schicken; ~ **for** kommen lassen <*person*>; sich (*dat*) schicken lassen <*thing*>. ~**er** *n* Absender *m.* ~**off** *n* Verabschiedung *f*

senile *a* senil

senior *a* älter; (*in rank*) höher ● *n* Ältere(r) *m/f;* (*in rank*) Vorgesetzte(r) *m/f.* ~ **citizen** *n* Senior(in) *m(f)*

seniority *n* höheres Alter *nt;* (*in rank*) höherer Rang *m*

sensation *n* Sensation *f;* (*feeling*) Gefühl *nt.* ~**al** *a,* **-ly** *adv* sensationell

sense *n* Sinn *m;* (*feeling*) Gefühl *nt;* (*common* ~) Verstand *m;* **make** ~ Sinn ergeben ● *vt* spüren. ~**less** *a,* **-ly** *adv* sinnlos; (*unconscious*) bewusstlos

sensible *a,* **-bly** *adv* vernünftig; <*suitable*> zweckmäßig

sensitiv|e *a,* **-ly** *adv* empfindlich; (*understanding*) einfühlsam. ~**ity** *n* Empfindlichkeit *f*

sensual *a* sinnlich. **-ity** *n* Sinnlichkeit *f*

sensuous *a* sinnlich

sent *see* **send**

sentence *n* Satz *m;* (*Jur*) Urteil *nt;* (*punishment*) Strafe *f* ● *vt* verurteilen

sentiment *n* Gefühl *nt;* (*opinion*) Meinung *f;* (*sentimentality*) Sentimentalität *f* ~**al** *a* sentimental. ~**ality** *n* Sentimentalität *f*

sentry *n* Wache *f*

separable *a* trennbar

separate¹ *a,* **-ly** *adv* getrennt, separat

separat|e² *vt* trennen ● *vi* sich trennen. ~**ion** *n* Trennung *f*

September *n* September *m*

septic *a* vereitert

sequel *n* Folge *f*; (*fig*) Nachspiel *nt*

sequence *n* Reihenfolge *f*

serenade *n* Ständchen *nt* ●*vt* ~ **s.o.** jdm ein Ständchen bringen

seren|e *a*, **-ly** *adv* gelassen. **~ity** *n* Gelassenheit *f*

sergeant *n* (*Mil*) Feldwebel *m*; (*in police*) Polizeimeister *m*

serial *n* Fortsetzungsgeschichte *f*; (*Radio, TV*) Serie *f*. **~ize** *vt* in Fortsetzungen veröffentlichen/ (*Radio, TV*) senden

series *n inv* Serie *f*

serious *a*, **-ly** *adv* ernst; <*illness, error*> schwer. **~ness** *n* Ernst *m*

sermon *n* Predigt *f*

servant *n* Diener(in) *m(f)*

serve *n* (*Tennis*) Aufschlag *m* ●*vt* dienen (+ *dat*); bedienen <*customer, guest*>; servieren <*food*>; verbüßen <*sentence*>; **it ~s you right!** das geschieht dir recht! ●*vi* dienen; (*Tennis*) aufschlagen

service *n* Dienst *m*; (*Relig*) Gottesdienst *m*; (*in shop, restaurant*) Bedienung *f*; (*transport*) Verbindung *f*; (*maintenance*) Wartung *f*; (*set of crockery*) Service *nt*; (*Tennis*) Aufschlag *m*; **~s** *pl* Dienstleistungen *pl*; (*on motorway*) Tankstelle und Raststätte *f*; **in the ~s** beim Militär; **out of/in** <*machine:*> außer/in Betrieb ●*vt* (*Techn*) warten

service: ~ **area** *n* Tankstelle und Raststätte *f*. ~ **charge** *n* Bedienungszuschlag *m*. **~man** *n* Soldat *m*. ~ **station** *n* Tankstelle *f*

serviette *n* Serviette *f*

servile *a* unterwürfig

session *n* Sitzung *f*

set *n* Satz *m*; (*of crockery*) Service *nt*; (*of cutlery*) Garnitur *f*; (*TV, Radio*) Apparat *m*; (*Math*) Menge *f*; (*Theat*) Bühnenbild *nt*; (*Cinema*) Szenenaufbau *m*; (*of people*) Kreis *m* ●*a* (*ready*) fertig, bereit; (*rigid*) fest; <*book*> vorgeschrieben; **be ~ on doing sth** entschlossen sein, etw zu tun ●*v* (*pt/pp* **set**, *pres p* **setting**) ●*vt* setzen; (*adjust*) einstellen; stellen <*task, alarm clock*>; festsetzen, festlegen <*date, limit*>; aufgeben <*homework*>; zusammenstellen <*questions*>; [ein]fassen <*gem*>; einrichten <*bone*>; legen <*hair*>; decken <*table*> ●*vi* <*sun:*> untergehen; (*become hard*) fest werden. ~ **back** *vt* zurücksetzen; (*hold up*) aufhalten; (Ⅱ *cost*) kosten. ~ **off** *vi* losgehen; (*in vehicle*) losfahren ●*vt* auslösen <*alarm*>; explodieren lassen <*bomb*>. ~ **out** *vi* losgehen; (*in vehicle*) losfahren ●*vt* auslegen; (*state*) darlegen. ~ **up** *vt* aufbauen; (*fig*) gründen

settee *n* Sofa *nt*, Couch *f*

setting *n* Rahmen *m*; (*surroundings*) Umgebung *f*

settle *vt* (*decide*) entscheiden; (*agree*) regeln; (*fix*) festsetzen; (*calm*) beruhigen; (*pay*) bezahlen ●*vi* sich niederlassen; <*snow, dust:*> liegen bleiben; (*subside*) sich senken; <*sediment:*> sich absetzen. ~ **down** *vi* sich beruhigen; (*permanently*) sesshaft werden. ~ **up** *vi* abrechnen

settlement *n* (*see* **settle**) Entscheidung *f*; Regelung *f*; Bezahlung *f*; (*Jur*) Vergleich *m*; (*colony*) Siedlung *f*

settler *n* Siedler *m*

set-up *n* System *nt*

seven *a* sieben. **~teen** *a* siebzehn. **~teenth** *a* siebzehnte(r,s)

S

seventh a siebte(r,s)

seventieth a siebzigste(r,s)

seventy a siebzig

several a & pron mehrere, einige

sever|e a (-r, -st,) **-ly** adv streng; <pain> stark; <illness> schwer. ~ity n Strenge f; Schwere f

sew vt/i (pt sewed, pp sewn or sewed) nähen

sewage n Abwasser nt

sewer n Abwasserkanal m

sewing n Nähen nt; (work) Näharbeit f. ~ **machine** n Nähmaschine f

sewn see sew

sex n Geschlecht nt; (sexuality, intercourse) Sex m. ~ist a sexistisch

sexual a, **-ly** adv sexuell. ~ **intercourse** n Geschlechtsverkehr m

sexuality n Sexualität f

sexy a (-ier, -iest) sexy

shabby a (-ier, -iest), **-ily** adv schäbig

shack n Hütte f

shade n Schatten m; (of colour) [Farb]ton m; (for lamp) [Lampen]schirm m; (Amer: window-blind) Jalousie f ● vt beschatten

shadow n Schatten m ● vt (follow) beschatten

shady a (-ier, -iest) schattig; (🚹 disreputable) zwielichtig

shaft n Schaft m; (Techn) Welle f; (of light) Strahl m; (of lift) Schacht m

shaggy a (-ier, -iest) zottig

shake n Schütteln nt ● v (pt shook, pp shaken) ● vt schütteln; (shock) erschüttern; ~ **hands with s.o.** jdm die Hand geben ● vi wackeln; (tremble) zittern. ~ **off** vt abschütteln

shaky a (-ier, -iest) wackelig; <hand, voice> zittrig

shall v aux we ~ see wir werden sehen; **what** ~ **I do?** was soll ich machen?

shallow a (-er, -est) seicht; <dish> flach; (fig) oberflächlich

sham a unecht ● n Heuchelei f ● vt (pt/pp shammed) vortäuschen

shambles n Durcheinander nt

shame n Scham f; (disgrace) Schande f; **be a** ~ schade sein; **what a** ~! wie schade!

shame|ful a, **-ly** adv schändlich. ~less a, **-ly** adv schamlos

shampoo n Shampoo nt ● vt schamponieren

shan't = shall not

shape n Form f; (figure) Gestalt f ● vt formen (into zu). ~less a formlos; <clothing> unförmig

share n [An]teil m; (Comm) Aktie f ● vt/i teilen. ~holder n Aktionär(in) m(f)

shark n Hai[fisch] m

sharp a (-er, -est), **-ly** adv scharf; (pointed) spitz; (severe) heftig; (sudden) steil; (alert) clever; (unscrupulous) gerissen ● adv scharf; (Mus) zu hoch; **at six o'clock** ~ Punkt sechs Uhr ● n (Mus) Kreuz nt. ~en vt schärfen; [an]spitzen <pencil>

shatter vt zertrümmern; (fig) zerstören; ~ed <person:> erschüttert; (🚹 exhausted) kaputt ● vi zersplittern

shave n Rasur f; **have a** ~ sich rasieren ● vt rasieren ● vi sich rasieren. ~r n Rasierapparat m

shawl n Schultertuch nt

she pron sie

shears npl [große] Schere f

shed[1] n Schuppen m

shed[2] vt (pt/pp shed, pres p shedding) verlieren; vergießen <blood, tears>; ~ **light on** Licht bringen in (+ acc)

sheep n inv Schaf nt. ~-**dog** n Hütehund m

sheepish *a*, **-ly** *adv* verlegen
sheer *a* rein; (*steep*) steil; (*transparent*) hauchdünn
sheet *n* Laken *nt*, Betttuch *nt*; (*of paper*) Blatt *nt*; (*of glass, metal*) Platte *f*
shelf *n* (*pl* **shelves**) Brett *nt*, Bord *nt*; (*set of shelves*) Regal *nt*
shell *n* Schale *f*; (*of snail*) Haus *nt*; (*of tortoise*) Panzer *m*; (*on beach*) Muschel *f*; (*Mil*) Granate *f* ● *vt* pellen; enthülsen <*peas*>; (*Mil*) [mit Granaten] beschießen. ~ **out** *vi* 🄵 blechen
shellfish *n inv* Schalentiere *pl*; (*Culin*) Meeresfrüchte *pl*
shelter *n* Schutz *m*; (*air-raid* ~) Luftschutzraum *m* ● *vt* schützen (**from** vor + *dat*) ● *vi* sich unterstellen. ~**ed** *a* geschützt; <*life*> behütet
shelve *vt* auf Eis legen; (*abandon*) aufgeben
shelving *n* (*shelves*) Regale *pl*
shepherd *n* Schäfer *m* ● *vt* führen
sherry *n* Sherry *m*
shield *n* Schild *m*; (*for eyes*) Schirm *m*; (*Techn & fig*) Schutz *m* ● *vt* schützen (**from** vor + *dat*)
shift *n* Verschiebung *f*; (*at work*) Schicht *f* ● *vt* rücken; (*take away*) wegnehmen; (*rearrange*) umstellen; schieben <*blame*> (**on to** auf + *acc*) ● *vi* sich verschieben; (🄵 *rush*) rasen
shifty *a* (**-ier, -iest**) (*pej*) verschlagen
shimmer *n* Schimmer *m* ● *vi* schimmern
shin *n* Schienbein *nt*
shine *n* Glanz *m* ● *v* (*pt/pp* **shone**) ● *vi* leuchten; (*reflect light*) glänzen; <*sun:*> scheinen ● *vt* ~ **a light on** beleuchten
shingle *n* (*pebbles*) Kiesel *pl*
shiny *a* (**-ier, -iest**) glänzend
ship *n* Schiff *nt* ● *vt* (*pt/pp* **shipped**) verschiffen

ship: ~**building** *n* Schiffbau *m*. ~**ment** *n* Sendung *f*. ~**per** *n* Spediteur *m*. ~**ping** *n* Versand *m*; (*traffic*) Schifffahrt *f*. ~**shape** *a & adv* in Ordnung. ~**wreck** *n* Schiffbruch *m*. ~**wrecked** *a* schiffbrüchig. ~**yard** *n* Werft *f*
shirt *n* [Ober]hemd *nt*; (*for woman*) Hemdbluse *f*
shit *n* (*vulg*) Scheiße *f* ● *vi* (*pt/pp* **shit**) (*vulg*) scheißen
shiver *n* Schauder *m* ● *vi* zittern
shoal *n* (*fish*) Schwarm *m*
shock *n* Schock *m*; (*Electr*) Schlag *m*; (*impact*) Erschütterung *f* ● *vt* einen Schock versetzen (+ *dat*); (*scandalize*) schockieren. ~**ing** *a* schockierend; (🄵 *bad*) fürchterlich
shoddy *a* (**-ier, -iest**) minderwertig
shoe *n* Schuh *m*; (*of horse*) Hufeisen *nt* ● *vt* (*pt/pp* **shod**, *pres p* **shoeing**) beschlagen <*horse*>
shoe: ~**horn** *n* Schuhanzieher *m*. ~**lace** *n* Schnürsenkel *m*. ~**string** *n* **on a** ~**string** 🄵 mit ganz wenig Geld
shone *see* **shine**
shoo *vt* scheuchen ● *int* sch!
shook *see* **shake**
shoot *n* (*Bot*) Trieb *m*; (*hunt*) Jagd *f* ● *v* (*pt/pp* **shot**) ● *vt* schießen; (*kill*) erschießen; drehen <*film*> ● *vi* schießen. ~ **down** *vt* abschießen. ~ **out** *vi* (*rush*) herausschießen. ~ **up** *vi* (*grow*) in die Höhe schießen/<*prices:*> schnellen
shop *n* Laden *m*, Geschäft *nt*; (*workshop*) Werkstatt *f*; **talk** ~ 🄵 fachsimpeln ● *vi* (*pt/pp* **shopped**, *pres p* **shopping**) einkaufen; **go** ~**ping** einkaufen gehen
shop: ~ **assistant** *n* Verkäufer(in) *m(f)*. ~**keeper** *n* Ladenbesitzer(in) *m(f)*. ~**lifter** *n* Ladendieb *m*. ~**lifting** *n* Ladendiebstahl *m*

S

shopping n Einkaufen nt; (articles) Einkäufe pl; do the ~ einkaufen. ~ bag n Einkaufstasche f. ~ centre n Einkaufszentrum nt. ~ trolley n Einkaufswagen m

shop-window n Schaufenster nt

shore n Strand m; (of lake) Ufer nt

short a (-er, -est) kurz; <person> klein; (curt) schroff; a ~ time ago vor kurzem; be ~ of ... zu wenig ... haben; be in ~ supply knapp sein ● adv kurz; (abruptly) plötzlich; (curtly) kurz angebunden; in ~ kurzum; ~ of (except) außer; go ~ Mangel leiden

shortage n Mangel m (of an + dat); (scarcity) Knappheit f

short: ~bread n ≈ Mürbekekse pl. ~ circuit n Kurzschluss m. ~coming n Fehler m. ~ cut n Abkürzung f

shorten vt [ab]kürzen; kürzer machen <garment>

short: ~hand n Kurzschrift f, Stenographie f. ~list n engere Auswahl f

short|ly adv in Kürze; ~ly before/after kurz vorher/danach. ~ness n Kürze f; (of person) Kleinheit f

shorts npl Shorts pl

short: ~-sighted a kurzsichtig. ~-sleeved a kurzärmelig. ~-story n Kurzgeschichte f. ~-tempered a aufbrausend. ~-term a kurzfristig. ~ wave n Kurzwelle f

shot see shoot ● n Schuss m; (pellets) Schrot m; (person) Schütze m; (Phot) Aufnahme f; (injection) Spritze f; (attempt) Versuch m; like a ~ [] sofort. ~gun n Schrotflinte f. ~-put n (Sport) Kugelstoßen nt

should v aux you ~ go du solltest gehen; I ~ have seen him ich hätte ihn sehen sollen; I ~ like

ich möchte; this ~ be enough das müsste eigentlich reichen; if he ~ be there falls er da sein sollte

shoulder n Schulter f ● vt schultern; (fig) auf sich (acc) nehmen. ~-blade n Schulterblatt nt

shout n Schrei m ● vt/i schreien. ~ down vt niederschreien

shouting n Geschrei nt

shove n Stoß m ● vt stoßen; ([] put) tun ● vi drängeln. ~ off vi [] abhauen

shovel n Schaufel f ● vt (pt/pt shovelled) schaufeln

show n (display) Pracht f; (exhibition) Ausstellung f, Schau f; (performance) Vorstellung f; (Theat, TV) Show f; on ~ ausgestellt ● v (pt showed, pp shown) ● vt zeigen; (put on display) ausstellen; (put on display) vorführen <film> ● vi sichtbar sein; <film:> gezeigt werden. ~ in vt hereinführen. ~ off vi [] angeben ● vt vorführen; (flaunt) angeben mit. ~ up vi [deutlich] zu sehen sein; ([] arrive) auftauchen ● vt deutlich zeigen; ([] embarrass) blamieren

shower n Dusche f; (of rain) Schauer m; have a ~ duschen ● vt ~ with überschütten mit ● vi duschen

show-jumping n Springreiten nt

shown see show

show: ~-off n Angeber(in) m(f). ~room n Ausstellungsraum m

showy a protzig

shrank see shrink

shred n Fetzen m; (fig) Spur f ● vt (pt/pp shredded) zerkleinern; (Culin) schnitzeln. ~der n Reißwolf m; (Culin) Schnitzelwerk nt

shrewd a (-er, -est), -ly adv klug. ~ness n Klugheit f

shriek n Schrei m ● vt/i schreien

shrill a, -y adv schrill

shrimp n Garnele f, Krabbe f
shrink vi (pt shrank, pp shrunk) schrumpfen; <garment:> einlaufen; (draw back) zurückschrecken (from vor + dat)
shrivel vi (pt/pp shrivelled) verschrumpeln
Shrove n ~**Tuesday** Fastnachtsdienstag m
shrub n Strauch m
shrug n Achselzucken nt ● vt/i (pt/pp shrugged) ~ [one's shoulders] die Achseln zucken
shrunk see shrink
shudder n Schauder m ● vi schaudern; (tremble) zittern
shuffle vi schlurfen ● vt mischen <cards>
shun vt (pt/pp shunned) meiden
shunt vt rangieren
shut v (pt/pp shut, pres p shutting) ● vt zumachen, schließen ● vi sich schließen; <shop:> schließen, zumachen. ~ **down** vt schließen; stilllegen <factory> ● vi schließen. ~ **up** vt abschließen; (lock in) einsperren ● vi 🔲 den Mund halten
shutter n [Fenster]laden m; (Phot) Verschluss m
shuttle n (Tex) Schiffchen nt
shuttle service n Pendelverkehr m
shy a (-er, -est), -**ly** adv schüchtern; (timid) scheu. ~**ness** n Schüchternheit f
siblings npl Geschwister pl
Sicily n Sizilien nt
sick a krank; <humour> makaber; be ~ (vomit) sich übergeben; be ~ of sth 🔲 etw satt haben; I feel ~ mir ist schlecht
sick|ly a (-ier, -iest) kränklich. ~**ness** n Krankheit f; (vomiting) Erbrechen nt
side n Seite f; on the ~ (as sideline) nebenbei; ~ by ~ nebeneinander; (fig) Seite an Seite; take ~s Partei ergreifen

(with für) ● attrib Seiten- ● vi ~ with Partei ergreifen für
side: ~**board** n Anrichte f. ~-**effect** n Nebenwirkung f. ~**lights** npl Standlicht nt. ~**line** n Nebenbeschäftigung f. ~-**show** n Nebenattraktion f. ~-**step** vt ausweichen (+ dat). ~**walk** n (Amer) Bürgersteig m. ~**ways** adv seitwärts
siding n Abstellgleis nt
siege n Belagerung f; (by police) Umstellung f
sieve n Sieb nt ● vt sieben
sift vt sieben; (fig) durchsehen
sigh n Seufzer m ● vi seufzen
sight n Sicht f; (faculty) Sehvermögen nt; (spectacle) Anblick m; (on gun) Visier nt; ~**s** pl Sehenswürdigkeiten pl; at first ~ auf den ersten Blick; lose ~ of aus dem Auge verlieren; know by ~ vom Sehen kennen ● vt sichten
sightseeing n go ~ die Sehenswürdigkeiten besichtigen
sign n Zeichen nt; (notice) Schild nt ● vt/i unterschreiben; <author, artist:> signieren. ~ **on** vi (as unemployed) sich arbeitslos melden; (Mil) sich verpflichten
signal n Signal nt ● vt/i (pt/pp signalled) signalisieren; ~ **to s.o.** jdm ein Signal geben
signature n Unterschrift f; (of artist) Signatur f
significan|ce n Bedeutung f. ~**t** a, -**ly** adv (important) bedeutend
signify vt (pt/pp -ied) bedeuten
signpost n Wegweiser m
silence n Stille f; (of person) Schweigen nt ● vt zum Schweigen bringen. ~**r** n (on gun) Schalldämpfer m; (Auto) Auspufftopf m
silent a, -**ly** adv still; (without speaking) schweigend; remain ~ schweigen

S

silhouette n Silhouette f; (picture) Schattenriss m ● vt be ∼d sich als Silhouette abheben

silicon n Silizium nt

silk n Seide f ● attrib Seiden-

silky a (-ier, -iest) seidig

sill n Sims m & nt

silly a (-ier, -iest) dumm, albern

silver a silbern; <coin, paper> Silber- ● n Silber nt

silver: ∼-plated a versilbert. ∼ware n Silber nt

similar a, -ly adv ähnlich. ∼ity n Ähnlichkeit f

simmer vi leise kochen, ziehen ● vt ziehen lassen

simple a (-r, -st) einfach; <person> einfältig. ∼-minded a einfältig

simplicity n Einfachheit f

simpli|fication n Vereinfachung f. ∼fy vt (pt/pp -ied) vereinfachen

simply adv einfach

simulate vt vortäuschen; (Techn) simulieren

simultaneous a, -ly adv gleichzeitig

sin n Sünde f ● vi (pt/pp sinned) sündigen

since
● preposition
····▸ seit (+ dat). he's been living here since 1991 er wohnt* seit 1991 hier. I had been waiting since 8 o'clock ich wartete* [schon] seit 8 Uhr. since seeing you seit ich dich gesehen habe. how long is it since your interview? wie lange ist es seit deinem Vorstellungsgespräch?
● adverb
····▸ seitdem. I haven't spoken to her since seitdem habe ich mit ihr nicht gesprochen. the house has been empty ever since das Haus steht seitdem leer. he has since remarried er hat danach

wieder geheiratet. long since vor langer Zeit
● conjunction
····▸ seit. since she has been living in Germany seit sie in Deutschland wohnt*. since they had been in London seit sie in London waren*. how long is it since he left? wie lange ist es her, dass er weggezogen ist? it's a year since he left es ist ein Jahr her, dass er weggezogen ist
····▸ (because) da. since she was ill, I had to do it da sie krank war, musste ich es tun

❗ *Note the different tenses in German

sincere a aufrichtig; (heartfelt) herzlich. ∼ly adv aufrichtig; Yours ∼ly Mit freundlichen Grüßen

sincerity n Aufrichtigkeit f

sinful a sündhaft

sing vt/i (pt sang, pp sung) singen

singe vt (pres p singeing) versengen

singer n Sänger(in) m(f)

single a einzeln; (one only) einzig; (unmarried) ledig; <ticket> einfach; <room, bed> Einzel- ● n (ticket) einfache Fahrkarte f; (record) Single f; ∼s pl (Tennis) Einzel nt ● vt ∼ out auswählen

single: ∼-handed a & adv allein. ∼ parent n Alleinerziehende(r) m/f

singly adv einzeln

singular a eigenartig; (Gram) im Singular ● n Singular m

sinister a finster

sink n Spülbecken nt ● v (pt sank, pp sunk) ● vi sinken ● vt versenken <ship>; senken <shaft>. ∼ in vi einsinken; (🄸 be understood) kapiert werden

sinner n Sünder(in) m(f)

sip n Schlückchen nt ●vt (pt/pp **sipped**) in kleinen Schlucken trinken

siphon n (bottle) Siphon m. ~ **off** vt mit einem Saugheber ablassen

sir n mein Herr; **S~** (title) Sir; **Dear S~s** Sehr geehrte Herren

siren n Sirene f

sister n Schwester f; (nurse) Oberschwester f. ~**-in-law** n Schwägerin f

sit v (pt/pp **sat**, pres p **sitting**) ●vi sitzen; (sit down) sich setzen; <committee:> tagen ●vt setzen; machen <exam>. ~ **back** vi sich zurücklehnen. ~ **down** vi sich setzen. ~ **up** vi [aufrecht] sitzen; (rise) sich aufsetzen; (not slouch) gerade sitzen

site n Gelände nt; (for camping) Platz m; (Archaeol) Stätte f

sitting n Sitzung f; (for meals) Schub m

situat|e vt legen; **be ~ed** liegen. ~**ion** n Lage f; (circumstances) Situation f; (job) Stelle f

six a sechs. ~**teen** a sechzehn. ~**teenth** a sechzehnte(r,s)

sixth a sechste(r,s)

sixtieth a sechzigste(r,s)

sixty a sechzig

size n Größe f

sizzle vi brutzeln

skate n Schlittschuh m ●vi Schlittschuh laufen. ~**r** n Eisläufer(in) m(f)

skating n Eislaufen nt. ~**-rink** n Eisbahn f

skeleton n Skelett nt. ~ **key** n Dietrich m

sketch n Skizze f; (Theat) Sketch m ●vt skizzieren

sketchy a (-ier, -iest), -**ily** adv skizzenhaft

ski n Ski m ●vi (pt/pp **skied**, pres p **skiing**) Ski fahren or laufen

skid n Schleudern nt ●vi (pt/pp **skidded**) schleudern

skier n Skiläufer(in) m(f)

skiing n Skilaufen nt

skilful a, -**ly** adv geschickt

skill n Geschick nt. ~**ed** a geschickt; (trained) ausgebildet

skim vt (pt/pp **skimmed**) entrahmen <milk>

skimp vt sparen an (+ dat)

skimpy a (-ier, -iest) knapp

skin n Haut f; (on fruit) Schale f ●vt (pt/pp **skinned**) häuten; schälen <fruit>

skin: ~**-deep** a oberflächlich. ~**-diving** n Sporttauchen nt

skinny a (-ier, -iest) dünn

skip[1] n Container m

skip[2] n Hüpfer m ●v (pt/pp **skipped**) vi hüpfen; (with rope) seilspringen ●vt überspringen

skipper n Kapitän m

skipping-rope n Sprungseil nt

skirmish n Gefecht nt

skirt n Rock m ●vt herumgehen um

skittle n Kegel m

skive vi 🆃 blaumachen

skull n Schädel m

sky n Himmel m. ~**light** n Dachluke f. ~**scraper** n Wolkenkratzer m

slab n Platte f; (slice) Scheibe f; (of chocolate) Tafel f

slack a (-er, -est) schlaff, locker; <person> nachlässig; (Comm) flau ●vi bummeln

slacken vi sich lockern; (diminish) nachlassen ●vt lockern; (diminish) verringern

slain see **slay**

slam v (pt/pp **slammed**) ●vt zuschlagen; (put) knallen 🆃; (🆃 criticize) verreißen ●vi zuschlagen

slander n Verleumdung f ●vt verleumden

slang n Slang m. ~**y** a salopp

slant n Schräge f; **on the ~** schräg ●vt abschrägen; (fig) färben <report> ●vi sich neigen

S

slap n Schlag m ●vt (pt/pp **slapped**) schlagen; (put) knallen 🗊 ●adv direkt

slapdash a 🗊 schludrig

slash n Schlitz m ●vt aufschlitzen; [drastisch] reduzieren <prices>

slat n Latte f

slate n Schiefer m ●vt 🗊 heruntermachen; verreißen <performance>

slaughter n Schlachten nt; (massacre) Gemetzel nt ●vt schlachten; abschlachten <men>

Slav a slawisch ●n Slawe m/ Slawin f

slave n Sklave m/ Sklavin f ●vi ~ [away] schuften

slavery n Sklaverei f

slay vt (pt slew, pp slain) ermorden

sledge n Schlitten m

sleek a (-er, -est) seidig; (well-fed) wohlgenährt

sleep n Schlaf m; go to ~ einschlafen; put to ~ einschläfern ●v (pt/pp slept) ●vi schlafen ●vt (accommodate) Unterkunft bieten für. ~er n Schläfer(in) m(f); (Rail) Schlafwagen m; (on track) Schwelle f

sleeping: ~-bag n Schlafsack m. ~-pill n Schlaftablette f

sleep: ~less a schlaflos. ~-walking n Schlafwandeln nt

sleepy a (-ier, -iest), -ily adv schläfrig

sleet n Schneeregen m

sleeve n Ärmel m; (for record) Hülle f. ~less a ärmellos

sleigh n [Pferde]schlitten m

slender a schlank; (fig) gering

slept see sleep

slew see slay

slice n Scheibe f ●vt in Scheiben schneiden

slick a clever

slid|e n Rutschbahn f; (for hair) Spange f; (Phot) Dia nt ●v (pt/pp slid) ●vi rutschen ●vt schieben. ~ing a gleitend; <door, seat> Schiebe-

slight a (-er, -est), -ly adv leicht; <importance> gering; <acquaintance> flüchtig; (slender) schlank; not in the ~est nicht im Geringsten; ~ly better ein bisschen besser ●vt kränken, beleidigen ●n Beleidigung f

slim a (slimmer, slimmest) schlank; <volume> gering; (fig) gering ●vi eine Schlankheitskur machen

slim|e n Schleim m. ~y a schleimig

sling n (Med) Schlinge f ●vt (pt/ pp slung) 🗊 schmeißen

slip n (mistake) Fehler m, 🗊 Patzer m; (petticoat) Unterrock m; (paper) Zettel m; give s.o. the ~ 🗊 jdm entwischen; ~ of the tongue Versprecher m ●v (pt/pp slipped) ●vi rutschen; (fall) ausrutschen; (go quickly) schlüpfen ●vt schieben; ~ s.o.'s mind jdm entfallen. ~ away vi sich fortschleichen. ~ up vi 🗊 einen Schnitzer machen

slipper n Hausschuh m

slippery a glitschig; <surface> glatt

slipshod a schludrig

slip-up n 🗊 Schnitzer m

slit n Schlitz m ●vt (pt/pp slit) aufschlitzen

slither vi rutschen

slog n [hard] ~ Schinderei f ●vi (pt/pp slogged) schuften

slogan n Schlagwort nt; (advertising) Werbespruch m

slop|e n Hang m; (inclination) Neigung f ●vi sich neigen. ~ing a schräg

sloppy a (-ier, -iest) schludrig; (sentimental) sentimental

slosh vi 🗊 schwappen

slot n Schlitz m; (TV) Sendezeit f ● v (pt/pp **slotted**) ● vt einfügen ● vi sich einfügen (**in** in + acc)

slot-machine n Münzautomat m; (for gambling) Spielautomat m

slouch vi sich schlecht halten

slovenly a schlampig

slow a (-er, -est), -ly adv langsam; be ~ <clock:> nachgehen; **in** ~ motion in Zeitlupe ● adv langsam ● vt verlangsamen ● vi ~ **down**, ~ **up** langsamer werden. ~**ness** n Langsamkeit f

sludge n Schlamm m

slug n Nacktschnecke f

sluggish a, -ly adv träge

sluice n Schleuse f

slum n Elendsviertel nt

slumber n Schlummer m ● vi schlummern

slump n Sturz m ● vi fallen; (crumple) zusammensacken; <prices:> stürzen; <sales:> zurückgehen

slung see **sling**

slur vt (pt/pp **slurred**) undeutlich sprechen

slurp vt/i schlürfen

slush n [Schnee]matsch m; (fig) Kitsch m

slut n Schlampe f 🔢

sly a (-er, -est), -ly adv verschlagen ● n **on the** ~ heimlich

smack n Schlag m, Klaps m ● vt schlagen ● adv 🔢 direkt

small a (-er, -est) klein ● adv **chop up** ~ klein hacken ● n ~ **of the back** Kreuz nt

small: ~ **ads** npl Kleinanzeigen pl. ~ **change** n Kleingeld nt. ~**pox** n Pocken pl. ~ **talk** n leichte Konversation f

smart a (-er, -est), -ly adv schick; (clever) schlau, clever; (brisk) flott; (Amer 🔢: cheeky) frech ● vi brennen

smarten vt ~ **oneself up** mehr auf sein Äußeres achten

smash n Krach m; (collision) Zusammenstoß m; (Tennis) Schmetterball m ● vt zerschlagen; (strike) schlagen; (Tennis) schmettern ● vi zerschmettern; (crash) krachen (**into** gegen). ~**ing** a 🔢 toll

smear n verschmierter Fleck m; (Med) Abstrich m; (fig) Verleumdung f ● vt schmieren; (coat) beschmieren (**with** mit); (fig) verleumden ● vi schmieren

smell n Geruch m; (sense) Geruchssinn m ● v (pt/pp **smelt** or **smelled**) ● vt riechen; (sniff) riechen an (+ dat) ● vi riechen (**of** nach)

smelly a (-ier, -iest) übel riechend

smelt see **smell**

smile n Lächeln nt ● vi lächeln; ~ **at** anlächeln

smirk vi feixen

smith n Schmied m

smock n Kittel m

smog n Smog m

smoke n Rauch m ● vt/i rauchen; (Culin) räuchern. ~**less** a rauchfrei; <fuel> rauchlos

smoker n Raucher m; (Rail) Raucherabteil nt

smoking n Rauchen nt; 'no ~' 'Rauchen verboten'

smoky a (-ier, -iest) verraucht; <taste> rauchig

smooth a (-er, -est), -ly adv glatt ● vt glätten. ~ **out** vt glatt streichen

smother vt ersticken; (cover) bedecken; (suppress) unterdrücken

smoulder vi schwelen

smudge n Fleck m ● vt verwischen ● vi schmieren

smug a (smugger, smuggest), -ly adv selbstgefällig

smuggl|e vt schmuggeln. ~**er** n Schmuggler m. ~**ing** n Schmuggel m

S

snack n Imbiss m. ~-bar n Imbissstube f

snag n Schwierigkeit f, 🔲 Haken m

snail n Schnecke f; at a ~'s pace im Schneckentempo

snake n Schlange f

snap n Knacken nt; (photo) Schnappschuss m ● attrib <decision> plötzlich ● v (pt/pp snapped) ● vi [entzwei]brechen; ~ at (bite) schnappen nach; (speak sharply) [scharf] anfahren ● vt zerbrechen; (say) fauchen; (Phot) knipsen. ~ up vt wegschnappen

snappy a (-ier, -iest) (smart) flott; make it ~! ein bisschen schnell!

snapshot n Schnappschuss m

snare n Schlinge f

snarl vi [mit gefletschten Zähnen] knurren

snatch n (fragment) Fetzen pl ● vt schnappen; (steal) klauen; entführen <child>; ~ sth from s.o. jdm etw entreißen

sneak n 🔲 Petze f ● vi schleichen; (🔲 tell tales) petzen ● vt (take) mitgehen lassen ● vi ~ in/out sich hinein-/hinausschleichen

sneakers npl (Amer) Turnschuhe pl

sneer vi höhnisch lächeln; (mock) spotten

sneeze n Niesen nt ● vi niesen

snide a 🔲 abfällig

sniff vi schnüffeln ● vt schnüffeln an (+ dat)

snigger vi [boshaft] kichern

snip n Schnitt m ● vt/i ~ [at] schnippeln an (+ dat)

snippet n Schnipsel m; (of information) Bruchstück nt

snivel vi (pt/pp snivelled) flennen

snob n Snob m. ~bery n Snobismus m. ~bish a snobistisch

snoop vi 🔲 schnüffeln

snooty a 🔲 hochnäsig

snooze n Nickerchen nt ● vi dösen

snore vi schnarchen

snorkel n Schnorchel m

snort vi schnauben

snout n Schnauze f

snow n Schnee m ● vi schneien; ~ed under with (fig) überhäuft mit

snow: ~ball n Schneeball m. ~drift n Schneewehe f. ~drop n Schneeglöckchen nt. ~fall n Schneefall m. ~flake n Schneeflocke f. ~man n Schneemann m. ~plough n Schneepflug m

snub n Abfuhr f ● vt (pt/pp snubbed) brüskieren

snub-nosed a stupsnasig

snuffle vi schnüffeln

snug a (snugger, snuggest) behaglich, gemütlich

snuggle vi sich kuscheln (up to an + acc)

so adv so; so am I ich auch; so I see das sehe ich; that is so das stimmt; so much the better umso besser; if so wenn ja; so as to um zu; so long! 🔲 tschüs! ● pron I hope so hoffentlich; I think so ich glaube schon; I'm afraid so leider ja; so saying/doing, he/she … indem er/sie das sagte/tat, … ● conj (therefore) also; so that damit; so what! na und! so you see wie du siehst

soak vt nass machen; (steep) einweichen; (🔲 fleece) schröpfen ● vi weichen; <liquid:> sickern. ~ up vt aufsaugen

soaking a & adv ~ [wet] patschnass 🔲

soap n Seife f. ~ opera n Seifenoper f. ~ powder n Seifenpulver nt

soapy a (-ier, -iest) seifig

soar vi aufsteigen; <prices:> in die Höhe schnellen

sob n Schluchzer m ● vi (pt/pp
sobbed) schluchzen
sober a, **-ly** adv nüchtern;
(serious) ernst; <colour> gedeckt.
~ up vi nüchtern werden
so-called a sogenannt
soccer n [✗] Fußball m
sociable a gesellig
social a gesellschaftlich; (Admin,
Pol, Zool) sozial
socialis|m n Sozialismus m. **~t** a
sozialistisch ● n Sozialist m
socialize vi [gesellschaftlich]
verkehren
socially adv gesellschaftlich;
know **~** privat kennen
social: ~ security n Sozialhilfe f.
~ worker n Sozialarbeiter(in)
m(f)
society n Gesellschaft f; (club)
Verein m
sociolog|ist n Soziologe m. **~y** n
Soziologie f
sock n Socke f; (kneelength)
Kniestrumpf m
socket n (of eye) Augenhöhle f;
(of joint) Gelenkpfanne f; (wall
plug) Steckdose f
soda n Soda nt; (Amer) Limonade
f. **~ water** n Sodawasser nt
sodden a durchnässt
sofa n Sofa nt. **~ bed** n
Schlafcouch f
soft a (-er, -est), **-ly** adv weich;
(quiet) leise; (gentle) sanft; ([✗]
silly) dumm. **~ drink** n
alkoholfreies Getränk nt
soften vt weich machen; (fig)
mildern ● vi weich werden
soft: ~ toy n Stofftier nt. **~ware** n
Software f
soggy a (-ier, -iest) aufgeweicht
soil¹ n Erde f, Boden m
soil² vt verschmutzen
solar a Sonnen-
sold see **sell**
soldier n Soldat m ● vi **~ on**
[unbeirrbar] weitermachen
sole¹ n Sohle f

sole² n (fish) Seezunge f
sole³ a einzig. **~ly** adv einzig und
allein
solemn a, **-ly** adv feierlich;
(serious) ernst
solicitor n Rechtsanwalt m/
-anwältin f
solid a fest; (sturdy) stabil; (not
hollow, of same substance)
massiv; (unanimous) einstimmig;
(complete) ganz
solidarity n Solidarität f
solidify vi (pt/pp -ied) fest werden
solitary a einsam; (sole) einzig
solitude n Einsamkeit f
solo n Solo nt ● a Solo-; <flight>
Allein- ● adv solo. **~ist** n
Solist(in) m(f)
solstice n Sonnenwende f
soluble a löslich
solution n Lösung f
solvable a lösbar
solve vt lösen
solvent n Lösungsmittel nt
sombre a dunkel; <mood> düster
some a & pron etwas; (a little) ein
bisschen; (with pl noun) einige;
(a few) ein paar; (certain)
manche(r,s); (one or the other)
[irgend]ein; **~ day** eines Tages; I
want **~** ich möchte etwas/ (pl)
welche; will you have **~** wine?
möchten Sie Wein? do **~**
shopping einkaufen
some: ~body pron & n jemand;
(emphatic) irgendjemand. **~how**
adv irgendwie. **~one** pron & n =
somebody
somersault n Purzelbaum m [✗];
(Sport) Salto m; turn a **~** einen
Purzelbaum schlagen/einen
Salto springen
something pron & adv etwas;
(emphatic) irgendetwas; **~**
different etwas anderes; **~** like this
so etwas [wie das]
some: ~time adv irgendwann ● a
ehemalig. **~times** adv manchmal.

S

~**what** adv ziemlich. ~**where** adv irgendwo; <*go*> irgendwohin

son n Sohn m

song n Lied nt. ~**bird** n Singvogel m

son-in-law n (pl ~**s-in-law**) Schwiegersohn m

soon adv (**-er, -est**) bald; (*quickly*) schnell; **too ~** zu früh; **as ~ as possible** so bald wie möglich; ~**er or later** früher oder später; **no ~er had I arrived than …** kaum war ich angekommen, da …; **I would ~er stay** ich würde lieber bleiben

soot n Ruß m

sooth|e vt beruhigen; lindern <*pain*>. ~**ing** a, **-ly** adv beruhigend; lindernd

sophisticated a weltgewandt; (*complex*) hoch entwickelt

sopping a & adv ~ **[wet]** durchnässt

soppy a (**-ier, -iest**) 🗓 rührselig

soprano n Sopran m; (*woman*) Sopranistin f

sordid a schmutzig

sore a (**-r, -st**) wund; (*painful*) schmerzhaft; **have a ~ throat** Halsschmerzen haben ● n wunde Stelle f. ~**ly** adv sehr

sorrow n Kummer m

sorry a (**-ier, -iest**) (*sad*) traurig; (*wretched*) erbärmlich; **I am ~** es tut mir Leid; **she is** or **feels ~ for him** er tut ihr Leid; **I am ~ to say** leider; ~**!** Entschuldigung!

sort n Art f; (*brand*) Sorte f; **he's a good ~** 🗓 er ist in Ordnung ● vt sortieren. ~ **out** vt sortieren; (*fig*) klären

sought *see* seek

soul n Seele f

sound[1] a (**-er, -est**) gesund; (*sensible*) vernünftig; (*secure*) solide; (*thorough*) gehörig ● adv **be ~ asleep** fest schlafen

sound[2] n (*strait*) Meerenge f

sound[3] n Laut m; (*noise*) Geräusch nt; (*Phys*) Schall m;

(*Radio, TV*) Ton m; (*of bells, music*) Klang m; **I don't like the ~ of it** 🗓 das hört sich nicht gut an ● vi [er]tönen; (*seem*) sich anhören ● vt (*pronounce*) aussprechen; schlagen <*alarm*>; (*Med*) abhorchen <*chest*>

soundly adv solide; <*sleep*> fest; <*defeat*> vernichtend

soundproof a schalldicht

soup n Suppe f

sour a (**-er, -est**) sauer; (*bad-tempered*) griesgrämig, verdrießlich

source n Quelle f

south n Süden m; **to the ~ of** südlich von ● a Süd-, süd- ● adv nach Süden

south: **S~ Africa** n Südafrika nt. **S~ America** n Südamerika nt. ~**-east** n Südosten m

southerly a südlich

southern a südlich

southward[s] adv nach Süden

souvenir n Andenken nt, Souvenir nt

Soviet a <*History*> sowjetisch; ~ **Union** Sowjetunion f

sow[1] n Sau f

sow[2] vt (pt **sowed**, pp **sown** or **sowed**) säen

soya n ~ **bean** Sojabohne f

spa n Heilbad nt

space n Raum m; (*gap*) Platz m; (*Astr*) Weltraum m ● vt ~ **[out]** [in Abständen] verteilen

space: ~**craft** n Raumfahrzeug nt. ~**ship** n Raumschiff nt

spacious a geräumig

spade n Spaten m; (*for child*) Schaufel f; ~**s** pl (*Cards*) Pik nt

Spain n Spanien nt

span[1] n Spanne f; (*of arch*) Spannweite f ● vt (pt/pp **spanned**) überspannen; umspannen <*time*>

span[2] *see* spick

Span|iard n Spanier(in) m(f). ~**ish** a spanisch ● n (*Lang*)

Spanisch *nt*; **the ~ish** *pl* die Spanier

spank *vt* verhauen

spanner *n* Schraubenschlüssel *m*

spare *a* (*surplus*) übrig; (*additional*) zusätzlich; <*seat, time*> frei; <*room*> Gäste-; <*bed, cup*> Extra- ● *n* (*part*) Ersatzteil *nt* ● *vt* ersparen; (*not hurt*) verschonen; (*do without*) entbehren; (*afford to give*) erübrigen. **~ wheel** *n* Reserverad *nt*

sparing *a*, **-ly** *adv* sparsam

spark *n* Funke *m*. **~[ing]-plug** *n* (*Auto*) Zündkerze *f*

sparkl|e *n* Funkeln *nt* ● *vi* funkeln. **~ing** *a* funkelnd; <*wine*> Schaum-

sparrow *n* Spatz *m*

sparse *a* spärlich. **~ly** *adv* spärlich; <*populated*> dünn

spasm *n* Anfall *m*; (*cramp*) Krampf *m*. **~odic** *a*, **-ally** *adv* sporadisch

spastic *a* spastisch [gelähmt] ● *n* Spastiker(in) *m(f)*

spat *see* spit²

spatter *vt* spritzen; **~ with** besprotzen mit

spawn *n* Laich *m* ● *vt* (*fig*) hervorbringen

speak *v* (*pt* spoke, *pp* spoken) ● *vi* sprechen (**to** mit) **~ing!** (*Teleph*) am Apparat! ● *vt* sprechen; sagen <*truth*>. **~ up** *vi* lauter sprechen; **~ up for oneself** seine Meinung äußern

speaker *n* Sprecher(in) *m(f)*; (*in public*) Redner(in) *m(f)*; (*loudspeaker*) Lautsprecher *m*

spear *n* Speer *m* ● *vt* aufspießen

spec *n* **on ~** 🔲 auf gut Glück

special *a* besondere(r,s), speziell. **~ist** *n* Spezialist *m*; (*Med*) Facharzt *m*/-ärztin *f*. **~ity** *n* Spezialität *f*

special|ize *vi* sich spezialisieren (**in** auf + *acc*). **~ly** *adv* speziell; (*particularly*) besonders

species *n* Art *f*

specific *a* bestimmt; (*precise*) genau; (*Phys*) spezifisch. **~ally** *adv* ausdrücklich

specification *n* & **~s** *pl* genaue Angaben *pl*

specify *vt* (*pt/pp* -ied) [genau] angeben

specimen *n* Exemplar *nt*; (*sample*) Probe *f*; (*of urine*) Urinprobe *f*

speck *n* Fleck *m*

speckled *a* gesprenkelt

spectacle *n* (*show*) Schauspiel *nt*; (*sight*) Anblick *m*. **~s** *npl* Brille *f*

spectacular *a* spektakulär

spectator *n* Zuschauer(in) *m(f)*

speculat|e *vi* spekulieren. **~ion** *n* Spekulation *f*. **~or** *n* Spekulant *m*

sped *see* speed

speech *n* Sprache *f*; (*address*) Rede *f*. **~less** *a* sprachlos

speed *n* Geschwindigkeit *f*; (*rapidity*) Schnelligkeit *f* ● *vi* (*pt/pp* sped) schnell fahren ● (*pt/pp* speeded) (*go too fast*) zu schnell fahren. **~ up** (*pt/pp* speeded up) ● *vt/i* beschleunigen

speed: **~boat** *n* Rennboot *nt*. **~ing** *n* Geschwindigkeitsüberschreitung *f*. **~ limit** *n* Geschwindigkeitsbeschränkung *f*

speedometer *n* Tachometer *m*

speedy *a* (**-ier**, **-iest**), **-ily** *adv* schnell

spell¹ *n* Weile *f*; (*of weather*) Periode *f*

spell² *v* (*pt/pp* spelled or spelt) ● *vt* schreiben; (*aloud*) buchstabieren; (*fig: mean*) bedeuten ● *vi* richtig schreiben; (*aloud*) buchstabieren. **~ out** *vt* buchstabieren; (*fig*) genau erklären

S

spell³ n Zauber m; (words)
Zauberspruch m. **~bound** a wie
verzaubert

spelling n (of a word)
Schreibweise f; (orthography)
Rechtschreibung f

spelt see **spell²**

spend vt/i (pt/pp **spent**) ausgeben;
verbringen <time>

spent see **spend**

sperm n Samen m

sphere n Kugel f; (fig) Sphäre f

spice n Gewürz nt; (fig) Würze f

spicy a würzig, pikant

spider n Spinne f

spik|e n Spitze f; (Bot, Zool)
Stachel m; (on shoe) Spike m. **~y**
a stachelig

spill v (pt/pp **spilt** or **spilled**) ●vt
verschütten ●vi überlaufen

spin v (pt/pp **spun**, pres p
spinning) ●vt drehen; spinnen
<wool>; schleudern <washing>
●vi sich drehen

spinach n Spinat m

spindl|e n Spindel f. **~y** a
spindeldürr

spin-drier n Wäscheschleuder f

spine n Rückgrat nt; (of book)
[Buch]rücken m; (Bot, Zool)
Stachel m. **~less** a (fig)
rückgratlos

spin-off n Nebenprodukt nt

spinster n ledige Frau f

spiral a spiralig ●n Spirale f ●vi
(pt/pp **spiralled**) sich hochwinden.
~ staircase n Wendeltreppe f

spire n Turmspitze f

spirit n Geist m; (courage) Mut m;
~s pl (alcohol) Spirituosen pl; in
low **~s** niedergedrückt. **~ away**
vt verschwinden lassen

spirited a lebhaft; (courageous)
beherzt

spiritual a geistig; (Relig) geistlich

spit¹ n (for roasting) [Brat]spieß
m

spit² n Spucke f ●vt/i (pt/pp **spat**,
pres p **spitting**) spucken; <cat:>

fauchen; <fat:> spritzen; **it's
~ting with rain** es tröpfelt

spite n Boshaftigkeit f; in **~ of**
trotz (+ gen) ●vt ärgern. **~ful** a,
-ly adv gehässig

splash n Platschen nt; (🔊 drop)
Schuss m; **~ of colour** Farbfleck
m ●vt spritzen; **~ s.o. with sth**
jdn mit etw bespritzen ●vi
spritzen. **~ about** vi planschen

splendid a herrlich, großartig

splendour n Pracht f

splint n (Med) Schiene f

splinter n Splitter m ●vi
zersplittern

split n Spaltung f; (Pol) Bruch m;
(tear) Riss m ●v (pt/pp **split**, pres
p **splitting**) ●vt spalten; (share)
teilen; (tear) zerreißen ●vi sich
spalten; (tear) zerreißen; **~ on
s.o.** 🔊 jdn verpfeifen. **~ up** vt
aufteilen ●vi <couple:> sich
trennen

splutter vi prusten

spoil n **~s** pl Beute f ●v (pt/pp
spoilt or **spoiled**) ●vt verderben;
verwöhnen <person> ●vi
verderben. **~sport** n
Spielverderber m

spoke¹ n Speiche f

spoke², **spoken** see **speak**

spokesman n Sprecher m

sponge n Schwamm m ●vt
abwaschen ●vi **~ on**
schmarotzen bei. **~-bag** n
Waschbeutel m. **~-cake** n
Biskuitkuchen m

sponsor n Sponsor m;
(godparent) Pate m/Patin f ●vt
sponsern

spontaneous a, **-ly** adv spontan

spoof n 🔊 Parodie f

spooky a (-ier, -iest) 🔊
gespenstisch

spool n Spule f

spoon n Löffel m ●vt löffeln.
~ful n Löffel m

sporadic a, **-ally** adv sporadisch

sport n Sport m ●vt [stolz]
tragen. **~ing** a sportlich

sports: ~ **car** n Sportwagen m. ~
coat n, ~ **jacket** n Sakko m.
~man n Sportler m. **~woman** n
Sportlerin f

sporty a (-ier, -iest) sportlich

spot n Fleck m; (place) Stelle f
(dot) Punkt m; (drop) Tropfen m;
(pimple) Pickel m; **~s** pl (rash)
Ausschlag m; **on the ~** auf der
Stelle ●vt (pt/pp spotted)
entdecken

spot: ~ **check** n Stichprobe f.
~less a makellos; (𝕀 very clean)
blitzsauber. **~light** n
Scheinwerfer m; (fig)
Rampenlicht nt

spotted a gepunktet

spouse n Gatte m/Gattin f

spout n Schnabel m, Tülle f ●vi
schießen (from aus)

sprain n Verstauchung f ●vt
verstauchen

sprang see spring²

sprawl vi sich ausstrecken

spray¹ n (of flowers) Strauß m

spray² n Sprühnebel m; (from
sea) Gischt m; (device) Spritze f;
(container) Sprühdose f;
(preparation) Spray nt ●vt
spritzen; (with aerosol) sprühen

spread n Verbreitung f; (paste)
Aufstrich m; (𝕀 feast) Festessen
nt ●v (pt/pp spread) ●vt
ausbreiten; streichen <butter,
jam>; bestreichen <bread,
surface>; streuen <sand,
manure>; verbreiten <news,
disease>; verteilen <payments>
●vi sich ausbreiten. ~ **out** vt
ausbreiten; (space out) verteilen
●vi sich verteilen

spree n 𝕀 **go on a shopping ~**
groß einkaufen gehen

sprightly a (-ier, -iest) rüstig

spring¹ n Frühling m ●attrib
Frühlings-

spring² n (jump) Sprung m;
(water) Quelle f; (device) Feder f;
(elasticity) Elastizität f ●v (pt
sprang, pp sprung) ●vi springen;
(arise) entspringen (from dat)
●vt ~ **sth on s.o.** jdn mit etw
überfallen

spring: **~-cleaning** n
Frühjahrsputz m. **~time** n
Frühling m

sprinkl|e vt sprengen; (scatter)
streuen; bestreuen <surface>.
~ing n dünne Schicht f

sprint n Sprint m ●vi rennen;
(Sport) sprinten. **~er** n
Kurzstreckenläufer(in) m(f)

sprout n Trieb m; [Brussels] **~s**
pl Rosenkohl m ●vi sprießen

sprung see spring²

spud n 𝕀 Kartoffel f

spun see spin

spur n Sporn m; (stimulus)
Ansporn m; **on the ~ of the
moment** ganz spontan ●vt (pt/pp
spurred) ~ **[on]** (fig) anspornen

spurn vt verschmähen

spurt n (Sport) Spurt m; **put on a
~** spurten ●vi spritzen

spy n Spion(in) m(f) ●vi
spionieren; ~ **on s.o.** jdm
nachspionieren. ●vt (𝕀 see)
sehen

spying n Spionage f

squabble n Zank m ●vi sich
zanken

squad n Gruppe f; (Sport)
Mannschaft f

squadron n (Mil) Geschwader nt

squalid a, **-ly** adv schmutzig

squall n Bö f ●vi brüllen

squalor n Schmutz m

squander vt vergeuden

square a quadratisch; <metre,
mile> Quadrat-; <meal>
anständig; **all** ~ 𝕀 quitt ●n
Quadrat nt; (area) Platz m; (on
chessboard) Feld nt ●vt (settle)
klären; (Math) quadrieren

S

squash n Gedränge nt; (drink) Fruchtsaftgetränk nt; (Sport) Squash nt ●vt zerquetschen; (suppress) niederschlagen. ~y a weich

squat a gedrungen ●vi (pt/pp squatted) hocken; ~ in a house ein Haus besetzen. ~ter n Hausbesetzer m

squawk vi krächzen

squeak n Quieken nt; (of hinge, brakes) Quietschen nt ●vi quieken; quietschen

squeal n Kreischen nt ●vi kreischen

squeamish a empfindlich

squeeze n Druck m; (crush) Gedränge nt ●vt drücken; (to get juice) ausdrücken; (force) zwängen

squiggle n Schnörkel m

squint n Schielen nt ●vi schielen

squirm vi sich winden

squirrel n Eichhörnchen nt

squirt n Spritzer m ●vt/i spritzen

St abbr (Saint) St.; (Street) Str.

stab n Stich m; (① attempt) Versuch m ●vt (pt/pp stabbed) stechen; (to death) erstechen

stability n Stabilität f

stable¹ a (-r, -st) stabil

stable² n Stall m; (establishment) Reitstall m

stack n Stapel m; (of chimney) Schornstein m ●vt stapeln

stadium n Stadion nt

staff n (stick & Mil) Stab m ●(& pl) (employees) Personal nt; (Sch) Lehrkräfte pl ●vt mit Personal besetzen. ~-room n (Sch) Lehrerzimmer nt

stag n Hirsch m

stage n Bühne f; (in journey) Etappe f; (in process) Stadium nt; by or in ~s in Etappen ●vt aufführen; (arrange) veranstalten

stagger vi taumeln ●vt staffeln <holidays>; versetzt anordnen <seats>; I was ~ed es hat mir die

Sprache verschlagen. ~ing a unglaublich

stagnant a stehend; (fig) stagnierend

stagnate vi (fig) stagnieren

stain n Fleck m; (for wood) Beize f ●vt färben; beizen <wood>; ~ed glass farbiges Glas nt. ~less a <steel> rostfrei

stair n Stufe f; ~s pl Treppe f. ~case n Treppe f

stake n Pfahl m; (wager) Einsatz m; (Comm) Anteil m; be at ~ auf dem Spiel stehen ●vt ~ a claim to sth Anspruch auf etw (acc) erheben

stale a (-r, -st) alt; <air> verbraucht. ~mate n Patt nt

stalk¹ n Stiel m, Stängel m

stall n Stand m; ~s pl (Theat) Parkett nt ●vi <engine:> stehen bleiben; (fig) ausweichen ●vt abwürgen <engine>

stalwart a treu ●n treuer Anhänger m

stamina n Ausdauer f

stammer n Stottern nt ●vt/i stottern

stamp n Stempel m; (postage ~) [Brief]marke f ●vt stempeln; (impress) prägen; (put postage on) frankieren ●vi stampfen. ~ out vt [aus]stanzen; (fig) ausmerzen

stampede n wilde Flucht f ●vi in Panik fliehen

stance n Haltung f

stand n Stand m; (rack) Ständer m; (pedestal) Sockel m; (Sport) Tribüne f; (fig) Einstellung f ●v (pt/pp stood) ●vi stehen; (rise) aufstehen; (be candidate) kandidieren; (stay valid) gültig bleiben; ~ still stillstehen; ~ firm (fig) festbleiben; ~ to reason logisch sein; ~ in for vertreten; ~ for (mean) bedeuten ●vt stellen; (withstand) standhalten (+ dat); (endure) ertragen; vertragen

<climate>; (put up with)
aushalten; haben <chance>; ~
s.o. a beer jdm ein Bier
spendieren; I can't ~ her 🔲 ich
kann sie nicht ausstehen. ~ by vi
daneben stehen; (be ready) sich
bereithalten ● vt ~ by s.o. (fig)
zu jdm stehen. ~ down vi (retire)
zurücktreten. ~ out vi
hervorstehen; (fig) herausragen.
~ up vi aufstehen; ~ up for
eintreten für; ~ up to sich
wehren gegen

standard a Normal- ● n Maßstab
m; (Techn) Norm f; (level) Niveau
nt; (flag) Standarte f; ~s pl
(morals) Prinzipien pl. ~ize vt
standardisieren; (Techn) normen

stand-in n Ersatz m

standing a (erect) stehend;
(permanent) ständig ● n Rang m;
(duration) Dauer f. ~-room n
Stehplätze pl

stand: ~-offish a distanziert.
~point n Standpunkt m. ~still n
Stillstand m; come to a ~still zum
Stillstand kommen

stank see stink

staple¹ a Grund-

staple² n Heftklammer f ● vt
heften. ~r n Heftmaschine f

star n Stern m; (asterisk)
Sternchen nt; (Theat, Sport) Star
m ● vi (pt/pp starred) die
Hauptrolle spielen

starboard n Steuerbord nt

starch n Stärke f ● vt stärken. ~y
a stärkehaltig; (fig) steif

starling n Star m

start n Anfang m, Beginn m;
(departure) Aufbruch m; (Sport)
Start m; from the ~ von Anfang
an; for a ~ erstens ● vi anfangen,
beginnen; (set out) aufbrechen;
<engine:> anspringen; (Auto,

Sport) starten; (jump)
aufschrecken; to ~ with zuerst
● vt anfangen, beginnen; (cause)
verursachen; (found) gründen;
starten <car, race>; in Umlauf
setzen <rumour>. ~er n (Culin)
Vorspeise f; (Auto, Sport) Starter
m. ~ing-point n Ausgangspunkt
m

startle vt erschrecken

starvation n Verhungern nt

starve vi hungern; (to death)
verhungern ● vt verhungern
lassen

state n Zustand m; (Pol) Staat m;
~ of play Spielstand m; be in a ~
<person:> aufgeregt sein ● attrib
Staats-, staatlich ● vt erklären;
(specify) angeben

stately a (-ier, -iest) stattlich. ~
home n Schloss nt

statement n Erklärung f; (Jur)
Aussage f; (Banking) Auszug m

statesman n Staatsmann m

static a statisch; remain ~
unverändert bleiben

station n Bahnhof m; (police)
Wache f; (radio) Sender m;
(space, weather) Station f; (Mil)
Posten m; (status) Rang m ● vt
stationieren; (post) postieren.
~ary a stehend; be ~ary stehen

stationery n Briefpapier nt;
(writing materials) Schreibwaren
pl

station-wagon n (Amer)
Kombi[wagen] n

statistic n statistische Tatsache f.
~al, -ly adv statistisch. ~s n &
pl Statistik f

statue n Statue f

stature n Statur f; (fig) Format nt

status n Status m, Rang m

statut|e n Statut nt. ~ory a
gesetzlich

staunch a (-er, -est), -ly adv treu

stave vt ~ off abwenden

stay n Aufenthalt m ● vi bleiben;
(reside) wohnen; ~ the night

S

übernachten. **~ behind** vi
zurückbleiben. **~ in** vi zu Hause
bleiben; (*Sch*) nachsitzen. **~ up**
vi <*person:*> aufbleiben

steadily adv fest; (*continually*)
stetig

steady a (-ier, -iest) fest; (*not
wobbly*) stabil; <*hand*> ruhig;
(*regular*) regelmäßig;
(*dependable*) zuverlässig

steak n Steak nt

steal vt/i (pt **stole**, pp **stolen**)
stehlen (**from** dat). **~ in/out** vi
sich hinein-/hinausstehlen

stealthy a heimlich

steam n Dampf ● vt (*Culin*)
dämpfen, dünsten ● vi dampfen.
~ up vi beschlagen

steam engine n Dampfmaschine
f; (*Rail*) Dampflokomotive f

steamer n Dampfer m

steamy a dampfig

steel n Stahl m

steep a, **-ly** adv steil; (🛈
exorbitant) gesalzen

steeple n Kirchturm m

steer vt/i (*Auto*) lenken; (*Naut*)
steuern; **~ clear of** s.o./sth jdm/
etw aus dem Weg gehen. **~ing** n
(*Auto*) Lenkung f. **~ing-wheel** n
Lenkrad nt

stem¹ n Stiel m; (*of word*) Stamm
m

stem² vt (pt/pp **stemmed**)
eindämmen; stillen <*bleeding*>

stench n Gestank m

stencil n Schablone f

step n Schritt m; (*stair*) Stufe f;
~s pl (*ladder*) Trittleiter f; **in ~**
im Schritt; **~ by ~** Schritt für
Schritt; **take ~s** (*fig*) Schritte
unternehmen ● vi (pt/pp **stepped**)
treten; **~ in** (*fig*) eingreifen. **~ up**
vt (*increase*) erhöhen, steigen;
verstärken <*efforts*>

step: **~brother** n Stiefbruder m.
~child n Stiefkind nt. **~daughter**
n Stieftochter f. **~father** n
Stiefvater m. **~-ladder** n

Trittleiter f. **~mother** n
Stiefmutter f. **~sister** n
Stiefschwester f. **~son** n
Stiefsohn m

stereo n Stereo nt; (*equipment*)
Stereoanlage f. **~phonic** a
stereophon

stereotype n stereotype Figur f

steril|e a steril. **~ize** vt
sterilisieren

sterling a Sterling-; (*fig*) gediegen
● n Sterling m

stern¹ a (-er, -est), **-ly** adv streng

stern² n (*of boat*) Heck nt

stew n Eintopf m; **in a ~** 🛈
aufgeregt 🛈 schmoren; **~ed**
fruit Kompott nt

steward n Ordner m; (*on ship,
aircraft*) Steward m. **~ess** n
Stewardess f

stick¹ n Stock m; (*of chalk*) Stück
nt; (*of rhubarb*) Stange f; (*Sport*)
Schläger m

stick² v (pt/pp **stuck**) ● vt stecken;
(*stab*) stechen; (*glue*) kleben; (🛈
put) tun; (🛈 *endure*) aushalten
● vi stecken; (*adhere*) kleben,
haften (**to** an + dat); (*jam*)
klemmen; **~ at it** 🛈 dranbleiben;
~ up for 🛈 eintreten für; **be stuck**
nicht weiterkönnen; <*vehicle:*>
festsitzen, festgefahren sein;
<*drawer:*> klemmen; **be stuck with**
sth 🛈 etw am Hals haben. **~ out**
vi abstehen; (*project*) vorstehen
● vt hinausstrecken;
herausstrecken <*tongue*>

sticker n Aufkleber m

sticking plaster n Heftpflaster nt

sticky a (-ier, -iest) klebrig;
(*adhesive*) Klebe-

stiff a (-er, -est), **-ly** adv steif;
<*brush*> hart; <*dough*> fest;
(*difficult*) schwierig; <*penalty*>
schwer; **be bored ~** 🛈 sich zu
Tode langweilen. **~en** vt steif
machen ● vi steif werden. **~ness**
n Steifheit f

stifl|e vt ersticken; (fig) unterdrücken. **~ing** a be ~ing zum Ersticken sein

still a still; <drink> ohne Kohlensäure; **keep ~** stillhalten; **stand ~** stillstehen ●adv noch; (emphatic) immer noch; (nevertheless) trotzdem; **~ not** immer noch nicht

stillborn a tot geboren

still life n Stilleben nt

stilted a gestelzt, geschraubt

stimulant n Anregungsmittel nt

stimulat|e vt anregen. **~ion** n Anregung f

stimulus n (pl -li) Reiz m

sting n Stich m; (from nettle, jellyfish) Brennen nt; (organ) Stachel m ●v (pt/pp stung) ●vt stechen ●vi brennen; <insect:> stechen

stingy a (-ier, -iest) geizig, 🄸 knauserig

stink n Gestank m ●vi (pt stank, pp stunk) stinken (**of** nach)

stipulat|e vt vorschreiben. **~ion** n Bedingung f

stir n (commotion) Aufregung f ●v (pt/pp stirred) vt rühren ●vi sich rühren

stirrup n Steigbügel m

stitch n Stich m; (Knitting) Masche f; (pain) Seitenstechen nt; **be in ~es** 🄸 sich kaputtlachen ●vt nähen

stock n Vorrat m (**of** an + dat); (in shop) [Waren]bestand m; (livestock) Vieh nt; (lineage) Abstammung f; (Finance) Wertpapiere pl; (Culin) Brühe f; (plant) Levkoje f; **in/out of ~** vorrätig/nicht vorrätig; **take ~** (fig) Bilanz ziehen ●a Standard- ●vt <shop:> führen; auffüllen <shelves>. **~ up** vi sich eindecken (**with** mit)

stock: ~broker n Börsenmakler m. **S~ Exchange** n Börse f

stocking n Strumpf m

stock: ~market n Börse f. **~- taking** n (Comm) Inventur f

stocky a (-ier, -iest) untersetzt

stodgy a pappig [und schwer verdaulich]

stoke vt heizen

stole, stolen see **steal**

stomach n Magen m. **~-ache** n Magenschmerzen pl

stone n Stein m; (weight) 6,35kg ●a steinern; <wall, Age> Stein- ●vt mit Steinen bewerfen; entsteinen <fruit>. **~-cold** a eiskalt. **~-deaf** a 🄸 stocktaub

stony a steinig

stood see **stand**

stool n Hocker m

stoop n walk with a ~ gebeugt gehen ●vi sich bücken

stop n Halt m; (break) Pause f; (for bus) Haltestelle f; (for train) Station f; (Gram) Punkt m; (on organ) Register nt; **come to a ~** stehen bleiben; **put a ~ to sth** etw unterbinden ●v (pt/pp stopped) ●vt anhalten, stoppen; (switch off) abstellen; (plug, block) zustopfen; (prevent) verhindern; **~ s.o. doing sth** jdn daran hindern, etw zu tun; **~ doing sth** aufhören, etw zu tun; **~ that!** hör auf damit! ●vi anhalten; (cease) aufhören; <clock:> stehen bleiben ●int halt!

stop: ~gap n Notlösung f. **~over** n (Aviat) Zwischenlandung f

stoppage n Unterbrechung f; (strike) Streik m

stopper n Stöpsel m

stop-watch n Stoppuhr f

storage n Aufbewahrung f; (in warehouse) Lagerung f; (Computing) Speicherung f

store n (stock) Vorrat m; (shop) Laden m; (department ~) Kaufhaus nt; (depot) Lager nt; **in ~** auf Lager; **be in ~ for s.o.** (fig) jdm bevorstehen ●vt aufbewahren; (in warehouse)

S

lagern; (*Computing*) speichern.
~-room n Lagerraum m
storey n Stockwerk nt
stork n Storch m
storm n Sturm m; (*with thunder*)
Gewitter nt ●vt/i stürmen. **~y** a
stürmisch
story n Geschichte f; (*in
newspaper*) Artikel m; (🛈 *lie*)
Märchen nt
stout a (**-er, -est**) beleibt; (*strong*)
fest
stove n Ofen m; (*for cooking*)
Herd m
stow vt verstauen. **~away** n
blinder Passagier m
straggl|e vi hinterherhinken. **~er**
n Nachzügler m. **~y** a strähnig
straight a (**-er, -est**) gerade;
(*direct*) direkt; (*clear*) klar;
<*hair*> glatt; <*drink*>; pur; **be ~**
(*tidy*) in Ordnung sein ●adv
gerade; (*directly*) direkt,
geradewegs; (*clearly*) klar; **~
away** sofort; **~ on** or **ahead**
geradeaus; **~ out** (*fig*)
geradeheraus; **sit/stand up ~**
gerade sitzen/stehen
straighten vt gerade machen;
(*put straight*) gerade richten ●vi
gerade werden; **~ [up]** <*person:*>
sich aufrichten. **~ out** vt gerade
biegen
straightforward a offen; (*simple*)
einfach
strain n Belastung f; **~s** pl (*of
music*) Klänge pl ●vt belasten;
(*overexert*) überanstrengen;
(*injure*) zerren <*muscle*>; (*Culin*)
durchseihen; abgießen
<*vegetables*>. **~ed** a <*relations*>
gespannt. **~er** n Sieb nt
strait n Meerenge f; **in dire ~s** in
großen Nöten
strand[1] n (*of thread*) Faden m; (*of
hair*) Strähne f
strand[2] vt **be ~ed** festsitzen
strange a (**-r, -st**) fremd; (*odd*)
seltsam, merkwürdig. **~ly** adv

seltsam, merkwürdig; **~ enough**
seltsamerweise. **~r** n Fremde(r)
m/f
strangle vt erwürgen; (*fig*)
unterdrücken
strap n Riemen m; (*for safety*)
Gurt m; (*to grasp in vehicle*)
Halteriemen m; (*of watch*)
Armband nt; (*shoulder ~*) Träger
m ●vt (*pt/pp* **strapped**) schnallen
strapping a stramm
strategic a, **-ally** adv strategisch
strategy n Strategie f
straw n Stroh nt; (*single piece,
drinking*) Strohhalm m; **that's the
last ~** jetzt reicht's aber
strawberry n Erdbeere f
stray a streunend ●n
streunendes Tier nt ●vi sich
verirren; (*deviate*) abweichen
streak n Streifen m; (*in hair*)
Strähne f; (*fig: trait*) Zug m
stream n Bach m; (*flow*) Strom m;
(*current*) Strömung f; (*Sch*)
Parallelzug m ●vi strömen
streamline vt (*fig*) rationalisieren.
~d a stromlinienförmig
street n Straße f. **~car** n (*Amer*)
Straßenbahn f. **~lamp** n
Straßenlaterne f
strength n Stärke f; (*power*) Kraft
f; **on the ~ of** auf Grund (+ *gen*).
~en vt stärken; (*reinforce*)
verstärken
strenuous a anstrengend
stress n (*emphasis*) Betonung f;
(*strain*) Belastung f; (*mental*)
Stress m ●vt betonen; (*put a
strain on*) belasten. **~ful** a
stressig 🛈
stretch n (*of road*) Strecke f;
(*elasticity*) Elastizität f; **at a ~**
ohne Unterbrechung; **have a ~**
sich strecken ●vt strecken;
(*widen*) dehnen; (*spread*)
ausbreiten; fordern <*person*>; **~
one's legs** sich (*dat*) die Beine
vertreten ●vt sich erstrecken;
(*become wider*) sich dehnen;

<person:> sich strecken. **~er** *n* Tragbahre *f*

strict *a* (-er, -est), **-ly** *adv* streng; **~ly speaking** streng genommen

stride *n* [großer] Schritt *m*; **take sth in one's ~** mit etw gut fertig werden ● *vi* (*pt* **strode**, *pp* **stridden**) [mit großen Schritten] gehen

strident *a*, **-ly** *adv* schrill; *<colour>* grell

strife *n* Streit *m*

strike *n* Streik *m*; (*Mil*) Angriff *m*; **be on ~** streiken ● *v* (*pt/pp* **struck**) ● *vt* schlagen; (*knock against, collide with*) treffen; anzünden *<match>*; stoßen auf (+ *acc*) *<oil, gold>*; abbrechen *<camp>*; (*impress*) beeindrucken; (*occur to*) einfallen (+ *dat*); **~ s.o. a blow** jdm einen Schlag versetzen ● *vi* treffen; *<lightning:>* einschlagen; *<clock:>* schlagen; (*attack*) zuschlagen; *<workers:>* streiken

striker *n* Streikende(r) *m/f*

striking *a* auffallend

string *n* Schnur *f*; (*thin*) Bindfaden *m*; (*of musical instrument, racket*) Saite *f*; (*of bow*) Sehne *f*; (*of pearls*) Kette *f*; **the ~s** (*Mus*) die Streicher *pl*; **pull ~s** 🛈 seine Beziehungen spielen lassen ● *vt* (*pt/pp* **strung**) (*thread*) aufziehen *<beads>*

stringent *a* streng

strip *n* Streifen *m* ● *v* (*pt/pp* **stripped**) ● *vt* ablösen; ausziehen *<person, clothes>*; abziehen *<bed>*; abbeizen *<wood, furniture>*; auseinander nehmen *<machine>*; (*deprive*) berauben (*of gen*); **~ sth off sth** etw von etw entfernen ● *vi* (*undress*) sich ausziehen

stripe *n* Streifen *m*. **~d** *a* gestreift

stripper *n* Stripperin *f*; (*male*) Stripper *m*

strive *vi* (*pt* **strove**, *pp* **striven**) sich bemühen (**to** zu); **~ for** streben nach

strode *see* **stride**

stroke[1] *n* Schlag *m*; (*of pen*) Strich *m*; (*Swimming*) Zug *m*; (*style*) Stil *m*; (*Med*) Schlaganfall *m*; **~ of luck** Glücksfall *m*

stroke[2] ● *vt* streicheln

stroll *n* Bummel *m* 🛈 ● *vi* bummeln 🛈. **~er** *n* (*Amer: pushchair*) [Kinder]sportwagen *m*

strong *a* (-er, -est), **-ly** *adv* stark; (*powerful, healthy*) kräftig; (*severe*) streng; (*sturdy*) stabil; (*convincing*) gut

strong: **~hold** *n* Festung *f*; (*fig*) Hochburg *f*. **~-room** *n* Tresorraum *m*

strove *see* **strive**

struck *see* **strike**

structural *a*, **-ly** *adv* baulich

structure *n* Struktur *f*; (*building*) Bau *m*

struggle *n* Kampf *m*; **with a ~** mit Mühe ● *vt* kämpfen; **~ to do sth** sich abmühen, etw zutun

strum *v* (*pt/pp* **strummed**) ● *vt* klimpern auf (+ *dat*) ● *vi* klimpern

strung *see* **string**

strut[1] *n* Strebe *f*

strut[2] *vi* (*pt/pp* **strutted**) stolzieren

stub *n* Stummel *m*; (*counterfoil*) Abschnitt *m*. **~ out** *vt* (*pt/pp* **stubbed**) ausdrücken *<cigarette>*

stubble *n* Stoppeln *pl*

stubborn *a*, **-ly** *adv* starrsinnig; *<refusal>* hartnäckig

stubby *a*, (-ier, -iest) kurz und dick

stuck *see* **stick**[2]. **~-up** *a* 🛈 hochnäsig

stud *n* Nagel *m*; (*on clothes*) Niete *f*; (*for collar*) Kragenknopf *m*; (*for ear*) Ohrstecker *m*

student *n* Student(in) *m(f)*; (*Sch*) Schüler(in) *m(f)*

S

studio n Studio nt; (for artist)
Atelier nt
studious a lerneifrig; (earnest)
ernsthaft
stud|y n Studie f; (room)
Arbeitszimmer nt; (investigation)
Untersuchung f; ~ies pl Studium
nt ● v (pt/pp studied) ● vt
studieren; (examine) untersuchen
● vi lernen; (at university)
studieren
stuff n Stoff m; (🔲 things) Zeug nt
● vt vollstopfen; (with padding,
Culin) füllen; ausstopfen
<animal>; (cram) [hinein]stopfen.
~ing n Füllung f
stuffy a (-ier, -iest) stickig; (old-
fashioned) spießig
stumbl|e vi stolpern; ~e across
zufällig stoßen auf (+ acc).
~ing-block n Hindernis nt
stump n Stumpf m ● ~ up vt/i 🔲
blechen. ~ed a 🔲 überfragt
stun vt (pt/pp stunned) betäuben
stung see sting
stunk see stink
stunning a 🔲 toll
stunt n 🔲 Kunststück nt
stupendous a, -ly adv enorm
stupid a dumm. ~ity n Dummheit
f. ~ly adv dumm; ~ly [enough]
dummerweise
sturdy a (-ier, -iest) stämmig;
<furniture> stabil; <shoes> fest
stutter n Stottern nt ● vt/i
stottern
sty n (pl sties) Schweinestall m
style n Stil m; (fashion) Mode f;
(sort) Art f; (hair~) Frisur f; in ~
in großem Stil
stylish a, -ly adv stilvoll
stylist n Friseur m/ Friseuse f.
~ic a, -ally adv stilistisch
suave a (pej) gewandt
subconscious a, -ly adv
unterbewusst ● n
Unterbewusstsein nt
subdivi|de vt unterteilen. ~sion n
Unterteilung f

subdue vt unterwerfen. ~d a
gedämpft; <person> still
subject¹ a be ~ to sth etw (dat)
unterworfen sein ● n
Staatsbürger(in) m(f); (of ruler)
Untertan m; (theme) Thema nt;
(of investigation) Gegenstand m;
(Sch) Fach nt; (Gram) Subjekt nt
subject² vt unterwerfen (to dat);
(expose) aussetzen (to dat)
subjective a, -ly adv subjektiv
subjunctive n Konjunktiv m
sublime a, -ly adv erhaben
submarine n Unterseeboot nt
submerge vt untertauchen; be ~d
unter Wasser stehen ● vi
tauchen
submission n Unterwerfung f
submit v (pt/pp -mitted, pres p
-mitting) ● vt vorlegen (to dat);
(hand in) einreichen ● vi sich
unterwerfen (to dat)
subordinate¹ a untergeordnet ● n
Untergebene(r) m/f
subordinate² vt unterordnen (to
dat)
subscribe vi spenden; ~ to (fig);
abonnieren <newspaper>. ~r n
Spender m; Abonnent m
subscription n (to club)
[Mitglieds]beitrag m; (to
newspaper) Abonnement nt; by ~
mit Spenden; <buy> im
Abonnement
subsequent a, -ly adv folgend;
(later) später
subside vi sinken; <ground:> sich
senken; <storm:> nachlassen
subsidiary a untergeordnet ● n
Tochtergesellschaft f
subsid|ize vt subventionieren. ~y
n Subvention f
substance n Substanz f
substandard a unzulänglich;
<goods> minderwertig
substantial a solide; <meal>
reichhaltig; (considerable)
beträchtlich. ~ly adv solide;
(essentially) im Wesentlichen

substitut|e *n* Ersatz *m*; (*Sport*) Ersatzspieler(in) *m(f)* ● *vt* ~**e A for B** B durch A ersetzen ● *vi* ~**e for s.o.** jdn vertreten. ~**ion** *n* Ersetzung *f*

subterranean *a* unterirdisch

subtitle *n* Untertitel *m*

subtle *a* (**-r, -st**), **-tly** *adv* fein; (*fig*) subtil

subtract *vt* abziehen, subtrahieren. ~**ion** *n* Subtraktion *f*

suburb *n* Vorort *m*. ~**an** *a* Vorort-. ~**ia** *n* die Vororte *pl*

subway *n* Unterführung *f*; (*Amer: railway*) U-Bahn *f*

succeed *vi* Erfolg haben; <*plan:*> gelingen; (*follow*) nachfolgen (+ *dat*); I ~**ed** es ist mir gelungen; he ~**ed in escaping** es gelang ihm zu entkommen ● *vt* folgen (+ *dat*)

success *n* Erfolg *m*. ~**ful** *a*,**-ly** *adv* erfolgreich

succession *n* Folge *f*; (*series*) Serie *f*; (*to title, office*) Nachfolge *f*; (*to throne*) Thronfolge *f*; **in** ~ hintereinander

successive *a* aufeinander folgend

successor *n* Nachfolger(in) *m(f)*

succumb *vi* erliegen (**to** *dat*)

such
● *adjective*
····▸ (*of that kind*) solch. **such a book** ein solches Buch; so ein Buch 🔟. **such a person** ein solcher Mensch; so ein Mensch 🔟. **such people** solche Leute. **such a thing** so etwas. **no such example** kein solches Beispiel. **there is no such thing** so etwas gibt es nicht; das gibt es gar nicht. **there is no such person** eine solche Person gibt es nicht. **such writers as Goethe and Schiller** Schriftsteller wie Goethe und Schiller

····▸ (*so great*) solch; derartig. **I've got such a headache!** ich habe solche Kopfschmerzen! **it was such fun!** das machte solchen Spaß! **I got such a fright that …** ich bekam einen derartigen *od* 🔟 so einen Schrecken, dass …

····▸ (*with adjective*) so. **such a big house** ein so großes Haus. **he has such lovely blue eyes** er hat so schöne blaue Augen. **such a long time** so lange

● *pronoun*
····▸ **as such** als solcher/solche/ solches. **the thing as such** die Sache als solche. (*strictly speaking*) **this is not a promotion as such** dies ist im Grunde genommen keine Beförderung

····▸ **such is: such is life** so ist das Leben. **such is not the case** das ist nicht der Fall

┊····▸ **such as** wie [zum Beispiel]

suchlike *pron* 🔟 dergleichen

suck *vt/i* saugen; lutschen <*sweet*>. ~ **up** *vt* aufsaugen ● *vi* ~ **up to s.o.** 🔟 sich bei jdm einschmeicheln

suction *n* Saugwirkung *f*

sudden *a*, **-ly** *adv* plötzlich; (*abrupt*) jäh ● *n* **all of a** ~ auf einmal

sue *vt* (*pres p* **suing**) verklagen (**for** auf + *acc*) ● *vi* klagen

suede *n* Wildleder *nt*

suet *n* [Nieren]talg *m*

suffer *vi* leiden (**from** an + *dat*) ● *vt* erleiden; (*tolerate*) dulden

suffice *vi* genügen

sufficient *a*, **-ly** *adv* genug, genügend; **be** ~ genügen

suffocat|e *vt/i* ersticken. ~**ion** *n* Ersticken *nt*

sugar *n* Zucker *m* ● *vt* zuckern; (*fig*) versüßen. ~ **basin, ~-bowl** *n* Zuckerschale *f*. ~**y** *a* süß; (*fig*) süßlich

suggest vt vorschlagen; (*indicate, insinuate*) andeuten. ~**ion** n Vorschlag m; Andeutung f; (*trace*) Spur f. ~**ive** a, **-ly** adv anzüglich

suicidal a selbstmörderisch

suicide n Selbstmord m

suit n Anzug m; (*woman's*) Kostüm nt; (*Cards*) Farbe f; (*Jur*) Prozess m ● vt (*adapt*) anpassen (**to** dat); (*be convenient for*) passen (+ dat); (*go with*) passen zu; <*clothing:*> stehen (**s.o.** jdm); **be** ~**ed for** geeignet sein für; ~ **yourself!** wie du willst!

suit|able a geeignet; (*convenient*) passend; (*appropriate*) angemessen; (*for weather, activity*) zweckmäßig. ~**ably** adv angemessen; zweckmäßig

suitcase n Koffer m

suite n Suite f; (*of furniture*) Garnitur f

sulk vi schmollen. ~**y** a schmollend

sullen a, **-ly** adv mürrisch

sultry a (**-ier, -iest**) <*weather*> schwül

sum n Summe f; (*Sch*) Rechenaufgabe f ● vt/i (*pt/pp* summed) ~ **up** zusammenfassen; (*assess*) einschätzen

summar|ize vt zusammenfassen. ~**y** n Zusammenfassung f ● a, **-ily** adv summarisch; <*dismissal*> fristlos

summer n Sommer m. ~**time** n Sommer m

summery a sommerlich

summit n Gipfel m. ~ **conference** n Gipfelkonferenz f

summon vt rufen; holen <*help*>; (*Jur*) vorladen

summons n (*Jur*) Vorladung f ● vt vorladen

sumptuous a, **-ly** adv prunkvoll; <*meal*> üppig

sun n Sonne f ● vt (*pt/pp* sunned) ~ **oneself** sich sonnen

sun: ~**bathe** vi sich sonnen. ~**bed** n Sonnenbank f. ~**burn** n Sonnenbrand m

Sunday n Sonntag m

sunflower n Sonnenblume f

sung *see* sing

sunglasses npl Sonnenbrille f

sunk *see* sink

sunny a (**-ier, -iest**) sonnig

sun: ~**rise** n Sonnenaufgang m. ~**-roof** n (*Auto*) Schiebedach nt. ~**set** n Sonnenuntergang m. ~**shade** n Sonnenschirm m. ~**shine** n Sonnenschein m. ~**stroke** n Sonnenstich m. ~**-tan** n [Sonnen]bräune f. ~**-tanned** a braun [gebrannt]. ~**-tan oil** n Sonnenöl nt

super a Ⅰ prima, toll

superb a erstklassig

superficial a, **-ly** adv oberflächlich

superfluous a überflüssig

superintendent n (*of police*) Kommissar m

superior a überlegen; (*in rank*) höher ● n Vorgesetzte(r) m/f. ~**ity** n Überlegenheit f

superlative a unübertrefflich ● n Superlativ m

supermarket n Supermarkt m

supernatural a übernatürlich

supersede vt ersetzen

superstiti|on n Aberglaube m. ~**ous** a, **-ly** adv abergläubisch

supervis|e vt beaufsichtigen; überwachen <*work*>. ~**ion** n Aufsicht f; Überwachung f. ~**or** n Aufseher(in) m(f)

supper n Abendessen nt

supple a geschmeidig

supplement n Ergänzung f; (*addition*) Zusatz m; (*to fare*) Zuschlag m; (*book*) Ergänzungsband m; (*to newspaper*) Beilage f ● vt ergänzen. ~**ary** a zusätzlich

supplier n Lieferant m

supply n Vorrat m; **supplies** pl (Mil) Nachschub m ●vt (pt/pp -ied) liefern; ~ s.o. with sth jdn mit etw versorgen

support n Stütze f; (fig) Unterstützung f ●vt stützen; (bear weight of) tragen; (keep) ernähren; (give money to) unterstützen; (speak in favour of) befürworten; (Sport) Fan sein von. ~er n Anhänger(in) m(f); (Sport) Fan m

suppose vt annehmen; (presume) vermuten; (imagine) sich (dat) vorstellen; **be ~d to do sth** etw tun sollen; **not be ~d to** 🔢 nicht dürfen; **I ~ so** vermutlich. ~dly adv angeblich

supposition n Vermutung f

suppress vt unterdrücken. ~ion n Unterdrückung f

supremacy n Vorherrschaft f

supreme a höchste(r,s); <court> oberste(r,s)

sure a (-r, -st) sicher; **make ~** sich vergewissern (of gen); (check) nachprüfen ●adv (Amer 🔢) klar; ~ **enough** tatsächlich. ~**ly** adv sicher; (for emphasis) doch; (Amer: gladly) gern

surf n Brandung f

surface n Oberfläche f ●vi (emerge) auftauchen

surfboard n Surfbrett nt

surfing n Surfen nt

surge n (of sea) Branden nt; (fig) Welle f ●vi branden; ~ **forward** nach vorn drängen

surgeon n Chirurg(in) m(f)

surgery n Chirurgie f; (place) Praxis f; (room) Sprechzimmer nt; (hours) Sprechstunde f; **have ~** operiert werden

surgical a, **-ly** adv chirurgisch

surly a (-ier, -iest) mürrisch

surname n Nachname m

surpass vt übertreffen

surplus a überschüssig ●n Überschuss m (of an + dat)

surpris|e n Überraschung f ●vt überraschen; **be ~ed** sich wundern (at über + acc). ~**ing** a, **-ly** adv überraschend

surrender n Kapitulation f ●vi sich ergeben; (Mil) kapitulieren ●vt aufgeben

surround vt umgeben; (encircle) umzingeln; ~**ed by** umgeben von. ~**ing** a umliegend. ~**ings** npl Umgebung f

surveillance n Überwachung f; **be under ~** überwacht werden

survey[1] n Überblick m; (poll) Umfrage f; (investigation) Untersuchung f; (of land) Vermessung f; (of house) Gutachten nt

survey[2] vt betrachten; vermessen <land>; begutachten <building>. ~**or** n Landvermesser m; Gutachter m

survival n Überleben nt; (of tradition) Fortbestand m

surviv|e vt überleben ●vi überleben; <tradition:> erhalten bleiben. ~**or** n Überlebende(r) m/f; **be a ~or** nicht unterzukriegen sein

susceptible a empfänglich/ (Med) anfällig (to für)

suspect[1] vt verdächtigen; (assume) vermuten; **he ~s nothing** er ahnt nichts

suspect[2] a verdächtig ●n Verdächtige(r) m/f

suspend vt aufhängen; (stop) [vorläufig] einstellen; (from duty) vorläufig beurlauben. ~**ders** npl (Amer: braces) Hosenträger pl

suspense n Spannung f

suspension n (Auto) Federung f. ~ **bridge** n Hängebrücke f

suspici|on n Verdacht m; (mistrust) Misstrauen nt; (trace) Spur f. ~**ous** a, **-ly** adv misstrauisch; (arousing suspicion) verdächtig

S

sustain vt tragen; (*fig*) aufrechterhalten; erhalten <*life*>; erleiden <*injury*>

sustenance n Nahrung f

swagger vi stolzieren

swallow¹ vt/i schlucken. **~ up** vt verschlucken; verschlingen <*resources*>

swallow² n (*bird*) Schwalbe f

swam see **swim**

swamp n Sumpf m ●vt überschwemmen

swan n Schwan m

swank vi 🗊 angeben

swap n 🗊 Tausch m ●vt/i (*pt/pp* **swapped**) 🗊 tauschen (**for** gegen)

swarm n Schwarm m ●vi schwärmen; **be ~ing with** wimmeln von

swat vt (*pt/pp* **swatted**) totschlagen

sway vi schwanken; (*gently*) sich wiegen ●vt (*influence*) beeinflussen

swear v (*pt* **swore**, *pp* **sworn**) ●vt schwören ●vi schwören (**by** auf + *acc*); (*curse*) fluchen. **~-word** n Kraftausdruck m

sweat n Schweiß m ●vi schwitzen

sweater n Pullover m

Swed|e n Schwede m/Schwedin f. **~en** n Schweden nt. **~ish** a schwedisch

sweep n Schornsteinfeger m; (*curve*) Bogen m; (*movement*) ausholende Bewegung f ●v (*pt/pp* **swept**) ●vt fegen, kehren ●vi (*go swiftly*) rauschen; <*wind:*> fegen

sweeping a ausholend; <*statement*> pauschal; <*changes*> weit reichend

sweet a (-er, -est) süß; **have a ~ tooth** gern Süßes mögen ●n Bonbon m & nt; (*dessert*) Nachtisch m

sweeten vt süßen

sweet: ~heart n Schatz m. **~ness** n Süße f. **~ pea** n Wicke f. **~-shop** n Süßwarenladen m

swell n Dünung f ●v (*pt* **swelled**, *pp* **swollen** or **swelled**) ●vi [an]schwellen; <*wood:*> aufquellen ●vt anschwellen lassen; (*increase*) vergrößern. **~ing** n Schwellung f

swelter vi schwitzen

swept see **sweep**

swerve vi einen Bogen machen

swift a (-er, -est), **-ly** adv schnell

swig n 🗊 Schluck m

swim n **have a ~** schwimmen ●vi (*pt* **swam**, *pp* **swum**) schwimmen; **my head is ~ming** mir dreht sich der Kopf. **~mer** n Schwimmer(in) m(f)

swimming n Schwimmen nt. **~-baths** npl Schwimmbad nt. **~-pool** n Schwimmbecken nt; (*private*) Swimmingpool m

swimsuit n Badeanzug m

swindle n Schwindel m, Betrug m ●vt betrügen. **~r** n Schwindler m

swine n (*pej*) Schwein nt

swing n Schwung m; (*shift*) Schwenk m; (*seat*) Schaukel f; **in full ~** in vollem Gange ●v (*pt/pp* **swung**) ●vi schwingen; (*on swing*) schaukeln; (*dangle*) baumeln; (*turn*) schwenken ●vt schwingen; (*influence*) beeinflussen

swipe n 🗊 Schlag m ●vt 🗊 knallen; (*steal*) klauen

swirl n Wirbel m ●vt/i wirbeln

Swiss a Schweizer, schweizerisch ●n Schweizer(in) m(f); **the ~** pl die Schweizer. **~ roll** n Biskuitrolle f

switch n Schalter m; (*change*) Wechsel m; (*Amer, Rail*) Weiche f ●vt wechseln; (*exchange*) tauschen ●vi wechseln; **~ to** umstellen auf (+ *acc*). **~ off** vt

ausschalten; abschalten
<engine>. ∼ **on** *vt* einschalten
switchboard *n* [Telefon]zentrale
f
Switzerland *n* die Schweiz
swivel *v* (*pt/pp* **swivelled**) ● *vt*
drehen ● *vi* sich drehen
swollen *see* **swell**
swoop *n* (*by police*) Razzia *f* ● *vi*
∼ **down** herabstoßen
sword *n* Schwert *nt*
swore *see* **swear**
sworn *see* **swear**
swot *n* 🔲 Streber *m* ● *vt* (*pt/pp*
swotted) 🔲 büffeln
swum *see* **swim**
swung *see* **swing**
syllable *n* Silbe *f*
syllabus *n* Lehrplan *m*; (*for
exam*) Studienplan *m*
symbol *n* Symbol *nt* (**of** für). ∼**ic**
a, **-ally** *adv* symbolisch ∼**ism** *n*
Symbolik *f*. ∼**ize** *vt*
symbolisieren
symmetr|ical *a*, **-ly** *adv*
symmetrisch. ∼**y** *n* Symmetrie *f*
sympathetic *a*, **-ally** *adv*
mitfühlend; (*likeable*)
sympathisch
sympathize *vi* mitfühlen
sympathy *n* Mitgefühl *nt*;
(*condolences*) Beileid *nt*
symphony *n* Sinfonie *f*
symptom *n* Symptom *nt*
synagogue *n* Synagoge *f*
synchronize *vt* synchronisieren
synonym *n* Synonym *nt*. ∼**ous** *a*,
-ly *adv* synonym
synthesis *n* (*pl* **-ses**) Synthese *f*
synthetic *a* synthetisch
Syria *n* Syrien *nt*
syringe *n* Spritze *f*
syrup *n* Sirup *m*
system *n* System *nt*. ∼**atic** *a*, **-ally**
adv systematisch

tab *n* (*projecting*) Zunge *f*; (*with
name*) Namensschild *nt*; (*loop*)
Aufhänger *m*; **pick up the** ∼ 🔲
bezahlen
table *n* Tisch *m*; (*list*) Tabelle *f*; **at
[the]** ∼ bei Tisch. ∼**-cloth** *n*
Tischdecke *f*. ∼**spoon** *n*
Servierlöffel *m*
tablet *n* Tablette *f*; (*of soap*)
Stück *nt*
table tennis *n* Tischtennis *nt*
tabloid *n* kleinformatige Zeitung
f; (*pej*) Boulevardzeitung *f*
taciturn *a* wortkarg
tack *n* (*nail*) Stift *m*; (*stitch*)
Heftstich *m*; (*Naut & fig*) Kurs *m*
● *vt* festnageln; (*sew*) heften ● *vi*
(*Naut*) kreuzen
tackle *n* Ausrüstung *f* ● *vt*
angehen *<problem>*; (*Sport*)
angreifen
tact *n* Takt *m*, Taktgefühl *nt*. ∼**ful**
a, **-ly** *adv* taktvoll
tactic|al *a*, **-ly** *adv* taktisch. ∼**s**
npl Taktik *f*
tactless *a*, **-ly** *adv* taktlos. ∼**ness**
n Taktlosigkeit *f*
tag *n* (*label*) Schild *nt* ● *vi* (*pt/pp*
tagged) ∼ **along** mitkommen
tail *n* Schwanz *m*; ∼**s** *pl* (*tailcoat*)
Frack *m*; **heads or** ∼**s**? Kopf oder
Zahl? ● *vt* (🔲 *follow*) beschatten
● *vi* ∼ **off** zurückgehen
tail: ∼**back** *n* Rückstau *m*. ∼ **light**
n Rücklicht *nt*
tailor *n* Schneider *m*. ∼**-made** *a*
maßgeschneidert
taint *vt* verderben
take *v* (*pt* **took**, *pp* **taken**) ● *vt*
nehmen; (*with one*) mitnehmen;
(*take to a place*) bringen; (*steal*)
stehlen; (*win*) gewinnen;

(*capture*) einnehmen; (*require*) brauchen; (*last*) dauern; (*teach*) geben; machen <*exam, subject, holiday, photograph*>; messen <*pulse, temperature*>; ~ **sth to the cleaner's** etw in die Reinigung bringen; **be** ~**n ill** krank werden; ~ **sth calmly** etw gelassen aufnehmen ● vi <*plant:*> angehen; ~ **after s.o.** jdm nachschlagen; (*in looks*) jdm ähnlich sehen; ~ **to** (*like*) mögen; (*as a habit*) sich (*dat*) angewöhnen. ~ **away** vt wegbringen; (*remove*) wegnehmen; (*subtract*) abziehen; **'to** ~ **away'** 'zum Mitnehmen'. ~ **back** vt zurücknehmen; (*return*) zurückbringen. ~ **down** vt herunternehmen; (*remove*) abnehmen; (*write down*) aufschreiben. ~ **in** vt hineinbringen; (*bring indoors*) hereinholen; (*to one's home*) aufnehmen; (*understand*) begreifen; (*deceive*) hereinlegen; (*make smaller*) enger machen. ~ **off** vt abnehmen; ablegen <*coat*>; sich (*dat*) ausziehen <*clothes*>; (*deduct*) abziehen; (*mimic*) nachmachen ● vi (*Aviat*) starten. ~ **on** vt annehmen; (*undertake*) übernehmen; (*engage*) einstellen; (*as opponent*) antreten gegen. ~ **out** vt hinausbringen; (*for pleasure*) ausgehen mit; ausführen <*dog*>; (*remove*) herausnehmen; (*withdraw*) abheben <*money*>; (*from library*) ausleihen; ~ **it out on s.o.** Ⓘ seinen Ärger an jdm auslassen. ~ **over** vt hinüberbringen; übernehmen <*firm, control*> ● vi ~ **over from s.o.** jdn ablösen. ~ **up** vt hinaufbringen; annehmen <*offer*>; ergreifen <*profession*>; sich (*dat*) zulegen <*hobby*>; in Anspruch nehmen <*time*>; einnehmen <*space*>; aufreißen

<*floorboards*>; ~ **sth up with s.o.** mit jdm über etw (*acc*) sprechen

take: ~**-away** n Essen nt zum Mitnehmen; (*restaurant*) Restaurant nt mit Straßenverkauf. ~**-off** n (*Aviat*) Start m, Abflug m. ~**-over** n Übernahme f

takings npl Einnahmen pl

talcum n ~ **[powder]** Körperpuder m

tale n Geschichte f

talent n Talent nt

talk n Gespräch nt; (*lecture*) Vortrag m ● vi reden, sprechen (**to/with** mit) ● vt reden; ~ **s.o. into sth** jdn zu etw überreden. ~ **over** vt besprechen

talkative a gesprächig

tall a (-er, -est) groß; <*building, tree*> hoch. ~ **story** n übertriebene Geschichte f

tally vi übereinstimmen

tame a (-r, -st), **-ly** adv zahm; (*dull*) lahm Ⓘ ● vt zähmen. ~**r** n Dompteur m

tamper vi ~ **with** sich (*dat*) zu schaffen machen an (+ *dat*)

tampon n Tampon m

tan a gelbbraun ● n Gelbbraun nt; (*from sun*) Bräune f ● v (*pt/pp* tanned) ● vt gerben <*hide*> ● vi braun werden

tang n herber Geschmack m; (*smell*) herber Geruch m

tangible a greifbar

tangle n Gewirr nt; (*in hair*) Verfilzung f ● vt ~ **[up]** verheddern ● vi sich verheddern

tank n Tank m; (*Mil*) Panzer m

tanker n Tanker m; (*lorry*) Tank[last]wagen m

tantrum n Wutanfall m

tap n Hahn m; (*knock*) Klopfen nt; **on** ~ zur Verfügung ● v (*pt/pp* tapped) ● vt klopfen an (+ *acc*); anzapfen <*barrel, tree*>; erschließen <*resources*>; abhören <*telephone*> ● vi klopfen. ~

dance n Stepp[tanz] m ● vi
Stepp tanzen, steppen
tape n Band nt; (adhesive)
Klebstreifen m; (for recording)
Tonband nt ● vt mit Klebstreifen
zukleben; (record) auf Band
aufnehmen
tape-measure n Bandmaß nt
taper vi sich verjüngen
tape recorder n Tonbandgerät nt
tar n Teer m ● vt (pt/pp tarred)
teeren
target n Ziel nt; (board)
[Ziel]scheibe f
tarnish vi anlaufen
tarpaulin n Plane f
tart[1] a (-er, -est) sauer
tart[2] n ≈ Obstkuchen m;
(individual) Törtchen nt; (⊠
prostitute) Nutte f ● vt ~ oneself
up 🗉 sich auftakeln
tartan n Schottenmuster nt;
(cloth) Schottenstoff m
task n Aufgabe f; take s.o. to ~
jdm Vorhaltungen machen. ~
force n Sonderkommando nt
tassel n Quaste f
taste n Geschmack m; (sample)
Kostprobe f ● vt kosten,
probieren; schmecken <flavour>
● vi schmecken (of nach). ~**ful** a,
-ly adv (fig) geschmackvoll.
~**less** a, **-ly** adv geschmacklos
tasty a (-ier, -iest) lecker
tat see **tit**[2]
tatters npl in ~s in Fetzen
tattoo n Tätowierung f ● vt
tätowieren
tatty a (-ier, -iest) schäbig; <book>
zerfleddert
taught see **teach**
taunt n höhnische Bemerkung f
● vt verhöhnen
taut a straff
tawdry a (-ier, -iest) billig und
geschmacklos
tax n Steuer f ● vt besteuern; (fig)
strapazieren. ~**able** a

steuerpflichtig. ~**ation** n
Besteuerung f
taxi n Taxi nt ● vi (pt/pp taxied,
pres p taxiing) <aircraft:> rollen.
~ **driver** n Taxifahrer m. ~ **rank**
n Taxistand m
taxpayer n Steuerzahler m
tea n Tee m. ~-**bag** n Teebeutel
m. ~-**break** n Teepause f
teach vt/i (pt/pp taught)
unterrichten; ~ s.o. sth jdm etw
beibringen. ~**er** n Lehrer(in)
m(f). ~**ing** n Unterrichten nt
tea: ~-**cloth** n (for drying)
Geschirrtuch nt. ~**cup** n
Teetasse f
teak n Teakholz nt
team n Mannschaft f; (fig) Team
nt; (of animals) Gespann nt
teapot n Teekanne f
tear[1] n Riss m ● v (pt tore, pp
torn) ● vt reißen; (damage)
zerreißen; ~ oneself away sich
losreißen ● vi [zer]reißen; (run)
rasen. ~ **up** vt zerreißen
tear[2] n Träne f. ~**ful** a weinend.
~**fully** adv unter Tränen. ~**gas** n
Tränengas nt
tease vt necken .
tea: ~-**set** n Teeservice nt. ~
shop n Café nt. ~**spoon** n
Teelöffel m
teat n Zitze f; (on bottle) Sauger
m
tea-towel n Geschirrtuch nt
technical a technisch;
(specialized) fachlich. ~**ity** n
technisches Detail nt; (Jur)
Formfehler m. ~**ly** adv technisch;
(strictly) streng genommen. ~
term n Fachausdruck m
technician n Techniker m
technique n Technik f
technological a, **-ly** adv
technologisch
technology n Technik f
teddy n ~ **[bear]** Teddybär m
tedious a langweilig
tedium n Langeweile f

T

teenage a Teenager-; ~ **boy/girl** Junge m/Mädchen nt im Teenageralter. ~**r** n Teenager m

teens npl the ~ die Teenagerjahre pl

teeter vi schwanken

teeth see tooth

teeth|e vi zahnen. ~**ing troubles** npl (fig) Anfangsschwierigkeiten pl

teetotal a abstinent. ~**ler** n Abstinenzler m

telecommunications npl Fernmeldewesen nt

telegram n Telegramm nt

telegraph pole n Telegrafenmast m

telephone n Telefon nt; **be on the** ~ Telefon haben; (be telephoning) telefonieren ● vt anrufen ● vi telefonieren

telephone: ~ **booth** n, ~ **box** n Telefonzelle f. ~ **directory** n Telefonbuch nt. ~ **number** n Telefonnummer f

telephoto a ~ **lens** Teleobjektiv nt

telescop|e n Teleskop nt, Fernrohr nt. ~**ic** a (collapsible) ausziehbar

televise vt im Fernsehen übertragen

television n Fernsehen nt; **watch** ~ fernsehen; ~ **[set]** Fernseher m Ⓣ

tell vt/i (pt/pp told) sagen (s.o. jdm); (relate) erzählen; (know) wissen; (distinguish) erkennen; **the time** die Uhr lesen; **time will** ~ das wird man erst sehen; **his age is beginning to** ~ sein Alter macht sich bemerkbar. ~ **off** vt ausschimpfen

telly n Ⓣ = television

temp n Ⓣ Aushilfssekretärin f

temper n (disposition) Naturell nt; (mood) Laune f; (anger) Wut f; **lose one's** ~ wütend werden ● vt (fig) mäßigen

temperament n Temperament nt. ~**al** a temperamentvoll; (moody) launisch

temperate a gemäßigt

temperature n Temperatur f; **have** or **run a** ~ Fieber haben

temple¹ n Tempel m

temple² n (Anat) Schläfe f

tempo n Tempo nt

temporary a, **-ily** adv vorübergehend; <measure, building> provisorisch

tempt vt verleiten; (Relig) versuchen; herausfordern <fate>; (entice) [ver]locken; **be** ~**ed** versucht sein (**to** zu). ~**ation** n Versuchung f. ~**ing** a verlockend

ten a zehn

tenaci|ous a, **-ly** adv hartnäckig. ~**ty** n Hartnäckigkeit f

tenant n Mieter(in) m(f); (Comm) Pächter(in) m(f)

tend vi ~ **to do sth** dazu neigen, etw zu tun

tendency n Tendenz f; (inclination) Neigung f

tender a zart; (loving) zärtlich; (painful) empfindlich. ~**ly** adv zärtlich. ~**ness** n Zartheit f; Zärtlichkeit f

tendon n Sehne f

tenner n Ⓣ Zehnpfundschein m

tennis n Tennis nt. ~**-court** n Tennisplatz m

tenor n Tenor m

tense a (**-r, -st**) gespannt ● vt anspannen <muscle>

tension n Spannung f

tent n Zelt nt

tentative a, **-ly** adv vorläufig; (hesitant) zaghaft

tenterhooks npl **be on** ~ wie auf glühenden Kohlen sitzen

tenth a zehnte(r,s) ● n Zehntel nt

tenuous a schwach

tepid a lauwarm

term n Zeitraum m; (Sch) ≈ Halbjahr nt; (Univ) ≈ Semester nt; (expression) Ausdruck m; ~**s**

pl (*conditions*) Bedingungen pl; **in the short/long ~** kurz-/langfristig; **be on good/bad ~s** gut/nicht gut miteinander auskommen

terminal a End-; (*Med*) unheilbar ● n (*Aviat*) Terminal m; (*of bus*) Endstation f; (*on battery*) Pol m; (*Computing*) Terminal nt

terminat|e vt beenden; lösen <*contract*>; unterbrechen <*pregnancy*> ● vi enden

terminology n Terminologie f

terminus n (pl **-ni**) Endstation f

terrace n Terrasse f; (*houses*) Häuserreihe f. **~d house** n Reihenhaus nt

terrain n Gelände nt

terrible a, **-bly** adv schrecklich

terrific a 🄵 (*excellent*) sagenhaft; (*huge*) riesig

terri|fy vt (pt/pp **-ied**) Angst machen (+ dat); **be ~fied** Angst haben. **~fying** a Furcht erregend

territorial a Territorial-

territory n Gebiet nt

terror n [panische] Angst f; (*Pol*) Terror m. **~ism** n Terrorismus m. **~ist** n Terrorist m. **~ize** vt terrorisieren

terse a, **-ly** adv kurz, knapp

test n Test m; (*Sch*) Klassenarbeit f; **put to the ~** auf die Probe stellen ● vt prüfen; (*examine*) untersuchen (**for** auf + acc)

testament n Testament nt

testify v (pt/pp **-ied**) ● vt beweisen; **~ that** bezeugen, dass ● vi aussagen

testimonial n Zeugnis nt

testimony n Aussage f

test-tube n Reagenzglas nt

tether n **be at the end of one's ~** am Ende seiner Kraft sein ● vt anbinden

text n Text m. **~book** n Lehrbuch nt

textile a Textil- ● n **~s** pl Textilien pl

texture n Beschaffenheit f; (*Tex*) Struktur f

Thai a thailändisch. **~land** n Thailand nt

Thames n Themse f

than conj als

thank vt danken (+ dat); **~ you [very much]** danke [schön]. **~ful** a, **-ly** adv dankbar. **~less** a undankbar

thanks npl Dank m; **~!** 🄵 danke! **~ to** dank (+ dat or gen)

that
  pl **those**
● adjective
····▶ der (m), die (f), das (nt), die (pl); (*just seen or experienced*) dieser (m), diese (f), dieses (nt), diese (pl). **I'll never forget that day** den Tag werde ich nie vergessen. **I liked that house** dieses Haus hat mir gut gefallen
● pronoun
····▶ der (m), die (f), das (nt), die (pl). **that is true** das ist nicht wahr. **who is that in the garden?** wer ist das [da] im Garten? **I'll take that** ich nehme den/die/das. **I don't like those** die mag ich nicht. **is that you?** bist du es? **that is why** deshalb
····▶ **like that so. don't be like that!** sei doch nicht so! **a man like that** ein solcher Mann; so ein Mann 🄵
····▶ (*after prepositions*) da …. **after that** danach. **with that** damit. **apart from that** außerdem
····▶ (*relative pronoun*) der (m), die (f), das (nt), die (pl). **the book that I'm reading** das Buch, das ich lese. **the people that you got it from** die Leute, von denen du es bekommen hast. **everyone that I know** jeder, den ich kenne. **that is all that I have** das ist alles, was ich habe
● adverb

T

····▶ so. **he's not that stupid** so blöd ist er [auch wieder] nicht. **it wasn't that bad** so schlecht war es auch nicht. **a nail about that long** ein etwa so langer Nagel

····▶ (*relative adverb*) der (*m*), die (*f*), das (*nt*), die (*pl*). **the day that I first met her** der Tag, an dem ich sie zum ersten Mal sah. **at the speed that he was going** bei der Geschwindigkeit, die er hatte

● *conjunction*

····▶ dass. **I don't think that he'll come** ich denke nicht, dass er kommt. **we know that you're right** wir wissen, dass du Recht hast. **I'm so tired that I can hardly walk** ich bin so müde, dass ich kaum gehen kann

····▶ **so that** (*purpose*) damit; (*result*) sodass. **he came earlier so that they would have more time** er kam früher, damit sie mehr Zeit hatten. **it was late, so that I had to catch the bus** es war spät, sodass ich den Bus nehmen musste

thatch *n* Strohdach *nt*. **~ed** *a* strohgedeckt

thaw *n* Tauwetter *nt* ● *vt/i* auftauen; **it's ~ing** es taut

the *def art* der/die/das; (*pl*) die; **play ~ piano/violin** Klavier/Geige spielen ● *adv* **~ more ~ better** je mehr, desto besser; **all ~ better** umso besser

theatre *n* Theater *nt*; (*Med*) Operationssaal *m*

theatrical *a* Theater-; (*showy*) theatralisch

theft *n* Diebstahl *m*

their *a* ihr

theirs *poss pron* ihre(r), ihrs; **a friend of ~** ein Freund von ihnen; **those are ~** die gehören ihnen

them *pron* (*acc*) sie; (*dat*) ihnen

theme *n* Thema *nt*

themselves *pron* selbst; (*refl*) sich; **by ~** allein

then *adv* dann; (*at that time in past*) damals; **by ~** bis dahin; **since ~** seitdem; **before ~** vorher; **from ~ on** von da an; **now and ~** dann und wann; **there and ~** auf der Stelle ● *a* damalig

theology *n* Theologie *f*

theoretical *a*, **-ly** *adv* theoretisch

theory *n* Theorie *f*; **in ~** theoretisch

therap|ist *n* Therapeut(in) *m(f)*. **~y** *n* Therapie *f*

there *adv* da; (*with movement*) dahin, dorthin; **down/up ~** da unten/oben; **~ is/are** da ist/sind; (*in existence*) es gibt ● *int* **~**, **~!** nun, nun!

there: ~abouts *adv* da [in der Nähe]; **or ~abouts** (*roughly*) ungefähr. **~fore** *adv* deshalb, also

thermometer *n* Thermometer *nt*

Thermos (P) *n* **~ [flask]** Thermosflasche *f*

thermostat *n* Thermostat *m*

these *see* **this**

thesis *n* (*pl* -ses) Dissertation *f*; (*proposition*) These *f*

they *pron* sie; **~ say** (*generalizing*) man sagt

thick *a* (-er, -est), **-ly** *adv* dick; (*dense*) dicht; <*liquid*> dickflüssig; (🄵 *stupid*) dumm ● *adv* dick; **in the ~ of** mitten in (+ *dat*). **~en** *vt* dicker machen; eindicken <*sauce*> ● *vi* dicker werden; <*fog:*> dichter werden; <*plot:*> komplizierter werden. **~ness** *n* Dicke *f*; (*density*) Dichte *f*; (*of liquid*) Dickflüssigkeit *f*

thief *n* (*pl* thieves) Dieb(in) *m(f)*

thigh *n* Oberschenkel *m*

thimble *n* Fingerhut *m*

thin *a* (thinner, thinnest), **-ly** *adv* dünn ● *adv* dünn ● *v* (*pt/pp* thinned) ● *vt* verdünnen <*liquid*> ● *vi* sich lichten

thing n Ding nt; (subject, affair) Sache f; ~s pl (belongings) Sachen pl; for one ~ erstens; just the ~! genau das Richtige! how are ~s? wie geht's? the latest ~ 🔡 der letzte Schrei

think vt/i (pt/pp thought) denken (about/of an + acc); (believe) meinen; (consider) nachdenken; (regard as) halten für; I ~ so ich glaube schon; what do you ~ of it? was halten Sie davon? ~ over vt sich (dat) überlegen. ~ up vt sich (dat) ausdenken

third a dritte(r,s) ●n Drittel nt. ~ly adv drittens. ~-rate a drittrangig

thirst n Durst m. ~y a, -ily adv durstig; be ~y Durst haben

thirteen a dreizehn. ~th a dreizehnte(r,s)

thirtieth a dreißigste(r,s)

thirty a dreißig

this a (pl these) diese(r,s); (pl) diese; ~ one diese(r,s); I'll take ~ ich nehme diesen/diese/ dieses; ~ evening/morning heute Abend/Morgen; these days heutzutage ●pron (pl these) das, dies[es]; (pl) die, diese; ~ and that dies und das; ~ or that dieses oder das da; like ~ so; ~ is Peter das ist Peter; (Teleph) hier [spricht] Peter; who is ~? wer ist das? (Teleph, Amer) wer ist am Apparat?

thistle n Distel f

thorn n Dorn m

thorough a gründlich

thoroughbred n reinrassiges Tier nt; (horse) Rassepferd nt

thorough|ly adv gründlich; (completely) völlig; (extremely) äußerst. ~ness n Gründlichkeit f

those see that

though conj obgleich, obwohl; as ~ als ob ●adv 🔡 doch

thought see think ●n Gedanke m; (thinking) Denken nt. ~ful a, -ly

adv nachdenklich; (considerate) rücksichtsvoll. ~less a, -ly adv gedankenlos

thousand a one/a ~ [ein]tausend ●n Tausend nt. ~th a tausendste(r,s) ●n Tausendstel nt

thrash vt verprügeln; (defeat) [vernichtend] schlagen

thread n Faden m; (of screw) Gewinde nt ●vt einfädeln; auffädeln <beads>. ~bare a fadenscheinig

threat n Drohung f; (danger) Bedrohung f

threaten vt drohen (+ dat); (with weapon) bedrohen; ~ s.o. with sth jdm etw androhen ●vi drohen. ~ing a, -ly adv drohend; (ominous) bedrohlich

three a drei. ~fold a & adv dreifach

thresh vt dreschen

threshold n Schwelle f

threw see throw

thrift n Sparsamkeit f. ~y a sparsam

thrill n Erregung f; 🔡 Nervenkitzel m ●vt (excite) erregen; be ~ed with sich sehr freuen über (+ acc). ~er n Thriller m. ~ing a erregend

thrive vi (pt thrived or throve, pp thrived or thriven) gedeihen (on bei); <business:> florieren

throat n Hals m; cut s.o.'s ~ jdm die Kehle durchschneiden

throb n Pochen nt ●vi (pt/pp throbbed) pochen; (vibrate) vibrieren

throes npl in the ~ of (fig) mitten in (+ dat)

throne n Thron m

throttle vt erdrosseln

through prep durch (+ acc); (during) während (+ gen); (Amer: up to & including) bis einschließlich ●adv durch; wet ~ durch und durch nass; read sth ~

T

etw durchlesen ● *a* <train>
durchgehend; **be ~** (finished)
fertig sein; (Teleph) durch sein
throughout prep **~ the country** im
ganzen Land; **~ the night** die
Nacht durch ● adv ganz; (time)
die ganze Zeit
throve see **thrive**
throw n Wurf m ● vt (pt **threw**, pp
thrown) werfen; schütten
<liquid>; betätigen <switch>;
abwerfen <rider>; (🅸 disconcert)
aus der Fassung bringen; 🅸
geben <party>; **~ sth to s.o.** jdm
etw zuwerfen. **~ away** vt
wegwerfen. **~ out** vt
hinauswerfen; (~ away)
wegwerfen; verwerfen <plan>. **~
up** vt hochwerfen ● vi sich
übergeben
throw-away a Wegwerf-
thrush n Drossel f
thrust n Stoß m; (Phys) Schub m
● vt (pt/pp **thrust**) stoßen; (insert)
stecken
thud n dumpfer Schlag m
thug n Schläger m
thumb n Daumen m ● vt **~ a lift**
🅸 per Anhalter fahren. **~tack** n
(Amer) Reißzwecke f
thump n Schlag m; (noise)
dumpfer Schlag m ● vt schlagen
● vi hämmern; <heart:> pochen
thunder n Donner m ● vi
donnern. **~clap** n Donnerschlag
m. **~storm** n Gewitter nt. **~y** a
gewittrig
Thursday n Donnerstag m
thus adv so
thwart vt vereiteln; **~ s.o.** jdm
einen Strich durch die Rechnung
machen
tick¹ n **on~** 🅸 auf Pump
tick² n (sound) Ticken nt; (mark)
Häkchen nt; (🅸 instant) Sekunde
f ● vi ticken ● vt abhaken. **~ off**
vt abhaken; 🅸 rüffeln
ticket n Karte f; (for bus, train)
Fahrschein m; (Aviat) Flugschein

m; (for lottery) Los nt; (for article
deposited) Schein m; (label)
Schild nt; (for library) Lesekarte
f; (fine) Strafzettel m. **~ collector**
n Fahrkartenkontrolleur m. **~
office** n Fahrkartenschalter m;
(for entry) Kasse f
tick|le n Kitzeln nt ● vt/i kitzeln.
~lish a kitzlig
tidal a **~ wave** Flutwelle f
tide n Gezeiten pl; (of events)
Strom m; **the ~ is in/out** es ist
Flut/Ebbe ● vt **~ s.o. over** jdm
über die Runden helfen
tidiness n Ordentlichkeit f
tidy a (-ier, -iest), **-ily** adv
ordentlich ● vt **~ [up]** aufräumen
tie n Krawatte f; Schlips m; (cord)
Schnur f; (fig: bond) Band nt;
(restriction) Bindung f; (Sport)
Unentschieden nt; (in
competition) Punktgleichheit f
● v (pres p **tying**) ● vt binden;
machen <knot> ● vi (Sport)
unentschieden spielen; (have
equal scores, votes) punktgleich
sein. **~ up** vt festbinden;
verschnüren <parcel>; fesseln
<person>; **be ~d up** (busy)
beschäftigt sein
tier n Stufe f; (of cake) Etage f; (in
stadium) Rang m
tiger n Tiger m
tight a (-er, -est), **-ly** adv fest;
(taut) straff; <clothes> eng;
<control> streng; (🅸 drunk) blau
● adv fest
tighten vt fester ziehen; straffen
<rope>; anziehen <screw>;
verschärfen <control> ● vi sich
spannen
tightrope n Hochseil nt
tights npl Strumpfhose f
tile n Fliese f; (on wall) Kachel f;
(on roof) [Dach]ziegel m ● vt mit
Fliesen auslegen; kacheln
<wall>; decken <roof>
till¹ prep & conj = **until**
till² n Kasse f

tilt n Neigung f ● vt kippen; [zur Seite] neigen <head> ● vi sich neigen

timber n [Nutz]holz nt

time n Zeit f; (occasion) Mal nt; (rhythm) Takt m; ~s (Math) mal; **at** ~s manchmal; ~ **and again** immer wieder; **two at a** ~ zwei auf einmal; **on** ~ pünktlich; **in** ~ rechtzeitig. (eventually) mit der Zeit; **in no** ~ im Handumdrehen; **in a year's** ~ in einem Jahr; **behind** ~ verspätet; **behind the** ~s rückständig; **for the** ~ **being** vorläufig; **what is the** ~? wie spät ist es? **wie viel Uhr ist es? did you have a nice** ~? hat es dir gut gefallen? ● vt stoppen <race>; **be well** ~**d** gut abgepaßt sein

time: ~ **bomb** n Zeitbombe f. ~**less** a zeitlos. ~**ly** a rechtzeitig. ~**-switch** n Zeitschalter m. ~-**table** n Fahrplan m; (Sch) Stundenplan m

timid a, **-ly** adv scheu; (hesitant) zaghaft

timing n (Sport, Techn) Timing nt

tin n Zinn nt; (container) Dose f ● vt (pt/pp tinned) in Dosen konservieren. ~ **foil** n Stanniol nt; (Culin) Alufolie f

tinge n Hauch m

tingle vi kribbeln

tinker vi herumbasteln (**with** an + dat)

tinkle n Klingeln nt ● vi klingeln

tinned a Dosen-

tin opener n Dosenöffner m

tinsel n Lametta nt

tint n Farbton m ● vt tönen

tiny a (**-ier, -iest**) winzig

tip¹ n Spitze f

tip² n (money) Trinkgeld nt; (advice) Rat m, Ⓘ Tipp m; (for rubbish) Müllhalde f ● v (pt/pp tipped) ● vt (tilt) kippen; (reward) Trinkgeld geben (**s.o.** jdm) ● vi kippen. ~ **out** vt auskippen. ~ **over** vt/i umkippen

tipped a Filter-

tipsy a Ⓘ beschwipst

tiptoe n **on** ~ auf Zehenspitzen

tiptop a Ⓘ erstklassig

tire vt/i ermüden. ~**d** a müde; **be** ~**d of sth** etw satt haben; ~**d out** [völlig] erschöpft. ~**less** a, **-ly** adv unermüdlich. ~**some** a lästig

tiring a ermüdend

tissue n Gewebe nt; (handkerchief) Papiertaschentuch nt

tit n (bird) Meise f

titbit n Leckerbissen m

title n Titel m

to

● preposition

····▸ (destinations: most cases) zu (+ dat). **go to work/the station** zur Arbeit/zum Bahnhof gehen. **from house to house** von Haus zu Haus. **go/come to s.o.** zu jdm gehen/kommen

····▸ (with name of place or points of compass) nach. **to Paris/ Germany** nach Paris/ Deutschland. **to Switzerland** in die Schweiz. **from East to West** von Osten nach Westen. **I've never been to Berlin** ich war noch nie in Berlin

····▸ (to cinema, theatre, bed) in (+ acc). **to bed with you!** ins Bett mit dir!

····▸ (to wedding, party, university, the toilet) auf (+ acc).

····▸ (up to) bis zu (+ dat). **to the end** bis zum Schluss. **to this day** bis heute. **5 to 6 pounds** 5 bis 6 Pfund

····▸ <give, say, write> + dat. **give/ say sth to s.o.** jdm etw geben/ sagen. **she wrote to him/the firm** sie hat ihm/an die Firma geschrieben

····▸ <address, send, fasten> an (+ acc). **she sent it to her brother** sie schickte es an ihren Bruder

T

····➤ (*in telling the time*) vor. **five to eight** fünf vor acht. **a quarter to ten** Viertel vor zehn

● *before infinitive*

····➤ (*after modal verb*) (*not translated*). **I want to go** ich will gehen. **he is learning to swim** er lernt schwimmen. **you have to** du musst [es tun]

····➤ (*after adjective*) zu. **it is easy to forget** es ist leicht zu vergessen

····➤ (*expressing purpose, result*) um … zu. **he did it to annoy me** er tat es, um mich zu ärgern. **she was too tired to go** sie war zu müde um zu gehen

● *adverb*

····➤ **be to** <*door, window*> angelehnt sein. **pull a door to** eine Tür anlehnen

····➤ **to and fro** hin und her

toad *n* Kröte *f*

toast *n* Toast *m* ● *vt* toasten <*bread*>; (*drink a ~ to*) trinken auf (+ *acc*). ~**er** *n* Toaster *m*

tobacco *n* Tabak *m*. ~**nist's [shop]** *n* Tabakladen *m*

toboggan *n* Schlitten *m* ● *vi* Schlitten fahren

today *n* & *adv* heute; ~ **week** heute in einer Woche

toddler *n* Kleinkind *nt*

toe *n* Zeh *m*; (*of footwear*) Spitze *f* ● *vt* ~ **the line** spuren. ~**nail** *n* Zehennagel *m*

toffee *n* Karamell *m* & *nt*

together *adv* zusammen; (*at the same time*) gleichzeitig

toilet *n* Toilette *f*. ~ **bag** *n* Kulturbeutel *m*. ~ **paper** *n* Toilettenpapier *n*

toiletries *npl* Toilettenartikel *pl*

token *n* Zeichen *nt*; (*counter*) Marke *f*; (*voucher*) Gutschein *m* ● *attrib* symbolisch

told *see* **tell** ● *a* **all** ~ insgesamt

tolerable *a*, -**bly** *adv* erträglich; (*not bad*) leidlich

toleran|ce *n* Toleranz *f*. ~**t** *a*, -**ly** *adv* tolerant

tolerate *vt* dulden, tolerieren; (*bear*) ertragen

toll *n* Gebühr *f*; (*for road*) Maut *f* (*Aust*); **death** ~ Zahl *f* der Todesopfer

tomato *n* (*pl* -**es**) Tomate *f*

tomb *n* Grabmal *nt*

tombstone *n* Grabstein *m*

tom-cat *n* Kater *m*

tomorrow *n* & *adv* morgen; ~ **morning** morgen früh; **the day after** ~ übermorgen; **see you** ~! bis morgen!

ton *n* Tonne *f*; ~**s of** 🛈 jede Menge

tone *n* Ton *m*; (*colour*) Farbton *m* ● *vt* ~ **down** dämpfen; (*fig*) mäßigen. ~ **up** *vt* kräftigen; straffen <*muscles*>

tongs *npl* Zange *f*

tongue *n* Zunge *f*; ~ **in cheek** 🛈 nicht ernst

tonic *n* Tonikum *nt*; (*for hair*) Haarwasser *nt*; (*fig*) Wohltat *f*; ~ **[water]** Tonic *nt*

tonight *n* & *adv* heute Nacht; (*evening*) heute Abend

tonne *n* Tonne *f*

tonsil *n* (*Anat*) Mandel *f*. ~**litis** *n* Mandelentzündung *f*

too *adv* zu; (*also*) auch; ~ **much/ little** zu viel/zu wenig

took *see* **take**

tool *n* Werkzeug *nt*; (*for gardening*) Gerät *nt*

tooth *n* (*pl* **teeth**) Zahn *m*

tooth: ~**ache** *n* Zahnschmerzen *pl*. ~**brush** *n* Zahnbürste *f*. ~**less** *a* zahnlos. ~**paste** *n* Zahnpasta *f*. ~**pick** *n* Zahnstocher *m*

top¹ *n* (*toy*) Kreisel *m*

top² *n* oberer Teil *m*; (*apex*) Spitze *f*; (*summit*) Gipfel *m*; (*Sch*) Erste(r) *m/f*; (*top part or half*) Oberteil *nt*; (*head*) Kopfende *nt*;

(*of road*) oberes Ende *nt*; (*upper surface*) Oberfläche *f*; (*lid*) Deckel *m*; (*of bottle*) Verschluss *m*; (*garment*) Top *nt*; **at the/on ~** oben; **on ~ of** oben auf (+ *dat*/ *acc*); **on ~ of that** (*besides*) obendrein; **from ~ to bottom** von oben bis unten ●*a* oberste(r,s); (*highest*) höchste(r,s); (*best*) beste(r,s) ●*vt* (*pt*/*pp* **topped**) an erster Stelle stehen auf (+ *dat*) <*list*>; (*exceed*) übersteigen; (*remove the ~ of*) die Spitze abschneiden von. **~ up** *vt* nachfüllen, auffüllen

top: ~ hat *n* Zylinder[hut] *m*. **~-heavy** *a* kopflastig
topic *n* Thema *nt*. **~al** *a* aktuell
topple *vt/i* umstürzen
torch *n* Taschenlampe *f*; (*flaming*) Fackel *f*
tore *see* **tear¹**
torment¹ *n* Qual *f*
torment² *vt* quälen
torn *see* **tear¹** ●*a* zerrissen
torpedo *n* (*pl* **-es**) Torpedo *m* ●*vt* torpedieren
torrent *n* reißender Strom *m*. **~ial** *a* <*rain*> wolkenbruchartig
tortoise *n* Schildkröte *f*. **~shell** *n* Schildpatt *nt*
tortuous *a* verschlungen; (*fig*) umständlich
torture *n* Folter *f*; (*fig*) Qual *f* ●*vt* foltern; (*fig*) quälen
toss *vt* werfen; (*into the air*) hochwerfen; (*shake*) schütteln; (*unseat*) abwerfen; mischen <*salad*>; wenden <*pancake*>; **~ a coin** mit einer Münze losen ●*vi* **~ and turn** (*in bed*) sich [schlaflos] im Bett wälzen
tot¹ *n* kleines Kind *nt*; (Ⓘ *of liquor*) Gläschen *nt*
tot² *vt* (*pt*/*pp* **totted**) **~ up** Ⓘ zusammenzählen
total *a* gesamt; (*complete*) völlig, total ●*n* Gesamtzahl *f*; (*sum*) Gesamtsumme *f* ●*vt* (*pt*/*pp* **totalled**); (*amount to*) sich belaufen auf (+ *acc*)
totalitarian *a* totalitär
totally *adv* völlig, total
totter *vi* taumeln
touch *n* Berührung *f*; (*sense*) Tastsinn *m*; (*Mus*) Anschlag *m*; (*contact*) Kontakt *m*; (*trace*) Spur *f*; (*fig*) Anflug *m*; **get/be in ~** sich in Verbindung setzen/in Verbindung stehen (**with** mit) ●*vt* berühren; (*get hold of*) anfassen; (*lightly*) tippen auf/an (+ *acc*); (*brush against*) streifen [gegen]; (*fig: move*) rühren; anrühren <*food, subject*>; **don't ~ that!** fass das nicht an! ●*vi* sich berühren; **~ on** (*fig*) berühren. **~ down** *vi* (*Aviat*) landen. **~ up** *vt* ausbessern
touch|ing *a* rührend. **~y** *a* empfindlich
tough *a* (**-er**, **-est**) zäh; (*severe, harsh*) hart; (*difficult*) schwierig; (*durable*) strapazierfähig
toughen *vt* härten; **~ up** abhärten
tour *n* Reise *f*, Tour *f*; (*of building, town*) Besichtigung *f*; (*Theat, Sport*) Tournee *f*; (*of duty*) Dienstzeit *f* ●*vt* fahren durch ●*vi* herumreisen
touris|m *n* Tourismus *m*, Fremdenverkehr *m*. **~t** *n* Tourist(in) *m(f)* ●*attrib* Touristen-. **~t office** *n* Fremdenverkehrsbüro *nt*
tournament *n* Turnier *nt*
tour operator *n* Reiseveranstalter *m*
tousle *vt* zerzausen
tow *n* **give s.o./a car a ~** jdn/ein Auto abschleppen ●*vt* schleppen; ziehen <*trailer*>
toward[s] *prep* zu (+ *dat*); (*with time*) gegen (+ *acc*); (*with respect to*) gegenüber (+ *dat*)
towel *n* Handtuch *nt*. **~ling** *n* (*Tex*) Frottee *nt*

T

tower n Turm m ● vi ~ **above** überragen. ~ **block** n Hochhaus nt. ~**ing** a hoch aufragend

town n Stadt f. ~ **hall** n Rathaus nt

tow-rope n Abschleppseil nt

toxic a giftig

toy n Spielzeug nt ● vi ~ **with** spielen mit; stochern in (+ dat) <food>. ~**shop** n Spielwarengeschäft nt

trace n Spur f ● vt folgen (+ dat); (find) finden; (draw) zeichnen; (with tracing-paper) durchpausen

track n Spur f; (path) [unbefestigter] Weg m; (Sport) Bahn f; (Rail) Gleis nt; **keep** ~ **of** im Auge behalten ● vt verfolgen. ~ **down** vt aufspüren; (find) finden

tracksuit n Trainingsanzug m

tractor n Traktor m

trade n Handel m; (line of business) Gewerbe nt; (business) Geschäft nt; (craft) Handwerk nt; **by** ~ von Beruf ● vt tauschen; ~ **in** (give in part exchange) in Zahlung geben ● vi handeln (in mit)

trade mark n Warenzeichen nt

trader n Händler m

trade: ~ **union** n Gewerkschaft f. ~ **unionist** n Gewerkschaftler(in) m(f)

trading n Handel m

tradition n Tradition f. ~**al** a, -**ly** adv traditionell

traffic n Verkehr m; (trading) Handel m

traffic: ~ **circle** n (Amer) Kreisverkehr m. ~ **jam** n [Verkehrs]stau m. ~ **lights** npl [Verkehrs]ampel f. ~ **warden** n ≈ Hilfspolizist m; (woman) Politesse f

tragedy n Tragödie f

tragic a, -**ally** adv tragisch

trail n Spur f; (path) Weg m, Pfad m ● vi schleifen; <plant:> sich ranken ● vt verfolgen, folgen (+ dat); (drag) schleifen

trailer n (Auto) Anhänger m; (Amer: caravan) Wohnwagen m; (film) Vorschau f

train n Zug m; (of dress) Schleppe f ● vt ausbilden; (Sport) trainieren; (aim) richten auf (+ acc); erziehen <child>; abrichten/(to do tricks) dressieren <animal>; ziehen <plant> ● vi eine Ausbildung machen; (Sport) trainieren. ~**ed** a ausgebildet

trainee n Auszubildende(r) m/f; (Techn) Praktikant(in) m(f)

train|er n (Sport) Trainer m; (in circus) Dompteur m; ~**ers** pl Trainingsschuhe pl. ~**ing** n Ausbildung f; (Sport) Training nt; (of animals) Dressur f

trait n Eigenschaft f

traitor n Verräter m

tram n Straßenbahn f

tramp n Landstreicher m ● vi stapfen; (walk) marschieren

trample vt/i trampeln

trance n Trance f

tranquil a ruhig. ~**lity** n Ruhe f

tranquillizer n Beruhigungsmittel nt

transaction n Transaktion f

transcend vt übersteigen

transfer[1] n (see transfer[2]) Übertragung f; Verlegung f; Versetzung f; Überweisung f; (Sport) Transfer m; (design) Abziehbild nt

transfer[2] v (pt/pp transferred) ● vt übertragen; verlegen <firm, prisoners>; versetzen <employee>; überweisen <money>; (Sport) transferieren ● vi [über]wechseln; (when travelling) umsteigen

transform vt verwandeln. ~**ation** n Verwandlung f. ~**er** n Transformator m

transfusion n Transfusion f

transistor n Transistor m

transit n Transit m; (of goods) Transport m; **in ~** <goods> auf dem Transport

transition n Übergang m. **~al** a Übergangs-

translat|e vt übersetzen. **~ion** n Übersetzung f. **~or** n Übersetzer(in) m(f)

transmission n Übertragung f

transmit vt (pt/pp transmitted) übertragen. **~ter** n Sender m

transparen|cy n (Phot) Dia nt. **~t** a durchsichtig

transplant[1] n Verpflanzung f, Transplantation f

transplant[2] vt umpflanzen; (Med) verpflanzen

transport[1] n Transport m

transport[2] vt transportieren. **~ation** n Transport m

transpose vt umstellen

trap n Falle f; (🄴 mouth) Klappe f; **pony and ~** Einspänner m ● vt (pt/pp trapped) [mit einer Falle] fangen; (jam) einklemmen; **be ~ped** festsitzen; (shut in) eingeschlossen sein. **~door** n Falltür f

trash n Schund m; (rubbish) Abfall m; (nonsense) Quatsch m. **~can** n (Amer) Mülleimer m. **~y** a Schund-

trauma n Trauma nt. **~tic** a traumatisch

travel n Reisen nt ● v (pt/pp travelled) ● vi reisen; (go in vehicle) fahren; <light, sound:> sich fortpflanzen; (Techn) sich bewegen ● vt bereisen; fahren <distance>. **~ agency** n Reisebüro nt. **~ agent** n Reisebürokaufmann m

traveller n Reisende(r) m/f; (Comm) Vertreter m; **~s** pl (gypsies) Zigeuner pl. **~'s cheque** n Reisescheck m

trawler n Fischdampfer m

tray n Tablett nt; (for baking) [Back]blech nt; (for documents) Ablagekorb m

treacher|ous a treulos; (dangerous, deceptive) tückisch. **~y** n Verrat m

tread n Schritt m; (step) Stufe f; (of tyre) Profil nt ● v (pt trod, pp trodden) ● vi (walk) gehen; **~ on/in** treten auf/ in (+ acc) ● vt treten

treason n Verrat m

treasure n Schatz m ● vt in Ehren halten. **~r** n Kassenwart m

treasury n Schatzkammer f; **the T~** das Finanzministerium

treat n [besonderes] Vergnügen nt ● vt behandeln; **~ s.o. to sth** jdm etw spendieren

treatment n Behandlung f

treaty n Vertrag m

treble a dreifach; **~ the amount** dreimal so viel ● n (Mus) Diskant m; (voice) Sopran m ● vt verdreifachen ● vi sich verdreifachen

tree n Baum m

trek n Marsch m ● vi (pt/pp trekked) latschen

trellis n Gitter nt

tremble vi zittern

tremendous a, **-ly** adv gewaltig; (🄴 excellent) großartig

tremor n Zittern nt; **[earth] ~** Beben nt

trench n Graben m; (Mil) Schützengraben m

trend n Tendenz f; (fashion) Trend m. **~y** a (-ier, -iest) 🄴 modisch

trepidation n Beklommenheit f

trespass vi **~ on** unerlaubt betreten

trial n (Jur) [Gerichts]verfahren nt, Prozess m; (test) Probe f; (ordeal) Prüfung f; **be on ~** auf Probe sein; (Jur) angeklagt sein

T

(for wegen); **by** ~ **and error** durch
Probieren

triang|le n Dreieck nt; (Mus)
Triangel m. ~**ular** a dreieckig

tribe n Stamm m

tribunal n Schiedsgericht nt

tributary n Nebenfluss m

tribute n Tribut m; **pay** ~ Tribut
zollen (**to** dat)

trick n Trick m; (joke) Streich m;
(Cards) Stich m; (feat of skill)
Kunststück nt ● vt täuschen, 🛈
hereinlegen

trickle vi rinnen

trick|ster n Schwindler m. ~**y** a
(-ier, -iest) a schwierig

tricycle n Dreirad nt

tried see try

trifl|e n Kleinigkeit f; (Culin)
Trifle nt. ~**ing** a unbedeutend

trigger n Abzug m; (fig) Auslöser
m ● vt ~ [**off**] auslösen

trim a (trimmer, trimmest) gepflegt
● n (cut) Nachschneiden nt;
(decoration) Verzierung f;
(condition) Zustand m ● vt
schneiden; (decorate) besetzen.
~**ming** n Besatz m; ~**mings** pl
(accessories) Zubehör nt;
(decorations) Verzierungen pl

trio n Trio nt

trip n Reise f; (excursion) Ausflug
m ● v (pt/pp tripped) ● vt ~ s.o.
up jdm ein Bein stellen ● vi
stolpern (on/over über + acc)

tripe n Kaldaunen pl; (nonsense)
Quatsch m

triple a dreifach ● vt
verdreifachen ● vi sich
verdreifachen

triplets npl Drillinge pl

triplicate n **in** ~ in dreifacher
Ausfertigung

tripod n Stativ nt

tripper n Ausflügler m

trite a banal

triumph n Triumph m ● vi
triumphieren (over über + acc).
~**ant** a, **-ly** adv triumphierend

trivial a belanglos. ~**ity** n
Belanglosigkeit f

trod, trodden see tread

trolley n (for food) Servierwagen
m; (for shopping) Einkaufswagen
m; (for luggage) Kofferkuli m;
(Amer: tram) Straßenbahn f

trombone n Posaune f

troop n Schar f; ~**s** pl Truppen pl

trophy n Trophäe f; (in
competition) ≈ Pokal m

tropics npl Tropen pl. ~**al** a
tropisch; <fruit> Süd-

trot n Trab m ● vi (pt/pp trotted)
traben

trouble n Ärger m; (difficulties)
Schwierigkeiten pl;
(inconvenience) Mühe f; (conflict)
Unruhe f; (Med) Beschwerden pl;
(Techn) Probleme pl; **get into** ~
Ärger bekommen; **take** ~ sich
(dat) Mühe geben ● vt (disturb)
stören; (worry) beunruhigen ● vi
sich bemühen. ~**-maker** n
Unruhestifter m. ~**some** a
schwierig; <flies, cough> lästig

trough n Trog m

troupe n Truppe f

trousers npl Hose f

trousseau n Aussteuer f

trout n inv Forelle f

trowel n Kelle f

truant n **play** ~ die Schule
schwänzen

truce n Waffenstillstand m

truck n Last[kraft]wagen m; (Rail)
Güterwagen m

trudge vi latschen

true a (-r, -st) wahr; (loyal) treu;
(genuine) echt; **come** ~ in
Erfüllung gehen; **is that** ~?
stimmt das?

truly adv wirklich; (faithfully)
treu; **Yours** ~ mit freundlichen
Grüßen

trump n (Cards) Trumpf m ● vt
übertrumpfen

trumpet n Trompete f. ~**er** n
Trompeter m

truncheon n Schlagstock m

trunk n [Baum]stamm m; (body) Rumpf m; (of elephant) Rüssel m; (for travelling) [Übersee]koffer m; (Amer: of car) Kofferraum m; ~s pl Badehose f

trust n Vertrauen nt; (group of companies) Trust m; (organization) Treuhandgesellschaft f; (charitable) Stiftung f ● vt trauen (+ dat), vertrauen (+ dat); (hope) hoffen ● vi vertrauen (in/to auf + acc)

trustee n Treuhänder m

trust|ful a, -ly adv, ~ing a vertrauensvoll. ~worthy a vertrauenswürdig

truth n (pl -s) Wahrheit f. ~ful a, -ly adv ehrlich

try n Versuch m ● v (pt/pp tried) ● vt versuchen; (sample, taste) probieren; (be a strain on) anstrengen; (Jur) vor Gericht stellen; verhandeln <case> ● vi versuchen; (make an effort) sich bemühen. ~ on vt anprobieren; aufprobieren <hat>. ~ out vt ausprobieren

trying a schwierig

T-shirt n T-Shirt nt

tub n Kübel m; (carton) Becher m; (bath) Wanne f

tuba n (Mus) Tuba f

tubby a (-ier, -iest) rundlich

tube n Röhre f; (pipe) Rohr nt; (flexible) Schlauch m; (of toothpaste) Tube f; (Rail 🔢) U-Bahn f

tuberculosis n Tuberkulose f

tubular a röhrenförmig

tuck n Saum m; (decorative) Biese f ● vt (put) stecken. ~ in vt hineinstecken; ~ s.o. in or up jdn zudecken ● vi (🔢 eat) zulangen

Tuesday n Dienstag m

tuft n Büschel nt

tug n Ruck m; (Naut) Schleppdampfer m ● v (pt/pp tugged) ● vt ziehen ● vi zerren (at an + dat)

tuition n Unterricht m .

tulip n Tulpe f

tumble n Sturz m ● vi fallen. ~down a verfallen. ~-drier n Wäschetrockner m

tumbler n Glas nt

tummy n 🔢 Bauch m

tumour n Tumor m

tumult n Tumult m

tuna n Thunfisch m

tune n Melodie f; out of ~ <instrument> verstimmt ● vt stimmen; (Techn) einstellen. ~ in vt einstellen; ● vi ~ in to a station einen Sender einstellen. ~ up vi (Mus) stimmen

tuneful a melodisch

Tunisia n Tunesien nt

tunnel n Tunnel m ● vi (pt/pp tunnelled) einen Tunnel graben

turban n Turban m

turbine n Turbine f

turbulen|ce n Turbulenz f. ~t a stürmisch

turf n Rasen m; (segment) Rasenstück m

Turk n Türke m/Türkin f

turkey n Truthahn m

Turk|ey n die Türkei. ~ish a türkisch; the ~ish die Türken

turmoil n Aufruhr m; (confusion) Durcheinander nt

turn n (rotation) Drehung f; (bend) Kurve f; (change of direction) Wende f; (Theat) Nummer f; (🔢 attack) Anfall m; do s.o. a good ~ jdm einen guten Dienst erweisen; take ~s sich abwechseln; in ~ der Reihe nach; out of ~ außer der Reihe; it's your ~ du bist an der Reihe ● vt drehen; (~ over) wenden; (reverse) umdrehen; (Techn) drechseln <wood>; ~ the page umblättern; ~ the corner um die Ecke biegen ● vi sich drehen; (~ round) sich umdrehen; <car:>

T

wenden; <*leaves:*> sich färben: <*weather:*> umschlagen; (*become*) werden; ~ **right/left** nach rechts/ links abbiegen; ~ **to s.o.** sich an jdn wenden. ~ **away** *vt* abweisen ● *vi* sich abwenden. ~ **down** *vt* herunterschlagen <*collar*>; herunterdrehen <*heat, gas*>; leiser stellen <*sound*>; (*reject*) ablehnen; abweisen <*person*>. ~ **in** *vt* einschlagen <*edges*> ● *vi* <*car:*> einbiegen; (🄸 *go to bed*) ins Bett gehen. ~ **off** *vt* zudrehen <*tap*>; ausschalten <*light, radio*>; abstellen <*water, gas, engine, machine*> ● *vi* abbiegen. ~ **on** *vt* aufdrehen <*tap*>; einschalten <*light, radio*>; anstellen <*water, gas, engine, machine*> ● *vi* abbiegen. ~ **out** *vt* (*expel*) vertreiben, 🄸 hinauswerfen; ausschalten <*light*>; abdrehen <*gas*>; (*produce*) produzieren; (*empty*) ausleeren; [gründlich] aufräumen <*room, cupboard*> ● *vi* (*go out*) hinausgehen; (*transpire*) sich herausstellen. ~ **over** *vt* umdrehen. ~ **up** *vt* hochschlagen <*collar*>; aufdrehen <*heat, gas*>; lauter stellen <*sound, radio*> ● *vi* auftauchen

turning *n* Abzweigung *f*. ~**-point** *n* Wendepunkt *m*

turnip *n* weiße Rübe *f*

turn: ~**-out** *n* (*of people*) Beteiligung *f*. ~**over** *n* (*Comm*) Umsatz *m*; (*of staff*) Personalwechsel *m*. ~**pike** *n* (*Amer*) gebührenpflichtige Autobahn *f*. ~**table** *n* Drehscheibe *f*; (*on record player*) Plattenteller *m*. ~**-up** *n* [Hosen]aufschlag *m*

turquoise *a* türkis[farben] ● *n* (*gem*) Türkis *m*

turret *n* Türmchen *nt*

turtle *n* Seeschildkröte *f*

tusk *n* Stoßzahn *m*

tutor *n* [Privat]lehrer *m*

tuxedo *n* (*Amer*) Smoking *m*

TV *abbr of* **television**

tweed *n* Tweed *m*

tweezers *npl* Pinzette *f*

twelfth *a* zwölfter(r,s)

twelve *a* zwölf

twentieth *a* zwanzigste(r,s)

twenty *a* zwanzig

twice *adv* zweimal

twig *n* Zweig *m*

twilight *n* Dämmerlicht *nt*

twin *n* Zwilling *m* ● *attrib* Zwillings-

twine *n* Bindfaden *m*

twinge *n* Stechen *nt*; ~ **of conscience** Gewissensbisse *pl*

twinkle *n* Funkeln *nt* ● *vi* funkeln

twin town *n* Partnerstadt *f*

twirl *vt/i* herumwirbeln

twist *n* Drehung *f*; (*curve*) Kurve *f*; (*unexpected occurrence*) überraschende Wendung *f* ● *vt* drehen; (*distort*) verdrehen; (🄸 *swindle*) beschummeln; ~ **one's ankle** sich (*dat*) den Knöchel verrenken ● *vi* sich drehen; <*road:*> sich winden. ~**er** *n* 🄸 Schwindler *m*

twit *n* 🄸 Trottel *m*

twitch *n* Zucken *nt* ● *vi* zucken

twitter *n* Zwitschern *nt* ● *vi* zwitschern

two *a* zwei

two: ~**-faced** *a* falsch. ~**-piece** *a* zweiteilig. ~**-way** *a* ~**-way traffic** Gegenverkehr *m*

tycoon *n* Magnat *m*

tying *see* **tie**

type *n* Art *f*, Sorte *f*; (*person*) Typ *m*; (*printing*) Type *f* ● *vt* mit der Maschine schreiben, 🄸 tippen ● *vi* Maschine schreiben, 🄸 tippen. ~**writer** *n* Schreibmaschine *f*. ~**written** *a* maschinegeschrieben

typical *a*, **-ly** *adv* typisch (**of** für)

typify *vt* (*pt/pp* **-ied**) typisch sein für

typing *n* Maschineschreiben *nt*
typist *n* Schreibkraft *f*
tyrannical *a* tyrannisch
tyranny *n* Tyrannei *f*
tyrant *n* Tyrann *m*
tyre *n* Reifen *m*

ugl|iness *n* Hässlichkeit *f*. **~y** *a*
(**-ier, -iest**) hässlich; (*nasty*) übel
UK *abbr see* **United Kingdom**
ulcer *n* Geschwür *nt*
ultimate *a* letzte(r,s); (*final*)
endgültig; (*fundamental*)
grundlegend, eigentlich. **~ly** *adv*
schließlich
ultimatum *n* Ultimatum *nt*
ultraviolet *a* ultraviolett
umbrella *n* [Regen]schirm *m*
umpire *n* Schiedsrichter *m* ● *vt/i*
Schiedsrichter sein (bei)
umpteen *a* 🔟 zig. **~th** *a* 🔟
zigste(r,s)
unable *a* **be ~ to do sth** etw nicht
tun können
unabridged *a* ungekürzt
unaccompanied *a* ohne
Begleitung; <*luggage*>
unbegleitet
unaccountable *a* unerklärlich
unaccustomed *a* ungewohnt; **be
~ to sth** etw (*acc*) nicht gewohnt
sein
unaided *a* ohne fremde Hilfe
unanimous *a*, **-ly** *adv* einmütig;
<*vote, decision*> einstimmig
unarmed *a* unbewaffnet
unassuming *a* bescheiden
unattended *a* unbeaufsichtigt
unauthorized *a* unbefugt
unavoidable *a* unvermeidlich

unaware *a* **be ~ of sth** sich (*dat*)
etw (*gen*) nicht bewusst sein. **~s**
adv **catch s.o. ~s** jdn überraschen
unbearable *a*, **-bly** *adv*
unerträglich
unbeat|able *a* unschlagbar. **~en**
a ungeschlagen; <*record*>
ungebrochen
unbelievable *a* unglaublich
unbiased *a* unvoreingenommen
unblock *vt* frei machen
unbolt *vt* aufriegeln
unbreakable *a* unzerbrechlich
unbutton *vt* aufknöpfen
uncalled-for *a* unangebracht
uncanny *a* unheimlich
unceasing *a* unaufhörlich
uncertain *a* (*doubtful*) ungewiss;
<*origins*> unbestimmt; **be ~** nicht
sicher sein. **~ty** *n* Ungewissheit *f*
unchanged *a* unverändert
uncharitable *a* lieblos
uncle *n* Onkel *m*
uncomfortable *a*, **-bly** *adv*
unbequem; **feel ~** (*fig*) sich nicht
wohl fühlen
uncommon *a* ungewöhnlich
uncompromising *a*
kompromisslos
unconditional *a*, **~ly** *adv*
bedingungslos
unconscious *a* bewusstlos;
(*unintended*) unbewusst; **be ~ of
sth** sich (*dat*) etw (*gen*) nicht
bewusst sein. **~ly** *adv* unbewusst
unconventional *a*
unkonventionell
uncooperative *a* nicht hilfsbereit
uncork *vt* entkorken
uncouth *a* ungehobelt
uncover *vt* aufdecken
undecided *a* unentschlossen; (*not
settled*) nicht entschieden
undeniable *a*, **-bly** *adv*
unbestreitbar
under *prep* unter (+ *dat/acc*); **~ it**
darunter; **~ there** da drunter; **~
repair** in Reparatur; **~**

construction im Bau; ~ age minderjährig ● *adv* darunter

undercarriage *n* (*Aviat*) Fahrwerk *nt*, Fahrgestell *nt*

underclothes *npl* Unterwäsche *f*

undercover *a* geheim

undercurrent *n* Unterströmung *f*; (*fig*) Unterton *m*

underdog *n* Unterlegene(r) *m*

underdone *a* nicht gar; (*rare*) nicht durchgebraten

underestimate *vt* unterschätzen

underfed *a* unterernährt

underfoot *adv* am Boden

undergo *vt* (*pt* -went, *pp* -gone) durchmachen; sich unterziehen (+ *dat*) <*operation, treatment*>

undergraduate *n* Student(in) *m(f)*

underground¹ *adv* unter der Erde; <*mining*> unter Tage

underground² *a* unterirdisch; (*secret*) Untergrund- ● *n* (*railway*) U-Bahn *f*. ~ **car park** *n* Tiefgarage *f*

undergrowth *n* Unterholz *nt*

underhand *a* hinterhältig

underlie *vt* (*pt* -lay, *pp* -lain, *pres p* -lying) zugrunde liegen (+ *dat*)

underline *vt* unterstreichen

underlying *a* eigentlich

undermine *vt* (*fig*) unterminieren, untergraben

underneath *prep* unter (+ *dat*/ *acc*) ● *adv* darunter

underpants *npl* Unterhose *f*

underpass *n* Unterführung *f*

underprivileged *a* unterprivilegiert

underrate *vt* unterschätzen

undershirt *n* (*Amer*) Unterhemd *nt*

understand *vt/i* (*pt/pp* -stood) verstehen; **I ~ that ...** (*have heard*) ich habe gehört, dass ... ~**able** *a* verständlich. ~**ably** *adv* verständlicherweise

understanding *a* verständnisvoll ● *n* Verständnis *nt*; (*agreement*)

Vereinbarung *f*; **reach an ~** sich verständigen

understatement *n* Untertreibung *f*

undertake *vt* (*pt* -took, *pp* -taken) unternehmen; ~ **to do sth** sich verpflichten, etw zu tun

undertaker *n* Leichenbestatter *m*; [firm of] ~**s** Bestattungsinstitut *n*

undertaking *n* Unternehmen *nt*; (*promise*) Versprechen *nt*

undertone *n* (*fig*) Unterton *m*; **in an ~** mit gedämpfter Stimme

undervalue *vt* unterbewerten

underwater¹ *a* Unterwasser-

underwater² *adv* unter Wasser

underwear *n* Unterwäsche *f*

underweight *a* untergewichtig; **be ~** Untergewicht haben

underworld *n* Unterwelt *f*

undesirable *a* unerwünscht

undignified *a* würdelos

undo *vt* (*pt* -did, *pp* -done) aufmachen; (*fig*) ungeschehen machen

undone *a* offen; (*not accomplished*) unerledigt

undoubted *a* unzweifelhaft. ~**ly** *adv* zweifellos

undress *vt* ausziehen; **get ~ed** sich ausziehen ● *vi* sich ausziehen

undue *a* übermäßig

unduly *adv* übermäßig

unearth *vt* ausgraben; (*fig*) zutage bringen. ~**ly** *a* unheimlich; **at an ~ly hour** 🄸 in aller Herrgottsfrühe

uneasy *a* unbehaglich

uneconomic *a*, **-ally** *adv* unwirtschaftlich

unemployed *a* arbeitslos ● *npl* **the ~** die Arbeitslosen

unemployment *n* Arbeitslosigkeit *f*

unending *a* endlos

unequal *a* unterschiedlich; <*struggle*> ungleich. ~**ly** *adv* ungleichmäßig

unequivocal *a*, **-ly** *adv* eindeutig
unethical *a* unmoralisch; **be ~** gegen das Berufsethos verstoßen
uneven *a* uneben; (*unequal*) ungleich; (*not regular*) ungleichmäßig; <*number*> ungerade
unexpected *a*, **-ly** *adv* unerwartet
unfair *a*, **-ly** *adv* ungerecht, unfair. **~ness** *n* Ungerechtigkeit *f*
unfaithful *a* untreu
unfamiliar *a* ungewohnt; (*unknown*) unbekannt
unfasten *vt* aufmachen; (*detach*) losmachen
unfavourable *a* ungünstig
unfeeling *a* gefühllos
unfit *a* ungeeignet; (*incompetent*) unfähig; (*Sport*) nicht fit; **~ for work** arbeitsunfähig
unfold *vt* auseinander falten, entfalten; (*spread out*) ausbreiten ● *vi* sich entfalten
unforeseen *a* unvorhergesehen
unforgettable *a* unvergesslich
unforgivable *a* unverzeihlich
unfortunate *a* unglücklich; (*unfavourable*) ungünstig; (*regrettable*) bedauerlich; **be ~** <*person:*> Pech haben. **~ly** *adv* leider
unfounded *a* unbegründet
unfurl *vt* entrollen
unfurnished *a* unmöbliert
ungainly *a* unbeholfen
ungrateful *a*, **-ly** *adv* undankbar
unhappiness *n* Kummer *m*
unhappy *a* unglücklich; (*not content*) unzufrieden
unharmed *a* unverletzt
unhealthy *a* ungesund
unhurt *a* unverletzt
unification *n* Einigung *f*
uniform *a*, **-ly** *adv* einheitlich ● *n* Uniform *f*
unify *vt* (*pt/pp* **-ied**) einigen
unilateral *a*, **-ly** *adv* einseitig
unimaginable *a* unvorstellbar

unimportant *a* unwichtig
uninhabited *a* unbewohnt
unintentional *a*, **-ly** *adv* unabsichtlich
union *n* Vereinigung *f*; (*Pol*) Union *f*; (*trade ~*) Gewerkschaft *f*
unique *a* einzigartig. **~ly** *adv* einmalig
unison *n* **in ~** einstimmig
unit *n* Einheit *f*; (*Math*) Einer *m*; (*of furniture*) Teil *nt*, Element *nt*
unite *vt* vereinigen ● *vi* sich vereinigen
united *a* einig. **U~ Kingdom** *n* Vereinigtes Königreich *nt*. **U~ Nations** *n* Vereinte Nationen *pl*. **U~ States [of America]** *n* Vereinigte Staaten *pl* [von Amerika]
unity *n* Einheit *f*; (*harmony*) Einigkeit *f*
universal *a*, **-ly** *adv* allgemein
universe *n* [Welt]all *nt*, Universum *nt*
university *n* Universität *f* ● *attrib* Universitäts-
unjust *a*, **-ly** *adv* ungerecht
unkind *a*, **-ly** *adv* unfreundlich; (*harsh*) hässlich
unknown *a* unbekannt
unlawful *a*, **-ly** *adv* gesetzwidrig
unleaded *a* bleifrei
unleash *vt* (*fig*) entfesseln
unless *conj* wenn … nicht; **~ I am mistaken** wenn ich mich nicht irre
unlike *prep* im Gegensatz zu (+ *dat*)
unlikely *a* unwahrscheinlich
unlimited *a* unbegrenzt
unload *vt* entladen; ausladen <*luggage*>
unlock *vt* aufschließen
unlucky *a* unglücklich; <*day, number*> Unglücks-; **be ~** Pech haben; <*thing:*> Unglück bringen
unmarried *a* unverheiratet. **~ mother** *n* ledige Mutter *f*

U

unmask vt (fig) entlarven
unmistakable a, **-bly** adv
unverkennbar
unnatural a, **-ly** adv unnatürlich;
(not normal) nicht normal
unnecessary a, **-ily** adv unnötig
unnoticed a unbemerkt
unobtainable a nicht erhältlich
unobtrusive a, **-ly** adv
unaufdringlich; <thing>
unauffällig
unofficial a, **-ly** adv inoffiziell
unpack vt/i auspacken
unpaid a unbezahlt
unpleasant a, **-ly** adv
unangenehm
unplug vt (pt/pp **-plugged**) den
Stecker herausziehen von
unpopular a unbeliebt
unprecedented a beispiellos
unpredictable a unberechenbar
unprepared a nicht vorbereitet
unpretentious a bescheiden
unprofitable a unrentabel
unqualified a unqualifiziert; (fig:
absolute) uneingeschränkt
unquestionable a
unbezweifelbar; <right>
unbestreitbar
unravel vt (pt/pp **-ravelled**)
entwirren; (Knitting) aufziehen
unreal a unwirklich
unreasonable a unvernünftig
unrelated a
unzusammenhängend; be ~
nicht verwandt sein; <events:>
nicht miteinander
zusammenhängen
unreliable a unzuverlässig
unrest n Unruhen pl
unrivalled a unübertroffen
unroll vt aufrollen ● vi sich
aufrollen
unruly a ungebärdig
unsafe a nicht sicher
unsatisfactory a unbefriedigend
unsavoury a unangenehm; (fig)
unerfreulich
unscathed a unversehrt

unscrew vt abschrauben
unscrupulous a skrupellos
unseemly a unschicklich
unselfish a selbstlos
unsettled a ungeklärt; <weather>
unbeständig; <bill> unbezahlt
unshakeable a unerschütterlich
unshaven a unrasiert
unsightly a unansehnlich
unskilled a ungelernt; <work>
unqualifiziert
unsociable a ungesellig
unsophisticated a einfach
unsound a krank, nicht gesund;
<building> nicht sicher; <advice>
unzuverlässig; <reasoning> nicht
stichhaltig
unstable a nicht stabil; (mentally)
labil
unsteady a, **-ily** adv unsicher;
(wobbly) wackelig
unstuck a come ~ sich lösen; (▯
fail) scheitern
unsuccessful a, **-ly** adv erfolglos;
be ~ keinen Erfolg haben
unsuitable a ungeeignet;
(inappropriate) unpassend; (for
weather, activity) unzweckmäßig
unthinkable a unvorstellbar
untidiness n Unordentlichkeit f
untidy a, **-ily** adv unordentlich
untie vt aufbinden; losbinden
<person, boat, horse>
until prep bis (+ acc); not ~ erst;
~ **the evening** bis zum Abend
● conj bis; not ~ erst wenn; (in
past) erst als
untold a unermesslich
untrue a unwahr; **that's** ~ das ist
nicht wahr
unused[1] a unbenutzt; (not
utilized) ungenutzt
unused[2] a be ~ **to sth** etw nicht
gewohnt sein
unusual a, **-ly** adv ungewöhnlich
unveil vt enthüllen
unwanted a unerwünscht
unwelcome a unwillkommen

unwell a be or feel ~ sich nicht wohl fühlen

unwieldy a sperrig

unwilling a, **-ly** adv widerwillig; be ~ to do sth etw nicht tun wollen

unwind v (pt/pp unwound) ● vt abwickeln ● vi sich abwickeln; (I relax) sich entspannen

unwise a, **-ly** adv unklug

unworthy a unwürdig

unwrap vt (pt/pp -wrapped) auswickeln; auspacken <present>

unwritten a ungeschrieben

up adv oben; (with movement) nach oben; (not in bed) auf; <road> aufgerissen; <price> gestiegen; be up for sale zu verkaufen sein; up there da oben; up to (as far as) bis; time's up die Zeit ist um; what's up? I was ist los? what's he up to? I was hat er vor? I don't feel up to it ich fühle mich dem nicht gewachsen; go up hinaufgehen; come up heraufkommen ● prep be up on sth [oben] auf etw (dat) sein; up the mountain oben am Berg; (movement) den Berg hinauf; be up the tree oben im Baum sein; up the road die Straße entlang; up the river stromaufwärts; go up the stairs die Treppe hinaufgehen

upbringing n Erziehung f

update vt auf den neuesten Stand bringen

upgrade vt aufstufen

upheaval n Unruhe f; (Pol) Umbruch m

uphill a (fig) mühsam ● adv bergauf

uphold vt (pt/pp upheld) unterstützen; bestätigen <verdict>

upholster vt polstern. ~**y** n Polsterung f

upkeep n Unterhalt m

upmarket a anspruchsvoll

upon prep auf (+ dat/acc)

upper a obere(r,s); <deck, jaw, lip> Ober-; **have the ~ hand** die Oberhand haben ● n (of shoe) Obermaterial nt

upper class n Oberschicht f

upright a aufrecht

uprising n Aufstand m

uproar n Aufruhr m

upset¹ vt (pt/pp upset, pres p upsetting) umstoßen; (spill) verschütten; durcheinander bringen <plan>; (distress) erschüttern; <food:> nicht bekommen (+ dat); **get ~ about sth** sich über etw (acc) aufregen

upset² n Aufregung f; **have a stomach ~** einen verdorbenen Magen haben

upshot n Ergebnis nt

upside down adv verkehrt herum; **turn ~** umdrehen

upstairs¹ adv oben; <go> nach oben

upstairs² a im Obergeschoss

upstart n Emporkömmling m

upstream adv stromaufwärts

uptake n slow on the ~ schwer von Begriff; **be quick on the ~** schnell begreifen

upturn n Aufschwung m

upward a nach oben; <movement> Aufwärts-; ~ **slope** Steigung f ● adv ~**[s]** aufwärts, nach oben

uranium n Uran nt

urban a städtisch

urge n Trieb m, Drang m ● vt drängen; ~ **on** antreiben

urgen|cy n Dringlichkeit f. ~**t** a, **-ly** adv dringend

urine n Urin m, Harn m

us pron uns; **it's us** wir sind es

US[A] abbr USA pl

usable a brauchbar

usage n Brauch m; (of word) [Sprach]gebrauch m

use¹ n (see use²) Benutzung f; Verwendung f; Gebrauch m; **be (of) no ~** nichts nützen; **it is no ~**

es hat keinen Zweck; **what's the ~?** wozu?

use[2] vt benutzen <*implement, room, lift*>; verwenden <*ingredient, method, book, money*>; gebrauchen <*words, force, brains*>; **~ [up]** aufbrauchen

used[1] a gebraucht; <*towel*> benutzt; <*car*> Gebraucht-

used[2] pt **be ~ to sth** an etw (acc) gewöhnt sein; **get ~ to sich** gewöhnen an (+ acc); **he ~ to say** er hat immer gesagt; **he ~ to live here** er hat früher hier gewohnt

useful a nützlich. **~ness** n Nützlichkeit f

useless a nutzlos; (*not usable*) unbrauchbar; (*pointless*) zwecklos

user n Benutzer(in) m(f)

usher n Platzanweiser m; (*in court*) Gerichtsdiener m

usherette n Platzanweiserin f

USSR abbr (*History*) UdSSR f

usual a üblich. **~ly** adv gewöhnlich

utensil n Gerät nt

utility a Gebrauchs-

utilize vt nutzen

utmost a äußerste(r,s), größte(r,s) ●n **do one's ~** sein Möglichstes tun

utter[1] a, **-ly** adv völlig

utter[2] vt von sich geben <*sigh, sound*>; sagen <*word*>

U-turn n (*fig*) Kehrtwendung f; **'no ~s'** (*Auto*) 'Wenden verboten'

vacan|cy n (*job*) freie Stelle f; (*room*) freies Zimmer nt; **'no ~cies'** 'belegt'. **~t** a frei; <*look*> [gedanken]leer

vacate vt räumen

vacation n (*Univ & Amer*) Ferien pl

vaccinat|e vt impfen. **~ion** n Impfung f

vaccine n Impfstoff m

vacuum n Vakuum nt, luftleerer Raum m ●vt saugen. **~ cleaner** n Staubsauger m

vagina n (*Anat*) Scheide f

vague a (-r, -st), **-ly** adv vage; <*outline*> verschwommen

vain a (-er, -est) eitel; <*hope, attempt*> vergeblich; **in ~** vergeblich. **~ly** adv vergeblich

valiant a, **-ly** adv tapfer

valid a gültig; <*claim*> berechtigt; <*argument*> stichhaltig; <*reason*> triftig. **~ity** n Gültigkeit f

valley n Tal nt

valour n Tapferkeit f

valuable a wertvoll. **~s** npl Wertsachen pl

valuation n Schätzung f

value n Wert m; (*usefulness*) Nutzen m ●vt schätzen. **~ added tax** n Mehrwertsteuer f

valve n Ventil nt; (*Anat*) Klappe f; (*Electr*) Röhre f

van n Lieferwagen m

vandal n Rowdy m. **~ism** n mutwillige Zerstörung f. **~ize** vt demolieren

vanilla n Vanille f

vanish vi verschwinden

vanity n Eitelkeit f

vapour n Dampf m

variable a unbeständig; (*Math*) variabel; (*adjustable*) regulierbar

variant n Variante f

variation n Variation f; (*difference*) Unterschied m

varied a vielseitig; <*diet:*> abwechslungsreich

variety n Abwechslung f; (*quantity*) Vielfalt f; (*Comm*) Auswahl f; (*type*) Art f; (*Bot*) Abart f; (*Theat*) Varieté nt

various a verschieden. **~ly** adv unterschiedlich

varnish n Lack m ● vt lackieren

vary v (*pt/pp* **-ied**) ● vi sich ändern; (*be different*) verschieden sein ● vt [ver]ändern; (*add variety to*) abwechslungsreicher gestalten

vase n Vase f

vast a riesig; <*expanse*> weit. **~ly** adv gewaltig

vat n Bottich m

VAT abbr (**value added tax**) Mehrwertsteuer f, MwSt.

vault¹ n (*roof*) Gewölbe nt; (*in bank*) Tresor m; (*tomb*) Gruft f

vault² n Sprung m ● vt/i **~ [over]** springen über (+ acc)

VDU abbr (**visual display unit**) Bildschirmgerät nt

veal n Kalbfleisch nt ● attrib Kalbs-

veer vi sich drehen; (*Auto*) ausscheren

vegetable n Gemüse nt; **~s** pl Gemüse nt ● attrib Gemüse-; <*oil, fat*> Pflanzen-

vegetarian a vegetarisch ● n Vegetarier(in) m(f)

vegetation n Vegetation f

vehement a, **-ly** adv heftig

vehicle n Fahrzeug nt

veil n Schleier m ● vt verschleiern

vein n Ader f; (*mood*) Stimmung f; (*manner*) Art f

velocity n Geschwindigkeit f

velvet n Samt m

vending-machine n [Verkaufs]automat m

vendor n Verkäufer(in) m(f)

veneer n Furnier nt; (*fig*) Tünche f. **~ed** a furniert

venerable a ehrwürdig

Venetian a venezianisch. **v~ blind** n Jalousie f

vengeance n Rache f; **with a ~** gewaltig

Venice n Venedig nt

venison n (*Culin*) Reh(fleisch) nt

venom n Gift nt; (*fig*) Hass m. **~ous** a giftig

vent n Öffnung f

ventilat|e vt belüften. **~ion** n Belüftung f; (*installation*) Lüftung f. **~or** n Lüftungsvorrichtung f; (*Med*) Beatmungsgerät nt

ventriloquist n Bauchredner m

venture n Unternehmung f ● vt wagen ● vi sich wagen

venue n (*for event*) Veranstaltungsort m

veranda n Veranda f

verb n Verb nt. **~al** a, **-ly** adv mündlich; (*Gram*) verbal

verbose a weitschweifig

verdict n Urteil nt

verge n Rand m ● vi **~ on** (*fig*) grenzen an (+ acc)

verify vt (*pt/pp* **-ied**) überprüfen; (*confirm*) bestätigen

vermin n Ungeziefer nt

vermouth n Wermut m

versatil|e a vielseitig. **~ity** n Vielseitigkeit f

verse n Strophe f; (*of Bible*) Vers m; (*poetry*) Lyrik f

version n Version f; (*translation*) Übersetzung f; (*model*) Modell nt

versus prep gegen (+ acc)

vertical a, **-ly** adv senkrecht ● n Senkrechte f

vertigo n (*Med*) Schwindel m

verve n Schwung m

very adv sehr; **~ much** sehr; (*quantity*) sehr viel; **~ probably** höchstwahrscheinlich; **at the ~**

most allerhöchstens ● a (*mere*) bloß; **the ~ first** der/die/das allererste; **the ~ thing** genau das Richtige; **at the ~ end/beginning** ganz am Ende/Anfang; **only a ~ little** nur ein ganz kleines bisschen

vessel n Schiff nt; (*receptacle & Anat*) Gefäß nt

vest n [Unter]hemd nt; (*Amer: waistcoat*) Weste f

vestige n Spur f

vestry n Sakristei f

vet n Tierarzt m /-ärztin f ● vt (*pt/pp* **vetted**) überprüfen

veteran n Veteran m

veterinary a tierärztlich. **~ surgeon** n Tierarzt m /-ärztin f

veto n (*pl* **-es**) Veto nt

VHF abbr (**very high frequency**) UKW

via prep über (+ acc)

viable a lebensfähig; (*fig*) realisierbar; <*firm*> rentabel

viaduct n Viadukt nt

vibrat|e vi vibrieren. **~ion** n Vibrieren nt

vicar n Pfarrer m. **~age** n Pfarrhaus nt

vice[1] n Laster nt

vice[2] n (*Techn*) Schraubstock m

vice[3] n Vize-; **~ chairman** stellvertretender Vorsitzender m

vice versa adv umgekehrt

vicinity n Umgebung f; **in the ~ of** in der Nähe von

vicious a, **-ly** adv boshaft; <*animal*> bösartig

victim n Opfer nt. **~ize** vt schikanieren

victor n Sieger m

victor|ious a siegreich. **~y** n Sieg m

video n Video nt; (*recorder*) Videorecorder m ● attrib Video-

video: **~ cassette** n Videokassette f. **~ game** n Videospiel nt. **~ recorder** n Videorecorder m

Vienn|a n Wien nt. **~ese** a Wiener

view n Sicht f; (*scene*) Aussicht f; Blick m; (*picture, opinion*) Ansicht f; **in my ~** meiner Ansicht nach; **in ~ of** angesichts (+ gen); **be on ~** besichtigt werden können ● vt sich (dat) ansehen; besichtigen <*house*>; (*consider*) betrachten ● vi (*TV*) fernsehen. **~er** n (*TV*) Zuschauer(in) m(f)

view: **~finder** n (*Phot*) Sucher m. **~point** n Standpunkt m

vigilan|ce n Wachsamkeit f. **~t** a, **-ly** adv wachsam

vigorous a, **-ly** adv kräftig; (*fig*) heftig

vigour n Kraft f; (*fig*) Heftigkeit f

vile a abscheulich

villa n (*for holidays*) Ferienhaus nt

village n Dorf nt. **~r** n Dorfbewohner(in) m(f)

villain n Schurke m; (*in story*) Bösewicht m

vindicat|e vt rechtfertigen. **~ion** n Rechtfertigung f

vindictive a nachtragend

vine n Weinrebe f

vinegar n Essig m

vineyard n Weinberg m

vintage a erlesen ● n (*year*) Jahrgang m. **~ car** n Oldtimer m

viola n (*Mus*) Bratsche f

violat|e vt verletzen; (*break*) brechen; (*disturb*) stören; (*defile*) schänden. **~ion** n Verletzung f; Schändung f

violen|ce n Gewalt f; (*fig*) Heftigkeit f. **~t** a gewalttätig; (*fig*) heftig. **~tly** adv brutal; (*fig*) heftig

violet a violett ● n (*flower*) Veilchen nt

violin n Geige f, Violine f. **~ist** n Geiger(in) m(f)

VIP abbr (**very important person**) Prominente(r) m/f

viper n Kreuzotter f

virgin a unberührt ● n Jungfrau f. ~ity n Unschuld f

virille a männlich. ~ity n Männlichkeit f

virtual a a ~ ... praktisch ein ... ~ly adv praktisch

virtue n Tugend f; (advantage) Vorteil m; by or in ~e of auf Grund (+ gen)

virtuoso n (pl -si) Virtuose m

virtuous a tugendhaft

virus n Virus nt

visa n Visum nt

visibility n Sichtbarkeit f; (Meteorol) Sichtweite f

visible a, -bly adv sichtbar

vision n Vision f; (sight) Sehkraft f; (foresight) Weitblick m

visit n Besuch m ● vt besuchen; besichtigen <town, building>. ~or n Besucher(in) m(f); (in hotel) Gast m; have ~ors Besuch haben

visor n Schirm m; (Auto) [Sonnen]blende f

vista n Aussicht f

visual a, -ly adv visuell. ~ display unit n Bildschirmgerät nt

visualize vt sich (dat) vorstellen

vital a unbedingt notwendig; (essential to life) lebenswichtig. ~ity n Vitalität f. ~ly adv äußerst

vitamin n Vitamin nt

vivacilous a, -ly adv lebhaft. ~ty n Lebhaftigkeit f

vivid a, -ly adv lebhaft; <description> lebendig

vocabulary n Wortschatz m; (list) Vokabelverzeichnis nt; learn ~ Vokabeln lernen

vocal a, -ly adv stimmlich; (vociferous) lautstark

vocalist n Sänger(in) m(f)

vocation n Berufung f. ~al a Berufs-

vociferous a lautstark

vodka n Wodka m

vogue n Mode f

voice n Stimme f ● vt zum Ausdruck bringen

void a leer; (not valid) ungültig; ~ of ohne ● n Leere f

volatile a flüchtig; <person> sprunghaft

volcanic a vulkanisch

volcano n Vulkan m

volley n (of gunfire) Salve f; (Tennis) Volley m

volt n Volt nt. ~age n (Electr) Spannung f

voluble a, -bly adv redselig; <protest> wortreich

volume n (book) Band m; (Geom) Rauminhalt m; (amount) Ausmaß nt; (Radio, TV) Lautstärke f

voluntary a, -ily adv freiwillig

volunteer n Freiwillige(r) m/f ● vt anbieten; geben <information> ● vi sich freiwillig melden

vomit n Erbrochene(s) nt ● vt erbrechen ● vi sich übergeben

voracious a gefräßig; <appetite> unbändig

votle n Stimme f; (ballot) Abstimmung f; (right) Wahlrecht nt ● vi abstimmen; (in election) wählen. ~er n Wähler(in) m(f)

vouch vi ~ for sich verbürgen für. ~er n Gutschein m

vowel n Vokal m

voyage n Seereise f; (in space) Reise f, Flug m

vulgar a vulgär, ordinär. ~ity n Vulgarität f

vulnerable a verwundbar

vulture n Geier m

wad *n* Bausch *m*; (*bundle*) Bündel *nt*. **~ding** *n* Wattierung *f*
waddle *vi* watscheln
wade *vi* waten
wafer *n* Waffel *f*
waffle[1] *vi* 🔲 schwafeln
waffle[2] *n* (*Culin*) Waffel *f*
waft *vt/i* wehen
wag *v* (*pt/pp* **wagged**) ● *vt* wedeln mit ● *vi* wedeln
wage *n*, & **~s** *pl* Lohn *m*
wager *n* Wette *f*
wagon *n* Wagen *m*; (*Rail*) Waggon *m*
wail *n* [klagender] Schrei *m* ● *vi* heulen; (*lament*) klagen
waist *n* Taille *f*. **~coat** *n* Weste *f*. **~line** *n* Taille *f*
wait *n* Wartezeit *f*; **lie in ~ for** auflauern (+ *dat*) ● *vi* warten (**for** auf + *acc*); (*at table*) servieren; **~ on** bedienen ● *vt* **~ one's turn** warten, bis man an der Reihe ist
waiter *n* Kellner *m*; **~!** Herr Ober!
waiting: ~-list *n* Warteliste *f*. **~-room** *n* Warteraum *m*; (*doctor's*) Wartezimmer *nt*
waitress *n* Kellnerin *f*
waive *vt* verzichten auf (+ *acc*)
wake[1] *n* Totenwache *f* ● *v* (*pt* **woke**, *pp* **woken**) **~ [up]** ● *vt* [auf]wecken ● *vi* aufwachen
wake[2] *n* (*Naut*) Kielwasser *nt*; **in the ~ of** im Gefolge (+ *gen*)
Wales *n* Wales *nt*
walk *n* Spaziergang *m*; (*gait*) Gang *m*; (*path*) Weg *m*; **go for a ~** spazieren gehen ● *vi* gehen; (*not ride*) laufen, zu Fuß gehen; (*ramble*) wandern; **learn to ~** laufen lernen ● *vt* ausführen

<*dog*>. **~ out** *vi* hinausgehen; <*workers:*> in den Streik treten; **~ out on s.o.** jdn verlassen
walker *n* Spaziergänger(in) *m(f)*; (*rambler*) Wanderer *m*/Wanderin *f*
walking *n* Gehen *nt*; (*rambling*) Wandern *nt*. **~-stick** *n* Spazierstock *m*
wall *n* Wand *f*; (*external*) Mauer *f*; **drive s.o. up the ~** 🔲 jdn auf die Palme bringen ● *vt* **~ up** zumauern
wallet *n* Brieftasche *f*
wallflower *n* Goldlack *m*
wallop *vt* (*pt/pp* **walloped**) 🔲 schlagen
wallow *vi* sich wälzen; (*fig*) schwelgen
wallpaper *n* Tapete *f* ● *vt* tapezieren
walnut *n* Walnuss *f*
waltz *n* Walzer *m* ● *vi* Walzer tanzen
wander *vi* umherwandern, 🔲 bummeln; (*fig: digress*) abschweifen. **~ about** *vi* umherwandern
wangle *vt* 🔲 organisieren
want *n* Mangel *m* (**of** an + *dat*); (*hardship*) Not *f*; (*desire*) Bedürfnis *nt* ● *vt* wollen; (*need*) brauchen; **~ [to have]** sth etw haben wollen; **~ to do sth** etw tun wollen; **I ~ you to go** ich will, dass du gehst; **it ~s painting** es müsste gestrichen werden ● *vi* **he doesn't ~ for anything** ihm fehlt es an nichts. **~ed** *a* <*criminal*> gesucht
war *n* Krieg *m*; **be at ~** sich im Krieg befinden
ward *n* [Kranken]saal *m*; (*unit*) Station *f*; (*of town*) Wahlbezirk *m*; (*child*) Mündel *nt* ● *vt* **~ off** abwehren
warden *n* (*of hostel*) Heimleiter(in) *m(f)*; (*of youth*

hostel) Herbergsvater *m*;
(supervisor) Aufseher(in) *m(f)*

warder *n* Wärter(in) *m(f)*

wardrobe *n* Kleiderschrank *m*;
(clothes) Garderobe *f*

warehouse *n* Lager *nt*; *(building)*
Lagerhaus *nt*

wares *npl* Waren *pl*

war: ~**fare** *n* Krieg *m*. ~**like** *a*
kriegerisch

warm *a* (-**er**, -**est**), -**ly** *adv* warm;
<welcome> herzlich; **I am** ~ mir
ist warm ● *vt* wärmen. ~ **up** *vt*
aufwärmen ● *vi* warm werden.
(Sport) sich aufwärmen. ~**-
hearted** *a* warmherzig

warmth *n* Wärme *f*

warn *vt* warnen (**of** vor + *dat*).
~**ing** *n* Warnung *f*; *(advance
notice)* Vorwarnung *f*; *(caution)*
Verwarnung *f*

warp *vt* verbiegen ● *vi* sich
verziehen

warrant *n* *(for arrest)* Haftbefehl
m; *(for search)*
Durchsuchungsbefehl *m* ● *vt*
(justify) rechtfertigen;
(guarantee) garantieren

warranty *n* Garantie *f*

warrior *n* Krieger *m*

warship *n* Kriegsschiff *nt*

wart *n* Warze *f*

wartime *n* Kriegszeit *f*

wary *a* (-**ier**, -**iest**), -**ily** *adv*
vorsichtig; *(suspicious)*
misstrauisch

was *see* **be**

wash *n* Wäsche *f*; *(Naut)* Wellen
pl; **have a** ~ sich waschen ● *vt*
waschen; spülen *<dishes>*;
aufwischen *<floor>*; ~ **one's
hands** sich *(dat)* die Hände
waschen ● *vi* sich waschen. ~
out *vt* auswaschen; ausspülen
<mouth>. ~ **up** *vt/i* abwaschen,
spülen ● *vi (Amer)* sich waschen

washable *a* waschbar

wash-basin *n* Waschbecken *nt*

washer *n (Techn)* Dichtungsring
m; *(machine)* Waschmaschine *f*

washing *n* Wäsche *f*. ~**-machine**
n Waschmaschine *f*. ~**-powder** *n*
Waschpulver *nt*. ~**-up** *n*
Abwasch *m*; **do the** ~**-up**
abwaschen, spülen. ~**-up liquid** *n*
Spülmittel *nt*

wasp *n* Wespe *f*

waste *n* Verschwendung *f*;
(rubbish) Abfall *m*; ~**s** *pl* Öde *f*
● *a <product>* Abfall- ● *vt*
verschwenden ● *vi* ~ **away**
immer mehr abmagern

waste: ~**ful** *a* verschwenderisch.
~ **land** *n* Ödland *nt*. ~ **paper** *n*
Altpapier *nt*. ~**-paper basket** *n*
Papierkorb *m*

watch *n* Wache *f*; *(timepiece)*
[Armband]uhr *f* ● *vt* beobachten;
sich *(dat)* ansehen *<film, match>*;
(keep an eye on) achten auf (+
acc); ~ **television** fernsehen ● *vi*
zusehen. ~ **out** *vi* Ausschau
halten (**for** nach); *(be careful)*
aufpassen

watch: ~**dog** *n* Wachhund *m*.
~**ful** *a*, -**ly** *adv* wachsam. ~**man** *n*
Wachmann *m*

water *n* Wasser *nt*; ~**s** *pl*
Gewässer *nt* ● *vt* gießen *<garden,
plant>*; *(dilute)* verdünnen ● *vi*
<eyes:> tränen; **my mouth was**
~**ing** mir lief das Wasser im
Munde zusammen. ~ **down** *vt*
verwässern

water: ~**-colour** *n* Wasserfarbe *f*;
(painting) Aquarell *nt*. ~**cress** *n*
Brunnenkresse *f*. ~**fall** *n*
Wasserfall *m*

watering-can *n* Gießkanne *f*

water: ~**-lily** *n* Seerose *f*. ~
logged *a* be ~**logged** *<ground:>*
unter Wasser stehen. ~ **polo** *n*
Wasserball *m*. ~**proof** *a*
wasserdicht. ~**-skiing** *n*
Wasserskilaufen *nt*. ~**tight** *a*
wasserdicht. ~**way** *n*
Wasserstraße *f*

watery *a* wässrig
watt *n* Watt *nt*
wave *n* Welle *f*; (*gesture*)
Handbewegung *f*; (*as greeting*)
Winken *nt* ● *vt* winken mit;
(*brandish*) schwingen; wellen
<*hair*>; ~ one's hand winken ● *vi*
winken (to *dat*); <*flag*:> wehen.
~length *n* Wellenlänge *f*
waver *vi* schwanken
wavy *a* wellig
wax *n* Wachs *nt*; (*in ear*) Schmalz
nt ● *vt* wachsen. ~works *n*
Wachsfigurenkabinett *nt*
way *n* Weg *m*; (*direction*)
Richtung *f*; (*respect*) Hinsicht *f*;
(*manner*) Art *f*; (*method*) Art und
Weise *f*; ~s *pl* Gewohnheiten *pl*;
on the ~ auf dem Weg (to nach/
zu); (*under way*) unterwegs; a
little/long ~ ein kleines/ganzes
Stück; a long ~ off weit weg; this
~ hierher; (*like this*) so; which ~
(*Auto*) 'Vorfahrt beachten'; go out
in welche Richtung; (*how*) wie;
by the ~ übrigens; in some ~s in
gewisser Hinsicht; either ~ so
oder so; in this ~ auf diese
Weise; in a ~ in gewisser Weise;
lead the ~ vorausgehen; make ~
Platz machen (for *dat*); 'give ~'
of one's ~ (*fig*) sich (*dat*)
besondere Mühe geben (to zu);
get one's [own] ~ seinen Willen
durchsetzen ● *adv* weit; ~ behind
weit zurück. ~ in *n* Eingang *m*
way out *n* Ausgang *m*; (*fig*)
Ausweg *m*
WC *abbr* WC *nt*
we *pron* wir
weak *a* (-er, -est), -ly *adv* schwach;
<*liquid*> dünn. ~en *vt* schwächen
● *vi* schwächer werden. ~ling *n*
Schwächling *m*. ~ness *n*
Schwäche *f*
wealth *n* Reichtum *m*; (*fig*) Fülle *f*
(of an + *dat*). ~y *a* (-ier, -iest)
reich
weapon *n* Waffe *f*

wear *n* (*clothing*) Kleidung *f*; ~
and tear Abnutzung *f*, Verschleiß
m ● *v* (*pt* wore, *pp* worn) ● *vt*
tragen; (*damage*) abnutzen; what
shall I ~? was soll ich anziehen?
● *vi* sich abnutzen; (*last*) halten.
~ off *vi* abgehen; <*effect*:>
nachlassen. ~ out *vt* abnutzen;
(*exhaust*) erschöpfen ● *vi* sich
abnutzen
weary *a* (-ier, -iest), -ily *adv* müde
weather *n* Wetter *nt*; in this ~ bei
diesem Wetter; under the ~ 🆒
nicht ganz auf dem Posten ● *vt*
abwettern <*storm*>; (*fig*)
überstehen
weather: ~-beaten *a* verwittert;
wettergegerbt <*face*>. ~ forecast
n Wettervorhersage *f*
weave¹ *vi* (*pt/pp* weaved) sich
schlängeln (through durch)
weave² *n* (*Tex*) Bindung *f* ● *vt* (*pt*
wove, *pp* woven) weben. ~r *n*
Weber *m*
web *n* Netz *nt*. ~site *n* Website *f*
wed *vt/i* (*pt/pp* wedded) heiraten.
~ding *n* Hochzeit *f*
wedding: ~ day *n* Hochzeitstag
m. ~ dress *n* Hochzeitskleid *nt*.
~-ring *n* Ehering *m*, Trauring *m*
wedge *n* Keil *m* ● *vt* festklemmen
Wednesday *n* Mittwoch *m*
wee *a* 🆒 klein ● *vi* Pipi machen
weed *n* & ~s *pl* Unkraut *nt* ● *vt/i*
jäten. ~ out *vt* (*fig*) aussieben
weedkiller *n*
Unkrautvertilgungsmittel *nt*
weedy *a* 🆒 spillerig
week *n* Woche *f*. ~day *n*
Wochentag *m*. ~end *n*
Wochenende *nt*
weekly *a* & *adv* wöchentlich ● *n*
Wochenzeitschrift *f*
weep *vi* (*pt/pp* wept) weinen
weigh *vt/i* wiegen. ~ down *vt*
(*fig*) niederdrücken. ~ up *vt* (*fig*)
abwägen
weight *n* Gewicht *nt*; put on/lose
~ zunehmen/abnehmen

weight-lifting n Gewichtheben nt
weighty a (-ier, -iest) schwer; (important) gewichtig
weir n Wehr nt.
weird a (-er, -est) unheimlich; (bizarre) bizarr
welcome a willkommen; you're ~! nichts zu danken! you're ~ to (have) it das können Sie gerne haben ● n Willkommen nt ● vt begrüßen
weld vt schweißen. ~er n Schweißer m
welfare n Wohl nt; (Admin) Fürsorge f. W ~ State n Wohlfahrtsstaat m
well¹ n Brunnen m; (oil ~) Quelle f
well² adv (better, best) gut; as ~ auch; as ~ as (in addition) sowohl … als auch; ~ done! gut gemacht! ● a gesund; he is not ~ es geht ihm nicht gut; get ~ soon! gute Besserung! ● int nun, na
well: ~-behaved a artig. ~-being n Wohl nt
wellingtons npl Gummistiefel pl
well: ~-known a bekannt. ~-off a wohlhabend; be ~-off gut dransein. ~-to-do a wohlhabend
Welsh a walisisch ● n (Lang) Walisisch nt; the ~ pl die Waliser. ~man n Waliser m
went see **go**
wept see **weep**
were see **be**
west n Westen m; to the ~ of westlich von ● a West-, west- ● adv nach Westen. ~erly a westlich. ~ern a westlich ● n Western m
West: ~ Germany n Westdeutschland nt. ~ Indian a westindisch ● n Westinder(in) m(f). ~ Indies npl Westindische Inseln pl
westward[s] adv nach Westen

wet a (wetter, wettest) nass; <🔲 person> weichlich, lasch; '~ paint' 'frisch gestrichen' ● vt (pt/ pp **wet** or **wetted**) nass machen
whack vt 🔲 schlagen. ~ed a 🔲 kaputt
whale n Wal m
wharf n Kai m

what
● pronoun
····▸ (in questions) was. what is it? was ist das? what do you want? was wollen Sie? what is your name? wie heißen Sie? what? (🔲 say that again) wie?; was? what is the time? wie spät ist es? (indirect) I didn't know what to do ich wusste nicht, was ich machen sollte

! The equivalent of a preposition with **what** in English is a special word in German beginning with *wo-* (*wor-* before a vowel): for what? what for? = wofür? wozu? from what? wovon? on what? worauf? worüber? under what? worunter? with what? womit? etc. what do you want the money for? wozu willst du das Geld? what is he talking about? wovon redet er?

····▸ (relative pronoun) was. do what I tell you tu, was ich dir sage. give me what you can gib mir, so viel du kannst. what little I know das bisschen, das ich weiß. I don't agree with what you are saying ich stimme dem nicht zu, was Sie sagen

····▸ (in phrases) what about me? was ist mit mir? what about a cup of coffee? wie wäre es mit einer Tasse Kaffee? what if she doesn't come? was ist, wenn sie nicht kommt? what of it? was ist dabei?

● *adjective*

••••➤ *(asking for selection)* welcher (*m*), welche (*f*), welches (*nt*), welche (*pl*). **what book do you want?** welches Buch willst du haben? **what colour are the walls?** welche Farbe haben die Wände? **I asked him what train to take** ich habe ihn gefragt, welchen Zug ich nehmen soll

••••➤ *(asking how much/many)* **what money does he have?** wie viel Geld hat er? **what time is it?** wie spät ist es? **what time does it start?** um wie viel Uhr fängt es an?

••••➤ **what kind of ...?** was für [ein(e)]? **what kind of man is he?** was für ein Mensch ist er?

••••➤ *(in exclamations)* was für (+ *nom*). **what a fool you are!** was für ein Dummkopf du doch bist! **what cheek/luck!** was für eine Frechheit/ein Glück! **what a huge house!** was für ein riesiges Haus! **what a lot of people!** was für viele Leute!

whatever *a* [egal] welche(r,s) ● *pron* was ... auch; ~ **is it?** was ist das bloß? ~ **he does** was er auch tut; **nothing** ~ überhaupt nichts

whatsoever *pron & a* ≈ **whatever**
wheat *n* Weizen *m*
wheel *n* Rad *nt*; *(pottery)* Töpferscheibe *f*; *(steering* ~*)* Lenkrad *nt*; **at the** ~ am Steuer ● *vt (push)* schieben ● *vi* kehrtmachen; *(circle)* kreisen

wheel: ~**barrow** *n* Schubkarre *f*. ~**chair** *n* Rollstuhl *m*. ~**clamp** *n* Parkkralle *f*

when *adv* wann; **the day** ~ der Tag, an dem ● *conj* wenn; *(in the past)* als; *(although)* wo ... doch; ~ **swimming/reading** beim Schwimmen/Lesen

whenever *conj & adv* [immer] wenn; *(at whatever time)* wann immer; ~ **did it happen?** wann ist das bloß passiert?
where *adv & conj* wo; ~ **[to]** wohin; ~ **[from]** woher
whereabouts[1] *adv* wo
whereabouts[2] *n* Verbleib *m*; *(of person)* Aufenthaltsort *m*
whereas *conj* während; *(in contrast)* wohingegen
whereupon *adv* worauf[hin]
wherever *conj & adv* wo immer; *(to whatever place)* wohin immer; *(from whatever place)* woher immer; *(everywhere)* überall wo; ~ **possible** wenn irgend möglich
whether *conj* ob

which
● *adjective*

••••➤ *(in questions)* welcher (*m*), welche (*f*), welches (*nt*), welche (*pl*). **which book do you need?** welches Buch brauchst du? **which one?** welcher/welche/welches? **which ones?** welche? **which one of you did it?** wer von euch hat es getan? **which way?** *(which direction)* welche Richtung?; *(where)* wohin?; *(how)* wie?

••••➤ *(relative)* **he always comes at one, at which time I'm having lunch/by which time I've finished** er kommt immer um ein Uhr; dann esse ich gerade zu Mittag/bis dahin bin ich schon fertig

● *pronoun*

••••➤ *(in questions)* welcher (*m*), welche (*f*), welches (*nt*), welche (*pl*). **which is which?** welcher/ welche/welches ist welcher/ welche/welches? **which of you?** wer von euch?

••••➤ *(relative)* der (*m*), die (*f*), das (*nt*), die (*pl*); *(genitive)* dessen (*m, nt*), deren (*f, pl*); *(dative)*

dem (*m, nt*), der (*f*), denen (*pl*); (*referring to a clause*) was. **the book which I gave you** das Buch, das ich dir gab. **the trial, the result of which we are expecting** der Prozess, dessen Ergebnis wir erwarten. **the house of which I was speaking** das Haus, von dem *od* wovon ich redete. **after which** wonach; nach dem. **on which** worauf; auf dem. **the shop opposite which we parked** der Laden, gegenüber dem wir parkten. **everything which I tell you** alles, was ich dir sage

whichever *a & pron* [egal] welche(r,s); ~ **it is** was es auch ist

while *n* Weile *f*; **a long** ~ lange; **be worth** ~ sich lohnen; **it's worth my** ~ es lohnt sich für mich ● *conj* während; (*as long as*) solange; (*although*) obgleich ● *vt* ~ **away** sich (*dat*) vertreiben

whilst *conj* während

whim *n* Laune *f*

whimper *vi* wimmern; <*dog:*> winseln

whine *vi* winseln

whip *n* Peitsche *f*; (*Pol*) Einpeitscher *m* ● *vt* (*pt/pp* whipped) peitschen; (*Culin*) schlagen. ~**ped cream** *n* Schlagsahne *f*

whirl *vt/i* wirbeln. ~**pool** *n* Strudel *m*. ~-**wind** *n* Wirbelwind *m*

whirr *vi* surren

whisk *n* (*Culin*) Schneebesen *m* ● *vt* (*Culin*) schlagen

whisker *n* Schnurrhaar *nt*

whisky *n* Whisky *m*

whisper *n* Flüstern *nt* ● *vt/i* flüstern

whistle *n* Pfiff *m*; (*instrument*) Pfeife *f* ● *vt/i* pfeifen

white *a* (**-r, -st**) weiß ● *n* Weiß *nt*; (*of egg*) Eiweiß *nt*; (*person*) Weiße(r) *m/f*

white: ~ **coffee** *n* Kaffee *m* mit Milch. ~-**collar worker** *n* Angestellte(r) *m*. ~ **lie** *n* Notlüge *f*

whiten *vt* weiß machen ● *vi* weiß werden

whiteness *n* Weiß *nt*

Whitsun *n* Pfingsten *nt*

whiz[z] *vi* (*pt/pp* whizzed) zischen. ~-**kid** *n* 🅸 Senkrechtstarter *m*

who *pron* wer; (*acc*) wen; (*dat*) wem ● *rel pron* der/die/das, (*pl*) die

whoever *pron* wer [immer]; ~ **he is** wer er auch ist; ~ **is it?** wer ist das bloß?

whole *a* ganz; <*truth*> voll ● *n* Ganze(s) *nt*; **as a** ~ als Ganzes; **on the** ~ im Großen und Ganzen; **the** ~ **of Germany** ganz Deutschland

whole: ~**food** *n* Vollwertkost *f*. ~-**hearted** *a* rückhaltlos. ~**meal** *a* Vollkorn-

wholesale *a* Großhandels- ● *adv* en gros; (*fig*) in Bausch und Bogen. ~**r** *n* Großhändler *m*

wholly *adv* völlig

whom *pron* wen; **to** ~ wem ● *rel pron* den/die/das, (*pl*) die; (*dat*) dem/der/dem, (*pl*) denen

whopping *a* 🅸 Riesen-

whore *n* Hure *f*

whose *pron* wessen; ~ **is that?** wem gehört das? ● *rel pron* dessen/deren/dessen, (*pl*) deren

why *adv* warum; (*for what purpose*) wozu; **that's** ~ darum

wick *n* Docht *m*

wicked *a* böse; (*mischievous*) frech, boshaft

wicker *n* Korbgeflecht *nt* ● *attrib* Korb-

wide *a* (**-r, -st**) weit; (*broad*) breit; (*fig*) groß ● *adv* weit; (*off target*) daneben; ~ **awake** hellwach; **far**

and ~ weit und breit. **~ly** adv weit; <known, accepted> weithin; <differ> stark

widen vt verbreitern; (fig) erweitern ● vi sich verbreitern

widespread a weit verbreitet

widow n Witwe f. **~ed** a verwitwet. **~er** n Witwer m

width n Weite f; (breadth) Breite f

wield vt schwingen; ausüben <power>

wife n (pl **wives**) [Ehe]frau f

wig n Perücke f

wiggle vi wackeln ● vt wackeln mit

wild a (-er, -est), **-ly** adv wild; <animal> wild lebend; <flower> wild wachsend; (furious) wütend ● adv wild; **run ~** frei herumlaufen ● n **in the ~** wild; **the ~s** pl die Wildnis f

wilderness n Wildnis f; (desert) Wüste f

wildlife n Tierwelt f

will¹

● auxiliary verb
   past **would**

····▶ (expressing the future) werden. **she will arrive tomorrow** sie wird morgen ankommen. **he will be there by now** er wird jetzt schon da sein

····▶ (expressing intention) (present tense) **will you go?** gehst du? **I promise I won't do it again** ich verspreche, ich machs nicht noch mal

····▶ (in requests) **will/would you please tidy up?** würdest du bitte aufräumen? **will you be quiet!** willst du ruhig sein!

····▶ (in invitations) **will you have/ would you like some wine?** wollen Sie/möchten Sie Wein?

····▶ (negative: refuse to) nicht wollen. **they won't help me** sie wollen mir nicht helfen. **the car**

won't start das Auto will nicht anspringen

····▶ (in tag questions) nicht wahr. **you'll be back soon, won't you?** du kommst bald wieder, nicht wahr? **you will help her, won't you?** du hilfst ihr doch, nicht wahr?

····▶ (in short answers) **Will you be there? — Yes I will** Wirst du da sein? — Ja

will² n Wille m; (document) Testament nt

willing a willig; (eager) bereitwillig; **be ~** bereit sein. **~ly** adv bereitwillig; (gladly) gern. **~ness** n Bereitwilligkeit f

willow n Weide f

will-power n Willenskraft f

wilt vi welk werden, welken

wily a (-ier, -iest) listig

win n Sieg m ● v (pt/pp **won**; pres p **winning**) ● vt gewinnen; bekommen <scholarship> ● vi gewinnen; (in battle) siegen. **~ over** vt auf seine Seite bringen

wince vi zusammenzucken

winch n Winde f ● vt **~ up** hochwinden

wind¹ n Wind m; (🔊 flatulence) Blähungen pl ● vt **~ s.o.** jdm den Atem nehmen

wind² v (pt/pp **wound**) ● vt (wrap) wickeln; (move by turning) kurbeln; aufziehen <clock> vi <road:> sich winden. **~ up** vt aufziehen <clock>; schließen <proceedings>

wind: **~ instrument** n Blasinstrument nt. **~mill** n Windmühle f

window n Fenster nt; (of shop) Schaufenster nt

window: **~-box** n Blumenkasten m. **~-cleaner** n Fensterputzer m. **~-pane** n Fensterscheibe f. **~-shopping** n Schaufensterbummel m. **~-sill** n Fensterbrett nt

windpipe n Luftröhre f
windscreen n, (Amer) **windshield** n Windschutzscheibe f. **~wiper** n Scheibenwischer m
wind surfing n Windsurfen nt
windy a (-ier, -iest) windig
wine n Wein m. **~bar** n Weinstube f. **~glass** n Weinglas nt. **~list** n Weinkarte f
winery n (Amer) Weingut nt
wine-tasting n Weinprobe f
wing n Flügel m; (Auto) Kotflügel m; **~s** pl (Theat) Kulissen pl
wink n Zwinkern nt; **not sleep a ~** kein Auge zutun ●vi zwinkern; <light:> blinken
winner n Gewinner(in) m(f); (Sport) Sieger(in) m(f)
winning a siegreich; <smile> gewinnend. **~post** n Zielpfosten m. **~s** npl Gewinn m
wint|er n Winter m. **~ry** a winterlich
wipe n **give sth a ~** etw abwischen ●vt abwischen; aufwischen <floor>; (dry) abtrocknen. **~ out** vt (cancel) löschen; (destroy) ausrotten. **~ up** vt aufwischen
wire n Draht m
wiring n [elektrische] Leitungen pl
wisdom n Weisheit f; (prudence) Klugheit f. **~ tooth** n Weisheitszahn m
wise a (-r, -st), **-ly** adv weise; (prudent) klug
wish n Wunsch m ●vt wünschen; **~ s.o. well** jdm alles Gute wünschen; **I ~ you could stay** ich wünschte, du könntest hier bleiben ●vi sich (dat) etwas wünschen. **~ful** a **~ful thinking** Wunschdenken nt
wistful a, **-ly** adv wehmütig
wit n Geist m, Witz m; (intelligence) Verstand m; (person) geistreicher Mensch m;
be at one's ~s' end sich (dat) keinen Rat mehr wissen
witch n Hexe f. **~craft** n Hexerei f
with prep mit (+ dat); **~ fear/cold** vor Angst/Kälte; **~ it** damit; **I'm going ~ you** ich gehe mit; **take it ~ you** nimm es mit; **I haven't got it ~ me** ich habe es nicht bei mir
withdraw v (pt -drew, pp -drawn) ●vt zurückziehen; abheben <money> ●vi sich zurückziehen. **~al** n Zurückziehen nt; (of money) Abhebung f; (from drugs) Entzug m
wither vi [ver]welken
withhold vt (pt/pp -held) vorenthalten (from s.o. jdm)
within prep innerhalb (+ gen) ●adv innen
without prep ohne (+ acc); **~ my noticing it** ohne dass ich es merkte
withstand vt (pt/pp -stood) standhalten (+ dat)
witness n Zeuge m/ Zeugin f ●vt Zeuge/Zeugin sein (+ gen); bestätigen <signature>
witticism n geistreicher Ausspruch m
witty a (-ier, -iest) witzig, geistreich
wives see **wife**
wizard n Zauberer m
wizened a verhutzelt
wobb|le vi wackeln. **~ly** a wackelig
woke, woken see **wake**¹
wolf n (pl wolves) Wolf m
woman n (pl women) Frau f. **~izer** n Schürzenjäger m
womb n Gebärmutter f
women npl see **woman**
won see **win**
wonder n Wunder nt; (surprise) Staunen nt ●vt/i sich fragen; (be surprised) sich wundern; **I ~** da frage ich mich; **I ~ whether she is**

ill ob sie wohl krank ist? **~ful** *a,* **-ly** *adv* wunderbar

won't = will not

wood *n* Holz *nt;* (*forest*) Wald *m;* **touch ~!** unberufen!

wood: **~ed** *a* bewaldet. **~en** *a* Holz-; (*fig*) hölzern. **~pecker** *n* Specht *m.* **~wind** *n* Holzbläser *pl.* **~work** *n* (*wooden parts*) Holzteile *pl;* (*craft*) Tischlerei *f.* **~worm** *n* Holzwurm *m*

wool *n* Wolle *f* ●*attrib* Woll-. **~len** *a* wollen

woolly *a* (**-ier, -iest**) wollig; (*fig*) unklar

word *n* Wort *nt;* (*news*) Nachricht *f;* **by ~ of mouth** mündlich; **have a ~ with** sprechen mit; **have ~s** einen Wortwechsel haben. **~ing** *n* Wortlaut *m.* **~ processor** *n* Textverarbeitungssystem *nt*

wore *see* **wear**

work *n* Arbeit *f;* (*Art, Literature*) Werk *nt;* **~s** *pl* (*factory, mechanism*) Werk *nt;* **at ~** bei der Arbeit; **out of ~** arbeitslos ●*vi* arbeiten; <*machine, system:*> funktionieren; (*have effect*) wirken; (*study*) lernen; **it won't ~** (*fig*) es klappt nicht ●*vt* arbeiten lassen; bedienen <*machine*>; betätigen <*lever*>. **~ off** *vt* abarbeiten. **~ out** *vt* ausrechnen; (*solve*) lösen ●*vi* gut gehen, Ⅰ klappen. **~ up** *vt* aufbauen; sich (*dat*) holen <*appetite*>; **get ~ed up** sich aufregen

workable *a* (*feasible*) durchführbar

worker *n* Arbeiter(in) *m(f)*

working *a* berufstätig; <*day, clothes*> Arbeits-; **be in ~ order** funktionieren. **~ class** *n* Arbeiterklasse *f*

work: **~man** *n* Arbeiter *m;* (*craftsman*) Handwerker *m.* **~manship** *n* Arbeit *f.* **~shop** *n* Werkstatt *f*

world *n* Welt *f;* **in the ~** auf der Welt; **think the ~ of s.o.** große Stücke auf jdn halten. **~ly** *a* weltlich; <*person*> weltlich gesinnt. **~-wide** *a & adv* weltweit

worm *n* Wurm *m*

worn *see* **wear** ●*a* abgetragen. **~-out** *a* abgetragen; <*carpet*> abgenutzt; <*person*> erschöpft

worried *a* besorgt

worry *n* Sorge *f* ●*v* (*pt/pp* **worried**) ●*vt* beunruhigen; (*bother*) stören ●*vi* sich beunruhigen, sich (*dat*) Sorgen machen. **~ing** *a* beunruhigend

worse *a & adv* schlechter; (*more serious*) schlimmer ●*n* Schlechtere(s) *nt;* Schlimmere(s) *nt*

worsen *vt* verschlechtern ●*vi* sich verschlechtern

worship *n* Anbetung *f;* (*service*) Gottesdienst *m* ●*vt* (*pt/pp* **-shipped**) anbeten

worst *a* schlechteste(r,s); (*most serious*) schlimmste(r,s) ●*adv* am schlechtesten; schlimmsten ●*n* **the ~** das Schlimmste

worth *n* Wert *m;* **£10's ~ of petrol** Benzin für £10 ●*a* **be ~ £5** £5 wert sein; **be ~ it** (*fig*) sich lohnen. **~less** *a* wertlos. **~while** *a* lohnend

worthy *a* würdig

would *v aux* **I ~ do it** ich würde es tun, ich täte es; **~ you go?** würdest du gehen? **he said he ~n't** er sagte, er würde es nicht tun; **what ~ you like?** was möchten Sie?

wound[1] *n* Wunde *f* ●*vt* verwunden

wound[2] *see* **wind**[2]

wove, woven *see* **weave**[2]

wrangle *n* Streit *m*

wrap *n* Umhang *m* ●*vt* (*pt/pp* **wrapped**) **~ [up]** wickeln; einpacken <*present*> ●*vi* **~ up**

warmly sich warm einpacken.
~**per** n Hülle f. ~**ping** n
Verpackung f
wrath n Zorn m
wreath n (pl **-s**) Kranz m
wreck n Wrack nt ● vt zerstören;
zunichte machen <plans>;
zerrütten <marriage>. ~**age** n
Wrackteile pl; (fig) Trümmer pl
wren n Zaunkönig m
wrench n Ruck m; (tool)
Schraubenschlüssel m; (fig) be a ~
(fig) weh tun ● vt reißen; ~ **sth
from s.o.** jdm etw entreißen
wrestl|e vi ringen. ~**er** n Ringer
m. ~**ing** n Ringen nt
wretch n Kreatur f. ~**ed** a elend;
(very bad) erbärmlich
wriggle n Zappeln nt ● vi
zappeln; (move forward) sich
schlängeln; ~ **out of sth** Ⅰ sich
vor etw (dat) drücken
wring vt (pt/pp **wrung**) wringen;
(~ **out**) auswringen; umdrehen
<neck>; ringen <hands>
wrinkle n Falte f; (on skin)
Runzel f ● vt kräuseln ● vi sich
kräuseln, sich falten. ~**d** a
runzlig
wrist n Handgelenk nt. ~**-watch** n
Armbanduhr f
write vt/i (pt **wrote**, pp **written**,
pres p **writing**) schreiben. ~ **down**
vt aufschreiben. ~ **off** vt
abschreiben; zu Schrott fahren
<car>
write-off n ≈ Totalschaden m
writer n Schreiber(in) m(f);
(author) Schriftsteller(in) m(f)
writhe vi sich winden
writing n Schreiben nt;
(handwriting) Schrift f; **in** ~
schriftlich. ~**-paper** n
Schreibpapier nt
written see write
wrong a, **-ly** adv falsch; (morally)
unrecht; (not just) ungerecht; **be**
~ nicht stimmen; <person:>
Unrecht haben; **what's** ~? was ist

los? ● adv falsch; **go** ~ <person:>
etwas falsch machen; <machine:>
kaputtgehen; <plan:> schief
gehen ● n Unrecht nt ● vt
Unrecht tun (+ dat). ~**ful** a
ungerechtfertigt. ~**fully** adv
<accuse> zu Unrecht
wrote see write
wrung see wring
wry a (**-er**, **-est**) ironisch;
<humour> trocken

Xmas n Ⅰ Weihnachten nt
X-ray n (picture)
Röntgenaufnahme f; ~**s** pl
Röntgenstrahlen pl ● vt röntgen;
durchleuchten <luggage>

yacht n Jacht f; (for racing)
Segeljacht f. ~**ing** n Segeln nt
yank vt Ⅰ reißen
Yank n Ⅰ Ami m Ⅰ
yap vi (pt/pp **yapped**) <dog:>
kläffen
yard¹ n Hof m; (for storage) Lager
nt
yard² n Yard nt (= 0,91 m)
yarn n Garn nt; (Ⅰ tale)
Geschichte f
yawn n Gähnen nt ● vi gähnen

year *n* Jahr *nt*; (*of wine*) Jahrgang *m*; **for ~s** jahrelang. **~ly** *a* & *adv* jährlich

yearn *vi* sich sehnen (**for** nach). **~ing** *n* Sehnsucht *f*

yeast *n* Hefe *f*

yell *n* Schrei *m* ● *vi* schreien

yellow *a* gelb ● *n* Gelb *nt*

yelp *vi* jaulen

yes *adv* ja; (*contradicting*) doch ● *n* Ja *nt*

yesterday *n* & *adv* gestern; **~'s paper** die gestrige Zeitung; **the day before ~** vorgestern

yet *adv* noch; (*in question*) schon; (*nevertheless*) doch; **as ~** bisher; **not ~** noch nicht; **the best ~** das bisher beste ● *conj* doch

Yiddish *n* Jiddisch *nt*

yield *n* Ertrag *m* ● *vt* bringen; abwerfen <*profit*> ● *vi* nachgeben; (*Amer, Auto*) die Vorfahrt beachten

yoga *n* Yoga *m*

yoghurt *n* Joghurt *m*

yoke *n* Joch *nt*; (*of garment*) Passe *f*

yolk *n* Dotter *m*, Eigelb *nt*

you *pron* du; (*acc*) dich; (*dat*) dir; (*pl*) ihr; (*acc, dat*) euch; (*formal*) (*nom & acc, sg & pl*) Sie; (*dat, sg & pl*) Ihnen; (*one*) man; (*acc*) einen; (*dat*) einem; **all of ~** ihr/ Sie alle; **I know ~** ich kenne dich/euch/Sie; **I'll give ~ the money** ich gebe dir/euch/Ihnen das Geld; **it does ~ good** es tut einem gut; **it's bad for ~** es ist ungesund

young *a* (**-er, -est**) jung ● *npl* (*animals*) Junge *pl*; **the ~** die Jugend *f*. **~ster** *n* Jugendliche(r) *m/f*; (*child*) Kleine(r) *m/f*

your *a* dein; (*pl*) euer; (*formal*) Ihr

yours *poss pron* deine(r), deins;

(*pl*) eure(r), euers; (*formal, sg & pl*) Ihre(r), Ihr[e]s; **a friend of ~** ein Freund von dir/Ihnen/euch; **that is ~** das gehört dir/Ihnen/ euch

yourself *pron* (*pl* **-selves**) selbst; (*refl*) dich; (*dat*) dir; (*pl*) euch; (*formal*) sich; **by ~** allein

youth *n* (*pl* **-s**) Jugend *f*; (*boy*) Jugendliche(r) *m*. **~ful** *a* jugendlich. **~ hostel** *n* Jugendherberge *f*

Yugoslavia *n* Jugoslawien *nt*

zeal *n* Eifer *m*

zealous *a*, **-ly** *adv* eifrig

zebra *n* Zebra *nt*. **~ crossing** *n* Zebrastreifen *m*

zero *n* Null *f*

zest *n* Begeisterung *f*

zigzag *n* Zickzack *m* ● *vi* (*pt/pp* **-zagged**) im Zickzack laufen/ (*in vehicle*) fahren

zinc *n* Zink *nt*

zip *n* ~ **[fastener]** Reißverschluss *m* ● *vt* ~ **[up]** den Reißverschluss zuziehen an (+ *dat*)

zip code *n* (*Amer*) Postleitzahl *f*

zipper *n* Reißverschluss *m*

zodiac *n* Tierkreis *m*

zone *n* Zone *f*

zoo *n* Zoo *m*

zoological *a* zoologisch

zoolog|ist *n* Zoologe *m*/gin *f*. **~y** Zoologie *f*

zoom *vi* sausen. **~ lens** *n* Zoomobjektiv *nt*

Summary of German grammar

Regular verbs

Most German verbs are regular and add the same endings to their stem. You find the stem by taking away the **-en** (or sometimes just **-n**) from the end of the infinitive. The infinitive of the verb, for example **machen**, is the form you look up in the dictionary. The stem of **machen** is **mach-**. There are six endings for each tense, to go with the different pronouns:

ich = *I*   du = *you*   er/sie/es = *he/she/it*
wir = *we*   ihr = *you*   sie/Sie = *they/you (polite form)*.

Present tense

For example, *I make, I am making,* or *I do make*:

infinitive	ich	du	er/sie/es	wir	ihr	sie/Sie
machen	mache	machst	macht	machen	macht	machen

Imperfect tense

For example, *I made, I was making,* or *I used to make*:

infinitive	ich	du	er/sie/es	wir	ihr	sie/Sie
machen	machte	machtest	machte	machten	machtet	machten

Future tense

For example, *I will make* or *I shall make*. This is formed by using the present tense of **werden**, which is the equivalent of *will* or *shall*, with the infinitive verb: **ich werde machen**.

infinitive	ich	du	er/sie/es	wir	ihr	sie/Sie
werden	werde	wirst	wird	werden	werdet	werden

Perfect tense

For example, *I made* or *I have made*. For most German verbs the perfect is formed by using the present tense of **haben**, which is the equivalent of *have*, with the past participle: **ich habe gemacht**. Some verbs take **sein** instead of **haben**, and these are all marked (***sein***) in the dictionary. They are mainly verbs expressing motion and involving a change of place:

he drove to Berlin today = er ist heute nach Berlin gefahren

Or they express a change of state, and this includes verbs
meaning to happen (**geschehen**, **passieren**, **vorkommen**):

he woke up = er ist aufgewacht

infinitive	ich	du	er/sie/es	wir	ihr	sie/Sie
haben	habe	hast	hat	haben	habt	haben
sein	bin	bist	ist	sind	seid	sind

Irregular verbs and other forms

Some German verbs are irregular and change their stem or
add different endings. All the irregular verbs that appear in
the dictionary are given in the section *German irregular
verbs* on pages 601–606.

The subjunctive

This is a form of the verb that is used to express speculation,
doubt, or unlikelihood. It is rarely used in English (*if I were
you* instead of *if I was you* is an exceptional example), but is
still used in both written and spoken German.

Present tense

infinitive	ich	du	er/sie/es	wir	ihr	sie/Sie
machen	mache	machest	mache	machen	machet	machen
sein	sei	sei(e)st	sei	seien	seid	seien

Imperfect tense

For regular verbs this is the same as the normal imperfect
forms, but irregular verbs vary.

infinitive	ich	du	er/sie/es	wir	ihr	sie/Sie
machen	machte	machtest	machte	machten	machtet	machten
werden	würde	würdest	würde	würden	würdet	würden
sein	wäre	wär(e)st	wäre	wären	wär(e)t	wären

The imperfect subjunctive of **werden** is used with an
infinitive to form the conditional tense. This tense expresses
what would happen if something else occurred.

he would go = er würde gehen
I wouldn't do that = das würde ich nicht machen

Reflexive verbs

The object of a reflexive verb is the same as its subject. In
German, the object is a reflexive pronoun. This is usually in
the accusative (I wash = **ich wasche mich**). The reflexive

pronouns of some verbs are in the dative (I imagine = **ich stelle mir vor**), and these are marked in the English–German part of the dictionary with (*dat*).

infinitive	ich	du	er/sie/es	wir	ihr	sie/Sie
sich waschen	wasche mich	wäschst dich	wäscht sich	waschen uns	wascht euch	waschen sich
sich vorstellen	stelle mir vor	stellst dir vor	stellt sich vor	stellen uns vor	stellt euch vor	stellen sich vor

The passive

In the passive form, the subject of the verb experiences the action rather than performs it: he was asked = **er wurde gefragt**. In German, the passive is formed using parts of **werden** with the past participle:

PRESENT PASSIVE	*it is done*	es wird gemacht
IMPERFECT PASSIVE	*it was done*	es wurde gemacht
FUTURE PASSIVE	*it will be done*	es wird gemacht werden
PERFECT PASSIVE	*it has been done*	es ist gemacht worden

When forming the perfect passive, note that the past participle of **werden** becomes **worden** rather than **geworden**.

Separable verbs

Separable verbs are marked in the German–English part of the dictionary with the label *sep*. In the perfect tense, the **ge-** of the past participle comes between the prefix and the verb, for example **er/sie/es hat an**ge**fangen**.

Articles

There are two articles in English, the definite article *the* and the indefinite article *a/an*. The way these are translated into German depends on the gender, number, and case of the noun with which the article goes.

There are three genders of nouns in German: masculine (**der Mann** = the man), feminine (**die Frau** = the woman), and neuter (**das Buch** = the book). There are two forms of number: singular (**der Baum** = the tree) and plural (**die Bäume** = the trees). And there are four cases, which show the part a noun plays in a sentence: nominative, accusative, genitive, and dative.

Definite article

the = der/die/das, (*plural*) = die

	SINGULAR			PLURAL
	masculine	feminine	neuter	all genders
NOMINATIVE	**der** Mann	**die** Frau	**das** Buch	**die** Bäume
ACCUSATIVE	**den** Mann	**die** Frau	**das** Buch	**die** Bäume
GENITIVE	**des** Mannes	**der** Frau	**des** Buches	**der** Bäume
DATIVE	**dem** Mann	**der** Frau	**dem** Buch	**den** Bäumen

Indefinite article

a/an = ein/eine/ein. This article can only be singular.

	masculine	feminine	neuter
NOMINATIVE	**ein** Mann	**eine** Frau	**ein** Buch
ACCUSATIVE	**einen** Mann	**eine** Frau	**ein** Buch
GENITIVE	**eines** Mannes	**einer** Frau	**eines** Buches
DATIVE	**einem** Mann	**einer** Frau	**einem** Buch

Nouns

In German, all nouns start with a capital letter: **das Buch** = the book.

Gender

There are three genders of nouns in German: masculine (**der Mann** = the man), feminine (**die Frau** = the woman), and neuter (**das Buch** = the book). These three examples are logical, with masculine for a male person, feminine for a female person, and neuter for an object. But it is not always like this with German nouns. Gender is sometimes determined by a noun's ending. For example, **das Mädchen** (= the girl) is neuter rather than feminine, simply because the ending **-chen** is always neuter.

The gender of German nouns is given in the dictionary. There are some general rules regarding the gender of groups of nouns, but individual genders must be checked by looking them up.

Masculine nouns

- male persons and animals: **der Arbeiter** = worker; **der Bär** = bear
- 'doers' and 'doing' instruments ending in **-er** in German: **der Gärtner** = gardener; **der Computer** = computer
- days, months, and seasons: (**der**) **Montag** = Monday

- words ending in **-ich**, **-ig**, and **-ling**: **der Honig** = honey; **der Lehrling** = apprentice
- words ending in **-ismus**, **-ist**, and **-ant**.

Feminine nouns

- female persons and animals: **die Schauspielerin** = actress; **die Henne** = hen; the feminine form of professions and animals is made by adding **-in** to the masculine (**der Schauspieler/die Schauspielerin** = actor/actress)
- nouns ending in **-ei**, **-ie**, **-ik**, **-in**, **-ion**, **-heit**, **-keit**, **-schaft**, **-tät**, **-ung**, **-ur**: **die Gärtnerei** = gardening; **die Energie** = energy
- most nouns ending in **-e**: **die Blume** = flower; note that there are many exceptions, including **der Name** = name, **der Käse** = cheese, **das Ende** = end.

Neuter nouns

- names of continents, most countries, and towns: (**das**) **Deutschland** = Germany; (**das**) **Köln** = Cologne
- nouns ending in **-chen** and **-lein** (indicating *small*): **das Mädchen**, **das Fräulein** = girl.
- most (but not all!) nouns beginning with **Ge-** or ending in **-nis**, **-tel**, or **-um**: **das Geheimnis** = secret; **das Zentrum** = centre
- infinitives of verbs used as nouns: **das Lachen** = laughter; **das Essen** = food.

Compound nouns

When two nouns are put together to make one compound noun, it takes the gender of the second noun:

der Brief + die Marke = die Briefmarke.

Plural

There are no absolutely definitive rules for the plural forms of German nouns. Plurals generally add an ending (**der Freund**, **die Freunde**), and change a vowel to an umlaut (**der Gast**, **die Gäste**; **das Haus**, **die Häuser**). Feminine words ending in **-heit**, **-keit**, and **-ung** add **-en** to make the plural (**die Abbildung**, **die Abbildungen**).

The plurals of all nouns are given in the German–English part of the dictionary.

Case

There are four cases, which show the part a noun plays in a sentence: nominative, accusative, genitive, and dative. The noun's article changes according to the case, and the ending of the noun changes in some cases:

	SINGULAR		
	masculine	feminine	neuter
NOMINATIVE	der Mann	die Frau	das Buch
ACCUSATIVE	den Mann	die Frau	das Buch
GENITIVE	des **Mannes**	der Frau	des **Buches**
DATIVE	dem Mann	der Frau	dem Buch

	PLURAL		
	masculine	feminine	neuter
NOMINATIVE	die Männer	die Frauen	die Bücher
ACCUSATIVE	die Männer	die Frauen	die Bücher
GENITIVE	der Männer	der Frauen	der Bücher
DATIVE	den **Männern**	den Frauen	den **Büchern**

The nominative is used for the subject of a sentence; in sentences with **sein** (to be) and **werden** (to become), the noun after the verb is in the nominative.

the dog barked = der Hund bellte
that is my car = das ist mein Wagen

The accusative is used for the direct object and after some prepositions (listed on page 597):

she has a son = sie hat einen Sohn

The genitive shows possession, and is also used after some prepositions (listed on page 597):

my husband's dog = der Hund meines Mannes

The dative is used for the indirect object. Some German verbs, such as **helfen**, take only the dative. The dative is also used after some prepositions (listed on page 596):

she gave the books to the children = sie gab den Kindern die Bücher

The following sentence combines all four cases:

der Mann gibt der Frau den Bleistift des Mädchens = *the man gives the woman the girl's pencil*
der Mann *is the subject* (*in the nominative*)
gibt *is the verb*
der Frau *is the indirect object* (*in the dative*)
den Bleistift *is the direct object* (*in the accusative*)
des Mädchens *is in the genitive* (*showing possession*).

Adjectives

An adjective is a word qualifying a noun. In German, an adjective in front of a noun adds endings that vary with the noun's gender, number, and case. Adjectives that come after a noun do not add endings.

With the definite article

Adjectives following **der/die/das** take these endings:

	SINGULAR masculine	feminine	neuter	PLURAL all genders
NOMINATIVE	der rote Hut	die rote Lampe	das rote Buch	die roten Autos
ACCUSATIVE	den roten Hut	die rote Lampe	das rote Buch	die roten Autos
GENITIVE	des roten Hutes	der roten Lampe	des roten Buches	der roten Autos
DATIVE	dem roten Hut	der roten Lampe	dem roten Buch	den roten Autos

Some German adjectives follow the pattern of the definite article, and adjectives after them change their endings in the same way as after **der/die/das**. For example, **dieser/diese/dieses** (= this):

	SINGULAR masculine	feminine	neuter	PLURAL all genders
NOMINATIVE	dieser	diese	dieses	diese
ACCUSATIVE	diesen	diese	dieses	diese
GENITIVE	dieses	dieser	dieses	dieser
DATIVE	diesem	dieser	diesem	diesen

Other common examples are:

jeder/jede/jedes = *every, each*   solcher/solche/solches = *such*
jener/jene/jenes = *that*   welcher/welche/welches = *which*
mancher/manche/manches = *many a, some*

With the indefinite article

Adjectives following **ein/eine/ein** take these endings:

	SINGULAR masculine	feminine	neuter
NOMINATIVE	ein roter Hut	eine rote Lampe	ein rotes Buch
ACCUSATIVE	einen roten Hut	eine rote Lampe	ein rotes Buch
GENITIVE	eines roten Hutes	einer roten Lampe	eines roten Buches
DATIVE	einem roten Hut	einer roten Lampe	einem roten Buch

Some German adjectives follow the pattern of the indefinite article, and adjectives after them change their endings in the same way as after **ein/eine/ein**. They are:

dein = *your*   kein = *no*
euer = *your*   mein = *my*
Ihr = *your*   sein = *his/its*
ihr = *her/their*   unser = *our*

These adjectives can also go with plural nouns: no cars = **keine Autos**. All genders take the same endings in the plural:

	PLURAL all genders
NOMINATIVE	keine roten Autos
ACCUSATIVE	keine roten Autos
GENITIVE	keiner roten Autos
DATIVE	keinen roten Autos

Without an article

Adjectives in front of a noun on their own, without an article, take the following endings:

	SINGULAR masculine	feminine	neuter	PLURAL all genders
NOMINATIVE	guter Wein	frische Milch	kaltes Bier	alte Leute
ACCUSATIVE	guten Wein	frische Milch	kaltes Bier	alte Leute
GENITIVE	guten Weins	frischer Milch	kalten Biers	alter Leute
DATIVE	gutem Wein	frischer Milch	kaltem Bier	alten Leuten

Adjectives as nouns

In German, adjectives can be used as nouns, spelt with a capital letter: **alt** = old, **ein Alter** = an old man, **eine Alte** = an old woman.

With the definite article (**der/die/das**), these nouns take the following endings:

	SINGULAR masculine	feminine	PLURAL both genders
NOMINATIVE	der Fremde	die Fremde	die Fremden
ACCUSATIVE	den Fremden	die Fremde	die Fremden
GENITIVE	des Fremden	der Fremden	der Fremden
DATIVE	dem Fremden	der Fremden	den Fremden

The feminine noun refers to a female stranger or foreigner.

With the indefinite article (**ein/eine/ein**), these nouns take the following endings:

| | SINGULAR | | PLURAL |
	masculine	feminine	both genders without an article
NOMINATIVE	ein Fremder	eine Fremde	Fremde
ACCUSATIVE	einen Fremden	eine Fremde	Fremde
GENITIVE	eines Fremden	einer Fremden	Fremder
DATIVE	einem Fremden	einer Fremden	Fremden

Comparative and superlative

In English, the comparative of the adjective *small* is *smaller*, and of *difficult* is *more difficult*. The superlatives are *smallest* and *most difficult*. In German, there is just one way to form the comparative and superlative: by adding the endings -**er** and -(**e**)**st**:

small, smaller, smallest = klein, kleiner, der/die/das kleinste

Many adjectives change their vowel to an umlaut in the comparative and superlative:

cold, colder, coldest = kalt, kälter, der/die/das kälteste

Some important adjectives are irregular:

big, bigger, biggest	= groß, größer, der/die/das größte
good, better, best	= gut, besser, der/die/das beste
high, higher, highest	= hoch, höher, der/die/das höchste
much, more, most	= viel, mehr, der/die/das meiste
near, nearer, nearest	= nah, näher, der/die/das nächste

Comparative and superlative adjectives take the same endings as basic adjectives:

a smaller child	= ein kleineres Kind
the coldest month	= der kälteste Monat

Adverbs

In German almost all adjectives can also be used as adverbs, describing a verb, an adjective, or another adverb.

she sings beautifully = sie singt schön

Some words, such as **auch** (= also), **fast** (= almost), **immer** (= always), and **leider** (= unfortunately) are used only as adverbs:

she is very clever = sie ist sehr klug

Comparative and superlative

The comparative is formed by adding -**er** to the basic adverb,

and the superlative by putting **am** in front of the basic adverb
and adding the ending -(e)sten:

clearly, more clearly, most clearly   = klar, klarer, am klarsten

Some important adverbs are irregular:

soon, earlier, at the earliest	= bald, früher, am frühesten
well, better, best	= gut, besser, am besten
willingly, more willingly, most willingly	= gern, lieber, am liebsten

Pronouns

Pronouns are words—such as *he, which,* and *mine* in
English—that stand instead of a noun.

Personal pronouns

These pronouns, such as he/she/it = **er/sie/es**, refer to
people or things.

	I	you	he/it	she/it	it	we	you	they	you
NOMINATIVE	ich	du	er	sie	es	wir	ihr	sie	Sie
ACCUSATIVE	mich	dich	ihn	sie	es	uns	euch	sie	Sie
DATIVE	mir	dir	ihm	ihr	ihm	uns	euch	ihnen	Ihnen
	me	*you*	*him/it*	*her/it*	*it*	*us*	*you*	*them*	*you*

The genitive form is not given, because it is so rarely used.

In German there are two forms for you, **du** and **Sie**. **Du** is less
formal and is used when speaking to someone you know well,
a child, or a family member. When speaking to a person or a
group of people you do not know very well, use the polite
form, **Sie**.

German pronouns agree in gender with the noun they refer
to. In the nominative case, *it* might be translated by **er** or **sie**,
as well as **es**:

it (the pencil) is red = er (der Bleistift) ist rot
it (the rose) is beautiful = sie (die Rose) ist schön
it (the car) is expensive = es (das Auto) ist teuer

Possessive pronouns

The possessive pronouns are:

mine = meiner/meine/mein(e)s   *ours* = unserer/unsere/unser(e)s
yours (informal singular) =   *yours (informal plural)* =
   deiner/deine/dein(e)s   eurer/eure/eures
his = seiner/seine/sein(e)s   *theirs* = ihrer/ihre/ihr(e)s
hers = ihrer/ihre/ihr(e)s   *yours (polite)* = Ihrer, Ihre, Ihr(e)s
its = seiner/seine/sein(e)s

They all take endings like **meiner/meine/mein(e)s**, as follows:

	SINGULAR masculine	feminine	neuter	PLURAL all genders
NOMINATIVE	meiner	meine	mein(e)s	meine
ACCUSATIVE	meinen	meine	mein(e)s	meine
GENITIVE	meines	meiner	meines	meiner
DATIVE	meinem	meiner	meinem	meinen

As can be seen in the table, in the neuter form an **-e-** can be added (making **meines**). This applies to all the possessive pronouns, but the extra **-e-** is rare.

Relative pronouns

These pronouns are used to introduce and link a new clause. In English they are *who*, *which*, *that*, and *what*. In German they are **der**, **die**, or **das**, depending on the noun referred to:

	SINGULAR masculine	feminine	neuter	PLURAL all genders
NOMINATIVE	der	die	das	die
ACCUSATIVE	den	die	das	die
GENITIVE	dessen	deren	dessen	deren
DATIVE	dem	der	dem	denen

Relative pronouns can be left out in English, but never in German:

the book (that) I'm reading = das Buch, das ich lese

They agree in gender and number with the noun they refer back to:

the man who visited us = der Mann, der uns besucht hat (**der** is masculine singular)

But the case of the pronoun depends on its function in the clause it introduces:

the pencil I bought yesterday = der Bleistift, den ich gestern gekauft habe

(**den** is masculine singular, but accusative because it is the object of the clause it introduces)

Interrogative pronouns

These pronouns are used to ask questions:

who? = wer?
what? = was?
which? = welcher/welche/welches?

Wer changes as follows:

NOMINATIVE	wer?
ACCUSATIVE	wen?
GENITIVE	wessen?
DATIVE	wem?

Reflexive pronouns
The object of a reflexive verb is the same as its subject. In German, the object is a reflexive pronoun. This is usually in the accusative (I wash = **ich wasche** mich). The reflexive pronouns of some verbs are in the dative (I imagine = **ich stelle** mir **vor**).

Indefinite pronouns
These pronouns do not refer to identifiable people or objects. In German, many indefinite pronouns, such as **etwas** (= something) and **nichts** (= nothing), never change. But some do take endings:

	someone	no one
NOMINATIVE	jemand	niemand
ACCUSATIVE	jemanden	niemanden
DATIVE	jemandem	niemandem

The genitive case is rarely used.

Prepositions
Prepositions are small words like *in*, that stand in front of a noun or pronoun. In German, the noun following a preposition always has to be in one of three cases—dative, accusative, or genitive.

Prepositions can be prefixes and form separable verbs:

to walk along the street = die Straße entlanggehen
he is walking along the street = er geht die Straße entlang

In the dictionary, the case governed by a preposition is given:

mit (+ *dat*) *means* mit *always takes the dative case.*

The most common case used after prepositions is the dative. The following prepositions always take the dative:

aus	mit	von
außer	nach	zu
bei	seit	

Some prepositions always take the accusative:

bis	entlang	gegen	um
durch	für	ohne	

Some prepositions always take the genitive:

anstatt	während
trotz	wegen

There is a group of prepositions that can take the dative or the accusative, depending on the sentence. They are:

an	in	unter
auf	neben	vor
hinter	über	zwischen

If the phrase containing one of these prepositions describes position—where something is happening—the dative case is used:

she sat in the kitchen = sie saß in der Küche

But if the phrase containing the preposition describes movement—motion towards something—the accusative follows:

she went into the kitchen = sie ging in die Küche

Some forms of the definite article are usually shortened when used with prepositions:

am (an dem); **ans** (an das); **aufs** (auf das); **beim** (bei dem); **durchs** (durch das); **fürs** (für das); **im** (in dem); **ins** (in das); **ums** (um das); **vom** (von dem); **zum** (zu dem); **zur** (zu der).

Conjunctions

Conjunctions are small words, such as *and* = **und**, which join clauses together in a sentence.

These common conjunctions link clauses together:

aber = *but*
denn = *for*
oder = *or*
sondern = *but (on the contrary)*
und = *and*

These conjunctions do not change normal word order in the two clauses:

ich gehe, und er kommt auch = *I am going, and he is coming too*

But there are many other conjunctions that send the verb to the end of the subordinate clause:

als = *when*, = *as*	daß = *that*	weil = *because*
bevor = *before*	ob = *whether*	
bis = *until*	während = *while*	
da = *since* .	wenn = *when*, = *if*	

er konnte nicht in die Schule gehen, *weil* er krank war = *he couldn't go to school, because he was ill*

Word order

The basic rule for German word order is that the verb comes second in a sentence. The subject of the sentence usually comes before the verb:

meine Mutter fährt am Freitag nach Köln = *my mother is going to Cologne on Friday*

When the verb is made up of two parts, such as in the perfect and the future tenses, the auxiliary verb comes second in the sentence, while the past participle (in the perfect) or infinitive (in the future tense) goes to the end:

wir haben sehr lang gewartet = *we waited a very long time*
sie wird sicher bald kommen = *she is sure to turn up soon*

Past participles and infinitives go to the end in other sentences too:

ich kann dieses Lied nicht leiden = *I can't stand this song*
du musst hier bleiben = *you must stay here*

When a sentence starts with a subordinate clause, the verb stays in second place:

da ich kein Geld hatte, blieb ich zu Hause = *since I had no money, I stayed at home*

In the clause itself, the verb goes to the end:

er konnte nicht in die Schule gehen, weil er krank war

The relative pronouns **der**, **die**, and **das**, as well as a number of conjunctions, send the verb to the end of the clause:

der Junge, der hier wohnt = *the boy who lives here*

When separable verbs separate, the prefix goes to the end:

der Film fängt um acht Uhr an = *the film starts at 8 o'clock*

In questions and commands, the verb is usually first in the sentence:

kommst du heute Abend? = *are you coming this evening?*
komm schnell rein! = *come in quickly!*

When there are a number of phrases in a sentence, the usual order for the different elements is 1 time, 2 manner, 3 place:

wir fahren heute mit dem Auto nach München = *we are driving to Munich today* (*time* = heute; *manner* = mit dem Auto; *place* = nach München)

German irregular verbs

1st, 2nd, and 3rd person present are given after the infinitive, and past subjunctive after the past indicative, where there is a change of vowel or any other irregularity.

Compound verbs are only given if they do not take the same forms as the corresponding simple verb, e.g. *befehlen*, or if there is no corresponding simple verb, e.g. *bewegen*.

An asterisk (*) indicates a verb which is also conjugated regularly.

Infinitive	Past tense	Past participle
abwägen	wog (wöge) ab	abgewogen
ausbedingen	bedang (bedänge) aus	ausbedungen
backen (du bäckst, er bäckt)	buk (büke)	gebacken
befehlen (du befiehlst, er befiehlt)	befahl (beföhle, befähle)	befohlen
beginnen	begann (begänne)	begonnen
beißen (du/er beißt)	biss (bisse)	gebissen
bergen (du birgst, er birgt)	barg (bärge)	geborgen
bewegen²	bewog (bewöge)	bewogen
biegen	bog (böge)	gebogen
bieten	bot (böte)	geboten
binden	band (bände)	gebunden
bitten	bat (bäte)	gebeten
blasen (du/er bläst)	blies	geblasen
bleiben	blieb	geblieben
bleichen*	blich	geblichen
braten (du brätst, er brät)	briet	gebraten
brechen (du brichst, er bricht)	brach (bräche)	gebrochen
brennen	brannte (brennte)	gebrannt
bringen	brachte (brächte)	gebracht
denken	dachte (dächte)	gedacht
dreschen (du drischst, er drischt)	drosch (drösche)	gedroschen
dringen	drang (dränge)	gedrungen

Infinitive	Past tense	Past participle
dürfen (ich/er darf, du darfst)	durfte (dürfte)	gedurft
empfehlen (du empfiehlst, er empfiehlt)	empfahl (empföhle)	empfohlen
erlöschen (du erlischst, er erlischt)	erlosch (erlösche)	erloschen
erschrecken (du erschrickst, er erschrickt)	erschrak (erschäke)	erschrocken
erwägen	erwog (erwöge)	erwogen
essen (du/er isst)	aß (äße)	gegessen
fahren (du fährst, er fährt)	fuhr (führe)	gefahren
fallen (du fällst, er fällt)	fiel	gefallen
fangen (du fängst, er fängt)	fing	gefangen
fechten (du fichtst, er ficht)	focht (föchte)	gefochten
finden	fand (fände)	gefunden
flechten (du flichtst, er flicht)	flocht (flöchte)	geflochten
fliegen	flog (flöge)	geflogen
fliehen	floh (flöhe)	geflohen
fließen (du/er fließt)	floss (flösse)	geflossen
fressen (du/er frisst)	fraß (fräße)	gefressen
frieren	fror (fröre)	gefroren
gären*	gor (göre)	gegoren
gebären (du gebierst, sie gebiert)	gebar (gebäre)	geboren
geben (du gibst, er gibt)	gab (gäbe)	gegeben
gedeihen	gedieh	gediehen
gehen	ging	gegangen
gelingen	gelang (gelänge)	gelungen
gelten (du giltst, er gilt)	galt (gölte, gälte)	gegolten
genesen (du/er genest)	genas (genäse)	genesen
genießen (du/er genießt)	genoss (genösse)	genossen
geschehen (es geschieht)	geschah (geschähe)	geschehen
gewinnen	gewann (gewönne, gewänne)	gewonnen
gießen (du/er gießt)	goss (gösse)	gegossen
gleichen	glich	geglichen
gleiten	glitt	geglitten
glimmen	glomm (glömme)	geglommen
graben (du gräbst, er gräbt)	grub (grübe)	gegraben
greifen	griff	gegriffen

Infinitive	Past tense	Past participle
haben (du hast, er hat)	hatte (hätte)	gehabt
halten (du hältst, er hält)	hielt	gehalten
hängen[2]	hing	gehangen
hauen	haute	gehauen
heben	hob (höbe)	gehoben
heißen (du/er hießt)	hieß	geheißen
helfen (du hilfst, er hilft)	half (hülfe)	geholfen
kennen	kannte (kennte)	gekannt
klingen	klang (klänge)	geklungen
kneifen	kniff	gekniffen
kommen	kam (käme)	gekommen
können (ich/er kann, du kannst)	konnte (könnte)	gekonnt
kriechen	kroch (kröche)	gekrochen
laden (du lädst, er lädt)	lud (lüde)	geladen
lassen (du/er lässt)	ließ	gelassen
laufen (du läufst, er läuft)	lief	gelaufen
leiden	litt	gelitten
leihen	lieh	geliehen
lesen (du/er liest)	las (läse)	gelesen
liegen	lag (läge)	gelegen
lügen	log (löge)	gelogen
mahlen	mahlte	gemahlen
meiden	mied	gemieden
melken	molk (mölke)	gemolken
messen (du/er misst)	maß (mäße)	gemessen
misslingen	misslang (misslänge)	misslungen
mögen (ich/er mag, du magst)	mochte (möchte)	gemocht
müssen (ich/er muss, du musst)	musste (müsste)	gemusst
nehmen (du nimmst, er nimmt)	nahm (nähme)	genommen
nennen	nannte (nennte)	genannt
pfeifen	pfiff	gepfiffen
preisen (du/er preist)	pries	gepriesen
raten (du rätst, er rät)	riet	geraten
reiben	rieb	gerieben
reißen (du/er reißt)	riss	gerissen
reiten	ritt	geritten
rennen	rannte (rennte)	gerannt
riechen	roch (röche)	gerochen
ringen	rang (ränge)	gerungen
rinnen	rann (ränne)	geronnen

Infinitive	Past tense	Past participle
rufen	rief	gerufen
salzen* (du/er salzt)	salzte	gesalzen
saufen (du säufst, er säuft)	soff (söffe)	gesoffen
saugen*	sog (söge)	gesogen
schaffen[1]	schuf (schüfe)	geschaffen
scheiden	schied	geschieden
scheinen	schien	geschienen
scheißen (du/er scheißt)	schiss	geschissen
schelten (du schiltst, er schilt)	schalt (schölte)	gescholten
scheren[1]	schor (schöre)	geschoren
schieben	schob (schöbe)	geschoben
schießen (du/er schießt)	schoss (schösse)	geschossen
schlafen (du schläfst, er schläft)	schlief	geschlafen
schlagen (du schlägst, er schlägt)	schlug (schlüge)	geschlagen
schleichen	schlich	geschlichen
schleifen[2]	schliff	geschliffen
schließen (du/er schießt)	schloss (schlösse)	geschlossen
schlingen	schlang (schlänge)	geschlungen
schmeißen (du/er schmeißt)	schmiss (schmisse)	geschmissen
schmelzen (du/er schmilzt)	schmolz (schmölze)	geschmolzen
schneiden	schnitt	geschnitten
schrecken* (du schrickst, er schrickt)	schrak (schräke)	geschreckt
schreiben	schrieb	geschrieben
schreien	schrie	geschrie[e]n
schreiten	schritt	geschritten
schweigen	schwieg	geschwiegen
schwellen (du schwillst, er schwillt)	schwoll (schwölle)	geschwollen
schwimmen	schwamm (schwömme)	geschwommen
schwinden	schwand (schwände)	geschwunden
schwingen	schwang (schwänge)	geschwungen
schwören	schwor (schwüre)	geschworen
sehen (du siehst, er sieht)	sah (sähe)	gesehen
sein (ich bin, du bist, er ist, wir sind, ihr seid, sie sind)	war (wäre)	gewesen

Infinitive	Past tense	Past participle
senden[1]	sandte (sendete)	gesandt
sieden	sott (sötte)	gesotten
singen	sang (sänge)	gesungen
sinken	sank (sänke)	gesunken
sitzen (du/er sitzt)	saß (säße)	gesessen
sollen (ich/er soll, du sollst)	sollte	gesollt
spalten*	spaltete	gespalten
spinnen	spann (spönne, spänne)	gesponnen
sprechen (du sprichst, er spricht)	sprach (spräche)	gesprochen
sprießen (du/er sprießt)	spross (sprösse)	gesprossen
springen	sprang (spränge)	gesprungen
stechen (du stichst, er sticht)	stach (stäche)	gestochen
stehen	stand (stünde, stände)	gestanden
stehlen (du stiehlst, er stiehlt)	stahl (stähle)	gestohlen
steigen	stieg	gestiegen
sterben (du stirbst, er stirbt)	starb (stürbe)	gestorben
stinken	stank (stänke)	gestunken
stoßen (du/er stößt)	stieß	gestoßen
streichen	strich	gestrichen
streiten	stritt	gestritten
tragen (du trägst, er trägt)	trug (trüge)	getragen
treffen (du triffst, er trifft)	traf (träfe)	getroffen
treiben	trieb	getrieben
treten (du trittst, er tritt)	trat (träte)	getreten
triefen*	troff (tröffe)	getroffen
trinken	trank (tränke)	getrunken
trügen	trog (tröge)	getrogen
tun (du tust, er tut)	tat (täte)	getan
verderben (du verdirbst, er verdirbt)	verdarb (verdürbe)	verdorben
vergessen (du/er vergisst)	vergaß (vergäße)	vergessen
verlieren	verlor (verlöre)	verloren
verzeihen	verzieh	verziehen
wachsen[1] (du/er wächst)	wuchs (wüchse)	gewachsen
waschen (du wäschst, er wäscht)	wusch (wüsche)	gewaschen
wenden[2]*	wandte (wendete)	gewandt
werben (du wirbst, er wirbt)	warb (würbe)	geworben

Infinitive	Past tense	Past participle
werden (du wirst, er wird)	wurde (würde)	geworden
werfen (du wirfst, er wirft)	warf (würfe)	geworfen
wiegen[1]	wog (wöge)	gewogen
winden	wand (wände)	gewunden
wissen (ich/er weiß, du weißt)	wusste (wüsste)	gewusst
wollen (ich/er will, du willst)	wollte	gewollt
wringen	wrang (wränge)	gewrungen
ziehen	zog (zöge)	gezogen
zwingen	zwang (zwänge)	gezwungen